The Author

Eugene L Rasor taught British and European history at Emory and Henry College for thirty-three years, retiring in 1997. He has compiled other naval bibliographies including ones on the battle of Jutland and the war in the Pacific.

THE
Seaforth
BIBLIOGRAPHY

A guide to more than 4,000 works on
British naval history
55BC – 1815

EUGENE L RASOR

Seaforth
PUBLISHING

To
John B Hattendorf

Copyright © Eugene L Rasor 2004

This paperback edition first published in Great Britain in 2008 by
Seaforth Publishing,
Pen & Sword Books Ltd,
47 Church Street,
Barnsley S70 2AS

British Library Cataloguing in Publication Data
A catalogue record for this book is available from the British Library

ISBN 978 1 84832 002 4

First published in 2004 by Praeger Publishers as
English/British Naval History to 1815

Printed and bound in Great Britain by Cpod, Trowbridge, Wiltshire

Contents

Acknowledgments

This work is a comprehensive historiographical and bibliographical survey of the most important scholarly and printed materials about the naval and maritime history of England and Great Britain from earliest times to 1815; a "prequel" to Eugene Rasor, <u>British Naval History since 1815: A Guide to the Literature</u> in the Garland <u>Military History Bibliographies</u> series, vol. 13. New York: Garland Publishing, 1990, xxi, 841 pages, 3125 bibliographical entries, 507 pages of historiographical narrative. That bibliography was not annotated. Robin Higham was the overall editor of the series.

For <u>English/British Naval History to 1815: A Guide to the Literature</u>, the bibliography is annotated, 913 pages (373 pages of historiographical narrative) and **4124** annotated bibliographical entries. This survey will provide a major reference guide for students and scholars at all levels. It incorporates evaluative, qualitative, and critical analysis processes, the essence of historical scholarship. Each one of the **4124** annotated entries is evaluated, assessed, analyzed, integrated, and incorporated into the historiographical narrative section, the essence of historiographical scholarship.

Each of my thirteen other works published by Greenwood Press, <u>The Battle of Jutland</u>, <u>The Spanish Armada</u>, <u>The Falklands/Malvinas Campaign</u>, <u>The Southwest Pacific Campaign</u>, <u>The Solomon Islands Campaign</u>, <u>The China-Burma-India Campaign</u>, <u>MacArthur</u>, <u>Mountbatten</u>, <u>Balfour</u>, <u>Churchill</u>, <u>TITANIC</u>, and, forthcoming, <u>William Gladstone</u> and <u>Benjamin Disraeli</u>, have similar formats: a comprehensive historiographical narrative section (about half of the total number of pages) followed by an annotated bibliography section. More recent ones have included a section on lists, as does this one. Critical analysis and qualitative assessments are featured.

The dedication is to John B. Hattendorf. No person in the Anglo-American world has done more as an advocate for English/British naval and maritime history; Anglo-American because he has contributed significantly in both worlds, holding a most prestigious chair at the U.S. Naval War College, a

Doctor of Philosophy from Oxford University, and recipient of the distinguished Caird Medal from the National Maritime Museum, Greenwich, among much else, as presented below in the introduction.

A historiographer-bibliographer is most reliant and appreciative of assistance from institutional and university libraries such as the British Library, the Institute of Historical Research, London, Cambridge, Oxford, and Edinburgh; in the United States, university libraries such as Virginia, Virginia Tech, Duke, North Carolina, North Carolina State, Maryland, Emory and Henry College, the Library of Congress, and the John Carter Brown Library. All of these institutions have provided essential assistance for scholarly research.

Likewise, a large number of persons have provided continuing support and assistance. That has been vital and much appreciated. Nothing could have happened without Claire Franklin Rasor. David Baber put it all together. Cynthia Harris, Tod Myerscough, and Jane Lerner oversaw it from Greenwood. Continued support, even after retirement, has been generously provided from Jack Roper and Emory and Henry College. Most appreciated support, continued encouragement, and assistance has been provided by John Hattendorf, to whom this work is dedicated. Others include Alan Aberg, Quince Adams, Richard Bateman, Daniel Baugh, Colin Baxter, Keith Bird, Tom Davis, Harry Dickinson, W.A.B. Douglas, Mrs. Paul Franklin, Michael Galgano, Barry Gough, Richard Harding, R.E.G. Harris, Robin Higham, John Hutcheson, Bruce Kinzer, Roger Knight, Andrew Lambert, Malcolm Lester, Michael Partridge, Alan Pearsall, Andy Rasor, Neel and Iris Rich, Rosemary Ricketts, Nicholas Rodger, Jon Sumida, Spencer Tucker, Fred van Hartesveldt, John and Vivienne Vickers, Anne Sharp Wells, Colin White, Glyndwr Williams, Alan Wilt, David R. Woodward, Charles and Betty Young, and the late Christopher Lloyd, Bryan Ranft, and Bryan Ricketts.

Abbreviations

Adm. - Admiral
AHR – American Historical Review
AmNep – American Neptune
Balt – Baltimore
Bull – Bulletin of . . . .
b/w – black and white
comp – compiler or compiled
diss – dissertation
DNB – Dictionary of National Biography
D.Phil – Doctor of Philosophy
ed – editor or edited
EHR - English Historical Review
FRHS – Fellow of the Royal Historical Society
FRS – Fellow of the Royal Society
fwd – foreword
HCA – High Court of the Admiralty
HisTod – History Today
illus – illustrations by
IHR – Institute of Historical Research
intro – introduction
JHUP – Johns Hopkins University Press
J – Journal
JRUSI – Journal of the Royal United Services Institute
LHA – Lord High Admiral
MHQ – Military History Quarterly
MM – Mariner's Mirror
MSS – manuscript
NASOH – North American Society of Oceanic History
NHS – Naval History Symposium

NIP – Naval Institute Press
NMM – National Maritime Museum
n.p. – no publisher
NRS – Navy Records Society
NWCR – Naval War College Review
NY – New York
Ph.D. – Doctor of Philosophy
Phil – Philadelphia
pp. – pages
PRO – Public Record Office
pseud – pseudonym
publishers – abbreviated names
RHS – Royal Historical Society
RN – Royal Navy
SOTL – ship-of-the-line
SNR – Society for Nautical Research
State - official abbreviations
trans – translated by
Trans – Transactions of the . . . .
Universities - by first name
UP – University Press
USN – United States Navy
USNA – United States Naval Academy
USNIP – United States Naval Institute Proceedings
Wash - Washington

PART I.

HISTORIOGRAPHICAL NARRATIVE

Chapter 1

Introduction

This work is a comprehensive historiographical and bibliographical survey of the most important scholarly and printed materials about the naval and maritime history of England and Great Britain from earliest times to 1815.

This chapter will introduce the history and background of English/British naval and maritime history. The topics in each of the following paragraphs represent those chapter titles in subsequent chapters of this historiographical narrative section.

The dedication is to a major contributor to maritime and naval history, John B. Hattendorf, Ernest J. King Professor of Maritime History and Director of the Advanced Research Program, U.S. Naval War College, Newport, RI, and, former Director, Graduate Courses in Maritime History, Frank Munson Institute of American Maritime Studies, Mystic, CT. He has served as a professor at the war college since 1983. Born in Illinois in 1941, Hattendorf has a BA, Kenyon College, Masters Degree, Brown University, and Doctor of Philosophy, Pembroke College, Oxford University; a veteran of the U.S. Navy. He has been a prolific author and writer. Over twenty of his works are incorporated herein [**1550-1570**], plus co-authorship of conference proceedings and works about Patrick O'Brian, also included herein. He has submitted 20 entries for the <u>New Dictionary of National Biography</u> [**2631**], for example, on George Byng, Viscount Torrington, George Rooke, and Clowsdisley Shovell. Hattendorf is recipient of the Caird Medal from the National Maritime Museum, Greenwich, December 2000, the Caird Lecture: "The Anglo-French Naval Wars, 1689-1815." Among his works not described in this historiographical-bibliographical survey are a biography of Stephen B. Luce, a survey of maritime strategy, and an edition of the diary of an American naval attache in Britain, 1940-1941.

A. HISTORICAL BACKGROUND AND OVERVIEW

The English/British have always been known as "the sailor race" with "hearts of oak"; the Royal Navy as the "Senior Service" and "first line of defense," it is and has been "British and Best." It facilitated the motto: "the sun never set on the British Empire." The Royal Navy has exerted a powerful influence on Great Britain, its Empire, Europe, and, ultimately, the world, especially at its height, the period of Pax Britannica between about 1800 and 1920. The Royal Navy, RN, has been seen in that past as a legendary force permeated by an enduring heritage and tradition unchallenged and unassailable and with an unprecedented series of glorious leaders. It was credited with saving the country, if not civilization, during the Wars of the French Revolution and Napoleon and it was the first line of defense during the 19th and 20th centuries. Perhaps the American naval officer-historian, Alfred Thayer Mahan [**2328, 2329**], said it best when he concluded that "those far distant, storm-beaten ships" foiled the determination of Napoleon to dominate the world, and, later, perhaps, the same could be said for Adolf Hitler. Great victories have been achieved: over the Spanish Armada, over the Dutch, and the unprecedented series identified with Admiral Lord Horatio Nelson: Cape St. Vincent of 1797, the Nile of 1798, Copenhagen of 1801, and, the ultimate annihilation, Trafalgar of 1805.

On the other hand, the Royal Navy has been depicted as "a paper tiger," "a myth," and a backward, barbaric, "drowsy, inefficient, moth-eaten" force suffering from Byzantine intrigues and disgraceful unreadiness. At one point, the American colonies were lost when the RN failed to sustain a land army. Extreme problems of corruption, impressment, punishment, drunkenness, mutiny, and neglect have plagued the RN for centuries. There were occasions of decline, especially in the early 17th century after the glorious victory over the Spanish Armada, in the aforementioned American Revolution, and in the late 19th century. Conditions aboard ship were scandalously squalid. Wages on the lower deck were unchanged between the mid-17th through the mid-19th centuries.

There has been some debate about the actual beginnings of the RN, even when there was an English naval force. The new Naval History of Britain by N.A.M. Rodger [**3110**] began during the Anglo-Saxon period, in 660 AD. The old standard of William Laird Clowes [**669**] began with the Romans.

Naval and maritime matters of the British Isles can be traced back two millennia to Celtic and Roman times. Julius Caesar, commander of a Roman army conquering Gaul, conducted amphibious forays across the English Channel into southeastern England twice, in 55 and 54 BC. The Romans invaded and settled Roman Britain beginning in 43 AD. Hadrians Wall and similar land defenses were constructed in the north. In the south along the English Channel, a system of forts called the Saxon Shore were constructed to defend Britain from attack and invasion from Germanic peoples of what is now Denmark and northern Germany, especially the Frisians, Angles, Saxons, and Jutes. About

400 AD, Anglo-Saxon England superseded Roman Britain. Subsequent "enemies" have varied over time. The Vikings were the first serious threat. The Irish and Scots, even the Welsh, have for short moments in ancient times exerted themselves at sea, usually the local sea. The Normans from northern France successfully invaded in 1066. "France" was a geographic expression until after 1000. Spain, Burgundy, some Italian states, the various Dutch republics, Denmark, Norway, Sweden, Russia, and, in recent times, of course, Germany, have fought England/Britain. Portugal consistently was an ally. Venice had the first and longest "standing navy" with its famous arsenal to sustain it. Genoa was a close second.

Navies began as assemblies of merchant ships "impressed" by the king as a feudal obligation. There is some dispute about the role of the 9th-century King Alfred and the navy. In general, the Vikings enjoyed domination throughout their era, from about 800 to 1100 AD. About 1050, King Edward the Confessor designated certain ports on the English Channel for "ship service." Later that group would be known as the Cinque Ports, the first semblance of an English navy. Perhaps, "navy royal" would be an appropriate term for naval forces, which assembled on occasion up through the 16th and 17th centuries. A naval administration which included finance, bases, dockyards, victualling, and permanent provisions for personnel was essential before the term "Royal Navy" rightly could be used.

The Tudor dynasty of the 16th century consciously advanced the process. King Henry VII encouraged exploration and commerce, provided for a dry dock, and established financial management institutions. Henry VIII and Elizabeth I built up permanent fleets. The Spanish Armada of 1588 was successfully prevented from invasion, a great national propaganda victory. Britain was formative in the development of "maritime enterprise," a combination of naval operations, privateering, exploration, commerce, and colonization, all of which expanded worldwide. Such global hegemony has been variously characterized: sea power, sea mastery, naval supremacy, maritime enterprise, and sea empire.

Smuggling, piracy, and, even more so, privateering, must rank high as contributing to and influencing naval developments leading to the modern Royal Navy. So must merchant and fishing enterprises. All were "schools" for seamen, who could be "impressed" into the navy during times of declared emergency or war.

The structural organization of the Royal Navy consisted of the Admiralty, the executive authority and central administration located at Admiralty House at the bottom of Trafalgar Square and the top of Whitehall in London. The civilian head in modern times, sometimes a member of the cabinet, responsible to the government and to Parliament, was the First Lord of the Admiralty. The professional head was the First Sea Lord with a varying number of Sea Lords comprising a Navy Board, responsible for the day-to-day operation of the fleets and shore establishment. Fleets were organized geographically, for example, Home, Mediterranean, North American, West Indian, and Far Eastern. In the Middle Ages and early modern period, Trinity House was the institution responsible for navigation, navigating aids, lighthouses, and channel marking.

The shore establishment consisted of the various naval bases, the Royal Dockyards, victualling yards, and shore service personnel. These were located all over the world. The Royal Dockyards were major industrial centers responsible for shipbuilding and maintenance. Victualling was a huge undertaking. Ordnance was supplied by a joint agency with the army. England had the best and most advanced gunfounding industry in the world. During the age of fighting sail, provision for the supply of wood, especially oak wood, became a matter of strategic survival of state, as would be the case later with the matter of access to unlimited and unhampered supplies of coal, then oil. First native wood was utilized and the supply was exhausted. Then the areas of Eastern Europe, the shores of the Baltic Sea, and North America were exploited. All of this essential process was documented by Robert Albion [**29**]. The huge quantities of wood had to be seasoned, the masts stored in ponds in the dockyards. Obviously, all of this, for wood, coal, and oil, over time, entailed massive commitment of resources just to ensure secure and unlimited access to these vital fuel sources.

Social history has become increasingly important. For the navy that included environmental conditions on the lower deck and personnel matters. Among the factors involved were recruitment practices. For centuries, that was impressment, a notorious process of virtual kidnapping. The government felt it had to maintain that option, even into the 19th century, to guarantee a supply of experienced seamen for mobilization for war. Again, the security of the state was at stake. Thousands and thousands of individual human tragedies, if not the origin of wars, can be traced to the practice of impressment in the Royal Navy. For normal circumstances, an early practice of recruitment was a "hire and discharge" system. An important reform of the mid-19th century, good for the navy and the seaman, was called long-term service. Other factors were discipline and legal provision for Courts Martial. Flogging was a common punishment for centuries. Mutinies, most notorious being those of 1797, occurring in the midst of the Wars of the French Revolution and Napoleon, were disruptive.

Life and status aboard ship were divided into the quarterdeck for officers and the lower deck for enlisted men, and, later, much later, women. The Royal Marines have always been attached to the navy. Marines comprised about one-quarter of the crew on large ships. Impressment meant a continuous shortage of seamen for the lower deck. For the quarterdeck, officers typically came from the upper classes. The supply was usually excessive. In peacetime, officers were put on "half-pay," a kind of limbo status, which ensured they would be available for mobilization for war.

Types of naval ships have evolved. Nautical archaeological techniques have informed us about details of early ships of northern Europe which operated in the North Sea, English Channel, Irish Sea, and Atlantic Ocean. Outstanding examples were SUTTON HOO, a 7th-century ship burial, wrecks of the Spanish Armada explored off the northern and western coasts of Scotland and Ireland, and VASA, a 17th-century Swedish warship. Findings of nautical archaeology also have led to revised interpretations. For example, revised conclusions have been reached about the guns aboard Spanish and English ships during the Armada campaign. Findings also determined that architectural design and construction were different for ships operating in the Mediterranean and those operating in the Atlantic. Spanish ships of the Armada built in Mediterranean shipyards were much more likely to break up and sink during stressful circumstances than those built in Spanish Atlantic shipyards.

Nevertheless, the earliest warships were basically merchant ships occasionally called up or "impressed" for war. Examples of early types were carracks and galleons. Galleys requiring oars were less used by the English but were often successful against the English. Early modern types included sloops, frigates, the "eyes" of the fleet, and ships of the line, early battleships. Designation was dependent on the number of guns in the broadside, for example, between up to 130 and down to 64, further subdivided into "rates," first-, second-, third-, and fourth-.

Naval tactics also have evolved. In the age of fighting sail, line-of-battle became the standard naval battle formation. The Admiralty issued rigid "Fighting Instructions" mandating tactical formations and battle maneuvers.

Strategic methods utilized by Britain have included blockade, close and distant. For centuries during the age of sail, this meant close blockade, a process of maintaining continuous watch opposite major ports of the enemy. That entailed a massive commitment of logistical, materiel, and personnel requirements during all seasons of the year.

Civil and criminal law and legal codes were found to be inapplicable under the international and unique conditions of the sea. Specialized judges and courts were set up, Vice-Admiralty Courts and Admiralty Law, dealing with such matters as piracy, prizes and prize law, wages and conditions for seamen, smuggling, collisions, wrecks, and insurance. The British Admiralty created model institutions basically copied by the rest of the world.

"The sailor race" with "hearts of oak" has been led by great monarchs and leaders. Kings and queens became increasingly conscious of sea power and its advantages for the unique situation for the British Isles. Kings Harold Godwinson, William I, Richard I, Henry V, Henry VII, Henry VIII, Queen Elizabeth I, and, of course, the king groomed for the navy, William IV, have been singled out. The navy remained loyal to Parliament during the Civil War, perhaps a decisive factor in the defeat and execution of King Charles I.

The age of fighting sail was characterized by gigantic national heroes, the foremost being Admiral Viscount Horatio Nelson. There has been an unequaled series of great professional naval commanders, including Francis Drake, Richard Grenville, Edward Hawke, George Rodney, Lord St. Vincent,

Cuthbert Collingwood, Edward Pellew, and after this period, Lord "Jackie" Fisher, John Jellicoe, David Beatty, A.B. Cunningham, and Lord Louis Mountbatten. Great First Lords have included George Anson, Lord Barham, and Winston Churchill.

Admiral Lord Horatio Nelson has become the epitome of British naval history, the idol, symbol, and icon of extraordinary influence. He was and is celebrated and commemorated with numerous portraits and statues, notably in Trafalgar Square, London; also in Edinburgh and Portsdown Hill, above Portsmouth. His memory is perpetuated by the Nelson Society and the 1805 Club. There are Nelson Galleries at the National Maritime Museum, Greenwich, and the Royal Naval Museum, Portsmouth, a Nelson Museum in Monmouth, and a famous Nelson Collection at Lloyd's of London. Biographies and studies of Nelson have proliferated. Professional associations and societies have joined to sponsor the Nelson Decade. The "decade" is 1995 to 2005, corresponding with the decade of the greatest achievements of Nelson during the period 1795-1805. Nelson's flagship at the battle of Trafalgar of 1805 was HMS VICTORY, restored, still in commission, and the object of much public interest at the Portsmouth Naval Base. Also at Portsmouth are MARY ROSE and HMS WARRIOR. Anchored on the Thames River near Tower Bridge is HMS BELFAST, a cruiser of World War II, now attached to the Imperial War Museum. All of these are ships of the British navy, which are constant and living reminders of a magnificent tradition.

A full-scale, multi-volume, scholarly, semi-official Naval History of Britain is in progress, the first in a hundred years. Volume I is out, The Safeguard of the Sea, by N.A.M. Rodger [3110], one of the most famous British naval historians. Among other things, Rodger [3117] was author of the best-selling Wooden World, about 18th-century naval society. There were hardback and paperback editions of Safeguard of the Sea. The project was sponsored by the National Maritime Museum, NMM, of Greenwich and the professional Society for Nautical Research, SNR, and Navy Records Society, NRS. Interestingly, the previous standard, The Royal Navy: A History, seven volumes, 1897-1903, edited by William Laird Clowes [669], has been reprinted by a new publishing house, which has concentrated on British naval works, Chatham Publishers of London. The Royal Navy included essays by Alfred Thayer Mahan [2328-2333] and by the then sitting president of the United States, Theodore Roosevelt [3137], who wrote on the War of 1812.

It is operations during the past 500 years which have made the Royal Navy great, beginning with the defeat of the 130-ship, "Invincible," Spanish Armada of 1588. The 17th century brought some setbacks, decline, civil war, and revolution. Nevertheless, the navy played a decisive role in its support of Parliament during the 1640s. Three Anglo-Dutch wars involved hard but ultimately victorious fights for the navy. Those wars were formative for the navy and the nation.

In the 18th century during the Seven Years' War, there were the great victories at Quiberon Bay of November 1759, Admiral Edward Hawke destroying 7 French ships of the line under the most severe conditions of weather, geography, and darkness, plus 2 successful amphibious campaigns thousands of miles from base, Havana and Manila, in June and October of 1762. Overcommitment worldwide was one explanation for the series of single-ship defeats during the American Revolution, and, ultimately, the loss of the American colonies.

One hundred fifteen was the total number of British ships of the line operated by the Royal Navy with no losses during a quarter-century of the ultimate period of sailing-ship warfare, the Wars of the French Revolution and Napoleon, 1793-1815. Major battles were fought against the French, Spanish, Dutch, and Danes. Victories were increasingly annihilation: Cape St. Vincent and Camperdown of 1797, the Nile of 1798, Copenhagen of 1801, and, the ultimate, Trafalgar, 21 October 1805. During the Trafalgar campaign, 1803-1805, Admiral Nelson led the long search for Admiral Villeneuve throughout the Mediterranean Sea, across to the West Indies, and back. It was over a century before the Royal Navy was seriously threatened again.

All of these matters will be elaborated upon in the following chapters. Among prominent themes will be forts of the Saxon Shore, the Cinque Ports, the "navigation institution," Trinity House, the Royal Observatory, Vice-Admiralty Courts and the High Court of the Admiralty, development of the Admiralty, search for the Northwest Passage, ship burials such as SUTTON HOO, events of the Nelson Decade, the ages of exploration, and development of the Royal Navy.

Throughout, some comparisons and juxtapositions will be pursued to inform better and learn more about the Royal Navy, its evolution and developments: Vikings, Scandinavia, Normandy, Gascony, Venice, Genoa, Portugal, Spain, the Netherlands, France, Denmark, the Ottoman Empire, Barbary States, North American colonies, and the United States of America.

Chapter 2

Purpose, Scope, Format, and Features

A. PURPOSE

English/British Naval History to 1815: A Guide to the Literature, a volume in the Bibliographies and Indexes in Military Studies series of Greenwood Press, is a complete reference, research, and information guide for use of all levels of general readers, students, and scholars and all persons interested in English/British naval and maritime history. It is a comprehensive survey and a critical review of the literature. The "literature" includes all important published and related materials about English/British naval history to the year 1815. It is a historiographical and bibliographical survey of standard, popular, and official histories, monographs, important articles in journals and periodicals, anthologies, conference, symposium, and seminar papers, guides, bibliographies, documents, doctoral dissertations, and master's theses. The emphasis is on the broadest possible coverage.

It is a purposeful and planned "pre-quel" to Eugene Rasor [**3012**], British Naval History since 1815: A Guide to the Literature in the Garland Military History Bibliographies series, volume 13, 1990, xxi, 841 pages, 3125 bibliographical entries, 507 pages of historiographical narrative. That bibliography was not annotated. Robin Higham [**1627**] was the overall editor of that series. For English/British Naval History to 1815: A Guide to the Literature, the bibliography is annotated. There are **3988** annotated bibliographical entries, plus items **3989** to **4124** in the Addendum. As far as can be determined, nothing as extensive, comprehensive, and up-to-date as this historiographical-bibliographical survey has been published.

B. SCOPE

It is important to incorporate historical background, context, comparison, perspective, linkage, origins, developments, and relationships. The narrative and listings below present the maximum scope and broadest coverage.

Topics covered are references, resource centers, histories, historians, naval wars, operations, and battles, related maritime matters, piracy and privateering, the law of the sea, warships, personalities – naval officers, human resources – the lower deck, the Admiralty, administration, logistics, victualling, discipline, shipbuilding, dockyards, naval ports, exploration and discovery, geographic regions, nautical archaeology, nautical dictionaries, nautical fiction, art, music, and cyberspace. The final chapter presents gaps in the literature and recommended research to be accomplished. Not covered, but perhaps should have been, are topics of empire, imperialism, colonialism, India and the East India Company, commerce, trade, monopoly companies, maritime entrepreneurs, commercial enterprise, fishing, whaling, and coastal shipping, and the Atlantic Slave Trade. Many of these areas were covered in Eugene Rasor [**3012**], British Naval History since 1815: imperialism (chapter 8, pp. 255-306), trade, commerce, and the merchant marine (chapter 7A-7F, pp. 225-45), fishing and whaling, (chapter 7G, pp. 246-48), and the slave trade (chapter 9, pp. 309-15). These maritime operations produced the vital "schools for seamen" and sources for "manning" the navy, and the investment, which was essential for exploration, discovery, and privateering, ventures. In turn, the navy provided the protection and security for the merchant, companies, fishing, and whaling fleets and their operations, advancement, and expansion.

A variety of types of publications are also included. Official and published documents, publication series, nautical fiction, and doctoral dissertations are all incorporated. A list of pertinent master's theses are added in Appendix I. Examples of documents include all of the publications of the Navy Records Society, over 140 works and counting, many of the publications of the Hakluyt Society, published proceedings from the American Naval History Symposia, Anglo-French and Anglo-Dutch conferences of naval historians, conferences celebrating important anniversaries and special events, for example, several commemorations of the quadricentennial of the Spanish Armada and the Longitude conference at Harvard University, and festschrift, collections of articles in honor or in memory of an important scholar.

The use of "English/British" in the title is to signify official, national, and regional transitions, specifically England and Wales up to 1603 when the dual kingdoms of England and Scotland were united under a single monarch, up to 1707, when those kingdoms were united, and up to 1800 when Ireland was incorporated. The naval histories of Scotland, Ireland, and that unique phenomenon, the Dalriada Kingdom, will be covered. 1815, an important watershed in British and European history, is the terminal date. Eugene Rasor

[**3012**], <u>British Naval History since 1815</u>, 1990, picks up the coverage for 1815 and after.

The subject of English/British naval and maritime history is blessed with numerous professional journals and periodicals in which discussion, analysis, interpretation, revision, and products of research can be presented and discussed. These are listed in Part II., the Descriptive Lists section. As with journals and periodicals, English/British naval and maritime history can be pursued, advanced, and enthused about by participation in related associations, societies, symposia, and conferences. These are listed in Part II. **See item a.**

C. FORMAT

<u>English/British Naval History to 1815: A Guide to the Literature</u> is a historiographical-bibliographical survey. Critical analysis is an important feature. It is divided into three major sections, Part I, the Historiographical Narrative section, Part II, the Descriptive Lists section, and Part III, the Annotated Bibliography section. This historiographical-bibliographical survey will be guided by a number of principles. As suggested, the subject is extraordinary, so an additional technique will be incorporated: descriptive listing. Indeed, that will be a third section, above and beyond the usual two sections, historiographical survey and annotated bibliography. Other than that, it will be in the same format as the eleven other published and two further contracted works the author has done or is doing for Greenwood Press.

The format is presented in three parts. The annotated bibliography section contains **3988** numbered entries plus entries **3989** to **4124** attached after item **3988** in the Addendum. Each and every one of those original annotated entries is incorporated, critically analyzed, evaluated, integrated, and set in context in the historiograpical narrative section.

As noted, the moment a draft of a historiographical-bibliographical work is completed, it becomes obsolete. Inevitably, new and additional works come to the attention of the author. In the case of <u>English/British Naval History to 1815</u>, several months intervened between submission of a final draft and the acceptance of the manuscript. Only then was it possible to proceed with the final steps, the making of the Author Index and the Subject Index. So, the 136 annotated bibliographical entries in the Addendum, items numbered **3989** to **4124**, are new and additional works which came to the attention of the author in that interval of several months. It was not possible to incorporate them into Part I, the Historiographical Narrative Section. They are added in the Addendum for the purpose of making this work as up-to-date as possible.

Each of the sections depends upon the other. Because the 8 categories (**a.** through **h.**), in the descriptive lists section incorporate so many individual items that do not lend themselves to being integrated and analyzed, they will stand by themselves as a separate and additional section, complementing the narrative. The descriptive lists section further demonstrates the vast expansion of the subject, the extraordinary interest in the subject, and the wide variety of approaches and categories associated with it.

The Historiographical Narrative section incorporates critical analysis, critiques, evaluation, assessment, and integration into the overall literature. A conscious effort has been made to demonstrate analytical and qualitative judgments. In each of the chapters and subdivisions, the best, most useful, most praiseworthy works are reviewed early in the presentations, generally in some detail. Lesser complementary and supplementary works are included but with less emphasis and comment. Every one of the **3988** numbered entries in the Annotated Bibliography section is incorporated, integrated, and placed in context in the Historiographical Narrative section, and, occasionally, in the Descriptive Lists section. The exception is items **3989-4124** found in the Addendum, added after item **3988**.

Works cited in the Historiographical Narrative section, in most cases, include the name of the author followed immediately by a bracket within which is a number in **bold** print, for example, "Christopher Lloyd **[1745]**." That is then followed by the title. Titles of books are underlined in the text and in the Annotated Bibliography section. Then, a date is included. That date is the earliest date of publication. If further editions have appeared, they are listed chronologically in the Annotated Bibliography section under the number in **bold** print. An example: "Christopher Lloyd **[1745]**, The Nation and the Navy, 1954, incorporated a traditional narrative approach." That book was published in 1954 and had subsequent editions in 1961 and 1965. That latter information would be found by going to the number "**1745**" in the Annotated Bibliography section.

To avoid some repetition, most first and last dates of births-deaths and some for events have been allocated to the Annotated Bibliography section, thus, not repeated in the Historiographical Narrative section.

The Annotated Bibliography section brings together **4124** annotated entries. It is structured alphabetically so that, in most cases, the first letter of the last name of the author is the key to the entry. The Addendum is alphabetized separately. In Part II, the 8 categories, **a.** through **h.**, are structured in descriptive list form. The individual items under each category are numbered consecutively with a right-hand parenthesis only, for example, "23)." That allows maximum opportunity to display the magnitude of different items associated with English/British naval history to 1815.

D. CROSS REFERENCING AND INDEXES

Within this work, several methods of assistance to the reader are utilized. Five will be described. First, the Table of Contents is detailed with many titled subdivisions for easy access by subject, for example, about 75 titled subdivisions in the chapter covering wars, campaigns, and battles chronologically, from Roman times to the 1820s. Second, brackets are used extensively in Part I. and, when appropriate, in Part II. As noted above, every pertinent citation in the Historiographical Narrative section is designated by a bracketed numbered entry usually followed by the date of publication, all taken from Part III., the Annotated Bibliography section. The entry numbers are in **bold** print, for example, "written by Tom Pocock [**3493**], 1999" or "according to Christopher Lloyd [**1455**], 1978."

A third way of cross-referencing uses the device of **bold print: "See ___,"** presenting numbers, capital letters, and numbers, and in some cases, lower-case letters for categories in Part II, the Descriptive Lists section, from a pertinent chapter, section, subdivision and/or category where the reader can go to find further or related information or elaboration on that subject. See the table of contents. Parts I and Part II are divided into chapters, sections, subdivisions, and, in the case of Part II, categories. Examples of this cross-referencing device are: **See 4., B., 2. and d., See 18., C., 12. and m.**, or **See 20., A.** These direct the reader to that Arabic numbered chapter, capital lettered section, and Arabic numbered subsection and, also, a lower-case lettered category from Part II. The numbers within each category are designated, for example, "16)." or "6)."

The fourth method of cross-referencing is the index. The nature of this historiographical-bibliographical survey is different from that of the traditional narrative history, monograph, and biography. There are two indexes that follow this work, Author-Person and Subject. Because persons incorporated in this survey were authors, and, on occasion, subjects of works, all persons have been included in the Author-Person Index. For some listings, abbreviated titles are used instead of author names.

A fifth method of assisting the reader concerns juxtaposition. As a number of items for one subject are presented the entries are qualitatively presented, that is, the best, most scholarly works, are listed first, followed by lesser works on the same topic in the hundreds of chronological, geographical, and topical categories.

E. LIMITATIONS

There is an important limitation in attaining the objectives of maximum scope and the broadest coverage: the historiographer-bibliographer is limited to what has been published. This is not a monograph, biography, or a book of history but a historiographical-bibliographical survey of the literature. The last chapter will point out a large number of gaps and recommend further research, study, and writing, which are needed to fill those gaps.

The limitation of what and how much has been published has guided the structure of the Contents. For example, because so much has been published about Nelson and about William Bligh and the mutiny on the BOUNTY of 1789, a single chapter, "Special Emphasis," has been set aside for them. In the next chapter, "Other Personalities – Officers," organization and priority were determined by the productivity of publication, a virtual quantitative assessment, for example, great leaders such as Drake, Raleigh, Pepys, and Blake have been the subjects of numerous studies. By contrast, such leaders as Hawke, Pellew, and Collingwood have been neglected, receiving little coverage. These and others are included later in the chapter under "Miscellaneous." In a later chapter, "Exploration and Discovery," the coverage of Captain James Cook so far exceeded all else that Cook is covered early in that chapter. As suggested in the final chapter on "Gaps," deficiencies about coverage of some great leaders, including several of the famous "Band of Brothers" close to Nelson, need to be rectified.

F. FEATURES

Goals and objectives of this historiographical-bibliographical survey have be enriched and furthered by incorporation of numerous scholarly conferences, symposia, and anniversary commemorations and celebrations. Scholars convene, read and critique papers, and publish their findings. In the Annotated Bibliography section, these are cited under the name of the editor. Participants are the most prominent and expert scholars and incorporate and report on the latest research and interpretations. Examples include past events of the Nelson Decade, 1995-2005, plans and events for Trafalgar 200, the quadricentennial of the Spanish Armada, 1988, the bicentennial of the founding of Australia, and many more, all included below.

Biographies and biographical studies of great and prominent naval and maritime figures are also numerous and constitute large parts of the historiographical narrative and annotated bibliography sections. As noted above, the extent and priority of coverage are factors of how much has been published about each. Specifically, biographies and biographical studies of:

1) Horatio Nelson – over 80
2) William Bligh and the mutiny - over 60
3) Francis Drake – over 40
4) Walter Raleigh and Samuel Pepys – over 20
5) Thomas Cochrane – over 10
6) Robert Blake and all subsequent ones listed – single digits
7) John Hawkins
8) George Monck
9) William Dampier
10) George Anson
11) Edward Vernon
12) Edward Hawke
13) George Rodney
14) Richard Howe
15) John Jervis, Earl of St. Vincent
16) William Sydney Smith
17) Cuthbert Collingwood

Incorporated is a systematic search and report of Ph.D. dissertations and Master's Degree theses, representing the cutting edge of scholarly research. Included are about 200 Ph.D. dissertations and over 30 Master's Degree theses, the former being properly integrated into the literature and the theses being listed separately in Appendix I. As noted, Part II, Descriptive Lists, add detail and elaboration in an abbreviated format.

Chapter 3

General References

A. BIBLIOGRAPHIES

A place to begin research on English/British naval history or any other topic related to military and naval history is Hardin Craig [**783**], <u>A Bibliography of Encyclopedias and Dictionaries Dealing with Military, Naval, and Maritime Affairs</u>, the latest edition, 1971. Then, go to <u>The American Historical Guide to Historical Literature</u> [**64**], particularly valuable because it has been updated, 1931, 1949, 1961, and 1995; the latest editor was Mary Beth Norton, there were 27,000 entries compiled by over 200 scholar-experts, and the entries were qualitatively listed, that is, the best, most scholarly works are listed first in the hundreds of chronological, geographical, and topical categories.

For British military and naval history, the best, most extensive historiographical-bibliographical surveys were Robin Higham [**1627**], <u>A Guide to the Sources of British Military History</u>, 1971, for the Conference on British Studies, and Gerald Jordan [**1836**], <u>British Military History: A Supplement to Robin Higham's Guide to the Sources</u>, 1988. These two works contained a total of 1250 pages, describing thousands of entries. Scholar-experts wrote historiographical essays, for example, Daniel Baugh, Roger Knight, and Alan Pearsall on the Royal Navy before 1714 and Christopher Lloyd on the navy of the 18th century and on health in the navy. Broader coverage was found in another sequential set. Robert Albion [**30**], <u>Naval and Maritime History</u>, 1973, and Benjamin Labaree [**1984**], <u>A Supplement to Robert G. Albion's "Naval and Maritime History</u>," 1988, both annotated bibliographies with a total of over 7000 entries. Two older, prominent British naval historians produced bibliographies: Geoffrey Callender [**547**] for the Historical Association, 1924-1925, and George Manwaring [**2355**], 1930, reprinted in 1970. For comparison, see Anthony Bruce [**481**], <u>A Bibliography Military History</u>, 1981, covered the army up to 1660, 3280 entries.

The "prequel" to this present historiographical-bibliographical publication was Eugene Rasor [3012], British Naval History since 1815: A Guide to the Literature, published by Garland in its Military History Bibliographies series in 1990: xxi, 841 pages, 3125 bibliographical entries, 507 pages of historiographical narrative. The renowned bibliographer, Robin Higham [1627], was the general editor of that series. The bibliography was not annotated and the focus was on publications since about 1960, considered the period of the "new military history." Every one of the 3125 bibliographical entries was incorporated, critically analyzed, evaluated, compared, and integrated into the overall literature. Two differences included in the present "prequel" were annotation of the 3988 entries in the bibliography and inclusion of the literature from modern times, that is, since the 18th century. In "Historical Background" (3012, pp. 7-12), a number of "pre-1815" works of note were introduced, for example, works of Kenneth Andrews [104-117], David Quinn [2973-2989], G.V. Scammell [3233-3238], Jeremy Black [327-336], Marcus Rediker [3037], N.A.M. Rodger [3103-3117], Roger Morriss [2566-2576], and Daniel Baugh [237-242]. Rasor [3010-3017] has also published similar historiographical-bibliographical, reference works on naval subjects, all for Greenwood Press. Most pertinent for this volume was The Spanish Armada of 1588: Historiography and Annotated Bibliography, vol. 9 of Bibliographies of Battles and Leaders series, 1993, xviii, 278 pp., 1125 annotated entries. The Falklands/Malvinas Campaign: A Bibliography, vol. 6 of Bibliographies of Battles and Leaders series, 1991, xvi, 196 pp., 554 annotated entries, included coverage beginning in the 18th century. Also, there was The Battle of Jutland: A Bibliography, vol. 7 of Bibliographies of Battles and Leaders series, 1991, xiv, 178 pp., 538 annotated entries; and, most recently, The TITANIC: Historiography and Annotated Bibliography, vol. 53 of Bibliographies and Indexes in World History series, 2001, xvi, 238 pp., 674 annotated entries, a total of 930 items described.

Four books described and surveyed naval publications and libraries of the early modern period: Maurice Cockle [689], Bibliography of Military Books Up to 1642 and of Contemporary Foreign Works, 1900, introduced by Charles Oman; Harry Skallerup [3335], Books Afloat and Ashore: A History of Books, Libraries and Reading among Seamen during the Age of Sail, 1974, applicable to America; Thomas Adams [18, English Maritime Books: Relating to Ships and Their Construction and Operation at Sea Printed before 1801, 1993, listing 3800 items, and John Parker [2756], Books to Build an Empire: A Bibliographical History of English Overseas Interests to 1620, 1966, listing 267 titles.

More generally, for medieval warfare, there were two recent contributions: Everett Crosby [807], Medieval Warfare: A Bibliographical Guide, 2000, and David Nicolle [2645], Medieval Warfare Source Book, 1996, a second volume projected. For the 17th and early 18th centuries, Colin Steele [3436] surveyed the bibliography of Iberian writing, which described the New World and was then translated into English. Translators included Samuel

Purchas, Richard Hakluyt, and John Stevens. The objective was to stimulate exploration and colonization. Alan Day [**886**], Search for the Northwest Passage, 1986, was an annotated bibliography, 5160 entries covering exploration, geography, and history.

As might be expected, the Wars of the French Revolution and Napoleon were well covered: Donald Horward [**1678**], Napoleonic Military History: A Bibliography, 1986, in Garland's Military History Bibliographies series, vol. 19, with 7131 items; two by Ronald Caldwell [**544, 545**], The Era of the French Revolution, 2 vols., 1990, with 48,000 entries, and The Era of Napoleon, 2 vols., 1991; Leigh Whaley [**3823**], The Impact of Napoleon, 1800-1815: An Annotated Bibliography, 1997, 480 annotated entries; Jack Meyer [**2503**], An Annotated Bibliography of the Napoleonic Era, 1987, 1754 entries, all books, and Clive Emsley [**1044**], The Longman Companion to Napoleonic Europe, 1993, the latter more of a reference guide. Whaley counted over 400,000 works on Napoleon.

Several bibliographies covered the obvious leaders. Three were for Horatio Nelson: Leonard Cowie [**780**], Lord Nelson: A Bibliography, 1990, in Bibliographies of British Statesmen series, vol. 7, with 1344 entries; an older one, John Knox Laughton [**2042**], The Bibliography of Nelson, 1894, an enormous compilation, and an article by Tom Pocock [**2867**], "Lord Nelson: A Selected Bibliography," 1990, covering about 200 biographies. Benjamin Draper [**962**] compiled a manuscript version, Drake Bibliography, 1979, with 600 annotated entries; two for Walter Raleigh, Christopher Armitage [**136**], 1987, with 1967 entries, and T.N. Brushfield [**491**], 1886, reprinted in 1968, 330 annotated entries, and two for James Cook, both originally published in 1928 with updated editions: Maurice Holmes [**1659**], Captain James Cook, RN: A Bibliographical Excursion and M.K. Beddie [**269**], Bibliography of Captain James Cook, RN, F.R.S., Circumnavigator, the latter with 4824 entries, Cook being especially popular in Australia. Seven bibliographies covered prominent writers associated with the navy: John Hattendorf [**1552**], A Bibliography of the Works of Alfred Thayer Mahan, 1993; P.N. Furbank [**1216**], A Critical Bibliography of Daniel Defoe, 1998; Philip Gosse [**1330**], A Bibliography of the Works of Captain Charles Johnson, 1927; Theodore Ehrsam [**1026**], A Bibliography of Joseph Conrad, 1969; Robert Madison [**2324**], an article on James Fenimore Cooper, 1997; A.E. Cunningham [**830**], Patrick O'Brian, 1994, and Michael Sadlier [**3204**], an article on Frederick Marryat, among others, 1922.

Bibliographies of events included Kenneth Andrews [**110**], an article on English voyages to the Caribbean in the late 16th century, 1974; W. Calvin Dickinson [**929**], The War of Spanish Succession, 1702-1713: A Selected Bibliography, 1996, with 808 annotated entries; three about the War of 1812: one by Dwight Smith [**3357**], The War of 1812: An Annotated Bibliography, 1985, with 1400 entries, and two by John Fredriksen [**1186, 1187**], Free Trade and Sailors' Rights: A Bibliography of the War of 1812, 1997, with over 6000 entries, and <u>War of 1812: Eyewitness Accounts: An Annotated Bibliography</u>, 1997, with 850 sources; Victor Crittenden [**804**], <u>A Bibliography of the First Fleet</u>, 1982, with 966 items, and Robert Bergerson [**304**], <u>Vinland Bibliography</u>, 1997. Significant for his virtual obsession was L.G. Carr Laughton [**2056**], "A Bibliography of Nautical Dictionaries," 1911; see elsewhere. In the 1980s, Walter Minchinton [**2520**] published <u>History of the Northern Seas: A Select Bibliography of Works</u>. The maritime journal, <u>Mariner's Mirror</u>, publishes an annual bibliography, edited by M. Patrick [**2379**].

B. NAVAL ENCYCLOPEDIAS

Two massive, multi-volume publication projects are in progress and are pertinent and contributory to English/British naval history. Spencer Tucker [**3656**], Biggs Professor of Military History at Virginia Military Institute, was general editor of <u>The Encyclopedia of Naval Warfare</u>, 3 hardback volumes, over 1500 articles by scholar-experts, projected to be published by ABC-Clio in 2002. John Hattendorf [**1566**], Ernest King Professor of Maritime History at the U.S. Naval War College, was general editor of <u>The Oxford Companion of Maritime History</u>, 4 vols., projected for 2005, seen as broader in scope and more extensive than the Tucker work. It will be divided by sections; individual sections under directors, for example, Roger Knight, Andrew Lambert, N.A.M. Rodger, and Glyn Williams. British naval history will be featured in both works. A third publication was completed: Anthony Bruce [**482**], <u>An Encyclopedia of Naval History</u>, 1998, with over 1000 articles.

<u>Sea Battles: A Reference Guide</u> by Michael Sanderson [**3217**] presented 250 naval battles in alphabetical order preceded by a chronology; coverage was from 494 BC to 1944. The first pertinent one was a battle off Dover in 1217; others highlighted included Sluys, Winchelsea, Brest, Spithead, and those of the three Dutch wars. Illustrations were exclusively from the NMM. Two other encyclopedias were Graham Blackburn [**339**], <u>Illustrated Encyclopedia of Ships, Boats, Vessels and Other Water-Borne Craft</u>, 1978, describing with illustrations a variety of types of craft, "Advice Boat" to "Zulu," a Scottish fishing boat, and H.B. Mason [**2454**], <u>Encyclopedia of Ships and Shipping</u>, 1908. The contribution of Oxford University Press continued: Peter Kemp [**1866**], <u>The Oxford Companion to Ships and the Sea</u>, 1988, with 3700 entries, and Jonathan Raban [**2993**], <u>The Oxford Book of the Sea</u>, 1992, an anthology. Selections included Hakluyt, Purchas, Defoe, Anson, Falconer, Cooper, Dana, and Melville.

C. NAVAL BIOGRAPHIES

Naval biography was covered well for the late 18th and early 19th centuries. Officers only were included. Most extensive, under these limitations, was William O'Bryne [**2684**], A Naval Biographical Dictionary, 2 vols., 1849, reprinted in 2000, touting coverage of "every living officer in Her Majesty's Navy" at that time. James Ralfe [**3003**], The Naval Biography of Great Britain, 4 vols., incorporated memoirs of naval officers during the reign of George III, 1760-1820, thirty per volume, for example, Rodney, Howe, Hood, Duncan, St. Vincent, and Nelson. These were published in the 1820s. John Marshall [**2417**], published Royal Naval Biography, 4 vols., there being numerous editions. Explanations for these and other memoirs were found in George Egerton [**1021**], Political Memoir: Essays on the Politics of Memory, 1994. A chapter, "Rulers of the Waves," cited a series, for example, Phineas Pett, inevitably, Pepys, John Charnock, Marshall, Ralfe, and O'Bryne. The prolific writer of naval biography, John Knox Laughton [**2055**], published Studies in Naval History: Biographies of Admirals, Naval Administrators, Naval Architects, and Naval Historians in the "Dictionary of National Biography," 1887. Somewhat related, both covering the age of sail, were an essay by William Hunt [**1737**] on nautical autobiography and R.C. Bell [**284**], describing diaries.

Naval biography was incorporated in the massive project in progress, The New Dictionary of National Biography [**2631**], forthcoming from Oxford University Press. H.C.G. Matthew, the original editor, died in 1999 and was replaced by Brian Harrison. All entries of The Dictionary of National Biography [**930**], 1911-1996, 22 vols. plus 1st-11th supplements, c.36,500 biographical essays, c.45,000 pages, 32 million words, were to be rewritten plus new essays will be added, especially of neglected women. 2004 was the anticipated date of publication of the New DNB, a massive undertaking described in an article by Harrison [**1533**]. 9500 contributors and a staff of 50 employees were involved. A CD-ROM version [**930**] of the original was published in 2000. As noted above, British naval historian John Knox Laughton personally wrote over 900 naval biographical essays for the original. Authors in the process of rewriting agreed that he had his own agenda and his essays were biased and neglected crucial aspects of the lives of those about whom he wrote, especially non-naval factors.

The Naval Chronicle [**2605**], 1799-1818, published twice a year, incorporated mini-biographies of British naval officers, including a short autobiography by Horatio Nelson [**2620**].

D. CHRONOLOGIES

Specialized as to region but covering all of modern time was Wars of the Americas: A Chronology of Armed Conflict in the New World, 1492 to the Present by David Marley [2393]. Divided into eight chronological parts, this useful reference guide presented hundreds of conflicts in a large, encyclopedic format.

The Royal Navy Day by Day by R.E.A. Shrubb [3312] was an extensive, informative, handy publication stressing naval heritage and anniversaries. Coverage was 700 years of British naval history, a day-by-day diary commemorating the major events and personalities. Mini-biographies appeared on appropriate days, battles and technical advances were noted, and 440 events were illustrated.

E. STATISTICS

Michael Clodfelter [663], Warfare and Armed Conflicts, 2 vols., 1992, was a statistical reference guide to casualties, individual persons and military and naval units, in warfare, 1618-1991. Examples in table form:
Beachy Head, July 1690: English-Dutch, 56 ships, 12 lost, French,78 ships, 0 lost;
La Hogue-Barfleur, May 1692: English-Dutch, 99 ships, 0 lost, French, 44 ships, 15 lost;
Quiberon Bay, November 1759: British, 23 ships, 2 lost, French, 21 ships, 7 lost;
Camperdown, October 1797: British, 16, 0 lost, Dutch, 15 ships, 9 lost;
the Nile, August 1798: British, 13 ships, 0 lost, French, 13 ships, 11 lost, and
Trafalgar, October 1805: British, 27 ships, 0 lost, French-Spanish, 33 ships, 20 lost.

F. DISSERTATIONS AND THESES

Scholarly productivity originally began with academic requirements and attaining proper status and qualification. The initiation, the cutting edge of academic endeavors has traditionally been at two levels, a lower level progressing to the highest, the ultimate, level. The Master's Degree thesis and the Doctor of Philosophy dissertation are incorporated in the Annotated Bibliography section as "Ph.D. diss" and in Appendix I. as "MA thesis." The dissertation has been described as "ultimate" because, in the ancient tradition of "masterpiece" for guild status, the dissertation must be unique, something never researched and covered. It must be an original contribution, registered as such. Qualified readers then certify it.

This work will recognize the importance of these scholarly endeavors. Over thirty pertinent Master's Degree theses are listed in Appendix I. Ph.D. dissertations have been incorporated in the proper place, in alphabetical order by the last name of the author in the Annotated Bibliography section and integrated into the Historiographical Narrative section at the appropriate place, always identified as a dissertation. About 200 dissertations have been cited.

Since Master's Degree theses have not been integrated into the text, a few examples from the list in Appendix I. will be reviewed. Richard Blake, 1980, researched aspects of religion in the RN, something much needed. **See 22.** This was noted as a "gap" in the literature. Another gap about religion and the navy also concerned chaplains, the subject of the thesis of J. Curry, 1955. E.A. Buchanan, 1996, wrote of maritime Scotland, 10,000 BC to 1018 AD. The great economic historian, Eleanor Carus Wilson [**589**], 1926, wrote about the early overseas trade of Bristol in the 15th century. Philip MacDougall [**2240-2244**], 1983, followed up his study of Chatham Dockyard with scholarly publications. Michael Steer, 1971, wrote on that decisive activity, the blockade of Brest.

Chapter 4

Resource Centers

Best entree to research and resource centers would be Janet Foster [**1163**], British Archives: A Guide to Archive Resources in the United Kingdom, 1995. Information and addresses of Record Offices, National Libraries, museums, universities, and colleges were in 1200 entries organized alphabetically by towns. For the general topic, go to Rita Bryon [**498**], Maritime Information: A Guide to Libraries and Sources of Information in the United Kingdom, 1993, sponsored by the Maritime Information Association. Included were 800 institutions, their addresses, telephone and fax numbers, and instructions on access.

A. OFFICIAL ARCHIVES AND DEPOSITORIES

1. The Public Record Office

The first archive to consult for naval and maritime history of England/Britain was the Public Record Office, PRO, since 1997, centrally located at Kew, about ten miles out from the center of London. All government records were housed and were available there. Indicative of its importance, several publications described it, its holdings, and its services: Guide to the Public Record Office [**1420**], a microfiche publication, 1999; John Cantwell [**571**], The Public Record Office, 1838-1958, 1991; G.H. Martin [**2433**], The Records of the Nation, 1990; Anne Crawford [**790**], "The Public Record Office," 2000; Montagu Giuseppi [**1289**], Guide to the Contents of the Public Record Office, 3 vols., 1923-1969; J.H. Collingridge [**706**], Catalogue of an Exhibition of Naval Records at the Public Record Office, 1950, and under Great Britain, Public Record Office [**1373-1377**], Summary of Records, 2 vols., 1962-1969. Its origins were traced to the PRO Act of 1838; it was the "repository of legal memory and fount of historical knowledge" of Great Britain. An online catalogue was available in 2002. Specifically for Admiralty records, again go to Great Britain, Public Record Office, and search for List of Admiralty Records, Admiralty Digests: Heads and Sections, and Admiralty Digests (IND Numbers by Year). N.A.M. Rodger [**3104, 3112**], a former official at the PRO and currently writing the quasi-official history of the navy of Britain, has two reference aids for the researcher: The Armada in the Public Records, 1988, and Naval Records for Genealogists, 1989. Related was another aid for genealogists: Christopher Watts [**3793**], My Ancestor Was a Merchant Seaman: How Can I Find Out More about Him?, 1991. Sources suggested were tax, legal, trade, port books, register of ships, Trinity House, and Lloyd's of London. David Dobson [**943**], Scottish Maritime Records, 1600-1850: A Guide for Family Historians, 1996, was a guide to records for genealogists in Scotland; topics included the Royal Navy, merchant marine, fishing, whaling, smuggling, pirates, privateering, and court records.

2. The British Library

Formerly the British Museum Library, the British Library recently moved several blocks to a new, purpose-built facility near King's Cross Station.

Patricia Fara [**1075**], 1997, described the origins of the British Museum, first opened in 1759, the first in Europe owned for and by the public. The Royal Society oversaw its development, especially its president, Joseph Banks. **See 17., E.** P.R. Harris [**1530**], A History of the British Museum Library, 1998, described the library of record for Britain. There was a massive collection of printed books and an enormous collection of manuscripts. Notable was The Harleian Miscellany: Or, a Collection of Scarce, Curious, and Entertaining Pamphlets and Tracts, as Well in Manuscript as in Print, Found in the Late Earl of Oxford's Library [**1517**], 8 vols., acquired in the late 18th and early 19th centuries by the British Museum Library. This famous collection came from the library of Robert and Edward Harley, Earls of Oxford and included pertinent materials from the 16th century, for example, the marriage of Mary Tudor and Philip of Spain and the Spanish Armada.

3. The National Archives of the United States and the Library of Congress

A complete survey of archival records of all agencies of the U.S. Government was found in The Guide to Federal Records in the National Archives of the United States [**1419**], 3 vols., 1996, 2500 pp. Pertinent information on English/British naval history was housed here. Equally massive were the collections of the Library of Congress, the library of record for the United States, Washington, DC.

4. Institutions of Higher Education

British institutions of higher education have traditionally facilitated advancement of British naval history. That continued, but the individual contributions have altered. In August 1999, the University of London announced appointment of a chair, the professorship of Naval History, the first such designated appointment for over half a century; Oxford and Cambridge once having such chairs which lapsed. The first holder of the London chair, professor in the War Studies Department, King's College, was Andrew Lambert [**2001-2009**], the prolific and acclaimed British naval historian.

Other British universities stressing naval and maritime studies and achieving impressive results were Exeter, Hull, Greenwich, Bristol, Plymouth, and St. Andrews. All have academic centers and degree programmes focusing on these areas.

The Institute of Historical Research has endured and contributed. On the occasion of its seventy-fifth anniversary, Steven Smith [**3370**] in an article and Debra Birch [**321**] in a book published accounts. A multi-storey reference library providing a variety of services such as publications, seminars, courses, and special projects, the Institute of Historical Research was located in the Senate House of the University of London, adjacent to the British Museum. There were 4000 members and 500 seminars a year. It sponsored the annual Anglo-American Historians Conference; in July 2001, the 71st conference, the theme was "The Sea."

B. LIBRARIES

Peter Fox [**1174**] in a book of 1998 described the history and collections of the Cambridge University Library, a central, massive, major university library at Cambridge. Its holdings in current and bound periodicals were particularly impressive. Other university libraries included London, Oxford, Edinburgh, Exeter, East Anglia, Greenwich, Hull, Aberdeen, and St. Andrews in Britain.

Admiralty Library
The old Admiralty Library has moved to its own separate building at the Portsmouth Naval Base and has ties to the Royal Naval Museum there.

Bodleian Library
This ancient resource center of Oxford University holds numerous primary, secondary, and manuscript sources. The famous Oxford professor-historian, C.H. Firth [**1104**], described "Papers Relating to the Navy in the Bodleian Library," 1913, for example, the Rawlinson Papers acquired in 1755, which contained log books and naval journals which had belonged to Samuel Pepys.

John Carter Brown Library, Providence, RI
In America, on the campus grounds of Brown University, Providence, RI, but
not officially part of the university, was the John Carter Brown Library where a
unique and massive collection of materials was housed, all about early maritime
history. Maritime History: A Preliminary Hand-List of the Collection in the John
Carter Brown Library, Brown University [2383], 1985, described the holdings in
1176 entries. Subject sections included navigation, sailing directions, shipping,
health, piracy, shipwrecks, navies, warfare, dictionaries, bibliographies, and, a
special area, Sir Francis Drake.

Pepysian Library, Magdalene College, Cambridge
A unique resource collection was originally accumulated by Samuel Pepys
[2815-2818] who intended to write a major history of the Royal Navy. Much of
the material was what would be later considered official and placed in the PRO.
It was now held at Pepys' college at the University of Cambridge, Magdalene
College. First, there was Catalogue of the Pepys Library of Magdalene College
[2815] originally arranged by Pepys himself and in the process of publication,
projected for at least 7 vols. Second was J.R. Tanner [3563], A Descriptive
Catalogue of the Naval MSS. in the Pepysian Library, 5 vols., a publication of
the NRS. The library consisted of 3000 volumes. It has been described as "an
inexhaustible mine of miscellaneous information about sea affairs."

Royal United Services Institution Library
An older institution, which has dealt with military and naval history matters for
almost two centuries, was the Royal United Services Institution and its library,
located at Whitehall Yard in London. Shelford Bidwell [316] described its
history and services.

Lloyd's of London
Perhaps surprisingly, Lloyd's of London was the site of an important, specialized
resource center, in addition to its role as registrar and insurer of maritime
shipping and intelligence worldwide since its founding in 1691; Lloyd's List
since 1734. Elaboration of those details was found in Antony Brown [470],
Hazard Unlimited: The Story of Lloyd's of London, 1978, Rupert Jarvis [1794],
"Sources for the History of Ships and Shipping," 1958, and Frank Murphy
[2586], a short article, 1967. Lloyd's maintained a unique feature as described in
detail by Warren Dawson [885], its librarian, The Nelson Collection at Lloyd's:
A Description of the Nelson Relics and the Transcript of the Autograph Letters
and Documents of Nelson and His Circle and the Other Naval Papers of
Nelson's Period, 1932. The Nelson Room was a strong-room located in the
Lloyd's Building since 1931. In the 1790s, Lloyd's presented a silver plate
service in honor of his victories at the Nile and Copenhagen. That has
subsequently been obtained by Lloyd's and expanded to include swords, medals,

telescopes, Trafalgar vases, portraits, letters, and documents from Nelson, his captains, and Admiral Rodney.

Archives General de Simancas
Spanish encouragement and impetus to expand research and publication among its holdings related to the Spanish Armada during the time of the quadricentennial, 1988, was productive and successful. Catalogos del Archivo General de Simancas [**594**] was an instance.

C. MUSEUMS

Maritime museums were important centers of interest and research. Many incorporated libraries, reading rooms, manuscript collections, maps, and prints. First, go to Martin Evans [**1059**], Maritime Museums: A Guide to the Collections and Museum Ships in Britain and Ireland, 1998, Keith Wheatley [**3824**], National Maritime Museum Guide to Maritime Britain, 1991, and Robert Smith [**3366**], The Naval Institute Guide to Maritime Museums of North America, 1990. Martin introduced 250 maritime museums and 400 historic ships, all open to the public. Wheatley divided Britain into ten regions, describing hundreds of places and institutions of interest, for example, docks, dockyards, preserved ships, replicas, and museums. Smith presented a directory and information on locations of 300 museums, for example, Vancouver and Key West. The National Maritime Museum, Greenwich and the Royal Naval Museum, Portsmouth, were among the sponsors of the Nelson Decade [**2624**] and Trafalgar 200.

For maximum effectiveness and efficiency, announcement has been made creating the Maritime Collection Initiative of the United Kingdom, UKMCI. It was an institution which coordinated collections and designated "lead" museums: Aberdeen Maritime Museum for the oil and gas industry; the National Fisheries Heritage Centre, Grimsby, for fishing; the MARY ROSE Trust for maritime archaeology; the Merseyside Maritime Museum for North Atlantic liner trade and emigration; the National Maritime Museum, Greenwich, for navigation and exploration, and National Maritime Museum, Cornwall, in Falmouth, for modern environment issues.

1. The National Maritime Museum, Greenwich

In the spring of 1999, Queen Elizabeth II and Prince Philip officially opened the large new entrance gallery of the National Maritime Museum, NMM, of Greenwich. It was located in part of the old royal palace at Greenwich and included the famous Greenwich Observatory, the location of the zero meridian, and the exquisite Queen's House. Since the 1920s, NMM has conducted an expansive programme as museum, educational, media, research and astronomical institutions. Within a stone's throw was the Millennium Dome, not attached to NMM, where exhibitions were held. There was an extensive collection of books, periodicals, prints, and manuscripts held in the Reading Room and related offices. Kevin Littlewood [2147], Of Ships and Stars: Maritime Heritage and the Founding of the National Maritime Museum, Greenwich, 1998; Basil Greenhill [1390], The National Maritime Museum, 1982; K.F. Lindsay-MacDougall [2139], A Guide to the Manuscripts at the National Maritime Museum, 1960; R.J.B. Knight [1963], Guide to the Manuscripts in the National Maritime Museum, 2 vols., 1977-1980; Michael Sanderson [3216], National Maritime Museum Catalogue of the Library, 2 vols., 1968-1970, and National Maritime Museum [2604], Catalogue of the Library of the National Maritime Museum, 5 vols., 1971, were pertinent publications. The initiative for founding the museum came from the SNR. Important personalities of its history included Geoffrey Callender [547-557], R.C. Anderson [79-98], C. Northcote Parkinson [2759-2774], and Basil Greenhill [1385-1392]. The NMM sponsored a project, which sought out British naval papers available in North America, the work of Roger Morriss [2571], originally suggested by John Hattendorf. 116 libraries responded positively, describing individual holdings, for example, Duke, Michigan, Yale, Harvard, JCB at Brown, the Folger, the Library of Congress, and the Peabody and the Mystic Seaport Museums. In all, there were 1190 items.

2. The Royal Naval Museum

The Royal Naval Museum at Portsmouth within the Portsmouth Naval Base also was undergoing expansion and provided impressive services. A new combined naval-Admiralty library was in a nearby, refurbished building. It has sponsored an ambitious publication programme. Matthew Sheldon [3297], Guide to the Manuscript Collection of the Royal Naval Museum, 1997, described one of its services.

3. Other Maritime Museums

The Merseyside Maritime Museum of Liverpool also rated commendation. J.G. Read [3033] described its holdings. The institution included ports, archives, and a Maritime Records Center.

Christopher Alexander [37] described the unique MARY ROSE Museum sponsored by the MARY ROSE Trust. There the MARY ROSE was displayed, having been raised after spectacular achievement of a nautical archaeology project in 1982; MARY ROSE sank in 1545. Thousands of extraordinary artifacts were housed in the nearby MARY ROSE Museum, all within the Portsmouth Naval Base.

David Goddard [1305] described the less successful Exeter Maritime Museum, which focused on working boats and was sponsored by the

International Sailing Craft Association. It opened in 1969 with 23 boats on display in a harbor at Exeter.

In the United States, a notable maritime museum was the Mariners' Museum [2380] of Newport News, VA., founded in 1930. A folio-size guide described its history, holdings, and fabulous location that included a lake and fish collection. The Mariners' Museum was the site where a major project of nautical archaeology is being conducted: artifacts, including tons of iron and an early steam engine, from the expedition on the USS MONITOR, sunk 31 December 1862 off the Outer Banks of North Carolina, were being identified, analyzed, and preserved. Plans were ongoing to create a USS MONITOR Center at the Museum. Other exhibitions and topics such as Nelson and TITANIC have been featured. See 18., A.

Mystic Seaport Museum, Salem, MA. and its associated Frank E. Munson Institute of American Maritime Studies were described by Jennifer Hardy [1511] and Benjamin Labaree [1983]. Guide to the Oral History Collections at Mystic Seaport Museum, 1992, by Fred Calabretta [541], catalogued 218 oral history interviews and included the Munson Lectures, 1955-1972.

D. INSTITUTIONS, ORGANIZATIONS, ASSOCIATIONS, AND SOCIETIES

British naval history has been pursued and advanced by associations, societies, symposia, and conferences. See item b.

1. The Navy Records Society

The Navy Records Society was a premier institution leading in the development of English/British naval history studies and research. The Navy Records Society, NRS, was founded in 1893 by a number of prominent leaders in the rising movement for naval history, for example, John Knox Laughton [2041-2055]. Beginning in 1894, NRS published annual volumes of collections of primary documents and papers related to English/British naval history, volume # 142 being a recent one and others are forthcoming. These were hefty tomes demonstrating the essence of historiography and historical research, publication of primary sources. See Appendix II. In 1993, The Centenary of the Navy Records Society was published by A.B. Sainsbury [3208]. At the same time the Centenary Volume, British Naval Documents, 1204-1960, edited by John Hattendorf [1553], R.J.B. Knight, A.W.H. Pearsall, N.A.M. Rodger and Geoffrey Till, was published, volume 131, almost 1200 pages, a total of 535 documents incorporated, organized in the same six topical categories over seven chronological periods, 1204-1960. Examples of the topical categories were introduction, strategy, operations, administration, weapons, and personnel. It was dedicated to the Lord High Admiral, Queen Elizabeth II.

On occasion, five times thus far, a volume, The Naval Miscellany, has been published by the NRS: 1. John Knox Laughton [**2048**], 1902, vol. 20; 2. Laughton [**2049**] again, 1912, vol. 40; 3. W.G. Perrin [**2828**], 1928, vol. 63; 4. Christopher Lloyd [**2164**], 1952, vol. 92, and N.A.M. Rodger [**3111**], 1984, vol. 125. As the title noted, items were various, for example, letters of Vernon and Nelson, a letter from a mutineer at the Nore, instructions to James Cook, a report on the bombardment of Copenhagen in 1807, letters between Nelson and Hood, instructions from Philip II to the commander of the Armada, a treatise on management of the Royal Dockyards, and an account of naval landings on the coast of France in 1758.

The pertinent volumes of Publications of the Navy Records Society were incorporated in the appropriate place in this Historiographical Narrative section. All volumes were listed in proper alphabetical order using the last name of the editor in the Annotated Bibliography section; each entry of a volume of NRS was preceded by "[NRS ___]," the blank being the volume number, #1 through # 140s. **See Appendix II**. A complete listing in numerical order, # 1 through # 140s, plus some forthcoming volumes is included. Most of the Publications of the Navy Records Society were pertinent to the years before 1815. A few were applicable for the period after 1815: all authors were editors; this listing was in alphabetical order: J. Beeler [**273**], Milne Papers, forthcoming; E. Grove [**1410**], Defeat of Attack on Shipping, # 137; two by P. Halpern [**1460, 1461**], Keyes Papers, # 117, 121, and 122 and Royal Navy in the Mediterranean, # 126; P. Kemp [**1867**], Papers of John Fisher, #s 102 and 106; Nicholas Lambert [**2009**], The Submarine Service, 1900-1918, 2001, # 142; E. Lumby [**2203**], Policy in the Mediterranean, # 115; T. Patterson [**2790**], Jellicoe Papers, #s 108 and 111; B.Ranft [**3006**], Beatty Papers, #s 128 and 132; S. Roskill [**3148**], Documents of the Naval Air Service, # 113; W. Rowbotham [**3154**], Naval Brigades in Indian Mutiny, # 87; three by M.Simpson [**3323, 3324, 3325**], Anglo-American Naval Relations, # 130, Cunningham Papers, # 140, and Somerville Papers, # 134; two by D. Smith [**3354, 3355**], Russian War, #s 83, 84, and 85 and Second China Wars, # 95; J. Sumida [**3517**], Pollen Papers, # 124; D. Syrett [**3539**], Battle of the Atlantic, # 139, and N. Tracy [**3637**], Collective Naval Defence, # 136.

2. The Society for Nautical Research

The Society for Nautical Research has focused on different approaches from NRS. The two organizations complement each other. The Society for Nautical Research, SNR, was founded in 1910. Three articles in Mariner's Mirror, the journal founded and sponsored by the SNR, described its origins and activities: Alan Moore [**2533**] in 1955, R.C. Anderson [**84**] in 1961, and A.B. Sainsbury [**3209**] in 1994. As early as 1904, Leonard Carr Laughton [**2056-**

2066], son of John Knox Laughton, Michael Oppenheim [**2710-2712**], and others discussed formation of a nautical antiquarian society. A longtime objective of L.C. Laughton [**2064**] was creation of the universal nautical dictionary, yet to be fulfilled. He was so dedicated to that end that he wanted to call SNR the Jal Society, named for Augustin Jal [**1772-1774**], the French formulator of an important nautical dictionary in the mid-19th century. **See 19.** A committee was formed and the SNR began in 1910, the first issue of Mariner's Mirror [**2378**], then to be monthly, came out in 1911 with Laughton as editor. Clements Markham [**2384-2385**] hosted the first Annual General Meeting, about 30 attending. It was the SNR in the 1920s that was most instrumental in saving HMS VICTORY and its "Save the VICTORY" campaign has maintained that historic ship over the decades. **See 8., A., 6.** Mariner's Mirror [**2378**], now a quarterly, has remained the best journal of and for naval and maritime history in the world. Michael Duffy [**971-978**] of the University of Exeter and Richard Harding [**1491**-1496] of the University of Westminster were recent editors. The SNR launched the initiative leading to creation of the National Maritime Museum, Greenwich. Another product of the SNR was the ongoing Bethel Watercraft Project, the work of John Bethel [**312**], a register and description of all watercraft.

3. Other Associations

Mention of Augustin Jal called to mind other institutions dedicated to famous naval personalities of the past. Two were the Nelson Society and the 1805 Club. Their objectives were to perpetuate the achievements and memory of Horatio Nelson. Richard Cavendish [**599**] described the Nelson Society, founded in 1981, which currently has about 500 members. It sponsors a quarterly journal, The Nelson Dispatch, annual lectures, and an annual commemoration service at 1:25 PM, 21 October, on the quarterdeck of HMS VICTORY, the time and place where Nelson was shot. It was a major sponsor of the Nelson Decade [**2624**] and Trafalgar 200. **See 8., A., 7.**

A separate society, the 1805 Club, has formed. Its focus has been preservation of Nelson-related monuments and graves. Its publication was Trafalgar Chronicle: Year Book of the 1805 Club.

Similarly, there was the Hakluyt Society, founded in 1846, like the NRS, publisher of volumes of primary sources on exploration and maritime achievements in the tradition of its namesakes, the two Richard Hakluyts of the 16th and early 17th centuries. R.C. Bridges [**438**], Compassing the Vaste Globe of the Earth: Studies in the History of the Hakluyt Society, 1996, commemorated the 150th anniversary of its founding. **See 17., A.** Publications of the Hakluyt Society, over 300 scholarly, primary works on voyages and travel have been published: 100 volumes in the first series, to 1898, 181 volumes in the second series, to 1995, and 44 volumes in the Extra series. Recent presidents have been Glyndwr Williams, D.B. Quinn, and Harold Smedley.

The Pepys Club perpetuated the memory and achievements of Samuel Pepys, the diarist and great administrator of the Royal Navy in the 17th century.

Other societies of mention were the Royal Society, the Royal Geographical Society, the Institute of Nautical Archaeology, the Nautical Archaeology Society, the International Congress of Maritime Museums, the Maritime History Group of the Memorial University of Newfoundland, the Maritime Historical Studies Centre of the University of Hull, the Maritime History Institute of the University of Greenwich, the Munson Institute of Maritime History of the Mystic Seaport Museum, the Naval Dockyards Society, and U.S. Naval Institute. **See item b.**

E. CONFERENCES, SYMPOSIA, EXHIBITIONS, AND <u>FESTSCHRIFT</u>

English/British naval and maritime history has been celebrated, reviewed, and advanced in a variety of venues and special publications, one-time and in series.

Conferences and symposia can be as a general interest, usually scholarly, event or, on occasion, in a series every year or every other year, or celebrating or commemorating special occasions. Examples of all of these will be presented. The heartbeat of the profession can be found among these products.

One-time conferences and celebrations of anniversaries occurred routinely. Their published proceedings can be found throughout this publication. Examples of ongoing ones were the Naval History Symposium, held every odd-numbered year at the U.S. Naval Academy, Annapolis, MD. Two others have periodic meetings in Britain and elsewhere: the Anglo-French Naval Historians Conference and the Anglo-Dutch Maritime Historians Conference.

Exhibitions, usually sponsored by museums or libraries, have been another way to celebrate special persons and events. Often, a catalogue, generally a detailed and scholarly undertaking, accompanied and supported the exhibition.

Finally, students, colleagues, and friends of outstanding scholars join, present, and publish academic papers in honor of or to memorialize that scholar, the German term, <u>festschrift</u>, describing the process. As well, here can be found the best products of the profession.

It is impossible to describe, to even list, all of the published papers and essays in these collections. Dozens of them have been cited throughout this Historiographical Narrative section. Hundreds have been included in the Annotated Bibliography section.

To illustrate the importance, the scholarly contributions, the extent, and the depth of these collections, examples will be presented, seemingly an arbitrary process. Others are described in later chapters.

In most cases, the editor is listed as author.

1. The Naval History Symposium

Since the mid-1970s, the Department of History of the U.S. Naval Academy, Annapolis, MD, has sponsored an international naval history conference every odd-numbered years, for example, number 14 was 23-25 September 1999 and number 15 was scheduled for 12-14 September 2001, but was cancelled after events of 11 September. It is anticipated that number 16 and number 17 will occur in September or October, 2003 and 2005. The proceedings of these symposia have been published. What is known about details of these symposia is as follows.

Naval History Symposium: as scheduled: examples of pertinent papers and published articles in the proceedings are included.

[NHS 1] dir: Arnold Shapack [**3290**]. Summary of papers published, 1973.

[NHS 2] No information.

[NHS 3] dir: Robert Love, proceedings published, 1980.
27-28 October 1977.
R. Seager on Mahan
Eugene Rasor on manning in the RN
A.Z. Freeman on "Wooden Walls" during the reign of Edward I
Ronald Pollitt on Elizabethan naval administration

[NHS 4] dir: Craig Symonds [**3533**], proceedings published, 1979.
25-26 October 1979.
N.A.M. Rodger on British naval thought
Rudy Bauss on Rio as a strategic base in the 18th century
Scott Harmon on the USN and suppression of the slave trade
Timothy Runyan on merchantmen as men-of-war in medieval England
Carl Christie on the RN and the Walcheren expedition of 1809

[NHS 5] No information.

[NHS 6] dir: Daniel Masterman [**2461**], proceedings published, 1987.
29-30 September 1983.
Michael Jones on logistics of Anglo-Saxon invasions
Donald Pollitt on the Armada
James Bradford on the papers of John Paul Jones
Barry Lord on armed schooners in the War of 1812
Daniel Baugh on the Blue-Water strategy over 4 centuries
Arthur Gilbert on mutinies in the 18th century.

[NHS 7] dir: William Cogar [**690**], proceedings published, 1988.
November 1986.
John Morrison on the trireme
Sari Horstein on convoys and strategy in the 17th century
Alan Jamieson on Caribbean strategy in the 18th century
Edward Miller on the MONITOR project, nautical archaeology
Gerald Jordan on the Trafalgar centennial

Ronald Carpenter on Mahan
    [NHS 8] dir: William Cogar [**691**], proceedings published, 1989.
24-25 September 1987.
Philip Callaghan on "The Myth of Trafalgar"
Donald Horward on Admiral Berkeley during the Peninsular campaign
John Talbott on cooper sheathing for the RN
Patricia Crimmin on the RN in the Levant, 1783-1815
David Williams on the British government and merchant seamen
separate papers by William Dudley, David Skaggs, and Barry Gough on the campaigns in the Lakes during the War of 1812
sessions on nautical archaeology and the quadricentennial for the Spanish Armada
    [NHS 9] dir: William Roberts [**3082**], proceedings published, 1991.
18-20 October 1989.
William Still on CSS ALABAMA and nautical archaeology
Julian Gwyn on naval power and the sieges of Louisbourg
John Brittain on Baltic naval operations in the 18th century
A.B. Sainsbury on the RN in the Dardanelles in 1807
Kenneth Breen on Rodney in the West Indies in 1781
Roger A. Morriss on Cockburn and the Chesapeake campaign of 1813
    [NHS 10] dir: Jack Sweetman [**3530**], proceedings published, 1993.
11-13 September 1991.
Gordon Rudd on joint operations during the War of 1812
Mark Grimsley on Henry Morgan and irregular naval warfare
Donald Graves on the RN and "the Military Revolution"
Gerald Jordan and John McErlean on amphibious operations during the 1780s and 1790s
Gordon Harrington on American action against the East India Company
    [NHS 11] dir: Robert Love [**2191**], proceedings published, 2001.
21-23 October 1993.
David Skaggs on James Fenimore Cooper and the battle of Lake Erie
Jorge Ortiz Sotelo on the British naval station and Peru in the early 19th century
a session on nautical archaeology
    [NHS 12] dir: William Cogar [**692**], proceedings published, 1997.
26-27 October 1995.
Roger Knight on sources for British naval history
Roger Morriss on British naval papers in North America
David Sylvester on "Medieval Reservists" of the English navy
Paul Walsh on the struggle for Ireland, 900-1200
Robert Glass on naval courts martial during the 17th century
Peter LeFevre on English naval propaganda in the 17th century
H.W. Dickinson on training British naval officers
Richard Harding and Michael Palmer on amphibious operations during the age of sail

[NHS 13] dir: William McBride [**2223**].

2-4 October 1997.

Christopher George on Cockburn in the Chesapeake, 1813

Gregory Ripple on English reaction to John Paul Jones, 1778-1779

Joseph Zarzynski on the sunken fleet of 1758 as time capsules

an additional session on nautical archaeology

Kelly DeVries on naval gunnery of the 15th century

James Pritchard on Franco-Dutch warfare in the West Indies in the 1670s

Julian Gwyn on prize vessels and the Halifax Vice Admiralty Court

[NHS 14] dir: Craig Symonds [**3534**] and Randy Blano, proceedings published, 2001.

23-25 September 1999.

Richard Harding on British naval intelligence during the 18th century

Patrick Jennings on operations of the RN on Lake Michigan, 1770s and 1780s

Eugene Rasor on British naval historiography

Andrew Lambert on early British naval historians

Daniel Baugh on British naval and political history

C.W. Koburger on French naval historiography

Donald Petrie on naval prize court records

Tyrone Martin on flogging in the USN

Joshua Smith on privateering during the War of 1812

[NHS 15] dir: William Roberts [**3083**].

12-14 September 2001 – CANCELLED.

proposed papers:

Richard Stewart on the English expedition to the Isle of Rhe in 1627

Adam Siegel on naval operations against Cadiz

Mark Danley on defense against amphibious operations in the 18th century

[NHS 16] Proposed for 2003 [**2606**].

[NHS 17] Proposed for 2005 [**2607**].

2. The Anglo-French Naval Historians Conference

These are periodic conferences consisting of meetings, papers are read, and proceedings are published, for example, Guerres ed Paix [**1418**], 1986: papers included a tribute to J.S. Bromley and John Hattendorf on George Byng; Francais et Anglais en Mediterranee [**1175**], 1992: Roger Morriss on maintaining a fleet in the Mediterranean; Peter LeFavre [**2097**], Guerres Maritimes, 1996: Michael Duffy on the Plymouth dockyard and Christie Pfister on privateering from Dunkirk, and Philippe Haudrere [**1573**], Les Flottes des Compagnies des Indes, 1996: Brian Lavery on the East India Company ships as warships and Andrew Lambert on building warships of teak in Bombay.

3. Anglo-Dutch Maritime Historians Conference

Since the late 1950s, Anglo-Dutch maritime historian conferences have been held periodically. Examples were London, September 1966 and Leiden in 1976. Examples included J.S. Bromley [**450**], Britain and the Netherlands in Europe and Asia, 1968: J.R. Jones on old rivalries and Bromley on impressment, and A.C. Duke [**984**], Britain and the Netherlands, 1977: Bromley on the search for an alternative to impressment.

4. Other Conferences and Symposia

As noted, these academic and professional gatherings can be seen as the advanced guard for the profession.

There have been a variety.

The U.S. Naval War College and Yale University have jointly sponsored several important conferences, the key initiators being, respectively, John Hattendorf and Paul Kennedy. An example was John Hattendorf [**1554**], Doing Naval History, 1995, the published proceedings: Volker Berghahn on the importance of domestic politics and Mark Shulman calling for an American equivalent to the Navy Records Society.

Examples of other conferences were Anne Bang-Andersen [**194**], The North Sea, 1985: A.N. Ryan on trade in the North Sea during the Continental System; Walter Minchinton [**2519**], Britain and the Northern Seas, 1988, from the 4th Conference of the Association for the History of the Northern Seas: David Aldrich on Anglo-Baltic trade; The American Revolution and the Sea [**65**], 1974, for the 14th International Conference of the International Commission for Maritime History: R.J.B. Knight on the performance of the Royal Dockyards and David Syrett on the RN and suppression of revolt; Sarah Palmer [**2740**], Charted and Uncharted Waters, 1982, the proceedings from a conference on British maritime history: J.S. Bromley on seamen of the RN after 1688; Abigail Siddall [**3315**], Actes du 7e Colloque International d'Histoire Militaire, 1984: A.W.H. Pearsall on George Anson; Timothy Runyan [**3174**], Ships, Seafaring and Society, 1987, from the Great Lakes Historical Society: Runyan on the organization of Royal fleets in medieval England and Mary Miller on naval stores and Anglo-Russian encounters; Frederick Allis [**51**], Seafaring in Colonial Massachusetts, 1980: Joseph Frese on smuggling, the RN, and the Customs Service, and Lewis Fischer [**1107**], Shipping and Trade, 1750-1950, 1990, from the International Congress of Economic History: David Starkey on manning problems when war begins.

5. Exhibitions

Any number of these exhibitions could be presented; most usually accompanied by scholarly-developed guides and catalogues.

Helen Wallis [**3744**], 1979, described an exhibition of maps associated with the circumnavigation of Francis Drake in the late 1570s, a secret voyage at the time. The British Library sponsored the quadricentennial exhibition. The inimitable A.L. Rowse [**3157**], 1952, introduced an exhibition of "Historical Relics of Sir Francis Drake."

A number of major exhibitions supported the quadricentennial of the Spanish Armada. **See 7., F., 4.-7.** A century previously, there were exhibitions: W.H.Wright [**3966, 3968**], "The Armada Tercentary Exhibition," 1888, and Catalogue of the Exhibition of Armada and Elizabethan Relics, 1888.

6. Festschrift

Any number could be cited. In each case, pertinent articles are cited as examples: Charles Carter [**584**], From the Renaissance to Counter-Reformation: Essays in Honour of Garrett Mattingly, 1965: Lamar Jensen on Franco-Spanish diplomacy and the Armada; Christopher Harper-Bill [**1523**], Studies in Medieval History: Presented to R. Allen Brown, 1989: Nicholas Hooper on the Anglo-Saxon navy; P.G.W. Annis [**122**], Sea Studies: Essays in Honour of Basil Greenhill, 1983: R.J.B. Knight on civilians and the navy, 1660-1832; Ian Wood [**3931**], People and Places in Northern Europe: Essays in Honour of Peter Hayes Sawyer, 1991: Wood on the Franks and SUTTON HOO; Fredrick Krantz [**1976**], History from Below: Studies in Popular Protest and Popular Ideology in Honour of George Rude, 1985: J.S. Bromley on Caribbean freebooters and other essays by Eric Hobsbawm and Christopher Hill; William Aiken [**23**], Conflict in Stuart England: Essays in Honour of Wallace Notestein, 1960: Aiken on the Admiralty in conflict and commission, and Facts and Factors in Economic History: Articles by Former Students of Edwin F. Gay [**1068**], 1932, a longtime professor at Harvard: F.C. Dietz on English public finance and the national state and A.P. Usher on Spanish ships in the 16th and 17th centuries.

F. JOURNALS AND PERIODICALS

Articles in professional and association journals and periodicals were among the best, most scholarly, most detailed sources of information, as demonstrated by the hundreds included in the Annotated Bibliography section of this work and incorporated into the Historiographical Narrative section. Dale Steiner [**3441**], Historical Journals, introduced the subject. More specific details were found in Michael Unsworth [**3699**], Military Periodicals, a useful guide to military and naval journals. Three exceptions to these traditional professional journals and periodicals were included first: The Naval Chronicle [**2605**], Brassey's Naval Annual [**425**], and The Naval Review [**2608**]. The first was directly pertinent to the pre-1815 period; the second and third were published later but, on occasion, have references to events and operations before 1815.

The Naval Chronicle
A unique journal [**2605**] applicable to the greatest era of English/British naval history, 40 volumes published twice a year between 1799 and 1818; the editors included Joyce Gold, James Clarke, and John M'Arthur. It had a magazine format and was aimed at the interests of contemporaneous naval officers and their families. Included were action reports, officer biographical memoirs, professional discussions, letters, stories, and anecdotes. There was little about nor of interest to the ordinary seaman. The third volume, 1800, included "A Sketch of My Life" by Horatio Nelson [**2620**]. There was no index. In 1999, Stackpole and Chatham publishers reprinted extracts in five volumes; an index was added. Nicholas Tracy was editor.

Brassey's Naval Annual
Titled variously [**425**] over the years, for example, The Naval Annual, Brassey's Naval Annual, Brassey's Naval and Shipping Annual, and Brassey's Annual: The Armed Forces Yearbook, initiated in 1886 by Lord Brassey, later edited by T.A. Brassey, Earl Brassey, and H.G. Thursfield. It surveyed and chronicled naval and shipping events with topical articles; later, incorporating all of the armed forces.

The Naval Review
In 1912, Herbert Richmond, K.G.B. Dewar, and R.M. Bellairs, leaders of what they called the Naval Society, launched a quarterly, in-house journal [**2608**] for members only by subscription. The purpose was an independent forum to further the spread of professional thought and study among officers of the RN. Richmond was the author of many of the early articles; later articles were by Stephen Roskill and J.F.C. Fuller. James Goldrick compiled a list of authors for some of the volumes and an index of volumes 1-64, 1913-1976, has been published.
The following traditional professional journals and periodicals would be most likely to contain articles and other helpful information on English/British naval history. In Part II, Descriptive Lists, there is a list of additional pertinent journals and periodicals. **See item a.**

The Mariner's Mirror
The premier journal for this subject was Mariner's Mirror [**2379**], sponsored by the Society for Nautical Research and founded in 1911. In 2001, Chatham Publishers announced the entire run of Mariner's Mirror [**2378**] was to be available on CD-ROM, every issue from 1911 to 2000, 45, 000 pages, 11,000 indexed articles, and 2000 illustrations.

The American Neptune
In North America was a quarterly journal since 1941, the name coming from Atlantic Neptune, an 18th-century collection of British Admiralty surveys of

northeastern North America. Samuel Eliot Morison [**2549-2553**] was a founding president. Sometime editor, Timothy Runyan [**3170**] summarized the history of The American Neptune in an article in 1991.

Proceedings of the Naval Institute
Sponsored by the U.S. Naval Institute, Annapolis, MD, this monthly journal was of primary interest to naval officers. Articles about English/British naval history were frequently included.

The Journal of Military History
Sponsored by the Society for Military History; previously Military Affairs, this quarterly journal contained numerous articles related to English/British naval history.

The Times Literary Supplement
A publication of The Times of London, the TLS has been a weekly, newspaper format review of the literature and intellectual developments for decades. Derwent May [**2473**], Critical Times: The History of "The Times Literary Supplement," 2001, described its history and status, currently at a circulation of 35,000 per week.

Chapter 5

Naval Writers and Historians

The story of English/British naval writers and historians can be told by presenting a series of generations of English/British naval historians, not all of whom were British citizens, and concentrating on those who have produced histories for this pre-1815 period. All of the noted persons reviewed in this chapter will appear again and again in subsequent chapters. Robert Shenk [**3298**] wrote Guide to Naval Writing, 1990, focusing on the technical and the professional types of writing.

Several groupings will be presented.

True professionalization culminating in acceptable levels of scholarship was a slow process, not maturing until the second or third decade of the 20th century. For example, as early as 1875 in what would at that time be considered the "trade journal," The Journal of the United Services Institute, John Knox Laughton [**2053, 2047**] vowed to produce "scientific" history, then the trend in the tradition of the great German historian, Leopold von Ranke. Indeed, Laughton elaborated, urging "the National Study of Naval History" in a later article in Transactions of the Royal Historical Society, 1898. The general public should be educated about the decisive role of the Royal Navy in the history of the country. A quarter of a century later, his son, L. Carr Laughton [**2066**], in the fledgling Mariner's Mirror, recalled the contributions of his father and presented a critique of A.T. Mahan [**2328, 2329**].

Professional societies such as the Navy Records Society, founded in 1893, and the Society for Nautical Research, founded in 1910, and academic institutions such as the Royal Naval College, first at Portsmouth and then at Greenwich, nurtured the process.

Among the great historians were the two Richard Hakluyts, Samuel Purchas, Robert Southey, William James, Nicholas Harris Nicolas, Julian Corbett, A.T. Mahan, Herbert Richmond, Robert Albion, Samuel Eliot Morison, Michael Lewis, Christopher Lloyd, N.A.M. Rodger, J.C. Beaglehole, John B. Hattendorf, R.J.B. Knight, Daniel Baugh, David Quinn, Glyndwr Williams,

Michael Duffy, and Richard Harding. Either in this chapter, or, more likely, in subsequent ones, each of these contributors will figure prominently and citations of their works will appear at the appropriate time; for each, more than once.

Grouping English/British Naval Historians
The generations were as follows.

A. THE PROTO-NAVAL HISTORIANS

William James, Sir John Barrow, and Nicholas Harris Nicolas.
Those three, James [**1783-1784**], Barrow [**219-225**], and Nicolas [**2639-2643**] maintained great interest in the Royal Navy and published some of the earliest histories and biographies. Andrew Lambert [**2001**] wrote of this generation and their contributions.

B. THE EARLIEST QUASI-PROFESSIONALS

The Colombs, the Laughtons, Alfred Thayer Mahan, Julian Corbett, Herbert Richmond, Geoffrey Callender, and C. Northcote Parkinson. Corbett, Mahan, Richmond, and Parkinson will receive special treatment.
The earliest professionals writing naval history were the Colombs, brothers, John and Philip; the Laughtons, father and son, John Knox and L.G. Carr, and Alfred Thayer Mahan. All were thinkers about and formulators of naval strategy and tactics, emphasizing naval history as the basis. The Colombs and the Laughtons influenced Mahan, Corbett, and Richmond. Mahan, of course, was an American naval officer, President of the U.S. Naval War College at Newport and later President of the American Historical Association. He wrote his major treatises on sea power and naval warfare based on his somewhat idiosyncratic historical study of the British navy in the 17th and 18th centuries. Barry Gough [**1339**] wrote an essay on Philip Colomb [**708**], "The Influence of Sea Power upon History," 1990. The security of England rested on command of the sea; history proved it. Between 1863 and 1899, P. Colomb wrote 30 pieces on this topic.
Corbett [**747-761**] refined and corrected the concepts of sea power articulated by Mahan. Richmond [**3058-3066**], a sailor-scholar, was the most intellectual of the historians and was instrumental in reforms in education of officers. Callender [**547-557**], the first director of the National Maritime Museum, Greenwich, in the late 1930s, also served as Professor of History, Royal Naval College, Greenwich. Laughton, father and son, Sir John Knox [**2041-2055**], and L. Carr [**2056-2066**]; J.K. Laughton taught at the Royal Naval College, first at Portsmouth, then at Greenwich; pursued the study of naval history as a vehicle for the development of naval doctrine; personally wrote 926

entries in the <u>Dictionary of National Biography</u> [**930**], about 3% of the entire publication, 35,000 entries; influenced the Colombs, Bridge, Corbett, and Stephen Luce who influenced Mahan; retired from the Royal Navy, 1885, and a founder of the NRS, 1893. Laughton was the focus of Andrew Lambert [**2002, 2006, 2001**], <u>Foundations of Naval History: Sir John Knox Laughton, the Royal Navy, and the Historical Profession</u>, 1998. Lambert is preparing a volume of the papers of John Knox Laughton, a publication of the NRS. Elsewhere, Lambert [**2005**] called Laughton "Our Naval Plutarch."

1. Julian Stafford Corbett

Corbett was not a naval officer. He first studied law, wrote three naval novels, a dozen works of naval history, and edited six volumes for the NRS, of which he was a founding member. Before World War I, he was principal adviser to Admiral Lord John Fisher. During the war, he became the official naval historian of World War I. Issues of interest to Corbett were naval staff organization and war plans, the Dardanelles campaign, and the battle of Jutland. Corbett formulated what has become the most influential theory of naval grand strategy and sea power.

The standard biography of Corbett was by Donald Schurman [**3254**], subtitled <u>Historian of British Maritime Policy from Drake to Jellicoe</u>, 1981. Essays about the influence of Corbett, for example, on the significance of naval history and on amphibious operations were by John Hattendorf [**1550**], John Gibson [**1272**], Peter Stanford [**3418**], and Liam Cleaver [**654**]. William C.B. Tunstall [**3662**] edited the catalogue of the Corbett papers. Herbert Richmond [**3065**] wrote an obituary. Corbett raised the study of naval history to a new level, Richmond concluded. There is a Julian Corbett Prize Essay in Modern Naval History awarded by the Institute of Historical Research, University of London. **See item g.** A summary of the essay is published in <u>Historical Research</u>, the journal of the Institute of Historical Research.

Both Corbett and Mahan stressed securing sea communications and denying them to potential enemies. However, in contradistinction to the "blue-water" orthodoxy and big-battle determinism of Mahan, Corbett was an advocate of limited war stressing blockade, amphibious warfare, and coordination of forces, deemed "the British way of warfare"; combining continental and maritime strategies and utilizing naval, military, economic, and diplomatic resources in a comprehensive policy.

2. Alfred Thayer Mahan

An American naval officer, Mahan [**2328-2333**] made his reputation from his intense study of British naval history. Biographies of Mahan were by William Puleston [**2966**], 1939, and Robert Seager [**3264, 3265**], 1977, who also edited his letters and papers in three volumes, 1975. Selections of important

essays were edited by John Hattendorf [**1560**], 1991, in the Classics of Sea
Power series. Kenneth Moll [**2524**], Richard Smith [**3364**], and Richard Unger
[**3689**] wrote about Mahan as historian and Bates Gilliam [**1287**] did a
dissertation. In a book and an article Jon Sumida [**3515, 3516**] reread all of the
works of Mahan and touted rehabilitation of his reputation in Inventing Grand
Strategy and Teaching Command: The Classic Works of Alfred Thayer Mahan
Reconsidered, 2000 and 2001. Richard Turk [**3666**] described a fascinating
relationship, The Ambiguous Relationship: Theodore Roosevelt and Alfred
Thayer Mahan, 1987. Both wrote naval history and were Anglophiles, Mahan
more than Roosevelt in both instances. Both became presidents of the American
Historical Association.

3. Herbert Richmond

    Barry Hunt [**1735**], Sailor-Scholar: Admiral Sir Herbert Richmond,
1871-1946, 1982, followed the career of this "unique phenomenon in the
Victorian-Edwardian navy: a professionally competent and successful officer
who was also an intellectual." Richmond [**3058-3066**] founded the in-house
professional journal, Naval Review [**2608**], in 1913. Arthur Marder [**2373**],
Portrait of an Admiral: The Life and Papers of Sir Herbert Richmond, 1952, was
an older study. Richmond [**3061**] himself addressed the Navy Records Society,
20 October 1939, praising J. Laughton for originating the methods of modern
research on naval history.

4. C. Northcote Parkinson

    Parkinson [**2759-2774**] was more famous for "economic laws." He was
a professor and naval historian. Richard Harding [**1496**] placed Parkinson, as
potentially in this group. Parkinson won the Julian Corbett Prize in 1936;
"Begotten by Sir John Knox Laughton, fostered by the Admiralty, and reared
beneath the colonnades at Greenwich." Parkinson was biographer of Pellew,
wrote two books on trade and war in the Far East, and wrote nautical fiction,
including a "biography" of Horatio Hornblower. **See 20., C. and 20., D.**

C. PROFESSORS AS HISTORIANS

    Michael Lewis, Christopher Lloyd, and Bryan Ranft.
    For the 1940s through 1980s, also operating from the Department of
History, Royal Naval College, Greenwich, were the prolific British naval
historians, Michael Lewis [**2118-2129**], Christopher Lloyd [**2149-2174**], and
Bryan Ranft [**3006-3008**]. Ranft, who died in 2001, also taught at King's
College, University of London. Ranft, among other things, was credited with

reviving the Navy Records Society. Their numerous works were reviewed in the appropriate places in following chapters.

D. FULL-TIME PROFESSIONAL HISTORIANS

Arthur Marder and Stephen Roskill.

Equally prolific were Arthur Marder [**2373**], an American professor, and Stephen Roskill [**3148-3149**], an officer in the Royal Navy and later a fellow at Churchill College, Cambridge University. These were giants of the field, highly esteemed and internationally renowned. Their presence was overwhelming. At one point, a raging controversy erupted between them and Ranft wrote an essay calling for peace. All of their works related to the post-1815 period and both were featured prominently in Rasor [**3012**], British Naval History since 1815, 1990, along with details about the controversy.

E. THE CURRENT LEADERS

Andrew Lambert, Daniel Baugh, John Hattendorf, N.A.M. Rodger, James Goldrick, and Glyndwr Williams.

The current leaders are Andrew Lambert [**2001-2008**], protégé to Ranft, John Knox Laughton Professor of Naval History, operating from the War Studies Department, King's College, University of London; Daniel Baugh [**237-242**] from Cornell University; John Hattendorf [**1550-1570**], the Ernest King Professor at the U.S. Naval War College; N.A.M. Rodger [**3103-3117**] has moved to the University of Exeter having formerly filled a research-publishing position sponsored by the National Maritme Museum; James Goldrick [**1314**], another true sailor-scholar, is a senior officer in the Royal Australian Navy, and Glyn Williams [**3872-3880**] is a senior professor at Queen Mary and Westfield College, University of London.

Andrew Lambert [**2002, 2004**] has concluded a biographical study of John Knox Laughton and will contribute a Nelson biography to the Nelson Decade [**2624**], and Baugh [**237, 238, 240**] is seen as the definitive historian of naval administration, notably in the 18th century. Hattendorf [**1561, 1554, 1558, 1563**] has been most enthusiastic in leading a crusade to advance the importance of naval and maritime history. See his recent edition of Maritime History, two volumes, the product of two summer National Endowment for the Humanities Institutes, 1992-1993, held at the John Carter Brown Library, Brown University, Providence, RI. Among the presenters were noted British naval historians, for example, Tony Ryan, Baugh, Rodger, Williams, and Roger Knight, former Deputy Director, National Maritime Museum, Greenwich, and now a professor at the University of Greenwich. Maritime History will be used as a textbook for academic courses. As noted elsewhere, Rodger [**3110**], a prolific historian, is writing the new standard history of the British navy. Goldrick, a serving officer, published an important study of the Royal Navy during the early months of World War I, pointing out that moment as the true beginning of modern naval warfare, in three dimensions, underwater, surface, and air. Williams [**3872, 3875, 3877**] has continued to be the expert on the age of exploration and circumnavigation.

F. THE NEXT GENERATION

Michael Duffy, Richard Harding, and Harry Dickinson.
The next and future generation included Duffy and Harding, past and present editors of <u>Mariner's Mirror</u>. Micheal Duffy [**971-978**], a prolific naval historian, has built up the naval and maritime studies programme at Exeter University into major prominence.

Richard Harding [**1491-1496**] of the University of Westminster, published an outstanding synthesis of the literature about sailing ship warfare. The origins of the Royal Navy involved armed merchant vessels for use as transports across the Channel. The evolution proceeded to the navy royal, the English navy, a standing navy, the emergence of an oceanic power, and culminating in the age of sail as the global hegemonic power, the time of the <u>Pax Britannica</u>. Harry Dickinson [**928**] was the recipient of the Julian Corbett Prize for Naval History for 1996 and is preparing a study of educational provisions for officers of the Royal Navy at the crucial time of the late 19th century. He was sometime professor at the Britannic Royal Naval College, Dartmouth, and has taught at the U.S. Naval Academy; more recently, attached to the War Studies Group, King's College, University of London.

G. OTHER NAVAL HISTORIANS

Others deserving recognition were Paul Halpern [**1460-1461**] of Florida State University, prolific on the naval situation of the pre-war and World War I periods in the Mediterranean area; Roger Morriss [**2566-2576**], Jonathan Coad [**671-676**], and Philip MacDougall [**2240-2244**] on the Royal Dockyards, the largest and most complicated "industry" of Great Britain for centuries; Martin Carver [**590-592**] on describing the excavation of the SUTTON HOO ship burial, a naval craft of the 7th century, and Jan Glete [**1298-1300**] of the University of Stockholm on three works of comparison of naval forces in the early modern period.

H. WRITING NAVAL HISTORY

An introduction to professional history writing about the armed forces can be found in David Charters [**623**], Military History and the Military Profession, 1992, 15 essays and a bibliography by the most eminent scholars, for example, W.A.B. Douglas on Mahan, Corbett, and Richmond; Daniel Baugh on Michael Lewis and N.A.M. Rodger, and other pertinent essays by Robin Higham and Eric Grove. Reference has been made to John Hattendorf [**1554**], Doing Naval History, 1995, the published proceedings to a U.S. Naval War College-Yale University jointly sponsored conference. The subtitle, Essays toward Improvement, defined the objective, which was carried out impressively. An older survey on writing naval history was by Jacques Barzun [**229**]. Andrew Lambert [**2001**], professor of naval history at the King's College, London, had a piece on three pioneers of what he dubbed "the heroic age": William James, John Barrow, and Nicholas Harris Nicolas; C. Northcote Parkinson [**2764**] on what he dubbed "the Greenwich historians": John Knox Laughton, Geoffrey Callender, and Michael Lewis; David Syrett [**3538**] on conflicting interpretations of British and American historians; William Dudley [**969**] on naval historians of the War of 1812: James Fenimore Cooper, Theodore Roosevelt, and Mahan, and Oliver Warner [**3763**], English Maritime Writing: Hakluyt to Cook, 1958, which included Raleigh, Dampier, Rogers, Defoe, and Anson.

Not known as a professional naval writer nor a naval historian but well known as a naval biographer, among other things, Poet Laureate and "the third" Lake District Poet, was Robert Southey [**3396-3398**], one of the best known biographers of Horatio Nelson. Mark Storey [**3461**] has a recent biography and one is projected by W.A. Speck [**3403**]. Storey called him "one of the most enigmatic figures in English literature." His Life of Nelson began as a review of new books on Nelson. In an article of 1830 in Edinburgh Review, Thomas Babington Macaulay [**2222**] proclaimed the biography as "the most perfect and most delightful of his works." Kenneth Curry [**838**] wrote a reference guide.

Another known literary figure deserved inclusion here: Daniel Defoe [**895-897**], author of Robinson Crusoe and a novel on pirates. Some attributed A General History of the Pyrates [**1813**], 1724, to Defoe. Biographies were by Maximilian Novak [**2653**], 2001, Paula Backscheider [**169**], 1989, and Richard West [**3821**], 1997, the last entitled The Life and Strange Surprising Adventures of Daniel Defoe. W.R. Owens [**2719**] edited his political and economic writings, 8 vols. so far, the project planned to run to 44 vols. On the question of authorship of A General History of Pyrates [**1813**], P.N. Furbank [**1215-1217**] credited Charles Johnson [**1813**] as the correct author. Defoe did write anonymously and in a checklist of 1960, J.R. Moore attributed it to Defoe; Furbank was not convinced. Johnson [**1813**] will appear as the author in a later chapter. See 12., C.

Robert Albion [**27-31, 1984**] made his reputation as historian with his study of the timber problem of the RN. He was also a noted bibliographer. The biography was by Benjamin Labaree [**1982**], 1975.

Samuel Eliot Morison [**2549-2553**], was, at one time, the official naval historian for the U.S. Navy during World War II, 15 volumes being the product, considered a classic. Morison won two Pulitzer Prizes for his biographies of John Paul Jones and Christopher Columbus. His 2-volume survey of Atlantic exploration was most pertinent here. Samuel Eliot Morison's Historical World: In Quest of a New Parkinson, 1991, by Gregory Pfitzer [**2839**] and Sailor Historian, 1977, by Emily Morison Beck [**267**] were biographical studies.

Equally esteemed was Gerald Graham [**1357-1362**], a Canadian. Albion, Morison, and Graham taught at Harvard, Graham later as Rhodes Professor at King's College, London. A biographical account was John Flint [**1128**], "Professor Gerald Graham, 1903-1988," 1989.

In an article in 1998, Elizabeth Malcolm [**2339**] paid tribute to David Quinn [**2973-2989**], "Ireland's greatest living historian," the historician of English expansionism. Quinn died in 2002.

Walter Minchinton [**2521**] presented the career of Michael Oppenheim [**2710-2712**], noted for his history of Admiralty administration.

Another prolific and endearing historian focusing on Irish maritime history was "Old Man of the Sea," John de Courcy Ireland [**1748-1755**], interviewed by David Sheehy [**3296**].

Not known as a naval historian, but deserving inclusion was C.R. Boxer [**396-407**], His biography, Charles R. Boxer: An Uncommon Life: Soldier, Historian, Teacher, Collector, Traveller, 2001. was by Dauril Alden [**32**].

Chapter 6

Histories of the English/British Navy

This chapter will be organized as follows. Coverage will begin with a short listing of when various historians traced the origins of the English/British navy and who was nominated as the "father" of the Royal Navy. No agreement and many suggestions for times and "fathers" have been volunteered. The qualitative assessment of premier histories, a chronological review of less distinguished histories, other pertinent and related naval histories, and historiographical surveys of the state of English/British naval history will follow.

A. WHEN AND WHO?

A chronological sequence of names attributed to English/British "navies" will adhere to the following somewhat speculative, but, nevertheless, informative, nomenclature: Roman fleets, Anglo-Saxon fleets, ships of the Cinque Ports, King's Ships, navy-maritime ships, Navy Royal, and Royal Navy.

When to begin? Who was the "father" of the Royal Navy?
In the latest and most authoritative naval history of Britain, Safeguard of the Sea, N.A.M Rodger [3110] began in 660 AD, the early Anglo-Saxon period and credited Henry VIII with establishing a permanent navy designed for war. However, Rodger refused to designate him as "founder" or "father" of the Royal Navy.

The old standard, William Laird Clowes [669] began in Roman times and the "Royal Navy" originated in the 16th century. E. Keble Chatterton [624] began with the Roman invasions, 50s BC and 40s AD.

Anglo-Saxon times were favored by David Howarth [1695], 450 AD, and J.R. Hill [1630], the 8th century. Christopher Lloyd [2171] began with the Vikings. King Alfred and the late 9th century were favored by Warren Tute [3677]; Matthew Strickland [3474], saw Alfred as "founder of the Royal Navy";

Peter Kemp [**1862**] credited Alfred with producing the first true navy, and Gregory Clark [**646**] began with Alfred and designated Henry VIII as "father."

John Leyland [**2131**] opened with "the Conqueror's Sea Power," thus 1066. The authoritative and prestigious centennial volume of the Navy Records Society, edited by John Hattendorf [**1553**], 1993, began with 1204. David Hannay [**1482**] began in 1217. Geoffrey Marcus [**2368**] began with "the medieval prelude" to the Tudors, more specifically, 1380 as the origin of English "maritime enterprise." Henry VIII was "the founder of the Royal Navy." C.L. Kingsford [**1939**] identified Henry V as creator of the navy as a national fighting force, about 1420.

Charles Derrick [**912**] contended the origins of the Royal Navy were in the 1530s; that meant Henry VIII as "father." Thomas Butcher [**526**] began with the Tudors.

Paul Kennedy [**1882**] began with the Stuarts about 1600, the time "the rise" began. A.T. Mahan [**2329**] began his influential study with 1660. Michael Lewis [**2125**] saw the fathers as Alfred, Edward III, Henry V, and Henry VIII; Charles II brought in the modern Royal Navy. Norman Davies [**875**] thought "Navy Royal" transformed into "Royal Navy" during the reign of Charles II.

For the 19th-century British naval historians, politics may have been uppermost. For example, in his biography of Admiral George Cockburn whose career spanned the period 1793-1848, Roger Morriss [**2569**] devoted a section on the politics of the early histories of the RN, summarized as follows: Chamier [**609-613**], Whig, William James [**1784**], Tory, Brenton [**430**], Tory, and Briggs [**439**], Whig; Cockburn suffered from the Whig bias of contemporaneous historians. And these historians tended to attack each other. **See 5., C. and 5., D.**

B. THE PREEMINENT HISTORIES

In this regard, the best news has been that a full-scale, multi-volume, scholarly, semi-official <u>Naval History of Britain</u> was in progress, the first in a hundred years. This one is by a single author, one of the most prolific and distinguished British naval historians of recent times, N.A.M. Rodger [**3103-3117**]. Volume I is out, <u>The Safeguard of the Sea</u> [**3110**], 1997. Among other things, Rodger was author of the best-selling <u>Wooden World</u> [**3117**], about 18th-century naval society. There were hardback and paperback editions of <u>Safeguard of the Sea</u>. The project was sponsored by the NMM, SNR, and NRS. Volume II, covering 1649-1815 and featuring Nelson's navy, is projected for 2002; no estimate as yet about subsequent volumes, projected to be a total of three. Volume III will feature Victoria's Empire. Rodger presented more than a naval history; "a naval slice of national history." The feature was synthesis of a vast literature, Rodger enjoying a formidable command of published sources and primary research reports. Approaches as he described them were policy, strategy and naval operations, finance and administration, logistics, materiel, ships, and personnel. Welsh, Scottish, and Irish sea powers were given full coverage, plus Anglo-Saxon and Dalriada naval operations. The formidable costs to sustain sea power were clearly demonstrated; appreciation, or, more likely, lack of appreciation, of sea power was assessed for each of noted monarchs, for example, Harold Godwinson, William I, Edward I, Henry V, Henry VII, Henry VIII, Elizabeth I, and James IV of Scotland. Rodger placed Harold Godwinson ahead of Alfred and Henry V as better appreciating concepts of sea power. All of this was supported by a series of appendices, for example, a list of warships, rates of pay, a chronology, a glossary, and 150 pages of notes and bibliography, the latter with pertinent, informative, critical, and knowledgeable annotation. Will this one stand for a hundred years? A good start was evident.

Interestingly, the previous standard, The Royal Navy: A History, 7 vols., 1897-1903, edited by William Laird Clowes [**669**], has been reprinted, 1996-1997, by a new publishing house, which has concentrated on British naval works, Chatham Publishers of London. The reprint was in paperback and affordable. The Royal Navy included substantial essays by Alfred Thayer Mahan and by Theodore Roosevelt who wrote on the War of 1812. Among other contributors were Clements Markham and H.W. Wilson. Coverage began with the Roman period and covered up to the death of Victoria in 1901. The project was on a massive scale, almost 4500 pages, nothing having been attempted to that degree before or since. At the time, Laird Clowes was naval correspondent for The Times and Roosevelt, who had written a naval history of the War of 1812 at age 24, was Police Commissioner of New York. Among the idiosyncrasies, the choice of the Duke of Medina Sidonia to command the Armada "was an extremely bad one," the didacticism of the account of the War of 1812 written by Roosevelt, and it was "large, rather over-factual" as described by Michael Lewis later. Andrew Lambert [**2007**] published some reflections on Laird Clowes on the occasion of the reprint by Chatham. Clowes repeated the "black legend" of intrigue and assassination by Nelson at Naples, all unsubstantiated. See **8., A., 2.**

The next major effort was Geoffrey Marcus [**2365-2371**] who launched his projected multi-volume A Naval History of England [**2368**], two volumes being published, The Formative Centuries and The Age of Nelson, 1961-1971, dedicated to J.A. Williamson and Robert Albion, respectively. A third volume was to be titled The Empire of the Sea, 1815-1918. Marcus lamented that there was no equivalent to John Fortescue [**1162**], A History of the British Army, 13 volumes, 1899-1930. Not only were subsequent volumes not forthcoming, but a projected The Great Armada also failed to appear. Marcus [**2367, 2371**] did publish other works on British naval history and on the TITANIC. What was completed has been praised as balanced, accurate, and perceptive. It was "a naval history set in a maritime aspect." The second volume of Mahan [**2328-2329**] had effectively ended with Trafalgar in 1805, so coverage of the Peninsular war, the greatest combined operation in British history up to that time, was neglected. Marcus favored the exploits of Edward Pellew. In a footnote, Marcus noted that HMS VICTORY flew the flags of Keppel, Kempenfelt, Hardy, Howe, Geary, Hood, Hyde Parker, and Nelson. A further strength was a substantial bibliography. In 1975, Marcus [2367] focused on life on the lower deck during the 18th and early 19th centuries in Hearts of Oak, 1975.

Paul Kennedy [1880-1883], Dilworth Professor of History, Yale University, previously at the University of East Anglia, became famous, some might say, notorious, for his The Rise and Fall of Great Powers [1883]. That book created quite a stir. Kennedy presented a deterministic survey of great powers which rose and fell, for example, Portugal, Spain, the Dutch, French, British, and, finally, the Americans. The common factor in "rise and fall" was imperial, economic, and strategic overstretch. He predicted "the Pacific Rim" would be the future "Great Power." Equally brilliant in conception and structural analysis was The Rise of Anglo-German Antagonism [1881]. He concentrated on their imperial, naval, cultural, religious, and dynastic competitions.

Kennedy [1882] began as a British naval historian, earlier publishing a history of British sea power in the Mahanian tradition, The Rise and Fall of British Naval Mastery, now republished half a dozen times since 1976. As with his other works, the perspective was the broadest and the approaches were strategic, economic, social, comparative, and interdisciplinary. As might be expected, it was more than traditional naval history. He began in 1600 and it was touted as "the first detailed examination of the history of British sea power since A.T. Mahan's classic" of 1890. Mahan [2328-2329] was hyperbolic and out of step with later, more solid interpretations of Julian Corbett [759] and Herbert Richmond [3066]. The sea power thesis of Mahan was rejected, Kennedy favoring the "far more prescient geopolitical theories of Halford Mackinder." Kennedy opted for "naval mastery" as preferable to sea power used by Mahan or naval supremacy or maritime ascendancy, favorite descriptive terms of Gerald Graham [1357-1362].

C. THE EARLIEST HISTORIES OF THE ENGLISH/BRITISH NAVY

The above histories of the RN were the most prominent contemporary efforts. The earliest attempts began with William James [1784], The Naval History of Great Britain: From the Declaration of the War by France in 1793 to the Accession of George IV, 6 vols., 1822-1824, with subsequent variations. James died in 1827 and Frederick Chamier, C.T. Wilson, and York Powell updated later editions, up to 1902. James was an attorney who traveled abroad, even detained as an enemy alien in Philadelphia during the War of 1812. Among his researches was a thorough investigation of HMS GUERRIERE vs. USS CONSTITUTION, James determining that the latter was larger and more heavily armed; going further, he concluded that no American ship captured a British one of similar force, whereas the opposite occurred more than once. Such "facts" later upset American naval historians. He contributed to The Naval Chronicle [**2605**]. Later, T.A. Brassey [**424**], editor of Brassey's Naval Annual [**425**], sponsored an index prepared by C.G. Toogood, a publication of the NRS, 1895.

James raised the ire of American naval historians and obviously agitated Edward P. Brenton [**430**] who published The Naval History of Great Britain from the Year, 1783 to 1836, 5 vols., 1823-1825, again with various subsequent editions. It was dedicated to King William IV. The period covered was similar to that of James. Brenton accused James of plagiarism and making errors, "but only to be expected by writers who are uninformed. . . and [one who is] a mere landsman." Tory and Whig bias was also involved. In 1823, George Montagu [**2528**] published a 60-page diatribe denouncing Brenton, his "incorrect statements and unjust insinuations" concerning the conduct of Admiral G. Montagu.

William Goldsmith [**1316**], The Naval History of Great Britain: From the Earliest Period with Biographical Notices, 1825, was a substantial tome.

A History of the Royal Navy from the Earliest Times to the Wars of the French Revolution, 2 vols., 1847, was by Nicholas Harris Nicolas [**2641**], who set out to fill gaps left by James [**1784**] and in preparation for what would be Clowes [**669**]. Nicolas conducted extensive primary research, for example, at the PRO. James had stressed the military; Nicolas expanded coverage to civil and military, for example, including trade, ship design, manning, pay, discipline, navigation, and law.

Next was Charles Yonge [**3974**], A History of the British Navy, 3 vols., 1863-1866, one of the first efforts at full coverage, again heading toward Clowes [**669**].

In 1911, in the first volume of Mariner's Mirror, L. Carr Laughton [**2058**] studied Nathaniel Boteler [**369**] and his Six Dialogues, 1634, touted as an early history, the dialogs being between the Lord High Admiral and a captain at sea.

Virtually unrecognized and with a curious title was an early attempt, Charles Derrick [**912**], Memoirs of the Rise and Progress of the Royal Navy, 1806. Derrick began with the arrival of the Romans. At the same time was William Burney [**515**], The British Neptune: Or, A History of the Achievement of the Royal Navy: From the Earliest Period to the Present Day, 1807.

D. ENGLISH/BRITISH NAVAL HISTORIES OF THE 20th CENTURY

Becoming more substantial was E. Keble Chatterton [**624**], The Story of the British Navy: From the Earliest Times to the Present Day, 1911, beginning with the time before the Norman Conquest. He described the "Classis Britannia," the Roman defense system based at Boulogne, Dover, and Lyme. Alfred and Edgar the Peaceable built impressive fleets. At about the same time,

Frank Fox [**1169**] wrote <u>The Story of the British Navy: The Ramparts of Empire</u>. Nelson was the crowning achievement. In 1914, John Leyland [**2131**] published <u>The Royal Navy: Its Influence in English History and in the Growth of Empire</u>, touted as a "little Manuel," a general overview.

David Hannay [**1482**], <u>A Short History of the Royal Navy, 1217-1815</u>, 2 vols., 1897-1909, was praised by many and became a popular account. Also popular was Geoffrey Callender [**554**], <u>The Naval Side of British History</u>, 2 vols., 1924, taking a glorified and patriotic approach, for example, over dramatizing with Drake's game of bowls and the death scene in the cockpit of HMS VICTORY.

William C.B. Tunstall [**3660**], <u>The Anatomy of Neptune: From King Henry VIII to the Present Day</u>, 1936, incorporated documents, prose, and verse. For juveniles, there were Peter Kemp [**1869**], <u>The True Book about the Royal Navy</u>, 1959, and Walter Brownlee [**480**], <u>The Navy that Beat Napoleon</u>, 1982. For naval cadets, there were Geoffrey Callender [**556**], <u>Sea Kings of Britain</u>, 2 vols., 1907; William C.B. Tunstall [**3665**], <u>The Realities of Naval History</u>, 1936, prepared for what was called the Osborne-Dartmouth Scheme and specifically to refute "all the foolishness in Callender's <u>Sea Kings</u>"; Thomas Butcher [**526**], <u>The Navy</u>, 1973, a short, balanced overview, and Gregory Clark [**646**], <u>Britain's Naval Heritage</u>, 1981. For adults, Peter Kemp [**1862**] contributed <u>History of the Royal Navy</u>, 1969. For Kemp, the first true navy was that of Alfred. There was also Grant Unden [**3687**], <u>British Ships and Seamen: A Short History</u>, 2 vols., 1969; a volume for each.

The equivalent textbook used in American naval history courses was E.B. Potter [**2923**], <u>Sea Power: A Naval History</u>, 1960, co-authored by Chester Nimitz; with an abridged edition of 1981. Its predecessor was William Stevens [**3449**], <u>A History of Sea Power</u>, 1920, half of which featured the RN and included only mention of John Paul Jones.

A curious approach was by Evelyn Berckman [**299**], <u>Creators and Destroyers of the English Navy: As Related by the State Papers Domestic</u>, 1974. She categorized monarchs, for example, the creators were Elizabeth I, Charles I, and Charles II; the destroyers were James I and Oliver Cromwell; the selections even more curious.

The two noted academic professional historians, consecutive professors of naval history at the Royal Naval College, Greenwich, each producing a series of histories: Michael Lewis [**2125, 2123, 2126**], <u>The Navy of Britain</u>, 1948, <u>The History of the British Navy</u>, 1957, and <u>The Navy in Transition, 1814-1864</u>, 1965, the last effectively continuing where Hannay [**1482**] left off; Christopher Lloyd [**2172, 2163, 2171**], <u>A Short History of the Royal Navy, 1805-1918</u>, 1942, <u>The Nation and the Navy</u>, 1954, and <u>Ships and Seamen: From the Viking Kings to the Present Day</u>, 1961.

David Howarth [**1695**], <u>Sovereign of the Seas: The Story of Britain and the Sea</u>, 1974, divided naval history into five parts beginning in 450 AD: obscurity, awakening, mastery, rivalry, and supremacy; the product was well written and elegantly presented. Oliver Warner [**3756**], The British Navy: A Concise History, 1975, was dedicated to Arthur Marder, "historian of the navy renewed by Lord Fisher." The True Glory: The Story of the Royal Navy over a Thousand Years, 1983, by Warren Tute [**3677**], saw the beginning in the 890s; after the Crown and the Law, the Royal Navy exerted more influence on the daily lives of its people than other institutions. D.P. Capper [**575**], Moat Defensive: A History of the Waters of the Nore Command, 55 BC to 1961, 1963, covered the traditional periods, for example, Roman, Cinque Ports, Dutch wars, press gangs and the mutinies; the Buoy of the Nore was the chief rendezvous of the RN throughout the days of sail. Richard Humble [**1724**], Before the DREADNOUGHT: The Royal Navy from Nelson to Fisher, 1976, was a general, superficial survey of the RN of the 19th century.

Politics resumed with Richard Humble [**1726**] who wrote The Rise and Fall of the British Navy, 1986, partly as a critique to excessive demobilization during the regime of Margaret Thatcher.

E. ILLUSTRATED HISTORIES

Folio sizes, profusely illustrated were popular and attractive productions. Most impressive was J.R. Hill [**1630**], a Rear Admiral, RN and sometime chairman of SNR, who was the general editor of The Oxford Illustrated History of the Royal Navy, 1995, folio size and fourteen essays by the best experts, for example, Susan Rose, John Hattendorf, J.D. Davies, Daniel Baugh, Andrew Lambert, James Goldrick, and Eric Grove. Antony Preston [**2945**] produced History of the Royal Navy, 1983, profusely illustrated and a post-Falklands/Malvinas campaign assessment. The prolific writer, John Winton [**3921**] produced An Illustrated History of the Royal Navy, 2000, sponsored by the Royal Naval Museum, Portsmouth, beginning with "the earliest times."

Illustrated histories covering "the industrial revolutions," updated, came from Anthony Watts [**3791, 3792**], Pictorial History of the Royal Navy, 2 vols., 1970-1971, and The Royal Navy: An Illustrated History, 1995. John Wells [**3810**], The Royal Navy: An Illustrated Social History, 1994, focused on the sociology of maritime communities within the officer class during the last 200 years of the history of the RN; anecdotal.

For the Osprey Men-at-Arms series, Robert Wilkinson-Latham [**3863**], The Royal Navy, 1790-1970, 1977, the focus was the development of uniforms of the RN.

F. THE GREAT BATTLES APPROACH

With this approach, one would always start with the classic compilation: Edward Creasy [**792**], Fifteen Decisive Battles of the World, 1851 and numerous subsequent editions. Pertinent battles were Hastings, the Armada, Saratoga, and Waterloo. In 1993, the prolific military historian, John Keegan [**1849**], has presented his nominations of fifteen battles to update Creasy: pertinent were Lepanto, the Armada, Quiberon Bay, Virginia Capes, Camperdown, the Nile, Copenhagen, Trafalgar, and Navarino. Another nomination, Famous Sea Battles, 1981, was by David Howarth [**1691**]: pertinent of the sixteen listed were the Armada and Trafalgar. HMS REVENGE and the dramatic "suicide" battle led by Richard Grenville against a Spanish fleet in 1591 was included in two listings: John Guttman [**1428**], Defiance at Sea: Stories of Dramatic Naval Warfare, 1995, and, more significantly, Alexander McKee [**2292**], Against the Odds: Battles at Sea, 1591-1949, 1991; in addition, Robert Blake in 1657, Barfleur in 1692, and John Paul Jones in 1776 were included.

An opposite approach was that of Geoffrey Regan [**3043**], The Guinness Book of Naval Blunders, 1993, which cited the WHITE SHIP tragedy, loss of MARY ROSE, the Dutch in the Medway of 1667, Beachy Head of 1690, Toulon of 1744, the Armada of 1779, and Navarino of 1827.

More specifically for the English/British navy were two older, extensive listings. Archibald Duncan [**987**], The British Trident: Or, Register of Naval Actions, 6 vols., 1805-1809, a total of 2,150 pages that describe these battles. Volume IV included a short biography of Nelson. The second was Joseph Allen [**45**], Battles of the British Navy, 2 vols., 1842 and subsequent editions.

David Thomas [**3592, 3591**], A Companion to the Royal Navy, 1988, and Battles and Honours of the Royal Navy, 1999, were in handbook format featuring chapters on the badges and battle honors of ships, descriptions of each battle, and a naval chronology.

Great Battles of the Royal Navy: As Commemorated in the Gunroom, BRNC, Dartmouth, 1994, by Eric Grove [**1411**], consisted of 25 essays by experts describing 25 battles, each with a colored painting from the Britannia Royal Naval College, for example, Sluys, the Armada, Quiberon Bay, and Trafalgar.

G. GENERAL NAVAL HISTORIES

One interested in general naval history would do well to start with Clark Reynolds [**3050**], Navies in History, 1998, an outstanding overview of naval history from earliest times to the present. Special essays were featured, for example, on the Armada, the Four Days' Battle, "fleet-in-being," Mahan, and Corbett. Elsewhere, Reynolds [**3051**] reviewed the history and significance of the "traders," for example, the Venetians, Genoans, the Dutch, and the English. Older and more extensive but with a narrower focus was John Southworth

[**3399**], War at Sea, 3 vols., 1967-1970: The Ancient Fleets, The Age of Sail, and The Age of Steam.

Philip de Sousa [**3395**], Seafaring and Civilization: Maritime Perspectives on World History, 2001, was a recent general synthesis incorporating broad themes: navigation, trade, empire, food, and health.

H. THE AGE OF FIGHTING SAIL

Here, a virtual genre has emerged of overly dramatized, profusely illustrated surveys of the age of fighting sail, perhaps a product of or stimulation for the popular nautical fiction associated with the Nelson era, for example, O'Brian, Forester, and Kent. As with biographies of Nelson, there seems to be a rush to publish. **See 20., B., 20., C., and 20., D.**

A good place to start would be Richard Harding [**1492**], The Evolution of the Sailing Navy, 1509-1815, 1995, an analytical approach incorporating a synthesis of the latest research. About 1500, armed merchant vessels ferrying expeditions across the Channel were transformed into full-time warships because the heavy cannon required larger and specialized ships. Brian Lavery [**2077**], Nelson's Navy: The Ships, Men and Organisation, 1793-1815, 1989, presented an impressive, comprehensive guide to all aspects of the RN. David Lyon [**2218**], Sea Battles in Close-Up: The Age of Nelson, 1996, folio size profusely illustrated, was sponsored by the NMM.

The most recent contributions were by Andrew Lambert [**2008**], War at Sea in the Age of Sail, 2000, Bernard Ireland [**1747**], Naval Warfare in the Age of Sail: War at Sea, 1756-1815, 2000, and Nicholas Blake [**346**], The Illustrated Companion to Nelson's Navy, 1999, all lavishly illustrated.

C. Northcote Parkinson [**2759**] contributed Britannia Rules: The Classic Age of Naval History, 1793-1815, 1977. Parkinson stressed extraordinary leadership as decisive, admirals in battle and others providing victualling, dockyard services, even Gilbert Blane who finally succeeded in reducing scurvy.

Nathan Miller [**2515**], Broadsides: The Age of Fighting Sail, 1775-1815, 2000, was produced purposely to provide background to the fictional works. It stressed American aspects. Nevertheless, one man dominated and epitomized this era, Horatio Nelson; his life was used as a framework. Historic Sail: The Glory of the Sailing Ship from the 13th to the 19th Century [**1638**], 2000, included detailed color drawings of a variety of ship types.

Veres Laszlo [**2034**], The Story of Sail, 1999, featured 1000 exquisite drawings illustrating 6000 years of evolution of sailing ships, for example, the Blackwall frigate, packet ship, and scientific ships. Donald G.F.W. Macintyre [**2268**], The Adventure of Sail, 1530-1914, 1970, was lavishly illustrated.

Brian Tunstall [**3659**], Naval Warfare in the Age of Sail: The Evolution of Fighting Tactics, 1650-1815, 1990, a revival of the work of the son-in-law of

Julian Corbett. Tunstall, who died in 1970, set out to complete the famous works of Corbett [**747-761**]; Nicholas Tracy completed the process. The focus was sailing-ship tactics, fighting instructions, and signaling.

Philip Bosscher [**367**], The Heyday of Sail, 1995, was in The History of the Ship series. Frank Bowen [**392**], Wooden Walls in Action, 1951, covered naval battles, 1340-1866. C.S. Forester [**1141**] entitled his history of the War of 1812, The Age of Fighting Sail, 1956.

Oliver Warner [**3773**], Nelson and the Age of Fighting Sail, 1963, was aimed at the juvenile market; the great American Admiral Chester Nimitz was consultant.

In an article of 1988, Dwight Robinson [**3090**] touted the contribution of the coasting fleet around the British Isles as the secret of British power in the age of sail.

At first glance, the dissertation and associated book by Alex Roland [**3135, 3134**] might appear to be a stretch: Underwater Warfare in the Age of Sail, 1974 and 1978, covering the period 1578-1866, pointing to developments in mines, torpedoes, and submarines. It seemed to be "magic" and some linked it to the devil.

I. THE NAVY, EMPIRE, EUROPE, AND EUROPEAN HEGEMONY

The navy as most instrumental in imperial expansion was the focus of two works by Peter Padfield [**2731, 2729**], Tides of Empire: Decisive Naval Campaigns in the Rise of the West, 4 vols. projected, 2 published, 1979-1982, and Maritime Supremacy and the Opening of the Western Mind: Naval Campaigns that Shaped the Modern World, 1588-1782, 1999; and James Stokesbury [**3458**], Navy and Empire, 1983, mostly anecdotal with little analysis. Padfield insisted that maritime supremacy was the key to dominance. The campaigns included the Armada, the Dutch Golden Age, Sole Bay, Finisterre of 1747, Chesapeake Bay of 1781, and the Saints of 1782. Archibald Lewis [**2112**], European Naval and Maritime History, 300-1500, 1986, presented the theme that sea power held together empires for centuries.

Correct with the times and latest trends were the global approaches. The eminent American historian and founder of the world history movement, William McNeill [**2319**] wrote a long essay, The Age of Gunpowder Empires, 1450-1800, 1989, sponsored by the American Historical Association. Continuing the global perspective, Geoffrey Scammell [**3238**], The World Encompassed: The First European Maritime Empires, c. 800-1650, 1981, described the unparalleled expansion of Western Europe, citing a chronological sequence of nine empires culminating with the English. An equally distinguished historian, J.H. Parry [**2782**], contributed The Establishment of European Hegemony, 1415-1715: Trade and Exploration in the Age of the Renaissance, 1961; the "tools" were charts, ships, and guns. Most recently,

George Raudzens [**3020**] presented a synthesis, Empires: Europe and Globalization, 1492-1788, 1999. The process was facilitated by the development of the fully rigged, cannon-armed oceanic vessel.

J. THE SEA, THE OCEAN, SEAFARERS, AND REGIONS

The sea has attracted many historians. The famous J.H. Parry [**2783**], Romance of the Sea, 1981, presented the history of seafaring sponsored by the National Geographic Society. The format was spectacular with color photos, some double-page. The contribution of Richard Armstrong [**140**] was A History of Seafaring, 3 vols., 1967-1969, folio size, individual titles being The Early Mariners, The Discoverers, and The Merchantmen. David Howarth [**1693**] added The Men-of-War to The Seafarers series, 1978.

The distinguished J.A. Williamson [**3899**] presented the Ford Lectures of 1939-1940 at Oxford University, The Ocean in English History. He featured the "propagandists," for example, the Hakluyts, Purchas, and Raleigh.

During the summers of 1992 and 1993, John Hattendorf [**1561**] directed National Endowment for the Humanities Summer Institutes at the John Carter Brown Library, Providence, RI. Over 40 lectures by 17 experts were presented and were here collected in 2 vols.: Maritime History, 1996-1997, The Age of Discovery and The Eighteenth Century. The experts included N.A.M. Rodger, Roger Knight, Tony Ryan, Glyn Williams, Daniel Baugh, Karel Davids, and Thomas Philbrick.

Regional studies have included The Narrow Seas: A History of the English Channel, Its Approaches, and Its Immediate Shores, 400 BC-AD 1945, 1959, by Reginald Hargreaves [**1512**], a fascinating survey; features included the Cinque Ports and the Thames Estuary. Michael Duffy [**975**], sometime editor of Mariner's Mirror and head of maritime studies at the University of Exeter, formulated The New Maritime History of Devon, 2 vols., 1992-1994, 32 expert writers presenting its history from earliest times; a model local history featuring maritime developments. The project began with an essay by Michael Oppenheim of 1900, originally for the Victorian County History. No area of the British Isles was more affected by the sea. A.G. Jamieson [**1792**], A People of the Sea: The Maritime History of the Channel Islands, 1986, was lavishly illustrated, featuring the period from 1680 to 1730 when privateering thrived; smuggling thrived throughout.

Ronald Hope [**1665**], A New History of British Shipping, 1990, was an impressive, scholarly reference work covering from 3000 BC to the present. Themes included Celts, Anglo-Saxons, Vikings, merchant adventurers, privateers, war and expansion, and, later, the decline.

The great C.R. Boxer [**406, 400**] collected a series of accounts of shipwrecks over history, The Tragic History of the Sea, 1959, and Further Selections from the Tragic History of the Sea, 1968, for the Hakluyt Society.

K. OTHER ENGLISH/BRITISH AND FOREIGN FORCES

For purposes of comparison and contrast, some other English/British forces will be presented. An introductory overview of the early periods can been obtained from the two great classics by Charles Oman [**2705, 2706**]. Their feature was encyclopedic coverage: A History of the Art of War in the Middle Ages, 2 vols., 1898, and A History of the Art of War in the Sixteenth Century, 1937.

More extensive, more respected, and more judgmental than the 7-volume history of the RN of Laird Clowes [**669**] was John Fortesque [**1162**], A History of the British Army, 13 vols., 1899-1930. A sample judgment was his assessment of the British attack on Washington and Baltimore in 1814, from vol. 10: "a useless and almost wicked sacrifice" for no object except to bring prize-money to the RN; unfortunately, not the first nor the last disaster attributable to the same cause.

Closest to the navy, actually, part of it, was the Royal Marines. In 1664, a time of mobilization and shortage of naval personnel, Charles II assigned 1200 soldiers to the RN as "The Duke of York and Albany's Maritime Regiment of Foot"; evolving into the Royal Marines. Commander of a Commando force during the Falklands-Malvinas campaign of 1982, Julian Thompson [**3605**], wrote The Royal Marines: From Sea Soldiers to Special Forces, 2000, which covered from the 18th century. Some short histories of the Royal Marines were by A. Cecil Hampshire [**1473**], G.W.M. Grover [**1412**], and A.P. Willasey-Wilsey [**3867**]. A dissertation by A.J. Marini [**2381**] compared British Marines, 1746-1771, with the U.S. Marines, 1798-1818. His theme was creation of institutional bureaucracies. Paul Harris Nicolas [**2644**], Historical Record of the Royal Marine Forces, 1845, described a limited chronological period. J.A. Lowe [**2193**, 1990, has more extensive coverage but limited it to the Portsmouth Division of the Royal Marines.

There were three accounts of HM Coastguard, which began in the 17th century as coast watchers and an anti-smuggling force: the official history by William Webb [**3800**], 1976; others by Frank Bowen [**389**], 1928, and Bernard Scarlett [**3239**], 1971. It evolved into a naval reserve force.

Emil Sigwart [**3316**] wrote the history of the Royal Fleet Auxiliary, 1969, covering the period 1760-1968. It was the supply and victualling force.

The Post Office Packet Service has maritime and naval connections; its history between 1793 and 1815 was by Arthur Norway [**2652**].

For purposes of comparison and contrast, some other navies will be presented. Most threatening for the longest period during the pre-1815 period was the French navy. During the long series of wars, sometimes dubbed "the Second Hundred Years' Wars," the only two antagonists of dozens, for example, Denmark, Sweden, Spain, Portugal, the Dutch, Prussia, Bavaria, Russia, and several Italian states, which, when war was in progress, were consistently on opposite sides: England/Britain and France. The old standard was Charles de La

Ronciere [**2031**], Histoire de la Marine Francaise, 6 vols., 1899-1932, the equivalent of Clowes [**669**]. In English, there was E.H. Jenkins [**1797**], A History of the French Navy, 1973, featuring Richelieu, Colbert, the Dutch wars, Barbary pirates, and guerre de course. Another was Philippe Masson [**2459**], Histoire de la Marine Francaise, 2 vols., 1981-1983. **See 12., B.**

There were too many histories of the U.S. Navy to consider, but that of James Fenimore Cooper [**737**], The History of the Navy of the United States, 2 vols., 1839, was pertinent for several reasons. For decades it was used as a textbook for American naval cadets and the account of the War of 1812 remained controversial; Oliver Hazard Perry and Jesse Duncan Elliot sued Cooper.

D.J. Hastings [**1548**], The Royal Indian Navy, 1612-1950, 1944, documented a parallel development with the RN.

L. PERTINENT GENERAL HISTORIES

Again, for context, background, and special emphases, several general histories of England/Britain should be reviewed. A good place for any student and researcher to begin would be David Hume [**1729**], The History of England from the Invasion of Julius Caesar to the Revolution of 1688, various editions beginning in 1754, 6 to 8 vols. Hume was seen as a Tory historian. Another classic was James A. Froude [**1207**], History of England from the Fall of Wolsey to the Defeat of the Spanish Armada, 12 vols., 1856-1870. Lawrence James [**1780**], The Rise and Fall of the British Empire, 1994, devoted much emphasis on origins to piracy in the 16th century, "a strong cord, whose fibres were greed and fearlessness, linked the Elizabethan sea rover, the eighteenth-century naval captain hungry for prize money, and the early Victorian soldier in the process of looting."

Most recently, a series of "Churchillian" approaches have emerged, copying Winston Churchill [**637**], A History of the English-Speaking Peoples, 4 vols., 1956-1958, originally written in 1936 but put away during the duration of World War II and his Prime Ministership. Copying Churchill, indeed, using extensive quotes from History of the English-Speaking Peoples, was Christopher Lee [**2089**], This Sceptered Isle, 55 BC-1901, 1997, in support of a BBC-Radio-4 series of the same name. Supporting a BBC-TV-1 and BBC-TV-2 series of six hours presented in the fall of 2001 was Simon Schama [**3242**], A History of Britain, 2 vols., 2000-2001. The role of Scotland was emphasized.

Of these broad national histories, the one most pertinent to this historiographical-bibliographical survey was Norman Davies [**875**], The Isles: A History, 1999, almost 1200 pages. Its strength was full coverage of England, Ireland, Scotland, and Wales, all part of "the isles." Its approach was the opposite of Anglocentrism. Extensive coverage included the invasions by Julius

Caesar, the Irish-Scots of Dalriada, the Angles of Northumbria, and the Danish empire of Cnut.

M. THE STATE OF ENGLISH/BRITISH NAVAL HISTORY

Begin with John Hattendorf [**1570**], UBI SUMUS?: The State of Naval and Maritime History, 1994, 33 essays by the most noted experts assessing the state of naval history in 29 countries: for Great Britain, N.A.M. Rodger; for Australia, James Goldrick; for Ireland, John de Courcy Ireland, and for Sweden, John Glete. W.J.R. Gardner [**1250**] assessed the state in 1995, reviewing significant books by J.R. Bruijn, Richard Harding, and Jan Glete and praising N.A.M. Rodger, Daniel Baugh, Michael Duffy, and John Hattendorf.

In 1999, N.A.M. Rodger [**3115**] reviewed recent books on the RN of the 18th century. He recalled Mahan, Corbett, J.K. Laughton, and Richmond followed by a long lull. Then, about 1960, quality and quantity increased, over 250 books about the 18th century alone since 1970. Broadened perspectives emerged, for example, administration, the dockyards, and logistics. The significance of privateering was now properly appreciated.

In 2001, Peter LeFevre [**2099**] reviewed several prominent books just published; the authors were Peter Padfield [**2729**], Clark Reynolds [**3050**], Jan Glete [**1299**], and Richard Harding [**1495**]. He was pleased with the collective output but called for publication of some noted dissertations, for example, Andrew Thrush [**3619**] and William Cogar [**693**]. Other gaps concerned the area of finance, funding for the navy, and the role of the Navy Treasurer.

In 2001, Eugene Rasor [**3011**] surveyed the historiography of the RN, concluding that interest was increasing. The essay was broad-based and included an extensive assessment supported by lengthy footnotes.

In 2001, Margarette Lincoln [**2135**] recalled W. Laird Clowes [**669**], Royal Navy, "the magisterial 6-volume" [sic] history. Clowes lamented that excessive hagiography and too much on battles characterized naval history. In a segue, she announced that interest was increasing: two conferences were featured in London in a week in July 2001.

Increasingly popular was the writing of counterfactual history, "What If?" The Spanish Armada has been a favorite topic. J.C. Squire [**3413**], If, or History Rewritten, 1931, was an older collection, reprinted in 1964. Prominent persons contributed, for example, Winston Churchill on the American Civil War. Several were about the Armada. More recently, Robert Cowley [**781**], 1999, editor of Military History Quarterly or MHQ, collected 24 examples of counterfactual history by prominent historians, for example, John Keegan, Niall Ferguson, Geoffrey Parker, and Steven Ambrose.

In articles elsewhere, Geoffrey Parker [**2751**], 1976, Colin Martin [**2424**], 1988, and Felix Barker [**205**], 1988, speculated about alternative, for example, if the Spanish had invaded and if the forces of Parma had coordinated properly with the Armada. Jonathan North [**2651**], The Napoleon Options, 2000, collected ten essays about decisive moments when Napoleon could have opted for alternative actions, for example, success in Egypt and in Ireland. Simon Leys [**2132**], The Death of Napoleon, 1989, touted "alternative history" in his popular counterfactual history: Napoleon escaped from the control of the British.

On the occasion of the 40th anniversary of the Journal of Transport History, 1993, David Williams [**3871**] assessed the progress of maritime history, pleased that interest was increasing, for example, opening of the MARY ROSE Museum and restoration of HMS WARRIOR; the return of GREAT BRITAIN to Bristol; adding to the already popular HMS VICTORY and CUTTY SARK.

Chapter 7

Chronological Periods: Naval Wars and Prominent Battles

What follows is a historiographical-bibliographical survey based on a chronological presentation and featuring naval wars and battles over time. Various ways can be used to divide this history. The following periodization of English/British history will be used:

Celts of Northern Europe – 800-50 BC
Roman Britain – 43-410 AD
Kingdom of Dalriada – c. 500-800 AD
Anglo-Saxon England – c. 600-1066
Vikings and Danes – 800-1100
Norman England – 1066-1154
Angevin England – 1154-1216
Medieval period – 10th to 15th centuries
Wales, Ireland, Scotland - various
Lancastrians and Yorkists – 1399-1485
Tudor England – 1485-1603
Stuart era – 1603-1714
Civil War and Cromwellian Period – 1640s and 1650s
Hanoverian-Windsor Britain – 1714 -present

Instead of a separate Chronology, a long list of dates in time, the periods of English/British naval history will be subdivided into major segments, some of which will be identified with the important feature of the period, for example, Julius Caesar and the invasion by Rome, King Alfred and the Anglo-Saxons, William the Conqueror and the Normans, and Richard I and the Crusades.

A. ROMAN BRITAIN

1. Julius Caesar

The future Roman Emperor, Julius Caesar [**538, 539**], himself, wrote of his famous campaign in what was called Gaul, the future area of France. Caesar recalled his "British expeditions" in 55 and 54 BC, for the purpose of pacifying Celtic native tribes there. Two large amphibious operations were undertaken and Caesar led forays through the southeast of England. Other descriptions of the two expeditions were Stephen Ridd [**3068**], Julius Caesar in Gaul and Britain, 1995; John Peddie [**2806**], Invasion: The Roman Invasion of Britain in the Year 43 and the Events Leading to Their Occupation of the West Country, 1997, Peter Ellis [**1038**], Caesar's Invasion of Britain, 1978, Francis Vine [**3729**], Caesar in Kent, 1886, Barry Burnham [**516**], Invasion and Response: The Case of Roman Britain, 1979, and Rice Holmes [**1661**], Ancient Britain and the Invasion of Julius Caesar, 1907. Vine described details of the two expeditions, for example, the Romans progressed along Watling Street, probably as far as Chertsey on the Thames River. Archaeological evidence has confirmed more details. Caesar oversaw construction of fleets of warships and transports, twice. There were 80 in the first and about 200 ships in the second expedition. They sailed from Boulogne. Weather interfered and caused disruption and losses. A century passed before the Claudian invasion, beginning in 43 AD. At that time the Roman Legions advanced along three fronts: to Lincoln, to the Midlands, and to the Southwest.

2. Invasion

The expeditions by Julius Caesar and subsequent Roman invasion and settlement were recounted by Malcolm Todd [**3629**], Roman Britain, 55 BC-AD 400: The Province Beyond the Ocean, 1997, Graham Webster [**3801**], The Roman Invasion of Britain, 1980, and Donald Dudley [**968**], The Roman Conquest of Britain, AD 43-57, 1965. Roman shipping and naval organization were explained by Chester Starr [**3428**], The Roman Imperial Navy, 31 BC-AD 324, 1941, Joan Taylor [**3582**], Roman Shipping and Trade, 1978, and in an article by D.B. Saddington [**3203**], 1990. On the northern frontier, three flotillas operated, each named for pertinent provinces, for example, classis Germanica for the Rhenish fleet and classis Britannica for the Channel. The latter consisted of transports and galleys plus associated support such as coastal forts and lighthouses. Later the entire system was called "the Saxon Shore," as described by Stephen Johnson [**1818**], The Roman Forts of the Saxon Shore, 1976.

B. ANGLO-SAXON ENGLAND

From about 400 AD until the Norman Conquest of 1066, Anglo-Saxon England superseded Roman Britain; the feature in the literature was King Alfred the Great who reigned from 871-899, technically as King of Wessex. Also, the Vikings-Danes were coming!

The student and researcher would do well to first consult John Haywood [**1585**], Dark Age Naval Power: A Reassessment of the Frankish and Anglo-Saxon Seafaring Activities, 1991. These pre-Viking Age seafarers of Germanic origin have been underestimated. From the study of numismatics, archaeology, and literary evidence, Haywood asserted that their maritime achievements were impressive in warfare, piracy, migration, and trade. They adopted use of sailing vessels, perhaps as early as the second century. Other scholars had assigned much of this credit to the Vikings and were skeptical about sailing ship use.

Two works presented preliminary aspects. Archaeological boat finds near the shores indicated that the primary route of immigration into the British Isles was across the North Sea from Denmark and northern Germany as described by Sean McGrail [**2259**], Maritime Celts, Frisians and Saxons, 1990, papers from an archaeological conference. Bernard Bachrach [**167**], 1990, speculated about the ubiquitous legendary King Arthur of the early Anglo-Saxon period, interjecting a naval connection. His thesis was that the location of battles associated with Arthur suggested that he was a notable naval commander.

For the Anglo-Saxon period, a good place to begin study was James Campbell [**567**], The Anglo-Saxons, 1982, a general survey. Among other things, Campbell described various fleets: Roman, Alfred's, and Viking. The ships of Alfred were a new design, "long ships of 60 oars," but it was unlikely that Alfred was "founder." The English were a maritime people and sea approaches were from three directions, meaning three different developments: the North Sea focusing on the east coast and Scandinavian connections, for example, the age of SUTTON HOO; the Irish Sea featuring monastic connections, for example, Iona, and the Channel, involving advanced Continental connections. Edward Gifford [**1274**], 1996, analyzed the performance of Anglo-Saxon ships. Trade was more extensive than previously reported. Half-scale models of the SUTTON HOO ship in Suffolk and the Graveney-find ship in Kent had been constructed and experimental tests could be made. The results were reported.

History and interpretations about the Anglo-Saxons were much in flux. For one thing, debate has arisen about a primary source for this chronological period, The Anglo-Saxon Chronicle, which covered about six centuries.

Another controversy concerned feudalism and institutional structure. Warren Hollister [**1655**], Anglo-Saxon Military Institutions on the Eve of the Norman Conquest, 1962, included a chapter on the navy, its institutional basis, and tactics and strategy. For Hollister, the key was the fyrd, a medieval tenure based on territorial obligations to provide ships and perform sea duty, especially for certain coastal towns, later designated as the Cinque Ports. The ship fyrd was similar to the land fyrd, about which more was known: one soldier per 5 hides. The naval obligation may have been one ship per 300 hides. The typical ship required a crew of 60 men. By the time of King Edward the Confessor and King Harold Godwinson, fleets were well established; Godwinson assembled and commanded a large force around the Isle of Wight in anticipation of the Norman invasion in the summer of 1066. Apparently, the time obligation was exhausted and Godwinson was forced to demobilize it. The Anglo-Saxon fyrd was also described in detail by Richard Abels [4, 5] in a dissertation and book, 1982 and 1988. He distinguished the landfyrd and scypfyrd. Nicholas Hooper [1664], 1978, elaborated. For the post-Norman Conquest period, Michael Powicke [2937], 1962, described similar military obligations.

1. King Alfred

The literature about Alfred abounded, as did the myths and legends such as "founder of the British navy." The Victorians were said to be suffering from Alfred-mania. Alfred Smyth [3375], 1996, elaborated, noting that the military-naval reputation of Alfred was documented in the Anglo-Saxon Chronicle. Interpretations by Frank Stenton [3444] dominated for too long. Anglo-Saxon England [120] was the applicable journal for this chronological period; vol. 28, 1999, being devoted to King Alfred and his shipbuilding innovations. Was he "founder of the British navy?"

Examples of corrective ventures included David Sturdy [3478], Alfred the Great, 1995, which touted debunking the myths. Alfred Smyth [3376], King Alfred the Great, 1995, caused much controversy. John Peddie [2805], Alfred: Warrior King, 1999, analyzed his military reputation as he fought the Vikings. Much was about his "newly founded navy" which fought inshore and in river estuaries; his ships being "of superior size." More generally, Richard Abels [3], Alfred the Great: War, Kingship, and Culture in Early England, 1998, was intended to restore the military-naval reputation of Alfred, for example, Alfred designed and operated an innovative warship against the Vikings. In an article of 1942, Francis Magoun [2326] repeated a description of a naval battle between the fleet of Alfred of nine ships versus a Danish fleet of six ships, deemed the first English naval engagement. Anglo-Norman Warfare, 1992, by Matthew Strickland [3474], covered warfare over several centuries. The "founder of the Royal Navy" was Alfred. The Anglo-Saxon Chronicle described "new model ships" participating in a battle of 896, plus, Alfred had been victorious in other sea confrontations with the Vikings: 875, 882, and 885.

2. The Vikings

Also called Norse, Norsemen, Northmen, Normans, and Danes, the Vikings were advanced maritime people. They conducted extensive pirate-plunder raids over an extraordinarily broad area including all of the British Isles and were able to colonize Scotland, Ireland, the Isle of Man, the Northern Isles, and much of England, among many other places. The latest survey of the Norsemen was by Eric Christiansen [**631**], 2002.

Meantime, the Vikings were coming! They were much to be feared. As noted, they roamed all over the Northern Seas and beyond. They first appeared in the British Isles in 778. These came from what is now Denmark and Norway. Their Danelaw continued until the Norman Conquest. Shallow-draft vessels meant they could navigate up river estuaries. Religious centers, especially valuable religious symbols and objects, were favorite items to plunder.

The Vikings were the subjects of an expansive literature. P.H. Sawyer [**3230**], a premier scholar, wrote <u>Kings and Vikings: Scandinavia and Europe, AD 700-1100</u>, 1982, summarizing the age of the Vikings. Sources were scarce, and the exploits of the Vikings have been distorted and exaggerated. Their violence was no worse than the English, Franks, and Friscians. Vikings settled. Alliances with locals were made, including one with the Archbishop of York. Place names and the Danelaw have endured. The rulers maintained fleets at the expense of the natives. Paddy Griffith [**1400**], <u>The Viking Art of War</u>, 1995, placed more emphasis on Vikings as traders and settlers. W.G. Collingwood [**707**], <u>Scandinavian Britain: Account of the Viking Age</u>, 1908, described the early Viking raids. Settlements were established in Wales, Cheshire, Lancaster, Cumberland, the Isle of Man, and the Orkneys. Eastern Ireland was settled by 830. Eric John [**1810**], 1977, called it the Three Hundred Years' War, the Vikings vs. the Anglo-Saxons. He focused on one reign, King AEthelred, about 1010, and a battle, Maldon, both of which were relatively well documented. Simon Keynes [**1928**], 1980, described the process of granting lands and privileges within the Viking-Danish Empire. N.A.M. Rodger [**3106**], 1995, elaborated on further Danish processes imposing monetary taxes on the English to pay for Danish fleets: the geld. Alfred Smyth [**3377**], <u>Scandinavian Kings in the British Isles, 850-880</u>, 1977, focused on an earlier, formative phase of Viking expansion. Henry Loyn [**2197-2199**], 1976-1977, produced three works about the Vikings in Britain and Wales.

Stephen Pollington [**2877**], <u>The Warrior's Way: England in the Viking Age</u>, 1989, pointed out that it was a violent era. That battle of Maldon of 991 was featured, the primary source being a long poem. The Vikings with a fleet of 93 ships invaded and attacked an Anglo-Saxon army. AEthelraed the Unready was king. Maldon was a town in Essex on the Blackwater estuary. Two accounts described the battle of Maldon: D.G. Scragg [**3263**], 1981, and Janet Cooper [**743**], 1993, the latter being papers from a conference on the occasion of the millennium of the battle. <u>Ships and Men of the Late Viking Age</u>, 2001, by Judith

Jesch [**1808**], was a critical survey, fleets, sailing, and battles, covering the 10th and 11th centuries.

King Cnut and the Danish Empire were covered by M.K. Lawson [**2082**], Cnut: the Danes in England in the Early Eleventh Century, 1993, noting it consisted of Denmark, Norway, and most of southern England and headed by Cnut who ruled from 1017-1035, the high point of Viking rule, and Alexander Rumble [**3169**], The Reign of Cnut: King of England, Denmark, and Norway, 1994. The grants, fiefdoms, and the geld meant accumulation of a fleet by Cnut and his successors of 150 to 200 ships, each with 60 oars; with a total carrying capacity of 10,000 men, plus land forces Rumble characterized as "a standing army."

C. NORMAN ENGLAND

The Norman period, 1066-1154, superseded the Anglo-Saxon period. A case can be made that the year 1066 in England was decisive, perhaps the most decisive in British history. Remember the historical satire by Walter Sellar [**3270**], 1066 and All That: A Memorable History of England, 1931. Anglo-Saxon England ended and Norman England began in l066.

1. William the Conqueror, the Conquest

On January 4, King Edward the Confessor died with no direct heir. Harold Godwinson of Wessex claimed the English throne, his coronation conducted on 5 January. With a more authentic claim, William, Duke of Normandy, began massive preparations for invasion of England from his realm of Normandy, across the Channel. Yet another claimant was Tostig, brother of Harold, and his supporter, King Harald Hardrada of Norway. They invaded England in the north and captured York. Thus, there were at least three claimants and, during 1066, there were three battles and two invasions. The dispute was resolved by force of arms, the decisive battles being Stamford Bridge in September, a victory for King Harold, and Hastings, fought on 14 October, and a defeat for Harold, who was killed. William proceeded to secure his new kingdom, arriving in London by a circuitous route for his coronation on 25 December. Recent writing has given more credit to Harold, especially as a naval commander. The Anglo-Saxon fleet was a viable force and had been mobilized during the summer of 1066, operating off the Isle of Wight, an excellent location to attack an invasion fleet from Normandy. Apparently its term of service expired and Harold was forced to let it go. The preparations by William and his supporters and retainers in Normandy were on a massive scale.

The old standard account plus a reprint of the third volume was E.A. Freeman [**1189, 1190**], The History of the Norman Conquest: Its Causes and Its

Results, 6 vols., 1867-1879, 1974, notoriously biased for the Anglo-Saxons and against the Normans and French, for example, conjuring up the "Norman Yoke" and insisting on calling the Anglo-Saxons the "English," in the process creating myths and praising "English liberties" and superior government.

Five works were based on the year 1066: by Denis Butler [**530**], 1066: The Story of a Year, 1966; David Howarth [**1696**], 1066: The Year of the Conquest, 1977; Rupert Furneux [**1218**], Invasion: 1066, 1966; Frank McLynn [**2315**], 1066: The Year of the Three Battles, 1998, N.A.M. Rodger [**3114**], "The Norman Invasion of 1066," 1994, and Richard Glover [**1303**], "English Warfare in 1066." Rodger stressed the complexity of events of the year. Glover described the army of Godwinson victorious at Stamford Bridge and defeated at Hastings.

A substantial, recent account shifted the traditional focus: Kelly De Vries [**923**], The Norwegian Invasion of England in 1066, 1999. The "other invasion" was described and the Scandinavian perspective was stressed. King Harald Hardrada of Norway invaded England in the north, captured York, and fought two battles against Harold Godwinson, Fulford Gate and Stamford Bridge.

The Norman Conquest was a popular title: by Donald Matthew [**2467**], 1966, Kenneth Setton [**3280**], 1966, H.R. Loyd [**2196**], 1967, and two by R. Allen Brown [**473, 472**], 1968 and 1984. The army of William followed the Continental military system centered on cavalry. Transport across the Channel would be a massive undertaking. Numbers varied wildly; perhaps, the army consisted of 7000, of which 3000 were mounted knights. Each knight must have four horses; so, at least 12,000 horses had to be transported. Elisabeth Van Houts [**1686**], "The Ship List of William the Conqueror," 1987, described naval preparations, which began on 5 January and continued through August. The extant ship list was an account of the magnates, the number of ships, knights service owed to William, and details about the provisions to be carried. 776 ships were listed. Another source said 696. That one claiming 10,000 ships can be discounted. Jean Laporte [**2030**], 1967, elaborated.

Christine Grainge [**1362**], "The Pevensey Expedition: Brilliantly Executed Plan or Near Disaster?", 1993, described the preparations and execution of the campaign. The flotilla set out from Dives Estuary. The ships were of Viking design, double ended open boats with a single mast and square sail, clearly depicted in the Bayeux Tapestry. Conditions of wind and tide in the Channel proved decisive. William was forced to wait for the proper conditions. Harold had to release the Anglo-Saxon fleet, which could not remain mobilized indefinitely. J. Neumann [**2629**], 1988, analyzed the hydrographic aspects of the campaign, for example, tides, tidal data, winds, and weather factors. Chroniclers and the Bayeux Tapestry were informative. Storms and sinkings were recalled.

David Douglas [**950, 951, 952**] has contributed three pertinent works: The Norman Achievement, 1969, The Norman Fate, 1976, and a biography, William the Conqueror, 1967. The "achievement" recounted extraordinarily expansive activities of the Normans, conquest of England being one, plus invasions of Scotland, Wales, Spain, and around into the Mediterranean, conquering Sicily and southern Italy, all between 1050-1100. The Conquest of England was a "crusade" sanctioned and supported by the Pope. Older biographies of William the Conqueror were by E.A. Freeman [1191], 1888, and the ubiquitous Frank Stenton [3444], 1908.

Harold Godwinson has been neglected. Ian Walker [3739], Harold: The Last Anglo-Saxon King, 2000, has filled the gap. Frank Barlow [208], 2002, presented a recent survey of the dynasty, the Godwins. Harold and William: The Battle for England, 1064-1066, 2001, reviewed the fateful conflict. The traditional depiction of Edward the Confessor was considerably altered: seen as crafty and manipulative and definitely not celibate. He banned the Godwinsons and designated William as his heir. Harold took an oath to William and was restored as Earl of Wessex. Earl Tostig was a brother. In 1066, Harold was able to assemble a substantial fleet in the Channel but was forced to disband it in September. Then the battles; Stamford Bridge was a great success. Perhaps Harold overestimated his capabilities and those of his army because Hastings proved fatal to both. Stephen Morillo [2546], The Battle of Hastings, 1996, described the battle in traditional and unapologetic "drum and trumpet" fashion. The debate over numbers of troops on either side continued.

Unlike the Anglo-Saxon period, primary sources for the Norman period were numerous. R. Allen Brown [472] counted 202, for example and especially, the extraordinary Bayeux Tapestry, plus The Anglo-Saxon Chronicle, charters, surveys, and seals. Brown [471] also edited a special edition, Volume XI, 1988, of Anglo-Norman Studies, a journal devoted to the period. It published the proceedings of the annual Battle Conference, the first being held in 1978. Michael Altschul [62], 1969, surveyed for the Conference on British Studies. Two works described unique sources: Elisabeth van Houts [1685], The "Gesta Normannorum Ducum" of William of Jumieges, Oderic Vitalis, and Robert of Turigni, 2 vols., 1995, and R.H.C. Davis [882], The "Gesta Guillelmi" of William of Poitiers, 1998, both in the Oxford Medieval Texts series. These were first hand accounts by participants.

Marjorie Chibnall [627] reviewed some of the controversies in The Debate on the Norman Conquest, 1999. In the 16th century, an ongoing controversy over feudalism, its degree, whether it was Anglo-Saxon and/or Anglo-Norman in origin and practice, raged. Reference has been made to the "Norman Yoke" and superior "English [read Anglo-Saxon] liberties," the question of "national identity," and interpretations of events depicted in the Bayeux Tapestry. See 21., B., 1.

2. Richard I, the Crusades

Rare were the sources identifying naval factors associated with the Crusades, far-off events. We know more about the Third Crusade, 1189-1192. Jerusalem had been conquered in 1099; Jerusalem fell to Saladin in 1187.

European monarchs took to the cross to recover Jerusalem. While Count of Poitou, Richard signaled his intention in 1187; he and King Philip Augustus of France departed for the Third Crusade in 1190; a "great English fleet" being assembled, 33 from the Cinque Ports plus others, and set out, first to Italy. Frederick Barbarossa died in 1190, en route to the Holy Land. In April 1191, Philip arrived at Acre; 8 June, Richard to Acre, and 12 October, the English fleet to Acre. Tripoli and Tyre were occupied; Acre was successfully besieged. Philip became ill and departed, August; Richard became ill and departed, and a shipwreck en route in October resulted in the capture of Richard.

A good introduction and overview was given by Susan Rose [**3144**], in "Islam versus Christendom: The Naval Dimension, 1000-1600," 1999. There was a dissertation, "Some Aspects of Maritime Activity and Use of Sea Power in Relation to the Crusading States, 1096-1169," by S.M. Foster [**1164**], 1978. Further developments were described by Peter Edbury [**1013**], The Conquest of Jerusalem and the Third Crusade, 1998, Thomas Archer [**133**], The Crusade of Richard I, 1189-1192, 1889, and Geoffrey Regan [**3044**], Lionhearts: Saladin, Richard I, and the Era of the Third Crusade, 1998, reviewing the campaigns of Saladin and Richard. James Reston [**3047**], Warriors of God: Richard the Lionheart and Saladin the Third, 2001, unfortunately, was overly popularized and pretentious, for example, Richard was described as "the greatest Arab-slayer on earth." John Pryor [**2960**], Commerce, Shipping and Naval Warfare in the Medieval Mediterranean, 1987, included essays on transports for horses for the Crusaders and naval architecture for those transports.

A dissertation stressed the Arab perspective, "Richard the Lion Heart and Salah Ad-Din Al-Ayyubi: A Historical Comparative Study," by AlJouharah B.S.B. AlMayman [**54**]. They were the most notable figures of the Crusade era and both represented respective images of chivalry. An article assessing the role of Saladin in the naval history of the eastern Mediterranean Sea was by A.S. Ehrenkreutz [**1023**], 1955. Before the Third Crusade, the Egyptian-Byzantine fleet dominated; the arrival of the navy of the Crusaders shifted the balance. The Egyptian fleet of Saladin, previously as many as 80 ships, mostly galleys, was eliminated. The fleet of Richard established a base on Cyprus and led in the siege of Acre. Saladin died in 1193 and Arab naval power never recovered.

Hans Mayer [**2480**], presented details of the return voyage of Richard I in October 1192 and his capture: "A Ghost Ship Called FRANKENEF: King Richard I's German Itinerary" 2000. En route from Acre to Corfu and to Ragusa, Richard was captured and held for ransom.

3. The Cinque Ports

Most, not all, historians agreed that the equivalent to the Royal Navy during the early Middle Ages was an impressed fleet by Royal decree from certain designated ports along the southeast coast of England, called the Cinque Ports, each receiving an appropriate charter from the Crown. The purpose was defense of the coasts and cross-Channel passage. A ship fyrd obligation was the basis, service being limited to fifteen days per year. Service meant provision of a ship and an appropriate crew. It was an ancient prerogative of the Crown. First noted, 1150-1190, by the 13th century, they were granted monopolistic privileges in exchange for building and equipping ships. For example, records noted that Henry II granted charters to Dover, Hastings, Sandwich, Romney, Hythe, Rye, and Winchelsea; later, up to 39 ports.

An older history was Montagu Burrows [**522**], Cinque Ports in the Historic Towns series, 1888; seven being included: Sandwich, Dover, Hythe, Romney, Hastings, Winchelsea, and Rye. Technically, the last two were "Ancient Towns." In addition, there were eight "Corporate Members" and 24 "Non-corporate Members," a total of 39 ports obliged to provide ships and personnel. Status was granted in charters. A substantial treatise was Katherine Murray [**2588**], The Constitutional History of the Cinque Ports, 1935. The Domesday Book contained descriptions. In the 13th century, a Confederation was established, the office of Warden was created, later as Admiral, and Admiralty Courts were set up. Decline began in the 14th century.

Margaret Brentnall [**429**], 1972, presented a summary of the historical background. A similar article was by F.W. Brooks [**454**], 1929. Edward Body [**358**], Cinque Ports and Their Lords Warden: History in Verse and Prose, 1979, was a unique presentation. Recent Lord Wardens included Winston Churchill and Queen Elizabeth, the Queen Mother. Timothy Runyan [**3173**], 1977, investigated administrative records. In the 12th and 13th centuries, naval forces came from the Cinque Ports. The "ancient custom" was 57 ships to serve 15 days per year. By the 14th century, the King's Ships were more common, over 50 can be identified about 1350. They were kept near the Tower or at the Cinque Ports. At one point, the Cinque Ports and Yarmouth came to blows in a series of conflicts, for example in 1293 and the mid-14th century, as described by F.W. Brooks [**455**], 1933.

Count on N.A.M. Rodger [**3113**], 1996, to clarify the situation. It was hard to determine actual time periods of significant use. Charters of the 11th and 12th centuries described obligations and privileges. Operations for sustained amounts of time became increasingly difficult while opponents, for example, France, Castile, Genoa, and Portugal, were able to operate warships at will, mostly galleys, along English coasts. F.W. Brooks [**456**] was the best source, describing these early warships. **See 11., D.**

4. Treaties and Expansion

Several general studies were devoted to military warfare during the Anglo-Norman period and through the medieval period. A good place to gain an introduction to the region, the sea, the peoples, and their activities was Archibald Lewis [**2113**], The Northern Seas: Shipping and Commerce in Northern Europe, AD 300-1100, 1958. So much more was known due to archaeology and numismatics. The Vikings were seen in a different light. The Anglo-Saxons, the Danish Sea Empire, the expansive Normans, the Frisians, the Carolingians, the Flemings, and the French were all described. The old standard on this subject for the Norman period was John Beeler [272], Warfare in England, 1066-1189, 1966. The most important military innovation of the Normans was the castle. There were land and sea fyrds. Warren Hollister [1656], The Military Organization of Norman England, 1965, pointed out unique factors of Norman feudalism, for example, the military household, knight's fee, castle service, scutage, mercenaries, and anticipation of the Cinque Ports.

Stephen Morillo [2547, 2548] has a dissertation and book, Warfare under the Anglo-Norman Kings, 1066-1135, the dissertation, 1066-1154, 1985 and 1994. Features were the feudal fyrd, the ship fyrd, mercenaries, and, of course, the decisive system of motte and bailey castles. Some naval campaigns were described, for example, William attacking Scotland in 1072 and in 1088, and a battle off Rochester. Tactics were described.

Michael Prestwich [2947], Armies and Warfare in the Middle Ages: The English Experience, 1996, was a scholarly synthesis, which included naval forces and logistics. Siege warfare predominated. The Third Crusade was the only one where an English monarch led a considerable contingent of English forces. A later, innovative tactic was massing of ranks of archers, which would prove so effective and successful in the Hundred Years' War. The Crecy campaign of 1346 involved a fleet, sailing from Portsmouth and, later, involved in the siege of Calais, which surrendered in August 1347. There was a chapter on the navy. Vessels were small and they must remain within close proximity to land. An open sea battle was practically impossible. Naval support was essential for all military operations, in France, the Low Countries, Ireland, Scotland, and Wales, for example, the island of Anglesey must be captured to overawe Wales. The ship types included galleys, balingers, cogs, hulks, and carrocks. Kings who assembled fleets included Henry II, Henry III, estimated at 288 ships; Richard I, John, Edward I, estimated at 300 ships, Edward III, estimated at 360 ships, and Henry V. Pieter Emmer [1042] contributed pertinent essays: The Organization of Interoceanic Trade in European Expansion, 1450-1800, 1996. Factors were the Dutch, Amsterdam as world entrepot, and the English East India Company as "a pre-modern multinational organization." Two works were on naval history, Susan Rose [3145], Medieval Naval Warfare, 2002, and John Hattendorf [1568], Power and Domination: Europe and the Sea in the Middle Ages and the Renaissance, to be published by Boydell.

In these earliest years during the transition from galleys to galleons to ships of the line, warships exclusively for warfare were rare. More common were merchant ships, which, on occasion, were converted for use in naval campaigns of the moment. They then reverted to merchant status and resumed their primary responsibility: trade. Certain areas of trade and commerce became particularly important, strategically important. They were bases for exploration, commercial and imperial expansion, and colonization. Among other things, they were essential in furthering English/British initiatives toward world hegemony. Four of these will be pursued: the Italian connections, the quasi-colonial status of Gascony in the 14th and 15th centuries, the strategically important trade and commerce in the Baltic-East European area, and the unique place of Bristol as a base for exploration and commerce.

In addition to these formative factors for naval, military, imperial, and commercial expansion, contacts, friendly and unfriendly, with certain rising states were influential, for example, Italian states such as Venice, Genoa, and Florence, and Iberian states such as Castile and Portugal. The English learned from them, exploited their forces for English purposes, and fought against them either as direct enemies or as contracted forces for traditional enemies, for example, France hiring galleys from Genoa.

Paul Kennedy [1883] and Geoffrey Scammell [3238], among others, have expounded upon long term developments of European hegemonic expansion, Kennedy presenting the process as chronological, a rise and fall dynamic. First there was Venice to be superseded by Portugal, then Spain, then the Dutch Republics, and finally, the English/British. Later, of course, the United States arose, and, in the view of Kennedy, will fall. Lessor players were Genoa, Florence, Sweden, and France. At one point, China was a potential participant but circumstances evolved so that that potential was never realized. The Arabs may have had an opportunity, again aborted. For one thing, they were quashed by the violent Portuguese. As far as the English/British were concerned, these developments were precursors and models for their own move toward global hegemony based upon naval supremacy. The culmination was Pax Britannica.

D. THE ISLES

Norman Davies [875] entitled his revisionist, anti-Anglo-centrist history of all of the British Isles, The Isles, 1999, noting "British Isles" became an obsolete term when Ireland left the Commonwealth.

1. Dalriada

As noted, Norman Davies [875] has a new history of the British Isles, which aggressively eschewed Anglo-centrism and N.A.M. Rodger [3110] in Safeguard of the Sea, brought the maritime kingdom of Dalriada out of obscurity. Dalriada was the Irish-Scottish naval kingdom. The origins of "Dal Riata" were obscure and in dispute. In about 500 AD in what was now County Atrim and County Down in Ireland, Fergus Mor, the dynastic leader of Dal Riata, moved from Ireland to the western isles of Scotland. They expanded into the Lords of the Isles of the Western Highlands and Hebrides. A Celtic naval power was established there between the 6th and 8th centuries. It was the sea that unified their scattered territories. St. Columba of Iona referred to them, and a famous sanctuary and holy burial ground of kings was established at Iona. The warships were oared vessels, about 14 oarsmen and smaller than Viking ships. Archaeologists have uncovered a series of fortress sites but, unfortunately, no ship remains. Their enemies were the Picts and the Celtic Britons. Then the Vikings invaded. The Romans called these peoples Scotti and that name endured, evolving into the kingdom of Scotland.

Ronald Williams [3890], The Lords of the Isles: The Clan Donald and the Early Kingdom of the Scots, 1984, John Bannerman [196], Studies in the History of Dalriada, 1974, and H.M. Chadwick [603], Early Scotland: The Picts, the Scots and Welsh of Southern Scotland, 1974, reviewed the history of Dalriada. Barbara Crawford [791], Scandinavian Scotland: Scotland in the Early Middle Ages, 1987, described the disposition of Dalriada; the Vikings came, invaded, and dominated here and the Isle of Man from the 8th century to the 1060s.

2. Ireland

The true isle was Ireland. Irish sea connections, ill served by historians, remained a neglected area. In the early 14th century, the Bruce brothers, Edward and Robert, were involved in Scotland and Ireland, recounted by Sean Duffy [979], 1991. In a dissertation, Duffy [980], 1993, recounted a series of expeditions by Irish kings to control the Irish Sea. The history of that region, 850-1254, was reviewed by J.T. Maple [2363], 1985. The Viking connection, a major one, was reviewed by Howard Clarke [648], 1998; and operations with the English in the 13th and 14th centuries, in a dissertation by James Lydon [2207], 1955. Michael McCaughan [2227], The Irish Sea: Aspects of Maritime History, 1989, stressed the perspectives of the Irish and Ulsterites. Thomas Bartlett [228], A Military History of Ireland, 1996, was a professional, scholarly survey of 1500 years of activity. The distinguished historian, John de Coursey Ireland [1749], wrote Ireland and Irish Maritime History, 1986, covering 8000 years. Aidan McIvor [2274], A History of the Irish Naval Service, 1994, began with Celtic invaders and covered subsequent ones: Vikings, Henry II, Oliver Cromwell, William III, and the French; the history of a maritime country.

3. Scotland

A recent short survey covering from 500 BC to the present, Maritime Scotland, 2000, by Brian Lavery [2074], provided a good introduction. More substantial was T.C. Smout [3374], Scotland and the Sea, 1992, a series of random essays by experts. In the 3rd century, Rome invaded Scotland by sea. Centuries later, the Jacobites used the sea to get in and out of Scotland. Scottish

contacts with Scandinavia and the Baltic trade were stressed. More specific was
A.R.G. McMillan [**2316**], "The Admiral of Scotland," 1923. McMillan lamented
the neglect of Scottish maritime history and presented instances of designated
"Admirals" and "Lord High Admirals" in Scottish history, for example, in the
13th, 15th, and 17th centuries. "Making the Empire British: Scotland in the
Atlantic World, 1542-1717," 1997, by David Armitage [**137**], stressed expansive
Scottish maritime connections.

Other developments around the Irish Sea were recounted by John
MacInnes [**2266**], "West Highlands Sea-Power in the Middle Ages," 1972. R.A.
MacDonald [**2236**], The Kingdom of the Isles: Scotland's Western Seaboard, c.
1000-c. 1336, 1997, was about the McSorley Clan who drove out the Vikings
and established a Lordship of the Isles, a maritime empire with links to
Scotland, Ireland, England, and Norway. They spoke Gaelic and communicated
and transported among the lochs, rivers, and firths. R.R. Davies [**877**] edited
eight papers, The British Isles, 1100-1500, 1988, stressing connections. One
paper described an invasion of Ireland in 1315 by Scots. Yet a later period was
the topic of a dissertation by James Hill [**1632**], "Continuity in Celtic Warfare:
Strategy, Tactics, and Logistics of the Highland Scots and Irish, 1595-1763,"
1985.

More general was Norman MacDougall [**2239**], Scotland and War, AD
790-1918, 1991. It included an essay on GREAT MICHAEL, the massive
warship of King James IV who reigned from 1496-1513. MacDougall [**2238**],
James IV, 1989, then elaborated on that specific reign and its naval connections.
James was obsessive; in 1506, he launched a fleet-building programme for
defense of Scotland. In alliance, Louis XII of France provided expert assistance,
38 warships were built or otherwise acquired, campaigns were launched against
Denmark and England, and, finally, all led to bankruptcy and collapse. James
was killed in the battle of Flodden. Two dissertations were applicable: F.W.
Robertson [**3084**], 1934, and Darlene Hall [**1458**], 1998.

Two works, covering two different times, linked sea power on both
sides in Anglo-Scottish conflicts, in 1296-1328 and 1513-1550, respectively:
W.S. Stanford Reid [**3045**] and Gervase Phillips [**2848**]. In the first case,
Scottish sea power aided in the resistance to English invasion; in the second,
English logistics and success were facilitated by extensive use of naval
transports.

4. Wales

Sources on the history of Wales were not plentiful; those on maritime
Wales less so. The Welsh Wars of Edward I, 1901, by John Morris [**2555**], was
a pioneering study. The Normans began the conquest of Wales. Edward I
consolidated the process. Blockade, for example, of Conway Castle from the
land, meant naval transports were required for logistical purposes. In an article
of 1986, Poul Holm [**1657**] described Welsh-Irish-Viking connections, for

example, with Gruffydd who in 1079 attempted to conquer northern Wales aided by a fleet of thirty ships of Norse-Irish mercenaries. That failed, but Gruffydd returned later with another fleet from Waterford. A.D. Carr [**581**], Owen of Wales: The Era of the House of Gwynedd, 1990, included an account of a Welsh admiral and soldier of fortune of the 14th century, Owain Llawgoch ap Thomas ap Rhodri.

E. THE MIDDLE AGES

1. WHY EUROPE; WHY ENGLAND/BRITAIN?

Some speculated about what might have been. European hegemony over the rest of the world from 1500 on was not foreordained. Ancient and early modern China was an advanced society with much potential. Even as late as the mid-15th century, enormous battle fleets roamed the South China Sea and ventured in great expeditions into the Indian Ocean, the Persian Gulf, and along the eastern coasts of Africa. The Portuguese "gunned" their way in there half a century later. Why not China?

Gang Deng [**908, 909**], Chinese Maritime Activities and Socioeconomic Development, c. 2100 BC-1900 AD, 1997, and in an article, 1995, presented the long history of Chinese maritime activities, evaluated the phenomenon, and presented explanations about its demise. Gang Deng insisted that the much-touted voyages of Zheng He of the early 15th century were merely a continuation of previous, similar operations. In the end, China failed to adapt to the changing world economy. Louise Levathes [**2110**], When China Ruled the Seas: The Treasure Fleet of the Dragon Throne, 1405-1433, 1994, focused upon Zheng He or He Zheng, who commanded a series of seven naval campaigns from China down through the Indian Ocean to the eastern coasts of Africa. The fleet consisted of over 300 ships, some over 400 feet long and 160 feet wide, with nine masts, and manned by a total of 30,000 sailors. Piracy was suppressed, diplomacy and exploration were conducted, and booty was collected. China then turned inward and became isolated for centuries. In Bruce Swanson [**3523**], The Eighth Voyage of the Dragon: A History of China's Quest for Seapower, 1982, the title alluded to the effort at naval expansion in the 19th century but the first five chapters were about the seven expeditions of the early 15th century. Andrew Sleeswyk [**3343**], 1996, speculated and clarified about ship dimensions, particularly those of the fleet of Zheng He, concluding that any wooden ship over 300 feet long would be vulnerable to collapse.

2. Italy

China turned inward. The Italian states turned outward, both overland and through the Mediterranean, out the Straits of Gibraltar, and to the Northern

Seas. Venice and Genoa were the leaders. Southampton, Sandwich, and London were major English stops and centers. In an article and book, A.A. Ruddock [3165, 3164], 1944 and 1950, recounted the activities of the Italian trading fleets with England; items included luxury goods and carpets in return for wool, for example from the Cotswolds and Cistercian monasteries of Yorkshire. Banking services were added. The Italian city-states, notably Venice, Genoa, and Florence, became rivals with the caravan trade from the East; their route being Constantinople, Aleppo, Damascus, Alexandria, thence Venice or Genoa to northern Europe by sea. Costs of this sea route were one-fourth those of the overland trade route. Southampton, Sandwich, and, especially, London were terminals. Enclaves of Italian merchant-bankers settled in these cities. The high point of this relationship was 1300-1460.

William Jordan [1838], Order and Innovation in the Middle Ages, 1976, was a series of disparate essays by experts, for example, A.R. Lewis on northern sea power: Venetian, Genoese, and Catalan galleys spread Italian influence to northern Europe, for example, to Southampton and Bruges, and T. Ruiz on Castilian merchants in England, 13th and 14th centuries. H.G. Rawlinson [3023], 1926, focused on the Flanders galleys, a thriving trade between England and the Italian states, 1327-1532. The activity was elaborated upon: finance with Florence, ships, munitions, and mercenaries with Genoa, and Oriental wares with Venice. These Flanders fleets included commercial galleys manned by 180 oarsmen, a number of whom were buried in churchyards of Southampton. M.E. Mallett [2347], 1962, described the high point of the Florentine-English trade, at its height in the1460s; alum from Italy in exchange for English wool.

Venice was first. Exerting pioneer, innovative, and formative influence on these matters was Venice, especially the unique Venice Arsenal. Tours of the ancient and formative industrial complex can be taken today.

The premier historian of Venice was Frederic Lane [2017-2022]. First there was a dissertation and a related book, Venetian Ships and Shipbuilding of the Renaissance, both 1934; later, a synthesis, Venice: A Maritime Republic, 1973, plus two related contributions, 1934 and 1966. Shipbuilders of the state-owned Venice Arsenal, a huge industrial facility with highly advanced labor relations and administrative and financial practices, dominated from at least the 12th through the 17th centuries. It produced model and powerful galleys in the 13th century and great galleons in the 16th century, in addition to large numbers of traditional merchant ships.

The preeminent historian, William McNeill [2320] contributed Venice: The Hinge of Europe, 1081-1797, 1974, describing the rise and fall of Venetian influence, especially in maritime matters. Other works were by David Nicolle [2646], The Venetian Empire, 1200-1670, 1989, and John Martin [2434], Venice Reconsidered: The History and Civilization of an Italian City-State, 1297-1797, 2000. Garry Willis [3905], Venice: Lion City: The Religion of Empire, 2001, described the Venetian fleet as the most sophisticated in Europe, noting Venetian hegemony as comparable to ancient Athens, and using contemporaneous art to illustrate his claims. M.E. Mallett [2347], The Military Organization of a Renaissance State: Venice, c. 1400 to 1617, 1984, noted the move away from feudal organization to permanent forces, a "standing" army and navy.

More specifically, Ennio Concina [712], L'Arsenale della Repubblica di Venezia, 1984, and Robert Davis [884], Shipbuilders of the Venetian Arsenal, 1991, described the greatest manufacturing complex in early modern Europe. Joseph Black [337], 1998, elaborated. At its height, the navy consisted of 3000 warships and 36,000 seamen. It was the Venetian navy that played the decisive role in the defeat of the Turks at the famous battle of Lepanto in 1571. The Arsenal was established in 1124 and expanded to 60 acres employing 16,000 workers. Included were drydocks and cannon casting and forging, rope, sail, and gunpowder facilities. Alethea Weil [3804], 1910, described the Venetian navy.

The chief commercial and naval competitor of Venice, across the Italian peninsula on the west coast, was Genoa. As with Venice, Genoa developed into an expansive commercial empire and naval power in the Mediterranean and out into the Atlantic Ocean and in Northern Europe. Its dealings with northern European powers, trade and war, were more extensive than those of Venice, but not as early. It was the home of Christopher Columbus.

The equivalent of Frederic Lane [2021] for Genoa was Steven Epstein [1052], Genoa and the Genoese, 958-1528, 1996. Other contributors were Eugene Byrne [534], Genoese Shipping in the Twelfth and Thirteenth Centuries, 1930, and a dissertation and forthcoming book by T.A. Kirk [1947, 1948], 1996. A dissertation by W.E. Burnham [517] gave details on the sea route and related activities between Genoa and England. Frederic Cheyette [626], 1970, elaborated on an incident of 1332 involving seventy Genoese and other galleys off the coast of southern France. Was it piracy or naval conflict, there being no distinction at the time? France had hired such galleys in wars against Edward I of England. The incident was a precedent in the development of Admiralty court jurisdiction. **See 15., B.**

3. Portugal

An early modern "special relationship" could characterize Anglo-Portuguese relations and connections. Sea power and imperial hegemony shifted from the Mediterranean Sea out into the Atlantic during the 15th century; much of the initiative and impetus of the transformation coming from the Iberian peninsula, especially from Portugal, seen as the first modern colonial empire; with some irony, it also lasted the longest period of time. In addition, the Anglo-Portuguese alliance was long lasting.

The inimitable C.R. Boxer [402, 399, 398] described it best: The Portuguese Seaborne Empire, 1415-1825, 1969, Four Centuries of Portuguese Expansion, 1415-1825, 1961, and The English and the Portuguese-Brazil Trade,

1660-1780, 1981. B.W. Diffie [**937, 936**], Prelude to Empire, 1960, and
Foundations of the Portuguese Empire, 1415-1580, 1977, described
preliminaries and foundations laid by Prince Henry, the Navigator and Vasco da
Gama; even Christopher Columbus, a Genoese, made a "Portuguese" voyage for
Spain, having been trained in navigation there. In a dissertation of 1968, Bentley
Duncan [**990**], "Uneasy Allies: Anglo-Portuguese Commercial, Diplomatic and
Maritime Relations, 1642-1662," presented a slightly different view. The
Portuguese received the initial credit in Ocean Traders, 1989, by Michael
Marshall [**2418**], in an instructive book about trade supported by an impressive
folio format. **See 17., F.**

4. In the Baltic Sea

For England/Britain, the Eastern trade was particularly, strategically
important. The area was the source of essential naval stores, wood and other
products necessary to sustain sailing ship warfare, for example, pitch, tar, tallow,
hemp, wax, and flax. Access was an additional problem for the English/British.
The narrow straits providing access from the North Sea to the Baltic were
vulnerable, especially because Denmark and Sweden could and did dominate
that access. For example, two battles of Copenhagen, 1801 and 1807, were
fought for secure access, among other things. **See 7., I., 9.**

There was a large literature. Coverage was from the 13th through the
18th centuries. Walter Minchinton [**2518**], The Baltic Grain Trade, 1985, was
enlightening about the essence of the trade and the international competition
over it. In this case, it was food: grain. By the 13th century, the Baltic was
becoming the grainery of Europe, England entering the market in the 14th
century, others later. The Hanseatic League was initially involved, Danzig being
the export center. Later, control shifted to the Low Countries and Amsterdam
had become the dominant center by the 16th century. Anglo-Dutch competition
ensued. **See 7., G., 6.**

Oliver Warner [**3776**], The Sea and the Sword: The Baltic, 1630-1945,
1964, was a succinct overview. The comparison between Baltic naval stores in
the days of sail and Middle Eastern oil in modern times was stressed. The great
R.C. Anderson [**93**], Naval Wars in the Baltic, 1522-1850, 1910, presented a
chronological survey of a series of naval wars. Stewart Oakley [**2657**], War and
Peace in the Baltic, 1560-1990, 1992, an updated survey, recalled frequent
conflicts and the rise and fall of Sweden. Russia superseded Sweden. Interests of
England/Britain, the Dutch, and France remained high. D.G. Kirby [**1944, 1943**]
has two pertinent and related works: Northern Europe in the Early Modern
Period: The Baltic World, 1492-1772, 1990, and The Baltic World, 1772-1993:
Europe's Northern Periphery in an Age of Change, 1995. Kirby noted that the
most crucial items of trade were grain and naval stores; touting his "Baltic
World" as comparable to the "Mediterranean World" of Fernand Braudel [**426**].

The evolutionary process was agrarian to industrial and with a trade-based structure.

Formative was Goran Rystad [**3199**], In Quest of Trade and Security: The Baltic in Power Politics, 1500-1990, 2 vols., 1994, a series of pertinent essays by experts, for example, about Britain by Stewart Oakley and Andrew Lambert and about Sweden by Jan Glete. Arthur Attman [**60**], The Struggle for Baltic Markets: Powers in Conflict, 1558-1618, 1979, delineated the powers: Sweden, Poland, Russia, and Denmark. More broadly, Attman [**156**] wrote of the Russian market in world trade, 1500-1860. A research project is in progress, "Navies, the Baltic Sea and Western European Politics, 1523-1990," by John Hattendorf [**1565**]. Jill Lisk [**2142**], reviewed The Struggle for the Supremacy in the Baltic, 1600-1725, 1967.

Denmark arose as the "gatekeeper" in and out of the Baltic; M. Bellamy [**286**] has a dissertation on Danish naval administration and shipbuilding, especially in the 17th century. Actually, English and Scottish shipwrights were called in. A dissertation of 1957 on Sweden and the maritime powers, 1698-1702, was by Edward Natharius [**2603**]. A series of shifting alliances involving England, the Netherlands, Denmark, Sweden, and Russia were reviewed.

Several works focused on the role on England/Britain in the Baltic world. The earliest period was covered by John Fudge [**1211**], Cargoes, Embargoes, and Emissaries: The Commercial and Political Interaction of England and the German Hanse, 1450-1510, 1995, in this monograph which presented details of the trade, the ports, commercial and political arrangements, and drastic change which ensued. England and the Hanseatic League fought a war, 1469-1474, and concluded the Treaty of Utrecht. Pertinent English ports at this time were on the east coast, for example, Hull, Lynn, Boston, Ipswich, and, of course, London with its Steelyard. A little later coverage was by Henryk Zins [**3984**], England and the Baltic in the Elizabethan Era, 1967, originally in Polish, describing the long struggle with the Hanseatic League. It was precisely this struggle and this area that the English/British gained vital experience in trade organization, for example, the Eastland Company and the Russia Company. Joseph Malone [**2349**], "England and the Baltic Naval Stores Trade in the Seventeenth and Eighteenth Centuries," 1972, reviewed the influence of sea power on history and the influence of naval stores on sea power. The 17th century was reviewed by J.K. Fedorowicz [**1081**], England's Baltic Trade in the Early Seventeenth Century, 1980, featuring the English shipping and trade in and out of the Baltic and Sven-Erik Astrom [**154**], From Cloth to Iron: The Anglo-Baltic Trade in the Late Seventeenth Century, 2 vols., 1963-1965. The next century: H.S.K. Kent [**1913**], War and Trade in the Northern Seas: Anglo-Scandinavian Economic Relations in the Mid-Eighteenth Century, 1973, surveyed Mercantilist policies and noted that the British navy depended on Norwegian timber and Swedish iron, pitch, and tar. Parliamentary initiatives to force a shift to British colonial sources generally failed, especially with timber and iron.

There was a dissertation on the Scottish connection: T.O. Smout [**3373**], "The Overseas Trade of Scotland with Particular Reference to the Baltic and Scandinavian Trade, 1660-1707," 1959. 300 ships were involved. David Aldridge [**35**], 1972, completed a dissertation about Admiral John Norris and naval expeditions into the Baltic, 1715-1727.

George Cawston [**600**], The Early Chartered Companies, 1296-1858, 1896, was an early work presenting chronological developments, for example, establishment of the Russia and the Eastland Companies. M.S. Anderson [**73**], Britain's Discovery of Russia, 1553-1815, 1958, was an early survey of the origins of the Russia Company. The late 16th century was the focus of T.S. Willan [**3864**], The Early History of the Russia Company, 1553-1603, 1956. It all began as a search for the Northeast Passage to "Cathay." Sebastian Cabot oversaw an early voyage led by Hugh Willoughby and Richard Chancellor. In 1555, a charter was concluded for the Russia Company. A quarter of a century later, the Eastland Company for the Baltic trade was chartered. **See 17., I.**

5. Gascony

Maritime activity and sea power also evolved around the Gascony connection in southwest France, the relationship being a factor in early Anglo-French competition and the Hundred Years' War. Southampton was an important center-terminal for the Italian connection, and for the wine trade with Gascony about the same time. Ships from Bordeaux and Bayonne exchanged wine for wool. To secure its "empire" in France during the 14th century, England constructed a series of "barbicans" along the entire French coast from Calais out to Brittany and around and down to Bayonne, an extensive and costly defense system. For a time, the English king held the additional title, Duke of Guyenne.

M.G.A. Vale [**3715**], English Gascony, 1399-1453, 1970, provided background. Gascony was acquired by England in a marriage arrangement at the time of the Lancastrian succession in 1399 and it was lost after French invasions in the mid-15th century. Trade involved wine, woad and other dyes, and wool. M.K. James [**1781, 1782**], in an article, 1951, and Studies in the Medieval Wine Trade, 1971, expounded upon the wine trade of Gascony, a prominent sector of commerce during the 14th and 15th centuries; detailed statistics were included.

6. Bristol

Across England/Britain from east to west, we find an even earlier dynamic activity, this one less associated with war. For several centuries, Bristol, in the west, was the second city of the land and a prominent port for trade and, especially, for exploration ventures.

It was David Harris Sacks [**3200-3202**] who has been the great advocate of the prominent role of Bristol in early trade and exploration, especially his The Widening Gate: Bristol and the Atlantic Economy, 1450-

1700, 1991, plus a 3-vol. dissertation and 2-vol. book, Trade, Society and Politics in Bristol, 1500-1640, 1985 and 1987. He dubbed Bristol "the navel of the world." The "widening gate" was capitalism, attained by incorporating social, political, and religious dimensions into an economic whole. The symbol on the city coat-of-arms was a gate. It became an Atlantic entrepot. John Cabot set out from Bristol exploring North America in 1497. Others searched for the Northwest Passage. Other surveys included J.W. Sherbourne [3301], The Port of Bristol in the Middle Ages, 1965, the great economic historian, E.M. Carus-Wilson [589], The Overseas Trade of Bristol in the Late Middle Ages, 1967, and in a dissertation by Anita Beetham Fisher [276], "The Merchants of Medieval Bristol, 1350-1500," 1987.

7. The Hundred Years' War

Dynastic conflict led to a series of major campaigns between England and France. It has been called the Hundred Years' War. Earlier, a naval disaster precipitated English dynastic chaos as described by Tony Brett-Jones [434], "The White Ship Disaster," 1999: on 25 November 1120 in an oft-repeated cross-Channel voyage, the BLANCHE NEF or WHITE SHIP, 50 oars with a single mast-sail, was ferrying about 300 persons, including many Norman nobles, from Barfleur along the seventy miles to Portsmouth. King Henry I had gone on in another ship; the future king, Stephen, had been aboard but went on in another ship, and the only heir of Henry, William of Aetheling, age 18, was aboard. It was a calm night and apparently many were drunk. WHITE SHIP struck Quilleboeuf rock and all but one person perished. It was seen as a preventable accident. In the mid-12th century, civil war ensued until a compromise was concluded. Most agree that the course of English/British history was changed.

Among the essays in Michael Prestwick [2949], Thirteenth-Century England, 1997, was "Richard I, Galley-Warfare and Portsmouth: The Beginnings of the Royal Navy." Prestwick [2951, 2948, 2950] also sorted out the financial details, which facilitated campaigns of Edward, I, II, and III, for example, conquering Wales and expeditions to Gascony and Scotland, in a dissertation and two books, 1968, 1972, and 1980. Describing operations bordering on piracy, Henry Cannon [570], presented "The Battle of Sandwich and Eustace the Monk, 1217," 1912. A turncoat Englishman, Eustace was able to wreak havoc against the English. There was a dissertation and article on war preparation and naval activities, 1199-1307, 1970 and 1972, by Michael Weir [3807, 3806]. English and Gascon naval forces were deployed against France. Portsmouth was the base and specific administrative departments of war were being developed. **See 14., B.**

The ostensible cause of the Hundred Years' War was dynastic: on the death of Charles IV of France, Edward III claimed succession. Factors included the ambitions of Edward III, the disposition of Gascony, and developments in

Scotland, Castile, and the Low Countries. War, of course, was not continuous. Christopher Allmand [**53**] set out chronological divisions: 1337-1360, 1360-1398, 1398-1422, and 1422-1453.

The old standard was Edouard Perroy [**2830**], The Hundred Years' War, 1945, a synthesis of a half century of scholarship; actually written in French during the German occupation of France as Perroy hid from the Gestapo. Jonathan Sumption [**3518**], The Hundred Years' War, I.: Trial by Battle and II.: Trial by Fire, 2 vols., 1990 and 1999, was a narrative history with more forthcoming; coverage only to 1369 in these two volumes; destined to be the new definitive account. Christopher Allmand [**53**], The Hundred Years' War: England and France at War, c. 1300-c. 1450, 1988, touted "total history." Naval objectives and naval forces were included. The bibliography was especially strong. Desmond Seward [**3285**], The Hundred Years' War: The English in France, 1337-1453, 1978 with a new edition of 2001, devoted some commentary to invasion and naval matters. Ships were cogs and galleys; France maintained a dockyard with Genoese expertise in producing galleys. Kenneth Fowler [**1168**], The Hundred Years' War, 1971, was a series of essays by noted scholars, for example, C.F. Richmond on the war at sea.

Individual aspects were covered, including naval battles. In an article of 1964, M.M. Postan [**2922**] investigated the costs of the war concluding that the English profited but the net balance was negative. The largest operation was the Crecy-Calais campaign of 1346-1347. Most expensive were naval forces: warships, barges, and transports. The great 19th-century naval historian, Nicholas Harris Nicolas [**2642, 2643**] presented what he called The Roll of Arms, 1829, a survey of forces under Henry III, and Edward II and III. War Cruel and Sharp: English Strategy under Edward III, 1327-1360, 2000, was by Clifford Rogers [**3125**]. The English prevailed during this first phase.

Especially enlightening were the dissertation and article by Timothy Runyan [**3171, 3172**], 1972 and 1986, an extensive study of the ships and fleets of the Anglo-French, 1337-1360, including the battle of Sluys and its consequences. Featured were issues of control of the seas, in this case, the Channel, piracy, convoys, and "a prosopographical study" of all known English ships, 1291 of them. Of those identified, 31 were king's ships, 467 came from specified ports, and 271 were foreign.

By the late 1330s, there was a French invasion threat resulting in the naval battle of Sluys, June 1340. Sluys was the port of Bruges. Edward III commanded 200 English ships, from which longbowmen rained arrows down on the French fleet, which was enhanced by galleons hired from Genoa. The French fleet was in three formations and contained 40,000 men. The French fled. 25,000 Frenchmen died. The French invasion threat ended for a time. These events were recounted in amateur fashion by Harry Maihafer [**2335**], 1990, and in scholarly fashion by Kelly DeVries [**921**], 1995, who reviewed and analyzed dozens of different accounts of the battle.

The Crecy campaign and the siege of Calais were a complicated series of events and operations in 1346 and 1347. An Anglo-Gascon force in Gascony was being threatened by a French force. Edward III chose to invade Normandy. 32,000 men were transported in 738 ships, all described by Yuval Harari [1486], 1999, and Alfred Burne [514], 1955. Naval aspects from the French perspective were described by Charles de la Ronciere [2032], 1900.

Later naval developments, 1330s-1380s, were reviewed in a dissertation by J.R. Alban [25], 1976, and in two works by James W. Sherbourne [3300, 3302], 1967 and 1994. Extensive military campaigns required much shipping. There were 40 King's Ships. Other vessels were impressed by the crown. 57 came from the Cinque Ports; others were foreign-hired. A strength of Sherborne was detail on the actual costs of naval warfare. The Black Prince led some expeditions, recounted by H.J. Hewitt [1613], 1958.

More broadly, Peter Russell [3179], studied the English intervention in Spain and Portugal, specifically in Navarre and Castile, Aragon, Portugal, and Gascony. These powers had galley fleets, which, on occasion, attacked the English. Galley expertise came from Genoa. The English had few galleys in the 14th century. The typical galley of the period was described in detail. In 1377, the Castile-Portuguese-French alliance assembled at least 13 galleys plus French warships and wreaked havoc along the south and southeast coast. Parliament responded, assisting the new king, Richard II, with aid to build fortresses and a fleet. In 1380, Charles V of France died and the alliance with Castile lapsed.

The naval battle of L'Espangols sur Mer, 1350, was against the Spanish; again, Edward III was in command of the English and 24 Spanish ships were destroyed or captured.

J.W. Sherborne [3299], 1969, analyzed the battle of La Rochelle and the naval war of the 1370s; the English lost heavily but were the consequences serious and long lasting? Some say yes, Sherborne downplayed any limitations on future English operations. The article was enlightening on the extent, operations, and resiliency of English naval forces. La Rochelle extended over two days in June 1372. Probably about 20 English ships of a convoy under the Earl of Pembroke, including three warships; 14 English ships were lost, defeated by 12 Castilian galleys; fire was a factor, some English ships being burned. Peter Russell [3179] placed much emphasis on the fact that there was little wind, thus the galleys enjoyed a crucial advantage. Historians disputed the consequences; whether the English lost control of the Channel for over a decade or not.

"The Crecy war" covered early decades; in "the Agincourt war," the battle was in 1415 and command was by Henry V. Operations moved to the 15th century. Accounts were by Christopher Hibbert [1619], 1964, Alfred Burne [513], 1976, and the older, classic account by Nicholas Harris Nicolas [2640], 1827. Christopher Allmand [52], Henry V, 1992, was an extensive new biography, which included a section on the navy. Naval forces played an important role in the campaigns and Henry took a personal interest in its developments; Southampton being the shipbuilding center. Henry was the favorite king of William Shakespeare. R.A. Newhall [**2633**], The English Conquest of Normandy, 1416-1424: A Study in Fifteenth-Century Warfare, 1924, reviewed finance, organization, logistics, and conquest.

Susan Rose [**3146**], The Navy of the Lancastrian Kings: Accounts of the Inventories of William Soper, Keeper of the King's Ships, 1422-1427, 1982, a publication of the NRS, introduced details of a higher level of naval organization and administration. Features included activities in Southampton and dealings with Italian merchants and bankers. David Loades [**2178**], has an article, "The King's Ships and the Keeper of the Seas, 1413-1480," 1991. In a dissertation of 1963 and articles of 1964 and 1967, C.F. Richmond [**3057, 3056, 3055**], described naval operations of the early 15th century, the most activity, a fine fleet of 30 ships, being under Henry V, 1417-1421, then neglect for most of the rest of the century. John Rainey [**3000**], 1987, has a dissertation on the defense of Calais through the 15th century, maintaining a key strategic base for the Lancastrian empire.

In a book of 1925 and an article of 1928, E.L. Kingsford [**1940, 1939**], observed the beginnings of English maritime enterprise in the 15th century, stressing the important role of sea power in the process. It was Henry V who created "the navy as a national fighting force" and the distinction between piracy and legitimate trade blurred; letters of marque facilitated indiscriminant reprisals; privateers to freebooters to plunderers. In conclusion: "the enterprise of the West-country pirates of the 15th century was the school of English seamen: they were the forerunners of the Elizabethans." Before Drake, "the arch-pirate," there were Prendergast, Pay, and Hawley.

In a collection of papers, Eileen Power [**2935**], 1933, assessed trade in the 15th century; the century itself was neglected, trade even more so. It was the century of transformation from medieval England to England of the Tudors and Stuarts with worldwide connections and imperial aspirations. Featured were the wool trade, the role of Bristol, relations with the Hanseatic League, and the Iceland trade.

F. THE 16th CENTURY

1. The Tudor Navy

During the Tudor period, 1485-1603, much praise has been heaped upon the Tudor dynasty as the first to grasp the implications of supremacy on the seas and as instigators of the process of commercial and colonial expansion and empire. Smuggling, piracy, and encouragement, indeed, direct participation, in privateering were other factors. **See 12., A., 12., C., and 12., D.** Among these factors associated with sea power and expansion were claims of sovereignty of the Narrow Seas, enactment of the first Navigation Acts, and construction of a permanent drydock at Portsmouth in 1496. The Cinque Ports were superseded by East Anglian and West Country ports, for example, Bristol. The first Tudor king, Henry VII, authorized voyages of exploration by John Cabot from Bristol and negotiated an alliance with Spain, sealed by marriage of his heir, Arthur, to Catherine of Aragon. Arthur died before Henry VII and Henry VIII married Catherine immediately after the death of his father. Under Henry VIII, in 1514, the Corporation of Trinity House of Deptford was founded, and in 1545, a Navy Board was created.

By far the best overall introduction of English/British naval history during this formative Tudor period was the trilogy of R.B. Wernham [**3814, 3813, 3817**]: Before the Armada: The Emergence of the English Nation, 1485-1588, 1966, After the Armada: Elizabethan England and the Struggle for Western Europe, 1588-1595, 1984, and The Return of the Armadas: The Later Years of the Elizabethan War against Spain, 1595-1603, 1994. In the early phase Spain replaced France as chief rival. By 1585, France was engulfed within herself in a civil war of religion. England and Spain went to war, which eventually sapped the wealth, manpower, and good temper of England. That would be a factor contributing to the alienation between government and people, court and country, in the next period. Meantime, in 1585, Elizabeth deployed a force of 7000 soldiers to aid the Dutch in rebellion against Spain. The war was increasingly an affair of navies. After the Armada, an effort was made to finish the destruction of Spanish naval power; the Drake-Norris expedition to Lisbon of 1589. It turned into a debacle. In the early 1590s, the English were primarily concerned that Spain would acquire bases in Brittany or Normandy from which to launch invasion. Spain threatened Scotland and Ireland. A successful campaign in Brittany prevented completion of a Spanish base. The Dutch and French, finally resolving the religious civil war, were occasional allies. Spanish armadas deployed again in 1596 and 1597; both were scattered by storms; the latter called "the Invisible Armada." An Irish rebellion aided by Spain was crushed at Kinsale in 1601. At one point, a "Grand Alliance" against Spain was discussed: England, France, the Netherlands, Denmark, and Italian and German states. James I made peace in 1604.

Elaine Fowler [**1167**], 1965, contributed a Folger Library booklet on English sea power under the early Tudors. David Grummitt [**1416**] did a dissertation on Calais, 1485-1547, 1996. It continued as a strategic base until "lost" by Queen Mary Tudor. Ronnie Day [**888**] has a dissertation about the navy under the early Tudors, 1485-1547. His conclusion: the foundations of the Royal Navy were laid at this time. Shipbuilding campaigns, permanent facilities, and technological advances were achieved. "The Navy under Henry VII," 1918, was by C.S. Goldingham [**1313**] and presented a restrained view. Henry was interested in consolidation and defense, not expansion. His navy was to supply transport and secure his throne. Henry VII conducted a campaign, the Breton wars, 1489-1491, recounted by John Currin [**836**], 2000. A force of 66 ships, many impressed and mercenary, was assembled. In a dissertation of 1995, John

Currin [**835**] reviewed European politics, diplomacy, and war under Henry VII. Maritime activity under Henry VII was the subject of a dissertation by W.E.C. Harrison [**1535**], 1931.

A recent survey by Arthur Nelson [**2617**] covered The Tudor Navy: The Ships, Men and Organization, 1485-1603, 2000, a "Navy Royal." Ship lists were included. M.A. Spont [**3411**] collected letters and papers relating to the war with France, 1512-1513, a publication of the NRS, 1897. Henry VIII abandoned his father's policy of restraint and launched naval campaigns against France. Charles Cruickshank [**815**], Henry VIII and the Invasion of France, 1990, described the campaign. Henry was anxious to prove himself and landed a large force at Calais.

Alexander McKee [**2295**] assessed "Henry VIII as Military Commander," 1991, concluding that his miscalculations were political, not military. In July 1545, a major confrontation of naval forces, 235 French and 104 English ships, occurred at Portsmouth. French landings on the Isle of Wight led to burning and pillaging. C.T. Witherby [**3928**] described one operation, The Battle of Bonchurch, 1962. L.G. Carr Laughton [**2057**], 1916, recounted a descent on, and the burning of, Brighton by French ships and galleys in 1545.

Elizabeth Bonner [**363**], 1996, recounted French diplomatic and naval operations in Scottish waters in the late 1540s: a siege of St. Andrews castle and a major victory by French naval forces led by Captain-General of Galleys Leone Strozzi. French mariners and pilots provided essential details about the Scottish coastline. A Franco-Scottish alliance resulted. Mary Queen of Scots and a Scottish-French union were factors.

J.D. Alsop [**57**] studied the role of the navy during the succession crisis of 1553. The Duke of Northumberland opted for Lady Jane Grey and mobilized several warships. Seamen mutinied and the effort collapsed. Between 1963-1970, Tom Glasgow [**1291**] wrote ten articles, "The Royal Navy in the French Wars of Mary and Early Elizabeth I, 1557-1564," recounting its growth and expansion. In the late 1530s, Pope Paul III issued the Excommunication decree prompting Henry VIII to commence defensive measures and expansion of the navy. Events of the 1550s and 1560s led to sustained developments and increased operations. Elizabeth succeeded in 1558. Ireland continued to be a problem. Ships were needed for transport and logistics and to overawe rebels. These operations were conducted in the 1560s as recounted by Tom Glasgow [**1293**], 1966.

David Raine [**2999**] introduced Sir George Somers, 1984, a West Country seaman who was involved with that extraordinary circle of Sea Dogs, Hawkins, Drake, Grenville, Raleigh, and Gilbert. Somers provided ships, funding, and organization in naval operations and in colonization ventures.

In the European context, Geoffrey Scammell [**3236**], Ships, Oceans and Empire, 1995, a collection of 14 of his essays, reviewed the profound and wide-ranging consequences of European expansion, elaborating on the earlier works of Quinn [**2976**], Andrews [**116**], and Boxer [**397, 402**]. One essay was on the

Hakluyts. For England, Henry VIII established a large state navy, privateering expanded, Navigation Acts were enacting culminating in the Act of 1651, eating fish was mandated in 1564, encouraging fishing fleet expansion and the fishing fleet was "the nursery of seamen" for the navy, and impressment as the recruiting device became well established. For Europe, unfortunately, the associated arrogance and racism stimulated the Atlantic slave trade.

2. Anglo-Spanish Relations

"Singeing the King's Beard" was how Francis Drake summarized operations against the Spanish. The Spanish treasure fleet, great silver mines in America, the Manila Galleon, the dreaded pirate, "El Draco," Spanish exclusivity and monopolies, and Spanish imperial developments, and the Black Legend, Spanish initiatives in forcing Catholicism back on the English, and threats against Elizabeth and vows to place Mary Queen of Scots on the English throne were all aspects of deteriorating Anglo-Spanish relations during the 16th century. Recall that Henry VII concluded an alliance, sealed by a marriage between his heir, Arthur, and Catherine of Aragon, daughter of Ferdinand and Isabella. In 1585, open war broke out. Christobal Real [3034], 1941, presented the Spanish perspective on "El Corsario Drake."

The Spanish empire was the subject of several important works: a classic by J.H. Parry [2784], The Spanish Seaborne Empire, 1966; the old standard in English, Roger Merriman [2500], The Rise of the Spanish Empire in the Old World and the New, 4 vols., 1918-1934, the fourth volume being Philip the Prudent, placing Philip II in a global context; Bohdan Chudoba [635], Spain and the Empire, 1519-1643, 1952; the noted expert, J.H. Elliott [1035], Spain and Its World, 1989; another noted expert, Jonathan Israel [1761], Conflict of Empire: Spain, the Low Countries and the Struggle for World Supremacy, 1585-1713, 1997; Paul Hoffman [1649], The Spanish Crown and the Defense of the Caribbean, 1535-1585: Precedent, Partimonialism, and Royal Parsimony, 1980, and Alan Gallay [1227], Colonial Wars of North America, 1512-1763, 1996.

R.A. Stradling [3467, 3466, 3468] contributed three related studies, Europe and the Decline of Spain: Study of the Spanish System, 1580-1720, 1981, The Armada of Flanders: Spanish Maritime Policy and European War, 1568-1668, 1992, and Spain's Struggle for Europe, 1598-1668, 1994. Stradling described the naval dimension of the tenacious struggle of Spain to maintain European hegemony. The armada of Flanders was based at Dunkirk and a related work was about the army of Flanders. The first work included an excellent bibliography. There were two similar dissertations: Richard Boulind [378], "The Strength and Weaknesses of Spanish Control in the Caribbean, 1520-1650," 1965 and Harold Bensusan [297], "The Spanish Struggle against Foreign Encroachment in the Caribbean, 1675-1697," 1970.

Anglo-Spanish relations were initially based on trade and commerce and deteriorated seriously after mid-century as described by Gordon Connell-

Smith [**716,718**] in a dissertation, "Anglo-Spanish Trade in the Early Tudor Period," 1950, and a book, Forerunners of Drake: A Study of English Trade with Spain in the Early Tudor Period, 1954, and J.L. Wright [**3965**], Anglo-Spanish Rivalry in North America, 1971. The "forerunners" were Elizabethan merchant seamen who resorted to privateering and piracy. Increasingly, the object of English, and also Dutch, French, and other mariners, was Spanish treasure, either in treasure fleets, transport overland, stored in colonial ports, or in the gold and silver mines. The famous "Manila Galleon" made an annual voyage across the Pacific from Acapulco to the Spanish capital in the Philippines and return. Timothy Walton [**3748**], The Spanish Treasure Fleets, 1994, recounted the history of 200 years of Spanish convoys, including a chapter on finds from nautical archaeology. The Spanish port of Seville administered the worldwide process. It was Philip II who initiated the "flota system." Two works were by Robert Marx [**2446, 2442**], The Treasure Fleets of the Spanish Main, 1968, and The Capture of the Treasure Fleet, 1977, the latter about the Dutch adventurer, Piet Heyn who capture the "flota"; five days being required to unload the gold, silver, and other booty.

The treasure fleet was the object of the famous "last fight of the REVENGE" of 1591 in which the heroic Richard Grenville and his crew sacrificed themselves against a large Spanish force; that was the title of two accounts of the action by Edmund Goldsmid [**1315**], 1886, and Peter Earle [**1007**], 1992. The noted English historian, A.L. Rowse [**3159, 3160**] wrote Sir Richard Grenville and the REVENGE: An Elizabethan Hero, 1937, and "Sir Richard Grenville's Place in English History," 1957. Walter Raleigh [**3002**] and Alfred Lord Tennyson glorified the event. In 1591, an English force of 22 naval and privateer ships in the Azores searching for the flota confronted a convoy escort of 53 Spanish warships. All of the English ships escaped except REVENGE, which fought five of the Spanish ships and surrendered; Grenville died and REVENGE sank.

The Manila-Acapulco galleon was a favorite subject. William Schurz [**3255**], The Manila Galleon, 1939, was about Spanish maritime commerce to the Philippines, 1565-1815, 1572-1814 in another source. William McCarthy [**2226**], 1995, elaborated on the far base of the Manila-Acapulco galleon phenomenon, the Cavite Yards. There were three galleons, two en route and a third in reserve, each year. They were expensive to build and turned out to be of poor quality. The preeminent historian of Pacific exploration, Glyndwr Williams [**3873**], "Commodore Anson and the Acapulco Galleon," 1967, described its capture near the Philippines in the 1740s, bringing Anson fame, fortune, and quick promotion. Dennis Flynn [**1130**], European Entry into the Pacific: Spain and the Acapulco-Manila Galleons, 2001, highlighted the role of this treasure ship in attracting Europeans into the Pacific.

Stanley Stein [**3439**], Silver Trade and War, 2000, was about "the bridge between medieval to modern times." An older study about global financial consequences was Earl Hamilton [**1463**], American Treasure and the

Price Revolution in Spain, 1501-1650, 1934. The entry of massive amounts of treasure via Seville precipitated the price revolution and transformed economic and social institutions in Europe.

Anti-Spanish feelings in Britain were fueled by "the Black Legend" introduced by William Maltby [**2352**], The Black Legend, 1968. Spain represented anti-Catholicism and anti-Papism in England. Englishmen, especially sailors and merchants, had been victims of the notorious Inquistion. There were rumors that an Inquisition Court was aboard the Armda fleet. In the end, victory over the Armada symbolized the moral and military superiority of the English. Albert Close [**664**], 1913, was particularly vehemently anti-Catholic, for example, England was saved by a Divine Hand and the defeat of the Armada was "a great sermon preached to the Popish and Protestant nations." C.F.T. Brooke [**453**], 1942, described pre-Armada propagandist poetry in England, stimulating the anti-Spanish feelings. Plots, conspiracies, and Mary Queen of Scots were prominent themes.

Arnold Meyer [**2502**], England and the Catholic Church under Queen Elizabeth, 1916, presented the religious, political, and commercial background to Anglo-Spanish relations. Factors included expansion of the English navy, plots against Elizabeth, aid to the Dutch, alliance between the Pope and Spain, and "sea dog" deployment against Spanish colonies in the Americas. Albert Loomie [**2187**] elaborated about Catholics in England, for example, would/could they aid Spanish invasion efforts and did Philip II anticipate collaboration from them? More of the flavor of the 19th century and the "Black Legend" can be seen in Thomas Lathbury [**2040**], The Spanish Armada, A.D. 1588: Or, the Attempt of Philip II and Pope Sixtus V to Reestablish Popery in England, 1840. Scotland and the Armada was the subject of J.D. Mackie [**2307**], 1914. Factors included Mary Queen of Scots, claims by Philip II of succession to the English throne and, even, the Scottish throne if James VI could be disinherited, fears of the Scots of enforcing Catholicism upon them, and the "double game" played by James. The popular and prolific British writer, Arthur Bryant [**492**], The Elizabethan Deliverance, 1980, was among the worst, glorifying the English victory and perpetuating the anti-Spanish image. Bryant bragged that he was "the New Elizabethan." Also all wrong was Robert Marx [**2441**], The Battle of the Spanish Armada, 1965: the Spanish fleet, so much more powerful and larger, "was defeated so badly that Spain could never again rule the oceans."

Mythology abounded. Bertrand Whitehead [**3842**], Brags and Boasts, 1994, was about propaganda during 1588, a systematic campaign lasting 9 months in England and in Spain. Here were the origins of many myths about the Armada, for example, Drake's game of bowls and the Tilbury speech of Elizabeth. Susan Frye [**1210**], 1992, wrote about the myth of the speech of Elizabeth at Tilbury. There was no reliable eyewitness. The "speech" was noted first in the 17th century. Estimates of the number of troops ranged from 8000 to 100,000. The myth conveniently covered up the facts of political, national, and religious lack of unity. As part of the quadricentennial, "Exploding the Myths,"

1988, was a joint Anglo-Spanish exhibition, purposely didactic, to teach lessons: "to teach humility to the English and tolerance to the Spaniards." David Cressy [**795**], 1989, described the development of the Protestant calander and the rhythm of the year. The defeat of the Armada and the Gunpowder Plot of 1605 meant "miraculous deliverance" and commemorations such as bonfires, bell-ringings, and patriotic prayers.

3. War

Garrett Mattingly [**2468**], The Armada, best presented the European diplomatic background and context leading up to the Armada campaign. The Armada fleet was assembling and being prepared after the Anglo-Spanish war began in 1585. These were the circumstances when the Cadiz Expedition of Francis Drake struck in 1587. It has been famously characterized as "singeing King Philip's beard." With a force of 25 ships only four of which were Crown ships, Drake wreaked havoc. Fifty Spanish ships were burned and much other damage occurred, recounted by Geoffrey Callender [**553**], 1918. Samuel Southworth [**3400**], Great Raids in History: From Drake to Desert One, 1997, recounted 19 decisive small-unit actions over the past 400 years, for example, Drake at Cadiz. Michael Oppenheim [**2711**], The Naval Tracts of Sir William Monson, 5 vols., 1902-1914, a publication of the NRS, collected documentary coverage of Tudor Sea Dogs in the form of narratives, for example, Drake, John Hawkins, Frobisher, Howard, and Raleigh.

4. The Armada

The Spanish Armada was seen as one of the most important events during early modern Western history. English privateers and illegal commercial forces had been attacking Spanish imperial forces and possessions before and after war began between Spain and England in 1585. France was distracted by religious civil war. Philip II of Spain, himself a former monarch of England, began planning for his "Enterprise of England." England must stop these depredations and be returned to the "true" religion, Catholicism.

There was an extensive historiographical-bibliographhical survey: Eugene Rasor [**3016**], The Spanish Armada of 1588: Historiography and Annotated Bibliography, 1993, 1114 annotated bibliographical entries and over 80 pages of historiographical narrative. One would do well to commence study of the Anglo-Spanish War and the Spanish Armada with Garrett Mattingly [**2468, 2469**], The Armada, 1959, winner of the Pulitzer Prize in History. Mattingly was also the author of The "Invincible" Armada and Elizabethan England, 1963, a Folger Library Booklet. There has been universal praise for the Mattingly survey. He presented the broadest European approach and was best on diplomatic matters and on background. For Philip, the decisive event was the execution of Mary, Queen of Scots, in February 1587, in England. Mary was a

Catholic and former Queen of France and Scotland. She became the center of a series of plots to eliminate Queen Elizabeth and replace her with Mary, an heir in her own right. Papal sanction was obtained. The Papacy supported the campaign, thus, a crusade.

Philip ordered the assembly of a large fleet from sources all over Europe, eventually 130 of the largest naval and maritime ships in the world of the 16th century. This assembly included ships from the Mediterranean, Baltic, and Adriatic Seas, especially from Ragusa, Venice, Genoa, Rostock, and Spanish and Portuguese ports. It has been determined that the latter, built for the unique conditions of the Atlantic Ocean, were more likely to survive the rigorous conditions of the long ocean voyage than those ships built to operate within the Mediterranean or Baltic Seas. Colin Martin in Patrick Gallagher [1226] elaborated on this matter. J. Casado Soto [3392] confirmed what others have contended: Spanish ships built in the Mediterranean suffered a higher loss-rate than ships built on the Atlantic coast, for example, ten of the famous "Twelve Apostles," built in Ragusa on the Adriatic coast, were lost.

Cesareo Fernandez Duro [1092], Armada Espanola, 9 vols., 1877-1903, was the exhaustive history of the Armada and the role of Philip II, by the preeminent Spanish naval historian and Columbus scholar. Fernandez Duro died in 1908. J.A. Froude [1206], Froude's "Spanish Story of the Armada" and Other Essays, 1892, was credited with reviving interest in the Armada. He depended much on Fernandez Duro. Froude was judgmental: Medina Sidonia was incompetent, Drake and Hawkins were pirates, and Elizabeth was reluctant to mobilize sufficient forces. David Howarth [1698], The Voyage of the Armada: The Spanish Story, 1981, focused on how and why the Spanish deployed the Armada; Philip II, "this strange obsessive monarch," was primarily responsible.

King Philip II has been extensively studied, then and now. The old standard biography was Luis Cabrera de Cordoba [537], 4 vols., 1619. A recent full biography was Henry Kamen [1841], Philip of Spain, 1997, depicting him as "normal" instead of as a Machiavellian monarch in the Escorial demonized by Protestants; the revolt of the Netherlands was more important than religion. The prolific American scholar, Geoffrey Parker [2753], 1978, has a biography. Philip assembled the greatest empire up to that day and was constantly at war, for example, against the Turks, Barbary pirates, the Netherlands, the French, and the English. The famous British scholar-historian of the 19th century has a substantial biography: Martin Hume [1730], Philip II of Spain, 1897, touted as "ala Ranke," that is, the "scientific" approach. Philip and England was the subject of a piece by Manuel Alverez [63], 1954. The product of the quadricentennial was Ricardo Cerezo Martinez [601], 1988, a useful general survey of Philip and the Armada.

John Lynch [2212], 1961, analyzed the relationship between Philip and the Pope. He noted that the objectives of Philip were political and popes were generally suspicious of him. Protestantism had little to fear from any Spanish-Papal alliance.

The consecutive Spanish commanders have received much attention. The Marquis of Santa Cruz was the obvious choice but he died 9 February 1588. Enrique Herrera Oria [**1609**], Felipe II Y el Marques de Santa Cruz en la empresa de Inglaterra, 1946, described the relationship between Philip and Santa Cruz. Documents from Archivo del General Simancas were incorporated.

The Seventh Duke of Medina Sidonia, Lord General of the King's Fleet, was appointed to replace Santa Cruz. Assessments have varied wildly. An extensive biography was by Peter Pierson [**2854**], Commander of the Armada: The Seventh Duke of Medina Sidonia, 1989, who insisted that Medina Sidonia did not deserve the bad reputation; under the circumstances, he was the obvious and an excellent choice as commander. There was no disgrace after the Armada, indeed, he rose in stature as a senior statesman. On the other hand, J.A. Froude [**1206**] depicted him as ignorant, inexperienced, and incompetent as a naval commander. Much cited was a letter from Medina Sidonia pleading incapacity, poor health, subject to seasickness, in debt, and with no knowledge of the sea. The standing orders of Medina Sidonia to the fleet have been published, 1588, edited by Alonso Perez de Guzman [**1430**]. I.A.A. Thompson [**3602**], 1969, speculated about the appointment. Some saw it as a "gross aberration" and "crowning blunder" of Philip II. He was the premier duke of the realm, very wealthy, an experienced naval commander with campaigns in North Africa and against Portugal. No official in Spain at the time expressed surprise at the appointment. Unfortunately, Medina Sidonia was Captain-General of the Coast of Andalusia in 1596 when an Anglo-Dutch expedition sacked Cadiz

A summary account was by Jean Mariejol [**2376**], The Master of the Armada: The Life and Reign of Philip II, 1933, also called the first modern king. Mariejol volunteered judgments: Philip defended Catholicism in Spain and in France and formulated the grand design against England; Medina Sidonia was "absolutely ignorant about anything to do with the sea" and incompetent, and Santa Cruz would have exploited opportunities and invaded England.

Edward Grierson [**1398**], The Fatal Inheritance: Philip II and the Spanish Netherlands, 1969, recounted details and consequences of the Dutch rebellion against Spain; factors were Philip, "bigoted idealist," the military commanders, Alva and Parma, the Prince of Orange, and direct intervention by Elizabeth and English forces. The best study of this key feature in the problems of Philip II was by the great Pieter Geyl [**1270**], Revolt of the Netherlands, 1550-1609, 1932.

Each of the Spanish ships was packed with sailors, soldiers, nobles, priests, provisions, and arms for attacking and invading England. The objective was to gain control of the English Channel to facilitate the amphibious invasion by the veteran Spanish army that had been campaigning in the Netherlands under the command of the Duke of Parma.

Preliminary events associated with the war were recounted: Conyers Read [**3032**], 1933, on the incident in 1568 when Elizabeth seized the Spanish pay ships of the Duke of Alva, effectively pocketing 85,000 pounds in 155 chests. Another source of funds for the Elizabethan navy was levies, substitution of money payments in lieu of impressment of ships, the process called "ship money," as demanded in 1588, 1596, and 1603. Charles I expanded the process in the 1630s with enormous consequences. This was recounted in A Study of Elizabethan Ship Money, 1588-1603, 1920, by Ada Lewis [2111]. O.F.G. Hogg [1650], 1966, reviewed the extensive process of mobilization of national resources in preparation. Included was a list of the source of 187 ships and 15,410 sailors, for example, 34 from the Crown, 33 from Drake, 10 from the Lord High Admiral, 34 from the City, and 15 transports. An extensive article detailing contingency planning was by Ronald Pollitt [2879], 1984. Three accounts dealt with the role and contributions of Robert Cecil, Lord Burghley by Burghley [510], 1588, W.F. Tilton [3625], 1896, and F.E. Dyer [1001], 1925. M.A. Flower-Smith [1129], 1990, described preparations for the English land forces. John Nolan [2649], 1991, and Lindsay Boynton [409], 1967, described the Great Muster of 1588, a massive undertaking.

Several regional studies were pertinent: T.N. McGurk [2265], 1970, on preparations and mobilizaton in Kent; J.R. Scott [3261], 1877, with an actual pay-list of these forces; John Roberts [3075], 1988, in Devon, and William Noble [2647], 1896, in Huntingdonshire.

Opposing the Spanish Armada was an accumulated naval and maritime force of almost 200 English vessels and thousands of members of trained bands and militia assembled for defense. The overall commander was Admiral Lord Howard of Effingham. Other commanders were John Hawkins and Francis Drake.

The Armada campaign was divided into chronological periods. In April 1588, Spanish ships began departing ports and assembling. Delays meant recall for refitting at Carunna, a northern port, in June. On 20 July the Armada entered the English Channel and proceeded down the Channel, maintaining a kind of half-moon formation. The English rushed out from Plymouth, gained "the weather gage," establishing themselves down wind in an advantageous formation, and began attacking the Spanish daily until the Armada was off Calais on 28 July. Little obvious damage was inflicted during this phase.

Here, obviously, the Spanish communication and planning broke down. The Armada had passed the port where Parma was assembling his army. Prevailing winds in the Channel precluded a return to that port. Meantime, the English released fire ships into the Calais anchorage, forcing the Armada ships to flee out into the North Sea. The Battle of Gravelines ensued, the English causing considerable structural damage to the Spanish ships. The English were forced to break off the fight and return to port to replenish.

Patrick Williams [3889], Armada, 2000, was a recent appraisal. The popular writer, Alexander McKee [2294], From Merciless Invaders: The Defeat of the Spanish Armada, 1963, incorporated over a hundred eyewitness accounts and supported a BBC programme of 1954. It was "a narrative of adventure" and, in a later edition, a chapter was added describing nautical archaeological expeditions off the Irish coast. There was an article and book, The Elizabethan Navy and the Armada of Spain, 1949 and 1975, by David Waters [**3781, 3782**]. Included were analyses of the capabilities of warships and the strategies from both sides: "the fact that Philip II actually made an invasion attempt places him in a class above that of other possible emulators such as Louis XIV, Napoleon, and Hitler." Waters also included some original documents from the archives of the NMM. Stephen Usherwood [**3705**], The Great Enterprise: The History of the Spanish Armada, 1982, called the campaign "the first world war," a new kind of warfare. A.M. Hadfield [**1443**], Time to Finish the Game: The English and the Armada, 1964, touted capturing the life and passion of the fortnight; one focus was the Duke of Parma. The American Heritage contribution, folio size and beautifully illustrated, was Jay Williams [**3882**], The Spanish Armada, 1966. Time-Life in The Seafarers series, produced Bryce Walker [**3737**], The Armada, 1971, also folio size and nicely illustrated. J.R. Hale [**1452**], The Story of the Great Aramda, 1910, was the product of Nelson publishers. Lorna Rea [**3031**], contributed The Spanish Armada, 1933. The Osprey Elite series account was John Tincey [**3627**], The Armada Campaign 1588.

Two early NRS publications presented original documents associated with the Armada: the very first two volumes, John Knox Laughton [**2054**], State Papers Relating to the Defeat of the Spanish Armada, 2 vols., 1894 and 1895, and the eleventh volume, Julian Corbett [**755**], Papers Relating to the Navy during the Spanish War, 1585-1587, 1898. Enrique Herrera Oria [**1610**], La Armada Invencible, 1929, contributed original documents published from the noted Spanish archive, Archivo General de Simancas.

Another documentary series, this one more for young people, was Roger Hart [**1537**], Battle of the Spanish Armada, 1973. Also for young people were Walter Buehr [**501**], The Spanish Armada, 1962, Cyril Hodges [**1645**], The Spanish Armada: The Story of Britain, 1967, and Christopher Falkus [**1072**], The Spanish Armada, 1972. Burt Hirschfeld [**1637**], 1966, contributed a superficial, fictionalized survey, which incorporated gross hyperbole. Gathered together as a textbook to demonstrate research techniques and methods in history was Taylor Littleton [**2146**], The Spanish Armada, 1964, a collection of source materials, for example, accounts of English privateering operations, the execution of Mary, Queen of Scots, Hakluyt narratives, and the memoir of Petruccio Ubaldino. Fifty research topics were suggested.

Variations of statistics can be reviewed: numbers of ships: Peter Kemp [**1859**] and Colin Martin [**2428**], 130 Spanish vs. 197 English; David Thomas [**3593**], 128 Spanish vs. 192 English; Roger Whiting [**3848**], 128 Spanish, and J. Casado Soto [**3392**], 127 Spanish. The number of Spanish losses: Mattingly [**2468**]: 44, David Thomas [**3593**]: 60 to 65, Laughton [**2054**]: 65, Whiting [**3848**]: 63. J. Casado Soto [**3392**] presented much detail about Spanish forces. 127 ships left Carunna; 24 warships, 44 armed merchantmen, 38 auxiliaries, and 21 hulks, 7667 sailors, 10,459 soldiers. The Armada losses: fate of 8 ships unknown, 3 damaged, 4 lost in combat, 28 lost to weather, 5 abandoned before the action, and 92 survived.

Foreign language accounts added more perspectives. A major Spanish study of the Armada was Bauer Landauer [**2011**], <u>Consideraciones sobre la politica naval de Espana en el siglo XVI</u>, 1926. W.F. Tilton [**3626**], <u>Die Katastrophe der Spanischen Armada, 31 Juli-8 August 1588</u>, 1894, in German, featured exhaustive documentation. Fernando Lozano [**2200**], <u>Los Medios Navales de Alejandro Farnesio, 1587-1588</u>, 1989, focused on the Duke of Parma, commander of Spanish forces operating against the Dutch revolt, including details about his "fleet" or shipping, 17 royal warships and 170 barges. Yet, at the crucial time when the Armada arrived, only three were manned. The enthusiasm of Parma was obviously low. A famous memoir in two parts was by Petrucci Ubaldino [**3683, 3684**], 36 folio leaves in Spanish dated 15 April 1589, the original in the British Museum. Jose Casado Soto [**3392**], 1988, in Spanish, described in detail the Spanish ships, shipbuilding, design, measurements, size, and manpower. J. Kretzmar [**1978**], <u>Die Invasion Projecte der Katolishchen Machte gegen England zur Zeit Elisabeths</u>, 1892, in German, incorporated pertinent documents from the extensive Vatican Archives in Rome.

Reactions from afar have been noted: Edwin Pears [**2799**], 1893, on English initiatives to urge the Ottoman Empire to assist by attacking the Spanish in the Mediterranean "on religious grounds, Protestants and Moslems hatred of idolatry"; a more general assessment, <u>Islam and Britain, 1558-1685</u>, 1998, recounted numerous connections; John Elder [**1030**], 1920, on the Catholic situation in Scotland and failure by the Spanish to exploit opportunities; Edward Armstrong [**138**], 1897, on assessments of the chances of Armada success by Venetian observers, and three accounts by De Lamar Jensen [**1804-1806**], 1957, 1964, and 1988, about French pro-Spanish machinations identified with Bernardino de Mendoza of the Catholic League. Jensen observed that Armada plans were "the worst-kept secret in Europe." In two accounts, John de Courcey Ireland [**1751, 1754**], 1963 and 1978, recounted details of a set of foreign-built ships impressed into Spanish service. Called "the Twelve Apostles," and there may have been a dozen more, these galleons were built in Ragusa, now Dubrovnik, on the Dalmatian coast, a famous maritime and shipbuilding center. One was the famous Tobermory Galleon, SAN JUAN BAUTISTA; ten of the twelve were lost. J. Casado Soto [**3392**] confirmed this finding.

The distinguished social historian of the Tudor-Stuart period, Lawrence Stone [**3459**], made observations in 1944 while on an American destroyer: England emerged inglorious but undefeated; the villains were Walsingham, Drake, and Leicester. Howard deserved more credit.

5. The Armada – Nautical Archaeology

Another factor in extraordinary opportunities for obtaining the best, detailed information has been a series of expeditions in nautical archaeology. A number of the Armada wrecks off the northern and western coasts of Scotland and Ireland have been investigated during the 1970s and 1980s using advanced and sophisticated nautical archaeological techniques. An enormous amount has been learned about guns, provisions, and Spanish social and cultural life from these expeditions. **See 18., D.**

Most extensive and authoritative was Colin Martin [**2428**], The Spanish Armada, 1988, reporting on expeditions sponsored by the University of St. Andrews with thanks to the City of Derry Sub-Aqua Club. Included were details on Spanish guns, gun carriages, ammunition, and daily life and routine. Robert Hardie [**1489**] wrote of The Tobermory Argosy, 1912.

The most extensive study of guns and gunnery of the Armada campaign had been by Michael Lewis [**2118, 2119**], Armada Guns: Comparative Study of English and Spanish Armaments, 1961, but much was revised later. The contribution in The British Battle series was Michael Lewis [**2128**], The Spanish Armada, 1960, brief and authoritative for its time. It included his analysis of Armada guns. Spanish guns had serious flaws: poor materials, shoddy construction, bubbles within the metal, irregular bores, and various types of shot including stone. Some guns had not been fired. Colin Martin [**2422**], 1983, did a St. Andrews dissertation on these matters. Two accounts analyzed comparative measurement methods: L. Carr Laughton [**2059**], 1958, and Colin Martin [**2429**]; the conclusions being that the size of individual Spanish and English ships were similar, correcting the older view that Spanish ships were so much larger than the English.

6. The Armada – Off Scotland and Ireland

The Armada had been forced to "escape." Prevailing winds were such that the Spanish had no choice but to continue up the North Sea, on around northern Scotland, and down the western coast of Ireland en route back to Spain, August through October. The greatest losses occurred here. A major Atlantic storm drove many of the weakened and exhausted ships ashore. It was estimated that as many as 50 of the 130 Spanish ships were lost, over 20,000 of the 31,000 men died. As many as 20 ships crashed in a major storm off the northwest coast of Scotland and west coast of Ireland. Three were near Sligo. Estimates vary: about 6000 Spanish were involved in the wrecks; 3750 died on site, as many as 1500 were executed or killed, about 750 survived, and as many as 30 escaped to Scotland and ultimately home on a French ship. Debate has persisted about actions of local Irish, the Queen's officials and armed forces, and the survivors.

Niall Fallon [**1073**], The Armada in Ireland, 1977, presented an assessment by a journalist after visiting every wreck site. It was a combination of folklore and topography. William Spotswood-Green [**3412**], 1908, wrote of Armada ships on the Kerry coast. Evelyn Hardy [**1510**], Survivors of the Armada, 1966, described connections between Ireland and Spain. An important one was religion. Spanish losses were due to weather and stories of numerous

Irish progeny from Spanish sailor-survivors were not true: how could starved, shipwrecked, emaciated, half-dying men begat numerous descendants?

John de Courcey Ireland [**1751, 1755, 1753**], 1963, 1967 and 1990, clarified several issues about events on the Irish coast and reviewed the Hardy [**1510**] account. He reminded us again about ships built and manned from Ragusa; 300 Ragusan widows were created. Laurence Flanagan [**1121**], Ireland's Armada Legacy, 1988, reviewed wreck sites and nautical archaeological expeditions on sites, for example, led by Robert Stenuit and Sydney Wignall. **See 18., D.** Artifacts were described in detail, now on display in the Ulster Museum, Belfast. Included were jewelry, rings, over 400 gold coins, forks, guns, and musical instruments. T.P. Kilfeather [**1930**], Ireland: Graveyard of the Spanish Armada, 1967, touted "a story of stark tragedy." In addition to weather problems, Spanish charts were out of date. Kevin Danaher [**851**], 1956, summarized Armada losses on the Irish coast, presenting a map pointing out 26 wreck sites. David Quinn [**2988**], 1984, explained the disposition of some survivors. A local English official took about a hundred survivors into custody with the intention to collect ransom. Some of those escaped, including Captain Cuellar [**823**]. Jose de Yturriaga [**3979**], "Attitudes in Ireland towards the Survivors of the Spanish Armada," 1990, sometime Spanish ambassador to Ireland, contended that massacres by Irish natives have been exaggerated. Paula Martin [**2436**], 1988, described the disposition of other Spanish prisoners.

Martin Hume [**1731**], 1897, summarized known information then about the disposition of Spanish wrecks: 2 off Dutch coast, 5 off the French coast, 2 off the Scottish Hebrides, and at least 32 in the North Atlantic. There was confusion over names: 9 were called SAN JUAN and 8, CONCEPCION.

About 400 Spanish prisoners were left in Torbay as a result of Drake capturing a Spanish ship on the second day of the Channel operation. Important factors remained concerning Catholicism, Spain, and Ireland. R.A. Stradling [**3469**], The Spanish Monarchy and Irish Mercenaries: The Wild Geese in Spain, 1618-1668, 1994. During the 17th century, thousands of Irish mercenaries were recruited by Spain to fight its European wars; they were called "wild geese."

7. The Armada – Literature and Anniversaries

Interest in the Armada has persisted. The English touted divine intervention. More recently, Spanish initiatives have meant more balanced and scholarly interpretations from scholars. A survey of the Armada in literature and a series of celebrations will be reviewed, especially the inordinate number of products from the quadricentennial in 1988. Output from that was extraordinary.

Douglas Sladen [**3342**], The Spanish Armada: A Ballad of 1588, 1888, described "The Armada off Devon" which began: "Now glory be to the Lord in Heaven" and ended: "our glorious victory." Leicester Bradner [**422**], 1944, collected poems on the Armada. There were surprisingly high numbers of them. W.H.K. Wright [**3970**], 1874, described a historical poem on the Armada. Pine's tapestries were depicted. **See 21., B.** Thomas Deloney [**907**], 1912, was an English contemporaneous balladeer especially famous for his "The Queenes Visiting of the Campe at Tilbury" of 1588. In another written before the event, he warned in explicit language, that if the Spanish landed, they would sack, burn, cut throats, rape, smite babies, and dethrone and kill the queen. Miller Christy [**634**], 1919, elaborated on the Tilbury visit. M.A. Flower-Smith [**1129**], 1990, analyzed "The Able and the Willynge," written to encourage mobilization in defense of the Armada. Samuel Clarke [**650**], recalled England's Remembrancer: Containing a True and Full Narrative of the Spanish Invasion of 1588, 1657, in a series of tracts.

In 1988, the quadricentennial of the Armada was celebrated and extraordinary international cooperation characterized events, especially Anglo-Spanish activities. The Spanish opened their archives and encouraged scholarly research and publication with significant productive results.

Most impressive was Felipe Fernadez-Armesto [**1091, 1090**], The Spanish Armada: The Experience of War in 1588, and an article, "Exploding the Myths," both 1988. Fernandez-Armesto observed that hyperbole was prevalent on both sides: the English interpretations touted Protestant wind, chauvinism, and a pride in achievement, which was unjustified, and the Spanish exaggerated the extent of defeat and catastrophic decline. Factors included the "Black Legend," English claims of Spanish cruelty and fanaticism, the Whig interpretation, and Protestant apologetics of moral superiority. Fernandez-Armesto also used the catalogue of a joint Anglo-Spanish Armada Exhibition to urge balance: "to teach humility to the English and tolerance to the Spaniards." The weather was a major influence, as well. His conclusions: weather, lack of a secure port, failure of the overall English strategy, and ultimate Spanish escape were most influential. Medina Sidonia was the correct choice for command. The Spanish were not "defeated" nor were the English "victorious." The Spanish continued to conduct major naval campaigns against the English until peace in 1604. Certainly, at the time, events were not seen as apocalyptic; Spain did not "decline" and England did not "rise."

Roger Whiting [**3848**], The Enterprise of England: The Spanish Armada, 1988, reassessed the situation in light of recent evidence and scholarly research, for example, nautical archaeology, the result being a balanced assessment, demythologizing, for example, making Drake less heroic and rehabilitating Howard and Medina Sidonia. In an article of 1990, M.J. Rodriguez-Salgado [**3120, 3121**] described the "Gran Armada teams," officially sponsored to search Spanish archives and produce extensive scholarly analysis.

Other products of the quadricentennial celebrations were Peter Kemp [**1859**], The Campaign of the Spanish Armada, 1988, nicely illustrated and with a focus on naval aspects; Peter Padfield [**2726**], Armada: A Celebration of the 400th Anniversary of the Defeat of the Spanish Armada, 1588-1988, 1988, a large, folio size book with traditional coverage, including the anachronistic "defeat" in the subtitle; Duff Hart-Davis [**1541**], Armada, 1988, profusely illustrated and purely traditional in approach; David Thomas [**3593**], The Illustrated Armada Handbook, 1988; Robert Milne-Tyte [**2517**], Armada!: The Planning, the Battle, and After, 1988; Nathaniel Harris [**1529**], The Armada: The Decisive Battle, 1987, in A Day that Made History series, utilizing a question and answer format; David Anderson [**69**], The Spanish Armada, 1988, a large, attractive, illustrated format aimed at young persons, sponsored by the NMM, and Merle Chacksfield [**602**], Armada 1588, 1988, relapsing into some romanticized rhetoric.

Simon Adams [**16, 15, 14**], all 1988, has written extensively, for example, "The Lurch into War: The Spanish Armada," a review article, and The Armada Campaign of 1588. One article insisted that the English were surprised throughout. The English Heritage celebrated the quadricentennial with a colorful, folio size pamphlet, Armada 1588, 1988, by Alison Plowden [**2862**]. Themes were the growing Catholic threat, photos of forts built by Henry VIII to defend from it, and "the Navy Royal."

W.H.K. Wright [**3967**], Britain's Salamis: Or, the Glorious Fight of 1588, 1888, was a tercentennial product.

During the quadricentennial, several conferences, symposia, and exhibitions were held. Patrick Gallagher [**1226**], God's Obvious Design: Papers for the Spanish Armada Symposium, Sligo, 1988, 1988, touted it as the most international of these conferences; scholars from Ireland, Scotland, England, Spain, and Holland. Three of the wrecks were near Sligo. Themes included the weather, Dutch participation, Parma, wrecks on the Irish coast, guns, and creation of myths. Included was a translation of the escaped eyewitness, Francisco de Cuellar [**823**], the translated version by Hugh Allingham [**50**]. I.A.A. Thompson [**3603**] concluded that the Armada was not a battle fleet but an armed convoy. Its primary purpose was to transport soldiers. M.J. Rodriguez-Salgado [**3121**], England, Spain and the Gran Armada, 1585-1604, 1991, was published papers from the Anglo-Spanish conference held in London and Madrid in 1988, sponsored by the International Commission of Historical Sciences. Jeff Doyle [**959**], England and the Spanish Armada, 1990, was the proceedings of a conference, University of New South Wales, August 1988. M.J. Rodriguez-Salgado [**3120**], Armada, 1588-1988: An International Exhibition to Commemorate the Spanish Armada, 1988, was the extensive official catalogue of the most important exhibition associated with the quadricentennial, this displayed at the NMM, 20 April-4 September 1988, then on to the Ulster Museum, Belfast, 12 October 1988-8 January 1989. It was the largest, most ambitious exhibition ever at the NMM. Over 400 items came from afar: Spain, Austria, the Vatican, and the U.S.

The quadricentennial, 1988, was the occasion for several historiographical surveys. Douglas Knerr [**1953**], "Through the Golden Mist," 1989, noted that the Armada was shrouded in myth and legend, the struggle between light and darkness, the beginning of Armageddon, and subject to competing Whig and Tory interpretations. God favored the English, Elizabeth was glorious, the nation was united, Medina Sidonia was a bumbling amateur out of his element and a "craven coward," and Spain was "defeated" never to rise again. Such were the interpretations, reinforced by the Victorians. Then, revision: Armada guns, their size, number, and capabilities, were incorrectly presented. The Duke of Medina Sidonia was courageous, talented, and "sound." Garrett Mattingly [2468] put it all in a European context.

John Hattendorf [1557], 1990, reviewed the literature. The quadricentennial was lavishly celebrated: bonfires, ceremonies, exhibitions, symposia, and much publication, new, original, and reprints. "Two magnificent studies" came from Wernham [3814, 3813]. 20 Spanish wrecks had been identified, some excavated. The NRS reissued pertinent collections. Spanish research was mobilized and archives mined. Rodger [3104] published pertinent documents from the PRO.

"1588 and All That," 1989, was the review of some of the literature of the quadricentennial by J.R. Hale [1453]. There was no epic battle nor clear-cut victory or defeat.

Wallace MacCaffrey [2224], 1989, observed a trend toward de-mythologizing with the advent of new research and evidence. Instead of the ultimate light-darkness apocalypse, it was a single campaign in a war of complex origins and development. Certainly, contemporaries did not see it as ultimate and final.

Geoffrey Parker [2751, 2755], 1976 and 1988, and Colin Martin [2424], 1988, have speculated extensively, for example, counter-factual presentations and assessments. An example was "Why the Armada Failed," recounting the greatest naval disaster in Spanish history. Why? Some answers came from nautical archaeology: eight Spanish ships had been excavated since 1968. The original plan was for 286 ships, 60,000 men, supported by the forces of Parma in a cross-Channel invasion. Pope Sixtus was to pay a third of the costs. Spanish guns and gunnery were subject to fatal flaws. Philip II was guilty of many failures.

8. After the Armada

Literature about the aftermath was as follows: Martin Hume [1732], The Year after the Armada: And Other Historical Studies, 1896, recounting some of the aftermath. The Spanish first announced a great victory but that was soon corrected. Francisco de Cuellar [823], 1895, wrote a letter of 4 October 1589 to Philip II, a dramatic account of his famous escape.

In England, a campaign was launched aimed at destroying what was left of Spanish naval power, led by Francis Drake and John Norris. Numerous problems were experienced. Drake took 20 ships off to the Azores with no results. All failed, as recounted by C.S. Goldingham [1311], 1918. Goldingham cited "parsimony of the Queen" as one cause, but that has been disputed. The premier historian of Tudor diplomacy and naval policy, R.B. Wernham [3815,

3816], reviewed this campaign in a publication for the NRS, <u>The Expedition of Sir John Norris and Sir Francis Drake to Spain and Portugal, 1589</u>, 1988, and in an article, "Queen Elizabeth and the Portugal Expedition," 1951. Naval forces, the Queen, and English investors supported an operation as a counter to the Armada and to attack the Lisbon-Brazil trade. Unfortunately, it was characterized by disobeying orders, botched operations, lost opportunities, and great expense. In the article, Wernham exonerates Elizabeth who had been blamed for lack of financial backing and unenthusiastic support: not so, contended Wernham.

Another counter-armada operation was a major expedition of 120 ships and 6000 soldiers against Cadiz in 1596: Alan Haynes [**1580**], 1973, two by Paul Hammer [**1467, 1468**], both 1997, and Stephen Usherwood [**3704**], 1983. Anglo-Dutch intelligence indicated Spanish preparation for another armada. The commanders were Lord Howard of Effingham and the Earl of Essex. The Dutch sent 24 ships. The Spanish defenders were commanded by the Duke of Medina Sidonia. Cadiz was sacked, but little else was achieved.

The novelist, Winston Graham [**1363**], <u>The Spanish Armadas</u>, 1972, recounted the Armada of 1588 plus several other Spanish naval attempts, for example, in 1596 and 1597. Other works described an English operation in 1594 against Brest to prevent establishment of a Spanish base there, by John Nolan [**2648**], 1995; an account of the campaign culminating in a Spanish-Irish rebel surrender at Kinsale in 1602, ending an effort by Spain to aid a major Irish rebellion led by Hugh O'Neill, the history was by John Silke [**3317**], 1970, and an account of the final Anglo-Spanish peace by Robert Kenny [**1886**], 1970. The impact of that peace on Anglo-Spanish relations in the Caribbean was studied by Kenneth Andrews [**105**].

Later Anglo-Spanish relations, in this case, naval relations, in the 18th century were reviewed by John Harbron [**1487**], 1990, and Jeremy Black [**327**], 1991. Coverage of Anglo-French antagonisms have been overemphasized at the expense of Anglo-Spanish relations. Contemporaries appreciated that the Spanish navy was a real force that could threaten the British. Harbon stressed the expertise, men, and materiel, which had and would continue to make Spain a formidable naval foe even as late as the battle of Trafalgar. **See 7., I., 11.**

G. THE 17th CENTURY

1. The Navy of the Early Stuarts

Elizabeth, the last of the Tudors, died in 1603 with no heirs. Succession was undisputed, to the Stuarts from Scotland, James I. Peace was negotiated with Spain in 1604. The navy was neglected. In the 1630s, the Ship Money controversy raised its head. By the 1640s, Civil War broke out.

Elizabeth Milford [**2510**], "The Navy at Peace: The Activities of the Early Jacobean Navy, 1603-1618," 1990, described routine peacetime operations: patrol of "the Narrow Seas," transport of important persons, and anti-pirate voyages. James I was blamed for neglect when the Dutch chased ten Spanish ships into Dover harbor and attacked them there in 1605. Christopher Penn [**2808**], The Navy under the Early Stuarts and Its Influence on English History, 1913, recalled "gloom, despair, and pessimism" and "low times," even "naval chaos," 1614-1619, during the early decades. Much hyperbole was in evidence. Important incidents included Algiers in 1620, Cadiz in 1625, Re in 1627, La Rochelle, and the imposition of Ship Money. Privateering was abolished and prizes were declared illegal.

The most prominent naval figure during these decades was the Lord Admiral, George Villiers, First Duke of Buckingham, a favorite of James I and Charles I. His career was described by Roger Lockyer [**2180**], 1981. The Second Duke, a later Privy Counsellor who opposed James, Duke of York and Samuel Pepys, was described in a dissertation by B.C. Yardley [**3973**], 1989.

The reign of Charles I was most identified with deteriorating relations between the Crown and Parliament, increasingly led by powerful merchants. War with Spain exacerbated the problems of Charles. Melvin Wren [**3960**], 1950, described serious problems resulting in a demand to impress 20 ships from London. Authorities, taxpayers, and crews rioted and mutinied. Robin Swales [**3522**], 1977, cited earlier instances for the use of Ship Money. Kenneth Andrews [**114**], Ships, Money and Politics: Seafaring and Naval Enterprise in the Reign of Charles I, 1991, assessed Caroline maritime enterprise. The threat from pirates increased. When Parliament refused funds, Charles levied this antiquated imposition, Ship Money. The first Ship Money Fleet, 25 ships, 19 of which were Crown ships, appeared in 1635, described by Florence Dyer [**1005**], 1937. An article and a dissertation described the navy under Charles I, 1988 and 1990, by Brian Quintrell [**2991**] and Andrew Thrush [**3619**].

Naval, maritime, and fishing forces at this time experienced volatility: mutinies, coercion by the Dutch and French, and harassment by North African corsairs and Channel pirates. A dissertation, "Ship Money during the Personal Rule of Charles I: Politics, Ideology and the Law, 1634-1640," 1991, was by A.A. Gill [**1281**]. Ship Money became political as more objections arose. "The Ship Money Case and William Fiennes, Viscount Saye and Sale," 1977, by Nelson Bard [**202**], cited one case; John Hampden was more prominently involved.

The war with Spain had ended. The French Religious Civil War of the late 16th century had been resolved. Now, under the early Stuarts, France was the enemy; Carleton Cunningham [**832**] has a dissertation, "Anglo-French Trade, War and Diplomacy in the Early Stuart Age," 1998. Naval operations during the early Stuart period were described: in a dissertation by Stephen Stearns [**3431**], 1967, operations against Cadiz and Re, the latter an island near La Rochelle, both operations being utter failures; two articles by Thomas Cogswell [**696,**

697], 1984 and 1986, on La Rochelle, and contemporaneous apologetics for Buckingham on the expedition to Re by Edward Herbert, Lord Herbert of Cherbury [**1605**], 1656.

2. The Rise of Maritime Hegemony

A consequence of the Armada campaign and Spanish failure was projection of English/British rise. Naval, maritime, commercial, imperial, and colonial hegemony were among the results. Success in preventing the Spanish Armada invading and a number of moves of expansion of trade, exploration expeditions, and enterprise activities laid the foundation. Formative, a turning point, decisive, and foundational were pertinent terms describing the situation.

Merchants and the Crown initiated commercial "reaching out" campaigns, for example, to the Baltic and Russia, to the Mediterranean and the Levant, out into the Atlantic and Newfoundland, and down toward Iberia and out to the island groups of the South Atlantic. Essential to it all was the matter of smuggling, piracy, plunder, and privateering, in addition to fishing and coastal trade, all sanctioned and invested in by the Crown and high officials, being established as "schools for seamen." Coincident were declines and disruptions in the wool and cloth trades, initial steps in establishing the slave trade, and religious rectifications. Earliest examples of ship money and navigation acts were also contributory factors.

All of these matters were best articulated in David Quinn [**2976**], England's Sea Empire, 1550-1642, 1983: a survey both of English naval power and early modern external trade plus the earliest experiments overseas and with colonization and touted as the first such study to combine these topics. The broad perspective was presented by Frederic Mauro [**2470**], L'Expansion Europeenne, 1600-1870, 1964. Walter Oakeshott [**2655**], Founded upon the Seas: A Narrative of Some English Maritime and Overseas Enterprises during the Period 1550-1616, 1942, recounted exploits of Elizabethan and Jacobean seamen and summarized essential issues, for example, the search for the Northeast and Northwest Passages, early voyaging of Hawkins and Drake, the Armada and related campaigns, English and Spanish, early advances in navigation and ventures in exploration, and ventures by Raleigh in colonization.

What was the contribution of the navy in all of this? I.R. Mather [**2465**] answered that in a dissertation, "Role of the Royal Navy in the English Atlantic Empire, 1660-1720," 1995, presenting statistical details of warships, size and type, which stations, convoying operations, and areas of activity, all facilitating the expansion of empire. The inimitable A.L. Rowse [**3158**], The Expansion of Elizabethan England, 1955, appreciated the key role of sea power in the process. Two phenomena facilitated the process: ship money and navigation acts. The former was identified with King Charles I in the 1630s and the latter seemingly emerged in the 1650s: not so. Precedents for both appeared earlier. Both have been linked to a Mercantile System. In a work about the repeal of the Navigation

Laws in 1849, Sarah Palmer [**2741**], 1990, defined them. They were based on the simple premise that maritime power and national defense depended on ability to man the navy with skilled men, which in turn relied on the merchant marine as supply or "nursery of seamen." They dominated for 200 years.

Lawrence Harper [**1522**], The Navigation Laws: A Seventeenth-Century Experiment in Social Engineering, 1939, noted that Adam Smith had praised them as acts to encourage trade and domestic shipping and seamen; the earliest efforts had been under Richard II and Henry VI; preference for the coal trade in 1620; the best known legislation was in 1651; modified in 1660, and sustained for 200 years. G.N. Clark [**645**], "The Navigation Act of 1651," 1923, brought up a series of "debatable points": links to the First Dutch War, the extent of enforcement, and the actual impact on English shipping and trade. James Farnell [**1078**], 1964, elaborated on the historiography and their implications. The classic act of 1651 was linked to English nationalism, domination of "the Narrow Seas," and was a factor precipitating the First Dutch War.

Later, debate on the navigation acts as one of the causes of the American Revolution arose: Oliver Dickerson [**926**], The Navigation Acts and the American Revolution, 1951 and Larry Sawers [**3229**], 1992, who reviewed the implications of the navigation acts. Did they cause the American Revolution? Sowers thought the answer was yes.

Some concluded that they were less a burden on the colonies than claimed at the time. In Anglo-Irish Trade, 1660-1800, 1968, Louis Cullen [**824**] noted that the navigation acts did not apply to Irish trade. Similar observations were made about Scottish trade, 1651-1791, by Eric Graham [**1356**]; the Act of Union resolving problems. The great economic historian J.H. Clapham [**641**] wrote of "The Last Years of the Navigation Acts," 1910, in the 19th century; officially in 1849 but more likely in the 1820s. That thesis was supported by the great naval historian, Gerald Graham [**1361**], Sea Power and British North America, 1783-1820, 1941. The British failed properly to assess the situation. The War of 1812 was a tragic mistake for all concerned. **See 7., I., 14.** The famed "nursery of seamen" rationale was negotiated away in a compromise in 1822.

It was the rise of the concepts of free trade and free navigation which led to repeal, as presented by the noted maritime authority, Sarah Palmer [**2741**], Politics, Shipping and the Repeal of the Navigation Laws, 1990. Protectionism ended and the British were first with these changing initiatives.

Other observations on these matters were as follows. Nicholas Tracy [**3635**], Attack on Maritime Trade, 1991, noted that A.T. Mahan [**2328, 2329**] saw "a maritime strategy" as decisive: the composition was a "holy trinity": shipping, colonies, and the navy. A type of naval activity was investigated, aided by nautical archaeological expeditions on shipwrecks. Samuel Margolin [**2374, 2375**], "Guardships on the Virginia Station, 1667-1767," 1995, documented campaigns to reduce maritime lawlessness, in this case, in the Chesapeake region on what was designated as the Virginia Station. Patrols against smuggling, piracy, and customs fraud achieved mixed results; a spectacular success was a victory against the pirate, Blackbeard. Yet another factor was the importance of Antwerp and its access from the sea as the premier European, if not world, entrepot during the early modern period. That history was reviewed by the great S.T. Bindoff [**318**], The Scheldt Question to 1839, 1945; the Scheldt was originally closed in 1585, greatly benefiting the Dutch rise to hegemony.

3. The Thirty Years' War

Some designated a series of military campaigns, mostly on the Continent, between 1618-1648, as the Thirty Years' War; some presented other delineations. Two solid histories by that title were by C.W. Wedgwood [**3802**], 1938, and Geoffrey Parker [**2754**], 1984, though neither acknowledged naval activities. However, W.P. Guthrie [**1425**], "Naval Actions of the Thirty Years' War," 2001, saw them as the last flourish of old naval tactics prior to the new of the Anglo-Dutch Wars. **See 7., G., 6.**

Jon Kepler [**1918**], "Fiscal Aspects of the English Carrying Trade during the Thirty Years' War," 1972, noted the neutrality of England but increasing competition with the Dutch. English merchants exploited the lucrative opportunities to carry contraband, money, and troops for the various antagonists; the Crown also benefited by increased customs receipts, especially for Charles I when Parliament refused funding and, later, when Parliament needed funds to oppose the Royalists.

4. The Navy and the Civil War

The English Civil War, the English Revolution, the Puritan Revolution, the English Republic, the Protectorate, the Commonwealth, rule of the Major Generals, rule by Oliver Cromwell, the Interregnum, and the period of "no king" were all terms describing England beginning in the late 1630s, war with Scotland, through the Restoration of 1660 when Charles II returns to England as King. The King, Charles I, and Parliament increasingly conflicted after Parliament was dismissed in 1629 and not recalled until 1640, "the eleven years of tyranny," first the Short Parliament, and then the Long Parliament. The "First" Civil War began in 1642, the "second" in 1647, and the culmination was the trial of Charles I in December 1648 and his beheading early in 1649. Oliver Cromwell was the most identifiable leader until his death in 1658; Charles II was recalled in 1660. The navy consistently supported Parliament, a decisive factor.

Some overviews have been contributed: John Kenyon [**1915**], The Civil Wars: A Military History of England, Scotland, and Ireland, 1638-1660, 1998, Edward Razzell [**3030**], The English Civil War, 5 vols., 1996, Graham Seel [**3267**], English Wars and the Republic, 1637-1660, 1999, and J.R. Powell

[**2924**], <u>Documents Relating to the Civil War, 1642-1648</u>, 1963, a publication of the NRS.

Bernard Capp [**574**], <u>Cromwell's Navy: The Fleet and the English Revolution, 1648-1660</u>, 1989, lamented the gap of naval history during this period; the New Model Army was prominently reported. The navy brought international prestige to the Commonwealth and Cromwell exploited it. Religion played an important role in the navy, Chatham being a prominent center. Naval officers, for example, Monck and Lawson, exerted decisive political influence related to the Rump Parliament and the Restoration. There was a good history in German, Hans-Christopher Junge [**1839**], <u>Flottenpolitic und Seemacht: Die Entstehung der Englischen Seemacht Wahrend der Herrschaft Cromwells</u>, 1980. J.R. Powell [**2926**], <u>The Navy of the English Civil War</u>, 1962, was an older survey. The navy continued to be decisive and Warwick, who became Lord High Admiral, was the hero. J.K. Laughton [**2055**] had virtually ignored the role of the navy in the Civil War in his pertinent entries in the DNB [**930**]: "a coach and four" could be driven through that gap. John Battick [**235**], <u>Cromwell's Navy and the Protectorate, 1653-1658</u>, 1967, was a dissertation: Cromwell appreciated the connection between sea power and diplomacy.

Donald Kennedy [**1875, 1873**] wrote a dissertation and article on the navy and Parliament and on the English naval revolt of 1648. Kennedy was revisionist on the revolt; others such as Oppenheim, Robinson, and Gardiner cited pay and "narrow personal jealousies" as the cause; Kennedy cited ideological rationales and political arguments as primary concerns of naval leaders of the revolt. The navy and contemporary politics were reviewed in a dissertation by R. McCaughey [**2228**], 1983. Stephen Greenberg [**1383**], 1991, presented details on the navy and its opting for Parliament, an almost unanimous choice. The loyalty of the seamen was crucial and naval support was decisive. He described "an early modern media blitz" as Parliamentary leaders such as John Pym and Warwick formulated a sophisticated "propaganda machine." Charles Firth [**1105**], 1926, historian of the army of the Civil War, wrote an article on the sailors of the Civil War.

Charles Maples [**2364**], "Parliament's Admiral: The Parliamentary and Naval Career of Robert Rich, Second Earl of Warwick, during the Reign of Charles I," 1975, was a dissertation recounting the career of Warwick. Warwick was moderate in Parliament and in religion but became increasingly alienated over the personal rule of Charles I. He was a privateer, having his own fleet of privateers; dramatically, in1642, he presented them to Parliament; then, in 1648 when the fleet mutinied, he again stepped in and restored the fleet to Parliament. His influence was equally effective in Scottish relations.

M.L. Baumber [**245, 243**], 1971 and 1989, presented two articles on the Navy and the Civil War in Ireland in the 1640s. The essential Chester-Dublin access across the Irish Sea was patrolled and blockaded, preventing a Royalist army from crossing into England.

It was a splendid era of Blake, Monck, Penn, and Lawson. **See 9., D.** Hugh Rogers [**3127**], Generals-at-Sea, 1992, presented more than the title suggested. The title described the commanders of the navy during the Civil War and the First and Second Dutch Wars, for example, Robert Blake, Richard Deane, Edward Montagu, Earl of Sandwich, George Monck, William Penn, and Prince Rupert. Together, they revolutionized naval tactics and introduced Fighting Instructions. **See 16., C.** There was a chapter on each of the important battles in the Dutch Wars. R.C. Anderson [**98**] contributed three consecutive articles on the Royalists at sea, 1928-1935, mostly on the operations of Prince Rupert, the Royalist naval commander. John Lynch [**2211**], 1998, wrote an article on Royalist naval power and logistics. For a time, Bristol remained under Royalist control.

In the run-up to the Civil War, Oliver Cromwell and the Puritans fulfilled commercial and imperial ambitions with a religious twist, called the Western Design. Earlier, the Providence Island venture had been the initiative of the Puritan leaders, for example, John Pym, Lord Saye and Sale, and Warwick; the goal was a Godly Republic. It was used as a base for anti-Spanish attacks and privateering led by Warwick. It was seen as a model for future English colonial expansion, all described by Karen Kupperman [**1979**], 1993. Stanley Taylor [**3583**], The Western Design: An Account of Cromwell's Expedition to the Caribbean, 1965, described the later grandiose scheme, begun in 1654. William Penn and Robert Venebles commanded. Barbados, St. Christopher, and Santo Domingo were unsuccessfully attacked in a kind of guerrilla warfare; Jamaica was retained. In a dissertation, Liam O'Melinn [**2709**], 1991, linked these operations to formative colonial government processes. The plantation owners remained loyal to Charles I and the Puritans dispatched a fleet and armed forces to demand support; Charles II at the Restoration continued this oppressive subordination. O'Melinn concluded that the Civil War led to greater restrictions on all of the English colonists.

A curious relationship required inclusion. D.F. Allen [**40**], "The Order of St. John and Cromwell's Navy, 1649-1660," 1993, explained that the famous Order of Hospitalers, founded in the 12th century, was traditionally protected by France and Spain. In the mid-17th century, those powers were at war and the Commonwealth government stepped in to play that role.

5. In the Mediterranean Sea

The entry into the Baltic Sea and the rationales have been reviewed. **See 7., E., 4.** Similarly, English/British entry into the Mediterranean Sea facilitated rise and expansion. For an introduction, go to the influential classic, The Mediterranean and the Mediterranean World in the Age of Philip II, 2 vols., 1949, by Fernand Braudel [**426**], which presented a global perspective incorporating Marxist and structuralist methodologies stressing interactions and relationships of politics, culture, commerce, climate, weather, war, and peace.

Traditional features such as national boundaries and many "political" aspects were rarely considered.

Not directly involving the English/British but seen as formative with wide ranging implications and often juxtaposed with the Armada just 17 years later was the major battle of Lepanto, 7 October 1571. It was fought off the west coast of Greece, Christians vs. Muslims, for example, the Holy League of Venice, the Papacy, and Spain vs. the Ottoman Empire; the last great galley battle. The Christians won but little changed in the area for centuries, as recounted by Andrew Hess [**1612**], 1972, and Geoffrey Parker [**2748**], 1978.

The great Julian Corbett [**749**], England in the Mediterranean, 1603-1713, 1904, covered the Stuart period, focusing on the rise and expansion of the English/British presence in the Mediterranean. It was a formative period, and this study was important. Peter Dietz [**935**], The British in the Mediterranean, 1994, ticked off specific places of increasing involvement including initial dates for naval and military interest: Tangier-1662, Gilbraltar-1704, Minorca-1708, Malta-1790s, Egypt-1798, and Cyprus-later. Commercial connections began in the 16th century; Hakluyt [**1446-1451**] recalled such as early as 1511 followed soon by the Levant and the Venice Companies. Later there would be added Corfu, the Ionian Islands, Suez, and Palestine.

Gigliola Pagano de Divitiis [**2732**], English Merchants in Seventeenth-Century Italy, 1997, observed the factors effecting the shift from the Mediterranean city-states of Venice, Genoa, and Florence to the entrepots of Northern Europe, Amsterdam and London. He concluded that English success was due to English naval superiority. Privateering, piracy, and war contributed to the transformation, the move of the center of gravity from the Mediterranean to Northern Europe. **See 7., E., 2.**

The strategic island of Malta and its owners, the Knights of St. John, became increasingly important as noted by Ernle Bradford [**411**], 1961.

T.S. Willan [**3865**], 1955, focused on Anglo-Turkish relations and trade in the Levant area of the eastern Mediterranean, all documented early by the Hakluyts [**1446-1451**]. Daniel Goffman [**1309**], Britons and the Ottoman Empire, 1642-1660, 1998, described chronology and a later connection; early contact and the Levant Company were in the 1580s, then others, for example, Venice, Genoa, and France, stepped in, and, finally, in the mid-17th century, the English returned. A classic survey on the eastern Mediterranean was R.C. Anderson [**94**], Naval Wars in the Levant, 1559-1853, 1952; themes included Lepanto, Malta, Crete, Venetian interests, and the entre of Russia into the area.

Expansion and extension of geographic and imperial responsibilities increasingly characterized the navies of Charles II and William III. In the process, the importance of the Spanish Main diminished and that of the Mediterranean increased. A standard account for the Mediterranean was by Julian Corbett [**749**].

Tangier was a marriage gift to Charles II, that possession providing a naval base and added obligations for the navy. W.F. Monk [**2527**], Britain and the Western Mediterranean, 1953, elaborated. Alternative bases were sought, for example, Gibraltar and Minorca. First, bases were needed to oppose Barbary pirates, later to maintain blockade of Toulon and other French interests. These factors contributed to expansion of British sea power. Many naval officers served there. Accusations that various plots leading to the Revolution of 1688 initiated there was the subject of an article by Peter LeFevre [2101], 1987. George Byng and Pepys were mentioned and, apparently, in November 1688, a decision was made that the navy would not oppose the invasion of William of Orange.

A three-part article by W.B. Rowbotham [3153], "The Algerine War in the Time of Charles II," 1964, described naval ventures into the Mediterranean to suppress piracy against merchant ships and slave taking. The pirates were from Tripoli, Tunis, Algiers, and Sallee, Algiers being the initial objective by a force commanded by John Narbrough during the late 1670s; Arthur Herbert led a revived campaign in the early 1680s.

Increasing commercial traffic into the Mediterranean demanded greater activity from the navy, especially to convoy the Mediterranean trade. John Ehrman [1025], 1949, wrote of such an operation in 1693, forcing the navy to abandon a planned attack on the enemy port of Brest.

Looking ahead to the situation in the Mediterranean half a century later, Daniel Panzac [2743], 1998, surveyed a slice of time, 1736-1739, and assessed the overall picture. Its importance had diminished. There persisted the old relationships: Venice, Malta, the Ottoman Empire, and rising Naples; the totality of their navies were involved. Relatively new arrivals, Britain, France, and Spain, sent minor parts of their navies. Extensive and detailed comparisons of all of them were made: size, age, firepower, crew size, wages, budgets, ship-building capacities, and diet. Similarly, Perfidious Albion: The Origins of Anglo-French Rivalry in the Levant, 1972, by John Marlowe [2394], focused on future implications of French expansion resulting from the Peace of Paris of 1763, for example, into Egypt and Syria; each saw the other as conspiratorial.

6. The Anglo-Dutch Wars

In the 17th century the Dutch or United Provinces catapulted into a dominating, hegemonic, and global superpower based on commercial, naval, and imperial expansion. It was an extraordinary achievement. In the chronological dynamic, Portugal and Spain had been superseded. In 1648, concluding the Eighty Years' War, freedom from Spain and the Habsburgs was achieved. The new state was the United Provinces of the Free Netherlands, seven provinces that broke away from Spain. The "Netherlands" and the "Dutch" were terms to describe the new entity. Maritime and naval powers provided the foundation for it all.

The aspiring and rising competitor was England/Britain. The relationships between them were highly competitive. The English assisted them in their rebellion against Spain. The Dutch aided England during the Armada and Anglo-Spanish war. Relations deteriorated during the 17th century. Ultimately, four wars, Anglo-Dutch Wars, occurred: First, 1652-1654, Second, 1665-1667, Third, 1672-1674, and, under different circumstances, the Fourth, 1780-1784. The Dutch eventually fell and the English rose. The wars were primarily naval wars, hard-fought and deadly on both sides. Modern naval tactics and warship design were transformed. Fighting Instructions [751] were formulated. France joined one side or the other, on occasion. Both countries were Protestant and in 1688, the Stadholder of Holland, William of Orange, became King William III of England. G.J.A. Raven [3022] summed up: even with this "special relationship," Anglo-Dutch relations were "always tense, usually sour, and only very rarely warm." An immediate cause was a traditional demand by the English in the Channel that all ships lower their flags in saluting English sovereignty, the ruler of "the Narrow Seas." The Dutch refused and war ensued. The English Navigation Law of 1651 was another cause.

Jonathan Israel [1763], The Dutch Republic: Its Rise, Greatness, and Fall, 1477-1806, 1995, followed the trajectory suggested in the title and in the previous paragraph. Much can be learned about the history of the Dutch or United Provinces. Commerce, finance, shipping, and technology were stressed; also, politics, economics, culture, art, and religion. Israel [1762] elaborated in Dutch Primacy in World Trade, 1585-1740, 1989. It was based on "bulk trades" and "rich trades" which projected the Dutch into unprecedented hegemony. The older standard was Pieter Geyl [1269], The Netherlands in the Seventeenth Century, 2 vols., 1936. The classic was C.R. Boxer [397], The Dutch Seaborne Empire, 1600-1800, 1965. A prominent Dutch scholar, Karel Davids [862], stressed a wider perspective: Miracle Mirrored: The Dutch Republic in European Perspective, 1995.

Background can be found in George Edmundson [1017], Anglo-Dutch Rivalry during the First Half of the Seventeenth Century, 1911. "Competing Cousins: Anglo-Dutch Trade Rivalry," 1988, was an essay by Jonathan Israel [1760]. "The Sound Trade and the Anglo-Dutch Conflicts, 1640-1654," 1947, was a dissertation by H.A. Hansen [1485]. Other works on Anglo-Dutch relations were Jaap Bruijn [485], Anglo-Dutch Mercantile Marine Relations, 1700-1850, 1991; an article, "Dutch and English Merchant Shipping in the Seventeenth Century," 1930, by Violet Barbour [198]; a dissertation by Lucile Deen [894], 1936, and a NMM pamphlet by Ralph Davis [881], 1975. More substantial was Charles Wilson [3908], Profit and Power: England and the Dutch Wars, 1957. Anglo-Dutch commercial relations during the early 18th century were reviewed in a dissertation by D.J. Ormrod [2714], 1977. More extensive on the same subject was a dissertation published by Garland: Hugh Dunthorne [993], 1986.

What was the role of religion? An answer in a dissertation and book was by Steven Pincus [2857, 2856], Protestantism and Patriotism, 1990 and

1996, contending that ideology and religion played as important or more important roles in the conflict as competition in trade and imperialism.

Jaap Bruijn [486], The Dutch Navy of the Seventeenth and Eighteenth Centuries, 1993, described the beginnings: in the 1560s, Sea Beggars opposed the sea forces of the Duke of Alva and Philip II. They evolved into regional naval organizations. Bruijn contended that the Dutch developed the first "standing navy" in the world. J.R. Jones [1830], "The Dutch Navy and National Survival in the Seventeenth Century," 1988, saw it as the first maritime power but vulnerable. C.R. Boxer [401], 1954, wrote of one of the great Dutch naval commanders, killed in the first war: M.H. Tromp, chief antagonist to Robert Blake. **See 9., D., 4.**

For the British, a "standing navy" was introduced during the reign of Charles II. Roger Hainsworth [1445], The Anglo-Dutch Naval Wars, 1652-1674, 1998, recounted the wars in a narrative history, a good introduction but undue coverage on the First and little on the Third Wars. Unanticipated were the capabilities of the English navy under the Commonwealth; the pendulum would swing back and forth throughout, victory and defeat. J.R. Jones [1829], The Anglo-Dutch Wars of the Seventeenth Century, 1996, came to several conclusions: weather was important; it was worse then than now; no new technology was introduced; English ships had heavier guns and superior gunners, proving decisive; the Dutch had fewer manning problems, and English finances were in chaos while the Dutch effectively stayed "in the black."

Anglo-Dutch relations during the 1640s before the First War were reviewed: Simon Groenveld [1404], "The English Civil Wars as a Cause of the First Anglo-Dutch War, 1640-1652," 1987. The relationship changed drastically, twice. The Dutch perspective on the First War and a war with Sweden was reviewed in Phil Ballhausen [186], Der Erste Englische-HollandischeSeekrieg, 1652-1654 sowie der Schwedisch-Hollandische Seekrieg, 1658-1659, 1923.

The impact on the Scottish marine was reviewed by Eric Graham [1356]. During the process of the three wars, the Scots were able to exploit privateering opportunities, slowly. James Grant [1368], 1914, assessed "the Old Scots navy" at the end of this period and stressed the importance of sea power for Scotland, a publication of the NRS.

Three publications of the NRS applied: Samuel Gardiner [1248], Letters and Papers Relating to the First Dutch War, 6 vols., 1898-1930; Julian Corbett [761], Views of the Battles of the Third Dutch War, and R.C. Anderson [88], Journals and Narratives of the Third Dutch War, 1946. Two works were produced for the NMM in pamphlet format: C.R. Boxer [396], The Anglo-Dutch Wars of the Seventeenth Century, 1652-1674, 1974, and Alan Pearsall [2801], The Second Anglo-Dutch War, 1665-1667, 1967, the latter as a catalogue for an exhibition. The inimitable Boxer [407, 403, 405, 404] has four other related additions in article form: "The Tromps and the Anglo-Dutch Wars, 1652-1674," 1953; "Public Opinion and the Second Anglo-Dutch War, 1664-1667," 1966;

"The Third Dutch War in the East," 1930, and "Some Second Thoughts on the Third Anglo-Dutch War, 1672-1674," 1969.

For the fourth Anglo-Dutch War, 1780-1784, the occasion was the War of the American Revolution and deteriorating Anglo-Dutch relations. H.M. Scott [**3259**], 1988, focused on Dutch politics. The machinations of the British ambassador exaggerated the disputes.

Individual events of the Anglo-Dutch Wars have been covered, sporadically and irregularly, unfortunately. The battle of Portland, February 1652, involved Monck, Deane, and Penn and a total of about 80 ships, described by R.C. Anderson [**82**], 1953. The Four-Days battle, June 1666, off the mouth of the Thames in the Second War, was a particularly bloody one: 2000 dead and wounded and 2000 prisoners, ten ships; covered in the standard work by H.A. van Foreest [**3722**], partly in Dutch and English; in an article by Philippus Bosscher [**368**], 1967, and, most extensively in a large book, A Distant Storm, 1996, by Frank Fox [**1170**]. Even so, this was not the decisive battle of the Second War. Fox [**1173**] also wrote on the warships.

More substantial coverage was about the famous and catastrophic Dutch attack up the Thames estuary and into the Medway where English warships at the Chatham Dockyard were devastated, May-June 1667, in the Second War. P.G. Rogers [**3131**], The Dutch in the Medway, 1970, and Anthony Bailey [**173**], "Inferno on the Medway," 1997, and related accounts of Dutch attacks by Alvin Coox [**746**], 1949, and Frank Hussey [**1740**], 1983, were presentations. Dutch admiral Michiel de Ruyter led 80 ships, burned some, and carried off other English warships, previously put in ordinary by Charles II. On top of this humiliation, plague and fire had devastated the English. The diary of Samuel Pepys [**2817**] was a great source for it all.

Eric Gruber von Arni [**1415**], 2001, presented an intriguing study on English army-navy relations during the First War. The perennial naval problem was manning. On occasion, army manpower was mobilized, "soldiers-at-sea." These relationships were described and reviewed.

In the Third War, the Dutch attacked New York and environs, formerly New Netherlands, and other British and French possessions in America, for example, Newfoundland fisheries and tobacco plantations in Virginia. Ronald Shomette [**3308**], Raid on America, 1988, was an extensive account. After this war, an Anglo-Dutch alliance against the French was concluded, described by Clyde Grose [**1406**], 1924. Carl Ekberg [**1028**], The Failure of Louis XIV's Dutch War, 1979, and G.N. Clark [**643**], 1923, focused on the Franco-Dutch War of 1672-1678, part of which, of course, was the Third Anglo-Dutch War. Charles Boxer [**404**], 1969, wrote of "second thoughts" about this Third War.

Beginning in 1959, Anglo-Dutch Historical Conferences have assembled, for example, in September 1966, the third in London, and in 1976, the sixth in Leiden. The proceedings were published, respectively: J.S. Bromley [**450**], Britain and the Netherlands in Europe and Asia, 1968, and A.C. Duke

[984], Britain and the Netherlands, 1977. Among the essays was J.S. Bromley, "Away from Impressment."

7. The Navy and the Restoration

The influential treatise on sea power, The Influence of Sea Power upon History, 1890, by A.T. Mahan [2328, 2329], in which the British navy was the model, commenced with 1660; the sequel ended with 1812. Mahan stressed the strategy of the "blue-water" navy, that is, a large, modern, powerful, compact fleet able to overawe any enemy at any time in any place. Antony Preston [2946], 1987, edited a version of the first volume plus 45 pages of the second, to 1805.

Generals-at-sea played important roles in the period after the death of Oliver Cromwell in 1658. A naval force deployed across the Channel to escort Charles II back to England for the Restoration in 1660. Arthur Tedder [3584], The Navy of the Restoration, 1916, described this very period. Baron Tedder stressed the important role played by the navy.

The Restoration navy has been designated by some as "the first English standing navy." The Second and Third Anglo-Dutch Wars were fought during this period. Some of the historians, revisionists all, were determined to overcome "the tyranny" of the Pepysian view. That concept was illustrated by Leslie Wilcox [3855], Mr. Pepys' Navy, 1966. The day-to-day administration of the Restoration navy was presented. Arthur Bryant [494] credited Pepys as "the savior of the navy." This account was about naval affairs and the handling of them by Pepys. Samuel Pepys [2817] and writings about him told the detailed story of the Restoration navy. **See 9., D., 16.** Was it self-serving and self-aggrandizement?

J.D. Davies [871, 872], Gentlemen and Tarpaulins: The Officers and Men of the Restoration Navy, 1991, concentrated on the personnel, the title coming from a Pepysian phrase. In an article, Davies elaborated on machinations of Parliament and a crisis over religion. Specifically, in the book, four groups were delineated as constituted in 1660: those from the Interregnum fleet, exiled Cavaliers or Royalists, "tarpaulins" or former warrant officers, and young gentlemen. As might be expected under the circumstances, divisiveness prevailed. Because they were persons of the Restoration, pejorative images of fragmentation, drunkenness, and dilettantism persisted. Not so, contended Davies, who rehabilitated them. Too long have the views of Pepys been the only measure, for example, by Arthur Bryant [495] and J.R. Tanner [3568]. Professionalism in the naval service emerged. The "old salts" from the navy of Cromwell sustained and reformed it.

In the article, Davies focused on the impact and reaction of conversion to Catholicism of James, Duke of York, then Lord High Admiral, heir, and future king. It was the crucial time of the Popish Plot and Exclusion Crisis, the navy being in the thick of the crises. Parliament feared Catholics and pro-French enthusiasts would take over the navy.

Perhaps, more than any other period of English/British history, the personalities of the monarchs directly affected the navy: Charles II and, more importantly, James II, sometime Duke of York, Lord High Admiral, and veteran land and naval commander. Charles II was son of the executed King and spent the time of the Interregnum in exile on the Continent. Returning to England at the Restoration in 1660; he died in 1685 with no legitimate children. Thus, succession went to his brother, the Duke of York, becoming King James II. James had married Anne Hyde and there were two daughters, Mary and Anne, brought up as Protestants. Ordinarily, these details may not appear important. However, in this case and in the event, both daughters succeeded. In 1669, James converted to Catholicism. Later, a widower, he married a French Catholic princess who, in the spring of 1688, bore a son. That signaled Catholic monarchs forever. But it was not to be.

Parliament was alarmed when James converted and other perceived Catholic threats emerged. The Test Act was passed, effectively excluding Catholics from all offices. James was forced to withdraw and the navy was placed in Commission under a Navy Board. Pepys was Clerk. Before Charles died in 1685, a series of Exclusion crises and an attempted rebellion caused disruption and uncertainty. All failed and James succeeded, presumably for a short reign, then his Protestant daughters would succeed. Then, the son was born.

As with Davies [**871-874**], Sari Hornstein [**1676**], The Restoration Navy and English Foreign Trade, 1674-1688, 1990, set out to revise the Pepysian evaluations of the navy as ineffective and divided. Pepys exaggerated any weaknesses so as to enhance his own contributions. Hornstein selected the postwar period, after the Third Anglo-Dutch War, a time of peace. She focused on the Mediterranean trade, the possession of Tangier from 1661-1684, and the operations of the navy there, for example, against the Barbary corsairs and facilitating diplomatic initiatives. Three or four dozen English ships were stationed there representing a model for maritime defense. It ran convoys, protected trade, and defeated the threats. The navy developed from a personal force of the monarch to an institution of the state.

Frank Fox [**1172**], Great Ships: The Battlefleet of King Charles II, 1980, used fabulous paintings, drawings, and schematics to illustrate the ships; 250 illustrations in a magnificent production. Characteristics, armament, and histories of each ship and details about the artists were included.

During the Restoration, the navy evolved into the largest spending department and, counting the dockyards, the largest industry; for the first time, the navy was seen as truly "British," and "Britannia" as an image first appeared. James, Duke of York, was Lord High Admiral. David Davies [**870**], 'A Lover of the Sea and Skilful in Shipping': King Charles II and His Navy, 1992, demonstrated the interest of Charles II in the navy. Lionel Glassey [**1297**], The

Reigns of Charles II and James VII and II, 1997, presented ten essays elaborating upon and revising the history of the Restoration and the Revolution of 1688.

The Yale English Monarch series biography of James II was by John Miller [**2514**], 2000, but there was little on James as naval commander and naval head. More pertinent in that regard were a dissertation and book by John Callow [**561, 562**], The Making of King James II, 1998 and 2000, concentrating on his early career. He was a brilliant soldier, then an astute naval commander, leading the battlefleet into two battles. Then, in the view of Callow, venereal disease and other problems created degeneration. Even in the 1670s, he was callous, obstinate, and inept and that persisted through the 1680s. Jock Haswell [**1549**], James II: Soldier and Sailor, 1972, was not a satisfactory presentation. More informative was The Memoirs of James II: His Campaigns as Duke of York, 1652-1660, 1962, edited by Arthur Sells [**3272**]. Better and more complete coverage, if dated, was F.C. Turner [**3670**], James II, 1948.

8. The Navy and the Revolution of 1688

The Revolution of 1688, the Glorious or Bloodless Revolution, altered the succession. James II had ruled from 1685-1688. He was forced to leave England as Stadholder William of Orange, husband of Mary Stuart, invaded England. Parliament met and decreed that the throne was vacant and Mary II and William III should occupy it jointly, a unique situation. Mary died first in 1694, William continued to rule until his death in 1702, and was succeeded by Queen Anne. She died in 1714 with no direct heirs; succession went to the next Protestant candidate, the Hanover dynasty of Germany. As noted, James II was forced to flee to the Continent as William of Orange landed an invasion force from the Netherlands at Torbay, precipitating the Revolution of 1688. James and his heirs become the Jacobite pretenders, threatening to return during the 18th century.

Three good surveys covered events: J.R. Jones [**1831**], 1972 and two by Eveline Cruickshank [**818, 819**], 1989 and 2000. The Army, James II and the Glorious Revolution, 1980, by John Childs [**628**], and "The Anxieties of an Admiral: Lord Dartmouth and the Revolution of 1688," 1962, by M.J. Syndenham [**3536**], described the actions, or lack of them, of the armed forces. Dartmouth, a Protestant and naval commander, was the pivotal figure at this crucial time, moved the English fleet to Harwich where it was immobilized. Meantime, William landed on the eastern coast of Cornwall.

On the occasion of the tercentennial of the Revolution, Charles Wilson [**3909**] edited 1688: The Seaborne Alliance and Diplomatic Revolution, 1988, the proceedings of an international symposium, Greenwich, October 1988. Prince Charles wrote the introduction. Twelve papers covered pertinent English, Dutch, and related events associated with 1688.

Loyalists to James II and the later Stuart pretenders were called Jacobites, especially prominent in Scotland. The French supported on occasion. F.J. McLynn [2314], "Sea Power and the Jacobite Rising of 1745," 1981, clarified the role of the RN: blockade of Scotland and denying passage to French invasion forces. John Gibson [1273], Ships of the '45: The Rescue of the Young Pretender, 1967, mined new sources and recounted operations of the RN in Scottish waters, and, in the process, de-romanticized some of the story of Bonnie Prince Charlie.

In June 1988, a conference celebrating the tercentennial of the Revolution of 1688 was held at the Royal Naval College of Holland; the proceedings, Navies and Armies: The Anglo-Dutch Relationship in War and Peace, 1688-1988, 1990, were published by G.J.A. Raven [3022]. A tercentennial conference was held at the British Academy, 10 April 1989: The Anglo-Dutch Moment: Essays on the Glorious Revolution and Its World Impact, 1991, edited by Jonathan Israel [1759]; among the 16 essayists were Geoffrey Parker, J.R. Jones, K.N. Chaudhuri, Hugh Trevor-Roper, and Blair Warden, for example, Parker and Israel compared the Spanish Armada of 1588 and Dutch Armada of 1688.

9. Tsar Peter the Great

A unique event was the basis for a digression. Hegemonic competition and technological and naval advances in the Netherlands and in England/Britain attracted interest abroad. "Backward" Russia was impressed and the ambitious new Tsar, Peter the Great, acted with dispatch, personally leading a large entourage in a technology- and talent-seeking venture to the West, as described in James Thomas [3596], "Peter the Great and the Quest for Knowledge: The Great Embassy to Western Europe, 1697-1698," 1998. William of Orange and his succession to the throne of England were factors. The "Embassy" consisting of 250 persons led by an incognito "Petr Mikhailov" or "Peter McIloff," set off from Muscovy via Riga, Berlin, to Amsterdam in March 1697. European shipbuilding was a particular attraction. On 7 January 1798, Peter arrived in London and set up temporary residence on Norfolk Street. William and Peter became fast friends and he presented Peter with a fast British warship. Peter visited Portsmouth where a naval review, mock battle, and tour of the naval base occurred. He left London on 2 May. Eventually, four ships were required to transport the Western goods and over 800 craftsmen back to Russia.

Anthony Cross [809], Peter the Great through British Eyes, 2000, celebrated the tercentennial by reviewing the visit and the English literature, then and now, about event; views, perceptions, myths, and depictions in poetry and drama, all uniformly favorable about the great "Europeanizer." Biographies of Peter the Great were: an older one by M.S. Anderson [75], 1969, a brief one by Stephen Lee [2092], 1993, and a substantial one by Robert Massie [2458], 1981.

Cyrian Bridge [**436**], 1899, presented the history of the Russian fleet during the reign of Peter the Great, a publication of the NRS. In a dissertation and book, Edward Phillips [**2846, 2847**], The Founding of Russia's Navy, 1990 and 1995, described the fleet and operations, especially to the south to face the threat from the Ottoman Empire; all obviously stimulated and a consequence of the Embassy of 1697-1698.

Another consequence was increased Anglo-Russian trade. George Barany [**197**], 1986, described an Entente Cordiale signed by Peter and William III, who met at Utrecht, 1697. Russians came to Britain, recounted by Anthony Cross [**808**], 1980. Trade increased, recounted by Herbert Kaplan [**1843**], 1995.

10. The Wars of King Louis XIV

As was the case of "miscellaneous" officers in the chapter on personalities, as events get closer to modern times, the literature about these wars and battles has increased. **See 9., E.** These wars of Louis XIV commenced what some have called the Second Hundred Years' War, the first being the Anglo-French wars, 1320s-1450s. **See 7., E., 7.** In the New World, this series of wars had different names, on occasion, and typically had commenced a year or two before formal war began in Europe; perpetuating a concept called "no peace beyond the line," that is, fighting could occur in the colonies without warfare being declared elsewhere. As suggested in the following chronology, alliances between and among the various European powers, particularly the Big Five, Britain, France, Prussia, Russia, and Austria, changed and shifted frequently. The only consistent observation: when war was being fought, Britain and France were always on opposite sides.

The chronology of the Second Hundred Years' War was as follows. Some titles were various.

1688-1697-Nine Years' War or War of English Succession or King William's War
1700 or 1702-1713 or 1714-War of Spanish Succession or Queen Anne's War
1715 – death of King Louis XIV
1739-War of Jenkins's Ear
1740-1748-War of Austrian Succession or King George's War
1748-1756-"Diplomatic Revolution"-before: Britain and Austria vs. France and Prussia; after: Britain and Prussia vs. France and Austria
1756-1763-Seven Years' War or French and Indian War
1775-1783-War of the American Revolution or War for American Independence
1792-1815-Wars of the French Revolution and Napoleon, Britain joining in 1793

The 18th was the formative century for eventual naval domination by the British navy. France maintained a respectable navy but, increasingly during the century, it was subjected to fatal administrative, logistical, and financial deficiencies. The zenith of the Dutch navy had been in the 17th century.

However, its commercial maritime forces remained formidable. The century was the high point of sailing ship warfare. Sailing ship and related ordnance designs had evolved making line-of-battle the optimum tactical formation for naval battles. The "battleship" of the century, reaching its zenith, was the Ship of the Line, SOTL; tactics of battle delineated in detail in published "Fighting Instructions," to be rigidly followed.

John Lynn [2215], The Wars of Louis XIV, 1667-1714, 1999, was a comprehensive study of four decades of French warfare, a costly endeavour with enormous consequences for France and the future of French monarchy. H.M. Scott [3260], 1992, described the period. In a study projected for 2004, John Hattendorf [1551] will publish The Anglo-French Wars, 1688-1815. Recall that in his two-volume treatise on sea power, A.T. Mahan [2328, 2329] cited the British navy and this period as the model and ultimate. Jeremy Black [331], The British Navy and the Use of Naval Power in the Eighteenth Century, 1988, reported the conclusion from a conference: the Royal Navy was the essential factor in the making of the first global power.

As suggested, this was the decisive time of the rise of British hegemony. Several writers focused on the 1690s and early 1700s, the era of William III and the Duke of Marlborough as antagonists of Louis XIV, as formative and decisive: Ragnhild Hatton [1572], William III and Louis XIV, 1968. One essay by Tony Ryan noted a consistency during the next century: creation of the "Western Squadron" to blockade the major French naval base at Brest on the Brittany peninsula; the strategy initiated by Admiral Vernon and executed by Anson, Hawke, St. Vincent, and William Cornwallis.

Global hegemony was one dimension. These factors were described as the development of the "fiscal-military state," a phrase initiated by John Brewer [435]. See 13., A. D.W. Jones [1825] elaborated in War and Economy in the Age of William III and Marlborough, 1988. During this epic battle between Britain and France, Britain gained Great Power status. It was war that was the boost to growth and advancement of the economy.

Equally decisive during the Nine Years' War was the French strategy, challenge, and response. French formulators at the time included Seignelay, Colbert, and Pontchartrain. Success in the battle of Beachy Head looked encouraging but the results at Barfleur and La Hogue were setbacks; the response was a shift from a main fleet strategy to guerre de course, a strategy of commerce destruction by naval vessels and privateers, all described by Geoffrey Symcox, [3532], 1974. See 12., B. An Anglo-Dutch alliance against the French who were supporting James and the Jacobite cause and who were supporting a massive privateering campaign was described by G.N. Clark [644], 1923.

The old standard accounts were a dissertation and two books by Edward Powley [2938-2940], The English Navy in the Revolution of 1688, 1920, and The Naval Side of King William's War, 1972. Much narrative detail of events but little analysis was featured. The cross-Channel invasion of William and the Irish campaign "against Popery" were stressed. The latter culminated with the fateful victory of William at the Boyne, 14 July 1692, still celebrated in Northern Ireland every summer. More recent and extensive was John Ehrman [**1024**], The Navy in the War of William III, 1689-1697, 1953, an outstanding scholarly monograph. Covered were administration, logistics, the dockyards, and operations. Philip Aubrey [**157**], The Defeat of James Stuart's Armada, 1692, 1979, reviewed in too much detail events after 1688.

Naval battles ensued in the 1690s. The battle of Beachy Head, June-July 1690: the French defeated an Anglo-Dutch fleet but failed to follow up after the battle. The Dutch lost 17 ships and 2000 men; the English, 2 ships and 350 men. E. Taillemite [**3560**], 1992, has an account in French. C.D. Lee [**2088**], "The Battle of Beachy Head: Lord Torrington's Conduct," 1995, concluded that Torrington was responsible for the defeat. Peter LeFevre [**2098**], 1994, contributed to the debate over the competence of Lord Torrington. Torrington was subsequently court martialled. Bias was demonstrated on all sides in the Torrington court martial.

Two subsequent battles were related: after Beachy Head, the French threatened invasion: the battle of Barfleur, 19 May 1692, and La Hogue, 20 May 1692. An Anglo-Dutch fleet defeated the French, destroying 15 ships. The invasion threat eased. One long-term consequence of these battles was the creation of the Royal Naval Hospital, Greenwich, later the Royal Naval College and the NMM, commissioned by Queen Mary II to care for the wounded from the battles of Barfleur and La Hogue. Christopher Wren was the architect.

H. THE 18th CENTURY

1. The War of Spanish Succession

The wars of Louis XIV continued. In 1655, acquisition of Jamaica in the Western Design drew English commerce and naval interests to Spanish America. **See 7., G., 4.** It was a base for English merchants in the Spanish trade, a factor in the origins of the War of Spanish Succession. The plot thickened. Complications arose within and among factions involved, for example, Jamaican planters, the English Royal Africa Company, pirates, privateers, and Spanish authorities. With the death of the heirless Spanish king in 1700, a French candidate was put forward. The Austrian Habsburgs, supported by the British, put forward a competing candidate.

Curtis Nettels [**2628**], 1931, attempted to sort out pertinent factors. The Spanish colonies required large numbers of slaves and Spain had no slave trade station in Africa. Jamaica developed into the primary source for the supply of slaves. In return, English merchants received silver and gold. The asiento was the Spanish-controlled monopoly for the importation of slaves. Beginning in 1676, asiento was awarded, first to a group from Seville, then to the Dutch, Portuguese, and French, all the while using Jamaica as chief supplier. In addition, pirates and privateers used Jamaica as a base. Henry Morgan was the prince of English pirates and in 1680, he became Governor of Jamaica. **See 12., E.** The English also benefited from a large, illegal trade in goods with Spanish colonists. In 1700, the French gained the asiento. The English feared a combined Spanish-French effort to exclude them, drawing England into the War of Spanish Succession.

John Hattendorf [**1556, 1555**], to whom this historiographical-bibliographical study is dedicated, produced a dissertation and book, England in the War of Spanish Succession, 1979 and 1987, in the tradition of Julian Corbett [**759**], focusing on the war as a factor in the development of a national grand strategy. The role of Queen Anne was stressed.

The navy of Queen Anne was the subject of three pieces: R.D. Merriman [**2498**], 1961, in a publication of the NRS; J.H. Owen [**2718**], War at Sea under Queen Anne, 1938, and Ruth Bourne [**386**], Queen Anne's Navy in the West Indies, 1939, the latter two complementing each other. The roles of the navy were convoying and attacking enemy bases, for example, Barcelona, Toulon, and Dunkirk; more successfully and significantly, Admiral George Rooke took Gibraltar in 1704. **See 14., J.**

Henry Kamen [**1842, 1840**] contributed two studies, The War of Spanish Succession in Spain, 1700-1715, 1969, and "The Destruction of the Spanish Silver Fleet at Vigo in 1702," 1966. The former was a survey highlighting some domestic problems; the latter described an Anglo-Dutch naval attack off the northwest coast of Spain immediately after the war began. The treasure fleet was guarded by allied French warships, all of which were lost along with the treasure. Kamen wondered if the real loss to Franco-Spanish interests was as serious as contemporaries claimed. He thought not.

Douglas Coombs [**735**], 1953, assessed the conduct of the Dutch in alliance with the English during this war. A generation or two earlier they were deadly enemies. He concluded that relations were a complex interplay of engrained hostility and a growing consciousness of common interests. Hugh Dunthorne [**993, 994**], "The Alliance of the Maritime Powers, 1721-1740", 1978 and 1986, were a dissertation and book covering these matters.

Two works described individual actions: H.T. Dickinson [**927**], 1965, on the capture of Minorca in the Mediterranean in 1708 to be used as a base for the navy, and Gerald Graham [**1362**], 1953, on the Walker Expedition to Quebec in 1711, a publication of the NRS.

2. The War of Jenkins's Ear

Spain again. The asiento was defined above. A conflict involving it was ostensibly the immediate cause of the War of Jenkins's Ear, England vs. Spain,, which escalated into the War of Austrian Succession, Europe wide. The name of the war and the circumstances were a curiosity. The ear of Jenkins, an English captain trading illegally in the Caribbean, was cut off as a symbolic lesson by

Spanish authorities in 1731. Jenkins appeared before Parliament waving his festered ear back and forth in 1739 so as to foment war. The ploy succeeded. Anti-Walpole "politics" were also a factor. Simultaneously, demands and operations expanded in the Caribbean, as articulated by Christian Buchet [**500**], 1994, and Norton Moses [**2577**], 1966. Jamaica and the Leeward Islands were cases in point. Between 1689-1763, European powers deployed 74 expeditions to the West Indies, obviously an active theater of naval and imperial operations.

Some prominent historians contributed important studies. The old standard was Herbert Richmond [**3063**], The Navy in the War of 1739-1748, 3 vols., 1920. The great naval officer-strategist-college professor-historian presented his magnum opus. Military and naval campaigns were reviewed; each was complicated, and there were many failures. Poor leadership prevailed on both sides. It was a time of experimentation, especially in amphibious warfare, and, presumably, learning from mistakes. An older assessment, "The Causes of the War of Jenkins's Ear, 1739," 1909, was by the great diplomatic historian, Harold Temperley [**3586**]. Richard Pares [**2746**], War and Trade in the West Indies, 1739-1763, 1936, incorporated two colonial wars in his coverage, the West Indies now seen as the most valuable colonial area. The emphasis was economic. It was the age of Mercantilism. "Naval war in those days was a branch of business." He began with a diplomatic review of 1739-1741. The Spanish Guarda-Costa set out to enforce the asiento and saw English commercial endeavors and shipping in the area as illegal smuggling. For the long term coverage, other themes emerged: English sugar plantations and political connections in London, Mercantilism, English imperial ambitions, neutral rights, embargoes, prizes, convoys, and Anson in the Pacific. George Nelson [**2618**], "Contraband Trade under the Asiento, 1730-1739," 1945, delved into the heart of the matter in a brilliant expose. The British South Sea Company, its officers in London, colonists in Jamaica, and naval authorities, all conspired in a massive trade in slaves and illegal merchandise. Bribery prevailed and, in order to maximize the amount of illegal goods, some legal slave ships carried small numbers of slaves while crew members blackened their faces to fool Spanish authorities.

In an article and a more recent book, Philip Woodfine [**3935, 3934**], 1967 and 1998, presented political and historiographical analyses of the controversy leading to the war and an operation during it. The Anglo-Spanish crisis began in 1737. Woodfine was especially informative about internal personality conflicts within the Spanish court. Then, London merchants pressed Parliament to react to Spanish "depredations" against English trade. Recall that asiento made any such trade breaking the Spanish monopoly illegal, as interpreted by Spanish authorities. Woodfine elaborated on an incident, the expedition to the West Indies and attack on Cartagena, led by Admiral Vernon and General Wentworth. The impact of disease had been devastating. Herbert Richmond [**3063**] and J.W. Fortesque [**1162**] wrote about it. Tobias Smollett [**3372**] was a participant and incorporated his experience in his novel, Roderick

Random. **See 20., E.** Parliament had intervened, determined to reverse the perceived pacifist machinations of the Walpole ministry. Julian de Zulueta [**3987**], 1992, elaborated on the devastating health problems experienced during the campaign and placed the blame on Vernon. Frank Lewis [**2116**], 1940, studied some correspondence bearing on this expedition against Cartagena. See the dissertation and a more general study of amphibious warfare by Richard Harding [**1493, 1494**].

A broader survey in a dissertation, "War at Sea in the West Indies, 1739-1748," 1963, was by John Oglesby [**2689**], citing the Vernon expedition of 1739-1740 and the Knowles attack on Havana in 1748, the former a failure and the latter a success. Such operations demonstrated the extreme importance of the West Indies in the maritime struggle, Oglesby concluded.

3. The War of Austrian Succession

Two general surveys, The War of Austrian Succession, 1993 and 1995, respectively by Reed Browning [**479**] and M.S. Anderson [**76**], properly noted the European continental issues and conflicts, for example, Prussia seizing Silesia from Austria, conflicts over Italy, and conflicts over the Low Countries. Also important were conflicts in the West Indies involving Britain vs. France and Spain.

Some operations were presented. Raymond Baker [**177**], A Campaign of Amateurs: The Siege of Louisbourg, 1745, 1978, obviously confirmed the thesis of Herbert Richmond [**3064**] about poor leadership. Edward Hawke had participated in the battles of Toulon, 1744, commanded at Ushant or the second battle of Finisterre, 1747, where six French warships and 38 ships of the convoy were taken or sunk. Hawke replaced Admiral Byng in 1756, he being court-martialled and shot in Portsmouth, January 1757. In 1757, Hawke led in the attack on Rochefort. He was in the battle of the Isle of Aix, 1757. Vice Admiral Peter Warren was an important naval leader in operations in North America during this period, illustrating that crucial decisions were being made outside London, the thesis of Julia Gwyn [**1433**], The Royal Navy and North America: The Warren Papers, 1973, a publication of the NRS.

Arthur Buffington [**504**], 1940, presented a revision of the traditional view that the British campaign in Canada in 1746 was insignificant; in fact, it was the beginning of the conquest of all of Canada. Later, the annexation of Canada led to the American Revolution. The failure of 1746 was not important as imperial or strategic, but political: the rise of the Newcastle-Bedford-Pitt nexus. The great Canadian naval historian, W.A.B. Douglas [**956**], 1973, completed a dissertation summarizing operations of the British navy in Nova Scotia, 1713-1766. A dissertation by Joseph Devine [**918**], 1968, studied the role of the British colonies of North America in operations, for example, expeditions to Cartegena in 1741, Louisbourg in 1745, and Canada in 1746; a total of 14,000

American colonists participated. This was a factor in deteriorating colonial relations.

French amphibious operations, among the largest of the century, failed and did not engage an enemy but were devastated due to poor planning, mismanagement, malnutrition, and rough weather. Especially enlightening was the account of these two expeditions to North America of 1746. The noted French naval historian, James Pritchard [**2954**], wrote an award-winning analysis focusing on administration, political corruption, and medical findings: Anatomy of a Naval Disaster, 1995. It was about the French answer to the Anglo-American capture of Louisbourg of 1745. Plans included recovery of lost territories plus the ravaging of the coast of New England from Maine to Boston. The largest French operation prior to the American Revolution, a fleet of 64 ships with 11,000 soldiers, set out in June for Nova Scotia. Apparently, no intelligence or normal preparation existed. A hurricane, devastating health problems of scurvy, hunger, disease, and gross mismanagement, plus later cover-up, all occurred. Similar problems plagued an effort to reinforce. 8,000 died, including two naval commanders, one definitely a suicide, and most of the ships never returned. In addition, catastrophic disease struck the native Micmac Indians after exposure to the Europeans. From his intensive research, Pritchard also concluded that French naval gunnery tactics at this time were the same as the British, shoot solid shot low into the hulls of the enemy.

Pritchard [**2956**] was the historian of the mid-18th-century French navy: Louis XV's Navy, 1748-1762: A Study of Organization and Administration, 1987, a brilliant structural analysis of naval administration; the administrators were not the cause of the decline. That was due to national fiscal, financial, political, bureaucratic, and business failures. The focus was administration in the great tradition of Daniel Baugh [**237**] for the British navy. A dissertation by R.D. Bourland [**383**], 1978, reviewed and assessed French naval administration during the War of Austrian Succession; the responsible minister was Jean de Maurepas. The Maurepas Papers were deposited at Cornell University.

While on the French navy, the chief antagonist of the British throughout the First and the Second Hundred Years' Wars, 1320s-1815, H.M. Scott [**3258**], 1979, wrote of the Duke of Choiseul, chief minister to Louis XV, who formulated a plan of revival to be effected simultaneously with revival of the Spanish navy. Both plans were launched; both failed. A key aspect of the Spanish effort was described in some detail by David Marley [**2387**], 1994.

4. The Seven Years' War

Assessments of the Seven Years' War, 1756-1763, included "the First World War," "the First Global War," the first war with global perspectives, and the conclusion of the process catapulting Britain into hegemonic global dominance for a century and a half. The context was the Seven Years' War:

Britain and Prussia vs. France, Austria, and Spain; the Family Compact of 1761 which brought Spain into the war.

Tom Pocock [**2864**], Battle for Empire: The Very First World War, 1756-1763, 1998, was a popular narrative of the war. Operations outside of Europe were stressed. A recent survey of one aspect of the Seven Years' War has made an important impact, including an academic forum of five scholars critiquing it: Fred Anderson [**70, 71**], Crucible of War, 2000, which concentrated on its impact in North America where it began and where much of the war was fought. The first engagement was in Ohio in 1754, George Washington leading a force of Virginia colonists to confront French and some Indians there. A critic assessed this work as the new paradigm for understanding the Seven Years' War. Rupert Furneaux [**1219**], The Seven Years' War, 1973, presented the British perspective in a short survey.

The British Admiralty was in the midst of reform led by Lord Anson laying the foundation for modern British sea power. A pertinent feature was a more efficient and productive system of logistical supply for the blockading Western Approaches Squadron. By contrast, the French navy of King Louis XV was subjected to crippling financial problems. The stage was set by William Nester [**2627**], Britain, France, and the Imperial Struggle for North America, 1607-1775, 2 vols., 2000. The second volume, covering 1756-1775, was entitled: The First Global War, "the world's first truly world war," nine years of carnage, 1754-1763. Harrison Bird [**322**] recounted The French and Indian War, 1754-1763, 1965, the battle for a continent.

Julian Corbett [**750**], England in the Seven Years' War: A Study in Combined Strategy, 2 vols., 1907, was the classic study by the preeminent authority on the strategy of sea power. Richard Harding [**1491**], 1991, has the latest and best survey on amphibious operations of the 18th century.

Traditional history surveys have placed William Pitt, the Elder, Lord Chatham, in the forefront as formulator of a brilliant, highly successful, preconceived scheme, "Pitt's Plan." The result of the plan was "Bells of Victory," signifying celebration of a series of great victories, especially in 1759, the "Year of Victory." Marie Peters [**2832, 2833**], 1998 and 1993-1994, has a biography and a two-part article. Recent revisionists have demolished that traditional picture. Pitt was not a great dictator, the "plan" was articulated after the fact, true credit should go to various leaders and departments, for example Anson, Newcastle, and the Admiralty, and Pitt was frequently ill and absent, for example, manic depression, 1767-1768 and 1775-1777. The thesis of Peters: the strength and effectiveness of Pitt was management of the House of Commons; when he went to the House of Lords as Lord Chatham his career collapsed. Pitt had no great vision of how to fight the war nor of imperial expansion. Eric McDermott [**2234**], "The Elder Pitt and His Admirals and Generals," 1956, elaborated. E.J.S. Frazer [**1185**], "The Pitt-Newcastle Coalition and the Conduct of the Seven Years' War, 1757-1760," 1976, in a dissertation, stressed the connections between domestic policy and the making of war policy.

Deserved or not, Pitt has been identified with "conjunct operations," amphibious landings, usually at remote locations and sometimes with no intention in establishing a bridgehead. These were recounted by Richard Middleton [2506], 1993, and W.K. Hackmann [1441], 1969, in a dissertation. These coastal expeditions hit Rochefort, 1757, St. Malo, 1758, Cherbourg, 1758, and Belle Isle, 1761. One objective was to disrupt French defenses and keep them off guard. The French navy failed to stop them.

Comparison and juxtaposition were the methodologies used by John McNeill [2318], Atlantic Empires of France and Spain: Louisbourg and Havana, 1700-1762, 1985. The dispositions of these two imperial centers, French and Spanish, respectively, both subject to numerous attacks by the British, were instructive. As a result, French and Spanish naval authorities consistently feared the British navy and, by 1700, French and Spanish naval thinkers conceded "command of the sea" to them; to avoid battle whenever possible.

For the British, 1759 was "the year of victories," or "annus mirabilis": Ticonderoga, Louisbourg, Quebec, and Quiberon Bay. Other prominent operations were against Minorca, a failure, Martinique, Belle Isle, Manila, and Havana. Manila and Havana were returned to Spain in the peace negotiations.

"The bells never stopped ringing." Among the most significant victories of 1759 was the battle of Quebec, the land battle on the Plains of Abraham resulting in a British victory under General James Wolfe. Getting the British force to the site of the battle was the great achievement of the navy under Admiral Saunders. Two accounts celebrated the bicentennial: Christopher Lloyd [2152] and C.P. Stacy [3415]. Loss of Quebec effectively meant loss of Canada, which surrendered to the British in September 1760.

The great naval victory of the war was the battle of Quiberon Bay, 20-21 November 1759. The location was on the west coast of Brittany, France. The antagonists were the Western Approaches Squadron of Great Britain and the Brest Squadron of France, commanded respectively by Admiral Edward Hawke and Marshal de Conflans. The battle squadrons confronted each other in unusual conditions: confined waters during a gale with wind blowing toward the shore and at night. Geoffrey Marcus [2371], Quiberon Bay in the British Battles Series, 1960, presented extensive background. Much credit was given to Anson and reforms he introduced at the Admiralty; Marcus compared Anson to Pepys.

The circumstances: commanding the Western Approaches Squadron of 23 ships from HMS ROYAL OAK, 100 guns, Hawke was blockading Brest in 1759. The French attempted a breakout from Brest during a westerly gale on the afternoon of 20 November. The chase involved 44 warships close inshore in a melee, the dramatic battle of Quiberon Bay. The battle resumed the next morning. The French fleet was annihilated; the British lost HMS RESOLUTION and HMS ESSEX, 350 men; the French lost 5 ships and several more were stranded, 2500 men. The leadership of Hawke under such extraordinary conditions was described as "incomparably the finest thing of its sort in our naval history."

Other operations were recounted. Herbert Richmond [**3064**] edited Papers Relating to the Loss of Minorca in 1756, 1913, a publication of the NRS. That loss led to the court martial and execution of Admiral Byng, as Voltaire observed, "to encourage the others."

The French had failed miserably at amphibious operations. By contrast, brilliance was demonstrated during the capture of Manila by forces of the RN and British Army in 1762 during the Seven Years' War; 15 sailing warships and 2000 men. It was a model of amphibious operations. However, word of the capture reached Europe after peace had been concluded; Manila was returned to Spain in 1764. In an article and book, Nicholas Tracy [**3636, 3640**], 1969 and 1995, described the successful British expedition against Manila in 1762: operating thousands of miles from base and seen as a model for army-navy cooperation.

The operation that has received the most attention was the expedition against Havana in 1762, the largest amphibious operation of the war; also called "combined" and "conjunct" operations. In two articles and a book, David Syrett [**3540, 3546, 3556**], 1969, 1972, and 1970, noted that the Havana expedition of 16,000 soldiers with supporting naval forces succeeded against this primary Spanish base; again disease savaged the participants. The book was a publication of the NRS. The Siege of Havana, 1762, 1931, was by Francis Hart [**1536**]. Sonia Keppel [**1919**], 1981, presented background and details of the Havana expedition based on memoirs of three Keppel brothers who participated. David Marley [**2388**], 1992, recounted an incident, which was advantageous to the British: a Spanish message warning Havana authorities of possible attack was intercepted.

J.M. Hitsman [**1642**], 1954, has an article of the ubiquitous Louisbourg, this on the assault of 1758; the beginning of the end of French rule in North America.

Barry Gough [**1336**], 1992, assessed the impact of the Peace of Paris of 1763: British mercantile interests pressured for provisions beneficial to them and the results favored them in a dramatic fashion. Herbert Richmond [**3062**], The Navy in India, 1763-1783, 1921, was a substantial tome by this imminent authority on operations in India for two decades after the Peace of Paris.

In two articles by Nicholas Tracy [**3639, 3638**], 1974 and 1975, gunboat diplomacy was applied, that is, an armed show of force to overawe the members of the Bourbon Family Compact, France and Spain. Four incidents after the war called for a show of force to protect British interests and territorial claims: the Falkland Islands, Honduras, Turks Island in the Bahamas, and Gambia. War was avoided.

Clennell Wilkinson [**3857**], 1997, wrote a dissertation on the administration of the peacetime navy between the end of the Seven Years' War and the beginning of the War of the American Revolution, a time of political instability. The navy declined. The causes were internal and unusually bad weather. Parliament was concerned and installed Sandwich as First Lord of the

Admiralty. He initiated proper rectifications. Unfortunately for Sandwich, war resumed and he was blamed for unpreparedness.

5. The War of the American Revolution

Also called the War for American Independence, this was the one war of the century, which the British "lost." Blame and accusations about loss of the American colonies have persisted: Lord North, Sandwich, and George III. One need only check the long list Thomas Jefferson ticked off in the Declaration of Independence.

Aspects before the American Revolution were introduced. Neil Stout [**3463, 3462**], in a dissertation and book, The Royal Navy in America, 1760-1775, 1962 and 1973, focused on enforcement of British colonial policies, for example, action against illegal trade and the Sugar, Stamp, and Townshend Acts; thus, the RN was a cause of the Revolution. Impressment was not an important issue at this time. More recently and more broadly, Peter Marshall [**2419**], The British Atlantic Empire before the American Revolution, 1980, assessed the imperial system, which created a European North America. Institutions and adaptation to change were stressed.

A recent, broad, comprehensive survey, good for introduction, was Stephen Conway [**727**], The War of American Independence, 1995. He saw it as a "world war," the first modern war, and a beginning, the first war of a new order. An older, extensive history, A Naval History of the American Revolution, 2 vols., 1913, by Gardner Allen [**41**], presented the American perspective. The various naval operations, including those in the lakes, "a cruise around the British Isles," and disposition of naval prisoners, were reviewed.

Inevitably, A.T. Mahan [**2331**] weighed in: The Major Operations of the Navies in the War of American Independence, 1913. Mahan had also written the pertinent essay in the 7-vol. history of the Royal Navy by William Laird Clowes [**669**]. Blockade of French and American ports should have been more rigorously pursued. Sandwich and incompetent admirals were blamed. A captain in the Royal Navy, W.M. James [**1785**], wrote The British Navy in Adversity, 1926, taking up where Mahan left off. Failure was due to lack of preparation and poor leadership. It was folly to permit British sea forces to have decayed to such depths. The distinguished historian, Gerald Graham [**1357, 1360**], focused on imperial developments in North America in two works, Empire of the North Atlantic, 1950, and The Royal Navy in the War of the American Revolution, 1976, the latter a pamphlet for the NMM on the occasion of the American bicentennial. A short survey profusely and beautifully illustrated using the collection of the NMM was by Robert Gardiner [**1245**], Navies and the American Revolution, 1996.

Piers Mackesy [**2305**], The War for America, 1963, stressed the interplay between strategy and politics from the British perspective. Increasingly, naval power became decisive and the army played a secondary role. Britain had no allies. In the ultimate battle, "the fight for the Chespeake," "the world turned upside down." For the first time in a hundred years, a British naval force was decisively defeated by France.

Daniel Baugh [**241**], 1992, produced a brilliant analysis. British naval obligations suddenly exceeded availability of resources. The threats in Europe and India were dramatically increasing. The build-up of the French naval forces was not anticipated. The British response to the situation in America was late. Nicholas Tracy [**3641**], Navies, Deterrence, and American Independence: Britain and Seapower in the 1760s and 1770s, 1988, was more about strategy, diplomacy, and departments. A system of deterrence was developed, gradually escalating the naval responses. However, it was too little, too late.

David Syrett [**3554, 3553**] produced two broad assessments, The Royal Navy in North American Waters, 1989, and The Royal Navy in European Waters, 1998. Syrett was prone to make historical analogies, for example, with Rommel, Eisenhower, Stonewall Jackson, and Bataan. To the point, the RN was unprepared, was overwhelmed from the beginning, was never able to recover; was oblivious of amphibious operations, had no effective strategy, and was forced to maintain major forces at home because of the French threat. In Europe, the colonists were supported by France, Spain, and the Netherlands. The Mediterranean had to be abandoned. Infighting among admirals and with generals proved fatal. There was praise for Sandwich and Rodney. The Maritime Dimensions of the American Revolution [**2382**], 1977, was a short piece from the Naval Historical Division in Washington, the proceedings from a session of the Organization of American Historians, April 1976, celebrating the bicentennial. Papers were by David Syrett and Frank Mevers.

Stephen Conway [**726**], 1997, reviewed the politics of British military and naval mobilization. Parliament and British public opinion were seriously divided. Was it civil war or illegal rebellion? What about the Irish? Then, France, Spain, and the Netherlands entered precipitating a threat of invasion. Lord North was blamed "for aggression against our bretheren and best friends." Threat of invasion was obviously real. The Other Armada: The Franco-Spanish Attempt to Invade Britain, 1960, was by Temple Patterson [**2792**]. Extensive and expensive operations were launched by the French and Spanish. Fatal were French bankruptcy, procrastination, and serious delays, for example, a French force waited six weeks at sea for a Spanish force to join it.

John Tilley [**3624**], The British Navy and the American Revolution, 1987, in haphazard fashion focused on British politicians and naval commanders only on the North American station, for example, Thomas Graves and Samuel Hood. Ships and Seamen of the American Revolution, 1969, by Jack Coggins [**694**], described and personally illustrated in a blue color the ships, crews, weapons, equipment, tactics and actions of the war. Examples included privateers, prison hulks, and even the "sub-marine" of David Bushnell. The war was fought mainly on land but won on the sea. Individual opinions of British officers were collected from correspondence. The editor was Marion Balderston

[**181**], The Lost War, 1975. Most saw British victory as inevitable. Most were clearly bitter against "the rebels," especially those in Boston. Much correspondence was devoted to the patronage system and "interests." **See 14., K.**

Nathan Miller [**2516**], Sea of Glory: A Naval History of the American Revolution, 1974, was strictly from the perspective of the colonists, a history of the Continental Navy, published for the bicentennial. By 1778, it had expanded into a worldwide maritime conflict. J.K. Kelly [**1855**] did a dissertation, "The Struggle for American Seaborne Independence as Viewed by John Adams," 1973, presenting the view by Adams that the cause was enforcement of the Navigation Acts. As a diplomat, Adams urged the French to gain command of the sea. He was infuriated by British impressment practices. For 25 years, Adams championed the cause of American seaborne independence.

Individual operations were covered. Inevitably, the spectacular attacks of John Paul Jones were included, for example, by John Walsh [**3746**], Night of Fire, 1978, and Thomas Schaeper [**3241**], John Paul Jones and the Battle of Flamborough Head, 1989, fought in September 1779. A dissertation by Allen Begnaud [**277**], "British Operations in the Caribbean and the American Revolution," 1966, described this major theater of naval activity. American privateers and French naval forces created disruption. The battle of the Saints of 1782 meant British recovery but too late to retain North America. A.G. Jamieson [**1793**] did a dissertation, "War in the Leeward Islands, 1775-1783," 1981, an impressive study. Ronald Hurst [**1738**], The Golden Rock: An Episode of the American War of Independence, 1996, was about St. Eustatius Island, a Dutch possession in the West Indies. It was the first foreign territory to officially recognize the United States in 1781. Barbara Tuchman [**3654**], The First Salute, presented the dynamic event in her inimitable style. The British were not amused and Rodney led an attack, one source describing it as "rape." It was recaptured by the French. Civil actions against Rodney and others actually recovered their prize money. Stephen Conway [**725**], 2001, described the celebrations in Britain after the victory of Rodney at the Saints in 1782, a demonstration by the public for "a resurgent Britain."

"The British Navy and the Siege of Quebec, 1775-1776,", 1980, by W.H. Whiteley [**3846**], described this rarity, British operations that were successful: American forces invaded, Quebec was besieged, and the RN played a major role in the successful relief. Sandwich was praised by George III for saving this part of North America. Such was not the case in other operations of the RN in the "lower colonies," each case followed by the author: failure to blockade the Delaware River, by George Comtois [**711**], 1980; failure around Long Island, by William Calderhead [**543**], 1976; failure in a siege of Rhode Island, by John Millar [**2511**], 1979, and scuttling of HMS MENTOR at Pensacola to prevent capture, by James Servies [**3279**], 1982.

Ultimate failure of the RN precipitated the defeat of Lord Cornwallis and his surrender at Yorktown in September 1781. British army commanders had rightly come to expect extrication by the RN when problems arose.

Command of the sea was a given, if command of the land was not. This case was the spectacular exception. Forces of the RN, for example, under Hyde Parker and Kempenfelt, were committed by threats from the French and Dutch in Europe; Rodney and Hood were busy in the West Indies. American leaders and the French were planning for a concentration of land and naval forces in the Chesapeake area, unbeknownst to the British. Concentration of forces was finally achieved and the British were overwhelmed. The RN squadron under Thomas Graves was defeated by the powerful French squadron arriving from the Caribbean commanded by Admiral de Grasse, albeit a year or two late. The battle was actually a minor affair. No ships were sunk. Graves was forced to withdrew to the north. Thus, no navy was at the Chesapeake to extract the large land force of Cornwallis, stranded and surrounded at Yorktown. He surrendered, and the rest, as they say, was history. These events were described by Thomas Fleming [**1125**], 1963, Harold Larrabee [**2033**], 1964, Randolph Adams [**13**], 1931, and William Willcox [**3868**], 1946.

And what of the French navy? De Grasse won at the Chesapeake but lost at the Saints. The historian to answer the question was Jonathan Dull [**985, 986**], in a dissertation and a book, The French Navy and American Independence, 1972 and 1975, in which he incorporated the diplomatic situation and the economic consequences. The French jumped at the opportunity to aid the American colonists: clandestine aid in 1776, war in 1778, the Spanish recruited in 1780, and success in 1781, all instigated by Count Vergennes. Charles Lewis [**2114**], Admiral de Grasse and American Independence, 1945, and Carl Tourquist [**3633**], The Naval Campaigns of Count de Grasse during the American Revolution, 1781-1783, 1942, covered the naval career of this famous French admiral.

And what of the Continental Navy? Chester Hearn [**1589**], George Washington's Schooners, 1995, described 8 ships and their exploits: harassing British supply lines and forcing the evacuation of Boston. In a dissertation, Stephen Powers [**2936**], "The Decline and Extinction of the American Naval Power, 1781-1787," 1965, recounted its demise: the Confederation failed to fund it.

And what of other nations? The response of some neutrals was to be fateful. In 1780, a series of efforts of neutral states, a League of Armed Neutrality, was launched. Participants opposed British aggressive enforcement against trade with its enemies by neutral states. Participants at this time and during several revivals later were Russia, Sweden, Denmark, and Prussia. Isabel de Madariaga [**2323**], 1962, presented the Russian perspective. In a later iteration, 1800-1801, Denmark was attacked by the RN: the battle of Copenhagen, over these issues, as described by Arne Feldbaek [**1082**], 1980. See 7., I., 9.

Paul Nelson [**2622**], 1978, presented a historiographical assessment of the British conduct of the war, including commentary and critiques on pertinent works of George Bancroft, G.O. Trevelyan, John Fortescue, George Beer, L.H.

Gipson, Lewis Namier, Piers Mackesy, and David Syrett. Did America win? Did Britain lose? Most agreed that the war was lost in the early years due to inferior bureaucrats in London and poor strategic planning.

Joseph Fewster [**1094**], 1988, recalled a crisis in Anglo-American relations in the 1790s: problems leading to the mission of John Jay. The British continued to seize American merchant ships.

I. THE WARS OF THE FRENCH REVOLUTION AND NAPOLEON

1. The Wars of the French Revolution and Napoleon

So much of the French Revolution had to do with internal crises in France developing for at least a century before the summer of 1789. Economic and social causes and the bankruptcy of the Crown were important factors. Early events leading to the outbreak of the Wars of the French Revolution and Napoleon had to do with the leaders of the French Revolution desiring to spread the revolution, threatening her eastern neighbors; the war actually began in April of 1792 involving France against Prussia and Austria.

Inevitably, Britain was drawn into the war. The ostensible pretext for British entry was the trial and execution of the King Louis XVI of France, December 1792-January 1793. As was the case in the Second Hundred Years' War, most of the European powers became involved. First, Second, Third, and Fourth Coalitions, consecutive alliances assembled against France, were initiated by the British; all failed except the Fourth. That alliance defeated Napoleon and proceeded to formulate the peace settlement, called the Versailles or Paris Peace Settlement. It technically lasted until the outbreak of World War I in August 1914. The Treaty of Amiens, 1802, introduced a year of peace. When war was in progress, Britain and France were on opposite sides. All other great powers, for example, Prussia, Russia, and Austria, plus Spain, Portugal, the Netherlands, Sweden, Denmark, and Italian states varied from neutrality to pro-British to pro-French during the period, 1792-1815.

The sequence was as follows: the First Coalition – 1793-1797, the Second Coalition – 1798-1801, the Third Coalition – 1803-1807, and the Fourth Coalition – 1814, evolving into the Quadruple Alliance, then the Quintuple Alliance, into the 1820s. Charles Esdaile [**1054, 1055**], The Wars of Napoleon, 1995, and The French Wars,1792-1815, 2001, presented excellent syntheses and overviews. He subdivided into 7 coalitions, the final one being the Waterloo campaign. An overly chauvinistic and flowery general survey of the period from the British perspective was the popular trilogy by Arthur Bryant [**496**], 1942-1950, purposely concocted to stir patriotism and determination against Hitler and the Nazis: Years of Endurance, Years of Victory, and Age of Elegance.

Some statistics were as follows: a comparison of forces: the RN in 1794 and the French in 1789: SOTLs – British 146, French 71; 50-gun ships –

British 21; Frigates – British 176, French 64; Sloops – British 303, French 80; Total – British 646, French 215. An early survey of the RN was John Jenkins [**1799**], The Naval Achievements of Great Britain: From the Year 1793 to 1817, 1817, dedicated to Lord St. Vincent.

Paul Webb [**3799**], writing about the League of Armed Neutrality and crises before 1793, noted that this time, thanks to the pressures exerted by William Pitt, the Younger, the RN was prepared: in 1793, a hundred SOTLs were ready for war. However, an early campaign signified otherwise: Michael Duffy [**972, 977**], 1971 and 1976, described a failed expedition attacking Dunkirk, August-September 1793. The aim was protecting the Low Countries and overthrowing the revolution. In the political fallout, the usual scapegoats were blamed; Duffy contended that weakness and deterioration of the allied coalition was the cause. In addition, the sometime editor of Mariner's Mirror, did a dissertation on British war policy and the alliance with Austria, 1793-1801. Elsewhere, Duffy [**978**], Soldiers, Sugar, and Seapower, 1987, covered British amphibious expeditions to the West Indies during the early years of the war. This colonial area was among the most important in the world for both, "a precious money-box." Both sides suffered heavily from disease, casualties up to 70 per cent. After trial and error, the British finally prevailed.

Another of the fabulous Chatham Pictorial Histories series was Robert Gardiner [**1240**], Fleet Battle and Blockade: The French Revolutionary War, 1793-1797, 1997, for the NMM.

In August 1799, an operation was launched: Coleman Williams [**3870**], "The Role of the British Navy in the Helder Campaign, 1799," 1985, was a dissertation about this joint Anglo-Russian campaign during the war of the Second Coalition; Admiral Duncan again commanding the North Sea fleet. The campaign failed but that was not the fault of the RN.

The prolific Jeremy Black [**328**], 2000, published a bicentennial assessment, "Britain in 1800," which surveyed the situation at that point. Britain was at war. Nelson was the hero of the day.

And what of the French? Navies of the Napoleonic Era, 1980, a complement to a work on the armies, was by Otto von Pivka [**2860**], describing the ships and sailors, the mutinies, the great battles, and each of the national navies, a total of fourteen. William Cormack [**772, 773, 771**], 1991, 1995, and 1996, in a dissertation, article, and book, wrote of a French dilemma associated with its navy stemming from the Revolution during the years, 1789-1794. What was the impact of the revolution beginning in 1789 on the French navy? The answer was chaos. In Toulon where Royalists were in control, it surrendered to the British. In Brest, there was mutiny. In the West Indies, the problem of legitimate authority arose, whether to follow royalists or republicans, the navy symbolizing authority and it was divided. Mutinies occurred on several ships. The problem intensified as war with Britain loomed. Paddy Griffith [**1399**], 1998, analyzed warmaking by France, 1789-1802, with a chapter on the navy. Considerable time was required to overcome the early purges. The total force of the French navy in 1789 was about 66% of that of the RN. French warships were deemed to have superior design but the state of readiness made it virtually unusable. He also concluded that during this period, Napoleon was a failure. An imperial perspective was the theme of Paul Fregosi [**1192**], Dreams of Empire: Napoleon and the First World War, 1792-1815, 1989. As a result, Britain doubled her empire and France sacrificed hers. One theme was the grandiose scheme of Napoleon to conquer Egypt, the Middle East, and, ultimately, India and China. In 1815, 500 years of Anglo-French warfare came to an end.

Creator of Parkinson's Law, C. Northcote Parkinson [**2774, 2771, 2773, 2772**] conducted his earliest scholarship about activities in the Far East during this period: a dissertation and three books, reinforcing the idea of "world war": "War and Trade in the Far East," 1935, War in the Eastern Seas, 1793-1815, 1954, and variations on trade in the Far East, 1937 and 1948. At the time he published, Parkinson lamented: "Maritime history has never taken its rightful place as a subject for investigation." **See 5., H.**

Another peripheral area has drawn attention. Edward Ingram [**1746**], 1982, described the threat of Napoleon and his Oriental ambitions, even after defeat of his Egyptian campaign. Some British failures in the eastern Mediterranean emboldened him. An alliance was concluded with Persia in 1807. The security of India was threatened. The great frigate captain, Edward Pellew, commanded British forces to secure the Strait of Hormuz.

Not peripheral was the Mediterranean Sea. The Mediterranean remained an important theater throughout the quarter-century of war. One of the earliest and most important campaigns was the siege of Toulon in 1793. Royalists controlled this vital base of the French fleet in the Mediterranean. They invited the British to take over, all described by J. Holland Rose [**3139**], 1922, and Stephen Usherwood [**3706**], 1972. Sidney Smith played an important role. Napoleon Bonaparte, a young artillery officer, made his initial reputation when the French pro-revolutionary forces recaptured Toulon.

A.B. Rodger [**3102**], The War of the Second Coalition, 1798 to 1801, 1964, noted how badly the war was progressing for Britain: withdrawal from the Mediterranean, naval mutinies, and defeats. Then the spectacular victories at Camperdown and Cape St. Vincent turned things around and attracted allies.

The best survey of the period after Amiens was Piers Mackesy [**2306**], The War in the Mediterranean, 1803-1810, 1957. The return of the RN exemplified one advantage of sea power. Because of the presence of the RN, Napoleon was forced to deploy 3600 cannon in 900 coastal batteries manned by 13,000 gunners, and the French trade was disrupted in the process. Overseeing British operations during this period after the death of Nelson was Collingwood.

The ubiquitous Sidney Smith appeared again in a campaign near Naples in 1806. His naval force ferried troops from Sicily to participate in the British land victory over the French at Maida, recounted by John Stewart [**3453**]. The British intervened and occupied Sicily to protect Mediterranean bases, 1806-1815, recounted by John Rosselli [**3151**], 1956.

For much of the early phase, Russia allied with Britain. Russian naval and military forces being sent into the Mediterranean, as described by in a dissertation and a book by Norman Saul [**3221, 3222**], 1965 and 1970. Russia was the traditional protector of the Knights of St. John of Malta. Napoleon sacked and occupied Malta en route to Egypt in 1798. The story of the Knights was told by H.J.A. Sire [**3329**], 1994. They originated from the Knights of St. John and the Knights Hospitallers during the Crusades. Emperor Charles V gave them Malta in 1530. Christopher Hibbert [**1620**], 1970, wrote of Napoleon and the Knights. **See 7., C., 2. and 7., E., 2.**

Russia joined the Third Coalition and sent a fleet and forces into the Mediterranean. One phase was covered by William Flayheart [**1123**], Counterpoint to Trafalgar: The Anglo-Russian Invasion of Naples, 1805-1806, 1992, albeit that the title was confusing. Allegedly, Napoleon ordered Villeneuve to sea because of this threat to the French in Italy. Malta was again involved. The joint expedition against Naples failed. In 1807, the Treaty of Tilsit effectively removed Russia from the Mediterranean.

One lesser role of the Russian navy in the Mediterranean was of interest, described by D.F. White [**3840**], 1947. A Russian squadron was in the Adriatic in 1800 as the French occupied Italy. Nelson, Lord and Lady Hamilton, and the Neapolitan royal entourage were forced to flee. A Russian frigate conveyed them to Trieste and safety, August 1800. Nelson and the Hamiltons then proceeded overland to Vienna, Prague, and, eventually, to London. **See 8., A., 2.**

2. The Glorious First of June

Oliver Warner [**3764**], The Glorious First of June, 1961, described the battle, the first great naval engagement of the war: Sunday, 1 June 1794, 430 miles west of Ushant out in the Atlantic, the furtherest from shore of any major battle in the age of sail. Richard Howe was commander. Peter Duncan [**992**], 1999, observed the bicentennial of the battle. Michael Duffy [**973**], 2001, led a recent assessment of the battle, the British celebrated annihilation of French warships; the French, perhaps more legitimately, celebrated the successful arrival of this essential grain convoy at Brest. In a dissertation and book, William Cormack [**772, 773**], 1991 and 1995, presented the French situation. Its navy was devastated as a consequence of the revolution. Experienced Royalist officers had been dismissed. Radicalism among the sailors effected operations. The revolutionary government diverted some French warships to other operations.

3. The Battle of Camperdown

An invasion scheme initiated by the French in the mid-1790s, and, again, later in the early 1800s, involved allies of the French, for example, Spain, the Dutch, Denmark, Sweden, and some Italian states. To eliminate one of those threats was one rationale for the confrontation between the British and the Dutch in 1797. Off the Dutch coast, against the Dutch fleet, October 1797, Adam Duncan, who had just dealt successfully with the naval mutinies of the Nore, was the victor. Accounts were by Christopher Lloyd [**2170**], 1963, Neil Duncan [**991**], 1995, and Patricia Crimmin [**801**], 1981.

4. The Blockade of Brest

The Western Squadron was one of the great success stories of this period, increasingly upgraded in importance in the literature. Maintaining this "close blockade" continuously was a massive undertaking. The purpose was blockade of the main French naval base of Brest on the Atlantic coast of the Brittany peninsula. Hawke was its commander at the battle of Quiberon Bay. **See 7., H., 4.** The support bases were Plymouth and some Cornwall ports. Lord St. Vincent was credited with perfecting the process. Fresh water was the most critical and most expensive item.

Richard Saxby [**3231**], 1992, described the process and some problems encountered. Roger Morriss [**2568**], The Channel Fleet and the Blockade of Brest, 1793-1801, 2001, provided extensive coverage of what has increasingly been seen as a formative and decisive operation. "Thrust and Counter," 1989, was how the process was carried out in an assessment by William Avery [**161**]. The French escaped on occasion, for example, attempted in 1759, and successfully in 1799. The French had capable leaders but were deficient in personnel; the British enjoyed efficient personnel but lacked leadership. Michael Steer [**3437**], 1990, featured description of the victualling process for the Western Squadron, 1793-1805. The results were much improved health conditions for the crews. In a publication of the NRS, John Leyland [**2130**], 2 vols., 1899-1902, described resumption of "the great blockade," 1803-1805. Among the collection of papers from a colloquium, the Sorbonne, September 1984, edited by Martine Acerra [**7**], 1985, was a paper by A.N. Ryan on the blockade of Brest, 1689-1805.

5. Nelson's Navy

Horatio, Lord Nelson became noted for tactical innovation, the "Nelson Touch", charismatic leadership, his "Band of Brothers", strategic perceptions, and devotion to duty, the "Immortal Memory." Nelson will be treated elsewhere, in a chapter exclusively about him and William Bligh, and again, in the chapter on Nautical Fiction. **See 8., A. and 20., C.**

Nicholas Tracy [**3642**], Nelson's Battles: The Art of Victory in the Age of Sail, 1996, was profusely illustrated and set the four famous battles in context: St. Vincent, 1797, the Nile, 1798, Copenhagen, 1801, and Trafalgar, 1805. The strengths of Nelson were listed: innovative tactics, charismatic leadership, and devotion to duty. All was "the Nelson Touch." There was Nelson's War, 1976, by Peter Padfield [**2730**], "the great turning point of history" and "the beginning of Pax Britannica"; Nelson's Battles, 1965, by Oliver Warner [**3774**], especially the Nile, Copenhagen, and Trafalgar; Nelson's Navy, 1993, by Philip Haythornthwaite [**1583**], in the Osprey Elite series; Logs of the Great Sea Fights, 1794-1805, 1899, by T.S. Jackson [**1767**], a publication of the NRS, a collection of the actual official descriptions from records at the PRO; James Hewitt [**1614**], Eye-Witnesses to Nelson's Battles, 1972, and Richard Woodman [**3952**], The Sea Warriors: Fighting Captains and Frigate Warfare in the Age of Nelson, 2001. The inimitable Robert Gardiner [**1246**], Nelson against Napoleon: From the Nile to Copenhagen, 1798-1801, 1997, was another of the exquisite series for the NMM. Timothy Jenks [**1802**] has a recent dissertation, "Naval Engagements: Patriotism, Cultural Politics, and the Royal Navy, 1793-1815," 2001.

Nelson led some lesser campaigns. In 1797, he led an assault on Santa Cruz de Teneriffe. Michael Nash [**2600**], 1984, described this amphibious assault. R.E.G. Harris [**1531**], 1998, reported on a joint Anglo-Spanish bicentennial re-enactment of the events at Teneriffe on 24 July 1997. Tom Pocock [**2868**] described a more obscure operation, Nelson and the Campaign in Corsica, 1994. Both events were celebratory for the Nelson Decade [**2624**].

A double-take may be a reaction after just reading the above, then reading Edward Ingram [**1745**], "Illusion of Victory: Nile, Copenhagen, and Trafalgar Revisited," 1984. Ingram began by reviewing the debate over whether El Alamein or Stalingrad was the turning point of World War II, then he proceeded to other "sleights of hand," "conjuring tricks," and "defeats passed off as victories." These were the "myths" of the battles of Nelson perpetuated by Mahan [**2328, 2329**], Parkinson [**2759**], and Paul Kennedy [**1882**]. These were myths of the "Mercantilist School," that British sea power caused the Industrial Revolution and was the chief product of it. So, reexamine the three great victories. They did nothing to defeat Napoleon who was able to rebuild the battlefleet and the results created serious problems for the British subsequently related to the League of Armed Neutrality and Continental System. Plus, Nelson was notorious as a troublesome and tiresome subordinate, muddling in politics, and creating a sensational scandal with his private life. All was hyperbole. The victories were illusions. See 7., I., 6.-11.

6. The Battle of Cape St. Vincent

14 February 1797, sometimes called the St. Valentine's Day victory, just off the extreme southwest corner of the Iberian peninsula, 27 Spanish SOTL vs. 15 British SOTL commanded by John Jervis, who gained a peerage and took the name of this battle as Lord St.Vincent. Four Spanish ships were captured. The move of Nelson, leaving the British line of battle to break the Spanish line, was the feature and, presumably, decisive event.

Accounts were by M.A.J. Palmer [**2735**], 1991, Stephen Howarth [**1699**], 1998, and Colin White [**3831**], 1997. Howarth reported on the Bicentennial International Naval Conference, Portsmouth, 15 February 1997, sponsored by the SNR, the Nelson Society, and the 1805 Club, one of the early celebrated events of the Nelson Decade [**2624**]. Christopher Lloyd [**2170**], St. Vincent and Camperdown, 1963, produced a standard account of this battle and Camperdown.

7. The Egyptian Campaign

It was defeat of the Spanish navy at Cape St. Vincent on 14 February and the Dutch navy at Camperdown in October, both in 1797, which meant those allied fleets could not assist in supporting a French invasion of Britain. Thus, Napoleon turned his attention to other areas.

An inordinate number of works described the rationale, aims, and objectives of the Egyptian campaign of Napoleon, 1798-1801. After giving up on an invasion plan of Britain, Napoleon assembled a large force at Toulon, 180 ships including 13 SOTL and 42 frigates, departing on 19 May 1798. The official French history of the campaign was by Marquis de la Jonquiere [**1833**], 5 vols., 1910. Henry Laurens [**2067**], Expetition d'Egypte, 1987, was a solid, scholarly study. Christopher Lloyd [**2167**], The Nile Campaign: Nelson and Napoleon in Egypt, 1973, covered events from the time of the capture of Malta by Napoleon to the defeat of the French at Alexandria in 1801. Malta was recovered and became an issue in the peace negotiations and in the resumption of the war.

Other accounts were Joseph Moiret [**2523**], 2001; Michael Barthorp [**226**], 1978, a short but clear account; J.C. Herold [**1608**], 1962, a long but popular account; P.G. Elgood [**1031**], 1931, an older account of the period, 1798-1799, in Egypt; Robert Tignor [**3622**], 1975, a translation from an Arabic account about the French occupation of Egypt, and Nathan Schur [**3252**], Napoleon in the Holy Land, 1999, describing later parts of the campaign. Napoleon was en route to conquer the Ottoman Empire. Next would be Persia and India, following the exploits of Alexander the Great. J.B. Kelly [**1854**], Britain and the Persian Gulf, 1795-1880, 1968, was a scholarly survey of British interests and activities here. One reason for initial British initiatives was concern about the Napoleonic threat to India. The French army made it to Acre. The RN captured the French siege train, stranding the French army. Sidney Smith was commander of the British forces, which defeated the French at Acre. After two months, the French were forced to retreat back to Egypt. The British army under George Abernathy, with support of the RN under Lord Keith, eventually defeated the French at Aboukir, 1801.

Piers Mackesy [**2303**], British Victory in Egypt, 1801: The End of Napoleon's Conquest, 1995, was actually the third volume of an excellent trilogy by Mackesy. Again, the RN played a prominent role. British success meant the end of French control of the area and an advantageous stance for the British in the upcoming peace negotiations.

A unique and enduring feature of this Egyptian campaign of Napoleon was Mission Civilisatrice, the addition of about 500 intellectuals, experts in archaeology and anthropology, and scientists, effectively, proto-Egyptologists, as recounted by Henry Laurens [2068], Les Origines Intellectuelles de l'expedition d'Egypte, 1987. Because the British eventually defeated the French in Egypt, the famous Rosetta Stone made its way to the British Museum where it can be seen today.

8. The Battle of the Nile

Not knowing where Napoleon and the task force were going, with his squadron of SOTLs and transports, Nelson had searched desperately all over the Mediterranean, just missing it on 22 June 1798 off Crete. He finally arrived at Alexandria on 1 August at 5:30 in the afternoon and found the French battle fleet in Aboukir Bay, 15 miles east of Alexandria. The circumstances and the response of the British were extraordinary. The brilliance of Nelson, the obvious preparations made between him and his captains, his "Band of Brothers," and the adroit exploitation of the situation, all contributed to making the result of this battle of the Nile the greatest sea battle of annihilation ever.

It was late in the afternoon. The 13 French SOTL were anchored in a north-south line just east of the shore and the wind was from the north. Some of the French crews were ashore obtaining water and provisions. The ships had anchored fairly close to the shore, but, in the event, obviously, not close enough, because the ships of Nelson were able to engage the French on both sides, between the shore and the French line and on the other side of the French line, the essence of concentration. HMS CULLODEN ran aground entering the Bay and remained out of the action. The British started at the top and slowly made their way down the line, doubling up alongside each French ship in turn. Since the wind was from the north, French ships down the line were unable to move northward to assist. Of the 13 French SOTL, 11 were captured or destroyed. At 10:05 PM, the French flagship, L'ORIENT, in the middle of the line, caught fire and blew up in a spectacular explosion seen and heard in Alexandria. The last two French ships were able to get underway and escape.

Brian Lavery [2076], Nelson and the Nile, 1998, confirmed it as the most decisive naval victory of its age in this bicentennial commemoration study; the epitome of the concept of "the Band of Brothers" Nelson cultivated. This defeat for Napoleon had enormous strategic consequences. Another account was by Oliver Warner [3755], 1960. Some bicentennial publications included: in French, by Michael Battesti [234], 1998; Richard Cavendish [597], 1998, noting that it was this battle which established the reputation of Nelson. Marianne Czisnik [843] elaborated: "Nelson and the Nile: The Creation of Admiral Nelson's Public Image," 2002. The London Gazette Extraordinary proclaimed the victory as unprecedented. Two plays were soon in production at Covent Garden. Portraits proliferated. The artists were obviously oblivious of his person, one even depicting the left arm as missing. Commemorative memorabilia included Wedgwood vases, urns, and jugs and wax models and pottery. Tom Malcolmson [2343], 1998, noting that a chart of Aboukir Bay recently had been found among records at the PRO and, apparently, Nelson and his captains were informed of the details of the Bay. Laura Foreman [1137], 1999, presented details of the battle and details of recent nautical archaeological expeditions at the site of the battle of the Nile, all lavishly illustrated. Ian Germani [1267], 2000, did a short piece on "imagining the battle of the Nile," illustrative of the escalation of ferocity of international conflict.

Nelson was awarded a peerage and made Baron of the Nile. Napoleon escaped back to France in a fast frigate and led a coup of the French government. His army was left stranded and was ultimately defeated. **See 9., D., 13.**

9. The Battles of Copenhagen, 1801 and 1807

Denmark was seen by the British as an aggressive neutral. Denmark was a potential ally of the French. Denmark controlled access into the Baltic Sea, an area vital to the maintenance of British sea power, hegemony, and containment of France. **See 7.,, E., 4.** The Danish fleet, a formidable force, was potentially available in some Grand Design of Napoleon.

An introduction about the circumstances can be found in Dudley Pope [2895], The Great Gamble: Nelson at Copenhagen, 1972, April 1801, presenting informative detail of the rationale of the campaign which related to the League of Armed Neutrality. He contended that Nelson recognized that Russia, not Denmark, was the objective. The battle was extremely hard fought. In the midst of the battle, the commander, Hyde Parker, signaled Nelson to withdraw, Signal Number 39, "discontinue action." Nelson acknowledged it and disobeyed it. Kenneth Langmaid [2029], The Blind Eye, 1972, focused on the "enlightened disobedience" of Nelson during this battle, and Langmaid contended, in subsequent similar events.

For reasons noted above, the RN returned and attacked Copenhagen in 1807. Two accounts of the background and the battle were by the well-known naval historian, A.N. Ryan [3193, 3196], both 1953, a controversial attack. Denmark was a neutral state at the time. The Tilsit agreement between Tsar Alexander I and Napoleon was concluded and the the the British reacted; to neutralize the Danish fleet before it could come to the aid of the French. Sven Trulsson [3653], 1976, reviewed Anglo-Swedish relations and the reactions of Sweden, Norway, and Russia to the attack on Copenhagen in 1807.

The attack on Copenhagen by the RN in 1807, a surprise attack on a state neutral at the time, was to have repercussions. The noted naval historian of the German navy, Jonathan Steinberg [3440], wrote "The Copenhagen

Complex," 1966. At the time of Anglo-German naval antagonism a century later, German propagandists warned of <u>Kopenhagen</u>, a past event and a present fear; playing up the utter ruthlessness of the British who would likely attack Kiel or Wilhelmshaven without warning.

10. The Campaign of Trafalgar

From hindsight, and in the mythology which emerged as a result of spectacular events in the autumn of 1805, the culmination of a series of movements over half of the world would come down to the meeting of two battle fleets off the extreme southwest corner of the Iberian peninsula, Cape Trafalgar. Annihilation of the enemy was followed immediately by the death of Horatio Nelson. The myth was launched. British naval, imperial, and global hegemony would be unsurpassed and unthreatened for over a century. Nelson did it. A.T. Mahan [**2328, 2329**] summed it up best: "Those far distant, storm-beaten ships, upon which the [Napoleonic] Grand Army never gazed, stood between it and the dominion of the world."

After the Treaty of Amiens broke down and war resumed in 1803, Napoleon formulated another grandiose plan to invade the British Isles, his Grand Design. Massive movement of fleets of France and its allies were involved. The aim was a familiar one: to concentrate these naval forces in the English Channel, gain command of the sea, and escort thousands of barges and other transports filled with troops to invade. A large Franco-Spanish fleet concentrated after breaking out of the blockades. The commander was French Admiral Pierre Villeneuve. As in the Egyptian campaign, Nelson frantically searched for it. It sailed across the Atlantic to the Caribbean and back, Nelson following.

Julian Corbett [**747**], <u>The Campaign of Trafalgar</u>, 2 vols., 1910-1919, was the classic account of the campaign. Corbett relied heavily on the Edouard Desbriere [**914**] account. Edouard Desbriere [**914**], <u>Trafalgar: The Naval Campaign of 1805</u>, 2 vols., 1907, was a French expert writer who described the elaborate invasion planning and presented the French and Spanish perspectives of the campaign.

Alan Schom [**3248**], <u>Trafalgar: Countdown to Battle, 1803-1805</u>, 1992, saw the battle of 21 October 1805 as the culmination of 29 months of an extensive naval campaign to prevent a French invasion of Britain. Credit for the contributions of Admiral William Cornwallis have been overshadowed by Nelson. Elsewhere in a letter in <u>History Today</u>, March 1991, Schom pointed out and persuasively argued that "five egregious errors" were made in the description of the battle by John Keegan [**1850**], <u>The Price of Admiralty</u>, 1988.

Dudley Pope [**2892**], <u>England Expects</u>, alternate title, <u>Decision at Trafalgar</u>, 1959, reviewed the long campaign leading to the battle. Chapter titles included "the Emperor's Plan," "the Great Chase," "the Nelson Touch," and "the Great Gale." Robert Gardiner [**1237**], <u>The Campaign of Trafalgar, 1803-1805</u>,

1997, was another of the exquisite series for the NMM, this one covering the high point of naval power under sail.

Rene Maine [2336], Trafalgar: Napoleon's Naval Waterloo, 1957, was translated from French and presented details of events leading to the battle. There were questionable assertions, for example, that the battle ended the threat to Britain, that it even ended the Napoleonic Empire, that the British fleet personnel were subject to "dysentery, typhus, cholera, and abominable food," and that Trafalgar was directly comparable to Operation Sea Lion, the invasion plan of Hitler in 1940.

More correctly, J. Holland Rose [3141], 1922, appraised the status of the fleet of Nelson in the years before the battle, praising the extraordinarily low health problems and excellent conditions on the lower decks.

On the occasion of the centennial of the death of Nelson, an account of the campaign was published by Henry Newbolt [2632], the official historian of the naval phase of World War I: The Year of Trafalgar, 1905. Newbolt recounted "events which led up to it" and included 26 poems, some by him; others by William Wordsworth, Walter Scott, Thomas Hardy, and D.G. Rossetti. It was dedicated to Julian Corbett. Some critics claimed it perpetuated the Nelson cult.

Trafalgar overshadowed another battle. On 22 July 1805, the British squadron under Robert Calder fought the combined Franco-Spanish fleet under Villeneuve. Two Spanish SOTLs were captured, a tactical victory. Calder chose not to renew the battle on 23 July. The British authorities questioned that decision. Calder was court martialled, found guilty, and censured. This was recounted by Oliver Warner [3761], 1969, and Nicholas Tracy [3644], 1991.

11. The Battle of Trafalgar

Finally, on 21 October 1805, the Franco-Spanish fleet which Nelson had chased to the Caribbean and back, came out from Cadiz and the two forces met off Cape Trafalgar. The Franco-Spanish fleet was in a rough north-south line and the British, divided into two lines led by Nelson and Collingwood, respectively, came at the allied line from the west, breaking it in two places. The wind was such that all ships of the allied fleet north of the breaking points were unable to engage in the early phases of the battle.

Statistics of the battle were as follows:
The British: 27 SOTL, broken down: 3-100 guns, 4-98 guns, 1-80 guns, 15-74 guns, and 3-64 guns; 4 frigates and 2 auxiliaries; no losses.
The Franco-Spanish fleet: 33 SOTL: 18 French and 15 Spanish; 15 sunk or destroyed, 8 captured; 10 escaped to Cadiz but were unfit for service.

Oliver Warner [3777], Trafalgar, 1959, described the battle in detail; Nelson was the great hero. Other accounts were by David Howarth [1697], Trafalgar: The Nelson Touch, 1969; D.G.F. Macintyre [2271], Trafalgar: Nelson's Great Victory, 1968; eye-witness accounts collected by Edward Fraser

[**1179**], 1906; Stuart Legg [**2103**], 1966; John Terraine [**3590**], 1975, and Thomas Huskisson [**1739**], 1985. William Laird Clowes [**669, 670**], historian of the RN, wrote Trafalgar Refought, 1905. R.H. Mackenzie [**2301**], The Trafalgar Roll: The Ships and the Officers, 1913, described the histories of the 33 ships of the RN present and the careers of 850 officer-participants of the battle. William Drummond [**967**], The Battle of Trafalgar: An Heroic Poem, 1807, was an extensive poem originally read to the Literary Society of Belfast. A.H. Taylor [**3570**], 1950, included copies of the plans Nelson formulated and shared with his captains, an aspect of "the Nelson Touch." The Jackdaw portfolio for the battle [**236**], 1963, was on of the better ones for young researchers.

Several works focused on the Spanish. John Harbron [**1488**], Trafalgar and the Spanish Navy, 1988, presented an extensive analysis of the Spanish navy. A traditional view was incompetence and consistent decline; not so, claimed Harbron. Spanish sea power revived and excelled. Julian Zulueta [**3988**], 1980, presented the Spanish perspective. Nelson and Collingwood both had praised Spanish SOTLs and their sailors. SANTISIMA TRINIDAD, a 4-decker, was the largest such ship ever. English guns were no better than the Spanish but the English gun carriages were superior and rate of fire was better. Similar observations have been made about Spanish Armada ships of 1588. Bernard Cornwell [**774**] presented Sharpe's Trafalgar: Spain 1805, 2001. Ronald Quirk [**2992**], 1998, analyzed the reaction of the Spanish people during the century after Trafalgar; a kind of rhythm: minimizing the impact to outrage, hand-wringing, and retaliation. Nelson continued to be admired, but Napoleon and the French were increasingly blamed.

David Howarth [**1692**] did a short piece, "The Man Who Lost Trafalgar," 1971, about Villeneuve. Napoleon had secretly ordered Villeneuve to leave Cadiz and engage the RN. Villeneuve was captured and taken to England, released, returned to Rennes, and committed suicide; with 6 knife wounds, some claimed a secret assassination by Napoleon. Later, Napoleon claimed Villeneuve disobeyed orders to remain at Cadiz; thus, the defeat was the fault of Villeneuve.

England Expects, 1972, by Roger Hart [**1538**], and Alan Villiers [**3724**], 1965, were for juveniles.

Bernard Claxton [**652**], Trafalgar and Jutland: A Study in the Principles of War, 1985, supported a war college analysis of the two battles illustrating principles of war.

Clemence Dane [**853**], 1940, described in fictional form Trafalgar Day, 1940, under the circumstances of war and imminent invasion.

The prolific military historian, meaning land warfare, John Keegan [**1850**], ventured one time into naval history; The Price of Admiralty: The Evolution of Naval Warfare, 1988, presenting his interpretations of the battles of Trafalgar, Jutland, Midway, and the battle of the Atlantic, in the end predicting the end of surface ship warfare. There was no scholarly apparatus and reviewers were not kind: Keegan was unfamiliar with the literature of naval history and the book was riddled with errors. In introducing Trafalgar, he praised 4 offensive minded commanders: Rodney, Howe, Duncan, and Nelson. Closest to Nelson subsequently was Chester Nimitz.

12. The Treaty of Tilsit of 1807 and the Continental System

When Napoleon and Tsar Alexander I met at Tilsit in 1807, there was an appearance of dividing up the world, Napoleon encouraging Alexander to "go east." The distinguished historian, Herbert Butterfield [**531**], The Peace Tactics of Napoleon, 1806-1808, 1929, assessed Napoleon as being at his high point of power and influence at this time. Napoleon then issued the Berlin and Milan Decrees, creating the Continental System, a kind of reverse blockade against the British. If he could not invade, if he could not defeat the British directly, then he would attack the British with economic warfare. The old standard was Eli Heckscher [**1594**], The Continental System: An Economic Interpretation, 1922, which began with an overview of Anglo-French economic warfare since the 1680s. About the same time, Frank Melvin [**2494**], Napoleon's Navigation System, 1919, surveyed the system.

In an impressive and persuasive test of the actual effectiveness, Silvia Marzagalli [**2447**], Les Boulevards de la Fraude: Le Negoce maritime et le Blocus continentale, 1806-1813, 1999, conducted a statistical analysis of three ports: Bordeaux, Hamburg, and Leghorn. There was, in fact, little change in each and the system failed. To counter it, the British established entrepots: Malta, Gibraltar, and Heligoland. A.N. Ryan [**3194**], 1959, wrote of the trade in the Baltic, 1808-1813. A major role of the RN was to keep this essential trade open. The Danes and Norwegians used privateers against British trade and British merchants suffered. Nevertheless, success was achieved by the RN; operations included protection of convoys, surface raiders, and exploitation by smuggling, false papers, and corruption of French customs officials. A RN squadron was sent into the Baltic every year, 1808-1813.

13. The Pensular Campaign and After

As noted more than once, Trafalgar may have been the ultimate but it was not the end. The Peninsular campaign, British and Spanish opponents of Napoleon and the French take-over of Spain, fought a massive and long campaign from 1807-1814. The Duke of Wellington made his reputation here. Napoleon exerted every effort to end it, to no avail. The land phases have been stressed; naval support and amphibious operations less so.

A good introduction from the British perspective was Roger Parkinson [**2775**], The Peninsular War, 1973. The old classic was William Napier [**2597**], History of the War in the Peninsula and the South of France, 1807-1814, 5 vols., 1828-1840. The great standard was Charles Oman [**2707**], A History of the Peninsular War, 7 vols., 1902-1930. Coverage was chronological and extensive. David Gates [**1258**], The Spanish Ulcer: History of the Peninsular War, 1985, was a good 1-vol. study. It included a section on sea power and the logistical difficulties. Michael Glover [**1301**], The Peninsular War, 1807-1814: A Concise Military History, 1974, did not cover naval aspects. Ian Fletcher [**1126**], The Peninsular War, 1998, featured memoir-correspondence. With numerous illustrations and insufficient narrative, Jean Tranie [**3645**], Napoleon's War in Spain: The French Peninsular Campaigns, 1807-1814, 1982, presented a year-by-year account of the campaign, Napoleon's "Spanish ulcer." Napoleon himself came, November 1808-January 1809, but to no avail. He sent his best generals and most experienced forces, again to no avail.

The naval-amphibious aspects of the campaign have been covered. A dissertation by T.M.O. Redgrave [**3036**], described the logistical arrangements of Wellington during the campaign. The role of the RN has been presented, albeit inadequately. Christopher Hall [**1457**], 1993, described the RN in the campaign. The peninsula had 1500 miles of coastline, poor roads, and was open to bombardment by the RN. Responsibilities included protection of supply ships, for example, in 1809, the RN protected 34 separate convoys to Iberia. Donald Horward [**1677**], 1978, wrote about the influence of British sea power upon the Peninsular campaign. Henry Shore [**3309**] wrote a series of 15 articles, "The Navy in the Peninsular War," 1912-1914.

Individual operations were recounted. Thomas Barker [**207**], 2000, described a failed amphibious operation against Fort Fuengirola in 1810. A monocausal analysis was insufficient. Poor naval-military cooperation and communication, lack of surprise, and misuse of gunboats were among the causes. Christopher Hibbert [**1621**] described Corunna, 1961, in the British Battles series, an important battle on the Spanish coast in 1809. James Herson [**1611**], 1998, completed a dissertation on the siege of Cadiz, 1810-1812, a successful joint operation which contributed directly to the defeat of the French. Julian Corbett [**754**], 1922, wrote a short piece just before his death on Napoleon and the RN after Trafalgar. Britain and the Defeat of Napoleon, 1807-1815, 1996, by Rory Muir [**2582**], described thrust and countertrust.

David Syrett [**3552**], 1979, has a piece on the RN after Trafalgar, 1805-1814. Operations included support and defense of the Peninsular campaign. Donald Stephenson [**3447**], 1948, described problems experienced by the Mediterranean fleet under Collingwood in continuing the blockade. Collingwood had received insufficient recognition for this type of operation. Most of his career of 50 years in the RN had been spent on blockade operations. **See 22.**

Other operations and campaigns were as follows. The RN was pulled into remote areas in this "first world war": Edward Ingram [**1746**], 1982, reviewed the consequences of the conquest of India: a French strategic threat being a Franco-Persian alliance. In 1807-1808, Pellew had to contend with this regional crisis around the Strait of Hormuz. John Grainger [**1365**], 1993, wrote of an expedition of 1806 off Cape Town in southern Africa invading the Dutch colony: 7 warships in a convoy of 120 ships carrying 6000 soldiers; the naval commander was Home Popham. A similar expedition had occurred in 1795; the colony was returned to the Dutch and now this second expedition. The Cape Colony was retained by the British after the war.

John Grainger [1366], The Royal Navy in the River Plate, 1806-1807, 1996, a publication of the NRS, was about a British attack on the Spanish Viceroyalty, later Argentina and Uruguay. Hugh Popham was the naval commander, the attack was repulsed, but the operation weakened Spanish control and encouraged rebellion later. Fortescue [1162], the army historian, dismissed it as a semi-piratical filibuster campaign. Ian Fletcher [1127] covered the same expedition, entitled The Waters of Oblivion, 1991.

W.Y. Carman [578], 1941, analyzed some paintings and accounts of the British capture of Martinique in 1809: a British naval force including 10,000 troops under the command of Cochrane.

The Walcheren Expedition of 1809 was an invasion of the Low Countries in the Scheldt area, partly to distract the campaign of Napoleon against the ally of Britain, Austria. Dismal failure was the result. Characterizations were "a gallant failure" and "fiasco." The force was devastated by disease, among other problems. It was recounted by Gordon Bond [361], 1979, Antony Brett-James [433], 1963, and in a dissertation by C.A. Christie [633], 1979.

14. The War of 1812

"Unnecessary war," "stupid war," "a blunder-filled episode," "our most obscure war," "how a war ought not to be conducted," "causes shrouded in mystery," and "neglected war" were descriptive terms used then and now about the Anglo-American conflict, fought at sea, on the lakes, in Canada, in the South, in the Chesapeake Bay and Washington, and, finally, after peace had been concluded, in an invasion attempt on New Orleans. There was no mention of impressment and free trade, seen by most as primary causes, in the peace treaty.

The British navy continued to have large commitments fighting the Wars of the French Revolution and Napoleon when war broke out between the United States and Britain, the War of 1812, lasting until 1815. Early on, it was clear there were insufficient British forces available to meet this new threat. The newly independent colony had struggled for several decades. Maritime and naval conflicts were increasingly experienced between the new nation and France and Britain in the run-up to actual war. It could have gone either way.

Never have so many prominent persons entered the fray of writing histories of the war, for example, William James [1783], James Fenimore Cooper [737], Henry Adams [12], George Bancroft [193], C.P. Stacey [3414], Theodore Roosevelt [3137], A.T. Mahan [2332], Bradford Perkins [2820], C.S. Forester [1141], and Walter Lord [2188], plus Julius Pratt, Samuel Flag Bemis,

Thomas A. Bailey, George Dangerfield, Samuel Eliot Morison, and Henry Steele Commager.

A crisis of 1794 involved Anglo-American relations. Over 50 American merchant ships were seized at Martinique. Crews were abused, some being impressed. Prize money was claimed by the British captains. Long delays were experienced in the adjudication of claims of the ship owners. The John Jay mission to London negotiated these issues. Malcolm Lester [**2109**], 1954, did a dissertation on diplomatic problems between America and Britain resulting from RN operations in American waters, 1793-1802. For example, American merchantmen were detained at Halifax and American sailors were impressed. The issue of American prisoners of war was introduced by Francis Cogliano [**695**], 2001.

The French factor was equally important. In preparation was Donald Hickey [**1625, 1623**] with an account of the Quasi-War with France, 1798-1800, a companion volume to his War of 1812. Another preliminary incident contributing to the deterioration of relations was the USS CHESAPEAKE vs. HMS LEOPARD affair, 22 June 1807, off Hampton Roads. Three Americans were killed and 4 were impressed, 3 of whom were American citizens, 2 of those were Black Americans. Comprehensive coverage and a synthesis was Spencer Tucker [**3657**], Injured Honor: The CHESAPEAKE-LEOPARD Affair, 1996, called "the preliminary salvo of the War of 1812." Observations and conclusions included: America was more unified for war after this than in 1812 and the subsequent American court martial of Captain Barron and its findings caused serious divisions among American officers; 7 duels were fought in the next year and in 1820, Barron killed Stephen Decatur in a duel. Internal feuds among the officers of CHESAPEAKE did not help matters. John Emmerson [**1043**], 1955, noted that it was a minor incident in naval history and that the consequences had been exaggerated and misunderstood. The English captain exceeded his instructions and the American captain also demonstrated despicable conduct. Another account was in a dissertation by Edward Gaines [**1223**], 1960.

Tucker [**3658**], The Jeffersonian Gunboat Navy, 1993, described the American policy to protect its shores: construction of 172 gunboats. Tucker was more sympathetic to the effort than most, for example, they were useful against the Barbary corsairs and in the preliminaries to the battle of New Orleans.

Much has been written about the origins and causes of the War of 1812. Warren Goodman [**1318**], 1941, surveyed what he called the changing interpretations. Most important were protection of national honor and neutral maritime rights. Too many stressed non-maritime matters. The declaration of war of June 1812 denounced British practices of violating the American flag, seizing American seamen, harassing the Atlantic coast, and plundering commerce. Others stressed expansionist ambitions for Canada, for Florida, for more Western lands, British exploitation of American Indians, Anglophobia, and Manifest Destiny. Reginald Horsman [**1673, 1674**], 1961 and 1969, contributed books on the causes and the war, praised as particularly accurate. Look carefully at the situation in Europe and the British dilemma in the decade before the war: fighting for her life, in desperate need of sailors, and to prevent American aid to its enemies. "Western expansion" has been overemphasized. The diplomacy was well covered. Another contribution was by Bradford Perkins [**2820**], 1962.

Donald Hickey [**1623, 1624**] contributed an interesting sequence, The War of 1812: The Forgotten Conflict, 1990, and "The War of 1812: Still a Forgotten Conflict?", 2001. In the decade between publications, Hickey admitted that coverage had increased, especially of military and naval aspects, counting 75 new works: perhaps less "forgotten." The famous Heath Pamphlet series, now dated, was George Taylor [**3579**], 1963, which reviewed the historiography.

The old standard account of the war was Henry Adams [**12**], The War of 1812, 1944, taken from his 9-volume history of the United States, 1890. Maritime rights and American expansionist ambitions for Canada were important causes. For reference, there was an Encyclopedia of the War of 1812, 1997, by David Heidler [**1595**]. Other accounts were as follows: Glenn Tucker [**3655**], Poltrons and Patriots: A Popular Account of the War of 1812, 2 vols., 1954; Harry Coles [**702**], The War of 1812, 1963, a lively survey, and J.K. Mahon [**2334**], The War of 1812, 1972, which sought balance.

The Canadian perspective was presented by Mackay Hitsman [**1643**], The Incredible War of 1812, 1965, containing apologetics on the impressment issue and sympathy for American loyalists.

The naval war was seen as most important, and perhaps, most controversial. William James [**1783**], 1817, presented the British perspective, biased and provocative, and generating extensive reaction, for example, "irritating reading," "glaring inaccuracies," and "his venomous hatred of America." Theodore Roosevelt [**3137**], The Naval War of 1812, 1882, had done his senior thesis at Harvard on the naval war and expanded it. Later he wrote the pertinent section in the 7-vol. British naval history by William Laird Clowes [**669**]. Roosevelt aggressively "corrected" the British version by William James [**1783**] and the American version by James Fenimore Cooper [**737**]. The U.S. Naval War College adopted it as a text. The war on the Lakes was well covered.

Alfred Thayer Mahan [**2332**], Sea Power in Its Relation to the War of 1812, 2 vols., 1905, saw "Free Trade and Sailors' Rights" as the major causes. He ticked off the consecutive legislative and other actions, for example, Navigation Acts, Berlin Decree, CHESAPEAKE-LEOPARD Affair, Orders-in-Council, Embargo Act, and Non-Intercourse Act.

Creator of Horatio Hornblower, C.S. Forester [**1141**], The Age of Fighting Sail: The Story of the Naval War of 1812, 1956, presented a popular account of the naval war. The popular writer about TITANIC and other events, Walter Lord [**2188**], surveyed the war in The Dawn's Early Light, 1972, observing "America during trying times."

Another of the exquisite productions of the Chatham Pictorial Histories series for the NMM was contributed: Robert Gardiner [**1244**], The Naval War of 1812, 1998. The extensive documentary history, William Dudley [**970**] produced The Naval War of 1812, 4 vols., 1985-____, with more to be published. Some conclusions from this official history were: the greatest contribution of the USN was in the Lakes campaigns, discussion of impressment, and between 1796-1812, 9991 American seamen were impressed.

James Jacobs [**1770**], 1969, touted itself as "a compact history." There was no fleet action during the war, only single-ship encounters. James Barnes, [**211**], Naval Actions of the War of 1812, 1896, recounted 19 battles each supported by a painting in color; the narrative was ultra-patriotic pro-American. The Fight for a Free Sea, 1920, by Ralph Paine [**2733**], was filled with hyperbole, for example, it was "the greatest armed conflict of all time" and "a great American victory."

Strategy and British efforts at amphibious warfare were the features of C.J. Bartlett [**227**], "Gentlemen vs. Democrats," 1944. Were the British guided by a coherent strategy or merely opportunism? Plans of Cochrane and Cockburn were reviewed. The attack on Washington provoked outrage in Parliament. Fortesque [**1162**] declared the New Orleans campaign as "a childish piece of folly." After the fact, a debate about whether the strategy of blockade was superior to amphibious coastal attacks occurred; blockade was deemed most effective. Joseph Goldenberg [**1310**], 1984, did a piece on the British naval blockade of New England, seemingly so successful, but, in a closer look, illustrative of serious problems: insufficient naval forces, discipline, drunkenness, suicides, treacherous weather, and resort to impressment. Those problems were elaborated upon by Barry Lohnes [**2182**], 1973, citing the Halifax squadron as an example. Problems included neglect by the Admiralty and Parliament, mediocre commanders, and unseaworthy ships. The journal of Lieutenant Henry Napier, RN, of HMS NYMPHE, a participant in the blockade in 1814 was edited by Walter Whitehill [**3843**], 1939.

One incident during that blockade campaign was The Battle of Stonington, 1990, recounted by J. T. De Kay [**898**]; the subtitle: Torpedoes, Submarines, and Rockets in the War of 1812. The RN attacked this seaport town in Connecticut. The squadron was commanded by Thomas Hardy, Nelson's flag captain. The town was bombarded for several days with little damage. Factors were smuggling, rockets, torpedoes of Fulton, and a submarine of Bushnell.

During operations in the Chesapeake Bay area in 1813-1814, four Maryland towns were plundered and burned, ships were attacked, Washington, and Alexandria, Virginia, were sacked, the Capitol and White House were burned, and Baltimore was attacked, albeit, unsuccessfully. Anthony Pitch [**2859**], The Burning of Washington, 1998, described in detail the operation of the British attack on Alexandria, occupation of Washington, burning of public buildings, bombardment of Ft. McHenry, and the failed attack on Baltimore. The campaign of 1813-1814 by the RN in the Chespeake Bay wreaked havoc, George Cockburn being the planner and commander. That fact was confirmed in A. Cockburn [**687**], 1911, a secret letter being discovered among the Cockburn papers at the Library of Congress. Perhaps the title was aptly chosen: Terror on the Chesapeake, 2000, by Christopher George [**1265**]. Joseph Whitehorne [**3844, 3845**], The Battle of Baltimore, 1814, 1997, and While Washington Burned, 1993, covered more than the operation against Baltimore and Washington.

Some ship-to-ship battles were presented. The literature was not balanced: 4 on the USS CHESAPEAKE vs. HMS SHANNON battle: by Hugh Pullen [**2967**], 1970, Kenneth Poolman [**2884**], 1961, H.J.G. Garbett [**1233**], 1913, and Peter Padfield [**2727**], 1968, with a biography of Captain Broke of CHESAPEAKE.

Ira Dye [**998**], The Fateful Cruise of the ARGUS, 1994, was actually in 3 parts: mini-biographies of Captain William Henry Allen of USS ARGUS and Captain John Fordyce Maples of HMS PELICAN, and an account of the battle between them off St. David's Head on the Welsh coast of Britain. ARGUS was defeated, Allen died, the ARGUS crew were sent to the Dartmoor Prison, and Maples was promoted. Additional interest was added because the two captains were veterans, for example, of CHESPEAKE-LEOPARD, UNITED STATES-MACEDONIAN, Copenhagen, and Trafalgar.

15. The War on the Lakes

Much attention in recent decades has been devoted to filling gaps in this important sector of the War of 1812. In the beginning, the British enjoyed decisive superiority, therefore the rate of shipbuilding became the focus and, ultimately, was to determine the outcome.

A good place to begin was the work of David Skaggs [**3334, 3333**], The Sixty Years' War for the Great Lakes, 1754-1814, 2001, and A Signal Victory: The Lake Erie Campaign, 1997, describing the long struggle beginning before the American Revolution. Key figures during the War of 1812 were Oliver Hazard Perry, the American commander, and Robert Barclay, for the British. Their forces, 9 American vs. 6 British, met 10 September 1813. After a 3-hour battle, Perry famously to William Henry Harrison concluded: "We have met the enemy and they are ours."

Other accounts were by Gerard Altoff [**61**], 1990, Bil Gilbert [**1277**], 1995, and an older standard by George Bancroft [**193**], 1891. The Canadian military historian, C.P. Stacey [**3414**], 1958, compared the situation; the British suffered, probably fatally, because supply lines were too long. Robert Malcomson [**2341, 2342**], 1990 and 1998, elaborated on the battle of Lake Erie and the campaign on Lake Ontario. Max Rosenberg [**3147**], 1950, and C. Winton-Clare [**3924**], 1943, described "the shipbuilder's war" on the Great Lakes. Patrick Wilder [**3856**], The Battle of Sackett's Harbor, 1994, recounted the decisive event in the struggle for Lake Ontario, an American victory. The Fleet in the Forest, 1943, by Carl Lane [**2016**], presented a fictional account of the battle of Lake Erie.

W.J. Welsh [**3812**], War on the Great Lakes, 1991, reported the proceedings of a symposium, September 1988, commemorating the 175th anniversary of the battle of Lake Erie. Operations on the lessor lakes were also important: Navies in the Mountains, 1962, by Harrison Bird [**323**], was the title of the work describing operations on Lakes Champlain and George.

16. Napoleon Bonaparte and Exile

Who was the enemy during the mid- and final-phases of the Wars of the French Revolution and Napoleon? As noted elsewhere, Napoleon Bonaparte first made his military reputation in the successful campaign to recover Toulon from the Royalists and the British in 1793. In 1797, he was successful as commander of a campaign in northern Italy. Then, he launched the Egyptian Campaign, anticipating grandiose Oriental conquests. **See 7., I.**

As might be expected, the literature about Napoleon in these various statuses was massive. Adam Gopnik [**1325**], 1997, surveyed some of that literature: an estimate of 45,000 biographies of Napoleon. Most French accounts glorified him; most English ones were critical, "a deformed megalomaniacal dwarf." More solid and a classic was the Dutch historian Pieter Geyl [**1268**], Napoleon For and Against, 1949, an outstanding historiographical survey of how Napoleon has been depicted over time.

The noted British historian of Napoleoniana, David Chandler [**615**], 2001, has a new biography. So does a noted British historian, Correlli Barnett [**212**], 1997. An English biography was by Frank McLynn [**2313**], 1997, sympathetic and resorting to the psychological approach. The British were responsible for the collapse of the Peace of Amiens and the British jailor, Hudson Lowe, was depicted negatively. Alan Schom [**3246**], Napoleon Bonaparte: A Life, 1997, was less sympathetic for Napoleon. Philip Haythornthwaite [**1582**], Napoleon: The Final Verdict, 1996, focused on his role as a soldier. F.M. Kircheisen [**1945**], Napoleon, 1931, presented the German perspective. The occupation of Prussia by Napoleon stimulated a dramatic recovery; it was the Germans who tipped the balance at the battle of Waterloo.

Charles Esdaile [**1055**], The Wars of Napoleon, 1995, provided an excellent overview. The pre-eminent authority on Napoleon contributed the standard survey: David Chandler [**614**], The Campaigns of Napoleon: The Mind and Method of History's Greatest Soldier, 1966. Henry Lachouque [**1987**], Napoleon's Battles, 1963, presented a French account, curiously omitting the Egyptian Campaign. Christopher Herold [**1607**], The Age of Napoleon, 1963, was a popular survey of the period, which David Gates [**1257**], The Napoleonic Wars, 1997, surveyed chronologically.

War resumed in 1803, Napoleon now as Emperor, planning his Grand Design, concentration of the French and allied fleets in the Channel to gain control of the sea so a massive invasion army could land. Edouard Desbriere [**913**], Projets de Debarquement aux Isles Britanniques, 4 vols., 1900-1902, presented a detailed history of French invasion plans, 1793-1805, the final one culminating in Trafalgar. Donald Come [**710**], 1952, described a series of efforts, beginning in 1793. Control of the sea was essential. As Napoleon gained success and notoriety in the mid-1790s, more plans were initiated. These were abandoned in 1797 and Napoleon launched the Malta-Egyptian campaign, apparently fulfilling an obsession of Napoleon to conquer the Orient. In progress for Westview Press was Frederick Schneid [**3244**], Napoleon's Grand Strategy. H.F.B. Wheeler [**3826**], Napoleon and the Invasion of England, 2 vols., 1908, was an early survey. Later, Carola Oman [**2703, 2702, 2701**], biographer of Nelson, wrote Britain against Napoleon, 1942, obviously relating those times with the time she was writing.

J. Holland Rose [**3140**], 1924, wrote about Napoleon and sea power. The RN gained from centuries of experience and an accumulated body of naval doctrine whereas the French navy suffered from purges after the revolution. Napoleon had no appreciation for sea power. With the Continental System, he hoped to control the sea from the land. Other accounts were A.A. Thomazi [**3598**], Napoleon et ses marins, 1950, and Philippe Masson [**2460**], Napoleon et la Marine, 1968, reviewing his relations with the French navy.

Richard Glover [**1302**], Britain at Bay: Defence against Bonaparte, 1973, concluded that Napoleon definitely intended to invade Britain, 1803-1805. Barges, the harbors, and pertinent roads were prepared. After Trafalgar, Napoleon persevered. Plans resumed, ports were prepared, a shipbuilding programme was launched, the goal being 150 SOTL. Revival of the French fleet after Trafalgar and the ambitious shipbuilding programme were confirmed by Richard Glover [**1304**], 1967. Another invasion plan proceeded: fleets of Denmark, Sweden, Russia, Spain, and Portugal were to join the French fleet. But, one after the other, those allied fleets were neutralized or destroyed. Lawrence Sondhaus [**3390**], 1989, confirmed that Napoleon launched a massive warship building programme, in his case, in Venice. Other shipbuilding centers included Amsterdam, Antwerp, Cherbourg, Brest, and Toulon.

E.H.S. Jones [**1826**], The Invasion that Failed: The French Expedition to Ireland, 1796, 1950, noted that Bantry Bay was the objective and that the Irish leader, Theobald Wolfe Tone, was implicated. The invasion force was dispersed in a storm and the British were unable to intercept it. A further invasion attempt also failed in 1798, defeated by the RN. Wolfe Tone died in 1798. John de Courcey Ireland [**1750**], 1987, wrote of Irish-French connections in general during this time.

Immediately after resumption of war in 1803, a flotilla from the Batavian Privateer Company, led by Jean Jacques de Saint-Faust, set out to invade "North Britain," the Orkney and Shetland Islands, one of the complex of operations of the Grand Design of Napoleon. The aim was disruption of the fishing fleets and commerce. The expedition failed. R.P. Fereday [**1087**], 1995, unearthed details of this obscure example of guerre de course in practice.

A review article, "Britain and Napoleon," 1998, was by Brendan Simms [**3320**], including five books, most about invasion and Napoleon. And from the exquisite Chatham Pictorial Histories series for the NMM came The

Victory of Seapower: Winning the Napoleonic War, 1998, by Richard
Woodman [3955].

Back to the War of the French Revolution and Napoleon, the role of the
RN at the end of the war was significant. Napoleon himself contributed to that
phenomenon, choosing to surrendered to the British navy, twice. In 1814, after
all was lost for his Empire, he rushed to the French coast and gave himself up to
a British naval captain. After Waterloo in 1815, he did the same. He obviously
felt that option gave optimum chances for his security and survival. In the
events, that proved to be correct, twice. In the end, as had been the case in 1814,
Napoleon rushed to the French coast and gave himself up, in this instance at
Rochefort to HMS BELLERPHON, thence via England to HMS
NORTHUMBERLAND to St. Helena.

R.F. Delderfield [903], Imperial Sunset: The Fall of Napoleon, 1813-
1814, 1968, was a popular approach and anecdotal. Katherine MacDonogh
[2237], 1994, wrote a piece on Napoleon at Elba and his return to power in
February 1815; was he assisted by the British? Britain was informed and
connived at the escape, MacDonogh claimed. Alan Schom [3247], Napoleon's
Road to Waterloo, 1992, presented details, too much so, of the time between the
return to power and the battle, June 1815. Napoleon abdicated, the second time,
on 22 June 1815. Henry Lachouque [1986] wrote of The Last Days of
Napoleon's Empire, 1966. M.J. Thornton [3610], Napoleon after Waterloo,
1968, described the days after abdication: to HMS BELLERPHON which sailed
to Torbay, Devon, July 1815, transferred to HMS NORTHUMBERLAND,
commanded by George Cockburn, and the one-month voyage to St. Helena.
William Warden [3749], 1816, published an extensive series of letters from
HMS NORTHUMBERLAND and St. Helena by the ship's surgeon who
conversed with Napoleon aboard and during the first months at St. Helena.

Gerald Graham [1358], "Napoleon's Naval Gaolers," 1978, noted that
the RN saw him as a potential threat, especially after Elba. The Vienna
Settlement provided that the British were responsible. An isolated location was
sought. St. Helena belonged to the East India Company and a contract was
concluded with the company providing for incarceration of Napoleon at British
expense, actually 400,000 pounds a year, 1815-1821. St. Helena was 1000 miles
west of the African coast and 1750 miles north of the Cape of Good Hope. An
older, comprehensive study was Barry O'Meara [2708], Napoleon at St. Helena,
2 vols., 1822.

Gilbert Martineau [2438, 2437], 1968 and 1971, described events as
Napoleon rushed to the coast and negotiated with the British about his surrender,
provisions for his exile, and his life at Longwood House on St. Helena.
Martineau claimed Napoleon died of cancer. Desmond Gregory [1396],
Napoleon's Jailor: Lt. Gen. Sir Hudson Lowe, 1996, contained two chapters on
St. Helena. He was recommended by Wellington. In the event, it was a dead end
to his career.

Frank Giles [**1279**], <u>Napoleon Bonaparte: England's Prisoner</u>, 2001, was a recent account. Giles rehabilitated Hudson Lowe. He had to deal with all of the court intrigue at Longwood. Julia Blackburn [**341**], <u>The Emperor's Last Island: A Journey to St. Helena</u>, 1991, recounted his bleak existence there. Jean Kauffmann [**1846**], <u>The Dark Room at Longwood</u>, 1999, described the last days of the life of Napoleon. Kauffmann actually visited St. Helena to gain perspective.

The death of Napoleon on 5 May 1821 has become a matter of continuing controversy up to the present day, more so in France than Britain. For example, hair samples have been scientifically analyzed. Ben Weider [**3803**], <u>Assassination at St. Helena Revisited</u>, 1978, insisted he was poisoned with arsenic by Bourbon interests beginning in 1805 and continuing at St. Helena. Weider insisted that the British acted to prolong the life of Napoleon. Guards surrounded Longwood at all times, unaware that the culprit was inside the household.

17. Lord Cochrane and South America

One consequence of the Wars of the French Revolution and Napoleon was a series of independence movements in South America; rebellions against Spain and Portugal. The British had cultivated commercial and political interests there for decades, the South American Station of the RN becoming increasingly important and active on the Atlantic and Pacific sides. Ordinarily, these facts would not be seen as justifying recognition and coverage herein. There was naval activity at all of the geographic British naval stations. There was more to it off the coasts of South America.

British officers, extraordinarily, the ubiquitous Thomas Cochrane, 10th Earl of Dundonald, and large numbers of British sailors were recruited by the rebel leaders in several states. These factors were described by David Cubitt [**822**], "The Manning of the Chilean Navy in the War of Independence," 1977. Some Americans also were recruited. Nevertheless, manning remained a serious problem among all of these rebel navies. **See 10., C.**

Overviews were by Robert Harvey [**1546**], <u>Liberators</u>, 2000, and Robert Albion [**27**], "British Shipping and Latin America," 1951. As the monopolies of Spain and Portugal became more tenuous, British merchants stepped in. The inimitable Gerald Graham [**1359**] surveyed the role of the RN: <u>The Navy and South America, 1807-1823</u>, 1962, a publication of the NRS. Naval commanders increasingly acted as diplomats on the spot. Barry Gough [**1343**], 1990, described activities on the South American Station, 1808-1837. Robert Harvey [**1545**], 2000, presented a recent survey. This time the British supported independence movements. In a dissertation, J. Ortiz-Sotelo [**2715**], presented a case study of a British naval station, in this case, the South American Station and its operations off the coast of Peru on the Pacific side. Protection and furthering of British trade were its functions.

Thomas Cochrane, 10th Earl of Dundonald [**685**], 1859, presented his version of his "services in the liberation of Chile, Peru, and Brazil." "That quirky genius," Lord Cochrane was "hired" as commander of these operations by the rebel governments. It has been Brian Vale [**3708-3714**] who has covered these events most thoroughly and extensively: Independence or Death: British Sailors and Brazilian Independence, 1996, and its complement, War Betwixt Englishmen: Brazil against Argentina on the River Plate, 2000, A Frigate of King George, 2001; plus 3 articles elaborating on Cochrane and various machinations with the Brazilian navy, two in 1971 and 1973. Vale effectively presented a case study of these operations, the "frigate" was HMS DORIS, 36 guns, which was stationed off Chile in the mid-1820s. Jose de San Martin of Argentina first recruited Cochrane but they fell out over money. Cochrane was involved with the navies of Chile and Peru. Then, in 1822, he became Commander-in-Chief of the Brazilian navy. Later, Cochrane also was recruited to command the Greek navy. Cochrane was interested in prize money and serious disputes developed over that issue subsequently. **See 9., D., 15.**

Chapter 8

Special Emphasis

In preparing this historiographical-bibliographical survey, the original intention was to include a chapter on "Personalities," the great officers in the history of the RN, at this point. However, in appraising the extent and magnitude of the literature, it became increasingly clear that two personalities stood out, over and above all others in the extent and amount of publications devoted to them. Admittedly, much was myth, legend, and exaggeration. It was immaterial that the mutiny under consideration may have been relatively insignificant, at that time and later. That incident took on a realm of its own and expanded beyond any expectation. So, this chapter, "Special Emphasis," was inserted here. The personalities, of course, were Horatio Lord Nelson and William Bligh. While covering them, the ships most identified with each also will be presented: respectively, HMS VICTORY and HM Bark BOUNTY. For the general public, these four items may be the best known aspects of English/British naval history.

A. HORATIO NELSON

1. Biographies and Studies

Admiral Lord Horatio Nelson, 1758-1805; Nelson signed himself "Nelson and Bronte," "Duke of Bronte" being a title awarded to him from the King of the Two Scilies. It was of questionable provenance. More importantly, a number of descriptive and memorable phrases have become traditional nomenclature: phrases which have persisted included, quotation marks excluded, The Nelson Touch, The Immortal Memory, The Durable Monument, Band of Brothers, Duty, Character, and Brilliant Tactician.

Burnham Thorpe in East Anglia was the birthplace of Nelson. His father was a struggling parish priest. His mother died when Nelson was 9 years old. Her brother, Captain Maurice Suckling, took over responsibility, serving as "interest" in support of the naval career of Nelson. The family history, The Nelsons of Burnham Thorpe, 1911, was by Mary Eyre Matcham [**2464**], covering 1787-1842. Admiral Nelson was simply one of the family. There was a chapter, "Trouble at Home and Merton Place." Anecdotal accounts were exaggerated further by writers during the 19th century, the stuff of legends, for example, the polar bear encounter, climbing the pear tree, being fearless, and extreme devotion to duty.

When the RN returned to the Mediterranean in the late 1790s, Lord St. Vincent sent a squadron commanded by Nelson in. After the battle of the Nile, 1 August 1798, Nelson spent increasing amounts of time in Naples, then the capital of the Kingdom of the Two Sicilies. His host was Lord William Hamilton, the British ambassador. The hostess was Lady Emma Hamilton. Complications ensued.

In 1799, Nelson became identified with the notorious Prince Carraciolo incident at Naples. Carraciolo was executed after a revolutionary revolt against the Neapolitan regime. Nelson was accused, by Southey [**3396**], among others, of involvement and duplicity, "the only blot on Nelson's career." Callender, editor of the edition of 1922, exonerated Nelson, his conduct being "above reproach."

The matters of Lady Emma Hamilton and Horatia, the daughter of Nelson and Emma Hamilton, remained controversial for a century, a kind of chronological rhythm. For decades, denial and cover-up prevailed. Few would believe that Horatia was the daughter of Emma Hamilton and Nelson; Horatia herself insisted she was not the daughter. Then, about 1850, still quite controversial for the rest of the century, more and more recognition that she was the daughter prevailed.

Details of the great battles and other naval operations were found elsewhere. **See 7., I., 5.-11.** Also, see the Nelson Decade [**2624**].

During the battle of Trafalgar, Nelson was shot fatally by a sniper from the rigging of a near-by enemy ship. Nelson was taken to "the cockpit," a place still much revered aboard HMS VICTORY, where he died, but not until he was informed of the magnitude of the great victory. The body was placed in a barrel full of spirits to preserve it. HMS PICKLE was the dispatch vessel which brought the news of Trafalgar and the death of Nelson to Britain; subsequently, "Pickle Night" has been celebrated.

After the battle, there was a terrific storm. HMS VICTORY made it to Gibraltar where temporary repairs were effected. On 5 November, she set sail for Britain. She arrived at the Nore on 23 December. At Greenwich, the body was laid in state in the Painted Hall, 4-7 January 1806. On 8 January, the body was placed on a barge and sailed up the Thames. The funeral was held at the Cathedral of St. Paul, 9 January 1806, and laid to rest in an elaborate marble casket directly under the crossing in the Crypt, where it can be seen today. The marble sarcophagus in which Nelson was laid was, in fact, originally prepared for Cardinal Wolsey who died in disgrace in the late 1520s.

Biographies of Nelson have appeared in their dozens since 1805, or earlier, and more are anticipated during the culmination of the Nelson Decade [**2624**]; several publishers have announced individual contributions in progress. At the annual Anglo-American Historians Conference at the Institute of Historical Research, July 2001, with its theme of "the Sea," a joke was shared: who there was NOT preparing a new biography of Nelson?

In the following section, concerning biographies of Nelson, special brackets will appear twenty times, followed by the entry number of the piece by Michael Nash among a series of essays in Colin White [**3833**], The Nelson Companion, 1995, for example: "[Number 7, **3833**]." Nash presented his appraisal of the top 20 biographies of Nelson in numerical order, 1 through 20. The rationales and priorities were not always clear.

To demonstrate the importance of the continuing interest in Nelson, prominent professional associations have oriented themselves around Nelson and "the immortal memory": the Society for Nautical Research, 1910; and its Save the VICTORY Fund, 1920s to the present; the Nelson Society, founded in 1981; its journal, The Nelson Dispatch, and the 1805 Club, founded 1990; its journal, The Trafalgar Chronicle. These three and other institutions have prepared and are executing a massive campaign to perpetuate and expand interest in Nelson, the Nelson Decade [**2624**] and Trafalgar 200. **See 8., A., 7. and items a. and b.**

Three recent publications would be good places to begin. Colin White [**3833**], The Nelson Companion, 1995, sponsored by the Royal Naval Museum, Portsmouth, profusely illustrated, reviewed the development of "the Nelson cult" and set the stage for preparation for the Nelson Decade [**2624**]. Seven experts wrote about their expertise, for example, Tom Pocock, Flora Fraser, Michael Nash, Richard Walker, and Felix Pryor. Included was the listing of the "Top Twenty" biographies by Michael Nash and a listing of Nelson "places," for example, HMS VICTORY, the Nelson Galleries at the NMM and the RNM, Lloyd's Nelson Collection, and Burnham Thorpe; Merton Place was demolished in 1846.

Second, David Harris, The Nelson Almanac: A Book of the Days Recording Nelson's Life and the Events that Shaped His Era, 1998, presented a popular format during the 18th and 19th centuries. Harris was a former commanding officer of HMS VICTORY who edited a series of essays, one at the beginning of each month of the calandar-almanac, for example, by Stephen Howarth, Tom Pocock, A.N. Ryan, Fiona Fraser Thomson, Anthony Cross, Robin Neillands, and Derek Allen.

And third, Dean King [**1933**], "Everyman Will Do His Duty": An Anthology of Firsthand Accounts from the Age of Nelson, 1997, co-edited by John Hattendorf, contained 22 articles by 17 authors, e.g., battle of the First of June, Cape St. Vincent, battle of Trafalgar, and an interview with Nelson.

In an anthology edited by Colin White [**3833**], Michael Nash estimated that there were over a thousand biographies of Nelson. Relying on his historiographical assessments, Nash formulated a listing of the top 20 biographies. As noted previously, Tom Pocock [**2867**], 1990, collected a bibliography on biographies of Nelson, citing about 200. **See 3., A.** In 1998, Gerald Jordan [**1837**] noted that there were more biographies of Nelson than any other figure in British history; they continued to appear.

There was an autobiography, of sorts: Horatio Nelson [**2620**], "A Sketch of My Life," in The Naval Chronicle [**2605**], vol. 3, 1800, a memoir he submitted to The Naval Chronicle [**2605**] at the request of John M'Arthur.

[Number 6, **3833**] Best known and most praised, worthy or not, was Robert Southey [**3396, 3398**] The Life of Nelson, 2 vols. 1813, 7th ed., 1844, 13th ed., 1867, claimed as the last to be corrected by the author, to a total of over 100 editions and reprints. Publishers included Murray, Gibbings, Cassell, Heinemann, Routledge, Constable, and Dent. A series of editors have commented: F.C. Rivington, David Hannay, Geoffrey Callender, Henry Newbolt, E.R.H. Harvey, Robert Madison, Carola Oman, Alan Palmer, and Eric Grove. It was by the then Poet Laureate and was seen as one of the most successful biographies of all time. The biography originated from a review of four works about Nelson in the Quarterly Review [**3398**], February 1810. The reviews were of Charnock [**622**], Harrison [**1534**], Churchill [**636**], and Clarke [**649**]. The publisher, John Murray, urged Southey to expand this into a biography. The brother of Southey, Thomas, a naval officer, assisted in the technical aspects. The biases of Southey were obvious: anti-Napoleon and anti-Emma Hamilton. The conservative bias of Southey was contrasted to the radicalism of a prominent competitor, Thomas Babington Macaulay [**2222**], who wrote for the Edinburgh Review; all reviewed by W.A. Speck [**3404**], 2001. The Callender edition was best at correcting the numerous errors made by Southey. Elsewhere, Callender assessed Southey as "a rich, perhaps inexhaustible mine of noxious Nelsonian fallacies." One recent edition was in the Classics of Naval Literature series.

David Eastwood [**1010**], "Patriotism Personified: Robert Southey's Life of Nelson Reconsidered," 1991, described its history, an instant classic with enduring popularity. Southey created a Nelson acceptable to the Establishment when, in fact, his life was an enigma, was not a typical figure like Wellington, never quite conformed, deserted his wife, and served his country but on his own terms. Michael Nash [**2601**], 1991, wrote an article "to chronologize" the various editions of Southey: the best was the Dent Edition of 1922, edited by Geoffrey Callender. Commentaries on English biography were by Joseph Reed [**3040**] who noted it was widely read but factually inaccurate.

In his history of the British navy, 1847, Nicholas Harris Nicolas [**2641**] contended that Nelson had not received his due and proceeded to list his attributes: ardent loyalty, genuine patriotism, a conscientious sense of duty, the highest professional skill, a most generous disposition, the kindest heart, and the noblest aspirations. No mention was made of Emma Hamilton.

[Number 12, **3833**] John Knox Laughton [**2051**], The Nelson Memorial: Nelson and His Companions in Arms, 1896, was dedicated to Earl Nelson, a direct heir. An extensive bibliography was included. This edition became notorious because on the frontispiece, the "England Expects" flag signal was presented but the wrong flags were displayed; the wrong signal book had been used. The mistake was followed by others and not corrected until 1908. An abbreviated version by Laughton [**2050, 2052**], Nelson, 1895, in the English Men of Action series, came out at the same time and the entry by Laughton [**2055**], 1993, for the DNB [**930**] has been extracted and published, about 30 pages.

Henry Baylis [**2330**], The True Account of Nelson's Famous Signal, 1905, corrected Laughton. Correlli Barnett [**213**], the distinguished naval historian and controversial historian of modern British developments, used the signal as title of his naval history of the Second World War, Engage the Enemy More Closely, 1991.

[Number 13, **3833**] Alfred Thayer Mahan [**2330**], The Life of Nelson: The Embodiment of the Sea Power of Great Britain, 2 vols., 1897, was seen as the best on the professional life of Nelson but with unfortunate digressions about Emma Hamilton. Mahan himself had commanded sailing warships and was world renowned as a strategic thinker and analyst. As noted in "Lord Nelson: Master of Command," 1988, by Michael Palmer [**2735**], Mahan saw in Nelson "all that was right with the Royal Navy." Gerald Jordan [**1837**], "Mahan's Life of Nelson," 1998, noted that it remained the standard professional study of Nelson, yet his two Influence of Sea Power [**2328, 2329**] books outsold and have endured longer than the biography of Nelson.

[Number 16, **3833**] Carola Oman [**2703**], Nelson, 1946, was the most substantial of the older biographies. It opened with an extensive bibliographical essay. Oman conducted extensive research, learning more about persons associated with the early life of Nelson, for example, a Canadian girl with whom he was close, his captain, William Locker, William Cornwallis, and, even Prince William Henry, over whom he served and the future King William IV. She described the evolution of the relations with Emma Hamilton: hostess, nurse, confidante, and lover. In a new introduction to the edition of 1996, Stephen Howarth [**1694**], himself a biographer of Nelson, saw this biography as so important that "the entire canon of Nelson historiography is either pre-Oman or post-Oman." As noted, Michael Nash declared it "as incomparably the best modern biography" of Nelson. A variation was Carola Oman [**2702**], Lord Nelson, 1954, in the Brief Lives series.

[Number 18, **3833**] Three works were by Oliver Warner [**3778, 3775, 3772, 3771**]: Victory: The Life of Nelson, 1958, A Portrait of Lord Nelson, 1958, and Nelson, 1975, the two former being bicentennial commemorations of the birth of Nelson and the latter being a masterly biography, knowledgeable, readable, and generous; some saw Warner as the best of the post-World War II biographers. The Portrait work surveyed the portraits of Nelson. Later, Richard Walker [**3741**] updated that survey.

[Number 20, **3833**].Tom Pocock [**2866**], Horatio Nelson, 1987, was one of several Nelson studies by Pocock, seen as a foremost authority on Nelson since the 1980s; this a "warts and all" biography, for example, stressing the vanity, greed, and cruelty to his wife of Nelson. Pocock computed the time Horatia, born 5 February 1801, was conceived: concluding the event occurred aboard HMS FOUDOYANT. Another Pocock [**2869**] entry was Nelson and His World, 1968, which followed the pertinent events and personalities in the life of Nelson, for example, Burnham Thorpe, schools attended, the funeral, Captain Maurice Suckling, Emma Hamilton, and Horatia. Tom Pocock [**2874**], The Young Nelson in the Americas, 1980, recounted the formative period of his career. Nelson gained his captaincy at age 21. His service then was on an expedition to the Caribbean. Among other things, Nelson met Fanny Nesbit, his future wife.

[Number 3, **3833**] David Howarth [**1694**], Nelson: The Immortal Memory, 1988, was co-authored by his son, Stephen. The Howarths were anxious to explain how and why Nelson became the epitome of sea power in the age of sailing ship warfare and such a model of naval leadership. The answers: supreme confidence, brilliant strategic insight, immense moral courage, and affection of his brother officers for him.

There was a biography in 1801 "by a neighbor", a Norwich printer, J. Payne [**2797**], Memoir of the Life of Admiral Lord Nelson. John Charnock [**622**], Biographical Memoirs of Lord Viscount Nelson, 2 vols., 1802, included an edition published before the death of Nelson, subsequent editions were in 1806 and 1810. One source was the correspondence between Nelson and his mentor, Captain William Locker.

Archibald Duncan [**989, 988**], The Life of Horatio Lord Viscount Nelson, 1805, was earliest to press after the death. A supplement was A Correct Narrative of the Funeral of Horatio Lord Viscount Nelson, 1806.

[Number 1, **3833**] Francis William Blagdon [**343**], Graphic History of the Life, Exploits and Death of Horatio Nelson, 1806, was an immediate best-seller at the time, 50,000 copies at six pence each. It featured good coverage of the funeral and anecdotes, for example, Nelson and the polar bear and Nelson himself explaining "the Nelson Touch" to his captains. It had a mediocre narrative but excellent engravings, including color.

[Number 2, **3833**] James Harrison [**1534**], The Life of Horatio, Lord Viscount Nelson, 2 vols., 1806, allegedly was commissioned, even "dictated," by Emma Hamilton with a specific agenda: to establish her claims on the government, Harrison seen as "a hireling." Lady Nelson was singled out and "disgraced by disparaging and unjust allusions." As noted, Nash placed it at number 2; Carola Oman saw it as "lowest in esteem" of the Nelson biographies; David Hannay called it "one of the most nauseous of known books," and J.K. Laughton assessed it as "a pack of lies."

[Number 17, **3833**] Frederick Lloyd [**2175**], 1806, touted his biography as "an accurate and impartial life"; pirated in an American edition credited to William Bolton.

T.O. Churchill [**636**], The Life of Lord Nelson, Duke of Bronte, 1808, was illustrated with engravings and curious use of that obscure title, "Duke of Bronte." Nicolas [---] condemned it: "a wretched compilation, intended as a vehicle of some equally wretched engravings."

[Number 5, **3833**] James Clarke [**649**], 1809, and John M'Arthur, The Life and Services of Horatio, Viscount Nelson, 2 vols., 1809 and a later 3-vol. edition, 1840, was touted as "the official life" and was filled with anecdotes. They had access to family papers. The tome weighed 21 pounds. Documents and various original manuscripts were incorporated with inadequate connecting narrative. The authors were editors of the valuable Naval Chronicle [**2605**]. Laughton [**2050**] was critical: "ponderous" and error-prone. Southey [**3396**] denounced it. Nevertheless, this became the most important source for many subsequent studies, including those of Southey and Laughton. Stephen Howarth noted that Clarke-M'Arthur were "constrained by mores and morals of their age" and, thus, avoided the relationships with Emma Hamilton.

[Number 9, **3833**] Thomas James Pettigrew [**2838**], Memoirs of the Life of Vice-Admiral Lord Viscount Nelson, 2 vols., 1849, had an expose quality, openly asserting that Horatia was the daughter of Nelson and Emma Hamilton. Pettigrew acquired letters from Emma Hamilton. There were accusations that she forged the handwriting of Nelson and doctored the letters. Critics saw it as better suited for "the School of Scancal" and "to stamp the memory of Nelson with infamy." The publication created a sensation, especially the insistance by Pettigrew that Horatia was, in fact, the daughter of Nelson and Emma Hamilton. It precipitated a series of letters, for and against, in The Times. Scandal continued and intensified after this work.

[Number 7, **3833**] Anonymous, The Letters of Lord Nelson to Lady Hamilton, 2 vols., 1814, contained the most intimate correspondence from Nelson to Emma Hamilton, with clarifications about Horatia. Again, it created a sensation, much revulsion, and a huge scandal. Again, accusations of forgeries abounded. In fact, some were not genuine. Who supplied them? Probably Francis Oliver, secretary to William Hamilton. Oliver and Emma Hamilton increasingly disagreed after the death of William Hamilton; more likely him than Emma Hamilton or Harrison.

Two other works came out in the mid-19th century: Francis Rivington [**3073**], Life of Horatio Lord Viscount Nelson, 1822, and Joseph Allen [**46**], Life of Viscount Nelson, 1852.

[Number 10, **3833**] John Cordy Jeffreson [**1795**], Lady Hamilton and Lord Nelson: A Historical Biography, 2 vols., 1888, was a novelist who relied heavily on the Morrison [**2562, 2563**] manuscripts. Jeffreson touted sorting out the Nelson-Emma Hamilton relationship. He also wrote a long account [**1796**], Queen of Naples and Lord Nelson, 2 vols., 1889.

An anonymous publication, actually by Matthew Barker [**206**], calling himself "The Old Sailor," The Life of Nelson, 1836, was praised by Nicolas [**2639**] as "the fullest collection of facts and anecdotes." The Barker Collection was described by J.K. Laughton [**2041**], 1913.

[Number 8, **3833**] Nicholas Harris Nicolas [**2639**], The Dispatches and Letters of Vice-Admiral Lord Nelson, 7 vols., 1844-1846, was a massive collection completed in 1846, a total of 3500 documents. Nicolas had full access to the essential manuscripts held by the niece of Nelson, Lady Bridport. Eventually Parliament authorized purchase of Nelson correspondence and papers; the ultimate collection in the then British Museum totaled 92 vols.; the exception was no access to the Clarke-M'Arthur collection, at least at first. Horatia was able to convince Nicolas that she was not the daughter of Nelson. Carola Oman, Oliver Warner, and Stephen Howarth assessed it as the most important work on Nelson of the 19th century. Callender saw it as the noblest memorial to the personality of Nelson. Chatham Publishers reprinted all seven volumes, 1997-1998.

[Number 11, **3833**] Alfred Morrison [**2562, 2563**], The Collection of Autograph Letters and Historical Documents Formed by Alfred Morrison, 13 vols., 1883-1897, included the Nelson and Hamilton Papers and a catalogue. This was a collector of autographs and letters referred to as "Morrison," a wealthy man and prominent collector. It included the collection of letters purchased in 1886 from Finch Hatton, heir to Sir William Hamilton. Morrison died in 1897 and his collection, 3300 lots, was auctioned by Sotheby's in 1919. The sale lasted 18 days and brought in 150,600 pounds.

G. Lathom Browne [**477**], Nelson: The Public and Private Life of Horation Viscount Nelson as Told by Himself, His Comrades, and His Friends, 1891, had earlier produced a biography of Wellington. Browne refused to believe that Horatia was the daughter of Nelson and Emma Hamilton.

[Number 14, **3833**] Charles Beresford [**303**], Nelson and His Times, 2 vols., 1897, was an early account profusely illustrated in folio size, including 450 pictures, several color prints, and incorporating much rhetorical glorification of Nelson. Beresford was a colorful, controversial Irish lord-naval officer-member of Parliament, who, incidentally, led powerful opposition to Lord Jacky Fisher in the early 1900s.

Trafalgar-death centennial publications were as follows: William Clark Russell [**3183, 3181**], The Life of Nelson in a Series of Episodes, 1905, and Horatio Nelson and the Naval Supremacy of England: A Biography, 1923, in the Heroes of the Nation series, presenting graphic descriptions of the primary battles and was enlightening on the notorious Carraciolo affair at Naples; Clara Gye [**1435**], 1905, "his life as told by himself," and James Thursfield [**3618**], Nelson and Other Studies, 1909, was a series of essays including a centennial tribute to Nelson. There was "no intention to rival Southey" [**3396**].

Arthur Corbett-Smith [**762**], Nelson: The Man, 1926, was highly critical of his personal life: chapter titles included: "Nelson Goes Berserk,"

"Nelson's Love for Emma," and "Nelson Descended into Hell." The effort of George Aston [**153**], <u>Nelson</u>, 1927, was for <u>Benn's Sixpenny Library</u> series.

[Number 17, **3833**] G.P.B. Naish [**2594**], <u>Nelson's Letters to His Wife</u>, 1958, a publication of the NRS, contained documents including letters to his wife and information about the problems within the marriage, plus some other documents concerning the navy. One source was the Nelson Museum, Monmouth.

C.S. Forester [**1155, 1138**], <u>Nelson</u>, 1929, later assessed this contribution as coming from his "hack biographer" days. It was the "unacknowledged prototype" for his Hornblower novels; 27 incidents in the ten novels directly linked to the life of Nelson. There was an edition in 2001.

[Number 15, **3833**] Clennell Wilkinson [**3858**], <u>Nelson</u>, 1931, set out to make Nelson more human, noting frequent ill-health, among the first to treat Nelson-Emma Hamilton sympathetically as a great romance, and including many anecdotes.

Mark Kerr [**1921**], <u>The Sailor's Nelson</u>, 1932, utilized the letters of Nelson to his friend and mentor, Captain Locker; "there is more to Nelson than the 'Lady Emma' side of the story." It was "the unique charm of our best-loved hero, . . . and the greatest war strategist and tactition in history but also foremost leader of men amongst the warriors of the world." William Cuthbert Brian Tunstall [**3664**], <u>Nelson</u>, 1933, was in the <u>Brief Lives</u> series.

C.J. Britton [**446**], <u>New Chronicles of the Life of Lord Nelson</u>, 1947, touted "a useful notebook of facts of Nelsoniana." His aim was to set the record straight, for example, there was no "blind eye," only that the right eye had ceased to function; the "yo-yo" analogy of Nelson being manipulated by Napoleon as he frantically sought the enemy fleet on a wild goose chase to the West Indies, 1803-1805, was "an utterly preposterous legend," and the dedication was to Emma, Lady Hamilton, "whose faults the Country remembered, and whose loving charms and the dead voice of DUTY the nation forgot."

Ranalt Capes [**573**], <u>Poseidon: A Personal Study of Admiral Lord Nelson</u>, 1947, bordered on expose. "At sea he was master of his fate. Ashore he was at the mercy of his emotions." Capes touted a psychological approach, apologetics on why he was vulnerable to Emma Hamilton.

W.M. James [**1786**], <u>The Durable Monument: Horatio Nelson</u>, 1948, was actually Admiral Sir William Milbourne James, GCB, who, at one time, used HMS VICTORY as his flagship when he was Commander-in-Chief, Portsmouth, during World War II, "a remarkable experience." Russell Grenfell [**1397**, <u>Horatio Nelson</u>, 1949, with various subtitles, assessed in the introduction by Stephen Roskill as "the best and fairest short biography." George Naish [**2593**], <u>Nelson and Bronte: An Illustrated Guide to His Life and Times</u>, 1959, was a collection of materials from the NMM prepared "for the less informed." Arthur Bryant [**493, 496**], <u>Nelson</u>, 1970, was actually selections from his trilogy on the Wars of the French Revolution and Napoleon.

[Number 19, **3833**] Geoffrey Bennett [**293**], Nelson the Commander, 1972, was by a professional naval officer and stressed the naval achievements of Nelson.

Christopher Lloyd [**2165**], Nelson and Sea Power, 1973, in Men and Their Times series, covered professional and personal matters. Roy Hattersley [**1571**], Nelson, 1974, in The Great Commanders series, was by a member of the Cabinet in a Labor Government who, in the early 1970s, had been a visiting fellow at Harvard University. Ernle Bradford [**412**], Nelson: The Essential Hero, 1977, was a popular biography consisting of 37 chapters and an index.

David Walder [**3735**], Nelson: A Biography, 1977, was praised when it was published; included an extensive historiographical survey. Richard Hough [**1684**] published a biography in 1980. Christopher Hibbert [**1622**], Nelson: A Personal History, 1994, as the subtitle implied, devoted much to Nelson and Emma Hamilton and was informative about the death of Nelson, the voyage home, and the funeral. An addendum described the "fate" of 80 related persons, including two pages on Emma Hamilton. Pieter Van der Merwe [**3719**], Nelson, 1995, was in the Great Leader series for the NMM.

Roger Morriss [**2572**], Nelson: An Illustrated History, 1995, co-edited by Brian Lavery and Stephen Seuchar, was another impressive production for the NMM; as was Roger Morriss, [**2573**], Nelson: The Life and Letters of a Hero, 1996, both exquisitely illustrated. Terry Coleman [**701**], Nelson: The Man and the Legend, 2001, was a recent addition about the man and the myth.

Leo Marriott [**2397**], What's Left of Nelson?, 1995, was a curious title for a biography.

And forthcoming to commemorate the Nelson Decade and Trafalgar 200 were: R.J.B. Knight [**1965**], [Nelson: A Bicentennial Biography], the contribution to the celebration by Penguin, projected for 2005; Brian Lavery [**2075**], projected 30,000 words published by the British Library and Andrew Lambert [**2004**], Professor of Naval History, King's College, University of London. Related was Colin White [**3836**], 2001, who described his Nelson Letters Project, sponsored by the NMM and the RNM. 550 previously unpublished letters have been accumulated to add to the published ones.

A series of foreign contributions were as follows: in French, Paul E.D. Forgues [**1157**], 1860, a standard biography and Jacques de Langlade [**2024**], Nelson: Biographie, 1990, concentrating on the battles, and in German: Friedrich Kircheisen [**1946**], Nelson: The Establishment of British World Dominion, 1931, "dedicated to the German Navy." Touting "a complete picture": "his hitherto spotless name he besmirched through his brutal behavior in Naples and his undignified relations with Lady Hamilton." And for juveniles there was Frank Knight [**1957**], The Hero, 1969.

2. Operations and Naval Career

The most controversial and the most commented upon of all of the activities of Nelson concerned Naples and the Kingdom of the Two Sicilies during the period 1798-1801. Here was where he met and romanced with Emma Hamilton. Here was where he was a chief British contact with the royal family of the kingdom. Here was where the sensational case of Francesco Caracciolo, an admiral who was executed during a Jacobin revolutionary movement. Caracciolo was accused of collaboration with the French. Southey [3396] was most accusatory in this matter, claiming Nelson instigated the execution because of his jealousy about the superior seamanship of Caracciolo. The NRS felt compelled to enter the frey with H.C. Gutteridge [1427], Nelson and the Neapolitan Jacobins: Documents Relating to the Suppression of the Jacobin Revolution at Naples, June 1799, 1903, with apologetics for Nelson. F.P. Badham [170], Nelson at Naples: A Journal for June 10-31, 1799 Refuting Recent Misstatements of Captain Mahan and Professor J.K. Laughton, 1900, was another account rising to the defense of Nelson. Accusatory of Nelson, the Hamiltons, and the royal family was Constance Stocker [3457], Naples in 1799, 1903. The background of The French in Italy, 1796-1799, 1957, was provided by Augus Heriot [1606].

An overview and background of the matter of the royal family of Naples was Harold Acton [8], The Bourbons of Naples, 1734-1825, 1956. Nelson had first called at Naples in 1793 at the time of the siege of Toulon. He returned in triumph immediately after the battle of the Nile.

Denis Orde [2713], Nelson's Mediterranean Command, 1997, was a broader view of British naval strategy and a series of threats of invasion, for example in the late 1790s and the early 1800s. The intricacies of command and commanders of the Mediterranean fleet were reviewed. Similarly, the activities of Russia and the Russian fleet entering the Mediterranean as ally of the British were dealt with in A.E. Sokol [3387], 1949. This involved Nelson as diplomat. Ludovic Kennedy [1879], alternate titles: Nelson's Band of Brothers and Nelson and His Captains, 1951, set the relationships of his captains in context. Frank Hoffman [1648], 1996, assessed Nelson as a "littoral leader," rather than a naval strategist of the "blue-water school." He functioned best in the littorals, peripheral areas such as in riverine warfare, amphibious operations, and in opportunities requiring innovation, initiative, and adaptability.

Other aspects of the career of Nelson were covered. "Nelson's Uncle: Captain Maurice Suckling, RN," 2002, was introduced by David Syrett [3548]. The naval officer of the 18th century required "interest" and Suckling provided that for the young Nelson. Brian Kirby [1942], 1989, recounted naval operations in the mid-1780s in the Caribbean. Nelson commanded a small warship enforcing the Navigation Acts, in the process seizing several American merchant ships. Were his actions overzealous?

Cecil Isaacson [**1757**], 1991, wrote of several matters. Nelson was on half-pay during the five years before 1793. On a tombstone in Fahan, Ireland was recorded the death of Midshipman Horatio Nelson of Burnham Thorpe, 1793-1811. He was not kin. E. Hallam Moorhouse [**2540**], 1913, wrote of Nelson in England. Louis Hodgkin [**1646**], 1991, wrote of Nelson and Bath. While on shore, Nelson made a foray into the west, surveying in the Forests of Dean. Edward Gill [**1285**], Nelson and the Hamiltons on Tour, 1987, described the investigation of forests by Nelson in 1802, accompanied by the Hamiltons. R.J.B. Knight [**1966**], 2001, clarified some controversy about those activities, revising the rationale for these matters and correcting misconceptions about availability of oak wood conveyed by Robert Albion [**29**].

3. Letters, Journals, Literature, Art, and Assessments

Colin White [**3832, 3836**], coordinating the Nelson Decade [**2624**] and Trafalgar 200, described his forthcoming project, The Collection Edition of Nelson Letters.

Joseph Callo [**560**], Nelson Speaks: Admiral Lord Nelson in His Own Words, 2001, was a collection of excepts from his letters and dispatches. E. Hallam Moorhouse [**2539**], "Nelson as Seen in His Letters," 1911, included profound assessments from extensive study and knowledge about Nelson. Geoffrey Rawson [**3025**], published Letters from Lord Nelson, 1949. Less extensive and more specific was Rawson [**3027**], Nelson's Letters from the Leeward Islands, 1953, selections from manuscripts held by the PRO and British Museum. These were descriptive of activities of Nelson in the 1780s.

John Knox Laughton [**2045**] published Letters and Despatches of Viscount Nelson, 1886, selected from the Nicolas [**2639**] collection. Two other collections were by William Clark Russell [**3184, 3185**], Nelson's Words and Deeds, 1890, and Pictures from the Life of Nelson, 1897. Clarence Dane [**852**], The Nelson Touch: An Anthology of Lord Nelson's Letters, 1942, touted "devastating frankness" about his life from Nelson himself and the only unbiased and consistent view of Nelson. He concluded with the famous "Nelson Prayer" of 21 October 1805.

Gilbert Hudson [**1714, 2626**], Nelson's Last Diary, September 13-October 21, 1805, 1917, edited the authoritative version acquired from the Probate Registry, Somerset House. It was this document in which Nelson urged that Emma Hamilton and Horatia be provided for by king and country.

Felix Pryor [**2959**], The Fabor Book of Letters, 1988, contained a newly discovered letter from Nelson to Emma Hamilton, 29 January 1800, the first love letter; also subsequent love letters and the last one, 20 October 1805. A.N.L. Munby [**2583**], The Cult of the Autograph Letter in England, 1962, included a section on letters of Nelson-Emma Hamilton, for example, T.J. Pettigrew [**2838**] purchased some from Emma Hamilton and Morrison [**2562**] accumulated a large collection which was eventually auctioned by Sotheby's, bringing in a huge sum. Joshua White [**3841**], <u>Memoirs of the Professional Life of Horatio Nelson, Viscount and Baron Nelson</u>, 1806, informed little.

Gerald Jordan [**1835**], 1989, wrote about admirals as heroes. Anniversaries, processions, and parades were symbols and rituals, for example, in the cases of Vernon and Nelson, to bolster the government in power. Nelson became a popular cult figure. Then, the scandal of the tour across Europe in 1800 of Nelson and the Hamiltons. The establishment ostracized Nelson but not the rest of the nation.

4. The Funeral and Memorials

The standard work on the death was William Beatty [**262**], <u>The Death of Lord Nelson: The Authentic Narrative</u>, 1807, by the surgeon of HMS VICTORY describing first hand the death of Nelson, events preceding it and after it.

Timothy Jenks [**1800**], 2000, described the funeral, 9 January 1806, "the apotheosis of Nelson." Harry Garlick [**1252**], 2000, made observations about state funerals and "the theatre of power." An example was that of Nelson. Rodney Mace [**2322**], <u>Trafalgar Square</u>, 1976, described its evolution: in 1839, the Nelson Memorial Competition resulted in the winning design by William Railton. The reliefs at the base depict Cape St. Vincent, the Nile, Copenhagen, and Trafalgar; the statue was by Edward Baily. A series of subsequent major demonstrations in the square were described in some detail. **See item f.**

Margaret Gatty [**1260**], <u>Recollections of the Life of the Rev. A.J. Scott, DD, Lord Nelson's Chaplain</u>, 1842, was the daughter of Scott, Chaplain of HMS VICTORY. P.K. Crimmin [**803**], 1997, tapped a collection of documents at the Wellcome Institute which detailed operations of the British Mediterranean fleet, 1796-1805. The focus was on health, mostly about victualling. All was enlightening about daily life and conditions.

G.S. Parsons [**2786**] had served with Nelson at Naples and recounted <u>Nelsonian Reminiscences</u>, 1843, reprinted by Chatham in its <u>Sailors' Tales</u> series, 1998. Included was an early description of Emma Hamilton; "divine Emma captivated all." The flag-captain of Nelson at the Nile, Edward Berry [**306**], published his memoirs of the occasion, 1798, originally anonymously, "By an Officer of Rank in the Squadron." Yet another former commanding officer of HMS VICTORY, this during the 1980s, Charles Addis [**22**], wrote of <u>The Men Who Fought with Nelson in HMS VICTORY at Trafalgar</u>, 1988.

And there were the numerous accounts of the extensive wounds experienced by Nelson, their circumstances, the results, and the effects on him. A good beginning was P.D.G. Pugh [**2964**], <u>Nelson and His Surgeons</u>, 1968, a product from a conference of the British Orthopedic Association and an exhibition, Royal Naval Hospital, Haslar, April 1967, summarizing the illnesses, wounds, and modern analyses of them. 25 surgeons treated him during his career thus his health was well documented. His early health problems were "ague," common to the marshy areas of East Anglia, and malaria, caught in the West Indies. Nelson was blinded but did not lose his right eye. After the battle of Santa Cruz de Tenerife, his right arm was amputated, the result of a grapeshot wound to his elbow. His step-son, Josiah Nisbet, applied a tourniquet which probably saved his life. The exhibition included the bullet-ball which killed him, a uniform coat pierced by a bullet, and death masks. Leslie LeQuesne [**2106**], 1955, summarized his wounds.

D'Arcy Power [**2934**], 1932, and H.T.A. Bosanquet [**366**], 1952, wrote of the amputation operation of July 1797. Sydney Fremantel [**1193**], 1950, described the first writing by Nelson with his left hand, a dispatch describing the attack written the next day. T.C. Barras [**217**], 1986, wrote of the lost eye in a journal of the Ophthalmological Society. Edith Keate [**1847**], 1936, wrote of the mystery of the coat of Nelson, "A Story of Greenwich."

After the battle of Copenhagen and before Nelson returned to the Mediterranean in pursuit of the combined French-Spanish fleet in 1803, he purchased Merton Place, an ancient priory estate of 160 acres. He returned for a short time just before setting off for Trafalgar in the fall of 1805. It was demolished in the mid-19th century; the location was near the current South Wimbledon Tube Station. Nelson lived there with the Hamiltons and Horatia. William Hamilton died in April 1803. This period was depicted as idyllic in the life of Nelson. The only sign was a memorial garden and the Nelson pew in the Parish Church. Accounts included Peter Hopkins [**1667**], A History of Lord Nelson's Merton Place, 2000, Philip Rathbone [**3018**], Paradise Merton: The Story of Nelson and the Hamiltons at Merton Place, 1973, and William Henry Chamberlain [**608**], Reminiscences of Old Merton, 1923. A curious piece by John Webb [**3796**], 2001, speculated about whether Nelson was a Mason. It was error-prone and not convincing.

John Twells [**3678**], Nelson: The Golden Orb: A Sonnet History, 1995, was a life of Nelson in Elizabethan sonnet form, 218 sonnet couplets. Section titles of the seven parts included "Spanish Triumph," "Band of Brothers," "A Foreign Court," and "Long Chase."

Terence Rattigan [**3019**], "Bequest to the Nation: A Play," was a drama about Nelson, first at the West End Theatre, 1969. It originated from a TV script; later made into a movie. The setting was August-September 1805 and described Nelson-Emma Hamilton relations through the eyes of a nephew, George Matcham.

Colin White [**3835**], The Nelson Legend, reviewed the myths and legends. Marianne Czisnik [**842**] is preparing a dissertation, "Admiral Nelson: Image and Icon."

The premier authority on portraits of Nelson was R.J.B. Walker [**3740, 3741**], both 1998, in an article and a book, the latter for the Royal Naval Museum, including a catalogue of all known portraits. There were 140 illustrations, 40 in color. Portraits and Nelsoniana were the focus of Oliver Warner [**3771**], Lord Nelson: A Guide to Reading with a Note on Contemporary

Portraits, 1955. Michael Nash [**2599**], 1993, The Nelson Masks, was the proceedings of a symposium, Royal Naval Museum, Portsmouth, October 1992, investigating the three masks. Geoffrey Callender [**549**], 1941, presented details about the effigy of Nelson in Westminster Abbey, a draped figure of Nelson carved from wood, the head and left hand in wax.

Thomas Foley [**1131**], The Nelson Centenary, 1905, featured the Nelson family history. The British Museum [**444**], 1905, sponsored a special centennial exhibition of books, prints, and medals associated with Nelson; the catalogue was published. Over 110 pages, it was an invaluable source on Nelsoniana. A similar centennial exhibition and catalogue [**595**], 1905, came from the Royal United Services Institution.

Remembering Nelson: As Told to Lt. Commander John Lea, RN: A Record of Lily Lambert McCarthy, 1995, were recollections by one much influenced by the story of Nelson. She began collecting Nelsoniana; subsequently contributed to the RNM, Portsmouth.

There were a number of Nelson manuscript collections. At the NMM: K.F. Lindsay-MacDougall [**2140**], 1955, and R.J.B. Knight [**1964**], 2000. Knight described 12 collections, for example, papers of Nelson, Lady Nelson, and Emma Hamilton. James Baxter [**248**], 1929, described the collection of Nelson manuscripts held at the Harvard College Library. Elsewhere, the famous Nelson Room at Lloyd's of London has been described. In Monmouth, Wales, an entire museum was devoted to Nelson, the Nelson Museum. **See 4., B. and 4., C.**

Arnold White [**3830**], Nelson and the Twentieth Century, 1905, was a centennial assessment. It professed "to apply the spirit of Nelson's teaching to some problems of today." Included was seeming finality concerning Emma Hamilton: J.K. Laughton had proved beyond question that Emma Hamilton deserved no consideration and that Nelson was mistaken. Ronald Andidora [**101**], Iron Admirals: Naval Leadership in the Twentieth Century, 2000, cited the legacy of Nelson on the RN, then proceeded to recount the careers of his heirs of the 20th century, for example, Togo, Jellicoe, Spruance, and Halsey.

Joseph Callo [**558, 559**], Legacy of Leadership: Lessons from Admiral Lord Nelson, 2000, and "Nelson: Character Counts in Combat," 1995, reviewed the "qualities" of Nelson: physical and mental courage, aggressiveness, religious belief, patriotism, knowledge of the sea, and regard for subordinates; not a role model for personal conduct. Attributes of character were also stressed by Susan Harmon [---], 1989. George Matham [**2463**], Notes on the Character of Admiral Lord Nelson, 1861, was an early assessment. Two prominent persons of different generations joined in: William Wordsworth [**3959**], Character of the Happy Warrior: A Poem, 1913, and Caspar Weinberger [**3805**], "The Nelson Touch, 1987; that latter being the title by Walter Jerrold [**1807**], 1918.

For the Nelson Society, David Shannon [**3289**] collected Nelsoniana, 1999, an anthology of pieces from a magazine of the 19th century. Colin White [**3834**] has recently published The Nelson Encyclopedia, 2002, a comprehensive sourcebook. It was to be expected that Nelson would be incorporated in the multimedia movement: a CD-ROM with more promised: <u>Nelson and His Navy</u> [**2625**], a CD-ROM, 1996. Included were scenarios of the great battles and a virtual tour of HMS VICTORY.

A curious novel, <u>Losing Nelson</u>, 1999, was by Barry Unsworth [**3698**]. A Charles Cleasby became obsessed, re-enacted all of the great battles in his basement, and focused on four days in Naples, June 1799.

The Nelson example persisted. Ian Thorne [**3609**], 1997, saw Jackie Fisher as "the greatest admiral since Nelson." Colin Lyle [**2208**], 1995, lamented "A Nelsonian Jutland?" The "defeat" of Jellicoe did not have to be. It was "an unNelsonian tactical draw." Could Nelson have done better? Similarly, J.A. English [**1049**], 1979, wrote of "the Trafalgar syndrome: Jutland and the indecisiveness of modern naval warfare." It might have been another Trafalgar.

Inevitably, a battleship was named HMS NELSON, built in the 1920s and describe by Ronald Careless [**577**], 1985.

5. The Women

The best place to begin was Tom Pocock [**2870**], <u>Nelson's Women</u>, 1999, a product of the Nelson Decade [**2624**]. The sequence began with the mother and ended with the daughter. Three who were wooed in vain before Fanny Nisbet and Emma Hamilton were included.

An introductory survey was by the naval novelist, Showell Styles [**3500**], <u>Mr. Nelson's Ladies</u>, 1953, albeit romanticized but including only women before he became famous, thus, no Emma Hamilton: eight in all, for example, Lady Parker, an Indian girl, Chetuma, Virginia Simpson, Rose Andrews, and Fanny Nisbet, whom he married.

As can be seen by the emotion of the attacks for and against various works, the matter of the relationship between Nelson and Emma Hamilton remained controversial well into the 20th century. The "official" biographer, James Clarke [**649**], was accused of "improvising the style" and even falsifying evidence to protect reputations; concentrating on his "splendid public character," ignoring the last four years, and careful to "consider the susceptibilities of survivors."

Edith Keate [**1848**], <u>Nelson's Wife</u>, 1939, was a biography of Lady Nelson. They had met in 1787 and separated in 1801; she died in 1831. Her son by her first marriage was Josiah Nisbet. Her granddaughter destroyed most of her papers; her letters from Nelson were purchased by the British Museum. Patrick Delaforce [**901**], <u>Nelson's First Love: Fanny's Story</u>, 1988, was a combination of fact and fiction about Lady Nelson, with accounts of her son, Josiah, and William, the future King William IV.

Inevitably, Emma Hamilton has attracted interest. Walter Sichel [**3313, 3314**] was the first with a sympathetic and balanced biography, on the occasion of the centennial of the death of Nelson: <u>Emma, Lady Hamilton: From New and Original Sources and Documents</u>, 1905, and an edition of <u>Memoirs of Emma,</u>

Lady Hamilton, the Friend of Lord Nelson and the Court of Naples, originally published anonymously in 1815.

Hilda Gamlin [**1231, 1232**], Emma, Lady Hamilton, 1891, was an older biography, one of the last perpetuating the illusions of the relationship of the Hamiltons and of Nelson-Emma Hamilton. Dependent on the Morrison [**2562, 2563**] collection and support from the family of Lady Nelson, Gamlin declared that Nelson and Emma Hamilton were "just good friends." In Nelson's Friendships, 2 vols., 1899, completed after the death of Gamlin, William Hamilton, a widower, accepted Emma to Naples as his ward and to further her education. Then came the "wounded warrior" in need of affectionate attention; the happy Hamiltons providing kindness to the unhappy and ailing Nelson. Back home, after the breakup of Nelson's marriage, Emma Hamilton searched for a home and acquired Merton Place where Nelson spent the happiest years of his life. Lady Nelson was put in the worst light. Accusations of forged letters and papers abounded. Emma escaped to Calais and died. Horatia was smuggled back into England dressed as a boy, married Rev. Phillip Ward, and lived happily, having nine children and dying in 1881. Esther Hallam Moorhouse [**2541, 2538**], 1906 and 1912, produced two illustrated biographies. Also, profusely illustrated, 23 of 36 being of Emma, and undated, was Henry Schumacher [**3251**], Nelson's Last Love.

In the format of a novel was Lily Beck [**268**], The Divine Lady: A Romance of Nelson and Emma Hamilton, 1924. Owen Sherrard [**3303**], A Life of Emma Hamilton, 1927, featured poignancy; after 1805, Emma Hamilton was ostracized and died a tragic death abroad in 1815. Marjorie Bowen [**395**], Patriotic Lady: A Study of Emma, Lady Hamilton and the Neapolitan Revolution of 1799, 1935, was thoroughly researched, sympathetic, and balanced. Oliver Warner [**3762**], Emma Hamilton and Sir William, 1960, was a general account. Jack Russell [**3177**], Nelson and the Hamiltons, 1969, was a popularized, cut-and-paste effort; they met first in 1793, when Nelson had "all his body parts." Hugh Tours [**3634**], The Life and Letters of Emma, Lady Hamilton, 1963, vowed to present a true picture of "a life which has been sometimes over-glamorized, sometimes unnecessarily maligned." Norah Lofts [**2181**], Emma Hamilton, 1978, was informative about her early life. Colin Simpson [**3322**], Emma: The Life of Lady Hamilton, 1983, focused on the Neapolitan years. Flora Fraser [**1184**], Emma, Lady Hamilton, 1986, was the standard biography, alternate title, Beloved Emma.

Two French contributions were, in the Great Adventuress series, Joseph Turquan [**3674**], 1913, concentrating on the Naples period, and Georges Blond [**356**], 1976, on Nelson and Emma Hamilton.

"That Hamilton Woman," 1991, was an article by K.R.M. Short [**3311**] describing the occasion for the premier of the movie by that name in the U.S., 19 March 1941. The producer-director was Alexander Korda, Laurence Olivier played Nelson, and Vivien Leigh played Emma Hamilton. The article focused on the Anglo-American aspect and the propaganda effect at a time when Britain was under siege. An obvious analogy between 1805 and 1940 was played up. The occasion was a factor in the steady shift in American position to aid the British.

William Hamilton has been studied. Brian Fothergill [**1166**], Sir William Hamilton: Envoy Extraordinary, 1969, recounted the career of this archeologist-diplomat, British ambassador to Naples. Beginning in 1783, Emma was his mistress, then his wife. Ian Jenkins [**1798**], 1996, reported on an exhibition at the British Museum, "Vases and Volcanoes," displaying the collection of William Hamilton, especially his collection of Greek vases.

And Horatia Nelson, the daughter, 1801-1881: Winifred Gerin [**1266**], 1970, produced a scholarly biography, "a major work on a minor subject." Much was about Emma Hamilton, recounting in detail "her stubborn and unsuccessful attempts to establish herself with pensions and honors, . . . then her degeneration and death. Horatia became the devoted and faithful wife of the Rev. Phillip Ward, had nine children.

6. HMS VICTORY

In December 1758, Parliament passed provision for a programme of 12 SOTLs. The largest was a First Rate, 100 guns, 3 decks, dimensions in feet: 226 by 52 by 25, 2162 tons. Construction was at Chatham Dockyard, the 5th ship of the programme, cost: 63,000 pounds, the 7th ship named VICTORY. There was delay as the Seven Years' War ended. VICTORY was launched in 1765, immediately decommissioned, and recommissioned in 1778. VICTORY was flagship for Admirals Keppel, Charles Hardy, Kempenfelt, Hyde Parker, Nelson, and Saumurez. In 1824, the tradition of the annual Trafalgar Day dinner aboard began.

In June 1921, Prince Louis Mountbatten, former First Sea Lord and then President of the SNR, launched the campaign, creating the Save the VICTORY Fund supported by the VICTORY Advisory Technical Committee. In 1922, it was decided to restore VICTORY and place it in a permanent position in Drydock Number 2 at Portsmouth, the oldest surviving drydock in the world. VICTORY remains on the active list and as a flagship in the RN; and a very popular attraction among the historic ships at the Portsmouth Naval Base.

Alan McGowan [**2250**], HMS VICTORY: Her Construction, Career, and Restoration, 1999, was a large folio size with 90 pages of exquisite color pictures and line drawings, the latter by John McKay. An older standard was A.R. Bugler [**505**], HMS VICTORY: Building, Restoration, and Repair, 2 vols., 1966.

Others were Geoffrey Callender [**557**], The Story of HMS VICTORY, 1913, John McKay [**2287**], The 100-Gun Ship VICTORY, 1987, in The Anatomy of the Ship series, Noel Hackney [**1442**], HMS VICTORY: Classic Ships, 1970, Frederick Engholm [**1048**], The Story of HMS VICTORY, 1944, and Bertie Smith [3347], HMS VICTORY: Nelson's Flagship at Trafalgar, 1939.

Kenneth Fenwick [**1083**], HMS VICTORY, 1959, touted a "life and times" history. Peter Goodwin [**1321**], Countdown to VICTORY: 101 Questions and Answers about HMS VICTORY, was a history of the ship profusely illustrated. The author was curator of HMS VICTORY. A bicentennial article was by Oliver Warner [**3767**], "HMS VICTORY, 1765-1965," 1965. Instrumental in Save the VICTORY in the early 1920s was L.G. Carr Laughton [**2061**], 1924, who wrote about archival research of technical records in preparation for the restoration. Edward Fraser [**1180**], 1922, wrote a 5-part series recounting histories of 4 predecessors and supporting the restoration. Philip Watts [**3794**], 1923, wrote on the preservation question.

R.O. Morris [**2558**], "HMS VICTORY and the Society for Nautical Research," 1990, reviewed the history of VICTORY, built during the 1750s at Chatham Dockyard; fleet flagship, 1805-1815, then, inactive and permanently moored at Portsmouth. In April 1921, VICTORY was moved to Number 2 Drydock, to be her permanent berth. SNR launched a preservation and restoration campaign, the Save the VICTORY Fund, raising 80,000 pounds. The Fund has continued to the present.

7. The Nelson Decade

Somewhat related was a commemoration: the Nelson Decade [**2624**], an extensive, well organized, bicentennial programme of special events associated with Admiral Lord Nelson and sponsored jointly by, among others, the NMM, RNM, SNR, the Nelson Society, the 1805 Club, and the King George Fund. An Official Nelson Coordinating Committee, ONCC, has been formed to plan, direct, and execute events and activities. Colin White [**3831**-3837] was appointed chair.

The "decade" was 1995 to 2005, corresponding with the decade of the greatest achievements of Nelson during the period 1795-1805. Already celebrated, among other things, have been commemorations of the battle of Cape St. Vincent, 1797, the battle of the Nile, 1798, and the battle of Copenhagen, 1801.

Examples of publications coming from the Nelson Decade sponsorship were Colin White [**3837**], 1797, Nelson's Year of Destiny, 1998, sponsored by the RNM with the enthusiastic support of the 1805 Club, focusing on the battles of Cape St. Vincent, 14 February, and Santa Cruz de Tenerife in July. The latest, detailed versions of these events were presented. R.E.G. Harris [**1531**], 1998, reported on the bicentennial occasion at Teneriffe, a re-enactment of Santa Cruz, 24 July 1997. The restored cutter of HMS VICTORY was included. British and Spanish naval units participated.

"St. Vincent 200," [**3210**], 1998, was the proceedings of a bicentennial international naval conference, Portsmouth, 5 February 1997, sponsored by the SNR, the Nelson Society, and the 1805 Club.

When Nelson and the Hamiltons departed from Naples in 1800, they opted to travel overland across Europe to the Channel. They passed through Vienna and met Joseph Haydn, who entertained them. Otto Deutsch **[916]**, <u>Admiral Nelson and Joseph Haydn</u>, 2000, was a Nelson Decade publication sponsored by the Nelson Society. Deutsch wrote the piece in German in 1982.

Trafalgar 200, a Festival, will be the culmination. It is planned that the VICTORY sail will go up again, the original having been displayed at the International Festival of the Sea, Portsmouth, August 1998, sponsored by the SNR. Six months of celebratory events will conclude with 21 October 2005. Among these will be the International Festival of the Sea, 2005, again at the Portsmouth Naval Base where IFOS 1998 and IFOS 2001 have already been celebrated. Featured will be and have been, the tall ship parade, dozens of the large 3-masted sailing ships of the various nations, used, among other things, for training of midshipmen during the summer.

The Royal Naval Museum is sponsoring the Nelson Biography Project **[2623]** and the Nelson Letters Project **[3832]**, anticipating publication for the bicentennial of his death in 2005.

Nelson has become the epitome of British naval history, the idol, symbol, and icon of extraordinary influence. In addition to the Nelson Decade **[2624]**, he has been celebrated and commemorated with and numerous portraits and statues, notably in Trafalgar Square, London; also in Edinburgh, Dublin, since destroyed, and Portsdown Hill, above Portsmouth. His memory was perpetuated by the Nelson Society and the 1805 Club. There are Nelson Galleries at both the National Maritime Museum, Greenwich, and the Naval History Museum, Portsmouth; a famous Nelson Collection at Lloyd's of London. **See 21., E. and items b. and f.**

B. WILLIAM BLIGH

1. Biographies and Studies

William Bligh, 1754-1817, became famous, even notorious, as a victim of mutinies, especially that aboard HMS BOUNTY in 1789. Born in 1754, son of a customs officer, Plymouth, Bligh died in Kent in 1817. He entered the RN at age 16 and rose through the officer ranks to admiral. Bligh originally made a deserved reputation, especially as a seaman, navigator, cartographer, and explorer, under Captain James Cook. **See 17., B. and 17., D.**

The first of a series of mutinies affecting Bligh was aboard HMS BOUNTY. A call for transplanting breadfruit trees from Pacific islands to the West Indies as cheap and abundant food for plantation slaves led to the Admiralty selecting Bligh as captain of the expedition and HMS BOUNTY, an armed transport, departing in 1787. The sponsors wanted a scientist and naturalist to lead; the Admiralty insisted on a naval officer. The breadfruit was collected at Tahiti when mutiny led by Fletcher Christian resulted in Bligh and eighteen loyal crewmen of the total of 46 men being forced into a 23-foot boat which Bligh then commanded and navigated with renowned brilliance for 3600 miles, successfully reaching the island of Timor fifty days later. Bligh eventually led a second, successful breadfruit venture. He rose in rank and stature.

Inevitably, the personality and psychological motivations of Bligh have been analyzed. That personality was definitely volatile. "Tyrant," "paranoid," "bad language," "that bastard," "damned to everlasting fame" as one of the favorite villains of the public, and causing the death of Cook were recurring accusations. "The growth of the BOUNTY legend" was a curious phenomenon. The Bligh-Christian relationship, possible homosexuality, has come under scrutiny, for example by R.Hough [1680] and M.Darby [859]; Geoffrey Rawson [3024] linked Bligh to the death of Cook. See 17., B.

Other mutinies were as follows: mutinous activity: at Sourabaya and aboard HMS DEFIANCE, 1795, as a captain during the infamous mutiny at the Nore in 1797, and 1805-1810, as Governor of New South Wales. Then, a violent conflict with John MacArthur in 1808 resulted in a military rebellion against Bligh who was deposed and later exonerated and restored. He was elected to the Royal Society and promoted to admiral.

In the Gavin Kennedy [1876] biography, over 300 biographical sources were listed about Bligh.

William Bligh [350-355] himself wrote accounts of pertinent events and responded to attacks. The Mutiny on Board HMS BOUNTY, 1790, and The Log of HMS BOUNTY, 1787-1789, 2 vols., 1936, with various editions and commentaries, for example, by Edward Hughes, Richard Bowman, Owen Rutter, J.A. Edgell, and Earl Mountbatten. The original log, at the PRO, was 900 pages. Also, A Voyage to the South Seas, 1975, The Bligh Notebook: Rough Account of Lt. William Bligh's Voyage in the BOUNTY Launch from the Ship to Tofua and from Thence to Timor, 18 April to 14 June 1789, 2 vols., 1987, was his account, the original of 1790 in the National Library of Australia. He described the launch, provisions, and navigation for the 3600 mile journey in this 23-foot launch with 19 persons over a period of 48 days. The Log of HMS PROVIDENCE, 1791-1793, 1976, described the second breadfruit voyage, this one a success. An Answer to Certain Assertions, 1794, was the response of Bligh to a pamphlet by Edward Christian [629], brother of Fletcher Christian, "to clear my character." In addition, there was Mutiny on the BOUNTY: The Story of Captain Bligh, Seaman, Navigator, Surveyor and the BOUNTY Mutineers [2592],1991, a summary version from the State Library of New South Wales. Paul Brunton [490], Awake Bold Bligh!: William Bligh's Letters Describing the Mutiny on HMS BOUNTY, 1989, combined three personal letters he wrote after the mutiny; a bicentennial publication.

Gavin Kennedy [1876, 1877] wrote Bligh, 1978, and Captain Bligh: The Man and His Mutinies, 1989, the latter a bicentennial publication, anniversary of the mutiny on the BOUNTY. Kennedy was trained as an economist. The blurb in the former book vowed to rehabilitate "the BOUNTY bastard." Apologetics for Bligh, Gavin Kennedy stressed the emotional instability of Fletcher Christian as a cause of the mutiny. One basis of that alleged instability was Christian family finances; the squandering of a family inheritance by an elder brother forced Fletcher Christian to pursue an undesirable career in the Royal Navy. Elsewhere, Kennedy concluded that Bligh was a great man with a temper, guilty of foul language and vindictiveness.

George Mackaness [**2281, 2278, 2280, 2279**], The Life of Vice-Admiral William Bligh, 2 vols., 1931, A Book of the BOUNTY, William Bligh and Others, 1938, Fresh Light on Bligh, 1949, and Captain William Bligh's Discoveries and Observations in Van Dieman's Land, 1943, were a series of works by this Australian scholar. Owen Rutter [**3192**], Turbulent Journey: A Life of William Bligh, Vice-Admiral of the Blue, 1936, concluded that Bligh was not a sadist, not deliberately and wantonly cruel. He accumulated a large collection of Bountiana in the 1930s. Richard Humble [**1725**], Captain Bligh, 1976, stressed balance: three mutinies, yet look at the accomplishments: "arguably the best surveyor the Navy has ever produced," that incredible 3600 mile voyage in the open boat, and stellar performances at those two great slugging matches, Camperdown and Copenhagen.

Roy Schreiber [**3250**], The Fortunate Adversities of William Bligh, 1991, began by trying to explain the Bligh-BOUNTY phenomenon: "why this unwarranted success?" Bligh was talented and lucky. Despite three mutinies in the RN and one as governor of New South Wales, he was promoted continuously, ending as Vice-Admiral. Cook was more important, Nelson was a greater sailor. Without the mutiny on the BOUNTY, Bligh, the famous tyrant of the seas, would have been ignored. Villains were popular. Comparisons were made to the treatment of Richard III by Shakespeare and with Captain Queeg.

The title attracted attention: "That BOUNTY Bastard": The True Story of Captain William Bligh, 1976, by Kenneth Allen [**47**]. Nevertheless, apologetics prevailed: Bligh was competent, beloved, respected, and successful. Those terms appeared on his tombstone, nothing about any mutiny on the tombstone. J.E. Chandler [**616**], "Beloved, Respected and Lamented": A Story of the Mutiny of the BOUNTY, 1973, was the title coming from the description on the tombstone of Bligh, St. Paul's Parrish Church, Lambeth. To that end, Chandler set out to correct the distortions and restore the image of Bligh as a humane and brilliant seaman, Chandler contending that he would have been happy to sail under Bligh.

Geoffrey Rawson [**3024**], Bligh of the BOUNTY, 1930, was well-written and impartial, devoting 60 of 240 pages to the mutiny on the BOUNTY. Bligh was linked to the death of Cook. Also, there was Joyce Nicholson [**2637**], Man against Mutiny: The Story of Vice-Admiral William Bligh, 1961.

The popular naval historian-novelist, Richard Hough [**1680**], Captain Bligh and Mr. Christian: The Men and the Mutiny, 1972, purported to have discovered "the real motives of the mutineers on the BOUNTY": Bligh was upset over the heterosexual activities of Fletcher Christian, his homosexual lover, with female natives on Tahiti. Critics say that was pure speculation with no evidence of such relationships.

The biographer of James Cook presented a lecture which was published in 1967: J.C. Beaglehole [252], Captain Cook and Captain Bligh. Rupert Gould [1345], 1928, wrote a piece summarizing the notes by Bligh on the third voyage of Cook, "Cook's Last Voyage," Bligh being the ship's Master during the voyage. The original was three volumes.

For some reason, poetry was the vehicle for four accounts: Lord Byron [535], "The Island," 1822; William Beard [261], "Valiant Martinet": The Adventures on Sea and Land of Captain William Bligh, 1956; J.M. Couper [775], The Book of Bligh, 1969, and E.T.A. Hoffman [1647], Haimatochare, 1924. Surprisingly, Byron was sympathic for Bligh. Beard was 90 pages, Couper contained no commentary or explanation, just six chapters of verse, and Hoffman was part of an extensive German satire, one episode of which was the mutiny on the BOUNTY.

A.H. Taylor [3572], 1937, wrote a piece on Bligh at the battle of Camperdown, commanding officer of HMS DIRECTOR. His log of the battle was said to be the most complete and informative. Madge Darby [857], Captain Bligh in Wapping, 1990, was a local item.

For Bligh [352] subsequently, there was a second, successful, breadfruit voyage, recounted by Ida Lee [2090], 1974, and Douglas Oliver [2695].

And, then, there was another sensational mutiny, Governor Bligh of New South Wales, ousted by a coup led by George Johnston and John Macarthur in 1808. Herbert Evatt [1060], 1938, and Arthur Hawkey [1577], 1975, elaborated. The court martial of George Johnston [1821], 1811, lasted 13 days, May-June 1811. Johnston led 400 Australian militia in overthrowing the Governor of New South Wales in 1808, William Bligh. Bligh was forced to flee. Bligh returned in triumph and Johnston was tried for mutiny at Chelsea Hospital, London, found guilty, and was dismissed.

2. The Mutiny

This event was the most celebrated mutiny in the history of the RN, if not the world. Why was that so?

In 1775, the Society for West Indian Merchants called for introduction of the breadfruit tree in the West Indies, offering a "bounty" as an incentive. A 220-ton ship, BETHIA, 94 feet by 24 feet, was acquired, designated HM Bark BOUNTY, an armed transport, with a crew of 46 men. Naval officer William Bligh, a protégé of Captain James Cook, was ordered to lead the expedition. Notably, no Royal Marines were included in the crew. After arriving off Tahiti in October 1788, 1000 breadfruit trees were collected. On 28 April 1789, second officer Fletcher Christian led a successful mutiny aboard BOUNTY, expelling Bligh and eighteen others into an open 23-foot launch.

The incident created a sensation and the fascination has been sustained, curiously, even expanded, to the present day. Other mutinies were more violent and more extreme; why this one? **See 10., J.**

Christian led a total of 28 mutineers and Polynesian men and women aboard BOUNTY to Pitcairn Island. 13 of the 15 men soon died violently, Christian in 1793. BOUNTY was burned and sank on 23 January 1790 in what is now called Bounty Bay. The Admiralty was determined to track down the mutineers; Captain Edward Edwards of HMS PANDORA placed 12 he found in a notorious "box," 11 by 18 feet on deck, but PANDORA was wrecked, 30 crew and 4 mutineers died. Ultimately, in September 1792, 14 mutineers were court martialled, among the judgments, three being hanged and four acquitted.

The entire series of events generated inordinate interest, then and now. Inevitably, movie makers were attracted and featured notable actors: 5 movies, especially, 1935, 1962, and 1984, and the actors, Bligh: Charles Laughton, Trevor Howard, Anthony Hopkins, and Fletcher Christian: Clark Gable, Marlon Brando, and Mel Gibson.

As noted above, Bligh [**350-355**] himself wrote extensively on the mutiny. The then Secretary of the Admiralty and prolific biographer, John Barrow [**220**], was credited with launching the extraordinary interest in this particular mutiny; for the time and place, not really so unusual an incident. The Eventful History of the Mutiny and Piratical Seizure of HMS BOUNTY: Its Causes and Consequences, 1831, remained the standard and went through various editions, for example, by Cyprian Bridge, Stephen Roskill, Gavin Kennedy, the World Classics series, and a bicentennial edition. As with others, Barrow depended on the Morrison [**3190**] "journal" and Peter Heywood papers. It was comprehensive, including the subsequent voyage of HMS PANDORA and the disposition of those on Pitcairn Island.

Owen Rutter [**3190**] edited The Journal of James Morrison, Boatswain's Mate of the BOUNTY, 1935. Much was made of this "journal," purporting to be a "diary," but clearly written after the fact. Morrison was a survivor from HMS PANDORA. Morrison was tried for mutiny, found guilty, sentenced to death, but pardoned and returned to the service. Many of the accusations of foul language, rage, and abuse against Bligh were based on this source. Hastings Montgomerie [**2529**], The Morrison Myth, 1935, analyzed the Morrison journal. Morrison was in PANDORA's box, in irons, and barely survived the wreck, saving only his Tahiti sash. Barrow [**220**], among others, misquoted from the journal. The contemporaneous accounts of James Morrison was apologetics for Edward Christian, brother of Fletcher, and became the basis of an anti-Bligh literature.

Edward Christian [**629**], brother of Fletcher and a professor at Cambridge University, attacked Bligh in a pamphlet. Bligh [**350**] responded. A descendant, Glynn Christian [**630**], 1982, elaborated on Fletcher Christian. Dea

Birkett [**324**], 1997, and Trevor Lummis [**2204**], 1997, focused on Christian after the mutiny. The titles were enlightening, respectively, Fragile Paradise, Serpent in Paradise, and Life and Death in Eden.

Owen Rutter [**3189**] edited John Fryer of the BOUNTY, 1939, a version of the recollections of the daughter, Mary Ann Gamble

Irvin Anthony [**126**], The Saga of the BOUNTY: Its Strange History as Related by the Participants Themselves, 1935, collected various accounts: Bligh, Christian, Fryer, Morrison, Heywood, and Barrow. He stressed conflicting versions, for example, Fryer, not a mutineer, disliked Bligh, and Heywood insisted he saw Christian alive in England in 1809.

Owen Rutter [**3191, 3188**], The True Story of the Mutiny in the BOUNTY, 1936, and The Court Martial of the Bounty Mutineers, 1931, in the Notable British Trials series, were two other products from this prolific collector of "Bountyana" and founder of the journal, Studia Bountyana. Proceedings of the courts martial for mutiny and desertion for ten survivors were included; the dates were September-October 1792.

Other accounts were Alexander McKee [**2296**], HMS BOUNTY: The Truth about the Mutiny on the BOUNTY, 1962; Sam McKinney [**2308**], Bligh: True Account of Mutiny aboard His Majesty's Ship BOUNTY, 1989, a bicentennial publication, touted to pursue the truth, not "the comfortable moral judgments of Nordhoff [**2650**] and Hall" or the Hollywood stereotypes; D. Bonner Smith [**3356, 3351**], 1936 and 1937, added some information, praising the accounts of Owen Rutter [**3188-3192**]; John Toohey [**3632**], Captain Bligh's Portable Nightmare: From BOUNTY to Safety, 2000, an imaginative, virtual fictional account which focused on the voyage of the launch, the "portable nightmare," and Charles Nordhoff [**2650**], The BOUNTY Trilogy: Mutiny on the BOUNTY, Men against the Sea, and Pitcairn's Island, 1932, admittedly fiction, depicting Bligh as a flogger and nagger who forced a diet of pumpkins, sauerkraut, and salt pork.

3. HM Bark BOUNTY

HM Bark BOUNTY was the subject: John McKay [**2286**], The Armed Transport BOUNTY, 1989, in the important The Anatomy of the Ship series, which included detailed descriptions and schematic drawings; among the illustrations were pictures of two replicas made for BOUNTY movies, and C. Knight [**1954**], 1936, in an article, explained the name: West Indian merchants, desirous of introducing breadfruit in their colonies, offered a reward or "bounty" for achievement of the goal.

4. Literature and Assessments

Raymond Maloney [**2351**], 1996, observed the problem of determining the exact location of the mutiny. Pauline Ernst [**1053**], 1993, described book relics, for example a pamphlet and two bibles, from the BOUNTY.

A Nobel Prize winner, Derek Walcott [**3734**], The BOUNTY, 1997, structured his account with sixty poems. Sven Wahlroos [**3732**], Mutiny and Romance in the South Seas: A Companion to the BOUNTY Adventure, 1989, a bicentennial commemoration of the mutiny, was a synthesis of the latest literature, plus a psychological twist. Coverage was from the departure, Portsmouth, December 1787, to the death of Christian, Pitcairn Island, September 1793. Added was a BOUNTY encyclopedia.

Greg Dening [**910**], Mr. Bligh's Bad Language: Passion, Power, and Theatre on the BOUNTY, 1992, was touted as an "anthro-historical" viewpoint: treatment of the incident in art, literature, and especially, the theater. It was a deconstructionist approach. Bligh often berated the officers and the men, cursing, taking over the office of purser, and flogging; Bligh as bad guy, Fletcher Christian as good guy.

Madge Darby [**859, 858**], 1965 and 1966, contended that Midshipman Young caused the mutiny and replied to Rolf du Rietz concerning the causes of the mutiny. Rolf Du Rietz [**997**], 1965, reacted to Darby. The exchange was in the journal, Studia Bountyana.

H.S. Montgomerie [**2530**], William Bligh and the BOUNTY in Fact and Fable, 1937, was a reference guide reviewing all of the details of the mutiny. Amasa Delano [**902**], 1817, an American naval officer, described three famous voyages, one of which was BOUNTY.

Most mutineers and their entourage escaped to Pitcairn Island. The Admiralty was determined to hunt them down and punish them. PANDORA under Edwards was dispatched in 1790. After picking up the first group, PANDORA proceeded to search for others, running aground on the Great Barrier Reef, killing 34 including 4 mutineers. There followed another long voyage in an open boat, 1100 miles to Timor.

The disposition of the mutineers was treated by Diana Jolliffe [**1823**], The Mutineers of the BOUNTY and Their Descendants in Pitcairn and Norfolk Islands, 1870. Wilmon Menard [**2496**], 1991, summarized the aftermath: the disastrous voyage of HMS PANDORA, fictional accounts, movie depictions, and replicas. Other accounts were by Alfred McFarland [**2246**], 1884, Harry Shapiro [**3291**], 1936, and Walter Brodie [**447**], 1980. HMS PANDORA has been included in The Anatomy of the Ship series, 1991, by John McKay [**2288**], and by George Hamilton [**1464**], 1793.

BOUNTY and PANDORA have been discovered by expeditions of nautical archaeology: BOUNTY in 1957, recounted by Bengt Danielsson [**854**], 1962, and Luis Marden [**2372**], 1957; PANDORA in 1997 recounted by John McKay [**2288**], 1991.

Chapter 9

Other Personalities - Officers

Two chapters will be devoted to the great leaders, outstanding naval officers, and the officer corps as an entity and institution in English/British naval history to 1815. As explained in the previous chapter, there were two exceptions who required special emphasis. Because of the large number of written works about them, a separate chapter was devoted exclusively to them and to the ships most identified with them: Admiral Lord Horatio Nelson and HMS VICTORY and William Bligh and HM Bark BOUNTY.

The previous chapter and this chapter were linked. The same applies to this chapter and the next, "Human Resources." This chapter will focus exclusively on the naval officer and the next on the abode of the naval enlisted man, the lower deck, and his professional career. Women will also be covered.

For this chapter, some general comments on professionalization and officers of the royal family will be followed by individual listings of naval officers receiving considerable attention, in chronological order, followed by a long section on those naval officers not subjects of several works, also in chronological order. As always, so much depends on the amount of publication.

As noted, a separate chapter, "Special Emphasis," dealt with the most famous of the naval officers during this period, if not of all periods and all countries, Horatio, Lord Nelson. **See 8., A.** As expected, the literature on naval personalities abounded. Balance was not an obvious feature. Nelson clearly dominated. Next in the extent of treatment were Drake, Raleigh, Blake, and Thomas Cochrane, then, Lord St. Vincent, then, Edward Pellew, and then, Sidney Smith. Unfortunately, the "Band of Brothers," for example, Collingwood and Hardy, received short shrift; Troubridge, Foley, and others, even less. **See 22.**

A. THE PROFESSION OF NAVAL OFFICER

A good place to start might be Michael Lewis [**2120**], England's Sea Officers: The Story of the Naval Profession, 1939. Originally, naval officer meant function not rank; later rank became important. The origin was during the Commonwealth period, the "General-at-Sea." Later the colored flags, in order of precedence, red, white, and blue, designated seniority and steps in promotion of flag officers. In a dissertation, Robert Glass [**1296**], 1990, agreed with Lewis that the origin of the professional naval officer was after 1650. Sea officers developed a consciousness of common interests and were successful in achieving some independence, preventing political pressure from the government. Glass saw the period 1688-1697 as decisive.

The professional naval officer corps originated in Britain, the army officer corps in Prussia, the contention of the Dutch sociologist, Gerke Teitler [**3585**], The Genesis of the Professional Officer Corps, 1977. For naval officers the culmination was the 18th, for army officers, it was the 19th, century. Prosopography and a spotlight approach were in the dissertation, "The British Officer Corps, 1754-1783," 2 vols., 1988, by Mark Odintz [**2687**], biographical studies of 394 officers, albeit from army regiments. It was enlightening on the background, sources, patronage, career patterns, rewards, punishments, and the code of honor.

The entry rank of midshipman was studied by Charles Walker [**3738**], Young Gentlemen: The Story of Midshipmen from the Seventeenth Century to the Present Day, 1938.

R.C. Anderson [**81**], "English Flag Officers, 1688-1713," 1849, sorted out the ranking system of flag officers, that is, those commanders who flew flags of a certain color aboard their home ships. The origins stemmed from the line-of-battle formation divided into three parts: the center, admiral of the red, later full admiral; the van, admiral of the white, vice admiral, and the rear, admiral of the blue, rear admiral; for awhile, there were three colors for each of the ranks, thus, a total of nine flag officers.

David Syrett [**3542**], The Commissioned Sea Officers of the Royal Navy, 1660-1815, 1994, was an occasional publication of the NRS and an informative reference guide. Within was a complete list of all officers of the RN during the early modern period.

Much earlier were two works: John Campbell [**568**], Lives of the British Admirals, 4 vols., 1742-1785, began with the "early Britons before the Romans," then Saxons, Danes, Normans, and on up to the mid-18th century, and John Charnock [**621**], Biographia Navalis: Or, Impartial Memoirs of the Lives and Characters of Officers of the Navy of Great Britain, 6 vols., 1794-1798.

Naval Schools, cadets, midshipmen, and state-sponsored education were all parts of the preparation and training of naval officers of the RN. Unfortunately, little publication has been devoted to the subject as applicable to the pre-1815 period. **See 22.**

"School for seamen" was a favorite term for preparating men for the lower deck; applicable to the fishing and whaling fleets and coastal and merchant trades. What was the "school" for officers? Christopher Lloyd [**2169**], 1966, a sometime professor at the Royal Naval College and H.W. Dickinson [**928**], forthcoming, have and propose to answer the question; about the Royal Naval Colleges, first at Portsmouth, later moved to Greenwich. First opened in 1733 and reconstituted in 1806, moving to Greenwich in 1873. Dickinson, a winner of the Julian Corbett Prize, 1997, has been preparing a history of the education provision in the RN.

A. MacDermott [**2233**], 1965, described an early "cadet" institution: the Royal Adademy, Gosport, run by Dr. Burney, founded in 1791 and closed in 1904.

An article by Timothy Jenks [**1801**], 2001, was enlightening about naval officers and political service, a case study of the Westminster election to Parliament of 1796. Two seats were at stake, three candidates: Charles James Fox, Admiral Allan Gardner, and the Irish radical, John Horne Tooke. The election coincided with the second anniversary of the Glorious First of June. The government backed Gardner and patriotism, "king and country," and alarm about Irish radicals were themes played up during the campaign. Fox and Gardner were returned, the latter seen as the model for later "political admirals," an increasingly prominent feature of the 19th century.

Edgar Thompson [**3600**], 1975, wrote of the regulations about facial hair for officers. Shaving was mandatory and strictly enforced: the upper lip smooth and "three finger gangway" for the chin. No beards or moustaches were permitted until after the 1850s.

B. LISTING THE GREATS

Collections of mini-biographies of "the greats" of British naval officers were popular. Twenty years after his biography of Nelson, Robert Southey [**3396, 3397**] began publishing Lives of the British Admirals, 5 vols., 1833-1848, using a series of biographical studies to present the naval history of Britain. He cited Howard, John Hawkins, Drake, Cavendish, Grenville, and Raleigh, among others.

In a dissertation and a book, John Horsfield [**1672, 1671**], The Art of Leadership in War: The British Navy from the Age of Nelson to the End of World War II, 1977 and 1980, singled out models: St. Vincent, Nelson, Collingwood, Jellicoe, Beatty, Keyes, and A.B. Cunningham. Also, a long list of unique features made the RN hegemonic, for example, better leadership, more experience in battle, more time at sea, greater experience in gunnery, and more severe discipline.

A.T. Mahan [**2333**], Types of Naval Officers, Drawn from the History of the British Navy, 1902, was a study Mahan made in conjunction with his

Influence of Sea Power [**2328, 2329**] series. His models were Saumarez, Rodney, St. Vincent, Richard Howe, Hawke, and Pellew.

A recent excellent compilation was Peter LeFevre [**2100**], Precursors to Nelson: British Admirals of the Eighteenth Century, 2000, mini-biographies of 18 admirals, for example, Vernon, Anson, Hawke, Samuel Hood, Rooke, Richard Howe, Keith, Rodney, and St. Vincent. W.H. Fitchett [**1117**], Nelson and His Captains: Sketches of Famous Seamen, 1902, presented "character studies" of a number, for example, Thomas Troubridge, Edward Pellew, Thomas Hardy, Thomas Foley, and Edward Berry.

Oliver Warner [**3765, 3760**], Great Seamen, 1961, and Command at Sea, 1976, selected Drake, Anson, Hawke, Saunders, Howe, Cook, Bougainville, Nelson, Beatty, and A.B. Cunningham, among others.

John Knox Laughton [**2043**], From Howard to Nelson: Twelve Sailors, 1899, selected from the entries in the DNB [**930**]: Howard, Drake, Blake, Rooke, Anson, Hawke, Boscawen, Rodney, Howe, Hood, St. Vincent, and Nelson. William Cuthbert Brian Tunstall [**3663**], Flights of Naval Genius, 1930, selected Howe, Rodney, and Sydney Smith, among others. Marvin Albert [**26**], Broadsides and Boarders, 1958, covered the great captains during sailing ship warfare; Nelson was the greatest, also, Dutch Sea Beggars, English Sea Dogs, Generals-at-Sea, Hawke, Jones, Suffren, and Decatur. Frank Bowen [**390**], Men of the Wooden Walls, 1952, consisted of 70 potted mini-biographies of any and all, international in scope, except there were no seamen. Examples included Columbus, Sebastian Cabot, John Hawkins, Francis Drake, Marten Tromp, Colbert, Pepys, James II, Jean Bart, William Kidd, Blackbeard, and even Samuel Cunard. Jack Sweetman [**3529**], The Great Admirals: Command at Sea, 1587-1945, 1997, collected 19 essays, leadership in battle being a prerequisite, for example, Drake, Tromp, Blake, De Ruyter, Hawke, and Nelson, 6 being British, 4 American, 2 Dutch, 2 Japanese; 7 during the pre-1815 period. Henry Dorling [**949, 948**], Sea Ventures of Britain, 1925, and Men O'War, 1929, selected Hawkins, Frobisher, Drake, Dampier, Anson, Cook, St. Vincent, Cochrane, Marryat, Fisher, and Beresford.

George Washington's Opponents: British Generals and Admirals in the American Revolution, 1969, by George Billias [**317**], included Richard Howe, Gambier, Graves, Samuel Hood, and Rodney. Factors of failure included no clear strategy, lack of preparation, French naval initiatives, the League of Armed Neutrality, and poor naval leadership, Gambier being deemed the worst.

George Marindin [**2377**], Our Naval Heroes, 1901, included 20 short biographies with an introduction by Charles Beresford. Geoffrey Lowis [**2195**], Fabulous Admirals and Some Naval Fragments, 1957, was a curious compilation about "those who represented the unseen and unchallenged power of Great Britain." Phil Grabsky [**1348**], The Great Commanders, 1993, selected seven, including Caesar, Nelson, and Napoleon.

More specifically, for the 16th century: Bryan Bevan [**315**], The Great Seamen of Elizabeth I, 1971, included seamen, pirates,   and patrons, degenerating into gossipy snippets; the same title by Neville Williams [**3884**], 1972, and Peter Brimacombe [**442**], 2000, All the Queen's Men, about courtiers of Queen Elizabeth: Howard, Raleigh, and Essex were included; James Anthony Froude [**1205**], English Seamen in the Sixteenth Century, 1895, a series of lectures at Oxford, was later criticized as carelessly researched with excessive errors; two with similar titles: Elizabethan Sea Kings, 1895, by John Fiske [**1114**], and Elizabethan Sea-Dogs, by William Wood [**3933**], 1918: the latter praising Drake as leader in the English winning command of the sea, the first of modern admirals, and Helen Miller [**2513**], Captains from Devon: The Great Elizabethan Seafarers Who Won the Oceans for England, 1985, designating a "Devon confraternity": Raleigh, Grenville, the Hawkins family, Frobisher, Gilbert, and John Davis. Two stressed deeds more than men: H.R.F. Bourne [**384**], English Seamen under the Tudors, 2 vols., 1868, stressing enterprises more than biography, for example, voyaging, exploration, colonization, attacks on Spanish enterprises, and the Armada, and Douglas Bell [**282**], Elizabethan Seamen, 1936, stressing deeds, for example, "Ventures All," search for the Northwest Passage, circumnavigation, operations against the Spanish Main, and the birth of empire.

In the mid-17th century, Oliver Cromwell was determined to expand the Royal Navy, launch imperialist policies, acquire the proper respect internationally for England and its navy, and intensify the competition with the Dutch. He drew naval leadership from his trusted officers of the New Model Army, thus "Generals-at-Sea." The first Dutch war, the great Western Design, and overcoming the Royalist navy were his achievements. **See 7., G., 4.**

Michael Baumber [**243**], "Cromwell's Soldier-Admirals," 1989, introduced seven, for example, Blake, Deane, Edward Popham, William Penn, and Montague; only Penn was a career naval officer. C.E.L. Phillips [**2844**], Cromwell's Captains, 1938, was a study of four, including Robert Blake. Donald Kennedy [**1874**], 1960, recounted the process of selecting captains for the 18 warships and 24 merchant ships under the control of Parliament in 1642; only Protestants were eligible. R.C. Anderson [**91**], List of English Naval Captains, 1642-1660, 1964, an occasional publication of the SNR.

For the 18th century: John Creswell [**796**], British Admirals of the Eighteenth Century: Tactics in Battle, 1972, touted revisionism. Mahan [**2328, 2329**] and Corbett [**759**] assessed naval warfare in the 18th century as indecisive and limited by the Fighting Instructions [**751**]. Creswell disagreed. Just look at Quiberon Bay, the Saints, Cape St. Vincent, and Trafalgar.

C. THE ROLE OF THE MONARCHY

Douglas Bell [**283**], Seamen of Britain, 1943, noted that the first king to appreciate a navy was Alfred, then Richard I, and, finally, Henry VIII. Later, James, Duke of York, was a member of the royal family, brother to Charles II, and, in 1685, king in his own right; then, expelled in the Revolution of 1688, the first of the Jacobite pretenders. A longtime history textbook for British naval cadets was Geoffrey Callender [**556**], Sea Kings of Britain, 2 vols., 1907, the approach soon seen as "foolish" and simplistic.

Hilaire Belloc [**287**], James II, 1928, considered James, Duke of York, influential formulator of naval tactics and a naval commander during the Dutch wars. Catholic officers in the navy of James II were described by L. Gooch [**1317**], 1978. Most had been dismissed after 1673 when the Test Act was enforced; with James on the throne, they returned. James was warned that this was contrary to public opinion, but he ignored that. About 80 commissions were restored or given out the first time. Nevertheless, the navy was in no danger of being taken over by Catholics. King William III led a successful invasion of England, driving out James II. J.R. Bruijn [**489**] wrote "William III and His Two Navies," 1989.

Most of the examples in A.C. Hampshier [**1474**], Royal Sailors, 1971, were from the 20th century, including Earl Mountbatten and Prince Charles, but James, Duke of York was an early instance. Tom Pocock [**2872**], Sailor King: The Life of King William IV, 1991, unlike most biographies of William IV, Pocock covered his early life. He served in the RN, 1779-1790, including service under Nelson; becoming king at age 64 in 1830.

D. PROMINENT PERSONALITIES

To reiterate: this section and the next, "Miscellaneous," are based on quantity of publication. Those with the most coverage receive the priority of presentation and the more extensive surveys.

1. Francis Drake

Substantial coverage has been forthcoming about this popular naval hero and adventurer, known, feared, and loved by the Spanish as "El Draco." Little was known about his early life. He preyed exclusively on Spanish commerce and bases to the point of extreme notoriety. Then, 1577-1580, the circumnavigation voyage, the first Englishman to accomplish that deed. During that voyage the Thomas Doughty affair, a court martial and execution at sea, and "Nova Albion," the alleged anchorage around San Francisco, both have sustained enduring interest and controversy. In 1587, he led the successful raid on Cadiz, setting back preparations for the Spanish Armada and "singeing the King of Spain's beard." The next year, on Plymouth Hoe, as the Armada was sighted, there was "time to finish the game of bowls and beat the Spanish, too." A raid expedition in 1589 was not successful and during the last treasure hunt, 1595-1596, both Drake and John Hawkins died.

Elizabeth Douglas Fuller-Eliott-Drake [**1214**], Family and Heirs of Sir Francis Drake, 2 vol., 1911, sorted out the family background. Anthony Wagner [**3730**], Drake in England, 1963, traced the Drake family in Devon from the 14th century.

A count of over 325 biographies, over 50 of those published in the last 20 years, was made. Most consistently praised of the Drake biographies was Julian Corbett [**748, 758, 760**], Drake and the Tudor Navy: History of the Rise of England as a Maritme Power, 2 vols., 1898. A shorter effort, Sir Francis Drake, 1890, in the English Men of Action series and The Successors of Drake, 1900, were also by the great historian of British naval strategy. He cited Drake as "the controlling force" in the Tudor navy and the post-Drake period was "an irretrievable miscarriage" and splendid failure. Drake was obviously approved of by Corbett, no doubt, too much so.

Most recently, John Sugden [**3513**], Sir Francis Drake, 1990, was praised as definitive treatment of the psychological, social, and religious dimensions, especially religious, again, sympathetic toward Drake. John Cummins [**828**], Francis Drake: The Lives of a Hero, 1995, was a substantial recent biography with a good historiographical essay; for the quadricentennial of his death. Harry Kelsey [**1856**], Sir Francis Drake: The Queen's Pirate, 1998, featured wide-ranging research and stress on a dark side of Drake: "a deeply unpleasant, devious sadist and a coward in battle." It was enlightening on the personality of Drake who was patriotic, religious, adroit as navigator, and problematical as a leader; his fearsome reputation was actually created by his enemies, he typically abandoned and mistreated his friends. Spanish mythology created the piratical image; Kelsey questioned whether Drake even came close to California.

John Barrow [**225**], The Life, Voyages, and Exploits of Admiral Sir Francis Drake, 1843, was the first important biography. One feature was "Drake's Prayer," which originated from the Cadiz expedition of 1587. D. Bonner Smith [**3349**], 1950, reviewed the sources about it and questioned its authenticity.

J.A. Williamson [**3901, 3891, 3892**], Sir Francis Drake, 1951, The Age of Drake, 1938, was a short biography and work of general context by a noted authority. Earlier, 1928, Williamson reviewed the literature on Drake. Christopher Lloyd [**2173**], Sir Francis Drake, 1957, was short and undocumented. E.F. Benson [**296**], Sir Francis Drake, 1927, saw Drake as "the King of Sailors" and contained excessive errors, all the while attacking Froude [**1207**] for his errors. Lewis Gibbs [**1271**], The Silver Circle: Sir Francis Drake, A New Re-Appraisal, 1963, was critical of Drake, a bold, bad man and common pirate. George Thomson [**3606**], Sir Francis Drake, 1972, depicted Drake as a kind of inspired guerrilla leader. David Beers Quinn [**2987**], 1996, presented Drake as his contemporaries saw him, a publication for the Hakluyt Society. John Hampden [**1472**], Francis Drake, Privateer: Contemporary Narratives and

Documents, 1972, included contemporaneous assessments, including that of the nephew of Drake in 1626.

Others were as follows: profusely illustrated, folio size, was Hans Kraus [**1977**], Sir Francis Drake: A Pictorial Biography, 1970; A.E.W. Mason [**2450**], The Life of Francis Drake, 1941, an older, popular account by a novelist; Ernle Bradford [**414**], The Wind Commands Me: A Life of Sir Francis Drake, 1965, non-scholarly and medium-length; Douglas Bell [**281**], Drake, 1935; Alex Cumming [**826**], Sir Francis Drake and the GOLDEN HINDE, 1975, a short account; Richard Boulind [**377**], 1968, assessing the navigational skills of Drake, and Derek Howse [**1711**], 1980, about Drake's Nautical Almanac of 1546.

Mary Keeler [**1851**], 1981, described the voyage of Drake to the West Indies of 1585-1586, a publication of the Hakluyt Society. Pillage in the Caribbean and stops in Florida and Roanoke Island were in the itinerary. Henry Haslop [**1547**], 1587, edited a report by Drake to Lord Howard about the operations and attack on Cadiz of April-May 1587.

The famous and fatal "last voyage" of Drake and John Hawkins was recounted by Thomas Maynarde [**2485**], 1849, a Spanish account, and Kenneth Andrews [**111**], 1972, both for the Hakluyt Society. One goal was to capture Panama. That failed. As previously, Drake abandoned Hawkins at a crucial time. Both died during the voyage.

Peter Brimacombe [**442**], 1992, presented a tourist-type description of Plymouth Hoe, including some questionable assertions. Christopher Lloyd [**2154**], 1953-1955, and others, discussed the legendary game of bowls on Plymouth Hoe as the Spanish Armada was sighted, concluding that there was no evidence to confirm the event.

In Mariner's Mirror of the early 1920s, an exchange took place between Gregory Robinson [**3095**], 1921, and Geoffrey Callender [**548, 550**], 1921-1923. Robinson listed nostalgic myths about Drake and attacked Callender for his interpretations and apologetics. Callender devoted four articles defending Drake from various accusations, for example, exonerating Drake for the Doughty affair, defending his actions during the Armada campaign, and declaring him a privateer, not a pirate.

The Drake Manuscript [**961**], 1996, was published and analyzed: a 16th-century work with 137 colored illustrations of plants and animals of the Caribbean and French captions. Drake was mentioned but, apparently, for no valid reason.

There was the love-hate perspective from the Spanish: Cristobal Real [**3034**], El Corsario Drake y el Imperio Espanol, 1941; Fray Pedro Simon [**3321**], in Spanish, The English Pirate, 1627, by a contemporary observer; G. Jenner [**1803**], "A Spanish Account of Drake's Voyages," 1901, focusing on the Simon [**3321**] biography, noting that the death of Drake was celebrated by the Spanish, and A.K. Jameson [**1789**], "Some New Spanish Documents dealing with Drake," 1934, presenting details on reasons for failures of attacks by Drake.

Other foreign biographies included Leon Lemonnier [**2105**], Sir Francis Drake in the La Grande Legende de la Mer series, 1932, a French biography. Others in the series were Jean Bart, Raleigh, and Nelson. Walter Kirsch [**1950**], Francis Drake: Protestant, Patriot, Pirate, 1992, was a German biography.

Several were for juveniles: John Upcott [**3701**], Sir Francis Drake and the Beginnings of English Sea Power, 1927, in a school textbook format and two by Frank Knight [**1960, 1962**], That Rare Captain: Sir Francis Drake, 1970, and The Young Drake, 1962.

On the circumnavigation: the departure with secret orders to explore the Pacific Ocean and plunder Spanish ports was in December 1577, originally five ships. Problems with Thomas Doughty led to a court martial and the decision by Drake to execute Doughty. At the Straits of Magellan, one ship sank and three turned back, leaving only GOLDEN HINDE. Spanish ports were plundered and a search was made for the Northwest Passage. On 17 June 1579, "a faire and good Baye" was used for four weeks of rest and restoration. Thence across the Pacific and return to England via the Cape of Good Hope.

Accounts of the circumnavigation included Kenneth Andrews [**106**], 1967, David Quinn [**2974**], 1981, and Florence Dyer [**1002**], 1923. Norman Thrower [**3614**], Sir Francis Drake and the Famous Voyage, 1577-1580, 1984, reported the proceedings of a quadricentennial conference, June 1979, including eight essays, for example, by J.H. Parry, David Quinn, Kenneth Andrews, and Helen Wallis. Another feature of the quadricentennial celebrations was a special exhibition sponsored by the British Museum in London and, then, in Oakland, California, described by Sarah Tyacke [**3680**]. Derek Wilson [**3910**], 1977, in preparation for the quadricentennial, wrote a chronological narrative of the voyage, sorting out the political and diplomatic complexities. He noted that Drake was anxious to hurt the Spanish by plunder, not violence. Not one Spaniard was killed.

Henry Wagner [**3731**], Sir Francis Drake's Voyage around the World, 1926, placed the voyage in perspective. Alexander McKee [**2300**], The Queen's Corsair: Drake's Journey of Circumnavigation, 1577-1580, 1978, described Drake as "master thief of the unknown world." Zelia Nuttall [**2654**], 1914, analyzed documents, many of them Spanish, about the circumnavigation voyage, a publication of the Hakluyt Society.

Francis Drake [**960**], The World Encompassed, 1628, by a nephew of Drake, Sir Francis Drake, was probably written in 1595, republished in 1854 by the Hakluyt Society. The notes of Francis Fletcher, the chaplain of GOLDEN HINDE, among other participants, were used. Another edition was published by Richard Temple [**3587**], 1926.

Residents and tourist authorities of coastal California were attracted, probably excessively, about "Nova Albion" and the landing of Drake in 1579. George Davidson [**864, 863**], 1890 and 1908, wrote generally of Drake along the Northwest coast of America and his "anchorage." John Robertson [**3087**], 1926, noted the latitude of the landing, 38 degrees north.

Then, a Brass Plate, a Drake marker, was "accidentally discovered" in 1933 or 1936 or 1937, depending on your source; all was academic, it was a fake. Walter Starr [3429], "Drake Landed in San Francisco Bay in 1579: The Testimony of the Plate of Brass," 1962, and Adolph Oko [2692], "Francis Drake and New Albion," 1964, relied heavily of the "brass plate" evidence.

In preparation for the quadricentennial, the state of California sponsored the Sir Francis Drake Commission, 1975-1980, to investigate. The California Historical Society facilitated further debate. Marilyn Ziebarth [3982] "The Francis Drake Controversy: His California Anchorage, June 17-July 23, 1579," 1974, was a review. At least three points in California claimed to be the landing spot. In 1949, the Drake Navigation Guild was formed to investigate. A "brass plate" and "fort" were "discovered" at likely places. Warren Hanna [1476], 1979, reviewed the controversy. Raymond Aker [24], Discovering Francis Drake's California Harbor, 2000, claimed finality. Sponsored by the Drake Navigators Guild, Drake's Bay, Marin County, was "Nova Albion." S.E. Morison and Alan Villiers, among others, agreed.

2. Walter Raleigh

There have been several spellings: Ralegh and Raleigh, the former used by Raleigh and his family. Actually, Willard Wallace [3742] counted 73 contemporary spellings, including Dutch and Spanish. Raleigh was an important literary figure of the Elizabethan and Jacobin eras and a prominent naval, merchant, exploration, imperial, and colonial contributor, as well, the true "Renaissance man." A prose and poetry writer, courtier and onetime favorite of Queen Elizabeth, soldier in Ireland, colonizer, entrepreneur, naval commander, and initiator and leader of exploration and colonization voyages: 1585 to Virginia and 1595 and 1617 to Guiana. He was frequently out of favor with Elizabeth and James I, spending a total of 17 years in the Tower. In that second voyage to Guiana, to get out of the Tower, Raleigh promised huge rewards to king and country but the attempt of 1617 was a failure and resulted in a treason trial and his execution. Raleigh was a leader in the campaign against Cadiz of 1596. He was enthusiastic and saw the attack as revenge for his cousin, Richard Grenville, lost in an attack against the Spanish treasure fleet in the Azores aboard REVENGE in 1591. Raleigh [3002] wrote a dramatic account, The Last Fight of the REVENGE, 1615. See 7., F., 2. and 3.

Robert Lawson-Peebles [2083], "The Many Faces of Sir Walter Raleigh," 1998, reviewed the numerous images of Raleigh over time. There was an annotated bibliography by Christopher Armitage [136], 1987, with 1967 entries.

Two Victorian-period biographies remained important authorities: Edward Edwards [1018], The Life of Sir Walter Ralegh, 2 vols., 1868, a biography and collection of 157 letters and William Stebbing [3432], Sir Walter

Ralegh: A Biography, 1891, a substantial and much praised biography with a good historiographical essay.

A recent biography was by Raleigh Trevelyan [**3648**], 2001, touting extensive new material, especially from Spanish sources. Robert Lacey [**1985**], Sir Walter Ralegh, 1973, covered the sequences: rise, favor, fall, disgrace, favor regained, prison, and execution. Other biographies were Willard Wallace [**3742**], 1959, and Stephen Coote [**744**], A Play of Passion, 1993, the title of this biography coming from a poem by Raleigh. No scholarly apparatus was included in the efforts of Norman Williams [**3888**], 1962, and John Winton [**3923**], 1975, the latter with many illustrations.

The Twayne English Authors series biography was by Steven May [**2474**], 1989. A dissertation on the prose writings of Raleigh was by R.A. Davies [**876**], 1997. Ernest Strathmann [**3472, 3471**], 1951 and 1964, took an intellectual approach in a biography and an account of his last voyage.

Others included Milton Waldman [**3736**], Sir Walter Raleigh, 1928; W.A. Devereux [**917**], 1909, subtitled, An Historical Romance in the form of a novel; Jack Adamson [**19**], The Shepherd of the Ocean, 1969, a biography; Anna Beer [**274**], 1997, stressing how Raleigh was perceived by contemporaries, and A.L. Rowse [**3161**], Sir Walter Ralegh: His Family and Private Life, 1962, was informative.

By far the best on Raleigh as explorer and colonizer was David Quinn [**2984**], Raleigh and the British Empire, 1947, initiating the first attempt to settle English people in North America. Quinn [**2985**] also described The Roanoke Voyages, 2 vols., 1955-1967, a publication of the Hakluyt Society. A quadricentennial conference of the Virginia settlement was sponsored by Exeter University, May 1985, the papers being edited by Joyce Youings [**3975**], 1985. Papers included ones by David Quinn and Ian Friel. Charles Nicholl [**2635**], 1995, described the voyage of Raleigh in 1595. The account of the voyage became a popular travelogue, the mythical search for El Dorado. The Hakluyt Society also published William Strachey [**3465**], History of Travel into Virginia Britania, 1953. Strachey was secretary of the Virginia Company. These Virginia voyages had been initiated by Raleigh. Vincent Harlow [**1520**] recounted Ralegh's Last Voyage, 1932, the famous attempt to create a settlement at Orinoco. Failure meant the end of his career and, ultimately, his execution.

Raleigh [**3001**], A History of the World, 1614, written in prison, 1603-1616, was a detailed, erudite analysis, an evaluation of morals and politics, and a counter to Machiavelli. An analysis was by Jenny Wilson [**3912**], 1998.

Pierre Lefranc [**2102**], a Canadian scholar, initiated the project to publish the complete works, inviting Agnes Latham to join in the project. It later collapsed. Agnes Latham [**2036, 2035**], 1964 and 1999, wrote a short biographical study in the Writers and Their Works series and the definitive collection of the letters of Raleigh. Latham contained 228 letters including most published by Edwards [**1018**].

3. The Hawkins Dynasty

This Devon maritime family was especially prominent: William Hawkins, the elder, died 1554, Mayor of Plymouth and Member of Parliament; William II, an elder son, an Elizabethan Sea Dog; the son of William II, John Hawkins; a son of John, Richard, and, more obscure, William III, prominent in India.

Michael Lewis [2122], The Hawkins Dynasty: Three Generations of a Tudor Family, 1969, covered 130 years and 5 members of this Plymouth family whose wealth was based on the slave trade, piracy, privateering, trade, and merchant shipping. Lewis observed that it was odd that there was no commemoration of the Hawkins family in Plymouth, "not even a lowly pub." Mary Hawkins [1578], Plymouth Armada Heroes, 1888, with a genealogical study, played up the deeds of the Hawkins family during the campaign. J.A. Williamson [3896], The Observations of Sir Richard Hawkins, 1933, was about another member.

J.A. Williamson [3902], Sir John Hawkins, 1927, was a substantial biography. John Hawkins made his reputation and fortune in slave-trading voyages, three of them. The DNB [930] entry was critical of Hawkins for "enriching himself as a merchant, ship owner, and Admiralty official, whose integrity was suspected." Elsewhere, he was "the greedy, unscrupulous" father of the English slave trade. Williamson praised his contributions as a formative Admiralty administrator and criticized Drake for problems experienced by Hawkins. It was Corbett [748] who praised Drake so much. J.A. Williamson [3896], Hawkins of Plymouth: A New History of Sir John Hawkins and the Other Members of His Family Prominent in Tudor England, 1949, updated the biography of 1927. Philip Gosse [1331], Sir John Hawkins, 1930, was apologetics; Drake too long had overshadowed Hawkins and Hawkins was finally receiving the credit he deserved.

Richard Hakluyt [1447], The Hawkins' Voyages, 1878, a publication of the Hakluyt Society, described 3 voyages to Africa and the West Indies. Rayner Unwin [3700], The Defeat of John Hawkins: A Biography of His Third Slaving Voyage, 1960, noted this voyage and operations against the Spanish Main, 1567-1568, marked a turning point in English naval strategy, precipitating an upset in Anglo-Spanish relations. Simon Adams [17], 1990, wrote on the "reformation" of John Hawkins. While he was Treasurer of the Navy, 1577-1595, significant improvements were made in repair and preparedness of the fleet. This was the crucial time before the Armada.

4. Robert Blake

By far the most attractive of these Generals-at-Sea based on the literature was Robert Blake. Naval administrator and commander during the first

Dutch war, little was known about his early life or his early career. He led operations against Prince Rupert and the Royalist fleet.

An older biography recently revived, 2000,was Hepworth Dixon [**942**], Robert Blake: Admiral and General-at-Sea, 1852, the first scholarly biography. J.R. Powell [**2928, 2925, 2927**], 1933, 1937, and 1972, wrote a short and a substantial biography and edited the letters of Robert Blake for the NRS. David Hannay [**1477**], Admiral Blake, 1886, was in the English Worthies series. C.D. Curtis [**839**], Blake: General-at-Sea, 1934, touted him as "second only to Nelson in our naval history." Roger Beadon [**251**], Robert Blake, 1935, saw him as the chief architect of the of the Commonwealth navy, a navy which began as insignificant and ended as dominant. Michael Baumber [**244**], General-at-Sea Robert Blake and the Seventeenth-Century Revolution in Naval Warfare, 1989, lacked scholarship and used hyperbole. For juveniles, there was Frank Knight [**1955**], 1971, with a biography of Blake.

5. George Monck, 1st Duke of Albemarle

Older biographies were Julian Corbett [**753**], Monk, 1889, in the English Men of Action series, and Oliver Warner [**3766**], Hero of the Restoration: A Life of General George Monck, First Duke of Albermarle, 1936. J.K. Powell [**2929**], The Rupert and Monck Letter Book, 1666, 1989, a publication of the NRS, presented documents about operations during the second Dutch war. Monck had fought in the Bishop's War and spent two years in the Tower, shifted to the side of Parliament, and became General-at-Sea during the first Dutch war.

6. William Dampier

An early figure of prominence was William Dampier, voyager around the world, navigator, hydrographer, naturalist, proto-anthropologist, buccaneer against the Spanish Main, and capturer of the Manila Galleon.

William Dampier [**847, 848**], A New Voyage Round the World, 2 vols., 1697, and Voyage to New Holland, 1703, were followed by a series of editions, even to the present day; it became a famous, formative, influential, and model travel journal. It covered thirteen years and involved buccaneering, piracy, plunder, and mutiny. He was the first Englishman to Australia, 70 years before James Cook. **See 17., B.**

Anton Gill [**1282**], The Devil's Mariner: A Life of William Dampier, Pirate and Explorer, 1651-1715, 1997, was a comprehensive biographical study. Others included Christoper Lloyd [**2174**], William Dampier, 1966; Elizabeth Cockburn [**688**], William Dampier: Buccaneer-Explorer-Hydrograher, 1987; Joseph Shipman [**3307**], William Dampier: Seaman-Scientist, 1962; Clennell Wilkinson [**3860**], William Dampier, 1929, and William Russell [**3187**], William Dampier, 1889, in the English Men of Action series.

Joel Baer [**171**], 1996, wrote a short survey of early pirate and privateering operations and "filled a gap" about activities of Dampier during the 1690s. Dampier was present when Alexander Selkirk was set on Juan Fernandez Island and when he was picked up four years later; the inspiration for "Robinson Crusoe" by Daniel Defore [**897**] and Jonathan Swift. **See 20., A.**

7. George Anson

Like Anson a half century earlier, leading a voyage around the world, 1740-1744, an epic but gruesome voyage, wracked by scurvy. Like Anson, he captured the Manila Galleon, accumulated the most prize treasure in history, called at Canton, China, and wrote a popular journal of the voyage. Of the original eight ships which set out, only one completed the circumnavigation.

George Anson [**123**], A Voyage Round the World, 1748, became a best-seller. There was some dispute and confusion about authors and editors: Anson, Richard Walter, and Benjamin Robins. Later, there was an informative editor, Glyndwr Williams, 1974. Pascoe Thomas [**3597**], 1745, had an edition. Leo Heaps [**1588**], Log of the CENTURION, 1973, was the most complete eye-witness account of the voyage, based on the papers of Captain Philip Saumarez. As suggested, the best authority on this voyage was Glyndwr Williams [**3877, 3874**], The Prize of All the Oceans, 1999, and Documents Relating to Anson's Voyage Round the World, 1740-1744, 1967, the latter a publication of the NRS. New material was incorporated. A recent account, 2001, was by Chaplin Walter [**3747**].

Anson was a later, most effective First Lord of the Admiralty initiating a series of reforms: victualling, sanitary arrangements, a corps of Marines, coppering ship bottoms, design of frigates, and signal tactics.

The biographies included S.W.C. Pack [**2724**], Admiral Lord Anson, 1960; John Barrow [**222**], The Life of George Lord Anson, 1839, and Walter Vernon Anson [**124**], The Life of Admiral Lord Anson: The Father of the British Navy, 1697-1762, 1912.

8. Edward Vernon

Known as "Old Grog," the formulator of the daily rum ration, Vernon was seen at the time as "an imperial hero." After a series of defeats in the War of Jenkins's Ear, Vernon gained a victory at Porto Bello. In Parliament, he opposed Walpole and his administration.

Biographies included Cyril Hartemann [**1543**], The Angry Admiral: The Later Career of Edward Vernon, Admiral of the White, 1953, and Douglas Ford [**1136**], Admiral Vernon and the Navy, 1907, mostly hagiography. Ford touted rehabilitation from abuse by historians and Tobias Smollett [**3372**].

Bryan Ranft [**3008**], The Vernon Papers, 1958, a publication of the NRS, featured his involvement with operations, signals, administration, and discipline. Kathleen Wilson [**3913**], 1988, saw Vernon as a popular hero and representative of British imperial expansion.

9. Edward Hawke

Hawke had participated in the battles of Toulon, 1744, commanded at Ushant or the second battle of Finisterre, 1747, where six French warships and 38 ships of the convoy were taken or sunk. Hawke replaced Admiral Byng in 1756, he being court-martialled and shot in Portsmouth, January 1757. In 1757, Hawke led in the attack on Rochefort. He was in the battle of the Isle of Aix, 1757. Commanding the Western Approaches Squadron of 23 ships from HMS ROYAL OAK, 100 guns, he blockaded Brest in 1759, culminating in the breakout of the French from Brest during a westerly gale on the afternoon of 20 November and the battle of Quiberon Bay. The chase involved 44 warships close inshore in a melee. The battle resumed the next morning. The French fleet was annihilated; the Britsh lost HMS RESOLUTION and HMS ESSEX; the French lost 5 and several more were stranded. The leadership of Hawke under such extraordinary conditions was described as "incomparably the finest thing of its sort in our naval history." **See 7., H., 4.** Hawke moved up to First Lord, retiring due to ill health in 1771.

The standard biography was Ruddock Mckay [**2289, 2290**], Admiral Hawke, 1965, supported by The Hawke Papers, 1990, a publication of the NRS. An older biography was by Montagu Burrows [**523**], Life of Edward Lord Hawke, Admiral of the Fleet, 1883.

10. George Rodney

Famous for his campaigns of Gibraltar, against St. Eustatius, and the famous breaking of the line at the Saints in 1782, George Rodney was also accused of "corruption" and excessive zeal for prize money.

J.D. Spinney [**3409, 3410**], 1969 and 1982, has a biography and a reassessment of the actions of Rodney at the battle of the Saints, the latter, a bicentennial publication. The battle of the Saints was seen later as such an innovation and as formative, Rodney thought little of it at the time. He acted because of a shift in the wind. The enduring reputation of Rodney should be for his restoration of discipline and high professional standards. He was very popular with the lower deck, a group hard to please.

Other biographies were David Hannay [**1481**], Rodney, 1891, in the English Men of Action series, and Donald Macintyre [**2267**], Admiral Rodney, 1962, a non-scholarly biography. An early biography was by the son-in-law of Rodney, Godfrey Mundy [**2584**], The Life and Correspondence of the Late Admiral Lord Rodney, 2 vols., 1830.

For the Naval History Society of New York, Dorothy Barck [**200**], 2 vols., 1932, published the extensive letter-books and order-books of Rodney while he was commander in the West Indies, 1780-1782. Included were such matters as intelligence about privateers, protection of trade, convoys, and cruisers.

11. Richard Howe

"Black Dick Howe" was commander of the North American squadron, mid-1770s, and reached Admiral of the Fleet rank and gained an earldom. He was First Lord in the 1780s. In 1797, he was called back to negotiate during Nore mutinies, giving in to all of the demands of the seamen, who respected him: Hardin Craig [784], "Black Dick Howe, the Sailor's Friend," 1949.

John Barrow [223], 1838, penned a life. Nothing followed until the 1960s. Ira Gruber [1413, 1414], 1961 and 1972, has a dissertation on Admiral Richard Howe and a book on Admiral Howe and his brother, General William Howe, both commanders of forces during the War of the American Revolution. Why did they fail to restore British rule? The strategy was to mix force with persuasion. Admiral Howe insisted on conciliation but the ministers in London were unsympathetic. All failed. Gruber aimed to rehabilitate Richard Howe.

Troyer Anderson [100], The Command of the Howe Brothers during the American Revolution, 1936, a scholarly effort but tilted toward land operations. Military-naval and political aspects must be considered when evaluating the performance of the Howe brothers.

12. John Jervis, Earl of St. Vincent

"Nelson's dear lord" and "old oak" were endearing terms describing John Jervis, longtime commander of the Mediterranean fleet, disciplinarian extraordinaire, credited with saving the RN from mutiny in 1797. He was promoted to Admiral of the Fleet and made Earl of St. Vincent, named for his greatest victory, the battle of Cape St. Vincent, Valentine's Day, 1797. Later, he was First Lord at a crucial time.

There was no good modern biography. There was Charles Arthur [142], The Remaking of the English Navy by Admiral St. Vincent: The Great Unclaimed Naval Revolution, 1795-1805, 1986, not a biography. Idiosyncratic, exaggerated, irritating, overstated, and conspiracy theorist, the blurb gave a taste: "Up to this time, the English naval revolution has been hidden from historical testimony by the corrupt sovereign masters who were saved by it." It was the administration and strategic vision of St. Vincent during the late 1790s which made the victories of Nelson possible.

Evelyn Berckman [301], Nelson's Dear Lord: Portrait of St. Vincent, 1962, was another effort. William Milbourne James [1787], "Old Oak": The Life of John Jervis, Earl St. Vincent, 1950; King George III calling him "my old oak," was barely adequate. Owen Sherrard [3304], A Life of Lord St. Vincent,

1933, was another mediocre effort. Ruddock Mackay [**2291**], 1990, wrote of the early years, 1735-1759; George Anson was a sponsor; frigate captain by age 25.

David Bonner Smith [**3350**], Letters of Admiral of the Fleet the Earl of St. Vincent Whilst First Lord of the Admiralty, 1801-1804, 2 vols., 1922-1927, a publication of the NRS, was organized by regional fleets, for example, Baltic, Channel, Mediterranean, and West Indian.

13. William Sydney Smith

If Nelson had a competitor, it would be Sidney Smith. Nelson called him "Swedish Knight," which was correct because he did receive a Swedish knighthood. Collingwood was not amused with Smith and Napoleon called him "half mad." Smith was in command of the naval force which destroyed the siege train of the French Egyptian army at Acre, ending Napoleonic dreams of conquering the Orient, as Alexander the Great had done. He did serve in the Swedish and the Turkish navies on occasion. Also, he was at Toulon in 1793 and in a Paris jail in 1798, from which he made a dramatic escape.

Tom Pocock [**2873**], A Thirst for Glory: The Life of Admiral Sir Sydney Smith, 1996, reviewed his characteristics: impulsive, tactless, insubordinate, and with fanciful ideas, but also imaginative, generous, and energetic, all comparable to Nelson. Another biography was by Lord Edward Frederick Russell of Liverpool [**3175**], Knight of the Sword: The Life and Letters of Admiral Sir William Sydney Smith, 1964. John Barrow [**221**], the son of the Naval secretary, wrote a biography, 2 vols., 1848.

Peter Shankland [**3288**], Beware of Heroes: Admiral Sir Sydney Smith's War against Napoleon, 1975, featured his campaign in the eastern Mediterranean in the late 1790s. An excellent historiographical survey was included, reviewing and "correcting" many of the adverse appraisals of Smith by historians, including A.T. Mahan, Herbert Richmond, David Bonner Smith, and J. Holland Rose.

14. Cuthbert Collingwood

Ever in the shadow of Nelson, second in command in the Mediterranean and at Trafalgar, Cuthbert Collingwood succeeded Nelson as commander, 1805-1810. He was rarely ashore during the first decade of the 19th century. In the DNB [**930**] entry, Laughton dismissed him as "mediocre," not deserved and not the first time Laughton was wrong.

Oliver Warner [**3770, 3759**], The Life and Letters of Vice-Admiral Lord Collingwood, 1968, and a piece on the character of Collingwood, 1969, the protege of Nelson, second in command at Trafalgar. He was ten years older than Nelson. Collingwood maintained the highest standards of professional leadership and duty.

William Clark Russell [**3182**], The Life of Admiral Lord Collingwood, 1895, was another biography and Edward Hughes [**1715**], 1957, edited the letters of Collingwood.

15. Thomas Cochrane, 10th Earl of Dundonald

Seen as most Nelson-like, the model for Marryat, G.A. Henty, Horatio Hornblower, Jack Aubrey, and other characters in nautical fiction of the Nelson era. **See 20., A.-D.** He was from a Scottish noble family and overall, had a notorious naval, political, and financial career. He failed in politics and was actually drummed out of the RN and the House of Commons for shady financial dealings; later reinstated. There were continuous financial issues in other venues, especially over prize money, even, and especially, when he commanded navies of Latin America, Chile and Brazil, later Greece, with offers from Spain, Peru, Mexico, and Malta. **See 7., I., 17.** He was buried in Westminster Abbey.

His autobiography [**684**], 2 vols., 1860. A. Cochrane [**683**], The Fighting Cochranes: A Scottish Clan over Six Hundred Years of Naval and Military History, 1983, was about the family by the 14th Earl of Dundonald.

A recent biography was Robert Harvey [**1545**], Cochrane: The Life and Exploits of a Fighting Captain, 2000, touting him as the greatest naval commander in history; his life was all action. Other biographies: Christopher Lloyd [**2159**], Lord Cochrane: Seaman, Radical, Liberator, 1947; Donald Thomas [**3594**], Cochrane: Britannia's Last Sea-King, 1978, an uncritical biography; J.P.W. Mallalieu [**2344**], Extraordinary Seaman, 1958, a popular biography; Ian Grimble [**1402**], The Sea Wolf, 1978; Warren Tute [**3676**], Cochrane: A Life of Admiral the Earl of Dundonald, 1965; Eric Twitchett [**3679**], Life of a Seaman: Thomas Cochrane, 10th Earl of Dundonald, 1931; John Fortescue [**1161**], Dundonald, 1895, in the English Men of Action series; an Argentine study in Spanish by Eros Siri [**3330**], 1979; for juveniles, Frank Knight [**1958**], Rebel Admiral, 1968; John Sugden [**3512**], 1981, in a dissertation on his early career; David Cubitt [**821**], 1974, on his exploits in the Chilean navy; F.C. Lynch [**2210**], 1975, and Peter McCormick [**2231**], 1997, pointed out specific connections between Cochrane and episodes of the career of Jack Aubrey, hero of the novels of Patrick O'Brian [**2660-2683**].

16. Samuel Pepys

Like Drake, but for different reasons, Samuel Pepys has attracted much interest. He was noted most widely for his famous diary and as a naval administrator. At the Admiralty, the titles of Pepys were Clerk of the Acts and Secretary to the Commission; in 1673 after passage of the Test Act, James, Duke of York, a Catholic, was forced out as Lord High Admiral, and the Admiralty was placed in Commission. He was Master of Trinity House. Pepys led reforms: victualling, exams for lieutenant, professionalization of the naval officer, an effective pay system, and oversaw a major warship building programme, 30 SOTL. Pepys himself collected extensive papers preparing to write a history of the navy and a history of the Dutch wars. That never materialized but those papers and his library went to Magdalene College, Cambridge, where there is currently a Pepysian Library. **See 4., B.** Pepys attended, 1651-1653. He was President of the Royal Society.

Pepys was most famous for Samuel Pepys [**2815-2818**], Diary, 11 vols., various editions, for example, 1893-1899, 1970-1983, and 1995; editors included Henry Wheatley and Robert Latham; covered the years 1660-1669, age 26-36, the formative period of his life, and he stopped because he feared he was going blind. He died, age 70, in 1703. Also published were Letters and the Second Diary, 1932, and Concise Pepys Diary, 1997. The diary, 3100 pages in the original, recounted the period of the second Dutch war, the Dutch in the Medway, the Great Plague of 1665, and the Great London Fire of 1666. **See 7., G., 6.** There were variations on the diary: Percival Hunt [**1736**], 1958, and Robert Latham [**2037-2039**], 1985 and 1988.

Joseph R. Tanner [**3565, 3568, 3566, 3567**], Mr. Pepys, 1925, Samuel Pepys and the Royal Navy, 1920, the Lees Knowles lectures of 1919, Pepys' Memoirs of the Royal Navy, 1679-1688, 1906, and Private Correspondence, 2 vols., 1926-1929, was the doyen of Pepysian scholars.

Arthur Bryant [**495, 494**], Samuel Pepys, 3 vols., 1933-1938, and Pepys and the Revolution, 1979, was based on the scholarly study of Tanner [**494, 495**], indeed, Bryant inherited the notes of Tanner, indeed, the Bryant biography was unfinished, ending exactly where the notes of Tanner ended, Tanner dying in 1931 before completing his biography. Thus, the last 14 years of the life of Pepys were not covered. Bryant took the Tory view, rehabilitating Charles II and James II. The titles: I: The Man in the Making, II: Years of Peril, and III: The Savior of the Navy.

Richard Ollard [**3699**], Pepys: A Biography, 1974, was elegantly written. A recent entry, Stephen Coote [**745**], Samuel Pepys: A Life, 2001, credited Pepys with inventing the British civil service. Geoffrey Trease [**3646**], Samuel Pepys and His World, 1972, featured profuse illustration. Bryan Ranft [**3007**], 1952, wrote a piece on the political career of Pepys; he served in the House of Commons, 1660-1688, so as to best represent the navy.

Others were Ivan Taylor [**3581**], Samuel Pepys, 1967, in the English Authors series; John Hearsey [**1590**], Young Mr. Pepys, 1973, lacked analysis; Cecil Emden [**1041**], Pepys Himself, 1963, focused on his character; Hallam Moorhouse [**2542**], Samuel Pepys: Administrator, Observer, Gossip, 1909, and most unsatisfactory, Vincent Brome [**449**], The Other Pepys, 1993, dwelling on the vulgar, the unscrupulous, the financial scandals, and the disordered sex life of Pepys.

A limited focus were Edward Chappell [**620**], The Tangier Papers of Samuel Pepys, 1935, a publication of the NRS, which demonstrated the Whig-

Tory factions and their effects on the navy, and Robert Latham [**2038**], Samuel Pepys and the Second Dutch War, 1995, a publication of the NRS, was enlightening on the bureaucracy of the navy.

Almost equally famous as diarist was John Evelyn [**1061**], Diary, 6 vols., 1906. The Pepys-John Evelyn relationship was presented by Guy de la Bedoyere [**271, 270**], Particular Friends: The Correspondence of Samuel Pepys and John Evelyn, 1997, and an abridged edition of the Evelyn diary, 1993, represented exchange of correspondence over 40 years; both were involved with the Royal Society and Evelyn was Commissioner of the Sick and Wounded, especially concerned about the casualties from the Dutch wars.

E. MISCELLANEOUS

"Miscellaneous" has nothing to do with importance. As with all of this historiographical-bibliographical survey, coverage depended of what and how much has been published about the subject, or, in this case, about the officer-personality. Mass does not equal fame or significance. The immediate previous personality, Thomas Cochrane, 10th Earl of Dundonald, has 14 entries, whereas, Cuthbert Collingwood, second in command to Nelson and his successor for years as commander of the Mediterranean fleet during the height of the Napoleonic war, has only 3, as does Edward Hawke, one of the most brilliant commanders of the Seven Years' War. Some of these anomalies will be pointed out in the chapter on Gaps in the Literature. **See 22.**

A long, descriptive listing of individual pieces on naval personalities follows, in chronological order.

Charles Howard of Effingham, Earl of Notingham

Howard was a brilliant administrator when he was Lord High Admiral, 1587-1603. He led the preparation and mobilization for defense against the Spanish Armada and attacks on Spanish ports, trade, and colonies. He has had a bad press, "corrupt" being the most-used description. Robert Kenny [**1885**] wrote Elizabeth's Admiral: The Political Career of Charles Howard, Earl of Nottingham, 1536-1624, 1970, and Donald Farmer [**1077**], 1965, did a dissertation on Howard, lamenting at best, neglect, or at worst, derogatory interpretations, of his accomplishments. There was a contemporaneous account, Petrucci Ubaldini [**3685**], Lord Howard of Effingham and the Spanish Armada, 1919, written about 1600.

Edward Montague, 1st Earl of Sandwich

R.C. Anderson [**87**], 1929, for the NRS, and Richard Ollard [**2696**], 1994, were accounts of the naval career of Edward Montagu, first Earl of Sandwich, admiral and general-at-sea, active under Cromwell and during the first decade of the Restoration. He led naval operations in the Mediterranean.

Robert Rich, 2nd Earl of Warwick

Privateer extraordinaire, commander of fleets of privateers in the early 17th century; when privateering became illegal under James I, Warwick turned to piracy. He was an opponent of Charles I and served as Lord High Admiral of the Parliamentary navy during the Civil War. His interventions were decisive more than once. Frank Craven [788], 1930, described his exploits. Warwick operated fleets of privateers. Nelson Bard [201] was noted as preparing a biography.

William Penn

Lucie Street [3473], An Uncommon Sailor: A Portrait of Sir William Penn: English Naval Supremacy, 1986, credited Penn with revolutionizing naval warfare. He was active in the Dutch wars. He was the father of the founder of Pennsylvania, Charles II rewarding the son for the achievements of the father.

Thomas Allin

R.C. Anderson [89], The Journals of Sir Thomas Allin, 1660-1678, 1939-1940, a publication of the NRS, was about the Four Days' Battle during the Anglo-Dutch Wars, plus service in Algiers and in the Mediterranean.

Prince Rupert, Count Palantine, Duke of Bavaria

Prince Rupert was nephew to Charles I, an army and naval commander, known as the "mad Cavalier." He led the Royalist fleet during the Civil War and served as admiral after the Restoration. He commanded fleets in the Second and Third Dutch wars and was instrumental in the development of the Fighting Instructions [751] for the RN. Frank Kitson [1951], Prince Rupert, 2 vols., 1994-1996, was a substantial, authoritative, scholarly biography, the first volume on "soldier" and the second on "admiral and general-at-sea. Clennell Wilkinson [3859] wrote Prince Rupert, the Cavalier, 1935. J.R. Powell [2929] wrote of Monke and Rupert.

Richard Holmes

Richard Ollard [2698], Man of War: Sir Richard Holmes and the Restoration Navy, 1968, an obscure cavalry, turned naval, officer. He originally served under Prince Rupert in the Royalist navy during the Civil War, and continued in the navy of the Restoration. Ollard noted the assessment of a wag: "cursed beginner of two Dutch wars." He was assistant administrator of the navy under Samuel Pepys. He led the raid recovering New York from the Dutch.

Henry Mainwaring

The Life and Works of Henry Mainwaring, 2 vols., 1920-1921, a publication of NRS, was by George Manwaring [2360]. Henry Mainwaring [2337] operated against and wrote about pirates, was a Brother, then a Master, of Trinity House, and contributed The Seaman's Dictionary, composed, 1620-1623, published in 1644. He was an early authority on seamanship and nautical terms and wrote Discourse on Pirates, 1618.

Henry Teonage
George Manwaring [**2356**], Diary of Henry Teonage: Chaplain on Board HMS ASSISTANCE and ROYAL OAK, 1675-1679, 1927, was the journal of this naval chaplain of the 17th century.

John Benbow
William Benbow [**290**], Brave Benbow: The Life of Vice-Admiral John Benbow, 1653-1702, 1987, fought a famous battle against the French which was thwarted by mutinous captains.

Arthur Herbert, Earl of Torrington
Peter LeFevre [**2096, 2095**], 1990, has produced an article and was preparing a biography on Arthur Herbert, Earl of Torrington, commander of Anglo-Dutch naval forces off Beachy Head, defeated by the French. A court martial for refusal to fight the enemy acquitted him.

John Leake
Geoffrey Callender [**552**], The Life of Sir John Leake, Rear-Admiral of Great Britain, 1920, a publication of the NRS, was about naval operations of 1690s.

Woodes Rogers
Woodes Rogers [**3132**] was a circumnavigator, most famous or infamous, for depositing and recovering Alexander Selkirk on a remote Pacific island for 4 years as recounted by Bryan Little [**2144**], Crusoe's Captain: Being the Life of Woodes Rogers, Seaman, Trader, Colonial Governor, 1960, and George Manwaring [**2362**], Woodes Rogers: Privateer and Governor, 1928.

Peter Warren
In a dissertation and a book, Julian Gwyn [**1431, 1432**], The Enterprising Admiral: The Personal Fortune of Admiral Sir Peter Warren, 1972 and 1974, focused on the finances of this early 18th-century admiral. His wealth came from prize money, a new kind of entrepreneurship with global perspectives. He was influential all over the empire: New York, Boston, Charleston, Dublin, and London. **See 15., C.**

Edmund Lechmere
John West [**3820**], A Captain in the Navy of Queen Anne, 1970, in the Then and There series, was about Edmund Lechmere.

George Rooke

Oscar Browning [478] and John Hattendorf [1559], The Journal of Sir George Rooke: Admiral of the Fleet, 1700-1702 and 1700-1704, 1897 and forthcoming, publications of the NRS. Rooke was noted for the famous naval campaign in the Mediterranean culminating in the capture of Gibraltar.

Cloudesley Shovell

Simon Harris [1532], Sir Cloudesley Shovell: Stuart Admiral, 2000, wrote of this unfortunate soul, best known for the disaster of the Scilly Islands in 1707 when the flagship, ASSOCIATION, and 3 others ran up on the rocks, killing over 2000. It was Shovell who made the decision to proceed during the night, all based on estimates of set and drift.

George Byng, Lord Torrington

J.L. Cranmer-Byng [786], Pattee Byng's Journal, 1718-1720, 1950, a publication of the NRS, recounted events of the Sicilian campaign led by George Byng, Lord Torrington, a decisive victory over the Spanish fleet at Cape Passaro.

John Byng

William Cuthbert Brian Tunstall [3661], The Byng Papers, 3 vols., 1930-1932, a publication of the NRS, included George Byng, Viscount Torrington and his son, John Byng, covering operations in the War of Spanish Succession. The father rose to First Lord and the son, John Byng, was court martialled and executed after the battle of Minorca.

Stephen Martin

Clements Markham [2384], Life of Stephen Martin, 1666-1740, 1895, a publication of the NRS, served in the merchant and naval services, 1686-1714, ultimately as flag captain during the War of Spanish Succession.

James Tregenen

Christopher Lloyd [2160], 1959, edited the memoir of James Tregenen during the late 18th century, a publication of the NRS. Tregenen was a midshipman on the third voyage of Cook, wrote a pamphlet on corporal punishment, and later served in the Russian navy of Catherine the Great.

Augustus Hervey

Michael Holmes [1660], Augustus Hervey: A Naval Casanova, 1996, focused on other achievements, 1740-1760s, Hervey being a notorious philanderer and rake, depicted as the most dashing British naval officer. He served with John Byng at Minorca and gave evidence at the court martial. Other duties were with the blockade of Brest and capture of Havana. He won 9,000

pounds in prize money. He was later naval commissioner and member of Parliament.
George Pocock

Richard Simpson [**3326**], 1951, did a dissertation on Admiral Sir George Pocock, his naval career spanning the 1740s-1760s.

Home Riggs Popham

Hugh Popham [**2918**], <u>A Damned Cunning Fellow: The Eventful Life of Rear-Admiral Sir Home Popham, 1762-1820</u>, 1991, described the inventor of a method of signaling and experimenter with submarine design; Richard Waite [**3733**], 1945, a dissertation-biography of Home Riggs Popham.

Edward Pellew, 1st Viscount Exmouth

Pellew was deemed the frigate captain <u>extraordinaire</u>. Edward Pellew, Viscount Exmouth, was a contemporary of Admiral Lord Nelson, best known for his great victories against superior warships in frigate battles. He later was commander-in-chief of the Mediterranean fleet. In 1816, after the Wars of the French Revolution and Napoleon, he commanded the fleet which bombarded the Barbary capital of Algiers. The result was the release of over 3000 slaves. Born in 1757, Pellew grew up in Penzance, joining the Royal Navy in 1770. He died in 1833.

Pellew distinguished himself commanding a series of frigates and frigate squadrons, especially HMS INDEFATIGABLE. His victory against a French frigate in June 1793 was the first British victory of the Wars of the French Revolution and Napoleon. Later, several French prizes were taken. The French ship of the line, DROIT DE L'HOMME, 74 guns, was defeated in January 1797 by Pellew in another frigate.

C. Northcote Parkinson [**2762**], <u>Edward Pellew, Viscount Exmouth: Admiral of the Red</u>, 1934, was the standard biography.

George Cadogen

Robert Pearman [**2798**], <u>The Cadogans at War, 1783-1862</u>, 1990, began with George Cadogan who serviced under Pellew aboard that famous frigate, HMS INDEFATIGABLE.

Earl of Egmont

Clive Wilkinson [**3861**], 1998, wrote an article on the Earl of Egmont, stressing operations during the 1760s and presenting an outstanding introduction of the RN, 1715-1760s.

Andrew Hamond

William Moomaw [**2532**], 1956, did a dissertation on the naval career of Captain Andrew Hamond during the 1770s. <u>The Hamond Naval Papers,</u>

1766-1825 [**1471**], 1966, were on 3 rolls of microfilm, the originals were in the library of the University of Virginia.

Samuel, Lord Hood
    One of the naval commanders during the War of the American Revolution was Samuel Hood. Dorothy Hood [**1663**] wrote The Admirals Hood, 1911, included Samuel Viscount Hood and Alexander Viscount Bridport. David Hannay [**1478**], Letters Written by Sir Samuel Hood, Viscount Hood, 1781-1783, 1895, a publication of NRS, included a description of the battle of the Chesapeake.

James Gambier
    David Syrett [**3551**], "'This Penurious Old Reptile': Rear-Admiral James Gambier and the American War," 2001, was about the commander at New York during the American Revolution, a veteran of Louisbourg and Quiberon Bay.

John Montague, 4th Earl of Sandwich
    N.A.M. Rodger [**3109**], The Insatiable Earl: A Life of John Montagu, Fourth Earl of Sandwich, 1718-1792, 1993, produced the definitive biography, effectively rehabilitating Sandwich. The "Whig" historians and the DNB [**930**] entry besmirched the reputation of Sandwich: he was corrupt and was responsible for the defeat of the RN in the War of the American Revolution; his mistress, mother of five of his children, was murdered on the steps of Admiralty House; a gambler, and inventor of the sandwich. It was American historians who exaggerated the importance of the loss of America. Look at the "high politics" of the period, 1740s-1780s, when Sandwich was at the Admiralty. Sandwich was a distinguished, effective, and perceptive First Lord. His personnel appointments were brilliant. His reforms featured maintenance of warships, especially concerning timber and copper, and reform of the dockyards. To appreciate Sandwich, look at the global perspective: America may have been lost, but Canada, the West Indies, and India were saved, plus, he saved Handel for posterity. The older standard biography was George Martelli [**2420**], Jeremy Twitcher: A Life of the Fourth Earl of Sandwich, 1718-1792, 1962. There was a dissertation by Mary Wickwire [**3851**], 1963, which focused on the naval administration of Sandwich, 1771-1782.

John Paul Jones
    Clearly, the most notorious American opponent deserved a place here. Most pertinent was the series of operations led by Jones around the British Isles during the late 1770s, culminating in the battle of Flamborough Head on the northeast coast, BONHOME RICHARD vs HMS SERIPUS.

Samuel Eliot Morison [**2549**], <u>John Paul Jones: A Sailor's Biography</u>, 1959, gained the Pulitzer Prize for the biography. It was republished in <u>Classics of Naval Literature</u>.

Lincoln Lorenz [**2189**], <u>John Paul Jones: Fighter for Freedom and Glory</u>, 1943, was a comprehensive, scholarly biography. Augustus Buell [**503**], <u>Paul Jones: Founder of the American Navy</u>, 1900, was criticized for fabrication and glorification. Don Seitz [**3268**], <u>Paul Jones: His Exploits in English Seas during 1778-1780</u>, 1917, used contemporaneous newspapers as a source describing the operations. The preeminent American naval historian, James Bradford [**417, 416**], 1986, gathered the papers of John Paul Jones in ten reels of microfilm, the most important source on Jones. Jones was prominently included in his <u>Command under Sail</u>, 3 vols., 1985-1987, a collection of scholarly articles.

Pierre-Andre Suffren

A French opponent deserved consideration. Roderick Cavaliero [**596**], <u>Admiral Satan: The Life and Campaigns of Suffren</u>, 1994, was a recent biography of Pierre-Andre Suffren, a Knight in the Order of St. John of Malta most noted for command of five major naval battles in the Indian Ocean in the early 1780s, never defeated; his British naval antagonist was Edward Hughes. Allied with the Nabob of Mysore with the aim of destroying the realm of the British East India Company, his naval tactics were studied by Nelson. Napoleon regretted Suffren died in 1788, hoping he would be the French "Nelson"; the effort in India failed. Francois Caron [**579**], 1996, surveyed the great battles in a French study and questioned whether Suffren deserved his naval reputation. Most was based on one, final battle. He kept blaming his captains for cowardice. British East India trade was little affected and, most important, the French lost India.

Louis Rene de Latouche

A later French opponent was touted as "the Admiral who defied Nelson": Louis Rene de Latouche, the French admiral who led the French fleet during the preliminaries to what became the Trafalgar campaign, 1803-1805. **See 7., I., 10.** He had confronted Nelson, quite successfully, at Boulogne in 1801 and at Toulon in 1804; he died in August 1804, to be succeeded by Villeneuve. This was recounted by Rene Monaque [**2526**], 2000, who concluded: he died in August 1804, "otherwise the results at Trafalgar may have been different."

Thomas Masterman Hardy

"Kiss me, Hardy" were said to be the last words of Nelson at Trafalgar on 21 October 1805, talking to his flag-captain, Thomas Hardy, one of the Band of Brothers.

John Gore [**1327**], <u>Nelson's Hardy and His Wife</u>, 1935, was as close as we have to a biography. The wife was Louisa, Lady Hardy, afterwards Lady Seaford. Derek Severn [**3284**], 1977, wrote a short survey of his career.

Charles Cotton
Paul Krajeski [**1975, 1974**], <u>In the Shadow of Nelson: The Naval Leadership of Admiral Sir Charles Cotton, 1753-1812</u>, 2000, did a dissertation and book on this officer, prominent in the blockade during the Peninsular campaign and successor in 1810 to Collingwood as commander of the Mediterranean fleet.

George Cockburn
George Cockburn had a full career all the way to Admiral of the Fleet, from 1793-1848, deemed "Nelson's acolyte," serving with him in frigates in the 1790s. He was dubbed "predator of the Chesapeake" for formulating the plan for the Chesapeake campaign of 1814. In August 1815, HMS NORTHUMBERLAND rendezvoused with HMS BELLERPHON, and the prisoner, Napoleon Bonaparte was transferred, then en route to St. Helena. Cockburn was jailor of Napoleon, overseeing the exile on St. Helena during the first year. He was a reactionary Tory and anti-reformist as MP, thus, suffering from the Whig naval historians. He rose to the Navy Board and First Sea Lord. Interestingly, his papers wound up in the Library of Congress, Washington. **See 7., I., 14 and 16.**
A. James Pack [**2722**], <u>The Man Who Burned the White House: Admiral Sir George Cockburn, 1772-1853</u>, 1987, and Roger Morriss [**2569**], <u>Cockburn and the British Navy in Transition</u>, 1997, were biographies. "Transition" was demonstrated by themes in his career: professional conduct, management of seamen, and the politics of administration.

George, 2nd Earl Spencer
Julian Corbett [**756**], 4 vols., 1913-1924, a publication of the NRS, edited the papers of George, Second Earl Spencer, First Lord from 1794-1801. Events included Cape St. Vincent, the mutinies of 1797, Camperdown, the Nile, and Copenhagen.

Lord Keith
William Perrin [**2826**], <u>The Keith Papers</u>, 3 vols., 1927-1955, a publication of the NRS, presented letters and papers of Admiral Lord Keith, covering his career from the 1770s until retirement in 1815.

Charles Middleton, Lord Barham
John Talbott [**3561**], <u>The Pen and Ink Sailor: Charles Middleton and the King's Navy, 1778-1813</u>, 1998, wrote of Middleton, later Lord Barham, controller of the navy and First Lord during and after the Trafalgar campaign.

He was credited with preparing the RN for the Wars of the French Revolution and Napoleon. John Knox Laughton [**2046**] published his letters and papers, 3 vols., 1907-1911, a publication of the NRS. Barham was one of the national administrators who contributed to the making of the "fiscal-military state." **See 13., A.**

John Markham

Clements Markham [**2385**], 1904, a publication of the NRS, presented the correspondence of Admiral John Markham during the decade of the 1800s, a protege of St. Vincent and later, First Sea Lord under First Lord St. Vincent.

Anthony Gardner

R. Vesey Hamilton [**1466**], 1906, edited the journal of James Anthony Gardner, a commander, RN, 1775-1814, a publication of the NRS. Comparison with the fictional Roderick Random was noted.

William Dillon

Michael Lewis [**2124**], 1953, a publication of the NRS, presented the narrative of Vice-Admiral William Dillon, serving in the 1790s, in war and peace.

Edward Codrington

Jane Bourchier [**381**], 2 vols., 1873, edited the memoirs of Edward Codrington, an admiral, among other things, a veteran of the Glorious First of June.

John Moore

Carola Oman [**2703, 2704**], biographer of Nelson, wrote Sir John Moore, 1953, about the commander of the assault force of the Egyptian campaign of 1801.

Robert and Nicholas Tomlinson

J.G. Bullocke [**508**], The Tomlinson Papers, 1935, a publication of the NRS, presented the correspondence between Robert and Nicholas Tomlinson, naval officers, 1768-1796, for example, about manning without impressment and timber preservation.

George Berkeley

Brian De Toy [**915**], recounted the career of another naval leader in the Peninsular campaign, George Berkeley, "Wellington's admiral," in a dissertation, 1997. De Toy insisted that naval power was vital to the success of Wellington and lamented that it had been neglected by historians.

James Saumarez

A.N. Ryan [**3197**], The Saumarez Papers, 1968, was the only account about an admiral who deserved more: James Saumarez, veteran at the Saints, Cape St. Vincent, the Nile, the blockade of Brest, and finally, recounted in this collection, commander of the Baltic fleet, 1808-1810, in the flagship, HMS VICTORY. Saumarez was not a favorite of Nelson; he was more a protege of St. Vincent.

William Hoste

Tom Pocock [**2871**], Remember Nelson: The Life of Captain Sir William Hoste, 1977, played up the great role of frigate captains, Hoste being one of the finest. He operated in the Adriatic, neutralizing a series of key fortresses on the Dalmatian coast, "real Hornblower stuff." The title came from a flag signal initiated by Hoste as he led his ships into a battle in 1814. The monument to Hoste was next to that of Nelson in St. Paul's cathedral.

P.B.V Broke and Provo Wallis

John Brighton [**441, 440**], 1866 and 1892, wrote of naval commanders P.B.V. Broke and Provo Wallis.

Samuel Walters

C. Northcote Parkinson [**2768**], 1949, edited the journal of Samuel Walters, a lieutenant, RN, serving 1797-1810.

David Bartholomew

Conrad Dixon [**941**], 1993, recounted the career of David Bartholomew, who progressed from a victim of the press gang, veteran of several battles, promotion to acting lieutenant, and gaining expertise in navigation and amphibious warfare.

Bartholomew James

John Knox Laughton [**2044**], 1896. edited the journal of Bartholomew James, 1752-1828, a publication of the NRS.

Abraham Crawford

Abraham Crawford [**789**], 1999, kept a journal, subtitled A Quarter-Deck View of the War against Napoleon. Featured were operations in the Mediterranean, 1800-1815, the boredom of naval life for blockading squadrons, and the opposition to impressment by Crawford.

James A. Gordon

Bryan Perrett [**2822**], The Real Hornblower: The Life of Admiral of the Fleet Sir James Alexander Gordon, GCB: Last Governor of the Royal Naval Hospital, Greenwich, 1997, described the naval career of Gordon. Gordon was commander of a squadron of frigates in the Adriatic in 1808 which achieved spectacular victories over a larger squadron of Venetian-French frigates. He was commander of the squadron which attacked Alexandria, Virginia, during 1814 at the time Cockburn was burning the White House. He led the unsuccessful attack on Baltimore when Francis Scott Key wrote the "Star Spangled Banner." Other, more persuasive models for Hornblower were Saumarez, Pellew, Hoste, and Cochrane.

Maurice Hewson
    Antony Brett-James [**432**], 1981, recounted the escape from the French by Captain Maurice Hewson, 1803-1809.

T. Marmaduke Wybourn
    Sea Soldier, 2000, by Anne Petrides [**2836**], recounted the exploits of T. Marmaduke Wybourn, Royal Marines, who served under Nelson, Collingwood, Duncan, and Cockburn.

Fredrick Hoffman
    A. Beckford Bevan [**314**], A Sailor of King George: The Journal of Captain Frederick Hoffman, RN, 1793-1814, 1901, in the Classics of Naval Literature series, was about Hoffman, a veteran of 18 major battles, including Trafalgar, and spending 2 years as a Prisoner of War in a French prison.

Nisbet Willoughby
    M.H. Mason [**2456**], Willoughby the Immortal, 1969, recounted the naval career of Nisbet Willoughby, "the hero of Mauritius."

Sam Barrington, John Boteler, and Thomas Byam Martin
    Three publications of the NRS were about naval officers who began their careers just before 1815: David Bonner Smith [**3348, 3353**], 2 vols. and 1 vol., 1937-1941 and 1942, respectively, about the papers of Admiral Samuel Barrington and Captain John Harvey Boteler, and Richard Vesey Hamilton [**1465**], 3 vols., 1898-1903, who edited the papers of Admiral of the Fleet Thomas Byam Martin, a veteran of the blockade of Brest and the Baltic where he met Tsar Alexander I.

Chapter 10

Human Resources: The Lower Deck

The previous chapter, "Personalities," dealt with naval officers with the exception of Horatio Lord Nelson and William Bligh, those two rating a separate "Special Emphasis" chapter. This chapter, "Human Resources," will deal with the enlisted man and woman of the lower deck up until 1815; women, because a large number of recent works focused on women and the sea, for example, Female Tars, Women under Sail, She Captains, Hen Frigates, Iron Men, Wooden Women, and Women Sailors and Sailors' Women. In the parlance of the RN, the "lower deck" was the abode of the enlisted man; the "quarterdeck" was the identifiable location associated with the officer class. Each had his place, everyone knew his place, and, at least, during this period, there was little or no mobility from one to the other. In the previous chapter were found numerous individual, named persons, most being prominent, and all being involved in notable events. Hundreds of "personalities" were reviewed. In this chapter, many less individual persons were identifiable. "Lower deck" was a collective status. Some individuals will be covered, but, comparatively, very few.

     "Lower deck" was the abode of the enlisted person. Much has been written about life and condition on the lower deck. Themes included health factors, for example, scurvy and environmental conditions; discipline, punishment, for example, flogging; victualling, wages, recruitment, for example, manning and impressment; mutiny, the role of women, and sexuality, for example, sexually transmitted disease and homosexuality. Popularly designated collective names have arisen for symbolic members of enlisted forces, for example, Tommy Atkins for the British soldier, Digger for the Australian soldier, Jackboot for the German soldier, and Johnny Reb for the Confederate soldier. For the enlisted man of the RN, it was Jack Tar.

A. SOCIAL HISTORIES OF THE LOWER DECK

The student and the researcher would do well to introduce him or herself to the social history of the lower deck by going to Christopher Lloyd [**2149**], The British Seaman, 1200-1860: A Social Survey, 1968, documenting men of the lower deck, merchant and naval. The reader immediately will notice that conditions on the lower deck were described variously, some presenting worst case scenarios, some insisting the worst has been exaggerating, and some, the most scholarly in most cases, insisting that the lower deck was a microcosm of society in general.

For more specific periods, N.A.M. Rodger [**3117**], The Wooden World: An Anatomy of the Georgian Navy, 1986, has produced the most remarkable survey. The period 1755-1763 was the focus. Life and conditions on the lower deck were similar to life and conditions at large in Britain in the 18th century, a microcosm of society. Ashore, the RN was the largest industrial organization in the western world. He disagreed with the traditional stereotypes: naval discipline was harsh and oppressive, a floating concentration camp. What was true was that life was filled "with innumerable perils" and grog was "the sailor's best friend." Rodger does put the best light on the volatile issues: the press gang, punishment, mutiny, officer-enlisted relations, and the patronage system. All of this contrasted to Marcus Rediker [**3037**], Between the Devil and the Deep Blue Sea, 1987. **See 10., C. and D.**

H.W.F. Baynham [**250**], From the Lower Deck: The Old Navy, 1780-1840, 1969, was actually the first study of a trilogy, the second and third books applicable to the post-1815 era. Baynham produced an outstanding synthesis of writings, journals, diaries, and correspondence from the lower deck. Major concerns were impressment and punishment.

Peter Earle [**1009**], Sailors: English Merchant Seamen, 1650-1775, 1998, was about the lower decks of naval and merchant ships and their contribution in creating the world's greatest maritime and commercial power. He reconstructed everyday life. Life was "not short, nasty, and brutish." Many were literate and musically inclined. Mutiny was rare and homosexuality virtually unknown.

Michael Lewis [**2127**], A Social History of the Navy, 1793-1815, 1960, described themes, for example, officers and men, recruitment, promotion, rewards, and punishment.

Peter Kemp [**1858**], The British Sailor: A Social History of the Lower Deck, 1970, covered the extent of the modern navy and incorporated lengthy extracts from contemporary sources. There were the usual suspects, all bad: treatment, manning, pay, and food.

W.R. Thrower [**3616**], Life at Sea in the Age of Sail, 1972, was observations of a physician about medical and social problems of European seamen over time. Michael Mason [**2455**], The British Seafarers, 1980, profusely and beautifully illustrated, was a BBC production for the NMM.

Ernest Sanger [**3220**], Englishmen at War: A Social History in Letters, 1993, collected letters from British persons at war, 1500 to the present. Even though there were appalling conditions and harsh treatment, especially at sea, they remained loyal and supportive.

The 15th century and 18th century were studied by John Masefield [**2449, 2448**], 1905 and 1906, then Poet Laureate. The latter, Sea Life in Nelson's Time, became notorious for presenting the worst, most pessimistic view, for example, describing in detail flogging, running the gauntlet, keel hauling, and hanging. All was exaggerated, presenting the worst as normal. Dudley Pope [**2898**], Life in Nelson's Navy, 1981, perpetuated the Masefield fallacies, presenting the worst-case scenario.

John Laffin [**1988**], Jack Tar: The Story of the British Sailor, 1969, was a popularized account stressing the worst. Florence Dyer [**1003**], 1924, studied "the Elizabethan sailorman," untaught and untamed and subject to long, dangerous voyages. There were no hammocks until 1597. Conditions of overcrowding, lack of ventilation, bad food, fevers, and scurvy prevailed. Cheryl Fury [**1220, 1221**], 1998 and 2002, described the lives of Elizabethan seamen ashore. The sources were wills and parish records. It was followed Tides in the Affairs of Men: The Social History of Elizabeth Seamen, a history from below recognizing the contribution of these ordinary seamen for maritime expansion and ultimate global hegemony.

The title was uninformative, English Seamen and Traders in New Guinea, 1553-1565, 1992, by J.D. Alsop [**56**], but the sources and methodology were innovative: a total of 90 wills of seamen held at the PRO and the Guildhall Library. Extraordinary detail about shipboard life in the 16th century was revealed: terms of service, manning, possessions, indebtedness, social networks, and the common practice of private trading.

Donald Kennedy [**1872**], 1964, studied the common seamen of the early Stuart period. They formed a distinct group with peculiar characteristics and the Crown ignored their contributions, driving them into the hands of Parliament.

Charles LeGuin [**2104**], 1967, focused on the 17th century based on publications of the Hakluyt Society. Merchant crews were always larger than needed initially so as to fill in for the inevitable deaths; excess officers to prevent mutinies. Ronald Hope [**1666**], Poor Jack: The Perilous History of the Merchant Seaman, 2001, was an anthology, accounts of life at sea: from Hakluyt, Drake, Anson, Cook, Dana, and Conrad. W.J. Bolster [**360**], Black Jacks, 1997, was about African-American seamen in the age of sail, including those of British ships during colonial times. At the high point of their participation in 1815, they comprised 20% of crews.

Stan Hugill [**1721**], Sailortown, 1967, described the conditions of naval ports in a composite picture, illustrating how seamen spent their time ashore: whoring, boozing, and debauchery. But, all was not bad.

J.D. Davies [**874**], 1986, had a dissertation on political, religious, and social aspects of naval personnel, 1660-1689. The depiction by Pepys [**2817**] was not a true picture: much more than "gentlemen" and "tarpaulin" officers presiding over brutalized seamen.

The renowned nautical fiction writer, Patrick O'Brian [**2673**], wrote Men-of-War: Life in Nelson's Navy, 1974, with illustrations, an ideal companion to the Aubrey-Maturin novels [**2660-2683**]. There were interesting details, for example, tables of gunnery, victualling, prize distribution, sail plans, and cross-sections of hulls. Steve Pope [**2917**], Hornblower's Navy: Life at Sea in the Age of Nelson, 1998, was massive folio size, was based on Hornblower, "the most enduring military hero in British fiction," and nominated James Alexander Gordon as the model used by Forester. Curiously, Gordon was not listed among the "bright stars" of the era. There was a two-page schematic of HMS VICTORY. Edward Fraser [**1183**], The Sailors Whom Nelson Led, 1913, presented first-hand accounts. They were listed individually in a publication of the Nelson Society, The Men Who Fought with Nelson at Trafalgar [**2495**], 1989.

John de Courcy Ireland [**1752**], 1959, described Irish seamen in naval warfare, 1793-1815; how many and what they did.

Brian Lavery [**2081**], Shipboard Life and Organisation, 1731-1815, 1998, a publication of the NRS, reviewed regulations, instructions, discipline, punishment, and medical journals. Jon Lewis [**2117**], The Mammoth Book of Life before the Mast, 2001, was a collection of extracts of accounts from British and American seamen.

As with officers, there was provision for education of sorts at the level of the lower deck. F.B. Sullivan [**3514**], 1976, wrote about the professional schoolmaster; between 1712-1824, 394 of them served in the RN. Michael Lewis [**2126**] assessed the programme as a failure. Dan Turner [**3671**], The Cradle of the Navy, 1980, was about the Royal Hospital School at Greenwich and at Holbrook, 1694-1988, for the children of the pensioners. Sons automatically went into the RN. **See 17., O.**

Too little has appeared about the RN and religion during this period. **See 22.** Two aspects have been covered.

As with schoolmaster, chaplain was an assigned billet on ships of the RN. Gordon Taylor [**3580**], The Sea Chaplains, 1978, was a substantial, albeit, self-serving study, including a complete listing from 1626. They served a variety of roles, similar to a modern social worker, "Jehovah's ambassadors." Walter Scott [**3262**], 1935, has a dissertation on some early ones in the 17th century.

Seamen's missions was an international movement, there being a number of sponsors, for example, the Society for the Promotion of Christian Knowledge, the British and Foreign Sailors' Society, and the Bethel Movement. These activities were described in a book and article by Roald Kverndal [**1980, 1981**], 1986 and 1979, by Mary Walrond [**3745**], 1904, and in a dissertation by Alston Kennerley [**1884**], 1989.

Colin Howell [**1700**], <u>Jack Tar in History: Essays on the History of Maritime Life and Labour</u>, 1991, presented a series of essays from a conference in 1990. The themes were Marxist in the tradition of E.P. Thompson and George Rude: mass protest actions, opposition to impressment, mutiny as equivalent to strikes, and disagreement with N.A.M. Rodger [**3117**]. Conditions were more harsh than he depicted.

Margaret Creighton [**794**], 1985, did a dissertation based on a series of diaries on sailors at sea in the 19th century. She concluded that the participants were a subculture with much in common. Eugene Rasor [**3015**], <u>Reform in the Royal Navy: A Social History of the Lower Deck, 1850 to 1880</u>, 1976, covered these issues two generations later; some had not changed but reform was clear and obvious, for example, punishment returns forced reduction because of pressure from above and the continuous service system regularized recruitment and solved the manning problem.

The traditions of the lower deck in the American navy came from those of the RN. The spokesperson for that story was Harold Langley [**2026, 2028**] with a dissertation and a book, <u>Social Reform in the United States Navy</u>, 1960 and 1967, covering the period, 1798-1862. Corporal punishment was abolished in 1850 and the spirit ration in 1862. Ira Dye [**999**], 1973, conducted a profile of the seafarer of 1812 using American registration records and British records of American prisoners; 20 percent were Black.

An old "friendly address to the seamen of the British navy" was published by Charles Penrose [**2813**], 1820. David Phillipson [**2852**], <u>Band of Brothers: Boy Seamen in the Royal Navy, 1800-1956</u>, 1996, focused on training of the boy seaman rating, formerly officer servants. Excessive detail and an incorrect title marred the effort.

B. INDIVIDUAL ACCOUNTS OF LIFE ON THE LOWER DECK

The lower deck was more a collective phenomenon than the quarterdeck, identified more with prominent individuals, some outstanding and well-known leaders. Some members of the lower deck have been identified, perhaps more than one might expect.

H.G. Thursfield [**2617**], <u>Five Naval Journals, 1789-1817</u>, 1951, a publication of the NRS, included 5 recollections of naval service. Elliot Snow [**3380**], 1925, collected accounts from four seamen, for example, Charles Barnard and John Nicol.

John Nicol, Samuel Leech, Robert Hay, and Jacob Nagle became well-known and influential published recollections. An individual account of John Nicol [**2638**], 1802, described his career of 25 years in the RN and merchant and fishing services. The experiences varied: to Greenland, China, the first ship to Hawaii after the death of Cook, in the Second Fleet to Australia, at Cape St. Vincent and the Nile, victim of the press gang, and denied a pension. Dean King

[**1933**], "Everyman Will Do His Duty," 1997, was an anthology of 22 firsthand accounts by 17 participants of life aboard ship in the age of Nelson, for example, accounts of the First of June, Cape St. Vincent, Trafalgar, and an interview with Nelson. Jonathan Press [**2943**], 1976, recounted experiences of seamen from Bristol, in the 18th century the second port of the land. Subjects included pay, food, disease, mortality rates, privateering, and press gangs.

Samuel Leech [**2093**], 1851, served in the American and RN each more than once: taken prisoner and deserting. This became a standard account of the details of the punishment of flogging, influencing Richard Henry Dana [**850**]. Arbitrary actions of officers were also documented. **See 9., A.**

M.D. Hay [**1579**], Landsman Hay: The Memoir of Robert Hay, 1789-1847, 1953, edited the journal of his great grandfather, a naval veteran, victim of the press gang, who served under Pellew and Collingwood.

The Nagle Journal: The Diary and Life of Jacob Nagle, Sailor, 1775-1841, 1988, edited by John Dann [**855**], was by an American colonist who gained a variety of experiences: in the army of George Washington, a privateer, a prisoner of the British, to the RN, in the First Fleet, service under Nelson, and a victim of impressment and crimps.

C.S. Forester [**1139**], 1953, edited the 1000-page autobiography of John Netherell, impressed, a veteran of several shipwrecks, and a prisoner for 11 years in a French jail where he met Napoleon.

A 17th-century journal was that of James Yonge, a surgeon from Plymouth, participant in the war against Algiers and taken prisoner during the second Dutch war, edited by F.N.L. Poynter [**2941**], 1963. John Knox Laughton [**2062**], 1923, edited the journal of another surgeon, John Cunningham, on the South American station.

An early account was Jack Nastyface, 1836, by William Robinson [**3096**], a veteran of Trafalgar. He verified certain themes: general adoration of Nelson, "stains of wanton and torturing punishment so often unnecessarily resorted to, and the unnatural and uncivilized custom of impressment."

Leon Garfield [**1251**], 1972, wrote about John Theophilus Lee, a sailor in Nelson's navy, who experienced the mutinies of 1797, met Nelson and Emma Hamilton, and passed the exam for lieutenant.

William Richardson [**3053**], A Mariner of England, 1908, recounted the career of William Richardson, 13 years in the merchant service and 26 years in the RN, "from cabin boy to warrant officer," 1780-1819; twice a victim of impressment and a recipient of a flogging round the fleet. Vivid descriptions of life on the lower deck were featured. William Spavens [**3401**], 1796, was a Chatham pensioner, impressed into the navy and a veteran of Quiberon Bay. John Bechervaise [**266, 265**], 1839 and 1847, was "an old quartermaster" with 36 years of experience in the RN and merchant service. Richard Barnett [**214**], 1978, presented the memoir of John Stradley, a foundling who was impressed and served during the 1770s. James Durand [**995**], 1926, was an American impressed into the RN, experienced floggings in both navies, who criticized the arbitrariness of punishment practices. John Kilby [**1929**], 1972, experienced a variety of events: privateers during the American Revolution, in an English prison, prisoner exchange, and service aboard BONHOME RICHARD. The American nautical novelist, Richard Henry Dana [**850**], recounted his Two Years before the Mast, 1854. **See 20., E.**

C. RECRUITMENT, MANNING, AND IMPRESSMENT

Impressment universally was seen as an evil, but no one in authority cared to replace it; national security was at stake. Something like it must be available in times of emergency. It was never repudiated, but it was not resorted to after 1815. Impressment was carried out by the Impress Service ashore and by warships at sea and in foreign ports. It has been presented as a major cause of the War of 1812. For the RN, exaggerating the desperate need for increased recruitment, desertion was a perennial problem for centuries.

G.V. Scammell [**3235, 3237**], 1970 and 1987, was informative on the manning situation, 1550-1650, a time of formative and dramatic expansion of naval and merchant forces. The primary problem was manning. The Navigation Acts were passed. Nevertheless, the ancient practice of impressment proved to be most effective. "The tentacles of the press spread ever wider." Scammell concluded that this problem demonstrated the fragility of the modern state. It became exaggerated during wartime. And wartime caused the end of the early Stuarts and of Cromwell. Scammel also assessed manning of merchant ships in the 16th century. Much manpower was required because overmanning was necessary so as to replace those seamen who died or deserted on the voyage. **See 10., E. and G.**

J.S. Bromley [**452**], The Manning of the Royal Navy, 1974, a publication of the NRS, reviewed the literature on manning issues and described one solution, the continuous service system, implemented in the 1850s. "Pressing was only one improvised and unsatisfactory answer to a permanent and increasingly technical requirement." Impressment was "the most odious and unfair mode of conscription ever devised."

In a dissertation and a book, Stephen Gradish [**1351, 1350**], The Manning of the British Navy during the Seven Years' War, 1971 and 1980, described the government policy and process for producing 80,000 seaman at the outbreak of the war. Parliament and William Pitt were no help. Anson was given much credit, attacking the problem on a broad front, for example, increasing the bounty, increasing the press gangs, improving victualling and conditions, and upgrading health arrangements.

Richard Pares [**2745**], 1937, conducted a case study of manning in the West Indies where there was great loss of men due to disease and desertion to privateers and merchant ships. The navy was forced to rely on the press gang which upset the colonial government.

Christopher Lloyd [**2168**], 1967, wrote about impressment and the law, a rationale of its legality. J.R. Hutchinson [**1742**], <u>The Press-Gang Afloat and Ashore</u>, 1913, was well researched about the process in the 18th century.

<u>Mariners and Markets</u>, 1992, by Charles Kindleberger [**1932**], was an idiosyncratic review of recruiting techniques and marketing of seamen by private and government authorities, remembering always the "nursery of seamen" rationale. All European governments required an available supply of seamen in times of war. What techniques?, for example, quotas, bounties, Navigation Acts, a registration system, bans on emigration, and impressment. Elaboration on impressment: in 1796, the British extended the practice to the high seas, precipitating problems with the U.S.: at least 2500 Americans were involved.

Lewis Fischer [**1106**], 1994, reported on a conference in Milan in 1994 which discussed the Kindleberger [**1932**] book. The various forms and methods of marketing were reviewed and assessed.

Jon Kepler [**1917**], 1973, went back to the 1340s, reviewing the practice of mandatory supply of forces to the monarch, for example, to provide transport across the English Channel. The navy of Edward III was acquired by impressment. Responsibilities of the Cinque Ports declined as use of impressment increased. David Ellison [**1039**], <u>Pressganged</u>, 1994, recounted the experiences of an ordinary seaman, 1803-1805. James Reddie [**3035**], 1867, reviewed the issue of manning the navy.

James Stewart [**3451**], 1960, wrote a general survey of the press gangs. Norman McCord [**2229**], 1968, presented as a case study the formation of the Impress Service in the north, 1893-1815. G. Hinchliffe [**1636**], 1967, described impressment during the War of Spanish Succession, the sweep in 1708 leading to the Admiralty having to release many because of exempted occupations. On the matter of exemptions, John Armstrong [**139**], 2000, presented a case study of the effectiveness of the use of registers to exempt seamen from the coastal fleet.

Larry Neal [**2609**], 1978, wrote of the costs of impressment during the Seven Years' War, concluding they were high for "this medieval remnant of royal prerogatives." Paul Conner [**719**], 1967, wrote of a critique of impressment in the 1770s, there being no legal basis for it.

Charles Butler [**529**], 1824, speculated on the legality of impressment. The nautical novelist, Frederick Marryat [**2404**], 1822, wrote a short essay urging abolition of impressment for the navy. Also opposed was Anselm Griffiths [**1401**], <u>Impressment Fully Considered: With a View to Its Gradual Abolition</u>, 1826.

In a dissertation and an article, Daniel Ennis [**1051, 1050**], 1999 and 2000, searched for representations of impressment in British literature, for example, in <u>Roderick Random</u> by Smollett [**3372**]. As a comparison, Tom McGuffie [**2263**], 1956, described recruiting practices of the army during mobilization for the Wars of the French Revolution and Napoleon: quotas, bounties, Volunteer Acts, crimps, and army recruiting forces scouring the countryside.

In one essay in a series, Nicholas Rogers [3130], 1998, described resistance to naval impressment during the 18th century.

Impressment was one method. There were others. Clive Emsley [1045, 1046], North Riding Naval Recruits: The Quota Acts and the Quota Men, 1795-1797, 1978, illustrated the workings of quotas. He also wrote of the recruitment of petty officers, captains being so desperate that imprisoned men were requested.

Brian Dietz [934], 1991, described the Royal Bounty which began in the 15th century, at first to shipbuilders to produce ships appropriate for war. A list of bounty ships was included, 1560-1618, over 700 being listed.

All was not impressment and desertion. Roger Hart [1539], 1998, wrote of "Sea Fencibles," volunteers recruited between 1798-1810, as a kind of naval militia to defend against invasion of Britain. The Admiralty acquired 20 Dutch trawlers and other small vessels to be stationed in coastal towns and manned by locals. The Impress Service was forbidden to bother them. Nelson denounced them because they refused to augment his crews in some Channel operations.

G.H. Gardner [1249], 1871, was pleased that a naval reserve system for officers and enlisted men had replaced "the evils and inadequacy of impressment."

N.A.M. Rodger [3116], 1984, wrote a piece on stragglers and deserters during the Seven Years' War. Depiction by John Masefield [2449] of a beaten and broken Jack Tar must be revised. Desertion, yes, but the situation was more complex. Leave was granted frequently, most men were reliable, and most served for long periods of time.

Paul van Royen [3162---], 1997, presented a series of national essays written by experts on the maritime labor market and career patterns of seamen, the essays on the British by Sarah Palmer, Peter Earle, and Gordon Jackson.

Robert Schaeffer [3240], "The Chains of Bondage Broke: The Proletarianization of Seafaring Labor, 1600-1800," 1984, produced a dissertation comparing conditions during this time as equivalent to enslavement in galleys of the 16th century, for example, impressment, coercion, discipline, and reduction of costs by shippers and governments. Conclusion: it was successful mutiny in the late 18th century which set maritime labor along the path to free wages.

Procurement of oarsmen for French galleys in the 17th and 18th centuries was a case study by Paul Bamford [191], 1959. In expanding the French fleet, Colbert was presented with a dilemma. Use of slaves declined and use of prisoners, especially Huguenots, increased; by the 1690s, 12,000 oarsmen were operating.

D. IMPRESSMENT AND THE WAR OF 1812

The authoritative source was James Zimmerman [**3983**], Impressment of American Seamen, 1925. He discussed the issue as it related to Anglo-American relations and the War of 1812. Even after 1812, the British never renounced the right of impressment. In a dissertation, Scott Jackson [**1766**], 1976, reviewed the impressment issue in Anglo-American relations, 1787-1818. Other issues were settled, this one defied solution. The arguments and issues from the perspective of both sides were reviewed. George Selement [**3269**], 1973, reviewed the impressment issue. Barriers to resolution included British national security, American nationalism, differing definitions of neutrality, commercial rivalry, American domestic politics, and British seamen deserting to American ships. Anthony Steel [**3434, 3435**], 1949 and 1951, discussed the impressment issue. The British policy was once a British citizen, always a British citizen. An estimate of 10,000 American seamen were impressed. The issue was not included in the negotiations of a treaty of 1807 nor was it mentioned in the final Treaty of Ghent.

E.   HEALTH   FACTORS,   SCURVY,   AND   ENVIRONMENTAL CONDITIONS

The literature on these issues has been impressive and extensive. The Customs of Oleron urged provision for illness and disabilities.

Most of the literature on naval health issues during this period has been about scurvy, "the most malignant of all sea diseases." There was great and longtime difficulty in finding a cure of scurvy. Dr. James Lind contributed but even he failed to recognize the significance. Diet was increasingly seen as decisive, but what part: fresh vegetables, sauerkraut, malt, and various citrus fruits were candidates. The voyages of Anson, 1740-1744, and the three voyages of Cook, 1768-1780, were formative events in the progress of naval medicine, especially concerning scurvy. It was not until 1799 that lemon juice was directly linked to cure. **See 17., B.**

In the literature, most impressive was John Keevil [**1852**], Medicine and the Navy, 1200-1900, 4 vols., 1957-1963, organized chronologically and by subjects, originally urged by L.G. Carr Laughton, and sponsored by the Wellcome Trust. For health matters first, there were barber-surgeons and, later, surgeons came from the Society of Apothcaries. Naval hospitals and hospital ships followed, for example, Haslar near Portsmouth. The University of Edinburgh supplied many if not most of the naval surgeons. Keevil, himself a surgeon commander, died after the second volume and Christopher Lloyd and J.L.S. Coulter stepped in to complete volumes III and IV.

Christopher Lloyd [**1852, 2157, 2153, 2158**] was co-writer of Medicine and the Navy, and wrote three other pieces: The Health of Seamen: Selections from the Works of Dr. James Lind, Sir Gilbert Blane, and Dr. Thomas Trotter, 1965, a publication of the NRS; "Cook and Scurvy," 1979, and "Limes, Lemons, and Scurvy," 1965. The term "Limey" for British sailors first came from descriptive appellations from Australian mariners about this peculiar addition to the diet of British sailors.

Kenneth Carpenter [**580**], The History of Scurvy and Vitamin C, 1986, was the first modern survey. Originally it was called the explorer's sickness, noting both sea and land expeditions. Ten weeks seemed to be the decisive point. One claimed citrus fruit has been mentioned as early as the 14th century; that seemed to be remembered and forgotten several times before 1800. Vasco da Gama suggested oranges. Pepys mentions scurvy; Anson suffered devastating losses. Lind, Blane, Cook, and Nelson contributed. Vitamin C was discovered in 1905. Carpenter praised the Keevil [**1852**] study.

Eleanor Gordon [**1326**], 1984, reviewed the Anson circumnavigation, "the Royal Navy's worst outbreak,": 8 ships, 1955 men set out; 1 ship and 145 men returned. James Riley [**3069**], 1981, conducted a statistical study of mortality during voyages of the 18th century, 17,092 persons on 84 vessels. He concluded mortality rates were higher at sea than on land.

Francis Cuppage [**834**], James Cook and the Conquest of Scurvy, 1994, recounted experiments with anti-scorbutic plants, most successful in the second and third voyages. J.D. Alsop [**58, 59**], 1990 and 1993, wrote two pieces crediting the work of naval surgeons contributing to the process of curing scurvy. Leonard Wilson [**3914**], 1975, reviewed the clinical definition of scurvy and the discovery of Vitamin C.

James Lind [**2137, 2138**], Lind's Treatise on Scurvy, 1753, and an article, 1757, wrote of the means of curing sea diseases, notably scurvy. The treatise was dedicated to Anson. Louis Roddis [**3101**], James Lind: Founder of Nautical Medicine, 1950, was about "the Hippocrates of nautical medicine," who wound up as Physician, Royal Hospital at Haslar. J.Glass [**1294**], 1949, studied the early career of James Lind, a graduate from the University of Edinburgh. R.E. Hughes [**1718**], 1975, analyzed the scientific approach of Lind. H.V. Wyatt [**3972**], 1976, responded to Hughes, taking him to task for denigrating the work of Lind. A.P. Meicklejohn [**2488**], 1954, speculated about "the curious obscurity" of Lind.

The protege of Lind, Thomas Trotter [**3652**], wrote Medicina Nautica: An Essay on the Diseases of Seamen, 3 vols., 1797-1803, stressing reforms of the environment, for example, more ventilation below decks.

A.N. Ryan [**3195**], 1990, wrote of disease and sickness during the age of Drake. Guenter Risse [**3070**], 1988, conducted a study of the health of seamen in the 1790s, analyzing medical records in Edinburgh.

Health conditions on the lower deck were linked to ventilation, something considered in two articles by Arnold Zuckerman [**3986, 3985**], 1976 and 1987; it was the time of miasmatic theories: foul, damp, noxious air caused disease.

Naval sewage was a health factor. Joe Simmons [**3319**], <u>Those Vulgar Tubes: External Sanitary Accommodations</u>, 1997, described the most common method to dispose of human wastes at sea during the age of sail. Somewhat related were Roy Palmer [**2739**], 1973, and Thomas Oertling [**2688**], 1996, about "the water closet" and the evolution of the bilge pump, leak management.

As an event of the Nelson Decade [**2624**], the year 2000 event was a conference, <u>Health in the Royal Navy during the Age of Nelson</u> [**1587**], in July 2000, at the Institute of Naval Medicine, the papers being published.

J.C. Goddard [**1306**], 1992, reviewed the life of naval surgeons. Early naval surgeons came from the University of Edinburgh. Helen Dingwall [**938**], 1995, wrote the medical history of Edinburgh in the 17th century. J. Worth Estes [**1056**], 1998, edited a surgeon's log from frigates of the early 19th century. Records of 240 patients; 6.6% died. He knew of 1300 drugs listing over 100 remedies. Boog Watson [**3786**], 1972, edited the diary of naval surgeon Thomas Robertson. Graphic descriptions of medical complications after flogging were featured; Robertson intervened after 125 lashes in a sentence of 400, deeming it "malice and cruelty."

James Thomas [**3595**], "Jack Tar, Mr. Sawbones and the Local Community," was about the hospital at Haslar, Gosport, 1750-1800.

Harold Langley [**2025**], <u>A History of Medicine in the Early U.S. Navy</u>, 1995, covered the period 1794-1842, focusing on naval surgeons and the medical service. Again, the traditions and background were the same as the RN.

Joan Druett [**965**], <u>Rough Medicine: Surgeons at Sea in the Age of Sail</u>, 2001, was more limited than the title suggested; only 11 doctors of whaling ships were studied. Ernest Gray [**1371**], 1937, edited what he claimed was a diary of a surgeon's mate, John Knyveton, practicing in the early 1750's. In a review, Herbert Richmond assessed it as a forgery.

F. VICTUALLING, UNIFORMS AND WAGES

The NMM sponsored an international symposium, "Starving Sailors," April 1980, the papers being published, edited by James Watt [**3790**]. The theme was the influence of nutrition on naval and maritime history. Clearly, poor nutrition meant adverse physical and mental effects. Pepys made the connection and the mutineers of 1797 complained.

Leslie Busch [**525**], 1995, wrote of the diet of seamen of very long voyages. Scurvy was not the only problem. Iron deficiency and poor nutrition were also problems.

George Manwaring [**2357**], 1924, described the dress of British seamen in the 18th century. The Dutch war had demonstrated a need for uniform clothing and availability of "slop-clothing." The links to health and discipline were stressed. New regulations on "slops" were issued in 1706 and officers agreed to a naval uniform for themselves in 1746. Gerald Dickens [**925**], <u>The Dress of the</u>

British Sailor, 1957, was an illustrated pamphlet from the NMM. John Mollo [**2525**], Uniforms of the Royal Navy during the Napoleonic Wars, 1965, was an impressive production, folio size and profusely illustrated.

William May [**2478, 2479, 2475**], 1962, 1970, and 1974, was the authority on uniform badges, insignia, swords, and firearms for the navy, all described at length. Swords, badges, and buttons of officers were described by P.G.W. Annis [**121**], 1970, Derek Barker [**204**], 1977, Charles Ffoulkes [**1097**], 1967, and K.V. Burns [**518**], 1988.

An interesting twist to victualling, "slops," and uniforms was presented by Geoffrey Green [**1380, 1379**], The Royal Navy and Anglo-Jewry, 1740-1820, 1982 and 1989. It was a local study of Jewish merchants in Portsmouth, Plymouth, and Chatham, who gained permission to set up shops in the dockyard and go aboard the ships selling their wares.

A separate section could be justified about the drink of British seamen, the daily "grog" or rum ration, the name coming from the rum-water mixture decreed by Admiral Edward Vernon and named for his rain parka. It became routine in 1655. The percent of rum was steadily reduced over time, halved in 1824 and halved again in 1850, until it was abolished in 1970; abolished for officers in 1881 and warrant officers in 1918; the U.S. Navy in 1862. Other terms were spirit ration, Dutch Courage, and Nelson's Blood. A.J. Pack [**2723**], 1982, wrote its history. Ben Blee [**348, 347**], 1959 and 1989, and Lawrence Phillips [**2850**], 1970, summarized the history.

F.W. Brooks [**461**], 1945, wrote of wages in the 16th century; impressed seamen were paid 2 pence a day. Maxwell Schoenfeld [**3245**], 1965, wrote about the wages of seamen in the 17th century. Wages remained the same for decades and payment was unreliable. Wage tickets were substituted and circulated virtually as currency. Sailors were perpetual victims. Stephen Gradish [**1352**], 1978, wrote of wages in the 18th century, an Act of 1758 providing pay on a regular basis and allotments to families. Parliament would not grant increases until the mutinies of 1797.

G. DISCIPLINE AND PUNISHMENT

Among the stereotypes handed down in history and lore, none were more graphic and damning of authorities, from the Admiralty down to the captain and ship's officers, than the issues of discipline and punishment in the RN. The literature on punishments tended to be poorly founded.

The best studies focused on one naval station but were intensively researched, revisionist, and formative: a dissertation and book, Crime and Punishment in the Royal Navy, 1987 and 1989, by John Byrn [**532, 533**]. The station was the Leeward Islands, 1784-1812. The naval discipline system was seen as an extension of criminal law. The conclusion was that discipline in the navy was enforced in much the same way as criminal law ashore. The lower deck was not a chamber of horrors. The most common punishments were for drunkenness, neglect of duty, and desertion. Buggery was about 1%.

The literature on corporal punishment was not so solid. George Scott [3257], The History of Corporal Punishment: A Survey of Flagellation in its Historical, Anthropological and Sociological Aspects, 1948, was informative but from a yellow journalism and superficial approach. Sensationalized was Scott Claver [651], Under the Lash: A History of Corporal Punishment in the British Armed Forces, 1954, touting collections of statistics, instances of all types of punishments, unpublished accounts, and selections from the debates for and against corporal punishment, all overly dramatized, poorly organized, and exaggerated. Similar was Gilbert Oakley [2656], The History of the Rod and Other Corporal Punishments, 1964, a "D.Psy." and graduate of the Glasgow School of Art, describing with the use of choppy paragraphs, much bold type, and many exclamation points, "masochistic-sadistic impulses," none of which was backed by scholarly apparatus. Henry Salt [3212], The Flogging Craze, 1916, sponsored by the Humanitarian League, collected all of the arguments against the use of corporal punishment. England was the "stronghold of the flogging cult."

William Andrews [119, 118] had two presentations, Old-Time Punishments, 1890, and Bygone Punishments, 1899, contributions to social history. Charles Penrose [2814], Observations on Corporal Punishment, 1824, reviewed the issues. William Glascock [---] was the anonymous "An Officer of Rank" who wrote Naval Sketch-book, 2 vols., 1826, and he expressed strong feelings about pertinent issues, for example, vehement support for corporal punishment. Other parts of the work were reminiscent of The Naval Chronicle [2605].

Eugene Rasor [3014], 1972, did a dissertation on discipline matters in the RN in the mid-19th century. Reforms were put in place and the situation improved greatly.

Jane Litten [2143], 1998, reviewed the debate for and against flogging in the American navy in the mid-19th century, the issues being similar. S.F. DuPont saw flogging as essential, "the sheet anchor of discipline," and Robert Stockton opposed it. In a poll of captains of the USN taken in 1850, 76 favored corporal punishment and 7 opposed it. Nevertheless, Congress abolished it in 1850.

Alternative punishments were addressed. D.L. Howard [1688], 1966, did a short piece on the punishment of transportation and on imprisonment. See 17., W. Edgar Thompson [3599], 1972, described the practice of keelhauling, more identified with the Dutch navy.

The situation of naval prisoners of war has attracted writers. Edward Fraser [1182], 1914, studied British sailors and soldiers, prisoners of the French during the Wars of the French Revolution and Napoleon. Olive Anderson [78, 77], 1959 and 1960, wrote of the implications of the exchange of prisoners. Recovery of British prisoners from the French meant some relief for the manning problems. Formal exchanges with the French and Spanish, all for all, occurred in 1691, 1742, 1780, and 1782. Unfortunately, perhaps fortunately for them, many British prisoners freed managed to avoid return to service. Sheldon Cohen [698], Yankee Sailors in British Gaols 1995, recounted the life and experiences of 3000 American prisoners in British prisons. Robin Fabel [1067], 1989, wrote of the experiences of life of 6500 American prisoners, most from privateers, during the War of 1812. And then there was the matter of criminals being forced into, or given a choice of prison or the RN, as described by William Senior [3277], "The Navy as Penitentiary," 1930.

H. THE ROLE OF WOMEN

Women legally serving in the RN was not a issue in the pre-1815 period. Women were carried aboard ship legally, for example, nurses and wives. The literature has increased encouragingly over the past decade.

Suzanne Stark [3420, 3422], Female Tars: Women Aboard Ship in the Age of Sail, 1996 and 1997, was a book and article. Most were wives of warrant officers who were traditionally permanent appointments to a ship. Some prostitutes came aboard in port but few went to sea. A few cases of women in disguise have been cited, for example, Mary Lacy, Margaret Thompson, Mary Anne Talbot, and Elizabeth Bowden. During the manning crisis of the 1790s, army regiments supplemented some crews. Married soldiers "on the strength" were accommodated aboard ships, occasionally with wives and children, as described by W.B. Rowbotham [3155], 1961. Margaret Creighton [793], Iron Men, Wooden Women: Gender and Seafaring in the Atlantic World, 1700-1920, 1995, collected essays from experts, for example, Marcus Rediker on women pirates, Lisa Norling on women in sea fiction, and Diane Dugaw on wives of merchant and whaling ship captains. Less scholarly and more anecdotal were Joan Druett [966, 964], She Captains, 2000, tales of exploits of women aboard ships, and Hen Frigates, 1998, tales of wives of merchant captains. David Cordingly [768], Women Sailors and Sailors' Women, 2001, recounted superstitions about women aboard ship in nautical literature, for example, sirens and mermaids. In a dissertation, Dianne Dugaw [983], 1982, collected popular ballads about female warriors. Early ones came from broadsides in England in the 17th century. Matthew Stephens [3446] wrote of Hannah Snell: The Secret Life of a Female Marine, 1723-1792, 1997.

Basil Greenhill [1392], Women under Sail, 1970, was 8 case histories of women travelling or working aboard in the 19th century. Sources were their letters and journals.

I. SEXUALITY AND HOMOSEXUALITY

Many of the works on health, discipline, and punishment previously covered dealt with sexuality, prostitution, and sexually transmitted diseases. That latter problem was also a prominent one for seamen. Linda Merians [2497] collected 15 papers on "the secret malady," 1996. It was an interdisciplinary production featuring political, social, and cultural aspects. Evelyn Berckman [300], The Hidden Navy, 1973, summarized the backwaters of the RN: prostitutes, stowaways, conditions on prison hulks, and corruption in the dockyards.

Buggery had been a capital offense since 1533; the last execution was in 1835. It ceased to be a capital offense in 1861. B.R. Burg [509], Sodomy and the Perception of Evil: English Sea Rovers in the Seventeenth-Century Caribbean, 1983, was about homosexuals among pirates from a sociological perspective. Arthur Gilbert [1276, 1275], "Buggery and the British Navy, 1700-1861," 1976, was about the most serious offense, worst than murder. Prosecution was more prevalent in the navy than the army. Accusations and convictions declined sharply after 1815. Sources were court martial records each of which contained considerable detail. Gilbert recounted one, the AFRICAINE case of 1816 where 4 members of the crew were hanged for buggery and two others received 200 lashes each for "uncleanness." N.A.M. Rodger [3110, 3117] disagreed with Arthur Gilbert, assessing his research as useful but his conclusions were "tenacious misconceptions." Rodger concluded that homosexuality was an insignificant issue in the 18th century, about 20 cases among 100,000 men in the 1760s.

Hans Turley [3668], Rum, Sodomy and the Lash, 1999, linked piracy, an all male society, transgressions of English norms, and "unnatural desires." Pirates were romantic antiheroes. Turley saw the depiction of Burg [509] as "historically flawed." Works of Daniel Defoe [895-897] were also analyzed. A.D. Harvey [1544], 1978, conducted a study of the incidence of prosecution for sodomy in Britain, 1800-1835; numbers had increased, including naval courts martial for the offence; a total of 9 executions between 1797-1805.

A recent First Sea Lord, Louis Le Bailly [2086], 1996, made observations about homosexuality in the RN, questioning whether the fighting capabilities of naval forces might be affected. He recounted some "old salt" tales from the past.

J. MUTINY

Another "capital" offense among armed force personnel was mutiny. In 1797, there were two major mutinies, at Spithead, April-May, near Portsmouth, and the Nore, May, at the entrance to the Thames, plus a series of individual mutinies aboard ships continuing into 1802. Such incidents in time of war and at this crucial time when danger of invasion was imminent made them extremely serious events. The matters of "Reds" and revolutionary connections related to the mutinies of 1797 and later ones such as Invergordon in 1931 have been hotly debated. Pay and conditions were high on the list of grievances. Tyrannical officers, excessive punishment, impressment, and poor food were mentioned. How political were the issues and how much "outside agitation" was occurring were the debatable questions. A serious Irish revolt occurred the next year. Clearly, Spithead was moderate and the parties dealt with each other with mutual respect. The Nore was more radical and the outcome involved punitive measures, including hangings. Wages were increased and pay was on time after 1797.

Leonard Guttridge [**1429**], Mutiny: A History of Naval Insurrection, 1992, was a general survey, synthesis and case-book, for example, BOUNTY, "most romanticized"; Spithead where Valentine Joyce was leader who successfully negotiated with "Black Dick" Howe; the Nore where Richard Parker, "President of the Floating Republic" was eventually executed, and HERMIONE, "the most murderous."

Thomas Wintringham [**3925**], Mutiny: Being a Survey of Mutiny from Spartacus to Invergordon, 1936, an older survey, recounted mutinies in the RN, in the end concluding: English mutinies were different from French, Russian, and German "due only to the wealth, skill, and success of the English ruling class," knowing when to give way and grant concessions.

Lawrence James [**1779**], Mutiny: In the British and Commonwealth Forces, 1797-1956, 1987, was a solid, non-emotional survey; the chapter on the naval mutinies was entitled "The Worm in the Oak." In a dissertation and a book, Jonathan Neale [**2611, 2610**], The Cutlass and the Lash: Mutiny and Discipline in Nelson's Navy, 1985 and 1990, studied disputes and conflicts between officers and enlisted men during the period. Included was a chapter on forms of resistance from "murmuring" to "mutiny." John Bullocke [**507**], Sailors' Rebellion: A Century of Mutiny at Sea, 1938, treated a series of mutinies over the century, for example, WAGER, BOUNTY, Spithead, the Nore, and HERMIONE.

Most extensive and serious, under the circumstances, were the events of 1797. Conrad Gill [**1284**], The Naval Mutinies of 1797, 1913, was a comprehensive account. The causes were reviewed: discontent with conditions and political unrest, a fusion of social and political movements. James Dugan [**981**], The Great Mutiny, 1965, was a popularized account of the mutinies of 1797, over dramatized. Somehow, "the Red flag," Irish rebellion, and "1817," were incorporated, for whatever reasons. George Manwaring [**2358**], The Floating Republic: An Account of the Mutinies at Spithead and the Nore in 1797, 1935, was sympathetic to the mutineers and denounced the severity of the commanding officers, many of whom were forced off and never returned. Critics, for example, David Bonner Smith [**3352**], complained it was too sympathetic and too partial to the mutineers.

In a dissertation, Christopher Doorne [**947**], 1998, faced the mutiny-sedition-revolution head on. In 1797, the Admiralty feared revolution. The Irish were restless. Would there be traitorous assistance for a French invasion? Looking at court martial records and the petitions of the seamen, Doorne concluded that the authorities overestimated the threat of sedition. The seamen were concerned about pay and conditions rather than politics. David Bonner Smith [**3352**], 1935-1936, wrote an account of the mutinies and presented original documents.

William J. Neale [**2613**], History of the Mutiny at Spithead and the Nore, 1842, first published anonymously, proved to be controversial. Its accuracy was questioned, its attacks were deemed scurrilous, and it was too emotional. Michael Lewis [**2129**], Spithead, 1972, called it an informal history. Included was a summary of all of the courts martial. A. Temple Patterson [**2791**], 1968, and Richard Saxby [**3232**], 1993, wrote about the Spithead mutiny. Negotiations between the "Delegates" and Admiral Howe were cordial and the Delegates later sent him a letter of appreciation. Roger Wells [**3811**], Insurrection: The British Experience, 1795-1803, 1997, was more about rebellion but included a chapter on the mutinies of 1797. They occurred against a background of multi-dimensional political crisis, for example, peace and democracy movements. C. Fields [**1098**], 1917, described the role of the marines during the mutinies.

Bicentennial conferences were held for the Spithead and Nore mutinies; the proceedings were to be edited by Ann Coats [**678**]. Reassessments were presented. Christopher Lloyd [**2166, 2162**], 1960 and 1968, wrote supplementing the information about the mutiny at the Nore and aboard HMS NEREIDE. Correspondence from Midshipman A. Hardy was especially enlightening on the substance of the grievances at the Nore.

Other mutinies have been reviewed. An earlier mutiny, The WAGER Mutiny, 1964, was described by S.W.C. Pack [**2725**]: an incident during the voyage of Anson in the early 1740s. WAGER went aground and the survivors mutinied, killing the captain and abandoning others. A court martial of 1746 found no one guilty.

Both Dudley Pope [**2888, 2891**], 1963 and 1987, and J.D. Spinney [**3408, 3407**], 1955 and 1956, treated the mutinies of HMS HERMIONE and HMS DANAE. Pope, The Black Ship, was the complete story of the mutiny aboard HMS HERMIONE, a frigate, on 21 September 1797, several months after the larger incidents, this occurring in the West Indies. Ten of 14 officers were murdered, including the captain, Hugh Pigot. The mutineers then sailed the ship and gave it over to the Spanish enemy. It was "cut out" in a dramatic operation later. Spinney was more detailed about the mutineers being hunted down and hanged. It was "the worst mutiny in the history of the RN." Edgar Thompson [**3601**], 1967, presented the saga of one mutineer. Pope followed with an account of the mutiny aboard HMS DANAE in March 1800, entitled The Devil Himself. DANAE was in the Brest squadron. In this case the crew took the ship to the French and some remained. Little violence was involved. The complaint seemed to be over impressment. Only 3 of the 45 mutineers were ever captured; the rest disappeared. Loyal members were returned to Britain. Again, Spinney was based on Admiralty records.

Norman McCord [**2230**], 1968, wrote about a strike of seamen in the north in 1815, describing some anti-impressment agitation in 1803 and 1811. In 1815, ships had been "paid off" and unemployment was an important factor.

Frederic Smoler [**3371**], did a dissertation, "Emeute: Mutiny and the Culture of Authority in the Victorian Navy," 1994, analyzing the rhetoric and reality of discipline and noting unique aspects of naval discipline and authority.

Chapter 11

Warships

The Royal Navy was the final descriptive term; predecessors can be reviewed in a chronological sequence from early times: a modified merchant-ship service, "ship muster," forces of the Cinque Ports, King's Ships, warships from entrepreneurs to be chartered, fleets built from local taxes, "safeguard of the sea," a term of the 15th century, private naval warfare or privateers, a modern standing navy, the original one, Venice, the Navy Royal administered by the Council of Marine, 1500-1575, and the Royal Navy.

Types of warships also evolved and names depended on time of use, size, and later, use and number of guns. An example of a listing was galley, galleon, carrack, Ship of the Line (SOTL), frigate, and a series of smaller warships: sloops, corvettes, and brigs, bomb vessels, fireships, storeships, and ship's boats and cutters.

A. GENERAL SURVEYS

The literature was expansive. A good place to begin was the survey, E.H.H. Archibald [**134, 135**], The Fighting Ship in the Royal Navy, 1984, and The Wooden Fighting Ship in the Royal Navy, 1968, folio size and illustrated, featuring naval architecture. It began with the ships of King Alfred. William Hovgaard [**1687**], Modern History of Warships, 1920, was a standard reference guide, featuring naval architecture and covering up to 1919.

Romola Anderson [**99**], The Sailing Ship: Six Thousand Years of History, 1926, was a longtime standard, profusely illustrated and numerous editions, for example, 1927, 1948, 1963, 1969, 1971, and 1980. Robert Albion [**28**], Five Centuries of Famous Ships: From SANTA MARIA to the GLOMAR EXPLORER, 1978,was a good reference guide and included 150 ships.

Four publication series have been particularly contributory. The Anatomy of the Ship series [**66**] focusing on ship design and including extensive schematic drawings; History of the Ship series [**1639**], a 12-vol. series originally published by Conway Maritime; Richard Woodman [**3947**], The History of the Ship, 1997, a summary volume, folio size, profusely illustrated, and Basil Greenhill [**1391**] edited The Ship series, 10 vols., 1980-1981, sponsored by the NMM, a series of 60-page pamphlets. Included in the latter series were Alan McGowan [**2253, 2254**], The Ship, vols. III and IV, 1980-1981, on the development of the sailing ship, 1400-1820.

Bjorn Landstrom [**2015, 2014**], The Ship, 1961, and Sailing Ships in Words and Pictures, 1969, were surveys with magnificent illustrations. The great French naval historian, Martine Acerra [**6**], L'Empire Des Mers Des Galions aux Clippers, 1990, featured the Venice Arsenal, Lepanto, and the Armada. Ian Friel [**1198**], The Good Ship: Ships, Shipbuilding and Technology in England, 1200-1520, 1995, for the British Museum, documented English leadership in the development of the sailing ship, especially the multi-masted, ocean-going ship, merchant and war.

Donald G.F.W. Macintyre [**2269**], The Man-of-War, 1969, was a history of the combat vessel with 230 illustrations. Peter Kemp [**1863**], The History of Ships, 1978, was slick, folio size, with colored pictures on every page.

Basil Greenhill [**1387, 1386**], The Evolution of the Wooden Ship, 1985, incorporated detailed schematic drawings and featured "how-to-build" instructions, and The Evolution of the Sailing Ship, 1995, featured reprints of articles from Mariner's Mirror. Frank Howard [**1689**], Sailing Ships of War, 1400-1860, 1979, folio size with 400 illustrations, covered century by century, the 15th through the 19th.

Richard Hough [**1682**], Man O'War, 1979, featured individual famous ships, for example, BONHOME RICHARD and VICTORY. Douglas Browne [**476**], The Floating Bulwark, 1963, a general popular survey; the origins were 1514, the building of the great ship of Henry VIII at Erith. Robert Gardiner [**1247**], Warships of the Napoleonic Era, 1999, featured blueprint plans of all ship types. Most were British but other nationals were included. The source was from the curator of Ships Plans Collection, at the NMM. Charles Longridge [**2185**], The Anatomy of Nelson's Ships, 1955, was a reference guide to drawings and plans. These types of publications were usually aimed at model builders. Robert Malcolmson [**2342**], Warships of the Great Lakes, 1754-1834, 2001, was a technical history. These ships were built inland, from rowboats to 3-deckers.

John Lynn [**2214**], Tools of War, 1990, was a series of essays on weapons and tactics, 1445-1871, for example, William Maltby on the fact that advances in technology in gunnery forced adoption of the line of battle tactics.

B. NAVY LISTS

In modern times, the navy produced listings of all ships in commission. Variations and later collection of lists of past ships have been published. Great Britain, Admiralty, The Navy List [**1372**], an annual listing beginning in 1814, published details of all ships in commission.

J.J. Colledge [**703**], Ships of the Royal Navy: An Historical Index, 2 vols., 1969, contained 14,000 entries in alphabetical order, coverage from the 15th century. No illustrations were included but data on name, type, dimensions, dates, honors, and disposition was incorporated. David Lyon [**2217**], The Sailing Navy List: All the Ships of the Royal Navy Built and Captured, 1688-1860, 1993, super-folio size, included 300 illustrations of ships and ship plans, complementing Colledge [**703**]. There were 67 different types, for example adice boat, bark, yacht, and SOTL. R.C. Anderson [**90, 91, 92**], Lists of Men-of-War, 1959, in 2 parts, 1509-1649 and 1650-1700, covered all of the major powers, for example, Britain, France, Sweden, Denmark-Norway, and Germany. The 1766 Navy List [**3281**], 2001, was an extraordinary compilation, edited by E.C. Coleman. In effect, it was a snapshot of the RN: ships, officers, boards, Trinity House, and chaplains.

Halton Lecky [**2087**], The King's Ships, 1913, was an ambitious project, to be 6 vols., a complete history of all individual ships of the RN; 2 vols. were published. David Hepper [**1604**], British Warship Losses in the Age of Sail, 1650-1859, 1994, presented circumstances and details of every loss from all causes, a total of 1700. The source was court martial records. Every loss required that the responsible person face a court martial. It complemented Gosset [**1335**]. W.P. Gosset [**1335**], The Loss of Ships of the Royal Navy, 1793-1900, 1986, provided a chronological listing with indexes by name, geography, and court martial.

Selection of names of English/British warships was done by a special committee. Names were reused, for example, VICTORY:

#1: 1559, 800 ton, 34 guns, flagship of Captain John Hawkins during the Armada campaign

#2: 1618, a 2nd-rate, 42 guns

#3: 1675, a 1st-rate, 100 guns

#4: 1733, a 1st-rate, 110 guns

#5: 1765, a 1st-rate, 100 guns, and still on the active list.

Reused names were described in publications: VANGUARD by Peter Kemp [**1865**], 1951: nine different ones; ARK ROYAL by Michael Apps [**132**], 1976: four different ones; LONDON by Edward Fraser [**1181**], 1908, included details of the combat experiences, and WARSPITE by Iain Ballentyne [**185**], 2001.

For more details and many more ships, go to Thomas Manning [**2354**], British Warship Names, 1959, a dictionary of ship names. There was an official Ship Names Committee. Michael Seymour [**3287**], "Warship Names of the English Republic, 1649-1659," 1990, noted that at this formative time, dramatic expansion and symbolism influenced selections: changes of names included PRINCE to UNITY and WARWICK to COMMONWEALTH. The names changed again at the Restoration, for example, NASBY to CHARLES and SPEAKER to MARY.

C. INDIVIDUAL SHIPS AND SHIP TYPES

HMS VICTORY, perhaps the most famous of all British ships, if not of all the world, was treated elsewhere. Individual ships will also show up in the chapter on Nautical Archaeology. **See 8., A., 6. and 18.**

Sean McGrail [**2255, 2256**], Ancient Boats, 1983, and Ancient Boats in Northern Europe, 1987, were sponsored as archaeological ventures about earliest water transport, for example, plank boats, longboats, and hide boats. John Pryor [**2960**], 1984, presented details about transports during the time of the Crusades, for example, those supplied by Venice and Genoa. Basil Greenhill [**1389**], 2000, described "the mysterious hulc," first used by the Hanseatic League, similar to the cog. None have been found by nautical archaeology but they have been depicted on iconographical sources. Also persisting from ancient times was the lateen sail, described by I.C. Campbell [**566**], 1995.

Michael Swanton [**3528**], 1999, studied the ships of King Alfred as described in the Anglo-Saxon Chronicle, a new design of "long-ships." Similarly, King Harold maintained a fleet in the Channel at the time of the Norman Conquest. Most informative about ships of the medieval period was Richard Unger [**3689-3697**], for example, Cogs, Caravels and Galleons, 1994, in The History of the Ship series, and The Ship in the Medievel Economy, 1980, concluding that the development of ships made a significant contribution to a broad range of developments in European society. SUTTON HOO was 7th century; by the 8th century, sails were in use; by the 9th and 10th centuries, the Vikings were operating widely, and after the 11th century the Crusades facilitated the rise of the Italian city-states. In an article, 1992, Unger compared the total tonnages of European merchant fleets, 1300-1800, for example, the English increasing from 70,000 tons to 880,000 tons. He also described Dutch shipbuilding before 1800. Anton Brogger [**448**], The Viking Ships, 1951, was a comprehensive, illustrated history.

F.W. Brooks [**456**], The English Naval Forces, 1199-1271, 1933, was a scholarly and valuable contribution during this "Cinque Ports-to-King's Ships" transition era. A.D. Forte [**1160**], 1998, used iconography in Scottish legal records of the 15th century to identify ship types.

Ian Friel [**1199**], 1993, W.J.C Turner [**3673**], 1954, and M.W. Prynne [**2958**], 1968, all wrote about GRACE DIEU, the warship of Henry V, 1418-1439, the largest ship in northern Europe then and nothing equaled it for another 200 years. R.C. Anderson [**85**], "The GRACE DE DIEU, 1446-1486," 1919, was a ship of Edward IV, built on the Thames and used, for example, against the Scots in the 1480s.

Enlightening about the caravel, an important ship-type of the time, were two works about the ships of Christopher Columbus by Xavier Pastor [2787], 1992, in The Anatomy of the Ship series and on the occasion of the quincentennial, and Eugene Lyon [2219], 1993. Replicas were built more than once since 1892. Another caravel was MATTHEW, the ship of John Cabot for his voyage of 1497 from Bristol described by J.S. Dean [890], 1999; the replica was launched in 1995 and was the flagship for the International Festival of the Sea, Bristol, 1996. It then proceeded to duplicate the Cabot voyage to Newfoundland, beginning 2 May 1997. Similarly, two works on the MAYFLOWER, an early 17th century ship, were by William Baker [178], 1958, and Kate Caffrey [540], 1974, also with a replica which can be seen at the dock in Plymouth, MA. See item e.

Dorothy Burwash [524], English Merchant Shipping, 1460-1540, 1947, gathered much information and statistics, for example, types, sizes, volume of trade, and number of ships in various ports, for example, London, Bristol, and Southampton. The greatest influences were Genoese and Portuguese.

C.S. Knighton [1971], The Anthony Roll of Henry VIII's Navy, 2000, an occasional publication of the NRS, was extraordinary, a manuscript from the Pepys Library. In 1546, the naval official of the day, Anthony Anthony, compiled a Roll, a complete visual record of the ships of Henry VIII, 58 colored hand paintings of individual ships. Gregory Robinson [3093, 3091], 1934 and 1956, wrote of the HENRY GRACE A' DIEU or "the Great Harry" and of the Elizabethan ship.

K.V. Burns [520], Plymouth's Ships of War, 1972, featured Plymouth-built ships, beginning in the later 13th century; 26 of the 700 ships of Edward III were Plymouth-built; ultimately, over 200 warships were built here.

MARY ROSE was the subject of works by Alexander McKee [2299], 1973, and Ernle Bradford [413], 1982. She sank on 19 July 1545; she was discovered and raised in the 1970s, now on display alongside HMS VICTORY at the Portsmouth Naval Base. See 18., C. HMS TIGER or TYGRE was the name of a barque under Henry VIII and of the flagship of Richard Grenville later under Queen Elizabeth, as described by Tom Glasgow [1292], 1966.

T.W.E. Roche [3100], The GOLDEN HIND, 1973, recounted building of an authentic replica of the ship of Drake, built in Devon, sailing from Plymouth, retracing the original track of Drake to San Francisco. It was a carrack to galleon transition-type.

Geoffrey Parker [2749], "The DREADNOUGHT Revolution of Tudor England," 1996, described how the British developed a superior tactical doctrine and prevailed in the Armada campaign. This led to broadside warfare during the next two centuries. There was a DREADNOUGHT, 700 tons, launched in 1573. No record of any structural damage of English ships inflicted by Spanish guns during the Armada campaign can be found. R.J. Lander [2012], 1977, compared the numbers, sizes, and types of warships under the English and the Spanish during the Armada campaign. English ships were streamlined, fast, and could sail close to the wind; 197 for a total of 32,196 tons, an average of 170 tons. Spanish ships had high bulwarks and were awkward to handle; 130 for a total of 40,320 tons, an average of 320 tons.

In a dissertation and a book, Roger Smith [**3367, 3368**], Vanguard of Empire, 1989 and 1993, described the formative technological advances of the Iberian peninsula, Spain and Portugal, with Italian influences. Examples were the boxed compass, charts, sailing directions, rigging, and weapons. Much evidence came from nautical archaeology. Richard Unger [**3692**], 1978, described Dutch innovations. In a magisterial survey, Jaap Bruijn [**486**], 1993, described similar advances among the fleets of the East India Companies. All followed the lead of the Portuguese, especially Vasco da Gama. Companies were formed by the Dutch, English, French, Danish, Swedish, and even the Austrians from Ostend. The ships were armed and were equivalent to warships. Frank Fox [**1173**], 1998, wrote about hired men of war in the Anglo-Dutch wars.

For the 17th century, ROYAL SOVEREIGN and SOVEREIGN OF THE SEAS, designed by the Petts, were described, respectively by R.C. Anderson [**97**], 1913, L.G. Carr Laughton [**2065**], 1932, Jim Sephton [**3278**], and Thomas Heywood [**1618**], 1990. The last named book went into detail about the elaborate carvings and inscriptions throughout the ship, "one of the greatest of Renaissance art and pageantry" and "an eighth wonder of the world." Bernard Pool [**2883**], 1970, described the famous 30-ship building programme of 1677, initiated and overseen by Samuel Pepys. **See 9., D., 16.**

James Henderson [**1598**], Sloops and Brigs, 1972, recounted the history of these smallest warships, 1793-1815. Bomb vessels for shore bombardment were described collectively by Chris Ware [**3750**], 1994, covering 1687-1854, and individually: GRANADO of 1742 in The Anatomy of the Ship series by Peter Goodwin [**1319**], 1989, and SALAMANDRE of 1752 by Jean Boudriot [**370**], 1982. David MacGregor [**2262**], The Schooner, 2001, traced its development from 1600, a sleek, elegant, and romantic design.

Unexpectedly for a pre-1815 survey would be Dan Van Der Vat [**3720**], Stealth at Sea: The History of the Submarine, 1994, beginning in 1465 and later including such names as Leonardo, Keyser, Bushnell, and Fulton.

Ships and naval forces servicing the army were subjects by Hugh Rogers [**3128**], Troopships and Their History, 1963, beginning with trooplifting transports in the 17th century; Reg Cooley [**734**], The Unknown Fleet, 1993, sponsored by the Royal Naval Museum, counting 1100 ships in this service by 1945, and David Habesch [**1439**], The Army's Navy, 2001, beginning as transport barges under the Board of Ordnance of Henry VIII.

Other types have drawn less interest. J.J.S. Shaw [**3295**], The Hospital :Ship, 1936, traced its beginnings, 17th and 18th centuries. Graham Smith [**3358**], King's Cutters, 1983, were built to eliminate smuggling around the coasts. W.E.

May [**2476**], The Boats of Men-of-War, 1974, described boats of warships during the age of sail.

Tony Dalton [**846**], British Royal Yachts, 2001, folio size, contained illustrations of the yachts. The author was a former captain of HMY BRITANNIA. Sergio Bellabarba [**285**], The Royal Yacht CAROLINE, 1749, 1989, was for The Anatomy of the Ship series. It was the state yacht of George II, the most sumptuously decorated ship of all time.

W.B. Johnson [**1819**], The English Prison Hulks, 1957, were operated within the prison system, sometime used to house prisoner of war and as preliminary housing prior to transfer to convict ships. Locations included Woolwich, the Medway, Portsmouth, Plymouth, and Bermuda.

Individual ships were covered. Brian Lavery [**2071**], The Colonial Merchantman SUSAN CONSTANT, 1605, 1988, in The Anatomy of the Ship series, was one of 3 ships to Virginia, over a decade before MAYFLOWER. Kenneth Breen [**427**], 1970, wrote of the loss of HMS RAMILLES in 1782 in a storm in the North Atlantic. 600 lives were saved due to proper actions by the officers and Admiral Graves. Others included Vivian Stuart [**3477**], His Majesty's Sloop-of-War DIAMOND ROCK, 1978, and two by Peter Goodwin [**1324, 1323**], The 20-Gun Ship BLANDFORD, 1987, and The Naval Cutter ALERT, 1777, 1991, both in The Anatomy of the Ship series, were an early frigate and a versatile dispatch boat, respectively. David Syrett [**3543**] chose HM Storeship PORPOISE, 1780-1783, converted to an 18-gun warship.

VASA, 64 guns, 1400 tons, was a Swedish warship launched in 1627 during the Thirty Years' War. On its maiden voyage in Stockholm harbor, it sank during a sudden storm. It was raised in a nautical archaeology expedition in 1961 and was displayed at the National Maritime Museum, Stockholm, very much a representative warship of its time; all recounted by Anders Franzen [**1178**], 1962, Bengt Ohrelius [**2691**], 1962, and Bjorn Landstrom [**2013**], 1980. **See 18., F.**

The inimitable Jean Boudriot [**371, 373**] did two studies of BONHOMME RICHARD, 1987 and 1988, including an account of the battle with HMS SERAPIS off Flamborough Head in September 1779. She was originally an East Indiaman.

A Dictionary of the World's Watercraft [**932**], 2001, was a basic reference, 5600 entries, sponsored by the Mariner's Museum, Newport News.

D. GALLEYS, GALASSES, AND GALLEONS

Galleys, oared commercial and war ships, came from the Greeks and Romans, for example, triremes, quinqueremes, and polyremes. Their history, 2500 years, was longer than that of the sailing ship. An example was the GREAT GALLEY of Henry VIII built in 1515. Gallasses first appeared in England in 1546.

A good place to start would be John Guilmartin [**1422, 1421**], Gunpowder and Galleys, 1974, and an article, 1997, focusing on the Mediterranean in the 16th century. Armed conflict at sea was transformed. In 1500, the galley was dominant; by 1600, galleys were in decline. Mahan [**2328, 2329**] was not applicable here; Braudel [**426**] was. Trade was interlinked with armed conflict and there was no clear distinction between war and peace. Carlo Cipolla [**640**] explained the changes.

John Morrison [**2565**], The Age of the Galley, 1994, in History of the Ship series, observed that they operated in the Mediterranean from classical times. During medieval times they ventured out into the Atlantic and to northern Europe. Quand Voguaient Les Galeres [**2971**], 1990, was a history of oared and sail-powered galleys, for example, those of Venice, Malta, and France. Ennio Concina [**713**], Navis, 1990, in Italian, was about different types of ships, especially galleys, depicted in art and architecture. Michael Mallett [**2346**], The Florentine Galleys in the Fifteenth Century, 1967, described the organization of the galley system, including trade monopolies and voyages to Flanders and England. William Rodgers [**3119**], Naval Warfare under Oars, 1939, was a narrative history covering the Romans, Vikings, Crusades, and medieval campaigns and battles, for example, Damme of 1213, Dover of 1217, Sluys of 1340, Winchelsea of 1349, and Lepanto of 1571. Others were R.C. Anderson [**95**], Oared Fighting Ships, 1962, and Paul Bamford [**187**], Fighting Ships and Prisons, 1973, a history of French galleys under Louis XIV.

English galleys have attracted interest. F.W. Brooks [**458**], 1929, wrote about galleys under Kings John and Henry II. These were King's Ships, separate from ships of the Cinque Ports. R.C. Anderson [**83**], 1928 and J.T. Tinniswood [**3628**], 1949, were about galleys in the 13th and 14th centuries, these with 120 oars each. E.R. Adair [**10**], 1920, and J.E.G. Bennell [**292**], 1974, were about galleys in the 16th century. Sails were used more than previously on these oared vessels. Denis Rixon [**3074**], The West Highlands Galley, 1998, was about a Hebridean galley with Irish connections. D.C. McWhannell [**2321**], "The Galley of Argyle, " 2002, described West Highland galleys. They were based on Scandinavian vessels of the Viking era. They were used over 800 years and were key symbols of power. Unfortunately, no nautical archaeological finds have been made. Depictions were from heraldry, jewelry, grave stones, graffiti, and pub signs. McWhannell studied 78 different stone inscriptions which contained images of these galleys.

Peter Kirsch [**1949**], Galleon: The Great Ships of the Armada Era, 1988, originally in German, presented details of the construction, rigging, weapons, men, and battles. It was the most important large sailing ship of the era, first developed by Venice, thence to Portugal, Spain, and Britain. It was large and unwieldy. Carla Rahn Phillips [**2843, 2842**], Six Galleons for the King of Spain, 1986, and an article on advances of Spanish ship design were scholarly, comprehensive, and based on extensive research in Spanish archives. In the 1620s the Spanish Crown ordered 6 galleons. Phillips described the bureaucracy, infrastructure, strategic concepts, command structure, nautical sociology, and naval performance. She concluded that the Spanish war machine was more efficient and resilient than suspected. Alison McLeay [**2311**], The Tobermory Treasure, 1986, was about a Spanish galleon lost in Tobermory Bay, Isle of Mull of the Inner Hebrides, after the Armada. Richard Humble [**1727**], 1993, described a 16th-century galleon. David Marley [---], 1991, wrote of the last Manila galleon, captured in 1764 and taken to England. Frank Knight [**1956**], The Golden Age of the Galleon, 1976, wrote at the juvenile level.

E. THE SHIP OF THE LINE

The galleon evolved into the Ship of the Line, SOTL, the battleship of the age of fighting sail. It ruled the sea for 200 years.

The primary and most prolific authority on the SOTL was Brian Lavery [**2080, 2073, 2078, 2079**]. Two books, 3 vols., were general histories of the SOTL and three were about individual ships, INVINCIBLE, BELLONA, and VALIANT. INVINCIBLE was the first French 74-gun SOTL, captured at Finisterre in 1747, wrecked off Portsmouth in 1758, and the wreck was discovered in 1979. The last book supported an exhibition at the Wooden Walls Gallery, Chatham Historic Dockyard. Rory Quinn [**2990**], 1998, also wrote about HMS INVINCIBLE.

The brilliant French naval writer, Jean Boudriot [**374**], The Seventy-Four Gun Ship: A Practical Treatise on the Art of Naval Architecture, 4 vols., 1974-1978, produced this massive effort, divided into volumes on the hull, masts, rigging, manning, and shiphandling. It depicted the average '74 of 1780, not a specific one. There were detailed, fold-out plans. There were details on dockyards, administration, and shipboard life. This work has not been surpassed. The Ernest King Professor of Maritime History at the Naval War College, John Hattendorf [**1564**], 1991, reviewed some works of Boudriot plus other works.

David Davies [**869**], Fighting Ships: Ships of the Line, 1793-1815, 1993, focused on the ships of the long war, the battles, and the personnel. An older survey was Reginald Custance [**840**], The Ship-of-the-Line in Battle, 1912. Steve Martinsen [**2439**], 1994, described the French SOTL during the Napoleonic Wars. Napoleon set out to rejuvenate the French battle fleet. French warships were better built.

The Professor of Naval History, King's College, University of London, Andrew Lambert [**2003**], The Last Sailing Battle Fleet, 1991, described the era of the last sailing battleships, covering political, economic, tactical, and strategic areas. There were 100 SOTLs and 160 frigates.

A.H. Taylor [**3571**], 1958-1959, reviewed the design changes leading from the galleon to the SOTL, the design being consolidated by the 1670s. All was triumphantly vindicated at Trafalgar.

Other individual SOTLs have been covered. HMS VALIANT, 74 guns, was modeled from the French INVINCIBLE, and its construction and service were described by Brian Lavery [**2078**], 1991. HMS IMPLACABLE, 74-guns, had a spectacular career. Originally a French SOTL in the van at Trafalgar, thus out of the battle. She fled south but was captured on 2 November. Recommissioned in the RN as IMPLACABLE, she served in the Baltic, was at the blockade of Alexandria in 1839, and was scuttled in the English Channel in 1949. Her stern-main concourse was preserved and is featured in the new Neptune's Court at the NMM, all recounted by Richard Cavendish [**598**], 1999, and Beverly Butler [**528**], 1999. HMS AGAMEMNON, 64-guns, was "Nelson's favorite," serving at the Saints, the Nore mutiny, Copenhagen, and Trafalgar, all recounted by Anthony Deane [**892**], 1996. HMS ELEPHANT was the flagship of Nelson at Copenhagen in 1801, described by Eric Tushingham [**3675**], 2001. HMS BELLEROPHON, 74-guns, was designed by Thomas Slade, as was VICTORY, at the Glorious First of June, the Nile, and Trafalgar. Napoleon surrendered aboard her in 1815, all recounted by Colin Pengally [**2807**], 1966. ROYAL GEORGE was tragically sunk in August 1782 at anchor in flat calm at Spithead with 900 lost including Admiral Kempenfelt, all studied carefully by lawyer R.F. Johnson [**1817**], 1971, who disagreed with the findings of the court martial upon which St. Vincent and Adam Duncan were sitting. Thomas Birbeck [**320**], 1966, described HMS FOUDROYANT.

Rif Winfield [**3916**] described The 50-Gun Ship, 1997, developed in the 19th century as the need for SOTLs diminished.

F. FRIGATES

"The eyes of the fleet," "maids of all work," and the ships with the most glamorous and adventurous histories were frigates. They were used for reconnaissance; their features: smaller, faster, more nimble, heavily armed, maneuverable, 5th and 6th rates, two decks, 20 to 40 guns. Nelson often lamented that there were not enough of them, for example, as he was desperately searching for Napoleon all over the Mediterranean in the summer of 1798 and the enemy fleet of 1803-1805.

The most authoritative, fabulous, and prolific naval historian and publisher, Robert Gardiner [**1242, 1239, 1243, 1241, 1238**], favored the frigate and produced 5 major works. He favored the "true frigate," their technical aspects, and history. Maximum use of illustrations from the NMM added further to their quality and importance. The Frigates of the Napoleonic Wars, 2000, was a most sophisticated analysis of the frigate, describing its origins and development; The First Frigates: Nine-Pounder and Twelve-Pounder Frigates, 1748-1815, 1992, in The Anatomy of the Ship series, and The Heavy Frigate: Eighteen Pounder Frigates, 1994, presented as vol. I. Subsequent vols. for the 19th century did not appear. There were technical histories: "The Frigate Designs of 1755-1757," 1977, about the SOUTHAMPTON-class, "The First English Frigates," 1975, originated in 1739, and the 6th rate, 20-24 guns, copied from a captured French frigate, TYGRE, a superior design.

James Henderson [1597], The Frigates, 1970, was about the "lesser warships." Single ship actions were favored. The narrative was marred by colloquialisms and extraneous comparisons. Paul Webb [3797], 1996, assessed the frigate situation in the RN, 1793-1815. There were 166 available in 1793, 206 were captured during the war, and 257 were available in 1815.

James De Kay [899], Chronicles of the Frigate MACEDONIAN, 1809-1922, 1995, was about the most important prize taken by USS UNITED STATES, October 1812 off the Cape Verde Islands; a 5th rate, 38 guns. She was captured, restored, and recommissioned in the USN. David White [3838], The Frigate DIANA, 1988, in The Anatomy of the Ship series, followed its history, built in 1793, and design features; a total of 312 illustrations. M.K. Barritt [218], 1972, wrote about Nelson's frigates during that crucial period of search for Napoleon, May-August 1798. Brian Vale [3710], 2001, selected a frigate on the South American station in the early 1820s and presented its "life" in detail for a commission. French designs were favored by the British. Jean Boudriot [372], The History of French Frigates, 1650-1850, 1993, was a technical history, profusely illustrated, and with a complete list of French frigates. Andrew Thrush [3621], 1991 and Gregory Robinson [3094], 1929, described frigates of the 17th century. Thrush noted British frigates failed to perform well, for example, against Dunkirk privateers and against Dutch frigates. Daniel Harris [1524], 1990, wrote of "Chapman's frigates," designed by the naval architect, F.H. Chapman; the BELLONA-class, 40 guns.

In a dissertation and a book, T.N.R. Wareham [3571, 3572], The Star Captains, 1999 and 2001, concentrated on frigate captains, studying the careers of 700 captains. The best, most successful ones kept on active service for longer times and were less dependent on "interest." It was "an elite area of activity." See 14., K. The spy-fiction writer, Anthony Price [2952], The Eyes of the Fleet, 1990, wrote about frigates and frigate captains, 1793-1815. Unfortunately he did not seem to know the difference between fact and fiction; Hornblower was the 6th example of frigate captains. Others were Pellew, Pigot, Cochrane, Hoste, and Broke. Why Pigot?: murdered by his crew for brutality.

G. SHIPBUILDING AND SHIP MODELS

Shipbuilding, construction, and the important fittings such as rigging and masts have attracted interest. Shipwrights and naval architects used ship models extensively, the NMM and Science Museum maintaining an impressive collection. An important literature has arisen aimed at those interested in construction of ship models. Clubs and associations encouraged the process.

Meticulouslessness, concentration on detail, and perseverance were essential requirements for the model shipbuilder.

A.J. Holland [**1654**], Ships of British Oak, 1971, described wooden shipbuilding in Hampshire; James Dodds [**944**], Building the Wooden Fighting Ship, 1984, was a more general survey. A trilogy featured large folio size books profusely illustrated, and including much detail: Peter Goodwin [**1320**], The Construction and Fitting of the Sailing Man of War, 1987, James Lees [**2094**], The Masting and Rigging of English Ships of War, 1625-1860, 1979, and Brian Lavery [**2069**], Arming and Fitting of English Ships of War, 1600-1815, 1987. R.C. Anderson [**96**], The Rigging of Ships in the Days of the Spritsail Topmast, 1600-1720, 1926, for the Marine Research Society, was a classic on rigging. I.C. Campbell [**566**], 1995, described the lateen sail in world history and took a revisionist view. Europeans and Pacific islanders developed the lateen sail separately and individually, without copying Arab use.

R.C. Anderson [**80**], Catalogue of Ship Models, 1952, was for the NMM. John Franklin [**1177**], Navy Board Ship Models, 1650-1750, 1989, large folio size, illustrated 30 examples of the official ship models used by the Admiralty and dockyards; extraordinarily detailed. Geoffrey Laird Clowes [**666**], Sailing Ships, 2 vols., 1931-1932, presented their history and development based on the collection of ship models at the Science Museum.

A series of "How to" publications as guides and reference works were available: Milton Roth [**3152**], Ship Modeling from Stem to Stern, 1988; Charles Davis [**878**], Ship Models: How to Build Them, 1925; Philip Reed [**3041**], Modelling Sailing Men-of-War, 2000, a step-by-step manual; two by John Bowen [**394, 393**], Scale Model Warships, 1978, and Scale Model Sailing Ships, 1977; Lennarth Petersson [**2835**], Rigging Period Ship Models, 2000; Jack Needham [**2615**], Modelling Ships in Bottles, 1972; Tom Gorman [**1328**], Working Scale Model Merchant Ships, 2001, and Marvin Saville [**3227**], Hornblower's Ships, 2001, about the 11 scale model ships constructed for the TV mini-series. Those models and more were the themes of Norman Boyd [**408**], The Model Ship: Her Role in History, 2000, sponsored by the Woodbridge Antique Collectors.

Chapter 12

Piracy, Plunder, and Privateering.

Piracy has been ubiquitous in time, ancient to modern, and place, worldwide: in ancient times, Phoenicians, Greeks, Romans, and Carteginians; in the early middle ages, the Vikings; in the early modern period, French corsairs, English Sea-Dogs, and Dutch Sea Beggars operating on the Spanish Main and elsewhere; some piracy by American colonists, and the Barbary States during the 17th and 18th centuries. Other centers over time have been the Indian Ocean with a popular base at Madagascar; in modern times, in the South China Sea. Indeed, piracy in the Orient or East and the Occident or West has differed. Piracy in Chinese waters was at a peak about 1810. The structure and operations were based on confederation-fleets. Philippine pirate communities have been studied; unique because it was government sponsored. Piracy has revived there during the late 20th and early 21st centuries.

Piracy was robbery or predation on the high seas, extraterritorial violence, and nonstate violence. Variations have evolved: pirates, privateers, buccaneers, free booters, corsairs, "Sea-Dogs," "Sea Beggars," renegades, outlaws, and terrorists. There were distinctions: the pirate preyed on all without discrimination, the privateer only on certified designated enemies, the buccaneer was an adventurer in the Caribbean area who concentrated on Spanish depredations in the 17th and 18th centuries, corsairs were sea rovers of the Barbary States, usually Muslims, "Sea-Dogs" were Elizabethan adventurers, and "Sea Beggars" were patriotic Dutch rebels.

To place all of this in perspective, go to Janice Thomson [**3607**], Mercenaries, Pirates, and Sovereigns: State-Building and Extraterritorial Violence in Early Modern Europe, 1994, tracing the development of "global coercive capabilities" and nonstate violence. Thomson described when piracy evolved into privateering, when "violence was marketized, democratized, and internationalized," and when there was no competent authority to distinguish or protect from nonstate violence. England was first to issue letters of marque, in 1295, against Portugal. Later, in 1544, Henry VIII gave blanket authority for privateering. Later still, Elizabethan Sea Dogs plundered, destroyed, and extorted at will. Finally, state-sponsored prize courts legitimized it all.

The importance of Venice has been stressed. **See 7., E., 2.** Alberto Teneti [**3589**], Piracy and the Decline of Venice, 1580-1615, 1961, reviewed the various attackers of Venice, destroying its hegemonic position. The "final blow" was administered by the English, between 1580-1600. One factor was what the English saw as retaliation against Venice for supplying galleons to the Spanish Armada. "But the primary purpose was plunder."

The best English/British perspective was David Quinn [**2976**], England's Sea Empire, 1550-1642, 1983, presenting the history of Britain's imperial rise. He described syndicates of British merchants, businessmen, and court and naval officials cultivating an aggressive, distant commerce of "merchant adventurers" and "armed private marauders" leading to slave trading and sanctioning plunder. During this early modern period, the naval-maritime operations of English, French, Dutch, and other seamen whom we today call pirates and privateers were sanctioned and sponsored by governments and entrepreneurs; thus, the true origins of the Royal Navy and British hegemony.

Frank Sherry [**3305**], Raiders and Rebels: The Golden Age of Piracy, 1986, singled out the period 1690 to 1730 as "the golden age of piracy" worldwide, "the most intense outbreak of seaborne banditry ever recorded."

A. PRIVATEERS

Privateering was abolished by the Declaration of Paris of 1856 and has not been an issue since.

Some older accounts included Edward Statham [**3430**], Privateers and Privateering, 1910, a collection of accounts and an old classic, and C.W. Kendall [**1871**], surveying English privateering in Private Men-of-War, 1931.

Kenneth Andrews [**108, 109, 104, 107**], Elizabethan Privateering, 1964, another book, 1959, an article, 1951, and a dissertation, 1951, analyzed the context of English privateering, discussing various ventures, and the role of these matters in English/British overseas expansion. He praised the thesis of David Quinn [**2976**]. In 1585, seven English ships and their cargoes were seized in Spanish harbors. In response, the Lord High Admiral issued letters of reprisal. Drake and, eventually, hundreds of others responded and retaliated. Issuance of letters of reprisal expanded beyond control. The Crown and other entrepreneurs invested. This was not piracy and not official enterprise; the term privateering was not used until later. These "Sea-Dogs" were joined by French Huguenots, Dutch Sea Beggars, and other plunderers in attacking the Spanish and the Spanish Main, quasi-official reactions. Anti-Papism was an incentive. Trade and plunder were undistinguishable. Piracy evolved into privateering. It was the business of plunder, plus Protestantism and patriotism were added. Privateering became the "school" of oceanic experience. All was sanctioned by Admiralty Courts and prize courts.

Stephen Pistono [**2858**], 1975, pushed back to 1400. During the reign of Henry IV a "pirate war" raged in the Channel, a "school of English seamen." Henry was reluctant to punish because he needed those same ships and men to further his own operations against enemies. C.S.L. Davies [**867**], 1994, described the "sack of Bristol" of the mid-1480s as related to privateering-type operations. English, French, Bretons, and Flemish were participants; maybe even Christopher Columbus.

Gordon Connell-Smith [**717**], 1951, presented precursors. As noted by Kenneth Andrews [**108**], the Anglo-Spanish struggle was an important impetus to the development of English/British naval power. Those Elizabethan seamen inherited a tradition of hostility and contempt from the time of Henry VIII. Corbett [**748**] saw 1545 as the birth of English naval power, the "forerunners of Drake." In an article and a dissertation, John Appleby [**127, 128**], 1988 and 1983, recounted the voyage of ANNE OF DUBLIN in the 1550s and English privateering in general during the 1620s. The voyage degenerated into quasi-legal attacks on neutral shipping in the Channel; "outright piracy." The High Court of the Admiralty was the chief controlling agency. Florence Dyer [**1004**], 1935, described "reprisals" in the 16th century. Every government sanctioned obtaining redress for wrongs committed.

J.R. Bruijn [**487**], 1978, described Dutch privateering in the 1660s and 1670s. G.N. Clark [**644**], 1921, described reductions in English and Dutch privateering during the age of Jean Bart, the late 17th century.

W.R. Meyer [**2504, 2505**], 1981 and 1983, turned to statistics. Records of the High Court of the Admiralty revealed that 490 letters of marque were issued between 1688-1697, 1622 between 1702-1713. Commissions by colonial governors were not included. Meyer agreed that French privateering exceeded that of the English by far, corsairs from Dunkirk alone exceeded that of the English.

Violet Barbour [**199**], 1911, focused on the West Indies and "no peace beyond the line." Letters of marque seemed to legitimize uncontrolled depredations. First were French Huguenots from Rochelle and Dieppe, followed by the English: 3 voyages by John Hawkins in the 1560s, followed by reprisals from Drake and others. In a dissertation and an article, Nuala Zahadieh [**3981, 3980**], 1984 and 1990, elaborated on these privateering operations in the West Indies, specifically "business aspects" in Jamaica, this "frugal, prudential and hopeful trade," an "ideal start-up trade." This peaked about 1670, followed by planting and merchandizing colonial enterprise. Howard Chapin [**617, 618**], 1926 and 1928, reviewed colonial privateering, 1625-1725, and again, 1739-1748. Alan Jamieson [**1791**], 1983, wrote of American privateering in the West Indies during the American Revolution where they were aided by the French.

W.B. Johnson [**1820**], 1931, reviewed these extensive privateering operations in the Channel, "the home of privateering." It was a business venture for private individuals. J.W.D. Powell, [2930], <u>Bristol Privateers and Ships of War</u>, 1930, studied participation from Bristol from the 14th century, mostly during the 18th century. 900 ships were cited. William Dampier and Alexander Selkirk were Bristol privateers.

John Appleby [130], 1990, Jane Ohlmeyer [2690], 1990, Louis Cullen [825], 1958, and R.J. Raymond [3029], 1977, described the activities of the Irish involved in privateering and piracy. Peter Raban [2994], 1994, studied the Channel Islanders who were able to substitute privateering for normal trade during wartime, send back intelligence to the RN, and assist in blockading the French coast.

Susan Maxwell [2472], 1996, Richard Spence [3406], 1995, and Conrad Gill [1283], 1961, presented case studies, Henry Seckford, George Clifford, Earl of Cumberland, and Thomas Hall, the first two courtiers and privateers, Hall, a merchant and privateer. In a dissertation, an article, and a book, David Starkey [3424, 3425, 3423], 1985, 1988, and 1990, reviewed British privateering in the 18th century. After thorough study, Starkey concluded that privateering exerted a marked impact on Britain, especially playing a significant role in the wartime economy. There were 7000 commissions, 3000 prizes were captured, plus 3500 more by the RN.

In a dissertation, two articles, and a book, Carl Swanson [3524-3527], <u>Predators and Privateers</u>, 1979, 1982, 1985, and 1991, and variations, focused on American colonial operations, 1739-1748. After a quantitative and qualitative study, for example, 3973 prize actions in Vice Admiralty Courts, he concluded that privateering was a sound proposition, the basis of a political economy of mercantilism. Regular navies were expensive. The profit motive was attractive. At no cost to the government, the overseas trade of France and Spain were destroyed. Mahan [2328, 2329], Corbett [759], and Richmond [3066] dismissed it as peripheral. Gwyn [1431] and Baugh [237] recognized its true importance. J.F. Jameson [1790], 1923, reviewed the documents, letters of marque, profits and losses, and libel actions, 1630s-1760s. Stephen Fisher [1112], 1987, edited 6 seminar papers, for example, David Starkey on British and Dutch privateering and Colin Elliott on the entrepreneurial aspects of British privateering.

B. FRANCE AND <u>GUERRE DE COURSE</u>

English/British naval strategy was "blue-water"; France may have experimented with that, and probably preferred it, but other circumstances and persistent British victories forced an alternative strategy, concentrating on destroying the commerce of the enemy, <u>guerre de course</u>. The famous French naval-maritime strategy of the 17th and 18th centuries, <u>guerre de course</u>, was founded and sustained by pirates operating from such English Channel ports as St. Malo and Dunkirk.

J.S. Bromley [**451**], <u>Corsairs and Navies, 1660-1760</u>, 1987, was a series of essays focusing on privateering. "Corsairs" came from the French practice, <u>guerre de course</u>. He wrote of supra-national groups, all the irregular forces scouring the high seas belonging to official and unofficial associations or confraternities, including, as expected, Dutch, French, and English, but also including Channel Islanders, Jacobites, Turks, and Moors. Paul Bamford [**190**], 1954, reviewed French shipping in the North European trade, 1660-1789.

R.P. Crowhurst [**813, 814, 812**], <u>The French War on Trade: Privateering, 1795-1815</u>, 1989 and an article, 1982, presented revision: <u>guerre de course</u> was less a strategy, especially in its economic manifestation. French investors and merchants resorted to privateering as a substitute for regular commerce when that collapsed in wartime. <u>The Defence of British Trade, 1689-1815</u>, 1977, described the threat of French privateering which led the British to adopt convoys and other defenses. Andre Lespagnol [**2108**], 1995, in a French book, confirmed the Crowhurst thesis: playing up the economic basis of French privateering, featuring St. Malo as a case study. Ulane Bonnel [**362**], 1961, and Patrick Villiers [**3727**], 2000, both French books, featured a general survey and Dunkirk as a case study. John Clark [**647**] made an extensive study of La Rochelle and its economy in the 18th century. War interrupted normal trade and La Rochelle declined seriously.

The legacy of A.T. Mahan [**2328, 2329**] forced neglect of privateering as a formative basis in the development of British sea power and global hegemony. Revisionists have overcome this legacy and it has now received proper attention. J.S. Bromley [**451**] called it "the private war at sea." The French strategy of <u>guerre de course</u> was based upon privateering; St. Malo and Dunkirk were primary centers.

C. PIRACY

Piracy was a very popular subject, romanticized and even glorified. Privateers operated under proper commissions, legalized freebooting; piracy was illegal predation, plunder on the high seas. Over time it thrived on the Spanish Main, among the Barbary states of North Africa, the Persian Gulf, the Red Sea, the South China Sea, and the West of England. Most sources cited records of the High Court of the Admiralty documenting piratical operations on a massive scale.

Alexander Olivier Exquemeling [**1066**], <u>The Buccaneers of America</u>, 1678, also presented as John Esquemeling, was probably a Fleming or Hollander, making personal observations of piratical exploits in the Caribbean in the 1670s, the only authentic history of operations on "the Spanish Main."

Charles Johnson [**1813**], <u>A General History of the Robberies and Murders of the Most Notorious Pyrates</u>, 1724, was a popular contemporaneous survey with over 60 subsequent editions. Authorship has become controversial;

some claimed Daniel Defoe [**895-897**] was "Captain" Johnson. All agreed that the author had direct access, perhaps even personal experience. There were individual accounts, for example, Blackbeard, Vane, Spriggs, Anne Bonney, and Mary Read.

Daniel Defoe [**895-897**], The Life, Adventures, and Pyracies of the Famous Captain Singleton, 1720, and another work, 1962, were by a famous writer of the 18th century, informative with authentic details, presumably based on personal knowledge and contact with pirates. Some claim Defoe was the actual author of the account credited to Captain Charles Johnson [**1813**]. The Singleton work, a novel, incorporated psychological realism and domestic subjectivity. In 1988, P.N. Furbank [**1217**] insisted Defoe was not Johnson. Hans Turley [**3667**], "Piracy, Identity, and Desire in Captain Singleton," 1997, was an analysis of the Defoe [**895**] novel, "proto-psychology," as he dubbed it. Turley noted the homoerotic aspect of the relationship between Singleton and Quaker William.

The most attractive format, colorful and folio size, was one of three works by David Marley [**2390, 2387, 2391**], Pirates: Adventurers of the High Seas, 1995, others, 1994, and 1992, including essays in French and Spanish and a chronology. David Cordingly [**767, 765, 764**] contributed Under the Black Flag, 1995, and two works, Pirates, 1992 and 1996, the former a synthesis. Cordingly estimated that there were about 2000 pirates in the West at the height and even more in the South China Sea, 18th and 19th centuries. He reviewed "fact and fiction," popular images, such as walking the plank, peg-legs, parrots, flags, women pirates, and buried treasure, most of which were myth. His Pirates supported a major exhibition at the NMM. Kenneth Maxwell [**2471**], 1997, reviewed Under the Black Flag, noting that Henry Morgan had successfully sued Alexander Exquemeling [**1066**] for defamation of character. He further reviewed the history of piracy, especially in the Caribbean. Fernand Braudel [**426**], 1949, treated piracy as part of the process of economic exchange in the Mediterranean world in the 16th century.

C.L. Ewen [**1065**], 1949, introduced "organized piracy," a virtual business in England in the 16th century. Others included Philip Gosse [**1332, 1334, 1333**], The History of Piracy, 1932, The Pirates Who's Who, 1924, and an article, 1950; Patrick Pringle [**2953**], 1953; Hugh Rankin [**3009**], 1969; Frank Sherry [**3305**], 1986, describing the golden age of piracy, the 1690s-1720s, "the most intense outbreak of seaborne banditry ever recorded," and Neville Williams [**3885**], Captains Outrageous, 1961, touting coverage of 7 centuries of piracy, beginning with "Rovers" of the Cinque Ports, especially Winchelsea, in 1200.

Cyrus Karraker [**1845**], Piracy Was a Business, 1953, elaborated: piracy was a profession, occupation, and a policy. There were pirate syndicates in the West Country of England. David Starkey [**3426**], Pirates and Privateers, 1997, was the proceedings from a conference in Middleburg, Zeeland, once a privateering center. Noted experts read papers, for example, Robert Ritchie,

Marcus Rediker, Faye Kent, and Patrick Crowhurst. It touted a scientific study of predation and a global perspective. England was a "notorious nation of pirates" but was first to suppress it and to put tighter controls on privateers.

Jo Stanley [**3419**], Bold in Her Breeches, 1991, focused on women pirates over time beginning in the 5th century BC. Others were a 5th century Danish princess and a 16th century Irish woman, Grace O'Malley.

Jan Rogozinski [**3133**], Pirates!: Brigands, Buccaneers, and Privateers in Fact, Fiction and Legend, 1995, combined popular and scholarly accounts in the form of an encyclopedia, 1000 entries: lives, exploits, history, novels, plays, poems, ballads, and paintings. C.R. Pennell [**2809**], 2001, was an anthology of Bandits at Sea.

A.G. Course [**777, 778**], recounted Pirates of the Eastern Seas, 1966, and Pirates of the Western Seas, 1969, the former about Africa to Japan, the latter about Europe and America.

D. SMUGGLING AND PIRACY IN ENGLAND

Smuggling was notorious throughout the coastal areas of the British Isles, especially in the West. David Phillipson [**2853**], Smuggling: A History, 1700-1970, 1973, was a general survey. An older account was Henry Shore [**3310**], Smuggling Days and Smuggling Ways, 1892.

Neville Williams [**3886**], Contraband Cargoes, 1959, was the best history, covering 7 centuries from 1272, recognized as a profession during some of that time. The heyday was 1713-1775. G.D. Ramsay [**3004**], 1952, wrote of the smugglers' trade, a neglected aspect of British commercial development. It was a significant share of foreign trade. In a dissertation, Paul Muskett [**2590**], 1996, studied English smuggling in the 18th century. He pursued the themes of commercial activity, social crime, and policing.

Again, we turn to the preeminent Kenneth Andrews [**116, 112, 113**], Trade, Plunder and Settlement: Maritime Enterprise and the Genesis of the British Empire, 1480-1630, 1984. Andrews continued his insistence that piracy and privateering were fundamental elements contributing to the rise and hegemony of the English/British in sea power and colonialism. Some themes were aggressive drives by armed traders to break into the Atlantic trade and colonization of Spain and Portugal, bellicose imperialism, militant acquisitiveness, "forcible trade," poaching, plunder, piracy, patronage from the Crown and courtiers, and "powerful West Country interests." Individuals included Robert Cecil, Walsingham, the Hakluyts, Frobisher, Gilbert, the Hawkins family, Drake, and Grenville. In a second work, Andrews described an enterprise of Robert Cecil which he dubbed as privateering, but that was illegal and was covered up.

Neville Williams [**3887**] described The Sea Dogs: Privateers, Plunder and Piracy in the Elizabethan Age, 1975, these operating from the Isle of

Purbeck and Bristol. David Matthew [**2466**], 1924, wrote of pirates at the same time operating from the Cornwall and Welsh coasts, commercial ventures financed by capitalist landowners. C.J. Ford [**1135**], 1979, wrote of an Anglo-French pirate war in the early 15th century, merchants on both sides suffering badly. Ronald Moore [**3535**], 1960, has a dissertation on English piracy in the early 17th century. They had begun from the Cinque Ports and piracy had become a profession by Elizabethan times.

In a dissertation and a book, C.M. Senior [**3273, 3274**], A Nation of Pirates, 1973 and 1976, described the situation in the early 17th century. The Anglo-Spanish war suddenly ended so no more privateering. no more letters of marque, losses must be recouped, and piracy was "a growing menace fast gaining momentum," and remaining so for several decades.

Mike Powell [**2932**], 1993, studied a battle of 1784 at Mudeford, Devon. Customs officials from a revenue cutter were attacked and killed. C.L. Ewen [**1062, 1065**], 1939 and 1949, wrote of organized piracy around England and a documented narrative of an English pirate. Most were local and conducted their illegal and violent operations locally. The Channel Islands were perfect sites. A.G. Jamieson [**1792**], A People of the Sea, 1986, was about their history. Topics included privateering and smuggling. Gregory Cox [**782**], 1999, compelled to "correct" Jamieson as he wrote about Guernsey and St. Peter Port, 1680-1836.

In a dissertation and an article, Samuel Margolin [**2375, 2374**], 1992 and 1995, shifted to colonial "maritime lawlessness" in the Chesapeake area, 1650-1750: smuggling, wrecking, and piracy, all supported by the locals who obstructed enforcement efforts. In a dissertation, Robert Ayer [**162**], 1993, looked at maritime smuggling in colonial and national America to 1812. Opposition to governmental controls became part of the pattern of resistance by the colonists.

In a dissertation and a book, David Hebb [**1592, 1593**], Piracy and the English Government, 1616-1642, 1985 and 1994, was more about English victims of piracy, especially from the Barbary corsairs: 400 English vessels and 8,000 captives. The government responded with two expeditions, against Sallee and Algiers. All the while, English piracy was declining, thus, the English were more victims than perpetrators.

Focusing on Jack Tar and a century later was Marcus Rediker [**3037-3039**], Between the Devil and the Deep Blue Sea: Merchant Seamen, Pirates, and the Anglo-American Maritime World, 1700-1750, 1987, an award-winning survey representing the Marxist perspective. Included was a chapter, "Plunder and Social Banditry at Sea," recounting thousands of Anglo-American pirates attacking merchants and commerce which he described as the "process of social change and working class development" and maritime class-consciousness. Supplementing it was a dissertation and an article, "'Under the Banner of King Death': The Social World of Anglo-American Pirates, 1716 to 1726."

Kris Lane [**2023**], Pillaging the Empire, 1998, insisted that the pirates were not egalitarians as some recent writers have depicted them, for example, Drake and Henry Morgan were dictatorial. Lane concluded that it was primarily English property law rather than any Spanish reaction which ended piracy.

Individual case studies have abounded. Francis Drake, John Hawkins, and William Dampier were treated in detail elsewhere. **See 9., D., 1., 3., and 6.** Nelson Bard [**201, 203**], 1995, was about Robert Rich, 2nd Earl of Warwick, leader during the Civil War, who had his own privateering fleet and was instrumental in bringing the navy over to the side of Parliament. James Kelly [**1853**], 1998, was about Bartholomew Sharpe, buccaneer of the late 17th century. C.L. Ewen [**1062**], 1939, was about John Ward, the "arch-pirate" who "took the turban" and joined the Barbary corsairs.

Aubrey Burl [**511**], 1997, was about Bartholomew Roberts, "that great pyrate" of the early 18th century. Robert Lee [**2091**], 1974, tried but failed to rehabilitate Edward Teach or Blackbeard, "the famous knight of the black flag."

One of the best pirate biographies was Robert Ritchie [**3072**], 1986, about Captain William Kidd, one of the most colorful pirates. Kidd had lived a respectable life, wealthy, with a residence on Wall Street, New York. His famous ship was ADVENTURE. He was tried and executed, 1701. Jan Rogozinski [**3133**], 2001, wrote of Kidd and others.

Dudley Pope [**2897**], 1977, E.A. Cruickshank [**817**], 1935, H.R. Allen [**43**], 1976, and Susie Core [**769**], 1943, wrote of Henry Morgan, "knight and knave." Peter Earle [**1008**], The Sack of Panama, 1982, was an exploit of Morgan. Morgan was a governor of Jamaica and president of an Admiralty Court. He was arrested, apparently to appease the Spanish. Then, Charles II knighted him. He was buried at Port Royal, 4 years before the earthquake. **See 18., E.** J.C. Appleby [**131**], 1989, wrote of John Hippisley, a privateer during the early 17th century.

E. THE CARIBBEAN AND PIRACY

Jamaica was the English base, originally established as part of the Western Design of Oliver Cromwell in 1655. **See 7., G., 4.** The English pirate base in Jamaica was Port Royal, 6 forts, 300 cannon, 5000 white settlers, 3000 slaves, 500 ships annually. The situation was seen as even more spectacular because on 7 June 1692 an earthquake destroyed 15 of the 25 acres of the city.

Jenifer Marx [**2440**], Pirates and Privateers of the Caribbean, 1992, described the French corsairs as first, then the English Sea-Dogs and Dutch Sea Beggars. She wrote of the buccaneers, the Brotheren of the Coast, a roving sea republic. The death knell was the elimination of Jean Lafitte by the USN in the 1820s. Dingman Versteeg [**3723**], 1901, focused on Dutch Sea Beggars.

In a dissertation and a book, Peter Galvin [**1229, 1228**] Patterns of Pillage: A Geography of Caribbean-based Piracy in Spanish America, 1536-

1718, 1991 and 1999, conducted a geographical-historiographical survey, locations and writings about piracy by pirates and popular writers. The "pattern" was chronological as follows: corsairs, 16th century, buccaneers, 17th century, and free booters, 18th century. Kenneth Andrews [**115**], The Spanish Caribbean: Trade and Plunder, 1530-1630, 1978, recounted depredations against the Spanish colonies and trade by English and Dutch pirates. Clinton Black [**326**], 1989, and C.H. Haring [**1513**], 1910, wrote of French and English buccaneers in the West Indies. In a dissertation, Nuala Zahedieh [**3981**], 1984, recounted trade and plunder around Jamaica, 1655-1689. Simon Smith [**3369**], 1996, reviewed piratical activity, much based from Jamaica.

Robert Marx [**2444, 2445**], 1967 and 1973, described Port Royal in its heyday, "the most wicked city in the world," and reported on the nautical archaeological expedition after 1959. Michael Pawson [**2796**], 1975, wrote a history of Port Royal. Larry Gragg [**1354**], 2000, described the earthquake; 2000 died. **See 18., E.**

Peter Kemp [**1857**], Bretheren of the Coast, 1960, has these West Indian pirates transferring out into the Pacific, the "South Seas." Kenneth Poolman [**2885**], The SPEEDWELL Voyage, 1999, concerned this 22-gun privateer which operated in the Pacific. An albatross was shot and a series of crises ensued, an inspiration for a famous tale by Coleridge. There were mutinies and a shipwreck.

F. BARBARY CORSAIRS

The states of North Africa were attached to the Ottoman Empire and were Muslim: Algiers, seen as most powerful, Tunis, Tripoli, Malta, Morocco, and ports Sallee and Santa Cruz.

Godfrey Fisher [**1108**], Barbary Legend, 1957, was an excellent historical survey. G.N. Clark [**642**], 1944, summarized the history of the Barbary corsairs. M.S. Anderson [**74**], 1956, reviewed British relations with the Barbary states. Peter Earle [**1006**], Corsairs of Malta and Barbary, 1970, was best on the Maltese corsairs. Malta was Christian. Roger Perkins [**2821**], Gunfire in Barbary, 1982, recounted a battle between the British and Algiers in 1816. Pirates in North Africa were the subject of Nicholas Harding [**1490**], 2000, who described British intervention on the part of Hanover, dynastically linked to Britain, and C.R. Pennell [**2810**], 1989, who introduced a journal of an English consul of the region.

Roger Morriss [**2570**], 1998, introduced the journal of William Davidson, 1788-1789, which contained graphic descriptions of atrocities by Barbary corsairs. Were they authentic or propaganda? Morriss concluded the latter, to be used as a call to arms. Christopher Lloyd [**2155**], 1981, wrote a book with a twist: English pirates who "took the turban" and joined the Barbary corsairs. Pitcairn Jones [**1827**], Piracy in the Levant, 1827-1828, 1934, a publication of the NRS, from the papers of Admiral Edward Codrington, described later piracy.

The famous nautical novelist, C.S. Forester [**1142**] wrote <u>The Barbary Pirates</u>, 1953, a work for juveniles. Gardner Allen [**42**], <u>Our Navy and the Barbary Corsairs</u>, 1905, was about the American navy.

Chapter 13

The Navy, State-Building, and the Military Revolution

How and why did England/Britain become a big power? It could not have been land-based power. So, it must have been the naval and maritime factors which figured prominently in the rise. "State-building" has become an operative term describing the process. Developments in governmental efficiency, finance, taxation, and management contributed. Special war powers facilitated the process. Financing, mobilization, planning, and deployment of war-making forces was the key.

Somewhat related, an important debate has persisted since the 1950s over the "military revolution," seemingly not applicable to naval developments and focused on continental armies and land fortresses, especially those of France, Spain, and the Italian states. The European continent was the operative area. Others have insistently inserted naval forces as contributory to the military revolution and added Britain to the mix, not as peripheral but as central.

A. THE NAVY AND THE RISE OF THE NATION STATE

The best place to learn about the role of naval forces in state building, in the rise of the modern world, and the role of naval forces in the debate over the military revolution was the brilliant and formative contributions of a Swedish naval historian, Jan Glete [**1298-1300**]. Three works build on each other. Navies and Nations: Warships, Navies, and State Building in Europe and America, 1500-1860, 2 vols., 1993, was detailed and statistical comparisons. It was a systematic survey of quantitative data for 12 major and 40 minor navies. He placed navies in the center of the rise of the modern state. Warfare at Sea, 1500-1650: Maritime Conflicts and the Transformation of Europe, 1999, was at a more general level, yet still dynamic and formative. Technology, tactics, strategy, the mobility of resources, the monopolization of violence at sea, the Atlantic and the Baltic, and maritime wars were the themes. It began with

Portugal in Asia and covered through the era of global maritime warfare. Third was War and the State in Early Modern Europe: Spain, the Dutch Republic and Sweden as Fiscal-Military States, 1500-1660, 2002, in The War and History series. The focus was on the 16th and 17th centuries and the rise of permanent armies and navies.

Furthermore, the historical background and perspective can be found in three other works. A contribution to a textbook series was Wilfrid Prest [2944], Albion Ascendant: English History, 1660-1815, 1998, described state-building as the basis; from an insignificant island to superpower. Larry Addington [21, 20], The Patterns of War, 2 vols., 1984-1990, was an introductory review of the history of naval and land warfare from ancient times to the present. Finally, James Cable [536], The Political Influence of Naval Force in History, 1998, was an idiosyncratic survey of how governments used naval forces for political purposes. Included was China in the early 15th century.

However, the most comment has been reaction to John Brewer [435], The Sinews of Power: War, Money, and the English State, 1688-1783, 1989, a formative publication and a major contribution to the matter of state building. Brewer described the development and maturity of the fiscal-military state. Themes were the growing power of the central government, enhancing the ability of the government to wage war, military and civilian administration, and taxation and public finance, especially more efficient and effective methods of taxation. For England/Britain, formative were the Navigation Acts of 1651, 1660, and 1662 and the three Anglo-Dutch Wars. The result was the rise of global hegemony. The RN was the single most expensive item. Opposite conditions and trends occurred in France.

Often linked in the discussion was Linda Colley [705], Britons: Forging the Nation, 1707-1837, 1992, studied the making of a unified nation. Protestant and anti-French consciousness forged a national identity, "Britishness."

John Cookson [733], The British Armed Nation, 1793-1815, 1997, was a critique of the Brewer and Colley theses. Scotland and Ireland had been ignored as had local initiatives to cooperate with the central government. Mobilization of all forces was stressed. Self interest was more important than support for the central government. Continuing in the more modern period, Eric Evans [1058], The Forging of the Modern State: Early Industrial Britain, 1783-1870, 1983, observed the curious juxtaposition of aristocracy and industrialization.

Lawrence Stone [3460], An Imperial State at War: Britain from 1689 to 1815, 1994, edited a series of essays from a colloquium, Princeton University, November 1990. Papers included ones by Brewer, Colley, Daniel Baugh, and Stone. Brewer and Colley elaborated on their theses. Baugh wrote of use of "a grand marine empire."

James Wheeler [3827-3829], The Making of a World Power: War and the Military Revolution in Seventeenth-Century England, 1999, pushed the decisive period back to the 1620s-1650s, the wars of Charles I and the Civil War and Commonwealth. The New Model Army and "a standing navy" were factors. Expenses for dramatic increases in the navy and army created a demand for new methods of finance and administration. The Long Parliament implemented new taxes: excise, land, and sales. The result was a standing army and professional navy. In an article, a contribution to the debate on the military revolution, Wheeler cited the crisis of 1649 when the army and navy had to be reorganized, forcing changes in finance and administration. M.L. Baumber [247], 1996, wrote of Parliamentary naval politics in the 1640s.

Pushing further back in time, Mark Fissel [1116, 1115], 1991 and 1998, described English warfare in the 16th and early 17th centuries. Mobilization, impressment, logistics, and operations on the continent were featured. Thomas Woodrooffe [3956], Vantage at Sea: England's Emergence as an Oceanic Power, 1958, focused on the developments during the Anglo-Spanish War, 1585-1603. The Spanish Main and Spanish treasure were objects, then, overcoming the Armada.

This formative naval advance and the debates over military revolution and state-building can be understood better after the numerous analytical contributions of Jeremy Black [331, 329, 330, 332]: The British Navy and the Use of Naval Power in the Eighteenth Century, 1988, summarizing new interpretations of British naval history, Britain as a Military Power, 1688-1815, 1999, an essay, 2000, and European Warfare, 2 vols., 1994-1999. Black insisted on incorporating naval developments in the military revolution debate. He also stressed "the long eighteenth century" as formative and Britain as central. He warned against overemphasis on institutional and structural factors. Military history was more than an account of the accountants.

Earl Reitan [3046], Politics, War, and Empire: The Rise of Britain to a World Power, 1688-1792, 1994, was a more traditional interpretation. Nicholas Tracy [3643], 1972, did a dissertation on the RN as an instrument of foreign policy.

The old classic on these matters was Herbert Richmond [3066], Statesman and Sea Power: The Navy as an Instrument of Policy, 1558-1727, 1946, the Ford Lectures at Oxford, citing historical events to stress the need for a strong navy.

B. THE MILITARY REVOLUTION

In Michael Roberts [3081], Essays in Swedish History, 1966, Roberts repeated a lecture he gave at the Queen's University, Belfast, 1955, "The Military Revolution, 1560-1660." He insisted that a radical transformation in the art of war, a massive increase in the size of armies and changes in tactics and drill, had occurred in that period. The model was Gustavus Adlophus of Sweden.

Many challenges followed. Geoffrey Parker [**2752**], The Military Revolution: Military Innovation and the Rise of the West, 1500-1800, 1984, originally as the Lees Knowles Lectures at Cambridge University, critiqued and broadened the Roberts thesis. The preeminence of Sweden was questioned and the time line was moved back to the early 16th century. Look at developments in land warfare by France, the Dutch, and the Habsburgs. Parker included a chapter, "Victory at Sea," in which he presented a critique of A.T. Mahan [**2328, 2329**]. A key to the revolution was adoption of the gun and its use with ruthless skill in large sailing warships, for example, HENRY GRACE A' DIEU of 1509, 1000 tons, and MARY ROSE of 1511, 600 tons. GREAT MICHAEL of Scotland and VASA of Sweden were mentioned.

Others entered the frey. Michael Duffy [**974**], The Military Revolution and the State, 1500-1800, 1980, contributed an essay on the foundations of British naval power. Jeremy Black [**336**], A Military Revolution?, 1991, was a radical reassessment, stressing or adding a later period. There was also the "chicken-egg" analysis: did the absolutist state come before or after the military revolution? Clifford Rogers [**3123, 3124**], The Military Revolution Debate, 1993 and 1995, summarized the debate. After 40 years there was still no consensus. David Eltis [**1040**], The Military Revolutions in Sixteenth-Century Europe, 1995, reviewed the debate and analyzed how it applied to England and other countries. M.J. Braddick [**410**], 1993, wrote of the English military revolution, focusing on the 17th century, the New Model Army and the increase in the number and size of ships.

In Safeguard of the Sea, Rodger [**3110**, pp. 430-34] persuasively argued for a "naval revolution" in Britain. Military revolutions were more identified with absolutist monarchies. Naval revolution needed a system of government which involved maximum participation by interest groups whose money and skills were indispensable to sea power, for example, shipowners, seafarers, urban merchants, financiers, investors, managers, and skilled craftsmen. Only England and the Dutch enjoyed these features. Spain failed in the 16th century, France in the 18th, and Germany in the 20th.

A.J. Palmer [**2734**], 1997, stressed the decisive Anglo-Dutch wars and the transition to modern warfare at sea. George Raudzens [**3021**], 1999, speculated: "Military Revolution or Maritime Evolution?" Perhaps the decisive factor of European advantage was the oceanic transport monopoly, to go anywhere anytime.

Chapter 14

Administration, Logistics, Victualling, Shipbuilding, Dockyards, and Naval Ports

In state-building and the military revolution, naval version, organization, management, finance, taxation, and industrialization have been stressed as essential features. For England/Britain and the rise of the RN, organization and administration have been in transition, various changes over time. Some examples were as follows.

Keeper of the King's Ports and Galleys, c. 1200
Lord Warden of the Cinque Ports
Council of Marine
The Navy Board, 1540s
Lord High Admiral, e.g., 1600s, then that office was put in commission in 1673
Navy Committee of Parliament during the 1640s
Commissioners
Lords Commissioners of the Admiralty, c. 1700
Board of Commissioners
Navy Board
Admiralty and Board of the Admiralty
First Lord of the Admiralty
First Sea Lord of the Admiralty

For England/Britain, the navy became the largest "industrial enterprise" of the age, incorporating Admiralty administration, the Royal Dockyards, enormous forests and wood processing arrangements, mast ponds, shipbuilding and maintenance, bases, arsenals, logistical and victualling facilities, personnel requirements, strategic foreign bases and dockyards, and operations of thousands of ships varying from longboats to Ships of the Line of 60 to over 100 guns on two to three decks. Administration, logistics, and operations became increasingly complicated and elaborate. Squadrons or Stations were created all over the world. The "Shore Establishment" was a term which incorporated the naval dockyards, especially, Portsmouth, Chatham, and Plymouth, overseas bases, and the Victualling Board which was located at Weevil Yard. It was the largest industrial unit in Britain in the 18th century and probably in the Western World.

A. THE ADMIRALITY

A good, comprehensive, up-to-date history of the Admiralty is needed. **See 22.** An important contribution was N.A.M. Rodger [**3103**], The Admiralty, 1979, in the Offices of State series, a short but brilliant survey. Most was about the 19th century when "the RN had gained an empire but lost a role."

Oswyn Murray [**2589**], 1937-1939, a longtime secretary of the Admiralty, completed part of his history of the Admiralty, in 9 parts published posthumously. It was intended to be for the Offices of State series. Leslie Gardiner [**1236**], The British Admiralty, 1968, used a chronological framework over this history of 500 years, unfortunately, anecdotal and superficial. Some deserved achievements of the Admiralty were superb charts and sponsoring exploration voyages.

John Sainty [**3211**], Office Holders in Modern Britain: Admiralty Officials, 1660-1870, 1975, was a comprehensive listing of all officials.

Stanley Bonnett [**364**], The Price of Admiralty: An Indictment of the Royal Navy, 1805-1966, 1968, filled this "indictment" with rambling diatribes and bitterness; no balance and no purpose.

Richard Middleton [**2508**], 1970, spotlighted the mid-18th century, writing about William Pitt, the Elder, Anson, and the Admiralty. Naval officials were discredited because of loss of Minorca. Pitt brought in Anson and relied on him heavily, with great success.

Alan McGowan [**2251**], The Jacobean Commissions of Enquiry, 1608 and 1618, 1971, a publication of the NRS, was about investigations of scandals caused by embezzlement and corruption early in the 17th century.

John Appleby [**129**], 1985, introduced the "Irish Admiralty." In the 16th and 17th centuries, the "law maritime" must be administered and enforced. A separate Admiralty Court was set up and it experienced expansive growth.

Admiralty House, Whitehall, 1960, by Viscount Cilcennin [**638**], and "The Admiralty Buildings," 1940, by G.F. James [**1776**], described the headquarters of the Admiralty, provided in 1695 and located at the top of Whitehall where it enters Trafalgar Square, the official residence of the First Lord since 1786.

B. ADMINISTRATION

The model study of naval administration was by Daniel Baugh [**237, 238, 240**] in his book, British Naval Administration in the Age of Walpole, 1965, and in the article in the Lawrence Stone [**3460**] colloquium of 1990.

Baugh best articulated these matters, describing the dynamics of power and trade. There was also a dissertation, 1961, and Naval Administration, 1715-1750, 1977, a publication of the NRS. His thesis was that government and politics of the 18th century were naval administration writ large. The concept of national security expanded. It involved administration, the Admiralty, the Treasury, the Customs and Excise, victualling, the dockyards, and the sick and wounded office. These were the "sinews of power," a "New Model Navy." The Navigation Acts were essential features. The most persistent problem was manning. Parliament refused to raise wages and to fund a reserve manning system. Conscription in the form of impressment was the sole answer. Contributions of the empire have been ignored: nurseries of seamen, strategic naval bases, strategic materials, potential for trade, and favorable commodities.

To supplement Baugh, coverage at the same time, administration of the navy in the West Indies during wartime, 1739-1748, was Duncan Crewe [**799, 798**], Yellow Jack and the Worm, 1992, and a dissertation, 1978. The source most used was Muster Books of the ships which were statistically analyzed. The title came from yellow fever, the toredo worm, hurricanes, and desertion, those covering all of the problems of administration in a remote and hostile environment, for example, manning, victualling, health, naval stores, ordnance, and dockyards to sustain 60 ships, 20,000 sailors, and 8000 soldiers. Ruth Bourne [**385**], 1931, elaborated in a dissertation.

Focusing on an earlier century, but renowned as an older classic on the history of naval administration, was Michael Oppenheim [**2710, 2711**], A History of the Administration of the Royal Navy, 1509-1660, 1896, the chapters divided by the reigns, Henry VIII to Charles II. Use it carefully, but use it. Anti-government bias and unreliable quotations were weaknesses. Naval Accounts and Inventories of the Reign of Henry VII, 1896, a publication of the NRS, incorporated financial documents related to "the Kyngis Shipps," for example, ordnance stores, hired vessels, and construction of a dry dock.

David Loades [**2179**], The Tudor Navy, 1992, focused on administration, placing the navy in the proper political and administrative context, superseding Oppenheim [**2710**]. Loades tracked the Council of Marine Causes which evolved into the Navy Board. Themes were finance, victualling, manning, maintenance, and Crown subsidies.

C.S.L. Davies [**866**], 1965, described the naval administration under Henry VIII. The Keeper or Clerk of the Ships expanded to the Council of Marine, then, the Navy Board originated at this time. 47 warships were built during the reign and Woolwich yard was established. The first drydock had been built at Portsmouth under Henry VII.

In a dissertation and an article, Ronald Pollitt [**2880, 2878**], 1968 and 1974, studied naval administration during the preparation for and execution of, operations of the Armada campaign. Too much credit had been given to the commanders. The role of the bureaucracy was equally important and contributory to success. Involved were the Privy Council, Lord Treasurer, and the Navy Board.

Three dissertations focused on the early Stuarts. Norman Clayton [**653**], 1935, described naval administration, 1603-1628, to the death of Buckingham. Michael Young **3978, 3977**], 1971 and 1986, the latter a book, introduced John Coke, Deputy Treasurer of the Navy and Commissioner during the Buckingham regime. Donald Martin [**2430**], 1974, described the investigation commission of 1608. Massive corruption was uncovered but James I forgave the officials.

G.F. James [**1775**], 1936, described the evolution of administration, 1619-1714. As LHA, Buckingham was in charge. When he died, the office was placed in commission, and again in 1673. Admiralty officials during the period were named, for example, Pepys.

The period of the Interregnum, 1649-1660, attracted several studies: a book by Alfred Dewar [**924**], 1926, and dissertations by William Cogar [**693**], 1983, Wayne Hammond [**1470**], 1974, and R. McCaughey [**2228**], 1983, all described administration of the navy during this crucial time of transition. Parliament administered the navy until the Restoration. James Wheeler [**3828**], 1996, described naval finance during the Interregnum.

J.D. Davies [**873**], 1989, described the Admiralty Commission and the role of Pepys, 1674-1684. A dissertation by A. Turnbull [**3669**], 1975, focused on naval administration, 1660-1673, from the Restoration until the time James, Duke of York, was forced out due to the Test Act. Clennell Wilkinson [**3857**], 1997, in a dissertation, focused on governing the navy, 1763-1778, a time of peace. Much has been written about the alleged decline of the navy and the consequent loss of the American Revolution. The Earl of Sandwich has been blamed. Wilkinson concluded that the navy was never under funded, neglected, nor mismanaged.

The turn of the century during the reigns of William III and Anne was the period of study of James Johnson [**1816**], 1969, in a dissertation. He described relations between Parliament and the navy. A parliamentary diary of Richard Cocks dealing with naval affairs was edited by David Hayton [**1584**], 1996; it was "barbarous inhumanity" not to pay wages of seamen on time.

A dissertation by G.W. Morgan [**2544**], 1977, investigated the impact of war on the administration of all armed force offices during the 1740s. A dissertation by Roland Usher [**3703**], 1943, assessed the administration during the American Revolution. Problem areas were victualling, manning, and the transport service. As with the study by Wilkinson, the conclusion was that the civil administration did not cause the loss of the war. P.K. Crimmin [**800**], 1967, described the process of preparation of the naval estimates for the annual budget, 1783-1806, a process requiring cooperation between the Admiralty and the Treasury.

The equivalent of naval administration has been studied for earlier times. Military administration during the Norman period was described by Bernard Bachrach [**168**], 1985. "A plethora of logistic problems" faced William as he prepared to invade in the summer of 1066, for example, maintenance of 3000 horses and 14,000 men for a month awaiting a favorable wind. Harold had mobilized a fleet but had to let it go when time expired.

Most enlightening was W.R. Powell [**2933**], "The Administration of the Navy and the Stannaries, 1189-1216," 1956. Richard I had raised a large fleet of over 100 ships to accompany him on the Third Crusade. **See 7., C., 2.** King John devised a method to finance naval forces: apply the stannary tax, a tax on tin smelting and production directly to naval administration. F.W. Brooks [**459**], 1929, described the process of raising a fleet during the reigns of John and Henry III, the early 13th century. William de Wrotham, covered elsewhere, was prominent.

James Willard [**3866**], 1940, edited a series of papers on the period 1327-1336. Naval forces were administered by the Master of the King's Ships. Responsibilities included transporting the army, enforcing sovereignty over the narrow seas, and operations in the west, north, and in the Irish Sea. Mary Lyon [**2220**], 1983, described the wardrobe record of expenses for operations of Edward III, 1338-1340, in this case in Gascony as a diversion and close to Paris for the primary campaign. The culmination was the battle of Sluys, 1340. H.J. Hewitt [**1615**], The Organization of War under Edward III, 1338-1362, 1966, described men at sea, supplies, victuals, ports and facilities, and transport of troops. Again, an event was the English victory over the French at Sluys. **See 7., E.** C.F. Richmond [**3057**], 1963, in a dissertation, was a solid study of royal administration and the keeping of the sea, 1422-1485, up to the Tudor period.

John Briggs [**439**], Naval Administrations, 1827-1892, 1897, focused on his appraisal as clerk of the Admiralty for 44 years; anecdotal. A general overview can be found in Charles Clode [**662**], The Military Forces of the Crown, 2 vols., 1869.

A sample of the communications between the Admiralty and ships at sea was Nathaniel Boteler [**369**], 1634, a series of exchanges of discourse between the LHA and a captain at sea.

Comparatively, French naval administration was described by Donald Pilgrim [**2855**], 1969, in a dissertation, in this case, during the reign of Louis XIV in the 1680s. The French won at Beachy Head but failed to follow up and exploit the situation.

C. ADMINISTRATORS

The offices of administration at the Admiralty included commissioner, clerk, secretary, and First Lord, and later, First Sea Lord. Franklin Wickwire [**3850**], 1965, linked the office of Admiralty secretary in the 18th century to the British civil service. Samuel Pepys [**2817**] was covered elsewhere. **See 9., D., 16.**

F.B. Stitt [**3456**], 1991, and, in a dissertation, George Humphries [**1733**], 1953, studied the regime of George Anson, 1745-1762, a brilliant management success in the massive preparations of the navy for the Seven Years' War. Features included reform of the dockyards and the practice of half-pay for officers. Anson was best as motivator and manipulator.

The most study has been about the 4th Earl of Sandwich, First Lord, 1771-1782, the controversial period before and during the War of the American Revolution. N.A.M. Rodger [**3109**], 1993, J. H. Broomfield [**465**], 1965, G.R. Barnes [**210**], 4 vols., 1932-1983, a publication of the NRS, and dissertations by M.J. Williams [**3883**], 1962, and Clifford Morrison [**2564**], 1950, reviewed the administration. The general conclusions were that Sandwich was an able, determined administrator. Sandwich has been rehabilitated.

Roger Morriss [**2575**], 1983, studied the regime of John Jervis, the Earl of St. Vincent, noted for reforms, 1801-1804. However, Morriss concluded that St. Vincent was ignorant of the complexities of civil administration and a failure.

Bernard Pool [**2881**], 1965, and I.L. Phillips [**2849**], in a dissertation, studied the career of Charles Middleton, 1st Baron Barham, 1770s-1805, more successful. Opposite from St. Vincent, Middleton was never a flag officer at sea but was seen as a great administrator.

A.P. McGowan [**2252, 2249**], 1967, in a dissertation and an article, studied the 1st Duke of Buckingham, Lord High Admiral, 1618-1628. These were revisionist efforts to rehabilitate. There were failed expedition operations but some success at reform: welfare of seamen and an anti-pirate patrol. Violet Rowe [**3156**], 1970, studied Henry Vane during the 1640s-1650s, a brilliant parliamentarian and naval minister during the Civil War and Commonwealth period. He was instrumental in the build-up of the navy. Vane was executed as a regicide after 1660.

As noted elsewhere, F.W. Brooks [**462**], 1925, studied William de Wrotham, Keeper of the King's Ports and Galleys, appointed in 1204, the earliest office of naval administrator. Included were the King's Ships and ships from the Cinque Ports.

G.F. James [**1777, 1778**], 1937 and 1939, wrote about Josiah Burchett, secretary, 1695-1742, seen as worthy but less conspicuous than Pepys. Roger Merriman [**2499**], 1950, a publication of the NRS, reviewed the papers of Charles Sergison, secretary in the 1690s. Henry Snyder [**3384**], 1972, and Robert H. Irrmann [**1756**], 1946, in a dissertation, studied Edward Russell, Earl of Orford, about 1700, a controversial official. Much politics was involved, for example, early political party pressure tactics; the Whigs forced Orford onto the Admiralty. He had been a successful commander at the battle of La Hogue, 1692.

Howell Lloyd [**2176**], 1971, studied John Hawkins, c. 1590. Michael Alexander [**38**], 1975, wrote of the Lord Treasurer of Charles I, Richard Weston, Earl of Portland, 1577-1635, a leading member of the Admiralty Board.

Hardin Craig [**785**], 1970, studied Thomas Grenville, First Lord, 1806-1807, as a case study of the business of the First Lord.

Christopher Lloyd [**2161**], Mr. Barrow at the Admiralty: The Life of Sir John Barrow, 1764-1848, 1970, was biographer of Barrow, like Pepys, one of the important Admiralty administrators, secretary from 1804-1845, initiator of Arctic exploration, a founder of the Royal Geographical Society, and member of the Royal Society. Barrow and his son, John Barrow [**219-225**] wrote 12 books including The Mutiny on the BOUNTY and biographies of Anson and Howe. Barrow suggested St. Helena as a prison for Napoleon.

D. SHIPBUILDING, NAVAL ARCHITECTURE, AND NAVAL ARCHITECTS

An introduction to these matters would be Robert Winklareth [**3917**], Naval Shipbuilders of the World, 2000, which included a table demonstrating the evolution of warship types, for example, galley, galleass, cog, carrack, galleon, sloop, frigate, and SOTL. The chapter on Britain began with the fleet Alfred built in the 9th century. In 1420, Henry V ordered the first naval warships. Henry VIII established a series of government-owned and –operated shipyards.

Y.E. Ozveren [**2720**], "Shipbuilding, 1590-1790," 2000, used the "world-system" perspective to describe this crucial two centuries. New large industrial enterprises, shipyards, produced ocean-going shipping. The prototype warship was the galleon, first produced by the Venice Arsenal, soon to be challenged by Ragusa, then the Portuguese, Spanish, Dutch, French, and British. Key products were timber, tar, sailcloth, and iron. R.C. Anderson [**86**], 1925, paid proper tribute to Italian naval architects of the mid-15th century.

Manuel Fernandes [**1089**], 1616, in Portuguese, published a treatise on shipbuilding from the Lisbon Arsenal. 22 types of vessels were described. Blaise Ollivier [**2700**], Eighteenth-Century Shipbuilding, 1992, was yet another production of Jean Boudriot publishers: in 1737, Ollivier, the French Chief Constructor, conducted a secret tour of Dutch and English dockyards, and wrote this 360-page report, "the most important document written during the age of sail." Among the British yards visited were Portsmouth, Chatham, Woolwich, Deptford, Sheerness, and Plymouth. This seems to correct a traditional view: that French ship design was superior.

Westcott Abell [**2**], The Shipwright's Trade, 1948, was a superficial survey. The Petts and Deane were included. Frank Fox [**1171**], 1992, described the naval shipbuilding programme of 1664 as Anglo-Dutch relations deteriorated. Pepys and Deane were involved.

Philip Banbury [**192**] studied Shipbuilders of the Thames and Medway, 1971. Julian Gwyn [**1434**], 1988, described an effort to build warships in North America. The timber was inferior. Paul Webb [**3798**], 1977, wrote of that crucial decade, 1783-1793, before the French Revolution. A major programme of repair of SOTLs was initiated. This meant the battle fleet was in good shape in 1793; not so frigates. Credit was to Sandwich and Barham. **See 7., I., 1.**

B.F. Hills [**1635**], 1979, described a warship building yard at Sandwich in the late 18th century. Marmaduke Stalkartt [**3416**], Naval Architecture, 1787, 1991, was a spectacular reproduction of design plates, each 6 feet long, of warships of the day, for example, sloop, frigate, 44-gun, and 74-gun, published by Jean Boudriot, the deluxe edition costing 200 pounds.

Prominent naval architects included Phineas Pett, 1570-1638. A.W. Johns [**1811**], 1926, clarified that there were 7 by that name, 4 of which were naval architects. This one designed SOVEREIGN OF THE SEA for Charles I. W.G. Perrin [**2823**], 1918, published Pett's autobiography, a publication of the NRS. Other Petts, for example, born 1628 and builder of a frigate at Chatham; # 3, son of Peter, Master Shipwright at Deptford and Woolwich, 1630-1652; #4, b. 1619, captain of MARY ROSE during the Civil War, and others of less distinction. Geoffrey Callender [**555**], 1930, introduced the naval architect, Peter Pett.

Anthony Deane, c. 1670, was studied by A.W. Johns [**1812**], 1925, in a mini-biography of Deane, a favorite of Pepys. Brian Lavery [**2072**], 1981, presented the doctrine of naval architecture of Deane.

John Barnard [**209**], 1997, introduced the Barnard dynasty of shipbuilders, 4 successive generations from the 1690s-1850s.

Daniel Harris [**1525, 1526**], 1989 and 1997, wrote about F.H. Chapman, son of an officer of the RN, a Swede who designed a programme of 10 SOTLs and 10 frigates in the 1780s and Francis Sheldon, born in Chatham and later shipbuilder to Denmark and Sweden.

E. TECHNOLOGICAL ADVANCES

The source to begin would be Charles Singer [**3327**], A History of Technology, 6 vols., 1954, which included chapters on shipbuilding, gunnery, cartography, and navigation.

Matthew Strickland [**3474**], 1996, described military technology of the Anglo-Saxons. Harold commanded an advanced fleet off the Isle of Wight but time expired and it was sent to the Thames. Ian Friel [**1197**], 1990, in a dissertation, and Kelly DeVries [**922, 919**], 1992 and 1997, surveyed medieval technology, for example, shipboard gunpowder and the ship with multiple masts. Richard Unger [**3690**], 1991, reported on medieval iconography, depictions of ships and shipbuilding revealing details of the technology; 77 illustrations. Another source was the Bayeux Tapestry. **See 21., B., 1.**

An important technological advance was cooper sheathing, described by Randolf Cock [**686**], 2001, John Bingeman [**319**], 2000, and J.R. Harris [**1528**], 1966. It afforded protection from the worm and encrustations, universally adopted by the 18th century. Anson was credited with adoption for the RN in the 1760s; Sandwich made the decision to cooper the fleet in 1779. Cock called it "the finest invention in the world." Peter Goodwin [**1322**], 1998, wrote of use of iron in shipbuilding, 1660-1830.

F. TIMBER AND THE WOODEN WALLS

It was wood in the age of sail, coal, and later, oil, in the age of steam. National security depended on an adequate and readily available source and supply.

Here, Robert Albion [**29, 31**] for the British and Paul Bamford [**188, 189**] for the French were first in the field with formative theses. Albion, Forests and Sea Power: The Timber Problem in the Royal Navy, 1652-1862, 1926, and an article, 1952, were older classics. Supply of "the hearts of oak" in Britain became a crucial issue. The problem became a factor of commercial, colonial, and foreign policy. The crisis of lack of timber was an issue of national security. In a dissertation and a book, Bamford, Forests and French Sea Power 1660-1789, 1951 and 1956, described the depletion of French forests and the implications of dependency on overseas markets.

Oliver Rackham [**2996**], Trees and Woodland in the British Landscape, 1976, reviewed the history of forest management. Rackham questioned the Albion thesis. Albion reported numerous complaints from shipbuilders but where was the evidence? There was little use of foreign timber, except for masts, until after 1800. Supply was steady and reliable until then. "No war was lost for want of shipping." R.J.B. Knight [**1967, 1966**], 1986 and 2001, also revised Albion who had been overly critical of Pepys and Sandwich, calling the latter "the Lord of Misrule." Baltic masts were favored and few came from New England, for example, in 1779, 5000 from the Baltic, none from New England. For the French situation, James Pritchard [**2955**], 1988, revised Bamford [**188**] who exaggerated the timber issue and ignored more serious problems of finance and administration.

Blake Tyson [**3682**], 1987, presented a case study of oak, 1700-1703. There had been a census of oak trees on crown lands in 1663; increasing concerns emerged. Shipbuilding Timber for the British Navy [**3306**], 1993, was a reproduced Parliamentary enquiry of the 18th century; forests increasingly seen as strategic materials.

In a dissertation and a book, J.J. Malone [**2348, 2350**], Pine Trees and Politics, 1956 and 1964, and in a book by Arthur Lower [**2194**], 1973, described naval stores and forest policy in New England, 1691-1775, an example of the Navigation Acts in action. It was "Great Britain's woodyard."

Samuel Manning [**2353**], 1980, wrote of "the wooden economy," focusing on the sources of masts: Baltic and New England. Crown agents would go through the forests of New England marking potential mast-trees with "the King's Broad Arrow," a symbol. Unauthorized cutting of a marked tree meant a fine of 100 pounds. Patricia Crimmin [**802**], 1992, recounted official searches by the RN for oak timber in the Balkans, especially for ship repair, for example, at the Malta Dockyard.

G. THE ORDNANCE OFFICE AND NAVAL GUNNERY

The Ordnance Office originated under Edward I and was located in the Tower. It provided all the gunnery needs for all of the armed forces of England/Britain.

A good place to learn about ordnance and gunnery was Carlo Cipolla [**640**], Guns, Sails, and Empires, 1965, placing the origins of seaborne gunnery in the 14th century; by the 16th and 17th centuries, Europe had gained dominance over the world. The East was unable to resist the expansion. The Portuguese first proved that as true, described by Douglas Braid [**423**], 1992.

General histories of early periods were Sonia Hawkes [**1575**], Weapons and Warfare in Anglo-Saxon England, 1989, and Bert Hall [**1454**], Weapons and Warfare in Renaissance Europe, 1997. For the Anglo-Saxons, some evidence came from the SUTTON HOO ship burial. Gunpowder was decisive in the Renaissance. Frederic Robertson [**3085**], The Evolution of Naval Armament, 1921, traced the history of shipboard guns and gunnery.

Adrian Caruana [**588**], The History of English Sea Ordnance, 1523-1875, 1994, was a folio size, profusely illustrated production by Jean Boudriot. Smoothbore and muzzle-loading guns were described. England led in the revolution of naval ordnance. Unfortunately, the author knew little about naval history and historical research about guns. Richard Stewart [**3455**], The English Ordnance Office, 1585-1625, 1996, described its function: to procure, store, and supply all arms and armaments.

Andrew Thrush [**3620**], 1991, and H.C. Tomlinson [**3631, 3630**], 1975 and 1979, connected the Ordnance Office to the navy and analyzed the criticisms against it and the Navy Board. H.A. Baker [**175**], The Crisis of Naval Ordnance, 1983, recalled problems of shortage in the 1790s.

O.F.G. Hogg [**1651**], The Royal Arsenal, 2 vols., 1963, was the standard history. The origins were 11th century, officially founded in 1670 and located at Woolwich. C.J. Ffoulkes [**1096**], The Gun-Founders of England, 1937, was a history, beginning about 1250. Carel de Beer [**275**], 1991, described the art of gunfounding, casting bronze cannon, in the 18th century, a publication of Jean Boudriot. Melvin Jackson [**1765**], 1974, described the Verbruggen family of Holland who came to England and founded the Royal Brass Foundry at Woolwich. Included were 50 detailed foundry drawings copied from the originals.

The authority on gunpowder was Jenny West [**3819. 3818**], in a dissertation and a book, Gunpowder, Government and War in the Mid-Eighteenth Century, 1991. It was a monograph about the Ordnance Office, supplier of gunpowder to the armed forces of Britain; focusing on administration, logistics, government policies, and the development of a reliable and consistent supply of this essential element of modern warfare. Stephen Bull [**506**], 1989, a dissertation, and E.W. Bovill [**388**], 1947, were about gunpowder in England in the 16th and 17th centuries.

John Seller [**3271**], The Sea-Gunner, 1691, was an early reference guide for gunners. F.W. Brooks [**460**], 1928, and Kelly DeVries [**920**], 1990, wrote of the earliest examples of shipboard gunnery, in the 13th and 15th centuries. Robert Smith [**3365**], British Naval Armaments, 1989, was proceedings from a conference, for example, how the gun affected ship design and tactics and on the carronade.

Two introductory works were helpful about gunnery. Dudley Pope [**2896**], Guns, 1965, opened with the invention of gunpowder and featured naval ordnance. Peter Padfield [**2728**], Guns at Sea, 1972, was folio size, profusely illustrated, with much on English and European developments.

John Kenyon [**1916**], 1983, surveyed ordnance and munitions of the King's Ships in the 16th century. An early treatise on gunnery was William Bourne [**387**], The Arte of Shooting Great Ordnance, 1587.

Most interest in naval gunnery during past years has centered on guns of the Armada campaign. In 1942-1943 in a series of 8 articles, later a book, 1961, the distinguished naval historian, Michael Lewis [**2118, 2119, 2121**], published a study, Armada Guns, comparing the English and Spanish guns and gunnery. He had also written about the guns of Hawkins' flagship, JESUS OF LUBECK, during an attack on the Spanish of 1568. Among those correcting Lewis was I.A.A. Thompson [**3603, 3604**], 1967 and 1975. Lewis had created comparative tables to show the total Spanish weight of broadside was almost 20,000 vs. almost 15,000. Thompson questioned why so little battle damage occurred on both sides and the Spanish guns were smaller and had shorter range; the English had 1/3 greater, not 1/3 less: total firepower was almost 60% less than Lewis figured. In an article, Thompson concluded that Spain was administratively unprepared for the campaign. Charles Trollope [**3650, 3651**], 1994 and 1997, elaborated on English guns. They had been improved and standardized just before the Armada. Two culverins were described which had been recovered from the ship of Richard Grenville. Colin Martin [**2425**], 1994, wrote of incendiary weapons found on one of the Spanish Armada wrecks. See elsewhere about nautical archaeological evidence about Spanish guns and their inactivity. **See 18., D.**

N.A.M. Rodger [**3108, 3107**], 1975 and 1996, wrote about gunnery and the broadside which first came from Venice, not England. John Talbott [**3562**], 1989, described the carronade. Jan-Piet Puype [**2970**], 1990, described Dutch gunnery practice in the 17th century, the time of the Anglo-Dutch wars.

H. LOGISTICS, VICTUALLING, AND THE TRANSPORT SERVICE

John Lynn [2213], Feeding Mars: Logistics in Western Warfare from the Middle Ages to the Present, 1993, edited 12 essays from a conference, University of Illinois, October 1990. Included were studies of logistics during the Crusades, during the Hundred Years' War, and during the Spanish imperial era. During the Hundred Years' War, England was dependent on sea transport, the key factor in success or failure. That transport was obtained by impressment plus the ships from the Cinque Ports. See 7., C,m 3.

C.M. Gillmor [1288], 1984, studied cross-Channel logistics during the Norman invasion of 1066. William mobilized a fleet of transports and set out, a complicated logistical process. Recent findings from nautical archaeology indicated a diverse collection of ships, not just a standard class as some previously claimed; still no agreement on how many: between 675, or 1000, or 3000, or 11,000? A correct answer would shed light on the number of men in the Norman army, still in dispute, as well. Richard Stewart [3454], 1986, had a dissertation about the supply of arms in England, 1585-1625, noting that the situation deteriorated under the Stuarts.

Victualling was food supply. "Victuallers" were agents of the government, functioning from the 1650s; the Victualling Board was formed in 1683 and was based on Tower Hill. Other parts of the bureaucracy of logistics included the Office of the Sick and Hurt and Pursers, the latter located at Somerset House, at what is now Waterloo Bridge, completely remodeled in the last decade. In 1832, the Navy Board and Admiralty Office, along with the Purser, all moved to Whitehall.

As a model facility, Tony Aldous [34], 1994, wrote the history of the Royal William Yard, Plymouth, named for the "sailor king," William IV. It was a victualling complex: brewhouse, cooperage, bakery, slaughterhouse, and dock offices.

S.J. Burley [512], 1958, wrote of victualling Calais, 1347-1365, after the Crecy campaign. It was maintained as a naval base, then "the brightest jewel in the English crown." Records of supplies and victualling were extensive. In a dissertation, Paula Watson [3789], 1965, studied the victualling and other obligations, 1702-1714.

David Aldridge [36], 1964, presented a case study, victualling the 9 expeditions to the Baltic, 1715-1727. Extended operations in the Baltic were an innovation. He concluded that the victuallers met their obligations creditably. The main problems concerned beer, butter, and cheese; beer was replaced by wine.

David Syrett [3541, 3557, 3558], 1995-1997, investigated two aspects of the Victualling Board in 3 works: the supply of grain, 1775-1782, and the chartering of shipping, 1739-1748, and 1775-1782. Naval personnel increased from 35,000 to 101,000. One agent administered the supply which was fulfilled, but the agent gained a huge personal fortune in the process. Shipping to foreign areas was a major, costly process.

Christian Buchet [**499**], 1999, made an important contribution to naval history. It was French study of the British Victualling Board in the late 18th century. The Board was by far the largest buyer of agricultural products in Britain and the most centralized, efficient agricultural market in Europe.

The matter of transport was perennial. John Pryor [**2962**], 1982, described the process of transporting horses by sea during the Crusades, citing specific instances of operations. Bernard Bachrach [**166**], 1985, described the horse transports for the horses of William the Conqueror of 1066, the largest amphibious operation in Europe since the Roman Empire. R.H.C. Davis [**883**], 1989, wrote on the medieval warhorse, including its transportation by sea.

C.S.L. Davies [**868**], 1963, was a dissertation about supply services to the English armed forces, 1509-1550, featuring the Ordnance Office.

A noted controversy was the availability of transports for logistics to supply British forces before and during the American Revolution, a logistical responsibility of the Navy Board. Five works by David Syrett [**3547, 3545, 3549, 3543, 3550, 3555**], a dissertation, 1965, three case studies, 1965, 1967, and 1989, and a book, 1970, confirmed the problem, the crisis being in 1777.

Mary Condon [**714**], 1968, did a dissertation on the transport service, 1793-1802. Bernard Pool [**2882**], Navy Board Contracts, 1660-1832, 1966, was a detailed description of the process. Contracts involved shipbuilding, supply, refit, and repair. Unfortunately, no records could be found of contracts for shipbuilding in private yards. Ben Warlow [**3754**], 1984, wrote the history of the Supply and Secretariat Branch.

I. THE DOCKYARDS

The Royal Dockyards were the largest industrial organization in the nation. The locations have changed over time and many have been closed, some due to natural changes such as silting, some for postwar reductions, and some because of changes in technology and warship design. Portsmouth was first, the first dry dock came during the reign of Henry VII. Others followed: Deptford, Woolwich, Chatham, Plymouth, later Devonport, Sheerness, Rosyth, and some others. Foreign establishments included Malta, Gibraltar, Bermuda, and Singapore. The dockyards have been denounced perennially as corrupt, inefficient, and excessively expensive. Daniel Baugh [**237**], among others, have come to their defense and others have praised their productivity.

A general introduction can be found in H.M. Colvin [**709**], The History of the King's Works, 6 vols., 1963-1982, which included coverage of naval works and coastal defenses. Bruce Dietz [**933**], 2002, studied the earliest English docks and dockyards in the 16th and 17th centuries.

Most prolific of the dockyard historians was Philip MacDougall [**2240-2244**], Royal Dockyards, 1982, The Chatham Dockyard Story, 1981, another work on Chatham, 1999, an article about the Malta Dockyard, 1990, and observations about problems of access to dockyards over time, 2001. The general work was an attempt at synthesis but with little on foreign establishments. Portsmouth has remained as the most important. Those on the Thames were increasingly isolated because of changes in natural conditions. HMS VICTORY was built at Chatham. It closed in 1981 and recently has featured a museum.

Roger Morriss [**2574, 2566, 2576**], The Royal Dockyards during the Revolutionary and Napoleonic Wars, 1983, a dissertation, 1978, and an article, 1981, produced comprehensive coverage of this massive industrial complex during the wars. By 1809, the system was maintaining almost 1000 ships; by 1814, 15,000 workers in 6 yards. The article was about Samuel Bentham, Inspector General, who was commended for important management improvements.

Unfortunately, the dissertation of R.J.B. Knight [**1970, 1968, 1969**], "The Royal Dockyards in England at the Time of the American War of Independence," 1972, has not been published. There were two articles, 1975 and 1987: the incidence of pilfering in the dockyards and Portsmouth dockyard papers of the 1770s. Venality and peculation abounded but so did corruption in finance and administration.

Most focused were the works of Jonathan Coad: [**671-676**], The Royal Dockyards, 1690-1850, 1989, a general work, Historic Architecture of the Royal Navy, 1983, and three individual articles on historic architecture, Portsmouth, 1981, Chatham, 1982, and Devonport, 1983. The consistent themes were architecture, engineering, and landmark status. Coad favored the Royal William Victualling Yard, Plymouth, as the finest group of buildings owned by the RN. The approach was industrial archaeology. Features included the first drydock, early use of large machine tools, and large-span metal roofs.

Three works were by James Haas [**1436-1438**]: A Management Odyssey: The Royal Dockyards, 1714-1914, 1994, an article on task work, 1969, and an article on reforms in the 18th century, 1970. Haas has been a consistent critic of the performance of the dockyards: incompetently run, expensive, and corrupt. The reforms of Sandwich were praised, especially the introduction of task work for the shipwrights. Haas reviewed the 300 warships built at Portsmouth, including HMS DREADNOUGHT of 1905. Reform followed investigatory visitations but required cooperation between the Admiralty and Navy Board. A book on Portsmouth-built warships was by James Goss [**1329**], 1984.

Kenneth Lunn [**2205**], 1999, analyzed the dockyards and labor relations. Contributions included R.J.B. Knight on strikes, Philip MacDougall on disputes, and Roger Morriss on labor relations. D.C. Coleman [**699**], 1953, wrote on the dockyards of the late 17th century. Henry Kitson [**1952**], 1947, wrote about the early history of Portsmouth Dockyard. In the late 15th century, Henry VII ordered large warships and authorized the first drydock. K.V. Burns [519], 1984, wrote on the Devonport Dockyard. Richard Middleton [2509], 1991, recalled a reform programme of Anson. There was continuous conflict and competition between the Admiralty and the Navy Board, responsible for the dockyards. Ann Coats [677] studied dockyard-community relations at Portsmouth, 1650-1800, in a dissertation, 2000.

J. NAVAL PORTS AND BASES

There were dozens of them, all around the coasts of the British Isles and in numerous strategic foreign locations all over the world: "The sun never set on the British Empire." Again, coverage will be responsive to what has been published.

Strategically important since its acquisition in 1704 was the base at Gibraltar on the northern shore of the Straits of Gibraltar. It was the most written about of the foreign bases of the early modern period, "the Rock." Singapore may surpass Gibraltar in interest for the 20th century. Gibraltar has become symbolic for security and endurance. It has been a strategic bridgehead for north-south and east-west movements for centuries. It has been a key strategic British base of enormous significance for 3 centuries. The fall of the Singapore base in 1942 precipitated enormous consequences.

William Jackson [1769], The Rock of Gibraltarians, 1988, presented the long history; recounting the sieges, for example, number 13 in 1720, number 14 in 1780, and number 15 in 1969-1985. Tito Benady [289], 1992, was on the RN at Gibraltar. Its role has been various, sometimes competing with Malta and Minorca. Captured from the Spanish by George Rooke in 1704, it has been subject to siege by the French and, more recently, the Spanish. Spain still has not recognized British ownership and keeps the base isolated, as anyone who visits will readily discover. The sovereignty issue, an Anglo-Spanish problem, has continued to erupt, even into the 21st century. Stetson Conn [715], 1942, focused on Gibraltar and diplomatic relations in the 18th century. Spain drifted over to the French. Others were Alan Andrews [103], 1958, Tom McGuffie [2264], 1965, Jack Russell [3176], 1965, and John Drinkwater [963], 1905, on the siege, 1779-1783, "the Great Siege." Jac Weller [3808], 1971, wrote on Gibraltar and sea power. G.T. Garratt [1253], 1939, contributed a popular history at a time when a German-Italian alliance threatened.

Malta was originally the property of the Knights of St. John who acquired it after the Crusades. Napoleon occupied it in 1798. It has remained a British base since. Peter Elliott [1036], 1980, wrote a bicentennial history of Malta and its base. Desmond Gregory [1394], 1996, focused on Malta, 1793-1815. France and Russia had designs on the island, the Tsar claiming traditional protection of the Knights of St. John. It was a pawn in the Treaty of Amiens; in

1803, Britain reclaimed it. Quentin Hughes [**1717**], 1956, described some of the original structures.

Minorca was a base in the western Mediterranean. Desmond Gregory [**1395**], 1990, recalled British occupations of 1708 and 1802.

Halifax served for decades as the chief British base for North America; Marilyn Smith [**3361**], The King's Yard, 1985, described Halifax.

Back home, there was the ancient port of Dover. The ancient site would be Dover Castle, described by Jonathan Coad [**671**], 1995.

The oldest and still the largest operating base was Portsmouth. John Winton [**3922**], 1989, and J. Webb [**3795**], 1989, contributed histories. Richard Winslow [**3920**], 1988, described in an exaggerated and chauvinistic way Portsmouth during "the golden age of privateering, 1775-1815."

During the late middle ages, Southampton was a major port, especially for the Italian trade, galleys from Genoa and Venice, among others, calling there annually. Wine and wool were main products. A. Temple Patterson [**2789**], A History of Southampton, 1700-1914, 3 vols., 1966-1975; Colin Platt [**2861**], 1973, about the port and trade, 1000-1600; J.L. Wiggs [**3852**], 1955, a dissertation focusing on the 16th century, and J.B. Morgan [**2545**], 1958, reviewing the history, for example, as a naval center, 1414-1458, all providing good coverage.

Plymouth, on the southwest coast, was identified with Drake, the famous game of bowls, the Pilgrim Fathers, Cook, and Darwin. **See 7., F., 2.** F.W. Woodward [**3957**], Plymouth Defences, 1990, described forts and defenses of the dockyard at Devonport. W.H.K. Wright [**3969**], 1872, and Libby Purves [**2969**], 1992, provided verbal tours of "Plymouth Ho!" or Plymouth Hoe.

Dartmouth, near Plymouth, was described by Percy Russell [**3178**], 1950, with a history of the port and town.

At one time Yarmouth on the east coast had been a dockyard, noted by J.F. Fone [**1132**], 1992.

Foreign ports of call and bases were included. For centuries, Lisbon has been a major port of call of British merchant and warships. Stephen Fisher [**1111**], 1988, summarized the British connection there.

Susan Rose [**3143**], 2000, described the importance of Bayonne in the Duchy of Aquitaine and capital of Gascony, a possession of the English king and an important shipping and trade center, 1204-1420.

K. PATRONAGE, "INTEREST," AND CORRUPTION

Do these matters belong in a discussion of administration? Ask any officer and any official at the Admiralty. In memoirs, journals, correspondence, and in The Naval Chronicle [**2605**], these issues were ubiquitous. "Corruption" was an overused word, then and now. Themes were patronage-client relations, public and private interests, bribery, sale of offices, venality, and investigative commissions, for example, 1608 and 1618.

Unfortunately, no general survey or comprehensive account has been published. Nor have "interest" and "corruption" been properly defined. **See 22.**

Coverage has been "spotlight," limited to specific times and events. Linda Peck [**2804**], <u>Court Patronage and Corruption in Early Stuart England</u>, 1990, covered the early 17th century. Lionel Cranfield and John Coke, prominent officials, were featured. V. Vale [**3716**], 1956, cited a case of accusations of the sale of naval offices during the 1660s. J.R. Tanner [**3564**], 1896, reviewed a series of accusations, in 1638, 1659, and 1660, about corruption and abuses within the navy, a publication of the NRS. David Syrett [**3537**], 1999, presented a prominent case study of patronage in action, this by George Rodney in the West Indies in the 1780s. One of the most successful commanders of the 18th century maximized use of patronage, for example, promoting his son to master at age 15. The Admiralty did refuse to honor it later. J.W.E. Spear [**3402**], studied naval reform efforts, 1745-1763, in a dissertation. He concluded that a large number of reforms and innovations took place and that they were of lasting value. Brian Vale [**3710**], 2002, did a piece, a case study, on appointment, promotion, and "interest" within the South American Squadron in the early 1820s. It was a crucial time of competition for employment after demobilization. A kind of compromise had been reached, for example, about promotion to lieutenant: there was an Admiralty list and a local list of the squadron commander. Theoretically, selections alternated between the two.

Chapter 15

The Law of the Sea, Admiralty Courts, and the Prize Process

Maritime law and naval regulations were related but the latter also incorporated discipline and punishment procedures, covered elsewhere. **See 10., G.** Ancient tradition and precedent prevailed. The Laws of Oleron originated from the Gascon trade. That set of customs and traditions were adopted by the English and evolved into discipline regulations for naval and maritime forces.

The general standard on English law was William Holdsworth [**1653**], History of English Law, 12 vols., 1938, which included references to the Laws of Oleron, Courts of the Admiralty, and The Black Book of the Admiralty [**338**].

A. THE LAW OF THE SEA

The Black Book of the Admiralty: Momumenta Juridica [**338**], 4 vols., 1870-1876, was a collection of sources about legal texts on Admiralty law; the chief source for the study of maritime law. Originally compiled in the reign of Henry VI, some parts were earlier. The Laws of Oleron were included. Walter Ashburner [**144**], The Rhodian Sea-Law, 1909, was a source for medieval shipping practices, customs, and regulations, another contribution to the development of maritime law. In a dissertation, B.M.M. Allen [**39**], 1975, reviewed Anglo-American relations concerning maritime law, 1793-1815. The first Navigation Act, 1540, was also pertinent, as were later ones. **See 13., A.**

B. COURTS OF THE ADMIRALITY

It was an evolutionary process involving the High Court of the Admiralty, Vice-Admiralty Courts, Cinque Ports Admiralty Courts, Prize Law, and the Office of Lord High Admiral. Origins were in the 13th century. The practices and structures later spread to the colonies and the concepts and institutions were eventually adopted worldwide. Vice Admiralty Courts functioned in the colonies, the first in Jamaica. It remained the busiest for decades. The bases for these courts and their jurisdiction were the Laws of Oleron and the Black Book of the Admiralty [**338**].

Early on, common law and local customs and practices were deemed inadequate for application to the sea, seen as more "international." and beyond usual boundaries. Related were early security and defense matters. Special procedures and broader concepts were necessary. Early "Admirals," Crown appointments, oversaw these issues and were given responsibility. Cases before Admiralty Courts were broad. Vice Admiralty Courts functioned in the colonies. Based on the Laws of Oleron and The Black Book of the Admiralty [**338**]; practitioners before the court were from Doctors' Commons, a professional association, housed near the Cathedral of St. Paul. R.G. Marsden [**2414**], 1907-1908, described origins, "Vice-Admirals of the Coast." These were early "land admirals" appointed by the LHA to defend assigned sections of the coast, first noted in 1295. They filled in as the need developed to conduct tribunals for the trials of piracy and offenses at sea.

Examples of cases before Admiralty and Vice Admiralty Courts were piracy, privateering, slave cases, slave law, the slave trade, letters of marque and reprisal, prize law, salvage, maritime contracts, collisions, wages of seamen, nationalities, neutral rights, trading with the enemy, contraband, blockade, convoy, continuous voyage, and the Rule of '56.

Reginald Marsden [**2409-2414**] was prolific on these matters: for example, Select Pleas in the Court of Admiralty, 2 vols., 1892-1897, was an excellent introduction and overview. In a pamphlet, the activities of the court were reviewed, 1550-1650. There was a digest of cases, 1899. D.A. Gardiner [**1235**], 1932, wrote about belligerent rights on the high seas in the 14th century. Alwyn Ruddock [**3163**], 1949, reviewed the earliest records of the High Court of the Admiralty, 1515-1558, for example, cases of privateering and piracy.

L.M. Hill [**1633**], "The Admiralty Circuit of 1591," 1971, was informative about the High Court of the Admiralty, in this case on circuit led by Judge Julius Caesar. The goal, not achieved but important as a precedent, was to force local courts to submit to Crown courts. W.G. Perrin [**2827**], 1926, recounted the role of the Lord High Admiral in Admiralty Courts in the late 16th century. Evelyn Berckman [**302**], 1979, surveyed actions of Admiralty Courts against piracy in the 17th century. There was unprecedented growth in cases.

Susan Mowat [**2579**], 1997, studied Scottish Admiralty Courts, 1556-1830; cases on shipping and trade.

Henry Bourguignon [**382**], 1987, conducted a case study of one judge, William Scott, Lord Stowell, during 30 years early in the 19th century. His decisions filled over 10 volumes, most prize court judgments.

Maritime seamen could appeal to Admiralty Courts, for example against arbitrary treatment and non-payment of wages. George Steckley [**3433**], 1999, collected statistics on 60,000 wage appeals in the 17th century, all favorable to the seamen. F.L. Wiswall [**3927**], 1970, reviewed Admiralty Court jurisdiction and practice in the 19th century. There was parallel development of British and American Admiralty Courts.

Vice Admiralty Courts outside England/Britain was a related subject. Helen Crump [**820**], Colonial Admiralty Jurisdiction, 1931, surveyed the feelings about these courts by the colonists. These courts were created to enforce the Navigation Acts and maintain peace on the seas; early courts were set up in Massachusetts, Virginia, Maryland, and Bermuda. David Owen [**2717**], 1995, conducted a case study on the Maryland Vice Admiralty Court. Speedy, impartial justice was the practice but the colonists hated them. Just look at the Declaration of Independence. Michael Watson [**3788**], 1997, did a dissertation on the judges of Vice Admiralty Courts in colonial North America. Watson insisted that these courts did not enforce the Navigation Acts. Carl Ubbelohde [**3686**], 1960, surveyed the 11 Vice Admiralty Courts during the American Revolution. The colonists complained. There was no trial by jury, action was arbitrary, and judges were paid for percent of goods condemned. They enforced Navigation Acts. Michael Craton [**787**], 1971, reviewed Vice Admiralty Courts in the Caribbean; these dealing with many more cases than those in North America.

C. THE PRIZE PROCESS

As with Admiralty Courts, discipline, and customs of the sea, the prize process was regulated by The Black Book of the Admiralty [**338**]; allocation was specified by percentages and was adjudicated by the High Court of the Admiralty. Other origins were contributory. Two works of the early 17th century Dutch jurist, Hugo Grotius [**1408, 1409**] and William Murray, Lord Mansfield, as described by C.H.S. Fifoot [**1099**], 1936, articulated essential foundations for the development of prize law. There was the Naval Prize Fund. Awarding prize money continued until after the Second World War. One aspect adjudicated by the courts was condemnation of prizes, captured ships and material. There was also a prize bounty for captured enemy personnel and weapons. That was paid up to the end of the First World War.

The authoritative source on these complex matters was J.R. Hill [**1631**], The Prizes of War, 1998, which focused on the period 1793-1815. Activity was economic warfare and state sanctioned robbery. The rules of contraband and blockade were described. There was a separate chapter on the Cochranes and Judge William Scott was presented as a model. Less sympathetic was Donald Petrie [**2837**], The Prize Game: Lawful Looting on the High Seas in the Days of Fighting Sail, 1999, which reviewed the origins, rules of the sea, and later decline. Reginald Marsden [**2410, 2411**], Documents Relating to the Law and Custom of the Sea, 2 vols., 1915-1916, a publication of the NRS, was a chronological history concerning prize policies and some treaties. Parliament passed pertinent legislation during almost every war. Admiralty Courts increasingly dealt with prize adjudication; some cases of privateering, naval stores, pillage, and the Salute. As early as 1205, 1216, and 1217, cases arose concerning prizes, piracy, and rights of the Cinque Ports. Early prize jurisdiction and prize law were described, 1909. The Cinque Ports enjoyed early prize rights.

E.S. Roscoe [**3138**], A History of the English Prize Court, 1924, covered the territory; American Prize Courts evolved from the British. Peter Kemp [**1868**], Prize Money, 1946, was about the Naval Prize Fund. C.S. Goldingham [**1312**], 1919, and Tony Gutridge [**1426**], 1994, wrote of prize money, how it was important for recruitment and a powerful incentive for the officer class. Joseph Fewster [**1095**], 1983, wrote of prize money and an expedition to the West Indies, 1793-1794; 180,000 pounds was involved. In a dissertation and a book, Faye Kert [**1923, 1922**], Prize and Prejudice, 1997, reviewed all aspects and focused on the War of 1812, the last war in which commerce raiding or privateering played a major role.

D. NAVAL REGULATIONS, DISCIPLINE, AND COURTS MARTIAL

The Law of the Sea also concerned regulations, discipline, punishments, and due process of law, the latter accomplished by the legal institution of the armed forces, courts martial, a proceeding headed by a number of senior officers as judges and jury. For example, in the navy, every instance of loss of a ship and other similar occurrences must be followed by a court martial of the responsible party, usually the commanding officer. William Bligh was subjected to a court martial upon his return to Britain after the mutiny on the BOUNTY. He was exonerated and promoted. More notorious was the court martial of Admiral Byng after the battle of Minorca. He, of course, was found guilty and shot on a quarterdeck, "to encourage the others," as Voltaire characterized it. Again, the Laws of Oleron and The Black Book of the Admiralty [**338**] were the bases.

A general guide was Charles Clode [**661**], The Administration of Justice under Military and Martial Law, 1872. John Bald [**180**], 1991, traced the origins of some naval regulations to the 1530s, "the Booke of Orders for the Warre both by Sea and Land," by Thomas Audley. N.A.M. Rodger [**3105**], Articles of War: The Statutes which Governed Our Fighting Navies, 1661, 1749 and 1886, 1982, setting the scene for governance of the RN for 300 years. James Valle [**3717**], Rocks and Shoals: Naval Discipline in the Age of Fighting Sail, 1980, was the basic source for the USN; Anglo-American traditions were the same.

Four basic guides have evolved: Observations on the Preparation and Discipline of the British Navy [**2685**], 1837; William Hickman [**1626**], A Treatise on the Law and Practice of Naval Courts-Martial, 1851; Theodore

Thring [**3612**], A Treatise on the Criminal Law of the Navy, 1861, and David Hannay [**1480**], Naval Courts Martial, 1914.

The records of courts martial were official documents including transcriptions of all evidence and presentations. They were and are filed with Admiralty records and kept in the archives at the PRO. They have continued to be outstanding sources for historical research. At the PRO, they can be found: "Great Britain, Public Record Office, Admiralty Courts Martial Records, ADM 1" [**1373**].

James Snedeker [**3379**], A Brief History of Courts Martial, 1954, presented the background. An early case created a long-lasting sensation: Francis Drake vs Thomas Doughty, early in the voyage of circumnavigation of the late 1570s. Drake assembled the court martial and had Doughty executed. The brother of Doughty sued Drake later but the suit failed. Gregory Robinson [**3095**], 1921, presented the details and introduced the characters. William Senior [**3275, 3276**], 1921 and 1927, cited this case, among others. **See 9., D., 1.**

T.L. O'Beirne [**3658**] published Considerations on the Principles of Naval Discipline and Naval Courts-Martial, 1781, using the Keppel-Palliser case as a model. That case was elaborated upon by in a dissertation by David Wells [**3809**], 1957, and J.H. Broomfield [**464**], 1961. The battle of Ushant, July 1778, was another of those indecisive line-of-battle events. Augustus Keppel vs. Hugh Palliser were admirals accusing each other, all linked to national politics for and against the Sandwich regime at the Admiralty. The dispute divided and demoralized the RN. Keppel was acquitted. Another political-based court martial of the 18th century: P.A. Luff [**2202**], 1991, presented Mathews vs. Lastock stemming from the battle of Toulon in the 1740s, another of several indecisive battles which resulted in attempted prosecution. Acquittal on charges of cowardice was the verdict.

In the next war, no such reluctance was shown. In March 1757, John Byng was found guilty and executed, "to encourage the others," under similar circumstances, as reported by Dudley Pope [**2887**], At Twelve Mr. Byng Was Shot, 1962. In this case, Pope was sympathetic for Byng. Anson and Newcastle were criticized for making Byng a scapegoat for the failures of the Admiralty and ministry.

Henry Parry [**2779**], 1781, a clerk, presented minutes of a court martial in Jamaica of 1781 against John Mountray, commander of HMS RAMILLES, because a convoy to the West Indies was captured; Mountray was found guilty and dismissed. Just before Trafalgar on 22 July 1805, Admiral Robert Calder and his fleet met a French-Spanish fleet in the Mediterranean, capturing 2 Spanish warships. A court martial reprimanded Calder for insufficient action. **See 7., I., 10.**

Chapter 16

Strategy, Tactics, Communications, Intelligence, and Amphibious Operations

Several early rationales articulated the foundations and bases for commercial, naval, imperial, and cultural expansion ultimately leading to hegemonic domination of the world for England/Britain. An ongoing debate has ensued throughout the 20th century about British sea power and naval strategy.

A.T. Mahan [**2328, 2329**] launched the debate with his connected analyses of the influence of sea power upon history. The British were much flattered with Mahan and his theories, lionizing him and awarding him with honorary degrees, for example from Oxford and Cambridge. Mahan touted independent battle fleets roaming at will, the "blue-water" approach. But battle fleets were not enough for Julian Corbett [**759**] and later critics of Mahan. Another contrast of strategies for the British was "maritime" vs. "continental."

The premier introduction on the subject of strategy was Peter Paret [**2747**], The Makers of Modern Strategy, 1986, an update of a classic of 1941. This one was 28 essays by noted experts, for example, on strategists Mahan and Basil Liddell Hart.

A. SEA POWER

In 1436, "Libelle of Enlyshe Polycye" [**2133**] or "Libel of English Policy: A Poem on the Use of Sea-Power," was an anonymous treatise calling for commercial and naval supremacy, described by G.A. Holmes [**1658**], 1961, and F. Taylor [**3578**], 1940. The title came from Nicholas Throckmorton, then ambassador to France. "Libelle" meant "little book." Hakluyt [**1446-1451**] printed a copy, 1598. The language was jingoistic. Foreign merchants must be expelled. The benefits of sea power were touted. The siege of Calais was in progress and France and Burgundy were threatening alliance against England, especially threatening the wool trade. Piracy was denounced, for example, from Dunkirk and St. Malo. "Libel" was a political programme, farsighted and profound. Much of this was reviewed, among other things, in George Manwaring [**2359**], The Flower of England's Garland, 1936.

A century and a half later, John Dee [**893**], a polymath and advisor to Elizabeth I, defined the rights of trade, limits of empire, and repudiation of the division of the new world by Pope Alexander VI between Spain and Portugal. This became the basis of English policy as described by Ken MacMillan [**2317**], 2001. **See 7., G., 2.**

Sir Walter Raleigh [**3001**] summed it up originally: "Whosoever commands the sea commands trade; whosoever commands the trade of the world commands the riches of the world, and consequently, the world itself."

A.T. Mahan articulated the British strategy, in the oft-repeated treatise: "Those far-distant, storm-beaten upon which the Grand Army never looked, stood between it and the dominion of the world."

Some have dubbed variations of this "the British Way in Warfare." Michael Howard [**1690**], The British Way in Warfare, 1975, originally the Lees Knowles Lectures, 1966, stressed a peripheral strategy, the indirect approach, for example, the Mediterranean strategy in wars of the 17th and 18th centuries, the Dardanelles campaign in World War I, and the North African invasion in World War II. Howard claimed he was continuing and critiquing the analyses of Julian Corbett [**759**], Herbert Richmond [**3066**], Basil Liddell Hart [**2134**], and, later, Paul Kennedy [**1882, 1883**]. Kennedy insisted he was not diminishing the importance of sea power but saw the task of the RN as a negative: not to gain control but to avoid losing control of the shipping lanes. Hew Strachan [**3464**], 1983, elaborated.

John Hattendorf [**1550**], 1990, wrote of the Anglo-American way in maritime strategy, a concept to which he has contributed significantly. He reviewed the major sea powers in world history: Greece, Rome, Venice, Portugal, Spain, the Dutch, and France. All in all, the Anglo-American strand was the dominant one. Corbett [**759**] made the most effective abstract statement: to combine naval and maritime domination.

Geoffrey Till [**3623**], Seapower: Theory and Practice, 1994, was the proceedings from an international conference, Yale University, 1993. Essays included Jan Breemer on Trafalgar: the "mystique" of Trafalgar, the ultimate "decisive" battle, was more important than the actual battle.

Richard Harding [**1495**], Seapower and Naval Warfare, 1650-1850, 1998, was a major synthesis. Sailing battlefleets were the ultimate seapower.

Stephen Roskill [**3149**], The Strategy of Sea Power, 1962, the Lees Knowles Lectures, purposely reversed the titles used by Mahan [**2328, 2329**]. He traced the evolution of British sea power, most of it applicable to the 20th century. Peter Hore [**1669**], Seapower Ashore, 2000, was a collection of essays by prominent naval historians, for example, Tom Pocock, Michael Duffy, Colin White, and Andrew Lambert; 13 case studies. David Loades [**2177**], England's Maritime Empire: Seapower, Commerce and Policy, 1490-1690, 2000, concentrated on the formative period. A popular approach was Jean Stewart

[**3452**], The Sea Our Heritage, 1993, tracing the rise and fall of British sea power.

Stephen Gradish [**1349**], 1975, described a decisive strategy, the establishment of British sea power in the Mediterranean, 1689-1713. During two wars, the will of the Grand Alliance initiated by William III prevailed; thus, he changed British naval strategy. Quentin Hughes [**1716**], Britain in the Mediterranean and the Defence of Her Naval Stations, 1981, stressed the importance of these naval stations and their support to the RN, for example, Gibraltar, Malta, Minorca, and Corfu. These, in turn, had to have land defenses, fortifications, and an army to man them.

For another vital area, Donald Macintyre [**2270**], Sea Power in the Pacific, 1972, noted Britain was relatively late in this area, the Portuguese and Dutch had preceded them.

Daniel O'Connell [**2686**], The Influence of Law on Sea Power, 1975, supplemented Mahan who ignored international law. O'Connell articulated the bases for naval activities, for example, blockade, right of transit, the territorial sea, the sea bed, neutrality zones, and, most pertinent today, rules of engagement. The thesis was: use of naval forces meant more pressure, less danger, and more predictability than use of land and air forces. All was backed up by historical case studies.

Colin Gray [**1369**], The Leverage of Sea Power, 1992, stressed the strategic advantage of naval power in war. From the defeat of Xerxes, 480 BC, to the defeat of Soviet Russia in the Cold War, superior sea power provided the leverage critical for success. Failure to exploit sea power had proved fatal, for example, to Carthage, Napoleon, Germany, and Soviet Russia. In the 10 case studies cited, Venice, England and Spain, and Britain and France were pertinent here.

On a modern note, there was George Modelski [**2522**], Seapower in Global Politics, 1494-1993, 1988, reviewing the states achieving sea power in the long cycle: Portugal, the Dutch, Britain, and the U.S. Application for ancient times was covered by Chester Starr [**3427**], The Influence of Sea Power on Ancient History, 1988.

B. NAVAL STRATEGY

For naval strategy, good places to begin would be Donald Schurman [**3253**], The Education of a Navy, 1984, tracing the development of British naval strategy, 1867-1914, featuring the contributions of John and Philip Colomb, Mahan, J.K. Laughton, Corbett, and Richmond, and two works by Clark Reynolds [**3048, 3049**], Command of the Sea, 2 vols., 1974, and History and the Sea, 1989, presenting background and context.

Alfred T. Mahan [**2328, 2329**], The Influence of Sea Power upon History, 1660-1783, 1890 and The Influence of Sea Power upon the French

Revolution and Empire, 1793-1812, 2 vols., 1892, were the standards, highly influential at the time, for example, used as virtual textbooks for the U.S., Britain, and two other aspiring naval powers about 1900, Germany and Japan. Mahan touted what became known as the "blue-water strategy," large battle fleets roaming at will, exerting command of the sea.

Commentary on Mahan included William Livezey [2148], Mahan on Sea Power, 1981, concluding that Mahan was basically a publicist supporting expanded naval forces and merchant marine. An older, popular textbook, Allan Westcott [3822], Mahan on Naval Warfare, 1941, contained selections.

In retrospect, the counter-argument to Mahan was presented by Julian Corbett [759], Some Principles of Maritime Strategy, 1911, and that has become the accepted articulation of British naval strategy, if not strategy in general. At the time, Corbett was a prominent naval adviser to John Fisher, then First Sea Lord, preparing the RN during the crises leading to World War I; subsequently, Corbett wrote the official naval history of the war. This work was based on lectures Corbett gave to the Royal Naval War College. Corbett stressed the need for "combined operations," more than a battle fleet gaining control of the sea. Tenets were to secure sea communications and deny them to the enemy, utilize combined operations, practice limited war, and maintain command of the sea as an ongoing task exercised by smaller vessels. Like Mahan, Corbett [748, 749, 755, 758, 760, 753, 747] had written British naval history, especially during the time of the Tudors, the Armada, and Drake, plus a biography of Monck and analysis of Trafalgar. Corbett was a founding member of the SNR and contributed to the NRS. Citing Corbett, Michael Handel [1475], 2000, explained that Clausewitz and Sun Tzu were his guides, for example, stressing the importance of politics and of limited war.

Influencing Mahan and Corbett was Philip Howard Colomb [708], Naval Warfare, 2 vols., 1891, selections from articles. Certain laws governed naval warfare and less stress was placed on command of the sea.

Daniel Baugh [239, 241, 242], 1988, 1992, and 1998, analyzed the "blue-water strategy" of Britain in practice, praising Corbett and the strategy of the indirect approach. The "blue-water strategy" was practical, cost-effective, and mundane. Richmond [3063] and Paul Kennedy [1882] had best articulated British grand strategy. Baugh saw 1750 as a decisive transition from a continental to a global strategy and 1775-1777 as temporary failure when the French exploited the lapse.

John Hattendorf [1558, 1567, 1563, 1314] edited the proceedings of two conferences: The Influence of History on Mahan, 1991, a centennial celebration, and Policy and Strategy in the Mediterranean Sea, 2000, the third of the Naval War Conference-Yale University conferences. Hattendorf was co-editor with James Goldrick [1314], Mahan Is Not Enough: The Proceedings of a Conference on the Works of Sir Julian Corbett and Admiral Sir Herbert Richmond, 1993, the conference being at the Naval War College, September 1992. Naval and maritime topics were reviewed by several experts. Mahan,

Corbett, and Richmond were discussed, analyzed, and evaluated, to the advantage of Corbett and Richmond. Hattendorf also collected 16 of his own essays, Naval Strategy, 2000. Topics included Mahan, Corbett, the Anglo-American way in maritime strategy, and the U.S. Naval War College.

Paul Kennedy [1880], Grand Strategies in War and Peace, 1991, presented 10 essays by experts, for example, John Hattendorf, Michael Howard, and Dennis Showalter.

Editing proceedings from seminars at Exeter University, Michael Duffy [976], Parameters of British Naval Power, 1650-1850, 1992, presented a series of papers on the making of British naval strategy, for example, Duffy saw the Western Squadron blockading the French at Brest as the lynchpin of British naval strategy at that time. See 7., I., 4.

Barry Hunt [1734], 1984, reviewed the outstanding writers on naval strategy, for example, Mahan, Corbett, Theopile Aube, the Colomb brothers, and Richmond. David Jablonsky [1764], Roots of Strategy, 1999, cited Mahan and Corbett, and the strategists for air power, Douhet and Mitchell.

Barry Gough [1338], editor of American Neptune, was preparing A Guide to the Literature on Maritime Strategy and History.

The great British naval historian, William Laird Clowes [668], Four Modern Naval Campaigns, 1902, applied concepts of strategy and tactics to each. Basil Liddell Hart [2134], Strategy: The Indirect Approach, 1953, was an influential treatise. Due to the fear of the magnitude of destruction from modern weapons, direct confrontation must be avoided.

Colin Gray [1370], Seapower and Strategy, 1989, was a series of papers, for example, John Gooch comparing Mahan and Corbett. The French theorist Theopile Aube articulated a theory of commerce warfare.

Philip Pugh [2965], 1989, computed the actual costs of the various strategies, adding up the costs of warships and operations.

More specifically, Clifford Rogers [3125], 2000, analyzed the strategy of Edward III, 1327-1360, describing how the English won in the early decades of the Hundred Years' War; those great victories: Sluys, Crecy, and Calais. In dissertations, Thomas Greenhaw [1384], 1978, and T.J. Denman [911], 1985, studied the political debate over strategy, 1689-1712. In a dissertation, A.W. Massie [2457], 1988, wrote about a perennial strategic concern, defense of the Low Countries, in this case in the mid-18th century. Richard Middleton [2507], 1989, described British naval strategy, 1755-1762.

The strategic dilemma of the British during the late 1770s and early 1780s, losing the American colonies, called out for strategic analysis. Answering were David Syrett [3544], 1991: a choice between defense against invasion at home or save a colony, and William Willcox [3869], 1945: the British commanders were distracted by disputes among themselves over prize money and other extraneous matters, for example, Rodney vs. Clinton and Graves vs. Clinton. Then the French arrived in the Chesapeake.

Richard Buel [**502**], In Irons, 1998, described a successful strategy during the American Revolution. The RN virtually eliminated American commerce, occupied its ports, and destroyed its economy, thus, "in irons."

In other dissertations, Charles Arthur [**143**], 1966, analyzed the naval strategy, 1800-1801, citing the close blockade policy of St. Vincent as the key, and Piers Mackesy [**2302**], 1954, on the naval strategy, 1803-1810. In a dissertation and a book, Christopher Hall [**1456, 1455**], British Strategy in the Napoleonic War, 1803-1815, 1984 and 1992, analyzed key factors in the making of the strategy, for example, manning, money, subsidies, and the Continental System.

Naval strategy in peacetime were the themes of Sari Horstein [**1675**], 1985, in a dissertation, and in a forthcoming book by John Hattendorf [**1562**].

Strategies of opponents were informative and pertinent. In a dissertation and a book, Jacques Paviot [**2795, 2794**], described the naval policies of the Dukes of Burgundy, 1384-1482; often aggressive and threats to invade England. Geoffrey Parker [**2750**], The Grand Strategy of Philip II, 1998, was a synthesis of a lifetime of research and writing. Did Philip have such? It was "messianic imperialism" and it failed because all depended on him personally, the "lonely hermit of the Escorial." For the next generation after Philip II, Paul Allen [**48**], 2000, assessed the grand strategy of Spain, 1598-1621, "a bid for mastery" which failed due to "strategic overstretch," with the British as successors and beneficiaries.

In a dissertation, Charles Petersen [**2834**], 1975, compared and contrasted the strategies of friends-enemies in the 17th century, Denmark and Britain. Dynastic ties meant nothing. Steven Ross [**3150**], 1975, looked at French strategy in the 1790s.

C. NAVAL TACTICS

The basis of British naval tactics during the age of sail was "the Fighting Instructions," first consolidated by James, Duke of York and Prince Rupert in the 1660s; permanent instructions dated from 1703. Additions were made by Rooke, Vernon, Anson, Hawke, and Rodney. Nelson wrote memos in 1803 and 1805. "Signal Books" came in 1816. The line-of-battle was the structure and remained so through the 19th century.

A History of Naval Tactical Thought, 1956, was by Giuseppe Fioravanzo [**1101**], an Italian tactical expert. The basis of British naval tactics during the age of sail was Fighting Instructions, the origin and history of which was written by Julian Corbett [**751**], 1905, a publication of the NRS, the dates were 1530-1816. An early treatise was by Paul Hoste [**1679**], 1697, a French writer. He demanded rigid compliance, fearing a degeneration into melee. It included Order of Battle, Orders of Sailing, and Order of Retreat. The "Fighting Instructions" were influenced by this work.

John Clerk [**656**], <u>An Essay on Naval Tactics</u>, 2 vols., 1782-1797, was a study of British and French naval tactics. The line-of-battle was the tactic of the age of sail. Clerk claimed it was not effective. Look at Suffren in India. "Abandon the tyranny of the line." Concentrate on one part and break the enemy line. Nelson studied this work before Trafalgar. Raoul Castex [**593**], 1911, in French, reviewed the indecisiveness of the line of battle, commending Suffren and de Ruyter. Michael Palmer [**2736**], 1997, reviewed the Fighting Instructions of the RN and its impact on command and control: it exacerbated the problems and decentralized control. Nelson recognized that a large fleet could not be controlled in battle with signals, so, he stressed his "band of brothers" process, informing all before the battle. Geoffrey Regan [**3043**], 1993, ticked off "naval blunders," for example, those of John Byng, ROYAL GEORGE, and VASA.

S.S. Robison [**3097**], <u>A History of Naval Tactics</u>, 1942, was international coverage. Wayne Hughes [**1720**], <u>Fleet Tactics</u>, 1986, included a chapter on the age of fighting sail. Nelson was a peerless tactician, especially at the Nile. Corbett credited Kempenfelt for new orders and signals in 1780. L.G. Carr Laughton [**2060**], 1928, and R.A. Konstam [**1973**], 1988, wrote of gunnery and line-of-battle tactics.

D. A PERENNIAL FEAR: INVASION

Some scholars claimed that 1066 was the last successful invasion of the British Isles; not so. Look at 1485 and 1688. From pre-Roman times, a persistent problem was how to defend and how to prepare. Debate and discussion intensified later: were coastal defenses to be the priority or was the "blue-water" battle fleet sufficient? After the period of this study, Lord Palmerston created a scare, minimizing the security of battle fleets; so build elaborate coastal defenses.

From pre-Roman times, defense of the coasts all around the British Isles and especially the south and southeast coasts had been a priority. An excellent place to start would be James Williamson [**3895**], <u>The English Channel: A History</u>, 1959, comprehensive and authoritative. Hillas Smith [**3359**], 1994, was a more recent but shorter history.

B.M. Morley [**2554**], 1976, produced an informative pamphlet mapping the coastal defenses created by Henry VIII, castles, forts, and batteries along the southern coast. Michael Powell [**2931**], <u>Spithead: The Navy's Anvil</u>, 1977, was about the defenses of Portsmouth, a total of 623 guns sited from the Needles to Spithead.

Among the earliest systems of coastal defense, the Saxon Shore, as presented by D.A. White [**3839**], <u>Litus Saxonicum</u>, 1961. Anglo-Saxon fortifications were covered by David Hill [**1628**], 1996, describing defenses sponsored by King Alfred against the Danes. A.Z. Freeman [**1188**], 1967, described a programme of 1295, sponsored by Edward I who divided the coast into defense zones. The French attacked Winchelsea but were driven away.

Norman Longmate [**2183, 2184**], Defending the Island: From Caesar to the Armada, 1989, and Island Fortress: The Defence of Great Britain, 1603-1945, 1991, were related works reviewing invasion schemes and defenses against them, for example, fortifications, earthworks, and pillboxes. Dan Cruickshank [**816**], Invasion, 2001, was another survey, but superficial.

From the mid-14th century to the 1550s, Calais, on the Channel coast of France, was a foothold. David Grummitt [**1417**], 2000, wrote of the defense of Calais in the 15th century, specially the aspects of logistics and victualling which had to be done from England. Anne Curry [**837**], 1994, edited papers from a conference on arms and fortifications of the Hundred Years' War, Oxford, 1991, including reports of historical archaeologists.

Andrew Saunders [**3223**], English Heritage Book of Channel Defences, 1997, was a popular reference guide, partly to inform tourists, Harwick to the Scilly Isles, featuring coastal fortifications and naval yards and ports. Modern coastal defense measures included the unique Martello Towers, dozens of individual, usually rounded, forts along the southern and eastern coasts to defend against anticipated Napoleonic invasion. Later, these were greatly expanded, sited all over the world. They were recounted by William Clements [**655**], 1999.

The defenses were against invasion, the perennial problem. Herbert Richmond [**3059**], The Invasion of Britain, 1941, at a time when Hitler was threatening, reviewed past efforts, 1586-1918, for example by the Spanish, French, and Dutch, if William III in 1688 can be counted. Invasion was a matter of naval strategy.

F.J. McLynn [**2312**], Invasion, 1987, reviewed attempts from the Armada to Hitler. Claiming no success since 1066; many failures, for example, the Jacobites, several French expeditions such as 1744, 1759, 1779, and 1798, and Operation Sea Lion. Was this correct? What about 1485 and 1688?

An older effort was Henry Hozier [**1712**], 2 vols., 1876, touting his review as "a history of the past with lessons for the future." Margaret Bradley [**418**], 1994, cited a case study: Pierre Forfait toured Britain in the 1790s, returned to France, and convinced Napoleon that the only way to defeat the British was to invade. Napoleon made him Minister of the Navy and plans commenced. 2000 gunboats were constructed by 1801 but the order to execute never came.

J.L. Anderson [**72**], 1983, speculated about climate and favorable and unfavorable winds, for example in 1588 and in 1688. Weather was definitely extraordinary in 1588, and again in 1596, and again in 1597. In 1688, William of Orange was successful because of favorable wind patterns as he landed in the southwest. **See 7., F., 4.**

E. TRADE, DEFENSE OF COMMERCE, AND IMPERIAL DEFENSE

The chronological evolution of great entrepots during the time England/Britain was emerging was instructive: for a moment, Hamberg and Lubeck, during the time of the Hanseatic League, more significantly, Venice and Genoa, then Seville, then Lisbon, then Bruges, then Antwerp, then Amsterdam, and finally London.

From the time of the Tudors, if not before, English/British trade increased dramatically, to the point that it dominated the commerce of the entire world and most of the trade of others was carried in British bottoms. After much trial and error over time, it was determined that the best defense for overseas trade was the convoy system. After the Tudor period, increasing responsibilities of imperial defense emerged. Richard Pares [2744], 1938, wrote on colonial blockade, 1739-1763.

In a dissertation, an article, and a book, Patrick Crowhurst [811, 812, 810], The Defence of British Trade, 1689-1815, 1970, 1971, and 1977, noted that the biggest threat during this era was French privateers, especially from Dunkirk and St. Malo. The most serious threat was in the English Channel, less in other places. Convoys reduced losses. Insurance helped. Crowhurst described merchant-government cooperation as effective during the Seven Years' War, keeping losses under control. A.W.H. Pearsall [2800], 1989, wrote on the RN and trade protection, 1688-1714.

David Syrett [3550], 1976, reported on British trade convoys during the American Revolution. The system was disliked but it worked; insurance rates actually decreased. Three dissertations focused on convoy protection for British trade during the Wars of the French Revolution and Napoleon: M.W.B. Sanderson [3215], 1968, C. Dowling [958], 1965, and R.W. Avery [160], 1983.

William Jackson [1768], 1995, focused on defense of India and the Suez Canal. This was the Eastern Question. The early defenders were Nelson and Sydney Smith. By contrast, Edward Ingram [1746], 1994, in a incisive and provocative presentation, saw Russia as the great threat to the empire after the Napoleonic wars. Mahan and the victories of Nelson were irrelevant in these matters of the Great Game.

F. MARITIME INSURANCE

In the early modern period, Lloyd's Coffee House in the City coordinated marine insurance. Lloyd's was and is a confederation of insurance underwriters. Lloyd's List, a newsletter, provided vital information to the underwriters and to the maritime community all over the world. Then and now, London dominated the international market for insurance.

A good introduction can be found in Barry Supple [3519], 1970, a history of British insurance, 1720-1970, a fourth of which was about marine insurance. The earliest English policies were 1547-1563. Histories were by Charles Wright [**3961**], A History of Lloyd's, 1928, and Frederick Martin [**2431**], A History of Lloyd's and Marine Insurance in Great Britain, 1971. Frank Murphy [**2586**], 1967, described other contributions of Lloyd's: a registry of shipping, shipping intelligence, and a world center for shipping information. Patrick Crowhurst [**812**], 1977, insisted that marine insurance saved British commerce in wartime.

G. COMMUNICATIONS

Under the circumstances of early modern technology with no electrical or electronic capabilities, this primarily concerned signaling from ship to ship. Flags were the primary method. By 1815, the Admiralty had set up its own communication system, a series of shutter stations within visual sight of each other so brief messages could be sent along the line, Portsmouth to London. That was expanded later. Word of the battle of Trafalgar and death of Nelson was conveyed by dispatch ship, HMS PICKLE, rushing to Cornwall and the captain then rushing overland to London. **See 8., A., 4.**

Again, Julian Corbett [**757**] was formative here: Signals and Instructions, 1908, a publication of the NRS. Most was about the introduction and use of the new Signal Book. More decisive battles followed. Barrie Kent [**1912**], Signal!: A History of Signaling in the Royal Navy, 1993, was a history of naval communications.

Timothy Wilson [**3915**], Flags at Sea, 1986, was a detailed guide to flags flown at sea, based on the collection at the NMM. The Trafalgar signal of Nelson and the signal code of Marryat were illustrated. The old standard, W.G. Perrin [**2825, 2829**], British Flags, 1922, traced the history of the use of flags at sea, first used in the 17th century. Nelson's Signals, 1908, was an earlier pamphlet illustrating the flags used by Nelson at Trafalgar. The basis was the navy's Signal Book of 1804. Hilary Mead [**2486**], Trafalgar Signals, 1936, corrected the error made by Perrin [**2829**] concerning the coloring of flag # 4.

Thomas Holmes [**1662**], The Semaphore, 1983, described the Admiralty shutter and semaphore systems of communication overland, from Portsmouth to Admiralty headquarters, begun in 1796. Jack Broome [**463**], Make Another Signal!, 1973, had an agenda, apologetics for a notorious incident concerning the order to scatter to Convoy PQ-17 to Russia in 1942.

H. INTELLIGENCE

Historically, intelligence has been associated with the navy, although not exclusive to it.

Alison Plowden [**2863**], The Elizabethan Secret Service, 1991, and Alan Haynes [**1581**], Invisible Power, 1992, reviewed intelligence matters in the late 16th century, a world of secret agents, double agents, espionage, and complex conspiracies, some to eliminate Elizabeth, replacing her with a Catholic candidate, Mary, Queen of Scots. The central figure was Francis Walsingham. Simon Singh [**3328**], 1999, elaborated about the conspiracies involving Mary, Queen of Scots. Breaking codes and implicating Mary directly convinced Elizabeth to sign the death warrant.

In a dissertation and a book, Alan Marshall [**2416, 2415**], Intelligence and Espionage in the Reign of Charles II, 1991 and 1994, described operations, the post office being increasingly involved. Pepys and Deane were victims of plots. Kenneth Ellis [**1037**], 1958, described the activities of the post office in the 18th century: subsections included the Private Office, the Secret Office, and the Deciphering Branch. It operated a fleet of packet boats.

Spies uncovered a Jacobite invasion plan of 1708. A French naval officer was a double agent. Further plots were recounted in the '45 in Scotland. Hugh Douglas [**953**], 1999, wrote of these events. At the same time, J.D. Alsop [**55**], 1991, contended that British intelligence had been overrated during the War of Spanish Succession.

Roger Kaplan [**1844**], 1990, assessed British intelligence during the American Revolution. Naval intelligence was interested in movements of the French fleet but information was too slow. Intelligence was available but it was not centralized and there were too many other problems.

Alfred Cobban [**679**], 1954, wrote on the British Secret Service in France, 1784-1792. Steven Maffeo [**2325**], Most Secret and Confidential, 2000, surveyed intelligence in the age of Nelson, presenting case studies of naval intelligence, for example, Nelson at Copenhagen. The role of frigates was played up. Unfortunately, no archival research occurred, accounts were superficial, and, curiously, fictional works of C.S. Forester, to whom the book was dedicated, and Patrick O'Brian, were cited; Stephen Maturin was depicted as an experienced intelligence officer.

Michael Duffy [**971**], 1998, recounted the vicissitudes of Nelson in the run up to the battle of the Nile. Napoleon was en route somewhere, Spain had just entered the war, at home there was the distraction of an Irish revolt, and the Admiralty was unaware that a French invasion plan had been cancelled. With the intelligence he had, Nelson believed Napoleon was headed for the Levant. Nelson even arrived at Alexandria before the French and began looking further to the east. He returned to Alexandria and annihilated the French fleet in the battle of the Nile. **See 7., I., 8.**

Michael Durey [**996**], 1999, recounted a British intelligence success story: Sydney Smith and J.W. Wright were in Temple prison in Paris as prisoners of state, a higher status. Yet, Royalists assisted in the successful escape of both in 1798.

Bernard Porter [**2920**], 1989, surveyed the history of political espionage in Britain, 1790-1988. Again, there was no centralized agency during the early decades.

I. AMPHIBIOUS WARFARE

Alternative descriptive terms were combined operations and conjunct expeditions.

A good place to begin was Herbert Richmond [**3058**], Amphibious Warfare in British History, 1941, a short overview for the Historical Association. Case studies included Drake to the West Indies, 1585-1586, Pocock to Havana in 1762, and the attack on Copenhagen in 1807. Alfred Vagts [**3707**], Landing Operations, 1946, was a general overview and history. Julius Caesar, William I, and William III were amphibious generals. Bernard Fergusson [**1088**], The Watery Maze: The Story of Combined Operations, 1961, was a British history by a distinguished veteran. First was Rochefort in 1757, a fiasco. Wolfe was there and learned; then Louisbourg and Quebec. Most subsequent ones were unopposed until World War I.

John Creswell [**797**], Generals and Admirals, 1952, was about amphibious command. A dozen case studies were presented, for example, Cadiz in 1596 and Quebec in 1759, Wolfe and Saunders given equal credit. A great veteran and former Director of Combined Operations, Roger Keyes [**1924**], Amphibious Warfare and Combined Operations, 1943, the Lees Knowles Lectures, emphasized interservice cooperation and cited examples, again giving equal credit to Wolfe and Saunders at Quebec.

Simon Foster [**1165**], 1995, was a superficial set of case studies, for example, Quebec, where he reviewed the essentials of amphibious warfare, for example, surprise, superiority, speed, and cooperation.

Actual operations have been presented. Valentine Belfiglio [**279, 280**], 1998 and 1999, wrote separate accounts of the two cross-Channel ventures of Julius Caesar in 55 and 54 BC.

The authority for the 18th century was Richard Harding [**1493, 1494, 1491**], in a dissertation, an article, and a book, 1985, 1989, and 1991, about the expedition to the West Indies, 1740-1742, a sensational failure. Preparation and planning were good and much was learned for the future. Execution was a disaster. The political fallout was worse than professional failure. Later in the century, William Pitt the Elder had been given too much credit. Amphibious operations did not enjoy unity of command, intelligence was poor, and the results were too often exaggerated. David Syrett [**3546**], 1972, reviewed 11 amphibious operations, 1756-1783. Army-navy cooperation was outstanding and much was gained by the British.

Piers Mackesy [**2304**], 1978, reviewed problems of amphibious warfare, 1793-1815. Until 1807, little was accomplished. The revolt in Spain resolved a strategic dilemma. The Peninsular campaign was the solution. Charles Fedorak [**1080**], 1988, reviewed amphibious operations and the RN during the Wars of the French Revolution and Napoleon.

R.D. Layman [**2085**], 1979, the historian of the aircraft carrier, recounted some instances of shipboard aviation beginning in 1783, for example, kites, balloons, and towed aerial devices.

Chapter 17

Exploration, Discovery, Navigation, Cartography, and Science

English/British trade and commerce and its dramatic expansion to world domination have been reviewed. **See 7., G., 2.** Facilitating that process were significant advances in sea voyaging, navigation, hydrography, cartography, and the Greenwich Observatory. **See 17., O.-R.** Trinity House developed to create and maintain navigational aids and safe channels. Closely associated with all of that were spectacular achievements in exploration and discovery. Significantly facilitating exploration and discovery was the preparation, planning, sponsoring, and executing of numerous voyages by the Admiralty, state-sponsored enterprises. The results were major contributions to all of the sciences and literature and, of course, discovery and claims of vast amounts of new territories.

Unique and extraordinary were the stated purposes of these voyages sponsored by the RN: scientific, astronomical, and botanical research. Accompanying the voyages were scientists, astronomers, naturalists, and artists. Naturalists were to collect specimens, most notably, Joseph Banks and Charles Darwin, both premier scientists of their day. Direct products were collections for the British Museum, the Science Museum, and Kew Gardens. Artists were the equivalent of modern photographers. Can any venture anytime and anywhere surpass this extraordinary series of achievements and advances?

The Admiralty had sponsored major voyages for decades, objectives including searching for and mapping of new lands, scientific investigation, astronomical observations, searching for the Northeast and Northwest Passages, establishing territorial claims, and, in the case of Vancouver at Nootka Sound, re-establishing claims of territory over those of Spain. The Vancouver voyage of exploration covered the early 1790s and included Australia, New Zealand, and Tahiti, thence to the northwest coast of North America. As others had, he searched for the elusive Northwest Passage. He explored, mapped, and laid claim to Vancouver Island, among other places.

The organization of this chapter may appear to be backwards. Coverage of the exploration and discovery appears later. James Cook is first and the Cook voyages, relatively late chronologically in the period, immediately follow. The reason for this is consistent with previous priorities. The guide is magnitude of publication. Like Nelson and Bligh elsewhere, Cook has attracted the most interest and publication. **See 8., A. and B.**

A. THE HAKLUYT SOCIETY

A good place to begin for this chapter on exploration and discovery would be a description and history of the equivalent of a scholarly propaganda and expansionist agency based on activities and personalities of the 16th century and later, the famous Hakluyt Society founded in 1846.

There were two Richard Hakluyts. More important and contributory was Richard the younger, a minister and friend of Walter Raleigh, once Archdeacon of Westminster, and buried in Westminster Abbey. The elder was a cousin and a barrister, seemingly less important. Their interests were in voyages and discoveries and they were advocates for expansion of English trade, exploration, and colonization. They collected and published in what modern persons would describe as propaganda endeavors. It was a strategy of enterprise and, in their cases, chauvinistic and rabidly anti-Spanish. Samuel Purchas inherited the Hakluyt papers and continued the process but in a reduced and inferior fashion.

Richard Hakluyt [**1446-1451**] The Principal Navigations, 12 vols., 1589-1600; the modern edition was 20 vols.; Hakluyts Voyages, 1589, and The Portable Hakluyt's Voyages, 1965, included accounts of the Cabots, searches for the Northeast and Northwest Passages, early contact with the Russians, and the circumnavigation of Drake; Virginia Voyages from Hakluyt, 1973, and Original Writings of the Two Hakluyts, 2 vols., 1965. Some selections from the works of the Hakluyts were by William Hacke [**1440**], 1699, Eva Taylor [**3576**], 2 vols., 1935, and David Hawkes [**1574**], 1972. There was a dissertation and a book by G.B. Parks [**2777, 2778**], both 1928, a definitive biography. Parks concluded that the works of the Hakluyts demonstrated that Elizabethan enterprises overseas were undertaken after careful inquiry and preparation. They laid the groundwork for the beginnings of the British Empire. Edward Lynam [**2209**], Richard Hakluyt and His Successors, 1946, was a commemoration volume of the centennial of the Hakluyt Society. Mary Fuller [**1213**], Voyages in Print, 1995, was a delightful and sophisticated narrative, placing the voyages publicized by the Hakluyts and others in context. The fact that many failed was rhetorically manipulated: "protoimperial haplessness" and "profitless self-sacrifice" were descriptions. P.A. Neville-Singleton [**2630**], 1997, inventoried the books of the Hakluyts. Kenneth Andrews [**112**], 1951, described some new sources on the activities of the Hakluyts. Most helpful was David Beer Quinn

[**2980, 2979**], The Hakluyt Handbook, 2 vols., 1974, dedicated to R.A. Skelton, including an extensive bibliography. Quinn also wrote about the Hakluyts, 1990, their contacts and their influence. Francis Edgar [**1014**], 1964, was aimed at a juvenile audience.

Samuel Purchas [**2968**], Hakluyt Posthumous, 4 vols., 1613-1625, included much that had been left unpublished at the death of Richard Hakluyt, expanded into 20 vols., 1905-1907. L.E. Pennington [**2811**], The Purchas Handbook, 2 vols., 1997, was the same format as the Quinn [**2980**] work.

The Hakluyt Society was founded in 1846. An ambitious publication project followed: Hakluty Society publications: first series, 100 vols.; second series, 189 vols., and now into the third series, at least 4 vols. Many of the works surveyed above and below were publications of the Hakluyt Society. Publications of the Hakluyt Society included Michael Brennan [**428**], The Travel Diary of Robert Bargrave, Levant Merchant, 1647-1656, 1999.

B. JAMES COOK

If magnitude of publications continued to be the guide, as in the case of the chapter, "Special Emphasis," on Nelson and Bligh, then James Cook must appear early in this chapter on exploration and discovery, especially scientific voyages of exploration. The three famous voyages of Cook demonstrated a high regard for scientific advancement. Indeed, the ostensible rationale for the first voyage, co-sponsored by the Royal Society, was to observe the rare astronomical event, the transit of Venus.

Cook had been saved from the press gang by volunteering for the RN in 1755. His early experience at sea was in the coal trade. He was in the Saunder's fleet at Quebec, then as surveyor of the basin of Quebec, Nova Scotia, and Newfoundland. It was unusual for the Admiralty to select a warrant officer for such a major expedition as was being planned. The expedition was jointly sponsored by the Admiralty and the Royal Society. Cook was later elected to the Royal Society and was a Younger Brother, Trinity House. The three voyages were #1 - August 1768-July 1771 – HM Bark ENDEAVOUR – as Lieutenant, promoted to Captain; #2 – July 1772-July 1775 – RESOLUTION and ADVENTURE, and #3 – July 1777-October 1780 – RESOLUTION and DISCOVERY. Cook died, February 1779. He was murdered, Kealakekua Bay, Hawaii, 14 February 1779; a marker was placed on the spot. As a demonstration of the international importance and scientific emphasis, during the War of the American Revolution, Benjamin Franklin sent orders to American warships that the ships of the Cook voyage were immune from attack.

James Cook [**729-732**], The Voyages of Captain James Cook, 1949, presented details on the three voyages, and Seventy North to Fifty South, 1969, was about the third voyage.

J.C. Beaglehole [**257, 253**], The Life of Captain James Cook, 1974, originally sponsored by the Hakluyt Society, was the standard and definitive biography. Beaglehole began research in 1967 and died in 1971. He also wrote The Discovery of New Zealand, 1939. Frances Porter [**2921**], 1978, republished the account of the landings of Cook in New Zealand by Beaglehole.

John Barrow [**224**], Voyages of Discovery, 1860, reviewed the three voyages; George Young [**3976**], 1836, was on the life and voyages.

Alan Villiers [**3725**], Captain James Cook, 1967, a Penguin paperback; the subtitle of the English edition: The Seamen's Seaman: A Study of the Great Discoverer, was by a professional sailor who actually retraced the voyages.

Richard Hough [**1681**], 1994, placed the famous Nathaniel Dance portrait on the cover and played up the questions of the health of Cook just before his death; physical and mental decline and strangely slow movements on shore before his death. He could have escaped if he wanted to.

Robin Fisher [**1109**], 1979, edited the proceedings from a bicentennial conference, Simon Fraser University, 1978. One paper was on the extended conflict between the RN and Royal Society about exploration of the Pacific; in the early 1760s, Alexander Dalrymple began lobbying; then more conflict over who would lead the voyage. John Hawkesworth [**1576**] purposely ignored the role of Dalrymple. A paper by Glyn Williams was on "theoretical geography": Cook was to investigate theories about a large southern continent. The goal of the 3rd voyage was to find the Northwest Passage and to survey the coast of Alaska. Dagny Hansen [**1483**], 1993, placed the search for the Northwest Passage by Cook in an international context. Spain and Russia, were also searching. Christopher Lloyd [**2150**], 1952, described Cook as mentor: Bligh and Vancouver.

James Williamson [**3894**], Captain Cook and the Opening of the Pacific, 1946, concerned the Pacific Ocean: "the field was vast, the progress was slow." This huge area remained unclear until Cook cleared up the major uncertainties. Lynne Withey [**3929**], 1987, was also on Cook and exploration of the Pacific and was touted as the best popular biography of Cook for 20 years. This was the last great age of European sea exploration. Withey was critical of the "dark view" of Alan Moorehead [**2537**-]. **See 17., J.**

Oliver Warner [**3757**], Captain Cook and the South Pacific, 1963, was a beautiful production, profusely illustrated with color and aimed for juveniles; in consultation with J.C. Beaglehole; the Nathaniel Dance portrait was on the cover. Richard Humble [**1728**], The Voyages of Captain Cook, 1990, was a short survey. Martin Dugard [**982**], Farther than Any Man, 2001, was on the rise and fall of Cook. Alan Gurney [**1424**], 1997, reviewed voyages toward Antarctica, especially those of Cook and Halley.

Tom Stamp [**3417**], James Cook, Maritime Scientist, 1978, emphasized the Whitby connection and the fact that he was self-taught. Keith Snowden [**3382**], 1999, stressed the explorer role. John Robson [**3098**], Captain Cook's World, 2000, featured extensive maps illustrating the career of Cook.

The NMM and British Museum have featured publications and exhibitions: Basil Greenhill [**1388**], 1970, was a booklet format sponsored by the NMM; Roger Morriss [**2567**], 1997, was in the Great Explorers series, for the NMM and HM Bark ENDEAVOUR Trust, and Captain Cook and the South Pacific [**576**], 1979, for the British Museum, supporting a bicentennial exhibition. R.A. Skelton [**3338**], 1954, the annual lecture, SNR, stressed the his role as surveyor.

Others were: Oswald Brett [**431**], 1978, "an appreciation" in a short article; Julia Rae [**2998, 2997**], 1991, on the early years before 1768, and Captain James Cook Endeavours, 1997, commemorating a visit by the replica; Walter Besant [**308**], 1890, in the English Men of Action series, and Arthur Hugh Carrington [**583**], 1939, an older standard which used logs of the RN ships. Roy Schreiber [**3249**], 2001, reviewed recent literature on Cook.

For juveniles, there were Frank Knight [**1961**], 1964, Alistair MacLean [**2310**], 1972, hagiographic, and Roger Hart [**1540**], 1973.

Circumstances around the death of Cook have been disputed: Gavin Kennedy [**1878**], The Death of Captain Cook, 1978, noted some causes: carelessness and acceptance of "Godhead" status, and Richard Hough [**1683**], The Murder of Captain James Cook, 1979, heavily relying on Beaglehole, blamed the death of Cook on Bligh. **See 8., B., 4.** James Watt [**3790**], 1981, speculated that Cook earlier had contacted a parasitic infection from raw fish; thus, his health and judgment were increasingly impaired.

C. THE SHIPS OF THE COOK VOYAGES

HM Bark ENDEAVOUR was originally a collier to carry coal and was built in the hometown of Cook, Whitby. HMS ENDEAVOUR Trust was formed in Australia and the United Kingdom, sponsored, among others, by the SNR, the NMM, and the Hakluyt Society. A replica of ENDEAVOUR was built in the 1990s and toured around the world. In the BBC-PBS TV series, "Inspector Morse," written by Colin Dexter, in one of the last episodes, just before he "died," reluctantly revealed that his parents were admirers of James Cook and named him "Endeavour" Morse.

Peter Aughton [**158**], ENDEAVOUR, 1999, was in fact the tale of the first voyage. Aughton contended that subterfuge was used by the Admiralty. The published rationale of the first voyage, to measure the transit of Venus across the sun, was to cover up the true objective, to discover and claim terra Australis, further expanding the British empire and depriving it from potential enemies.

Others were Ray Parkin [**2758**], HM Bark ENDEAVOUR, 1997, a boxed set, Karl Marquardt [**2395**], Captain Cook's ENDEAVOUR, 1995, in The Anatomy of the Ship series, Antonia MacArthur [**2221**], His Majesty's Bark ENDEAVOUR, 1997, and R.O. Morris [**2560**], 1986.

Margarette Lincoln [**2136**], 1998, presented the proceedings of a conference, NMM, 1992, focused on the voyage of ENDEAVOUR II, the replica, traveling around the world. And, there is a CD-ROM, ENDEAVOUR [**1047**], 1999, sponsored by the NMM of Australia.

The other ships have not been the subjects of separate works.

D. THE JOURNALS OF THE VOYAGES

This itself was a story with many ramifications and complexities. Some of these journals became immediate best sellers. They exerted influence, for example, on the Enlightenment and on adventure literature, playing up Enlightenment themes such as the noble savage and idea of progress. Questions arose about authorship and manipulation of originals. For the Cook voyages, publication of the journal of the first voyage was 1773 and the others in the 1780s. Other journals of other pertinent voyages in time will be reviewed.

A good place to start on the subject of journals of voyages was a research and reference guide, Ian Nicholson [**2636**], Log of Logs: A Catalogue of Logs, Journals, Shipboard Diaries, Letters, and All Forms of Voyage Narratives, 1788-1988, for Australia, New Zealand, and Surrounding Oceans, 1989, in alphabetical order by ship name. Philip Edwards [**1020**], The Story of the Voyage, 1994, recounted sea narratives, for example, Dampier, Alexander Selkirk, Cook, Bligh, and the convicts. Ignore the anti-imperialist diatribes. Georg Steller [**3442**], 1988, presented the journal of a voyage with Bering to the northwest coast, 1741-1742.

Still, most important were the journals of James Cook [**729-732**], with various editions and editors, originally sponsored by the Hakluyt Society, 1955-1974, 5 vols., 4038 pages. Editors have been Williamson, Davidson, and Skelton; in the reissue of 2001, the Beaglehole [**257**] biography of Cook was included. There was a Penguin Classic edition, edited by Philip Edwards, 1999, 672 pages. J.C. Beaglehole [**258**] wrote "Some Problems of Editing Cook's Journals," 1957. The journals of Cook were never printed as he wrote them. He wrote down his assessments later and other accounts were integrated by editors. All was quite complicated.

Exquisite, spectacular, monumental, artistic, and superb production were some descriptions of Andrew David [**861**], The Charts and Coastal Views of Captain Cook's Voyages, 3 vols., 1988-1992, a publication of the Hakluyt Society, folio size, with hundreds of illustrations. There were some variations: J.C. Beaglehole [**255**], The ENDEAVOUR Journal of Joseph Banks, 2 vols., 1963; Frank Paluka [**2742**], The Three Voyages of Captain Cook, 1974, an elegant production with a short narrative, valuable footnotes, and a bibliography, and Sydney Parkinson [**2776**], 1984, a journal of the ENDEAVOUR voyage.

John Hawkesworth [**1576**], 3 vols., 1773, published the original journal of the first voyage, creating much controversy, then and now. The title mentions

Cook, Commodore Byron, Captain Wallis, and Captain Carteret. The journal of Banks [195] was used. Plus, much moralizing was inserted. Who wrote what? How much was authentic Cook? How much did Hawkesworth insert? J.L. Abbott [1], John Hawkesworth, 1982, was about the editing of the journals of Cook. In 1771, Lord Sandwich, First Lord of the Admiralty, instructed Hawkesworth to edit and publish. The product became a sensation. Hawkesworth was denounced for blasphemy and immorality. W.H. Pearson [2803], 1972, elaborated: Hawkesworth "converted the trustworthy impressions of honest navigators into demonstrations of enviable happiness of primitive societies." Pearson concluded that Hawkesworth aimed to increase sales and raise the status of explorers.

Johann Reinhold Forster [1159, 1158], 1982 and 1996, was the published journal, 4 vols., and observations during the second voyage. Forster was the replacement, hastily recruited, when Joseph Banks withdrew from the second voyage. John Elliott [1034], Captain Cook's Second Voyage, 1982, was the published journals of Lieutenants Elliott and Richard Pickersgill. George Manwaring [2361], 1931, published the journal of James Burney who was on the second and third voyages. Geoger Gilbert [1278], Captain Cook's Final Voyage, 1982, was the journal of this midshipman, 1776-1780.

Germaine Warkentin [3753], Critical Issues in Editing Exploration Texts, 1996, was essays by prominent editors, for example, Helen Wallis on John Hawkesworth and David Quinn on the Hakluyts. In a dissertation, Mary Fuller [1212], 1990, wrote on the process of recounting voyages during the Renaissance.

B. JOSEPH BANKS

Another extraordinary aspect of these matters of exploration and discovery were the contributions of Joseph Banks, the naturalist on the first Cook voyage. He was prepared to go on the second and insisted on a large entourage and command; the Admiralty refused and Banks withdrew. Later, he was patron and apologist for William Bligh; it was Banks who first suggested the breadfruit voyage. Banks was President of the prestigious Royal Society, 1778-1820, 42 years. He was instrumental in the establishment of Kew Gardens and the Natural History Museum of the British Museum. He was dubbed "father of Australia." His extensive library was given to the British Museum.

Joseph Banks [195], The Papers of Joseph Banks, 1993, was original documents on 34 reels of microfilm.

Harold Carter [585, 586], Sir Joseph Banks, both 1987, was a substantial biography, definitive, plus a guide to biographical and bibliographical sources. T.H. Watkins [3785], 1996, was on Banks and "the greening of the empire." Banks was instrumental in expanding the natural sciences, for example, exotic plants and animals. The famous nautical fiction writer, Patrick O'Brian [**2669**], wrote <u>Joseph Banks: A Life</u>, 1987, linking Banks with naval figures, for example, Cook, Bligh, and Flinders.

George Mackaness [**2282**], 1936, focused on the relations of Banks with Australia. In a dissertation, David MacKay [**2283**], 1969, linked Joseph Banks to exploration and economic development of the British empire.

The matter of the Enlightenment was elaborated upon by John Gasciogne [**1255, 1256**], <u>Joseph Banks and the English Enlightenment</u>, 1994, and <u>Science in the Service of Empire</u>, 1998. Banks exemplified so many characteristics of the Enlightenment and was an advocate of the advancement of science. **See 17., G.**

F. THE AGE OF DISCOVERY

More to the general theme of exploration and discovery were studies, summaries, and assessments of the age of discovery.

The esteemed J.H. Parry [**2780, 2785, 2781**] completed a trilogy: <u>The Age of Reconnaissance</u>, 1963, <u>Trade and Dominion</u>, 1971, and <u>The Discovery of the Sea</u>, 1975. The stages of imperial expansion were described. David Arnold [**141**], 1983, contributed a pamphlet on the age of discovery. Dan O'Sullivan [**2716**], 1984, surveyed the age of discovery. H.R. Trevor-Roper [**3649**], 1968, reviewed the age of expansion, 1559-1660. J.N.L. Baker [**176**], 1931, wrote a general survey on the history of geographical discovery and exploration. A.P. Newton [**2634**], <u>The Great Age of Discovery</u>, 1932, recounted the major voyages of exploration. Robert Silverberg [**3318**], <u>The Longest Voyage</u>, 1972, was about the circumnavigators in the age of discovery, including Drake and Cavendish. Woodes Rogers [**3132**], <u>A Cruising Voyage Round the World</u>, 1712, was his journal. David Divine [**940**], <u>The Opening of the World</u>, 1973, folio size and lavishly illustrated, was about the great age of maritime exploration. John Parker [**2757**], <u>Merchants and Scholars</u>, 1965, surveyed the history of exploration and trade. Edward Heawood [**1591**], 1965, wrote a general survey of the history of geographical discovery in the 17th and 18th centuries; the chronological sequence began with Portugal, followed by Spain, the Dutch, England, and France. Percy Sykes [**3531**], 1961, recounted the history of exploration. Richard Bohlander [**359**], <u>World Explorers and Discoverers</u>, 1992, was a biographical dictionary; 313 mini-biographies of explorers.

G. THE ENLIGHTENMENT, MYTHS, AND APOTHEOSIS

Reference has been made about the impact of the voyages of Cook and others on the ideas evolving into the famous Enlightenment in Europe in the late 17th and 18th centuries. The journals of those voyages, authentic and original, and contrived and manipulated, exerted enormous influence and created much controversy. In addition, debate has raged about events associated with exploration of the Pacific Ocean, cross-cultural contact, the death of Cook, and "the apotheosis."

Less controversial was the bicentennial celebration of the first voyage, a commemorative address by R.A. Skelton [**3337**], 1969, and Hugh Cobbe [**680**], Cook's Voyages and the Peoples of the Pacific, 1979, both for the British Museum. "James Cook Commemoration," [**1788**], 1979, reported a special service, Westminster Abbey, 11 February 1979, arranged by the NMM: the navy prayer and Drake's prayer were included.

The premier authority on these matters, Glyndwr Williams [**3878**], 1979, reviewed the matter of the influence of these voyages on philosophical speculation at the time of the Enlightenment: had man progressed or regressed? There was "a Pacific craze," a search for "the noble savage" and bitter reaction from religious leaders. Joseph Banks and John Hawkesworth had contributed. **See 17., D.** Bernard Smith [**3346, 3345**], Imagining the Pacific, 1992, and European Vision of the South Pacific, 1768-1850, 1985, stressed art, science, and an unspoiled civilization; exotic peoples, places, flora, and fauna all depicted by artists, art in the service of science. The influence of all of this on Europeans at the time was monumental, for example, on Darwin, Coleridge, Turner, and Constable. In a dissertation, Clara Lesher [**2107**], 1937, studied the South Sea islanders as depicted in English literature.

Alan Frost [**1204**], Pacific Empires, 1999, collected 13 essays in honor of Glyn Williams, balanced critiques on Cook and the subsequent literature, for example, Beaglehole [**257**] created the hero, about the origins of the hydrographic office, and the strategic and commercial consequences of these voyages. Jillian Robertson [**3086**] produced The Captain Cook Myth, 1981, with emphasis on the Australian connection.

With an agenda, the noted Australian journalist, Alan Moorehead [**2537**], contributed The Fatal Impact, 1966. He stressed the tragic consequences of the invasion of the South Pacific. There were separate parts: Tahiti, Australia, and Antarctica. It has been characterized as a "dark view" of the Euro-Polynesian encounter with a strident stance. Included were consequences up to the 1840s, for example, the sensation of the BOUNTY mutiny, Coleridge's "Ancient Mariner," Herman Melville, and Gaugin.

Another famous journal, associated later with the Enlightenment, was Louis-Antoine de Bougainville [**375**], 1772, describing his famous circumnavigation, a French voyage. In a dissertation, Stephen Turner [**3672**], 1995, studied cultural encounters, in this case, Cook and the Maori of New Zealand, "a state of nature."

Gananath Obeyesehere [**2659**], The Apotheosis of Captain Cook: European Mythmaking in the Pacific, 1992, launched major debate and controversy, a broad, intricate, and complex argument: topics included mythology around Cook and his death, violence in the modern world, and Sri Lanka, the native country of the author. It countered "Eurocentric" interpretations. It was Europeans, not Hawaiians, who made Cook a god. To Hawaiians, Cook was just a chief. There was a "destructive side" of Cook. History itself was a tool of domination, how one group controlled another.

Marshall Sahlins [**3206, 3205**], How "Natives" Think: About Captain Cook, For Example, 1995, was a direct response to and critique of Obeyesehere [**2659**]. There was an earlier article, 1981, and a book, Islands of History, 1985, by Sahlins [**3207**], which launched the debate. The controversy was limited only to anthropologists. Cook was a god to the Hawaiians and his return upset his divinity; thus, the assassination. The Apothesis was "a flimsy historical case," all "humbug." Jonathan Friedman [**1195**], 1985, and Clifford Geertz [**1264**], reviewed the debate, "Culture War," 1995. These were divisive issues of anthropology.

H. EXPLORATION AND DISCOVERY: THE ATLANTIC OCEAN

Much exciting literature has been devoted to exploration and discovery in the Atlantic by English/British. There were Brendan, Madoc, and other mythological, legendary, and actual figures.

The Irish cleric, Brendan, had founded three monasteries. Allegedly, about 570 AD, he set out, eventually reaching Newfoundland in a curragh, a boat covered in animal skins. A"test" voyage was successfully made by Tim Severin [**3282**] in the mid-1970s. Madoc allegedly went to North America in 1170; Columbus was 1492.

Paul Butel [**527**], The Atlantic, 1999, was a chronological narrative, introductory and an economic approach. Alan Villiers [**3726**], The Western Ocean, 1957, reviewed the history of the North Atlantic. Boies Penrose [**2812**], Travel and Discovery in the Renaissance, 1952, was a general review of the important voyages and supporting data, for example, maps, navigation, and ship design, plus an excellent survey of the literature. Barry Cunliffe [**829**], 2001, surveyed the Atlantic and its peoples, in support of a series on BBC Radio 4. Archaeological findings were the evidence; all reminiscent of Braudel [**426**].

John Allen [**44**], North American Exploration, 3 vols., 1997, noted that the quadricentennial of the discovery by Columbus was celebratory to the extreme, for example, at the Chicago World's Fair, while the quincentennial degenerated into controversy and accusations: genocide, institutional racism, moral decadence, and Columbus as villain, all obvious revisionism. The first volume was most pertinent: pre-Columbian discoveries, for example, the Irish cleric, Brendan and Welsh prince Madoc, and the Norse; the search for the Northwest Passage, and the map of John Dee staking English claims, 1580.

There was tenuous evidence that Christopher Columbus gained experience in northern European waters. Elaboration on Columbus, "then and now," was by Miles Davidson [**865**], 1997, reviewing much of the literature. David Quinn [**2973**], 1992, speculated about gaps in the life of Columbus. He left Genoa about 1475. Did he travel as a merchant to Southampton and Bristol, as many did at that time? Fishermen from these places and elsewhere proceeded to Iceland. Some speculation has stimulated interest. Ian Wilson [**3911**], 1991, wondered whether men of Bristol reached America before Columbus. In 1492, Columbus departed from Rio Saltes estuary, the favorite haunt of the Bristolians.

The premier historian of Atlantic voyages was Samuel Eliot Morison [**2549-2553**], with the authoritative general survey, an abridgement, and an award-winning biography of Columbus and abridgement. The European Discovery of America, 2 vols., 1971 and 1978, was divided into "northern" and "southern" voyages, including commentary and opinion on all of the big questions. Morison castigated "the academic tribe of armchair admirals and library navigators." Beginning with the Irish and going up to 1600, Morison concluded that at least 10 pre-Columbian voyages were pure legend, for example, Phoenicians to America, "Welsh Indians" to America, and a Welsh prince in 1170. The Vinland Map was based on dubious evidence. See 17., R. The three Frobisher voyages cost stockholders 20,000 pounds and were complete failures, characterized by "stupidity" and "skulduggery." Sebastian Cabot was not a favorite. Morison personally followed the routes of the Columbus voyages and wrote the best biography, 2 vols., 1942 and 1956.

Equally distinguished were the works of David Quinn [**2973-2989**], most prolific on early exploration to North America: North America from Earliest Discovery to First Settlement, 1971; England and the Discovery of North America, 1974; New American World, 1979; The English New England Voyages, 1983, and European Approaches, 1998. He recounted a "triangular trade" of the 15th century: Bristol to Iceland to Portugal. The English were the first to plant viable settlements. Quinn was critical of Morison [**2551**] for rejecting out of hand so many pre-Columbian voyages. C.H. Clough [**665**], The European Outthrust and Encounter, 1994, was a collection of 11 papers dedicated to David Quinn.

W.P. Cumming [**827**], The Discovery of North America, 1971, began with the Irish explorers, followed by the Norse, John Cabot, Drake, and others. Original narratives and drawings were included. Geoffrey Ashe [**145, 146**], Land to the West, 1962, and The Quest for America, 1971, were about pre-Columbian voyages such as that of St. Brendan, attributable to "an unknown author." Ashe traced the origins and noted a pre-Columbian site in Newfoundland. T.J. Oleson [**2694**], 1964, described the early voyages, 1000-1632, mythical and actual, for example, St. Brendan, Icelandic sagas, Madoc, the search for "Brasil," Cabot, and Frobisher. Frederick Pohl [**2875, 2876**], 1961 and 1974, described pre-Columbian voyages. The "Zeno documents," claims of early voyages, were reviewed. Roger Morris [**2557**], Atlantic Seafaring, 1992, covered ten centuries of exploration and trade and presented details of the techniques of sailing and navigation. An older classic was John Fiske [**1113**], Discovery of America, 1893. G.V. Scammell [**3233**], 1986, described English

ventures to the Atlantic islands, the Azores, Canaries, and others, 1450-1650.
Bristol had a special relationship and privateers found productive hunting. **See
7., E., 6.** James Williamson [**3897, 3900**], 1913 and 2 vols., 1922, reviewed the
history of British expansion, including armed trade and reprisals. The former
included a chapter on the role of the navy. I.A.A. Wright [**3962-3964**], 1929,
1932, and 1951, wrote about English voyages to the Spanish Caribbean in the
16th century, all publications of the Hakluyt Society. W.G. Perrin [**2824**], 1929,
described a voyage to the West Indies by Nathaniel Butler in the early 17th
century, a publication of the NRS.

And do not forget the Vikings. Kirsten Seaver [**3266**], The Frozen
Echo, 1996, was about Norse voyages, 1000-1500. The Norse established a
settlement in Greenland and Bristol merchants sustained it to the late 15th
century. Hjalmar Holand [**1652**], Norse Discoveries and Explorations in
America, 982-1362, 1940, described Norsemen sites and artifacts. William
Fitzhugh [**1120**], The Vikings: The North Atlantic Saga, 2000, was the
exhibition catalogue for an ambitious and popular exhibition, the National
Museum of Natural History of the Smithsonian Institution, Washington, opening
in April 2000; a millennium commemoration of the voyage of Leif Erikson.
Scandinavians had been upset over the exaggerated emphasis on the
"Discovery" celebrations, the quincentennial of the Columbus Encounter in
1992. One reason for this exhibition was to appease them. Penepole Johnstone
[**1822**], 1999, reported on celebrations in Newfoundland; new evidence of
discovery. In 1001, Vikings settled at a site, L'Anse aux Meadow.

William Goetzmann [**1308**], An Atlas of North American Exploration,
1998, lavishly illustrated, reviewed the voyages. Glyndwr Williams [**3875**],
1966, wrote of the expansion of Europe during the 18th century.

Now to review some of the myth-voyages. St. Brendan was an Irish
monk of the 6th century; the accounts coming from the 8th century. Paul
Chapman [**619**], The Man Who Led Columbus to America, 1973, was about the
legendary voyage of St. Brendan, concluding that it was possible but not proven.
Columbus had access to the account. John de Courcy Ireland [**1748**], 1989,
elaborated on sources of the St. Brendan voyage. As he has done to "prove"
sailing ventures, Tim Severin [**3282**], The Brendan Voyage, 1978, chronicled his
construction of a oxhide boat, the curragh, which he then sailed to the Hebrides,
Sheep Island, the Faroes, Iceland, and Greenland in the mid-1970s.

The myth-voyage of the Welsh Prince Madoc was even more tenuous.
Ellen Pugh [**2963**], Brave His Soul, 1970, speculated about Prince Madoc but
not convincingly.

Other accounts of the English to America in pre-Columbian times
included Geoffrey Marcus [**2366, 2365**], 1956 and 1980, recounting the first
English voyage to Iceland, first to fish and then to trade, a precursor to the
Cabots. In a broader study, Marcus speculated about the capabilities of these
early voyagers, for example, the Norse, Irish, and Bristol merchants. How and

where did they travel?: magnetic compass, dead reckoning, Faeroes, Iceland, Greeenland, and Vinland voyages.

Anthony McFarlane [**2247**], The British in the Americas, 1480-1815, 1992, was a synthesis of the literature. The first efforts were from Bristol in the 1480s in search of "Brasil." Kenneth Andrews [**117**], The Westward Enterprise, 1978, reviewed English activities, 1480-1650. These collected essays were in honor of David Quinn. David Birmingham [**325**], 2000, recounted a series of European ventures into the Atlantic, 1400-1600, including those of the Normans, English, and Dutch. In a dissertation, William Sewell [**3286**], 1971, described English contacts with North America, for example, Cabot, Frobisher, Drake, and John Davis. A similar work focused exclusively on the British: Peter Bradley [**419**], 1999. He elaborated on the expeditions, the sponsors, companies, boats, losses, and prizes. In a dissertation, Ruth McIntyre [**2273**], 1948, studied the role of merchants in promoting discovery and colonial enterprise, especially the financing. Franklin McCann [**2225**], 1952, described English discovery of America in 1585.

Myth was not a factor in the cases of John and Sebastian Cabot, but there were other problems. Peter Pope [**2916**], The Many Landfalls of John Cabot, 1997, described them at Newfoundland, Labrador, Cape Breton Island, Maine, and Belle Isle. Sebastian systematically misappropriated the legacy of his father. A quincentennial publication was by Manuel Gaibrois [**1222**], 1997, lamenting the lack of sources and information about John Cabot. Added to the problem were the alleged inflated claims of son, Sebastian. Brian Cuthbertson [**841**], 1997, was about John Cabot and his MATTHEW, a quincentennial occasion, lavishly produced. P.L. Firstbrook [**1102**], 1997, described "the voyage of the MATTHEW." Unfortunately, little evidence existed about the Cabots and the exaggerations of Sebastian have exacerbated the problem. That was discussed by G.P. Winship [**3919**], 1898. The Cabot-Bristol connection has received attention from all of the best academics: James Williamson [**3903, 3904, 3893**], 1929, 1937, and 1962; R.A. Skelton [**3336**], 1962, David Quinn [**2986**], Sebastian Cabot and Bristol Exploration, 1968, and Bryan Little [**2145**], 1983. Bernard Fardy [**1076**], John Cabot, 1994, described his discovery of Newfoundland in a popular account. A MATTHEW replica has revived interest. **See item e.**

John Dee was a fascinating figure. John Dee [**893**], 1991, described his library and manuscripts; the originals were at the Bodleian Library on 40 microfilm reels. Accounts were by Peter French [**1194**], John Dee: The Life of an Elizabethan Magus, 1972; Gerald Suster [**3520**], John Dee, 1986, noting that Dee was regarded as the most learned Englishman of his time, and Eva Taylor [**3575**], 1929, describing the role of Dee in the planning of the circumnavigation of Drake in the late 1570s. In dissertations, Deborah Harkness [**1515, 1514**], 1994, plus a book, 1999, and Robert Barone [**215**], 1989, evaluated the reputation of John Dee. Harkness stressed the occult aspect: Dee was a navigator, astronomer, astrologer, and alchemist who talked to the angels.

Less has come out about John Day. A.A. Ruddock [**3166**], 1966, studied John Day of Bristol who wrote of transatlantic voyages of the late 1490s.

Similarly, John Davis [**879**], 1992, reviewed the voyages of Gilbert, Frobisher, Dee, and his 3 voyages of the 1580s. Davis and Cavendish were linked.

Better known was Humphrey Gilbert. David Quinn [**2989**], 2 vols., 1940, a publication of the Hakluyt Society, described the colonization enterprises, for example, grandiose plans of 1576 and 1578; to Newfoundland in 1583. All degenerated into piracy close to home.

Better documented were the tragic exploits of Martin Frobisher. Thomas Symons [**3535**], "Meta Incognita, 2 vols., 1999, described the Arctic expeditions of Frobisher, 1576-1578. Glyn Williams characterized them as a semi-tragic, semi-comic fiasco. George Best [**311**], 1938, described the three voyages of Frobisher, searching for the Northwest Passage. James McDermott [**2235**], 2001, dubbed him "the Queen's privateer: "a hugely endearing rogue."
A nautical novelist, William McFee [**2248**], 1928, presented an account.

More expansive were the exploits of Thomas Cavendish, a series of voyages, including a circumnavigation, in the 1580s and 1590s. He hoped to open trade with the Philippines and China. David Quinn [**2981**], 1975, recounted the last voyage, 1591-1592. R.F. Hitchcock [**1640, 1641**], 1994 and 2001, questioned the role of John Davis in the last voyage. Cavendish accused him of deserting.

Best known to contemporary Americans was Henry Hudson. Donald Johnson [**1814**], 1993, reviewed the four voyages, 1607-1611. G.M. Asher [**147**], 1860, a publication of the Hakluyt Society, wrote about Henry Hudson. C.L.E. Ewen [**1064**], 1938, elaborated on the murder of Henry Hudson who had been set adrift by his crew. A replica of HALF MOON was built by the Dutch in 1909 and another in 1989. **See item e.** Hudson searched for the Northeast and the Northwest Passages. After a long, frustrating voyage, his crew set him adrift and returned home.

Last Voyages, 1988, by Philip Edwards [**1019**], presented original narratives of them for Cavendish, Hudson, and Raleigh, 1591-1618.

In a dissertation, I.R. Mather [**2465**], 1995, analyzed the role of the RN in the Atlantic imperial activities, 1660-1720. Duties and contributions included convoying merchantmen and providing security. The conclusion was that the RN provided a foundation for the expansion of empire.

I. THE NORTHWEST PASSAGE

An enduring quest was initiated to bypass the Spanish-Portuguese monopoly sanctioned by the Papacy in the late 15th century, to the northwest around the Americas or to the northeast around northern Asia. It began with John and Sebastian Cabot. Martin Frobisher tried in the late 16th century. Others were John Davis, Henry Hudson, and William Baffin. It was an enduringly popular story and peculiarly English/British.

Ann Savours [**3228**], <u>The Search for the North West Passage</u>, 1999, focused on British efforts from the late 16th century until success in the 20th century; in reality, "a chimera." Glyn Williams [**3872**], <u>The British Search for the Northwest Passage in the Eighteenth Century</u>, 1962, for the Royal Commonwealth Society, presented some background. In the 16th century, Robert Thorne, a Bristol merchant, urged action followed by 60 years of searching sponsored by the government, nobles, and merchants, for example, three voyages by Frobisher, Davis, Hudson, and then a pause. In a dissertation, Fulmer Mood [**2531**], studied the influence of Robert Thorne on English maritime expansion, 1527-1607. Edward Struzik [**3476**], <u>Northwest Passage</u>, 1991, was about the quest for a route to the East, many sponsored by the RN. Miller Graf [**1353**], <u>Arctic Journeys</u>, 1992, recounted the searches. Demonstrated were the saga, motivations, perseverance, illusion, and false hopes; unfortunately, no scholarly apparatus. Ernest Dodge [**946**], <u>Northwest by Sea</u>, 1961, featured a chronological survey beginning with John Cabot in 1497. James Delgado [**904**], <u>Across the Top of the World</u>, 1999, large folio size, profusely illustrated, was about the quest for the Northwest Passage.

In a dissertation and a trilogy, Barry Gough [**1342, 1341, 1337, 1340**], 1969, 1971, 1980, and 1992, concentrated on operations of the RN and events on the northwest coasts of North America: Drake, Anson, Cook, and Vancouver. William Barr [**216**], <u>Voyages to Hudson Bay in Search of a Northwest Passage, 1741-1747</u>, 2 vols., 1994-1995, a publication of the Hakluyt Society, described searches, mandated by Parliament and sponsored by the Northwest Committee. Pierre Berton [**307**], <u>The Arctic Grail</u>, 1988, was a catchy title about the search, concentrating on events of the 19th century.

J. EXPLORATION AND DISCOVERY: THE PACIFIC OCEAN

For European exploration and discovery, the Pacific Ocean was a formidable barrier, more exotic, more remote, and more enticing. It was "the East," "the Great South Sea," "<u>El Mar del Sur</u>," and the Spanish Lake, where the Acapulco-Manila treasure galleon made its annual transit. Drake, Dampier, and Anson were in hot pursuit. In practice, science and the scientific disciplines were all further advanced as a result of these voyages of exploration and discovery; and most of these were state-sponsored voyages; most English/British. They all exerted influence on philosophical thought. **See 17., D.-G.**

Glyndwr Williams [**3876, 3880**], <u>The Great South Sea</u>, 1997, brilliantly presented English voyages and encounters, 1570-1750, the story of a series of obsessions: glory, gold, adventure, and exotic peoples; the noble savage. From earliest times, the Cabots and Frobisher searched for "the East." That search influenced literature, for example, Hakluyt, Swift, Defoe, and Coleridge. In the

Caird Lecture at the NMM, 1996, Williams recounted officially-sponsored English voyages over 200 years, for example, Dampier, Cook, and Vancouver; Banks as the "guiding light."

Derek Howse [**1701**], Background to Discovery, 1990, reviewed Pacific exploration, the proceedings from seminars at UCLA, dedicated to J.H. Parry. Presentations were by Daniel Baugh, Glyn Williams, Howse, and N.A.M. Rodger, the last not published. Important points were made. The voyages stimulated literature, for example, Defoe and Swift. Beginning in the 1760s, the British resumed exploration previously abandoned by the Spanish and the Dutch. It was state sponsored, it was "protective maritime imperialism." The Cook voyages established salient features of the Pacific and answered most geographical questions. The scientists, Banks and Solander, added much to human knowledge. Unfortunately, no scientists were on the third voyage or on the Vancouver voyage, a step backward.

A precursor was Alexander Dalrymple [**845**], 1767, recounted his voyage, formative for hydrography, cartography, and imperialism. Dalrymple was a candidate to command the ENDEAVOUR expedition of Cook.

Roger Morris [**2559**], Pacific Sail, 1987, exquisitely illustrated by maritime artists, described the voyages of Western ships in the Pacific. Jonathan Lamb [**1990**], collected an anthology, Exploration and Exchange, 2000. Ernest Dodge [**945**], 1971, surveyed exploration of the Pacific.

David Miller [**2512**], Visions of Empire, 1996, proceedings from a conference on Banks, described how Europeans depicted the peoples and plants of the Pacific: how botany and natural history were shaped by imperial, political, and cultural frameworks. Cook and Banks contributed significantly, for example, Banks as "agent of empire." **See 17., E.** The great biographer of Cook, J.C. Beaglehole [**257, 254**], 1934, wrote a book and a pamphlet on science and the voyages: expansion of mathematics, chemistry, botany, zoology, physics, astronomy, geography, and physiology; advances in instruments: quadrant, sextant, and chronometer. The South Kensington branch of the British Museum included the Banksian Herbarium.

Diana Souhami [**3394**], 2001, and Ralph Woodward [**3958**], 1969, wrote of Alexander Selkirk and Juan Fernandez Islands west of southern South America. Selkirk was marooned there for four years and was the model for Robinson Crusoe by Daniel Defoe [**897**].

Peter Bradley [**420, 419**], The Lure of Peru, 1989 and 1993, recounted early interest in "the South Sea," the west coast of South America, especially the Potosi silver mines of Peru, Aztec treasure, and Inca craftsmanship. Buccaneers, Dutch, French, and English were attracted, for example, Drake and Cavendish. Robert King [**1938**], 1986, wrote of "ports of shelter and refreshment," the strategic naval dimension, 1786-1808. In the late 18th century, that was more important than penal colonies. Alex Calder [**542**], Voyages and Beaches, 1999, was about Pacific encounters, 1769-1840, the proceedings of a seminar, University of Auckland, 1993.

Rod Edmond [**1016**], <u>Representing the South Pacific</u>, 1997, elaborated on how the Pacific was represented by explorers, missionaries, travelers, writers, and artists. An example was the extensive descriptions of the peoples and nature of Tahiti, which influenced developments during the Enlightenment and Romanticism. The events of the mutiny on the BOUNTY, the open boat voyage by Bligh, the search for the mutineers, and their trials stimulated extraordinary interest and much myth. **See 8., B.**

David Mackay [**2285**], <u>In the Wake of Cook</u>, 1985, discussed the aftermath, for example, the fur trade, food for slaves, advances in science, and penal colonies. George Henderson [**1596**], <u>The Discovery of the Fiji Islands</u>, 1933, was about explorers, for example, Tasman, Cook, and Bligh. Frank Horner [**1670**], <u>Looking for La Perouse</u>, 1995, was about a French effort but with British implications. A French explorer, Jean La Perouse, led a 2-ship exploration voyage in the late 1780s and disappeared. The French conducted a massive search mission, exploring at the same time. Bligh was in the area at the time. The French mission was later arrested and taken to England where Captain Rossel remained at the Hydrographic Office. Catherine Gaziello [**1263**], 1984, elaborated.

K. THE SCIENCE OF NAVIGATION

Haven-finding art was how the great authority, Eva Taylor [**3573**], called it. It had to do with the elements of open sea voyages: sun, stars, winds, tides, currents, and sea patterns. Instruments to measure them were developed and refined. Astronomy and mathematics facilitated advances. In England, it was Trinity House, Gresham College, and the chartered trading companies, which fostered the scientific applications to navigation. Nautical science related to the development of navigation. "Geography" was broadly defined, encompassing "navigation," nautical theory, voyaging, and surveying. Richard Hakluyt, the younger, was the self-proclaimed propagandist for expansion of exploration and trade. Formative was the voyage of John Dee [**893**] in 1583 associated with the Tudor initiatives for trade and discovery; the consultant was Richard Hakluyt [**1450**]; the first printing of <u>Principal Voyages</u> was 1589. **See 7., G., 2.**

J.E.D. Williams [**3881**], 1992, traced the origin and development of navigational science. Dead reckoning was first, then instruments such as the astrolabe, sextants, and cross-staffs followed. Derek Howse [**1704**], <u>Five Hundred Years of Nautical Science, 1400-1900</u>, 1981, sponsored by the NMM, was the proceedings of the 3rd annual conference for the history of nautical science and hydrography. Two of the four categories were navigation and hydrography and wooden ships and sailing.

Eva Taylor [**3573, 3577, 3674**], Grand Dame of the history of navigation, wrote <u>The Haven-Finding Art</u>, 1956, about these matters: open sea voyages and the natural elements to be measured and exploited. Astronomy and mathematics facilitated advances. In England, it was Trinity House, Gresham College, and the chartered trading companies, which fostered the scientific applications to navigation. There were two works, 1930 and 1934, on geography in the 16th and 17th centuries. Geography was broadly defined: voyages, maps, and navigation. Her work featured analyses of geographical thought and nautical theory.

David Waters [**3780**], The Art of Navigation in England in Elizabethan and Early Stuart Times, 1958, presented a brilliant survey of the technical contributions of the English, ticking off the great navigators, Hawkins, Drake, Hudson, and Baffin, and describing a series of navigational aids, all profusely illustrated. W.G.L. Randles [**3005**], Geography, Cartography and Nautical Science in the Renaissance, 2000, was a collection of his papers, some in French, focusing on the great discoveries and how they transformed the world. The ubiquitous W.E. May [**2477**], 1973, reviewed the history of marine navigation. Joseph Hewson [**1616**], 1951, wrote the history of the practice of navigation.

An inferior effort was Duane Cline [**660**], Navigation in the Age of Discovery, 1990, focusing on the 17th century and touting the MAYFLOWER voyage as the model. History of Seamanship, 1971, by Douglas Phillips-Birt [**2851**], was the title but the subject matter included sailing, navigation, instruments, chronometer, and mechanical advances. Lawrence Wroth [**3971**], The Way of the Ship, 1937, surveyed the literature of navigational science, based on the holdings of the John Carter Brown Library and supporting an exhibition.

Some, but not all, credit a Portuguese prince for launching modern advances in the science of navigation: Prince Henry the Navigator, actually the great-grandson of Edward III and first cousin to Henry V. A recent biography, 2000, was by Peter Russell [**3180**], a revisionist interpretation not sympathetic: his interests in Portuguese expansion were limited and his personal expertise in navigation was nil. An earlier effort was C.R. Beazley [**264**], 1901, the traditional interpretation, overdrawn and exaggerated. R.A. Skelton [**3340**], 1960, produced the catalogue of an exhibition at the British Museum, September 1960, the quincentennial of the death of Prince Henry. Featured were 326 items demonstrating feats of Portuguese nautical science and cartography.

Accounts of earlier efforts included, in a dissertation and an article, Geoffrey Marcus [**2370, 2369**], 1955 and 1953, reviewed ocean-going navigation of the Norsemen; Sean McGrail [**2258**], 1983, described cross-Channel navigation about 1000 AD, and G.V. Scammell [**3234**], 1982, credited advances, 1400-1600, with the founding of the first global maritime empires.

The next period, 1650-1900, was the focus of Margaret Deacon [**889**], Scientists and the Sea, 1971, about oceanography. In a dissertation, Stephen Beaumont [**263**], 1971, linked navigational advances to the scientific revolution.

He concluded that progress in theory exceeded advances in instrumentation, for example, the problem of longitude. **See 17., M.**

Development of the compass facilitated the process. Frederic Lane [**2017**], 1963, wrote of the development of the compass and its impact, for example, more voyages could be made throughout the year. Amir Aczel [**9**], The Riddle of the Compass, 2001, touted it as "the invention that changed the world," but with some questionable assertions, for example, ignoring that the compass was a Chinese invention. A.E. Fanning [**1074**], 1986, traced the history of the Compass Department of the Admiralty, "Steady as She Goes." The decade of the 1790s saw important advances. John Harland [**1516**], 1984, reviewed shiphandling and seamanship.

Another example of the Scottish Enlightenment was presented by David Gavine [**1262**], 1990. Astronomy and mathematics were basic parts of education in Scotland, leading to advances in navigation. **See 10., E.**

L. TRINITY HOUSE

Navigation, navigational aids, coastal and estuary sailing, and pilotage were the responsibilities of a formative agency in use of the sea for the English/British. The initial responsibilities applied to various ports around the British Isles; responsibilities such as buoyage and beaconage, light houses, dredging channels, and facilitating the pilot service. For London, it was at Deptford, for navigation of the Thames; others arose at Hull, Exeter, and Plymouth.

G.G. Harris [**1527**], 1969, and Alwyn Ruddock [**3167**], 1950, wrote of the Trinity House at Deptford in the 16th century, a medieval guild, designated as a corporation with members as Masters, Elder Bretheren, and Younger Bretheren: "the cradle of the RN." There were other Trinity Houses at other ports. Prominent members have been Samuel Pepys and Winston Churchill. Other accounts were Hilary Mead [**2487**], Trinity House, 1947, and Richard Woodman [**3949**], Keepers of the Sea, 1983. F.W. Brooks [**457**], 1942, printed the First Order Book of the Hull Trinity House. Ian Cameron [**563**], 2002, commended the Royal National Lifeboat Institution for 175 years of service.

M. TIME AND THE SEARCH FOR LONGITUDE

The desperate need for solution, the agonizing slowness, "political" complications, and the perseverance of one man told the fascinating story of time and the search for longitude. At sea, with the proper instruments, latitude can be easily determined. On land, latitude and longitude can be easily determined. However, at sea, determination of longitude was complicated, seemingly impossible. Some claimed a solution after tortuous calculation processes. What was needed was a solution to the problem of accurate time, an accurate clock, or, at least, a clock which could compare its time to Greenwich Mean Time.

Deserved publication recognition should include Longitude, 1995, by Dava Sobel [**3386, 3385**], a major best seller. It helped popularize the complicated story of the process. The subtitle was informative: The True Story of a Lone Genius Who Solved the Greatest Scientific Problem of His Time. John Harrison and the timekeeper he invented, called "H-4," solved the problem of determining longitude at sea. The impetus was the smashing of an entire squadron of ships of the RN on the rocks of the Scilly Isles in 1707 with loss of four ships and 2000 lives due to an error in navigation. In 1714, Parliament passed the Longitude Act, offering an incentive reward of 20,000 pounds. Ms. Sobel, who was inspired to write after participation in a navigation colloquium at Harvard University [**102**], has also published Illustrated Longitude, 1998.

That very Longitude Symposium, Harvard University, November 1993, the tricentennial of the birth of John Harrison, was reported by William Andrewes [**102**], The Quest for Longitude, 1996. Included were four papers on Harrison plus 14 other papers. William Laycock [**2084**], The Lost Science of John "Longitude" Harrison, 1976, commemorating the bicentennial of his death, featured a detailed description of the mechanism of the chronometer, especially the gears. Humphrey Quill [**2972**], John Harrison, 1966, wrote of "the man who found longitude." A short biography of Harrison, 1993, was by Jonathan Betts [**313**].

Eric Forbes [**1134**], 1974, wrote a short piece, linking the solution to the longitude problem to the birth of scientific navigation. Derek Howse [**1706, 1703**], Greenwich Time and the Discovery of the Longitude, 1980, sponsored by the NMM, presented a broader view, for example, describing other clockmaker-contributors and documenting previous offers of a prize to solve the problem, for example, by Philip II in 1567 and Philip III in 1598. Howse also wrote Clocks and Watches, 1969.

Carlo Cipolla [**639**], Clocks and Culture, 1967, was a survey, 1300-1700. Rupert Gould [**1347, 1346**], The Marine Chronometer, 1923, traced its history and development. Gould wrote about "Harrison and his Timekeepers," 1935. Cook took one Harrison chronometer on a 3-year voyage and Bligh had a modified version on his open-boat voyage. Raymond Ashley [**149**], 1991, wrote about the search for longitude, again, state-supported research. The solution was the chronometer, the key being mathematical precision.

Particularly fascinating was the work of the distinguished Italian novelist, Umberto Eco [**1012**], The Island of the Day Before, 1995, depicting Roberto on DAPHNE in 1643. Longitude was the key factor, all dealt with in brilliant fashion. Critics have compared it to Gulliver's Travels and Candide.

All four of the Harrison chronometers have been restored and have been displayed in the Time Gallery, at the NMM. From December 1999-September 2000, the NMM sponsored an exhibition, "The Story of Time," housed in the Queen's House, designed by Indigo Jones. Kristen Lippincott [2141], The Story of Time, 1999, was the catalogue, lavish, elegant, beautiful, and profusely illustrated. Umberto Eco wrote the preface.

N. THE WEATHER

The effects of the weather and meteorological factors during the age of sail were more direct and potentially devastating than later for the age of steam. Sources for these long term studies were systematic and recorded weather observations, logs of ships, and diaries and journals. The products were "synoptic reconstruction" maps for particular times.

Hubert Lamb [1989], 1991, for the Danish Meteorological Institute, studied historic storms across northern Europe, 1509-1990, a total of 166 being analyzed, 11 in the 16th century. Among the worst was the "Armada" gales of August-September 1588.

K.S. Douglas [954, 955], 1978 and 1979, conducted a fascinating study of weather observations during the summer and fall of 1588 around the British Isles, sponsored by the University of East Anglia Climate Research Unit. This was facilitated by records of systematic weather observations by Tycho Brahe at his laboratory, Uranienborg, between Denmark and Sweden. On 8 August, a dramatic shift in the wind saved the Armada ships from running ashore off Zeeland; then, about 20 September a great Atlantic gale drove ships ashore in northern Scotland and western Ireland. John Christianson [632], 2000, made a study of "Tycho's Island," details about his "observatory" and collection of data, 1570-1601.

J. Holland Rose [3142], 1936, asked whether weather caused the failure of the Armada? Previously, "Protestant wind" had been credited. Rose answered "no." He counted five times when wind actually aided the Spanish, for example, off Plymouth and off Zeeland. See 7., F., 4. and 6.

John Tyrrell [3681], 1996, analyzed the weather around Ireland in December 1796, when France tried to invade at Bantry Bay, using "synoptic reconstruction." Yes, the weather drove the French away, but it also denied the British from attempting battle. Dennis Wheeler [3825], 1991, analyzed weather the next year, 1797. A mutiny had disrupted blockade operations by Admiral Duncan. Then on 10 October, he feared changes might favor the Dutch, so he hurried into battle, successfully.

O. GREENWICH

The current arrangement combined three features: the Royal Observatory atop the hill of Greenwich Park, the NMM, including the exquisite Queen's House, and the old Greenwich Palace, designed by Christopher Wren, formerly a royal palace, the naval pensioners' hospital, and the Royal Naval College, and now, among other things, home of the University of Greenwich.

Eric Forbes [1134], Greenwich Observatory, 3 vols., 1975, on the occasion of the tricentennial, presented an extensive history. The roles of the Astronomers Royal, for example, Flamsteed, Halley, Bradley, and Maskelyne, were featured.

Clive Aslet [151, 150], The Story of Greenwich, 1999, wrote the history, opening with an account of the funeral of Nelson. The official ceremonies began with Nelson lying in state in the Painted Hall beginning on Christmas Day, 1805. Derek Howse [1707, 1705], 1973 and 1975, published a guide to the old Royal Observatory and linked Francis Place to its early history. Christopher Lloyd [2156], 1969, traced the development of related features: a palace to hospital to college. Richard Ollard [2697], 1955, focused on the Royal Naval Hospital.

T.D. Bridge [437], 1996, surveyed the past statuses and history. In 1415, the Duke of Gloucester was awarded 200 acres by Henry V. Henry VIII was born in the old Palace of Placentia and Drake was knighted there. In 1884, the International Meridian Conference, Washington, DC, searched for a universal reference point to measure longitude and time. Paris made a bid, but Greenwich was selected. Greenwich Mean Time was officially established. Other features were the Zero Meridian or prime meridian, time signals, and the time ball. A recent guide was Iris Bryce [497], Remember Greenwich, 1995.

P. THE ASTRONOMER ROYAL

Functioning from the Royal Observatory, Greenwich was the Astronomer Royal, early ones being John Flamsteed and Edmond Halley.

Francis Willmoth [3906], Flamsteed's Stars, 1997, reported proceedings of a conference at the NMM, Greenwich, 1995, "Flamsteed at Greenwich." Flamsteed set the standard for 300 years. Alan Cook [728], 1998, produced a good biography of Edmond Halley. Halley had encouraged Isaac Newton to publish Principia and was a friend to Pepys. Halley published the first meteorological chart of trade winds and general patterns of the prevailing winds worldwide. Norman Thrower [3615], 1980, recounted scientific voyages led by Halley during the late 1690s, a publication of the Hakluyt Society.

Derek Howse [1709], Nevil Maskelyne, 1989, was the 5th Astronomer Royal, 46 years of the late 18th and early 19th centuries. He insisted on the lunar-distance method of obtaining longitude. It was favored because expensive and bulky chronometers could not be obtained by most ships. This led to some "political" disputes involving John Harrison and his chronometers. See 17., M.

Q. HYDROGRAPHY

The British Hydrographic Office was established in 1795. Later, Francis Beaufort was deemed "father of British hydrography." It had to do with the development of surveys for charts, sailing directions, "rutters of the sea," "waggoners," and many other publications and guides to aid in navigation; in the 20th century, called Admiralty Pilots.

Archibald Day [887], The Admiralty Hydrographic Service, 1967, traced developments from 1795 and described hydrographic surveys. John Edgell [1015], Sea Surveys, 1965, sponsored by the NMM, was about the contributions of Britain to Hydrography. Nothing has equaled them. And all of it was immediately made available to seamen throughout the world.

Alexander Dalrymple [845] was an early hydrographer with formative influence; described in a dissertation and book by Howard Fry [1208, 1209], 1967 and 1970. Alfred Friendly [1200], Beaufort of the Admiralty, 1977, was the definitive biography of Francis Beaufort, Hydrographer of the Navy during the early 19th century, responsible for the Beaufort Scale and exploration of the Arctic, including searching for the Northwest Passage. **See 17., I.** He appointed Charles Darwin as naturalist.

In a dissertation by Robert Brown [474], 1972, and a book by Edmond Burrows [521], 1979, were descriptions of the accomplishments of W.F.W. Owen, a productive Hydrographer who focused on surveys of the African coast. Admiralty Hydrography was elaborated upon by Mary Blewitt [349], 1957, and Trevor Blore [357], 1962.

David Waters [3784, 3783], 1967 and 1989, wrote about sailing directions, variously called "waggoners," "rutters of the sea," and the English Pilot. A.B. Taylor [3569], 1980, wrote about Scottish Rutters, which were achieved with assistance from the French.

Albert Loomie [2186], 1963, wrote about Spanish coastal surveys to aid the pilots during the Armada campaign, for example, of Falmouth, Dartmouth, Torbay, Poole, the Isle of Wight, and Portsmouth.

R.A. Skelton [3339], 1955, featured charts and views drawn during the Cook voyages, a publication of the Hakluyt Society.

R. CARTOGRAPHY

The origins were Chinese; for Europe, the Spanish were the best at first, later, the Dutch. Salient dates were as follows:

1490 – first sailing directions, from Italy

1528 – first English sailing directions

1539 – first English chart

1564 – first Mercator chart

1588 – first "Mariner's Mirror," Zuider Zee to Gibraltar

1671 – English Pilot
1714 – Longitude Act

The standard history is still in progress, a monumental project: J.B. Harley [**1518, 1519**], The History of Cartography, ___ vols., 1987-___, projected to be 6 vols., at least 8 books. The scope was global. Harley elaborated in a book, 2001. Leo Bagrow [**172**], 1951, wrote a history of cartography, much praised.

Jerry Brotton [**466**], 1997, credited the Portuguese and the Ottoman Empire with formative advances in the 15th century. Robert Baldwin [**182**], 1997, saw the period 1440-1640 as decisive in the expansion of Europe.

The prolific Jeremy Black [**334, 335**] has two recent contributions, Maps and History, 1997, and Maps and Politics, 1997, describing historical atlases and political links, for example, stressing the subjectivity of maps and that Mercator projected Eurocentric perceptions: more recent applications: exaggeration of the size of the Soviet Union as a tool of Cold War advocates.

Arthur Robinson [**3088**], Marine Cartography in Britain, 1961, noted Hakluyt initiated a call for improved charts and maps; later Pepys lamented the gaps. Surveying techniques and operations were described. Peter Whitfield [**3847**], 1998, was about maps in the history of exploration, illustrated with holdings from the British Library. A.N. Porter [**2919**], The Atlas of British Overseas Expansion, 1991, reproduced 140 maps, for example, those of John Cabot, Frobisher, Raleigh, Cook, and Livingston. Jules Sottas [**3393**], 1912, elaborated on an atlas used by Drake, now in a French archive. Lesley Cormack [**770**], 1997, described the contributions of English universities in charting the empire; geography classes encouraged students to view their country in a global context.

George Ritchie [**3071**], The Admiralty Chart, 1967, stressed surveys of the 19th century, a follow-on of those of Cook. Very important in many respects was the early decision to share the products, the charts, with the world. They early gained the reputation for accuracy and trustworthiness. Safe navigation for all was the goal. Roger Morris [**2561**], 1996, recalled 200 years of the Admiralty charts and surveys. Some examples of these Admiralty surveys for charts included Herbert Beals [**259**], The Last Temperate Coast, 1991, concerning exploration of northwest America, accounts of 13 surveys; Jill Kinahan [**1931**], By Command of Their Lordships, 1992, about surveys of the Namibian coast, 1795-1895, and William Huddart [**1713**], 1990, about his ancestor, Joseph Huddart, conductor of important surveys, 1777-1808. He was a Fellow of Trinity House and was elected to the Royal Society.

Derek Howse [**1710, 1708, 1702**], The Sea Chart and Handlist of Manuscript Sea Charts and Pilot Books, 1973, based his surveys on the collection at the NMM. A separate book, 1991, told the story of English buccaneers who obtained secret Spanish charts in 1681. These assisted later explorers of the Pacific.

Best known, perhaps, most notorious, of map controversies has been the ongoing saga of the Vinland Map, originally purchased for $300,000 by Mellon from an anonymous seller and contributed to Yale University. Its history before 1957 was unknown.

The map was dated 1440 and was touted as the earliest depiction of North America. R.A. Skelton [**3341**], The Vinland Map and the Tartar Relation, 1965, first published the map and concluded that it was authentic. Whether Columbus knew of it was another matter. S.E. Morison [**2551**] had serious reservations about its authenticity. In 1965, Yale University announced that its Vinland Map might be a fake. Wilcomb Washburn [**3779**], 1971, reported the proceedings of a conference, Smithsonian Institution, 1966, published by the Newberry Library and dedicated to Skelton who had just died in an auto accident. Michael Richey [**3054**], 2000, elaborated on the role of Eva Taylor who consistently insisted on forgery. Geoffrey Gathorne-Hardy [**1259**], 1921, wrote earlier on "the Vinland sagas."

S. GEORGE VANCOUVER AND MATTHEW FLINDERS

George Vancouver was a protégé of Cook and British explorer of the Pacific Ocean, especially the coasts of North America. The origins of Vancouver were obscure, probably born in 1758, entering the Royal Navy at age 13. He was a young officer on the second and the third of the famous voyages of Cook. He was in the West Indies squadron of Admiral George Rodney at the battle of the Saints in 1782. Vancouver had a reputation as rigid disciplinarian. An incident involving flogging three times of young Lord Camelford created a sensation. Vancouver died at Petersham in 1798. The Camelford affair had tarnished his reputation and ruined his career.

George Vancouver [**3718**], A Voyage of Discovery to the North Pacific and Round the World, 1791-1795, 4 vols., 1984, a publication of the Hakluyt Society, was his account. An older biography, 1931, was by George Godwin [**1307**]. Brenda Gillespie [**1286**], 1992, wrote about "the triumphs and torments" of Vancouver in a curious format, "creative non-fiction" with no scholarly apparatus. His early life and development of his career were featured by E.C. Coleman [**700**], 2001.

Other accounts about Vancouver included Bern Anderson [**67**], Surveyor of the Sea: The Life and Voyages of Captain George Vancouver, 1960, and John Naish [**2595**], 1994, writing of the achievements of Vancouver. Roderick Haig-Brown [**1444**], 1956, wrote a popular biography.

Robin Fisher [**1110**], Vancouver's Voyage: Charting the Northwest Coast, 1791-1795, 1992, was proceedings of a conference on exploration and discovery, Simon Fraser University, April 1992, a bicentennial occasion. The voyage contributed much to hydrography.

John Naish [**2596**], 1996, wrote a collective biography of Vancouver, Joseph Whidbey, and Peter Puget, all explorers of the Pacific northwest coast during an expedition in the early 1790s.

Matthew Flinders was a protégé of Joseph Banks, serving with Bligh on his second voyage. Flinders commanded INVESTIGATOR and set off in July 1801, charting the southern and eastern coasts of Australia.

Geoffrey Ingleton [**1743**], Matthew Flinders, 1986, described him as "navigator and chartmaker." James Mack [**2275**], 1966, was an excellent biography. Ernestine Hill [**1629**], My Love Must Wait, 1941, was a fictional version of the life of Flinders. Magde Darby [**856**], 2000, reproduced the journal of Flinders during the voyage of HMS PROVIDENCE, 1791-1793, the second breadfruit voyage of Bligh; Geoffrey Rawson [**3026**], 1946, another journal of the voyage of HMS FRANCIS, 1798.

Anthony Brown [**468**], 2001, wrote on two pioneers of Pacific exploration, Flinders and Nicholas Baudin, "ill-starred captains."

T. JOHN BARROW

British Admiralty Secretary and promoter of Arctic exploration, born in 1746 in Ulverston in the Lake District, dying in London in 1848, Barrow was a noted and long time civil servant. Early in his career, he participated in diplomatic and cartographic missions to China and to southern Africa, remaining a noted expert on these areas. For over 40 years, until 1845, he served as Secretary of the Admiralty, now depicted in the tradition of Samuel Pepys and Sir Joseph Banks. He sponsored searches for the Northwest Passage and Arctic exploration, for example, of Parry, Ross, and Franklin. He was a founder of the Royal Geographical Society and served fifty years in the Royal Society. In Arctic regions, Point Barrow, Cape Barrow, and the Barrow Straits were all named for him.

John Barrow [**219, 222, 223**] chronicled an expedition into the Arctic region. His best known writing [**220**], still in print, was the authoritative account of the mutiny on HMS "BOUNTY." Barrow wrote biographical studies of Lord Anson, Lord Howe, and Tsar Peter the Great and almost 200 articles, anonymous at the time, for The Quarterly Review.

Christopher Lloyd [**2161**], Mr. Barrow of the Admiralty: The Life of Sir John Barrow, 1764-1848, 1970, was the standard biography. Fergus Fleming [**1124**], Barrow's Boys, 1998, described the regime of Barrow at the Admiralty, literally sending naval expeditions to the ends of the earth. Barrow was a protégé of Joseph Banks at the Royal Society.

U. CHARLES DARWIN AND THE BEAGLE

Another of the famous scientific voyages sponsored by the state and overseen by the Admiralty, was the voyage of HMS BEAGLE, 1831-1836, admittedly after the period of this book but included because it was the culmination of the series of voyages sponsored by the state with the purpose of advancement of science, a hydrographic expedition. The naturalist on that voyage was Charles Darwin. Darwin and Robert Fitzroy, the captain of BEAGLE, met in 1831.

Alan Moorehead [2536], Darwin and the BEAGLE, 1969, recounted the famous voyage. HMS BEAGLE, 1997, in The Anatomy of the Ship series, was by Karl Marquardt [2396]. HMS BEAGLE, 1995, was by Keith Thomson [3608] and touted as "biography of a ship." Other accounts were by Lois Darling [860], 1984, on HMS BEAGLE and Fitzroy of the BEAGLE, 1968, by Harold Mellersh [2490]. Robert Fitzroy was commanding officer during the 1830s and was a weather expert. It was his idea to take a naturalist.

Richard Keynes [1925, 1927, 1926], two 1979 and 1988, wrote about Darwin and the BEAGLE, including reproductions of original drawings during the voyage and reproduction of the diary of Darwin. Not satisfactory was Richard Marks [2386], Three Men of the BEAGLE, 1991. Marsden Horden [1668], 1989, reviewed the 3rd voyage of BEAGLE, 1837-1843.

V. AUSTRALIA AND NEW ZEALAND

The search for Terra Australis Incognita took several centuries. It was the mysterious "southern continent" searched for by Cook and others. An ongoing debate has concerned the rationale or rationales for British initiatives in the 1750s and 1760s. What were the priorities?: relief for the penal system, establishment of a strategic naval base system, territorial expansion, prevention of potential enemies for territorial expansion, scientific advancement, for example, measuring the transit of Venus, source for key naval stores, to replace America, the lost colony, reasons of hydrography, and reasons of cartography. The Royal Society favored the science-transit rationale and the Admiralty seemed to agree. But, there must have been more to it than that.

William Eisler [1027], The Furtherest Shore, 1995, recounted the history of images of Australia from the middle ages, from England, the Dutch, and Spain. Simon Ryan [3198], 1996, reviewed how explorers depicted Australia. It was a critique of the methodology of exploration through textual analysis. It was "the antipodes in the European imagination."

Glyndwr Williams [3879], "Terra Australis" to Australia, 1988, traced the discovery through cartographical depictions, 145 plates illustrating the development: the Dieppe Map, Java la Grande, Portuguese, French, English, and Dutch navigators. Thomas Perry [2831], The Discovery of Australia, 1982, reproduced a series of maps and charts of navigators and explorers. Gunter Schilder [**3243**], Australia Unveiled, 1975, recounted the activities of Dutch navigators, 1606-1644. Lawrence Fitzgerald [**1118**] "Java la Grande": The Portuguese Discovery of Australia, 1984, described the discovery in 1521. The territory was depicted in a 16th century map, the Dieppe Map. Was it speculation, a hoax, or fantasy? Kenneth McIntyre [**2272**], The Secret Discovery of Australia, 1977, was about Portuguese ventures. Helen Wallis [**3743**], "Did the Portuguese Discover Australia?", 1988, noted that maps of the 16th century depicted what became Australia. Trevor Jacobs [**1771**], Southland: The Maritime Exploration of Australia, 1988, recounted exploration by Portugal, the Dutch, France, and Britain. Andrew Sharp [**3293**], The Discovery of Australia, 1963, confirmed that it was a slow process and remained controversial.

John Bach [**165**], The Maritime History of Australia, 1976, covered up to 1975. Australia was a creature of maritime enterprise, at least to Europeans, an extension of British sea power. An earlier account was Gerold Wood [**3930**], The Discovery of Australia, 1922, a standard for decades. Ged Martin [**2432**], The Founding of Australia, 1978, reviewed the series of rationales for the original settlement: penal colony, naval station, trading base, and a source of flax and naval timber. Alan Atkinson [**155**], 1997, was the first of a projected trilogy about Europeans in Australia, this about the first three decades. In the early 1970s, as a memorial to J.C. Beaglehole, a New Zealander, the New Zealand Historical Places Trust sponsored erection of markers at Cook sites around the coast.

W. CONVICT VOYAGES AND PENAL COLONIES

Australia was seen by the authorities first and foremost as another penal colony and plans were immediately put into effect to transport convicts there on a large scale, the so-called First Fleet and Second Fleet. The First Fleet arrived at Botany Bay, 18 January 1788, now a southern suburb of Sydney. They soon moved to Fort Jackson, a few miles to the north. The first governor was Arthur Phillip of New South Wales. He saw the convicts as servants of the state and enforced rigid discipline and hard labor. A later governor was William Bligh. There was a rebellion in 1808 that drove Bligh away. **See 8., B.**

A.G.L. Shaw [**3294**], Convicts and the Colonies, 1966, and Robert Hughes [**1719**], The Fatal Shore, 1986, were histories of the transportation of convicts to Australia, 1787-1868. In 1775, America refused to accept any more; the prison hulks were filled. Roger Ekirch [**1029**] confirmed this: Bound for America, 1987, about transportation to the American colonies, 1718-1775. A decision was made to set up penal colonies: New South Wales, Norfolk Island, Van Diemen's Land, and Moreton Bay. A total of 160,000 were transported.

Victor Crittenden [**805**], 1981, and Jonathan King [**1937**], 1983, described the voyage of the First Fleet, 1787-1788, which founded Australia.

Stops along the way were Teneriffe, Rio, Capetown, through the Indian Ocean, and to Botany Bay. There were 11 ships carrying a total of 1300 persons. Alan Frost [**1203, 1201, 1202**], Convicts and Empire, 1980, and Arthur Phillip, 1987, summarized the history of the colony and presented a biography of its first governor. Frost insisted that imperial and naval logistical reasons were uppermost; a penal colony was secondary. Frost was preparing a history of British maritime expansion in the Indian and Pacific Oceans, 2002. Paul Carter [**587**], The Road to Botany Bay, 1987, described the founding of the colony. Watkin Tench [**3588**], 1979, reported on the first four years of the new colony, eventually, Sydney. Norval Morris [**2556**], 2001, described Alexander Maconochie, a captain of the RN, who developed the penal colony on Norfolk Island, part of the subtitle being . . . the Roots of Modern Prison Reform.

John Cobley [**681, 682**], 1965 and 1970, conducted a statistical study of the crimes and the convicts, 1788-1792. Of the 778 convicts in the First Fleet, most were habitual offenders; not one political prisoner. No information accompanied them as to the length of sentence. Other accounts were L.L. Robson [**3099**], The Convict Settlers of Australia, 1965, and Charles Bateson [**233**], The Convict Ships, 1787-1868, 1959. The ships were inspected, certified, and contracted by the Admiralty. The voyage was 13,000 miles and required 6 months in sailing ships; a total of 163,000 men and women prisoners were transported; 122,620 men and 24,960 women, plus other felons. A voyage-by-voyage account with details, for example, disease, floggings, murders, mutinies, and shipwrecks, was included. In a dissertation, W. Oldham [**2693**], 1933, described the administration of the system of transportation of British convicts, 1763-1793. John Moore [**2534**], The First Fleet Marines, 1987, was about the military to protect the colony.

Individual recollections included Suzanne Rickard [**3067**], 2001, an edition of a diary of George Barrington, a notorious thief and settler of New South Wales; Colleen McCullough [**2232**], Morgan's Run, 2000, a fictionalized, romanticized account of an actual First Fleet convict, Richard Morgan, sequels being promised, and M.D. Nash [**2598**], The Last Voyage of the GUARDIAN, 1989, was the journal of Edward Riou. This latter one was the story of a disaster. GUARDIAN, 44-gun frigate on her maiden voyage, was the first supply ship sent out to New South Wales, 1789-1791, with food and provisions for the next two years. She never arrived, causing a crisis and starvation. This was the story of why she did not arrive: she got past Capetown and hit an iceberg. Some launches abandoned the ship; Riou and 60 crew-convicts stayed and sailed back to Capetown for repairs. In a sensationalized, speculative account, Sian Rees [**3042**], The Floating Brothel, 2001, recounted the voyage of LADY JULIANA, with 237 female convicts, to New South Wales.

Chapter 18

Nautical Archaeology

Variously described as nautical archaeology, underwater archaeology, and maritime archaeology and called "the last great frontier on earth," nautical archaeology was a relatively new discipline much stimulated by a series of spectacular achievements from exploration expeditions during the last three decades. As with any scholarly and scientific discipline, sophisticated and highly technical processes and approaches were involved. Inevitably, purposeful associations, professional journals, and academic institutions have emerged. Diving clubs provided personnel for the expeditions. Leaders have included Colin Martin, Peter Marsden, Robert Stenuit, Margaret Rule, and Robert Ballard. Sources other than archaeological "digs" and nautical archaeological expeditions come from iconography, images of ships and ship types from illuminated manuscripts, stone and woodcarvings such as on church or cathedral pews and facades, fine metallic work, seals, coins, and graffiti.

What has dramatically stimulated the discipline since the 1980s was the search, discovery, and consequent publicity of the TITANIC, sunk off Newfoundland in a disaster of monumental proportions in 1912. The movie made about TITANIC added to the interest.

Three early cases were formative, if less spectacular to the public. VASA was a 1200-ton Swedish warship just completed when she sank in Stockholm harbor in 1628. She was raised in 1961 and was displayed in a purpose-built museum. Second was a find of archaeology, in this case, excavation of a land site containing a ship burial. SUTTON HOO was discovered in 1939 on an estate near Woodbridge in Suffolk, in 1993 presented to the National Trust. The conclusion of Rupert Bruce-Mitford [**483, 484**] of the British Museum was that the "burial," there was no body, was for Raedwald, King of East Anglia who died about 625 AD. Artifacts of extraordinary quality and beauty were and are on permanent display in the British Museum. The third was MARY ROSE, a four-masted carrack, 600 tons, built in 1509 at the new shipbuilding facility at Portsmouth, flagship of the Navy Royal of King Henry

VIII. She capsized and sank while the King was observing in the Solent outside Portsmouth harbor in July 1545. Discovered in the 1960s, a long, expensive, technical process encouraged and sponsored by Charles, Prince of Wales, to raise the ship concluded successfully in October 1982. Again, thousands of artifacts were displayed in a purpose-built museum. The ship remains were on display behind continuously spraying water at the Portsmouth Naval Base directly next to HMS VICTORY.

Examples of other finds included wrecks of the Spanish Armada from 1588 off the northern and western coasts of Scotland and Ireland; GRIFFIN, an East Indiaman built on the Thames in 1748, sunk off the Philippine Islands in 1761; HMS BOUNTY of mutiny fame; USS MONITOR, off the coast of the Outer Banks, North Carolina; the Confederate submarine H.L. HUNLEY, sunk in February 1864 and raised from Charleston Harbor in August 2000, to be displayed after several years of restoration paid for by Friends of the HUNLEY; several notorious pirate ship wrecks from Madagascar to Cape Cod, including the ships of Blackbeard and Captain Kidd, and two underwater sea ports of former historic importance which have been the objects of study, Dunwich, Suffolk and Port Royal, Jamaica.

Informative, even startling, findings and conclusions have been revealed. Examples included revision of details about guns and gunnery and about structural construction and survivability of the ships of the Spanish Armada. **See 7., F., 5.**

These developments were exemplified by a proliferation of professional institutions and journals, academic programmes at major universities, and prominent personalities. Institutions included the Nautical Archaeology Society, the Institute of Nautical Archaeology at Texas A&M University, the Archaeological Research Centre of the National Maritime Museum at Greenwich, and Sub-Aqua Clubs for divers. Among the best-known academic institutions were Texas A&M and St. Andrews Universities. Professional journals included The International Journal of Nautical Archaeology, founded in 1972, and The Nautical Research Journal. Books were published in the Plenum Series in Underwater Archaeology.

A. NAUTICAL ARCHEOLOGY

As might be expected, the literature has proliferated. George Bass [**231, 232**], A History of Seafaring: Based on Underwater Archaeology, 1972, with over 500 illustrations, and Ships and Shipwrecks of the Americas, 1988, with 357 illustrations, were both basic guides. Martin Dean [**891**], Archaeology Underwater: The Nautical Archaeology Society Guide to Principles and Practice, 1992, was a sanctioned handbook by the prestigious association. The society coordinated recording, fixing positions, and publishing. The Dean handbook described 33 historic wreck sites in and around the British Isles.

James Delgado [**905**], Encyclopedia of Underwater and Maritime Archaeology, 1997, folio size and illustrated, listed hundreds of wreck sites in alphabetical order; over 500 entries written by 150 experts. Valerie Fenwick [**1086, 1084, 1085**], 1972, 1978, and 1998, Historic Shipwrecks, and accounts of boat finds, focused on sites around Britain. Since a registration act of 1973, 47 wreck sites have been designated; two pages per designation.

Basil Greenhill [**1385**], The Archaeology of Ships and Boat, 1976, featured a wide and deep scope, chronological and geographic; a survey of boat finds. Peter Throckmorton [**3613**], History from the Sea: Shipwrecks and Archaeology, from Homer's ODYSSEY to the TITANIC, 1970, covered all of the important finds with maximum information. The oldest British find was TRIAL, 1622, an East Indiaman off the west coast of Australia; this updated Bass [**231, 232**]. An alternate subtitle was "the unharvested sea." The Throckmorton study included a wreck chart illustrating the location of 34 wrecks of East Indiamen, including those of the British, Portuguese, Dutch, Danes, and Swedes.

Jeremy Green [**1381**], Maritime Archaeology, 1990, was a technical handbook, superseding Muckelroy [**2580, 2581**]. Lawrence Babits [**164**], Maritime Archaeology, 1998, was a textbook on nautical archaeology containing 50 articles reviewing the past history, noting the increase in interest and activity, and presenting examples: CSS HUNLEY, TITANIC, and ARIZONA. Richard Gould [**1344**], Shipwreck Anthropology, 1983, was a series of essays by experts, for example, on wrecks of the Armada. Shipwrecks were the equivalent of "documents." Robert Marx [**2443**], The History of Underwater Exploration, 1978, was a general survey.

Sean McGrail [**2255-2260**] has been a major contributor: Ancient Boats, 1983, an explanation of maritime archaeology, Ancient Boats in Northern Europe: The Archaeology of Water Transport to A.D. 1500, 1987, The Archaeology of Medieval Ships and Harbours in Northern Europe, 1979, papers from an international conference, Bremerhaven, and Studies in Maritime Archaeology, 1997, a collection of 36 articles, 1975-1995; critical of the NMM for closing its archaeological unit. An older standard, Keith Muckelroy [**2580, 2581**], 1978 and 1980, were a technical guide and an atlas of the submerged sites throughout the world.

Mensum Bound [**379, 380**], 1995 and 1998, featured the archaeology of ships of war, for example, GRACE DIEU, MARY ROSE, PANDORA, CSS ALABAMA, and restorations such as HMS VICTORY. D.J. Blackman [**342**], Marine Archaeology, 1973, was the proceedings of a conference, University of Bristol, April 1971. Sessions featured the MARY ROSE and Armada wrecks.

For juveniles, there was Christopher Lampton [**2010**], Underwater Archaeology, 1988, described new technology.

P.R.V. Marsden [**2406, 2408, 2407**], 1966, 1974, and 1997, described a ship from the Roman period found near Blackfriars Bridge, London, and AMSTERDAM, a Dutch East Indiaman found off Hastings. J.R. Steffy [**3438**],

Wooden Ship Building and the Interpretation of Shipwrecks, 1994, super-folio size and profusely illustrated with drawings and pictures, was a technical handbook, an aid to the analysis of ship and boat construction, and, thus, discovery. E.E. Rice [**3052**], The Sea and History, 1996, in a unfocused collection, recounted changes over eons of time, for example, caused by changing levels in the sea and what ancient wrecks can tell us.

The most active, well-known, and dynamic participant was Robert Ballard [**184, 183**], Explorations, 1995, and The Eternal Darkness, 2000, two autobiographical works recounting his extensive experience in deep-sea exploration, for example, TITANIC, the Roman vessel, ISIS, BISMARCK, and LUSITANIA, more recently, PT-109.

Lucien Basch [**230**], 1972, presented an overview about ancient wrecks. Thorleif Sjovold [**3331**], 1963, described the Oseberg find and several other important Viking ships, three especially well preserved. R.C. Anderson [**79**], 1934, described the Bursledon ship, probably GRACE DIEU, the ship of Henry V, struck by lightening and buried in 1439. H. Lovegrove [**2192**], 1964, described two old vessels at Rye, Sussex. Gillian Hutchinson [**1741**], Medieval Ships and Shipping, 1994, in the Archaeology of Medieval Britain series, was a synthesis of recent research. Ian Friel [**1196**], 1983, elaborated on medieval ships.

William Fitzhugh [**1119**], 1993, reported on an expedition to study artifacts and cultural items from the three Frobisher voyages of the 1570s. Charles Daggett [**844**], 1990, reported on the expedition for the GRIFFIN, a British East Indiaman, sunk in the Philippines in 1761; 40,000 of the 125,000 pieces of porcelain were recovered. Dennis Callegari [**546**], 1994, reported on the expedition to recover cannon and anchor from HMS ENDEAVOUR, thrown overboard when she went aground in 1770 on, appropriately, Endeavour Reef.

Barry Clifford [**659, 657, 658**], 1993, 1999, and 2000, reported about expedition projects, wrecks discovered and analyzed: 1985, WHYDAH, sunk in a storm off Cape Cod, 1717, and ADVENTURE, a galley-sailing ship, 34-guns, late 1690s, the ship of William Kidd, off Madagascar. Wayne Lusardi [**2206**], 2000, described a shipwreck in the Beaufort Inlet, North Carolina discovered in 1996: probably QUEEN ANNE'S REVENGE, the ship of Blackbeard, lost in 1718.

John Sands [**3218**], 1983, described details of "Yorktown's captive fleet," combining conventional research with nautical archaeology, all for the Mariner's Museum of Newport News.

Terence Grocott [**1403**], 1997, described the shipwrecks of the Wars of the French Revolution and Napoleon, including a chronicle of incidents, for example, 1967 British merchant ships were lost, as per Lloyd's List. In 1999, a French expedition [**939**] reported nautical archaeological analysis of the sunken French fleet in Aboukir Bay.

Norman Brouwer [**467**], International Register of Historic Ships, 1985, updated in 1999, sponsored by the World Ship Trust, described 800 ships, for example, HMS VICTORY, HMS FOUDROYANT, CUTTY SARK, and HOLLAND I. Colin Elliott [**1033**], 1981, described Britain's preserved historic ships and where to find them. Michael Jones [**1828**], Historic Warships, 1993, was a directory of 140 museums and memorials worldwide; entries for 144 ships in 25 countries, for example, VASA, HMS VICTORY, U-505, and MARY ROSE. Veryan Heal [**1586**], 1988, published an illustrated guide to historic vessels.

Colin Martin [**2427**], Scotland's Historic Shipwrecks, 1998, was essays by experts in nautical archaeology, especially about six historic sites, including the Tobermory galleon; for each: background, incident, salvage efforts, and current status. Because the scientific preservation was so delicate, complicated, and ongoing, the technical report about CSS HUNLEY, 1998, by Larry Murphy [**2587**], was of interest. She was discovered in Charleston harbor in 1995, raised, and was being prepared for public display.

B. SUTTON HOO SHIP BURIAL

One find of archaeology, in this case, excavation of a land site containing a ship burial, was SUTTON HOO, discovered in 1939 on an estate near Woodbridge in Suffolk, in the 1990s presented to the National Trust. The location was the Edith May Pretty estate near the River Deben. Excavation began in the late 1930s, was ceased during the war, and resumed afterwards. It was among a series of 17 burial mounds. The ship was about 90 by 14 by 5 feet. The 60-odd artifacts were part pagan and part Christian. There were 37 coins, none dated after 613 and each from different mints.

R.L.S. Bruce-Mitford [**483, 484**], The SUTTON HOO Ship Burial, 3 vols. in 4 books, 1975-1983, was the definitive report. Publication was sponsored by the overseeing agency of the expedition and display of the spectacular artifacts, the British Museum. There was also a guidebook, 1947.

M.O.H. Carver [**590, 591, 592**] produced three works, again, all sponsored by the British Museum: The Age of Sutton Hoo: The Seventh Century in North-Western Europe, 1989, Sutton Hoo: Burial Ground of Kings?, 1998, and a bulletin, 1993. Bruce-Mitford [**483**] was brought up to date. Angela Evans [**1057**], 1986, folio size with color illustrations, was also sponsored by the British Museum.

Calvin Kendall [**1870**], Voyage to the Other World, 1992, was the proceedings from a conference celebrating the 50th anniversary of the find. Robert Farrell [**1079**], 1992, was a summary after 50 years. Roland Allen [**49**], 1997, presented some interpretations in the context of Anglo-Saxon times. P.N. Cameron [**564**], 1982, Charles Green [**1378**], 1963, Bernice Grohskopf [**1405**], 1963, and Michael Pearson [**2802**], 1993, elaborated. An early description was by C.W. Phillips [**2845**], 1940. An entire issue of Antiquity [**3521**], 1940, was devoted to the find. H.M. Chadwick [**604**], 1940, speculated about whom was the burial for, some disagreeing that it was Raedwald. Francis Magoun [2327], 1954, and Jess Bessinger [310], 1958, were bibliographical essays. Albany Major [2338], 1924, presented a critical analysis of the practice of ship burials, not strictly a Viking practice. The earliest discovery was 5th century. Angus Wilson [3907], Anglo-Saxon Attitudes, 1956, was a fictional account of the mysterious discovery of a tomb at "Melphan." Andrew Davies adapted it for TV in the 1990s.

C. MARY ROSE

One of the most important of all of nautical archaeological finds was MARY ROSE, located at Spithead, the great anchorage opposite Portsmouth and the Isle of Wight.

Margaret Rule [3168], The MARY ROSE, 1982, introduced the "flagship of Henry VIII," told its story, and the story of discovery and recovery of the wreck, now at Portsmouth naval base with its own separate museum. The Prince of Wales, personally involved in diving and recovery, wrote the foreword. Between 1979-1982, 25,000 dives were conducted. Alexander McKee and the Southsea Branch of the British Sub-Aqua Club led in the recovery: McKee [2298, 2297], How We Found the MARY ROSE, 1982, and a history, 1968.

D. WRECKS OF THE SPANISH ARMADA

Major nautical archaeological expeditions have focused on a number of wrecks of the Spanish Armada. Estimates vary: 51 of 130 ships were lost; 20,000 of 30,656 men were lost.

Examples were LA GIRONA; 12,000 artifacts were recovered including 1276 coins, jewels, gold chains, and crucifixes, this expedition was led by Robert Stenuit, a Belgian diver. EL GRAN GRIFON was a supply hulk at Fair Isle, led by Colin Martin. LA TRINIDAD VALENCERA was a 1100-ton Venetian merchant ship, the expedition was led by the Derry Sub-Aqua Club.

Colin Martin [2428, 2423, 2421, 2422, 2426] has published extensively: The Spanish Armada, 1988, incorporating much new information from nautical archaeological researches; Full Fathom Five: Wrecks of the Spanish Armada, 1975, the title from Shakespeare; detailed searches and discoveries of three wrecks from Spanish ships, 1979 and 1972. Colin Martin pointed out obvious and decisive differences in ship construction between those from the Mediterranean and those from the Atlantic: loss rate, 80% vs. 10%, respectively; 26 of the former were lost off the west coasts of Scotland and Ireland. Concerning the guns: the barrels were bored incorrectly and the shot was old, brittle, badly made, and poorly cast. See 7., F., 5.

Robert Stenuit [**3445**], 1972, Sydney Wignall [**3854, 3853**], 1968 and 1982, and Laurence Flanagan [**1122**], 1985, described experiences in "searching for Spanish treasure," and the findings. Reappraisals had to be made about Spanish ordnance and gunnery tactics.

Colin Elliott [**1032**], 1987, anticipating the quadricentennial, established an "Armada Trail," a series of sites beginning in Cornwall via Plymouth and the hillside beacons, around the coasts of Scotland and Ireland. An older account was W.S. Green [**1382**], 1906, describing what was known then about the Spanish wrecks on the Irish coast.

E. TOWNS AND NAVAL ARCHEOLOGY

Dulwich on the East Anglia coast and Port Royal, a notorious pirate base in Jamaica were important towns subjected to nautical archaeological expeditions.

Robert Marx [**2445**], Port Royal Rediscovered, 1973, was about this old English port used by pirates, southern coast of Jamaica, destroyed by earthquake in 1692, and rediscovered 1965. D.L. Hamilton [**1462**], 1984, reported on Port Royal, Jamaica. T.W. Courtney [**779**], 1974, reported on the excavations at the Royal Dockyard, Woolwich, in the early 1970s.

F. VASA

The Swedish galleon, 1300 tons, 64 guns, which suddenly sank on its maiden voyage in the harbor of Stockholm in 1628, was an important model for a warship of the early days of sail. It was an important model on permanent display described by Roy Saunders [**3225**], Raising the VASA, 1962. "VASA under Attack," 2002, by Magnus Sandstrom [**3219**], presented alarming evidence of "chemical attack," that is, sulfuric acid destroying the wood from the inside.

Chapter 19

Nautical Dictionaries

Nautical dictionaries were more significant than the name might indicate initially. "Dictionary" was the favorite term over time, beginning in the 17th century. Perhaps a more appropriate explanation would incorporate other terms such as glossary, encyclopedia, manual, sea slang, euphemisms, idioms, ancient and medieval ship practices and routine, and a specialized, even unique, vocabulary. Included were technical terms and phrases employed in the construction, equipment, furniture, machinery, movements, navigation, gunnery, and military operations of a ship and detailed information on the various types of ships. A chronological sequence can be demonstrated, each step intending to improve and elaborate upon its predecessor. English and French languages have dominated. Each one had various titles and numerous later editions.

Early ones were by John Smith [**3360**], Governor of Virginia, A Sea Grammar, 1626. Henry Mainwaring [**2337**], The Sea-man's Dictionary, 1644, was the first in English and included 17th century terms, phrases, and nautical descriptions. It remained the standard until William Falconer [**1071**] and the best as a research source. John Aspley [**152**], "Speculum Nauticum," 1642, was an early collection. Jacques Savary des Bruslons [**3226**], Universal Dictionary of Trade and Commerce, 2 vols., 1707, was a French contribution translated into English. It contained much pertinent information, for example, countries, ports, and commodities.

William Falconer [**1071**], Universal Marine Dictionary or A New Universal Dictionary of the Marine, 1750, with numerous subsequent editions, the latest, 1974, has remained the model. Falconer incorporated themes from the 18th century. English and French sea terms were included but there was bias, for example, "retreat" was defined as "a French maneuver," not a proper term for British use. Falconer relied on Pierre Bouguer [**376**], French hydrographer, 1760. William Mountaine [**2578**], The Seaman's Vade-Mecum and Defensive War at Sea, 1756, incorporated a variety of helpful information and regulations.

Most important was Augustin Jal [**1772-1774**], Archeologie navale, 2 vols., 1840, Glossaire nautique, 2 vols., 1848, and another 2-vol. work, 1873, was first to scholarly consider naval aspects. Jal was a pre-eminent French naval historian and launched the project to produce a modern polyglot dictionary. In 1836, The United Services Journal called for a "Nautical Dictionary or Cyclopaedia of Naval Science and Nomenclature." The article noted that Falconer [**1071**] was "imperfect and out of date." William Henry Smyth [**3378**], 1867, L.R. Hammersly [**1469**], 1881, and H.B. Mason made contributions. William Clark Russell [**3186**], 1883, collected sea terms and their definitions. Heinrich Paasch [**2721**] published Paasch's Illustrated Marine Dictionary, 1885, collecting German and French terms.

In 1910, L.G. Carr Laughton [**2064**], son of the naval historian, John Knox Laughton, initiated a major campaign to create what he termed a nautical encyclopedia incorporating all terms related to seamanship. He saw that as the primary objective of the newly created Society for Nautical Research. Laughton even wanted to name the new professional organization the Jal Society. The journal of the Society was Mariner's Mirror. During its first year, he wrote an article, 1911, and included a tentative list, A through Z. He collected more but was never satisfied that he had enough entries. Laughton, who died in 1955, was continuously disappointed in the lack of progress in achieving the goal he had set.

A. Ansted [**125**], A Dictionary of Sea Terms, 1917, has been updated on occasion and was still in print. W.A. McEwen [**2245**], Encyclopedia of Nautical Knowledge, 1953, featured maritime lore, the practical and theoretical aspects, and the historical. Rene De Kerchove [**900**], International Maritime Dictionary, 1961, was a collection of English, French, and German terms. John Rogers [**3129**], Origins of Sea Terms, 1984, was sponsored by the Mystic Seaport Museum. Rick Jolly [**1824**], Jackspeak, 1989, was a recent guide to "slanguage" in the RN: notes on slang, euphemisms, and idioms.

In a dissertation, G.C. Johnson [**1815**], 1949, studied military and naval terms in the Norman and Anglo-Saxon chronicles. Bertil Sandahl [**3214**], Middle English Sea Terms, 3 vols., 1951-1982, presented details on medieval ships and reprinted essential documents. Most recent contributions of dictionaries and encyclopedias have been by Peter Kemp [**1860**], 1980, Frank Bowen [**391**], 1929, A.G. Course [**776**], 1962, Gershorn Bradford [**415**], 1972, and Graham Blackburn [**340**], 1981. In progress, was Historical Nautical Dictionary by Laurence Urdang [**3702**]. The subtitle explained: "seafaring words in everyday speech": When a Loose Cannon Flogs a Dead Horse, There's the Devil to Pay, 1996, by Olivia Isil [**1758**]. Interestingly, Dean King [**1936**] has edited A Sea of Words, 1995, definitions of over 3000 words and phrases used by the naval fiction writer, Patrick O'Brian [**2660-2683**], in his twenty Aubrey-Maturin novels. See 20., B.

Specialized collections included Grant Uden [**3688**], A Dictionary of British Ships and Seamen, 1981, a partial collection of heritage and history,

Archibald Campbell [**565**], <u>Customs and Traditions of the Royal Navy</u>, 1956, and Eric Booth or Talbot-Booth [**365**], 1942, collecting some manners, customs, and privileges of the RN. He was a prolific writer of these types of guides.

Chapter 20

Nautical Fiction

Nautical fiction has been an increasingly popular literary phenomenon. Naval fiction was based on naval and maritime history and has been popular and attractive from the days of Homer and "Beowulf" through those of William Shakespeare, Frederick Marryat, James Fenimore Cooper, Herman Melville, C.S. Forester, Ernest Hemingway, Patrick O'Brian, Herman Wouk, Ian Fleming, and Tom Clancy. The Nelson era, the 1790s through the 1810s, especially noteworthy, has produced an enormous outpouring, a veritable genre in itself, intensively exploited with high quality works and some not so worthy.

One inspiration for Nelson-era fiction writers was <u>The Naval Chronicle</u> [**2605**], originally forty volumes published twice a year, 1799-1818, during and after the period of the Wars of the French Revolution and Napoleon. It was the high point of sailing ship warfare. C.S. Forester [**1138**] admitted that he began his interest and research in the Nelson era by reading <u>The Naval Chronicle</u>. Chatham Publishers has reprinted an abridgement in five volumes. It contained details of naval operations, activities, and personnel. Nelson [**2620**] himself wrote a short autobiography for it.

The era with the most interest was the period Admiral Lord Nelson achieved fame and an incredible series of major victories against the Spanish, French, and Danes, the Dutch also being involved. Nelson clones, Nelson surrogates, and fiction about the Nelson era have become increasingly popular: at least twenty separate authors and a conservative count of at least 100 separate works. **See item h.**

A. NAUTICAL FICTION

Fiction based on British naval history has been expansive. Notable were works featuring British naval operations and activities during the period of the Nelson Decade [**2624**]. **See 8., A., 7.**

A good place to begin would be the prolific bibliographer, Myron Smith [**3362**], Sea Fiction Guide, 1976, which had 2525 entries. Charles Lewis [**2115**], Books of the Sea, 1943, a reference guide, reviewed the salient works, for example, Defoe, Swift, Smollett, Marryat, Cooper, Corbett, Clowes, and Fred T. Jane. The greatest sea story was Samuel Taylor Coleridge, "The Rime of the Ancient Mariner," 1798.

Charles Robinson [**3089**] The British Tar in Fact and Fiction: The Poetry, Pathos, and Humour of the Sailor's Life, 1909, was a nostalgic panegyric. Herbert Richmond [**3060**], "The Naval Officer in Fiction," 1945, surveyed some novels of the 19th century and how they depicted naval officers; clearly, Marryat [**2398-2405**] was best. Robert Glass [**1295**], 1994, analyzed the image of the sea officer in English literature.

C. Northcote Parkinson [**2767**], Portsmouth Point: The Navy in Fiction, 1948, was an anthology of passages from 35 naval novels written between 1826-1848, authors from "the school of Captain Marryat [**2405**]," who was influenced by Smollett [**3372**]. Parkinson [**2766**], himself, wrote a fictitious biography of "Viscount Hornblower, 1776-1857," which was reviewed by the prestigious Times Literary Supplement as non-fiction.

H.F. Watson [**3787**], The Sailor in English Fiction and Drama, 1550-1800, 1931, broke down the chronology into three periods: 1600-1642, 1660-1760, and 1760-1802, and featured voyage narratives. Anne Treneer [**3647**], The Sea in English Literature, 1926, began with Beowulf [**298**], comparable to "the Odyssey." The Hakluyts contributed significantly and there were poetry and ballads about the Spanish Armada. **See 7., F., 7.** Frank Knight [**1959**], The Sea Story, 1958, called itself a guide to nautical literature.

Frank Adam [**11**], Hornblower, Bolitho and Co.: Krieg unter Segeln in Roman and Geschichte, 1987, was a fascinating and comprehensive review of nautical fiction with the focus on events, 1775-1815. A chronological table placed the fictional heroes in context; "especially busy" was 1798-1800. Olaf Hartelie [**1542**], 1911-1920, produced a series of articles on naval novelists, for example, Marryat, Chamier, Neale, and Glascock.

James Winnefeld [**3918**], 1996, reviewed modern naval fiction, most cases being in the post-1815 period, for example, Monsarrat, Wouk, McLean, and Clancy, the latter "incomplete" because his characters lacked development. Patrick O'Brian [**2660-2683**] was best for the age of sail. Douglas Reeman under the name Alexander Kent [**1887-1911**] "falls short."

There were anthologies. Brandt Aymar [**163**], Men at Sea, 1988, touted the best stories of all time, a companion to Ernest Hemingway, Men at War, 1939. Mike Ashley [**148**], The Mammoth Book of Men O'War, 1999, collected 18 stories, for example, O'Brian, Forester, Kent, Woodman, Styles, and Melville. A.C. Spectorsky [**3405**], The Book of the Sea, 1954, was a collection, for example, Cook, Dampier, Hakluyt, Conrad, and Masefield.

Others were Peter Kemp [**1864**], <u>A Hundred Years of Sea Stories</u>, 1955, and George Solley [**3389**], <u>Short Stories of the Sea</u>, 1984, the latter divided into 5 sections.

Many have placed the famous Anglo-Saxon poem as an early sea story: <u>Beowulf</u> [**298**], the original manuscript not published until 1815. There was a recent translation by Seamus Heaney, 2000. Frank Kermode [**1920**], "The Geat of Geats," was a review of the new translation of <u>Beowulf</u>, 2000, "King of the Geats." Beowulf has been linked to the king of the SUTTON HOO ship burial. **See 18., B.** Previous translations were by Longfellow, William Morris, and J.R.R. Tolkien.

Another classic, Daniel Defoe [**897**], <u>Robinson Crusoe</u>, 1719, was based on the true story of Alexander Selkirk, a Scottish sailor marooned on a Pacific island. **See 17., J.** Maximillian Novak [**2653**], <u>Daniel Defoe: Master of Fiction</u>, 2001, noted that 547 works were attributed to Defoe, a rabid Protestant and competitor of Jonathan Swift.

Swift was a sea author. Anne Gardiner [**1234**], 1991, described the context for writing <u>Gulliver's Travels</u>, 1726, an anti-Dutch work. Many actual episodes were recounted, for example, Japanese pirates supported by the Dutch killed Englishmen.

Tobias Smollett [**3372**], <u>The Adventures of Rodrick Random</u>, 1748, was about experiences on the lower deck of the RN; Random was impressed at Wapping; the lower deck was "a claustrophobic hell," and among the experiences was the circumnavigation of Anson in the 1740s. Daniel Ennis [**1051**], 2000, wrote an article about impressment as depicted in Smolett [**3372**], <u>Roderick Random</u>, published in 1748, among the "unpleasantries" of the navy: martinet captains, flogging, and disease were others.

Alan Chester [**625**], <u>Brother Captain</u>, 1964, was about the Dampier voyage to the South Sea, 1698-1701.

Most important and formative was the "Marryat School." Frederick Marryat [**2398-2405**] and two other naval captains contributed to these endeavors in the 1820s and 1830s. Marryat was "the grand ole man of the naval novel." Marryat joined the Royal Navy after the battle of Trafalgar and was at St. Helena when Napoleon died. The model for Marryat was Admiral Lord Cochrane, under whom he served. His naval novels, written later, were autobiographical. In 1822, he wrote a pamphlet opposing impressment.

Frederick Marryat [**2398-2405**] was prolific: <u>Works</u>, 5 vols., 1849, included 10 novels. Examples were <u>Mr. Midshipman Easy</u>, 1836, <u>Peter Simple</u>, 2 vols., 1902, best of all, <u>Frank Mildmay</u>, <u>The King's Own</u>, 1896, <u>Jacob Faithful</u>, and <u>Masterman Ready: Or the Wreck of the Pacific</u>, 1901.

Tom Pocock [**2865**], <u>Captain Marryat: Seaman, Writer, and Adventurer</u>, 2000, was an outstanding new biography; crediting Marryat with inventing the genre of sea novels. Maurice Gautier [**1261**], <u>Captain Fredrick Marryat</u>, 1973, in French, was scholarly and definitive, especially good on his personal life. Others were Oliver Warner [**3758**], <u>Captain Marryat</u>, 1953,

Christopher Lloyd [**2151**], Captain Marryat and the Old Navy, 1939, and David Hannay [**1479**], Life of Frederick Marryat, 1889, in the Great Writers series.

Another of the Marryat school was Frederick Chamier [**609-613**] who wrote The Life of a Sailor, 3 vols., 1832; Ben Brace, 2 vols.,1836, about service with Nelson; Jack Adams: The Mutineer, 1836, an account of the mutiny on HMS Bounty; The Arethusa: A Naval Story, 1837, about press gangs, and The Spitfire: A Tale of the Sea, 3 vols., 1840. Chamier supported impressment and corporal punishment.

P.J. Van der Voort [**3721**], The Pen and the Quarter Deck, 1972, was a biography of Chamier. Chamier openly copied the novels of Marryat; had a mediocre career in the RN and as an author.

The third of this group was William Glascock [**1290**]. He wrote didactic sea novels.

A fourth author was usually included, William Johnson Neale [**2612-2614**], author of Paul Periwinkle, or The Pressgang, 3 vols., 1841, and Gentleman Jack, 3 vols., 1837. Marryat and Neale allegedly had a fistfight in Trafalgar Square, Marryat striking Neale with a cane, claiming he libeled a favorite admiral.

Later, there was Joseph Conrad [**723-724**], The Mirror of the Sea, 1906, the last section containing a tribute to Nelson, and The Nigger of the NARCISSUS: A Tale of the Forecastle, 1914, about a Black sailor who was the dominant personality on this sailing ship.

Oliver Warner [**3769**], Joseph Conrad, 1950, was a biography; Conrad was born in Poland and adopted Britain as his home. Owen Knowles [**1972**] published The Oxford Reader's Companion to Conrad, 2000. F.G. Cooper [**736**], 1940, wrote about Conrad: the sea was his world during the 1870s and 1880s, he served in 13 vessels, rising to Master.

Nelson clones, Nelson surrogates, and fiction about the Nelson era have become increasingly popular. The first, The Post Captain or The Wooden Walls Manned, by John Davis [**880**], was published in 1805, the year of the battle of Trafalgar and the death of Nelson. It was touted as "a comic, saucy novel about the sailing navy written by one of its midshipmen." It appeared as Trafalgar was being celebrated. Elaboration on this point is illustrated in Part II, Lists. **See item h.**

Actual fiction about Horatio Nelson, "imaginative reconstruction," seemingly a fad, was by Pauline Hunter Blair [**344, 345**], The Nelson Boy, 1999, and A Thorough Seaman, 2000.

Inevitably, Emma Hamilton has attracted fiction writers. Susan Sontag [**3391**], The Volcano Lover: A Romance, 1992, was actually about William Hamilton, the volcano lover, but the Nelson-Emma Hamilton relationship was incorporated: the first kiss: "a fat lady and the short man with one arm." Bernard Capes [**572**], The Extraordinary Confessions of Diana Please, 1904, depicted Nelson-Emma Hamilton relations at Naples, 1798-1799. **See 8., A., 5.**

Perhaps, not usually appreciated as fiction and perhaps more appropriately covered in the chapter on Special Emphasis was Charles Nordhoff [**2650**], The BOUNTY Trilogy, 1932, co-authored by James Norman Hall. The three parts were Mutiny on the BOUNTY, Men against the Sea, and Pitcairn's Island. It included a fictious narrative by Roger Byam, actually Peter Heywood. The full story of all was told. **See 8., B.**

B. PATRICK O'BRIAN

Today, for naval fanatics, indeed, cultists, there are now twenty Aubrey-Maturin novels by Patrick O'Brian [**2660-2683**], praised by some as the best fiction of the 20th century. When O'Brian died in January 2000, he was said to have been writing the 21st novel. He has had a highly dedicated following, perhaps more so in North America than in Britain. All are in paperback. Various guides and explanatory aids to this series have been published, including a "gastronomic companion" devoted to pertinent cuisine from the novels and a CD-recording of period music. The strengths were minute details about seamanship and all aspects of the world of the early 19th century, the Nelson era; featuring politics, language, recreations, diet, furniture, ideas, manners, and, of course, the details of sailing ships. The New York Times declared them "the greatest historical novels ever written"; 3 ½ million copies in print.

The O'Brian novels about Captain Jack Aubrey-Dr. Stephen Maturin:

1. Master and Commander, 1969
2. Post Captain, 1972
3. HMS SUPRISE, 1973
4. The Mauritius Command, 1977
5. Desolation Island, 1978
6. The Fortune of War, 1979
7. The Surgeon's Mate, 1980
8. The Ionian Mission, 1981
9. Treason's Harbor, 1983
10. The Far Side of the World, 1984
11. The Reverse of the Medal, 1986
12. The Letter of Marque, 1988
13. The Thirteen-Gun Salute, 1989
14. The Nutmeg of Consolation, 1991
15. The Truelove, 1992
16. Wine-Dark Sea, 1993
17. The Commodore. 1994
18. The Yellow Admiral, 1997
19. The Hundred Days, 1998
20. Blue at the Mizzen. 1999

Also:

Men-of-War: Life in Nelson's Navy, 1974

Pablo Ruiz Picasso: A Biography, 1976

Joseph Banks, 1987

and Golden Ocean, about an Irish midshipman on the voyage of circumnavigation by Anson, 1740s.

As expected, the literature about O'Brian has flourished. Dean King [**1933-1936**], Patrick O'Brian: A Life Revealed, 2000, was not an authorized biography. O'Brian was a private person and "not the man he claimed to be." His name was Russ, he was not Irish, he abandoned his family, remarried, and moved to France. Harbors and High Seas: An Atlas and Geographical Guide to the Aubrey/Maturin Novels of Patrick O'Brian, 1996, was a companion guide for the O'Brian novels, maps and geographical descriptions, and A Sea of Words: A Lexicon and Companion for Patrick O'Brian's Seafaring Tales, 1995, another companion guide with definitions of 3000 words and phrases. John Hattendorf was co-author.

A.E. Cunningham [**830, 831**], Patrick O'Brian: Critical Appreciations and Bibliography, 1986 and 1994, was a survey and Anthony Brown [**469**], 1999, described the persons, animals, ships and cannon in the novels using a dictionary format, A to Z. Anne Grossman [**1407**], Lobscourse and Spotted Dog: Gastronomic Companion to the Aubrey/Maturin Novels, 1997, described the historical dishes of early 19th-century naval cuisine. These authors were variously known as "priestesses of the cult," "O'Brianites," and "Amiable Sluts." All of the concoctions and their strange names were here. Frank Snyder [**3383**], 1994, described some of the historical background and ticked off other, inferior, Nelson clones. "An Author I'd Walk the Plank For," 1991, was the title of an introduction of O'Brian by Richard Snow [**3381**]. Robert Jones [**1832**], 1994, presented an overview of the Aubrey-Maturin novels. A review was by Charles McGrath [**2261**], 1993. The Patrick O'Brian 1995 Calendar [**2788**], 1995, was a fabulous production; cover illustrations were featured each month. Noted as forthcoming was David Lyon [**2216**], The Patrick O'Brian Companion.

C. C.S. FORESTER

For those less interested in the complexities of sailing ship warfare, the dozen Horatio Hornblower novels of C.S. Forester [**1138-1156**] were attractive. There was the movie of 1951 starring Gregory Peck. Interest has been boosted with the showing of the four-part, eight-hour TV mini-series, "Hornblower" on British television and A&E in America in 1998 and 1999, starring Ioan Gruffudd. More are projected. There was a Hornblower Companion, and Sutton Publishers has reprinted C. Northcote Parkinson [**2766**], The Life and Times of Horatio Hornblower, which, incidentally, the esteemed Times Literary Supplement reviewed as non-fiction biography when it first came out. Forester created his Hornblower from reading <u>The Naval Chronicle</u> [**2605**] and <u>The Gazette</u> from the period. There was a C.S. Forester Society. There was a course, "Horatio Hornblower's Navy," in the Morning Lecture Series, October-November 1999; themes included life at sea, the Hornblower novels, naval intelligence, and naval prizes. The originals began as serialized articles in <u>Argosy Magazine</u>. Forester was unequalled in describing single-ship actions.

The Forester works were as follows:

1.-3. <u>Captain Horatio Hornblower</u>, 1939, 1967

> <u>Beat to Quarters</u>
> <u>Ship of the Line</u>
> <u>Flying Colors</u>

4. <u>The Commodore</u>, 1945

5. <u>Lord Hornblower</u>, 1945

6. <u>Mr. Midshipman Hornblower</u>, 1950

7. <u>Lieutenant Hornblower</u>, 1951

8. <u>Hornblower and the Atropos</u>, 1953

9. <u>Hornblower and the Hotspur</u>, 1962

10. <u>Admiral Hornblower in the West Indies</u>, 1963

11. <u>Hornblower and the Crisis</u>, 1967, incomplete, Forester died prior to completion

<u>The Hornblower Companion: An Atlas and Personal Commentary on the Writing of the Hornblower Saga</u>, 1964

Also:

<u>The African Queen</u>

<u>The Good Shepherd</u>,

<u>The Ship</u>.

<u>The Gun</u>.

<u>Payment Deferred</u>; Jeffrey Dell [**906**] based a play on <u>Payment Deferred</u>, 1934

<u>The Age of Fighting Sail: The War of 1812</u>.

<u>Hunting the BISMARCK</u>.

and the original choice to be official biographer of Earl Mountbatten of Burma; after death of Forester, Philip Ziegler was selected.

C.S. Forester [**1152**], <u>Long before Forty</u>, 1967, was a memoir. Sanford Sternlicht [**3448**], <u>C.S. Forester</u>, 1981, a biography in the <u>Twayne's English Authors</u> series, saw Forester as writing escapist fiction. He compared Forester and Ian Fleming: Hornblower was the hero of the generation of World War II; James Bond of the generation of the cold war. <u>African Queen</u> was his best novel. Forester [**1155**] wrote a biography of Nelson.

C. Northcote Parkinson [**2766**], <u>The Life and Times of Horatio Hornblower</u>, 1970, explained, tongue in cheek, that this biography was based on previously unknown papers discovered in the attic of the executor of the Hornblower estate. Often asked was "Who Was Hornblower?," 1999, as did John Grainger [**1367**]. Hornblower first appeared in 1937. Forester relied on <u>The Naval Chronicle</u> [**2605**]. In the set, Hornblower appeared only at Cape St.

Vincent and, even then, he was captured before the battle. Two possibilities were Cochrane and Home Riggs Popham. Colin Bogg of the C.S. Forester Society nominated Edward Pellew. Bryan Perret [**2822**] had a nomination. **See 9.,D.**

D. OTHER NELSON SURROGATES

In addition to the Aubrey-Maturin [**2660-2683**] and the Hornblower [**1138-1156**] novels, there has accumulated a long list of lesser Nelson surrogates. A more complete summary can be found in Part II, Lists. **See item h.** From Part III, the Annotated Bibliography section, there are as follows: Nicholas Ramage by Dudley Pope [**2886-2915**], Richard Bolitho by Alexander Kent [**1887-1911**], Nathaniel Drinkwater by Richard Woodman [**3937-3955**], Matthew Lamb by Kenneth Maynard [**2481-2484**], George Abercrombie Fox by Adam Hardy [**1497-1509**], Richard Delancey by C. Northcote Parkinson [**2759-2774**], Michael Fitton by Showell Styles [**3479-3511**], John Justice by Anthony Forrest, Percival Merewither by Ellis K. Meacham, Alan Lewrie by Dewey Lambdin [**1991-2000**], Charles Oakshott by Robert Challoner [**605-613**], George Markham by Tom Connery [**720-722**], and Charles Cleasby by Barry Unsworth [**3698**]. Even the notorious lover of Nelson, Lady Emma Hamilton, is included in a novel by Bernard Capes [**572**]. More recently, an American has contributed. William P. Mack [**2276-2277**], Captain Kilburne, 1999, Fergus Kilburne being a Scotsman. Mack, a former commander of the Seventh Fleet of the USN, also wrote six naval novels about destroyers during World War II, some with his son, William P. Mack, Jr. All of these were just for the Nelson era.

For the Nelson era, there were two by the famous novelist of the late Victorian era who influenced young men: G.A. Henty [**1601-1603**], By Conduct and Courage, 1905, and At Aboukir and Acre, 1898. The Mutiny Run, 1994, depicted the mutiny at the Nore and the battle of Camperdown, by Frank Eccles [**1011**]. In Spanish, there was Trafalgar, 1870, by Benito Galdos [**1224**], anti-French and with admiration for Nelson. An example of nautical fiction from the War of 1812 was Clifford Alderman [**33**], Wooden Ships and Iron Men, 1964, depicting service in the RN and USN.

E. OTHER NAUTICAL FICTION

Sea fiction from other eras and other places deserved mention, especially those by authors known better for other accomplishments. One was the famous Daniel Defoe [**895-897**] who wrote Robinson Crusoe and Captain Singleton. Robert Louis Stevenson [**3450**], The Black Arrow, 2001, took place during the Wars of the Roses. For the 16th century, there was William Laird Clowes [**667**] who edited the seven-volume definitive history of the RN and wrote The Captain of the MARY ROSE, 1892. Equally notable is the foremost naval strategist, Julian S. Corbett [752], who wrote of Drake in the West Indies, For God and Gold, 1887. Less well known was Keith Roberts [3076] who wrote Pavane, 1968, a counterfactual attempt: the Spanish Armada succeeded, Queen Elizabeth was assassinated, and the subsequent world was turned upside down. **See 7., F., 2.-8.**

Other nautical fiction for different eras will be reviewed in chronological order. For the Norman Conquest, there was Hope Muntz [2585], The Golden Warrior, 1949, the story of William and Harold.

As with biographies, Francis Drake attracted extensive interest in nautical fiction: Herbert Strang [3470], A Mariner of England, 1908; Leonard Wibberley [3849], The King's Beard, 1952; Ralph Smith [3363], The Dragon in New Albion, 1953; James Wood [3932], The Queen's Most Honorable Pirate, 1961; Louise Kent [1914], He Went with Drake, 1961, and the ubiquitous, prolific G.A. Henty [1603], Under Drake's Flag, 1883. For Walter Raleigh, there was George Garrett [1254], Death of the Fox, 1971.

The Spanish Armada was popular: Augustin Filon [1100], Renegat, 1894; Joseph Hocking [1644], A Flame of Fire, 1903, and Georgette Heyer [1617], Beauvallet, 1929. For piracy, there was Arturo Perez-Reverte [2819], The Nautical Chart, 2002, about a search for treasure.

F. AMERICAN NAUTICAL FICTION

American sea fiction has had outstanding contributors. Herman Melville [2491-2493] wrote Moby Dick, Billy Budd, and White-Jacket, featuring the merchant marine, whaling fleets, and the RN. Peter Neill [2616], American Sea Writing, 2000, was an anthology of 64 selections. Bert Bender [291], Sea-Brothers, 1988, summarized American nautical fiction, for example, Melville and Hemingway.

James Fenimore Cooper [737-742] was an early example: The Pilot, 1824, depicted John Paul Jones and the American Revolution, The Red Rover, 1827, The Water Witch: Or the Skimmer of the Seas, 1830, depicted smuggling in the 18th century, The Two Admirals, 1842, and Ned Myer: Or a Life before the Mast, 2 vols., 1843, was a social commentary on life on the lower deck, based on the experiences of a friend, Ned Meyers.

Thomas Philbrick [2841], James Fenimore Cooper and the Development of American Sea Fiction, 1961, noted Cooper and Melville were influenced by Tobias Smollett [3372] and Marryat [2398-2405]. Mary Cunningham [833], James Fenimore Cooper: A Reappraisal, 1954, was a series of critiques of Cooper, for example as nautical novelist and as naval historian. Alan Dyer [1000], James Fenimore Cooper, 1991, was a bibliography and critique. Harold Langley [2027], 1997, analyzed the nautical fiction of Cooper. David Skaggs [3332], 1995, commented on the writing of Cooper about the battle of Lake Erie. James Beard [**260**] published Letters and Journals, 6 vols., 1960-1968.

Richard Henry Dana [**849-850**], The Seaman's Friend, 1873, described practical seamanship in detail. About Dana were Robert Metzdorf [**2501**], An Autobiographical Sketch, 1815-1842, 1953, Robert Lucid [**2201**], The Journal of Richard Henry Dana, 3 vols., 1968, Robert Gale [**1225**], 1969, a biography in the Twayne's U.S. Authors series, and Samuel Shapiro [**3292**], 1961, biography.

Most impressive and most challenging was Herman Melville [**2491-2493**], Moby Dick: Or the Whale, 2 vols., 1851, the classic, highly dramatic and profoundly intellectual nautical novel, Billy Budd, 1891, placed at the time of the mutinies of 1797, a young seaman struck a petty officer, and White-Jacket: Or the World in a Man-of-War, 1892, just as informative about life on the British lower deck as American.

Charles Anderson [**68**], Melville in the South Seas, 1939, demonstrated how much Melville was dependent on the writings of others, for example, the story of the whaleship, ESSEX, and the account of the Somers mutiny of 1842. Benjamin Britten [**445**] produced an opera based on Billy Budd, produced at the Metropolitan Opera, June 1998. Howard Vincent [**3728**], Twentieth-Century Interpretations of "Billy Budd," 1970, was a collection of reviews, for example, by W.H. Auden, Albert Camus, and E.M. Forster. Thomas Scorza [**3256**], 1979, presented an analysis of "Billy Budd," interpreting it as a critique of the whole of modern politics; the subtitle: The Limits of Politics and Modernity.

Timothy Severin [**3283**] has published In Search of "Moby Dick, 2000. Severin set out to "find" Moby Dick, recounting the tragedy of ESSEX, a Nantucket whaling ship destroyed by a sperm whale in 1820. Melville had made whaling voyages and read about ESSEX. Severin personally made a 6000 mile quest, participating in a hunt for sperm whales in the Far East. Sena Naslund [**2602**], Ahab's Wife, 1999, was inspired by Moby Dick [**2492**], interjecting the female, liberal, Protestant perspective. Very popular in the year 2000 was Nathaniel Philbrick [**2840**], In the Heart of the Sea: The Tragedy of the Whaleship ESSEX.

Chapter 21

Art, Literary Products, the Media, and Cyberspace

A. ART AND DESIGN

Marine painting was another genre in itself, for example, look at the massive collection at the NMM.

Oliver Warner [**3768**], <u>An Introduction to British Marine Painting</u>, 1948, nicely illustrated, persented the scope and artists, for example, the Thames Group and Northern painters. Both J.M.W. Turner and John Constable did HMS VICTORY at Trafalgar. Peter Kemp [**1861**], <u>The Great Age of Sail</u>, 1986, large folio size with over 200 illustrations, featured maritime art and photography from the collections of the NMM. Rina Prentice [**2942**], 1994, described the decorative art collection at the NMM, the largest nautical-oriented collection in the world. Most extensive were Nelson relics. Hans Jurgen Hansen [**1484**], <u>Art and the Seafarer</u>, 1968, large folio size with exquisite artistic illustrations, reviewed the arts and crafts of sailors and shipwrights, for example, ship portraits, ship models, wood-carving, scrimshaw, and ornamentation. **See 10., A. and B.** J.W. Henderson [**1599**], a noted collector, produced <u>Marine Arts and Antiques: Jack Tar</u>, 1999, depicting life on the lower deck by art, for example, paintings, drawings, sea-chests, illustrated log books, postcards, and ephemera.

F.B. Crockett [**806**], <u>Early Sea Painters, 1660-1730</u>, 1996, for the Peabody Essex Museum, traced the beginning of maritime painting to William van de Veldes, father and son, invited over from Holland by Charles II; 100 examples, 60 in color, were included. Richard Unger [**3690**], 1998, collected a series of his essays. One was about marine painting and the history of shipbuilding. Works of art were sources for detail; fortunately Dutch painters were best at attention to detail. David Joel [**1809**], 2000, wrote about Charles Brooking, a British maritime painter of the 18th century. Dutch painters were his primary influence.

Significant were the official naturalist-artists of the voyages of Cook. Outstanding examples were Rudiger Joppien [**1834**], <u>The Art of Captain Cook's</u>

Voyages, 3 vols., 1985-1988, folio size and lavishly illustrated, over 1200 pages. D.J. Carr [**582**], 1983, for the British Museum, wrote a biography of Sydney Parkinson, artist on ENDEAVOUR. He died late in the voyage. **See 17., D.**

Graphically and poignantly symbolic of the old and the new was one of the most famous naval paintings, The Fighting TEMERAIRE, 1995, at the National Gallery. It was described and illustrated by Judy Egerton [**1022**], painted in 1839 by J.M.W. Turner. This veteran of Trafalgar was in tow by a steam tug in a haze, en route to her last berth to be broken up. A negative image of the RN resulted from a famous painting, "Raft of the MEDUSA." In 1816, this frigate ran aground off the coast of North Africa. Most of the 1100 passengers perished. A painting depicting agonizing events reminded all about the scandal; recounted by Alexander McKee [**2293**], 1976.

Bernard Smith [**3344**], The Art of the First Fleet and Other Early Australian Drawings, 1988, included 241 plates of art by persons of the First Fleet; celebrating the bicentennial of the foundation of New South Wales. A dozen oil paintings of the seven ships of John Paul Jones from the U.S. Naval Academy Museum were presented by William Gilkerson [**1280**], 1987.

For the Aberdeen Maritime Museum, T.I. Gunn-Graham [**1423**], 1996, reproduced a painting of a Scottish 60-gun warship of the 1660s. Lillian Martin [**2435**], 2001, with 150 illustrations, presented the art and archaeology of Venetian ships.

Unique were the drawings of John White who flourished in the 1580s and depicted early colonial North Carolina and Virginia. Paul Hulton [**1723, 1722**], 1964 and 1984, produced two books with exquisite illustrations, sponsored by the British Museum.

L.G. Carr Laughton [**2063**], Old Ship Figure-heads and Sterns, 1925, described the development of naval ship ornamentation in spectacular fashion, for example, SOVEREIGN OF THE SEA. Figure-heads were abolished in 1894; the Admiralty discouraged elaborate stern galleries, between 1703-1817, issuing 23 orders regulating them.

From the art collection of the NMM were a series of battle scenes beautifully produced in color in Nicholas Pocock, 1986, by David Cordingly [**763, 766**], for example, battles of Rodney and Nelson. Cordingly, 1997, also produced maritime prints and drawings of ships and seascapes.

Geoffrey Callender [**551**], 1932, wrote about the famous portrait of Francis Drake, a Dutch engraving of the 16th century by Hondius.

Numismatics was the basis of "The First British Navy," 1971, by C.E. Dove [**957**], a study of Roman coins, many of which depicted ships. Romans needed small, cheap vessels to supplement the defense system, the Saxon Shore. Thus, these coins contained the earliest representations of a British naval vessel.

B. TAPESTRIES

One tapestry stands out above all others pertinent to this study, the Bayeux Tapestry, and most of the following works elaborate on it.

However, also spectacular but, unfortunately, no longer extant, were the massive set of tapestries hanging in the House of Lords: "representing the several engagements between the English and Spanish fleets, the ever memorable year MCLXXXVIII," 1739, the engravings by Philip Morant [2543]. They were designed by C. Vroom, purchased by James I, given to the House of Lords, and burned in 1834 in the great fire which engulfed Parliament.

1. The Bayeux Tapestry

Originally commissioned by Odo, Bishop of Bayeux, brother of William I, executed in Canterbury, and completed in 1077, the Bayeux Tapestry was wool weave on bleached linen, 8 colors, depicting over 70 incidents, on view today at Bayeux, France. The "politics" and controversy have persisted.

Hilaire Belloc [287], 1914, depicted the complete work in color. Frank Stenton [3443], 1957, included extensive commentary and 150 illustrations. Others were Lewis Thorpe [3611], 1973, David Bernstein [305], 1986, folio size, Shirley Brown [475], 1988, featuring a history and annotated bibliography, Richard Wissolik [3926], 1990, reviewing the scholarship about it, Theodore Rabb [2995], 1997, noting that Halley's Comet of February 1066 was included, and Richard Gameson [1230], 1997.

C. LITERATURE

Nautical fiction was covered in its own chapter. **See 20.**

For poetry and ballads, a good place to begin would be George Solley [3388], Moods of the Sea: Masterworks of Sea Poetry, 1981, an anthology, for example, works of William Wordsworth, John Donne, and Rudyard Kipling. William Falconer [1070] wrote Shipwreck: A Poem, 1762, a popular poem of the time. He was one of three survivors from the wreck of HMS BRITANNIA off Greece.

A.F. Falconer [1069] wrote Shakespeare and the Sea, 1964, noting that Shakespeare was well informed about maritime enterprise. J.O. Halliwell [1459], 1866, found ballads or poems Shakespeare wrote about the Spanish Armada.

Thomas Campbell [569], 1891, wrote a ballad about the victory by Nelson at Copenhagen, "Ballad of the Baltic."

Chris Hillier [1634], The Devil and the Deep, 1997, was a guide to nautical myths and superstitions, describing their origins and meanings. Cynthia Behrman [278], Victorian Myths of the Sea, 1977, divided these myths into three types: self-image, seamen, and the navy. She had an agenda: these old myths were finally recognized and appreciated "only when, in fact, the seeds of its destruction were being sown." The English people enjoyed superior rights to decide the destiny of seafaring countries. The RN was "God's agent on the ocean."

A different agenda concerned some pertinent British films. Michael Bennett [**295**], 1997, wrote about use of British films to strengthen the Anglo-American alliance in the late 1930s, for example, showing "Mutiny on the BOUNTY," "Fire over England," and "That Hamilton Woman."

D. MUSIC

Ever popular was nautical music.

Charles Firth [**1103**], Naval Songs and Ballads, 1908, a publication of the NRS, was structured to illustrate the history of the RN by presenting hundreds of songs and ballads; there were notes explaining the origin and details. David Proctor [**2957**], Music of the Sea, 1992, for the NMM, presented sea songs and shanties, international in scope. Roy Palmer [**2738**], The Valiant Sailor: Sea Songs and Ballads and Prose Passages Illustrating Life on the Lower Deck in Nelson's Navy, 1973, featured descriptions of the bad conditions afloat and ashore, a kind of love-hate perspective. An American scholar, Stuart Frank [**1176**], collected The Book of Pirate Songs, 1998: 62 songs and ballads divided into 6 sections. Benjamin Britten [**445**] turned "Billy Budd" by Herman Melville [**2491**] into an opera, for example, performed at the Metropolitan Opera, June 1998.

E. CEREMONY

No one has equalled the English/British art of ceremony and celebration. Mention has been made of the celebration of Nelson and the State Funeral. **See 8., A., 4.**

David Saunders [**3224**], Britain's Maritime Memorials and Momentoes, 1996, was a gazeteer of maritime memorials, counting 1400 of them, for example, sites of shipwrecks, lifeboat losses, and monuments, locating them by reference to the Ordnance Survey maps.

S. Rodgers [**3118**], 1983, completed a dissertation on the symbolism of ship launching in the RN. More on the level of the lower deck were two traditions. Henning Henningsen [**1600**], Crossing the Equator, 1961, described an important ceremony, a ritual or custom for all seamen of all categories who first cross the equator. Suzanne Stark [**3421**], 1991, wrote about pets aboard ship, for example, the nanny goat on the voyages of Cook; to supply milk for the coffee of the officers. Cats helped reduce the population of rats. Cuthbert Collingwood, who spent much of his life at sea, had his favorite dog, Bounce.

F. THE INTERNET

The information in cyberspace has become limitless and offered opportunities for pursuit of English/British naval history at all levels. The societies and museums have web sites and provided research and educational opportunities. Obrianites and Gunroom Forum members created "chat rooms" to discuss Aubrey-Maturin novels [**2660-2683**]. The persistent problem was how to determine what is valulable and authentic and what was not. Again, as with published materials, one must apply critical analysis and discrimination.

Journals and periodicals are now available on the internet, for example, Journal for Maritime Research, an electronic journal sponsored by the National Maritime Museum, Greenwich since 1999, and The International Journal of Naval History, 2001, a new online journal supported in America by the Naval Historical Center, Washington. **See item a.**

Chapter 22

Gaps and Research Needed

Even though there are **4124** annotated entries, much more needs to be researched, pursued, and published about English/British naval and maritime history. What is needed is a number of research projects leading to purpose-studies followed by publication of results, findings, and revisions. A wide range of opportunities are open. The list of possibilities is long.

1) Administration. A serious lack of administrative histories of English/British naval history have persisted. Daniel Baugh [**237**] has covered the 18th century. There are other gaps. Richard Harding [**1492**] lamented the lack of comparative examinations of administrative practices in the navy and contemporary large-scale private organizations, for example for the 17th century.

2) The Admiralty. A good, comprehensive, up-to-date history of the Admiralty is much needed.

3) Finance. Like administration, coverage is far behind other areas. The work of Jon Sumida on naval finance in the early 20th century would be the model to follow for studies of the earlier periods.

4) Admiralty Clerks and Secretaries. We know much, perhaps too much, about Samuel Pepys, and, later, about John Barrow. What about others?; for example, Josiah Burchet, Thomas Corbett, and Evan Nepean? What about the offices themselves? What powers, duties, and influence did they have and wield?

5) Education and Training for Officers and the Lower Deck. A serious lack of published sources on these topics has persisted. Ideally, a separate section, if not a designated chapter, should be devoted to this essential and vital

subject. The published literature was insufficient. Schooling, training exercises, training routines, preparation for battle, cadet, midshipmen, and young officer schools, testing, and examinations, training at the level of the lower deck, and descriptions of any connections to the colleges and universities, are a few of areas which require research and publication. J.S. Bromley [452] called for a history of naval training ships. Harry Dickinson [928] is pursuing some of these issues. More is needed.

6) Sea Travel, 500-1500 AD. Sea travel, logistics, transport of persons, material, and horses, and crossing the Channel, North and Irish Seas, official missions; there being a general neglect of systematic and purpose-studies of these matters.

7) The Crusades. How did English crusaders get to the Holy Land and back? What transports? What naval forces? What naval activities? What naval defenses? What about supplies and logistics? Again, there is a general neglect of systematic and purpose-studies of these matters.

8) The Norman Conquest and Anglo-Saxon Defenses. Coverage of the origins, types of ships and transports, construction, sailing qualities, handling, especially in bad weather, capabilities, and disposition of the massive fleet of William the Conqueror has been haphazard, often dependent on the iconography of the Bayeux Tapestry. No one can agree on the number of men and horses. Similar gaps appear in the fleet of Harold. Purpose-studies are needed and a comprehensive survey would greatly assist our understanding.

9) The Navigation Acts and Ship Money. Much of what has been published is out of date and not comprehensive on both of these topics. These are key issues in state-building, to which a chapter is devoted. **See 13., A.** When did each begin and why? When was the need recognized? When was the first one passed ? How many were there? What did they accomplish? Why did they pass? Why were they abolished? There is no agreement on those questions. They need to be placed in context. Purpose-studies are needed.

10) Ireland, Scotland, Wales, and Dalriada. Some progress has been made, but much needs to be done to elaborate upon and adequately cover sea connections and naval aspects of these "states" and kingdoms.

11) Impressment. Richard Harding [1492] called for a comprehensive and up-to-date study. A gap exists: the dominant view of impressment drawn from official sources has yet to be presented. Everybody hated the practice and it was universally denounced, but never renounced.

12) The Role of the Treasurer. The Royal Treasurer and other financial officers and their power over and relations with the navy have never been clarified. Explanations and purpose-studies are needed.

13) Anglo-Dutch Wars. The individual battles of these wars were important at the time and exerted a great influence on future naval tactics. More publications about individual battles are needed. Current coverage is haphazard and sketchy.

14) The Revolution of 1688. William of Orange successfully invaded the British Isles and became king, all the while, there being a legitimate monarch with a legitimate male heir. John Locke, in his inimitable way, explained the political and dynastic aspects. What about the naval aspects? We need to know more about the Dutch forces and fleet. What and where was the RN? How could this happen? Were there conspiracies in remote Tangier? Purpose-studies of these matters are needed.

15) Jacobite Operations. Naval operations associated with the Jacobite cause after the Revolution of 1688 and subsequent events, for example, the '15 and the '45, are other gaps in the literature. Purpose-studies are needed.

16) The Royal Dockyards. In the last decade, much has been accomplished, especially the general history, architecture, facilities, and specific yards, for example, Portsmouth, Plymouth, and Chatham. Now, look at infrastructure, organization, finance, the role and effectiveness of commissioners, workforce relationships, efficiency, and corruption. Roger Knight [1970] gave us a taste in a spotlight effort. More needs to be done.

17) Sociological Studies. Sociology-based studies of the English/British naval officer class are deficient. Better ones have appeared for other services, for example, Donald Bittner for officers of the Royal Marines, Peter Karsten for the American naval officer class, Holger Herwig for the German naval officer class, and Ronald Hood for the French naval officer class. Where is the study for the English/British naval officer class? Similar observations of deficiencies could be made about enlisted men.

18) Religion and Chaplains. Studies are needed on the matter of religion, the service of chaplains, divine services, religious literature, hymns and hymnals, and rituals of the established religion of the realm. Divine services were required by regulation. Obviously, these were deemed important matters. Purpose-studies are needed. For example, religion was a factor in the navy before, during, and after the Civil War. James, Duke of York was forced out as Lord High Admiral because he was a Catholic. What effect did all of that have on the navy?

19) The Role of Women. Again, some progress is being made, but for this subject, there are always gaps to be filled.

20) The Matters of Patronage, "Interest," and Corruption. Unfortunately, no general survey or comprehensive account has been published. "Interest" and "Corruption" are ubiquitous terms. What does each mean? They need to be defined and elaborated upon. Purpose-studies would help.

21) Horatio Nelson. Oliver Warner [**3771**] claimed all had been said that needed to be said about Nelson. That is a dangerous thing to say about any topic of history, even if there have been hundreds of biographies. The most prominent authority, Tom Pocock [**2866**] pointed out several gaps: Nelson and prize money, recruitment, radicalism, trade, and the monarchy; the latter Pocock himself professed to be studying.

22) John Jervis, Earl St. Vincent. Still there is no adequate biography of this key naval figure, mentor of Nelson, commander of the Mediterranean Fleet, "savior" from the mutinies of 1797, and First Lord at a crucial time.

23) Prominent "Band of Brothers." Imbalance is the problem. Most of them have been neglected: Collingwood and Hardy received short shrift; Troubridge, Foley, and others, even less.

24) Neglect of Others. Imbalance is again the problem about other prominent naval leaders. Examples are Charles Howard, George Rooke, Woodes Rogers, Edward Pellew, George Cockburn, Charles Middleton, William Hoste, and James Saumarez.

25) Propaganda. Research and study are needed about the role of propaganda and public opinion related to naval and maritime affairs during these early centuries. The Naval Chronicle [**2605**], 1790s to about 1820, fulfilled some of these needs for that limited time. The impact and influence of other newsletters and songs, ballads, poems, tracts, broadsides, prints, gossip, and graffiti need to be studied.

26) The Second, Third, and Fourth Anglo-Dutch Wars. There is a need to update the histories with purpose-studies. The First War has been covered adequately; not so subsequent ones, especially the Fourth.

PART II.

DESCRIPTIVE LISTS

Descriptive Lists

This section, Descriptive Lists, is described in Chapter 2 on Format and Scope. **See 2.**

a. JOURNALS AND PERIODICALS
The following journals and periodicals would most likely contain pertinent articles to English/British Naval History.

1) <u>Albion: A Quarterly Journal Concerned with British Studies</u>. Boone: Appalachian State University, since 1969. Ed: Michael Moore.

2) <u>American Historical Review</u>. Bloomington: Indiana University. 5 times a year since 1895.

3) <u>American Neptune: Quarterly Journal of Maritime History</u>. Salem: Peabody Essex Museum, since 1941. A former editor, Timothy Runyan [---], reviews the first 50 years. An anthology, <u>Thirty Years of "American Neptune"</u> was published in 1972.

4) <u>Anglo-Norman Studies: Proceedings of the Annual Battle Conference</u>. Rochester: Boydell, since 1978.

5) <u>Banksia: Journal of the Joseph Banks Society</u>, since 1980.

6) <u>English Historical Review</u>. London: Longman. 5 times a year since 1886.

7) <u>Great Circle: Journal of the Australian Association for Maritime History</u>. Semiannual. Victoria: AAMH, since 1980.

8) Historical Journal, formerly Cambridge Historical Journal. Quarterly. Cambridge: Cambridge UP, since 1923.

9) Historical Research: The Bulletin of the Institute of Historical Research. London: IHR, since 1923. Notice of the Julian Corbett Prize Essay.

10) International Journal of Maritime History: Journal of the International Maritime Economic History Association. St. Johns: Memorial University. 2 times a year since 1989.

11) International Journal of Nautical Archaeology and Underwater Exploration: The Journal of the Council for Nautical Archaeology. Quarterly. London: Academic Press, since 1972.

12) The International Journal of Naval History. An online journal supported in America by the Naval Historical Center, Washington, 2001.

13) Journal of British Studies: The Journal of the Conference of British Studies. Quarterly. Chicago: Chicago University Press, since 1961.

14) Journal for Maritime Research. An electronic journal sponsored by the National Maritime Museum, Greenwich since 1999.

15) The Journal of Military History: The Journal of the Society for Military History. Formerly Military Affairs. Quarterly. Lexington: Marshall Library, since 1937.

16) Mariner's Mirror: The Journal of the Society for Nautical Research. Quarterly. Oxford: Alden Press, since 1911.

17) Naval War College Review: The Journal of the U.S. Naval War College. Monthly. Newport: USNWC, since 1948.

18) Nelson Dispatch: The Journal of the Nelson Society. Annual. Portsmouth: Nelson Society, since 1981.

19) Northern Mariner; Le Marin du Nord: Journal of the Canadian Nautical Research Society. Quarterly. St. Johns: Memorial University, since 1991.

20) Proceedings of the Naval Institute. Monthly. Annapolis: Naval Institute, since 1875.

21) Royal United Services Institution: The Journal of the Royal United Services Institution for Defence Studies. Quarterly. London: RUSI, since 1857.

22) Shipmodeler: Official Organ of the Ship Model Makers Club. 10 times a year. NY: SMC, since 1931.

23) Studia Bountyana. A periodical since 1965.

24) Times Literary Supplement (TLS). Weekly. London: Times Newspaper.

25) Trafalgar Chronicle: Yearbook of the 1805 Club. Annual. Portsmouth: 1805 Club.

26) Warship: A Quarterly Journal Devoted to the Design, Development and Service History of the World's Fighting Ships. Annual. London: Conway Maritime, since 1977.

b. ASSOCIATIONS AND SOCIETIES
The following associations and societies would most likely have special interests in English/British Naval History. The listing is to demonstrate the magnitude of interests. Some associations and societies obviously have not remained active.

1) American Friends of the Hakluyt Society
2) Anson Society
3) Association for the History of the Northern Seas, founded 1974.
4) Australian Association for Maritime History, founded 1978. Journal: Great Circle.
5) Canadian Nautical Research Society
6) Chatham Dockyard Historical Society
7) Captain Cook Study Unit; publishes Cook's Log.
8) Center for Marine Resources, Texas A&M University
9) Centre for Maritime Historical Studies, University of Exeter
10) Centre for Maritime Research, National Maritime Museum, Greenwich
11) The C.S. Forester Society
12) The 1805 Club
13) Greenwich Maritime Institute, University of Greenwich
14) Hakluyt Society
15) HM BARK ENDEAVOUR Foundation
16) HMS VICTORY Foundation (sponsors Save the VICTORY Fund)
17) Institute of Marine Studies, University of Plymouth
18) Institute of Maritime Archaeology, St. Andrews University, Scotland
19) Institute of Nautical Archaeology, Texas A&M University
20) International Commission for Maritime History
21) International Congress of Maritime History
22) International Congress of Maritime Museums
23) International Maritime Economic History Association

24) International Napoleon Society
25) International Women of the Sea Network. Sponsored by NMM.
26) Linschoten Vereeniging. Equivalent of the Hakluyt Society for the Dutch.
27) International Women of the Sea Network
28) John Carter Brown Library, Brown University, Providence, RI
29) Marine Research Society. Based at Salem, MA.
30) Maritime Historical Studies Centre, University of Hull
31) Munson Institute of Maritime History, Mystic Seaport Museum, Mystic, CT.
32) Nautical Archaeology Society
33) Naval Dockyard Society
34) Naval History Symposium, U.S. Naval Academy, Annapolis, MD
35) Navy Records Society.
36) Nelson Society
37) North American Society for Oceanic History (NASOH)
38) Pepys Club. To honor Samuel Pepys.
39) Royal Geographical Society
40) Royal United Services Institution
41) Save the VICTORY Fund, sponsored by the Society for Nautical Research.
42) Society for the History of Discoveries
43) Society for Military History
44) Society for Nautical Research
45) Sutton Hoo Society
46) Trinity House
47) U.S. Naval Institute

c. MUSEUMS

The following are museums most likely to collect and display items pertinent to English/British Naval History.

1) Collection of Nelsoniana by Mrs. Lilly McCarthy, deemed "Queen of Nelsonians"
2) Exeter Maritime Museum, Exeter
3) Merseyside Maritime Museum, Liverpool
4) Mariner's Museum, Newport News, VA
5) MARY ROSE Museum, Portsmouth
6) Mystic Seaport Museum, Salem, MA
7) National Maritime Museum, Greenwich
8) National Maritime Museum of Australia
9) Nelson Collection, Lloyd's of London Headquarters Building
10) Nelson Museum, Monmouth
11) Royal Naval Museum, Portsmouth

d. PUBLISHERS AND PUBLICATION SERIES

Another demonstration of the interest and importance of English/British Naval History is the magnitude of publication. The following list contains publishers noted for pertinent titles and equally pertinent publication series.

1) The Anatomy of the Ship series. NIP and Conway Maritime.

2) Archon Books, Shoe String Press

3) Arms and Armour

4) Batsford British Battles series.

5) Blueprint series. Chatham Publishing.

6) Brassey's

7) Capstan Press series. Hamden: Merritt Communication

8) Chatham Pictorial Histories, co-sponsored by the National Maritime Museum, Greenwich.

9) Chatham Publishing

10) Classics of Nautical Fiction series. McBooks Press, Ithaca, NY.

11) Classics on Naval Literature series. Naval Institute Press, Annapolis, MD.

12) Classics of Sea Power series. Naval Institute Press, Annapolis, MD.

13) Conway Maritime

14) Exeter Maritime Studies series. Exeter University Press.

15) Fontana History of Europe War and Society series

16) Golden Hind series

17) Greenwood Press Bibliographies of _____ series. Greenwood Press, Westport, CT.

18) HarperCollins

19) Heart of Oak Sea Classics series. Holt Publishers, NY.

20) <u>History of the Ship</u> series

21) Jane's

22) <u>Library of Naval Biography</u> series. Naval Institute Press, Annapolis, MD.

23) McBooks Press, Ithaca, NY.

24) <u>Maritime History, 1475-1815</u> series. From the collection of the John Carter Brown Library, Providence, RI.

25) <u>Maritime Monographs and Reports</u> series. From NMM.

26) <u>National Maritime Museum Papers</u> series. From NMM.

27) <u>Naval Academy</u> series. Sponsored by the Naval History Museum, Portsmouth.

28) Naval Institute Press, Annapolis, MD.

29) <u>Nelson Library</u> series

30) <u>Plenum Series in Underwater Archaeology</u>. Texas A&M Institute of Nautical Archaeology.

31) <u>Publications of the Hakluyt Society</u>

32) <u>Publications of the Navy Records Society</u>

33) Routledge

34) <u>Sailors' Tale</u> series. Chatham Publishers.

35) <u>Sea Battles in Close-Up</u> series. Naval Institute Press, Annapolis, MD.

36) <u>Seafarers</u> series. Time-Life Publishers.

37) <u>Studies in Maritime History</u> series. University of South Carolina Press, Columbia.

38) Texas A&M University Press, College Station, TX.

39) <u>Warships</u>. Conway Publishing.

40) <u>Warships of the Royal Navy</u> series. Hugh Evelyn, London.

41) <u>Yale English Monarch</u> series. Yale University Press, New Haven.

e. REPLICAS
In the last several decades a number of replicas of historic ships have been constructed. Some have made highly publicized voyages.

1) AMISTAD
2) BOUNTY launch
3) BRENDAN
4) Christopher Columbus's ships, NINA, PINTA, and SANTA MARIA
5) USS CONSTITUTION
6) USS CONSTELLATION
7) DUYFKEN
8) ENDEAVOUR
9) HMS FOUDROYANT
10) GOLDEN HIND
11) HALF-MOON
12) ICELANDER (ISLENDINGUR)
13) MARY ROSE
14) MATTHEW
15) MAYFLOWER
16) HMS ROSE
17) SUTTON HOO
18) HMS VICTORY
19) HMS VICTORY's cutter

f. MONUMENTS AND MEMORIALS

1) The Temple at Kymin. A monument site dedicated to naval events, dedicated in 1794; included The Roundhouse and the Temple; a commemoration to the battle of the Nile was added; Nelson visited the site, 25 July 1802.

2) Nelson monuments. Interestingly, no sign of Nelson at Burnham Thorpe.

3) Statue by Flaxman in the South Transcept of St. Paul's Cathedral.

4) Effigy at Westminster Abbey by Catherine Andras.

5) Trafalgar Square, London, completed in 1846, architect, William Railton and statue by E.H. Bailey; the panels on the plinth were depictions of the four great battles: St. Vincent, the Nile, Copenhagen, and Trafalgar.

6) Carlton Hill, Edinburgh, towering over the city diagonally across from Edinburgh Castle, a neo-Gothic tower shaped like an upside down telescope.

7) Portsdown Hill. 150 foot granite obelisk begun in 1807; paid for by veterans of the battle of Trafalgar.

8) The Bull Ring, High Street, Birmingham.

9) A memorial at Liverpool.

10) A monument at Dublin; originally equivalent to the monuments in London and Edinburgh; in 1966, the statue was blown up and demolished by the Irish Republican Army.

11) A Doric column at Mortreal.

12) A monument in Barbados.

13) Monument to James Cook, Whitby, his hometown.

g. LECTURES AND AWARDS

1) Anderson Medal. In Memory of R.C. Anderson. Awarded by the Society for Nautical Research for significant publications in maritime matters. Winners include Richard Walker and Michael Partridge.

2) Annual Lecture of the Society for Nautical Research

3) Caird Medal and Lecture. Annual. Awarded by NMM. Winners include Glyndwr Williams, John de Courcy Ireland, and John B. Hattendorf.

4) Corbett Prize. Julian S. Corbett Prize in Modern Naval History. Every 2 years. Sponsored by the University of London on the advice of the Institute of Historical Research; announced in Historical Research. Winners include G. Connell-Smith, James A. Williamson, A.P. McGowan, Andrew Thrush, and H.W. Dickinson

5) Ford Lectures, Oxford University

6) Keith Matthews Award. For books on maritime matters. Awarded by the Canadian Nautical Research Society.

7) Lees Knowles Lectures, Cambridge University

8) Munson Lectures, Mystic Seaport Museum

9) Nelson Birthday Lecture. Sponsored by the Nelson Society.

h. FICTIONAL HEROES OF THE NELSON ERA
It has become a genre if not an industry: fictional seamen during the period, 1775-1815, the Nelson era. The following is a list.

1) Horatio Hornblower by Forester
2) George Abercrombie Fox by Adam Hardy
3) Richard Bolitho by Alexander Kent
4) Richard Delancey by C. Northcote Parkinson
5) Nicholas Ramage by Dudley Pope
6) Nathaniel Drinkwater by Richard Woodman
7) Matthew Lamb by Kenneth Maynard
8) Jack Aubrey and Dr. Stephen Maturin by Patrick O'Brian
9) Michael Fitton by Showell Styles
10) John Justice by Anthony Forrest
11) Percival Merewither by Ellis K. Meacham
12) Charles Oakshott by Robert Challoner.
13) Fergus Kilburnie by William P. Mack
14) George Markham by Tom Connery
15) Alan Lewrie by Dewey Lambdin
16) Lord Charles Oakshott by Robert Challoner

Or put another way, a summary of Nelson era novels:

1) Capes, Bernard – Diane Please – 1 re Lady Hamilton
2) Challoner, Robert – Lord Charles Oakshott – at least 4
3) Chamier, Frederick – Ben Brace, a servant to Nelson
4) Connery, Tom – George Markham – 1 in 2000, more promised
5) Davis, John – The Post Captain - 1805
6) Forester, C.S. - Horatio Hornblower – 11 novels
7) Hardy, Adam – George Abercrombie Fox
8) Kent, Alexander – Richard Bolitho – 24 novels
9) Lambdin, Dewey – Alan Lewrie – 5 novels
10) Mack, William P. – Fergus Kilburnie – (6 previous ones on WWII)
11) Marryat, Frederick – model was Lord Cochrane – 4

12) Maynard, Kenneth – Matthew Lamb – at least 4
13) Meacham, Ellis K. – Percival Merewither
14) Neale, William Johnson – two in the period
15) O'Brian, Patrick – Aubrey-Maturin novels – 20, working on 21 at his death
16) Parkinson, C. Northcote – Richard Delancy and Horatio Hornblower "biography"
17) Pope, Dudley – Nicholas Ramage – at least 14
18) Styles, Showell – Michael Fitton –
19) Unsworth, Barry – Charles Cleasby
20) Woodman, Richard – Nathaniel Drinkwater – at least 6

PART III.

ANNOTATED BIBLIOGRPAHY

This work is a comprehensive historiographical and bibliographical survey of the most important academic and printed materials about the naval and maritime history of England and Great Britain from earliest times to 1815; a "prequel" to Eugene L. Rasor [**3012**], <u>British Naval History since 1815: A Guide to the Literature</u>, New York: Garland Publishing, 1990, xxi, 841 pages, 3125 bibliograhical entries, 507 pages of historiographical narrative. That bibliography was not annotated.

For <u>English/British Naval History to 1815: A Guide to the Literature</u>, a volume in the <u>Bibliographies and Indexes in Military Studies</u> series of Greenwood Press, there are three parts and a series of appendixes: the historiographical narrative section, a lists section, and the annotated bibliography section. The purpose of the survey is to provide a comprehensive reference guide for students and scholars at all levels. It incorporates evaluative, qualitative, and critical analysis processes, the essence of historical scholarship.

1 Abbott, John L. <u>John Hawkesworth: Eighteenth-Century Man of Letters</u>. Madison: U Wisc P, 1982, xvii, 241 pp. Hawkesworth, 1720-1773, among other "occupations," controversial historian-editor of the first voyage of Captain Cook, published in 1773.

2 Abell, Westcott S. <u>The Shipwright's Trade</u>. Cambridge: Cambridge UP, 1948, 1962, 1981, xiii, 218 pp. An undistinguished survey of the development of shipbuilding from dug-outs to iron-steam-steel, e.g., Vikings, Phineas Pett, Anthony Deane, and East Indiamen.

3 Abels, Richard P. <u>Alfred the Great: War, Kingship, and Culture in Early England</u>. <u>The Medieval World</u> series. London: Longman, 1998, xviii, 373 pp. By a historian at the U.S. Naval Academy; elaborated on naval aspects and clarified "myths," e.g., Alfred designed warships and he and his brother commanded during naval battles against the Danes; "father of the Royal Navy" is a stretch; noted that the first American warship was USS ALFRED and on the 1000th anniversary of his death, HMS ALFRED, an armored cruiser, was commissioned.

4 -------. "Leadership and Military Obligation in Anglo-Saxon England." Ph.D. diss, Columbia, 1982. The basis for the next entry.

5 -------. <u>Lordship and Military Obligation in Anglo-Saxon England</u>. Berkeley: U Cal P, 1988, xii, 313 pp. An important entry in the debate over feudal obligations, e.g., the matter of <u>landfyrd</u> and <u>schypfyrd</u>, the latter possibly being feudal tenure for sea defense.

6 Acerra, Martine and Meyer, Jean. <u>L'Empire des Mers: Des Galions aux Clippers</u>. London: Nathan, 1990, 282 pp. A brilliant study of the development of shipping, naval and merchant, by the noted French naval historian; focused on the carrack and clipper and incorporated Lepanto, the Armada, and advances in Northern Europe.

7 Acerra, Martine, ed. <u>Les Marines de Guerre Europeennes, XVII-XVIIIe Siecles</u>. Paris: UP Paris-Sorbonne, 1985, 436 pp. Madam Acerra edited a series of papers from a colloquium at the Sorbonne in 1984, e.g., Roger Knight on maintenance of the Royal Navy, A.N. Ryan on the blockade of Brest, Brian Lavery on the revolution in naval tactics, and David Lyon and Richard Unger on warships.

8 Acton, Harold. <u>The Bourbons of Naples, 1734-1825</u>. London: Methuen; London: Prion, 1956, 1957, 1963, 1974, 1998, xviii, 731 pp. Nelson was in and out of Naples in the 1790s, e.g., the spectacular entry after the battle of the Nile; his consistent hosts were Lord and Lady Hamilton.

9 Aczel, Amir D. <u>The Riddle of the Compass: The Invention that Changed the World</u>. NY: Harcourt, 2001, 240 pp. Contends the invention of the magnet compass was "the most important technological invention since the wheel; possibly invented by Flavio Gioia of Italy, more likely, by the Chinese c. 1000 AD.

10   Adair, E.R."English Galleys in the Sixteenth Century." , <u>EHR</u>, 35 (October 1920): 497-512. Details about these Mediterranean-type warships, e.g., Henry VIII had galleys built in operations against the French, 1543-1544; others used in 1550s.

11   Adam, Frank. <u>Hornblower, Bolitho and Co.: Krieg unter Segeln in Roman and Geschichte</u>. Frankfort: Ullstein, 1987, 1992, 204 pp. Fascinating and comprehensive review of nautical fiction in the Nelson era; emphasis on events, 1775-1815; reviews fictional seamen: Hornblower by Forester, George Abercrombie Fox by Adam Hardy, Richard Bolitho by Alexander Kent, Richard Delancey by C. Northcote Parkinson, Nicholas Ramage by Dudley Pope, Nathaniel Drinkwater by Richard Woodman, Matthew Lamb by Kenneth Maynard, Jack Aubrey and Dr. Stephen Maturin by Patrick O'Brian, Michael Fitton by Showell Styles, John Justice by Anthony Forrest, and Percival Merewither by Ellis K. Meacham; others, not included in this book: Charles Oakshott by Robert Challoner and Fergus Kilburnie by William Mack.

12   Adams, Henry. <u>The War of 1812</u>. Harrisburg: Infantry Journal; NY: Cooper, 1944, 2000, vii, 377 pp. Ed: H.A. Weerd, intro: John Elting; Adams, 1838-1918, the distinguished historian-autobiographer, from his larger 9-vol. U.S. history; a classic study.

13   Adams, Randolph G. "A View of Cornwallis's Surrender at Yorktown." <u>AHR</u>, 37 (October 1931): 25-49. Presents the many "interacting" causes for the surrender; for once "the British failed to muddle through."

14   Adams, Simon L. <u>The Armada Campaign of 1588</u>. <u>New Appreciations in History</u> # 13. London: Historical Association, 1988, 24 pp. A Historical Association pamplet reviewing the literature.

15   -------. "The Gran Armada: 1988 and After: Review Article." <u>History</u>, 76 (June 1991): 238-49. Reviews 18 English and Spanish works associated with the Quadricentennial.

16   -------. "The Lurch into War: The Spanish Armada." <u>History Today</u>, 38 (May 1988): 18-25. A new interpretation: the English fleet departed Plymouth prematurely and was unprepared for battle in the Channel.

17   -------. "New Light on the 'Reformation' of John Hawkins: Notes and Documents." <u>EHR</u>, 105 (January 1990): 96-111. Revised assessment of the naval administration of Hawkins.

18   Adams, Thomas R. and Waters, David W., comps. <u>English Maritime Books Relating to Ships and Their Construction and Operation at Sea Printed before 1801</u>. Providence: John Carter Brown; London: NMM, 1993, 1995, xl, 837 pp. A bibliographical compilation of 3800 items under 26 topics and presenting the contemporaneous body of knowledge about ships and maritime history.

19   Adamson, Jack H. and Folland, H.F. The Shepherd of the Ocean: An Account of Sir Walter Raleigh and His Times. Boston: Gambit, 1969, 464 pp. A biography.

20   Addington, Larry H. The Patterns of War since the Eighteenth Century. Bloomington: Indiana UP, 1984, 1994, xiv, 370 pp. Dedicated to Theodore Ropp; a synthesis of the many changes in war since the late 18th century, e.g., from dynastic to national warfare and for naval warfare, Jeune Ecole, Mahanite, and technical developments.

21   -------. The Patterns of War through the Eighteenth Century. Bloomington: Indiana UP, 1990, xii, 161 pp. A "prequel" surveying ancient to neoclassical naval and land warfare, e.g., the Norman Conquest, the Crusades, Hundred Years' War, and England's rise to naval supremacy.

22   Addis, Charles P. The Men Who Fought with Nelson in HMS VICTORY at Trafalgar. London: Nelson Society, 1988, 144 pp. By a former commanding officer of VICTORY; describes personnel.

23   Aiken William A. and Henning, Basil D., eds. Conflict in Stuart England: Essays in Honour of Wallace Notestein. London: Cape; NY: New York UP, 1960, 271 pp. Various essays; see Aiken, "The Admiralty in Conflict and Commission, 1679-1684," describing the evolution of Admiralty structure and the impact on operations.

24   Aker, Raymond and Porten, Edward von der. Discovering Francis Drake's California Harbor. Palo Alto: Drake Navigators Guild, 2000, vi, 73 pp. A fascinating investigation, following a complex research project over 4 decades by dedicated investigators; the Drake Navigators Guild set out to prove the California landfall of Drake in 1579 was Drake's Bay, Marin County, and, after disproving many other claims, succeeded in doing so, e.g., the notorious "plate" was proved a fake and original descriptions could only be the site, "Nova Albion."

25   Alban, J.R. "National Defence in England, 1337-1389." Ph.D. diss, Liverpool, 1976. A useful survey including naval aspects.

26   Albert, Marvin H. Broadsides and Boarders: An Account of the Great Captains Who Fought with Cannon under Sail, and of their Battles. NY: Appleton; London: Harrap, 1958, x, 360 pp. Popular and superficial; Nelson was the greatest, 1 of 6 chapters devoted to him; other topics, e.g., Sea Beggars, Sea Dogs, Generals-at-Sea, Hawke, Jones, and Suffren.

27   Albion, Robert G. "British Shipping and Latin America, 1806-1914." J Economic History, 11 (Fall 1951): 361-74. Re the origins, e.g., John Hawkins forcing merchants to buy his slaves, that and later incursions breaking the Spanish and Portuguese monopolies.

28   -------. Five Centuries of Famous Ships: From the SANTA MARIA to the

GLOMAR EXPLORER. NY: McGraw, 1978, ix, 435 pp. Fwd: Benjamin Labaree; a useful reference guide presenting over 150 ships.

29 -------. Forests and Sea Power: The Timber Problem of the Royal Navy, 1652-1862. Harvard Economic Studies, vol. 29. Cambridge: Harvard UP; Hamden: Archon; Annapolis: NIP, 1926, 1965, 2000, 512 pp. Intro: Timothy Bean; by the famous "Boats," professor at Harvard; a pre-eminent study, one of the most influential in naval historiography; supply of proper timber increasingly became a problem for the Royal Navy, a '74 SOTL requiring 3000 loads of timber or 60 acres of oaks 100 years old, plus ongoing maintenance demanded enormous supplies; alternatives to disappearing domestic supplies were the Baltic and North America; the logistical situation and its strategic impact have been compared to the decision to adopt oil for propulsion early in the 20th century; e.g., British naval attacks on Copenhagen in 1801 and 1807 were to exclude access to enemies; recent studies have questioned some assertions of Albion.

30 -------. Naval and Maritime History: An Annotated Bibliography. Alt. title: Maritime and Naval History. Mystic: Maritime Association, 1951, 1955, 1963, 1973, 380 pp. General reference guide originally for his "Ocean History" course; 1800 entries with some annotation, including almost 800 dissertations; see update by Benjamin Labaree.

31 -------. "The Timber Problem of the Royal Navy, 1652-1862." MM, 38 (February 1952): 4-22. An earlier version of the above.

32 Alden, Dauril. Charles R. Boxer: An Uncommon Life: Soldier, Historian, Teacher, Collector, Traveller. Lisbon: Oriente, 2000, 616 pp. A major biography of Boxer, 1904-2000, the great multilingual scholar and historian of maritime empires, among other attributes.

33 Alderman, Clifford L. Wooden Ships and Iron Men. NY: Walker, 1964, 134 pp. Juvenile fiction; re a young English sailor, Samuel Leech, who shifted to the American navy during the War of 1812.

34 Aldous, Tony. "Royal Recovery." HisTod, 44 (July 1994): 6-7. About the Royal William Dockyard, Plymouth, informative about facilities, e.g., victualling, brewhouse, cooperage, bakery, slaughterhouse, docks, and offices.

35 Aldridge, David D. "Admiral Sir John Norris and the British Naval Expeditions to the Baltic Sea, 1715-1727." Ph.D. diss, London, 1972. Recounted 6 expeditions commanded by an important figure in logistic issues and operations.

36 -------. "The Victualling of the British Naval Expedition to the Baltic Sea, 1715-1727." Scandinavian Economic History Review, 12 (1964): 1-25. An informative account of 9 expeditions into this new theater of operations of the RN; comanders included Norris, Byng, and Wager.

37 Alexander, Christopher, et al. The MARY ROSE Museum. NY: Oxford UP, 1995, 128 pp. The extensively illustrated account of the creation of this extraordinary museum, located within the Portsmouth Naval Base; MARY ROSE of the 16th century being raised in 1982 along with thousands of artifacts now on display.

38 Alexander, Michael V.C. Charles I's Lord Treasurer: Sir Richard Weston, Earl of Portland, 1577-1635. Chapel Hill: UNCP, 1975, xvi, 261 pp. Fwd: A.L. Rowse; re a leading member of the Navy Board of the 1620s; instrumental in reform and revival effort for the navy.

39 Allen, B.M.M. "Britain, the United States and Maritime Law, 1793-1815: A Study of Opinion on Some Problems Affecting Anglo-American Relations with Regard to Sea-Power." Ph.D. diss, London, 1975. Re Anglo-American legal relationships.

40 Allen, D.F. "The Order of St. John and Cromwell's Navy, 1649-1660." MM, 79 (May 1993): 142-54. An English intervention involving this ancient order traditionally protected by the French and Spanish.

41 Allen, Gardner Weld. A Naval History of the American Revolution. 2 vols. NY: Russell; Williamstown: Corner House, 1913, 1962, 1970, xii, 752 pp. "Aspects of our struggle for independence"; some connections to British naval operations, e.g., in the West Indies, on Lake Champlain, and along the east coast.

42 -------. Our Navy and the Barbary Corsairs. Boston: Houghton; Hamden: Archon, 1905, 1965, xiii, 354 pp. From the American perspective; informative on naval operations.

43 Allen, H.R. Buccaneer: Admiral Sir Henry Morgan. London: Barker, 1976, xii, 193 pp. Re the notorious pirate; Morgan buried at Port Royal and grave disappeared during earthquake.

44 Allen, John Logan, ed. North American Exploration. 3 vols. I: A New World Disclosed. II: A Continent Defined. III: A Continent Comprehended. Lincoln: U Neb P, 1997, xlvi, 1666 pp. A series of essays by experts, balanced and in-depth; e.g., voyages of Irish cleric, Brendon, Welsh prince, Madoc, the Norse, Columbus, John Dee, and the search for the Northwest Passage.

45 Allen, Joseph A. Battles of the British Navy: From AD 1000 to 1840. 2 vols. London: Baily; London: Bell, 1842, 1852, 1889-1890. An older survey.

46 -------. Life of Viscount Nelson. London: Routledge, 1852, xvi, 319 pp. Allen, 1810-1864, produced the last biography able to incorporate those who knew Nelson; a reaction to perceived defamation of the character of Nelson by those such as Pettigrew which was filled, it was claimed, with exposes and infamy, e.g., that the adopted daughter of Nelson was actually his daughter by Lady Hamilton; "the public have no right to pry too deeply into the sanctuary of private life" (p. ix).

47 Allen, Kenneth S. "That BOUNTY Bastard": The True Story of Captain William Bligh. London: Hale; NY: St. Martin, 1976, 1977, 224 pp. Revisionist apologetics, taking its cue from the grave marker, St. Paul's, Lambeth: FRS, Vice-Admiral, fought battles and died, beloved, respected and lamented, also that he was successful, e.g., the second breadfruit voyage; not forthcoming about the curious title.

48 Allen, Paul C. Philip III and the Pax Hispanica, 1598-1621: The Failure of the Grand Strategy. New Haven: Yale UP, 2000, xvi, 336 pp. From a Yale dissertation under Geoffrey Parker; a careful, scholarly study of the era after Philip II characterized by an English succession superseding the failed Habsburg bid for mastery; impressive bibliography.

49 Allen, Roland. "A Stag Stands on Ceremony: Evaluating Some of SUTTON HOO Finds." Bull John Rylands U Lib, 79 (Autumn 1997): 167-75. Analysis of symbols and depictions among the artifacts, e.g., a whetstone stag for kingship and various panels signifying wealth and status.

50 Allingham, Hugh. Captain Cuellar's Adventures in Cannaught and Ulster, 1588. London: Stock, 1897, 72 pp. Trans: Robert Crawford; the account of the Spanish escapee.

51 Allis, Frederick S. Seafaring in Colonial Massachusetts: A Conference Held by the Colonial Society of Massachusetts, 21-22 November 1975. Boston: Colonial Society, 1980, xviii, 240 pp. Series of papers, e.g., Joseph Frese on the role of the RN in smuggling; RN officers served as customs officials rewarded by a percentage of confiscations, all at odds with regular Customs Service officers.

52 Allmand, Christopher T. Henry V. Yale English Monarch series. London: Methuen; New Haven: Yale UP, 1992, 1997, xvi, 480 pp. A solid scholarly study; to de-mythologize Henry from the image presented by Shakespeare and set his rule in context; much experience in war, section of "the Navy": naval forces essential for medieval English warfare; Henry took personal interest; Southampton developed for shipbuilding.

53 -------. The Hundred Years' War: England and France at War, c.1300-c.1450. Cambridge: Cambridge UP, 1988, x, 207 pp. Touted as "total history," presenting English and French perspectives; section on the war at sea.

54 AlMayman, AlJouharah B.S.B. "Richard the Lion Heart and Salah Ad-Din Al-Ayyubi: A Historical Comparative Study." Ph.D. diss, Florida State, 1993, 267 pp. A "parallel biography" of these "two most notable figures of the Crusade era, Richard I and Saladin; details on operations and battles; both represented images of chivalry.

55   Alsop, J.D. "British Intelligence for the North Atlantic Theatre of the War of Spanish Succession." MM, 77 (May 1991): 113-18. Marlborough's "intelligence system" much acclaimed but limited and amateurish, e.g., about French ports.

56   Alsop, J.D. and Hair, P.E.H., eds. English Seamen and Traders in New Guinea, 1553-1565: The New Evidence of their Wills. Dyfed: Mellen, 1992, 392 pp. Innovative and productive use of wills of English seamen of the 16th century who died on the voyages; informative on shipboard life; involved 350 named seamen.

57   Alsop, J.D. "A Regime at Sea: The Navy and the 1553 Succession Crisis." Albion, 24 (Winter 1992): 577-90. Involved Northumberland and Lady Jane Grey; 9 crown ships mobilized but seamen reluctant to serve; effort collapsed, demonstrating difficulty of using navy for political ends.

58   -------. "Sea Surgeons, Health and England's Maritime Expansion: The West African Trade, 1553-1660." MM, 76 (August 1990): 215-21. A case study of problems of mortality, ill health, and incapacitation of seamen, especially serious in West African trade; important contributions of surgeons has been neglected.

59   -------. "Sickness in the British Mediterranean Fleet: The TIGER's Journal of 1706." War and Society, 11 (October 1993): 57-76. A case study of much illness and high mortality but surgeons responded by maintaining journals and recording data.

60   Altman, Artur. The Struggle for Baltic Markets: Powers in Conflict, 1558-1618. Gothenburg: Vetenskaps, 1979, 231 pp. Enlightening on products, mostly naval stores such as hemp, pitch, tar, and timber, and the fact of monetary imbalance which was made up with precious metals from the West to the Baltic states; prominent ports included Danzig, Rega, Viborg, Lubeck, and Archangel.

61   Altoff, Gerard. Oliver Hazard Perry and the Battle of Lake Erie. Put-in Bay: Perry, 1990, 1999, x, 99 pp. Recounts lake battles of 1813.

62   Altschul, Michael. Anglo-Norman England, 1066-1154. Conference on British Studies Bibliography. Cambridge: Cambridge UP, 1969, xii, 83 pp. 1800 annotated entries, including a section on military and naval history (pp. 46-49).

63   Alverez, Manuel F. Tres embajadores de Felipe II en Ingalterra. Madrid: Superior, 1954, 319 pp. A Spanish account, Philip and England.

64   American Historical Association Guide to Historical Literature. 2 vols. NY: Oxford UP, 1949, 1961, 1995, 2052 pp. Ed: Mary Beth Norton; the place to begin a bibliographical search; the most comprehensive and authoritative bibliography of all historical literature divided by sections, based on chronology, geographic area, and field; 27,000 entries in 48 sections; annotation by individual experts and items listed in qualitative order, i.e., the best first.

65 The American Revolution and the Sea: Proceedings of the Fourteenth International Conference of the International Commission for Maritime History. Greenwich: NMM, 1974. A series of published papers, e.g., Haffenden on New England and the RN, Roger Knight on the performance of the Royal Dockyards, and David Syrett on the role of the RN in suppressing rebellion.

66 The Anatomy of the Ship series. London: Conway; Annapolis: NIP, various, typically 128 pp. Illustrated with pictures and schematic line drawings; e.g., HMBark BOUNTY, frigate DIANA, royal yacht CAROLINE, naval cutter ALERT, HMS BELLONA, SUSAN CONSTANT, bomb vessel GRANADO, and ships of Christopher Columbus.

67 Anderson, Bern. Surveyor of the Sea: The Life and Voyages of Captain George Vancouver. Seattle: U Wash P, 1960, 1966, xii, 274 pp. From a Harvard diss; good on the description of the voyages and on problematical issues in the career of Vancouver, e.g., Camelford affair and the disappointing end of his career and his life.

68 Anderson, Charles R. Melville in the South Seas. NY: Columbia UP, 1939, 522 pp. Sponsored by the Modern Language Association; re the sources Melville relied on, his influence on naval reform movements, and plagerizing.

69 Anderson, David. The Spanish Armada. London: Macdonald; NY: Hampstead, 1988, 49 pp. For NMM; large folio size with color illustrations and narrative at clear, understandable level; some revision, e.g., downplays drama, sensation, and fateful interpretations and the Armada seen in Spain as one of many fleet mobilizations under Philip II and other episodes, settling nothing and not weakenilng Spain.

70 Anderson, Fred. Crucible of War: The Seven Years' War and the Fate of Empire in British North America, 1754-1766. London: Faber; NY: Knopf, 2000, xxv, 862 pp. "Retro" interpretation creating considerable scholarly reaction; revives global approach reminiscent of Francis Parkman and Lawrence Gipson concerning imperial expansion and pushes the issue of origins back earlier, to as early as 1450; in this case, the "first world war"; naval engagements emphasized; important factors: the strategy of William Pitt, Louisbourg, Quebec, Quiberon Bay, Havana, Manila, Bengal, and early conflicts involving American Indians; all being the beginning of the end of the British Empire; and all quite persuasive.

71 -------. "Forum on Fred Anderson's Crucible of War." Canadian J of History, 35 (December 2000): 473-506. 6 scholars react to the previous entry and Anderson responds.

72 Anderson, J.L. "Climatic Change, Seapower and Historical Discontinuity: The Spanish Armada and Glorious Revolution of 1688." The Great Circle, 5 (1983): 13-23. An intriguing comparative approach focusing on the impact of climate on events of 1588 and 1688 related to sailing ship warfare and naval engagements, e.g., climatic conditions of the late 16th century were extreme, affecting not only the famous Spanish Armada of 1588 but also subsequent attempts of 1596, 1597, and 1601.

73 Anderson, Matthew S. Britain's Discovery of Russia, 1553-1815. NY: St. Martin, 1958, vi, 245 pp. A scholarly presentation analyzing the impact of Russian expansionism on the English.

74 -------. "Great Britain and the Barbary States in the Eighteenth Century." Bull IHR, 29 (May 1956): 87-107. Posing a threat to commerce in the western Mediterranean; in the 18th century, Britain generally successful in maintaining good relations, e.g., with Morocco, Algiers, Tunis, and Tripoli.

75 -------. Peter the Great. NY: Longman, 1969, 1978, 1995, 2000, ix, 234 pp. A short, solid biography.

76 -------. The War of Austrian Succession, 1740-1748. Modern Wars in Perspective series. London: Longman, 1995, x, 248 pp. An important overview; factors include land, navy, colonies, and commerce.

77 Anderson, Olive. "The Establishment of British Supremacy at Sea and the Exchange of Naval Prisoners of War, 1698-1783." EHR, 75 (January 1960): 77-89. The RN saw return of its prisoners as yet another way to relieve manning problems, e.g., with France in1691 and 1780 and with Spain in 1742 and 1782.

78 -------. "The Impact on the Fleet of the Disposal of Prisoners of War in Distant Waters, 1689-1783." MM, 45 (1959): 243-49. Elaboration on the previous entry.

79 Anderson, Roger Charles. "The Bursledon Ship." MM, 20 (April 1934). By one of the most prominent naval historians, 1883-1976, a founder of SNR and President, 1913-1960, editor of Mariner's Mirror on and off, 1913-1946, for whom a major award, the Anderson Medal, is named; so self-conscious about his contributions that he used an alias, Winton Clare; this work a nautical archaeologist study about GRACE DIEU of Henry V, struck by lightening and burned in 1439.

80 -------. Catalogue of Ship Models. London: HMSO, 1952, 133 pp. For NMM, a listing of famous models.

81 -------. "English Flag Officers, 1688-1713." MM, 35 (October 1949): 333-41. Presenting the evolution of organizational structure, e.g., Center, Van, Rear and Red, White, Blue, respectively, each subdivided into divisions: admiral, vice admiral, and rear admiral; but soon outdated.

82 -------. "The English Fleet at the Battle of Portland." MM, 39 (August 1953): 171-77. Details about participants during this battle of the First Anglo-Dutch War, February 1652; 80 ships listed.

83 -------. "English Galleys in 1295." MM, 14 (July 1928): 220-41. New information fills gaps, an order to build 20 galleys at Newcastle, London, and Southampton.

84 -------. "The First Fifty Years." MM, 47 (1961): 3-16. Celebrating the SNR and its most spectacular achievement: restoration of HMS VICTORY; the campaign began in 1923, the VICTORY museum opening in 1938; important contributions from Caird and Callender.

85 -------. "The GRACE DE DIEU, 1446-1486." EHR, 34 (October 1919): 584-86. The warship of Edward IV, a veteran of the Scottish wars.

86 -------. "Italian Naval Architecture about 1445." MM, 11 (April 1925): 135-63. Details on Venetian galley shipbuilding; designs influential elsewhere.

87 [NRS 64]. Anderson, Roger Charles, ed. The Journal of Edward Montagu, First Earl of Sandwich, Admiral and General at Sea, 1659-1665. Publications of the Navy Records Society, vol. 64. London: NRS, 1929, 329 pp. Recounts his experiences and exploits, e.g., an expedition into the Sound, the Restoration, operations at Algiers and Tangier, and the battle of Lowestoff.

88 [NRS 86]. Anderson, Roger Charles, ed. Journals and Narratives of the Third Dutch War. Publications of the Navy Records Society, vol. 86. London: NRS, 1946, vi, 421 pp. A collection of various journals and descriptions of operations, e.g., the battle of Sole Bay and 3 battles in 1673.

89 [NRS 79 and 80]. Anderson, Roger Charles, ed. The Journals of Sir Thomas Allin, 1660-1678. 2 vols. Publications of the Navy Records Society, vols. 79 and 80. London: NRS, 1939-1940, xiv, 309 and lii, 272 pp. Journals from the Bodleian Library; recounts events of Dutch Wars; 4 Days Battle; to Algiers.

90 Anderson, Roger Charles. List of English Men-of-War, 1509-1649. The Society for Nautical Research Occasional Paper, # 7. Greenwich, SNR, 1959, 1974, 24 pp. An authoritative listing.

91 Anderson, Roger Charles, comp. List of English Naval Captains, 1642-1660. SNR Occasional Publication # 8. London: SNR, 1964, 44 pp. A authoritative listing.

92 Anderson, Roger Charles, et al., comps. Lists of Men-of-War, 1650-1700. 5 parts. London: SNR, 1935-1939, 1959, 24 pp. An international listing, e.g., English, French, Swedish, Danish-Norwegian, and German.

93 Anderson, Roger Charles. Naval Wars in the Baltic, 1522-1850. London: Edwards, 1910, 1969, x, 423 pp. Recounts chronologically the series of naval wars there during the sailing ship era.

94 -------. Naval Wars in the Levant, 1559-1853. Liverpool: Liverpool UP; Princeton: Princeton UP, 1952, 619 pp. An important survey; factors: Turks, Venetians, Russians, Malta, Corfu, Greece, and Syria; interesting conclusions: Lepanto seen to be less important and Russians in the Mediterranean more important.

95 -------. Oared Fighting Ships: From Classical Times to the Coming of Steam. London: Marshall, 1962, 1976, xiv, 99 pp. Covers 2500 years; origins were in the eastern Mediterranean, possibly Crete and not Egypt; triremes and polyremes; 2 chapters on English galleys, pointing out differences from Mediterranean galleys, e.g., no rams and different type of sail.

96 -------. The Rigging of Ships in the Days of the Spritsail Topmast, 1600-1720. Marine Research Society Publication # 14. Salem: Marine Research Society; NY: Dover, 1926, 1982, 1984, 1994, xiv, 278 pp. A classic on riggings of the 17th century, especially useful for modellers.

97 -------. "The ROYAL SOVEREIGN of 1637." MM, 3 parts, 3 (1913): 109-12, 168-70, 208-11. Launched in 1637 at Woolwich, designed and built by Peter Pett, the first 3-decker, 100 guns, destroyed in 1693; fought in First Anglo-Dutch War.

98 -------. "The Royalists at Sea." MM, a series, 14-21 (1928-1935): various. A series of articles in narrative form describing the naval operations of the Royalists during the 1640s and 1650s; a hopeless cause.

99 Anderson, Romola and Anderson, Roger Charles. The Sailing Ship: Six Thousand Years of History. London: Harrap, McBride; NY: Norton, Bonanza, 1926, 1927, 1929, 1948, 1963, 1969, 1971, 1980, 212 pp. The standard history, 134 detailed drawings; coverage from the ships of Egypt, Crete, Phoenicia, Greece, Rome, Northern Europe up through SOTL and the "last days."

100 Anderson, Troyer S. The Command of the Howe Brothers during the American Revolution. London: Oxford UP; NY: Octagon, 1936, 1971, 1972, vii, 368 pp. A scholarly study but overemphasis on land and political aspects, and ends prematurely in 1777.

101 Andidora, Ronald. Iron Admirals: Naval Leadership in the Twentieth Century. Contributions in Military Studies # 194. Westport: Greenwood, 2000, 208 pp. The model is the legacy of Nelson, his heirs of the 20th century.

102 Andrewes, William J. The Quest for Longitude. Cambridge: Harvard UP, 1996, 437 pp. 19 scholarly papers from the Longitude Symposium, Harvard, November 1993, the occasion of the tricentennial of the birth of John Harrison; 4 papers on him; influenced Dava Sobel.

103 Andrews, Alan. Proud Fortress: The Fighting Story of Gibraltar. London: Evans; NY: Dutton, 1958, 212 pp. Re the history of "the Rock."

104 Andrews, Kenneth R. "Appraisements of Elizabethan Privateersmen." MM, 37 (January 1951): 76-98. Use of PRO records of HCA; details about legal processes by the court.

105 -------. "Caribbean Rivalry and the Anglo-Spanish Peace of 1604." History, 59 (February 1974):, 1-17. Activities during Anglo-Spanish peace negotiations; the Spanish were concerned about ending privateering operations but that was not mentioned in the final peace of 1605.

106 -------. Drake's Voyages: A Re-assessment of Their Place in Elizabethan Maritime Expansion. NY: Scribner, 1967, 200 pp. Drake, 1543-1596, led "the heroic phase of English maritime enterprise" (p. 1) and plunder, violence, and marauding were prominent features; all the time "speechifying godliness"; the Spanish dubbed him "El Draque."

107 -------. "The Economic Aspects of Elizabethan Privateering." Ph.D. diss, London, 1951. Much detail and assessments; basis for these entries.

108 -------. Elizabethan Privateering: English Privateering during the Spanish War, 1585-1603. Cambridge: Cambridge, 1964, xvi, 297 pp. An exhaustive study based on his dissertation; details on prizes, prize courts, Admiralty courts, and smuggling; conclusion: continuing linkages between trading, privateering, naval warfare, buccaneering, and piracy to the point that boundaries remained blurred.

109 Andrews, Kenneth R., ed. English Privateering Voyages to the West Indies, 1588-1595. For the Hakluyt Society. Cambridge: Cambridge UP, 1959, xxviii, 421 pp. From HCA records and Spanish documents, narratives of 25 privateering voyages, late 16th century.

110 Andrews, Kenneth R. "English Voyages to the Caribbean, 1596 to 1604: An Annotated List: Notes and Documents." William and Mary Quarterly, 31 (April 1974): 243-54. During the Anglo-Spanish war; a synthesis of information known; description of voyages by ship-name and year.

111 Andrews, Kenneth R., ed. The Last Voyages of Drake and Hawkins. Publication of the Hakluyt Society, 2nd ser, vol. 142. Cambridge: Cambridge UP, 1972, xiv, 283 pp. Re the expedition of 1595, Plymouth to Panama; total failure and death for the leaders.

112 Andrews, Kenneth R. "New Light on Hakluyt." MM, 37 (October 1951): 299-308. Now able to check directly sources used by Hakluyt; conclusion: Hakluyt exaggerated, making Spanish look worse and English better.

113 -------. "Sir Robert Cecil and the Mediterranean Plunder." EHR, 87 (1972): 513-32. Cecil invested in privateering, in this case against Venice, and covered up the fact, thus, a government official sponsoring illegal plunder, all proven by use of

HCA records.

114 -------. Ships, Money and Politics: Seafaring and Naval Enterprise in the Reign of Charles I. Cambridge: Cambridge UP, 1991, ix, 240 pp. It is the time of Ship Money and the Ship Money fleet, the antagonists being North African corsairs and the Dutch; the navy failed to cope, racked by mutinies and disaffection; ultimately explaining why the navy opted for Parliament in the crucial 1640s.

115 -------. The Spanish Caribbean: Trade and Plunder, 1530-1630. New Haven: Yale UP, 1978, xi, 267 pp. The Spanish perspective; factors included maritime trade, colonies, the slave trade, defense, Hawkins, and plunder.

116 -------. Trade, Plunder and Settlement: Maritime Enterprise and the Genesis of the British Empire, 1480-1630. New York: Cambridge UP, 1984, ix, 394 pp. A brilliant and comprehensive synthesis describing the transformation of England based on commercial expansion, often involving aggression, the objects being Spanish and Portuguese, and, to the East, Russian enterprise, but with less aggression against them.

117 Andrews, Kenneth R., Canny, Nicholas P., and Hair, P.E.H., eds. The Western Enterprise: English Activities in Ireland, the Atlantic and America, 1480-1650. Detroit: Wayne State UP, 1978, 1979, xiv, 326 pp. Essays in honor of David Quinn; Quinn concentrated on English expansion and enterprise into the Atlantic.

118 Andrews, William. Bygone Punishments. London: Andrews, 1899, 311 pp. Andrews, 1848-1908, linked to the next entry; a summary of traditional punishment practices.

119 -------. Old-Time Punishments. London: Andrews; London: Muller, 1890, 1972, 251 pp. Elaboration of the previous entry.

120 Anglo-Saxon England, 28 (1999): 428 pp. Entire issue devoted to King Alfred, e.g., ship-building innovations and "founder of the British navy"??

121 Annis, Philip G.W. Naval Swords: British and American Naval Edged Weapons, 1600-1815. Harrisburg: Stackpole, 1970, 80 pp. An informed illustrated survey.

122 Annis, Philip G.W., ed. Sea Studies: Essays in Honour of Basil Greenhill. Greenwich: NMM, 1983. A series of essays, e.g., Roger Knight on civilians and the navy, 1660-1832.

123 Anson, George. A Voyage Round the World. . . . London: Oxford UP, 1748, 1928, 1970, 1974, xxv, 402 pp. Anson's voyage, 1739-1748; the account was a best-seller, various editors then and now, e.g., Richard Walter, Benjamin Robbins, William Laird Clowes, L.A. Wilcox, and Glyndwr Williams; major losses in ships and men, much scurvy; exploits included capture of the Manila galleon.

124 Anson, Walter Vernon. The Life of Admiral Lord Anson: The Father of the British Navy, 1690-1762. London: Murray, 1912, xx, 202 pp. A biography of the great explorer-buccaneer-Admiralty official; curious subtitle.

125 Ansted, A. A Dictionary of Sea Terms. Glasgow: Brown, 1917, 1928, 1985, 355 pp. An important addition under nautical dictionaries, updated occasionally, still timely.

126 Anthony, Irvin, ed. The Saga of the BOUNTY: Its Strange History as Related by the Participants Themselves. NY: Putnam, 1935, xiv, 358 pp. Accounts, often contradictory, by various participants, e.g., Bligh, Christian, Fryer, Morrison, also, Sir John Barrow.

127 Appleby, John C. "The ANNE OF DUBLIN: A Sixteenth-Century Man-of-War." Irish Sword, 17 (Summer 1988): 74-80. From HCA records, informative details on the voyage of this privateer during 1557; degenerated into piracy.

128 -------. "English Privateering during the Spanish and French Wars, 1625-1630." Ph.D. diss, Hull, 1983, 734 pp. An extensive survey.

129 Appleby, John C. and O'Dowd, Mary. "The Irish Admiralty: Its Organisation and Development, c.1570-1640." Irish Historical Studies, 24 (May 1985): 299-326. Defense of surrounding seas by the Admiralty in London; also must administer and enforce "law maritime"; in mid-16th century, delegated to Admiralty Court which expanded during the next centuries; duties included salvage, wrecks, pirates, sea-rovers, and wages.

130 Appleby, John C. "A Nursery of Pirates: The English Pirate Community in Ireland in the Early Seventeenth Century." International J Maritime History, 2 (June 1990): 1-27. Irish bases notorious as part of a network of plunder; privateering no longer legal and economic conditions deteriorated, forcing many into plunder.

131 -------. "A Pathway Out of Debt: Activities of Sir John Hippisley during the Early Stuart Wars with Spain and France, 1625-1630." AmNep, 49 (Fall 1989): 251-61. An informative case study demonstrating varying elements of patronage, plunder, and power in these ventures; a prominent crown official resorted to privateering to relieve his debts.

132 Apps, Michael. The Four ARK ROYALS. London: Kimber, 1976, 256 pp. Fwd: Michael Fell; a historical account of famous ships.

133 Archer, Thomas A. The Crusade of Richard I, 1189-1192. NY: Putnam; NY: AMS, 1889, 1912, 1978, xii, 395 pp. Several monarchs on Crusade, Richard, as Count of Poitou, vowed to go, actually departed in 1190 after he became king aboard "the great English fleet"; some details, 33 ships from Cinque Ports plus many others, transported to Acre; Richard shipwrecked and captured en route home.

134 Archibald, E.H.H. The Fighting Ship in the Royal Navy, AD 897-1984. Annapolis: NIP, 1984, 416 pp. A revised edition combined into a single volume; recounts material developments, naval architecture, and participation in battles covering over 1000 years.

135 -------. The Wooden Fighting Ships in the Royal Navy, AD 897-1860. London: Blandford; NY: Arco, 1968, 1970, 174 pp. Folio size with many illustrations; ships, pictures, and events from the time of Alfred to the mid-19th century.

136 Armitage, Christopher M. Sir Walter Ralegh: An Annotated Bibliography. Chapel Hill: UNCP, 1987, viii, 236 pp. For the America's Four Hundredth Anniversary Committee; Raleigh, 1552-1618; 1967 annotated entries.

137 Armitage, David. "Making the Empire British: Scotland in the Atlantic World, 1542-1717." Past and Present, 155 (May 1997): 34-63. Critique that historians of "British" Empire who ignore or neglect roles of Scotland and Ireland, e.g., Franco-Scottish alliance of 1540s.

138 Armstrong, Edward. "Venetian Despatches on the Armada and its Results." EHR, 12 (October 1897): 659-78. Sources of naval history; Venetian officials reported events, e.g., Drake's raid on Cadiz and delay of Armada.

139 Armstrong, John and Cutler, John. "The British Coastal Fleet in the Eighteenth Century: How Useful Are the Admiralty Registers of Protection from Impressment." AmNep, 60 (Siummer 2000): 235-51. A study of the development and effectiveness of lists of exemptions for impressment.

140 Armstrong, Richard. A History of Seafaring. 3 vols. I: The Early Mariners. II: The Discoverers. III: The Merchantmen. London: Benn; NY: Praeger, 1967-1969, 381 pp. A trilogy, folio size, illustrated; a superficial overview.

141 Arnold, David. The Age of Discovery, 1400-1600. Lancaster Pamphlets. London: Methuen, 1983, x, 43 pp. Places in global context; voyaging not unique to Europe, e.g., Arabs, Chinese, and, especially, the Polynesians.

142 Arthur, Charles B. The Remaking of the English Navy by Admiral St. Vincent: The Great Unclaimed Naval Revolution, 1795-1805. Lanham: UP of America, 1986, xi, 578 pp. Aim is to credit Sir John Jervis, Lord St. Vincent, and Sandwich with major reforms laying the foundation for British naval hegemony; idiosyncratic, excessive capitalization, exaggeration, and conspiracy theories mar the effort; exaggerated and unconvincing; elsewhere, this is the Nelson Decade.

143 -------. "The Revolution in British Naval Strategy, 1800-1801." Ph.D. diss, Harvard, 1966. The basis of the previous entry.

144 Ashburer, Walter. The Rhodian Sea-Law. Oxford: Clarendon; Union: Law Book, 1909, 2001, ccxcvi, 131 pp. Best on medieval shipping practice, especially on legal aspects; the foundation for maritime law.

145 Ashe, Geoffrey. <u>Land to the West: St. Brendan's Voyage to America</u>. NY: Viking, 1962, 352 pp. Dedicated to "unknown author of the <u>Navigatio Sancti Brendani</u>"; speculative; legend connects St. Brendan with Arthurian and Madoc stories; he was a prince from north Wales who went to sea exploring to the West in 1170.

146 Ashe, Geoffrey, <u>et al</u>. <u>The Quest for America</u>. NY: Praeger, 1971, 298 pp. Folio size, exquisite production, glossy color; a synthesis of pre-Columbian exploration, e.g., mythical, literary, archaeological, and historical evidence.

147 Asher, G.M., ed. <u>Henry Hudson, the Navigator: The Original Documents</u>. <u>Publications of the Hakluyt Society</u>, 1st ser, vol. 27. London: Hakluyt Society, 1860, ccxvii, 292 pp. An early production of the society, the voyages of Hudson.

148 Ashley, Mike, ed. <u>The Mammoth Book of Men O'War</u>. NY: Carroll; London: Robinson, 1999, xvi, 496 pp. Intro: Alexander Kent; an anthology of 18 excerpts from the period, 1790-1820, e.g., O'Brian, Forester, Woodman, Melville, and Styles; elsewhere, Nelson Decade period.

149 Ashley, Raymond E. "The Search for Longitude." <u>AmNep</u>, 51 (Fall 1991): 252-66. The solution to the ancient riddle was solved in the 18th century, the result of pure science and state-supported research.

150 Aslet, Clive. <u>Greenwich Millennium: The 2000-Year Story of Greenwich</u>. London: Fourth Estate, 1999, 64 pp. A pamphlet commemorating the events of the millennium at Greenwich.

151 -------. <u>The Story of Greenwich</u>. Cambridge: Harvard UP; London: Fourth Estate, 1999, 288 pp. The history of this "center of maritime expansion," the Observatory, Queen's House, the palace, and NMM; includes description of funeral of Nelson.

152 Aspley, John. <u>"Speculum Nauticum": A Looking-Glass for Sea-Men</u>. London: Godbin, 1642, 1655, 1668, 1678, 96 pp. An early nautical dictionary; the original in the Bodleian Library; "first set down by John Aspley"; numerous editions.

153 Aston, George G. <u>Nelson</u>. <u>Benn's Sixpenny Library</u>. London: Benn, 1927, 80 pp. A biography for juveniles.

154 Astrom, Sven-Erik. <u>From Cloth to Iron: The Anglo-Baltic Trade in the Late Seventeenth Century</u>. 2 vols. Helsingfors: Fennica, 1963-1965, 346 pp. Details on the Scandanavian trade of England.

155 Atkinson, Alan. <u>The Europeans in Australia: A History</u>. Vol. I: <u>The Beginning</u>. London: Oxford UP, 1997, xviii, 429 pp. The first volume of a projected trilogy, covers the first thirty years; topics include convict settlement and governorship of Bligh.

156 Attman, Arthur. "The Russian Market in World Trade, 1500-1860." Scandinavian Economic History Review, 29 (1981): 177-202. The story, including Vikings, Russians, Hanseatic League, and Novgorod; products, including flax, tar, and hemp, essential for shipbuilding; noted imbalance.

157 Aubrey, Philip. The Defeat of James Stuart's Armada, 1692. Leicester: Leicester UP, 1979, 194 pp. A detailed review of events, 1688-1692, consequences of the Revolution of 1688, e.g., escape of James II, landing of William, Beachy Head, and Barfleur.

158 Aughton, Peter. ENDEAVOUR: The Story of Captain Cook's First Great Epic Voyage. Gloucester: Windrush, 1999, 224 pp. A major exploratory and scientific voyage incorporating astronomers, naturalists, artists, and, secretly, explorers to map Australia.

159 Averley, Gwendoline. "English Scientific Societies of the Eighteenth and Early Nineteenth Centuries." Ph.D. diss, Council National Awards, U.K., 1989, 436 pp. The origins and development of these societies, e.g., the Royal Society.

160 Avery, R.W. "The Naval Protection of Britain's Maritime Trade, 1793-1802." D.Phil. diss, Oxford, 1983. Operations resulting from the French Revolution and its expansion.

161 Avery, William P. "Thrust and Counter." MM, 75 (November 1989): 333-48. Re naval operations during 1799, the British blockading Brest, the French escaped; the conclusion: the French had capable leaders, deficient personnel while the British had efficient personnel, lacked capable leaders.

162 Ayer, Robert C. "Shifty Seafarers, Shifting Winds: Governmental Policies toward Maritime Smuggling in North America from Colonization to the War of 1812." Ph.D. diss, Fletcher School, 1993, 425 pp. Maritime smuggling, governmental efforts to suppress, and resistance by colonists as factors in the revolution and new American government.

163 Aymar, Brandt, ed. Men at Sea: The Best Sea Stories of All Time from Homer to William F. Buckley, Jr. NY: Crown, 1988, 640 pp. Fictional and actual accounts of battles, shipwrecks, and mutinies.

164 Babits, Lawrence E. and Van Tilburg, Hans, eds. Maritime Archaeology: A Reader of Substantive and Theoretical Contributions. The Plenum Series in Underwater Archaeology. NY: Plenum, 1998, xx, 590 pp. An anthology of 50 articles for academic courses; dedicated to founders, Bass, Muckelroy, Ruppe, and Throckmorton; a history of nautical archaeology.

165 Bach, John. A Maritime History of Australia. London: Hamilton, 1976, xiv, 481 pp. Re the development period, 1788-1850; Australia was a creature of maritime enterprise, especially British sea power.

166 Bachrach, Bernard S. "On the Origins of William the Conqueror's Horse Transports." Technology and Culture, 25 (July 1985): 505-53. Details on the logistics for the largest amphibious operation since the Roman Empire, e.g., how William transported large groups of horses and influences of development, the Byzantines.

167 -------. "The Question of King Arthur's Existence and the Romano-British Naval Operations." Haskins Society J, 2 (1990): 13-28. Thesis: the location of Athur's battles suggests that he may have been a notable naval commander of 5th and 6th centuries.

168 -------. "Some Observations on the Military Administration of the Norman Conquest." Anglo-Norman Studies, 8 (1985): 1-27. Administrative factors, e.g., types, means, and terms of service, logistics, equipment, and manpower.

169 Backscheider, Paula R. Daniel Defoe: His Life. Balt: JHUP, 1986, 1989, xv, 671 pp. A biography in a series on 18th-century authors.

170 Badham, Francis P. Nelson at Naples: A Journal for June 10-30, 1799 Refuting Recent Misstatements of Captain Mahan and Professor J.K. Laughton. London: Nutt, 1900, viii, 48 pp. A contribution to the debate over the actions of Nelson at Naples.

171 Baer, Joel H. "William Dampier at the Crossroads: New Light on the 'Missing Years,' 1691-1697." International J Maritime History, 8 (December 1996): 97-117. Accounts of voyages and exploits of pirates were popular; Dampier broadened the subject matter.

172 Bagrow, Leo. History of Cartography. Berlin: Safari; London: Watts; Chicago: Precedent, 1951, 1964, 1966, 1985, 312 pp. Bagrow, 1881-1957, produced a formative work, originally in German.

173 Bailey, Anthony. "Inferno on the Medway." MHQ, 9 (Summer 1997): 50-59. A popularized account of the audacious naval raid by the Dutch.

174 Bailey, Chris H. Remembering Nelson. Portsmouth: Royal Naval Museum, forthcoming. Re the Nelsonian Collection of Lilly McCarthy at the Museum.

175 Baker, H.A. The Crisis of Naval Ordnance. Maritime Monographs and Reports # 56. London: NMM, 1983, 49 pp. Intro: Basil Greenhill, ed: P.G.W. Annis; new technology, especially new methods of smelting, led to advances, laying the foundation of the dramatic expansion of the 1790s; Barham credited.

176 Baker, J.N.L. A History of Geographical Discovery and Exploration. NY: Cooper Square; London: Harrap, 1931, 1937, 1945, 1967, 552 pp. An outstanding short general survey.

177 Baker, Raymond F. A Campaign of Amateurs: The Siege of Louisbourg, 1745. Ottawa: Parks, 1978, 150 pp. A government publication assessing the campaign.

178 Baker, William A. The New MAYFLOWER: Her Design and Construction. Barre: Barre, 1958, xviii, 164 pp. By the architect, constructed in the 1950s after a thorough study of ship design of the 17th century.

179 [NHS-14] Balano, Randy C. and Symonds, Craig, eds. New Interpretations in Naval History: Selected Papers from the Fourteenth Naval History Symposium. Annapolis: NIP, 2001, xiv, 433 pp. The 14th NHS, 23-25 September 1999; a selection of papers, e.g., Richard Harding on British naval historiography, Baugh on naval administration, and Vandervort on the French navy.

180 Bald, John. "Naval Regulations, c. 1530." HisTod, 41 (June 1991): 30. A one-page excerpt from the "Booke of Orders for the Warre both by Sea and Land" by Thomas Audley, commanded by Henry VIII.

181 Balderston, Marion and Syrett, David, eds. The Lost War: Letters from British Officers during the American Revolution. NY: Horizon, 1975, xi, 237 pp. Intro: Henry Steele Commager; letters from army and naval officers; some observations: general overconfidence demonstrated, victory being inevitable for the British and bitterness against the rebels, especially in Boston.

182 Baldwin, Robert. Navigation, Cartography and the Expansion of Europe, 1440-1640: Collection of Essays. Oxford: Headstart, 1997. An analysis of the contributions facilitating the expansion.

183 Ballard, Robert D. The Eternal Darkness: A Personal History of Deep-Sea Exploration. Princeton: Princeton UP, 2000, xii, 388 pp. A short history by a primary spokesman and practitioner, discoverer of TITANIC, LUSITANIA, BISMARCK, plus some ancient wrecks.

184 -------. Explorations: An Autobiography: My Quest for Adventure and Discovery Under the Sea. London: Weidenfeld, 1995, viii, 407 pp. A memoir by this extraordinary oceanographer-celebrity.

185 Ballentyne, Iain. WARSPITE: Warships of the Royal Navy. London: Pen and Sword, 2001. An account of this famous ship.

186 Ballhausen, Phil Carl. Der Erste Englische-Hollandische Seekrieg, 1652-1654 sowie der Schwedishch-Hollandische Seekrieg, 1658-1659. The Hague: Nijhoff, 1923. From the Dutch perspective; 2 wars, against the English and the Swedes.

187 Bamford, Paul W. Fighting Ships and Prisons: The Mediterranean Galleys of France. Minneapolis: U Minn P, 1973, x, 380 pp. Re naval operations in the Mediterranean in the 17th century and about galleys as "prisons."

188 -------. Forests and French Sea Power, 1660-1789. Toronto: Toronto UP, 1956, 240 pp. Re the timber problem as a phase of naval activity; involved a program to manage French forests sponsored by the navy; it ultimately failed; a study similar to that of Robert Albion for the British.

189 -------. "French Naval Timber: A Study of the Relation of Forests to French Sea Power, 1660-1789." Ph.D. diss, Columbia, 1951, 409 pp. The basis for the previous entry.

190 -------. "French Shipping in Northern European Trade, 1660-1789." J Modern History, 26 (September 1954): 207-19. Neglect by the French led to domination of the trade by Dutch, British, and Swedish shipping.

191 -------. "The Procurement of Oarsmen for French Galleys, 1660-1748." AHR, 65 (October 1959): 31-48. A case study of manpower procurement, sources being slaves and prisoners, including Huguenots; need for 12,000 at high point in 1690s.

192 Banbury, Philip. Shipbuilders of the Thames and Medway. Newton Abbot: David and Charles, 1971, 336 pp. A study of these important shipbuilders.

193 Bancroft, George. History of the Battle of Lake Erie and Miscellaneous Papers. NY: Bonner, 1891, 264 pp. By the great American historian, 1800-1891; an account of the lake battle.

194 Bang-Andersen, Arne, Greenhill, Basil, and Grude, Egil H., eds. The North Sea: A Highway of Economic and Cultural Exchange: Character, History. Oslo: Norwegian UP, 1985, 277 pp. A collection of essays, e.g., Ryan on trade between enemies at the time of the Continental System and others on warfare in the North Sea and Dutch sea power.

195 Banks, Joseph. The Papers of Sir Joseph Banks. Marlborough: Adam Matthew, 1993, Microfilm. On 34 reels from papers held at the British Library.

196 Bannerman, John. Studies in the History of Dalriada. Edinburgh: Scottish Academic, 1974, x, 178 pp. A series of papers about these fascinating people and time, the kingdom of Dal Riata about 500-800; based in Ireland and Scotland, thus, the sea unified them; the "navy" of the Celtic peoples; naval forces, mostly small oared ships, were described.

197 Barany, George. The Anglo-Russian Entente Cordiale of 1697-1698: Peter I and William III at Utrecht. NY: Columbia UP, 1986, viii, 101 pp. An international arrangement during the famous visit of Peter to the West, January-April 1698, including a meeting with William III when agreement of interests in military, technology, and commerce factors were reached.

198 Barbour, Violet. "Dutch and English Merchant Shipping in the Seventeenth Century." Economic History Review, 2 (January 1930): 261-90. Merchant ships and warships were similar; merchants were encouraged to build "stout" ships and man them well, for dual purposes; a basis for the Navigation Acts.

199 -------. "Privateers and Pirates of the West Indies." AHR, 16 (April 1911): 529-66. While it was being suppressed in European waters, piracy flourished in the West Indies; first were the French, then the English, later, the Dutch, and, increasingly, independent buccaneers, a piratical fraternity; it continued to rule through the 18th century.

200 Barck, Dorothy C., ed. Letter Books and Order-Book of George, Lord Rodney. 2 vols. NY: Naval History Society, 1932, xxiii, 932 pp. Rodney was a commander in the West Indies in the 1780s; topics include intelligence, convoys, and naval operations.

201 Bard, Nelson P. "'Might and Would Not': The Earl of Warwick's Privateering Expedition of 1627." AmNep, 55 (Winter 1995): 5-18. Warwick, 1584-1658, led a fleet in a suppression campaign.

202 -------. "The Ship Money Case and William Fiennes, Viscount Saye and Sele." Bull IHR, 50 (November 1977): 177-84. Charles I vowed to avoid calling Parliament and Fiennes obstructed some measures.

203 -------. [Biography of Robert Rich, 2nd Earl of Warwick]. In 1984, noted as in preparation; re one of the greatest privateers, e.g., sending out 4 fleets in the 1620s.

204 Barker, Derek. "British Naval Officers' Buttons, 1748-1975." MM, 63 (November 1977): 373-87. Re uniform arrangements; many illustrations.

205 Barker, Felix. "If Parma Had Landed." HisTod, 38 (May 1988): 34-41. Counterfactual history; English militia along the southern coast was half-trained and ill-equipped.

206 [Barker, Matthew H.] "By an Old Sailor." The Life of Nelson. London: Tegg, 1836, 1838, 1867, 486 pp. Barker, 1790-1846, a vivid writer of the sea; praise for the Nicholas biography; for the time, a comprehensive biography with many facts and anecdotes, some new.

207 Barker, Thomas M. "A Debacle of the Peninsular War: The British-Led Amphibious Assault against Fort Fuengirola, 14-15 October 1810." J Military History, 64 (January 2000): 9-52. Assessment of the campaign; problems of faulty collaboration between the army and navy and lack of surprise.

208 Barlow, Frank. The Godwins: The Rise and Fall of a Noble Dynasty. NY:

Longman, 2002, xiv, 141 pp. A recent study of the last of the Anglo-Saxon nobility-monarchy.

209 Barnard, John E. Building Britain's Wooden Walls: The Barnard Dynasty, 1697-1851. London: Nelson, 1997, 1998, 180 pp. Fwd: Jean Sutton; re 4 generations of shipwrights for the RN and East India Company.

210 [NRS 69, 71, 75, and 78]. Barnes, G.R. and Owen, J.H., eds. The Private Papers of John, Earl of Sandwich, First Lord of the Admiralty, 1771-1782. 4 vols. Publications of the Navy Records Society, vols. 69, 71, 75, and 78. London: NRS, 1932-1938, xxx, 456, xiv, 394, x, 333, and xii, 446 pp. The 5th volume was a "victim of World War II"; at the Admiralty during the 1740s and 1770s; including operational papers of the First Lord.

211 Barnes, James. Naval Actions of the War of 1812. London: Harper; London: Cornmarket, 1896, 1969, 263 pp. 19 essays, each about a naval engagement accompanied by a color painting; criticized as chauvinistic.

212 Barnett, Correlli. Bonaparte. London: Allen and Unwin, 1978, 1998, 224 pp. A short biography by the prolific author-scholar of British naval history.

213 -------. Engage the Enemy More Closely: The Royal Navy in the Second World War. London: Hodder; New York: Norton, 1991, xx, 1050 pp. The title comes from the final signal of Nelson to the British fleet at Trafalgar; the most provocative naval history of the war.

214 Barnett, Richard C. "The View from Below Deck: The British Navy, 1777-1781." AmNep, 38 (April 1978): 92-100. The memoir of John Stradley, 1757-1825, impressed seaman aboard HMS GRAFTON, '74.

215 Barone, Robert W. "The Reputation of John Dee: A Critical Appraisal." Ph.D. diss, Ohio State, 1989, 204 pp. Details about this fascinating figure.

216 Barr, William and Williams, Glyndwr, eds. Voyages to Hudson Bay in Search of a Northwest Passage, 1741-1747. 2 vols. Publications of the Hakluyt Society, 2nd ser, vols. 180 and 181. London: Hakluyt Society, 1994-1995, xxvii, 726 pp. Accounts of two exploration voyages sponsored by the Hudson Bay Company and the Northwest Committee; both failed and were subject to criticism.

217 Barras, T.C. "Vice-Admiral Lord Nelson's Lost Eye." Trans Ophthalmological Societies of the United Kingdom, 1986. Demonstrative of the variety of interest in Nelson.

218 Barritt, M.K. "Nelson's Frigates: May to August, 1798." MM, 58 (August 1972): 281-96. An important aspect of the British naval return to the Mediterranean in 1797; Nelson was desperate for information about French machinations in 1798, knowing Napoleon was leading a large force; "my want of frigates is extreme," he lamented; details on where the frigates were; noted how Mahan misinterpreted several incidents.

219 Barrow, John. <u>A Chronological History of Voyages into the Arctic Regions</u>. London: Murray; NY: Barnes, 1818, 1971, x, 379 pp. Intro: Christopher Lloyd; Barrow, 1764-1848, a prominent Admiralty official in the tradition of Samuel Pepys and propagandist in the tradition of Sir Joseph Banks; Secretary for over 40s years; founder of the Royal Geographical Society and member of the Royal Society for 50 years; land and sea points of Arctic named for him.

220 -------. <u>The Eventful History of the Mutiny and Piratical Seizure of HMS BOUNTY: Its Causes and Consequences</u>. London: Folio Society; Boston: Godine, 1831, 1845, 1876, 1914, 1931, 1980, 1989, xi, 356 pp. Series of editions and series of editors, e.g., Cyprian Bridge, Stephen Roskill, and Gavin Kennedy; semi-official and the most important of the early accounts; thorough about events before, during, and after the mutiny, including Pitcairn Island episodes.

221 -------. <u>The Life and Correspondence of Admiral Sir Sidney Smith</u>. 2 vols. London: Murray, 1848. An older life and times biography.

222 -------. <u>The Life of George Lord Anson, Admiral of the Fleet</u>. London: Murray, 1839, xxxiv, 484 pp. An older biography of Anson, an important circumnavigator, successful in battle, and brilliant administrator; use of preface to answer critics of his <u>Life of Howe.</u>

223 -------. <u>The Life of Richard Earl Howe</u>. London: Murray, 1838. The only full biography of Howe until the 1970s.

224 Barrow, John, ed. <u>Voyages of Discovery: Captain Cook</u>. NY: Dutton; Chicago: Academy, 1860, 1906, 1909, 1932, 1991, ix, 479 pp. An account of the 3 voyages.

225 Barrow, John. <u>The Life, Voyages, and Exploits of Admiral Sir Francis Drake, with Numerous Original Letters from Him and the Lord High Admiral to the Queen and Great Officers of State</u>. London: Murray, 1843, 428 pp. Barrow, 1808-1898, the son; an important, older biography.

226 Barthorpe, Michael. <u>Napoleon's Egyptian Campaign, 1798-1799</u>. <u>Men-at-Arms</u> series. London: Osprey, 1978, 40 pp. A brief, clear, reliable survey of the campaign.

227 Bartlett, Christopher J. "Gentlemen vs. Democrats: Cultural Prejudice and Military Strategy in Britain in the War of 1812." <u>War in History</u>, 1 (July 1944): 140-59. Re British government and Admiralty strategy and intervention in operations in America; the campaign of the RN, including blockade operations, attacks on Baltimore and Washington, and operations in the Great Lakes.

228 Bartlett, Thomas and Jeffery, Keith, eds. <u>A Military History of Ireland</u>. London: Cambridge UP, 1996, xxv, 565 pp. An introduction and 18 scholarly essays; 1500 years of varied military activity; most about armies but includes a little on Irish naval service and operations, for and against, e.g., the Bantry Bay operation and Irish officers in the RN.

229 Barzun, Jacques. Introduction to Naval History: An Outline with Diagrams and Glossary. Chicago: Lippincott, 1944, 246 pp. Notes from a introductory course.

230 Basch, Lucien. "Ancient Wreck and the Archaeology of Ships." International J Nautical Archaeology, 1 (1972): 1-58. An overview of the field.

231 Bass, George F., ed. A History of Seafaring: Based on Underwater Archaeology. London: Thames; NY: Walker, 1972, 320 pp. Folio size, illustrated; essays by experts, e.g., on Viking, Scandinavian, and Hanseatic League shipbuilding, Alexander McKee on British naval strategy, and on privateering.

232 -------, ed. Ships and Shipwrecks of the Americas: A History Based on Underwater Archaeology. London: Thames, 1988, 272 pp. Folio size, illustrated, including many in color; many authors from Texas A&M programme; re information from excavation of shipwrecks, e.g., a Norse site in Newfoundland, naval transports from the French and Indian War, and wrecks from the Great Lakes.

233 Bateson, Charles. The Convict Ships, 1787-1868. Glasgow: Brown, 1959, 355 pp. Re the "transportation fleet," ships transporting criminals to Australia, a 13,000 mile voyage taking 6 months; details, voyage by voyage, e.g., flogging records, ratio of men to women, mutinies, and health situation.

234 Battesti, Michele. La bataille d'Aboukir 1798: Nelson contrarie la strategie de Bonaparte. Paris: Economica, 1998, xxxiii, 263 pp. A French account of the campaign culminating in the battle of the Nile, on the occasion of the bicentennial.

235 Battick, John F. "Cromwell's Navy and the Foreign Policy of the Protectorate, 1653-1658." Ph.D. diss, Boston, 1967, 344 pp. A neglected topic; Cromwell appreciated sea power as an instrument of diplomacy; concluded Anglo-Dutch War and sent squadrons into Mediterranean and to the West Indies.

236 The Battle of Trafalgar. Jackdaw. London: Cape, 1963, portfolio. The famous educational packets, this one on Trafalgar and a formative one.

237 Baugh, Daniel A. British Naval Administration in the Age of Walpole. Princeton: Princeton UP, 1965, xvi, 557 pp. Baugh, 1938-____, the premier historian of British naval administration; focused on period, 1739-1748; the navy was an enormous organization and its administration was a microcosm of national administration; the most pressing problem was recruitment of seamen in wartime; features, e.g., reforms of Anson and Hawke blockading Brest; a very important and valuable study.

238 -------. "British Naval Administration in the War of 1739-1748." Ph.D. diss,

Cambridge, 1961. The basis for the previous entry.

239 -------. "Great Britain's Blue-Water Policy, 1689-1815." International History Review, 10 (February 1988): 33-58. An important article; "The British Way of Warfare," the title of over 30 books; re the making of British naval strategy; Corbett best articulated it, influenced by Clausewitz; defensive in Europe, aggressive overseas; better term is "Blue-Water Strategy," originating in the mid-17th century, e.g., the Anglo-Dutch War and Navigation Acts.

240 [NRS 120]. Baugh, Daniel A., ed. Naval Administration, 1715-1750. Publications of the Navy Records Society, vol. 120. London: NRS, 1977, xvi, 523 pp. The two studies of naval administration and other works by Baugh are the standard studies of naval administration, anytime and anyplace; takes up where Merriman left off, re the navy of Queen Anne.

241 Baugh, Daniel A. "The Politics of British Naval Failure, 1775-1777." AmNep, 52 (Fall 1992): 221-46. How could the pre-eminent naval power fail in North America?; proceeds to answer, e.g., budget cutbacks, timber shortages, poor officers, combination of European enemies; the sea-naval approach to the problem was overruled by government officials.

242 -------. "Withdrawing from Europe: Anglo-French Maritime Geopolitics, 1750-1800." International History Review, 20 (March 1998): 1-32. The culmination of 7 lengthy wars, perpetual rivalry at sea; about 1750, British policy changed: less emphasis on Europe and more on global and colonial concerns.

243 Baumber, Michael L. "Cromwell's Soldier Admirals." HisTod, 39 (October 1989): 42-47. Re Blake, Richard Deane, Edward Popham, Monck, Penn, James Disbrowe, and Edward Montagu.

244 -------. General-at-Sea: Robert Blake and the Seventeenth-Century Revolution in Naval Warfare. London: Murray, 1989, viii, 284 pp. Places Blake in category of Nelson and Drake; Blake began in the army, Cromwell shifted him to navy, and he achieved several naval victories; superficial, popular study; unconvincing.

245 -------. "The Navy and Civil War in Ireland, 1641-1643." MM, 57 (November 1971): 385-98. In 1641, rebellion in Ireland created distractions during the Civil War, Parliament being overextended; small ships secured the Dublin-Chester passage.

246 -------. "The Navy and the Civil War in Ireland, 1643-1646." MM, 75 (August 1989): 255-68. Another example of the Parliamentary navy influencing victory in the Civil War, its blockade being decisive in preventing invasion from Ireland.

247 -------. "Parliamentary Naval Politics, 1641-1649." MM, 82 (November 1996): 398-408. The navy was inevitably drawn into politics during the Civil War.

248 Baxter, James P. "The Nelson Manuscripts in the Harvard College Library." Harvard Library Notes, 22 (May 1919). Another Nelson collection.

249 Baylis, T. Henry. The True Account of Nelson's Famous Signal. London: N.p., 1905, 32 pp. Touts illustration of the correct flags; noted Laughton depiction in error.

250 Baynham, Henry W.F. From the Lower Deck: The Old Navy, 1780-1840. London: Hutchinson, 1969, 1970, 200 pp. First of a trilogy by this noted historian of the lower deck; individual recollections from 9 seamen, important issues being impressment, punishments, and changes taking place; accounts of Cape St. Vincent, the Nile, Trafalgar, and Navarino.

251 Beadon, Roger H. Robert Blake: Sometime Commanding All the Fleets and Naval Forces England. London: Arnold, 1935, 308 pp. Among the greatest of the English men of action, creator and chief architect of the Parliamentary navy; emphasis on character and achievements.

252 Beaglehole, John C. Captain Cook and Captain Bligh. Wellington: Victorian UP, 1967, 27 pp. Beaglehole, 1901-1971, from New Zealand; the authority on James Cook; this the W.E. Collins Lecture of 1967.

253 -------. The Discovery of New Zealand. London: Oxford UP, 1939, 1961. xvi, 160 pp. Describes an important event in the voyages of Cook.

254 -------. Eighteenth-Century Science and the Voyage of Discovery. Pamphlet of the Royal Society of New Zealand, n.d., 120 pp. Re Joseph Banks, the ENDEAVOUR voyage, his later voyage to Iceland, and associated advances in science, e.g., the transit of Venus, specimen collections, and navigation instruments.

255 -------. The ENDEAVOUR Journal of Joseph Banks, 1768-1771. 2 vols. Sydney: Angus, 1963, 984 pp. Banks went on the first voyage as chief naturalist, this being a major contribution.

256 -------. The Exploration of the Pacific. London: Black, 1934, 1947, 1966, xv, 410 pp. Exploration of the Pacific from Magellan to Cook, including the long search for "Terra Australis"; Balboa the first European to sight it, others included Magellan, Dampier, Bougainville, and Cook; this work stimulated his interest in Cook.

257 -------. The Life of Captain James Cook. Stanford: Stanford UP, 1974, 1992, xi, 760 pp. Captain James Cook, 1728-1779, combination sailor, explorer, navigator, and cartographer; the authoritative, acclaimed biography, massively researched, outstanding writing.

258 -------. "Some Problems of Editing Cook's Journals." Historical Studies, 8 (November 1957): 31-50. The journals were never printed as Cook wrote them and are more complex than most realized, e.g., multiple accounts of incidents.

259 Beals, Herbert K. The Last Temperate Coast: Maritime Exploration of Northwest America, 1542-1794: Map and Broadside. Portland: Oregon Historical Society, 1991. Recounts 13 sea exploratory endeavors, e.g., English, Spanish, French, Russian; 15 magnificent maps.

260 Beard, James F., ed. Letters and Journals of James Fenimore Cooper. 6 vols. Cambridge: Harvard UP, 1960-1968. A distinguished contribution to American literary scholarship; extenisve annotation, equivalent to a biographical study.

261 Beard, William. Valiant Martinet: The Adventures on Sea and Land of Captain William Bligh. London: Beard, 1956, 90 pp. Poetry about Bligh.

262 Beatty, William. The Death of Lord Nelson: The Authentic Narrative. London: Atheneum, 1807, 1825, 1894, 1895, 1985, 95 pp. Fwd: Charles Weston; the first-hand account by the surgeon of HMS VICTORY, his entry of 21 October 1805.

263 Beaumont, Stephen K. "Science and Navigation in England, 1660-1714." Ph.D. diss, Wisconsin, 1971, 475 pp. The place of advances in navigation in the scientific revolution; the theory was more advanced in England than the practice, due to poor instruments; advances during the Stuart period have been exaggerated.

264 Beazley, C. Raymond. Prince Henry the Navigator: The Hero of Portugal and of Modern Discovery, 1394-1460. NY: Barnes and Noble, 1901, 1968, 336 pp. An older but still reliable biography, hagiography.

265 Bechervaise, John. A Farewell to My Old Shipmates and Messmates: With Some Examples and a Few Hints of Advice By the Old Quartermaster. Portsea: Woodward, 1847, 107 pp. Dedicated to Admiral Sir William Parker; a first-hand memoir of conditions on the lower deck.

266 -------. Thirty-Six Years of a Seafaring Life: By an Old Quartermaster. Portsea: Woodward, 1839, 336 pp. First-hand memoir; praised by Baynham.

267 Beck, Emily Morison, ed. Sailor Historian: The Best of Samuel Eliot Morison. Boston: Houghton, 1977, 431 pp. Re the great Harvard historian, designated by President Franklin Roosevelt as official naval historian of World War II, prize-winning biographer, and historian of Atlantic exploration; excerpts from his writings.

268 Beck, Lily A. The Divine Lady: A Romance of Nelson and Emma Hamilton. NY: Dodd, 1924, 1925, viii, 417 pp. Pseud: E. Barrington; grandaughter of a midshipman serving in Nelson's fleet; a fictional account of the relationship.

269 Beddie, M.K., ed. Bibliography of Captain James Cook, RN, FRS, Circumnavigator. Sydney: Library, 1928, 1970, xvi, 894 pp. Occasion for the 2nd edition, the bicentennial of the discovery of Australia; 4824 annotated entries; Ms Beddie includes works by and about Cook, other associated personalities, e.g., Banks, Bligh, Vancouver, and Sandwich, monuments, and portraits.

270 Bedoyere, Guy de la, ed. The Diary of John Evelyn. Woodbridge: Boydell; Bangor: Headstart, 1993, 1995, 501 pp. Re John Evelyn, 1620-1706, abridged edition; see Evelyn for full publication; associated with Pepys.

271 -------, ed. Particular Friends: The Correspondence of Samuel Pepys and John Evelyn. RHS Studies in History series. London: Boydell, 1997, 350 pp. Chronological presentation of 40 years of correspondence; features, e.g., Anglo-Dutch Wars and naval reforms.

272 Beeler, John. Warfare in England, 1066-1189. Ithaca: Cornell UP, 1966, 506 pp. From a Cornell dissertation; a classic and authoritative description of feudal warfare in England, e.g., at Hastings, land and sea fyrds, use of sea transports, and naval aspects of campaigns in Wales.

273 [NRS ___]. Beeler, John F., ed. [The Papers of Admiral Alexander Milne.] Publications of the Naval Records Society, vol. ____. London: _____. (in 2001, noted as forthcoming). An edition of selected papers from this noted 19th-century admiral.

274 Beer, Anna R. Sir Walter Ralegh and His Readers in the Seventeenth Century: Speaking to the People. Early Modern Literature in History series. London: Macmillan, 1997, xii, 208 pp. Ralegh published 8 vols., including accounts of voyages and naval battles; emphasis on how Ralegh was perceived at the time.

275 Beer, Carel de. The Art of Gunfounding: The Casting of Bronze Cannon in the Late Eighteenth Century. Rotherfield: Boudriot, 1991, viii, 232 pp. Preface: Prince Bernhard of the Netherlands; definitive on the technology of bronze gunfounding, e.g., at Woolwich; 50 watercolor illustrations of the process.

276 Beetham Fisher, Anita Ley. "The Merchants of Medieval Bristol, 1350-1500." Ph.D. diss, Oregon, 1987, 575 pp. This merchant class stimulated developments and exploration of new trade routes; Bristol became the largest provincial English town; sources included wills, custom records, and deeds.

277 Begnaud, Allen E. "British Operations in the Caribbean and the American Revolution." Ph.D. diss, Tulane, 1966, 362 pp. West Indies a major theater of operations, the government having designated sugar as a high priority, but British resources overextended; American privateers and entry of French were further set-backs.

278 Behrman, Cynthia F. Victorian Myths of the Sea. Athens: Ohio State UP, 1977, x, 188 pp. "Myth" of superiority of RN traced back to earlier time when the English lorded it over all as "God's agents on the ocean."

279 Belfiglio, Valentine J. "Roman Amphibious Operations against Britain in 55 BC." Military and Naval History J, 7 (March 1998): 3-13. Re the 1st foray by Julius Caesar.

280 -------. "The Roman Amphibious Raid against Britain in 54 BC." Military and Naval History J, 8 (April 1999): 15-21. Re the 2nd, more substantial, foray by Julius Caesar.

281 Bell, Douglas H. Drake. London: n.p., 1935, 144 pp. A popular biography.

282 -------. Elizabethan Seamen. Phil: Lippincott, 1936, ix, 322 pp. A dramatic version of exploits, e.g., "Venturers All," circumnavigation, the Armada, and the Northwest Passage.

283 -------. Seamen of Britain. London: Nelson, 1943, vii, 288 pp. Credits Alfred, Richard I, and Henry VIII for furthering the development.

284 Bell, R.C., ed. Diaries from the Days of Sail. London: Barrie, 1974, 160 pp. Intro: Alan Villiers; individual reminiscences from the early 19th century.

285 Bellabarba, Sergio and Osculati, Giorgio. The Royal Yacht CAROLINE, 1749. The Anatomy of the Ship series. London: Conway; Annapolis: NIP, 1989, 120 pp. The state yacht of George II and George III, described as the most sumptuously decorated ship of all time; voyages to Hanover and back; 200 illustrations.

286 Bellamy, M. "Danish Naval Administration and Shipbuilding in the Reign of Christian IV, 1596-1648." Ph.D. diss, Glasgow, 1997. In the early 17th century, Denmark expanded its navy, then the largest in Europe; English and Scottish shipwrights brought in, e.g., David Balfour.

287 Belloc, Hilaire. The Book of the Bayeux Tapestry. NY: Putnam, 1914, xix, 176 pp. Belloc, 1870-1953, a prominent literary figure; depicts the entire tapestry in a series of color facsimiles; a contribution to the great debate over the Norman Conquest and battle of Hastings, raging since the 1890s.

288 -------. James II. Phil: Lippincott, 1928, 297 pp. Biography of James; as Duke of York, influenced naval tactics and administration.

289 Benady, Tito. The Royal Navy at Gibraltar. Liskeard: Maritime, 1992, 1993, xvi, 271 pp. A history of "the Rock" and the part it played in the development of the RN.

290 Benbow, William A. Brave Benbow: The Life of Vice-Admiral John Benbow, 1653-1702. Victoria: Brendah, 1987, 174 pp. Romanticized biography, commander of squadrons vs. the French.

291 Bender, Bert. Sea-Brothers: The Tradition of American Sea Fiction from

"Moby-Dick" to the Present. Phil: U Penn P, 1988, xiv, 267 pp. A review of 15 of the great American sea fiction writers, e.g., Melville, Crane, and Hemingway.

292 Bennell, J.E.G. "English Oared Vessels of the Sixteenth Century." MM, 60 (February and May 1974): 9-26, 169-86. An overview, including characteristics, administration, and manning.

293 Bennett, Geoffrey M. Nelson the Commander. London: Batsford; NY: Scribner, 1972, 322 pp.. Intro: Sir Peter Hill-Norton; by a captain, RN, and prolific naval historian; touts "a new angle," his achievements as a commander"; a few points of interest, e.g., enlightening on an episode concerning Malta and the Russians in 1799 and informative on Lady Nelson.

294 -------. "Royal Reviews at Spithead." HisTod, 27 (June 1977): 358-66. Accounts of a series of reviews at this large water near Portsmouth and Southampton, e.g., in 1512, 1627, 1665, 1687, 1783, and 1814, plus 9 during the reign of Victoria.

295 Bennett, Michael Todd. "Anglophilia on Film: Creating an Atmosphere for Alliance, 1935-1941." Film and History, 27 (1997): 4-21. Re pro-British film making and its influence in America, e.g., "Mutiny on the BOUNTY" and "That Hamilton Woman," the latter "a historical film which parallels the present."

296 Benson, E.F. Sir Francis Drake. Gold Hind series # 1. London: Lane; NY: Harper, 1927, viii, 315 pp. To correct Froude biography; 17 chapters and a bibliography; mediocre effort; features, e.g., chapters on the circumnavigation, Doughty, Cadiz, the Armada, and "Fall and Recovery."

297 Bensusan, Harold G. "The Spanish Struggle against Foreign Encroachment in the Caribbean, 1675-1697." Ph.D. diss, UCLA, 1970, 285 pp. Re Spanish defense measures which ultimately were effective.

298 Beowulf: A New Verse Translation. NY: Farrar, 2000, xxx, 211 pp. A new award-winning translation by Seamus Heaney; original manuscript not published until 1815 as Old English was restored; contemporary with SUTTON HOO.

299 Berckman, Evelyn. Creators and Destroyers of the English Navy: As Related by the State Papers Domestic. London: Hamilton, 1974, 212 pp. Arbitrarily designates, e.g., creators are Elizabeth, Charles I, and Charles II; destroyers are James I and Oliver Cromwell.

300 -------. The Hidden Navy. London: Hamilton, 1973, xiv, 159 pp. "Hidden" aspects of life in the RN, e.g., prostitution, stowaways, prison hulks, and curious situations in the Royal Dockyards.

301 -------. Nelson's Dear Lord: A Portrait of St. Vincent. NY: Macmillan, 1962, 274 pp. A biography.

302 -------. Victims of Piracy: The Admiralty Courts, 1575-1678. London: Hamilton, 1979, 134 pp. Research from records of Admiralty courts; incidents of English piracy increased after 1602, the victims being French, Venetian, Spanish, Breton, Flemish, and Hollanders.

303 Beresford, Charles and Wilson, HerbertW. Nelson and His Times. 2 vols. London: Harmsworth, 1897-1898. Beresford, 1846-1919, a colorful, controversial admiral and peer; folio size with over 450 small illustrations and large color prints, the first Nelson biography so illustrated; first serialized in Daily Mail; much rhetoric and chauvinism.

304 Bergerson, Robert, comp. Vinland Bibliography: Writings Relating to the Norse in Greenland and America. Tromsoo: Tromsoo UP, 1997, viii, 411 pp. From a Norwegian academic; re Scandinavian voyages of exploration to America.

305 Bernstein, David J. The Mystery of the Bayeux Tapestry. London: Weidenfeld, 1986, 272 pp. Folio size, pictorial account; enlightening on the Norman Conquest; noted the "politics" of the story of the tapestry.

306 [Berry, Edward.] "By an Officer of Rank in the Squadron." An Authentic Narrative of the . . . Squadron under the Command of Sir H. Nelson . . . of the Battle of the Nile. N.p, 1798, 46 pp. A memoir of the campaign by the flag-captain.

307 Berton, Pierre. The Arctic Grail: The Quest for the North West Passage and the North Pole, 1818-1909. NY: Viking; London: Penguin, 1988, 1990, xii, 672 pp. A choronological review of explorers; features, e.g., glorious successes, fatal failures, bravery, science, and cartography.

308 Besant, Walter. Captain Cook. English Men of Action series. London: Macmillan, 1890, 1894, vi, 191 pp. A biography in a series.

309 Besant, Walter and Rice, James. 'Twas in Trafalgar Bay. NY: 1873 Press, 2000. Besant, 1836-1901; naval fiction of the Nelson era.

310 Bessinger, Jess B. "The SUTTON HOO Ship Burial: A Chronological Bibliography." Speculum, 29 and 33 (1954 and 1958): 116-24 and 515-22. Re discovery of the 7th century ship burial, investigation of the artifacts, and their display in the British Museum; noted parallels with the poem "Beowulf."

311 Best, George. The Three Voyages of Martin Frobisher in Search of a Passage to Cathay and India by the North-west, AD 1576-1578. London: Argonaut, 1938. An account of the voyages.

312 Bethell, John. "Bethell Watercraft Project." A Project sponsored by the Society for Nautical Research. A comprehensive compilation of the history of watercraft under Water Information Resources; in 1999, a grant to Bethell to complete the project.

313 Betts, Jonathan. John Harrison. London: NMM, 1993, 1997, 24 pp. A pamphlet-biography of the chronometer maker.

314 Bevan, A. Beckford and Wolryche-Whitmore, H.B., eds. A Sailor of King George: The Journals of Captain Frederick Hoffman, RN, 1793-1814. Classics of Naval Literature series. Annapolis: NIP, 1901, 1998, 376 pp. Intro: Gerald Jordan; written in 1836, recollections of the Wars of the French Revolution and Napoleon; in 18 battles, e.g., Trafalgar.

315 Bevan, Bryan. The Great Seamen of Elizabeth I. London: Hale, 1971, 319 pp. Popularized; seamen, pirates, patrons, e.g., Gilbert, Ralegh, Grenville, Drake, Howard, and Cavendish; curious organization.

316 Bidwell, Shelford. "The Royal United Services Institute for Defence Studies, 1831-1991." JRUSI, 136 (Summer 1991): 68-72. A history of this important military association and research center founded in 1831.

317 Billias, George A., ed. George Washington's Opponents: British Generals and Admirals in the American Revolution. NY: Morrow, 1969, xxvii, 362 pp. A series of essays by experts, e.g., on William and Richard Howe, Samuel Hood, George Rodney, and Thomas Graves; noted British failure to adopt a clear strategy.

318 Bindoff, S.T. The Scheldt Question to 1839. London: Allen, 1945, 238 pp. An ongoing and vital issue in European history, sea access to Antwerp; in 1585, the Scheldt was closed.

319 Bingeman, John M., Bethell, John P., Goodwin, Peter, and Mack, Arthur T. "Copper and Other Sheathing in the Royal Navy." International J Nautical Archaeology, 29 (2000): 218-29. As anti-fouling and protection against "worms"; included a series of "logos" identifying different manufacturers.

320 Birbeck, Thomas T. The FOUDROYANT. Chepstow: Rural District, 1966, 116 pp. A descriptive account of this famous ship.

321 Birch, Debra J. and Horn, Joyce M., comps. The History Laboratory: The Institute of Historical Research, 1921-1996. London: IHR, 1996, viii, 203 pp. A history of the outstanding research center and library.

322 Bird, Harrison. Battle for a Continent: The French and Indian War, 1754-1763. NY: Oxford UP, 1965, ix, 376 pp. An extensive history of the war.

323 -------. Navies in the Mountains: The Battles on the Waters of Lake Champlain and Lake George, 1609-1814. NY: Oxford UP, 1962, vii, 361 pp. Naval activities and operations of the French, British, and Americans; ultimately, "the American Lake."

324 Birkett, Dea. Serpent in Paradise. NY: Doubleday; London: Picador, 1997, 296 pp. Ms. Birkett visited Pitcairn Island and researched about the disposition of the BOUNTY mutineers who settled there, especially Fletcher Christian; several descendants still live there; John Adams was the last survivor; sunken BOUNTY still there, plus a museum and library.

325 Birmingham, David. Trade and Empire in the Atlantic, 1400-1600. London: Routledge, 2000, vi, 99 pp. A brilliant survey of early modern exploratory and maritime enterprises, e.g., Vikings, Normans, Portuguese, English, French, and Dutch.

326 Black, Clinton V. Pirates of the West Indies. London: Cambridge UP, 1989, 136 pp. Re pirates, e.g., Henry Morgan and some women pirates; peak time here was 1714-1724 with about 5000 involved.

327 Black, Jeremy. "Anglo-Spanish Naval Relations in the Eighteenth Century." MM, 77 (August 1991): 235-58. Author of 30 books and concerned that military history has been neglected for the last 40 years; in this article, believes Anglo-French relations have overshadowed Anglo-Spanish; the Spanish were a genuine challenge to RN; series of crises.

328 -------. "Britain in 1800." HisTod, 50 (November 2000): 29-35. An assessment; Britain at war, Nelson was the hero, preparation for the Aboukir campaign the next year.

329 -------. Britain as a Military Power, 1688-1815. London: Routledge; NY: Garland, 1999, viii, 332 pp. A provocatively traditional approach, critical of the state-building structuralists and "accounts of the accountants"; naval and sea power incorporated in a major way; the most successful navy in the world with a large empire and efficient finanancial and administrative foundations; emphasis on leadership, morale, and fortune.

330 -------. "Britain as a Military Power, 1688-1815: Historiographical Essay." J Military History, 64 (January 2000): 159-78. Critique of Brewer, Kennedy, O'Brien, and Bowen, all with too much economics and politics; return to true military history, use of British army as model; more acceptable, e.g., Corbett, Harding, Hattendorf, Mackesy, and Muir.

331 Black, Jeremy and Woodfine, Philip, eds. The British Navy and the Use of Naval Power in the Eighteenth Century. Leicester: Leicester UP, 1988, 1989, xiv, 273 pp. 12 papers from a conference on uses of naval power in the 18th century in April 1987; e.g., Baugh on why RN lost the American Revolution, Jones on France, Woodfine on Spain, and Middleton on naval administration.

332 Black, Jeremy, ed. European Warfare, 1453-1815. Problems in Focus series. London: Macmillan, 1999, vii, 287 pp. Collected essays of major significance; most pertinent is Richard Harding on naval warfare.

333 Black, Jeremy. <u>European Warfare, 1660-1815</u>. <u>Warfare and History</u> series. London: UCL, 1994, x, 276 pp. A review of the debate over the Military Revolution beginning with the original Roberts essay of 1955, then Parker, Rogers, and Black, who pushes the time period back; praise for Glete.

334 -------. <u>Maps and History: Constructing Images of the Past</u>. New Haven, Yale UP, 1997, ix, 267 pp. On historical atlases; includes a carto-bibliography tracing general trends; praise for Harley.

335 -------. <u>Maps and Politics</u>. Chicago: Chicago UP, 1997, ix, 188 pp. Sees cartography as power and relates wars and political cartography; types of projection have caused problems and political contention.

336 -------. <u>A Military Revolution?: Military Change and European Society, 1550-1800</u>. <u>Studies in European History</u>. London: Macmillan, 1991, xiii, 109 pp. To re-examine the so-called Military Revolution; critique of Roberts and Parker; changes occurred earlier and then again, later.

337 Black, Joseph. "Saving the Lagoon." <u>HisTod</u>, 48 (April 1998): 10-16. Despite the title, an informative naval history of Venice, a great naval and trading power during the period from 1100 to the late 18th century, surrendering to Napoleon; at height, over 3000 warships and 36,000 seamen, plus hundreds of large merchant ships and galleys, all furnished and maintained by the Venice Arsenal, established in 1124, employing 16,000 by 1500, the largest industrial complex in Europe; a model for subsequent naval and imperial powers.

338 <u>The Black Book of the Admiralty or Monumenta Juridica</u>. 4 vols. London: Longman, 1871-1876. Ed: Travis Triss and published in the Rolls Series; an extensive collection of commentaries on maritime law and legal texts on Admiralty law in Latin, French, and English; originally compiled in the 15th century.

339 Blackburn, Graham. <u>The Illustrated Encyclopedia of Ships, Boats, Vessels and Other Water-Borne Craft</u>. Woodstock: Overlook, 1978, 447 pp. Types of craft in alphabetical order, Advice Boat to Zulu; plus a glossary, bibliography, and many illustrations.

340 -------. <u>The Overlook Illustrated Dictionary of Nautical Terms</u>. Woodstock: Overlook, 1981, 349 pp. A contribution to nautical dictionaries.

341 Blackburn, Julia. <u>The Emperor's Last Island: The Journey to St. Helena</u>. London: Secker; NY: Random House, 1991, 1992, 244 pp. An account of the last days of Napoleon, taken to St. Helena aboard a British warship and guarded by RN; 24 untitled chapters and bibliography.

342 Blackman, D.J., ed. <u>Marine Archaeology: Proceedings of the Twenty-Third Symposium of the Colston Research Society, Held at the University of Bristol, 4-8 April 1971</u>. London: Butterworth, 1973, x, 522 pp. A collection of published papers, e.g., Alexander McKee on the search for MARY ROSE, Colin Martin on the search for wrecks of the Armada, and Sidney Wignall on the controversy over Armada gunnery.

343 Blagdon, Francis W. Graphic History of the Life, Exploits and Death of Horatio Nelson. London: Orme, 1806, 72 pp. An early popular biography; excellent engravings, some in color, e.g., the funeral and Nelson and the polar bear; text less important.

344 Blair, Pauline Hunter. The Nelson Boy: An Imaginative Reconstruction of a Great Man's Childhood. Cambridge: Church Farm, 1999, x, 256 pp. A fascinating approach, combining known facts with plausible fiction or "reconstruction" as she describes it; little is known of his childhood; fills a gap.

345 -------. A Thorough Seaman: The Ship's Logs of Horatio Nelson's Early Voyages Imaginatively Explored. Cambridge: Church Farm, 2000, 211 pp. A sequel to the previous entry; based primarily on research in ship's logs; Nelson to the West Indies, Arctic, and Madras.

346 Blake, Nicholas and Laurence, Richard. The Illustrated Companion to Nelson's Navy. London: Chatham; Mechansburg: Stackpole, 2000, 207 pp. A recent publication, part of the Nelson Decade campaign; 500 illustrations; themes, e.g., "the true picture," RN, sailors, life aboard, fiction, and recipes "for real Jack Tar fare."

347 Blee, Ben W. "A Farewell to Dutch Courage." USNIP, 115 (February 1989): 64-69. History and abolition of grog ration in RN as of 1970.

348 -------. "The Story of Grog in the Royal Navy." USNIP, 85 (August 1959): 62-64. History of the rum ration in RN.

349 Blewitt, Mary. Surveys of the Seas: A Brief History of British Hydrography. London: MacGibbons, 1957, 168 pp. Fwd: Archibald Day; folio size, 69 charts; re the Hydrographic Office of the Admiralty; conducting marine surveys beginning in 1670, especially the "heroic age," 1750-1850; the RN led the world in this endeavor.

350 Bligh, William. An Answer to Certain Assertions Contained in the Appendix to a Pamphlet. . . . Charged with Mutiny on Board His Majesty's Ship BOUNTY. London: Nicol, 1794, 31 pp. Bligh, 1754-1817, responds to Edward Christian "to clear my character."

351 -------. The Log of HMS BOUNTY, 1787-1789. London: Golden Cockerel; Guilford: Genesis, 1936, 1975, 362 pp. Fwd: Earl Mountbatten; intro: Owen Rutter; comments: J.A. Edgell; a facsimile of the original in the PRO; editions vary in length.

352 -------. The Log of HMS PROVIDENCE, 1791-1793. Guilford: Genesis, 1976, 951 pp. Fwd: Earl Mountbatten; a facisimile of the original in the PRO; the 2nd breadfruit voyage.

353 -------. The Mutiny on Board HMS BOUNTY. [Various titles and editions]. London: Methuen; Glocester: Sutton, 1790, 1936, 1981, xxix, 283 pp. Ed: Richard Bowman; afterword: Milton Rugoff; the personal account and apologia of Lt. Bligh; a court martial found Bligh innocent, he was promoted to commander, and ultimately admiral.

354 -------. The Voyage of the BOUNTY Launch from the Ship to Tofua and from Thence to Timor, 28 April to 14 June 1789. [Various titles and editions]. London: Golden Cockerel; Sydney: Allen, 1934, 1987, xiv, 336 pp. Intro: Owen Rutter; ed: John Bach; a facsimile copy; the original notebook, 108 pp., is in the National Library of Australia; Bligh navigated this incredible voyage and managed provisions, 47 days, 3900 miles, 19 persons, in a boat 23 feet long.

355 -------. A Voyage to the South Seas. N.p., 1975, xix, 150 pp. An abridged account with illustrations.

356 Blond, Georges. La Beaute et La Gloire: Nelson et Emma Hamilton. Paris: Laffont, 1976, 455 pp. A French account, recounting the affair and disposition, e.g., "the sacrifice of Emma" and chronology at the end.

357 Blore, Trevor. "Admiralty Hydrography." USNIP, 88 (June 1962): 72-81. Founded in 1795, a history of operations, surveys, and administration.

358 Body, Edward. Cinque Ports and Their Lords Warden: History in Verse and Prose. Larkfield: Messenger, 1979, 1992, 36 pp. A literary piece on the Lords Warden and Constables of Dover.

359 Bohlander, Richard E., ed. World Explorers and Discoverers. NY: Macmillan; NY: DaCapo, 1992, 1998, xi, 532 pp. A series of 313 short biographies, from Abruzzi to Zheng He, e.g., James Cook and Verrazano.

360 Bolster, W. Jeffrey. Black Jacks: African American Seamen in the Age of Sail. Cambridge: Harvard UP, 1997, viii, 310 pp. From the 1740s to the 1860s; early ones were British, then, more and more Americans; by 1815, 20% of American seamen were Black, then numbers declined; includes individual pictures of many.

361 Bond, Gordon C. The Grand Expedition: The British Invasion of Holland in 1809. Athens: U Ga P, 1979, viii, 232 pp. The Walcheren expedition to the Scheldt, a dismal failure; analysis of causes and responsibilities; good on details but lacking grasp of strategic situation.

362 Bonnel, Ulane. La France, Les Etats-Unis et la guerre de course, 1797-1815. Paris: Latines, 1961, 489 pp. A comprehensive study of guerre de course, privateering warfare which was the basis of French naval strategy; brilliantly places it in the context of international economics.

363 Bonner, Elizabeth. "The Recovery of St. Andrews Castle in 1547: French Naval Policy and Diplomacy in the British Isles." EHR, 111 (June 1996): 578-98. The French conducted a siege, sending a fleet of galleys from the Mediterranean and Atlantic to assist; the English had neglected the navy; the defeat meant French domination of Scotland and a plan to combine the kingdoms of France and Scotland; Mary, Queen of Scots to rule.

364 Bonnett, Stanley. The Price of Admiralty: An Indictment of the Royal Navy. London: Hale, 1968, 272 pp. Unbalanced, poorly organized, and superficial judgments; over-zealous attack stressing instances of corruption, elitism, and horrendous conditions.

365 Booth, Eric Charles Talbot, ed. The Royal Navy: Some Account of Her Manners, Customs and Privileges. London: Sampson, 1942, 575 pp. A prolific popular author of general guides; a cultural history.

366 Bosanquet, H.T.A. "Lord Nelson and the Loss of His Arm." MM, 38 (August 1952): 184-94. Nelson lost his right arm while leading a landing party at Santa Cruz, 25 July 1797; after he was struck by a musket ball, amputation by the surgeon of HMS THESEUS.

367 Bosscher, Philip, ed. The Heyday of Sail: The Merchant Sailing Ship, 1650-1830. Conway History of the Ship series, vol. 5. London: Conway, 1995, 175 pp. A series of essays by experts, e.g., Christopher French describing the phenomenal growth of the British merchant marine from 300,000 tons in 1700 to 2.2 million tons in the 1830s and Ab Hoving on Dutch shipbuilding in its heyday.

368 Bosscher, Philippus M. "The Four Days' Battle: Some Remarks and Reflections." JRUSI, 112 (February 1967): 56-65. A Dutch account of this famous battle, the English loosing 10 ships; a total of about 7000 casualties, including 4500 dead.

369 Boteler, Nathaniel. Six Dialogues about Sea Services between an High Admiral and a Captain at Sea. Limited edition, 1634, 1685. Copies in the British Library; collected correspondence about naval affairs.

370 Boudriot, Jean and Berti, Hubert. The Bomb Ketch SALAMANDRE, 1752. Rotherfield: Boudriot, 1982, 1991, 144 pp. Trans: David Roberts; by the brilliant and prolific French antiquarian, publisher, and expert on sailing warships; the bomb ketch was a French invention of the 1680s first used against the Barbary corsairs.

371 Boudriot, Jean. The BONHOMME RICHARD, 1779. Paris: Boudriot, 1988, 63 pp. Trans: David Roberts; details, including 26 pages of schematic plans; formerly an East Indiaman refitted in 1779.

372 -------. The History of the French Frigates, 1650-1850. Paris: Boudriot, 1993, 416 pp. Trans: David Roberts; the usual highest standards; a technical history with a complete list; profusely illustrated.

373 Boudriot, Jean, ed. John Paul Jones and the BONHOMME RICHARD: A Reconstruction of the Ship and an Account of the Battle with HMS SERAPIS. Annapolis: NIP, 1987, 127 pp. Trans: David Roberts; large folio size profusely illustrated in color; a series of pertinent essays, e.g., Peter Reaveley illustrating the battle of Flamborough Head, Thomas Gilmer on its sailing qualities, and James Cheevers on naval uniforms; a comprehensive analysis.

374 Boudriot, Jean. The Seventy-Four Gun Ship: A Practical Treatise on the Art of Naval Architecture. 4 vols. Rotherfield: Boudriot; Annapolis: NIP, 1973-1977, 1986-1988, 1062 pp. Trans: David Roberts; a spectacular tour de force with a choice of a deluxe edition; hundreds of illustrations including fold-out schematic plans; re an "ideal" '74, not a particular one, to illustrate the French navy at its height in the 1780s; the 4 volumes focusing on hull construction, hull fittings, masts, sails, and rigging, and manning and shiphandling; a section on conditions aboard, health, punishments, and religion.

375 Bougainville, Louis-Antoine de. Journal of a Voyage Round the World. London: Nourse, 1772, 362 pp. Trans: J.R. Forster; by the famous French explorer.

376 Bouguer, Pierre. Trait d'optique sur la gradation de la lunniere. Paris: Guerin, 1760, xviii, 368 pp. By a French professor and royal hydrographer, a major authority on nautical dictionaries; praised by Falconer.

377 Boulind, Richard. "Drake's Navigational Skills." MM, 54 (November 1968): 349-72. An account about Drake and his navigational abilities, especially during the circumnavigation.

378 -------. "The Strength and Weakness of Spanish Control in the Caribbean, 1520-1650." Ph.D. diss, Cambridge, 1965. Re Spanish colonial defenses at this formative time.

379 Bound, Mensun, ed. The Archaeloogy of Ships of War. International Maritime Archaeology series # 1. Oswestry: Nelson, 1992, 1995, 192 pp. Folio size; proceedings, 24 papers from a conference at NMM, November 1992; excavations, e.g., GRACE DIEU, MARY ROSE, and a Cromwellian wreck, and restorations, e.g., VICTORY and WARRIOR.

380 -------, ed. Excavating Ships of War. International Maritime Archaeology series # 2. Oswestry: Nelson, 1998, 309 pp. 27 papers from a conference; more excavation projects described, many from the 18th century.

381 Bourchier, Jane B., ed. Memoirs of Admiral Sir Edward Codrington. 2 vols. London: Longman, 1873. By daughter, Lady Bourchier; covers 1770-1851, including battles, e.g., Glorious First of June and Navarino.

382 Bourguignon, Henry J. Sir William Scott, Lord Stowell: Judge of the High Court of the Admiralty, 1798-1828. Cambridge Studies in Legal History. Cambridge: Cambridge UP, 1987, xiv, 310 pp. A description of Admiralty Courts and the types of cases; Scott was a judge for 30 years; the law is based on the Laws of Oleron and the Black Book of the Admiralty.

383 Bourland, Richard D. "Maurepas and His Administration of the French Navy on the Eve of the War of Austrian Succession, 1737-1742." Ph.D. diss, Notre Dame, 1978, 504 pp. Maurepas, 1701-1781, naval secretary, 1725-1749, administering expansion of French navy under Louis XIV, but finances reduced and navy deteriorated.

384 Bourne, H.R. Fox. English Seamen under the Tudors. 2 vols. London: Bentley, 1868, 646 pp. Bourne, 1837-1919, emphasized operations and less on great admirals; review of predecessors, e.g., Cinque Ports and the Cabots; under Tudors, e.g., colonization projects and the Armada.

385 Bourne, Ruth M. "British Naval Administration in the West Indies." Ph.D. diss, Yale, 1931. The basis of the next entry.

386 -------. Queen Anne's Navy in the West Indies. New Haven: Yale UP, 1939, x, 334 pp. A critical appraisal of the navy, at odds with Mahan; informative on administration, conditions, and operations.

387 Bourne, William. The Arte of Shooting Great Ordnance. Amsterdam: Terraruur; NY: Da Capo, 1587, 1969, 94 pp. Bourne, ____-1583; an early manual for gunners.

388 Bovill, E.W. "Queen Elizabeth's Gunpowder." MM, 33 (July 1947): 179-86. An example of arms dealing in the 16th century; much to the objection of Portugal, England traded arms, e.g., pikes, lances, helmets, cannon, and ammunition, for sugar, and secretly, saltpetre, with Morocco.

389 Bowen, Frank C. His Majesty's Coastguard: The Story of this Important Naval Force from the Earliest Times to the Present Day. London: Hutchinson, 1928, 288 pp. By an older, traditional and popular naval historian; a history of the coast guard.

390 -------. Men of the Wooden Walls. NY: Staples, 1952, viii, 152 pp. 70 short biographical profiles, multi-national, e.g., Alfred, Cabot, Hawkins, Drake, Ralegh, Columbus, Tromp, Capt. Kidd, J.P. Jones, and Cunard.

391 -------. Sea Slang: A Dictionary of the Old-Timers' Expressions and Epithets. London: Sampson, 1929, 154 pp. Another contribution to the nautical dictionary.

392 -------. Wooden Wall in Action. London: Halton, 1951, viii, 144 pp. Accounts of naval battles, 1340-1866.

393 Bowen, John L., ed. Scale Model Sailing Ships. London: Conway, 1977, 1979, 192 pp. A guidebook.

394 -------, ed. Scale Model Warships. London: Conway, 1978, 192 pp. A guidebook.

395 Bowen, Marjorie. Patriotic Lady: A Study of Emma, Lady Hamilton and the Neapolitan Revolution of 1799. NY: Appleton; London: Bruce, 1935, 1970, xi, 349 pp. A biographical study; focus on the Neapolitan Jacobins; excellent bibliography.

396 Boxer, Charles R. The Anglo-Dutch Wars of the Seventeenth Century, 1652-1674. London: HMSO, 1974, vi, 68 pp. Boxer, 1904-2000, a prolific naval historian; this for NMM; conflict between Protestant maritime powers; issues, e.g., herring fishery, cloth markets, Muscovy trade, colonial rivalry, freedom of the seas, and definition of contraband.

397 -------. The Dutch Seaborne Empire, 1600-1800. The History of Human Society series. New York: Viking, 1965, 1989, xxvi, 326 pp. The standard; re its rise and fall; notes that a key was commercial-familial links all over the world.

398 -------. The English and the Portuguese Brazil Trade, 1660-1780: Some Problems and Personalities. Melbourne: La Trobe UP, 1981, 11 pp. A brief introduction to the commercial relationships.

399 -------. Four Centuries of Portuguese Expansion, 1415-1825: A Succinct Survey. Berkeley: U Cal P, 1961, 1969, 102 pp. From a series of lectures; a brilliant synthesis.

400 Boxer, Charles R., ed. Further Selections from the Tragic History of the Sea, 1559-1565. Publications of the Hakluyt Society, 2nd ser, # 132. Cambridge: Cambridge UP, 1968, x, 170 pp. A feature was didacticism, i.e., avoid the mistakes of predecessors.

401 Boxer, Charles R. "M.H. Tromp, 1598-1653." MM, 40 (1954): 33-54. The latest research; re the great antagonist of Blake; actually knighted by Charles I in 1642, thus, Sir Martin Tromp; James, Duke of York told Pepys that Tromp was the greatest seaman.

402 -------. The Portuguese Seaborne Empire, 1415-1825. The History of Human Society series. NY: Knopf, 1969, 1991, 456 pp. Re the first modern colonial empire and it lasted the longest time; launched the maritime expansion era; a lust for riches and passion for God.

403 -------. "Public Opinion and the Second Anglo-Dutch War, 1664-1667." HisTod, 16 (September 1966): 618-26. Commercial and colonial issues created conflict, all exaggerated by journalists and pamphleteers, e.g., John Selden.

404 -------. "Some Second Thoughts on the Third Anglo-Dutch War, 1672-1674." Trans RHS, 5th ser, 19 (1969): 67-94. A study of public opinion; relations deteriorated after treaty ending the 2nd war; English alliance with the French.

405 -------. "The Third Dutch War in the East." MM, 16 (October 1930): 343-86. Details on naval operations there.

406 Boxer, Charles R., ed. The Tragic History of the Sea, 1589-1622. Publications of the Hakluyt Society, 2nd ser, vol. 112. NY: Kraus, 1959, 1986, xiv, 297 pp. Narratives of shipwrecks of Portuguese East India Company vessels, 1589, 1593, and 1622.

407 Boxer, Charles R. "The Tromps and the Anglo-Dutch Wars, 1652-1674." HisTod, 3 (December 1953): 836-45. A review of the conflicts, e.g., English claim about sovereignty over "the Narrow Seas."

408 Boyd, Norman. The Model Ship: Her Roll in History. Woodbridge: Antique, 2000, 191 pp. A recent guide to the development and use of ship models; cited example of models built for TV "Hornblower" production.

409 Boynton, Lindsay. The Elizabethan Militia, 1558-1638. London: Routledge, 1967, xvii, 334 pp. Informative on this institution, especially the Great Muster and preparation for the Armada.

410 Braddick, M.J. "An English Military Revolution." Historical J, 36 (December 1993): 965-75. A historiographical survey; conclusion: some symptoms of a "military revolution."

411 Bradford, Ernle D.S. The Great Siege: Malta, 1565. NY: Harcourt, 1961, 1962, 1999, v, 256 pp. A episode involving the Knights of St. John, in this case vs. the Ottoman Empire as invader.

412 -------. Nelson: The Essential Hero. London: Macmillan; Ware: Wordsworth, 1977, 1999, xv, 368 pp. A popular biography with no scholarly apparatus.

413 -------. The Story of the MARY ROSE. London: Hamilton, 1982, 207 pp. For the MARY ROSE Trust; MARY ROSE, named for the sister of Henry VIII, sank at Spithead, Sunday, 19 July 1545, en route to counter the invading French.

414 -------. The Wind Commands Me: A Life of Sir Francis Drake. NY: Harcourt; London: Hodder, 1965, 251 pp. A popular biography.

415 Bradford, Gershorn. The Mariner's Dictionary. NY: Weathervane, 1972. A contribution to the nautical dictionary.

416 Bradford, James C., ed. Command under Sail. 3 vols. Annapolis: NIP, 1985-1987. A comprehensive biographical survey; coverage from 1775-1830, e.g., J.P. Jones.

417 -------, ed. The Papers of John Paul Jones. Cambridge: Chadwyck-Healey, 1986. 10 reels of microfilm and a printed guide; the authoritative basic source on Jones.

418 Bradley, Margaret. "Bonaparte's Plans to Invade England in 1801: The Fortunes of Pierre Forfait." Annals of Science, 51 (1994): 453-75. Forfait was Minister of Marine for Napoleon, issuing a decree in May 1801, preparing for invasion, e.g., a plan to construct a fleet of gunboats, 2000 of which were completed; plan never executed.

419 Bradley, Peter T. British Maritime Enterprise in the New World: From the Late 15th Century to the Mid-19th Century. Lewiston: Mellen, 1999, xix, 600 pp. A provocative, scholarly study; re British seaborne ventures and expeditions, including warlike activities; included sponsors, companies, ships, losses, and prizes.

420 -------. The Lure of Peru: Maritime Intrusion into the South Sea, 1598-1701. NY: St. Martin, 1989, xiii, 242 pp. Re the international struggle over Peru, especially Potosi, the great silver source, becoming the largest city of the Spanish empire, population of 160,000.

421 -------. "The Ships of the Armada of the Viceroyalty of Peru in the Seventeenth Century." MM, 79 (November 1993): 393-402. During his circumnavigation, Drake raided the convoy; accounts of later bullion convoys.

422 Bradner, Leicester. "Poems on the Defeat of the Spanish Armada." J English and Germanic Philology, 43 (October 1944): 447-48. Describes volumes of poetry, much English but more in Latin.

423 Braid, Douglas. "Ordnance and Empire: Portugal in the 15th and 16th Centuries." J Ordnance Society, 4 (1992): 55-66. An aspect of global history; advances in gunmaking, ship design, and navigation instruments as essential features of expansion of Portugal, in alliance with the English.

424 [NRS 4]. Brassey, T.A., ed. An Index to James' "Naval History," 1886 Edition: Prepared by C.G. Toogood. Publications of the Navy Records Society, vol. 4. London: NRS, 1895, vi, 188 pp. Brassey edited and Toogood prepared; a guide to the 6-vol. history which covers 1790s-1827; divided into 4 parts, e.g., ships, officers, and battles; insufficient information about the history and its author.

425 Brassey's Naval Annual. London: Clowes, 1886-present. A journal using various names and a series of editors since its beginning in 1886; carries articles and factual data on the modern navy and merchant service, later, the modern armed forces; some historical background and context.

426 Braudel, Fernand. The Mediterranean and the Mediterranean World in the Age of Philip II. 2 vols. New York: Harper, 1949, 1966, 1977, 1992, 1578 pp. A premier contribution to global history and world-system structures stressing interactions and relationships; environmental, cultural, and human events of the Mediterranean, 1550-1600; the great French "global" historian who claimed he wrote this while a prisoner of the fascists.

427 Breen, Kenneth. "The Foundering of HMS RAMILLIES." MM, 56 (May 1970): 187-97. RAMILLIES was lost in a storm, North Atlantic, 1782, 600 saved, credit to officers and Admiral Graves.

428 Brennan, Michael, ed. The Travel Diary of Robert Bargrave, Levant Merchant, 1647-1656. Publications of the Hakluyt Society. London: Hakluyt, 1999, xix, 288 pp. An early English merchant in the eastern Mediterranean.

429 Brentnall, Margaret. The Cinque Ports and Romney Marsh. London: Gifford, 1972, 1980, xii, 286 pp. A historical survey; chapters on the individual towns.

430 Brenton, Edward Pelham. The Naval History of Great Britain from the Year, 1783 to 1836. Various combinations: 5 and 2 vols. London: Colburn, 1822, 1823-1825, 1837. By a captain, RN; various editions, e.g., that of the 1820s had 5 vols.; the 1837 edition was touted as "new and greatly improved"; "whig" vs. "tory" biases; responds to critics in James's Naval History who "scalped" him; the new edition of James plagerizes and is uninformed, but only to be expected from a "mere landsman."

431 Brett, Oswald L. "Captain James Cook, RN, FRS: An Appreciation of the Man and His Voyages." Sea History, 11 (Summer 1978): 12-16. An overview of his contributions.

432 Brett-James, Antony, ed. Escape from the French: Captain Hewson's Narrative, 1803-1809. London: Hodder, 1981, 192 pp. Memoir of a British seaman, Maurice Hewson, 1786-1869.

433 Brett-James, Antony. "The Walcheren Failure." 2 parts. HisTod, 13 and 14 (December 1963 and January 1964): 811-20, 60-68. The expedition into the Scheldt of 1809; review of causes for the fiasco.

434 Brett-Jones, Tony. "The White Ship Disaster." Historian, 64 (Winter 1999): 23-26. On 25 November 1120, one of the largest ships afloat, struck rocks and sank in a calm sea on a quiet night a half mile from the shore near Barfleur, 1 of 300 survived; 3 victims were children of King Stephen, including the 18-year-old heir, William; a series dynastic crisis ensued.

435 Brewer, John. The Sinews of Power: War, Money and the English State, 1688-1783. Boston: Unwin; Cambridge: Harvard UP, 1989, 1990, xxii, 289 pp. Important revisionist interpretation on state-building and the political and economic institutions of the 18th century, e.g., the excise tax to finance naval expansion, navies being very expensive; the "blue-water strategy" was a commercial decision; recounts the conditions and changes which created the modern fiscal, military state; all of the changes were related to enhancing the ability of the government to wage war.

436 [NRS 15]. Bridge, Cyrian A.G., ed. History of the Russian Fleet during the Reign of Peter the Great: By a Contemporary Englishman, 1724. Publications of the Navy Records Society, vol. 15. London: NRS, 1899, xxvv, 161 pp. Describes creation of a naval force at St. Petersburg; its activities in the Baltic.

437 Bridge, T.D. "Greenwich: Need for Careful Thought." Army Quarterly and Defence J, 126 (July 1996): 258-59. At a crucial stage, decisions about the future of Greenwich; brief history of its past, the situation of its present, and the significance of its future.

438 Bridges, R.C. and Hair, P.E.H., eds. Compassing the Vaste Globe of the Earth: Studies in the History of the Hakluyt Society, 1846-1996. Publications of the Hakluyt Society, 2nd ser, vol. 183. Aldershot: Ashgate, 1996, xi, 336 pp. On the occasion of the 150th anniversary, founded in 1846, paying tribute to Richard Hakluyt; list of publications and officers, e.g., D.B. Quinn, Glyndwr Williams, Ann Savours, and Clements Markham; a history of the society; publications: 1st series, 100 vols. to 1898; 2nd series, 181 vols. to 1995, and 3rd series, vols. forthcoming.

439 Briggs, John Henry. Naval Administrations, 1827-1892: The Experience of 65 Years. London: Sampson, 1897, 339 pp. Ed: Lady Briggs; a memoir of 44 years as Clerk of the Admiralty, retiring in 1870; an anecdotal record of administrations.

440 Brighton, John G., comp. Admiral of the Fleet Sir Provo Wallis: A Memoir. London: Hutchinson, 1892, 299 pp. Born in Nova Scotia in 1791; began career in 1804; to 1876.

441 -------, comp. Admiral Sir P.B.V.Broke: A Memoir. London: S. Low, 1866, 488 pp. Journals and letters, some covering the 1st decade of the 19th century.

442 Brimacombe, Peter. All the Queen's Men: The World of Elizabeth I. NY: St. Martin, 2000, vii, 214 pp. Folio size, illustrated; profiles of statesmen, seafarers, explorers, and others, e.g., Drake.

443 -------. "Daring, Dashing Drake." In Britain (February 1992): 14-18. Focused on the attractions of Plymouth, the statue on the Hoe and, "as they say," playing bowls on that fateful day; a review is the career of Drake; some exaggeration.

444 British Museum. A Guide to the Manuscripts, Printed Books, Prints and Medals Exhibited on the Occasion of the Nelson Centenary. London: British Museum, 1905, viii, 107 pp. A feature of the centennial of the death of Nelson.; an invaluable reference source.

445 Britten, Benjamin. "Opera: Billy Budd." From the novel by Herman Melville. E.g., performances: Metropolitan Opera, June 1998 and on PBS, 8 PM, 3 June 1998.

446 Britton, C.J. New Chronicles of the Life of Lord Nelson. Birmingham: Cornish, 1947, viii, 125 pp. Fwd: Geoffrey Callender; a curious study, touting facts and a list of "Nelsoniana" published in 1813; dedicated to Emma, Lady Hamilton, "whose faults the Country remembered and whose loving charms and the dead voice of Duty the Nation forgot"; Callender sets out to correct "Nelsonian fallacies," e.g., Nelson lost an eye and was Napoleon's "yo-yo," i.e., he hood-winked Nelson into a wild chase to the West Indies; the Southey biography being "a rich, perhaps an inexhaustible, mine of noxious Nelsonian fallacies" (p. 6); appraisal of portraits and monuments.

447 Brodie, Walter. Pitcairn Island and the Islanders in 1850. London: Whitaker; NY: AMS, 1851, 1980, 260 pp. The story of the island since the BOUNTY mutineers arrived.

448 Brogger, Anton W. and Shetelig, Haakon. The Viking Ships: Their Ancestry and Evolution. London: Hurst, 1950, 1971, 192 pp. Trans: Katherine John; folio size, illustrated; a comprehensive guide and description by noted Norwegian archaeologists.

449 Brome, Vincent. The Other Pepys. London: Weidenfeld, 1993, 343 pp. A sensationalized pot-boiler; concentrates on sex and financial scandals; little after 1669 when the diary ends.

450 Bromley, John Selwyn. and Kossman, E.H., eds. Britain and the Netherlands in Europe and Asia: Papers Delivered to the Third Anglo-Dutch Historical Conference. NY: St. Martin, 1968, 264 pp. Conference organized by Boxer and Bindoff; Bromley, 1911-1985, an important naval social historian focusing on privateering; 11 papers by experts, e.g., J.R. Jones on old rivalries and contrasting attitudes.

451 Bromley, John Selwyn. Corsairs and Navies, 1660-1760. London: Hambledon, 1987, xxv, 517 pp. Preface: Alastair Duke; a collection of essays published posthumously; privateers and pirates comprised an international group belonging to the confraternity of oceans; Bromley, the historian of all of the irregular forces scouring the high seas, e.g., Dutch, French, English, and even Jacobites sponsored by James II; comprehensive and broad-based coverage, e.g., politics, war plans, economic designs, guerre de course, seaports, sailors, and logistics.

452 [NRS 119]. Bromley, John Selwyn, ed. The Manning of the Royal Navy: Selected Public Pamphlets, 1693-1873. Publications of the Navy Records Society, vol. 119. London: NRS, 1976, li, 409 pp. Excellent introduction about manning; a series of pamphlets outlining issues and problems of manning, a perennial situation.

453 Brooke, C.F. Tucker. "Some Pre-Armada Propagandist Poetry in England, 1585-1586." Proceedings of the American Philosophical Society, 85 (1942): 71-83. Presents evidence of growing anti-Spanish feeling, boosting morale, and glorification of Drake.

454 Brooks, Frederick W. "The Cinque Ports." MM, 15 (April 1929): 142-91. An important contributor to the early history of the navy, especially its administration; a extended history and description of this institution, seen as a precursor to the navy; ports named, eventually included 39 towns.

455 -------. "The Cinque Ports' Feud with Yarmouth in the Thirteenth Century." MM, 19 (January 1933): 27-51. This was an extraordinary conflict deteriorating into war twice.

456 -------. The English Naval Forces, 1199-1272. London: Brown; London: Pordes, 1933, 1962, xvi, 228 pp. Fwd: Geoffrey Callender; a scholarly assessment; themes, e.g., shipbuilding, navigation, crew, armament, types of ships, Cinque Ports, and King's Ships.

457 Brooks, Frederick W., ed. The First Order Book of the Hull Trinity House, 1632-1665. York: Beverley, 1942, xxxiv, 193 pp. Sponsored by the Yorkshire Archaeology Society; re this important naval institution.

458 Brooks, Frederick W. "The King's Ships and Galleys Mainly under John and Henry II." MM, 15 (January 1929): 15-48. This "King's own fleet" was distinct from the Cinque Ports' fleet; evolves into Navy Royal.

459 -------. "Naval Administration and the Raising of Fleets under John and Henry III." MM, 15 (October 1929): 351-90. Extensive coverage of a neglected subject: naval forces and administration, e.g., victualling, recruitment, upkeep, and armaments.

460 -------. "Naval Armaments of the Thirteenth Century." MM, 14 (April 1928): 115-31. Armaments before cannon, e.g., Greek fire, the ram, and stone-throwing engines.

461 -------. "A Wage Scale for Seamen, 1546." EHR, 60 (May 1945): 234-46. Records are lacking; clear that the scale was very complex; also describes rules and regulations of conduct.

462 -------. "William de Wrotham and the Office of Keeper of the King's Ports and Galleys." EHR, 40 (October 1925): 570-79. Aim of King John was to combine various sources of ships and place under central control; filling what is seen as the earliest office of naval administration which evolved into the Admiralty.

463 Broome, Jack. Make Another Signal! London: Kimber, 1955, 1973, viii, 255 pp. The history of naval signals and the significance of preciseness and clarity, e.g.,

Salamis, and Trafalgar; nothing in the edition of 1973 about a controversy around the edition of 1955.

464 Broomfield, J.H. "The Keppel-Palliser Affair, 1778-1779." MM, 47 (1961): 195-207. Augustus Keppel vs. Sir Hugh Palliser, a sensational case during the War of the American Revolution, demonstrating how important naval business and politics were in the halls of Parliament.

465 -------. "Lord Sandwich at the Admiralty Board: Politics and the British Navy, 1771-1778." MM, 51 (February 1965): 7-25. Sandwich was blamed by Whigs for losses during the War of the American Revolution; revisionism on Sandwich.

466 Brotton, Jerry. Trading Territories: Mapping the Early Modern World. London: Reaktion, 1997, 208 pp. Illustrated; a survey and analysis, e..g., the significant contributions of the Portuguese and Ottomans in the techniques and methodologies of mapmaking.

467 Brouwer, Norman J. International Register of Historic Ships. Annapolis: NIP; Peekskill: National Maritime; London: Chatham, 1985, 1993, 1999, viii, 392 pp. Illustrated; sponsored by the World Ship Trust; a list of over 1800 ships being preserved in 43 countries, e.g., MARY ROSE, VICTORY, and FOUDROYANT.

468 Brown, Anthony. Ill-starred Captains: Baudin and Flinders. London: Chatham, 2001, 512 pp. Illustrated; re Nicolas Baudin and Matthew Flinders, pioneers of exploration of the Pacific; operations interrupted by war.

469 Brown, Anthony Gary. Persons, Animals, Ships and Cannon in the Aubrey-Maturin Sea Novels of Patrick O'Brian. Jefferson: McFarland, 1999, vi, 342 pp. O'Brian noted as Anglo-Irish writer who kept his privacy; extensive dictionary (pp. 8-338).

470 Brown, Antony. Hazard Unlimited: The Story of Lloyd's of London. London: Davies, 1973, 1978, xi, 226 pp. Origin in a "coffee house" and developed into an insurance empire accepting all risks; details on technical aspects.

471 Brown, R. Allen, ed. Anglo-Norman Studies, XI: Proceedings of the Battle Conference, 1988. London: Arnold; London: Boydell, 1989, viii, 295 pp. Papers from the confernce, e.g., J. Neumann on the hydrography associated with the Norman invasion of 1066, i.e., tides, tidal streams, and the hydrodynamics of sailing ships of the era.

472 Brown, R. Allen. The Norman Conquest of England. Documents of Medieval History series, # 5. London: Arnold; Rochester: Boydell, 1984, 1995, xx, 181 pp. 202 primary sources plus commentary, e.g., from Anglo-Saxon, Norman, Old English, and Anglo-Norman sources; topics, e.g., charters, the Bayeux Tapestry, and seals.

473 -------. The Normans and the Norman Conquest. NY: Crowell; Dover: Boydell, 1968, 1984, 1997, 292 pp. Title varies; included naval aspects, e.g., the fyrd, the Norman fleet, the fleet assembled by Harold and its disposition, and the fleet of Harold Hardrada.

474 Brown, Robert T. "William Fitzwilliam Owen: Hydrographer of the African Coast, 1774-1857." Ph.D. diss, Syracuse, 1972, 355 pp. Owen, in RN, 1788-1854; series of surveys, e.g., 30,000 miles of African coastline during the 1820s; involved in anti-slave trade movement.

475 Brown, Shirley Ann. The Bayeux Tapestry: History and Bibliography. Dover: Boydell, 1988, xi, 186 pp. In fine arts collection; includes an annotated bibliography.

476 Browne, Douglas G. The Floating Bulwark: The Story of the Fighting Ship, 1514-1942. NY: St. Martin, 1963, 274 pp. An adequate, popular survey; begins with warships of Henry VIII.

477 Browne, George Lathom. Nelson: The Public and Private Life of Horatio, Viscount Nelson as Told by Himself, His Comrades, and His Friends. London: Unwin; London: Trident, 1891, 1999, xxxii, 472 pp. Use of Morrison collection and other sources; adamant that Horatia not his daughter; commentary on Caracciolo affair.

478 [NRS 9]. Browning, Oscar, ed. The Journal of Sir George Rooke: Admiral of the Fleet, 1700-1702. Publications of the Navy Records Society, vol. 9. London: NRS, 1897, xlvi, 272 pp. An "errata" of 1898 noted a large number of corrections; recounts operations against Cadiz and Vigo; some effective diplomacy relating to Denmark and Sweden.

479 Browning, Reed. The War of Austrian Succession. NY: St. Martin; Stroud: Sutton, 1993, 1995, xviii, 445 pp. Another recent contribution on these wars of the mid-18th century; comprehensive with a witty and engaging narrative; actually 4 wars; conclusion: a stand-off, the French prevailed on land, the British on the sea.

480 Brownlee, Walter. The Navy that Beat Napoleon. Topic Book. Cambridge: Cambridge UP, 1982, 52 pp. A pamphlet at the juvenile level; insightful and articulate on RN, strategy, and tactics.

481 Bruce, Anthony. A Bibliography of British Military History: From the Roman Invasion to the Restoration, 1660. NY: Saur, 1981, 349 pp. 3280 entries, a survey of printed sources.

482 Bruce, Anthony and Cogar, William. An Encyclopedia of Naval History. NY: Viking; London: Fitzroy Dearborn, 1989, 1998, viii, 440 pp. Folio size, illustrated; over 1000 alphabetical entries; re world naval history since the 16th century.

483 Bruce-Mitford, Rupert L.S., ed. The SUTTON HOO Ship Burial. 3 vols. in 4. London: British Museum, 1975-1984, 1442 pp. Coverage from all aspects by 35 authors; discovery in 1939 on the Edith May Pretty estate; possible identity of the king: Raedwald, a bretwalda of East Anglia; coins dated after 625; interesting juxtaposition of pagan and Christian artifacts.

484 -------, ed. The SUTTON HOO Ship Burial: A Provisional Guide. London: British Museum, 1947, 1972, 1979, 134 pp. The museum guide describing the collection and display.

485 Bruijn, Jaap R. and Bruyns, W.F.J. Morzer, eds. Anglo-Dutch Mercantile Marine Relations, 1700-1850. Amsterdam: Rijksmuseum, 1991, 134 pp. 10 papers from the symposium, "The Interchange," 12-13 October 1990, Amsterdam; themes, e.g., the interchanges, influences, and developments, English and Dutch seamen, and technology, economic, and financial factors.

486 Bruijn, Jaap R. The Dutch Navy of the Seventeenth and Eighteenth Centuries. Studies in Maritime History. Columbia: USCP, 1993, 1998, xviii, 258 pp. Fwd: Clark Reynolds; by a professor, University of Leiden; divided into parts chronologically: "Old," "New," and "2nd Rate" navies, 1500-1795; informative on the development, make-up, and influence of the Dutch republic; the Dutch had the first "standing navy."

487 -------. "Dutch Privateering during the Second and Third Anglo-Dutch Wars." Acta Historial Neerlandical, 11 (1978): 79-93. A summary of operations.

488 Bruijn, Jaap R. and Gaastra, Femme S., eds. Ships, Sailors and Spices: East India Companies and Their Shipping in the 16th, 17th and 18th Centuries. Amsterdam: NEHA, 1993, xi, 208 pp. 7 papers from a conference, University of Leiden, 1987; a comparative study of East India Companies, e.g., Portuguese, English, French, Danish, Swedish, Dutch, and the Ostend Company; themes, e.g., numbers transported, mortality, number and size of ships.

489 Bruijn, Jaap R. "William III and His Two Navies." Notes and Records of the Royal Society of London, 43 (1989): 119-20. A brief descriptive account.

490 Brunton, Paul, ed. Awake, Bold Bligh!: William Bligh's Letters Describing the Mutiny on HMS BOUNTY. Sydney: Allen; Honolulu: U Haw P, 1989, viii, 87 pp. A bicentennial publication presenting 3 personal letters by Bligh written after the mutiny.

491 Brushfield, T.N. A Bibliography of Sir Walter Ralegh, Knt. NY: Franklin, 1886, 1908, 1968, x, 181 pp. 330 annotated entries divided by topics, e.g., biographies, memoirs, and voyages.

492 Bryant, Arthur. The Elizabethan Deliverance. NY: St.Martin, 1980, 1982, 232 pp. Arthur Bryant, 1899-1985, prolific, popular, nationalist, and Royalist historian;

to be expected, glorified the decisive victory of the English and perpetuated an anti-Spanish image; proclaimed himself "the New Elizabethan."

493 -------. Nelson. London: Collins, 1970, 1972, 173 pp. Illustrations; emphasis on great battles; excerpts from other works of Bryant.

494 -------. Pepys and the Revolution. London: Collins, 1979, 264 pp. Focused on Pepys and 1688.

495 -------. Samuel Pepys. 3 vols. I: The Man in the Making. II: The Saviour of the Navy. III: The Years of Peril. London: Collins, 1933-1938, 1967, 1354 pp. Projected multi-volume, vol. III not completed, only up to 1689; Pepys, 1633-1703; this work seen as making the scholarly reputation but some now say it was not deserved; depended upon J.R. Tanner who died before completing a full biography, up to 1689; notes passed to Bryant; typical Tory bias favoring Charles II and James II.

496 -------. Years of Endurance, 1793-1802; Years of Victory, 1802-1812; Age of Elegance, 1812-1822. NY: Harper; London: Collins, 1942-1950, 1975, 384, 486, and 450 pp. Bryant's "super-patriotic trilogy"; the theme is the "war with Gallic tyranny"; seen as "history as wartime propaganda"; obviously written during World War II after his change of heart as pro-fascist.

497 Bryce, Iris. Remembering Greenwich. London: Greenwich College, 1995, 137 pp. A survey of its history.

498 Bryon, Rita V. and Bryon, Terence N., eds. Maritime Information: A Guide to Libraries and Sources of Information in the United Kingdom. London: Maritime Information Association, 1983, 1993, v, 222 pp. Fwd: Roger Knight; libraries, museums, archives, and other institutions; exactly 500 listed, Aberdeen. . . . to Zetland.

499 Buchet, Christian. Marine, Economie et Societe: Un exemple d'interaction: l'avitaillement de la Royal Navy durant la guerre de sept ans. Paris: Champion, 1999, 430 pp. Re victualling and reforms of the Victualling Board; compares operations of the 1690s to the time of Nelson in 1805; an enormous organization, the most centralized and efficient agricultural market in Europe; analysis of the market, contracts, and increased efficiency and effectiveness, especially from 1690 through the 1760s; a major contribution to naval history.

500 -------. "The Royal Navy and the Caribbean, 1689-1763." MM, 80 (February 1994): 30-44. A total of 74 expeditions to the Caribbean by European powers were conducted during the period; the British failed to appropriate Spanish and French possessions at first; for all, the main problem was sickness during long voyages, e.g., scurvy, typhus, and typhoid.

501 Buehr, Walter. The Spanish Armada. NY: Putnam, 1962, 96 pp. Illustrated; at juvenile level; excellent presentation.

502 Buel, Richard. In Irons: Britain's Naval Supremacy and the American Revolutionary Economy. New Haven: Yale UP, 1998, xi, 397 pp. Re the economic role of overseas commerce, placing it in international context, filling a gap; British blockaded, seized major ports, and produced worthless paper money, forcing American agriculture and commerce "in irons"; the impact of the RN on the American economy; weak on European aspects.

503 Buell, Augustus C. Paul Jones: Founder of the American Navy. NY, 1900. Most information fabricated; deceived many for years.

504 Buffington, Arthur H. "The Canada Expedition of 1746: Its Relation to British Politics." AHR, 45 (April 1940): 552-80. A neglected campaign; initiated by the elder Pitt and the Duke of Bedford; eventually led to annexation of Canada and, ultimately, to the American Revolution; not important as imperial or strategic campaign but as a political episode.

505 Bugler, Arthur R. HMS VICTORY; Building, Restoration and Repair. 2 vols. London: HMSO, 1966, xix, 382 pp. The authorized account; re the oldest ship in existence; restoration began in 1922; the 2nd volume is a case of 17 drawings.

506 Bull, Stephen B. "Gunpowder, Ordnance and Warfare: Britain, 1580-1655." Ph.D. diss, Wales, 1989. A survey.

507 Bullocke, John G. Sailors' Rebellion: A Century of Mutiny at Sea. London: Eyre, 1938, 318 pp. Recounts a series of mutinies in RN, beginning in 1702, e.g., HMS WAGER, HM Bark BOUNTY, Spithead, the Nore, and HMS HERMIONE.

508 [NRS 74]. Bullocke, John G., ed. The Tomlinson Papers: Selected from the Correspondence and Pamphlets of Captain Robert Tomlinson, RN and Vice-Admiral Nicholas Tomlinson. Publications of the Navy Records Society, vol. 74. London: NRS, 1935, xxx, 400 pp. Robert, 1733-1813 and Nicholas, 1764-1847; topics include timber problems and manning.

509 Burg, B.R. Sodomy and the Perception of Evil: English Sea Rovers in the Seventeenth-Century Caribbean. NY: NYUP, 1983, xxiv, 215 pp. Re homosexual contact between adult males; sociological approach; focused on an unusual group of Caribbean pirates; assesses the nature of pirate life and English naval life.

510 Burghley, William. The Spanish Invasion. 1588. A contemporaneous report by William Cecil, Lord Burghley, chief minister to Elizabeth I.

511 Burl, Aubrey. That Great Pyrate: Bartholomew Roberts and His Crew, 1718-1723. London: Alun, 1997, 254 pp. A popular study.

512 Burley, S.J. "The Victualling of Calais, 1347-1365." Bull IHR, 31 (May 1958):

49-57. The tradition in the middle ages: "armies live off the land," but for this campaign of Calais led by Edward III that was impossible; a year-long seige of 1347, associated with the Crecy campaign; required supply and victualling from England at great cost; able to maintain continental base at Calais for 200 years.

513 Burne, Alfred H. The Agincourt War: A Military History of the Latter Part of the Hundred Years' War from 1369 to 1453. Westport: Greenwood; Ware: Wordsworth, 1956, 1976, 1999, 359 pp. The basic objective of England: maintain dominion in France; performance of England waxed and waned; little scholarly apparatus and nothing on naval operations.

514 -------. The Crecy War: A Military History of the Hundred Years' War from 1337 to the Peace of Britigny, 1360. London: Eyre; London: Greenhill; Ware: Wordsworth, 1955, 1990, 1999, 366 pp. England enjoyed continued success during this phase, the first half of the war.

515 Burney, William. The British Neptune: Or, A History of the Achievement of the Royal Navy: From the Earliest Periods to the Present Day. London: Phillips, 1807, 490 pp. An early 19th-century history of RN.

516 Burnham, Barry C. and Johnson, Helen B., eds. Invasion and Response: The Case of Roman Britain. British Archaeological Reports # 73. Oxford: BAR, 1979, v, 365 pp. Folio size; papers from a conference, St. John's College, Cambridge, March 1979; focus on 43 AD, the Roman invasion and the response from native Britons.

517 Burnham, W.E. "The Opening of the Sea Route between Genoa and England and Its Development to the End of the Fourteenth Century." Ph.D. diss, Cambridge, 1977. Re the increasing relations with the Mediterranean.

518 Burns, K.V. Badges and Battlehonors of H.M. Ships. London: Maritime, 1988, 208 pp. Luxury production with full color illustrations on every page; a detailed history of RN ship names including badges and career summaries.

519 -------. The Devonport Dockyard Story. Liskeard: Martime, 1984, 126 pp. A history of this dockyard.

520 -------. Plymouth's Ships of War: A History of Naval Vessels Built in Plymouth between 1694 and 1860. Maritime Monographs and Reports # 4. Greenwich: NMM, 1972, 152 pp. Preface: G.P.B. Naish; naval forces at Plymouth first noted in 1287; 26 ships from Plymouth when Edward III besieged Calais in 1347; the "golden age": Drake, Hawkins, Gilbert, Frobisher; list of over 200 ships built there.

521 Burrows, Edmund H. Captain Owen of the African Survey: The Hydrographic Surveys of Admiral W.F.W. Owen on the Coast of Africa, 1774-1857. Rotterdam: Balkema, 1979, viii, 248 pp. 300 charts came from these surveys under this great hydrographic surveyor.

522 Burrows, Montagu. <u>Cinque Ports</u>. <u>Historic Towns</u> series. London: Longman, 1888, viii, 261 pp. Re the 7 head ports, technically 5 Cinque Ports and 2 Ancient Towns plus 8 corporate and 24 non-corporate members; status granted by charter; they declined after the 15th and 16th centuries

523 -------. <u>Life of Edward Lord Hawke, Admiral of the Fleet</u>. London: Allen, 1883, 1896, 1904, xii, 508 pp. A biography using official and family records.

524 Burwash, Dorothy. <u>English Merchant Shipping, 1460-1540</u>. Toronto: Toronto UP; Newton Abbot: David and Charles, 1947, 1969, 259 pp. An extensive study, intensively researched; features, e.g., types, sizes, navigation, volume of trade, and number of ships in various ports; London was main port followed by Southampton; English depended on Portugal and Genoa for scientific advances, navigation, and piloting; legal basis was Laws of Oleron.

525 Busch, Leslie C. and Busch, Briton C. "The Seaman's Diet Revisited." <u>International J Maritime History</u>, 7 (December 1995): 163-72. Scurvy, the "seaman's disease," was actually more complicated; more than lack of ascorbic acid; long voyages meant nutritional needs not satisfied.

526 Butcher, Thomas K. <u>The Navy</u>. London: Batsford, 1973, 95 pp. Illustrated; 500 years of history of the navy to instruct sea cadets; a balanced summary.

527 Butel, Paul. <u>The Atlantic</u>. <u>Seas in History</u> series. London: Routledge, 1999, xv, 330 pp. 1st in a series; a chronological narrative, e.g., Irish monks, Viking traders, Italians to islands, Portuguese-Bristol cooperative ventures, and Iberian expansion.

528 Butler, Beverley and Littlewood, Kevin. <u>IMPLACABLE: A Trafalgar Ship Remembered</u>. Greenwich: NMM, 1999, 31 pp. 74-gun SOTL, scuttled in 1949; the stern section was reconstructed and installed in the new Neptune Court, NMM.

529 Butler, Charles. "On the Legality of Impressing Seamen." <u>The Pamphleteer</u>, 23 (1824): 225-87. Later edition included comment by Lord Sandwich; a review, monarch by monarch, of the practice, 13th through the 18th centuries.

530 Butler, Denis. <u>1066: The Story of a Year</u>. London: Putnam, 1966, 328 pp. On the occasion of the 600th anniversary, a review of the crucial year; apologetics for Harold.

531 Butterfield, Herbert. <u>The Peace Tactics of Napoleon, 1806-1808</u>. Cambridge: Cambridge UP; NY: Octagon, 1929, 1972, 395 pp. A superb analysis of diplomacy at the high point of Napoleonic power, e.g., Tilsit and British defiance at Copenhagen.

532 Byrn, John D. "Crime and Punishment in the Royal Navy: Discipline on the Leeward Islands Station, 1784-1812." Ph.D. diss, Louisana State, 1987, 386 pp. The basis for the next entry.

533 -------. Crime and Punishment in the Royal Navy: Discipline on the Leeward Islands Station, 1784-1812. Naval History series. London: Scolar, 1989, x, 251 pp. Leeward Islands as case study; extensive analysis of logs of 73 ships; contends naval justice of the 18th century is similar to justice ashore and conditions on the lower deck have been misrepresented; in line with presentations of Rodger and Gilbert and at odds with J. Masefield and D.Pope.

534 Byrne, Eugene Hugh. Genoese Shipping in the Twelfth and Thirteenth Centuries. Monographs of the Medieval Academy # 5. Cambridge: Medieval Academy, 1930, ix, 159 pp. Informative on this influential naval and maritime power expanding its commerce, e.g., cargo, horses and bulk goods of the Crusaders; types of ships include galleys and sail plus a combination; Jal cites Genoa as a model; chapter on privateering.

535 Byron, George Gordon, Lord. "The Island: Or Christian and His Comrades: A Poem." Various editions, c. 1822. Byron, 1788-1822, the last work of the great Romantic poet; his perspective and dramatization of the mutiny on the BOUNTY and its aftermath; favorable to Bligh; "Awake Bold Bligh."

536 Cable, James. The Political Influence of Naval Force in History. London: Macmillan, 1998, viii, 213 pp. An assessement, including some musings, by a distinguished and prolific diplomat-naval historian; the "high noon" was 1690-1815, then peace, then the rise of new naval powers, the U.S. and Japan; earlier, da Gama had blasted a colonial path for Portugal; also cited China in the 15th century and French use of privateers.

537 Cabrera de Cordoba, Luis. Felipe Segunda, Rey de Espana. 4 vols. Madrid: n.p., 1619, 1876-1877. An extraordinary source by Cabrera de Cordoba, 1559-1623, a Spanish official in Italy; a rich source of information about Philip II and planning for the Armada.

538 Caesar, Julius. The Conquest of Gaul. Penguin Classic. NY: Panguin, 2001, 288 pp. Trans: S.A. Handford; intro: Jane Gardner; a new, popular edition.

539 -------. The Gallic Wars. Everyman's Library series. NY: Modern Library, various editions, e.g., 1953, 1957, xix, 363 pp. Trans: John Warrington and Moses Hadas, respectively; Caesar's account of his campaigns in the north, including "the first British expedition."

540 Caffrey, Kate. The MAYFLOWER. NY: Stein, 1974, 392 pp. Enlightening on ships of the 17th century; for general audience; details on the ship, the voyage, and the passengers.

541 Calabretta, Fred. Guide to the Oral History Collection at Mystic Seaport Museum. Mystic: MSM, 1992, 74 pp. Includes a catalogue, 218 oral history interviews, 1965-1991 and 93 Munson Lectures, 1955-1972; features, e.g., design of ships and ship construction.

542 Calder, Alex, Lamb, Jonathan, and Orr, Bridget, eds. Voyages and Beaches: Pacific Encounters, 1769-1840. Honolulu: U Haw P, 1999, viii, 344 pp. Papers from a seminar, University of Auckland, 1993, e.g., by J.G.A. Pocock and David Mackay; Pacific exploration.

543 Calderhead, William L. "British Naval Failure at Long Island: A Lost Opportunity in the American Revolution." New York History, 57 (July 1976): 321-38. A reassessment; an opportunity to trap George Washington on Long Island was lost.

544 Caldwell, Ronald J. The Era of the French Revolution: A Bibliography of the History of Western Civilization, 1789-1799. 2 vols. NY: Garland, 1985, 1990, 1448 pp. A massive compilation, 48,136 entries, some annotated, plus over 3000 serials; demonstrative of the interest in this period.

545 -------. The Era of Napoleon: A Bibliography of the History of Western Civilization, 1799- 1815. 2 vols. NY: Garland, 1991, xxi, 1447 pp. A continuation of the previous entry, again, some briefly annotated.

546 Callegari, Dennis. Cook's Cannon and Anchor: The Recovery and Conservation of Relics from HM Bark ENDEAVOUR. Kenthurst: Kangaroo, 1994, 96 pp. In June 1770, ENDEAVOUOR ran aground on Endeavour Reef; 200 years later, an expedition recovered the cannon and anchor.

547 Callender, Geoffrey A.R. Bibliography of Naval History. 2 parts. London: Historical Association, 1924-1925. Geoffrey Callender, the pre-eminent British naval historian of the 1920s and 1930s, Director of NMM; see his edition of Southey, Life of Nelson; this being short historiographical essays presenting and assessing contributions to the naval literature.

548 -------. "Drake and His Detractors." MM, 7 (March, April, May 1921): 66-74, 98-104, 142-53. A response to Gregory Robinson in an earlier article concerning the notorious Doughty affair; Callender defends Drake point by point; the controversy takes up much of the volume of 1921.

549 -------. "The Effigy of Nelson in Westminster Abbey." MM, 27 (October 1941): 307-13. Descriptions of statues and portraits of Nelson, e.g., in Westminster Abbey, carved in wood but the head and left hand are in wax; Hoppner and Devis portraits described.

550 -------. "Fresh Light on Drake." MM, 9 (January 1923): 16-28. A continuation of the controversy of 1921; new information from Spanish sources, dubbing Drake as pirate and corsair.

551 -------. "The Greenwich Portrait of Sir Francis Drake." MM, 18 (October 1932): 359-62. A Dutch engraving of the 16th century by Hondius, frontispiece for Corbett's biography; another oil painting by Janssen.

552 [NRS 52 and 53]. Callender, Geoffrey A.R., ed. The Life of Sir John Leake, Rear-Admiral of Great Britain by Stephen Martin-Leake. 2 vols. Publications of the Navy Records Society, vol. 52 and 53. London: NRS, 1920, clviii, 334 and x, 490 pp. Recounts important events, e.g., battles of Bantry Bay and La Hogue and the capture of Gibraltar.

553 Callender, Geoffrey A.R. "The Naval Campaign of 1587." History, 3 (July 1918): 82-91. An early contribution; re the raid on Cadiz by Drake, burning 50 ships being readied for the Armada and spreading panic, "singeing King Philip's beard."

554 Callender, Geoffrey A.R. and Hinsley, F.H. The Naval Side of British History. 2 vols. Boston: Little, Brown; London: Chistophers, 1924-1950, 1960, 409 pp. Chronological coverage; cites the origins of RN as the 16th century; emphasis on battles; review of legendary aspects, e.g., game of bowls, last words of Grenville, and death of Nelson.

555 Callender, Geoffrey A.R. The Portrait of Peter Pett and the SOVEREIGN OF THE SEAS. London: NMM; Newport: Yelf, 1930, 51 pp. For the Society for Nautical Research; history and description.

556 -------. Sea Kings of Britain. 2 vols. London: Longman, 1907, 1917, 1939. For a long time, used as introductory text for naval cadets, becoming a classic, but simplistic approach; saw naval history in terms of fleets, fighting instructions, and brilliant leadership.

557 -------. The Story of HMS VICTORY. London: Allan, 1913, 1914, 1920, 1929, 254 pp. A history, beginning with construction at Chatham in the mid-18th century, Trafalgar, and restoration project initiated by the Society for Nautical Research in 1921; Callender saw the process to date as frustrating and disappointing.

558 Callo, Joseph F. Legacy of Leadership: Lessons from Admiral Lord Nelson. NY: Hellgate, 2000, 136 pp. By an American admiral; a new assessment; reviewed 5 battles.

559 -------. "Nelson: Character Counts in Combat." USNIP, 121 (June 1995): 60-62. Observations about contrasts perceived in the character of Nelson: a brilliant tactician and victor but not a model in his personal life; listed his mythical characteristics.

560 -------. Nelson Speaks: Admiral Lord Nelson in His Own Words. London: Chatham; Annapolis: NIP, 2001, xxx, 216 pp. A collection of excerpts from letters and dispatches divided by themes, e.g., duty, combat, sea power, his wife, and Emma.

561 Callow, John. The Making of King James II: The Formative Years of a Fallen King. Stroud: Sutton, 2000, xi, 340 pp. A reappraisal of the public career of James

Stuart before becoming James II, e.g., as LHA and naval commander during 2 major battles; in 1669, converted to Catholicism and was deprived of all offices; thesis: there was only one James, not two, pre-1688 and post-1688, as some have depicted; James was callous, obstinate, self-serving, and inept thoughout.

562 -------. "The Noble Duke of York: James, Duke of York and Albany, the Early Modern Prince as Lord High Admiral, Imperialist and Entrepreneur, 1660-1685." Ph.D. diss, Lancaster, 1998. The basis of the previous entry.

563 Cameron, Ian. Riders of the Storm: The Story of the Royal National Lifeboat Institution. London: Weidenfeld, 2002, 256 pp. The RNLI, formed in the late 18th century, the first such service in the world; some anecdotal accounts.

564 Cameron, P.N. "Saxons, Sea and Sail." International J Maritime History, 11 (1982): 319-32. Assessment of archaeological discoveries, e.g., SUTTON HOO; informative on Anglo-Saxon sea travel.

565 Campbell, Archibald B. Customs and Traditions of the Royal Navy. Aldershot: Gale, 1956, 1986, 169 pp. A historical review.

566 Campbell, I.C. "The Lateen Sail in World History." J World History, 6 (Spring 1995): 1-23. Revisionist view; Arabs did not invent nor transmit the sail to Europe; the Pacific sail was developed independently.

567 Campbell, James, John, Eric, and Wormald, Patrick, eds. The Anglo-Saxons. Oxford: Phaidon; London: Penguin, 1982, 1991, 272 pp. Folio size; an excellent survey; informative on the period, e.g., Saxon Shore forts, end of Roman Britain, Christian kings, arrival of Vikings, ships of Alfred who was not the founder of RN, the Irish at Iona, and various sea links.

568 Campbell, John. Lives of the British Admirals: Containing a New and Accurate Naval History. 4 vols. Edinburgh: Donaldson, 1742-1785, 1666 pp. Campbell, 1708-1795, covers up to 1779; unusually full coverage, chronological, beginning with the "ancient Britons"; other chapters, e.g., the Danes, Normans, Henry VII, Elizabeth, Howard, Gilbert, Hawkins, etc.

569 Campbell, Thomas. "Battle of the Baltic" or "Copenhagen": A Ballad. London: Novello, 1891, 33 pp. Music by Charles Stanford; a ballad set to music; musical score included; re the battle of Copenhagen of 1801.

570 Cannon, Henry L. "The Battle of Sandwich and Eustace the Monk, 1217." EHR, 27 (October 1912): 649-70. Eustace the Monk was the "Channel master pirate"; formerly served under King John but deserted to King Louis, returning to successfully invade the Channel Islands.

571 Cantwell, John D. The Public Record Office, 1838-1958. London: HMSO, 1991, ix, 631 pp. A detailed monograph on the history, services, and facilities of the

PRO.

572 Capes, Bernard. The Extraordinary Confession of Diana Please. London: Methuen, 1904, viii, 301 pp. A fictional account, Lady Hamilton and Nelson at Naples, 1798-1799.

573 Capes, Ranalt. Poseidon: A Personal Study of Admiral Lord Nelson. London: Sidgwick, 1947, viii, 206 pp. Touted as balanced, "not a heroic biography and more than legend"; naval and personal life: "at sea he was master of his fate. Ashore he was at the mercy of his emotions"; an attempt at a psychological assessment.

574 Capp, Bernard. Cromwell's Navy: The Fleet and the English Revolution, 1648-1660. Oxford: Clarendon, 1989, 1993, xii, 420 pp. Re "the New Model Navy" to fill a historical gap; actually credit for naval build-up to Rump Parliament; the navy brought international prestige and Cromwell exploited it; deals with social issues, e.g., manning, retention, victualling, wages, health, and religion.

575 Capper, D.P. Moat Defensive: A History of the Waters of the Nore Command, 55 BC to 1961. London: Barker, 1963, xii, 251 pp. The Nore, a natural, large anchorage where the Thames enters the Channel, the Nore Buoy was a rendezvous point for RN during the days of sail; a survey, e.g., Romans, Cinque Ports, Press-Gang, and mutiny at the Nore.

576 Captain Cook and the South Pacific. London: British Museum, 1979, 249 pp. A supporting publication for a bicentennial exhibition.

577 Careless, Ronald. Battleship NELSON: The Story of HMS NELSON. London: Arms, 1985, 160 pp. A modern battleship named for Nelson, of the "Cherry-Tree Class," cut down as a result of the Washington Naval Conference of the early 1920s; a veteran of World War II.

578 Carman, W.Y. "The Capture of Martinique, 1809." J Society for Army Historical Research, 200 (Spring 1941): 1-4. Analysis of 3 watercolor drawings of Parker Gallery; determined to be about the Martinique operation led by Cochrane with 10,000 troops; secured British position in the West Indies.

579 Caron, Francois. La Guerre In comprise ou le Mythe de Suffren: La campaigne en Inde, 1781-1783. Vincennes: Service, 1996, xxx, 497 pp. Re French admiral Pierre-Andre Suffren, commander of French naval forces in the final campaign over domination of India in the 1780s; Caron questions the reputation of Suffren as undeserved, he had no plan and was a poor leader.

580 Carpenter, Kenneth J. The History of Scurvy and Vitamin C. London: Cambridge UP, 1986, viii, 288 pp. An important survey, comprehensive, on this "explorers' sickness"; chapters on scurvy in RN and on Cook; voyages of over 10 weeks meant problems; the citrus cure was known as early as the 14th century, but forgotten; Anson voyage ravaged; experiments of James Lind, 1716-1794, and

Gilbert Blane, 1749-1834, eased the problem.

581 Carr, Antony D. Owen of Wales: The End of the House of Gwynedd. Cardiff: U Wales P, 1990, 140 pp. Biography of a Welsh admiral and soldier of fortune, late 14th century.

582 Carr, D.J., ed. Sydney Parkinson: Artist on Cook's ENDEAVOUR Voyage. London: Croom, 1983, xv, 300 pp. For the British Museum; employed by Joseph Banks during the first voyage; died during the voyage.

583 Carrington, Arthur H. Life of Captain Cook. London: Sidgwick, 1939, 1967, ix, 324 pp. An important biography.

584 Carter, Charles H., ed. From the Renaissance to the Counter-Reformation: Essays in Honour of Garrett Mattingly. London: Cape, 1965, 437 pp. Essays honoring Mattingly; special praise for his The Armada and an article on Franco-Spanish diplomacy and the Armada.

585 Carter, Harold B. Sir Joseph Banks, 1743-1820. London: British Museum, 1988, xii, 671 pp. The definitive biography of this extraordinary figure: explorer, naturalist, collector, organizer, "Father of Australia," and President of the Royal Society for 42 years.

586 -------. Sir Joseph Banks, 1743-1820: A Guide to Biographical and Bibliographical Sources. Winchester: St. Paul, 1987, 328 pp. For the British Museum; a comprehensive survey of the papers, publications, and persons associated with Banks, an important contributor to natural history.

587 Carter, Paul. The Road to Botany Bay: An Essay in Spatial History. London: Faber, 1987, xxv, 384 pp. Re the exploration and settlement of Australia, especially Sydney and the First Fleet.

588 Caruana, Adrian B. The History of English Sea Ordnance. 2 vols. I: The Art of Evolution, 1523-1715. II: The Age of the System, 1715-1815. London: Boudriot, 1994-1997, 867 pp. Folio size, illustrated; a monumental study, a 3rd vol. is promised, III: The Age of Change, 1815-1875; and a 4th; the English led in the revolution in naval ordnance; advances in gunfoundering; knowledgable only about guns and barrels, only ignorant of the navy and of history.

589 Carus-Wilson, Eleanor M. The Overseas Trade of Bristol in the Later Middle Ages. Bristol: Record Society, 1937, 1967, vii, 347 pp. Coverage of important and early maritime enterprise and exploration.

590 Carver, Martin O.H., ed. The Age of SUTTON HOO: The Seventh Century in North-Western Europe. Rochester: Boydell, 1989, 1992, 424 pp. 24 papers from a conference at York on the occasion of the 50th anniversary of the discovery in East Anglia; essays, e.g., on Anglo-Saxon burial rites, "Beowulf," the situation in northwestern Europe in the 7th century; many questions remain, and probably will remain, unanswered.

591 Carver, Martin O.H. SUTTON HOO: Burial Ground of Kings? Phil: U Pa P; London: British Museum, 1998, xii 195 pp. More details about the find and its significance; description of the 61 artifacts: weapons, jewelry, and the ship; the burial was probably for King Raedweld of East Anglia who died in 624 AD, but there is no body; in adjoining mounds, executed, mutilated bodies were found

592 Carver, Martin O.H., ed. SUTTON HOO: Research Committee Bulletins, 1983-1993. Woodbridge: Boydell, 1993, various. Annual summaries of this 3rd stage of the excavation projects; there are 16 mounds; technical details.

593 Castex, Raoul V.P. Les Idees Militaires de la Marine du XVIIIeme siecle: De Ruyter a Suffren. Paris: Fournier, 1911. An astute and persceptive analysis of the age of fighting sail, noting the indecisiveness of line ahead tactics.

594 Catalogos del Archivo General de Simancas. A Handlist. A guide to these important archives and information on access to researchers; since the 1980s, more original sources made available; informative on Spanish perspectives of the Armada.

595 Catalogue of an Exhibition of Nelson Relics in Commemoration of the Battle of Trafalgar. London: RUSI, 1905. A centennial exhibition at the Royal United Services Institute in London.

596 Cavaliero, Roderick. Admiral Satan: The Life and Campaigns of Suffren. London: Taurus; NY: St. Martin, 1994, xix, 312 pp. A biography of Pierre-Andre Suffren, 1729-1788; Napoleon hoped he would be his "Nelson"; commander of French naval forces in the Indian Ocean during 5 ferocious battles; innovative tactics, abandoning line of battle.

597 Cavendish, Richard. "August 1, 1798: Battle of the Nile." HisTod, 48 (August 1998): 27. On the occasion of the bicentennial, the battle which established the reputation of Nelson, 15 miles east of Alexandria, French at anchor in Aboukir Bay; the victory left Napoleon and his army stranded.

598 -------. "The End of the IMPLACABLE: December 2, 1949." HisTod, 49 (December 1999): 54. An account of the official scuttle in the Channel, French and British flags flying; a survivor of Trafalgar; originally a French '74 SOTL, captured after Trafalgar and entered in the British fleet, retired in 1842; restored stern now in Neptune Court, NMM.

599 -------. "The Nelson Society: Articles of Association." HisTod, 41 (November 1991): 62-63. The Nelson Society, founded in 1981, about 500 members, quarterly journal, The Nelson Dispatch; annual commemorative ceremony, 21 October, on the quarterdeck of HMS VICTORY; toast "to the immortal memory"; a separate association, the 1805 Club.

600 Cawston, George. The Early Chartered Companies, 1296-1858. London: Arnold, 1896, xi, 329 pp. An older comprehensive survey of regulated and joint stock companies, included as introduction to the phenomenon, e.g., the Hanseatic League, Merchants of the Staple, Merchant Adverturers, the Russia Company, Levant Company, and East India Company; all influential in the earliest days of naval development.

601 Cerezo Martinez, Ricardo. Las Armadas de Felipe II. Madrid: San Martin, 1988, 440 pp. A Spanish account on the occasion of the Quadricentennial.

602 Chacksfield, Merle. Armada 1588. Guildford: Biddles, 1988, 160 pp. Fwd: Rodney Legg; a kind of didactic folk version; the campaign was the result of Spanish folly, the extent to which was not equalled until Hitler invaded Russia; "they wrote themselves out of world history."

603 Chadwick, H.M. Early Scotland: The Picts, the Scots and the Welsh of Southern Scotland. NY: Farrar, 1974, xxxii, 171 pp. Informative details about Dalriada, the Irish foundation of the kingdom, c.500-750 AD; originated in Ireland and expanded to western Scotland; links to St. Patrick and St. Colombo.

604 -------. "Who Was He?" Antiquity, 14 (March 1940): 76-87. The question concerns the identity of the king for SUTTON HOO: Raedwald, King of East Anglia, d. 624 AD; disagreement from others and, of course, no body was in the burial.

605 Challoner, Robert. Give Fire!: A Commander Lord Charles Oakshott Novel. London: Century, 1986, 204 pp. Challoner, 1924-1986, pseud., Michael Butterworth; Nelson era fiction, one of several featuring Charles Oakshott; this one re preliminaries to battle of the Nile, description of L'ORIENT blowing up.

606 -------. Into Battle: A Lord Charles Oakshott Novel. London: Century, 1987, 214 pp. Another in the series.

607 -------. Run Out the Guns. London: Century, 1984, 193 pp. Nautical fiction of Nelson era; re siege of Toulon and curious encounter with Captain Bonaparte.

608 Chamberlain, William Henry. Reminiscences of Old Merton. London: Mitchell, 1923, 1925, 56 pp. Illustrated; a description of Merton, the home of Nelson, near Wimbledon.

609 Chamier, Frederick. The Arethusa: A Naval Story. London: Routledge, 1837. Re press gangs; an agenda: for impressment and apologist for corporal punishment.

610 -------. Ben Brace: The Last of Nelson's AGAMEMNONs. 2 vols. Phil: Carey and Lea, 1836, 1840, 1850, 1896, 420 pp. Chamier, 1796-1870; contemporaneous naval fiction; an account of service with Nelson.

611 -------. Jack Adams: The Mutineer. 3 vols. London: Colburn; London: Routledge, 1838, 1873, 396 pp. Jack Adams, 1760-1829, a fictional figure in the story of the mutiny on the BOUNTY.

612 -------. The Life of a Sailor. 3 vols. London: Bentley, 1832. Nautical fiction; social side of the naval life.

613 -------. The Spitfire: A Tale of the Sea. 3 vols. London: Colburn, 1840. Nautical fiction.

614 Chandler, David G. The Campaigns of Napoleon: The Mind and Method of History's Greatest Soldier. London: Macmillan, 1966, 1172 pp. By a prominent authority on Napoleon and military strategy; a significant contribution.

615 -------. Napoleon. London: Cooper, 2001. A new biography by an important authority.

616 Chandler, J.E. "Beloved, Respected and Lamented": A Story of the Mutiny of the BOUNTY. Marlborough: Chandler, 1973, 45 pp. The title: the inscription on the gravestone of Bligh but others saw him as tyrant, cruel, and inhuman; to correct the distortions and restore the image of Bligh as a humane and brilliant seaman; blames Edward Christian for blackening the reputation of Bligh; includes details of the disposition of every crewman of BOUNTY.

617 Chapin, Howard M. Privateer Ships and Sailors: The First Century of American Colonial Privateering, 1625-1725. Toulon: Mouton, 1926, 256 pp. Privateering from the American colonies.

618 -------. Privateering in King George's War, 1739-1748. Providence: Johnson, 1928, 259 pp. Continuation of the previous entry.

619 Chapman, Paul H. The Man Who Led Columbus to America. Atlanta: Judson, 1973, xx, 202 pp. Re the legendary voyage of St. Brendan of Ireland; exhausted the sources but admits not proven.

620 [NRS 73]. Chappell, Edwin, ed. The Tangier Papers of Samuel Pepys. Publications of the Navy Records Society, vol. 73. London: NRS, 1935, liv, 372 pp. Papers from the Bodleian Library; reflects serious factions within RN at the time of the Revolution of 1688.

621 Charnock, John. Biographia Navalis: Or Impartial Memoirs of the Lives and Characters of Officers of the Navy of Great Britain. 6 vols. London: Faulder, 1794-1798. Charnock, 1756-1807, collects these biographical memoirs.

622 -------. Biographical Memoirs of Lord Viscount Nelson: With Observations,

Critical, and Explanatory. 2 vols. Boston: Etheridge; London: Symonds, 1802, 1806, 1810, 1968, 1978, vii, 350 pp. Formulated from collections of letters and memoirs, e.g., Captain Locker, an early patron.

623 Charters, David A., et al., eds. Military History and the Military Profession. Westport: Praeger, 1992, xvi, 242 pp. Fwd: Anne Foreman; a series of 15 essays by experts assessing the various fields, e.g., W.A.B. Douglas on naval history, Keith Jeffery on intelligence, Donald Schurman on naval strategy, and Eric Grove on modern navies.

624 Chatterton, E. Keble. The Story of the British Navy: From the Earliest Times to the Present Day. London: Mills, 1911, xiv, 371 pp. Illustrated; from Roman times through the late 19th century; early figures, e.g., Julius Caesar, Alfred, and Edgar the Peaceable.

625 Chester, M. Alan. Brother Captain: A Novel Reconstructing HMS RODBUCK's Voyage to the South Seas in 1698/1701 under Command of William Dampier. London: Davies, 1964, 259 pp. A fictional account of the Dampier voyage.

626 Cheyette, Frederic L. "The Sovereign and the Pirates, 1332." Speculum, 45 (January 1970): 40-68. Re Genoese galleys, the prominent naval and piratical force of the 14th century, mostly in the Mediterranean, but the French chartered them to fight against the English in northern Europe

627 Chibnall, Marjorie. The Debate on the Norman Conquest. Issues in Historiography. NY: Manchester UP, 1999, viii, 168 pp. A masterly summary of the historiography over 900 years, e.g., over "feudalism," the Bayeux Tapestry, the Anglo-Saxon Chronicle, and the Battle Conferences.

628 Childs, John C.R. The Army, James II and the Glorious Revolution. Manchester: Manchester UP, 1980, xix, 226 pp. A comprehensive survey of the military dimension of 1688, James having previously been LHA in England.

629 Christian, Edward. A Short Reply to Captain William Bligh's Answer. London: Deighton, 1795, 11 pp. A pamphlet, a response in the ongoing debate and accusations between Bligh and Christian.

630 Christian, Glynn. Fragile Paradise: The Discovery of Fletcher Christian, BOUNTY Mutineer. Boston: Little, Brown, 1982, 256 pp. Christian, 1764-1793; this is an apologia for Christian by a great, great, great grandson with an obvious agenda; not balanced and not an important contribution to Bountyana.

631 Christiansen, Eric. The Norsemen in the Viking Age. Oxford: Blackwell, 2002, xiii, 378 pp. A recent synthesis and assessment.

632 Christianson, John R. On Tycho's Island: Tycho Brahe and His Assistants,

1570-1601. Cambridge: Cambridge UP, 2000, xii, 451 pp. Brahe constructed and maintained the first observatory on the island of Hven in the Danish Sounds during the late 16th century; a pertinent feature: detailed and authoritative weather observations during the time of the Armada.

633 Christie, C.A. "The Walcheren Expedition of 1809." Ph.D. diss, Dundee, 1979. Re the failed campaign in the Scheldt.

634 Christy, Miller. "Queen Elizabeth's Visit to Tilbury in 1588." EHR, 33 (January 1919): 43-61. During June and July, 1588, the English militia mobilized at West Tilbury as defense for London; legend has it that Elizabeth went down and addressed the troops.

635 Chudoba, Bohdan. Spain and the Empire, 1519-1643. Chicago: Chicago UP; NY: Octagon, 1952, 1969, xi, 299 pp. An authentic presentation of the Spanish perspective often ignored by prominent English historians; apologetics for Philip II; Armada of 1588 was one of many episodes of Spanish history and much downplayed here.

636 Churchill, T.O. The Life of Lord Viscount Nelson, Duke of Bronte. London: Bensley, 1808, 1810, 1811, 154 pp. A popular biography at the time; engravings by W. Bromley; Nicolas assessed this as "a wretched compilation" with equally wretched engravings.

637 Churchill, Winston S. A History of the English-Speaking Peoples. 4 vols. New York: Dodd, Mead, 1956-1958, 1965, 1998, 1759 pp. Various editions and excerpts; Churchill wrote this classic in the late 1930s but put it aside during World War II; a "cosmic" view and highly ideosyncratic; Anglocentric.

638 Cilcennin, Viscount. Admiralty House, Whitehall. London: Country Life, 1960, 62 pp. Illustrated; by the First Lord of the Admiralty in the 1950s; re the official residence of the First Lord since 1786; description of furnishings and "picture" tour.

639 Cipolla, Carlo M. Clocks and Culture, 1300-1700. NY: Norton, 1967, 1978, 192 pp. A cultural history approach.

640 -------. Guns, Sails, and Empires: Technological Innovation and the Early Phases of European Expansion, 1400-1700. NY: Pantheon; Manhattan: Sunflower, 1965, 1989, 192 pp. A noted treatise; thesis: the West developed armaments and naval technology so advanced that the East could not resist; called it the "Vasco da Gama era," the dominance of maritime economies; emphasis on the contribution of sails and guns to European expansion and dominance.

641 Clapham, J.H. "The Last Years of the Navigation Acts." EHR 25 (July 1910): 481-501. By the noted economic historian; the Navigation Acts formally ended in 1849; look closer, the effect probably ended in the 1820s; a factor in the manning question.

642 Clark, George N. "The Barbary Corsairs in the Seventeenth Century." Cambridge Historical J, 8 (1944): 22-35. A review of causes and effects; among other things, a threat to the Levant trade, important to England, France, Holland, and Italian states.

643 -------. The Dutch Alliance and the War against French Trade, 1688-1697. Manchester: Manchester UP, 1923, 1971, xi, 160 pp. Noted commercial and military motivations; a formative period in the evolution of the war at sea.

644 -------. "English and Dutch Privateering under William III." MM, 7 (June and July 1921): 162-67, 209-17. A review of the use, problems of control, and the age of Jean Bart.

645 -------. "The Navigation Act of 1651." History, 7 (January 1923): 282-86. It forbade importation except in English ships, but other factors were influential; an assessment of those factors.

646 Clark, Gregory. Britain's Naval Heritage. London: HMSO, 1981, viii, 131 pp. Fwd: James Eberle; by the Curator, Royal Naval Museum; an introductory essay with traditional views; began with Alfred and Cinque Ports; "Father" was Henry VIII.

647 Clark, John G. La Rochelle and the Atlantic Economy during the Eighteenth Century. Balt: JHUP, 1981, xiv, 286 pp. A case study: the impact of war; French commercial ports of the 18th century declined, each war with Britain precipitating an economic crisis.

648 Clarke, Howard B., et al., eds. Ireland and Scandinavia in the Early Viking Age. Dublin: Four Courts, 1998, xxiii, 468 pp. Papers from a conference on the occasion of the 1200th anniversary of the first Viking raid, 795, at Dublin Castle, October 1995; nautical and other archaeologists, Viking studies experts, and early medievalists presented pertinent papers; re Scotland, Ireland, Irish Sea, monastaries, and settlement.

649 Clarke, James S. and M'Arthur, John M. The Life and Services of Horatio, Viscount Nelson: From His Lordships Manuscripts. 2 vols., later expanded to 3 vols. London: Cadell, 1809, 1810, 1840, 1902, 902 pp. Illustrated; Rev. Clarke and Dr. M'Arthur had previously collaborated on The Naval Chronicle; access to Nelson papers and approved by family and by Emma Hamilton; seen as the basis of most biographies; research of the authors was uncritical and anecdotal; documents and incidents were altered to protect reputations; J.K. Laughton assessed much of it as "irrelevant and doubtful matter"; nevertheless, essential and "official."

650 Clarke, Samuel. England's Remembrancer: Containing a True and Full Narrative of. . . . the Spanish Invasion of 1588. Historical and Biographical Tracts series, I., #1. London: n.p., 1657, 35 pp. An almost contemporaneous assessment.

651 Claver, Scott. Under the Lash: A History of Corporal Punishment in the British Armed Forces. London: Touchstream, 1954, 288 pp. Good points and not so good; broad discussion of punishments, campaigns of reform, statistics, documents, and personal experiences; poorly organized and sensationalized.

652 Claxton, Bernard D., et al. Trafalgar and Jutland: A Study in the Principles of War. Military History Monograph series # 85-2. Montgomery: USAF Command and Staff College, 1985, x, 86 pp. An in-house teaching aid; 3 faculty members assess and compare these naval battles based on principles of war.

653 Clayton, Norman. "Naval Administration, 1603-1628." Ph.D. diss, Leeds, 1935. A useful description.

654 Cleaver, Liam J. "The Pen behind the Fleet: The Influence of Sir Julian Stafford Corbett on British Naval Developments, 1898-1918." Comparative Strategy, 14 (January 1995): 45-57. How a relatively obscure naval historian influenced policy and decisions, e.g., Lord Jacky Fisher; who could put his writings into action.

655 Clements, William H. Towers of Strength: The Story of Martello Towers. Barnsley: Cooper, 1999, 192 pp. A fortification defense system built along the east and south coasts against invasion by Napoleon; others built later all over the world; an archaeological and historical study; a list of surviving ones.

656 Clerk, John. An Essay on Naval Tactics. 2 vols. London: Cadell, 1782, 1790, 1797, 1804. Clerk, 1728-1812, a Scottish laird from Eldin; a study of British and French naval tactics, e.g., the line of battle, used by the British for a century, was denounced as not effective, "the tyranny of the line"; for the French, praise for the tactics of Suffren in the Indian Ocean; advised concentrating on one part of the enemy line, preferably the rear, then a melee to finish off the remainder; Nelson studied this work.

657 Clifford, Barry. The Black Ship: The Quest to Recover an English Pirate Ship and Its Lost Treasure. London: Headline, 1999, viii, 311 pp. A nautical archaeology project; overdramatized titles.

658 -------. Expedition WHYDAH: The Story of the World's First Excavation of a Pirate Treasure Ship and the Man Who Found Her. Winter Springs: ISIS, 2000. A nautical archaeology project.

659 -------. The Pirate Prince: Discovering the Priceless Treasures of the Sunken Ship WHYDAH: An Adventure. NY: Simon, 1993, 222 pp. A nautical archaeology project.

660 Cline, Duane A. Navigation in the Age of Discovery: An Introduction. Rogers: Montfleury, 1990, 214 pp. Illustrated; a survey of questionable value; emphasis on the English, e.g., the voyage of MAYFLOWER; didactic and speculative; only a nod to the Portuguese and the Dutch.

661 Clode, Charles M. <u>The Administration of Justice under Military and Martial Law as Applicable to the Army, Navy, Marines, and Auxiliary Forces</u>. London: Murray, 1872, 1874, 412 pp. A quasi-official survey, including the Naval Code.

662 -------. <u>The Military Forces of the Crown: Their Administration and Government</u>. 2 vols. London: Murray, 1869, 804 pp. Focus on the army; some descriptions of conditions.

663 Clodfelter, Michael D. <u>Warfare and Armed Conflicts: A Statistical Reference to Casualty and Other Figures, 1618-1991</u>. 2 vols. London: McFarland, 1991-1992, liii, 1414 pp. A statistical record of casualties of modern warfare, chronologically by battles and campaigns, extensive detail, battle by battle, e.g., at 4-Days Battle, June 1666, English, 79 ships vs. Dutch, 84; losses, 4 ships each and at Trafalgar, British SOTL losses – 0; French/Spanish - 20; development of weapons.

664 Close, Albert. <u>The Defeat of the Spanish Armada</u>. London: Focus Christian Ministry, 1913, 1988, 47 pp. A curious and solely religious interpretation, grossly anti-Catholic; the Armada was a great sermon preached to the Popish and Protestant nations, England being saved by Divine Hands; the documents "give the lie to the view" that religion had no role.

665 Clough, Cecil H. and Hair, P.E.H., eds. <u>The European Outthrust and Encounter: The First Phase, 1400-1700: Essays in Tribute to David Beers Quinn on His 85th Birthday</u>. Liverpool: Liverpool UP, 1994, 348 pp. A <u>festschrift</u> to Quinn; 11 papers by noted experts, e.g., Drake in the Pacific, Anson at Canton, and the Portuguese in the Far East.

666 Clowes, Geoffrey S. Laird. <u>Sailing Ships: Their History and Development as Illustrated by the Collection of Ship-Models in the Science Museum</u>. 2 vols. London: HMSO, 1931-1932, 1952, 1959. Clowes, 1893-1937, presents results of the study of ship models.

667 Clowes, William Laird. <u>The Captain of the MARY ROSE: A Tale of To-morrow</u>. London: Tower, 1892, 1893, xvi, 308 pp. Sir William Laird Clowes, 1856-1905, was naval correspondent for "The Times"; wrote the definitive history of RN; a fictional account, includes imaginary battles.

668 -------. <u>Four Modern Naval Campaigns: Historical, Strategical, and Tactical</u>. London: Hutchinson, 1902, 1906, ix, 244 pp. A survey by this noted expert.

669 Clowes, William Laird, ed. <u>The Royal Navy: A History from the Earliest Times to the Present [later] to 1900</u>. 7 vols. London: S. Low; London: AMS; London: Chatham, 1897-1903, 1971, 1996-1997, 4357 pp. The standard and most extensive history of RN, although now dated; contributors include A.T. Mahan, Theodore Roosevelt, and Clements Markham; centennial reprint by Chatham in paperback.

670 Clowes, William Laird and Burgoyne, Alan H. <u>Trafalgar Refought</u>. <u>Active Service</u> series. London: Nelson, 1905. An example of the "new navalism" and the "cult of Nelson" on the occasion of the centennial.

671 Coad, Jonathan G. <u>Book of Dover Castle and the Defence of Dover</u>. London: Batsford, 1995, 128 pp. By the prolific and expert historian of the dockyards; a survey and illustration.

672 -------. "Historic Architecture of Chatham Dockyard, 1700-1850." <u>MM</u>, 68 (May 1982): 133-88. Chatham closed in 1984; accounts of historic buildings; numerous photos.

673 -------. "Historic Architecture of HM Naval Base Devonport, 1689-1850." <u>MM</u>, 69 (November 1983): 341-92. Originally Plymouth dockyard, expanded and named Devonport in 1823; numerous photos.

674 -------. "Historic Architecture of HM Naval Base Portsmouth, 1700-1850." <u>MM</u>, 67 (February 1981): 3-59. A history of the base and dockyard, e.g., victualling yard, Haslar Hospital, and HMS VICTORY; numerous photos.

675 -------. <u>Historic Architecture of the Royal Navy: An Introduction</u>. London: Gollancz, 1983, 1984, 160 pp. Fwd: Lord Lewin; illustrated; an outstanding example of industrial archaeology, dockyards and associated facilities, e.g., Portsmouth, Woolwich, Sheerness, Pembroke, Rosyth, Gibraltar, Halifax, Malta, and Singapore.

676 -------. <u>The Royal Dockyards, 1690-1850: Architecture and Engineering Works of the Sailing Navy</u>. London: Scolar, 1989, 410 pp. Illustrated; a major contribution of architecture, engineering works, and the shore establishment; remarkable and comprehensive.

677 Coats, Ann. "'The Oeconomy of the Navy and Portsmouth': A Discourse between the Civilian Administration of Portsmouth Dockyard and the Surrounding Communities, 1650-1800." D.Phil. diss, Sussex, 2000. Personnel, management, and community relationship matters associated with this major enterprise.

678 Coats, Ann and MacDougall, Philip, eds. <u>The 1797 Mutinies: Papers of the Spithead and Nore Conferences, 1997</u>. In 2001, noted as forthcoming; publication of the proceedings; a bicentennial occasion; conferences to reassess: some themes: "The Delegates: A Radical Tradition" and "The Admiralty's Retribution, or Restoration of Discipline."

679 Cobban, Alfred. "British Secret Service in France, 1784-1792." <u>EHR</u>, 69 (April 1954): 226-61. A detailed description of operations by this noted historian of France.

680 Cobbe, Hugh, ed. <u>Cook's Voyages and Peoples of the Pacific</u>. London: British

Museum, 1979, 143 pp. Folio size, illustrated; voyages, e.g., to New Zealand, Society Islands, Hawaii, and Nootka Sound.

681 Cobley, John. The Convicts, 1788-1792: A Study of a One-in-Twenty Sample. Studies in Australian and Pacific History # 3. Sydney: Wentworth, 1965, vii, 104 pp. A statistical survey of the convicts of the First Fleet.

682 Cobley, John, comp. The Crimes of the First Fleet Convicts. London: Angus, 1970, xv, 324 pp. A statistical study of 778 convicts, details about crimes; conclusion: most were repeat offenders, not one political convict.

683 Cochrane, A. The Fighting Cochranes: A Scottish Clan over Six Hundred Years and Naval and Military History. London: Quiller, 1983, 469 pp. By the 14th Earl of Dundonald; a family history with emphasis on service in the armed forces.

684 Cochrane, Thomas. The Autobiography of a Seaman. 2 vols. London: Bentley; London: Chatham, 1860, 2000, 917 pp. Intro: Richard Woodman; Lord Cochrane, 10th Earl of Dundonald, 1775-1860, one of the most dynamic naval officers of RN; eccentric, egoist, brilliant tactician, and scourge of the French navy; inspiration for naval fiction writers, e.g., Marryat, Forester, and O'Brian.

685 -------. Narrative of Services in the Liberation of Chile, Peru, and Brazil. London: Ridgeway, 1859. Recounts the exploits in these navies of South American revolting against Spain and Portugal during the early 19th century; biased; the so-called Cochrane-Earp-Jackson version.

686 Cock, Randolph. "'The Finest Invention in the World':The Royal Navy's Early Trials of Copper Sheathing, 1700-1770." MM, 87 (November 2001): 446-59. A detailed study of a series of experiments of sheathing underwater portions of ships to protect against "the worm," e.g., an extra layer of wood, lead, and copper; the Admiralty experimented during the mid-18th century, deciding to copper the fleet in 1779.

687 Cockburn, A. "Admiral Cockburn's Plan." Maryland Historical Magazine, 6 (March 1911): 16-19. From Cockburn papers at the Library of Congress; from a letter of 17 July 1814, he clearly originated the plan to attack Baltimore and Washington.

688 Cockburn, Elizabeth O. William Dampier: Buccaneer-Explorer-Hydrographer. 1987. A recent biographical study.

689 Cockle, Maurice J.D., ed. A Bibliography of Military Books Up to 1642: And of Contemporary Foreign Works. London: Holland, 1900, 1957, xl, 267 pp. Intro: Charles Oman; a bibliography of English and foreign books bearing on war.

690 [NHS 7]. Cogar, William B. and Sine, Patricia, eds. Naval History: The Seventh Symposium of the United States Naval Academy. Wilmington: Scholarly,

1988, 336 pp. (November 1986, USNA).

691 [NHS 8]. Cogar, William B., ed. New Interpretations in Naval History: Selected Papers from the Eighth Naval History Symposium. Annapolis: NIP, 1989, 320 pp. (24-25 September 1987, USNA).

692 [NHS 12]. Cogar, William B., ed. New Interpretations in Naval History: Selected Papers from the Twelfth Naval History Symposium. Annapolis: NIP, 1997, xxiv, 369 pp. (26-27 October 1995, USNA).

693 Cogar, William B. "The Politics of Naval Administration, 1644-1660." D.Phil. diss, Oxford, 1983, 324 pp. Re naval administration and politics during the Civil War and Commonwealth.

694 Coggins, Jack. Ships and Seamen of the American Revolution: Vessels, Crews, Weapons, Gear, Naval Tactics, and Actions of the War for Independence. Harrisburg: Stackpole, 1969, 224 pp. Illustrated by Coggins, all in blue color; the American Revolution was fought mainly on land but won at sea; features, e.g., submarine vessels, the navy on lakes, privateering, prison hulks, J.P. Jones, De Grasse to the Chesapeake, and tactics.

695 Cogliano, Francis D. American Maritime Prisoners in the Revolutionary War: The Captivity of William Russell. Annapolis: NIP, 2001, xii, 218 pp. A case study: William Russell from Massachusetts, captured on an American privateer, 1779; to Mill Prison, 1779-1782; returned to privateering and captured again; to prison hulk, JERSEY, in harbor of New York City; released.

696 Cogswell, Thomas. "Foreign Policy and Parliament: The Case of La Rochelle, 1625-1626." EHR, 99 (April 1984): 241-67. Buckingham and Charles I formulating imaginative policies; reviews Whig and revisionist interpretations.

697 -------. "Prelude to Re: The Anglo-French Struggle over La Rochelle, 1624-1627." History, 71 (February 1986): 1-21. Buckingham instigated an Anglo-French war and led an English force to Re; he and Charles I underrated the French.

698 Cohen, Sheldon S. Yankee Sailors in British Gaols: Prisoners of War at Forton and Mill, 1777-1783. Newark: U Del P; London: Cranbury, 1995, 278 pp. 3000 American sailors taken prisoner during the American Revolution; to British jails; details on life there, escapes, and hardships; some exaggeration.

699 Coleman, D.C. "Naval Dockyards under the Later Stuarts." Economic History Review, 2nd ser, 6 (December 1953): 134-55. During the late 17th century, expansion of Royal Dockyards, e.g., Portsmouth, Chatham, and Woolwich; seen as important industrial enterprise.

700 Coleman, E.C. Captain Vancouver: North-West Navigator. Whitby: Caedmon, 2001. A study of local origins of Vancouver, from King's Lynn; first service on 2nd

and 3rd voyages of Cook.

701 Coleman, Terry. Nelson: The Man and the Legend. London: Bloomsbury, 2001, xix, 352 pp. A recent biography; focus on the man and the myth.

702 Coles, Harry Lewis. The War of 1812. Chicago: Chicago UP, 1965, ix, 298 pp. An undistinguished survey.

703 Colledge, James J. The Ships of the Royal Navy: An Historical Index. 2 vols. Newton Abbot: David and Charles; Annapolis: NIP, 1969, 1987, 1989, 654 pp. Fwd: David Brown; a valuable reference guide; 14,000 entries; begins with the 15th century.

704 Collett, Bill. The Last Mutiny: The Further Adventures of Captain Bligh. NY: Norton, 1995, 304 pp. Creative fictional account; Bligh's story in the first person; " the most famous mutiny in history."

705 Colley, Linda. Britons: Forging the Nation, 1707-1837. New Haven: Yale UP; London: Vintage, 1992, 1994, 1996, xvi, 464 pp. A much-discussed interpretation about nationalism, state-building, and national identity.

706 Collingridge, J.H. Catalogue of an Exhibition of Naval Records at the Public Record Office. London: HMSO, 1950, 53 pp. A series of selected documents with excerpts, mostly cases.

707 Collingwood, W.G. Scandinavian Britain: Account of the Viking Age. Felinfach: Llanerch, 1908, 1993, 272 pp. A survey of the age, the first fleet of Danes to Dorchester in 778; continuous stream of invasions to the 12th century; much legend, sagas, poetry; Alfred fought naval battles against them in the 870s.

708 Colomb, Philip Howard. Naval Warfare: Its Ruling Principles and Practice Historically Treated. 2 vols. London: Allen; Annapolis: NIP, 1891, 1895, 1899, 1990. Intro: Barry Gough; P. Colomb, 1831-1899, produced the first reasonable British historical work on naval history; one of the early "educators" touting naval history, strategy, and the lessons to be learned.

709 Colvin, Howard M., ed. The History of the King's Works. 6 vols. London: HMSO, 1963-1982. Illustrated; a massive presentation, chronologically organized; re shore fortifications, harbor facilities, harbor works, royal palaces, prisons, Kew Gardens, and the British Museum.

710 Come, Donald R. "French Threat to British Shores, 1793-1798." Military Affairs, 16 (Winter 1952): 174-88. After abandoning a plan to invade Britain, the French with Napoleon in command, set out to conquer Malta and Egypt.

711 Comtois, George. "The British Navy in the Delaware, 1775-1777." AmNep, 40 (January 1980): 7-22. During the early years of the American Revolution, the

British forces were threatened by the French and American forces; British had large numbers of forces, but too scattered and failed to concentrate, a major mistake.

712 Concina, Ennio. L'Arsenale della Republica di Venezia. Milan: Electa, 1984, 243 pp. 330 illustrations; re the famous Venice Arsenal, the largest industry in Europe for several centuries; included a dockyard and shipbuilding facilities.

713 -------. Navis: l'Unianesimo sul mare, 1470-1740. Rotino: Einaudi, 1990, xviii, 220 pp. In Italian; more on the Venice Arsenal, ships, different types of ships, dockyards; depiction of ships in art and architecture.

714 Condon, Mary E.A. "The Administration of the Transport Service during the War against Revolutionary France, 1793-1802," Ph.D. diss, London, 1968. Details about this essential service in a continental war.

715 Conn, Stetson. Gibraltar in British Diplomacy in the Eighteenth Century. Yale Historical Publications, vol. 41. New Haven: Yale UP, 1942, 317 pp. A detailed, scholarly, and well-written monograph on the strategic and geopolitical significance of "The Rock."

716 Connell-Smith, Gordon. "Anglo-Spanish Trade in the Early Tudor Period." Ph.D. diss, London, 1950. Re this important early relationship.

717 -------. "Forerunners of Drake: Some Aspects of Privateering and Piracy during the French War of Henry VIII." Bull IHR, 24 (1951): 82-84. A description of the paper awarded the Julian Corbett Prize for 1949; the Anglo-Spanish struggle was an important impetus to the development of English naval power; Spanish Inquisition and Spanish persecution of English merchants and sailors generated contempt, hostility, and retaliation.

718 -------. Forerunners of Drake: A Study of English Trade with Spain in the Early Tudor Period. London: Longman; Westport: Greenwood, 1954, 1975, xxii, 264 pp. The background for increasing conflict with Spain; relations began with merchants and trade, later accelerating to privateering and piracy, "forerunners of Drake."

719 Conner, Paul. "'Maynard' Unmasked: Oglethorpe and Sharp versus the Press Gangs." Proceedings of the American Philosophical Society, 111 (August 1924): 199-211. "Maynard" was pseud. for Granville Sharp and James Oglethorpe; 4 letters in London periodical in 1777 opposing impressment; thesis: no legal basis.

720 Connery, Tom. Honor Be Damned: A Markham of the Marines Novel. London: Orion, 1998, 336 pp. A recent Nelson-era novel, George T. Markham is a Royal Marine involved in intrigue and romance.

721 -------. Honor Redeemed: A Markham of the Marines Novel. London: Orion; Wash: Regnery, 1998, 2000, 400 pp. This one re amphibious operations, Corsica; meets Nelson.

722 -------. A Shred of Honor. London: Orion, 1996, 288 pp. More adventures of Markham of the Marines.

723 Conrad, Joseph. The Mirror of the Sea and a Personal Record. NY: Harper, 1906, 1946, 1960, 1988, 226 pp. Conrad, 1857-1924, the great writer about the sea; includes a tribute to Nelson.

724 -------. The Nigger of the NARCISSUS: A Tale of the Forecastle. NY: Norton, 1914, 1928, 1979, xi, 370 pp. Ed: Robert Kimbrough; seen as one of finest sea stories in any language; re negro, James Wait, the dominant personality on a sailing ship; psychological analysis; last chapter meets Nelson.

725 Conway, Stephen. "'A Joy Unknown for Years Past': The American War, Britishness, and the Celebration of Rodney's Victory at the Saints." History, 86 (April 2001): 180-99. Rodney's victory at the Saints, April 1782; a discussion of the victory, its implications, effects on domestic politics, public opinion, celebrations, and a transformation of the concept of British identity; it was a long time coming!.

726 -------. "The Politics of British Military and Naval Mobilization, 1775-1783." EHR, 112 (November 1997): 1179-1201. The war was politically divisive in Parliament and in public opinion; details on recruitment, government initiatives, and reaction of the work force.

727 -------. The War of American Independence, 1775-1783. Modern War series. London: Arnold, 1995, xvi, 280 pp. Ed: Hew Strachan; a multi-disciplinary overview; places it in a global perspective, thus, a world war.

728 Cook, Alan H. Edmond Halley: Charting the Heavens and the Sea. Oxford: Oxford UP, 1998, xvii, 540 pp. Halley, 1656-1742, a scientific pioneer, contemporary of Newton and Pepys; like Pepys, the navy and navy concerns were paramount; noted need for surveys and charts to aid merchants and the navy; led scientific voyage into southern hemisphere, then Royal Astronomer at Greenwich.

729 Cook, James. The Journals of Captain Cook. Penguin Classic series. London: Penguin, 1999, xiv, 646 pp. Ed: Philip Edwards; Cook, 1728-1779, has been called the greatest of all explorers; an abridged version of all 3 voyages.

730 -------. The Journals of Captain James Cook on His Voyages of Discovery. 3 vols. in 4 books. I: ENDEAVOUR, 1768-1771. II: RESOLUTION and ADVENTURE. III: RESOLUTION and DISCOVERY. London: Hakluyt; Cambridge: Cambridge UP; Woodbridge: Boydell, 1955-1974, 2001, cclxxiv, 3352 pp. Various editions and editors, e.g., R.A. Skelton and J.C. Beaglehole; an exquisite, monumental production, folio size, illustrated, in a new edition; these 3 voyages of the late 18th century were the ultimate models of exploration, navigation, science, and cartography involving the RN; publication in association with the Hakluyt Society.

731 -------. <u>Seventy North to Fifty South: The Story of Captain Cook's Last Voyage</u>. NY: Prentice-Hall, 1969, xii, 370 pp. Ed: Paul W. Dale; further subtitle: <u>Wherein Are Discovered Numerous South Pacific Islands, the Hawaiian Islands, the Coast of North America, and Alaska</u>; as noted, this voyage explored the eastern Pacific and west coast of North America.

732 -------. <u>The Voyages of Captain James Cook: Round the World</u>. London: Cresset, 1949, xxii, 383 pp. Ed: Christopher Lloyd; an earlier abridged version of all 3 voyages.

733 Cookson, John E. <u>The British Armed Nation, 1793-1815</u>. Oxford: Clarendon, 1997, vi, 286 pp. Of the War and Society school; a comprehensive survey of mobilization of the armed forces; truly British, incorporating Scot and Irish dimensions, especially their significant military contributions, but little on navy; a critique of Brewer-Colley construct of the national, fiscal, military state.

734 Cooley, Reg. <u>The Unknown Fleet: The Army's Civilian Seamen in War and Peace</u>. Stroud: Sutton, 1993, 256 pp. Sponsored by the Royal Naval Museum; the history of civilian-manned sea-vessels from medieval times on the Thames to the present, e.g., for rescue and troop transport.

735 Coombs, Douglas. <u>The Conduct of the Dutch: British Opinion and the Dutch Alliance during the War of Spanish Succession</u>. The Hague: Nijhoff, 1958, 405 pp. From a London diss; demonstrates a transition in Anglo-Dutch relations, a complex interplay of engrained hostility and a growing consciousness of common interests.

736 Cooper, F.G. "Some Aspects of Joseph Conrad." <u>MM</u>, 26 (January 1940): 61-78. His greatest writing was of the sea; appreciations of Nelson.

737 Cooper, James Fenimore. <u>The History of the Navy of the United States</u>. <u>Classics of Naval Literature</u> series. 2 vols. Phil: Lea; NY: Literature House; Annapolis: NIP, 1839, 1856, 1970, 2001, 458 pp. Cooper, 1789-1851, an American fictional writer and naval historian; numerous editions, intensively researched, including oral history; contemporaneous controversy, including lawsuits by O.H. Perry and J.D. Elliot, over his interpretations of events of the War of 1812.

738 -------. <u>Ned Myers: A Life before the Mast</u>. <u>Classics of Naval Literature</u>. 2 vols. Phil: Lea; Annapolis: NIP, 1843, 1989, 304 pp. Intro: William Dudley; Edward Myers was a former shipmate of Cooper; nautical reminiscences and commentary on life on the lower deck.

739 -------. <u>The Pilot</u>. 1824. Re era of American Revolution and John Paul Jones

740 -------. <u>The Red Rover</u>. London: Bentley, 1827, 1834, 1970, 1989, 1997, viii, 451 pp. Re mid-18th century piracy.

741 -------. <u>The Two Admirals: A Tale</u>. Albany: SUNY, 1842, 1845, 1848, 1990, xlii, 511 pp. A sea novel; re dynastic conflicts during Stuart age, based on Southey's Life of Nelson; the admirals: Nelson and Collingwood.

742 -------. The Water Witch. London: Bentley, 1830, 1834, 1896, 1970, viii, 429 pp. Re smuggling in early 18th century.

743 Cooper, Janet, ed. The Battle of Maldon: Fiction and Fact. Rio Grande: Hambledon, 1993, xii, 265 pp. 13 papers from an international conference on the millennium of the battle, 991; the battle resulted from an early Danish raid on the Anglo-Saxons of Essex during the reign of AEthelraed the Unready; English overwhelmed by Danes; from a classic poem describing the battle; subjects, e.g., topographical changes, literature and culture of the time, and an overview of medieval warfare.

744 Coote, Stephen. A Play of Passion: The Life of Sir Walter Ralegh. London: Macmillan, 1993, xi, 419 pp. Ralegh, 1552-1618; voyages to America, 1585-1617; the true "Renaissance Man"; features the theatricality of the life of Ralegh; soldier, explorer, privateer, philosopher, courtier, poet, and imperialist.

745 -------. Samuel Pepys: A Life. NY: Palgrave, 2000, xiii, 386 pp. A recent biography; a clear, consistent, thorough portrait; focus on his administrative career as leading member of the Navy Board.

746 Coox, Alvin D. "The Dutch Invasion of England, 1667." Military Affairs, 13 (Winter 1949): 223-33. During the 2nd Anglo-Dutch war, a Dutch attack and invasion.

747 Corbett, Julian S. The Campaign of Trafalgar. 2 vols. London: Longman; NY: AMS, 1910, 1919, 1976, 534 pp. Corbett, 1854-1922, naval official, strategist, and historian, dramatically rehabilitated during recent decades, now seen as more important and influential than A.T. Mahan; a founder of NRS and the official naval historian of World War I; this work places the battle in context as the culmination of a long campaign; informative on Napoleon, Villeneuve, and Nelson; the Nelsonian plan, a masterstroke.

748 -------. Drake and the Tudor Navy: History of the Rise of England as a Maritime Power. 2 vols. NY: Longman; Brookfield: Gower, 1898, 1988, 924 pp. Intro: R.B. Wernham; Drake depicted as "the controlling force" of the Tudor navy, an unsurpassed master of amphibious warfare; included a tactical analysis of the Armada campaign; hagiographic.

749 -------. England in the Mediterranean, 1603-1713: A Study of the Rise and Influence of British Power within the Staits. 2 vols. London, 1904. An important contribution; an overview of the Mediterranean strategy.

750 -------. England in the Seven Years' War: A Study in Combined Strategy. 2 vols. London: Longman, 1907, 1918, 1992, 883 pp. Re William Pitt, the Elder, his strategy, and brilliant successes; the crucial period of English naval history.

751 [NRS 29]. Corbett, Julian S., ed. Fighting Instructions, 1530-1816. Publications of the Navy Records Society, vol. 29. London: NRS, 1905, xvi, 366 pp. Only a few original copies existed, then this important publication by NRS; effectively, the history of naval tactics beginning in the 1530s; the dominating tactical doctrine for all commanders to follow; contributions by Ralegh, Duke of York (James II), Anson, Hawke, Nelson, and Cochrane; demonstrates unique contribution of English developments; no borrowing from the Dutch, as some claimed; French also adopted; see Addendum to NRS 29 in NRS 35; discovery of a "trunk" at RUSI which contained a collection of Signal Books and Instructions.

752 Corbett, Julian S. For God and Gold. London: Macmillan, 1887. Contribution to nautical fiction; re fictional exploits of Drake; gaps in the evidence imaginatively filled in.

753 -------. Monk. English Men of Action series. London: Macmillan, 1889, vi, 221 pp. A short biography of George Monck, Duke of Albemarle, 1608-1670, a prominent General-at-Sea.

754 -------. "Napoleon and the British Navy after Trafalgar." Quarterly Review, 237 (April 1922): 238-55. Informative analysis by Corbett.

755 [NRS 11]. Corbett, Julian S., ed. Papers Relating to the Navy during the Spanish War, 1585-1587. Publications of the Navy Records Society, vol. 11. London: NRS, 1898, xlix, 363 pp. Collections relating to Drake in the West Indies, the Cadiz campaign of 1587, and miscellaneous papers.

756 [NRS 46, 48, 58, and 59]. Corbett, Julian S. and Richmond, H.W., eds. Private Papers of George, Second Earl Spencer, First Lord of the Admiralty, 1794-1801. 4 vols. Publications of the Navy Records Society, vols. 46, 48, 58, and 59. London: NRS, 1913-1924, xxiv, 417, vi, 518, xvi, 401, and viii, 320 pp. Reports and descriptions, e.g., Jervis in the Mediterranean, the mutinies at Spithead and the Nore, Duncan at Camperdown, and the battles of Cape St. Vincent and the Nile.

757 [NRS 35]. Corbett, Julian S., ed. Signals and Instructions, 1776-1794: With Addenda to Vol. 29. Publications of the Navy Records Society, vol. 35. London: NRS, 1908, xvi, 403 pp. A review of naval tactics during a period of transition, the old system of Fighting Instructions ending and the introduction of the new Signal Book; in 1782, Rodney broke the line at the Saints; extensive bibliography; see Addendum to NRS 29 in this volume; re discovery of a collection of Signal Books and Instructions.

758 Corbett, Julian S. Sir Francis Drake. English Men of Action series. London: Macmillan; Westport: Greenwood, 1890, 1898, 1968, 1970, vii, 209 pp. A short biography of Drake, called "the Reformation man."

759 -------. Some Principles of Maritime Strategy. Classics of Sea Power. London: Conway; Annapolis: NIP, 1911, 1972, 1987, 416 pp. Eds: Bryan Ranft (1972) and Eric Grove (1987); articulation of the basic strategic theories of Corbett, e.g., certain principles which were unchanging; emphasis on combined operations; the objective: secure sea communications and deny them to the enemy; based on lectures to the Royal Naval War College; this work seen as contribution of Corbett, making him "Britain's greatest maritime strategist."

760 -------. The Successors of Drake. London: Longman; NY: Franklin, 1900, 1916, 1968, xiv, 464 pp. Covers 1596-1605, a neglected period; more armadas and counter-armadas; more privateering; successors were soldiers, e.g., Ralegh, Essex, and Mountjoy.

761 [NRS 34]. Corbett, Julian S., ed. Views of the Battles of the Third Dutch War. Publications of the Navy Records Society, vol. 34. London: NRS, 1907. Documents elaborating on the Third Dutch War of the 1670s.

762 Corbett-Smith, Arthur. Nelson: The Man: A Portrait Study. London: Williams, 1926, xv, 364 pp. A popular biography, no scholarly apparatus; curious chapter titles, e.g., "goes beserk," "love for Emma," and "descended into hell."

763 Cordingly, David. Nicholas Pocock. Conway Maritime Artists series # 1. Annapolis: NIP, 1986, 120 pp. An exquisite production; Pocock began by illustrating logbooks as maritime captain, then paintings for NMM, e.g., battles of Nelson and Rodney.

764 Cordingly, David and Falconer, John. Pirates, Fact and Fiction: In Which the Authors Relate the History of Piracy from the Spanish Main to the China Seas. London: Collins, 1992, 128 pp. Folio size, slick, paperback production; to support exhibition, NMM, 1992-1995; delightful coverage of all aspects and personalities.

765 Cordingly, David, ed. Pirates: An Illustrated History of Privateers, Buccaneers and Pirates from the Sixteenth Century to the Present. London: Salamander, 1996, 255 pp. Illustrated; series of essays by experts, e.g., Marcus Rediker on a pirate's utopia, Dian Murray on Chinese pirates from the 15th century, and John Falconer on the Eastern Seas.

766 Cordingly, David. Ships and Seascapes: An Introduction to Maritime Prints, Drawings and Water Colours. London: Wilson, 1997, 160 pp. Folio size, illustrated, color and b/w; describes print-making, the Dutch school of maritime art, and depictions of naval battles, voyages, and shipwrecks; not up to the quality of other works.

767 -------. Under the Black Flag: The Romance and the Reality of Life among the Pirates. Boston: Little, Brown; NY: Random House, 1995, 1996, xiv, 338 pp. A follow-up to the exhibition, NMM, 1992-1995; an informative summary, sorting out times and places and fact from fiction; pirates, e.g., Kidd, Blackbeard, Lafitte, and

Morgan; high point in the West, 1650-1720, later in the 19th century in the East.

768 -------. <u>Women Sailors and Sailors' Women</u>. NY: Random House, 2001, 286 pp. Extensive research collection of anecdotal stories of women aboard ship; superstitions, women in ports, women disguised as men, and homosexuality; 3 great naval Casanovas: Nelson, J.P. Jones, and Augustus Hervey.

769 Core, Susie. <u>Henry Morgan: Knight and Knave</u>. NY: River, 1943, 222 pp. An undistinguished account.

770 Cormack, Lesley B. <u>Charting an Empire: Geography at the English Universities, 1580-1620</u>. Chicago: Chicago UP, 1997, xvi, 281 pp. Re the institutionalization and professionalization of geography and its influence in the making of the British empire; from the 16th century, an expanding world view; combination of factors stimulated the interest and pursuit, e.g., surveying, navigation, cartography, and popular travel; personalities, e.g., Hakluyt, Purchas, Mercator, and Camden.

771 Cormack, William S. "Legitimate Authority in Revolution and War: The French Navy in the West Indies, 1789-1793." <u>IHR</u>, 8 (February 1996): 1-27. The problem of proper authority in French colonial areas; included the navy: officers loyal to royalists, sailors to republicans; mutinies on several ships.

772 -------. "Revolution and Political Conflict in the French Navy, 1789-1794." Ph.D. diss, Queen's at Kingston, 1991, 534 pp. The basis of these entries.

773 -------. <u>Revolution and Political Conflict in the French Navy, 1789-1794</u>. Cambridge: Cambridge UP, 1995, xiii, 343 pp. Illustrated; the study of the impact of the French Revolution on the French navy, thus, political implications; first, degeneration into chaos, at Toulon, surrendered to the British and mutiny at Brest; then some revival; Glorious 1st of June not so serious a defeat.

774 Cornwell, Bernard. <u>Sharpe's Trafalgar: Spain 1805</u>. NY: HarperCollins, 2001, 293 pp. A survey of the situation in Spain and the reaction to the battle of Trafalgar.

775 Couper, John Mill. <u>The Book of Bligh</u>. Melbourne: Melbourne UP, 1969, 88 pp. 6 chapters in verse; no commentary or explanation.

776 Course, A.G. <u>Dictionary of Nautical Terms</u>. London: Arco, 1962, 216 pp. 1500 definitions but does not claim to equal the great dictionaries, e.g., Falconer, Smyth, and Paasch.

777 -------. <u>Pirates of the Eastern Seas</u>. London: Muller, 1966, viii, 263 pp. Presents the characteristics and history; European navies have intervened, mostly in the 19th century.

778 -------. <u>Pirates of the Western Seas</u>. London: Muller, 1969, 215 pp. A traditional survey, e.g., buccaneers of the West Indies, women pirates, and campaigns to eliminate; personalities: the usual suspects.

779 Courtney, T.W. "Excavations at the Royal Dockyards, Woolwich, 1972-1973." Post-Medieval Archaeology, 8 and 9 (1974 and 1975): 1-28, 42-102. Report from an excavation; description of building slips and other facilities from the 17th and 18th centuries.

780 Cowie, Leonard W., ed. Lord Nelson, 1758-1805: A Bibliography. Bibliographies of British Statesmen series, # 7. Westport: Meckler, 1990, viii, 192 pp. 1344 items, e.g., books, articles, portraits, caricatures; coverage of 17 contemporaries of Nelson; lists 31 NRS publications pertinent to Nelson.

781 Cowley, Robert, ed. What If?: The World's Foremost Historians Imagine What Might Have Been. NY: Putnam, 1999, 336 pp. In association with the 10th anniversary of MHQ; counterfactual history, an increasingly popular exercise; 24 essays, e.g., Parker on the Spanish Armada, if Spain had won and Horne on the opportunities and blunders of Napoleon.

782 Cox, Gregory Steven. St. Peter Port, 1680-1836. Woodbridge: Boydell, 1999, xxi, 145 pp. In the Channel Islands, an early modern entrepot; center of privateering; "to correct Jamieson, People of the Sea."

783 Craig, Hardin, comp. A Bibliography of Encyclopedias and Dictionaries: Dealing with Military, Naval and Maritime Affairs, 1577-1971. Houston: Fondren Library, 1960, 1965, 1971, 101 pp. Limited production for the library of Rice University; in chronological order, some annotation.

784 -------. "Black Dick Howe, the Sailor's Friend." MM, 35 (January 1949): 18-28. Re Admiral Richard Howe of the American Revolution, later First Lord; recalled in 1797 to deal with the great mutiny; compares to St. Vincent; sympathetic assessement.

785 -------. "The First Lord Opens His Mail: Thomas Grenville and Personnel Problems at the Admiralty, 1806-1807." Huntington Library Quarterly, 33 (February 1970): 175-86. From the Stowe papers at the library, 2500 pieces of correspondence; enlightening on business conducted at the Admiralty and problems of personnel.

786 [NRS 88]. Cranmer-Byng, J.L., ed. Pattee Byng's Journal, 1718-1720. Publications of the Navy Records Society, vol. 88. London: NRS, 1950, xxxii, 311 pp. Recounts operations in the Mediterranean, e.g., the campaign in Sicily and the battle of Cape Passaro.

787 Craton, Michael. "The Role of the Caribbean Vice Admiralty Courts in British Imperialism." Caribbean Studies, 11 (July 1971): 5-20. These courts were more numerous and handled more cases than in North America and were agents of naval policy; lists types of cases adjudicated.

788 Craven, W. Frank. "The Earl of Warwick, a Speculator in Piracy." Hispanic American Historical Review, 10 (1930): 457-79. After peace with Spain in 1604, privateers searched for alternatives; James I attempted to stop piracy but nobles profited; an example: Earl of Warwick.

789 Crawford, Abraham. Reminiscences of a Naval Officer: A Quarter-Deck View of the War against Napoleon. Sailors' Tale series. London: Chatham, 1851, 1999, ix, 304 pp. Intro: Tom Pocock; a quarterdeck journal of a captain, RN; operations in the Mediterranean, early 19th century; described naval life, the tedium and boredom of blockade duty; a critic of impressment.

790 Crawford, Anne. "The Public Record Office." History Today, 50 (March 2000): 26-27. An up-to-date description of the national archives and its purpose-built center at Kew; online catalogue to be completed by 2002.

791 Crawford, Barbara E. Scandinavian Scotland. Scotland in the Early Middle Ages # 2. Leicester: Leicester UP, 1987, xii, 274 pp. Re archaeological evidence of the Vikings and Viking settlements ; section on Dal Riada area; excavations of several fortresses.

792 Creasy, Edward S. Fifteen Decisive Battles of the World: From Marathon to Waterloo. Chicago: Henneberry; NY: Da Capo, 1851, 1894, 1910, 1960, 1987, 1996, 518 pp. Famous Creasy selection, e.g., Hastings and Spanish Armada.

793 Creighton, Margaret S. and Norling, Lisa, eds. Iron Men, Wooden Women: Gender and Seafaring in the Atlantic World, 1700-1920. Balt: JHUP, 1996, xvi, 293 pp. A series of 10 sketches; features, e.g., occupation, class, race, colonization, and cross-dressing women; women pirates, wives of seamen, and literary figures.

794 Creighton, Margaret S. "The Private Life of Jack Tar: Sailors at Sea in the Nineteenth Century." Ph.D. diss, Boston, 1985, 294 pp. Sources from diaries and letters of the New England area: conclusions: seamen came from local area.

795 Cressy, David. Bonfires and Bells: National Memory and the Protestant Calendar in Elizabethan and Stuart England. Berkeley: U Cal P; London: Weidenfeld, 1989, xiv, 271 pp. Celebrations of the calendar year in early modern England; chapter on the Armada, religious, royal, and civic occasions; features, e.g., the divine nature of the Protestant victory, beacons, bell ringing, and the "black legend," an anti-Spanish mentality.

796 Creswell, John. British Admirals of the Eighteenth Century: Tactics in Battle. London: Allen, 1972, 263 pp. A study of British admirals and battles; disagrees with Mahan and Corbett; Fighting Instructions less important; recounts cases, e.g., Byng, Quiberon Bay, Rodney, Chesapeake, and Trafalgar.

797 -------. Generals and Admirals: The Story of Amphibious Command. NY: Longman; Westport: Greenwood, 1952, 1976, viii, 192 pp. Emphasis on command relationships; 12 examples, e.g., Cadiz and the Scheldt.

798 Crewe, Duncan G. "British Naval Administration in the West Indies, 1739-1748." Ph.D. diss, Liverpool, 1978. An informative study; sources include ship's musters.

799 -------. Yellow Jack and the Worm: British Naval Administration in the West Indies, 1739-1748. Liverpool: Liverpool UP, 1993, x, 321 pp. The title themes are disease and rot in hot climates; comprehensive coverage, e.g., manning, health, victualling, logistics, dockyards, and ordnance.

800 Crimmin, Patricia K. "Admiralty Relations with the Treasury, 1783-1806: The Preparation of the Naval Estimates and the Beginnings of Treasury Control." MM, 53 (February 1967): 63-72. The budgeting process during a period of expensive and extensive war.

801 -------. "George Canning and the Battle of Camperdown." MM, 67 (November 1981): 319-26. This future Prime Minister met Duncan and interviewed him immediately after the battle in 1797.

802 -------. "'A Great Object with Us to Procure This Timber': The Royal Navy's Search for Ship Timber in the Eastern Mediterranean and Southern Russia, 1803-1815." International J Maritime History, 4 (December 1992): 83-115. Re agents searching for oak timber in the Balkans, purchases, and shipping to Malta; French and Spanish agents also searching.

803 -------. "Letters and Documents Relating to the Service of Nelson's Ships, 1780-1805: A Critical Report." Historical Research, 70 (February 1997): 52-69. Sources from the Wellcome Institute, official returns about administration of the Mediterranean fleet, 1790s-1800s; enlighted about health, food, transports, convoys, and condition of ships during the command of Nelson.

804 Crittenden, Victor. A Bibliography of the First Fleet. Canberra: Australian National UP, 1981, ix, 359 pp. Events associated with the First Fleet, 1785-1790; 966 annotated entries divided by topics, e.g., the settlement, convict theory, naval logistics, and commerce.

805 -------. The Voyage of the First Fleet, 1787-1788: Taken from Contemporary Accounts. Canberra: Mulini, 1981, v, 105 pp. An account of the voyage via Teneriffe, Rio, Capetown, and on to Botany Bay.

806 Crockett, F.B. Early Sea Painters, 1660-1730. NY: Antique, 1996, 160 pp. Folio size, 60 color and 50 b/w pictures; the history of British maritime painting from Willem van de Veldes, father and son, and others; an impressive collection.

807 Crosby, Everett U. <u>Medieval Warfare: A Bibliographic Guide</u>. NY: Garland, 1992, 2000, xv, 215 pp. Divided by categories, e.g., reference, arms, fortifications, strategy and tactics, war and the state, and art and literature.

808 Cross, Anthony G. <u>By the Banks of the Thames: Russians in Eighteenth-Century Britain</u>. Boston: Oriental, 1980, viii, 358 pp. A study of Anglo-Russian contacts stemming from the visit by Peter the Great; c. 400 Russians identified; special interests were science and the navy.

809 -------. <u>Peter the Great through British Eyes: Perceptions and Representations of the Tsar since 1698</u>. Annapolis: NIP, 2001, 172 pp. By a prolific writer on early modern Anglo-Russian relations; this re the visit of Peter for 3 months in 1698, how he was seen then and later.

810 Crowhurst, R. Patrick. "The Admiralty and the Convoy System in the Seven Years' War." <u>MM</u>, 57 (May 1971): 163-74. Re a radical change in the nature of British trade, e.g., the Navigation Acts, new markets, and French privateers; merchants and Admiralty cooperated and launched a convoy system.

811 -------. "British Oceanic Convoys in the Seven Years' War, 1756-1763." Ph.D. diss, London, 1970. Implementation of an effective and successful convoy system.

812 -------. <u>The Defence of British Trade, 1689-1815</u>. Folkstone: Dawson, 1977, 281 pp. The primary threat was French privateering; a general summary incorporating numerous aspects, e.g., convoys, insurance, Canada, and East Indies; specifics: main French port for privateering was St. Malo; for insurance, Lloyd's produced the solution.

813 -------. <u>The French War on Trade: Privateering, 1795-1815</u>. London: Scolar, 1985, 1989, xi, 395 pp. An alternate perspective, privateering as an ecnomic endeavor, not wartime strategy; privateering replacing trade as an occupation; study of several French ports.

814 -------. "Profitability in French Privateering, 1793-1815." <u>Business History</u>, 24 (March 1982): 48-60. French <u>guerre de course</u>, Jean Bart, and others; describes the business process: attraction of investors and shareholders, plans for the voyage, and profits and losses.

815 Cruickshank, Charles G. <u>Henry VIII and the Invasion of France</u>. Stroud: Sutton; NY: St. Martin, 1990, 1991, viii, 193 pp. Henry was anxious to prove himself; a large-scale invasion of France, in 1513, transporting a large army to Calais.

816 Cruickshank, Dan. <u>Invasion: Defending Britain from Attack</u>. London: Boxtree, 2001, 185 pp. Superficial review: "no more" invasions of Britain after the Romans and Vikings-Normans; focus on defenses, especially fortification casements.

817 Cruickshank, Ernest A. The Life of Sir Henry Morgan. Toronto: Macmillan, 1935, 448 pp. A biography of this English nobleman who turned to piracy, was captured and executed; his travels, exploits, and death.

818 Cruickshank, Eveline, ed. By Force or by Default?: The Revolution of 1688-1689. Edinburgh: Donald, 1989, xi, 196 pp. A series of essays, e.g., David Davies on James II, William of Orange, and the Admirals and Jeremy Black on foreign policy; counterfactual essay by Davies: if the English admirals had prevailed, no revolution.

819 Cruickshank, Eveline. The Glorious Revolution. British History in Perspective. series. NY: St. Martin, 2000, 126 pp. A recent study; a narrative of events.

820 Crump, Helen Josephine. Colonial Admiralty Jurisdiction in the Seventeenth Century. Imperial Studies for the Royal Empire Society, # 5. London: Longman, 1931, x, 200 pp. Details about the Vice-Admiralty Court jurisdiction and the system, all based on the Navigation Act of 1696, plus updates; the study included how they were perceived and accepted by the colonists: not well received; seen as interference and with no due process.

821 Cubitt, David J. "Lord Cochrane and the Chilean Navy,1818-1823." Ph.D. diss, Edinburgh, 1974. By use of the Cochrane papers, a study of his service as Commander-in-Chief of the Chilean navy.

822 -------. "The Manning of the Chilean Navy in the War of Independence, 1818-1823." MM, 63 (May 1977): 115-27. The social aspects of recruiting and manpower of the navy; sources were British and American seamen, some impressment, and some resort to criminals.

823 Cuellar, Francisco de. Spanish Armada Tracts: A Letter Written on October 4, 1589. NY: Richmond, 1895, xi, 109 pp. An eyewitness account of the campaign and his dramatic escape written by Cuellar to Philip II.

824 Cullen, Louis M. Anglo-Irish Trade, 1660-1800. NY: Kelley, 1968, vi, 252 pp. From a London diss.; a survey of the trade, shipping, Navigation Acts, smuggling, and insurance.

825 -------. "Privateers Fitted Out in Irish Ports in the Eighteenth Century." Irish Sword, 3 (Winter 1958): 171-77. A scholarly study; the Irish successfully operated as privateers against the English and the French.

826 Cumming, Alex A. Sir Francis Drake and the GOLDEN HIND, Norwich: Jerrold, 1975, 36 pp. A short overview.

827 Cumming, William Patterson, et al. The Discovery of North America. London: Elek, 1971, 304 pp. Folio size, illustrated; re the explorers, e.g., the Irish, the Norse, Cabot, Verrazzano, Cartier, and Drake; also, the search for the Northwest Passage.

828 Cummins, John. Francis Drake: The Lives of a Hero. NY: St. Martin; London: Weidenfeld, 1995, 1997, xv, 348 pp. A recent biography, de-mythologizing and stressing his navigational skills; thoroughly researched; an extensive bibliography and historiographical essay, noting 327 other biographies.

829 Cunliffe, Barry. Facing the Ocean: The Atlantic and Its Peoples 8000 BC-AD 1500. Oxford: Oxford UP, 2001, viii, 600 pp. Lavishly illustrated; in support of a Radio-4 series; demonstrates the "commonalities," North Africa to Scotland.

830 Cunningham, Arthur E., comp. Patrick O'Brian: A Bibliography of First Printings, and First British Printings. London: Thrommett, 1986, 28 pp. Re Patrick O'Brian, 1914-2000, published his first novel in 1952, the first naval stories in 1956; details on the first 11 Aubrey-Maturin novels.

831 Cunningham, Arthur E., ed. Patrick O'Brian: Critical Appreciations and Bibliography. London: British Library; New York: Norton, 1994, 176 pp. O'Brian is seen as one of the best storytellers of the age; 11 essays, e.g., J. Bayley, Charlton Heston, N.A.M. Rodger, B.Lavery, S.Bennett, R.Ollard, William Waldegrave, MP, and O'Brian himself; O'Brian's study of Banks makes Maturin more authentic; Americans did not like O'Brian at first, then enthusiasm.

832 Cunningham, Carleton S. "Anglo-French Trade, War and Diplomacy in the Early Stuart Age." Ph.D. diss, Virginia, 1998. A scholarly study of this crucial period for England.

833 Cunningham, Mary E., ed. James Fenimore Cooper: A Reappraisal. Cooperstown, 1954. See the Walter Muir essay on Cooper as naval historian.

834 Cuppage, Francis E. James Cook and the Conquest of Scurvy. Contributions in Medical Studies, # 40. Westport: Greenwood, 1994, x, 163 pp. By a physician who spent a year tracing the voyages and studying the botany; a fascinating medical study; during the 3 voyages, plants as anti-scorbutics were used to prevent scurvy; credit to James Lind and to Cook; Cook preferred sauerkraut and malt, the latter with no effect.

835 Currin, John M. "Henry VII and the Politics of Europe, 1485-1492: Diplomacy and War at the Accession of the Tudor Regime." Ph.D. diss, Minnesota, 1995. Tudor exploitation of the European situation.

836 -------. "The King's Army into the Partes of Bretaigne: Henry VII and the Breton Wars, 1489-1491." War in History, 7 (November 2000): 379-412. Henry VII was determined to prevent Brittany from falling into the hands of France; Henry had two ships built, impressed ships and sailors, and hired Spanish merchantmen; an English naval and army force of 66 ships and 1690 men to Brittany; a smaller expedition in 1491; the Breton Wars.

837 Curry, Anne and Hughes, Michael, eds. Arms, Armies and Fortifications in the

Hundred Years' War. Woodbridge: Boydell, 1994, xv, 221 pp. A series of papers from a conference, Oxford University, November 1991, e.g., Ian Friel on ships during the war and Hughes on raids on Hampshire and the Isle of Wight.

838 Curry, Kenneth. Robert Southey: A Reference Guide. Boston: Hall, 1977, xx, 95 pp. A biographical study; although a Lake Poet, his prose has endured better; about his biographies of Nelson and Wesley.

839 Curtis, C.D. Blake: General-at-Sea. Taunton: Wessex, 1934, xv, 200 pp. Fwd: Earl Jellicoe; Blake, 1598-1657, one of the earliest and most important naval commanders.

840 Custance, Reginald N. The Ship-of-the-Line in Battle. London: Blackwood, 1912, viii, 213 pp. Custance, 1847-1935, published these lectures given at the Royal Naval War College, Portsmouth.

841 Cuthbertson, Brian. John Cabot and the Voyage of the MATTHEW. Halifax: Formac, 1997, 72 pp. A lavish production; to commemorate the 500th anniversary of the voyage from Bristol, May 1497.

842 Czisnik, Marianne. ["Admiral Nelson: Image and Icon."]. Ph.D dissertation noted as "in progress"; by a German lawyer having completed an MA at Edinburgh University.

843 -------. "Nelson and the Nile: The Creation of Admiral Nelson's Public Image." MM, 88 (February 2002): 41-60. A fascinating study of the making of a "grand reputation"; began as unsurpassed praise of Nelson in the London Gazette Extraordinary reporting on the victory after the battle of the Nile; the news spread quickly and "icons" proliferated, e.g., portraits by painters who never saw Nelson, one even depicting the wrong arm removed.

844 Daggett, Charles and Shaffer, Christopher. Diving for the GRIFFIN. London: Weidenfeld, 1990, xii, 178 pp. An important case study of nautical archaeology and a link to hydrography; GRIFFIN was an East Indiaman sunk when she ran on rocks in the Philippines in 1761; Alexander Dalrymple, father of the Hydrographic Office, was commander of the convoy and in charge of navigation; illustrated.

845 Dalrymple, Alexander. An Account of the Discoveries Made in the South Pacifick Ocean. Sydney: Hordern, 1767, 1996, 103 pp. For the Australian NMM; the account of a voyage by Dalrymple, seen as father of the Hydrographic Office.

846 Dalton, Tony. British Royal Yachts. London: Halsgrove, 2001, 240 pp. Large folio size with 250 illustrations; a complete history by a veteran of HMY BRITANNIA.

847 Dampier, William. A New Voyage Round the World. London: Hummingbird; NY: Da Capo, 1697, 1699, 1703, 1709, 1729, 1906, 1927, 1968, 1970, 1998, 376 pp. Various titles and editions; eds: Albert Grey, John Masefield, N.M. Penzer, and Mark Beken; Dampier set out in 1679, the series of voyages lasting over 12 years, parts being sponsored by the Admiralty; involved were circumnavigation, exploration, scientific experimentation, advances in navigation and cartography, mutinies, extensive buccaneering and plunder, and a model for travel literature, later influencing Daniel Defoe and Jonathan Swift; Alexander Selkirk was cast off and rescued on Juan Fernandez Island, 4 years later, in the presence of Dampier; one section,"A Discourse on Wind," is still pertinent today.

848 -------. Voyage to New Holland. 1703, 1709. Further report of the voyage by Dampier; vindication and "to repudiate" journal account by W. Funnell.

849 Dana, Richard Henry. The Seaman's Friend: Containing a Treatise on Practical Seamanship. Boston: Little, Brown, 1873, 223 pp. Dana, 1815-1882, American writer, left Harvard for the sea service; the first to write factual sea tales; this work, details on seamanship and the law of the sea.

850 -------. Two Years before the Mast: A Personal Narrative of Life at Sea. NY: Harper; London: Low, 1854, 1869, 1980, 1986, 430 pp. Tends to idealize the merchant service.

851 Danaher, Kevin. "Armada Losses on the Irish Coast." Irish Sword, 2 (1956): 320-31. In September 1588, a severe storm struck the west coast of Ireland and Scotland; the Armada, 7 weeks at sea and having run the gauntlet of English gunfire, was returning to Spain via "the northern route"; estimated 26 ran onto the Scottish and Irish coasts, many marked on an excellent map; an unknown number of Spanish survivors were killed by Irish locals; some description by Cuellar.

852 Dane, Clemence, comp. The Nelson Touch: An Anthology of Lord Nelson's Letters. London: Heinemann, 1942, xviii, 285 pp. Pseud. for Winifred Ashton, writing early in World War II at time of a Nelson revival; a collection, mainly from Nicolas; includes autobiography; Nelson describes himself quite candidly.

853 -------. Trafalgar Day, 1940. London: Heinemann, 1940, 14 pp. A fictional commemoration under the conditions of wartime crisis, to boost morale.

854 Danielsson, Bengt. What Happened to the BOUNTY? London: Allen, 1962, 232 pp. Trans: Alan Tapsell; a popular account of the disposition describing the time from the mutiny to the settlement at Pitcairn Island; touts "thrilling events."

855 Dann, John C., ed. The Nagle Journal: A Diary of the Life of Jacob Nagle, Sailor, 1775-1841. NY: Weidenfeld, 1988, xxx, 402 pp. An extraordinary manuscript, the original at Clements Library, University of Michigan; re Jacob Nagle, 1762-1841; an American soldier captured by the British during the American Revolution; adventures in RN, including service under Nelson, and in merchant service; to 5 continents.

856 Darby, Madge. "Bligh's Discipline: Matthew Flinders's Journals of HMS PROVIDENCE, 1791-1793." MM, 86 (November 2000): 401-11. Flinders kept an account of the 2nd breadfruit voyage, serving under Bligh; many quotes.

857 -------. Captain Bligh in Wapping. London: Wapping Trust, 1990, 16 pp. An account of local history.

858 -------. The Causes of the BOUNTY Mutiny: A Short Reply to Mr. Rolf Du Rietz's Comments. Uppsala: Almqvist, 1966, 22 pp. From the Studia Bountyana of 1966; Darby presented a controversial theory about the cause, precipitating reaction; see Du Rietz's account.

859 -------. Who Caused the Mutiny on the BOUNTY? London: Angus, 1965, 128 pp. Presents a logical and thought provoking theory: the 3rd mate, Midshipman Young, was the cause; however, puts into question most other descriptions.

860 Darling, Lois. HMS BEAGLE, 1820-1870: Voyages Summarized, Research and Reconstruction. NY: Sea History, 1984, 12 pp. A short description of the famous ship of RN used for the expedition of Charles Darwin during the early 1830s; cited because an example of another exploration, scientific expedition sponsored by RN.

861 David, Andrew, Joppien, Rudiger, and Smith, Bernard, eds. The Charts and Coastal Views of Captain Cook's Voyages. 3 vols. I: The Voyage of the ENDEAVOUR, 1768-1771. II: The Voyage of the RESOLUTION and ADVENTURE, 1772-1775. III: The Voyage of the RESOLUTIOIN and DISCOVERY, 1776-1780. London: Hakluyt Society, 1988-1997, c. 1200 pp. Folio size, exquisite production monumental in extent, including hundreds of charts and drawings of coasts; supplements Beaglehole, The Journals, and other accounts.

862 Davids, Karel and Lucassen, Jan, eds. A Miracle Mirrored: The Dutch Republic in European Perspective. Cambridge: Cambridge UP, 1995, xix, 539 pp. From a year-long seminar, Netherlands Institute of Advanced Study, 1992-1993; a history of the Dutch Republic from international and interdisciplinary perspectives; features, e.g., the Dutch Revolt, religion, "the golden age," and comparisons with the British and Germans.

863 Davidson, George. Francis Drake on the Northwest Coast of America in 1579. San Francisco, 1908. An account by a local historian.

864 -------. Identification of Sir Francis Drake's Anchorage on the Coast of California in the Year 1579. San Francisco: Bacon, 1890, 58 pp. An account by a local historian; controversy about the location.

865 Davidson, Miles H. Columbus Then and Now: A Life Re-examined. Norman: U Okla P, 1997, xxx, 609 pp. Not a biography but a valuable asssessment of the literature and analysis of the evidence; de-mythologizes; reviews biographies, e.g.,

Noble, the Phillips, Morison, Sale, and Fernandez-Armesto; speculation about activities before the voyage of 1492, e.g., to England?

866 Davies, C.S.L. "The Administration of the Royal Navy under Henry VIII: The Origin of the Navy Board." EHR, 80 (April 1965): 268-86. Advances in ordnance meant increasing differences between merchant and warships; Henry inherited 5 warships and built 47; number of offices increased, from Clerk of the Ships to "council of marine" to Navy Board, thus, the Admiralty.

867 -------. "The Alleged 'Sack of Bristol': International Ramifications of Breton Privateering, 1484-1485." Historical Research, 67 (October 1994): 230-39. French sources but not any from Bristol describe an attack on Bristol, 1484; an aspect of England-France-Brittany relations; informative on role of Bristol in exploration amd commerce; did Columbus come?

868 -------. "Supply Services of English Armed Forces, 1509-1550." D.Phil. diss, Oxford, 1963. Important research reported, e.g., about the Ordnance Office, supplier for the army and navy.

869 Davies, David. Fighting Ships: Ships of the Line, 1793-1815. London: Constable; NY: Stackpole, 1996, 201 pp. Alt. title: Nelson's Navy; details of the ships, their operations, and their battles, e.g., Camperdown, the Nile, Copenhagen, and Trafalgar, "their last battle."

870 -------. 'A Lover of the Sea and Skilful in Shipping': King Charles II and His Navy. Huntingdon: Royal Stuart Society, 1992. Informative and enlightening on Charles and his love of the navy.

871 Davies, J.D. Gentlemen and Tarpaulins: The Officers and Men of the Restoration Navy. Oxford Historical Monographs. Oxford: Clarendon, 1991, 1992, 270 pp. A description of 4 types of officers, from the Commonwealth and from the Cavaliers; meant the navy was divided by old rivalries, and Pepys contributed to the divisiveness; defends them as professional, effective, and productive, contrary to claims of Macaulay, Tanner, Bryant, and Pepys, himself; focus on officers, but neglects and lacks understanding of the lower deck, the tarpaulins.

872 -------. "The Navy, Parliament and Political Crisis in the Reign of Charles II." Historical J, 36 (June 1993): 271-88. James, Duke of York, was LHA, and he was Catholic, a factor in Parliamentary and public criticism of the navy, 1670s and 1680s; naval personnel involved in various plots and crises.

873 -------. "Pepys and the Admiralty Commission of 1679-1684." Historical Research, 62 (February 1989): 34-53. Pepys, prominent administrator, 1684-1688, perpetuated the view of major reforms of the navy; a consequence was criticism of the Commission, criticism which was not deserved.

874 -------. "The Seagoing Personnel of the Navy, 1660-1689: Political, Religious, and Social Aspects." D.Phil. diss, Oxford, 1986, 298 pp. A study of the Restoration navy; thesis: Pepys depicted as too influential, a more balanced view is needed.

875 Davies, Norman. The Isles: A History. London: Macmillan, 1999, 2000, xlii, 1078 pp. A substantial, idiosyncratic, deconstructionist, and revisionist interpretation of the history of all of the British Isles from 600 BC to the present; to counteract Anglo-centric dominance; informative on Kingdom of Dal Riata featuring its naval prowess, the king evolving into the 1st king of Scotland; later transoceanic ventures of the Cabots and Bristol; other features: Gascony, Scottish naval ventures under James IV, Devonian explorers, "Navy Royal" to "Royal Navy" at the time of Charles II, and presents a series of naval heroes culminating with Nelson.

876 Davies, R.A. "Subjects of History: The Prose Writings of Sir Walter Ralegh, 1582-1603." Ph.D. diss, London, 1997. A focus on his writings before the death of Elizabeth; touts a historicist approach and critical analysis of these writings.

877 Davies, R.R., ed. The British Isles, 1100-1500: Comparisons, Contrasts and Connections. Edinburgh: Donald, 1988, 159 pp. 8 papers from a Colloquium, September 1986, Newtown, Powys; historians from "the 4 kingdoms"; see A. Duncan on the Scots invasion of Ireland, 1315.

878 Davis, Charles G. Ship Models, How to Build Them. Salem: Marine Research, 1925, xii, 139 pp. An older "how-to" guide.

879 Davis, John. The Seamans Secret. Maritime History series. Providence: JCB, 1633, 1992, unpaged. Intro: A.N. Ryan; Davis, 1550-1605, a 16th century explorer and adventurer; 3 voyages in the 1580s, each going further north; later to Dutch and, then, English East India Company as navigation expert; killed by pirates in the Far East.

880 Davis, John. The Post Captain or The Wooden Walls Manned. London: Tops'l Books, 1805, 1928, 1984, 159 pp. Ed: Colin Elliott; Davis, 1774-1854, midshipman, RN; the first novel about Nelson surrogates; comic novel about the navy, first appearing during celebration of Trafalgar; best seller; "the parent of all of our nautical novels"; 10 editions but Davis died forgotten and penniless.

881 Davis, Ralph. English Merchant Shipping and the Anglo-Dutch Rivalry in the Seventeenth Century. London: HMSO, 1975, iv, 36 pp. For NMM; illustrated; a pamphlet; Navigation Acts and expansion of English commerce led to inceasingly fierce Anglo-Dutch rivalry; a result was 3 Anglo-Dutch wars; sections on the ships, seamen, and politics.

882 Davis, R.H.C. and Chibnall, M.M., ed. The "Gesta Guillelmi" of William of Poitiers. Oxford: Clarendon, 1998, xlvii, 199 pp. An edition of a first-hand commentary, concentrating on the years 1066-1067 and on William I, by his chaplain; preparations for the Norman invasion.

883 Davis, R.H.C. The Medieval Warhorse: Origin, Development and Redevelopment. NY: Thames, 1989, 144 pp. A scholarly and readable study; includes descriptions of transport by sea.

884 Davis, Robert C. Shipbuilders of the Venetian Arsenal: Workers and Workplace in the Preindustrial City. Balt: JHUP, 1991, x, 270 pp. Re the greatest manufacturing complex in early modern Europe; built warships; a model for modern dockyard administration; founded in 1107 and lasting until the late 18th century, covered 60 acres, 2500 laborers.

885 Dawson, Warren R. The Nelson Collection at Lloyd's: A Description of the Nelson Relics and a Transcript of the Autograph Letters and Documents of Nelson and His Circle and the Other Naval Papers of Nelson's Period. London: Macmillan, 1932, xiv, 525 pp. For Lloyd's of London; a description of the famous and extensive collection still housed at the corporate headquarters at Lloyd's in the City; items, e.g., the Nelson Plate, the Trafalgar Vase, orders, swords, portraits, medals, letters, and documents.

886 Day, Alan E. Search for the Northwest Passage: An Annotated Bibliography. NY: Garland, 1986, xvi, 632 pp. 5160 annotated entries; divided into 9 chronological periods beginning in 1497.

887 Day, Archibald. The Admiralty Hydrographic Service, 1795-1919. London: HMSO, 1967, 377 pp. Fwd: Edmund Irving; the definitive history of maritime surveys; presents by period of individual hydrographers.

888 Day, Ronnie M. "Neptune's Forge: The Evolution of the Royal Navy under the Early Tudors, 1485-1547." Ph.D. diss, Texas Christian, 1971, 261 pp. A study of the navy and its development; conclusion: the early Tudors laid the foundation for RN, Henry VII providing and building technologically specialized warships and facilities.

889 Deacon, Margaret. Scientists and the Sea, 1650-1900: A Study of Marine Science. Aldershot: Ashgate, 1971, 1997, xl, 459 pp. The history of oceanography and marine biology; stressed links between rise of maritime affairs and emerging science.

890 Dean, J.S. "The New MATTHEW: Making a Ship, Bristol-Fashion." AmNep, 59 (Winter 1999): 51-59. The 3-masted, 50-ton caravel John Cabot sailed from Bristol in 1497 to explore the North Atlantic was MATTHEW, named for his wife, Mattia; the replica, laid down in 1992, launched in 1995, and set sail, 2 May 1997, 500 years to the day; to Newfoundland.

891 Dean, Martin, et al., eds. Archaeology Underwater: The Nautical Archaeology Society Guide to Principles and Practice. London: NAS, 1992, ix, 336 pp. Folio size, glossy, illustrated; an informative handbook and guide; focus on 33 mapped wrecks around the British Isles; much technical detail, e.g., search methods, fixing, recording, presenting, and publishing.

892 Deane, Anthony N. Nelson's Favourite: HMS AGAMEMNON at War, 1781-1809. London: Chatham; Annapolis: NIP, 1996, 320 pp. Re the 64-gun SOTL, veteran of the Saints, Copenhagen, and Trafalgar, and at the Nore in 1797; in 1809, aground off Uruguay, where she still lies; Nelson captain for 3 years in the mid-1790s.

893 Dee, John. The Books and Manuscripts of John Dee, 1527-1608. Renaissance Man: The Reconstructed Libraries of European Scholars, 1450-1700: Manuscripts from the Bodleian Library, Oxford. London: Matthew, 1991, 60 pp. Incorporated are 40 microfilm reels and a printed guide.

894 Deen, Lucile D. "Anglo-Dutch Relations from 1660 to 1668." Ph.D. diss, Radcliffe, 1936. A scholarly review of Anglo-Dutch relations.

895 Defoe, Daniel. The Life, Adventures, and Pyracies of the Famous Captain Singleton. Oxford: Oxford UP, 1720, 1990. Ed: Shiv Kumar; Defoe, 1660-1731, a well-known figure and writer of the early 18th century; this is a fictional account, the best of his descriptions of pirates; incorporates psychological realism and perceptiveness; another pirate work: General History of Pirates. London: Conway, 1724, 1955, 1990, 1992, 1998; an ongoing debate of authorship: attributed by most to Charles Johnson.

896 -------. Lives of the Most Notorious Pirates. London: Folio, 1962, 232 pp. Eds: Christopher Lloyd and Arthur Hayward; a contemporaneous survey.

897 -------. Robinson Crusoe. Alt. title: The Life and Strange Surprising Adventures of Robinson Crusoe of York, Mariner: Who Lived Eight and Twenty Years All Alone in an Uninhabited Island on the Coast of America. . . . Written by Himself. Penguin Classics. London: Ballantyne; NY: Sears; London: Penguin, 1719, 1810, 1948, 1972, 2001, 304 pp. Intro: Sir Walter Scott; Crusoe was the character based on Alexander Selkirk, a Scottish sailor forced to live on an isolated island, west of South America in the Pacific Ocean; gave story to Defoe; Selkirk returned to sea, died in 1721.

898 De Kay, James Tertius. The Battle of Stonington: Torpedoes, Submarines, and Rockets in the War of 1812. Annapolis: NIP, 1990, xvi, 218 pp. A curious incident: in 1814, a British naval attack on the town of Stonington, CT, bombarding with rockets; a study asking who, why, what, and how?; Nelson's Hardy was commander, Bushnell's submarine and Fulton's torpedo appeared.

899 -------. Chronicles of the Frigate MACEDONIAN, 1809-1922. NY: Norton, 1995, 336 pp. A British frigate of 1810, taken as prize after battle with UNITED STATES and entered into USN as "trophy ship."

900 De Kerchove, Rene. International Maritime Dictionary: An Encyclopedic

Dictionary of Useful Maritime Terms and Phrases. Princeton: Van Nostrand, 1948, 1961, 1018 pp. Incorporates terms in English, French, and German.

901 Delaforce, Patrick. Nelson's First Love: Fanny's Story. London: Bishopsgate, 1988, 242 pp. Some imaginary fiction, some fact; a first-person account by Lady Nelson of her life; valuable and informative.

902 Delano, Amasa. Narrative of Voyages: . . . Three Voyages around the World. Boston: House, 1817, 598 pp. A narrative description; includes an account of the mutiny on the BOUNTY.

903 Delderfield, Ronald F. Imperial Sunset: The Fall of Napoleon, 1813-1814. NY: Chilton; NY: Cooper Square, 1968, 2001, x, 300 pp. Popular history, anecdotal and superficial; background for the exiles, both of which involve RN.

904 Delgado, James P. Across the Top of the World: The Quest for the Northwest Passage. London: Checkmark, 1999, xii, 228 pp. Folio size, glossy, illustrated in color; for the British Museum; search for the Northwest Passage was a major initiative of the Admiralty for centuries beginning in 1576 with Martin Frobisher; a peculiarly British quest.

905 Delgado, James P., ed. Encyclopedia of Underwater and Maritime Archaeology. London: British Museum; New Haven: Yale UP, 1997, 1998, 493 pp. Folio size, glossy, illustrated in color; individual essays by 150 experts; a comprehensive reference guide on nautical archaeology, "the last great frontier on earth"; shipwrecks in alphabetical order, e.g., BOUNTY, MARY ROSE, Port Royal, and VASA.

906 Dell, Jeffrey F. Payment Deferred: A Play in a Prologue, Three Acts and an Epilogue: From the Novel by C.S. Forester. London: French, 1934, 90 pp. From one of the novels by Forester.

907 Deloney, Thomas. The Work of Thomas Deloney. Oxford: Clarendon, 1912, 1967, xliii, 600 pp. Ed: Francis Mann; Deloney, 1543-1600; includes his "Armada Ballads," e.g., about the visit of Elizabeth I to Tilbury and warnings of horrendous acts by the Spanish if they landed, e.g., sacking, raping, killing babies, cutting throats, and assassinating the queen.

908 Deng, Gang. Chinese Maritime Activities and Socioeconomic Development, 2100 BC-1900 AD. Westport: Greenwood, 1997, xxvi, 218 pp. A comprehensive summary of 4000 years of Chinese maritime history; informative as comparison with developments in the West, e.g., the famous voyages of Zheng He in the 15th century, piracy in the Far East, and discussion about the peak of advancement and, then, decline.

909 -------. "An Evaluation of the Role of Admiral Zheng He's Voyages in Chinese Maritime History." International J Maritime History, 7 (December 1995): 1-19.

Between 1405-1433, Zheng He commanded 7 expeditions with a large fleet; noted these voyages were not new and their significance has been exaggerated.

910 Dening, Greg. Mr. Bligh's Bad Language: Passion, Power and Theatre on the BOUNTY. Cambridge: Cambridge UP, 1992, 1994, xii, 445 pp. A "creative reading" of the mutiny; the title from a common critique of Bligh and his leadership; events as seen from native lore, British life, art, theater, and the cinema, e.g., stars playing Bligh: Laughton, Howard, and Hopkins; Christian: Gable, Brando, and Gibson.

911 Denman, T.J. "The Political Debate over War Strategy, 1689-1712." Ph.D. diss, Cambridge, 1985, 392 pp. A study of the politics of war strategy, "Wars of English and Spanish Succession."

912 Derrick, Charles. Memoirs of the Rise and Progress of the Royal Navy. London: Blacks, 1806, 309 pp. Traces the origins from the 1530s, credit to Henry VIII.

913 Desbriere, Edouard. Projets de Debarquement aux Isles Britanniques. 4 vols. in 5 books. Paris: Chapelot, 1900-1902. By the authoritative French historian; the most detailed history of the massive invasion plans for Britain.

914 -------. Trafalgar: The Naval Campaign of 1805. 2 vols. Paris: Chapelot; Oxford: Clarendon, 1907, 1933, 792 pp. Trans: Constance Eastwick; one of the most comprehensive surveys of the campaign by a noted French historian; includes reports from French and Spanish officers; Corbett used this for his account.

915 De Toy, Brian Mark. "Wellington's Admiral: The Life and Career of George Berkeley, 1753-1818." Ph.D. diss, Florida State, 1997, 660 pp. A scholarly study of this naval commander; informative on the role of the navy in the Peninsular campaign; a neglected aspect.

916 Deutsch, Otto Erich. Admiral Nelson and Joseph Haydn. Portsmouth: Nelson Society, 1982, 2000, 169 pp. Deutsch, 1883-1967, a German authority on Haydn and Schubert; a Nelson Decade publication; in 1800, Nelson and the Hamiltons travelled overland from Naples to Britain; en route, met and were entertained by Haydn in Vienna.

917 Devereux, William A. and Lovell, Stephen. Sir Walter Raleigh: An Historical Romance. London: Greening, 1909, 1910, vi, 319 pp. A fictional and romanticized biography.

918 Devine, Joseph A. "The British North American Colonies in the War of 1739-1748." Ph.D. diss, Virginia, 1968. American colonists increasingly participated in military operations, e.g., Louisbourg and Canadian campaigns; then, some territory returned to France at peace, upsetting colonists.

919 De Vries, Kelly R. "Catapults Are Not Atomic Bombs: Towards a Redefinition of 'Effectiveness' in Premodern Military Technology." War in History, 4 (November 1997): 454-70. A review in debate format of the controversy over the "Military Revolution," including naval aspects.

920 -------. "A 1445 Reference to Shipboard Artillery." Technology and Culture, 31 (October 1990): 818-29. Re early galley-mounted heavy guns; other evidence: guns aboard as early as 1336; 1st recorded sinking in 1513; few sources, thus, speculative.

921 -------. "God, Leadership, Flemings, and Archery: Contemporary Perceptions of Victory and Defeat at the Battle of Sluys, 1340." AmNep, 55 (Summer 1995): 223-42. Sluys, 24 June 1340; a historiographical analysis.

922 -------. Medieval Military Technology. Lewiston: Broadview, 1992, xi, 340 pp. Encyclopedic but no analysis; 4 parts, including medieval warships.

923 -------. The Norwegian Invasion of England in 1066. Warfare in History series, # 8. Woodbridge: Boydell, 1999, 352 pp. Re the "other" invasion of 1066, a victory for Harold over King Harald Hardrada of Norway, culminating in the battle of Stamford Bridge; all overshadowed by Norman invasion.

924 Dewar, Alfred C. "The Naval Administration of the Interregnum, 1641-1659." MM, 12 (October 1926): 406-30. A review of 3 functions: the Admiralty, administration, and finance; oversight by the Navy Committee of Parliament.

925 Dickens, Gerald. The Dress of the British Sailor. London: HMSO, 1957, 30 pp. By Admiral Sir Gerald Dickens; for NMM; a colorful pamphlet.

926 Dickerson, Oliver M. The Navigation Acts and the American Revolution. Phil: U Penn P; NY: Octagon, 1951, 1971, xv, 344 pp. An assessement of the British mercantile system, especially the Navigation Acts, and its impact on causes of the American Revolution.

927 Dickinson, H.T. "The Capture of Minorca, 1708." MM, 51 (August 1965): 193-204. Example of further strategic and commercial interest in the Mediterranean; need for an English base in addition to Gibraltar; its loss later was consequential.

928 Dickinson, Harold W. [The History of Educational Provision in the Royal Navy.] Dickinson noted as forthcoming, an essay was awarded the Julian Corbett Prize for Naval History in 1997.

929 Dickinson, W. Calvin and Hitchcock, Eloise R., comp. The War of Spanish Succession, 1702-1713: A Selected Bibliography. Bibliographies of Battles and Leaders series, # 15. Westport: Greenwood, 1996, xvi, 140 pp. 808 entries, some annotated, in 9 sections by subject; poorly organized and dated.

930 The Dictionary of National Biography, various editions: 63 vols., 1884-1900; later, 22 vols. plus Supplements # 1-11. London: Oxford UP, 1911-1996, about 36,500 biographical essays, c.45,000 pages. Eds: Leslie Stephen and Sydney Lee, et al.; Supplements cover up to 1990; Sir John Knox Laughton wrote over 900 entries, mostly on past naval leaders; The New Dictionary of National Biography. London: Oxford UP, forthcoming. Eds., H.C.G. Matthew, 1941-1999, then Brian Harrison; all 36,500 essays to be rewritten and new ones added; estimated to be 50,000 essays, 9500 contributors; The New DNB to be published in 2004 or 2005.

931 The Dictionary of National Biography on CD-Rom. London: Oxford UP, 2000, c. 32 million words. Entire DNB included on CD-Rom.

932 A Dictionary of the World's Watercraft: From Aak to Zumbra. London: Chatham, 2001, x, 676 pp. Fwd: Basil Greenhill; for the Mariner's Museum, Newport News; a basic reference guide, 5600 entries identifying worldwide watercraft, e.g., hides, rafts, and, the most entries, wooden plank built craft.

933 Dietz, Brian. "Dikes, Dockheads and Gates: English Docks and Sea Power in the 16th and 17th centuries." MM, 88 (May 2002): 144-54. The evolution of docks and dockyards; an early survey, 1698, was by Edmund Dummer; developments described for Portsmouth, Deptford, Chatham, and Woolwich.

934 -------. "The Royal Bounty and English Merchant Shipping in the Sixteenth and Seventeenth Centuries." MM, 77 (February 1991): 5-20. The bounty was offered to reward ship builders for ships "fit for service" as naval ships; origins in the 15th century; included list of over 700 ships receiving the bounty, 1560-1618.

935 Dietz, Peter. The British in the Mediterranean. Wash: Brassey, 1994, 1995, viii, 228 pp. The history of military and naval involvement, e.g., in Tangier, Gibraltar, Malta, and Cyprus; the first effective convoy system to protect against Barbary corsairs in the early 17th century.

936 Diffie, Bailey W. Foundations of the Portuguese Empire, 1415-1580. Minneapolis: U Minn P, 1977, 534 pp. Portugal was the first in advances in navigation, in exploration, and in imperial and comercial expansion.

937 -------. Prelude to Empire: Portugal Overseas before Henry the Navigator. Lincoln: U Neb P, 1960, 1963, 127 pp. Coverage of the period before the previous entry.

938 Dingwall, Helen M. Physicians, Surgeons and Apothecaries: Medicine in Seventeenth-Century Edinburgh. East Linton: Tuckwell, 1995, 262 pp. Medical history; many, if not most, of the naval surgeons were trained at Edinburgh.

939 "Divers Reveal Nelson's Blast from the Past." The Times, 28 June 1999: 12-13. An article by Richard Beeston; 18 French divers in a nautical archaeological project over a 3-year period; discovery of the sunken French fleet from the battle of the

Nile, August 1798; sponsored by the European Institute of Marine Archaeology, Paris.

940 Divine, David. <u>The Opening of the World: The Great Age of Maritime Exploration</u>. NY: Putnam, 1973, 272 pp. Folio size, illustrated; introductory survey, a chronological review of the early exploration states and advances in navigation and ship design; no scholarly apparatus.

941 Dixon, Conrad. "To Walk the Quarterdeck: The Naval Career of David Ewen Bartholomew." <u>MM</u>, 79 (February 1993): 58-63. An extraordinary career, from impressed seaman to Captain, RN; career began in 1790s; later expert in navigation and amphibious warfare.

942 Dixon, Hepworth. <u>Robert Blake: Admiral and General-at-Sea</u>. Ithaca: Regatta, 1852, 2000, 400 pp. Intro: Barry Gough; Dixon, 1821-1879, a naval historian producing the first scholarly biography of this important 17th century naval leader.

943 Dobson, David. <u>Scottish Maritime Records, 1600-1850: A Guide for Family Historians</u>. St. Andrews: N.p., 1996, 32 pp. A guide for various records, e.g., RN, merchant navy, fishermen, smuggling, pirates, slave trade, and court proceedings.

944 Dodds, James and Moore, James. <u>Building the Wooden Fighting Ship</u>. NY: Facts; London: Hutchinson, 1984, 128 pp. Illustrated with detailed drawings and schematics; comprehensive coverage, the '74 gun ship being the model, origins of timber, dockyards, shipbuilding.

945 Dodge, Ernest S. <u>Beyond the Capes: Pacific Exploration from Cook to the CHALLENGER, 1776-1877</u>. Boston: Little, Brown, 1971, 429 pp. An informative account of exploration of the Pacific.

946 -------. <u>Northwest by Sea</u>. NY: Oxford UP, 1961, xiv, 348 pp. A chronological presentation, including a table, of the voyages in search of the Northwest Passage, e.g., Cabot, Varrazano, Frobisher, Davis, Hudson, and Baffin; also English efforts to Northeast.

947 Doorne, Christopher J. "Mutiny and Sedition in the Home Commands of the Royal Navy, 1793-1803." Ph.D. diss, London, 1998. Research from Court-Martial records and petitions from seamen; an analysis of the causes of mutinies during the time of those of 1797, the Irish rebellion of 1798, and French invasion scares; the authorities touted radical activity and sedition; conclusion: the government exaggerated, most were over pay and conditions.

948 Dorling, Henry Taprell. <u>Men O'War: St. Vincent, Cochrane, Marryat, Fisher, Beresford</u>. London: N.p., 1929, 308 pp. Known as "Taffrail," a captain, RN, who wrote popular naval history and naval fiction; this a series of mini-biographies.

949 -------. <u>Sea Ventures of Britain</u>. London: Collins, 1925, xix, 316 pp. Illustrated;

accounts of famous voyages, e.g., Hawkins, Drake, Dampier, Anson, and Cook.

950 Douglas, David C. <u>The Norman Achievement, 1050-1100</u>. Berkeley: U Cal P, 1969, xvi, 271 pp. By a prominent scholar; a summary history of extraordinary expansion and achievement, from a small province in France to England, southern Italy, Sicily, and the eastern Mediterranean; a "holy war" sponsored by the Pope; achievements in culture, architecture, and religion.

951 -------. <u>The Norman Fate, 1100-1154</u>. Berkeley: U Cal P, 1976, 273 pp. Results and consequences from the previous entry.

952 -------. <u>William the Conqueror: The Norman Impact upon England</u>. Berkeley: U Cal P; New Haven: Yale UP, 1964, 1967, 1999, 488 pp. Fwd: Frank Barlow; an analysis of William and his achievements; section on preparations for the invasion and naval aspects, e.g., William's massive shipbuilding programme, at least 700 ships, and problems of the Anglo-Saxon fleet.

953 Douglas, Hugh. <u>Jacobite Spy Wars: Moles, Rogues and Treachery</u>. Stroud: Sutton, 1999, xviii, 269 pp. A survey of intelligence, 18th century; case studies, e.g., Jacobite invasion plan thwarted when French naval officer in English pay exposed the effort, 1708, and loyalty of Scottish Highlanders in '45 attempt.

954 Douglas, K.S., <u>et al</u>., <u>A Meteorological Study of July to October 1588: The Spanish Armada Storms</u>. Norwich: E Anglia UP, 1978, 76 pp. Folio size; results of an extraordinary study; Tycho Brahe recorded daily weather observations from Scandinavia; plus other tabulations, produced synoptic weather maps; conclusions about winds and weather explaining effects on Spanish ships, e.g., the "miraculous" shift of wind off Zeeland and, more importantly, the unprecedented storms in the Atlantic off Ireland.

955 Douglas, K.S. and Lamb, H.H. <u>Weather Observations and a Tentative Meterological Analysis of the Period May to July 1588</u>. Norwich: E Anglia UP, 1979, 39 pp. Elaboration of the previous entry.

956 Douglas, W.A.B. "Nova Scotia and the Royal Navy, 1713-1766." Ph.D. diss, Queen's, 1973. A history of the dealings of the Navy Board with the colony; e.g., shipbuilding and other matters.

957 Dove, C.E. "The First British Navy." <u>Antiquity</u>, 45 (March 1991): 15-20. The results of numismatic evidence and conclusions: Romans deployed scouting vessels from Britain to supplement the Saxon Shore fortifications, thus, the earliest representations of a British naval force.

958 Dowling, C. "The Convoy System and the West India Trade, 1803-1815." D.Phil. diss, Oxford, 1965. A scholarly study of the system.

959 Doyle, Jeff and Moore, Bruce, eds. <u>England and the Spanish Armada: Papers</u>

Arising from the 1988 Conference, ... University of New South Wales. . . .
Canberra: U NSW P, 1990, 196 pp. On the occasion of the 400th anniversary, e.g., a
paper debunking the myths, e.g., Drake and the game of bowls, the absolute victory
of the English, and the permanent decline of Spain.

960 Drake, Francis. The World Encompassed. Publication of the Hakluyt Society,
1st ser, vol. 16. London: Hakluyt Society, 1628, 1653, 1854, 1966, 195 pp. By the
nephew, Francis Drake; various eds: W.S.W. Vaux, N.M. Penzer, and Nicholas
Bourne; from firsthand sources; includes description of the voyage of
circumnavigation.

961 The Drake Manuscript. London: Deutsch, 1996, xxiv, 272 pp. Fwd: Patrick
O'Brian; intro: Verlyn Klinkenborg; illustrations; an interesting collection of
unknown origin, primarily about Renaissance "natural history": plants, animals, and
resources of the Spanish Caribbean; a "manuscript" similar to the famous drawings
of John White.

962 Draper, Benjamin P. Drake Bibliography, 1569-1979. MSS, 1979. A
compilation for libraries, 600 annotated entries plus essays, e.g., by N. Thrower on
Drake and Draper on Drake in California.

963 Drinkwater, John. A History of the Siege of Gibraltar, 1779-1783. London:
Murray, 1905, 375 pp. A siege during the War of the American Revolution.

964 Druett, Joan. Hen Frigates: Wives of Merchant Captains under Sail. NY:
Simon, 1998, 274 pp. Although about wives of American sea captains, it fills a gap
and demonstrates comparable ways of life; sources were letters, journals, and
diaries.

965 -------. Rough Medicine: Surgeons at Sea in the Age of Sail. London:
Routledge, 2000, x, 270 pp. Misleading title; touted as a "microstudy"; 11 surgeons
aboard whaling ships in the 1830s; useful and well-researched; informative on
pharmacological practices.

966 -------. She Captains: Heroines and Hellions of the Sea. NY: Simon, 2000, 304
pp. A series of tales about exploits of women, from antiquity to the present;
anecdotal; exaggerated and disappointing.

967 Drummond, William H. The Battle of Trafalgar: An Heroic Poem. Charleston:
Courier, 1807, 1979, 84 pp. By Rev. Drummond, 1778-1865; read to the Literary
Society of Belfast; reprinted by the American Antiquarian Society.

968 Dudley, Donald R. and Webster, Graham. The Roman Conquest of Britain, AD
43-57. Chester Spring: Dufour, 1965, 216 pp. An undistinguished history.

969 Dudley, William S. "Naval Historians of the War of 1812." Naval History, 4
(Spring 1990): 52-57. By the historian of the U.S. Naval Historical Center; re

Cooper, Mahan, and T. Roosevelt, all popular and all untrained as historians.

970 Dudley, William S., ed. The Naval War of 1812: A Documentary History. 4 vols., more forthcoming. Wash: GPO, 1985-1992, c. 3000 pp. Fwd: John Kane and Dean Allard; 2 vols. of the official collection of documents from the Naval Historical Center; among the most creditable U.S. operations were successes on the Lakes; discussion of background and importance of the issue of impressment.

971 Duffy, Michael. "British Naval Intelligence and Bonaparte's Egyptian Expedition of 1798." MM, 84 (August 1998): 278-90. By the prolific and productive professor at Exeter University, former editor of Mariner's Mirror; re reconnaissance and operational problems of RN maintaining surveillance of a sea 2000 miles long; Admiralty distracted by threats from Ireland; Spain entered the war; lack of information; Nelson learned Napoleon was leading a force, but where?; rushed east but just missed the French, searched further east, then, upon return to Alexandria, found the fleet at Aboukir Bay; battle of the Nile ensued.

972 -------. "British War Policy: The Austrian Alliance, 1793-1801." D.Phil. diss, Oxford, 1971. A scholarly study of an important phase in the coalitions against France; involved operations of RN in the Mediterranean.

973 Duffy, Michael and Morriss, Roger, eds. The Glorious First of June 1794: A Naval Battle and Its Aftermath. Exeter Maritime Studies. Exeter: Exeter UP, 2001, vii, 179 pp. The 1st naval engagement of the Wars of the French Revolution and Napoleon; British captured the largest number of French warships in 100 years but the vital French food convoy reached Brest safely; 8 expert appraisals from British and French scholars; with validity, both sides claimed victory.

974 Duffy, Michael, ed. The Military Revolution and the State, 1500-1800. Exeter Studies in History, # 1. Exeter: Exeter UP; NY: Humanities, 1980, 1981, 91 pp. A series of essays, e.g., by Duffy on the foundation of British naval power beginning in 1514, further growth, 1646-1659.

975 Duffy, Michael, et al., eds. The New Maritime History of Devon. 2 vols. I: From Early Times to the Late Eighteenth Century. II: From the Late Eighteenth Century to the Present. London: Conway, 1992-1994, 538 pp. A series of 36 essays by 32 experts; began as a work by Michael Oppenheim on regional maritime history and expanded; coverage of regional issues, e.g., cartography, trade, privateering, the Plymouth dockyard, and the landing of William of Orange at Torbay in 1688; Duffy and N.A.M. Rodger on aspects of RN and Devon.

976 Duffy, Michael, ed. Parameters of British Naval Power, 1650-1850. Exeter Maritime Studies, # 7. Exeter: Exeter UP, 1992, vi, 144 pp. A collection of 7 essays, e.g., David Davies and Jeremy Black on the development of naval strategy, Duffy on the Western Squadron as "lynchpin," N.A.M. Rodger on regional recruitment and resort to impressment.

977 Duffy, Michael. "A Particular Service: The British Government and the Dunkirk Expedition of 1793." EHR, 91 (July 1976): 529-44. An early war effort by the administration of William Pitt, the Younger: to aid Austria, expel the French revolutionary government, and restore the Bourbons by an invasion of Dunkirk; the defeat had significant consequences.

978 -------. Soldiers, Sugar, and Seapower: The British Expedition to the West Indies and the War against Revolutionary France. Oxford: Clarendon, 1987, viii, 420 pp. A major study of the Anglo-French military-naval warfare in the Caribbean; presents global context; integrates a series of issues: the ongoing conflict, profitability of the West Indies for Britain, slavery, deadly health conditions for armed force personnel, the resurgence of France, and the threat from Spain and Holland.

979 Duffy, Sean. "The Bruce Brothers and the Irish Sea World, 1306-1329." Cambridge Medieval Celtic Studies, 21 (1991): 55-86. A long article describing links or "Celtic Alliance" of the Irish Sea: Scotland, Ireland, the Isle of Man, and others.

980 -------. "Ireland and the Irish Sea Region, 1014-1318." Ph.D. diss, Trinity College, Dublin, 1993. Accounts of expeditions by Irish kings, part of the struggle for control of the Irish Sea; also English and Scots; Anglo-Norman invasions.

981 Dugan, James. The Great Mutiny. NY: Putnam; London: Deutsch, 1965, 1967, 510 pp. An over-dramatized version of the mutinies of 1797 and subsequent ones, linking all to revolutionaries, French and Irish; opens with storming the Bastille and includes a chapter, "the Red Flag."

982 Dugard, Martin. Farther Than Any Man: The Rise and Fall of Captain James Cook. NY: Pocket, 2001, xiv, 287 pp. A recent account of the exploits of Cook.

983 Dugaw, Dianne M. "The Female Warrior Heroine in Anglo-American Popular Balladry." Ph.D. diss, UCLA, 1982, 1069 pp. An impressive collection of ballads; origins from broadsides of the 17th century in the folksong tradition; focus on women in male dress.

984 Duke, A.C. and Tamse, C.A., eds. Britain and the Netherlands. The Hague: Nijhoff, 1977, 256 pp. Proceedings from the 6th Anglo-Dutch Historians Conference; the pertinent paper, # 8, is J.S. Bromley, the outstanding authority, on RN search for alternatives to impressment, 1696-1859, the solution being a kind of naval reserve; recounts "the evils of impressment" and describes it as "a badge of slavery."

985 Dull, Jonathan R. "The French Navy and American Independence: Naval Factors in French Diplomacy and War Strategy, 1774-1780." Ph.D. diss, California-Berkeley, 1972, 427 pp. The basis of the next entry.

986 -------. The French Navy and American Independence: A Study of Arms and Diplomacy, 1774-1787. Princeton: Princeton UP, 1975, xv, 437 pp. Touts as anti-Mahanian view, stressing diplomacy instead of battles and tactics; French authorities saw opportunities in intervening in the American Revolution; program of naval expansion achieved victory but led to bankruptcy and revolution; commendable bibliography.

987 Duncan, Archibald. The British Trident: Or, Register of Naval Actions. 6 vols. London: Cundee, 1805-1809, xxvi, 2159 pp. Originally 4 vols., increased to 6; coverage from 1588 to 1809; short biography of Nelson in vol. IV; superseded by Brenton and William James.

988 -------. A Correct Narrative of the Funeral of Horatio Lord Viscount Nelson. London: Cundee, 1806. A contemporaneous account.

989 -------. The Life of Horatio Lord Viscount Nelson: Baron of the Nile, etc. Alt. title: The Life of the Most Noble Lord Horatio Nelson. London: Cundee; London: Milner, 1805, 1870, vi, 327 pp. A contemporaneous biography.

990 Duncan, Bentley. "Uneasy Allies: Anglo-Portuguese Commercial, Diplomatic and Maritime Relations, 1642-1662." Ph.D. diss, Chicago, 1968, 162 pp. A scholarly study of an enduring alliance.

991 Duncan, Neil. Duncan of Campardown. Diss: Craig-Niven, 1995, 128 pp. Duncan, 1731-1804; on the occasion of the bicentennial of the mutiny and the battle; Duncan handled both situations brilliantly and successfully.

992 Duncan, Peter. "Admiral Howe and the Glorious First of June." Trafalgar Chronicle, 9 (1999): 29-63. Associated with the bicentennial of the battle; Richard Howe was commander.

993 Dunthorne, Hugh L. "The Alliance of the Maritime Powers, 1721-1740." Ph.D. diss, London, 1978, 346 pp. The basis for the next entry.

994 -------. The Maritime Powers, 1721-1740: A Study of Anglo-Dutch Relations in the Age of Walpole. NY: Garland, 1986, 360 pp. After a century of warfare, this maritime alliance joined the 2 major powers in the early 18th century.

995 Durand, James R. James Durand, an Able Seaman of 1812. New Haven: Yale UP, 1926, 139 pp. Ed: George Brooks; fwd: Herbert Satterlee; a memoir; served on USS CONSTITUTION and was impressed into RN; case study of floggings and being put "in irons" in both navies; notes arbitrariness of punishments.

996 Durey, Michael. "The British Secret Service and the Escape of Sir Sidney Smith from Paris in 1798." History, 84 (July 1999): 437-57. Revisionist: British secret service was effective during this war; escape of prominent British prisoners from Temple Prison with the assistance of French Royalists; review of spectacular career of Smith, a RN officer.

997 Du Rietz, Rolf. The Causes of the BOUNTY Mutiny. Uppsala: Almqvist, 1965, 59 pp. An account from Studia Bountyana; generated some controversy; see Madge Darby response.

998 Dye, Ira. The Fatal Cruise of the ARGUS: Two Captains in the War of 1812. Annapolis: NIP, 1994, 1995, xiii, 368 pp. A scholarly and dramatic account; the naval experiences of an American, William Allen, and a British, John Maples, naval captains who ultimately met in a single ship battle off St. David's Head in 1813; Maples, former service under Nelson, at Copenhagen and Trafalgar and Allen, in the CHESEAPEAKE-LEOPARD battle and others.

999 -------. "Seafarers of 1812: A Profile." Prologue, 5 (Spring 1973): 2-13. British impressment prompted the U.S. to keep detailed records of service of sailors; those records now exploited effectively in prosopographical studies.

1000 Dyer, Alan Frank, comp. James Fenimore Cooper: An Annotated Bibliography of Criticism. Bibliographies and Indexes in American Literature. Westport: Greenwood, 1991, xvii, 293 pp. 1943 annotated entries divided into categories, e.g., biographies, general studies, and literature of the sea.

1001 Dyer, Florence E. "Burghley's Notes on the Spanish Armada." MM, 11 (October 1925): 419-24. As an intelligence project, Cecil compiled an analysis of the Armada; conclusions: 130 ships, 8300 sailors, and 19,300 soldiers.

1002 -------. "Drake's Voyage of Circumnavigation: Some of the Original Sketches." MM, (July 1923): 194-201. See Drake Manuscript; a collection of drawings: animals, fish, birds, weapons, and maps.

1003 -------. "The Elizabethan Sailorman." MM, 10 (April 1924): 133-46. A collective analyis of assessments of these seamen, e.g., Drake called them "an unruly lot," others as "untaught and untamed," and instances of health, overcrowding, bad food, fevers, scurvy, and advent of surgeons.

1004 -------. "Reprisals in the Sixteenth Century." MM, 21 (April 1935): 187-97. The rationale for reprisals, a common practice, especially against increasing instances of piracy, of every government of the day.

1005 -------. "The Ship-Money Fleet." MM, 23 (April 1937): 198-209. Describes the result of the special tax implemented by Charles I in the 1630s.

1006 Earle, Peter. Corsairs of Malta and Barbary. London: Sidgwick; Annapolis: NIP, 1970, xii, 307 pp. An excellent study of these Mediterranean pirates.

1007 -------. The Last Fight of the REVENGE. London: Collins, 1992, 192 pp. Incorporates research in Spanish archives and de-mythologizing; re Richard

Grenville and REVENGE leading 22 English war and other ships vs. 53 Spanish in the Azores in 1591; the English escaped except for REVENGE which, facing 5 of the enemy, soon surrendered, Grenville later dying; Walter Ralegh and Alfred Lord Tennyson, among others, created myths.

1008 -------. The Sack of Panama: Sir Henry Morgan's Adventure on the Spanish Main. NY: Viking, 1982, 304 pp. Re operations of privateers and the epic attack and sack of Panama by Morgan in the 1660s; informative on prizes and prize courts.

1009 -------. Sailors: English Merchant Seamen, 1650-1775. London: Methuen, 1998, xii, 259 pp. An outstanding and comprehensive study of the English seaman during the formative period of English expansion; re life aboard ship, e.g., recruitment, pay, victuals, drinks, behavior, beliefs, superstitions, and naval service; revision: life was not nasty and brutish, mutinies and homosexuality were rare, and most were literate and loved music.

1010 Eastwood, David. "Patriotism Personified: Robert Southey's Life of Nelson Reconsidered." MM, 77 (May 1991): 143-49. Re that instant classic and its enduring popularity about England's greatest naval hero was a political statement; elaboration on a series of anomalies, e.g., not the life of a true Englishman, anti-establishment, and scandalous personal life, all covered up by Southey so Nelson could be presented as a patriotic hero.

1011 Eccles, Frank. The Mutiny Run. NY: St.Martin, 1994, 298 pp. Fictional account of mutiny at the Nore and some espionage.

1012 Eco, Umberto. The Island of the Day Before. NY: Harcourt, 1995, 515 pp. Trans: William Weaver; a brilliant and challenging intellectual fiction by this superb novelist, originally in Italian; re the problem of longitude in the 17th cen., concerns Roberto aboard DAPHNE, 1643, at the international dateline.

1013 Edbury, Peter W. The Conquest of Jerusalem and the Third Crusade: Sources in Translation. Brookfield: Ashgate, 1998, vi, 196 pp. In the 1180s and 1190s, crusaders of the Third Crusade, including Richard I and a naval contingent, fought Saladin attempting unsuccessfully to recover Jerusalem.

1014 Edgar, Francis. They Told Mr. Hakluyt: Being a Selection of Tales and Other Matters taken from Richard Hakluyt's "The Principal Navigations," "Voyages," "Traffics," and "Discourses of the English Nation." NY: St. Martin, 1964, ix, 150 pp. Excerpts for juveniles; subjects, e.g., search for the Northwest Passage, Cabot, Gilbert, and the Virginia Company.

1015 Edgell, John. Sea Surveys: Britain's Contribution to Hydrography. London: HMSO, 1965, 29 pp. For NMM; Edgell, Hydrographer of the Navy, 1932-1945; an informative pamphlet.

1016 Edmond, Rod. Representing the South Pacific: Colonial Discourse from Cook to Gauguin. Cambridge: Cambridge UP, 1997, xii, 309 pp. Intellectual and literary analysis; chapters on missionaries, traders, explorers, and mutineers; the persistent attraction was Terra Australis incognita, the unknown southern continent; reports by the first Europeans to Tahiti influenced the Enlightenment and Romanticism; other fateful events, e.g., mutiny on the BOUNTY, Bligh's voyage in the launch, Christian's search for paradise, and the death of Cook, "the God."

1017 Edmundson, George. Anglo-Dutch Rivalry during the First Half of the Seventeenth Century. Oxford: Oxford UP, 1911, 176 pp. The Ford Lectures of 1910; an older standard, especially good on cultural and social aspects; the naval rivalry was fiercely contested; chronological coverage.

1018 Edwards, Edward. The Life of Sir Walter Ralegh: Based on Contemporary Documents. 2 vols. London: Macmillan, 1868, 1444 pp. Books on "life" and "letters"; an undistinguished biography and collection of 157 letters of Ralegh.

1019 Edwards, Philip, ed. Last Voyages: Cavendish, Hudson, Ralegh: The Original Narratives. Oxford: Clarendon, 1988, xi, 268 pp. Selected narratives of 3 long, dangerous voyages, 1591-1618; essays presenting background; enlightening on English maritime history and overseas expansion.

1020 Edwards, Philip. The Story of the Voyage: Sea Narratives in Eighteenth-Century England. Cambridge: Cambridge UP, 1994, 255 pp. A survey and review of voyage literature, e.g., Dampier, Cook, Bligh, convicts of the First Fleet, and press-gangs; included short anti-imperialist diatribe.

1021 Egerton, George, ed. Political Memoirs: Essays on the Politics of Memory. London: Cass, 1994, viii, 350 pp. 19 chapters about political memoirs; pertinent is chapter 7, "Rulers of the Waves: British Naval Memoirs," e.g., Phineas Pett, Samuel Pepys, John Campbell, and John Charnock.

1022 Egerton, Judy. The Fighting TEMERAIRE: Making and Meaning. New Haven: Yale UP, 1995, 143 pp. Re J.M.W. Turner, Britain's greatest painter, and his famous painting of HMS TEMERAIRE being towed to her last berth; a veteran of Trafalgar; Turner emphasized the impact of the industrial revolution; symbolized the transition to a modern, industrial age.

1023 Ehrenkreutz, A.S. "The Place of Saladin in the Naval History of the Mediterranean Sea in the Middle Ages." J American Oriental Society, 75 (June 1955): 100-16. Changes in the naval situation was one impact of the Crusades, a transformation as Egypt and Byzantium were superseded by Saladin's naval power, between 1169-1191; the Norman fleet also operated successfully in the Mediterranean, e.g., in 1191, the fleet of Richard I met and defeated the fleet of Saladin.

1024 Ehrman, John. The Navy in the War of William III, 1689-1697: Its State and Direction. Cambridge: Cambridge UP, 1953, xiii, 710 pp. An outstanding monograph, chronicling the rapid naval expansion of England; re the ships, dockyards, logistics, and administration.

1025 -------. "William III and the Emergence of a Mediterranean Naval Policy, 1692-1694." Cambridge Historical J, 9 (1949): 269-92. A review of naval battles of the 1690s and their implications, e.g., Beachy Head, Barfleur, and La Hogue.

1026 Ehrsam, Theodore G., comp. A Bibliography of Joseph Conrad. Metuchen: Scarecrow, 1969, 448 pp. 2043 items, including works, 1857-1924, biographical and critical material, and films.

1027 Eisler, William L. The Furtherest Shore: Images of "Terra Australis" from the Middle Ages to Captain Cook. London: Cambridge UP, 1995, xi, 180 pp. Emphasis on Spanish, Dutch, and English sources imagining, exploring, observing, scientific researching, and mapping the continent.

1028 Ekberg, Carl J. The Failure of Louis XIV's Dutch War. Chapel Hill: UNCP, 1979, xix, 240 pp. The campaigns of 1672-1674 with emphasis on French activities during the Third Dutch War.

1029 Ekirch, A. Roger. Bound for America: The Transportation of British Convicts to the Colonies, 1718-1775. Oxford: Clarendon, 1987, 1990, 304 pp. Re the enforced migration of 50,000 convicts, all ending with the war; most to Maryland and Virginia; author convinced that most had committed crimes.

1030 Elder, John R. Spanish Influences on Scottish History. Glasgow: Maclehose, 1920, vii, 323 pp. The 16th century was crucial for Scotland, especially the consequences of the Reformation and the spectacular reign of Mary Stewart; potential for Catholicism was defeated; key factors were Spanish incompetence, the Armada, and subsequent "armadas."

1031 Elgood, P.G. Bonaparte's Adventure in Egypt. London: Oxford UP, 1931, vi, 262 pp. Re the Egyptian campaign of 1798-1799; good maps.

1032 Elliott, Colin. Discovering Armada Britain: A Journey in Search of the Sites, Relics and Remains which Tell the Story of the Defeat of the Spanish Armada 400 Years Ago. Newton Abbot: David and Charles, 1987, 176 pp. Illustrated; anticipating the Quadricentinnial, Elliott followed the Armada trail on land, beginning in Cornwall, Plymouth, hilltop beacons, travels of Queen Elizabeth, and Spanish wrecks along Scottish and Irish coasts.

1033 -------. Maritime Heritage: The Story of Britain's Preserved Historic Ships and Where to See Them. London: Tops'l, 1981, 64 pp. Details on the preserved ships and their locations.

1034 Elliott, John and Pickersgill, Richard. Captain Cook's Second Voyage: The Journals of Lieutenants Elliott and Pickersgill. Dover: Caliban, 1982, 1984, 250 pp.

Ed: Christine Holmes; 2 manuscripts from the voyage of RESOLUTION, 1772-1775.

1035 Elliott, John H. Spain and Its World, 1500-1700: Selected Essays. New Haven: Yale UP, 1989, xiv, 295 pp. Essays by the most noted authority in English of Spanish history, Sir John Elliott.

1036 Elliott, Peter. The Cross and the Ensign: A Naval History of Malta, 1798-1979. Annapolis: NIP, 1980, 217 pp. "Who controls Malta, controls the Mediterranean," and in modern times that has been Britain, supeseding the Knights of St. John and the French.

1037 Ellis, Kenneth. The Post Office in the Eighteenth Century: A Study in Administrative History. London: Oxford UP, 1958, 1969, xvi, 176 pp. An important institution, e.g., large fleet of packets, intelligence functions of the Secret Office, and the Deciphering Branch.

1038 Ellis, Peter B. Caesar's Invasion of Britain. NY: NYUP; London: Constable 1978, 1980, 1994, 144 pp. Folio size, illustrated; Caesar, conquering Gaul, invaded with a fleet of 80 ships across the Straits of Dover, Celtic tribes awaiting the Romans; in 55 and 54 BC, then a pause for over 90 years.

1039 Ellison, David, ed. Pressganged: The Letters of George Price of Southwark, alias "George Green": Ordinary Seaman in HM Sloop SPEEDY, 1803-1805. Royston: Ellison, 1994, vii, 71 pp. A memoir.

1040 Eltis, David. The Military Revolutions in Sixteenth-Century Europe. London: Tauris, 1995, 175 pp. A comprehensive review of the debate, even going back before Michael Roberts, e.g., Charles Oman and J.R. Hale, then Parker, Lynn, and Howard.

1041 Emden, Cecil S. Pepys Himself. Oxford: Oxford UP; Westport: Greenwood, 1963, 1980, xi, 146 pp. Emphasis on his character and personal qualities.

1042 Emmer, Pieter C. and Gaastra, Femme S., eds. The Organization of Interoceanic Trade in European Expansion, 1450-1800. Aldershot: Variorum, 1996, xxvi, 429 pp. A collection of 18 articles, e.g., Anglo-Dutch merchant shipping, Amsterdam as world entrepot, and East India Companies as "a pre-modern multinational organization."

1043 Emmerson, John, comp. The CHESAPEAKE Affair of 1807. Portsmouth: Emmerson, 1955, 223 pp. Re the CHESEPEAKE-LEOPARD affair, a minor incident but major political controversy; this compilation sorts out the complications and explains the consequences.

1044 Emsley, Clive. The Longman Companion to Napoleonic Europe. London: Longman, 1993, x, 327 pp. A useful reference guide, facts and figures and chronology.

1045 Emsley, Clive, <u>et al.</u>, eds. <u>North Riding Naval Recruits: The Quota Acts and the Quota Men, 1795-1797</u>. Northallerton: North Yorkshire County Council, 1978, 151 pp. Regional details about one of the recruiting measures.

1046 Emsley, Clive. "The Recruitment of Petty Offenders during the French Wars, 1793-1815." <u>MM</u>, 66 (1980): 199-208. The manpower problem led to extraordinary methods, e.g. Quota Acts, ballots, bounties, impressment, and recruiting criminals, this article on the latter.

1047 <u>ENDEAVOUR: Captain Cook's Journal, 1768-1771</u>. CD-ROM. 1999, 1 disc. For the National Library of Australia and the Australian National Maritime Museum; includes the handwritten journal and an annotated transcript and a simulated three-dimensional tour of the ship; a printed guide.

1048 Engholm, Frederick W. <u>The Story of HMS VICTORY</u>. London: Drummond, 1944, 55 pp. Illustrated, including unusual sketches; a history plus details on bombing damage of the area during World War II.

1049 English, J.A. "The Trafalgar Syndrome: Jutland and the Indecisiveness of Modern Naval Warfare." <u>NWCR</u>, 32 (May 1979): 60-77. By a Canadian officer; comparisons of Trafalgar and Jutland; cites Corbett, Mahan, and Marder on naval strategy; concludes Jutland was final but indecisive.

1050 Ennis, Daniel J. "Naval Impressment in Tobias Smollett's <u>Roderick Random</u>." <u>Albion</u>, 32 (Summer 2000): 232-47. The novel of 1748 realistictly depicting life aboard ship, e.g., impressment, floggings, and disease.

1051 -------. "Representations of Naval Impressment in Eighteenth-Century British Literature." Ph.D. diss, Auburn, 1999, 280 pp. A survey of the literature.

1052 Epstein, Steven A. <u>Genoa and the Genoese, 958-1528</u>. Chapel Hill: UNCP; London: Eurospan, 1996, 2001, xx, 396 pp. A scholarly and thoughtful study of this important Italian state, home of Columbus; early 13th century at height, a fleet as large as that of Venice; especially noted for war galleys.

1053 Ernst, Pauline F. <u>Book Relics from HMS BOUNTY</u>. Los Altos: Ernst, 1993, 42 pp. A pamphlet describing some surviving books; demonstrative of the enduring fascination.

1054 Esdaile, Charles J. <u>The French Wars, 1792-1815</u>. <u>Lancaster Pamphlet</u>. NY: Routledge, 2001, xvi, 95 pp. An excellent synthesis; global context; based on 7 coalitions during the period.

1055 -------. <u>The Wars of Napoleon</u>. <u>Modern Wars in Perspective</u> series. London: Longman, 1995, xii, 417 pp. A recent survey, global perspective; chapter on

"Perfidious Albion" and "facing up to Boney"; an extensive bibliographical essay.

1056 Estes, J. Worth. <u>Naval Surgeon: Life and Death at Sea in the Age of Sail</u>. Canton: Science, 1998, lx, 266 pp. Publication of the log of a surgeon aboard an American frigate in the Mediterranean, 1802-1803, previously captured by the British and freed; description of the life and times of a naval surgeon; over a tour of 435 days, 370 men aboard, data on 240 patients, 6.6% of whom died.

1057 Evans, Angela Care. <u>The SUTTON HOO Ship Burial</u>. London: British Museum, 1986, 1994, 127 pp. Folio size, illustrated; a detailed report of the 2nd stage of excavation, 1984-1992.

1058 Evans, Eric J. <u>The Forging of the Modern State: Early Industrial Britain, 1783-1870</u>. London: Longman, 1983, 1996, 486 pp. Growth of the modern state linked to industrialization; aristocratic government endured.

1059 Evans, Martin H. and West, Janet. <u>Maritime Museums: A Guide to the Collections and Museum Ships in Britain and Ireland</u>. London: Chatham, 1998, 96 pp. A compilation; introduction to 250 maritime museums and 400 historic ships; presented by area.

1060 Evatt, Herbert V. <u>Rum Rebellion: A Study of the Overthrow of Governor Bligh by John Macarthur and the New South Wales Corps</u>. Sydney: Angus; London: Dawson, 1938, 1955, 1968, 1971, xix, 365 pp. A detailed study of the circumstances and events in this sensational episode.

1061 Evelyn, John. <u>Diary</u>. 6 vols. NY: Bray; Oxford: Clarendon, 1906, 1951, 1955, xlviii, 3295 pp. Ed: E.S. de Beer; the definitive edition; Evelyn, 1620-1706, friend and fellow-diarist of Pepys; informative on Anglo-Dutch wars, the Royal Society, and administration of RN.

1062 Ewen, C.H. L'Estrange. <u>Captain John Ward: "Arch Pirate."</u> Paignton: Ewen, 1939, 16 pp. A pamphlet on this pirate.

1063 -------. <u>The Golden Chalice: A Documented Narrative of an Elizabethan Pirate</u>. Paignton: Ewen, 1939, 17 pp. A pamphlet about John Callice or Challis active in the 1570s and after; from records of LHA.

1064 -------. <u>The North-West Passage: Light on the Murder of Henry Hudson from Unpublished Documents</u>. London: Ewen, 1938, 8 pp. Hudson was set adrift and disappeared.

1065 -------. "Organized Piracy Round England in the Sixteenth Century." <u>MM</u>, 35 (January 1949): 29-42. Informative about domestic English pirates operating along coasts and about their methods of circumvention of laws, regulations, and the authorities; from records of HCA.

1066 Exquemeling, Alexandre Olivier. The Buccaneers of America. Classics of Naval Literature series. NY: Dover; Annapolis: NIP, 1678, 1684, 1698, 1951, 1967, 1993, li, 506 pp. Trans: John Exquemeling; various editions; translation of De Americaeneche Zee Roover; Exquemeling, fl. 1670s, a Dutch buccaneer of the West Indies who recounted his extensive experiences during the heyday of piracy, e.g., Henry Morgan storming Panama; authentic despite the fact that Morgan sued Exquemeling and won a settlement for defamation of character.

1067 Fabel, Robin F.A. "Self-Help in Dartmoor: Black and White Prisoners in the War of 1812." J Early Republic, 9 (Summer 1989): 165-90. Description of what life was like for 6500 POWs, most from American privateers.

1068 Facts and Factors in Economic History: Articles by Former Students of Edwin F. Gay. Cambridge: Harvard UP, 1932, x, 757 pp. A panel of editors, e.g., Arthur H. Cole; 34 essays in honor of this Harvard professor of economic history, e.g., Frederick Dietz on English public finance in the 16th century, A.P. Usher on Spanish ships and shipping of the 16th and 17th centuries, and Earl Hamilton on Spanish mercantilism.

1069 Falconer, Alexander F. Shakespeare and the Sea. NY: Ungar, 1964, xvi, 164 pp. Shakespeare was well informed about the sea and sea enterprises, e.g., storms, shipwrecks, pirates, Trinity House, voyages of exploration, and navigation.

1070 Falconer, William. Shipwreck: A Poem. N.p., 1762. Falconer, 1732-1769, credited with an early and most important nautical dictionary; a popular poem of the 18th century; based on personal experiences aboard HMS BRITANNIA, wrecked in a storm off Greece, 3 survivors, including Falconer who was later lost at sea.

1071 -------. Universal Marine Dictionary. Alt. titles: A New Universal Marine Dictionary and The Old Wooden Walls. London: Badcock; Newton Abbot: David and Charles; London: Macdonald; London: Chatham, 1750, 1769, 1789, 1804, 1815, 1930, 1970, 1974, 2002, viii, 864 pp. Various eds: J.W. Norie, William Burney, and Claude S. Gill; themes based on 18th century: shipbuilding, seamanship, discipline, glossary, and sea terms (English and French); some bias, e.g., "retreat" defined as "a French maneuver. . . not properly a term of British marine"; praise for Pierre Bougue as the supreme authority.

1072 Falkus, Christopher. The Spanish Armada. Panorama of History series. London: Pan, 1972, 64 pp. Illustrated; for juveniles, the series to portray major events in world history.

1073 Fallon, Niall. The Armada in Ireland. London: Stranford; Middletown: Wesleyan UP, 1977, 1978, x, 236 pp. By a journalist; re the role of Ireland in the Armada campaign; features, e.g., interviews with locals, visits to every wreck site, elaboration about the case of Cuellar, and myths and mysteries.

1074 Fanning, A.E. Steady as She Goes: A History of the Compass Department of the Admiralty. London: HMSO, 1986, xl, 463 pp. By the department director, 1960s and 1970s; magnet compasses came from China; focus on advances from the 18th century.

1075 Fara, Patricia. "The Application of Science: The Georgian British Museum." HisTod, 47 (August 1997): 39-45. The British Museum was authorized in 1753 "to studious and curious people"; large role of the Royal Society, especially Joseph Banks and Hans Sloane; in 1881, the Natural History Museum of Kensington was opened.

1076 Fardy, Bernard D. John Cabot: The Discovery of Newfoundland. St. Johns: Creative, 1994. A popular account.

1077 Farmer, Donald W. "Charles Howard of Effingham, Lord High Admiral of England: An Appreciative Re-evaluation." Ph..D. diss, Georgetown, 1965, 334 pp. Howard has been neglected and defamed; not deserved; a long, didactic treatise.

1078 Farnell, James E. "The Navigation Act of 1651, the First Dutch War, and the London Merchant Community." Economic History Review, 2nd ser, 16 (April 1964): 439-54. The programme of the Commonwealth Government to support and expand English shipping; the Dutch reacted.

1079 Farrell, Robert T. and de Vegvar, Carol N., eds. SUTTON HOO: Fifty Years After. Oxford: Miamill, 1992, 198 pp. 12 papers from a 50th anniversary conference, 1989; a series of assessments and revisions.

1080 Fedorak, Charles J. "The Royal Navy and British Amphibious Operations during the Revolutionary and Napoleonic Wars." Military Affairs, 52 (July 1988): 141-46. A study of amphibious campaigns.

1081 Fedorowicz, J.K. England's Baltic Trade in the Early Seventeenth Century: A Study in Anglo-Polish Commercial Diplomacy. Cambridge: Cambridge UP, 1980, xiii, 334 pp. From a Cambridge dissertation; re the Eastland Company and its development; details on imports and exports, e.g., naval stores.

1082 Feldbaek, Arne Ole. Denmark and the Armed Neutrality, 1800-1801: Small Power Policy in a World War. Copenhagen: Akademisk, 1980, 305 pp. Details on the league: Sweden, Russia, Prussia, and Denmark; its impact on the British; led to the battle of Copenhagen of 1801.

1083 Fenwick, Kenneth. HMS VICTORY. London: Cassell, 1959, xiv, 369 pp. Recounts the naval history of VICTORY, campaign by campaign; claimed as "the world's most famous ship"; short piece on earlier VICTORY, veteran of the Armada.

1084 Fenwick, Valerie. The Graveney Boat: A Tenth-Century Find from Kent. British Archaeology Reports, vol. 53. Greenwich: NMM, 1978, xix, 348 pp. Fwd:

Basil Greenhill; a series of essays re the discovery, excavation, recovery, and display of a boat in the Graveney Marshes in 1970.

1085 Fenwick, Valerie and Gale, Alison. Historic Shipwrecks: Discovered, Protected and Investigated. Stroud: Tempus, 1998, 1999, 160 pp. Details about the most important wreck sites in Britain, e.g., GRACE DIEU, MARY ROSE, and HMS COLOSSUS; a map notes 47 sites, 2-page description for each.

1086 Fenwick, Valerie, ed. Three Major Ancient Boat Finds in Britain. Monographs and Reports, # 6. Greenwich: NMM, 1972. One description is SUTTON HOO by Angela Evans.

1087 Fereday, R.P. Saint-Faust in the North, 1803-1804: Orkney and Shetland in Danger. Oxford: Tempus, 1995, 115 pp. Re an obscure and failed French expedition led by Jean de Saint-Faust to invade "North Britain"; to be a distraction for a major invasion across the Channel.

1088 Fergusson, Bernard E. The Watery Maze: The Story of Combined Operations. NY: Holt; London: Collins, 1961, 445 pp. Sir Bernard, later Lord Ballantrae; most is about the Combined Operations Headquarters formed in 1940; an introductory history of amphibious operations beginning with Rochefort in 1757, more importantly, Quebec in 1759, and others of the American Revolution and the Peninsular campaign, 1808-1814.

1089 Fernandes, Manuel. Livro de Tracas de Carpintaria. Lisbon: Facsimile, 1616, 1989, 150 pp. Intro: Rogerio d'Oliveira; for the Academia de Marinha; the most important treatise on shipbuilding, originally for the Lisbon Arsenal; details on design of 22 types of vessels; masts and spars.

1090 Fernandez-Armesto, Felipe. "Exploding the Myths." Apollo, 128 (July 1988): 49-50. A joint Anglo-Spanish exhibition of Armada artifacts and related items; a "total history" project, didactic: "to teach humility to the English and tolerance to the Spaniards."

1091 -------. The Spanish Armada: The Experience of War in 1588. London: Oxford UP, 1988, 1989, x, 300 pp. An important Quadricentennial project; purposely balanced presentation, contending Spanish interpretations exaggerated the extent of defeat and English ones were chauvinistic; elaboration on the latter: the "Black Legend" of Spanish cruelty and fanaticism, the Whig interpretation of good liberty vs. bad despotism, and Protestant apologetics, God on the side of England; conclusion: failure was due to the winds; defeat and victory not terms appropriate for this campaign.

1092 Fernandez Duro, Cesareo. Armada Espanola desde la union de los reinos de Castilla y de Aragon. 9 vols. Madrid: Museo Naval, 1877, 1972-1973, 4500 pp. A massive and exhaustive study; Fernandez Duro, 1830-1908, a Spanish naval captain and prolific maritime historian, researched in the Spanish royal archives; corrects misconceptions about Philip II and enlightens on other Spanish aspects.

1093 -------. La Armada Invencible. 2 vols. Madrid: Tipografico, 1884-1885, 1074 pp. Published these 199 letters and documents; important sources elaborating on the Spanish and the Armada.

1094 Fewster, Joseph M. "The Jay Treaty and British Ship Seizures: The Martinique Cases." William and Mary Quarterly, 45 (July 1988): 426-52. A crisis in Anglo-American relations in 1794 when RN ships seized over 50 American merchant ships, the attraction of prize money being a factor; John Jay negotiated a treaty resolving the issues.

1095 -------. "Prize Money and the Expedition of 1793-1794." J Imperial and Commonwealth History, 12 (October 1983): 1-28. Researched the issue and the practice during a British campaign to the West Indies, Jervis being one of the commanders; 80,000 pounds sterling was involved.

1096 Ffoulkes, Charles J. The Gun-Founders of England: With a List of English and Continental Gun-Founders from the Fourteenth to the Nineteenth Centuries. York: Shumway; Cambridge: Cambridge UP, 1937, 1969, xvi, 134 pp. A history of English cannon making, some experts shifted about to and from Europe; England led in the field.

1097 Ffoulkes, Charles J. and Hopkinson, E.C. Sword, Lance and Bayonet: A Record of the Arms of the British Army and Navy. London: Arms, 1967, xvi, 144 pp. The English Ordance Office supplied to the army and navy; a history of these small arms.

1098 Fields, C. "The Marines in the Great Naval Mutinies, 1797-1802." JRUSI, 62 (1917): 720-46. By a Royal Marine colonel; to clarify: whether Royal Marines participated with or against the mutineers.

1099 Fifoot, C.H.S. Lord Mansfield. Oxford: Oxford UP, 1936, vi, 266 pp. William Murray Mansfield, 1st Earl, 1705-1793, the pre-eminent authority on maritime law and formulator of prize procedures.

1100 Filon, Augustin. Renegat. Paris: Colin, 1894. A novel about the Armada.

1101 Fioravanzo, Giuseppe. A History of Naval Tactical Thought. Annapolis: NIP, 1956, 1979, x, 251 pp. Trans: Arthur Holst; by an Italian theorist; a conceptual approach; case studies of tactical thought about the progression of propulsion types, e.g., oars, sail, steam, etc.

1102 Firstbrook, Peter L. The Voyage of the MATTHEW: John Cabot and the Discovery of North America. London: BBC, 1997, 191 pp. The supporting book for a BBC-TV documentary about the replica and the re-enactment voyage.

1103 [NRS 33]. Firth, Charles H., ed. <u>Naval Songs and Ballads</u>. <u>Publications of the Navy Records Society</u>, vol. 33. London: NRS, 1908, cxxiv, 387 pp. A fabulous collection of hundreds of ballads and songs illustrating the history of RN, 16th century to the mid-19th century; a long, informative introduction; notes explain origins and details of each.

1104 Firth, Charles H. "Papers Relating to the Navy in the Bodleian Library." <u>MM</u>, 3 (August 1913): 225. A description of the holdings, e.g., log-books, naval journals, and some Pepys MSS within the Rawlinson Papers.

1105 -------. "Sailors of the Civil War, the Commonwealth and the Protectorate." <u>MM</u>, 12 (July 1926): 237-59. Firth calls for more study, research, and writing on RN during the Civil War; a review of the literature, demonstrating the neglect of this coverage.

1106 Fischer, Lewis R., ed. <u>The Market for Seamen in the Age of Sail</u>. <u>Research in Maritime History</u>, # 7. St. Johns: Memorial UP, 1994, xi, 166 pp. 8 papers from the 11th International Congress of Economic History, 1994, Milan; a contribution to an ongoing debate about the market for seamen during the age of sail; review of the issues, e.g., recruitment, supply and demand, wages, crimps, and government intervention.

1107 Fischer, Lewis R. and Nordvik, Helge W., eds. <u>Shipping and Trade, 1750-1950</u>. Pontefract: Lofthouse, 1990, xii, 325 pp. 16 papers from the 10th International Congress of Economic History, 1990, Louvain; e.g., David Starkey on British seafarers and war in the 18th century.

1108 Fisher, Godfrey. <u>Barbary Legend: War, Trade and Piracy in North Africa, 1415-1830</u>. Oxford: Clarendon; Westport: Greenwood, 1957, 1974, xii, 349 pp. Apologetics for the Barbary states: Algiers, Tunis, Tripoli, and Morocco; not "scourge of Christendom" and no worse than European pirates; early English encounters in 1580s; overstates the case.

1109 Fisher, Robin and Johnston, Hugh, eds. <u>Captain Cook and His Times</u>. Canberra: Australian National UP; Seattle: U Wash P, 1979, x, 278 pp. 12 papers from a conference on Cook's voyages, Simon Fraser University, 1978, celebrating a bicentennial of the 3rd voyage; e.g., medical aspects and consequences, Dalrymple and Cook, and an analysis of the works of Beaglehole.

1110 Fisher, Robin. <u>Vancouver's Voyage: Charting the Northwest Coast, 1791-1795</u>. Vancouver: Douglas, 1992, xi, 131 pp. Fabulous folio format; reviewed the voyage and its significance.

1111 Fisher, Stephen, ed. <u>Lisbon as a Port Town, the British Seaman, and Other Maritime Themes</u>. <u>Exeter Maritime Studies</u>, # 2. Exeter: Exeter UP, 1988, vii, 143 pp. 6 papers from a conference on maritime history, 1986; e.g., J.L. Anderson on the descent of William III on Devon in 1688 and Lewis Fischer on wage patterns of seamen.

1112 -------, ed. Studies in British Privateering, Trading Enterprise and Seamen's Welfare, 1775-1900. Exeter Papers in Economic History, # 17. Exeter: Exeter UP, 1987, xiv, 165 pp. 6 papers from a conference, e.g., David Starkey on 4th Anglo-Dutch war in the 1780s, Alston Kennerley on seamen's missions and sailor's homes, and Colin Elliott on entrepreneurial aspects of British privateering.

1113 Fiske, John. Discovery of America: With Some Account of Ancient America and the Spanish Conquest. 2 vols. Boston: Houghton; London: Macmillan, 1892, 1893. Fiske, 1842-1901; a classic study of discovery.

1114 -------. Elizabethan Sea Kings. 1895. Describes a stereotype of the 16th cen.

1115 Fissel, Mark C. English Warfare, 1511-1642. Warfare and History series. London: UCL, 1998, 2001, 352 pp. To place the wars in context; includes the era of the military revolution; issues, e.g., expeditions to the continent, impressment, mobilization, and logistics.

1116 Fissel, Mark C., ed. War and Government in Britain, 1598-1650. War, Armed Forces, and Society series. Manchester: Manchester UP, 1991 x, 293 pp. A series of essays, e.g., Andrew Thrush on ship money.

1117 Fitchett, W.H. Nelson and His Captains: Sketches of Famous Seamen. London: Smith, 1902, 322 pp. Fitchett, 1845-1928; character studies, e.g., of Berry, Riou, Blackwood, Troubridge, Pellew, Foley, and Hardy.

1118 Fitzgerald, Lawrence. Java La Grande: The Portuguese Discovery of Australia. Hobart: Publishers, 1984, xv, 140 pp. Illustrated; "an enigma": the Portuguese discovery c. 1521; land mass on some French maps of the 16th cen.

1119 Fitzhugh, William W. and Olin, Jacques S., eds. Archaeology of the Frobisher Voyages. Wash: Smithsonian, 1993, xiii, 271 pp. Folio size, illustrated; 14 articles by experts about expeditions of investigation re the 3 voyages of the late 1570s, exploring the North Atlantic and Frobisher Bay.

1120 Fitzhugh, William W. and Ward, Elisabeth I., eds. Vikings: The North Atlantic Saga. Wash: Smithsonian, 2000, 416 pp. Profusely illustrated; in support of an exhibition, National Museum of Natural History, 2000; on the occasion of the millennium of the voyage of Leif Eriksson; articles by experts; elaboration on various replicas, the Vinland Map, and "Kensington Stone."

1121 Flanagan, Laurence. Ireland's Armada Legacy. Dublin: Gill, 1988, 210 pp. Illustrated; Quadricentennial publication associated with the Ulster Museum; maps designating 14 wreck sites along the Irish coast; excavation expeditions, e.g., at site of GIRONA, 6000 hours of diving; catalogue of artifacts.

1122 Flanagan, Laurence, Martin, Colin, and Stenuit, Robert. <u>Tresors de l'Armada</u>. Burssels: Credit Communal, 1985, 1986, 207 pp. The findings of nautical archaeological operations.

1123 Flayhart, William H. <u>Counterpoint to Trafalgar: The Anglo-Russian Invasion of Naples, 1805-1806. Studies in Maritime History</u>. Columbia: USCP, 1992, 209 pp. During the 3rd coalition, 1803-1806; an Anglo-Russian expedition to Naples; Napoleon reacted vigorously on land and sea, in the former case, forcing withdrawal of the allies, and, in the latter, ultimately leading to the battle of Trafalgar.

1124 Fleming, Fergus. <u>Barrow's Boys</u>. London: Granta, 1998, xiv, 489 pp. Re John Barrow, 1764-1848, longtime Secretary of the Admiralty and founder of the Royal Geographical Society; the role of RN in peacetime; a popular and superficial account, error prone.

1125 Fleming, Thomas J. <u>Beat the Last Drum: The Siege of Yorktown, 1781</u>. NY: St.Martin, 1963, 375 pp. Extensive coverage of the Yorktown campaign; based on diaries, journals, and letters.

1126 Fletcher, Ian, ed. <u>The Peninsular War: Aspects of the Struggle for the Iberian Peninsula</u>. Staplehurst: Spellmount, 1998, 205 pp. A history of the campaign based on primary sources.

1127 Fletcher, Ian. <u>The Waters of Oblivion: The British Invasion of the Rio De La Plata, 1806-1807</u>. Tunbridge Wells: Spellmount, 1991, 172 pp. A neglected British operation, an invasion of this Spanish Viceroyalty producing many heroic acts, some defeats, and some brilliant feats.

1128 Flint, John. "Professor Gerald Sanford Graham, 1903-1988." <u>J Imperial and Commonwealth History</u>, 17 (May 1989): 297-300. A native of Canada, later professor at Harvard and Queen's University; historian of naval power and its relationship to empire.

1129 Flower-Smith, M.A. "'The Able and the Willynge': The Preparations of the English Land Forces to Meet the Armada." <u>British Army Review</u>, 95 (August 1990): 54-61. Describes the process.

1130 Flynn, Dennis O., <u>et al.</u>, eds. <u>European Entry into the Pacific: Spain and the Acapulco-Manila Galleons</u>. Aldershot: Ashgate, 2001, 384 pp. An important feature of trans-Pacific operations; ultimate influence on the world economy and the role of the Philippines in world and global history.

1131 Foley, Thomas. <u>The Nelson Centenary</u>. Norwich: East, 1905. Pseud: Florence Horatia Suckling; Nelson centennial; an authoritative family history, reprinted from <u>Norfolk Chronicle</u>.

1132 Fone, J.F. "The Naval Yard at Yarmouth in the Napoleonic Wars." Norfolk Archaeology, 41 (1992): 351-58. Yarmouth dockyards was created for operations during the Wars of the French Revolution and Napoleon.

1133 Forbes, Eric G. The Birth of Scientific Navigation: The Solving in the Eighteenth Century of the Problem of Finding Longitude at Sea. Greenwich: NMM, 1974, 25 pp. The history of solving the longitude problem; in 1714, Parliament offered a 20,000 pound sterling reward and set up a board to investigate solutions; later, Harrison's chronometer.

1134 Forbes, Eric G., Meadows, Arthur Jack, and Howse, Derek. Greenwich Observatory: The Story of Britain's Oldest Scientific Institution, the Royal Observatory at Greenwich and Herstmonceux, 1675-1975. 3 vols. I: Origins and Early History, 1675-1835. II: Recent History, 1836-1975. III: The Buildings and Instruments. London: Taylor, 1975, 512 pp. Folio size, illustrated; a comprehensive history of the Royal Observatory and contributions of the Astronomer Royal.

1135 Ford, C.J. "Piracy or Policy: The Crisis in the Channel, 1400-1403." Transactions of RHS, 5th ser, 29 (1979): 63-78. At a time of deteriorating Anglo-French relations, the incidence of piracy, banditry, and lawlessness in the Channel increased; conclusion: these acts were inspired by the governments of England and France, "unlicensed privateering" or pirate warfare.

1136 Ford, Douglas. Admiral Vernon and the Navy: A Memoir and Vindication. London: Unwin, 1907, xx, 322 pp. A conscious effort to rehabilitate Vernon, 1684-1757, who has had a bad press, it was contended; hagiography.

1137 Foreman, Laura and Phillips, Ellen B. Napoleon's Lost Fleet: Bonaparte, Nelson, and the Battle of the Nile. NY: Discovery, 1999. Intro: Frank Gaddis; folio size, lavishly illustrated, supporting TV presentation on Discovery Channel; incorporates recent nautical archaeology operations.

1138 [Hornblower career, chronological order, # 11 of 11]. Forester, Cecil Scott. Admiral Hornblower in the West Indies. Boston: Little, Brown, 1963, 1997. Forester, 1899-1966, the original and the most popular of the Nelson-era nautical fiction writers, ultimately 11 Hornblower novels and others related; Forester created Hornblower after reading The Naval Chronicle and The Gazette; themes: life at sea, ship construction, naval intelligence, naval prizes, and romance; Forester was unequalled in describing single-ship actions; originally serialized in Argosy Magazine, beginning in 1936; Forester was the original choice to be official biographer of Earl Mountbatten of Burma; after death of Forester, Philip Ziegler was selected; Parkinson's "biography" of Hornblower was reviewed in The Times Literary Supplement as non-fiction; the latest manifestations of the popularity: "Hornblower," TV Movie, ITV-Meridian and A&E TV, two 4-part, 8-hour TV series, from the 6th of 11 Horatio Hornblower novels of C.S. Forester, shown 1998 and 2001 in Britain and 1999 and 2001in U.S., starring Ioan Gruffudd; more TV dramas promised; "Horatio Hornblower Navy," a course in the Morning Lecture

Series, NMM, fall 1999, re "Admiral of the Fleet, Viscount Hornblower of Smallbridge, 1776-1857"; there is a C.S. Forester Society, noted in 1999.

1139 Forester, Cecil Scott, ed. The Adventures of John Wetherell. NY: Doubleday; London: Penguin, 1953, 1954, 1994, 1995, 379 pp. An edition of an autobiograpy written in 1834; experiences in RN, including impressment, several shipwrecks, and years in a French prison; link to notorious HMS HERMOINE mutiny

1140 Forester, Cecil Scott. The Adventures of Horatio Hornblower. New York: Barnes & Noble, 2000. A reprint of the 11 vols.

1141 -------. The Age of Fighting Sail: The Story of the Naval War of 1812. NY: Doubleday, 1956, 284 pp. Non-fiction; a survey of the naval war.

1142 -------. The Barbary Pirates. London: Macdonald, 1956, 185 pp. A short history.

1143 [Hornblower career, #s 6, 7, and 8]. -------. Captain Horatio Hornblower. Boston: Little, Brown., 1938, 1939, 1967, 1997, 1141 pp. Beat to Quarters. Ship of the Line. Flying Colors. The original introduction of Hornblower; in various editions and combinations.

1144 [Hornblower career, # 9]. -------. The Commodore. London: Joseph, 1945, 1997, 320 pp.

1145 [Hornblower career, # 5]. -------. Hornblower and the Atropos. London: Joseph, 1953, 1975, 1997, 302 pp.

1146 [Hornblower career, # 4]. -------. Hornblower and the Crisis. London: Joseph, 1950, 1967, 1997, 175 pp. Incomplete, Forester died prior to completion.

1147 [Hornblower career, # 3]. -------. Hornblower and the Hotspur. London: Joseph, 1962, 1965, 1967, 1997, 287 pp.

1148 -------. The Hornblower Companion: An Atlas and Personal Commentary on the Writing of the Hornblower Saga. Boston: Little, Brown, 1964, 1998, 1999, ix, 149 pp. Describes all of the main incidents of the Hornblower novels; how the novels were written and the context.

1149 -------. The Hornblower Novels of C.S. Forester. 11 vols. Cranbury, CT: Scholars, 1997. A paperback set.

1150 -------. The Indomitable Hornblower. Boston: Little, Brown, 1963, 998 pp. A combination-trilogy: Commodore, Lord. . ., and Admiral of the West Indies.

1151 [Hornblower career, # 2]. -------. Lieutenant Hornblower. Boston: Little, Brown, 1951, 1997.

1152 -------. Long before Forty. London: Joseph, 1967, 254 pp. A memoir by Forester.

1153 [Hornblower career, # 10]. -------. Lord Hornblower. Boston: Little, Brown, 1946, 1997, 322 pp.

1154 [Hornblower career, # 1]. -------. Mr. Midshipman Hornblower. Boston: Little, Brown, 1950, 1997, 310 pp.

1155 -------. Nelson. London: Bodley Head; Indianapolis: Bobbs-Merrill, 1929, 1944, 1946, 1952, 2001, 352 pp. Forester admitted this was written when he was a "hack" biographer, a prototype for the Hornblower novels; no scholarly apparatus; more literary than historical.

1156 -------. Young Hornblower. Boston: Little, Brown, 1960, 672 pp. A combination-trilogy: Mr. Midshipman. . ., Lieutenant. . ., and Hornblower of the Atropos.

1157 Forges, Paul E.D. Histoire de Nelson d'apres les Depeches officielles et ses Correspondances Privees. Paris, 1860. A standard French biography of Nelson.

1158 Forster, Johann Reinhold. Observations Made During a Voyage Round the World. London: Robinson; Honolulu: U Haw P, 1778, 1996, lxxviii, 446 pp. Ed: Nicholas Thomas; when Joseph Banks decided not to go on subsequent voyages, Cook recruited Forster as chronicler; fluent in 17 languages; Cook-Forster relations deteriorated; in fact, 3 accounts of the 2nd voyage: this, that of Cook, and that of the son of Forster; 4 introductory essays.

1159 -------. The RESOLUTION Journal of Johann Reinhold Forster, 1772-1775. 4 vols. Publications of the Hakluyt Society, 2nd ser, vols. 152-55. London: Hakluyt Society, 1982, xvii, 831 pp. Ed: M. Hoare; a daily diary of the 2nd voyage; much detail.

1160 Forte, A.D.M. "The Identification of the Fifteenth-Century Ship-Types in Scottish Legal Records." MM, 84 (February 1998): 3-12. Sources from Scottish archives; various depictions of ship-types.

1161 Fortescue, John W. Dundonald. English Men of Action series. London: Macmillan, 1895, 227 pp. A short biography of Cochrane by the noted army historian; M. Lewis praised it.

1162 -------. A History of the British Army. 13 vols. NY: Macmillan; NY: AMS, 1899-1930, 1976; Vol. III only. Mechanicsburg: Stackpole, 2001, 263 pp. Fortescue, 1859-1933, librarian at Windsor Castle and official historian; this standard history equivalent to Clowes for RN; biased and judgmental, e.g., in section on the Armada: "Elizabeth must bear the chief share of the blame. The woman who in her imbecile parsimony starved the fleet. . . . It was no thanks to the

Queen that the Spanish invasion was repelled" (I., p. 151) and the Baltimore campaign of 1813 in which the British suffered 290 casualties: ". . . useless and almost wicked sacrifice for no object except to bring prize-money to the Navy. . . . unfortunately, not the first nor the last disaster attributable to the same cause" (X., p. 149).

1163 Foster, Janet and Sheppard, Julia, eds. British Archives: A Guide to Archive Resources in the United Kingdom. NY: Stockton, 1982, 1984, 1989, 1991, 1995, lviii, 834 pp. Over 1200 entries describing archival resource centers; alphabetical listing by town location; centers, e.g., record offices, national libraries, college and university libraries, museums, and reading rooms.

1164 Foster, S.M. "Some Aspects of Maritime Activity and the Use of Sea Power in Relation to the Crusading States, 1096-1169." D.Phil. diss, Oxford, 1978, 444 pp. A scholarly study of naval activity.

1165 Foster, Simon. Hit the Beach!: Amphibious Warfare from the Plains of Abraham to San Carlos Water. London: Arms, 1995, 224 pp. Illustrated; a general description of features of amphibious campaigns, e.g., surprise, superiority, cooperation, and speed; then, 4 case studies, e.g. Quebec; not comprehensive and difficult reading to follow.

1166 Fothergill, Brian. Sir William Hamilton: Envoy Extraordinary. London: Faber, 1969, 1973, 459 pp. Hamilton had fought in the Seven Years' War, then, envoy to Naples; death of first wife, Emma as his mistress, then wife; Nelson to Naples; Hamilton recalled; Merton Place and death.

1167 Fowler, Elaine W. English Sea Power in the Early Tudor Period, 1485-1558. Folger Booklets series. Ithaca: Cornell UP, 1965, 73 pp. For the Folger Library; touted as the age of reconnaissance and age of empire; Cinque Ports superseded by East Anglia and West Country ports, especially Bristol; 1545: the creation of the Navy Board, was the birth of English naval power; the traditional, even outdated, version.

1168 Fowler, Kenneth, ed. The Hundred Years' War. Problems in Focus series. London: Macmillan, 1971, 210 pp. Essays by noted scholars, e.g., C.F. Richmond on the war at sea: series of French attacks along south coast, the battle of Sluys, a combined French-Spanish-Geneose attack by galleys on Portsmouth, and French and English hired Geneose, Castile, Aragon, and Portuguese galleys.

1169 Fox, Frank. The Story of the British Navy: The Ramparts of Empire. London: Black, 1910, 1913, vi, 271 pp. A traditional tale, Nelson being "the crowning achievement."

1170 Fox, Frank L. A Distant Storm: The Four Days' Battle of 1666. Rotherfield: Boudriot, 1996, xiii, 425 pp. Illustrated; a great epic battle fought off the entrance to the Thames, but not the decisive one of the 2nd Dutch War; this work is comprehensive: administration, ordnance, personnel, other navies, e.g., French and Danes.

1171 -------. "The English Naval Shipbuilding Programme of 1664." MM, 78 (August 1992): 277-92. As Anglo-Dutch relations deteriorated again, preparation for the navy; Pepys, Deane, and Christopher Pett involved.

1172 -------. Great Ships: The Battle Fleet of King Charles II. London: Conway, 1980, 208 pp. Folio size, a magnificent production, 250 illustrated, e.g., many beautiful paintings, detailed drawings, and schematics; marine artists introduced, most being Dutch, e.g., Willem Van de Veldes, father and son.

1173 -------. "Hired Men-of-War, 1664-1667." MM, 84 (February 1998): 13-25. Re use of hired warships, in this case, in the 2nd Dutch War; list of the ships.

1174 Fox, Peter, ed. Cambridge University Library: The Great Collections. Cambridge: Cambridge UP, 1998, 296 pp. Illustrated; one of the great central libraries; enormous collection; building has appearance of a huge fortress.

1175 Francais et Anglais en Mediterranee de la Revolution francaise a l'independence de la Grece, 1789-1830: IIIes Journees franco-britanniques d'histoire de la marine, Toulon, 14-16 November 1990. Vincennes: Marine, 1992, 330 pp. Anglo-French historians; 21 essays from a conference, in French and English; on naval competition in the Mediterranean, 18th and 19th centuries, e.g., British occupation of Toulon, the Egyptian campaign, and maintenance of a British fleet in the Mediterranean.

1176 Frank, Stuart. The Book of Pirate Songs. Sharon: Kendall Whaling Museum, 1998, viii, 124 pp. An excellent collection of 62 songs and ballads, e.g., democratic virtues touted, pirate lifestyles, and women in buccaneers' clothing; omits Gilbert and Sullivan and Robert L. Stevenson.

1177 Franklin, John. Navy Board Ship Models, 1650-1750. London: Conway; Annapolis: NIP, 1989, vi, 186 pp. Folio size, 300 illustrations; 26 examples of official ship models used by the Admiralty and dockyards.

1178 Franzen, Anders. The Warship VASA: Deep Diving and Marine Archaeology in Stockholm. Stockholm: Norstedt, 1962, 1966, 1974, 88 pp. Illustrated; by the director of the project to raise VASA, a project of the 1950s; built for service in 30 Years' War by Gustav II; launched in 1627 and sank on maiden voyage in Stockholm harbor in 1628.

1179 Fraser, Edward. The Enemy at Trafalgar: An Account of the Battle from Eye-Witnesses' Narratives. London: Hodder, 1906, xix, 436 pp. Descriptions from a collection of letters and dispatches from French and Spanish observers.

1180 -------. "HMS VICTORY." MM, 8 in 6 parts (1922): various. At the time SNR launched the campaign to preserve and rebuild, this series which covers the present ship and predecessors, e.g., of 1559, 1618, 1675, and 1733.

1181 -------. The LONDONs of the British Fleet: How They Faced the Enemy on the Day of Battle and What Their Story Means to Us Today. London: Lane, 1908, xiv, 455 pp. The story of HMS LONDONs.

1182 -------. Napoleon the Gaoler: Personal Experiences. . . of British Sailors and Soldiers during the Great Captivity. London: Methuen, 1914, x, 312 pp. Illustrated; a summary of the experiences of POWs.

1183 -------. The Sailors Whom Nelson Led: Their Doings Described by Themselves. London: Methuen, 1913, xii, 354 pp. Illustrated; a collection of records and reminiscences from subordinates of Nelson.

1184 Fraser, Flora. Emma, Lady Hamilton. Alt. title: Beloved Emma. NY: Knopf, 1986, 1987, x, 356 pp. A popular biography; born Emma Lyon in 1765; a fascinating story.

1185 Frazer, E.J.S. "The Pitt-Newcastle Coalition and the Conduct of the Seven Years' War, 1757-1760." D.Phil. diss, Oxford, 1976. A detailed analysis of the interaction between domestic politics and the formation of war policy.

1186 Fredriksen, John C. Free Trade and Sailors' Rights: A Bibliography of the War of 1812. Bibliographies and Indexes in American History, # 2. Westport: Greenwood, 1985, 1997, xiii, 399 pp. Over 6000 entries, most on U.S.; no annotation, no evaluation.

1187 -------. War of 1812 Eyewitness Accounts: An Annotated Bibliography. Bibliographies and Indexes in Military Studies, # 8. Westport: Greenwood, 1997, 328 pp. Over 900 sources listed, American, British, and Canadian; from letters, diaries, journals, and memoirs.

1188 Freeman, A.Z. "A Moat Defensive: The Coast Defense Scheme of 1295." Speculum, 42 (1967): 442-62. England was threatened from France, Scotland, Gascony, and Wales; Edward I prepared for defense by dividing coasts into defense zones and appointing local leaders to be responsible, a basis for future structures.

1189 Freeman, Edward A. The History of the Norman Conquest: Its Causes and Its Results. 6 vols. Chicago: Chicago UP, 1867-1879, 1974. A controversial account, e.g., accusation that Freeman applied 19th century geography to 11th century circumstances; criticism from J.H. Round.

1190 -------. The History of the Norman Conquest of England. Classics of British Historical Literature. Chicago: Chicago UP, 1879, 1974, 259 pp. Intro: J.W. Burrow; reprint of Vol. III of previous entry.

1191 -------. William the Conqueror. Twelve English Statesmen series. London: Macmillan, 1888, viii, 205 pp. An older biography; no scholarly apparatus.

1192 Fregosi, Paul. Dreams of Empire: Napoleon and the First World War, 1792-1815. London: Hutchinson, 1989, 373 pp. Focus on the expansionist objectives of Napoleon, e.g., the Egyptian campaign was the first step of a dream of conquering India and the Orient.

1193 Fremantel, Sydney. "Nelson's First Writing with the Left Hand." MM, 36 (July 1950): 205-11. At Santa Cruz in July 1797, Nelson lost his right arm in an operation he commanded, writing a note the next day.

1194 French, Peter J. John Dee: The World of an Elizabethan Magus. London: Routledge, 1972, xii, 243 pp. John Dee, 1527-1608, an Elizabethan explorer.

1195 Friedman, Jonathan. "Captain Cook, Culture and the World System." J Pacific History, 20 (July 1985): 191-201. Historical anthropology; a contribution to the debate over "the apotheosis of Cook" by Obeyesekere.

1196 Friel, Ian. "Archaeological Sources and the Medieval Ship: Some Aspects of the Evidence." International J Nautical Archaeology, 12 (1983): 41-62. A lesson about sources and interpretation.

1197 -------. "The Documentary Evidence for Maritime Technology in Late Medieval England and Wales." Ph.D. diss, Keele, 1990. Re construction, maintenance and equipment of ships, 1300-1500.

1198 -------. The Good Ship: Ships, Shipbuilding and Technology in England, 1200-1520. Balt: JHUP; London: British Museum, 1995, 208 pp. 70 illustrations; based on the previous entry; focused on the 3-masted, ocean-going sailing ship; places English developments in the context of European setting, demonstrating advances in ship construction, skeletal framing, and rigging by the English; much from nautical archaological evidence.

1199 -------. "Henry V's GRACE DIEU and the Wreck in the River Hamble near Bursledon, Hampshire." International J Nautical Archaeology, 22 (February 1993): 3-19. The 4th and last of the "great" ships of Henry V; conclusion: it was GRACE DIEU.

1200 Friendly, Alfred. Beaufort of the Admiralty: The Life of Sir Francis Beaufort, 1774-1857. London: Hutchinson; NY: Random House, 1977, 362 pp. The great Hydrographer of the Navy, originating the Beaufort Scale on wind force and Arctic exploration; an excellent biography.

1201 Frost, Alan. Arthur Phillip, 1734-1814: His Voyaging. Melbourne: Oxford UP, 1987, x, 320 pp. Exquisite production, maps, and illustrated; Phillip was commander of the First Fleet, settler of Botany Bay, and 1st Governor of New South

Wales; dual objective: convict colony and/or strategic base, ongoing matters of debate; voyage, May 1787-January 1788; no further supply or contact until arrival of Second Fleet, June 1790; conclusion: Phillip deserves more credit for founding Australia.

1202 -------. [British Maritime Expansion in the Indian and Pacific Oceans, 1764-1815]. In 2001, noted as "just completed."

1203 -------. Convicts and Empire: A Naval Question. Melbourne: Oxford UP, 1980, xv, 240 pp. 1787, a naval officer, Cook, to New South Wales; 1786, Pitt government plan to establish penal colony; as described in previous entry, Phillip to New South Wales, also a naval operation; to build naval base and exclude French and Dutch interventions, thus a strategic initiative.

1204 Frost, Alan and Samson, Jane, eds. Pacific Empires: Essays in Honour of Glyndwr Williams. Melbourne: Melbourne UP, 1999, viii, 334 pp. 13 papers from a conference, Simon Fraser University, April 1978, on Captain Cook; Beaglehole created "our hero" image of Cook; Williams credits Edmund Halley as the original; other papers on the Hydrographic Office, and an enduring search for a Cook image.

1205 Froude, James A. English Seamen in the Sixteenth Century: Lectures Delivered at Oxford. NY: Scribner; London: Longman, 1895, 1923, 309 pp. Intro: Ashley Froude; 9 lectures; reviews voyages of Hawkins and Drake; England as "sea cradle"; Froude criticized for negligent research and errors; Froude died shortly after these lectures.

1206 -------. Froude's Spanish Story of the Armada and Other Essays. Gloucester: Sutton, 1892, 1988, viii, 262 pp. Ed: A.L. Rowse; Froude biased against Tudors, saw Hawkins and Drake as pirates, and Medina Sidonia as effete; incorporated new Spanish sources; anxious to present Spanish perspective and "correct" some of his interpretations in the next entry; revived interest in Armada.

1207 -------. History of England from the Fall of Wolsey to the Defeat of the Spanish Armada. 12 vols. NY: Scribner, 1856-1870, 1893. The classic historical narrative of the period, 1529-1588; hero is Henry VIII; nationalistic, anti-Catholic, anti-Irish, anti-Elizabeth; notorious for vigorous judgments and for errors.

1208 Fry, Howard T. "Alexander Dalrymple: Cosmographer and Servant of the East India Company." Ph.D. diss, Cambridge, 1967. The basis of the next entry.

1209 -------. Alexander Dalrymple, 1737-1808, and the Expansion of British Trade. London: Cass, 1970, xxvii, 330 pp. Fwd: R.A. Skelton; Dalrymple shifted the focus from expansion through colonialism to expansion through trade; in the process, reshaped the pattern of British trade.

1210 Frye, Susan. "The Myth of Elizabeth at Tilbury." Sixteenth Century J, 23 (Spring 1992): 95-114. Questions if legendary appearance of Elizabeth and her speech to the forces at Tilbury ever occurred; reviews origins of the "myth" and sources for the event.

1211 Fudge, John D. <u>Cargoes, Embargoes, and Emissaries: The Commercial and Political Interaction of England and the German Hanse, 1450-1510</u>. Toronto: U Toronto P, 1995, xxi, 265 pp. Trade in the Middle Ages, the Hanse, a confederation of German towns; Anglo-Hanse trade altered radically; late 1460s, war and English shift to Cologne.

1212 Fuller, Mary C. "The Age of Expansion: Recounting Renaissance Voyages." Ph.D. diss, Johns Hopkins, 1990, 279 pp. Enterprises of the English in North and South America; records of discovery and narratives of the voyages.

1213 -------. <u>Voyages in Print: English Travel to America, 1576-1624</u>. Cambridge: Cambridge UP, 1995, xiii, 210 pp. A literary study; Hakluyt and voyages of Gilbert, Ralegh, and John Smith; need to demythologize; "protoimperial haplessness" and the psychodrama of nation-building; debunking?

1214 Fuller-Eliott-Drake, Elizabeth Douglas. <u>Family and Heirs of Sir Francis Drake</u>. 2 vols., London: Smith, 1911. The standard geneaological work on the Drake family.

1215 Furbank, P.N. and Owen, W.R. <u>The Canonisation of Daniel Defoe</u>. New Haven: Yale UP, 1988, viii, 210 pp. Questions some of Defoe "canon," e.g., Charles Johnson, author of pirate history, is not Defoe.

1216 ------- and -------. <u>A Critical Bibliography of Daniel Defoe</u>. London: Pickering, 1998, xxxvii, 319 pp. Continuation of the previous entry.

1217 ------- and -------. <u>Defoe De-Attributions: A Critique of J.R. Moore's Checklist</u>. London: Hambledon, 1994, xxxiv, 161 pp. Attributions of Moore in his <u>Checklist</u>, 1960, questioned; 570 titles "unrealistic"; conclusion: 252 items not Defoe's, especially not Johnson's <u>History</u>.

1218 Furneux, Rupert. <u>Invasion: 1066</u>. NY: Prentice-Hall, 1966, 288 pp. A popular account.

1219 -------. <u>The Seven Years' War</u>. <u>The British at War</u>. London: Hart, 1973, 208 pp. Seen as a turning-point in British history; features: "to encourage the others," Pitt, Louisbourg, Quebec, and Quiberon Bay.

1220 Fury, Cheryl A. "Elizabethan Seamen: Their Lives Ashore." <u>International J Maritime History</u>, 10 (June 1998): 1-40. A neglected topic; study of wills and parish records; to correct the image as drunken, debaunched, and ne'er-do-wells; in researching, noted emphasis on marriage, family, community, and retirement.

1221 -------. <u>Tides in the Affairs of Men: The Social History of Elizabethan</u>

Seamen, 1580-1603. Contributions in Military Studies, # 214. Westport: Greenwood, 2002, xii, 293 pp. During the age of maritime expansion, to use "history from below" approach; to study the lives of the seafaring community, e.g., pressures, health, and capabilities of the crew and the ships, civilian and war; meticulous research; adds depth and breadth; in the tradition of E.P. Thompson.

1222 Gaibrois, Manuel Ballesteros. Juan Caboto. Valladolid: Casa-Museo, 1997, 286 pp. Occasion of the quincentennial of Cabot voyage; little is known about Cabot; John disappeared and son, Sebastian, claimed his exploits; this a collection of most that is known.

1223 Gaines, Edwin M. "Outrageous Encounter: The CHESAPEAKE-LEOPARD Affair of 1807." Ph.D. diss, Virginia, 1960, 174 pp. A scholarly study as a case study of Anglo-American relations with emphasis on maritime grievances, e.g., impressment.

1224 Galdos, Benito P. Trafalgar. Madrid: N.p., c. 1870, 2001. A Spanish fictional account, still in print in 2001; demonstrates perceptions of the Spanish and the profound and enduring impact of the battle; anti-French, praise for Spanish heroes, and reverence for Nelson.

1225 Gale, Robert L. Richard Henry Dana, Jr. Twayne's U.S. Authors series. NY: Twyane, 1969, 190 pp. Emphasis on personal experiences of Dana.

1226 Gallagher, Patrick and Cruickshank, Don W., eds. God's Obvious Design: Papers for the Spanish Armada Symposium, Sligo, 1988. Woodbridge: Boydell; London: Tamesis, 1988, 1990, vii, 256 pp. Illustrated; an international quadricentennial symposium, Sligo being near the most important wreck site on the Irish coast; the title from a letter to Philip II announcing the death of Mary, Queen of Scots; scholars from Spain, Britain, Ireland, and Holland; a series of significant papers, e.g., on the extreme weather, details on the Spanish guns, "myths" of the Armada, observations about comparative survivability of Mediterranean- and Atlantic-built ships, and questions about "decisiveness"; includes the account of Cuellar.

1227 Gallay, Alan, ed. Colonial Wars of North America, 1512-1763: An Encyclopedia. Military History of the U.S., vol. 5. NY: Garland, 1996, xxxiii, 858 pp. 650 essays by 130 experts; topics: e.g., privateering, sea laws, "Western Design" of Oliver Cromwell, and 140 biographical studies.

1228 Galvin, Peter R. Patterns of Pillage: A Geography of Caribbean-Based Piracy in Spanish America, 1536-1718. NY: Lang, 1999, 271 pp. An imaginative discussion of the geographic context; presents pirate haunts and strongholds; accounts by pirates, e.g., Exquemeling and Dampier, and popular writers, e.g., Charles Johnson, R.L. Stevenson, and Philip Gosse; distinguished the terms describing piracy chronologically: corsairs, buccaneers, and freebooters, respectively, for 16th, 17th, and 18th centuries; good bibliography and maps.

1229 -------. "The Pirates' Wake: A Geography of Piracy and Pirates as Geographers in Colonial Spanish America, 1536-1718." Ph.D. diss, Louisiana State, 1991. The basis of the previous entry.

1230 Gameson, Richard, ed. The Study of the Bayeux Tapestry. NY: Boydell, 1997, xiii, 216 pp. An anthology, presenting 11 classic studies plus his own, an excellent synthesis.

1231 Gamlin, Hilda. Emma, Lady Hamilton: An Old Story Re-told. Liverpool: Howell, 1891, xii, 299 pp. An example of the "pre-expose" phase; insists as a fact that Emma-Nelson relationship was "just good friends."

1232 -------. Nelson's Friendships. 2 vols. London: Hutchinson, 1899, x, 753 pp. Preface: John Hargreaves; Mrs. Gamlin died in 1898, completion by Mary Hargreaves; denounced "certain scandalmongers" and a series of "forged letters" re Emma-Nelson relationship; Emma to Naples for her education and as "ward" of Hamilton; Horatia Nelson Ward was an adopted child; Lady Nelson depicted as villain.

1233 Garbett, H.J.G. "The SHANNON and the CHESAPEAKE." JRUSI, 57 (June 1913): 797-802. One of a series of British defeats early in the War of 1812; in previous decades rare for a defeat by RN, then a series.

1234 Gardiner, Anne B. "Swift on the Dutch East India Merchants: The Context of 1672-1673 War Literature." Huntington Library Quarterly, 54 (Summer 1991): 235-52. Gulliver's Travels, 1726, as an anti-Dutch diatribe; Gulliver's voyage to the Far East included many opportunities to denounce the Dutch.

1235 Gardiner, D.A. "The History of Belligerent Rights on the High Seas in the Fourteenth Century." Law Quarterly Review, 48 (1932): 521-46. Enlightening on the origins of the law of the sea and aspects of piracy and privateering.

1236 Gardiner, Leslie. The British Admiralty. London: Blackwood; Annapolis: NIP, 1968, 1970, 418 pp. By a RN veteran; light-hearted, idiosyncratic, superficial, and anecdotal with no scholarly apparatus; touted as administrative history of 500 years of chicanery and patronage over ability; covered chronologically.

1237 [Wars of the French Revolution and Napoleon, 1793-1815, vol. IV of 6]. Gardiner, Robert, ed. The Campaign of Trafalgar, 1803-1805. Chatham Pictorial Histories series, co-sponsored by the National Maritime Museum, Greenwich. London: Chatham, 1997, 192 pp. Super folio size, profusely illustrated in color; essays by experts; a superlative series, currently 6 vols.; celebrating the high point of naval power under the sail; Nelson a key figure in the essays; reproduction of over 1500 paintings, prints, and drawings; pertinent essays by experts throughout the series; features eyewitness accounts; Gardiner ed. of 5 of the 6, Richard Woodman of vol. V.

1238 Gardiner, Robert. "The First English Frigates." MM, 61 (May 1975): 163-72. Re the 6th-rate, from 20-24 guns; for commerce protection; the French were the first to build "true" frigates.

1239 Gardiner, Robert, ed. The First Frigates: Nine-Pounders and Twelve-Pounder Frigates, 1748-1815. London: Conway, 1992, 128 pp. One of a series on frigates by the premier authority; the first frigates were designed by the French; RN adopted; 5th and 6th rates, 2-decks, 20 to 44 guns; Nelson called them "the eyes of the fleet"; detailed drawings and schematics.

1240 [Wars of the French Revolution and Napoleon, 1793-1815, vol. II of 6]. Gardiner, Robert, ed. Fleet Battle and Blockade: The French Revolutionary War, 1793-1797. Chatham Pictorial Histories series, co-sponsored by the National Maritime Museum, Greenwich. London: Chatham; Annapolis: NIP, 1997, 192 pp. Another in this superb series.

1241 Gardiner, Robert. "The Frigate Designs of 1755-1757." MM, 63 (February 1977): 51-70. Fascinating account of the development of the design of frigates and frigate classes; conclusion: by the mid-1750s, a thoughtful and coherent policy of small cruiser design had emerged in RN.

1242 -------. Frigates of the Napoleonic Wars. London: Chatham; Annapolis: NIP, 2000, xv, 192 pp. Folio size, illustrated; an in-depth study of this legendary ship class by the premier expert on this subject; 3rd in a series on frigates, plus articles.

1243 -------. The Heavy Frigate: Eighteen-Pounder Frigates. London: Conway, 1994, 127 pp. Folio size, illustrated; the 2nd in the series on frigates; subsequent volumes are planned to follow on these heavy frigates, coverage of those of the 19th century; extensive collaboration with NMM.

1244 [Wars of the French Revolution and Napoleon, 1793-1815, vol. VI]. Gardiner, Robert, ed. The Naval War of 1812. Chatham Pictorial Histories series, co-sponsored by the National Maritime Museum, Greenwich. London: Chatham, 1998, 192 pp. Another in this superb series.

1245 [Wars of the French Revolution and Napoleon, 1793-1815, vol. I]. Gardiner, Robert, ed. Navies and the American Revolution, 1775-1783. Chatham Pictorial Histories series, co-sponsored by the National Maritime Museum, Greenwich. London: Chatham, 1996, 192 pp. Another in this superb series.

1246 [Wars of the French Revolution and Napoleon, 1793-1815, vol. III]. Gardiner, Robert, ed. Nelson against Napoleon: From the Nile to Copenhagen, 1798-1801. Chatham Pictorial Histories series, co-sponsored by the National Maritime Museum, Greenwich. London: Chatham, 1997, 192 pp. Intro: Roger Morriss; another in this superb series.

1247 Gardiner, Robert. Warships of the Napoleonic Era. Blueprint series. London:

Chatham; Annapolis: NIP, 1999, 160 pp. Folio size, illustrated; co-sponsor: NMM and its Ships Plan Collection; includes original draughts of each of the ship types.

1248 [NRS 13, 17, 30, 37, 41, and 66]. Gardiner, Samuel R. and Atkinson, C.T., eds. Letters and Papers Relating to the First Dutch War, 1652-1654. 6 vols. Publications of the Navy Records Society, vols. 13, 17, 30, 37, 41, and 66. London: NRS, 1899-1930, xx, 431, xx, 507, xviii, 452, xiv, 396, xvi, 429, and xiv, 379 pp. Atkinson took over as health of Gardiner declined; some complaints about poor translation from the Dutch; includes documents from the Dutch Admiralty; descriptions, e.g., series of incidents over "honoring" the flag; operations in the Channel and North Sea.

1249 Gardner, G.H. "On the Formation of Reserves of Officers and Seamen for the Royal Navy, and the Evils and Inadequacy of Impressment to Provide the Same." JRUSI, 15 (1871): 601-42. A review of the Reserve program; conclusion: impressment was a failure.

1250 Gardner, W.J.R. "The State of Naval History." Historical J, 28 (September 1995): 695-705. A review article, e.g., works of Jan Glete, Richard Harding, and J.R. Bruijn; praise for Rodger, Hattendorf, Goldrick, Friedman, Brown, and Lambert.

1251 Garfield, Leon. Child O'War: The True Story of a Boy Sailor in Nelson's Navy. NY: Holt, 1972, 128 pp. Illustrated; re John Theophilus Lee, to RN at age 5; met Nelson and Emma Hamilton; observed mutinies of 1797; written in 1836; edition assisted by David Proctor.

1252 Garlick, Harry. The Final Curtain: State Funerals and the Theatre of Power. Amsterdam: Rodopi, 2000, 252 pp. Case studies, e.g., funerals of George Monck, Nelson, Wellington, Lincoln, Churchill, John Kennedy, and Princess Diana; thesis: state funerals are a means by which the Establishment buttresses its power through propaganda; curious compilation; a clear pro-American bias.

1253 Garratt, G.T. Gibraltar and the Mediterranean. NY: Coward, 1939, 351 pp. A history of the fortress, somewhat superficial; written at the time of a serious fascist threat associated with the Spanish Civil War.

1254 Garrett, George P. Death of the Fox. NY: Doubleday, 1971, 739 pp. A fictional biography of Sir Walter Raleigh; 1 of a trilogy on the Elizabethan period.

1255 Gasciogne, John. Joseph Banks and the English Enlightenment: Useful Knowledge and Political Culture. Cambridge: Cambridge UP, 1994, xi, 324 pp. Banks, 1743-1820, naturalist on the 1st Cook voyage, later President, Royal Society for 40 years; a pioneer of and propagandist for science.

1256 -------. Science in the Service of Empire: Joseph Banks, the British State and the Uses of Science in the Age of Revolution. Cambridge: Cambridge UP, 1998, vii, 247 pp. Continuation of the previous entry; not a government minister but very influential; special interest in sheep and Kew Gardens; Sandwich was his patron, he was patron of Bligh.

1257 Gates, David. The Napoleonic Wars, 1803-1815. London: Arnold, 1997, xx, 304 pp. A history of Napoleon and his times; praise for the military brilliance of Napoleon; reviews the literature, counting 220,000 works on the topic; critical of Owen Connelly.

1258 -------. The Spanish Ulcer: A History of the Peninsular War. London: Allen; London: Pimlico, 1985, 1986, 2002, xiv, 557 pp. Touted as superseding the monumental Charles Oman history; chapter on sea power and on logistical difficulties.

1259 Gathorne-Hardy, Geoffrey M. The Norse Discoverers of America: The Wineland Sagas. Oxford: Clarendon, 1921, 1970, 304 pp. An important but dated history of Vinland voyages.

1260 Gatty, Margaret and Gatty, Alfred. Recollections of the Life of the Rev. A.J. Scott, DD, Lord Nelson's Chaplain. N.p., 1842, vii, 302 pp. Re the chaplain of HMS VICTORY by his daughter and son-in-law.

1261 Gautier, Maurice Paul. Captain Frederick Marryat: L'Homme et L'Oeuvre. Etudes Anglaises, #41. Paris: Dedier, 1973, 518 pp. The definitive biography, in French; scholarly; Marryat was quite popular in France.

1262 Gavine, David. "Navigation and Astronomy Teachers in Scotland outside the Universities." MM, 76 (February 1990): 3-12. Notable that Scotland took important initiatives, especially programmes in math, astronomy, and navigation; and elsewhere, medicine.

1263 Gaziello, Catherine. L'Expedition de Laperouse, 1785-1788: Replique francaise aux voyages de Cook. Paris: CTHS, 1984, 323 pp. Re the French equivalent to the Cook voyages.

1264 Geertz, Clifford. "Culture War." New York Review of Books, 42 (30 November 1995): 4-6. Coverage of the Obeyesekere vs Sahlins anthropological debates re Cook and Pacific exploration.

1265 George, Christopher T. Terror on the Chesapeake: The War of 1812 on the Bay. Shippensbury: White Mane, 2000, ix, 213 pp. A detailed account of British campaigns of 1813; deaths of Admiral Peter Parker and General Ross due to poor intelligence; noted other failures.

1266 Gerin, Winifred. Horatia Nelson. NY: Oxford UP, 1970, xiv, 350 pp. A biography of the daughter of Nelson, Horatia, 1801-1881; much on Emma Hamilton.

1267 Germani, Ian. "Combat and Culture: Imagining the Battle of the Nile." Northern Mariner, 10 (January 2000): 53-72. An instance of dramatic escalation of the ferocity of international conflict.

1268 Geyl, Pieter. Napoleon, For and Against. New Haven: Yale UP, 1949, 1965, 1976, 1986, 477 pp. Trans: Olive Renier; by the preeminent Dutch historian; a model and commendable approach to historiography, a series of excerpts for and against Napoleon over time, 1815-1940s.

1269 -------. The Netherlands in the Seventeenth Century. 2 vols. I: 1609-1648. II: 1648-1715. London: Benn, 1936, 1961, 1963. A definitive history by the best of historians.

1270 -------. Revolt of the Netherlands, 1556-1609. NY: Barnes, 1932, 1966, 1980. Coverage of the period before the previous entry; includes the crucial Elizabethan intervention.

1271 Gibbs, Lewis. The Silver Circle: Sir Francis Drake, A New Re-appraisal. London: Dent, 1963, 1964, xii, 168 pp. Pseud: Joseph W. Cove; a biography; critical of Drake as a bold, bad man, a common pirate; discussion of sources.

1272 Gibson, John D. "Sir Julian Corbett on Amphibious Operations." Marine Corps Gazette, 82 (March 1998): 68-73. Sees Corbett as the ultimate disciple of Clausewitz: war as the extension of politics; guerre de course preferable to "great battle" thesis; sea operations to facilitate land operations; a timely strategic theorist.

1273 Gibson, John S. Ships of the '45: The Rescue of the Young Pretender. London: Hutchinson, 1967, xviii, 172 pp. Preface: James Fergusson; the untold story of operations of RN in Scottish waters during the crisis; weak on scholarship.

1274 Gifford, Edwin and Gifford, Joyce. "The Sailing Performance of Anglo-Saxon Ships as Derived from the Building and Trials of Half-Scale Models of the SUTTON HOO and Graveney Ship Finds." MM, 82 (May 1996): 131-53. Anglo-Saxon use of the sea was more extensive than previously believed; the Romans regarded them as powerful and dangerous; capable of evaluating performance using these models based on actual ships.

1275 Gilbert, Arthur N. "The AFRICAINE Courts-Martial: A Study of Buggery and the Royal Navy." J Homosexuality, 1 (1974): 111-23. A case of 1816: 4 crewmen hanged for buggery and 2 punished with 200 lashes for "uncleanliness"; the last death sentence for buggery in RN was 1829.

1276 -------. "Buggery and the British Navy, 1700-1861." J Social History, 10 (Fall 1976): 72-98. Buggery was a capital offense in RN until the 1860s, the punishment seen as more serious than that for murder; only 1 instance of pardon in 150 years; from the records, fewer cases in the army and no instances of execution.

1277 Gilbert, Bil. "The Battle of Lake Erie." Smithsonian, 25 (January 1995): 24-32. 10 September 1813, Oliver Hazard Perry led Americans to victory.

1278 Gilbert, George. Captain Cook's Final Voyage: The Journal of Midshipman George Gilbert. Honolulu: U Haw P, 1982, viii, 158 pp. Ed: Christine Holmes; the 3rd voyage, RESOLUTION and DISCOVERY; search for the Northwest Passage, the "geographical chimera pursued by Englishmen"; Cook was killed; Bligh was a master.

1279 Giles, Frank. Napoleon Bonaparte: England's Prisoner. London: Constable, 2001, 206 pp. A controversial study of the life and death of Napoleon on St. Helena; description of how the British treated Napoleon; author aimed to rehabilitate Sir Hudson Lowe, gaoler of Napoleon.

1280 Gilkerson, William. The Ships of John Paul Jones. Annapolis: NIP, 1987, iv, 83 pp. Accounts of the 7 ships associated with Jones; painting of each.

1281 Gill, A.A.M. "Ship Money during the Personal Rule of Charles I: Politics, Ideology and the Law, 1634 to 1640." Ph.D. diss, Sheffield, 1991. The politics of ship money, its impact, and consequences.

1282 Gill, Anton. The Devil's Mariner: A Life of William Dampier, Pirate and Explorer, 1651-1715. London: Joseph, 1997, xx, 396 pp. Dampier, an explorer who propagandized successfully and was an expert navigator.

1283 Gill, Conrad. Merchants and Mariners of the Eighteenth Century. London: Arnold; NY: St. Martin, 1961, 176 pp. Re Thomas Hall who died in 1748; service in merchant marine, slave trade, and as privateer; life on the lower deck.

1284 -------. The Naval Mutinies of 1797. Manchester: Manchester UP, 1913, xix, 412 pp. From research in Admiralty records; a comprehensive account including Spithead and 3 phases at the Nore; conclusion: causes were social, discontent over conditions, and political, general unrest.

1285 Gill, Edward. Nelson and the Hamiltons on Tour. Stroud: Sutton, 1987, x, 112 pp. For the Nelson Museum of Monmouth; fwd: Keith Kissack; follows a tour of southern Wales by Nelson and the Hamiltons, 6 weeks in the summer of 1802, ostensibly to report on the state of timber in the Forest of Dean.

1286 Gillespie, Brenda G. On Stormy Seas: The Triumphs and Torments of Captain George Vancouver. Victoria: Horsdal, 1992, xvi, 298 pp. Fictionalized as if written by brother, John, a technique dubbed "creative non-fiction"; questionable; oblivious of the context of the voyages.

1287 Gilliam, Bates M. "The World of Captain Mahan." Ph.D. diss, Princeton, 1961, 224 pp. A scholarly appraisal; the historical analysis of Mahan was an attempt to compare early modern England to the situation of the U.S. in the 1890s with mixed results; Mahan stressed diplomacy.

1288 Gillmor, C.M. "Naval Logistics of the Cross-Channel Operation, 1066." Anglo-Norman Studies, 7 (1984): 105-31. Details on the preparations by William; construction and assembly of transports, route taken, and probable weather and wind conditions; sources vary on numbers, e.g., from 696 to 11,000.

1289 Giuseppi, Montagu S. Guide to the Contents of the Public Record Office. 3 vols. I: Legal Records. II: State Papers and Department Records. III: Documents Transferred, 1960-1966. London: HMSO, 1923-1969, 860 pp. A detailed description of holdings.

1290 [Glascock, William N.] Naval Sketch-Book: Or, the Service Afloat and Ashore. . . Interspersed with Copious Notes, Biographical, Historical, Critical and Illustrative. 2 vols. London: Colburn, 1826, 1835. "By an officer of rank," first published anonymously; includes chapters on discipline and punishment, e.g., he vehemently supported corporal punishment.

1291 Glasgow, Tom. "The Elizabethan Navy in Ireland, 1558-1603." Irish Sword, 7 (Winter 1966): 291-307. The primary role was transport of men and supplies, and for Ireland, arms and to overawe rebels.

1292 -------. "HMS TIGER." North Carolina Historical Review, 43 (Spring 1966): 115-21. The history of various ships by this name, e.g., flagship of Sir Richard Grenville on the occasion of a landing in North Carolina; the original, 1546, under Henry VIII.

1293 -------. "The Royal Navy. . . during the Reigns of the Tudors." MM, 49-59 (1963-1973): various. A series of 10 articles informative on RN, especially during the reigns of Henry VIII, Mary, and Elizabeth; types of warships, origins of the "Royal Navy," the office of LHA, the process of institutionalization, operations against the French, and oared vessels.

1294 Glass, J. "James Lind, MD: Eighteenth-Century Naval Medical Hygienist." J Royal Naval Medical Service, 35 (1949): 1-20, 68-86. The naval service of Surgeon's Mate James Lind; a study on health convinced him to revive a practice of the 16th century, citrus; later, a protege, Gilbert Blane, implemented the order of 1795, compulsory use of lemon juice.

1295 Glass, Robert E. "The Image of the Sea Officer in English Literature, 1660-1710." Albion, 26 (Winter 1994): 583-99. Re the navy as profession; "Jack Tar" moving up to officer status; the stereotype of naval serviceman.

1296 -------. "The Profession of Sea-Officer in Late Seventeenth-Century England." Ph.D. diss, California-Berkeley, 1990, 249 pp. The struggle for naval officers to gain professional status. Monograph promised.

1297 Glassey, Lionel K.J., ed. <u>The Reigns of Charles II and James VII and II</u>. London: Palgrave; NY: St. Martin, 1997, vi, 309 pp. 10 essays with revised interpretations, e.g., J.D. Davies on war and the armed forces: the navy was the true "British" force and James played a formative role; image of "Britannia" first used; the largest spending department and the dockyards as the largest industry.

1298 Glete, Jan. <u>Navies and Nations: Warships, Navies, and State Building in Europe and America, 1500-1860</u>. 2 vols. Stockholm: Almqvist, 1993, ix, 752 pp. One of the most significant works on naval history of the early modern period in several decades; an entry in the debate over the military revolution from a different approach; contends that the navy and the state are neglected while the army and the state are overemphasized; a global, structural, and comparative approach incorporating an assessment of 12 major and 40 minor navies of Europe and America over the long term, e.g., their size based on comparative statistics, their role in state-building, the production of warships, financial and economic factors, and powerful support of key interest groups, e.g., politicians and merchants; the first "modern" naval war, 1563-1570, in the Baltic Sea; neglect of maintenance of powerful naval forces could be fatal, e.g., Spain and the Dutch; many quantitative comparisons within 130 tables; 37 pages of notes, sources in 12 languages.

1299 -------. <u>War and the State in Early Modern Europe: Spain, the Dutch Republic and Sweden as Fiscal-Military States, 1500-1660</u>. <u>Warfare and History</u> series. London: Routledge, 2002, 304 pp. A contribution to the nation-building debate; the rise of permanent armies and navies; the models for Glete were Spain, the Dutch, and Sweden.

1300 -------. <u>Warfare at Sea, 1500-1650: Maritime Conflicts and the Transformation of Europe</u>. <u>Warfare in History</u> series. London: Routledge, 1999, 2000, viii, 231 pp. An approach considering such factors as technology, tactics, strategy, seamen, nations, and maritime wars; the connecting theme is use of violence at sea; the first maritime states were in the Baltic, then movement out into the Atlantic, then global, that final status as early as 1600-1650; conclusion: the key to transformation: permanent navies, centralized state power, and gun-armed warship technology; pertinent states were England, France, Portugal, Denmark-Norway, Sweden, and the Dutch; gun-foundry developments, chronologically: France, Burgundy, the Ottoman Empire, Venice, especially England, and the Dutch; interestingly, the chronological development of "great" ships: Normandy, France, Venice, and Scotland; extensive footnotes, sources in many languages.

1301 Glover, Michael. <u>The Peninsular War, 1807-1814: A Concise Military History</u>. Newton Abbot: David and Charles, 1974, 431 pp. A welcome, substantial but not overwhelming study; little on naval aspects; initiatives evolve, from French to balance to British.

1302 Glover, Richard G. <u>Britain at Bay: Defence against Bonaparte, 1803-1814</u>. London: Allen; NY: Barnes, 1973, 235 pp. A document-based analysis of British forces from recruitment to grand strategy, the motivating factor being the French invasion threat for which the French made massive preparations, e.g., boats, harbor facilities, infrastructure, and logistical arrangements; for the British, dependence on naval forces through Trafalgar, then offensive attacks, and, later, coastal defenses, e.g., Martello Towers and the Royal Military Canal; French created formidable naval forces supplemented by allies, e.g., Spain, Denmark, Holland, even Russia; neglected topic: renaissance of French battle fleet, e.g., SOTLs, from 34 in 1807 to 80 with 35 building in 1813; thus, danger to Britain remained past 1805, even 1808.

1303 -------. "English Warfare in 1066." EHR, 67 (January 1952): 1-18. A reassessment of opposing forces at the battle of Hastings; the traditional literature, e.g., Maitland, Davis, and Stenton, makes Norman victory inevitable but William did not believe that; one problem: the overconfidence of Harold after his own victory at Stamford Bridge.

1304 -------. "The French Fleet, 1807-1814: Britain's Problem and Madison's Opportunity." J Modern History, 39 (September 1967): 233-52. Challenges the "myth" of British command of the sea after the battle of Trafalgar; Madison praised for exploiting this situation.

1305 Goddard, David. "Exeter Maritime Museum: The Museum of the Evolved Boat." MM, 71 (May 1985): 201-14. The planning and opening of the museum, the focus: working boats; opened, June 1969, 23 boats on display.

1306 Goddard, J.C. "An Insight into the Life of Royal Navy Surgeons during the Napoleonic War." JRN Medical Service, 78 (1992): 27-36. General observations of the service.

1307 Godwin, George. Vancouver: A Life. NY: Appleton, 1931. An older biography.

1308 Goetzmann, William H. and Williams, Glyndwr. The Atlas of North American Exploration: From the Norse Voyages to the Race to the Pole. Norman: Okla UP, 1998, 224 pp. Lavishly illustrated; survey of the expeditions by award-winning scholars.

1309 Goffman, Daniel. Britons in the Ottoman Empire, 1642-1660. Seattle: U Wash P, 1998, xvi, 310 pp. Geneose, Venetians, and the French had preceded them; the Levant Company of 1581 set 3 trading factories and established relations; re traders, diplomats, and merchant ships.

1310 Goldenberg, Joseph A. "The Royal Navy's Blockade in New England Waters, 1812-1815." IHR, 6 (August 1984): 424-39. Touts as "a closer look"; the blockade by RN was not effective; the squadron from Halifax was unprepared, suffered from serious discipline problems, and resorted to impressment.

1311 Goldingham, C.S. "The Expedition to Portugal, 1589." JRUSI, 63 (August 1918): 469-78. The expedition was led by Drake and Norreys to attack Spanish naval forces and restore the Portuguese Pretender; all failed partly due to parsimony of Elizabeth.

1312 -------. "Naval Prize Money." JRUSI, 64 (1919): 98-104. Noted changes due to an act of 1918; presented history and background.

1313 -------. "The Navy under Henry VII." EHR, 33 (October 1918): 472-88. Previous reigns had meant deterioration; Henry VII expanded, building 6 ships, building the 1st drydock, and encouraging expansion of merchant ships.

1314 Goldrick, James and Hattendorf, John B., eds. Mahan Is Not Enough: The Proceedings of a Conference on the Works of Sir Julian Corbett and Admiral Sir Herbert Richmond. Newport: NWCP, 1993, viii, 405 pp. The works of Corbett and Richmond had been assigned at the War College for years; 14 essays from the proceedings of a conference, U.S. Naval War College, September 1992; essayists included James Goldrick, John Hattendorf, Clark Reynolds, Jon Sumida, and Barry Hunt.

1315 Goldsmid, Edmund M., comp. The Last Fight of the REVENGE and the Death of Sir Richard Grenville, AD 1591. 2 vols. Edinburgh: Private, 1886. An older, lengthy account of the battle.

1316 Goldsmith, William. The Naval History of Great Britain: From the Earliest Period with Biographical Notices. London: Jacques, 1825, 808 pp. An older, undistinguished history.

1317 Gooch, L. "Catholic Officers in the Navy of James II." Recusant History, 14 (1978): 276-80. The Test Act forbade Catholics to serve; 1686-1688, James appointed some Catholic officers to the navy, was warned, but ignored them; conclusion: the navy was never in danger of being taken over by Catholics.

1318 Goodman, Warren H. "The Origins of the War of 1812: A Survey of Changing Interpretations." Mississippi Valley Historical Review, 28 (1941): 171-86. A historiographical survey, e.g., Julius Pratt, Henry Adams, Louis Hacker, S.E. Morison, and H.S. Commager; reviews causes.

1319 Goodwin, Peter G. The Bomb Vessel GRANADO, 1742. The Anatomy of the Ship series. London: Conway, 1989, 125 pp. Illustrated; by the curator of HMS VICTORY, a nautical design engineer; a specialized ship was needed in preparation for the War of Jenkins's Ear; recounts design details and operational history.

1320 -------. The Construction and Fitting of a Sailing Man of War, 1650-1850. Alt. title: The Construction and Fitting of the English Man of War, 1650-1850. London: Conway; Annapolis: NIP, 1987, xii, 288 pp. Folio size, illustrated; a companion to the work of James Lee; much detail and drawings about construction, beams, bulkheads, and machinery.

1321 -------. Countdown to Victory: 101 Questions and Answers about HMS VICTORY. Portsmouth: Manuscript Press, 2000, 101 pp. Profusely illustrated; includes a history, details of armament, the crew, life aboard, Nelson, Trafalgar, and the restoration.

1322 -------. "The Influence of Iron in Ship Construction, 1660 to 1830." MM, 84 (February 1998): 26-40. A description and history.

1323 -------. The Naval Cutter ALERT, 1777. The Anatomy of the Ship series. London: Conway; Annapolis: NIP, 1991, 126 pp. Illustrated; cutters were versatile vessels, fast and well armed.

1324 -------. The 20-Gun Ship BLANDFORD. The Anatomy to the Ship series. London: Conway; Annapolis: NIP, 1987, 120 pp. Illustrated; a sixth-rate warship of the early 18th century; influenced the evolution of the frigate.

1325 Gopnik, Adam. "The Good Soldier: Critic at Large." New Yorker (24 November 1997): 106-14. A historiographical survey about Napoleon; estimated 45,000 biographical studies, those in French mostly hagiographic; English depictions, e.g., "deformed, megalomaniacal dwarf"; featured biography by Alan Schom; pertinent items, e.g., Toulon, Egyptian campaign, invasion plans, Trafalgar, and exiles.

1326 Gordon, Eleanor C. "Scurvy and Anson's Voyage Round the World, 1740-1744: An Analysis of the Royal Navy's Worst Outbreak." AmNep, 44 (Summer 1984): 155-66. The famous voyage, 3 years, 9 months; 8 ships and 1955 men set out; 1 ship and 145 men returned; conclusion: key factor was deficiency of fresh food; stimulated efforts at cure, e.g., James Lind.

1327 Gore, John. Nelson's Hardy and His Wife: Some Account of the Lives, 1769-1877. London: Murray, 1935, xvii, 252 pp. Re Thomas Masterman Hardy, flag-captain for Nelson; editing the extensive journals of Lady Hardy, later Lady Seaford.

1328 Gorman, Tom. Working Scale Model Merchant Ships. London: Chatham, 2001, 184 pp. About 250 illustrations; the standard reference work; comprehensive guide.

1329 Goss, James. Portsmouth-Built Warships, 1497-1967. Emsworth: Mason, 1984, 111 pp. Over 300 vessels, described in chronological order, SWEEPSTAKE to ANDROMEDA and including battleships, e.g., HMS DREADNOUGHT, ROYAL SOVEREIGN, and QUEEN ELIZABETH.

1330 Gosse, Philip H.G. A Bibliography of the Works of Captain Charles Johnson. London: Dulau, 1927. A listing of his works.

1331 -------. Hawkins: Scourge of Spain. Golden Hind series. London: Lane; NY:

Harper, 1930, xii, 290 pp. Re the great 16th-century naval warrior; touted as neglected and overshadowed by Drake and others; exploits in slave trade, depredations against Spain, and the Armada.

1332 -------. The History of Piracy. London: Cassell, 1932, 1954, x, 349 pp. A substantial survey, e.g., Barbary corsairs, Elizabethan and Jacobean pirates, and pirates of the West and East.

1333 -------. "Piracy." MM, 36 (October 1950): 337-49. Defines, operations in English seas, chronological sequences of rise and fall, and anecdotes.

1334 -------. The Pirates' Who's Who: Giving Particulars of the Lives and Deaths of the Pirates and Buccaneers. NY: Fanklin, 1924, 1968, 328 pp. An alphabetical listing with brief biographies, Aisa to Andrew Zekerman.

1335 Gosset, W.P. The Lost Ships of the Royal Navy, 1793-1900. NY: Mansell, 1986, x, 157 pp. A substantial reference guide, e.g., a chronological listing of ships lost from all causes, geographical index, and courts-maritial index.

1336 Gough, Barry M. British Mercantile Interests in the Making of the Peace of Paris, 1763: Trade, War, and Empire. Lewiston: Mellen, 1992, ix, 156 pp. An assessment of the treaty, its implications, and consequences; Britain gained much territory, creating a "global reach capability."

1337 -------. Distant Dominion: Britain and the Northwest Coast of North America, 1579-1809. Vancouver: UBCP, 1980, 190 pp. One of a trilogy on exploration and operations off the northwest coast.

1338 -------. A Guide to the Literature on Maritime Strategy and History. In 2000, noted as forthcoming; a proposed historiographical survey.

1339 -------. "The Influence of Sea Power upon History Revisited: Vice-Admiral P.H. Colomb, RN." JRUSI, 135 (Summer 1990): 55-63. Colomb was influential re navalism, the influence of history on sea power, and among those of the Mahan era; the security of Britain depended on command of the sea.

1340 -------. The Northern Coast: British Navigation, Trade, and Discoveries to 1812. Pacific Maritime Studies series, #9. Vancouver: UBCP, 1992, xiv, 279 pp. A general survey by the authority on the Pacific Northwest; the history of exploration and discovery, e.g., Drake, Anson, Cook, Vancouver, Spanish, and Russians; similar to Distant Dominion.

1341 -------. The Royal Navy and the Northwest Coast of North America, 1810-1914: A Study of British Maritime Ascendancy. Vancouver: UBCP, 1971, xvi, 294 pp. One of a trilogy; the ongoing presence of RN in the area was decisive, e.g., vs. competition with the U.S. and Russia.

1342 -------. "The Royal Navy and the Northwest Coast of North America, 1810-1910." Ph.D. diss, London, 1969. The basis of the previous entry.

1343 -------. "Sea Power and South America: The 'Brazils' or South American Station of the Royal Navy, 1808-1837." AmNep, 50 (Winter 1990): 26-34. Details on an important regional command.

1344 Gould, Richard A., ed. Shipwreck Archaeology. Albuquerque: UNMP, 1983, xiv, 273 pp. Sponsored by the School of American Research; a series of articles, e.g., Gould on the essentials of nautical archaeology and on the wrecks of the Armada.

1345 Gould, Rupert T. "Bligh's Notes on Cook's Last Voyage." MM, 14 (October 1928): 371-85. Re the 3rd voyage, the account annotated by Bligh, the Master; the notes are revealing.

1346 -------. "John Harrison and his Timekeepers." MM, 21 (April 1935): 115-39. From the annual lecture, SNR, 1935; the story of older methods of calculation, the huge reward offered by Parliament, and the timepieces developed by Harrison.

1347 -------. The Marine Chronometer: Its History and Development. London: Potter; Woodbridge: Antique, 1923, 1960, 1976, 1989, xvi, 401 pp. Fwd: Francis Dyson; re the problem of calculating longitude at sea and the contribution of John Harrison; also Cook and HMS BOUNTY.

1348 Grabsky, Phil. The Great Commanders: Alexander, Caesar, Nelson, Napoleon, Grant, Zhukov. London: Boxtree, 1993, 192 pp. Folio size, fabulous colored illustrations; fwd: David Chandler; stress on great generalship; 3 of the 5 pertinent to this study.

1349 Gradish, Stephen F. "The Establishment of British Seapower in the Mediterranean, 1689-1713." Canadian J History, 10 (1975): 1-16. Published posthumously, Gradish died 1974; reign of William incorporated expansion and containment of Louis XIV; re the Grand Alliance; RN blockade extended from Brest into the Mediterranean opposite Toulon; need for base led to Rooke taking Gibraltar.

1350 -------. The Manning of the British Navy during the Seven Years' War. Rochester: Boydell, 1980, 1997, ix, 235 pp. For RHS; a model of social history; emphasis on administration; need for 80,000 seamen for war; resorted to impressment because Parliament would not consider alternatives.

1351 -------. "The Manning of the British Navy during the Seven Years' War, 1755-1762." Ph.D. diss, Toronto, 1971. The basis for the previous entry.

1352 -------. "Wages and Manning: The Navy Act of 1758." EHR, 93 (January 1978): 46-67. At the time of mobilization, Parliament responded to some concerns, e.g., timely pay and allotments, but ignored others, e.g., low pay and uncertain length of service; conclusion: lack of action contributed to later mutinies of 1797.

1353 Graf, Miller. Arctic Journeys: A History of Exploration for the Northwest Passage. American University Studies, # 121. NY: Lang, 1992, vii, 377 pp. Re the great saga, time after time, from Irish monks to the Tudors and beyond; much illusion and false hope; an adequate study.

1354 Gragg, Larry D. "The Port Royal Earthquake." HisTod, 50 (September 2000): 28-34. Jamaica, June 1692, at the time, a most prosperous town, notorious for piracy; 2/3s of town disappeared into the sea, 2000 died; archaeological expedition of 1959 and after by Texan A&M.

1355 Graham, Eric J. "The Impact of Mercantilism and War on the Scottish Marine, 1651-1791." Ph.D. diss, Strathclyde, 1998. A study of the impact of this trading system of the era; themes, e.g., the Navigation Acts, warfare, smuggling, and navigation aids; the Act of Union resolved the conflicts.

1356 -------. "The Scottish Marine during the Dutch Wars." Scottish Historical Review, 61 (April 1982): 67-74. During the Dutch Wars, 1650s, 1660s, and 1670s, the Scottish were late in exploiting privateering opportunities against the Dutch, very slow in the 1650s but acceleration subsequently; the basis for recovery of the Scottish marine.

1357 Graham, Gerald S. Empire of the North Atlantic: The Maritime Struggle for North America. Toronto: Toronto UP, 1950, 325 pp. By the distinguished and prolific Canadian, Rhodes Professor at the University of London; a scholarly study of empire and sea power; the English exploitation of the Atlantic connection.

1358 -------. "Napoleon's Naval Gaolers." J Imperial and Commonwealth History, 7 (October 1978): 3-17. Re RN responsibility for "the Corsican ogre," to ensure he remained on St. Helena, 1815-1821; RN leased St. Helena from the East India Company; naval command was the Cape Station; annual cost, 400 thousand pounds sterling.

1359 [NRS 104]. Graham, Gerald S. and Humphreys, R.A., eds. The Navy and South America, 1807-1823: Correspondence of the Commanders-in-Chief. . . . Dedicated to Sir Charles Webster. Publications of the Navy Records Society, vol. 104. London: NRS, 1962, xxxiv, 394 pp. The Iberian monarchies were overthrown "freeing" colonies in South America; RN set up South American Station to deal with a complex situation, states declaring independence; demonstration of diplomatic capabilities of station admirals; Cochrane is ubiquitious.

1360 Graham, Gerald S. The Royal Navy in the War of American Independence. London: HMSO, 1976, 24 pp. For NMM; to support a bicentennial exhibition, NMM; a summary of operations and personnel.

1361 -------. Sea Power and British North America, 1783-1820: A Study in British Colonial Policy. Cambridge: Harvard UP; NY: Greenwood, 1941, 1969, 302 pp. The focus is on the operation of the Navigation Acts and the formative period of Anglo-American relations; British emphasis on its merchant marine as "a nursery for seamen."

1362 [NRS 94]. Graham, Gerald S., ed. The Walker Expedition to Quebec, 1711. Publications of the Navy Records Society, vol. 94. London: NRS, 1953, xx, 430 pp. An expedition to Canada during the War of Spanish Succession.

1363 Graham, Winston. The Spanish Armadas. London: Collins; NY: Doubleday, 1972, 1988, 288 pp. Folio size, illustrated, exquisite layout; a popular history by a noted novelist; an account of the Armada of 1588 and 3 attempts of 1596; opened with account of the ceremony of 1554 off the Isle of Wight welcoming Philip II as king-to-be of England.

1364 Grainge, Christine and Grainge, Gerald. "The Pevensey Expedition: Brilliantly Executed Plan or Disaster?" MM, 79 (August 1993): 261-73. From sources, e.g., Bayeux Tapestry and Anglo-Saxon Chronicle; details on operations of William in sailing across the Channel to Pevensey and the reactions of Harold and the Anglo-Saxon fleet.

1365 Grainger, John D. "The Conquest of the Cape, 1806." Army Quarterly and Defence J, 123 (July 1993): 316-22. Re the expeditionary force, 120 ships and 6000 men to capture the Cape Colony from the Dutch, commanded by Hugh Popham; actually the 2nd capture, the first in 1795.

1366 [NRS 135]. Grainger, John D, ed. The Royal Navy on the River Plate, 1806-1807. Publications of the Navy Records Society, vol. 135. Aldershot: Scolar, 1996, xiv, 384 pp. A documented study of RN in the River Plate area, a British attack on the Spanish Viceroyalty led by Hugh Popham; details on a extensive amphibious operation, 1800 troops landed and were repulsed; in the long run, aided independence from Spain and Popham was promoted to Vice Admiral.

1367 Grainger, John D. "Who Was Hornblower?" HisTod, 49 (October 1999): 32-33. First appeared in 1937; Forester had researched Naval Chronicle; conclusion: a combination of Cochrane and Home Riggs Popham.

1368 [NRS 44]. Grant, James, ed. The Old Scots Navy from 1689 to 1710. Publications of the Navy Records Society, vol. 44. London: NRS, 1914, lx, 448 pp. A history of the navy of Scotland; emphasis on the significance of sea power; a factor in Anglo-Scottish relations.

1369 Gray, Colin S. The Leverage of Sea Power: The Strategic Advantage of Navies in War. NY: Free Press, 1992, xii, 372 pp. Re the uses and practices of sea power; 10 case studies, e.g., Rome vs. Carthage, Venice, English vs. Spain, and English vs. France; also where the failure of sea power was fatal, e.g., Carthage,

Napoleon, Germany, and Russia.

1370 Gray, Colin S. and Barnett, Roger W., eds. Seapower and Strategy. Annapolis: NIP, 1989, xvi, 396 pp. A series of essays reviewing strategies of sea power, e.g., Theopile Auge for French commerce warfare, Mahan, first to formulate a general theory, and Corbett, less grand than Mahan but more sophisticated.

1371 Gray, Ernest A., ed. The Diary of a Surgeon in the Year 1751-1752 by John Knyveton, Surgeon's Mate, HMS LANCASTER. London: Appleton, 1937, 1942, xiv, 322 pp. Serious question about authenticity; a graphic description of life on the lower deck and medical work aboard ships of RN in the 18th century, e.g., press gang, summary justice, cruel and brutal punishments, scurvy, the horrors of war, and a plea for fresh air and improved ventilation.

1372 Great Britain. Admiralty. The Navy List. ___ vols. London: HMSO, various. The annual, or more frequently since 1814, listing of details of all ships of RN in commission.

1373 Great Britain. Public Record Office. Admiralty Court-Martial Records: Admiralty 1. London: PRO, various. The extensive records of all official courts-martial of RN; excellent source material.

1374 Great Britain. Public Record Office. Admiralty Digests: Heads and Sections. London: PRO, 1935. An explanation by the secretary about the organization of the individual heads and sections of the Admiralty Digests, the secretarial record of all correspondence and documents of RN; this bookkeeping aid is essential for primary research on RN.

1375 Great Britain. Public Record Office. Admiralty Digests: IND Numbers by Year. The massive notebooks maintained by the Admiralty clerks recording all correspondence and documents pertinent to RN, each volume in chronological order, year by year.

1376 Great Britain. Public Record Office. List of Admiralty Records Preserved in the Public Record Office. London: HMSO; NY: Kraus, 1904, 1963. A listing of the holdings of Admiralty Records at the PRO.

1377 Great Britain. Public Record Office. Summary of Records. 2 vols. I: High Court of the Admiralty. II: Admiralty Captured Enemy Documents and Departmental Records. London: HMSO, 1962-1969. A detailed explanation and listing of how all Admiralty records are filed and stored; an essential guide for access to records of RN.

1378 Green, Charles. SUTTON HOO: The Excavation of a Royal Ship-Burial. London: Merlin, 1968, 1988, 168 pp. Recounts the discovery of this remarkable ship burial; no body was present and identity of the king not determined.

1379 Green, Geoffrey L. "Anglo-Jewish Trading Connections with Officers and Seamen of the Royal Navy, 1740-1820." Jewish Historical Studies, 29 (1982): 97-122. Dickens noted Portsmouth was famous for mud, Jews, and sailors; poor Ashkenazi Jews developed tradesman businesses at naval bases.

1380 -------. The Royal Navy and Anglo-Jewry, 1740-1820: Traders and Those Who Served. Author published, 1989, 244 pp. The story of Jews in RN, e.g., shopkeepers at the dockyards, roving peddlers with official permission to board ships, and agents for prize money; obviously a neglected topic but of limited interest.

1381 Green, Jeremy N. Maritime Archaeology: A Technical Handbook. San Diego: Academic, 1990, xx, 282 pp. Illustrated; touted as superseding Muckelroy; sections on searching, recording, excavation, management, and research.

1382 Green, W. Spotswood. "The Wrecks of the Spanish Armada on the Irish Coast." Geographical J, 27 (1906): 429-48. A descriptive account.

1383 Greenberg, Stephen J. "Seizing the Fleet in 1642: Parliament, the Navy, and the Printing Press." MM, 77 (August 1991): 227-34. Little popular knowledge of RN and its activities was known; Parliament formulated publicity to attract seamen, e.g., an account by Warwick was printed and distributed; naval support proved decisive for Parliament in the Civil War.

1384 Greenhaw, Thomas D. "Factors Influencing Royal Naval Policy for the Mediterranean, 1702-1705." Ph.D. diss, Auburn, 1978, 187 pp. English to Mediterranean during War of Spanish Succession, but, at first, faced failure after failure; little cooperation from allies; incompetent leaders.

1385 Greenhill, Basil and Morrison, John. The Archaeology of Ships and Boats: An Introduction. London: Conway; Annapolis: NIP, 1976, 1995, 320 pp. Intro: W.F. Grimes; illustrated; by the longtime director of NMM; wide and deep scope, chronological and geographic; survey of boat finds from nautical archaeology; a synthesis of findings illustrating pertinent features of ships and boats from earliest times.

1386 Greenhill, Basil, ed. The Evolution of the Sailing Ship, 1250-1580. Keynote Studies: Mariner's Mirror. London: Conway, 1995, 264 pp. A collection of 70 articles from the first decades of publication; emphasis on the development of the ship.

1387 Greenhill, Basil. The Evolution of the Wooden Ship. NY: Facts; London: Batsford, 1985, 1989, 239 pp. Illustrated with drawings and schematics; presents the background and much detail on how to build wooden ships; for model builders.

1388 -------. James Cook, The Opening of the Pacific. London: HMSO, 1970, 32 pp. An illustrated booklet sponsored by NMM, commemorating the life and work of

Cook.

1389 -------. "The Mysterious Hulc." MM, 86 (February 2000): 3-18. A study of medieval ships; only iconographic evidence; types were keel, cog, and hulc.

1390 Greenhill, Basil, ed. The National Maritime Museum. London: Wilson, 1982, 144 pp. A colorful and informative book about NMM; 9 essays by experts, e.g., on navigation, paintings, hydrography, books, weapons, and astronomy.

1391 Greenhill, Basil, gen. ed. The Ship. 10 vol. series. London: HMSO, 1980-1981, 600 pp. I: Ships of the Ancient World by Sean McGrail. II: Long Ships and Round Ships by John Morrison. III: The Ship from 1550-1700. IV: The Ship, 1700-1820 by Alan McGowan V: Steam Tramps and Cargo Liners by Robin Craig. VI: Merchant Steamships, 1850-1970 by John Maber. VII: The Merchant Sailing Ship of the Nineteenth Century by Greenhill. VIII: Steam, Steel and Torpedoes: Warships of the Nineteenth Century by David Lyon. IX: DREADNOUGHT to Nuclear Submarine by Antony Preston. X: The Revolution in Merchant Shipping, 1950-1980 by Eugene Corlett. A series of 60-page illustrated pamphlets, each by a noted expert, covering the history of the ship.

1392 Greenhill, Basil and Gifford, Ann, comps. Women under Sail: Letters and Journals Concerning Women Travelling or Working in Sailing Vessels between 1829-1949. Newton Abbot: David and Charles, 1970, 1972, 213 pp. 8 first-person accounts of women immigrants, passengers, wives, daughters, and workers at sea; commentary about each; by husband and wife team.

1393 Greenwich Observatory: The Story of Britain's Oldest Scientific Institution, the Royal Observatory of Greenwich and Herstmonceux, 1675-1975. 3 vols. London: Taylor, 1975. On the occasion of the tricentenary, an extensive history of the observatory.

1394 Gregory, Desmond. Malta, Britain, and the European Powers, 1793-1815. Madison: Fairleigh Dickinson UP, 1996, xvii, 353 pp. The modern history of Malta; originally controlled by the Knights of St. John, a military-monastic order from the age of the Crusades; played an important role in Anglo-French conflict in the Mediterranean, e.g., Napoleon captured it en route to Egypt in 1798; it became a serious bone of contention before, during, and after the Peace of Amiens; concerned the national interests of Britain, France, and Russia.

1395 -------. Minorca, the Illusory Prize: The History of the British Occupation of Minorca between 1708 and 1802. Rutherford: Fairleigh Dickinson UP, 1990, 295 pp. The history of the strategic role of this island-naval base, the British occupying it by force on 3 occasions.

1396 -------. Napoleon's Jailor: Lt. Gen. Sir Hudson Lowe: A Life. Madison: Fairleigh Dickinson UP, 1996, 234 pp. Lowe, 1769-1844; commander of the forces guarding Napoleon, 1815-1821; had served in the Mediterranean, indeed, on

Corsica, and knew French and Italian.

1397 Grenfell, Russell. Horatio Nelson: A Short Biography. London: Faber, 1949, 1959, 1968, xvi, 247 pp. Ed: Stephen Roskill; a good, concise biography by an officer of RN; best on Nelson at sea.

1398 Grierson, Edward. The Fatal Inheritance: Philip II and the Spanish Netherlands. NY: Doubleday, 1969, xii, 390 pp. Re Spanish possession of the Low Countries and international developments, e.g., intervention by Elizabeth to aid rebellion and the Spanish campaign to put down rebellion, factors in the Armada campaign.

1399 Griffith, Paddy. The Art of War of Revolutionary France, 1789-1802. London: Greenhill, 1998, 304 pp. A critical re-evaluation of the French war machine, especially the rise of Napoleon; 12 chapters, # 11 on "The Navy"; the post-revolutionary purges devastated the French navy; essential was collaboration of Spain, the Dutch, the Danes, and others.

1400 -------. The Viking Art of War. London: Greenhill, 1995, 224 pp. A critical re-evaluation of the Vikings, stressing objectives of trading and settling.

1401 Griffiths, Anselm J. Impressment Fully Considered: With a View to Its Gradual Abolution. London: Norie, 1826, 262 pp. By an officer of RN; calling for alternatives.

1402 Grimble, Ian. The Sea Wolf: The Life of Admiral Cochrane. London: Blond, 1978, 2000, 433 pp. A biography; access to Dundonald papers; recounts service in navies of Britain, Chile, Peru, and Greece.

1403 Grocott, Terence. Shipwrecks of the Revolutionary and Napoleonic Eras. London: Chatham, 1997, xvi, 430 pp. An extensive chronicle of maritime tragedies using Lloyd's List, e.g., 1793-1816, a listing of British vessels, war and merchant, lost, e.g., from 1794-1800, 2967 merchant ships were lost.

1404 Groenveld, Simon. "The English Civil Wars as a Cause of the First Anglo-Dutch War, 1640-1652." Historical J, 30 (September 1987): 541-66. During this period, Anglo-Dutch relations changed dramatically, twice.

1405 Grohskopf, Bernice. The Treasure of SUTTON HOO: Ship-Burial for an Anglo-Saxon King. NY: Atheneum, 1963, 1970, xx, 168 pp. The story of the discovery, excavation, treatment, and display of this fantastic collection of artifacts; informative on the history of the Saxons and on "Beowulf."

1406 Grose, Clyde L. "The Anglo-Dutch Alliance of 1678. EHR, 39 (July 1924): 349-72. The backgrouond to the Anglo-Dutch alliance which included the marriage of William of Orange to Princess Mary; factors, e.g., the Catholicism of James, Duke of York, Anglo-French relations involving Charles II and Louis XIV, and future naval cooperation.

1407 Grossman, Anne C. and Thomas, Lisa Grossman. Lobscourse and Spotted Dog: A Gastronomic Companion to the Aubrey/Maturin Novels. NY: Norton, 1997, xxix, 304 pp. Fwd: Patrick O'Brian; by mother-daughter, "priestesses of the cult" or "O'Brianites" or "Amiable Sluts"; re early nineteenth-century naval cuisine, e.g., "Drowned Baby," white rats in onion sauce, and raised meat pie.

1408 Grotius, Hugo. De Jure Praedae. [The Law of Prize and Booty]. 1609, 1868. By the great Dutch jurist, 1583-1645, originally part of "the Freedom of the Seas" concept; full publication over 2 centuries later.

1409 -------. Mare Liberum. [Freedom of the Seas]. Oxford: Oxford UP, 1609, 1916. The single most influential book to support the doctrine of maritime prize under the law of nations.

1410 [NRS 137]. Grove, Eric J., ed. The Defeat of the Enemy Attacks on Shipping, 1939-1945. Publications of the Navy Records Society, vol. 137. Aldershot: Ashgate, 1997, xc, 380 pp. An edition of the Naval Staff History; describes the German campaign and its ultimate defeat.

1411 Grove, Eric J., ed. Great Battles of the Royal Navy: As Commemorated in the Gunroom, BRNC, Dartmouth. London: Arms; Annapolis: NIP, 1994, 1995, 288 pp. Fwd: Prince Philip; an illustrated historical tribute to RN; 25 essays on epic battles, e.g., Sluys, Armada, Quiberon Bay, Copenhagen, and Trafalgar; battles commemorated in the gunroom of Britannia Royal Naval College, Dartmouth.

1412 Grover, S.W.M. Short History of the Royal Marines. Aldershot: Gale, 1948, 68 pp. A brief history.

1413 Gruber, Ira D. "Admiral Lord Howe and the War for American Independence." Ph.D. diss, Duke, 1961, 487 pp. The basis of the next entry.

1414 -------. The Howe Brothers and the American Revolution. NY: Norton, 1972, 1975, ix, 396 pp. An analysis and explanation on the failure of the Howe brothers, Admiral Richard and General William; one factor was the continued effort at conciliation until too late; brothers blamed.

1415 Gruber von Arni, Eric. "Soldiers-at-Sea and Inter-Service Relations during the First Dutch War." MM, 87 (November 2001): 406-19. Reassessment of the administrative history of RN, 1509-1660, to "correct" Michael Oppenheim and others; army personnel were used to supplement seamen in times of shortage, they were used to enforce discipline, and army-navy rivalry intensified.

1416 Grummitt, David I. "Calais, 1485-1547: A Study in Early Tudor Government and Politics." Ph.D. diss, London, 1996. A study of the impact of Calais, the last English possession in France.

1417 -------. "The Defence of Calais and the Development of Gunpowder Weaponry in England in the Late Fifteenth Century." War in History, 7 (July 2000): 253-72. Victualler records proved informative; explanation of the unique survival of this English outpost.

1418 Guerres et Paix, 1660-1815. Vincennes: Historique, 1986, 1987, 328 pp. The proceedings of the Anglo-French Naval History Conference, Rochefort, March 1986; papers, e.g., a tribute to J.S. Bromley, John Hattendorf on George Byng, and W.R. Jones on literary images.

1419 The Guide to Federal Records in the National Archives of the United States. 3 vols. Wash: GPO, 1996, 2428 pp. The place to start research in the massive American national archives; over 400 chapters describing records of government agencies.

1420 Guide to the Public Record Office. Microfiche. London: PRO, 1999. A comprehensive reference guide listing the holdings, e.g., administration, record classes, and index.

1421 Guilmartin, John F. "The Galley in Combat: Tactical Exercises." MHQ, 9 (Winter 1997): 20-21. Revisionist; galley battles more than land-tactics at sea; tactics demanded technical acumen and sophistication.

1422 -------. Gunpowder and Galleys: Changing Technology and Mediterranean Warfare at Sea in the Sixteenth Century. Cambridge: Cambridge UP, 1974, xiv, 321 pp. In 1500, galleys were dominant in the Mediterranean but drastic change had occurred; traces developments in naval warfare; one factor was more powerful gunnery; theories of Mahan did not apply here.

1423 Gunn-Graham, T.I. "A Seventeenth-Century Warship Painting in the Aberdeen Maritime Museum." MM, 82 (May 1996): 159-64. Re the portrait of a Scottish warship, 60 guns.

1424 Gurney, Alan. Below the Convergence Voyages towards Antarctica, 1699-1839. NY: Norton, 1997, 315 pp. Re the renowned search for Terra Australis Incognita, the great southern continent, e.g., Halley and Cook; led to discovery of Antarctica.

1425 Guthrie, W.P. "Naval Actions of the Thirty Years' War." MM, 87 (August 2001): 262-80. The last flourish of old naval tactics; the Anglo-Dutch wars were to introduce the new; English naval forces at war against France and Spain.

1426 Gutridge, Tony. "Aspects of Naval Prize Agency, 1793-1815." MM, 80 (February 1994): 45-53. A study of prize money as recruitment device, especially for officers; explanation of procedures and legislation.

1427 [NRS 25]. Gutteridge, H.C., ed. Nelson and the Neapolitan Jacobins:

Documents Relating to the Suppression of the Jacobin Revolution at Naples, June 1799. Publications of the Navy Records Society, vol. 25. London: NRS, 1903, cxvii, 347 pp. Clarification of an important controversy, some say the most serious in the professional career of Nelson: Southey placed blame on Nelson for excessive action, including execution of a republican admiral, Francesco Caracciolo.

1428 Guttman, Jon. Defiance at Sea: Stories of Dramatic Naval Warfare. London: Arms, 1995, 192 pp. Illustrated; 14 individual engagements, e.g., REVENGE in 1591.

1429 Guttridge, Leonard F. Mutiny: A History of Naval Insurrection. Annapolis: NIP, 1992, x, 319 pp. A historical survey and synthesis of cases, e.g., "the world's most romanticized mutiny," the BOUNTY, also HERMIONE, Spithead, and the Nore.

1430 Guzman, Alonso Perez de, 7th Duke of Medina Sidonia. Orders Set Down by the Duke of Medina Sidonia, Lord General of the King's Fleet, to Be Observed in the Voyage toward England. London: Orwin, 1588, 16 pp. Trans: "T.P."; Guzman, 1550-1619, commander of the Armada; his orders to his fleet.

1431 Gwyn, Julian R.J. The Enterprising Admiral: The Personal Fortune of Admiral Sir Peter Warren. London: McGill-Queens UP, 1974, xvi, 292 pp. A fascinating study of the financial impact of war on naval officers; Warren gained his fortune from prize money and pursued entrepreneurial success; worth 160 thousand pounds sterling at death in 1752.

1432 -------. "The Personal Fortune of Admiral Sir Peter Warren." D.Phil. diss, Oxford, 1972. The basis of the previous entry.

1433 [NRS 118]. Gwyn, Julian R.J., ed. The Royal Navy and North America: The Warren Papers, 1736-1752. Publications of the Navy Records Society, vol. 118. London: NRS, 1973, xlvi, 464 pp. The North American Squadron was established in 1745 and expanded dramatically; Warren was a key figure.

1434 Gwyn, Julian R.J. "Shipbuilding for the Royal Navy in Colonial New England." AmNep, 48 (Winter 1988): 22-30. Some construction but native timber seen as inferior and colonists increasingly resisted; later shift to Canadian builders.

1435 Gye, Clara E.E., ed. Nelson: His Life as Told by Himself. N.p., 1905. An older biography; occasion on centenary of Trafalgar.

1436 Haas, James M. "The Introduction of Task Work in Royal Dockyards, 1775." J British Studies, 8 (May 1969): 44-68. A reform under the Sandwich administration; a reform which meant building and repairing a larger number of ships; an aspect of the history of trade unions, a conflict between tradition, efficiency, and corruption.

1437 -------. A Management Odyssey: The Royal Dockyards, 1714-1914. Lanham: UP America, 1994, vi, 243 pp. A study of administration; praise for Henry VIII and expansion, i.e., "the founder"; quality remained high but condemns the dockyards for poor management, high costs, weak direction, and corruption.

1438 -------. "The Royal Dockyards: The Earliest Visitations and Reform, 1749-1778." Historical J, 13 (June 1970): 191-215. Stresses high important and massive were the dockyards, the largest employer and industry; reform during the Sandwich administration.

1439 Habesch, David. The Army's Navy: British Military Vessels and their History since Henry VIII. London: Chatham, 2001, 240 pp. Re a fleet to support land forces, e.g., transport barges for the Board of Ordnance.

1440 Hacke, William. A Collection of Original Voyages: A Facsimile Reproduction. Providence: J.C. Brown Library, 1699, 1993, various. Intro: Glyndwr Williams; early English exploration of "South Seas," the Pacific off the coast of South America, e.g., Juan Fernandez Island; favorite of buccaneers, e.g., Basil Ringrose; Hacke a cartographer.

1441 Hackmann, William K. "English Military Expeditions to the Coasts of France, 1757-1761." Ph.D. diss, Michigan, 1969, 224 pp. An offensive strategy during Seven Years' War; cooperation of RN and army, e.g., Rochefort, St. Malo, Cherbourg, and Belle Isle; trial and error, increasing cooperation and success; nevertheless, Pitt not a strategic genius as depicted by some; credit to naval commanders, mixed results.

1442 Hackney, Noel C.L. HMS VICTORY. Classic Ships, Their History and How to Model Them series, # 1. London: Stephens, 1970, 96 pp. A shipbuilding programme for 12 STOL, first rate, 3-decks, 100 guns; 5th ship of that name; built at Chatham Dockyard; launched 1765, cost 63 pounds sterling.

1443 Hadfield, A.M. Time to Finish the Game: The English and the Armada. London: Phoenix, 1964, 228 pp. A popular study of the Armada campaign, before and during, she intends "to catch something of the secret of those days in time"; from the Netherlands, Spain, and England.

1444 Haig-Brown, Roderick L. Captain of the DISCOVERY: The Story of Captain George Vancouver. Toronto: Macmillan, 1956, 181 pp. Illustrations by Robert Banks; a short biography from the Canadian perspective.

1445 Hainsworth, Roger and Churches, Christine. The Anglo-Dutch Naval Wars, 1652-1674. Stroud: Sutton, 1998, 224 pp. Accounts of commercial and colonial rivalry and naval heroics; for the general reader.

1446 Hakluyt, Richard. Hakluyt's Voyages. Boston: Houghton, 1589, 1600, 1929, vi, 317 pp. Ed: Adrian Mott; Hakluyt, the younger, 1552-1616; Richard Hakluyt, an elder cousin, and Samuel Purchas, all propagandists for empire and commerce, didactic; collections of descriptive accounts of voyages, "the very papers of empire," e.g., Cabot, the Northeast Passage, Frobisher, Drake, and the Northwest Passage.

1447 -------. The Hawkins Voyages. Publications of the Hakluyt Society. London: Hakluyt Society, 1878. Ed: Clements Markham; an account of 3 voyages to the coasts of Africa and the West Indies.

1448 Hakluyt, Richard and Hakluyt, Richard. Original Writings of the Two Hakluyts. 2 vols. Cambridge: Cambridge UP, 1589, 1965, lx, 1035 pp. Eds: David B. Quinn and R.A. Skelton; selections from both Hakluyts, the Younger, 1552-1616, a preacher and the Elder, a lawyer; facsimile of the edition of 1589.

1449 Hakluyt, Richard. The Portable Hakluyt's Voyages. NY: Viking, 1965, xx, 522 pp. Ed: Irwin Blacker; selections for the general reader.

1450 -------. The Principal Navigations: Voyages, Traffics, and Discoveries of the English Nation. 12 vols. and other editions. Glasgow: MacLehose, 1589-1600, 1903-1905, 1965. An anthology; the collection was encouraged by government officials; emphasis on geography, commerce, economics, and the navy, e.g., an account of the Armada.

1451 -------. Virginia Voyages from Hakluyt. Oxford: Oxford UP, 1973, 195 pp. Eds: David B. Quinn and M. Alison; these voyages, 1584-1600, an example of overseas expansion.

1452 Hale, John Richard. The Story of the Great Armada. London: Nelson, 1910, 1913, vi, 350 pp. A full account and still useful.

1453 Hale, J.R. "1588 and All That." New York Review of Books (16 February 1989): 30-32. An extensive review of pertinent works related to the quadricentennial; noted that accounts about the Armada are a story, not an event or a place.

1454 Hall, Bert S. Weapons and Warfare in Renaissance Europe: Gunpowder, Technology, and Tactics. Johns Hopkins Studies in the History of Technology. Balt: JHUP; Estover: Plymbridge, 1997, xiii, 300 pp. Introduction of gunpowder from the 13th century; emphasis on technology, e.g., gun casting and gun carriages; an entry in the debate over the military revolution.

1455 Hall, Christopher D. British Strategy in the Napoleonic War, 1803-1815. Manchester: Manchester UP, 1992, xii, 239 pp. An assessment of British strategy from the perspective of the British Cabinet; recounts resources and commitment of forces and finances to ultimately defeat Napoleon; factors, e.g., shipbuilding, transportation, intelligence, amphibious operations, e.g., Walcheren, and continental commitment, e.g., the Peninsular campaign; noted resource and personnel shortages, e.g., wood supply and recruitment for army and navy.

1456 -------. "Factors Influencing British Strategic Planning and Execution during the Napoleonic Wars, 1803-1815." Ph.D. diss, Exeter, 1984, 362 pp. The basis of the previous entry.

1457 -------. "The Royal Navy and the Peninsular War." MM, 79 (November 1993): 403-18. Fills a gap, the role of the navy in the Peninsular campaign; 1500 miles of coastline, poor roads, and guerrilla operations made the navy role essential; convoy duties, bombardment of coast roads and shore, blockade, and troop movements.

1458 Hall, Darlene M. "The Navy of James IV of Scotland." Ph.D. diss, Pennsylvania State, 1998, 394 pp. A scholarly study of this extraordinary force.

1459 Halliwell, J.O. A Discovery that Shakespeare Wrote One or More Ballads or Poems on the Spanish Armada. London: Private, 1866. Halliwell, 1820-1889, researched and found writings of Shakespeare.

1460 [NRS 117, 121, and 122]. Halpern, Paul G., ed. The Keyes Papers. 3 vols. Publications of the Navy Records Society, vols. 117, 121, and 122. London: NRS, 1972-1981, xxiv, 547, xiv, 468, and xvi, 398 pp. The papers of the great admiral of World Wars I and II, active and involved in Gallipoli, Zeebrugge, and Combined Operations Headquarters.

1461 [NRS 126]. Halpern, Paul G., ed. The Royal Navy in the Mediterranean, 1915-1918. Publications of the Navy Records Society, vol. 126. London: NRS, 1987, xvi, 623 pp. By the noted expert on naval operations in the Mediterranean before and during World War I; primary documents.

1462 Hamilton, D.L. "Preliminary Report on the Archaeological Investigation of the Submerged Remains of Port Royal Jamaica, 1981-1982." International J Nautical Archaeology, 13 (February 1984): 11-26. A report of findings of this major nautical archaeology project.

1463 Hamilton, Earl J. American Treasure and the Price Revolution in Spain, 1501-1650. Harvard Economic Studies, # 43. Cambridge: Cambridge UP, 1934, 1965, 1970, xxxv, 428 pp. A classic in economic history; re the discovery, exploitation, production, and transportation of precious metals, especially gold and silver from Mexico and Peru, to Europe; central control was from Seville; the impact of this treasure on Europe; many tables and charts.

1464 Hamilton, George. A Voyage Round the World in His Majesty's Frigate PANDORA. Sydney: Hordern, 1793, 1998, xxxvii, 164 pp. Intro: Peter Gestner; by the surgeon; PANDORA was sent out to arrest the mutineers of BOUNTY in 1790; 14 were arrested; as search continued for Christian and 8 others, PANDORA was destroyed on the rocks; as with Bligh, a 1100 mile sailing to Timor in an open boat; return to England; court martial of mutineers.

1465 [NRS 12, 19, and 24]. Hamilton, R. Vesey, ed. Letters and Papers of Admiral of the Fleet Sir Thomas Byam Martin, GCB. 3 vols. Publications of the Navy Records Society, vols. 12, 19, and 24. London: NRS, 1898-1903, xxiv, 384, xvii, 416, and xxii, 399 pp. Vol. II was published before vol. I; Martin, 1773-1854; begins with service as a boy and young man; later operations, e.g., blockade of Brest, service in the Baltic where he met Tsar Alexander I; instrumental in saving Riga.

1466 [NRS 31]. Hamilton, R. Vesey and Laughton, John Knox, eds. Recollections of James Anthony Gardner, Commander, RN, 1775-1814. Publications of the Navy Records Society, vol. 31. London: NRS, 1906, xxii, 287 pp. Somewhat different; personal and social aspects of his career reminiscent of Roderick Random, including the crude language.

1467 Hammer, Paul E.J. "Myth-Making: Politics, Propaganda and the Capture of Cadiz in 1596." Historical J, 43 (September 1997): 621-42. An Anglo-Dutch expedition, seen as a counter-Armada; problems of command conflicts; another expedition in 1625 failed.

1468 -------. "New Light on the Cadiz Expedition of 1596." Historical Research, 70 (June 1997): 182-202. Recent research has added information; Essex had intelligence; the naval and some amphibious operations were successful, then, the city was abandoned.

1469 Hammersly, L.R., publisher. A Naval Encyclopaedia: Comprising a Dictionary of Nautical Words and Phrases, Biographical Notices and Records of Naval Officers; Special Articles of Naval Art and Science. . . together with Descriptions of the Principal Naval Stations and Seaports of the World. New York, 1881. Informative; emphasis is American.

1470 Hammond, Wayne N. "The Administration of the English Navy, 1649-1660." Ph.D. diss, British Columbia, 1974. Re the Interregnum; the navy was consistently loyal to Parliament and then, immediately acquiesced to the Restoration; the navy became engulfed in the political turmoil, financial support was diverted elsewhere and the situation deteriorated so that the Restoration offered hope.

1471 The Hamond Naval Papers, 1766-1825. Wilmington: Scholarly Resources, 1990. Microfilm, 3 rolls of 35mm, D3181; originally at the Library of the University of Virginia, 1966; re Captain Sir Andrew Snape Hamond, 1779-1862, e.g., commanding officer of HMS ROEBUCK, '44.

1472 Hampden, John, ed. Francis Drake, Privateer: Contemporary Narratives and Documents. London: Methuen, 1972, 286 pp. A collection with annotation of contemporary accounts, e.g., by the nephew and by Fletcher; not a biography.

1473 Hampshier, A. Cecil. The Royal Marines, 1664-1964. London: N.p., 1964, 77 pp. A history on the occasion of the tercentenary.

1474 -------. <u>Royal Sailors</u>. London: Kimber, 1971, 224 pp. Examples from the 17th century, e.g., James, Duke of York, brothers of George III, and William IV, who served under Nelson.

1475 Handel, Michael I. "Corbett, Clausewitz and Sun Tzu." <u>NWCR</u>, 53 (Autumn 2000): 106-24. Mahan followed Jomini, Corbett, Clausewitz; however, Corbett was closer to Sun Tzu, but never studied him; emphasis of 2 principles of Corbett: concentration of force and limited war; Corbett and Clausewitz appreciated the importance of politics in war.

1476 Hanna, Warren L. <u>Lost Harbor: The Controversy over Drake's California Anchorage</u>. Berkeley: U Cal P, 1979, xvii, 459 pp. A study in preparation for the quadricentennial; re the voyage of Drake along the west coast of North America during his circumnavigation; the anchorage, Nova Albion, during the summer of 1579, not identified nor has the mystery been solved; the debate was sponsored by the California Historical Society.

1477 Hannay, David. <u>Admiral Blake</u>. <u>English Worthies</u> series. NY: Appleton, 1886, viii, 194 pp. Hannay, 1853-1934, a journalist from England; a short biography of Blake emphsizing naval service, e.g., in the navy during the Commonwealth, operations against the Dutch, and operations in the Mediterranean.

1478 [NRS 3]. Hannay, David, ed. <u>Letters Written by Sir Samuel Hood, Viscount Hood, in 1781-1783</u>. <u>Publication of the Navy Records Society</u>, vol. 3. London: NRS, 1895, xlvii, 170 pp. Letters of Viscount Hood, e.g., describing the battle of the Chesapeake, Graves vs. de Grasse.

1479 Hannay, David. <u>Life of Frederick Marryat</u>. <u>Great Writers</u> series. London: Scott; NY: Gage, 1889, vii, 163 pp. A bibliography added by John Anderson; a biography of the naval officer and popular naval fiction writer.

1480 Hannay, David. <u>Naval Courts Martial</u>. Cambridge: Cambridge UP, 1914, 210 pp. A history and description.

1481 -------. <u>Rodney</u>. <u>English Men of Action</u> series. <u>The American Revolutionary</u> series. London: Macmillan; Boston: Gregg, 1891, 1903, 1910, 1920, 1972, vi, 222 pp. Intro: George Billias; a popular biography with no scholarly apparatus; obsolete.

1482 -------. <u>A Short History of the Royal Navy, 1217-1815</u>. 2 vols. London: Methuen, 1897-1909, 1914, xvi, 998 pp. A popular history by a journalist and writer of naval history; interesting date for the beginning.

1483 Hansen, Dagny B. "Captain James Cook's First Stop on the Northwest Coast: By Chance or by Chart?" <u>Pacific Historical Review</u>, 62 (November 1993): 475-84. A factor in Pacific exploration was the competition, e.g., with Spain and Russia; Cook to the coast, March 1778 at the 49th parallel, anchoring for a month; why that place at that time?

1484 Hansen, Hans Jurgen, ed. <u>Art and the Seafarer: A Historical Survey of the</u> <u>Arts and Crafts of Sailors and Shipwrights</u>. London: Faber, 1968, 297 pp. Trans: James and Inge Moore; folio size, many illustrations of art; on the architecture and ornamentation of ships, e.g., essay by E.H.H. Archibald; details for ship model enthusiasts.

1485 Hansen, Harold A. "The Sound Trade and the Anglo-Dutch Conflicts, 1640-1654." Ph.D. diss, UCLA, 1947. A review of a series of confrontations precipitating the 1st Dutch War.

1486 Harari, Yuval Noah. "Inter-frontal Cooperation in the Fourteenth Century and Edward III's 1346 Campaign." <u>War in History</u>, 6 (November 1999): 379-95. An analysis of the spatial scale of medieval wars, this the Hundred Years' War; in 1346, Edward III operated in Artois, Brittany, Normandy, and Gascony; was there a "grand strategy?"; a look at possibilities of communication, cooperation, and coordination.

1487 Harbron, John D. "Spain's Forgotten Naval Renaissance." <u>HisTod</u>, 40 (August 1990): 29-34. A revaluation of Spanish naval capabilities; survey of developments after 1588; examples of great ships, e.g., SANTISIMA TRINIDAD, 4-decker, made of teak wood and built in Havana in 1769; lost in storm after Trafalgar.

1488 -------. <u>Trafalgar and the Spanish Navy</u>. London: Conway; Annapolis: NIP, 1988, xiv, 178 pp. Illustrated, folio size; a re-evaluation of the operations and capabilities of the Spanish navy; conclusion: Spain was not in decline; the navy revived; 25 Spanish SOTL ships captured were incorporated into RN and actually preferred by British captains; presents details of the 15 SOTL at Trafalgar, their captains, and individual operations.

1489 Hardie, Robert P. <u>The Tobermory Argosy: A Problem of the Spanish Armada</u>. London: Oliver, 1912, vii, 67 pp. The saga of a Spanish ship which was sunk.

1490 Harding, Nicholas B. "North African Piracy, the Hanoverian Carrying Trade and the British State, 1720-1828." <u>Historical J</u>, 43 (March 2000): 25-47. An aspect of the "British composite state," i.e., combined England-Hanover; dealings with the pirates of North Africa and associated treaties linked both states.

1491 Harding, Richard. <u>Amphibious Warfare in the Eighteenth Century: The</u> <u>British Expedition to the West Indies, 1740-1742</u>. <u>Royal Historical Society Studies</u>, # 62. Woodbridge: Boydell, 1991, ix, 248 pp. By the editor of <u>Mariner's Mirror</u>; a thoroughly researched study of the Cartegana operation, a failure, but much was learned and corrected for future operations; Vernon was blamed, one problem being lack of interservice cooperation; but the operations and the politics were misunderstood and manipulated.

1492 -------. The Evolution of the Sailing Navy, 1509-1815. British History in Perspective series. London: Macmillan, 1995, ix, 181 pp. A synthesis of work of historians and nautical archaeologists, timely; development of a professional naval service and administrative structure; begins with the navy of the late middle ages, mostly armed merchant vessels, for use as transports across the Channel; designations: 1509-1603, navy royal; 1603-1642, English navy; 1642-1660, standing navy; 1660-1713, emergence of oceanic power; 1714-1815, oceanic supremacy; the navy was the largest single spending department of government and the largest organization of its kind in the world; conclusion: by 1815, at the end, RN was at the height: improved ships, tactics, management, administration, and public standing; due to Howe, Rodney, Keppel, Hughes, and Sandwich; outstanding historiographical survey.

1493 -------. "'A Golden Adventure': Combined Operations in the Caribbean, 1740-1742: A Re-examination of the Walpole Ministry's Response to War with Spain." Ph.D. diss, London, 1985. The basis of these entries.

1494 -------. "Sailors and Gentlemen of Parade: Some Professional and Technical Problems Concerning the Conduct of Combined Operations in the Eighteenth Century." Historical J, 32 (March 1989): 35-55. A scholarly reassessment of "conjunct operations," touted as the unique contribution of Pitt the Elder and praise for his choice of Wolfe, all perpetuated by Corbett; not so: divided command was not a problem in the 18th century and successes and failures have been exaggerated; actually, they were not so significant in the 18th century.

1495 -------. Seapower and Naval Warfare, 1650-1850. Warfare and History series. London: UCL; NY: Garland, 1998, 1999, xx, 356 pp. Another brilliant, scholarly synthesis; emphasis on the elements of sea power, e.g., sailing battlefleets and the SOTL.

1496 -------. [Unpublished paper]. "'there must be somewhere in England a place for an expert in maritime history': The Career of Cyril Northcote Parkinson, 1909-1993." Paper: Anglo-Ameican Historians Conference, 4-6 July 2001, Institute of Historical Research. Recounts the fascinating career of Parkinson, touting himself in the 1950s as Britain's only lecturer in maritime history; off to University of Singapore; formulated "Parkinson's Law" using RN as model, e.g., as ships decrease, admirals increase.

1497 Hardy, Adam. Battle Smoke. London: NEL, 1974, 126 pp. Hardy, 1921-___; nautical fiction series of the Nelson era; hero-seaman, George Abercrombia Fox, # 8.

1498 -------. Blood Beach. London: NEL, 1975, 110 pp. Fox, # 12.

1499 -------. Blood for Breakfast. London: NEL, 1974, 124 pp. Fox, # 6.

1500 -------. Boaders Away. London: NEL, 1975, 128 pp. Fox, # 10.

1501 -------. Close Quarters. London: NEL, 1977, 128 pp. Fox, # 13.

1502 -------. Court Martial. London: NEL, 1974, 124 pp. Fox, # 7.

1503 -------. Cut and Thrust. London: NEL, 1974, 126 pp. Fox, # 9.

1504 -------. Fireship. London: NEL, 1975, 126 pp. Fox, # 11.

1505 -------. Powder Monkey. London: NEL, 1973, 126 pp. Fox, # 5.

1506 -------. Press Gang. London: NEL, 1973, 112 pp. Fox, #3.

1507 -------. Prize Money. London: NEL, 1973, 120 pp. Fox, # 4.

1508 -------. Siege. London: NEL, 1972, 130 pp. Fox, # 1.

1509 -------. Treasure. London: NEL, 1972, 119 pp. Fox, # 2.

1510 Hardy, Evelyn. Survivors of the Armada. London: Constable, 1966, xiv, 186 pp. Dedicated to Garrett Mattingly; re links between Ireland and Spain, especially a common religion; but most of the survivors from the 2-dozen wrecks drowned or were slaughtered by locals; stories of Spanish progeny not true; weather was the decisive factor; included de Cuellar saga.

1511 Hardy, Jennifer K. "Mystic Seaport Museum." Historian, 55 (Spring 1993): 447-52. Originating from the Marine Historical Association in 1929; collects, preserves, and exhibits artifacts, traditions, and skills of maritime history; educational programmes.

1512 Hargreaves, Reginald. The Narrow Seas: A History of the English Channel, Its Approaches, and Its Immediate Shores, 400 BC-AD 1945. London: Sidgwick, 1959, 517 pp. The fascinating history of the Channel, e.g., the Cinque Ports and Thames Estuary.

1513 Haring, Clarence H. The Buccaneers in the West Indies in the Seventeenth Century. London: Methuen; Hamden: Archon, 1910, 1966, viii, 298 pp. Focused on French and English, e.g., Dampier and Wafer; distinguishes between freebooters, sea-rovers, buccaneers, privateers, pirates, corsairs, and filibusters, seen as a chronological sequence.

1514 Harkness, Deborah E. John Dee's Conversations with Angels: Cabala, Alchemy, and the End of Nature. Cambridge: Cambridge UP, 1999, xi, 252 pp. Dee, 1527-1608, polymath and occultist; revived interest in this contributor to science, navigation, astronomy, and the occult.

1515 -------. "The Scientific Reformation: John Dee and the Restitution of Nature." Ph.D. diss, California, Davis, 1994, 612 pp. The basis of the previous entry.

1516 Harland, John and Myers, Mark. <u>Seamanship in the Age of the Sail: An Account of the Shiphandling of the Sailing Man-of-War, 1600-1850</u>. London: Conway; Annapolis, NIP, 1984, 1987, 320 pp. Folio, profusely illustrated; impressive account and realistic, e.g., how a sailing warship actually handled.

1517 <u>The Harleian Miscellany: Or, a Collection of Scarce, Curious, and Entertaining Pamphlets and Tracts, as Well in Manuscript as in Print, Found in the Late Earl of Oxford's Library</u>. 8 vols. London: T. Osborne, 1744-1746, 1808-1811. Ed: T. Osborne; Earl of Oxford, 1689-1741; a unique and extensive collection of contemporaneous documents; coverage of the Armada.

1518 Harley, J.B., Woodward, David, et al., eds. <u>The History of Cartography</u>. Projected 6 vols. Chicago: Chicago UP, 1987-____, 2600 pp. An ambitious project, a multi-volume, illustrated, multi-disciplinary, general history with essays by the most prominent experts; monumental and comprehensive with global coverage, e.g., a map on wood from China of 300 BC; as of vol. II, 3rd part, 1998, 2600 pages; Vol. I, Part 1 and Vol. II, Parts 1, 2, and 3, with at least 4 more books projected.

1519 Harley, J.B. <u>The New Nature of Maps: Essays in the History of Cartography</u>. Balt: JHUP, 2001, 331 pp. Ed: Paul Laxton; intro: J.H. Andrews; an illustrated collection of essays by the noted historian who died in 1991.

1520 Harlow, Vincent T., ed. <u>Ralegh's Last Voyage</u>. London: Argonaut; NY: DaCapo, 1932, 1971, 379 pp. An old standard; re his failed attempt to capture the Orinoco basin; led to his imprisonment and execution.

1521 Harmon, Susan. "The Serpent and the Dove: Studying Nelson's Character." <u>MM</u>, 75 (February 1989): 43-51. A review of his character traits, e.g., leadership, courage, loyalty, and gratitude; Nelson at the battle of Copenhagen as case study.

1522 Harper, Lawrence A. <u>The Navigation Laws: A Seventeenth-Century Experiment in Social Engineering</u>. NY: Octagon, 1939, 1964, 503 pp. The original rationale was to enhance and expand English shipping and trade, also applicable to seamen; a review of precursors, the Act of 1651, and subsequent ones; the concept endured for 200 years; they accomplished their purpose.

1523 Harper-Bill, Christopher, et al., eds. <u>Studies in Medieval History: Presented to R. Allen Brown</u>. Rochester: Boydell, 1989, 382 pp. A collection of essays, e.g., Nicholas Hooper on the Anglo-Saxon navy; asks if Alfred was founder of RN in 890s?; there were earlier English naval activities, e.g., 851, and significant later ones, 1018 and 1040.

1524 Harris, Daniel G. "Chapman's Frigates." <u>Warship</u> (1990): 9-17. Chapman was a great naval architect; this concerning a series of 10 40-gun frigates of the BELLONA class; see next entry.

1525 -------. <u>F.H. Chapman: The First Naval Architect and His Work</u>. Annapolis:

NIP; London: Conway, 1989, 256 pp. The model naval architect; formulated ship design and a programme of the 1780s: 10 SOTL and 10 frigates.

1526 -------. "Francis Sheldon in Denmark, 1686-1690." MM, 83 (August 1997): 293-302. Sheldon, born 1612 in Chatham; a skilled shipbuilder; to Sweden and Denmark.

1527 Harris, G.G. The Trinity House of Deptford, 1514-1660. London: Athlone, 1969, xii, 310 pp. Originally the "Almes Hous of Depford"; the early "coast guard," responsible for providing pilots and maintaining channel markers, lighthouses, beacons, etc.; evolved from guilds of seamen; Pepys was Master of the Corporation twice; included a history of English trade.

1528 Harris, J.R. "Copper and Shipping in the Eighteenth Century." Economic History Review, 2nd ser, 19 (December 1966): 550-68. Copper sheathing to protect wooden hulls; Anson credited with implementing it in the 1760s.

1529 Harris, Nathaniel. The Armada: The Decisive Battle. A Day that Made History series. London: Dryad, 1987, 64 pp. At juvenile level; curious organization, beginning with the fireship raid at Calais; asks questions.

1530 Harris, P.R. A History of the British Museum Library, 1753-1973. London: BL, 1998, xx, 833 pp. Re the library of record for the British, one of the best research centers; a descriptive history.

1531 Harris, R.E.G. "The Nelson Bicentenary at Teneriffe: Spanish Celebration and British Commemoration." MM, 84 (February 1998): 88-92. An event of the Nelson Decade, a re-enactment of the events at Santa Cruz, 24 July 1997; Nelson played by Peter Goodwin, Curator of HMS VICTORY, the restored VICTORY cutter being used; Nelson lost his right arm; sponsorship by the Nelson Society and 1805 Club.

1532 Harris, Simon. Sir Cloudesley Shovell: Stuart Admiral. London: Spellmount, 2000, xv, 431 pp. Re the commander of the fleet which crashed onto the Scilly Isles, 22 October 1707; over 2000 lost; led to Longitude Act; a popular account with bias.

1533 Harrison, Brian. "National Biography for a Computer Age." HisTod, 51 (August 2001): 16-18. Details on The New DNB, projected for 2004 or 2005, by the editor who replaced Colin Matthew who died in 1999; estimated 50,000 new or rewritten entries, 9500 contributors.

1534 Harrison, James. The Life of Horatio Lord Viscount Nelson. 2 vols. London: Chapple, 1806, 904 pp. The biography sponsored by Lady Hamilton to support her case and claims; numerous disparagements against Lady Nelson; reviewers assessed it as "a pack of lies," by "a hireling," and "one of the most nauseous of known books."

1535 Harrison, W.E.C. "Maritime Activities under Henry VII." Ph.D. diss, London, 1931. A scholarly study of his initiatives.

1536 Hart, Francis Russell. The Siege of Havana, 1762. Boston: Houghton, 1931, 54 pp. An account of the amphibious operation.

1537 Hart, Roger. Battle of the Spanish Armada. Documentary History series. London: Wayland; NY: Putnam, 1973, 128 pp. For young readers, illustrated; begins with Drake at game of bowls; other exaggerations, e.g., ". . . the Armada struggled home to ignominy and disgrace."

1538 -------. England Expects. Documentary History series. London: Wayland, 1972, 128 pp. Illustrated; for young readers; battle of Trafalgar; "to portray seafaring life in the navy notorious for its press gangs, its flogging officers, and its grim life below decks."

1539 -------. "The Sea Fencibles of 1798-1801." Nelson Birthday Lectures, Portsmouth Public Library, 26 September 1998. Published lecture; armed auxiliary forces raised during the period 1790s and early 1800s; a corps of volunteers recruited to protect from invasion; initiated by Hugh Popham; seamen and officers but not in RN.

1540 -------. The Voyage of Captain Cook. An Eyewitness Book. London: Wayland, 1973, 96 pp. Illustrated; for juveniles; little narrative.

1541 Hart-Davis, Duff. Armada. London: Bantam, 1988, 256 pp. An illustrated, superficial account.

1542 Hartelie, Olaf. "Notes on Naval Novelists." MM, 1, 3, 6 (1911-1920): various. A series of 6 articles about naval novelists, e.g., Marryat, Chamier, Marsh, and Glascock.

1543 Hartemann, Cyril H. The Angry Admiral: The Later Career of Edward Vernon, Admiral of the White. London: Heinemann, 1953, 1957, 236 pp. Vernon, 1684-1757, an important naval leader in the pre-Nelson era.

1544 Harvey, A.D. "Prosecutions for Sodomy in England at the Beginning of the Nineteenth Century." Historical J, 21 (1978): 939-48. Use of legal and court-martial records; a history of prosecution for buggery, a capital offence since 1533; this article gathers statistics, e.g., 1797-1805, 9 executed; 1805-1815, 28 of 42 convicted were executed, the last execution was 1835; questioned the figures and "Freudian" link presented by Arthur Gilbert.

1545 Harvey, Robert. Cochrane: The Life and Exploits of a Fighting Captain. London: Constable, 2000, 332 pp. A recent biography of the "sea wolf," "the greatest naval commander in the history of the British navy. . . not even Nelson could surpass his genius in action"; also successful in Chile, Brazil, and Greece;

inspiration for Forester and O'Brian.

1546 -------. Liberators: Latin America's Struggle for Independence, 1810-1830. London: Murray, 2000, 561 pp. Recounts a series of revolutionary leaders, e.g., Bolivar, San Martin, and "the bravest and strangest," Cochrane, who brought his "Nelson Touch" to South America.

1547 Haslop, Henry. Newes ovt of the Coast of Spaine. The English Experience series, # 466. London: How; NY: Da Capo, 1587, 1972, 16 pp. A pamphlet; "The true Report . . . Sir Francis Drake, April-May 1587, to Lord Howard."

1548 Hastings, D.J. The Royal Indian Navy, 1612-1950. London: McFarland, 1944, 1988, x, 371 pp. An introduction and historical summary.

1549 Haswell, Jock. James II: Soldier and Sailor. London: Hamilton; NY: St. Martin, 1972, xii, 323 pp. An inadequate, apparently fictionalized biography intended as apologetics; most on Duke of York and land battles; no scholarly apparatus.

1550 Hattendorf, John B. "The Anglo-American Way in Maritime Strategy." NWCR, 43 (Winter 1990): 90-99. Begins with historical survey of maritime strategies; emphasis on "Anglo-American strand," the dominant one; Mahan and Corbett pointed to the model, the British navy in the 17th and 18th centuries; Corbett made the most effective abstract statement: establish control of shipping and use that control to affect events on land; combines naval and maritime, public and private, civilian and military.

1551 -------. The Anglo-French Naval Wars, 1688-1815. London: Addison, in preparation, forthcoming in 2004. To survey the series of naval wars; refuses to use phrase, "Second Hundred Years' War."

1552 Hattendorf, John B. and Hattendorf, Lynn C., comps. A Bibliography of the Works of Alfred Thayer Mahan. Historical Monograph series, # 7. Newport: NWCP, 1986, 1987, 1990, 1993, 150 pp. Mahan was prolific: books, translations, editions, articles, and pamphlets.

1553 [NRS 131]. Hattendorf, John B., Knight, R.J.B., Pearsall, A.W.H., Rodger, N.A.M., and Till, Geoffrey, eds. British Naval Documents, 1204-1960. Publications of the Navy Records Society, Vol. 131. Aldershot: Scolar, 1993, 1196 pp. Fwd: Prince Philip; for NRS, the special centennial volume, dedicated to the Lord High Admiral, Queen Elizabeth II; begins in 1204 with 7 chronological sections, each in the same 6 parts, to 1960; total of 23 contributors writing descriptions and background for the documents; an impressive selection.

1554 Hattendorf, John B., ed. Doing Naval History: Essays toward Improvement. Newport: NWCP, 1995, vi, 160 pp. Proceedings of a conference, Yale University, 1993, in the series of joint Yale-Naval War College conferences; papers on the state of naval history by noted experts, e.g., James Goldrich, N.A.M. Rodger, Paul Kennedy, Paul Halpern, Volker Berghahn, and Dennis Showalter; conclusion: incorporate the broadest themes of maritime history.

1555 Hattendorf, John B. England in the War of Spanish Succession: A Study of the English View and Conduct of Grand Strategy, 1702-1712. NY: Garland, 1987, xxiv, 408 pp. A broad strategic analysis elaborating on the work of Corbett; first to study this period on basis of broad strategy rather than campaigns, battles, and leaders.

1556 -------. "England in the War of Spanish Succession: A Study in the English View and Conduct of Grand Strategy, 1701-1712." D.Phil. diss, Oxford, 1979. The basis for the previous entry.

1557 -------. "1588: An Armada of Books." NWCR, 43 (Summer 1990): 107-13. A comprehensive historiographical survey of 13 works, examples of the vast literature, especially that celebrating the quadricentennial; described commemoration events, e.g., exhibitions, beacons, bonfires, ceremonies, conferences, reprints, and publications; noted significant new information from nautical archaeology.

1558 Hattendorf, John B., ed. The Influence of History on Mahan: The Proceedings of a Conference Marking the Centenary of Alfred Thayer Mahan's "Influence of Sea Power upon History". Historical Monograph series, # 9. Newport: NWCP, 1991, vii, 208 pp. Proceedings of the Mahan Centennial Conference, 1990, to evaluate the influence of Mahan; 15 essays by expert assessors, e.g., Barry Gough, Wayne Hughes, Holger Herwig, and Clark Reynolds; noted limitations of interpretations and judgments of Mahan; conclusion by Reynolds: the most articulate historical philosopher of sea power was Corbett.

1559 [NRS ___]. Hattendorf, John B., ed. The Journal of Admiral Sir George Rooke, 1700-1704. Publications of the Navy Records Society, vol. ___. London: NRS. In 2000, noted as in progress and forthcoming.

1560 Hattendorf, John B., ed. Mahan on Naval Strategy: A Selection of Essays by Alfred Thayer Mahan. Classics of Sea Power. Annapolis: NIP, 1991. A collection of essays.

1561 Hattendorf, John B., ed. Maritime History. 2 vols. I: The Age of Discovery. II: The Eighteenth Century and the Classic Age of Sail. Melbourne: Krieger, 1996-1997, xxxi, 635 pp. 41 essays from National Endowment for the Humanities Institutes, John Carter Brown Library, Providence, RI, summers of 1992 and 1993; by 17 internationally-known scholars, e.g., Hattendorf, Glyndwr Williams, Daniel Baugh, N.A.M. Rodger, Roger Knight, Karel Davids, and A.N. Ryan; comprehensive introduction to maritime history; themes: discoveries, expansions, navigation, commerce, cartography, colonialism, politics, personnel, logistics, dockyards, naval and imperial struggles of the eighteenth century.

1562 Hattendorf, John B. <u>Naval Force and Peacetime Deterrence: Case Studies from British Naval History on the Peacetime Use of Naval Force for Deterrence, 1700-1934</u>. London: Macmillan. Noted in 2001 as forthcoming.

1563 -------. <u>Naval History and Maritime Strategy: Collected Essays</u>. <u>Anvil</u> series. Melbourne: Krieger, 2000, x, 284 pp. 16 collected essays on interrelationships between naval history and maritime strategy; supported by documents.

1564 -------. "Naval War under Sail: Review of Jean Boudroit, <u>The Seventy-Four Gun Ship</u> and Other Works." <u>NWCR</u>, 44 (Summer 1991): 94-104. Review of the Boudroit work and 8 more related works.

1565 -------. "Navies, the Baltic Sea and Western European Politics, 1523-1990." Research project. A current research project, noted in September 2000.

1566 Hattendorf, John B., ed. <u>The Oxford Encyclopedia of Maritime History</u>. __ vols. NY: Oxford UP, forthcoming. Noted in 2000 as in preparation; section chief editors include Roger Knight, Andrew Lambert, Karel Davids, N.A.M. Rodger, and Glyn Williams; probably 4 vols.; a comprehensive survey.

1567 Hattendorf, John B., ed. <u>Policy and Strategy in the Mediterranean Sea: Past, Present and Future</u>. <u>Naval Policy and History</u> series, # 10. London: Cass, 2000, xxiv, 445 pp. Fwd: Paul Kennedy; from the 3rd Yale-NWC conference, this one at Malta, June 1997; on fundamental issues of maritime strategy and naval power in the Mediterranean, e.g., migration, environment, geography, technology, economics, rivalries, and international politics, all earlier dealt with by Fernand Braudel.

1568 Hattendorf, John B. and Unger, Richard W., eds. <u>Power and Domination: Europe and the Sea in the Middle Ages and the Renaissance</u>. Woodbridge: Boydell, forthcoming. Noted in 2001 as in preparation.

1569 Hattendorf, John B. "Sir Julian Corbett on the Significance of Naval History." <u>AmNep</u>, 31 (October 1971): 275-85. An appreciation of Corbett and his influence on the development of naval strategy.

1570 Hattendorf, John B., ed. <u>UBI SUMUS?: The State of Naval and Maritime History</u>. Newport: NWCP, 1994, x, 419 pp. From Yale-NWC conference, 1993, 33 essays; assessments for various countries, e.g., for Britain by N.A.M. Rodger, for Australia by James Goldrick, for Sweden by Jan Glete, for Japan by John de Courcy Ireland, and for the U.S. by Kenneth Hagan.

1571 Hattersley, Roy. <u>Nelson</u>. <u>The Great Commanders</u> series. London: Weidenfeld; London: Futura, 1974, 1976, 223 pp. Intro: Lord Chalfont; folio size; by a politician and former Minister of Defence; a biography of narrative and many colored pictures.

1572 Hatton, Ragnhild M. and Bromley, J.S., eds. <u>William III and Louis XIV: Essays, 1680-1720 by and for Mark A. Thomson</u>. Toronto: Toronto UP, 1968, xii, 332 pp. Intro: George Clark; essays, e.g., A.N. Ryan on William III and the blockade of Brest; Admiral Vernon initiated the policy of blockade of Brest as the 1st line of defense, the primary task for the "Western Squadron" and it persisted, e.g., led by Anson, Hawke, St. Vincent, and William Cornwallis.

1573 Haudrere, Philippe. <u>Les Flottes des Companies des Indes, 1600-1857</u>. Vincennes: Service, 1996, 346 pp. 26 papers from the 5th Anglo-French Conference, 15 in French and 11 in English; e.g., Brian Lavery on English East India Company ships as warships, 4 serving at the battle of Camperdown, Andrew Lambert on building British warships of teak in Bombay, and Nicholas Tracy on the Manila expedition of 1762.

1574 Hawkes, David F., ed. <u>Richard Hakluyt: Voyages to the New World: A Selection</u>. NY: Bobbs-Merrill, 1972, 201 pp. A popular edition of selections.

1575 Hawkes, Sonia C., ed. <u>Weapons and Warfare in Anglo-Saxon England</u>. Oxford: Oxford UP, 1989, vi, 213 pp. Papers from a conference, Oxford, 1987, multi-disciplinary and sanctioned by the Dark Ages Society; evidence from burials, including ship burials.

1576 Hawkesworth, John. <u>An Account of the Voyage Undertaken. . . . for Making Discoveries in the Southern Hemisphere. . . . by Commodore Byron, Captain Wallis, Captain Carteret, and Captain Cook. . . .</u> 3 vols. London: Strahan, 1773, 1775, 1809. A controversial edition of the 1st voyage of Cook, an amalgamation; impossible to determine who wrote what, Cook, Banks, or Hawkesworth.

1577 Hawkey, Arthur. <u>Bligh's Other Mutiny</u>. London: Angus, 1975, vi, 206 pp. What happened to Bligh after BOUNTY and the successful breadfruit voyage; the Nore mutiny of 1797, at Camperdown, at Copenhagen, a court martial on HMS WARRIOR, a court martial on HMS SAN JOSEF, and, finally, the imbroglio at New South Wales in 1808.

1578 Hawkins, Mary W.S. <u>Plymouth Armada Heroes: The Hawkins Family</u>. Plymouth: Brendon, 1888, viii, 189 pp. A geneological study, anecdotal accounts of deeds of ancestors.

1579 Hay, M.D., ed. <u>Landsman Hay: The Memoirs of Robert Hay, 1789-1847</u>. London: Hart-Davis, 1953, 248 pp. A memoir of lower-deck experiences, 1803-1811.

1580 Haynes, Alan. "The Cadiz Expedition, 1596." <u>HisTod</u>, 23 (February 1973): 161-69. Amid evidence of preparations for another Armada, Elizabeth authorized another raid on Spain, an Anglo-Dutch operation; to Cadiz, causing much damage but internal conflicts developed.

1581 -------. Invisible Power: The Elizabethan Secret Service, 1570-1603. Stroud: Sutton, 1992, xxi, 179 pp. Re a neglected subject, e.g., secret agents, intrigue, and plots; Shakespeare in Hamlet refers to such agents.

1582 Haythornthwaite, Philip, et al. Napoleon: The Final Verdict: A New Assessment of the Emperor. London: Arms, 1996, 320 pp. Fwd: David G. Chandler; a series of assessments by experts; emphasis on Napoleon as general.

1583 Haythornthwaite, Philip. Nelson's Navy. Osprey Elite series, # 48. London: Osprey, 1993, 64 pp. A series for military enthusiasts; a popularized survey.

1584 Hayton, David W., ed. The Parliamentary Diary of Sir Richard Cocks, 1698-1702. Oxford: Clarendon, 1996, lxvii, 345 pp. A journal from 4 Parliamentary sessions; informative on naval matters, e.g., a scandal over victualling of the expedition of 1595, delays in wages for seamen, and naval officers as Members of Parliament.

1585 Haywood, John. Dark Age Naval Power: A Reassessment of the Frankish and Anglo-Saxon Seafaring Activity. Boston: Routledge, 1991, xiv, 232 pp. Re pre-Viking Germanic sea operations, not counting trade, e.g., shipbuilding, piracy, coastal raids, and sea transport; conclusion: maritime achievements have been underestimated.

1586 Heal, Veryan. Britain's Maritime Heritage: A Guide to Historic Vessels. London: Conway, 1988, 128 pp. A reference guide, profusely illustrated.

1587 "Health in the Royal Navy during the Age of Nelson: Conference Papers." J Royal Navy Medical Service, 86 (2000). Papers from a conference, Institute of Naval Medicine, 1 July 2000; associated with the Nelson Decade activities.

1588 Heaps, Leo, ed. Log of the CENTURION: Based on the Original Papers of Captain Philip Saumarez on Board HMS CENTURION, Lord Anson's Flagship during His Circumnavigation, 1740-1744. London: Hart-Davis, 1973, 264 pp. A first-hand account of this important voyage.

1589 Hearn, Chester G. George Washington's Schooners: The First American Navy. Annapolis: NIP, 1995, 312 pp. The story of 85 ships assembled to oppose RN, predecessor to the Continental Navy; most operated from Boston to harrass the British.

1590 Hearsey, John E.N. Young Mr. Pepys. London: Constable; NY: Scribner , 1973, 1974, 306 pp. Touted as presenting context for the diaries, during the 1660s; no analysis and disappointing.

1591 Heawood, Edward. A History of Geographical Discovery in the Seventeenth and Eighteenth Centuries. NY: Octagon, 1912, 1965, 1969, xii, 475 pp. An excellent, if dated, general survey; the sequence was Portugal and Spain, consolidation, pause, Armada, Dutch, English, and French.

1592 Hebb, David D. "The English Government and the Problem of Piracy, 1616-1642." Ph.D. diss, London, 1985. The basis for the next entry.

1593 -------. Piracy and English Government, 1616-1642. Studies in Naval History. Aldershot: Scolar, 1994, xv, 303 pp. An assessment of the impact, e.g., loss of 400 merchant ships and 8000 seamen, and the response, e.g., James I initiated an international force, e.g., Venice, France, Spain, and Holland, to oppose corsairs in Algiers and Sallee; interestingly, English piracy, which itself had a notorious reputation, declined steadily during this period.

1594 Heckscher, Eli F. The Continental System: An Economic Interpretation. Oxford: Clarendon, 1922, xvi, 420 pp. Ed: Harald Westergaard; the classic study of the impact of the Continental System implemented by Napoleon, the culmination of Anglo-French commercial relations since 1680; by the noted economic historian.

1595 Heidler, David S. and Heidler, Jeanne T., eds. Encyclopedia of the War of 1812. Santa Barbara: ABC-Clio, 1997, xxxviii, 636 pp. A reference work, a series of essays by experts, A to Z.

1596 Henderson, George C. The Discovery of the Fiji Islands: Tasman, Cook, Bligh, Wilson, Bellingshausen. London: Murray, 1933, xviii, 324 pp. An older survey of voyages of discovery of the Fiji Islands.

1597 Henderson, James. The Frigates: An Account of the Lesser Warships of the War from 1789-1815. NY: Dodd; London: Cooper, 1970, 1994, 192 pp. A popular history at the juvenile level; accounts of battles and some mutinies; error prone.

1598 -------. Sloops and Brigs: An Account of the Smallest Vessels of the Royal Navy during the Great Wars, 1793-1815. London: Coles; Annapolis: NIP, 1972, 190 pp. Re these supporting warships, listed by name, losses, and rigging plans.

1599 Henderson, J. Welles and Carlisle, Rodney P. Marine Art and Antiques: Jack Tar: A Sailor's Life, 1750-1910. Woodbridge: Antique, 1999, 287 pp. Fwd: Walter Annenberg; large folio size, exquisite slick production; presentation of large, well-known collection on life of the seaman on the lower deck, e.g., paintings, drawings, pottery, sea-chests, ephemera, and log books; associated with the Independence Seaport Museum, Philadelphia.

1600 Henningsen, Henning. Crossing the Equator: Sailors' Baptism and Other Initiation Rites. Copenhagen: Munksgaard, 1961, 324 pp. An extensive, scholarly study of sea customs and rituals.

1601 Henty, George Alfred. At Aboukir and Acre: A Story of Napoleon's Invasion of Egypt. NY: Scribner, 1898, vi, 331 pp. By the prolific and popular author of didactic juvenile adventure literature; this on the Egyptian campaign.

1602 -------. By Conduct and Courage: A Story of the Days of Nelson. London: Blackie, 1905, 383 pp. Illus: William Rainey; another in the didactic juvenile literature; this one on Nelson.

1603 -------. Under Drake's Flag: A Tale of the Spanish Main. London: Blackie; NY: Scribner, 1912, 1922, 358 pp. Illus: Gordon Browne; juvenile fiction, re Drake.

1604 Hepper, David J. British Warship Losses in the Age of Sail, 1650-1859. Ratherfield: Boudriot, 1994, vi, 213 pp. An extraordinary reference guide; recounts the circumstances and details of the loss of 1700 British warships; most were accidental; from records of courts-martial.

1605 Herbert, Edward. The Expedition to the Isle of Rhe. London: Philobiblion, 1656, 1860. Ed: Lord Powis; by Lord Herbert of Cherbury; contemporaneous apologetics for Buckingham.

1606 Heriot, Augus. The French in Italy, 1796-1799. London: Chatto, 1957, 316 pp. An adequate study of the Napoleonic campaign in Italy; background for incidents while Nelson was in Naples.

1607 Herold, J. Christopher. The Age of Napoleon. Horizon Book. NY: Dell, 1963, 1965, 416 pp. An assessment for the general reader.

1608 -------. Bonaparte in Egypt. NY: Harper, 1962, xii, 424 pp. By the noted biographer of Napoleon; this campaign has broad implications, e.g., for French imperialism, cultural considerations, and demonstrations of sea power or the lack of it.

1609 Herrera Oria, Enrique. Felipe II Y el Marques de Santa Cruz en la empresa de Inglaterra. Madrid: Instituto Historico, 1946, 179 pp. Sources from Archivo General de Simancas; re preparations for the Armada.

1610 Herrera Oria, Enrique, ed. La Armada Invencible: Documentos procedentes de Archivo General de Simancas, 1587-1589. Valladolid: Archivo Historico, 1929. An edition of pertinent documents, before, during and after the Armada campaign.

1611 Herson, James P. "The Siege of Cadiz, 1810-1812: A Study in Joint and Combined Operations during the Peninsular War." Ph.D. diss, Florida State, 1998, 360 pp. A scholarly survey based on research in British, French, and Spanish archives; a 30-month siege; details of the operations; massive British support for its ally, Portugal.

1612 Hess, Andrew C. "The Battle of Lepanto and Its Place in Mediterranean History." Past and Present, 57 (November 1972): 53-73. Places the battle of 1571 in perspective; use of Ottoman sources; as with revisionism re the Armada, its significance has been exaggerated.

1613 Hewitt, H. James. The Black Prince's Expeditions of 1355-1357. Manchester: Manchester UP, 1958, ix, 226 pp. The famous exploits of Edward, Prince of Wales.

1614 Hewitt, H. James, ed. Eye-Witnesses to Nelson's Battles. Reading: Osprey, 1972, 206 pp. A collection of first-hand observations of all of the famous battles.

1615 Hewitt, H. James. The Organization of War under Edward III, 1338-1362. Manchester: Manchester UP; NY: Barnes, 1966, ix, 206 pp. Informative on naval aspects, e.g., defense from French attacks by privateers and galleys, operations at sea, transport of horses, logistics, and victualling.

1616 Hewson, Joseph B. A History of the Practice of Navigation. Glasgow: Brown, 1951, 1983, viii, 295 pp. A general summary.

1617 Heyer, Georgette. Beauvallet. London: Heinemann; NY: Longman, 1929, 1930, 1952, 1963, 1969, 1974, 1992, 244 pp. Nautical fiction; by the prolific writer of historical romances; re English pirates and the Armada.

1618 Heywood, Thomas. His Majesty's Royal Ship: A Critical Edition of Thomas Heywood's "A True Description of His Majesties Royale Ship". NY: AMS, 1990, xxxviii, 79 pp. Ed: Alan Young; a contemporaneous description of the extraordinary and elaborate decorations of the great warships of Charles I, e.g., SOVEREIGN OF THE SEAS of 1637, "undoubtedly the most complex industrial product that nation had ever produced."

1619 Hibbert, Christopher. Agincourt. Great Battles series. NY: Cooper; Gloucester: Windrush, 1964, 1968, 1978, 1998, 2000, xii, 176 pp. A popular account of the famous victory of 1415.

1620 -------. "Bonaparte and the Knights of Malta." HisTod, 20 (March 1970): 153-62. Relationships and antagonisms of the 1790s and 1800s.

1621 -------. Corunna. British Battles series. NY: Macmillan, 1961, 216 pp. A neglected battle during the Peninsular campaing in Spain in 1809.

1622 -------. Nelson: A Personal History. Boston: Addison: London: Viking, 1994, xix, 472 pp. A popular account; extensive description of the funeral; competent, chronological, excessive on domestic issues, and no analysis.

1623 Hickey, Donald R. The War of 1812: A Forgotten Conflict. Chicago: U Ill P, 1990, xvi, 457 pp. From the American perspective but broad coverage, well-balanced and well-researched; excellent survey of the literature and concedes many American interpretations grossly exaggerated.

1624 -------. "The War of 1812: Still a Forgotten Conflict?: Historiographical Essay." J Military History, 65 (July 2001): 741-69. Questions his own use of subtitle of book in previous entry; survey of 75 books on the war in the 1990s; T.

Roosevelt's remains the best on the naval war, Mahan best on naval strategy, and J.F. Cooper on the U.S. Navy.

1625 -------. [The Quasi-War with France]. Noted in 2001 as forthcoming, companion to The War of 1812; American problems with France in the 1790s.

1626 Hickman, William. A Treatise on the Law and Practice of Naval Courts-Martial. London: Murray, 1851, 319 pp. By a naval veteran presenting an overview of the history and proceedings.

1627 Higham, Robin, ed. A Guide to the Sources of British Military History. London: Routledge, 1971, xxi, 630 pp. For the Conference on British Studies; one of the best bibliographical surveys edited by the most eminent bibliographical scholar; 25 essays of critical analysis of the pertinent literature by experts, e.g., Daniel Baugh on RN to 1714, Christopher Lloyd on RN in the 18th century and on naval medicine; over 1300 publications incorporated; has been updated in an edition by Gerald Jordan.

1628 Hill, David and Rumble, Alexander R., eds. The Defence of Wessex: The "Burghal Hidage" and Anglo-Saxon Fortification. Manchester: Manchester UP, 1996, 1997, xx, 256 pp. Essays by experts about King Alfred and the defense against the Vikings, e.g., a document of the 10th century, a description of the web of fortresses, and the battle of Edington.

1629 Hill, Ernestine. My Love Must Wait: The Story of Matthew Flinders. London: Angus, 1941, 1950, 1972, 1981, 466 pp. Historical fiction about Flinders, 1774-1814, a naval explorer.

1630 Hill, J.R., ed. Oxford Illustrated History of the Royal Navy. Oxford Illustrated History series. London: Oxford UP, 1995, xvi, 480 pp. Folio size, lavishly illustrated; 14 essays by the best experts, e.g., Susan Rose, David Loades, John Hattendorf, Andrew Lambert, and Daniel Baugh; begins with Alfred but denies he was founder; notes evolution from "King's Ships" to RN.

1631 Hill, J.R. The Prizes of War: Prize Law and the Royal Navy in the Napoleonic Wars, 1793-1815. Stroud: Sutton, 1998, xx, 266 pp. For the Royal Naval Museum; re an important aspect of economic warfare, financial incentives and "state sanctioned robbery"; rules of contraband, blockade, prize agents, and Admiralty courts.

1632 Hill, James M. "Continuity in Celtic Warfare: Strategy, Tactics, and Logistics of the Highland Scots and Irish, 1595-1763." Ph.D. diss, Alabama, 1985. Involved maritime and naval operations; unusual to incorporate these factors at this time and this place.

1633 Hill, L.M. "The Admiralty Circuit of 1591: Some Comments on the Relations between Central Government and Local Interests." Historical J, 14 (March 1971):

3-14. Re aspects of privateering against Spain; an analysis of the background for the development of Admiralty courts.

1634 Hillier, Chris. The Devil and the Deep: A Guide to Nautical Myths and Superstitions. London: Coles, 1997, 120 pp. Cartoons by Owen Hill; a light-hearted survey of origins and meaning.

1635 Hills, B.F. "Shipbuilding for the Royal Navy at Sandwich in the Eighteenth Century." Archaeologia Cantiana, 94 (1979): 195-230. Archaeological evidence of shipbuilding facilities from the time of Nelson.

1636 Hinchliffe, G. "Impressment of Seamen during the War of Spanish Succession." MM, 53 (May 1967): 137-42. First-hand accounts of the injustices related to pressed men during the mobilization of 1708.

1637 Hirschfeld, Burt. The Spanish Armada: The Story of a Glorious Defeat. NY: Messner, 1966, 191 pp. A fictionalized account for juveniles; "ended in a glorious defeat that changed the course of history."

1638 Historic Sail: The Glory of the Sailing Ship from the 13th to the 19th Century. Annapolis: NIP; London: Greenhill, 2000, 208 pp. Folio size, lavishly illustrated; a series of essays by Stephen Howarth supported by 91 colored illustrations by Joseph Wheatley; a series of ship types depicted.

1639 History of the Ship Series. London: Conway Maritime Press; Annapolis: NIP, various. A superb series of detailed guides to individual ship types and classes, e.g., galley, cog, line-of-battle, big gun, and steam-powered; important series.

1640 Hitchcock, R.F. "Cavendish's Last Voyage: The Charges against Davis." MM, 80 (August 1994): 259-69. Cavendish led a 3-ship force, 1586-1588, and a 5-ship force, 1591-1593; during the 1st, much Spanish booty and during the 2nd, many problems including conflict with John Davis.

1641 -------. "Cavendish's Last Voyage: Purposes Revealed and Concealed." MM, 87 (February 2001): 5-14. Elaboration on the Cavendish-Davis controversy; re the failure of this voyage and recriminations.

1642 Hitsman, J. Mackay and Bond, C.C.J. "The Assault Landing at Louisbourg, 1758." Canadian Historical Review, 35 (December 1954): 314-40. A review of the implications and consequences, e.g., the foundation for the Saunders-Wolfe attack on Quebec and the end of French rule in North America.

1643 Hitsman, J. Mackay. The Incredible War of 1812: A Military History. Toronto: Toronto UP; Toronto: Brass, 1965, 1966, 1999, xxxii, 398 pp. Ed: Donald Graves; recently expanded and updated by Graves; presents the Canadian perspective; reviews the origins and causes; includes listing of all British and American naval forces and an extensive bibliography.

1644 Hocking, Joseph. <u>A Flame of Fire: Being the History of the Adventures of Three Englishmen in Spain at the Time of the Great Armada</u>. London: Cassell, 1903, 397 pp. Nautical fiction; Spain vs. England and the Armada.

1645 Hodges, C. Walter. <u>The Spanish Armada: The Story of Britain</u>. London: Oxford UP, 1967, 1968, 32 pp. An illustrated account for juveniles.

1646 Hodgkin, Louis. <u>Nelson and Bath</u>. Corsham: Nelson Society, 1991. Local interest about Nelson.

1647 Hoffman, E.T.A. "Haimatochare". Munich: Rosl, 1924. One part of an extensive satire in German verse or "verse theater," 11 vols. in all; this one re Bligh and the BOUNTY mutiny; places Bligh in the best light.

1648 Hoffman, Frank G. "A Littoral Leader." <u>USNIP</u>, 122 (October 1996): 60-66. Contends Nelson of the "immortal memory," not "blue-water" specialist; his operations were in the littoral, e.g., rivers, amphibious; he demostrated intitiative, innovation, and adaptability; not convincing.

1649 Hoffman, Paul E. <u>The Spanish Crown and the Defense of the Caribbean, 1535-1585: Precedent, Patrimonialism, and Parsimony</u>. Alt. title: <u>The Defense of the Spanish Caribbean</u>. Baton Rouge: LSUP, 1980, 1985, xiv, 312 pp. Thorough research in Spanish records; correction of myths and legends about Spanish competence and Drake causing Spanish decline; conclusion: Spanish colonization and defense were adequate and viable.

1650 Hogg, O.F.G. "England's War Effort against the Spanish Armada." <u>J Society of Army Historical Research</u>, 44 (March 1966): 25-43. At the time of threats from invasion from Napoleon and from Hitler, studies were made comparing mobilization of national resources; statistics on English naval forces: 187 ships from all sources manned by 15,410 vs. the Armada of 129 ships of which only 54 returned to Spain.

1651 -------. <u>The Royal Arsenal: Its Background, Origin and Subsequent History</u>. 2 vols. London: Oxford UP, 1963, xviii, 1560 pp. A brilliant and comprehensive study, the arsenal providing all guns and ammunition to all forces; origins in the 11th century, formalized in 1670.

1652 Holand, Hjalmar R. <u>Norse Discoveries and Explorations in America, 982-1362: Leif Erikson to the Kensington Stone</u>. Alt. title: <u>Westward from Vinland</u>. NY: Duell, 1940, 1969, x, 354 pp. An investigative report about various Norse discoveries, e.g.. Vinland and Kensington stone of Minnesota.

1653 Holdsworth, William S. <u>History of English Law</u>. 12 vols. London: Methuen, 1938. The standard survey including some naval-maritime aspects: the history of the Courts of the Admiralty, Laws of Oleron, and the Black Book.

1654 Holland, A.J. <u>Ships of British Oak: The Rise and Decline of Wooden Shipbuilding in Hampshire</u>. Newton Abbot: David and Charles, 1971, 204 pp. A survey of this important center which includes Southampton.

1655 Hollister, C. Warren. <u>Anglo-Saxon Military Institutions on the Eve of the Norman Conquest</u>. NY: Oxford UP, 1962, xiv, 170 pp. An important contribution to the "feudalism" debate by a noted authority; institutional matters, e.g., the fyrd, mercenaries, and 5-hide recruiting; includes a chapter on tactics and strategy and the Saxon navy.

1656 -------. <u>The Military Organization of Norman England</u>. Oxford: Clarendon, 1965, xiv, 319 pp. A continuation of the previous entry; re Norman institutions, e.g., the <u>fyrd</u> and Cinque Ports.

1657 Holm, Poul. "The Slave Trade of Dublin, Ninth to Twelfth Centuries." <u>Peritia</u>, 5 (1986): 317-45. The Vikings operated fleets in the Irish Sea which raided, followed by demands for ransom, tribute, and slave trading; Dublin had a slave market; also a Welsh-Viking-Irish connection, e.g., Gruffydd of the late 11th century.

1658 Holmes, G.A. "The 'Libel of English Policy.'" <u>EHR</u>, 76 (April 1961): 193-216. Presents the circumstances of its origin in the 1430s during a seige of Calais; a well-informed, jingoistic plea for protection and expansion of English trade, in this case, the threat to the wool trade from Burgundy and France.

1659 Holmes, Maurice. <u>Captain James Cook, RN: A Bibliographical Excursion</u>. NY: Franklin; London: Edwards, 1928, 1936, 1952, 1968, 103 pp. Some critical analysis in the bibliography; sorts out the various "voyage" publications; the literature on Cook almost equals that on Nelson.

1660 Holmes, Michael R.J. <u>Augustus Hervey: A Naval Casanova</u>. Durham: Pentland, 1996, 1997, xiv, 306 pp. The 1st full biography of Hervey, active during the mid-18th century as naval officer, e.g., at the Byng court-martial, blockade of Brest, capture of Havana, and earning 9,000 pounds sterling in prize money; self-proclaimed womanizer.

1661 Holmes, Rice. <u>Ancient Britain and the Invasions of Julius Caesar</u>. Oxford: Clarendon, 1907, 1936, xvi, 764 pp. A survey of Bronze and Iron Age Britain; chapter detailing operations by Caesar and his forces during both invasions, e.g., preparations, sea crossings, forays inland, and weather problems.

1662 Holmes, Thomas W. <u>The Semaphore: The Story of the Admiralty-to-Portsmouth Shutter Telegraph and Semaphore Lines</u>. Devon: Stockwell, 1983, 223 pp. In use from 1796-1847; actually 2 systems, a shutter replaced by a symphore system; a significant contribution to communication and to intelligence, to be replaced by the telegraph.

1663 Hood, Dorothy. The Admirals Hood. London: Hutchinson, 1911, 1942, 255 pp. Covers the period, 1724-1816; re Samuel Viscount Hood and Alexander Viscount Bridport.

1664 Hooper, Nicholas. "Anglo-Saxon Warfare on the Eve of the Conquest: A Brief Survey." Anglo-Norman Studies, 1 (1978): 84-93. Re the sources of forces for the Anglo-Saxons, e.g., household force and levy of freemen.

1665 Hope, Ronald. A New History of British Shipping. London: Murray, 1990, xiii, 533 pp. A vast work of reference intensively researched covering from 3000 BC to the present, from sailing ships of the Celts to the Cinque Ports to privateers to exploration to decline; presumably to supersede Ralph Davis.

1666 -------. Poor Jack: The Perilous History of the Merchant Seaman. London: Chatham, 2001, vi, 375 pp. Illustrated, an anthology of accounts of sea life in chronological order, e.g., from Hakluyt, Anson, Cook, Bligh, Conrad, and 20 autobiographies.

1667 Hopkins, Peter. A History of Lord Nelson's Merton Place. Morden: Merton, 2000, 47 pp. Re the 160 acres and buildings Nelson bought in 1801.

1668 Horden, Marsden. Mariners Are Warned! John Lort Stokes and HMS BEAGLE in Australia, 1837-1843. Melbourne: Melbourne UP, 1989, 359 pp. BEAGLE was an Admiralty survey ship, Stokes being on earlier ones; an example of exploration and scientific operations of RN.

1669 Hore, Peter, ed. Seapower Ashore: The Royal Navy and Land Warfare since 1799. Alt. Subtitle: 200 Years of Royal Navy Operations on Land. London: Chatham, 2000, 2001, 288 pp. Editor a Captain in RN; essays by experts, e.g., T. Pocock, A. Lambert, M. Duffy, and C. White, e.g., about Nelson at Calvi and Royal Naval Divisions.

1670 Horner, Frank. Looking for La Perouse: D'Entrecasteaux in Australia and the South Pacific, 1792-1793. Melbourne: Melbourne UP; Lancaster: Gazelle, 1995, xiv, 318 pp. The story of a French explorer and the subsequent search which involved some British connections during the 1780s and 1790s; enlightening about exploration of the Pacific.

1671 Horsfield, John A. The Art of Leadership in War: The Royal Navy from the Age of Nelson to the End of World War II. Contributions in Military History, # 21. Westport: Greenwood, 1980, 240 pp. An idiosyncratic assessment, selecting 7 "greats"; pertinent here are a "trinity," St. Vincent, Nelson, and, to a lesser degree, Collingwood, and, later, Jellicoe, Beatty, Keyes, and Cunningham; contending that the leadership qualities of that "trinity" can never be exceeded; impressive listing of prominent characteristics of them; deteriorates in coverage of the final 4.

1672 -------. "The Art of Leadership in War: The Royal Navy from the Age of

Nelson through World War II as a Case History." Ph.D. diss, California, Irvine, 1977, 301 pp. The basis of the previous entry.

1673 Horsman, Reginald. <u>The Causes of the War of 1812</u>. Phil: U Penn P; NY: Octagon, 1961, 1972, 345 pp. An American perspective; focuses on the issue of western expansion and neglects others, e.g., impressment and American trade with France.

1674 -------. <u>The War of 1812</u>. NY: Knopf, 1969, xvi, 286 pp. A survey with emphasis on the foreign policy aspects.

1675 Horstein, Sari R. "The Deployment of the English Navy in Peacetime, 1674-1688." Ph.D. diss, Leiden, 1985. The basis for the next entry.

1676 -------. <u>The Restoration Navy and English Foreign Trade, 1674-1688</u>. <u>Studies in Naval History</u>. Aldershot: Scolar, 1990, 1991, x, 293 pp. Re peacetime operations, a neglected topic; this scholarly study focuses on the Mediterranean and obligations concerning protection of trade there; to rehabilitate RN from bad image created by Pepys.

1677 Horward, Donald D. "The Influence of British Seapower upon the Peninsular War, 1808-1814." <u>NWCR</u>, 31 (Fall 1978): 54-71. A review of the joint land-sea operations in support of Wellington and his army; elsewhere, RN had experienced a series of failures but not in this campaign.

1678 Horward, Donald D., ed. <u>Napoleonic Military History: A Bibliography</u>. <u>Military History Bibliographies</u> series, vol.. 9. NY: Garland, 1986, xiii, 689 pp. A series of historiographical essays by noted experts, e.g., Steven Ross, Owen Connelly, John Gallagher; and Gordon Bond on "England at War, 1798-1815"; 7131 entries; estimate of 220,000 titles related to Napoleon.

1679 Hoste, Paul. <u>L'Art des Armees Navales ou Traite des Evolutions Navales</u>. Alt. title: <u>Naval Evolutions</u>. Lyon, 1697. Dedicated to Louis XIV; later translations into English: Charles O'Bryen and J.D. Boswall; French writings on naval tactics including demonstration-illustrations on 130 engraved plates; the basis of English Fighting Instructions; insistence on rigid compliance; avoid degeneration into melee.

1680 Hough, Richard A. <u>Captain Bligh and Mr. Christian: The Men and the Mutiny</u>. London: Hutchinson; NY: Dutton; London: Chatham, 1972, 1979, 1988, 2000, 320 pp. By the prolific naval historian, biographer, novelist, and writer about race cars; the blurb touts "a masterly and thrilling account" and "the best account"; illustrated; scholars are more critical: virtual fiction, e.g., dialogue and claims unsupported by documentation, e.g., a Bligh-Christian homosexual relationship.

1681 -------. <u>Captain James Cook: A Biography</u>. London: Hodder; NY: Norton, 1994, 1995, 1997, xx, 492 pp. An adequate biography but Beaglehole remains the standard; Hough did personally follow the route of the voyages; thesis: Cook was acting in a peculiar manner at the end and could have avoided death.

1682 -------. Man O'War: The Fighting Ship in History. NY: Scribner, 1979, 239 pp. Popularized coverage of a series of famous warships, e.g., ARK ROYAL, BONHOMME RICHARD, VICTORY, and ESSEX.

1683 -------. The Murder of Captain James Cook. Alt. title: The Last Voyage of Captain James Cook. London: Macmillan, 1979, 271 pp. Relies on Beaglehole account.

1684 -------. Nelson. London: Park Lane, 1980, 192 pp. An undistinguished biography.

1685 Houts, Elisabeth M.C. van, ed. The "Gesta Normannorum Ducum" of William of Jumieges, Oderic Vitalis, and Robert Torigni. Oxford Medieval Texts. 2 vols. Oxford: Clarendon, 1992-1995, 646 pp. Among the best original sources for events of the year 1066.

1686 Houts, Elisabeth M.C. van. "The Ship List of William the Conqueror." Anglo-Norman Studies, 10 (1987): 159-84. January-August 1066, preparations for the Norman Conquest; few details from sources; a text of December 1067, probably written before the conquest, is enlightening on logistics; describes the careful process of building the ships and fitting them with arms and provisions.

1687 Hovgaard, William. Modern History of Warships: Comprising. . . Naval Matters. London: Conway: Annapolis: NIP, 1920, 1971, xii, 501 pp. A standard reference guide; taken from extensive lectures on the history of warship design by this ship designer from Denmark who later taught at the Royal Naval College, Greenwich and Massachusetts Institute of Technology; descriptive of the development of large navies; divided by class of warship and nationality.

1688 Howard, D.L. "Transportation and Impressment." The Listener, 76 (17 November 1966): 722-24. A article about punishment of British convicts and manning of the navy.

1689 Howard, Frank. Sailing Ships of War, 1400-1860. Koblenz: Bernard; London: Conway, 1979, 1983, 254 pp. Large folio size, 400 pictures, some colored; a chronological survey, a chapter for each century, 15th-19th; in sequence: full rigged, galleons, SOTL, frigates, and sloops; annotated bibliography.

1690 Howard, Michael E. The British Way in Warfare: A Reappraisal. London: Cape, 1975, 24 pp. The Neale Lecture of 1974; reviews theories of modern strategists, e.g., Corbett and Richmond.

1691 Howarth, David A. Famous Sea Battles. Boston: Little, Brown, 1981, 185 pp. A companion to Famous Land Battles; 16 sea battles, 8 from the age of sail, e.g.,

Armada and Trafalgar.

1692 -------. "The Man Who Lost Trafalgar." MM, 57 (November 1971): 361-70. From a lecture to SNR aboard HMS VICTORY, 5 December 1970; re French Admiral Pierre Villeneuve, harshly judged by history and a scapegoat; not deserved; Napoleon issued secret orders to sail from Cadiz; Villeneuve captured and released; "suicide" by 6 knife wounds; a court martial would have exposed Napoleon's order.

1693 -------. The Men-of-War. Seafarers series. Alexandria: Time-Life, 1978, 176 pp. Exquisite folio size with fabulous illustrations, e.g., battles of Sluys, Armada, Anglo-Dutch wars, and famous ships: GREAT HARRY, SOVEREIGN OF THE SEAS, and VASA.

1694 Howarth, David A. and Howarth, Stephen. Nelson: The Immortal Memory. Alt. title: Lord Nelson.London: Dent; NY: Viking, 1988, x, 390 pp. Father, 1912- and son, 1953-; a popular biography with no scholarly apparatus; emphasis on his popularity, leadership, relations with Emma Hamilton, and the fate of Horatia; trivia, anecdotes, and many superlatives, e.g., the greatest of all naval officers.

1695 Howarth, David A. Sovereign of the Seas: The Story of Britain and the Sea. NY: Atheneum; London: Collins, 1974, 382 pp. A panoramic history based on chronological coverage in 5 parts, 450-1945: obscurity, awakening, mastery, rivalry, and supremacy; incorporates shipbuilding, navigation, cartography, and exploration; no scholarly apparatus.

1696 -------. 1066: The Year of the Conquest. London: Collins, 1977, 207 pp. A review of events of the year; clearly appreciates the technicalities of cross-Channel operations, e.g., navigation, wind, and weather.

1697 -------. Trafalgar: The Nelson Touch. London: Collins; NY: Atheneum; London: Windrush, 1969, 1997, 254 pp. A detailed description; no scholarly apparatus.

1698 -------. The Voyage of the Armada: The Spanish Story. London: Collins, 1981, 256 pp. Extensive use of Spanish sources; presents the background and rationale; Spanish operations of the campaign and the return home.

1699 Howarth, Stephen, ed. Battle of Cape St. Vincent, 200 Years: Selected Papers from the Bicentennial International Naval Conference, Portsmouth, England, 15 February 1997. Shelton: 1805 Club, et al., 1998, vii, 100 pp. A Nelson Decade event sponsored by SNR, the Nelson Society, and the 1805 Club; published papers from the conference.

1700 Howell, Colin and Twomey, Richard, eds. Jack Tar in History: Essays in the History of Maritime Life and Labour. Fredericton: Acadiensis, 1991, 276 pp. 17 papers from a conference, Halifax, Nova Scotia, October 1990; "Jack Tar," a subriquet from the 17th century; social history in the Marxist tradition of E.P.

Thompson and George Rude; essays, e.g., by Nicholas Rogers, James Pritchard, and Marcus Rediker; emphasis on mass protest actions, e.g., resistance against press gangs and Spithead and the Nore mutinies.

1701 Howse, Derek, ed. Background to Discovery: Pacific Exploration from Dampier to Cook. Berkeley: U Cal P, 1990, xvi, 210 pp. 6 essays presented at seminars sponsored by the Clark Memorial Library, UCLA; dedicated to J.H. Parry who planned the seminars and died in 1982; papers on exploration operations of the 18th century, e.g., Daniel Baugh on seapower and science, Glyndwr Williams on English voyages, and Howse; initiatives and stimulation in England by Defoe, Swift, Dampier, and Cook.

1702 Howse, Derek and Thrower, Norman J.W., eds. A Buccaneer's Atlas: Basil Ringrose's South Sea Waggoner. Berkeley: U Cal P, 1991, 1992, 336 pp. Fwd: D.B. Quinn; in 1681, Ringrose captured a Spanish ship and exploited its secret charts and waggoner, sailing directions; an intelligence project, all presented to Charles II; essential for later Pacific exploration.

1703 Howse, Derek and Hutchinson, B. Clocks and Watches of Captain James Cook, 1769-1969. London, 1969, 1970. A history of these clocks by a noted expert.

1704 Howse, Derek, ed. Five Hundred Years of Nautical Science, 1400-1900. Greenwich: NMM, 1981, xii, 408 pp. Proceedings of the 3rd International Reunion for the History of Nautical Science and Hydrography at NMM, September 1979; paper topics included weapons, navigation, hydrography, and sailing ships.

1705 Howse, Derek. Francis Place and the Early History of the Greenwich Observatory. NY: Science History, 1975, 64 pp. Place, 1647-1728, was a prominent intellectual of London with interests in astronomical observations.

1706 -------. Greenwich Time and the Discovery of the Longitude. Oxford: Oxford UP, 1980, 1990, 1997, 208 pp. Fwd: Martin Rees; for NMM; folio size, many illustrations; the millennium edition of 1997; Sobel gives too much credit to Harrison; others contributed, e.g., Arnold and Earnshaw.

1707 -------. Guide to the Old Royal Observatory, Greenwich. London: NMM, 1973, 1985, 23 pp. An informative pamphlet guide for tours.

1708 Howse, Derek and Billings, Pat, comps. Handlist of Manuscript Sea Charts and Pilot Books Executed before 1700. London: HMSO, n.d., 55 pp. A report from NMM related to its collections.

1709 Howse, Derek. Nevil Maskelyne: The Seaman's Astronomer. Cambridge: Cambridge UP, 1989, xiv, 280 pp. Fwd: Francis Graham-Smith; a biography of Britain's 5th Astronomer General, 1765-1811; preferred the lunar distance method for obtaining longitude; nemesis of Harrison.

1710 Howse, Derek and Sanderson, Michael. The Sea Chart: An Historical Survey Based on the Collection in the National Maritime Museum. NY: McGraw, 1973, 144 pp. Intro: G.S. Ritchie; survey of 60 representative charts, the earliest from 1420.

1711 Howse, Derek, ed. Sir Francis Drake's Nautical Almanac, 1546. London: Nothingham Court, 1980, 32 pp. An edition from the original at Magdalene College, Cambridge; Drake was an outstanding navigator.

1712 Hozier, Henry M. The Invasions of England: A History of the Past with Lessons for the Future. 2 vols. London: Macmillan, 1876. Recounts a series of invasions, pointing out lessons so as to be prepared and ready in the future.

1713 Huddart, William. Unpathed Waters: The Life and Times of Captain Joseph Huddart, FRS, 1741-1816. London: Quiller, 1990, vii, 200 pp. By a descendant; Huddart conducted surveys for charts around the British Isles and abroad, 1777-1808; an official of Trinity House; elected to the Royal Society.

1714 Hudson, Gilbert, ed. Nelson's Last Diary, September 13-October 21, 1805. London: Matthews; Kent: Kent State UP, 1917, 1971, 80 pp. The first accurate edition; original at the Probate Office, Somerset House.

1715 [NRS 98]. Hughes, Edward, ed. The Private Correspondence of Admiral Lord Collingwood. Publications of the Navy Records Society, vol. 98. London: NRS, 1957, xiv, 348 pp. From unpublished personal correspondence; informative on his character; Laughton had dismissed him as "mediocre"; not correct; now rehabilitated.

1716 Hughes, Quentin. Britain in the Mediterranean and the Defence of Her Naval Stations. Liverpool: Penpaled, 1981, 235 pp. Folio, paperback, profusely illustrated; over 400 years of strategic interest and operations; bases, e.g., Tangier, Malta, Gibraltar, Corfu, and Minorca.

1717 -------. The Building of Malta During the Period of the Knights of St. John of Jerusalem. London: Tiranti, 1956, xiii, 241 pp. Preliminaries to establishment of the British base.

1718 Hughes, R.E. "James Lind and the Cure for Scurvy: An Experimental Approach." Medical History, 19 (October 1975): 342-51. From his Treatise on Scurvy, 1753, but less aware of experimentation techniques.

1719 Hughes, Robert. The Fatal Shore: A History of the Transportation of Convicts to Australia, 1787-1868. NY: Knopf; London: Collins, 1986, 1987, xvi, 688 pp. Illustrated; Roberts is a critic, calling the process "the British Gulag in the South Pacific" highlighting the brutality and barbarism; thoroughly researched and well-written; 160 convicts were in the First Fleet.

1720 Hughes, Wayne P. Fleet Tactics: Theory and Practice. Annapolis: NIP, 1986, xvi, 316 pp. Fwd: Thomas Hayward; reviewed chronologically by periods, e.g., age of fighting sail, 1650-1805, featuring SOTL, Fighting Instructions, and Nelson as the peerless tactician; Corbett favored Kempenfelt; later periods covered.

1721 Hughill, Stan. Sailortown. London: Routledge, 1967, 360 pp. A social history approach describing seamen ashore; presenting a composite of ports, mostly British; overemphasis on whoring, brothels, debauchery, and drunkenness.

1722 Hulton, Paul, ed. America 1585: The Complete Drawings of John White. Chapel Hill: UNCP; London: British Museum, 1984, viii, 213 pp. Very large folio with 106 b/w and 77 color reproductions of the work of White, fl. 1580s; the first drawings of the New World, what is now Virginia and North Carolina; depictions, e.g., fish, birds, fruit, Eskimos, Indians, and villages.

1723 Hulton, Paul and Quinn, David B., eds. The American Drawings of John White, 1577-1590. 2 vols. London: British Museum, 1964, xi, 160 pp. A variation of the previous entry.

1724 Humble, Richard. Before the DREADNOUGHT: The Royal Navy from Nelson to Fisher. London: Macdonald, 1976, viii, 216 pp. A somewhat superficial overview of developments in the 19th century; presents Admiralty as too conservative and reluctant to change.

1725 -------. Captain Bligh. London: Barker, 1976, 212 pp. More stress on the accomplishments of Bligh, e.g., great seaman, explorer, navigator, surveyor, the extraordinary voyage in the open boat, the 2nd breadfruit voyage, and veteran of Camperdown and Copenhagen.

1726 -------. The Rise and Fall of the British Navy. London: Queen Anne, 1986, 255 pp. A historical survey, beginning in 1509, with an agenda, cold war rhetoric, and indictment of the post-World War II policies and actions, e.g., the Falklands campaign was "irrelevent," other actions were "a total waste" and only for "machismo."

1727 Humble, Richard and Bergin, Mark. A Sixteenth-Century Galleon. Inside Story series. NY: Simon, 1993, 48 pp. Details about this ship type.

1728 Humble, Richard. The Voyages of Captain Cook. Voyages series. NY: Watts, 1990, 32 pp. A short overview.

1729 Hume, David. The History of England from the Invasion of Julius Caesar to the Revolution of 1688. Various: 8, 6, and 1 vols. London; Chicago: Chicago UP; Indianapolis: Liberty, 1754-1791, 1975, 1983-1985. Fwd: William Todd; Hume, 1711-1776, a Scottish intellectual; 1778 was the latest edition to be corrected by Hume; one of the earliest scholarly histories; the so-called "Tory" interpretation.

1730 Hume, Martin A.S. <u>Philip II of Spain</u>. London; Westport: Greenwood, 1897, 1903, 1970, 325 pp. A biography in the "scientific" tradition, ala Ranke; Hume, 1847-1910, used vast resources available.

1731 -------. "Some Survivors of the Armada in Ireland." <u>Trans RHS</u>, 2nd ser, 11 (1897): 41-66. At least 32 of the Spanish ships foundered along the west coasts; English concerned about loyalty of Irish, especially fellow Catholics of Spanish; confusion and lack of information; 270 Spanish befriended by Scots and others to Scotland from Irish wrecks.

1732 -------. <u>The Year after the Armada: And Other Historical Studies</u>. Port Washington: Kennikat, 1896, 1970, xi, 388 pp. A summary of post-Armada events; Mendoza announced a Spanish victory, soon corrected; Spanish cry for vengeance; Medina Sidonia as scapegoat; plans for another armada; much on Philip II.

1733 Humphries, George P. "Admiral George Anson's Administration of the British Admiralty, 1745-1762." Ph.D. diss, Emory, 1953. A scholarly study and appraisal.

1734 Hunt, Barry D. "The Outstanding Naval Strategic Writers of the Century." <u>NWCR</u>, 37 (September 1984): 86-107. For the centennial issue; a review of Mahan, the Colombs, J.K. Laughton, and Corbett, the last being the most important.

1735 -------. <u>Sailor-Scholar: Admiral Sir Herbert Richmond, 1871-1946</u>. Waterloo: Wilfrid Laurier UP, 1982, 259 pp. A biographical study of this unique British naval officer, professor, and scholar; founder of <u>The Naval Review</u>, brilliant intellectual and often prescient; strategic analysis and important historian.

1736 Hunt, Percival. <u>Samuel Pepys in the Diary</u>. Westport: Greenwood, 1958, 1978, 178 pp. A review of the background and substance of the diary; events, e.g., the Restoration, his clerkship, and the great fire.

1737 Hunt, William. "Nautical Autobiography in the Age of Sail." <u>MM</u>, 57 (May 1971): 135-42. A survey of examples.

1738 Hurst, Ronald. <u>The Golden Rock: An Episode of the American War of Independence, 1775-1783</u>. London: Cooper; Annapolis: NIP, 1996, xviii, 254 pp. Re the island of St. Eustatius in the West Indies, important as a base during the American Revolution; originally a Dutch colony, seized by the British, the plunder seized by the French en route to Britain; involved prominent naval commanders, e.g., Rodney, Samuel Hood, and Cockburn.

1739 Huskisson, Thomas. <u>Eyewitness to Trafalgar</u>. London: Ellison, 1985, xii, 112 pp. Huskisson was aboard HMS DEFENCE.

1740 Hussey, Frank. <u>Suffolk Invasion: The Dutch Attack on Landguard Fort, 1667</u>. Lavenham: Dalton, 1983, xi, 188 pp. Many illustrations; during 2nd Dutch War, attack and landing at Landguard Fort on the Suffolk coast.

1741 Hutchinson, Gillian. Medieval Ships and Shipping. Archaeology of Medieval Britain series. Leicester: Leicester UP, 1994, xi, 219 pp. Fwd: Helen Clark; by the curator at NMM; sources from nautical archaeology; covers 1050-1500; chapter on ships in warfare; noted at least 700 ships for Norman Conquest and King John had at least 52 royal galleys.

1742 Hutchinson, J.R. The Press Gang Afloat and Ashore. London: Nash, 1913, viii, 349 pp. A well-researched but exaggerated survey; began in Anglo-Saxon times and evolved into the Impress System; sources from PRO.

1743 Ingleton, Geoffrey C. Matthew Flinders: Navigator and Chartmaker. Guildford: Genesis, 1986, xxiv, 467 pp. Fwd: Duke of Edinburgh; a biography of the late 18th century, early 19th century explorer.

1744 Ingram, Edward. Empire-Building and Empire-Builders: Twelve Studies. London: Cass, 1994, 1995, xvii, 231 pp. By the outspoken critic of traditional views of seapower; most of the 12 essays related to India and the Russian threat of the 19th century; but Nelson is included, yet his 3 great battles are dismissed as irrelevent; also dismisses Mahan; to Ingram, most important was the threat of Russia, replacing that of France; empire builders were Kipling, Forster, and Orwell.

1745 -------, "Illusion of Victory: The Nile, Copenhagen, and Trafalgar Revisited." Military Affairs, 48 (July 1984):140-43. The debunking contiues from the previous entry; the 3 were illusions and a sleight of hand; great myths created by Mahan, C. Northcote Parkinson, and, "most weightily," by Paul Kennedy; the 3 great battles prove the ineffectiveness of seapower and the inability to create decisive influence.

1746 -------. "A Scare of Seaborne Invasion: The Royal Navy at the Strait of Hormuz, 1807-1808." Military Affairs, 46 (April 1982): 64-68. Trafalgar failed to relieve from the threat of invasion; the French moved into the Eastern Mediterranean and concluded an alliance with Persia; this forced RN to enter and defend the Red Sea and Persian Gulf, denuding other important areas.

1747 Ireland, Bernard. Naval Warfare in the Age of Sail: War at Sea, 1756-1815. London: HarperCollins, 2000, 240 pp. A lavishly illustrated introduction to the development of a standing navy, from the time of Henry VIII, the Dutch Wars, and 18th-century wars.

1748 Ireland, John de Courcy and Sheehy, D., eds. Atlantic Visions. Dublin: Glendale, 1989. De Courcy Ireland, a revered and prolific naval historian; a series of essays, e.g., Mac Cana, "The Voyage of St. Brendan: Literary and Historical Origins" and D.B. Quinn on the Atlantic islands.

1749 Ireland, John de Courcy. Ireland and the Irish in Maritime History. Dublin: Glendale, 1986, xiv, 449 pp. To present the basis for Ireland as a place of maritime tradition for 8000 years; includes Vikings and Anglo-Normans.

1750 -------. "Irish Naval Connections in Brest in the Eighteenth and Nineteenth Centuries." Irish Sword, 17 (Summer 1987): 57-60. Description of extensive sources available in Brest, e.g., archives on the French navy and some Irish connections.

1751 -------. "Irish Naval Links with the Adriatic." Irish Sword, 6 (Winter 1963): 76-80. The Adriatic was famous for naval innovation, Dubrovnik, now Ragusa, and Venice being production facilities; some ships and men were aboard Armada wrecks along the Irish coast.

1752 -------. "Irish Seamen in the Naval Warfare of 1793-1815." Irish Sword, 4 (1959): 40-42. Recounts seamen and service in the wars.

1753 -------. "Note on the Spanish Armada." MM, 76 (May 1990): 173-75. To elaborate and clarify certain aspects at the quadricentennial: the international nature of the ships and men, Portuguese-built galleons were impressive for survival, and Medina Sidonia deserves more credit.

1754 -------. "Ragusa and the Spanish Armada." MM, 64 (August 1978): 251-62. Formerly Dubrovnik, and successful rival of Venice; contributed the "Twelve Apostles," plus as many as 20 more galleons built there, to the Armada; but 10 of 12 Ragusan-built ships sank; an impressive naval tradition for centuries.

1755 -------. "Review of Evelyn Hardy, Survivors of the Armada." Irish Historical Studies, 15 (March 1967): 317-22. Noted myths from the English, e.g., Armada almost totally destroyed and "Protestant Wind"; how decisive was the Armada campaign?; notes differing numbers of estimates of Spanish losses, e.g., Mattingly, 63, Waters, 44, Lewis, 51, and Petruccio Ubaldino, 32; Hardy careless errors.

1756 Irrmann, Robert H. "Edward Russell, Earl of Orford, 1653-1727, and the Administration of the Royal Navy to 1701." Ph.D. diss, Indiana, 1946, 185 pp. A scholarly study of this administrator.

1757 Isaacson, Cecil J. Nelson's "Five Years on the Beach" and the Other Horatio Nelson of Burnham Thorpe. Falkenham: Lancaster, 1991, 27 pp. Anecdotal; discovery of a grave in Fahan, Northern Ireland: "Thomas 'Horatio' Nelson, 1793-1811, Midshipman, RN, born, Burnham Thorpe, died, age 18"; no kin; and that Nelson had spent 5 years on half-pay.

1758 Isil, Olivia. When a Loose Cannon Flogs a Dead Horse There's the Devil to Pay: Seafaring Words in Everyday Speech. NY: McGraw, 1996. In the nautical dictionary tradition.

1759 Israel, Jonathan I., ed. The Anglo-Dutch Moment: Essays on the Glorious Revolution and Its World Impact. NY: Cambridge UP, 1991, xvi, 502 pp. Edited by the preeminent British historian of Dutch history; the proceedings of a conference at the British Academy, April 1989, on the tercentenary of the Revolution and Dutch involvement; contributors, e.g., Geoffrey Parker, J.R. Jones, H.R. Trevor-Roper, and K.N. Chaudhuri; 16 papers, e.g., on "Protestant Winds" and Armadas, Spanish of 1588 and Dutch of 1688, on English-Dutch-French competition in the Indian Ocean, and on the East India Companies.

1760 Israel, Jonathan I. "Competing Cousins: Anglo-Dutch Trade Rivalry." HisTod, 38 (July 1988): 17-22. 3 hard-fought wars in the 17th century based primarily on commercial rivalry; conclusion: from hindsight, all was an unmitigated failure for the English; it was the Glorious Revolution that transformed the situation.

1761 -------. Conflict of Empires: Spain, the Low Countries and the Struggle for World Supremacy, 1585-1713. London: Hambledon, 1997, xxv, 420 pp. 18 collected essays, e.g., on Anglo-Dutch competition, the Dutch and the Jews, and the Glorious Revolution; conclusion: in 1585, Spain was hegemonic; by 1713, "the sick man of Europe."

1762 -------. Dutch Primacy in World Trade, 1585-1740. Oxford: Oxford UP, 1989, 1990, 1992, xxi, 462 pp. The definitive treatment: for 200 years, the Dutch dominated world trade, an unprecedented hegemony, then a fatal and absolute decline; a critique of the Braudel thesis.

1763 -------. The Dutch Republic: Its Rise, Greatness, and Fall, 1477-1806. The Oxford History of Early Modern Europe. NY: Oxford UP, 1995, 1998, 1231 pp. A massive tome and definitive survey of a Golden Age without precedent; a bibliography of 57 pages.

1764 Jablonsky, David, ed. Roots of Strategy. Book 4: Mahan, Corbett, Douhet, Mitchell. Mechanicsburg: Stackpole, 1999, 533 pp. From a series on strategic thinkers, this one on sea and air power; introductory essays and excerpts, about 100 pages each.

1765 Jackson, Melvin H. and De Beer, Carel. Eighteenth-Century Gunfounding: The Verbruggens at the Royal Brass Foundry: A Chapter in the History of Technology. Wash: Smithsonian, 1974, 183 pp. Fwd: Basil Greenhill; the Verbruggens came from Holland bringing this advanced technology with them; to the Royal Arsenal, Woolwich; this book contains 50 extraordinary drawings, origins unknown, demonstrating the technical details of brass gunfounding; the originals held by NMM.

1766 Jackson, Scott T. "Impressment and Anglo-American Discord, 1787-1818." Ph.D. diss, Michigan, 1976, 518 pp. A comprehensive scholarly review of the backgrounds, rationales, and positions of both sides.

1767 [NRS 16 and 18]. Jackson, T. Sturges, ed. Logs of the Great Sea Fights, 1794-1805. 2 vols. Publications of the Navy Records Society, vols. 16 and 18. London: NRS, 1899-1900, xvi, 342 and vi, 343 pp. Sources from the PRO; logs of Masters and journals of Captains, e.g., battles of Cape St. Vincent, Camperdown,

Copenhagen, the Nile, and Trafalgar.

1768 Jackson, William Godfrey Fothergill. <u>The Pomp of Yesterday: The Defence of India and the Suez Canal, 1798-1918</u>. London: Brassey, 1995, x, 262 pp. Later Field Marshal Sir William Jackson and Lord Bramall; fundamental to British strategy was control over all access routes to India resulting in numerous conflicts for over 200 years; involved, e.g., Nelson, Sidney Smith, the Eastern Question, and the Great Game.

1769 -------. <u>The Rock of the Gibraltarians: A History of Gibraltar</u>. London: Associated, 1987, 1988, 384 pp. Jackson was Governor, 1978-1982; covers from ancient times to the present, e.g. 3 sieges between 1300-1460; # 13 in the 1720s, # 14, the "Great Siege," in the 1780s, and the 15th, 1969-1985.

1770 Jacobs, James R. and Tucker, Glenn. <u>The War of 1812: A Compact History</u>. <u>The Military History of the United States</u> series. NY: Hawthorne, 1969, 224 pp. A short, undistinguished account of this "stupid war."

1771 Jacobs, Trevor K. and Vellios, Jim. <u>Southland: The Maritime Exploration of Australia</u>. East Perth: Australian Education, 1988, 164 pp. A summary of the exploration efforts of the Portuguese, Dutch, French, and British.

1772 Jal, Augustin. <u>A. Du Quesne el la marine de son temps</u>. 2 vols. Paris, 1873. Augustin or Auguste Jal, 1795-1873, the pre-eminent and influential French naval historian who, in this and the next entries, presents the first scholarly consideration of ships and naval matters; so influential during turn-of-the-century Britain that founders of SNR almost called it The Jal Society.

1773 -------. <u>Archeologie navale: publiee par ordre des roi</u>. 2 vols. Paris, 1839, 1840. A continuation.

1774 -------. <u>Glossaire nautique: Repertoire polyglotte de terms de marine ancien et modernes</u>. Alt. title: <u>Nouveau Glossaire Nautique d'Augustin Jal</u>. 2 vols. Paris: Moutin, 1848, 1970, 1978, 1989, 1998, 612 pp. Various editions; described as "a polyglot dictionary" in alphabetical order by sections, e.g., "A-E," "G," etc.

1775 James, G.F. and Shaw, J.J. Sutherland. "Admiralty Administration and Personnel, 1619-1714." <u>Bull IHR</u>, 14 (1936 and 1937): 10-24, 166-83. At this time a Navy Board acted on behalf of and at the command of the LHA, all described by Pepys.

1776 James, G.F. "The Admiralty Buildings, 1695-1723." <u>MM</u>, 26 (October 1940): 356-74. The rapid expansion of the navy meant expanded facilities and the status of a department of state; in 1695, the Commissioners called for a new set of buildings at the top of Whitehall, the present location.

1777 -------. "Josiah Burchett, Secretary to the Lords Commissioners of the

Admiralty, 1695-1742." MM, 23 (1937): 477-98. Effectively, the successor to Pepys, not as colorful nor as perceptive, but as influential.

1778 -------. "Some Further Aspects of Admiralty Administration, 1689-1714." Bull IHR, 17 (1939): 13-27. A continuation; details on how business was conducted and the role of the Secretary of State.

1779 James, Lawrence. Mutiny: In the British and Commonwealth Forces, 1797-1956. London: Buchan, 1987, 276 pp. A survey of the incidents, e.g., "the Worm in the Oak" about naval mutinies, 1797-1806; other accounts are better.

1780 -------. The Rise and Fall of the British Empire. London: Little, Brown, 1994, 1996, xvi, 704 pp. An unusual naval slant, beginning with the "first Empire" of the late 16th century, notably the piracy, "a strong cord, whose fibres were greed and fearlessness, linked the Elizabethan sea rover, the 18th century naval captain hungry for prize money, and the early Victorian soldier in the process of looting"; 300 years of rise, 80 years of fall; much use of Admiralty records.

1781 James, Margery K. "Fluctuations in the Anglo-Gascon Wine Trade during the Fourteenth Century." Economic History Review, 2nd ser, 4 (1951): 170-96. An important medieval trade; records indicate fluctuations.

1782 -------. Studies in the Medieval Wine Trade. Oxford: Oxford UP, 1971, 232 pp. Ed: Elspeth Veale; intro: E.M. Carus-Wilson; re detailed statistics of the wine trade with Gascony in the 14th and 15th centuries.

1783 James, William. A Full and Correct Account of the Chief Naval Occurrences of the Late War between Great Britain and the United States of America. London, 1817. James, 1780-1827, had travelled in the West Indies and was actually detained as an enemy alien in Philadelphia in 1812; conducted considerable research, e.g., learning that American frigates were large and heavily armed; written to counteract the ultra-patriotic American interpretations and inaccuracies, in his view, of the War of 1812; conclusion: no American ship captured a British one of equal force and the opposite did occur, more than once; this account much criticized by American historians.

1784 -------. The Naval History of Great Britain: From the Declaration of the War by France in 1793 to the Accession of George IV. 6 vols. London: Macmillan; Harrisburg: Stackpole, 1822-1827, 1836-1837,1847, 1859, 1864, 1886, 1898, 1902, 2002, 2640 pp. Eds: Frederick Chamier, C.T. Wilson, and York Powell, each updating the history; new intro: Andrew Lambert; popularly known as "James's Naval History"; begins with 1488 with the construction of GREAT HARRY of Henry VII; Henry VIII instituted an Admiralty and a naval office; Chamier added coverage of Navarino and the Burma campaign.

1785 James, W.M. The British Navy in Adversity: A Study of the War of American Independence. London: Longman; London: Russell, 1926, 1970, 459 pp. By

Admiral Sir William James; a survey of naval operations with emphasis on fleet movements and battles, little on naval policies and strategy; now superseded; judgmental: English leaders and the admirals were weak and incompetent, a conclusion similar to that of Mahan.

1786 -------. The Durable Monument: Horatio Nelson. London: Longman, 1948, viii, 312 pp. James had actually used HMS VICTORY as his flagship as C-in-C, Portsmouth during World War II; an adequate biography but no scholarly apparatus; a brief historiographical survey in the Prologue.

1787 -------. "Old Oak" The Life of John Jervis, Earl St. Vincent. London: Longman, 1950, ix, 230 pp. The title comes from George III who called Jervis that; an adequate biography but the definitive biography has yet to be written.

1788 "James Cook Commemoration." MM, 65 (May 1979): 105-08. Re a special service at Westminster Abbey, Sunday, 11 February 1979, commemorating his life and achievements; Cook, killed in Hawaii, 14 February 1779; Basil Greenhill of NMM gave the address; the Naval Prayer and Drake's Prayer.

1789 Jameson, A.K. "Some New Spanish Documents Dealing with Drake." EHR, 49 (January 1934): 14-31. Re new sources, especially Spanish ones, about Drake, e.g., new details about the failed attacks by Drake.

1790 Jameson, John F. Privateering and Piracy in the Colonial Period: Illustrative Documents. Reprints of Economic Classics. London: Macmillan; NY: Kelley, 1923, 1970, 619 pp. A chronological survey, 1630s-1760s with supporting primary documents, e.g., letter of marque, profits and losses, and legal and constitutional issues; supplements Exquemeling.

1791 Jamieson, Alan G. "American Privateers in the Leeward Islands, 1776-1778." AmNep, 43 (January 1983): 20-30. Re American maritime activity during the American Revolution; some operations off the British Isles but more effective in the Caribbean; aided by the French; British forced to resort to convoys and Anglo-French relations deteriorated.

1792 Jamison, Alan G., ed. A People of the Sea: The Maritime History of the Channel Islands. London: Methuen, 1986, 1987, xxxvi, 528 pp. Illustrated; a series of essays by experts, e.g., J.S. Bromley and Barry Cunliffe; topics, e.g., privateering from the islands, smuggling, and harbor development.

1793 Jamieson, Alan G. "War in the Leeward Islands, 1775-1783." D.Phil. diss, Oxford, 1981. A substantial and definitive study.

1794 Jarvis, Rupert C. "Sources for the History of Ships and Shipping." J Transport History, 3 (November 1958): 212-34. A review of records and sources, e.g., government records, HCA, Lloyd's Registry, letters of marque, and Customs transactions.

1795 Jeaffreson, John C. Lady Hamilton and Lord Nelson: A Historical Biography. 2 vols. London: Hurst, 1888, 1897, xvi, 714 pp. Jeaffreson, 1831-1901, a novelist and inspector of manuscripts; based on the Morrison MSS, some of which was not published until later.

1796 -------. The Queen of Naples and Lord Nelson: An Historical Biography based on MSS in the British Museum and. . . amongst the Morrison MSS. 2 vols. London: Hurst, 1889, xxviii, 747 pp. Further biographical studies based on contemporary MSS.

1797 Jenkins, Ernest H. A History of the French Navy: From Its Beginnings to the Present Day. London: Macdonald, 1973, 364 pp. A history featuring Richelieu, Colbert, Dutch wars, Barbary pirates, guerre de course, and conflict with Britain; privateering and naval policies are indistinguishable; superficial coverage.

1798 Jenkins, Ian and Sloan, Kim. Vases and Volcanoes: Sir William Hamilton and His Collection. London: British Museum, 1996, 320 pp. In support of an exhibition at the British Museum, 1996; Hamilton was an archaeologist, collector, and British envoy to the Kingdom of the Two Sicilies; favored were Greek vases; he died in 1803.

1799 Jenkins, John. The Naval Achievements of Great Britain: From the Year 1793 to 1817. London: Comfort, 1817, 1998, 288 pp. Illustrated; dedicated to Lord St. Vincent; a contemporaneous history.

1800 Jenks, Timothy. "Contesting the Hero: The Funeral of Admiral Lord Nelson." J British Studies, 39 (October 2000): 422-53. The funeral, 9 January 1806, the "apotheosis"; planners and the government were anxious to exploit the popularity of Nelson, especially after Trafalgar, 21 October 1805; a state funeral and internment in St. Paul's in the Crypt immediately under the crossing.

1801 -------. "Language and Politics at the Westminster Election of 1796." Historical J, 44 (June 2001): 419-39. Naval officers in politics; Admiral Allan Gardner, the government-supported candidate in the Westminster election; others, C.J. Fox and John Horne Tooke; 2nd anniversary of the Glorious First of June played up; Gardner and Fox won.

1802 -------. "Naval Engagements: Patriotism, Cultural Politics, and the Royal Navy, 1793-1815." Ph.D. diss, Toronto, 2000. The basis for these entries.

1803 Jenner, G. "A Spanish Account of Drake's Voyages." EHR, 16 (January 1901): 46-66. Reviews Spanish accounts recently discovered; recounted how the Spanish celebrated at word of the death of Drake.

1804 Jensen, De Lamar. "Bernardino de Mendoza and the League." Ph.D. diss, Columbia, 1957, 293 pp. The basis of the next entry.

1805 -------. Diplomacy and Dogmatism: Bernardino de Mendoza and the French Catholic League. Cambridge: Harvard UP, 1964, 322 pp. A case study of Catholic-Protestant-Calvinist conflict; the Spanish ambassador to France was de Mendoza who coordinated action between extreme Catholics of the Holy League and Philip II and prevented any aid by Henry III of France to Elizabeth of England.

1806 -------. "The Spanish Armada: The Worst-Kept Secret in Europe." Sixteenth-Century J, 19 (Winter 1988): 621-42. Details on plans, preparations, and diplomatic maneuvers from the Spanish perspective; expense was a factor; Philip II demanded action to prevent further excess expense.

1807 Jerrold, Walter, ed. The Nelson Touch: Being a Little Book of the Great Seamen's Wisdom. London: Murray, 1918, xxv, 91 pp. Intro: H.W. Wilson; excerpts from writings of Nelson with emphasis on character.

1808 Jesch, Judith. Ships and Men of the Viking Age: The Vocabulary of Runic Inscriptions and Skaldic Verse. Woodbridge: Boydell, 2001, xiv, 330 pp. A survey of the period, 950-1100, including fleets, battles, and sailing qualities; critical analysis; emphasis on philology; sets vocabulary in context.

1809 Joel, David. Charles Brooking, 1723-1759 and 18th-Century British Maritime Painters. Woodbridge: Antique, 2000, 208 pp. An excellent survey of this maritime painter, native of Greenwich; 228 paintings; as with the Dutch painters, treated ships as works of art.

1810 John, Eric. "War and Society in the Tenth Century: The Maldon Campaign." Trans RHS, 5th ser, 27 (1977): 173-95. The time of Anglo-Saxons vs. Vikings, 300 years of war; reign of AEthelred II who died in 1008; Vikings attacked area around Southampton; Anglo-Saxon forces were mobilized, culminating in the battle of Maldon, a turning point.

1811 Johns, A.W. "Phineas Pett." MM, 12 (October 1926): 431-42. Several members of this famous family of naval constructors with the same name during the late 17th century.

1812 -------. "Sir Anthony Deane." MM, 11 (April 1925): 164-93. Re the most prominent naval constructor of the late 17th century, a close collaborator with Pepys who did not get along with the Petts; in the 1670s, Deane and Pepys to the Tower but later released; Deane hosted Peter the Great during his visit to Portsmouth.

1813 Johnson, Charles. A General History of the Robberies and Murders of the Most Notorious Pyrates. London: Conway; London: Routledge; Columbia: USCP, 1724, 1728, 1765, 1788, 1850, 1955, 1990, 1992, 1998. Eds: Philip Gosse, Manuel Schonhorn, and Arthur Hayward; an ongoing debate: attributed by some to Daniel Defoe; a contemporaneous survey; features, e.g. Blackbeard, Anne Bonny, and Mary Read; used in literature, e.g., R.L. Stevenson, Sir Walter Scott, and Hollywood movie makers.

1814 Johnson, Donald S., ed. Charting the Sea of Darkness: The Four Voyages of Henry Hudson. NY: McGraw; London: Kodansha, 1993, 1995, xiii, 242 pp. Re the 4 voyages of Hudson, 1607-1611; Hudson sailed for the Muscovy Company to seek the Northeast Passage, to the Kara Sea, then west to Delaware and up the Hudson River, and, finally, up to Hudson's Bay where he and 8 others were set adrift; in 1989, a replica of HALF MOON was built and sailed, now at Jersey City.

1815 Johnson, G.C. "The Military and Naval Terms in the Norman and Anglo-Saxon Chronicles of the Twelfth Century." Ph.D. diss, Leeds, 1949, ix, 410 pp. A scholarly study of the terminology.

1816 Johnson, J.A. "Parliament and the Navy, 1688-1714." Ph.D. diss, Sheffield, 1969. A scholarly study of relationships during and after the Glorious Revolution.

1817 Johnson, Roy F. The ROYAL GEORGE. London: Knight, 1971, 201 pp. Fwd: Earl Mountbatten; the flagship of Admiral Kempenfelt sank off Portsmouth, 1782, at anchor in a flat calm, 900 lost including women and children; Duncan and Jervis on court martial which deemed structural accident; Johnson disagrees and concludes incompetence and carelessness while heeling the ship; not convincing.

1818 Johnson, Stephen. The Roman Forts of the Saxon Shore. London: Elek, 1976, 1979, xii, 172 pp. As Germanic tribes began invading about the 3rd century, the Romans built a series of forts along the south and east coast, called the Saxon Shore; some ruins still exist and much evidence from archaeological digs.

1819 Johnson, William B. The English Prison Hulks. London: Phillimore, 1957, 1970, 205 pp. A temporary measure as prisons filled and before transportation was initiated; locations, e.g., Woolwich, Medway, Portsmouth, Plymouth, and Bermuda; revived in 1922-1925 for internment at Belfast.

1820 -------. Wolves of the Channel, 1681-1856. London: Wishart, 1931, xi, 309 pp. The "wolves" were privateers, all aspects being explained, e.g., the business side, tactics, bases, and practitioners, e.g., English, Scots, and French, calling it guerre de course.

1821 Johnston, George. A Charge of Mutiny: The Court Martial of Lt. Col. George Johnston for Deposing Governor William Bligh in the Rebellion of 26 January 1808. Canberra: National Library, 1988, xxiv, 490 pp. Ed: John Ritchie; a trial of 13 days, May-June 1811 at Chelsea Hospital, London; Bligh testified for 3 days; Bligh was deposed by Johnston and the New South Wales Corps; deliberation was 1 hour and Johnston was guilty, sentenced to be cashiered.

1822 Johnston, Penelope. "Newfoundland's Twin Celebrations." HisTod, 49 (December 1999): 7-8. Actually, several celebrations including sailing of a replica of a Viking ship, ISTENDINGUR, Iceland to L'Anse where Lief Eiriksson landed in 1001, and the archaeological discovery of the settlement in 1960.

1823 Jolliffe, Diana. The Mutineers of the BOUNTY and their Descendants in Pitcairn and Norfolk Islands. NY: Harper; London: Murray; NY: AMS, 1870, 1871, 1980, 377 pp. By Diana, Lady Belcher, 1805-1890; a study based on the journal of James Morrison.

1824 Jolly, Rick and Wilson, Tugg. Jackspeak: The Pusser's Rum Guide to Royal Navy Slanguage. Torpoint: Palamanando, 1989, 336 pp. By a surgeon commander; notes on slang, euphemisms, idioms; 3500 entries.

1825 Jones, D.W. War and Economy in the Age of William III and Marlborough. Oxford: Blackwell, 1988, xviii, 351 pp. A monograph about the Nine Years' War and War of Spanish Succession; the beginnings of the fiscal-military state.

1826 Jones, E.H.S. The Invasion that Failed: The French Expedition to Ireland, 1796. London: Blackwell, 1950, xvi, 256 pp. A French invasion operation under General Hoche to Bantry Bay, December 1796; to aid Wolfe Tone in Dublin; all failed, and again in 1797, and again in 1798.

1827 [NRS 72]. Jones, G. Pitcairn, ed. Piracy in the Levant, 1827-1828: Selected from the Papers of Admiral Sir Edward Codrington, KCB. Publications of the Navy Records Society, vol. 72. London: NRS, 1934, xxxvi, 325 pp. Codrington, 1770-1851; commander of ORION and TRAFALGAR; battle of Navarino.

1828 Jones, J. Michael. Historic Warships: A Directory of 140 Museums and Memorials Worldwide, with Histories. Jefferson: McFarland, 1993, xxv, 245 pp. A listing of 144 ships in 25 countries, e.g., MARY ROSE, VICTORY, and WARRIOR at Portsmouth and VASA at Stockholm; in alphabetical order by country.

1829 Jones, J.R. The Anglo-Dutch Wars of the Seventeenth Century. Modern Wars in Perspective series. NY: Longman, 1996, xi, 242 pp. An outstanding survey; recounts the 3 wars of the mid-17th century; assessed strengths and weaknesses of each; global implications; Mahan made much of them, illustrating his principles of sea power.

1830 -------. "The Dutch Navy and National Survival in the Seventeenth Century." International History Review, 10 (February 1988): 18-32. The 1st martime power and 1st bourgeois state but very vulnerable to the English and to French privateering; at war over 60 years in the 17th century.

1831 -------. The Revolution of 1688 in England. Revolutions in the Modern World series. NY: Norton; London: Weidenfeld, 1972, 1984, xx, 345 pp. A standard survey of the revolution.

1832 Jones, Robert C. "Patrick O'Brian's Aubrey/Maturin Novels: An Overview." Naval History, 8 (February 1994): 55-56. The novels present a grand tour of early 19[th-]century naval, diplomatic, and social world; also features intelligence and culture, e.g., music, food, and language.

1833 Jonquiere, Marquis de la. [in French] The Official History of the Egyptian Campaign of Napoleon Bonaparte. 5 vols. Paris: Ministry of War, 1910. The official history from the French government.

1834 Joppien, Rudiger and Smith, Bernard. The Art of Captain Cook's Voyages. 3 vols. I: The Voyage of the ENDEAVOUR, 1768-1771. II: The Voyage of the RESOLUTION and ADVENTURE, 1772-1775. III: The Voyage of the RESOLUTION and the DISCOVERY, 1776-1780. New Haven: Yale UP, 1985-1988, xxviii, 1431 pp. Very large folio size with magnificent colored illustrations, an impressive production; among the extraordinary features of the Cook voyages was the presence of professional artists of nature, e.g., Sydney Parkinson, Herman Sporing, Alexander Buchan, and William Hodges; sometime supervised by Joseph Banks.

1835 Jordan, Gerald and Rogers, Nicholas. "Admirals as Heroes: Patriotism and Liberty in Havoverian England." J British Studies, 28 (July 1989): 201-24. A study in political culture, symbolism, and ritual; the ceremonial aspects of anniversaries, processions, and parades of Georgian England; heroes were celebrated, e.g. Vernon and Nelson; the celebrations took on political and religious implications, e.g., anti-Walpole, anti-Catholic, pro-Pitt, anti-radical, and anti-Paine.

1836 Jordan, Gerald, ed. British Military History: A Supplement to Robin Higham's Guide to the Sources. Military History Bibliographies series, vol. 10. NY: Garland, 1988, xiv, 586 pp. 6400 entries, updating of the Higham Guide of 1970; experts writing historiographical essays, e.g., Daniel Baugh on the navy to 1714 and Roger Knight and Alan Pearsall on the navy after 1714.

1837 Jordan, Gerald. "Mahan's Life of Nelson." Northern Mariner, 8 (April 1998): 39-49. Contention: more biographies of Nelson than any other figure in British history; that of Mahan remains the standard though that was not his most popular book.

1838 Jordan, William C., et al., eds. Order and Innovation in the Middle Ages: Essays in Honour of Joseph R. Strayer. Princeton: Princeton UP, 1976, xii, 582 pp. Festschrift essays, e.g., A.R. Lewis, "Northern European Sea Power and the Straits of Gibraltar, 1031-1350 AD," and Teofilo Ruiz, "Castilian Merchants in England, 1248-1350"; Lewis noted the great transformation, Genoese, Venetian, Catalan, and Florentine galleys with regular annual schedules from the Mediterranean to Northern Europe, to Southampton and Bruges; but not opposite, i.e., rare for northern Europeans into the Mediterranean, indeed, no single European ship returned out of the Mediterranean; interesting alliance system, late 13th century: English-Flemish-Gascon vs. French-Genoese-Castilian, e.g., battles of Sluys and La Rochelle.

1839 Junge, Hans-Christoph. Flottenpolitik und Seemacht: Die Entstehung der

Englishen Seemacht Wahrend der Herrschaft Cromwells. Stuttgart: Klett-Cotta, 1980, 368 pp. An important study of the navy of the mid-17th century.

1840 Kamen, Henry A.F. "The Destruction of the Spanish Silver Fleet at Vigo in 1702." Bull IHR, 39 (November 1966): 165-73. An English-Dutch operation at the beginning of the War of Spanish Succession failed at Cadiz but attacked Spanish treasure fleet guarded by French SOTL at Vigo; conclusion: allies destroyed French and Spanish ships but no great benefit was achieved.

1841 -------. Philip of Spain. New Haven: Yale UP, 1997, xvi, 384 pp. Re the Machiavellian monarch in the Escorial, tyrant, bigot, and zealot, the depictions of the Black Legend and other myths; occasion of the quadricentennial of his death, an appraisal with emphasis on personal attributes and depiction of Philip as "normal."

1842 -------. The War of Succession in Spain, 1700-1715. Bloomington: Ind UP, 1969, xii, 436 pp. The perspective of Spain experiencing financial problems and internal revolts.

1843 Kaplan, Herbert. Russian Overseas Commerce with Great Britain during the Reign of Catherine II. Memoirs of the American Philosophical Society. Phil: APS, 1995, xxx, 309 pp. From British and Russian archives; Anglo-Russian relations stimulated British expansion, industrial revolution, and strategic considerations; products, especially naval stores, e.g., hemp, flax, tallow, and timber.

1844 Kaplan, Roger. "The Hidden War: British Intelligence Operations during the American Revolution." William and Mary Quarterly, 47 (January 1990): 115-38. Problems and obstacles of British commanders were overcome somewhat by an expansive intelligence network achieved by innovation and resourcefulness; but it was not enough.

1845 Karraker, Cyrus H. Piracy Was a Business. NY: Smith, 1953, 244 pp. A superficial survey of piracy, privateering, smuggling, wrecking, bootlegging, and racketeering, all historical, e.g., the Pirate Syndicate of the West Country of England and Barbary corsairs.

1846 Kauffmann, Jean-Paul. The Black Room at Longwood: A Voyage to St. Helena. London: Harvill, 1999, xviii, 297 pp. Trans: Patricia Clancy; by a French magazine writer who spent a week on St. Helena reviewing the last days of Napoleon.

1847 Keate, Edith M. The Mystery of Nelson's Coat: A Story of Greenwich. London: Eldon, 1936, 279 pp. Speculation on the disposition.

1848 -------. Nelson's Wife: The First Biography of Frances Herbert, Viscountess Nelson. London: Cassell, 1939, x, 303 pp. Dedicated to Julian Corbett; chronological coverage; depicts an admirable wife for an ordinary officer; the first crack was Nelson's visit to Naples after the Nile; critical of Emma Hamilton.

1849 Keegan, John. "The Parameters of Warfare." MHQ, 5 (Winter 1993): 36-43. Some see John Keegan as the best current military historian; his version of Fifteen Decisive Battles by Creasy, his list of 15 naval battles, e.g., Armada, Quiberon Bay, Virginia Capes, Camperdown, the Nile, Copenhagen, and Trafalgar.

1850 -------. The Price of Admiralty: The Evolution of Naval Warfare. NY: Viking; London: Hutchinson, 1988, 1989, 304 pp. A survey of the battle at sea, selecting 4: Trafalgar, Jutland, Midway, and the Atlantic; not well received, claiming Keegan unfamiliar with essentials and the literature; "replete with errors"; no scholarly apparatus.

1851 Keeler, Mary F. Sir Francis Drake's West Indian Voyage, 1585-1586. Publications of the Hakluyt Society, 2nd ser, vol. 148. London: Hakluyt Society, 1981, xiv, 358 pp. This voyage before the circumnavigation and before the Armada; raids in the Caribbean and on Florida, called at Roanoke.

1852 Keevil, John J. Lloyd, Christopher, and Coulter, J.L.S., eds. Medicine and the Navy, 1200-1900. 4 vols. Edinburgh: Livingston, 1957-1963. Intro: Henry Dale; sponsor: Wellcome Trust; Keevill died in mid-term; formerly a neglected subject, L.G. Carr Laughton calling to fill the gap in 1910, now fulfilled; extensive and comprehensive coverage in chronological sections per volume: 1200-1649, 1649-1714, 1714-1815, 1815-1900; themes, e.g., scurvy, James Lind, hygiene, ventilation, sea diseases, naval hospitals, nursing services, convict voyages, and Arctic voyages.

1853 Kelly, James. "The Pirate, the Ambassador and the Map-Maker." HisTod, 48 (July 1998): 49-55. An incident of 1682 involving HCA; buccaneer Bartholomew Sharpe and 2 others indicted for piracy and murder; the fact of secret Spanish charts and pilotage directions figured in the case.

1854 Kelly, J.B. Britain and the Persian Gulf, 1795-1880. Oxford: Clarendon, 1968, 1991, xiv, 911 pp. A comprehensive survey emphasizing diplomacy and political expansion; an early concern was Napoleonic ambitions in the Middle East; also naval operations against piracy and to secure route to India.

1855 Kelly, Joseph K. "The Struggle for American Seaborne Independence as Viewed by John Adams." Ph.D. diss, Maine, 1973, 431 pp. Adams identified the cause as the Navigation Acts, he having adjudicated several cases; he urged French naval intervention; he and son, J.Q. Adams, consistently opposed impressment and supported American seaborne independence.

1856 Kelsey, Harry. Sir Francis Drake: The Queen's Pirate. New Haven: Yale UP, 1998, xviii, 566 pp. From provincial obscurity to international celebrity; 6 major voyages and the Armada; flaws in his character, e.g., disloyalty to superiors, bully, poor leadership skills, and controversial execution of Thomas Doughty, intensively researched.

1857 Kemp, Peter Kemp and Lloyd, Christopher. <u>Bretheren of the Coast: The British and French Buccaneers of the South Sea</u>. NY: St. Martin, 1960, 1961, 248 pp. Kemp, a naval officer, former head of the Historical Branch, and prolific writer; this book on incursions into the Pacific, e.g., Morgan, Dampier, and Woodes Rogers; some themes, e.g., brotherhood and homosexuality.

1858 Kemp, Peter Kemp. <u>The British Sailor: A Social History of the Lower Deck</u>. London: Dent, 1970, 241 pp. Incorporates primary sources; themes, e.g., service, conditions, victualling, pay, punishment, prize money, recruiting, and scurvy.

1859 -------. <u>The Campaign of the Spanish Armada</u>. Oxford: Phaidon; NY: Facts, 1988, 176 pp. Quadricentennial publication, lavishly illustrated; traditional narrative, focusing on naval operations; dated.

1860 Kemp, Peter Kemp, ed. <u>The Encyclopedia of Ships and Seafaring</u>. NY: Crown; London: Stanford, 1980, 256 pp. Profusely illustrated; a series of comprehensive chapters by experts; ship and boat types, great men, e.g., TITANIC and HMS VICTORY.

1861 Kemp, Peter Kemp and Ormond, Richard. <u>The Great Age of Sail: Maritime Art and Photography</u>. Oxford: Phaidon; NY: Facts, 1986, 127 pp. Very large folio size, illustrated, magnificent production; from the largest collection in the world at NMM.

1862 Kemp, Peter Kemp, ed. <u>History of the Royal Navy</u>. NY: Putnam, 1969, 304 pp. A series of essays by experts, e.g., Lloyd, Ranft, and Warner; noted commendation of RN that Napoleon trusted it for his security, twice, as he surrendered; other themes, e.g., Cinque Ports, LHA, Alfred, Sluys, and Armada.

1863 Kemp, Peter Kemp. <u>The History of Ships</u>. London: Orbis, 1978, 288 pp. Fwd: Frank Carr; large folio size, colored pictures every page; a survey.

1864 Kemp, Peter Kemp, ed. <u>A Hundred Years of Sea Stories: From Melville to Hemingway</u>. London: Cassell, 1955, 287 pp. An anthology, selections from nautical fiction.

1865 Kemp, Peter Kemp. <u>Nine VANGUARDS</u>. London: Hutchinson, 1951, 236 pp. Survey of the history of these named warships.

1866 Kemp, Peter Kemp, ed. <u>The Oxford Companion to Ships and the Sea</u>. London: Oxford UP, 1976, 1988, vii, 971 pp. Outstanding reference guide, 4000 entries, a <u>potpourri</u> of maritime heritage, battles, ports, and biographical sketches; contributors, e.g., Arthur Marder, S.E. Morison, Padfield, and Skelton.

1867 [NRS 102 and 106]. Kemp, Peter Kemp, ed. <u>The Papers of Admiral Sir John Fisher</u>. 2 vols. <u>Publications of the Navy Records Society</u>, vols. 102 and 106. London: NRS, 1955-1964, xxviii, 411 and xii, 472 pp. From the extensive collection of Fisher papers; informative on one of the most influential and fascinating figures in British naval history.

1868 Kemp, Peter Kemp. Prize Money: A Survey of the History and Distribution of the Naval Prize Fund. Aldershot: Gale, 1946, 33 pp. A short survey in pamphlet format.

1869 -------. The True Book about the Royal Navy. London: Muller, 1959, 144 pp. Illus: David Cobb; an overview for juveniles.

1870 Kendall, Calvin B. and Wells, Peter S., eds. Voyage to the Other World: The Legacy of SUTTON HOO. Minneapolis: U Minn P, 1992, xix, 222 pp. 12 papers, conference proceedings, the 50th anniversary of the discovery; topics, e.g., links to the epic poem, "Beowulf," coins from diverse origins, and the significance of the ship burial.

1871 Kendall, Charles W. Private Men-of-War. London: Allan, 1931, ix, 308 pp. A useful survey of English privateering.

1872 Kennedy, Donald E. "The Crown and the Common Seamen in Early Stuart England." Historical Studies, 11 (April 1964): 170-77. To answer the question, why did the navy support Parliament in the Civil War?; the state and crown had alienated the seamen and rebuffed their patriotism, driving them into the hands of Parliament.

1873 -------. "The English Naval Revolt of 1648." EHR, 77 (April 1962): 247-56. The Julian Corbett Essay Award for 1958; stresses the political basis for the naval revolt of 1648; other historians attributed it to personal and economic causes; the seamen repeatedly referred to political concerns; upset with the soldiers as too radical.

1874 -------. "Naval Captains at the Outbreak of the English Civil War." MM, 46 (1960): 181-98. Process of selection for command of ships determined by Parliament, summer of 1642: only Protestants for the 18 warships and 24 merchant ships.

1875 -------. "Parliament and the Navy, 1642-1648: A Political History of the Navy during the Civil War." Ph.D. diss, Cambridge, 1959. The basis for the previous entries.

1876 Kennedy, Gavin. Bligh. London: Duckworth, 1978, xii, 420 pp. Kennedy, an economist, is editor of the Barrow account of the BOUNTY mutiny; the blurb touts "rehabilitation of the BOUNTY bastard"; Bligh made the villain from biased accounts of Morrison and Edward Christian; Kennedy not knowledgeable on naval matters; extensive bibliography.

1877 -------. Captain Bligh: The Man and His Mutinies. London: Duckworth; NY: Sheridan, 1989, 334 pp. On the occasion of the bicentennial of the mutiny, the 2nd account by Kennedy who expands coverage, e.g., praise of Bligh by Nelson and as navigator, cartographer, and election to the Royal Society, and recounted subsequent mutinies, e.g., the Nore and Governor of New South Wales, and at least 2 courts-martial; conclusion: Bligh was a great man but with a temper, foul language, and vindictiveness; discounts claims of homosexuality; some errors and absence of recent scholarship.

1878 -------. The Death of Captain Cook. London: Duckworth, 1978, 103 pp. Illustrated; presents details on the events leading up to the murder of Cook in Hawaii, 14 February 1779; causes: carelessness and acceptance of Godhead; discounts any blame on Bligh.

1879 Kennedy, Ludovic H.C. Nelson and His Captains. Alt. title: Nelson's Band of Brothers. London: Odhams; London: Collins, 1951, 1975, 1977, 353 pp. A popular account of Nelson and relationships with his subordinates.

1880 Kennedy, Paul M., ed. Grand Strategies in War and Peace. New Haven: Yale UP, 1991, 1992, x, 228 pp. 10 essays by experts, e.g., John Hattendorf on the War of Spanish Succession and J.H. Elliott on continental powers.

1881 Kennedy, Paul M. The Rise of Anglo-German Antagonism, 1860-1914. Boston: Unwin; NY: Ashfield, 1980, 1982, 1987, 616 pp. A brilliant history of relationships of these great powers, incorporating all the humanities and social sciences, e.g., history, language, religion, economics, psychology, and dynastic conflict; cited as an example of this broadened approach.

1882 -------. The Rise and Fall of British Naval Mastery. London: Allen, 1976, 1982, 1983, 1987, 1998, 405 pp. Kennedy, 1945-____, formerly at East Anglia, now at Yale in prestigious chair and with an increasingly international reputation; author of 10 major books; this earlier work a standard history of RN, broadly based using the social sciences; to place RN in a geopolitical perspective; a brilliant achievement; begins with the Tudors; notes that Mahan is no longer useful.

1883 -------. The Rise and Fall of Great Powers: Economic Change and Military Conflict from 1500 to 2000. NY: Random House, 1987, 1989, xxvi, 678 pp. A controversial cosmic survey of early modern and modern competition and conflict among a series of great powers, e.g., Iberian powers, the Dutch, British and America, each experiencing "imperial overstretch" as it rose and fell; a pattern demonstrated; deterministic.

1884 Kennerley, Alston. "British Seamen's Missions and Sailors' Homes, 1815-1970: Voluntary Welfare Provisions for Serving Seafarers." Ph.D. diss, Polytechnic South West, Australia, 1989, 386 pp. Reviews the many services and needs, e.g., recreation, medical care, schooling, religion, homes, and welfare.

1885 Kenny, Robert W. Elizabeth's Admiral: The Political Career of Charles Howard, Earl of Nottingham, 1536-1624. Balt: JHUP, 1970, xi, 354 pp. Re Lord

Howard of Effingham and Earl of Nottingham, LHA for 30 years; 3 chapters on the Armada; debate over "corruption"; no analysis.

1886 -------. "Peace with Spain, 1605." HisTod, 20 (March 1970): 198-208. On the death of Elizabeth, negotiations for ending the Anglo-Spanish war; Philip III to end crusading zeal against Protestant England.

1887 Kent, Alexander, pseud., Douglas Reeman. Beyond the Reef. Ithaca: McBooks, 2000, 352 pp. An example, # 19 of about two dozen nautical novels of the Nelson era in this series; featuring naval-officer hero, Richard Bolitho; plus 3 novels about the Royal Marines; some anthologies, e.g., Bolitho, 1993, The Bolitho Omnibus, 1991, and Captain Richard Bolitho, 1978; each of these a combination of 3 novels; Bolitho novels listed in alphabetical order with the chronological number added at the end of the entry; where known, dates of original and subsequent reprints.

1888 -------. Colours Aloft. London: Hutchinson, 1986, 304 pp. Bolitho, # 16.

1889 -------. Command a King's Ship. NY: Putnam, 1973, 352 pp. Bolitho, # 6.

1890 -------. Cross of St. George. London: Heinemann; Ithaca: McBooks, 1996, 2001, 320 pp. Bolitho, # 22.

1891 -------. The Darkening Sea. Ithaca: McBooks, 2000, 352 pp. Bolitho, # 20.

1892 -------. Enemy in Sight! NY: Putnam, 1970, 350 pp. Bolitho, # 10.

1893 -------. Flag Captain. NY: Putnam, 1971, 384 pp. Bolitho, # 11.

1894 -------. For My Country's Freedom. NY: Putnam; Ithaca: McBooks, 1997, 2000, 304 pp. Bolitho # 21.

1895 -------. Form Line of Battle. NY: Putnam, 1969, 1999, 352 pp. Bolitho, # 9.

1896 -------. In Gallant Company. NY: Putnam; Ithaca: McBooks, 1977, 1998, 2000, 320 pp. Bolitho, # 3.

1897 -------. Honour This Day. London: Heinemann; Ithaca: McBooks, 1987, 2000, 320 pp. Bolitho, # 17.

1898 -------. The Inshore Squadron. NY: Putnam; Ithaca: McBooks, 1977, 1979, 1999, 288 pp. Bolitho, # 13.

1899 -------. The Only Victor. Ithaca: McBooks, 2000, 384 pp. Bolitho, # 18.

1900 -------. Passage to Mutiny. NY: Putnam; Ithaca: McBooks, 1976, 1999, 352 pp. Bolitho, # 7.

1901 -------. Relentless Pursuit. Ithaca: McBooks, 2001, 367 pp. This about Adam Bolitho, carrying on the family tradition; Bolitho # 25.

1902 -------. Midshipman Bolitho, Midshipman. NY: Putnam; Ithaca: McBooks, 1975, 1976, 1998, 159 pp. Bolitho, # 1.

1903 -------. Second to None. Ithaca: McBooks, 2001, 352 pp. Bolitho, # 24.

1904 -------. Signal, Close Action! NY: Putnam; Ithaca: McBooks, 1974, 1999, 368 pp. Bolitho, # 12.

1905 -------. Sloop of War. NY: Putnam; Ithaca: McBooks, 1972, 1998, 352 pp. Bolitho, # 4.

1906 -------. Stand into Danger. NY: Putnam; Ithaca: McBooks, 1981, 1998, 288 pp. Bolitho, # 2.

1907 -------. Success to the Brave. NY: Putnam; Ithaca: McBooks, 1983, 2000, 284 pp. Bolitho, # 15.

1908 -------. Sword of Honour. NY: Putnam; Ithaca: McBooks, 1998, 2001, 320 pp. Bolitho, # 23.

1909 -------. To Glory We Steer. NY: Putnam; Ithaca: McBooks, 1968, 1998, 352 pp. Bolitho, # 5.

1910 -------. A Tradition of Victory. NY: Putnam; Ithaca: McBooks, 1981, 1998, 304 pp. Bolitho, # 14.

1911 -------. With All Despatch. London: Heinemann; Ithaca: McBooks, 1988, 1999, 320 pp. Bolitho, # 8.

1912 Kent, Barrie. Signal!: A History of Signalling in the Royal Navy. Hampshire: Hyden, 1993, viii, 371 pp. Fwd: Edward Ashmore; the history of communication in RN; earliest methods of visual signalling were flags, semaphore, and a shutter system.

1913 Kent, H.S.K. War and Trade in Northern Seas: Anglo-Scandinavian Economic Relations in the Mid-Eighteenth Century. Cambridge: Cambridge UP, 1973, xvi, 240 pp. Contends mercantilist policies; RN dependent on Norwegian timber and Swedish iron, pitch, and tar; unable to develop alternative sources, thus, increasingly dependent.

1914 Kent, Louise A. He Went with Drake. Boston: Houghton, 1961, 1964, 220 pp. Juvenile fiction depicting piracy, the Armada, and operations with Drake; the author of a series, He Went with. . . ., e.g., Columbus, Magellan, John Paul Jones, and Marco Polo.

1915 Kenyon, John P. and Ohlmeyer, Jane, eds. The Civil Wars: A Military History of England, Scotland, and Ireland, 1638-1660. Oxford: Oxford UP, 1998, xxiv, 391 pp. Wars of the 3 kingdoms; a chapter on naval operations by Bernard Capp; the navy defected to Parliament and Charles I formed a Royalist navy, mostly privateers; also chapter on logistics and supply.

1916 Kenyon, John P. "Ordnance and the King's Fleet in 1548. International J Nautical Archaeology, 12 (1983): 63-65. From original manuscripts; surveys of ordnance and munitions for warships of the mid-16th century.

1917 Kepler, Jon S. "The Effects of the Battle of Sluys upon the Administration of English Naval Impressment, 1340-1343." Speculum, 48 (January 1973): 70-77. Re the obligation to supply forces to the monarch, effectively the English navy of the 14th century; main task: transport to the continent and logistical support for the army; Sluys had strategic implications, giving England control of the Channel for 30 years, until defeat at La Rochelle.

1918 -------. "Fiscal Aspects of the English Carrying Trade during the Thirty Years' War." Economic History Review, 2nd ser, 25 (1972): 261-83. England was neutral; this article about the opportunities and consequences for English merchants, about the increase in customs receipts for Charles I as he ruled without Parliament, and about the benefits transfering to Parliament during the 1640s.

1919 Keppel, Sonia. Three Brothers at Havana, 1762. Salisbury: Russell, 1981, 120 pp. The Keppel brothers, Augustus, George, and William, played various command roles in operations associated with Pitt's Plan, e.g., Belleisle and Havana, both great successes.

1920 Kermode, Frank. "The Geat of Geats." NY Review of Books, 47 (20 July 2000): 18-21. Review of new translation of "Beowulf" by Seamus Heaney; more evidence of link to the Anglo-Saxon king and the SUTTON HOO ship burial.

1921 Kerr, Mark E.F. The Sailor's Nelson. London: Hurst, 1932, 288 pp. Intro: Earl Nelson; hagiography, e.g., "the unique charm of our best-loved hero. . . the greatest war-strategist and tactician in history but also as the foremost leader of men amongst the warriors of the world."

1922 Kert, Faye M. Prize and Prejudice: Privateering and Naval Prize in Atlantic Canada in the War of 1812. St. Johns: Marine History, 1997, viii, 253 pp. A study of privateering, trade, smuggling, specie, Prize Law, and Admiralty Law; a formative period in the development of international maritime law.

1923 -------. "Prize and Prejudice: Privateering and Naval Prize in Atlantic Canada in the War of 1812." Ph.D. diss, Leiden, 1997. The basis of the previous entry.

1924 Keyes, Roger T.B. Amphibious Warfare and Combined Operations. NY: Macmillan, 1943, 101 pp. The Lee Knowles Lectures; by sometime Director of

Combined Operations, Lord Keyes; emphasis on interservice cooperation; operations, e.g., Quebec of 1759 and Zeebrugge of 1918.

1925 Keynes, Richard Darwin, ed. The BEAGLE Record: Selections from the Original Pictorial Records and Written Accounts of the Voyage of HMS BEAGLE. Cambridge: Cambridge UP, 1979, xiv, 409 pp. Large folio size; another exquisite production, colorful and detailed sketches from the BEAGLE voyage, admittedly in the 1830s but an important one in the sequence of exploration and scientific advances sponsored by the Admiralty.

1926 -------, ed. Charles Darwin's BEAGLE Diary. London: Cambrige UP, 1988, 2001, xxix, 464 pp. The journal of Darwin during the 5-year voyage.

1927 Keynes, Richard Darwin. "Darwin and the BEAGLE." Proceedings of the American Philosophical Society, 123 (October 1979): 323-35. The Jayne Lecture; the influence and impact of the voyage on the development of the theories of Darwin.

1928 Keynes, Simon. The Diplomas of King AEthelred "the Unready," 978-1016: A Study in Their Use as Historical Evidence. Cambridge: Cambridge UP, 1980, xix, 295 pp. The equivalent of royal grants, about 1000 from the 7th-11th centuries; includes a description of the fleet of Cnut, about 200 ships each with 60 oars carrying a total of 10,000 men.

1929 Kilby, John. "The Narrative of John Kilby." Maryland History Magazine, 67 (Spring 1972): 21-53. Kilby shipped aboard privateers and was captured, held as POW in England, exchanged, to the crew of BONHOMME RICHARD as gunner, and wrote memoir in 1810; poorly edited when published in 1905; now corrected and more useful.

1930 Kilfeather, T.P. Ireland: Graveyard of the Spanish Armada. Tralee: Anvil, 1967, 142 pp. In September 1588, along the rugged northwest coast, an estimated 25 Armada ships wrecked with loss of life of 5000 men, some from drowning and some slaughtered by natives; no scholarly apparatus.

1931 Kinahan, Jill. By Command of Their Lordships: The Exploration of the Namibian Coast by the Royal Navy, 1795-1895. Windhoek: Namibian Trust, 1992, iv, 216 pp. Intro: R.J. Campbell; extracts of reports re surveying of the coasts; presents details of the process.

1932 Kindleberger, Charles P. Mariners and Markets. NY: Harvester, 1992, xvii, 109 pp. An underlying agenda opposed to economic and econometric historians; case study of the "market" for seamen during later days of sail: wages, "crimping," "shanghaiing," press gangs, desertion, mutiny; supply-demand process failed; not convincing.

1933 King, Dean and Hattendorf, John B., eds. "Every Man Will Do His Duty": An

Anthology of Firsthand Accounts from the Age of Nelson. NY: Holt, 1997, xxxvii, 425 pp. "For Patrick O'Brian"; maps: Adam Cooper; re the Nelson era; "from fiction to fact"; 22 factual excerpts from 17 authors demonstrating how adapted to fiction, e.g.., exploits of Nelson, Cockrane, and William Richardson; these were the inspirations for Forester, O'Brian, Kent, Parkinson, and Pope.

1934 King, Dean and Hattendorf, John B. Harbors and High Seas: An Atlas and Geographical Guide to the Aubrey/Maturin Novels of Patrick O'Brian. NY: Holt, 1995, 1996, 1998, 2000, xvi, 219 pp. Maps: William Clipson and Adam Cooper; a companion guide for the O'Brian novels, individual maps and geographical descriptions for each up to that time; informative on sources used by O'Brian.

1935 King, Dean. Patrick O'Brian: A Life Revealed. NY: Holt; London: Hodder, 2000, xviii, 397 pp. O'Brian died in January 2000; this biography verges on expose and clearly without the cooperation of O'Brian: aspects O'Brian obviously covered up, e.g., abandoned a wife and 2 children, the name change, not Irish, and fake degrees; much praise for the writing of O'Brian, perhaps too much; insisted O'Brian far superior to Forester.

1936 King, Dean, Hattendorf, John B., and Estes, J. Worth, eds. A Sea of Words: A Lexicon and Companion for Patrick O'Brian's Seafaring Tales. NY: Holt, 1995, 1997, xvii, 483 pp. An extensive companion guide to the O'Brian sea novels; definitions of 3000 words and phrases; an astounding compilation.

1937 King, Jonathan. The First Fleet: The Convict Voyages that Founded Australia, 1787-1788. Melbourne: Macmillan; London: Secker, 1982, 1983, 186 pp. A history of the First Fleet.

1938 King, Robert J. "'Ports of Shelter and Refreshment. . .': Botany Bay and Norfolk Island in British Naval Strategy, 1786-1808." Historical Studies, 22 (1986): 199-213. In the 1780s, the British decided to settle Australia; several contemporary concerns, e.g., disposition of convicts and deterioration of relations with Spain.

1939 Kingsford, C.L. "The Beginnings of English Maritime Enterprise in the Fifteenth Century." 2 parts. History, 13 (July and October 1928): 97-106 and 193-203. Recounts the earliest events in the development of a naval force, e.g., Cinque Ports, Sluys, hired ships, then Henry V and "the real creation of the navy as a national fighting force. . . founder of the royal navy"; then decay, Wars of the Roses; line between legitimate trade and piracy not clear; evolution to privateering; English piracy revived as commerce was controlled by foreign merchants of Italy and Spain; "the enterprise of the West-country pirates of the fifteenth century was the school of English seamen: they were the forerunners of the Elizabethans"; Edward III was "father of English commerce"; English ships into Mediterranean, 1457; Navigation Act of Richard II; conclusion: new spirit with emphasis on royal shipping led to the early navy.

1940 -------. Prejudice and Promise in Fifteenth-Century England. Oxford:

Clarendon; London: Cass, 1925, 1962, vi, 215 pp. The Ford Lectures; a determination to rehabilitate the 15th century, distorted by the prejudice of chroniclers and Tudor historians; features, e.g., a spirit of adventure and commercial enterprise manifested in West Country piracy, precursors of Drake, "the arch pirate," e.g., Prendergast, Harry Pay of Poole, and Hawkey; most active were Fowey and Dartmouth; the earliest systematic study of English piracy.

1941 Kingsley, Charles. Westward Ho!: Or, the Voyages and Adventures of Sir Amyas Leigh, Knight. . . of Devon, in the Reign of Her Most Glorious Majesty Queen Elizabeth, Rendered into Modern English. NY: Macmillan, 1855, 1896, 1902, 1986, 1989, 591 pp. A variety of editions, 1-, 2-, or 3-vol.; a famous novel by a militant Christian Socialist advocating muscular Christianity; this on exploits of Elizabethans vs Spain, e.g., Drake, Ralegh, Hawkins, and Grenville.

1942 Kirby, Brian S. "Nelson and American Merchantmen in the West Indies, 1784-1787." MM, 75 (May 1989): 137-47. During the mid-1780s, Nelson in the West Indies aboard HMS BOREAS, '28, to enforce Navigation Acts; some claim action of seizure of 4 American ships was overzealous.

1943 Kirby, David. The Baltic World, 1772-1993: Europe's Northern Periphery in an Age of Change. London: Longman, 1995, vii, 472 pp. Claims to do for the Baltic what Braudel did for the Mediterranean; the sequel to the next entry; the change was evolution from agrarian to industrial and trade-based structure plus the rise of nationalism.

1944 -------. Northern Europe in the Early Modern Period: The Baltic World, 1492-1772. London: Longman, 1990, xii, 443 pp. Places the Baltic in the European economy; features, e.g., the Dutch, Teutonic Order, the rise of Sweden, and grain and naval stores.

1945 Kircheisen, Friedrich Max. Napoleon. 2 vols. London: Howe; NY: Harcourt, 1931, 1932, xii, 761 pp. Trans: Henry St. Lawrence; abridged from the original 9 vols. by this German scholar; the product of a lifetime of study; the German perspective; thesis: Napoleon caused the rise of Germany which then defeated him; one fallacy was no long-term plan by Napoleon.

1946 -------. Nelson, Man and Admiral. Alt. title: Nelson: The Establishment of British World Dominion. NY: Duffield; London: Hutchinson, 1931, 288 pp. Trans: Frederick Collins; dedicated to "The German Navy"; by the German authority on Napoleon; a concise life of Nelson; touted as complete and balanced: his naval victories and his activities at the Court of Naples; ". . . his hitherto spotless name he besmirched through his brutal behavior in Naples and his undignified relations with Lady Hamilton."

1947 Kirk, T.A. "Genoa and the Sea: Ships and Power in Early Modern Mediterranean, 1559-1680." Ph.D. diss, European Union Institute, Florence, 1996. A scholarly study of these early operations.

1948 -------. [Genoa and the Sea]. In 1999, noted as a forthcoming book based on the previous entry.

1949 Kirsch, Peter. The Galleon: The Great Ship of the Armada Era. Annapolis: NIP, 1988, 1990, 224 pp. Trans: Rachel Magowan; profusely illustrated designed for model makers; the most important large sailing ship of the 17th century evolving into SOTL; ship design, e.g., techniques of construction, rigging, fittings, and armament; earliest ones from Venice.

1950 Kirsch, Walter P. Francis Drake: Protestant, Patriot, Pirat. Wien: Literatur, 1992, 125 pp. A popular biography in German; no scholarly apparatus.

1951 Kitson, Frank. Prince Rupert. 2 vols. I: Portrait of a Soldier. II: Admiral and General-at-Sea. London: Constable, 1994-1998, 1999, xxxii, 640 pp. Rupert, 1619-1682, a nephew of Charles I, an army and navy commander; volumes focus respectively on these phases; coverage of the commander of the Royalist fleet; later the equivalent of First Lord in the mid-1670s; veteran naval commander in the 2nd and 3rd Dutch wars; noted as developer of Fighting Instructions of RN.

1952 Kitson, Henry. "The Early History of Portsmouth Dockyard, 1496-1800." MM, 33 (October 1947): 256-65. A review of activities, e.g., the initiative of Henry VII for a permanent dry dock and orders for several large ships; soon shipbuilding superseded by the Thames.

1953 Knerr, Douglas. "Through the 'Golden Mist': A Brief Overview of Armada Historiography." AmNep, 49 (Winter 1989): 5-13. The Armada is shrouded in myth and legend: God favored the English, light vs darkness, Howard-Drake conflict, unflattrering depiction of Medina Sidonia, Whig view of English fleet inferior in numbers and firepower, and Michael Lewis on Armada guns.

1954 Knight, C. "H.M. Armed Vessel BOUNTY." MM, 22 (April 1936): 183-99. Illustrated; presents the background and occasion for the voyage: in 1775, the Society of West Indian Merchants petitioned for the introduction of breadfruit trees, offering a reward or "bounty"; BETHIA, 220T, was approved by Joseph Banks and accepted into RN.

1955 Knight, Frank. General-at-Sea: The Life of Admiral Robert Blake. London: Macdonald, 1971, 152 pp. For juveniles; Blake, 1599-1657.

1956 -------. The Golden Age of the Galleon. London: Collins, 1976, 96 pp. Illustrated; a prolific writer of naval history for juveniles; a review of voyages of Drake, Hawkins, privateers, and the Armada.

1957 -------. The Hero: Vice-Admiral Horatio Viscount Nelson. London: Macdonald, 1969, 157 pp. Illus: John Laurence; for juveniles.

1958 -------. Rebel Admiral: The Life and Exploits of Admiral Lord Cochrane,

Tenth Earl of Dundonald. London: Macdonald, 1968, 172 pp. For juveniles.

1959 -------. The Sea Story: Being a Guide to Nautical Reading from Ancient Times to the Close of the Sailing Ship Era. London: Macmillan, 1958, xii, 240 pp. A survey and guide to the literature.

1960 -------. That Rare Captain: Sir Francis Drake. London: Macdonald, 1970, 1979, 144 pp. For juveniles; a survey.

1961 -------. The Young Captain Cook. Famous Childhood series. London: Parrish, 1964, 127 pp. For juveniles.

1962 -------. The Young Drake. Famous Childhood series. NY: Roy, 1962, 1963, 126 pp. For juveniles; a survey.

1963 Knight, R.J.B., ed. Guide to the Manuscripts in the National Maritime Museum. 2 vols. I: The Personal Collections. II: The Public Records. London: Mansell, 1977-1980, lviii, 508 pp. NMM was established in 1934; describes 300 personal papers donated or purchased, e.g., Hawke and Nelson, and other holdings.

1964 Knight, R.J.B. "The National Maritime Museum's Collection of Written Nelson Material." Nelson Dispatch, 7 (January 2000): 27-29. A guide to the manuscripts held at NMM; 12 collections, e.g., papers of Lady Nelson and Lady Hamilton.

1965 -------. [Nelson: A Bicentennial Biography]. London: Penguin, projected for 2005. Penguin has projected this major biography as commemoration and celebration of the culmination of the Nelson Decade and Trafalgar 200.

1966 -------. "Nelson and the Forests of Dean." MM, 87 (February 2001): 88-92. Focus on documents and a critique of the Albion thesis; in this case, questions the claim that a "Timber Trust" manipulated timber production and prices.

1967 -------. "New England Forests and British Seapower: Albion Revisited." AmNep, 46 (Fall 1986): 221-29. A review of the issue of the timber shortage for Britain described by Albion, and for France by Bamford; revision, e.g., Pepys and Sandwich were competent, alleged corruption in dockyards not proven, and masts from the Baltic were preferred.

1968 -------. "Pilfering and Theft from the Dockyards at the Time of the American War of Independence." MM, 61 (August 1975): 215-28. Albion depicted the dockyards as corrupt, plagued by venality, peculation, and bare-faced roguery; revision based on intensive study of details, e.g., wages and wage-freeze, effect on prices, degrees of efficiency, and comparisons.

1969 Knight, R.J.B., comp. Portsmouth Dockyard Papers, 1774-1783: The American War. Portsmouth Record series, vol. 6. Portsmouth: City Council, 1987, lv, 196 pp. Calendars of these papers, letters, and orders, about 6000 pages; Portsmouth the largest of 6 dockyards at the time.

1970 Knight, R.J.B. "The Royal Dockyards in England at the Time of the American War of Independence." Ph.D. diss, London, 1972. A scholarly study of operations.

1971 Knighton, C.S. and Loades, David M., eds. The Anthony Roll of Henry VIII's Navy. Aldershot: Ashgate, 2000, xxi, 198 pp. For NRS, the BL, and Magdalene College, Cambridge; a significant publication: a series of inventories over time of the Royal ships, e.g., Great Ships, each depicted in a colored painting; details about rigging, guns, and flags, among other things; all supported by a series of essays by experts, e.g., Knighton, Loades, Ann Payne, and Stuart Vine.

1972 Knowles, Owen and Moore, Gene, eds. Oxford Reader's Companion to Conrad. Oxford: Oxford UP, 2000, xxxii, 429 pp. An extensive referenced guide to Joseph Conrad.

1973 Konstam, R.A. "Sixteenth-Century Naval Tactics and Gunnery." International J Nautical Archaeology, 17 (February 1988): 17-23. From nautical archaeology, details and corrections, e.g., rate of fire, arc of train, and loading muzzle loaders.

1974 Krajeski, Paul C. "Flags around the Peninsula: The Naval Career of Admiral Sir Charles Cotton, 1753-1812." Ph.D. diss, Florida State, 1998. A scholarly study of this naval commander; thesis: less glorious and less pretentious than Nelson, but still a model naval officer.

1975 -------. In the Shadow of Nelson: The Naval Leadership of Admiral Sir Charles Cotton, 1753-1812. Westport: Greenwood, 2000, xx, 219 pp. Fwd: N.A.M. Rodger; a biography of a naval officer with a solid but unremarkable career; to RN at age 18, at the Glorious First of June, blockades, and naval support in the Peninsular campaign.

1976 Krantz, Frederick, ed. History from Below: Studies in Popular Protest and Popular Ideology in Honour of George Rude. Montreal: Concordia UP, 1985, xvi, 408 pp. Intro: George Rude; a series of essays honoring Rude, e.g., Hobsbawm, Christopher Hill, and R.B. Rose; see J.S. Bromley, "Outlaws at Sea, 1660-1720: Liberty, Equality and Fraternity among the Caribbean Freebooters."

1977 Kraus, Hans P. Sir Francis Drake: A Pictorial Biography. Amsterdam: Israel, 1970, viii, 236 pp. Intro: David Waters and Richard Boulind; very large folio profusely illustrated; extensive bibliography.

1978 Kretzmar, J. Die Invasion Projecte der Katolischen Machte gegen England zur Zeit Elisabeths. Leipzig: Archiv, 1892. From the Vatican archives; a summary of plans and projects by Catholic powers to invade England of Elizabeth I.

1979 Kupperman, Karen Ordahl. Providence Island, 1630-1641: The Other Puritan

Colony. London: Cambridge UP, 1993, xiii, 393 pp. An extraordinary commercial venture of Puritan leaders, e.g., John Pym, Lord Saye, and Warwick; Providence Island off the coast of Nicaragua; became a model for English expansion and colonization, fulfilling the plan for a Godly English society; base for privateers against Spain; lasted through the 1630s, but failed.

1980 Kverndal, Roald. Seamen's Missions: Their Origin and Early Growth. Pasadena: Carey, 1986, 1997, xxviii, 903 pp. A substantial history of these missions on the occasion of the bicentennial of founding; served thousands all over the world with various types of services; sponsors were religious associations, e.g., Naval and Military Bible Society, Bethel Movement, and Agnes Weston.

1981 -------. "The 200th Anniversary of Organized Seamen's Missions, 1779-1979." MM, 65 (August 1979): 255-63. Celebrating these institutions.

1982 Labaree, Benjamin W., ed. The Atlantic World of Robert G. Albion. Middletown: Wesleyan UP, 1975, vi, 263 pp. On the occasion of the 50th anniversary of Forests and Sea Power, a series of essays, e.g., John Kemble on maritime history, A.R. Lewis on the medieval background, and Clark Reynolds on American Anglophobia.

1983 Labaree, Benjamin W. "The Frank C. Munson Institute of American Maritime Studies." AmNep, 45 (1985): 441-45. A description of the institute, its holdings, and its services.

1984 -------. A Supplement (1971-1986) to Robert Albion's Naval and Maritime History: An Annotated Bibliography. Mystic: Seaport Museum, 1988, viii, 232 pp. The original was mimeographed and supported courses of Albion; the edition of 1972, 5000 entries; this adds 2000 more, annotated.

1985 Lacey, Robert. Sir Walter Ralegh. London: Weidenfeld, 1973, 1974, 415 pp. A popular biography reflecting the latest research; sections: rise, favor, fall, disgrace, favor regained, captivity, and execution.

1986 Lachouque, Henry. The Last Days of Napoleon's Empire: From Waterloo to St. Helena. London: Allen, 1966, 299 pp. Trans: Lovett Edwards; an account of his last years.

1987 -------. Napoleon's Battles: A History of His Campaigns. London: Allen, 1963, 1967, 479 pp. Trans: Roy Monkcom; a survey of his battles and campaigns.

1988 Laffin, John. Jack Tar: The Story of the British Sailor. London: Cassell, 1969, xi, 212 pp. By the prolific popular military historian; one of a series, e.g., Tommy Atkins, Jackboot, and Digger; on the common seaman of Britain, 1500 to the present; a survey of life on the lower deck.

1989 Lamb, Hubert and Frydendahl, Knud. Historic Storms of the North Sea,

British Isles, and North West Europe. Cambridge: Cambridge UP, 1991, xi, 204 pp. By meteorologists who gather climate data from ships logs, diaries, and weather reports; described and analyzed 166 storms, e.g., 11 in the 16th century including the gales of August and September 1588 which struck the Armada, including maps for 13 and 16 August and 18 and 21 September; other notable storms: 1688, 1703, 1805, and 1944.

1990 Lamb, Jonathan, et al., eds. Exploration and Exchange: A South Seas Anthology, 1680-1900. Chicago: Chicago UP, 2000, xxv, 359 pp. Selections divided by category, e.g., Dampier, Anson, Cooks, Banks, Hawksworth, Defoe, and Smollett.

1991 Lambdin, Dewey. For King and Country: The Naval Adventures of Alan Lewrie. NY: Fine, 1994, 1098 pp. Nautical fiction series, life and adventures (usually bawdy) in RN in the late 18th century; naval officer hero: Alan Lewrie # 6.

1992 -------. The French Admiral: A Midshipman Alan Lewrie Adventure: A Novel. NY: Fine, 1989, 1990, 1999, 414 pp. Alan Lewrie # 2.

1993 -------. The Gun Ketch. NY: Fine, 1993, 312 pp. Alan Lewrie # 5.

1994 -------. HMS COCKEREL; An Alan Lewrie Naval Adventure. NY: Fine, 1995, 360 pp. Alan Lewrie, # 7.

1995 -------. Jester's Fortune: An Alan Lewrie Naval Adventure. NY: Dutton, 1999, 373 pp. Alan Lewrie, # 9.

1996 -------. The King's Captain: An Alan Lewrie Naval Adventure. NY: St. Martin; NY: Dunne, 2000, 2001, 358 pp. Alan Lewrie, # 10.

1997 -------. The King's Coat: The Naval Adventure of Alan Lewrie. NY: Fine; NY: Hall, 1989, 1999, 371 pp. Alan Lewrie, # 1.

1998 -------. The King's Commander: An Alan Lewrie Naval Adventure. NY: Fine, 1997, 374 pp. Alan Lewrie, # 8.

1999 -------. The King's Commission: An Alan Dewrie Naval Adventure. NY: Fine, 1991, xiii, 400 pp. Alan Lewrie, # 3.

2000 -------. The King's Privateer. NY: Fine, 1992, 360 pp. Alan Lewrie, # 4.

2001 Lambert, Andrew D. "British Naval History, 1812-1848: Three Pioneers in an Heroic Age." Unpublished Paper, 14th Naval History Symposium, 23-25 September 1999, USNA, Annapolis by the Laughton Professor of Naval History, King's College, University of London and the member, British Commission for Maritime History; re the origins of the discipline of naval history; 3 British pioneers: William James, John Barrow, and Nicholas Harris Nicolas.

2002 -------. The Foundations of Naval History: Sir John Knox Laughton, the Royal Navy, and the Historical Profession. London: Chatham, 1998, 256 pp. Laughton, 1830-1915, initiated the formal study of naval history to incorporate into naval education and training; Laughton was a founder of NRS; wrote 926 biographical entries for DNB; most are on naval persons and are biased; launched a successful campaign to rehabilitate Nelson; influenced Colomb, Corbett, and Luce who influenced Mahan.

2003 -------. The Last Sailing Battlefleet: Maintaining Naval Mastery, 1815-1850. London: Conway, 1991, x, 214 pp. Folio size, illustrated; re the design history of these last sailing battleships which sustained Pax Britannica and kept at a two-power standard.

2004 -------. [Nelson: A Biography]. Noted in 2001, preparing biography in support of the Nelson Decade and Trafalgar 200 commemorations.

2005 -------. "'Our Naval Plutarch': Sir John Knox Laughton and The Dictionary of National Biography." MM, 84 (August 1998): 308-15. Laughton, 1830-1915; "scientific" historian of the navy and teacher at the Royal Naval Colleges; wrote of "naval worthies" for The DNB, a total of 926 entries, almost 30,000 words, over 1000 pages; biased entries, now all being rewritten for The New DNB; entries generally overlong and unbalanced; Laughton anti-Tory.

2006 [NRS #___]. Lambert, Andrew, ed. The Papers of Sir John Knox Laughton. Publications of the NRS, vol. ___. London: NRS. In 2001, noted as forthcoming.

2007 Lambert, Andrew. "Reflections on A History of the Royal Navy: A History from the Earliest Times to 1900 by Sir W.L. Clowes." Naval Review, 85 (October 1997): 393-99. Chatham reprinted the 7 vols., 1996-1997, from the original, 1897-1903; a notable problem, Laird Clowes perpetuated the "black legend" of Nelson at Naples.

2008 -------. War at Sea in the Age of Sail. London, 2000. Lavishly illustrated; re 1650-1850; well-written survey.

2009 [NRS #142]. Lambert, Nicholas, ed. The Submarine Service, 1900-1918. Publications of the NRS, vol.. 142. Aldershot: Ashgate, 2001, xliv, 397 pp. Details about the formative period of the submarine and the role of Jacky Fisher in its development.

2010 Lampton, Christopher. Underwater Archaeology. A First Book series. NY: Watts, 1988, 96 pp. For juveniles; a brief survey of the essentials; gives examples, e.g., VASA, MARY ROSE, and TITANIC.

2011 Landauer, I. Bauer. Consideraciones sobre la politica naval de Espana en el Siglo XVI. Madrid, 1926. Considered one of the best of the studies of the Armada.

2012 Lander, R.J. "An Assessment of the Numbers, Sizes and Types of English and Spanish Ships Mobilised for the Armada Campaign." MM, 63 (November 1977): 359-64. Comparisons, e.g., English ships were fast, could sail close to the wind, had slim lines, and averaged 170 tons while the Spanish had high bulwarks, towering poops and forecastles, were more difficult to handle, and averaged 310 tons.

2013 Landstrom, Bjorn. The Royal Warship, VASA. Stockholm: Interpublishing, 1980, 1988, 160 pp. Trans: Jeremy Franks; fwd: Anders Franzen; very large folio size, color pictures, detailed schematics, an exquisite production; re the 17th century Swedish warship which sank on its maiden voyage, later raised and on display in Stockholm.

2014 -------. Sailing Ships in Words and Pictures from Papyrus Boats to Full-riggers. NY: Doubleday, 1969, 191 pp. Illustrated; a survey for the general reader; informative on the development of sailing ships, especially in Europe.

2015 -------. The Ship: A Survey of the History of the Ship. . . NY: Doubleday; London: Allen, 1961, xi, 309 pp. Trans: Michael Phillips; a pictorial survey from earliest times to the present; topics, e.g., Cinque Ports, HMS VICTORY, and SOTL.

2016 Lane, Carl Daniel. The Fleet in the Forest. NY: Armed Services, 1943, 443 pp. Nautical fiction, fleet of Perry, Lake Erie, 1812-1813.

2017 Lane, Frederic C. "The Economic Meaning of the Invention of the Compass." AHR, 68 (1963): 605-17. Lane, 1900-1984, the prolific historian of Venice in the Middle Ages; direction was important during sea voyages in the Mediterranean only in bad weather; the magnetic compass in 13th century meant more voyages and operations outside the Mediterranean, thus, more and extended voyages per year.

2018 -------. "Venetian Naval Architecture about 1550." MM, 20 (January 1934): 24-49. A study of craftsmen-builders of war galleys at the Venice Arsenal.

2019 -------. "Venetian Ships and Shipbuilding of the Renaissance." Ph.D. diss, Harvard, 1934. The basis for these entries.

2020 -------. Venetian Ships and Shipbuilders of the Renaissance. Balt: JHUP, 1934, 1993, ix, 285 pp. A comprehensive study of this unique industrial production center, the Venice Arsenal, a state-owned industry producing galleys, round ships, armaments, and all fittings; advanced shipwrights, guilds, timber supplies; the original and the model for other states.

2021 -------. Venice: A Maritime Republic. Balt: JHUP, 1973, 1977, xviii, 505 pp. A history up to 1797; Venice was the original maritime republic with many innovative characteristics, e.g., industrial enterprise, naval administration, dockyards, guilds, and dealings in personnel matters.

2022 -------. Venice and History: The Collected Papers of Frederic C. Lane. Balt: JHUP, 1966, 560 pp. A collection of articles, e.g., Venice, ships and shipbuilding, galleys, and diet and wages of seamen.

2023 Lane, Kris E. Pillaging the Empire: Piracy in the Americas, 1500-1750. NY: Sharpe, 1998, xxiv, 237 pp. A recent synthesis with a global perspective about "freethinking, rum-swilling, sexual rebellious cutthroats"; emphasis on victims of Spanish America; waves of attacks, e.g., French, English, Dutch, and other free-booters; conclusion: English property law, not any Spanish efforts, finally led to the demise of piracy; astute historiographical essay.

2024 Langlade, Jacques de. Nelson: Biographie. Paris: Renaissance, 1990, 442 pp. A French biography concentrating on the battles.

2025 Langley, Harold D. A History of Medicine in the Early U.S. Navy. Balt: JHUP, 1995, xxii, 435 pp. By the noted historian of the lower deck of the American navy; re the health, welfare, and safety of seamen; informative of the times; the development of a professional service to 1842.

2026 -------. "The Humanitarians and the United States Navy, 1798-1862." Ph.D. diss, Pennsylvania, 1960, 380 pp. The basis of these entries.

2027 -------. "Images of the Sailor in the Novels of James Fenimore Cooper." AmNep, 57 (Fall 1997): 359-70. Re the pioneer of American nautical fiction, didactic and moralizing; to celebrate and promulgate American maritime nationalism through fiction.

2028 -------. Social Reform in the United States Navy. Chicago: U Ill P, 1967, xii, 209 pp. The standard; informative as a model describing conditions on the lower deck and reform movements, e.g., recruiting, corporal punishment, rum ration, and living conditions.

2029 Langmaid, Kenneth J.R. The Blind Eye. London: Jarrolds, 1972, xxi, 166 pp. Featured the theme of "enlightened disobedience" which, it is contended, persists in Nelson, e.g. St. Vincent and Copenhagen.

2030 Laporte, Jean. "Les operations navales en Manche et Mer du Nord pendant l'annee 1066." Annales de Normandie, 17 (1967): 3-42. From a French journal; re naval operations during that formative year.

2031 La Ronciere, Charles de. Histoire de la Marine Francaise. 6 vols. Paris: Plon; Paris: Larousse, 1898-1932; abridged, 1934, vi, 408 pp. La Ronciere, 1870-1941, authored this monumental history of the French navy.

2032 -------. "L'Invasion Anglaise sous Charles VI: Dernieres battailles Navales." Revue des Questiones Historiques, 67 (1900): 56-80. Re the naval aspects of the Hundred Years' War.

2033 Larrabee, Harold A. Decision at the Chesapeake. NY: Potter, 1964, 1965, xvii, 317 pp. Re the background, political aspects, the battle, and the consequences of this battle off the Virginia Capes, 5 September 1781.

2034 Laszlo, Veres and Woodman, Richard. The Story of Sail. London: Chatham; Annapolis: NIP, 1999, 352 pp. A massive, folio size, exquisite production with 1000 scaled drawings of sailing ships over 6000 years; all types all over the world.

2035 Latham, Agnes M.C. and Youings, Joyce, eds. The Letters of Sir Walter Ralegh. Exeter: Exeter UP, 1999, lviii, 403 pp. Fwd: David Quinn; a project of 1930s revived in the 1990s; some correspondence describes naval operations, voyages, and colonization projects.

2036 Latham, Agnes M.C. Sir Walter Ralegh. Writers and their Works series, # 177. London: Longman, 1964, 43 pp. A bibliograhical survey.

2037 Latham, Robert and Latham, Linnet, eds. A Pepys Anthology: Passages from the Diary of Samuel Pepys. Berkeley: U Cal P, 1988, xii, 287 pp. Excerpts from the famous diary; Latham and William Matthews edited publication of the full diary; an informative introduction to Pepys.

2038 [NRS 133]. Latham, Robert, ed. Samuel Pepys and the Second Dutch War: Pepy's Navy White Book and Brooke House Papers. Publications of the Navy Records Society, vol. 133. London: Scolar, 1995, xxxix, 488 pp. From a memo book of the 1660s containing much detail on naval operations; enlightening on relationships within the Admiralty and Navy Board.

2039 Latham, Robert, ed. The Shorter Pepys: From the Diary of Samuel Pepys. Berkeley: U Cal P, 1985, xlix, 1096 pp. A substantial condensation of the diary.

2040 Lathbury, Thomas. The Spanish Armada, AD 1588: or, the Attempt of Philip II and Pope Sixtus V to Reestablish Popery in England. London: Parker, 1840, iv, 154 pp. From the extreme Protestant perspective.

2041 Laughton, John Knox. The Barker Collection: Manuscripts of and Relating to Admiral Lord Nelson. London: Chiswick, 1913, 50 pp. Laughton, father and son, Sir John Knox, 1830-1913, and L.G. Carr, 1880-1955, prominent and formative naval historians; this a description of a manuscript collection re Nelson.

2042 -------. The Bibliography of Nelson. London, 1894. An extensive compilation, actually too much and not helpful.

2043 Laughton, John Knox, ed. From Howard to Nelson: Twelve Sailors. Phil: Lippincott; London: Lawrence, 1899, viii, 476 pp. 12 essays by experts, e.g., Laughton on Howard, Bedford on Drake, Fremantle on Hawke, and Philip Colomb on St. Vincent and on Nelson.

2044 [NRS #6].Laughton, John Knox and Sulivan, J.Y.F., eds. Journal of Rear-Admiral Bartholonew James, 1752-1828. Publications of the Navy Records Society, vol. 6. London: NRS, 1896, xxvi, 402 pp. Sulivan was great-grandson of James whose career spanned the French Revolutionary Wars.

2045 Laughton, John Knox, ed. Letters and Despatches of Viscount Nelson. London: Longman, 1886, xx, 456 pp. Selections from the multi-volume collection of Nicolas.

2046 [NRS #32, 38, and 39]. Laughton, John Knox, ed. Letters and Papers of Charles, Lord Barham, Admiral of the Red Squadron, 1758-1813. 3 vols. Publications of the Navy Records Society, 32, 38, and 39. London: NRS, 1907-1911, lxvi, 422, xxii, 438, and xl, 413 pp. Re Charles Middleton, Lord Barham, sometime First Lord of the Admiralty.

2047 Laughton, John Knox. "The National Study of Naval History." Trans RHS, new ser., 12 (1898): 81-94. An early advocacy for the study of naval history; didactic and overly patriotic.

2048 [NRS 20]. Laughton, John Knox, ed. The Naval Miscellany. Publications of the Navy Records Society, vol. 20. London: NRS, 1902, xii, 463 pp. First in a series, e.g., letters from Vernon and Nelson, accounts of the battle of Quiberon Bay, an operation against Cadiz in 1596, and seizure of Helgoland in 1807.

2049 [NRS 40]. Laughton, John Knox, ed. The Naval Miscellany. Publications of the Navy Records Society, vol. 40. London: NRS, 1912, x, 430 pp. The second of these collections; the battle of Santa Cruz of 1656, on the mutiny at the Nore, the tactics of Jervis, voyages of Sebastian Cabot of 1526 and William Hawkins of the 1530s, and an escape plan for Napoleon.

2050 -------. Nelson. English Men of Action series. London: Macmillan, 1895, 1904, 1928, viii, 240 pp. A summary biography; assesses sources.

2051 -------. The Nelson Memorial: Nelson and His Companions in Arms. London: Allen, 1896, 1899, xvi, 351 pp. Dedicated to Earl Nelson; a survey placing Nelson in context with his contemporary peers; notorious error on frontispiece: the flags for the famous signal, "England expects. . . ," are incorrect, use of the wrong signal book.

2052 -------. The Pocket Life of Nelson: Being a Reprint of the Biographical Entry: Extracted from the DNB. Eugene: 1805 Club, 1993, viii, 27 pp. A "keepsake" for members of the 1805 Club.

2053 -------. "The Scientific Study of Naval History." JRUSI, 18 (1875): 508-27. A very early advocacy identified with the famous German School of Ranke.

2054 [NRS #1 and 2]. Laughton, John Knox, ed. State Papers Relating to the

Defeat of the Spanish Armada. 2 vols. Publications of the Navy Records Society, vols. 1 and 2. London: NRS, 1894-1895, 1900, 1981, lxxxiv, 365 and vi, 418 pp. The earliest and, for decades, the best collection of pertinent documents about the Armada; an introduction of 84 pages; notable among the documents and reports are strong religious feelings and motives; also prevalent are contemporaneous claims of massive damage and utter defeat of Armada ships during operations en route through the Channel and North Sea; also a contention that Medina Sidonia was "utterly ignorant of naval affairs"; overall, an impressive beginning despite later revision.

2055 Laughton, John Knox. Studies in Naval History: Biographies of Admirals, Naval Administrators, Naval Architects, and Naval Historians in "The Dictionary of National Biography". London: Longman, 1887, 469 pp. An extensive collection from DNB and many published elsewhere, e.g., on French naval heroes, e.g., Jean de Vienne, Colbert, and Jean Bart, plus John Paul Jones and Wilhelm Tegetthoff.

2056 Laughton, L.G. Carr, comp. "A Bibliography of Nautical Dictionaries." MM, 1 (March and August 1911): 84-89, 212-15. A complete listing; see elaboration in September 1911; a fixation of Laughton who was an advocate of the original and formative work of Jal.

2057 Laughton, L.G. Carr. "The Burning of Brighton by the French." Trans RHS, 3rd ser, 10 (1916): 167-73. Describes 2 attacks, 1514 and 1545, during Anglo-French wars; attacks by French galleys.

2058 -------. "Captain Nathaniel Boteler." MM, 1 (January 1911): 23-27. From the first issue of MM; re the naval author of Six Dialogues, 1634.

2059 -------. "English and Spanish Tonnage in 1588." MM, 44 (May 1958): 151-54. An effort to clarify; English and Spanish ships were close to the same size, the English being more heavily armed.

2060 -------. "Gunnery, Frigates and the Line of Battle." MM, 14 (October 1928): 339-63. An important contribution reviewing the history of naval tactics; the origin of frigates in the 17th century, a "ship under the line," or 5th or 6th rate.

2061 -------. "HMS VICTORY: Report to the VICTORY Technical Committee of a Search among the Admiralty Records." MM, 10 (April 1924): 173-211. At a crucial time, when investigations were conducted with the goal of restoring VICTORY; technical details re the hull, masts, sails, and armament.

2062 -------. "John Cunningham's Journal." MM, 9 (1923): 332-40. Cunningham, born 1771, served as surgeon; this journal aboard HMS CAMBRIDGE, 1824-1825, off South America.

2063 -------. Old Ship Figure-heads and Sterns: With Which Are Associated Galleries, Hanging Pieces, Catherades, and Divers Other Matters that Concern the

Grace and Countenance of Old Sail-Ships. London: Conway, 1925, 1991, xv, 281 pp. A beautiful production, folio size, profusely illustrated; the history of the development of ship ornamentation with emphasis on English ships, e.g., SOVEREIGN OF THE SEAS; the Admiralty was not enthusiastic, issuing 23 orders limiting them, and, in 1894, abolished them.

2064 -------. "The Project for a Nautical Encyclopedia." MM, 1 (September 1911): 245-46. The-for him-THE major, perhaps, only-objective of the newly formed Society for Nautical Research: "a complete and scholarly Nautical Encyclopedia or Dictionary"; to be "systematically taken in hand"; Laughton conducted an extensive collection but was never satisfied; SNR sponsored MM.

2065 -------. "The ROYAL SOVEREIGN, 1685." MM, 18 (April 1932): 138-50. A description of alterations, improvements, and repairs.

2066 -------. "The Writing of Naval History." MM, 10 (January 1924): 17-30. A survey of writing, e.g., William James, Mahan, and father, J.K. Laughton.

2067 Laurens, Henry L. L'Expedition d'Egypte, 1798-1801. Paris: Seuil, 1989, 1997, 595 pp. A recent full study in France with an extensive bibliography.

2068 -------. Les Origines Intellectualles de l'expedition d'Egypte. Istanbul: Isis, 1987, 257 pp. The Egyptian campaign of Napoleon was formative in that professional archaeologists and proto-Egyptologists purposely accompanied the forces and made extraordinary discoveries.

2069 Lavery, Brian. The Arming and Fitting of English Ships of War, 1600-1815. Annapolis: NIP, 1987, 1988, 320 pp. By a foremost authority on sailing warship design and architecture; comprehensive and profusely illustrated; one of a quartet, see James Lees, Peter Godwin, and Harland; the sailing warship was a complicated machine; detailed information for model-builders, nautical archaeologists, and historians.

2070 -------. Building the Wooden Walls: Design and Construction of the 74-Gun VALIANT. London: Conway; Annapolis: NIP, 1991, 224 pp. 130 illustrations; details of the SOTL, 1715-1810, as a sample; supports an exhibition, "Wooden Walls," at the Chatham Historic Dockyard Museum.

2071 -------. The Colonial Merchantman SUSAN CONSTANT, 1605. The Anatomy of the Ship series. London: Conway; Annapolis: NIP, 1988, 120 pp. One of the 3 ships to Virginia in 1607, a decade before MAYFLOWER.

2072 Lavery, Brian, ed. Deane's Doctrine of Naval Architecture, 1670. London: Conway; Annapolis: NIP, 1670, 1981, 128 pp. Re Anthony Deane, 1638-1721, foremost naval architect of the 17th century and favorite of Pepys; his treatise.

2073 -------, ed.. The Line of Battle: The Sailing Warship, 1650-1840. Historic Ship series. London: Conway, 1992, 208 pp. 13 essays by 8 experts producing a comprehensive reference work, e.g., frigates, sloops, brigs, corvettes, and ship decoration.; title is diverting.

2074 Lavery, Brian. Maritime Scotland. Historic Scotland series. Wash: Batsford, 2000, 128 pp. Re 5000 years of Scottish history with emphasis on maritime aspects.

2075 -------. [Nelson: A Biography]. London: British Library. Forthcoming. In 2001, noted as in preparation, to be c. 30,000 words; project associated with the Nelson Decade.

2076 -------. Nelson and the Nile: The Naval War against Napoleon, 1798. In alt. subtitle: . . . against Bonaparte, 1798. London: Chatham; Annapolis: NIP, 1998, 318 pp. Illustrated; for NMM and to support the Nelson Decade; the most decisive naval victory of its age; the story of the entire campaign.

2077 -------. Nelson's Navy: The Ships, Men and Organization, 1793-1815. London: Conway; Annapolis: NIP, 1989, 1990, 352 pp. Fwd: Patrick O'Brian; large folio size, 150 illustrations, 250 line drawings; a guide to the sailing navy at its height; chapters on life aboard, tactics, dockyards, and types of ships; social, technical, and historical background.

2078 -------. The Royal Navy's First INVINCIBLE, 1744-1758: The Ship, the Wreck, and the Recovery. Portsmouth: INVINCIBLE Conservation, 1988, x, 119 pp. Extra large folio size, illustrated; for the INVINCIBLE 1759 Committee; oversaw the discovery and recovery process; the French invented the '74; INVINCIBLE built at Rochfort, 1740s, captured by RN in 1747, aground and lost, Portsmouth, 1758, discovered and recovery, 1979.

2079 -------. The 74-Gun Ship BELLONA. The Anatomy of the Ship series. London: Conway; Annapolis: NIP, 1985, 120 pp. Re an early British "74"; built in 1760, the first of about 40.

2080 -------. The Ship of the Line. 2 vols. I: Development of the Battlefleet, 1650-1850. II: Design, Construction, and Fittings. London: Conway; Annapolis: NIP, 1983-1984, 426 pp. The standard reference work on SOTLs which dominated naval warfare for 200 years; in 1815, 214 SOTL on the list; a sophisticated, complex, expensive war machine requiring skilled labor to build and to operate; source of materials became a strategic problem.

2081 [NRS 138] Lavery, Brian, ed. Shipboard Life and Organisation, 1731-1815. Publications of the Navy Records Society, vol. 138. London: Ashgate, 1998, xxv, 656 pp. To fill gaps about social life on the lower deck, correcting myths and anecdotal conclusions; describes structure of naval discipline; from diaries, journals, and medical records.

2082 Lawson, M.K. Cnut: The Danes in England in the Early Eleventh Century.

London: Longman, 1993, 1994, xiii, 290 pp. From an Oxford dissertation; the 1st modern study; Cnut ruled his North Sea "empire," 1017-1035; Danish domination on land and sea.

2083 Lawson-Peebles, Robert. "The Many Faces of Sir Walter Raleigh." HisTod, 48 (March 1998): 17-24. Review of the several "images" of Raleigh over the centuries, e.g., "imperial dreamer," creator of a sea-going tradition, Renaissance man, epitome of chivalry, courtier, and prisoner; various spellings of name.

2084 Laycock, William. The Lost Science of John "Longitude" Harrison. Ashford: Wright, 1976, 159 pp. Harrison, 1693-1776, horologist and scientist; bicentennial of his death; explains the mechanism and gears of his clocks.

2085 Layman, R.D. To Ascend from a Floating Base: Shipboard Aeronautics and Aviation, 1783-1914. London: Associated, 1979, 271 pp. The "prehistory of naval aviation"; earliest aeronautics, e.g., in 1783, a man-lifting aerial vehicle and, later, balloons and kites.

2086 Le Bailly, Louis. "Rum, Bum and the Lash: Some Thoughts on the Problems of Homosexuality in the Royal Navy." JRUSI, 141 (February 1996): 54-58. By Admiral Sir Louis Le Bailly; some "Old Salt" stories; rum and the lash now gone; observations about homosexuality; will its presence affect fighting capabilities?

2087 Lecky, Halton S. The King's Ships. ____ vols. London: Muirhead, 1913-____. At least 2 vols. published, 6 projected; to provide a complete history of every ship of RN, e.g., I: ABOURKIR to BUSTARD and II: CADMUS to ENCOUNTER.

2088 Lee, C.D. "The Battle of Beachy Head: Lord Torrington's Conduct." MM, 80 (August 1994): 270-89. The battle, 30 June 1690, Anglo-Dutch vs. French; Dutch lost 17 ships, 2000 men, English, 2 ships, 350 men; Torrington blamed and court-martialed but not guilty; conclusion: Torrington was guilty.

2089 Lee, Christopher. This Sceptered Isle, 55 BC-1901: From the Roman Invasion to the Death of Queen Victoria. London: BBC; London: Penguin, 1997, 1998, xxviii, 643 pp. Another of the cosmic surveys, this to support a BBC programme; much use of quotes from Winston Churchill, History of the English-Speaking Peoples; cited because of gaps and errors related to English/British naval history, e.g., Harold Godwinson and Anglo-Saxons had no navy (sic), Trafalgar was fought 21 September 1805 (sic); Alfred as "father of British navy," and nothing on Scottish navy.

2090 Lee, Ida. Captain Bligh's Second Voyage to the South Sea. London: Longman, 1920, xix, 290 pp. Re the successful breadfruit voyage, HMS PROVIDENCE, 1791-1793.

2091 Lee, Robert E. Blackbeard the Pirate: A Reappraisal of His Life and Times.

Winston-Salem: Blair, 1974, 264 pp. To rehabilitate, placing Teach in the context of English law and colonial government; "Blackbeard, the famous knight of the black flag"; not convincing.

2092 Lee, Stephen J. Peter the Great. Lancaster Pamphlets. London: Routledge, 1993, x, 78 pp. Peter, 1689-1725, made a famous visit to western Europe, e.g., Portsmouth.

2093 Leech, Samuel. A Voice from the Main Deck: Being a Record of the Thirty Years Adventures of Samuel Leech. Boston: Tappan; London: Chatham, 1843, 1857, 1999, viii, 174 pp. "Adventures" in the British and American navies, 1811-1841; a unique service sequence; a popular work, influencing Melville and Dana, e.g., details on floggings and arbitrary actions of officers.

2094 Lees, James. The Masting and Rigging of English Ships of War, 1625-1860. Annapolis: NIP, 1979, 1984, 212 pp. Large folio size, profusely illustrated; one of a quartet, see Lavery, Godwin, and Harland; details on masts and rigging.

2095 LeFevre, Peter. [Arthur Herbert, Earl of Torrington: A Biography]. A biography of this late 17th century admiral; noted as in preparation.

2096 -------. "The Earl of Torrington's Court-Martial, December 1690." MM, 76 (August 1990): 243-49. The trial for refusal to fight the French fleet at Beachy Head; Torrington blamed for the defeat but acquitted.

2097 LeFevre, Peter, ed. Guerres Maritimes, 1688-1713: IVe Journees franco-britanniques d'histoire de la Marine. Vincennes: Historique, 1996, 305 pp. Proceedings from the 4th Anglo-French naval historians conference, Portsmouth, April 1992; papers, e.g., English navy of 1689 by David Davies, privateers of Dunkirk by Christian Pfister, the Plymouth Dockyard by Michael Duffy, the structure of European navies by Jan Glete, the Register Act of 1696 on manning by Gillian Hughes, and the battle of Barfleur by Patrick Villiers.

2098 LeFevre, Peter. "'Meer Laziness' or Incompetence: The Earl of Torrington and the Battle of Beachy Head." MM, 80 (August 1994): 290-97. Contribution to an ongoing debate about Torrington and Beachy Head; questions about bias.

2099 -------. "Naval History: Half Way There?" MM, 87 (February 2001): 98-103. An outstanding review essay summarizing the state and providing critical analysis; specifically, 4 "big themed" books: Padfield, Reynolds, Glete, and Harding; notes a series of gaps to be filled.

2100 LeFevre, Peter, ed. The Precursors of Nelson: British Admirals of the Eighteenth Century. London: Chatham, 2000, 352 pp. A series of biographical studies by experts, e.g., Daniel Baugh and Roger Knight; precursors, e.g., Vernon, Anson, Hawke, Hood, Howe, St. Vincent, Keith, Rodney, and Herbert.

2101 LeFevre, Peter. "Tangier, the Navy and Its Connection with the Glorious Revolution of 1688." MM, 73 (May 1987): 187-90. A fascinating conspiracy theory, touted by Brian Tunstall: Tangier was the possession, from the dowry of Catherine Broganza, and a base from which a naval conspiracy was launched; George Byng was leader; Pepys accused naval officers of being disloyal; 5 November 1688, decision by navy not to oppose landing by William of Orange.

2102 Lefranc, Pierre. Ralegh Ecrivain l'oeuvre et les idees. Quebec: Laval UP, 1968, 738 pp. Letters of Raleigh; project to publish complete works failed for lack of funding.

2103 Legg, Stuart, ed. Trafalgar: An Eyewitness Account of a Great Battle. NY: Day; London: Hart-Davis, 1966, 133 pp. Edited to present an exciting narrative of the battle; use of quotations, contemporary records, and eyewitness accounts.

2104 LeGuin, Charles A. "Sea Life in Seventeenth-Century England." AmNep, 27 (April 1967): 111-34. Social history, life aboard ships during voyages, e.g., number of crew must increase for longer voyages because of mortality; other matters, e.g., discipline, food, disease, and punishments.

2105 Lemonnier, Leon. Sir Francis Drake. La Grande Legende de la Mer series, vol. 20. Paris: La Renaissance, 1932, 255 pp. A popular French biography of Drake.

2106 LeQuesne, Leslie P. "Nelson's Wounds." Middlesex Hospital J, 55 (1955): 180-82. Some details from a medical perspective.

2107 Lesher, Clara. "The South Sea Islanders in English Literature, 1519-1798." Ph.D. diss, Chicago, 1937. The images in literatue, e.g., Cook voyages and Tahiti.

2108 Lespagnol, Andre. Entre L'Argent et La Gloire: La Course Malouine au Temps de Louis XIV. Vendome: Apogee, 1995, 190 pp. Enlightening on French privateering at its height, e.g., at St. Malo, 1692-1713; rationale and motivation not patriotism and glory as previously stressed but all economic: for profit.

2109 Lester, Malcolm. "Anglo-American Diplomatic Problems Arising from British Naval Operations in American Waters, 1793-1802." Ph.D. diss, Virginia, 490 pp. Scholarly study of British depredations by the Halifax station squadron, e.g., detention of American merchantmen and impressment of American seamen.

2110 Levathes, Louise. When China Ruled the Seas: The Treasure Fleet of the Dragon Throne, 1405-1433. NY: Simon; NY: Oxford UP, 1994, 1996, 264 pp. To counter contentions of absolute Western exclusivity and hegemony; in the 15th century, large fleets operated from China into the South China Sea, into the Indian Ocean, and to the coast of East Africa; Zheng He, 1371-1435, was commander of over 300 ships during 7 voyages; larger ships were 5 times larger than those of Columbus; then, suddenly, China went into isolation.

2111 Lewis, Ada H. A Study of Elizabethan Ship Money, 1588-1603. Phil: U Penn P, 1928, 116 pp. Beginning in 1588, the English crown impressed ships to defend the coast and the realm, expanded in 1596, and 1603; previous sources from the Cinque Ports and London dried up; increasingly, money payments were substituted; some opposition but that seriously increased in the 1630s when Charles I implemented Ship Money taxes.

2112 Lewis, Archibald R. and Runyan, Timothy J. European Naval and Maritime History, 300-1500. Bloomington: Ind UP, 1986, xiii, 192 pp. Lewis, 1914-1990, a prolific historian of medieval maritime and naval activities; a popular-level survey; the "players" during this period were the Byzantines, Vikings, Genoese, Venetians, Catalans, Hanseatic League, and Portugal; English and Dutch toward the end.

2113 Lewis, Archibald R. The Northern Seas: Shipping and Commerce in Northern Europe, AD 300-1100. Princeton: Princeton UP; Ann Arbor: Univ. Microfilms, 1958, 1976, xi, 498 pp. Divided by chronological periods, e.g., invasion, Carolingian, Viking, Alfred, Danish Sea Empire; involved were Romans, Germans, Irish, Anglo-Saxons, Friscians, Flemings, Normans, and French.

2114 Lewis, Charles Lee. Admiral de Grasse and American Independence. Annapolis: NIP, 1945, 404 pp. An account of the French naval intervention culminating in the battle of the Chesapeake.

2115 -------. Books of the Sea: An Introduction to Nautical Literature. Annapolis: NIP; Westport: Greenwood, 1943, 1972, vi, 318 pp. A review of English and American sea literature, poetry, novels, drama, and biography; actually, 20 chapters and 20 categories; features, e.g., Defoe, Smollett, Marryat, Cooper, Conrad, and even Julian Corbett, Laird Clowes, and Fred T. Jane; includes "top 10" list.

2116 Lewis, Frank R. "John Morris and the Carthagena Expedition, 1739-1740." MM, 26 (July 1940): 257-69. From correspondence of Morris to his brother, details on the preparations for, and operations of, the expedition; Morris died during the operation.

2117 Lewis, Jon E. The Mammoth Book of Life Before the Mast. London: Robinson, 2002, 492 pp. A collection of extracts of accounts; focus on Anglo-Americans during the Wars of the French Revolution and Napoleon.

2118 Lewis, Michael A. Armada Guns: A Comparative Study of English and Spanish Armaments. London: Allen, 1961, 243 pp. Lewis, 1890-1970, prolific and important naval historian, longtime professor, RNC, Greenwich; this a study of gunnery, now criticized as inaccurate and misleading.

2119 -------. "Armada Guns: A Comparative Study of English and Spanish Armaments." MM, 28 and 29 (January 1942-October 1943): within 41-289 and 3-231. These 8 articles the basis for the previous entry.

2120 -------. England's Sea Officers: The Story of the Naval Profession. London: Allen, 1939, 307 pp. A survey of officer status, its evolution, and types of officers, e.g., line, warrant, and engineers; once "General-at-Sea"; color of flags, e.g., red, white, and blue, in that order after 1653.

2121 -------. "The Guns of the JESUS OF LUBECK." MM, 22 (July 1936): 324-45. The ship of Hawkins in voyage of 1568 attacking San Juan de Ulua; an inventory and description of its guns.

2122 -------. The Hawkins Dynasty: Three Generations of a Tudor Family. London: Allen, 1969, 247 pp. The famous maritime family of Plymouth; 5 notable members in order, William, William, John, Richard, and William; slave ships, piracy, privateering, the epitome of "Elizabethan Sea Dogs"; curious that Plymouth has no monument to the Hawkins.

2123 -------. The History of the British Navy. Balt: Penguin, 1957, 1959, 1962, 287 pp. A short, broad history, a synthesis; in 3 parts, to 1660, to 1815, and to post-World War II.

2124 [NRS # 93 and 97]. Lewis, Michael A., ed. A Narrative of Professional Adventures by Sir William Henry Dillon, Vice-Admiral of the Red. 2 vols. Publications of the Navy Records Society, vols. 93 and 97. London: NRS, 1953-1956, xxxiv, 468 and xxix, 407 pp. Dillon, born 1780; in RN during time of peace but preparing for war; the Glorious First of June and Ireland in 1798 and 1799; later to Jamaica.

2125 Lewis, Michael A. The Navy of Britain: A Historical Portrait. London: Allen, 1948, 1949, 560 pp. A scholarly and thorough general history; "fathers" were Alfred, Edward III, Henry V, and Henry VIII; the "modern" RN from Charles II; good on impressment.

2126 -------. The Navy in Transition, 1814-1864. London: Hodder; Mystic: Verry, 1965, 287 pp. A social history approach; "the RN at its worst," especially manning and conditions on the lower deck.

2127 -------. A Social History of the Navy, 1793-1815. London: Allen, 1960, 467 pp. "There never was such a navy before and never will be again"; re officers and men, recruiting, promotion, rewards; great leaders, e.g., Howe, Hood, St. Vincent, Duncan, Nelson, and Collingwood.

2128 -------. The Spanish Armada. British Battle series. London: Macmillan; NY: Crowell, 1960, 1968, 240 pp. Touted as complementing Mattingly but lacks broad perspective; emphasis on ships, guns, officers, and men; no scholarly apparatus.

2129 -------. Spithead: An Informal History. London: Allen, 1972, 207 pp. Published posthumously; a general history of the area between Portsmouth and the Isle of Wight; includes coverage of the mutiny and subsequent courts-martial.

2130 [NRS 14 and 21]. Leyland, John, ed. Dispatches and Letters Relating to the Blockade of Brest, 1803-1805. 2 vols. Publications of the Navy Records Society, vols. 14 and 21. London: NRS, 1898-1902, lxvi, 369 and lvi, 390 pp. After resumption of the war in 1803; re "the great blockade"; 609 documents.

2131 Leyland, John. The Royal Navy: Its Influence in English History and in the Growth of Empire. Cambridge Manuals of Science and Literature series. Cambridge: Cambridge UP, 1914, x, 167 pp. A general overview about the sea and the making of England, e.g., ships, men, discovery, naval supremacy, and culminating with Nelson and Trafalgar.

2132 Leys, Simon. The Death of Napoleon. NY: Farrar, 1989, 1992, 129 pp. Trans: Patricia Clancy; a fictional account touting "alternative history" and received in Britain and France with enthusiasm; Napoleon escapes again.

2133 The Libelle of Englyshe Polycye: A Poem on the Use of Sea-Power, 1436. Oxford: Clarendon, 1436, 1926, lvi, 126 pp. Ed: George Warner; author unknown, possibly Adam Moleyns; this a careful edition with annotation, notes and a glossary; stressed its political and commercial advantage in order to secure command of the sea; earlier editions were by Hakluyt and in the Rolls Series.

2134 Liddell Hart, Basil H. Strategy: The Indirect Approach. NY: Praeger; NY: NAL, 1953, 1957, 1967, 1974, 426 pp. A classic survey, from 400 BC to the present; the fundamentals of strategy and of grand strategy; provocative and analytical.

2135 Lincoln, Margarette and Rigby, Nigel. "Reinventing Maritime History." HisTod, 51 (June 2001): 2-3. Recalled William Laird Clowes in the 1890s lamenting diverting of naval history by endless hagiographical accounts and battles; now, it has evolved into an academic discipline; British universities furthering the cause, maritime museums; occasion for the article: "Maritime History Week, July 2001: conference at NMM and Anglo-American conference at IHR with theme: "The Sea."

2136 Lincoln, Margarette, ed. Science and Exploration in the Pacific: European Voyages to the Southern Oceans in the Eighteenth Century. Rochester: Boydell, 1998, xix, 228 pp. On the occasion of ENDEAVOUR II, a conference, NMM, Greenwich, 1997; papers, e.g., Glyndwr Williams on ENDEAVOUR, John Gascoigne on Joseph Banks, Wayne Orchiston on Cook and astronomy, and Jackie Huggins on Cook and anthropology; ENDEAVOUR II on round-the-world cruise.

2137 Lind, James. An Essay on the Most Effective Means of Preserving the Health of Seamen in the Royal Navy. Edinburgh, 1757, 1762, 1774, xx, 363 pp. Lind, 1716-1794, from Edinburgh medical school; the early classic on naval medicine; how to prevent and cure sea diseases.

2138 -------. Lind's Treatise on Scurvy: A Bicentenary Volume. London: Millar;

Edinburgh: Edinburgh UP, 1753, 1757, 1953, xvi, 476 pp. Eds: C.P. Stewart and Douglas Guthrie; dedicated to Anson; a great medical classic; how scurvy can be prevented; time-lag, not adopted by the Admiralty for 40 years; Blane was the mouthpiece for Lind; daily allowance of lemon juice implemented in 1795.

2139 Lindsay-MacDougall, K.F. A Guide to the Manuscripts at the National Maritime Museum. Greenwich: NMM, 1960, 20 pp. A description of the scope of the collection and its special features.

2140 -------. "Nelson Manuscripts at the National Maritime Museum." MM, 41 (1955): 227-32. A guide to the Nelson papers.

2141 Lippincott, Kristen, ed. The Story of Time: Catalogue of the Exhibition. London: Holberton, 1999, 304 pp. Large folio size with beautiful color illustrations; exhibition in the Queen's House, NMM, December 1999-September 2000.

2142 Lisk, Jill. The Struggle for Supremacy in the Baltic, 1600-1725. NY: Funk, 1967, 1968, 232 pp. The crucial period of the competition; a general survey.

2143 Litten, Jane. "Navy Flogging: Captain Samuel Francis Du Pont and Tradition." AmNep, 58 (Spring 1998): 145-65. Re the mid-19th century USN but informative; the position of Du Pont: flogging was essential, "the sheet anchor of discipline"; others opposed it and, in 1850, Congress abolished corporal punishment.

2144 Little, Bryan D.G. Crusoe's Captain: Being the Life of Woodes Rogers, Seaman, Trader, Colonial Governor. London: Oldhams, 1960, 240 pp. Re Woodes Rogers who died in 1732; a biography.

2145 -------. John Cabot: The Reality. Bristol: Radcliffe, 1983, 36 pp. Gathered all known about Cabot.

2146 Littleton, Taylor D. and Rea, Robert R. The Spanish Armada. NY: American, 1964, viii, 145 pp. A description of source materials to aid in research projects for a 1st year college course; background and 1st-hand accounts.

2147 Littlewood, Kevin and Butler, Beverly. Of Ships and Stars: Maritime Heritage and the Founding of the National Maritime Museum, Greenwich. London: Athlone, 1998, xxiv, 275 pp. Fwd: Prince Philip; afterword: Roger Knight; an exhibition on NMM, 1927-1967; re the making of NMM, linked to SNR; founding fathers, e.g., R.C. Anderson, Callender, and Parkinson.

2148 Livezey, William E. Mahan on Sea Power. Norman: U Okla P; London: Eurospan, 1947, 1981, 1987, xii, 334 pp. A biographical study on the mind and influence of Mahan; conclusion: Mahan no longer influential.

2149 Lloyd, C. Christopher. The British Seaman, 1200-1860: A Social Survey.

London: Collins, 1968, 1970, 319 pp. Lloyd, 1906-1986, editor of Mariner's Mirror during the 1970s and longtime professor at RNC, Greenwich; the men of the lower deck, navy and maritime, e.g., conditions, impressment, manning, discipline, punishment, and victualling.

2150 -------. Captain Cook. London: Faber, 1952, 172 pp. A short biography; stress on his navigation and survey skills and brilliant success in training officers, e.g. Bligh, Vancouver, and Flinders.

2151 -------. Captain Marryat and the Old Navy. London: Longman, 1939, 286 pp. Marryat to RN after Trafalgar, served under Cochrane, at St. Helena when Napoleon died, wrote naval novels later, and much autobiographical material.

2152 -------. The Capture of Quebec. British Battle series. NY: Macmillan, 1959, 175 pp. Illustrated; an outstanding example of cooperation of army and navy.

2153 -------. "Cook and Scurvy." MM, 65 (February 1979): 23-28. Revised view: Cook quite inadvertently delayed introducing a cure, orange or lemon juice, known since 1753.

2154 Lloyd, C. Christopher, Carrington, C.E., and Waters, D.W. "Drake's Game of Bowls." MM, 39, 40, and 41 (1953-1955): various. A series of Notes and Queries, back and forth, about this famous legend; no contemporary accounts make mention of it.

2155 Lloyd, C. Christopher. English Corsairs on the Barbary Coast. London: Collins, 1981, 178 pp. Re Englishmen "who took the turban" and joined the Barbary corsairs; some Enlish and Dutch taught them about weapons and shipbuilding; included some individual cases.

2156 -------. Greenwich: Palace, Hospital, College. London: RNC, 1969, 39 pp. An introductory pamphlet and short history.

2157 [NRS 107]. Lloyd, C. Christopher, ed. The Health of Seamen: Selections from the Works of Dr. James Lind, Sir Gilbert Blane, and Dr. Thomas Trotter. Publications of the Navy Records Society, vol. 107. London: NRS, 1965, viii, 319 pp. Informative on the contributions and achievements of these great experts on health.

2158 Lloyd, C. Christopher. "Limes, Lemons, and Scurvy." USNIP, 91 (February 1965): 72-77. Traces origin of the term "Limey"; Australians called ships of RN "limejuicers" and a variation spread to the U.S.: "Limey" for "Brits."

2159 -------. Lord Cochrane: Seaman, Radical, Liberator: A Life of Thomas, Lord Cochrane, Tenth Earl of Dundonald. Hearts of Oak series. London: Longman; NY: Holt, 1947, 1998, 222 pp. Intro: John Hattendorf; a good biography.

2160 [NRS 101]. Lloyd, C. Christopher and Anderson, R.C., eds. A Memoir of James Trevenen, 1760-1790. Publications of the Navy Records Society, vol. 101. London: NRS, 1959, xiv, 250 pp. Service in RN and Russian navy; a midshipman on the 3rd voyage of Cook; to the navy of Catherine the Great.

2161 Lloyd, C. Christopher. Mr. Barrow of the Admiralty: A Life of Sir John Barrow, 1764-1848. London: Collins, 1970, 224 pp. The longtime influential secretary of the Admiralty, advocate of Arctic exploration, and founder of the Royal Geographical Society.

2162 -------. "The Mutiny of the NEREIDE." MM, 54 (August 1968): 245-52. Details of the incident.

2163 -------. The Nation and the Navy: A History of Naval Life and Policy. NY: Macmillan; London: Crosset, 1954, 1961, 1965, 314 pp. A short survey, 16th century to 1922.

2164 [NRS 92]. Lloyd, C. Christopher, ed. The Naval Miscellany. Publications of the Navy Records Society, vol. 92. London: NRS, 1952, xii, 502 pp. The 4th vol. of this series; documents from the Armada, including the instructions of Philip II to Medina Sidonia, Nelson-Hood letters, Congreve's Rockets, and correspondence of St. Vincent.

2165 Lloyd, C. Chistopher. Nelson and Sea Power. Men and Their Times series. London: English UP; NY: Verry, 1973, 156 pp. Features analysis and thoroughness; re his personal and professional life.

2166 -------. "New Light on the Mutiny at the Nore." MM, 46 (1960): 86-95. An eye-witness account by Midshipman A. Hardy of HMS NASSAU, May-June 1797; enlightening about grievances.

2167 -------. The Nile Campaign: Nelson and Napoleon in Egypt. Newton Abbot: David and Charles; NY: Barnes, 1973, 120 pp. A succinct, illustrated account; covers from Malta to Acre.

2168 -------. "The Press Gang and the Law." HisTod, 17 (October 1967): 683-90. A review of the history, evolution, and legalities.

2169 -------. "The Royal Naval Colleges at Portsmouth and Greenwich" MM, 52 (May 1966): 145-56. The development of officer education, from 1729 at Portsmouth, 1870-1920 at Greenwich.

2170 -------. St. Vincent and Camperdown. British Battle series. NY: Macmillan, 1963, 184 pp. An account of these 2 great battles, seen as a turning point in the tide of the long war.

2171 -------. Ships and Seamen: From the Vikings to the Present Day: A Short

History. Cleveland: World, 1961, 223 pp. A short general survey.

2172 -------. A Short History of the Royal Navy, 1805-1918. London: Methuen, 1942, 134 pp. An older survey of the long 19th century RN.

2173 -------. Sir Francis Drake. London: Faber, 1957, 144 pp. A short biography; no scholarly apparatus.

2174 -------. William Dampier. London: Faber, 1966, 161 pp. A short biography.

2175 Lloyd, Frederick. An Accurate and Impartial Life of the Late Lord Viscount Nelson. Lancaster: Fowler, 1806, 303 pp. An early, popular biography; pirated in the U.S. by William Bolton.

2176 Lloyd, Howell A. "Sir John Hawkins' Instructions, 1590." Bull IHR, 44 (May 1971): 125-28. A rare extant document, the Queen's instructions to Hawkins.

2177 Loades, David M. England's Maritime Empire: Seapower, Commerce and Policy, 1490-1690. London: Harlow, 2000. A general survey of the earliest 2 centuries.

2178 -------. "The King's Ships and the Keeping of the Seas, 1413-1480." Medieval History, 1 (1991): 93-104. Description of early operations and policies.

2179 -------. The Tudor Navy: An Administrative, Political and Military History. Studies in Naval History. Aldershot: Scolar, 1992, x, 317 pp. A general overview; depicts the navy as an integral part of the royal government; places the navy in political and administrative context; late in the reign of Henry VIII, a "standing navy."

2180 Lockyer, Roger. Buckingham: The Life and Political Career of George Villiers, First Duke of Buckingham, 1592-1628. London: Longman, 1981, 1984, xix, 506 pp. The favorite of James I who, among other important offices, served as LHA; coverage of some naval preparations, operations, and mutinies.

2181 Lofts, Norah R. Emma Hamilton. London: Joseph; NY: Coward, 1978, 192 pp. An adequate biography.

2182 Lohnes, Barry J. "British Naval Problems at Halifax during the War of 1812." MM, 59 (August 1973): 317-33. Headquarters of the North American Squadron; informative about problems of RN in American waters, e.g., neglect by the Admiralty, mediocre commanders, and unseaworthy ships.

2183 Longmate, Norman. Defending the Island: From Caesar to the Armada. London: Hutchinson; London: Grafton, 1989, 1990, x, 532 pp. "Invasion history"; a narrative survey of the situation over 16 centuries, e.g., Caesar, Romans, Saxons, Cnut, Normans, and the Armada.

2184 -------. Island Fortress: The Defence of Great Britain, 1603-1945. London: Hutchinson, 1991, 580 pp. A limited review, curiously starting with 1603; good on fortifications but poor overview; error-prone.

2185 Longridge, Charles J.N. The Anatomy of Nelson's Ships. London: Marshall; Annapolis: NIP, 1955, 1961, 1965, 1970, 1977, 1980, 1985, 283 pp. Revised: E. Bowness; detailed and elaborate ship plans, including 5 fold-outs; especially for model builders.

2186 Loomie, Albert J. "An Armada Pilot's Survey of the English Coastline, October 1597." MM, 49 (November 1963): 288-300. By a Catholic priest; from the Spanish archives; detailed descriptions of about 20 English ports and coastline for use of the commander of the Armada of 1597.

2187 -------. "The Armadas and the Catholics of England." Catholic Historical Review, 59 (October 1973): 385-403. Enlightening about the impact of Anglo-Spanish war on English Catholics; the religious civil war in France also was a factor.

2188 Lord, Walter. The Dawn's Early Light. NY: Norton; Balt: JHUP, 1972, 1994, 384 pp. The experiences of Americans during the War of 1812, e.g., British depredations along the coasts, especially Cockburn- and Parker-led forays into the Chesapeake area.

2189 Lorenz, Lincoln. John Paul Jones: Fighter for Freedom and Glory. Annapolis: NIP, 1943, xxii, 846 pp. A substantial and solid biography.

2190 [NHS 3]. Love, Robert W., ed. Changing Interpretations and New Sources in Naval History: Papers the Third United States Naval Academy Naval History Symposium. NY: Garland, 1980, 471 pp. (27-28 October 1977, USNA).

2191 [NHS 11]. Love, Robert W., et al., eds. New Interpretations in Naval History: Selected Papers from the Eleventh Naval History Symposium. Annapolis: NIP, 2001, 408 pp. (21-23 October 1993, USNA; delay in publication).

2192 Lovegrove, H. "Remains of Two Old Vessels Found at Rye, Sussex." MM, 50 (May 1964): 115-22. Nautical archaeology report; excavation project in 1963.

2193 Lowe, J.A., ed. Records of the Portsmouth Division of Marines, 1764-1800. Portsmouth Record series, # 7. Portsmouth: City Council, 1990, lxxv, 193 pp. To fill gaps in the history of the Royal Marines.

2194 Lower, Arthur R.M. Great Britain's Woodyard: British America and the Timber Trade, 1763-1867. Montreal: McGill-Queen's UP, 1973, xiv, 271 pp. A history of the timber trade, essential for shipbuilding.

2195 Lowis, Geoffrey L. Fabulous Admirals and Some Naval Fragments: Being a

Brief Account of Some of the Froth of These Characters. . . London: Putnam, 1957, 291 pp. Fwd: Denis Boyd; apparently written in the late 19th century, recollections, anecdotes, and "the lighter side" of RN and its personnel, "men who, however curious, set the world an example of justice, mercy and truth. . . ."; description of drinking and drunkenness, comparing civilians and naval personnel and late 18th and late 19th centuries.

2196 Loyn, Henry R. The Norman Conquest. London: Hutchinson, 1967, 1968, 1982, x, 212 pp. An adequate history.

2197 -------. The Vikings in Britain. Historical Association Studies. NY: St. Martin; Oxford: Blackwell, 1977, 1994, 175 pp. By a noted expert; a succinct history with explanations of the reasons for Scandinavian invasions, 800-1100.

2198 -------. "The Vikings in Britain." Historian, 61 (Spring 1999): 21-22. A survey of recent literature by the prolific historian of these matters; review of recent informative studies, e.g., place-names, density of settlements, archaeological finds, and proceedings of Viking Congresses, e.g., of 1993 and 1994; conclusion: the Northern Isles were heavily "Scandinavianized."

2199 -------. The Vikings in Wales. London: UCL, 1976, 22 pp. The Dorothea Coke Lecture; re spasmodic attacks on Wales but settlements were in Ireland; assesses recent archaeological and numismatic studies.

2200 Lozano, Fernando Riano. Los Medios Navales de Alejandro Farnesio, 1587-1588. Instituto de Historia y Cultura Naval, vol. VII. Madrid: Editorial Naval, 1989, 339 pp. An outstanding example of the products of Spanish archival research associated with the quadricentennial of the Armada, this on the situation with the forces of the Duke of Parma, e.g., the state of his "fleet" at Dunkirk, 17 royal warships and 170 barges; when the Armada arrived, only 3 warships were manned and Parma had lost confidence in the enterprise.

2201 Lucid, Robert F., ed. The Journal of Richard Henry Dana, Jr. I: 1815-1850. II: 1851-1858. III: 1859-1860. Cambridge: Belknap, 1968, 1155 pp. Re the personal journal, including time in England in 1856; observations about the voyage and RN.

2202 Luff, P.A. "Mathews vs Lastock: Parliament, Politics and the Navy in the Mid-Eighteenth-Century England." Parliamentary History, 10 (1991): 45-62. A survey of politics and patronage; in 1744, off Toulon, an indecisive engagement of the squadron of Mathews vs. French-Spanish; 4 captains were court-martialled but acquitted of charges of cowardice; Parliament investigated.

2203 [NRS 115]. Lumby, E.W.R., ed. Policy and Operations in the Mediterranean, 1912-1914. Publications of the Navy Records Society, vol. 115. London: NRS, 1970, xvi, 481 pp. Churchill to the Admiralty; debate over strategy and policy; Anglo-French negotiations; war and the GOEBEN-BRESLAU fiasco.

2204 Lummis, Trevor. Pitcairn Island: Life and Death in Eden. Aldershot: Ashgate, 1997, xlv, 173 pp. Christian led 28 mutineers and Tahitians there; 13 of 15 men soon died; murders, suicides, and racial differences; John Adams and 9 women with children established a society.

2205 Lunn, Kenneth and Day, Ann, eds. History of the Work and Labour Relations in the Royal Dockyards. London: Cassell; NY: Mansell, 1999, xxi, 200 pp. A series of essays by experts; the Royal Dockyards since 1660; the dockyards being one of the largest industries with an enormous labor force; essays, e.g., Roger Knight, Philip MacDougall, and Roger Morriss; on disputes, strikes, and disruptions.

2206 Lusardi, Wayne R. "The Beaufort Inlet Shipwreck." International J Nautical Archaeology, 29 (2000): 57-68. A nautical archaeological excavation and field studies, 1996-1999, off the coast of North Carolina; tentative identification: QUEEN ANNE'S REVENGE, the pirate flagship of Blackbeard, lost in 1718.

2207 Lydon, James F. "Ireland's Participation in the Military Activities of English Kings in the Thirteenth and Fourteenth Centuries." Ph.D. diss, London, 1955. A scholarly study of a neglected subject.

2208 Lyle, Colin. "A Nelsonian Jutland." JRUSI, 140 (February 1995): 56-60. A new look at the battle of Jutland of 1916, "Jellicoe's defeat," and "an Un-Nelsonian tactical draw"; compares with Nelson and Trafalgar; conclusion: Jellicoe could have achieved victory under certain conditions, e.g., more experience in fleet tactics and better nightime scouting.

2209 Lynam, Edward, ed. Richard Hakluyt and His Successors: A Volume Issued to Commemorate the Centenary of the Hakluyt Society. Publications of the Hakluyt Society, 2nd ser, vol. 93. London: Hakluyt Society, 1946, lxviii, 192 pp. The 100th anniversary commemoration of the Hakluyt Society.

2210 Lynch, F.C. "Admiral Lord Cochrane: A Hero for Today's Professionals." USNIP, 101 (February 1975): 63-73. A survey of his extraordinary career, including personal and financial matters; conviction for fraud meant being expelled from RN and Parliament, later to return; meantime to Latin American navies.

2211 Lynch, John. "Bristol Shipping and Royalist Naval Power during the English Civil War." MM, 84 (August 1998): 260-67. The Royalist forces were dependent on supply by sea, e.g., from agents based in Dunkirk; massive arms shipments in "blockade runners" to ports of the West; some captured by Parliamentary ships based at Milford Haven.

2212 -------. "Philip II and the Papacy." Trans RHS, 5th ser, 2 (1961). The traditional view: an "unholy" alliance to restore Protestantism in England; one outcome: the Armada; not so, the Papacy being suspicious of Philip and their conflicts and competition centered on France in the late 16th century.

2213 Lynn, John A., ed. Feeding Mars: Logistics in Western Warfare from the Middle Ages to the Present. Boulder: Westview, 1993, xii, 326 pp. An anthology of 12 essays from the Midwest Consortium on Military History, 1990, University of Illinois, e.g., Lynn critique of Van Creveld, Bernard Bachrach on the Crusades, John Guilmartin on the domination of the seas by Spain in the 16th century, and Timothy Runyan on naval logistics in the Hundred Years' War.

2214 -------, ed. Tools of War: Instruments, Ideas and Institutions of Warfare, 1445-1871. Urbana: U Ill P, 1990, xiv, 262 pp. An anthology from a conference, 1987, e.g., Simon Adams on the Military Revolution and William Maltby on sailing ship tactics.

2215 Lynn, John A. The Wars of Louis XIV, 1667-1714. Modern Wars in Perspective series. London: Longman, 1999, 421 pp. A comprehensive study; France was continuously at war for 4 decades, frequently with Britain; France achieved little and debts mounted.

2216 Lyon, David J. The Patrick O'Brian Companion. (in 1999, noted as forthcoming, but Lyon died in 2000).

2217 -------. The Sailing Navy List: All the Ships of the Royal Navy-Built and Captured, 1688-1860. London: Brassey, 1993, xv, 367 pp. Large folio size with 300 illustrations; a compilation, informative, and succinct, including the "fate" of each ship; incorporates 67 different types.

2218 -------. Sea Battles in Close-Up: The Age of Nelson. NMM series. London: Allen; Annapolis: NIP, 1996, 192 pp. Folio size, illustrated; to launch the Nelson Decade; battles, e.g., Quiberon Bay, Flamborough Head, the Nile, and Trafalgar.

2219 Lyon, Eugene. "The NINA, the SANTA CRUZ, and Other Caravels as Described in the Libro de Armadas and Other Spanish Records." AmNep, 53 (Fall 1993): 239-46. Details from Spanish archives; informative on ship-type details.

2220 Lyon, Mary, et al., ed. The Wardrobe Book of William de Norwell, 12 July 1338 to 27 May 1340. Brussels: Academies, 1983, cxxiii, 546 pp. The wardrobe book of Edward III of the late 1330s was part of the royal household; re military and naval administration; a series of campaigns, e.g., leading to Crecy and Poitiers, and against the Scots; successful battle of Sluys of 1340; this the last time the wardrobe coordinates operations.

2221 MacArthur, Antonia. His Majesty's Bark ENDEAVOUR: The Story of the Ship and Her People. London: HarperCollins, 1997, 86 pp. Re the famous ship of Cook; a replica was built and sailed.

2222 Macaulay, Thomas Babington. "Southey." Edinburgh Review (January 1830). Gushing praise for his Life of Nelson, "the most perfect and most delightful of his works," resulting in a revised edition in 1830.

2223 [NHS 13]. McBride, William and Reed, Eric, eds. New Interpretations in Naval History: Selected Papers from the Thirteenth Naval History Symposium. Annapolis: NIP, 1997, xiv, 341 pp. (2-4 October 1997, Annapolis, MD).

2224 MacCaffrey, Wallace T. "The Armada in Its Context: Review Article." Historical J, 32 (September 1989): 713-15. A historiographical survey of the literature associated with the quadricentennial and new information from nautical archaeology; new research has "de-mythologized" the Armada, no longer seen as the ultimate battle of darkness vs. light; certainly contemporaries in England and Spain did not see it as a decisive end and major watershed.

2225 McCann, Franklin T. English Discovery of America to 1585. NY: Crown, 1952, xiv, 246 pp. A survey of a series of voyages, e.g., beginning in 1509, revived in the late 1550s and early 1560s.

2226 McCarthy, William J. "The Yards at Cavite: Shipbuilding in the Early Colonial Philippines." International J Maritime History, 2 (December 1995): 149-62. Re the famous Manila galleon, 300 T, Acapulco to Manila across the Pacific, 1572-1814, 2 per year, and highly profitable; English privateers sought to capture its treasure, e.g., Drake and Anson.

2227 McCaughan, Michael and Appleby, John, eds. The Irish Sea: Aspects of Maritime History. Belfast: Institute of Irish Studies, 1989, x, 179 pp. Proceedings from an academic conference, Queen's University, Belfast, October 1986; papers, e.g., medieval trade and shipping, descriptions of the papers of HCA, findings of nautical archaeology, and smugglers of the 18th century.

2228 McCaughey, R. "The English Navy, Politics and Administration, 1640-1649." D.Phil. diss, Ulster, 1983. A scholarly study of the navy during the Civil War.

2229 McCord, Norman. "The Impress Service in Northeast England during the Napoleonic War." MM, 54 (May 1968): 163-80. A case study of an important recruiting force for RN, 1803-1815.

2230 -------. "The Seamen's Strike of 1815 in North-East England." Economic History Review, 2nd ser, 21 (1968): 127-43. One consequence of demobilization of 1815, "paying off" ships of RN, leading to agitation in ports, especially in the Northeast; these events seen as economic, the seamen obviously having no political motives, but that changed by 1820.

2231 McCormick, Peter. "The Improbable Thomas Cochrane." MHQ, 8 (Spring 1997): 94-101. Links Cochrane to nautical fiction, e.g., Marryat was inspired from service under him; O'Brian used him as the model for Jack Aubrey; others, G.A. Henty and C.S. Forester.

2232 McCullough, Colleen. Morgan's Run. NY: Simon, 2000, 604 pp. Re Richard Morgan, an actual historic person incorporated in this fictional account of the voyage of the First Fleet; much sex; sequels promised.

2233 MacDermott, A. "Dr. Burney's Royal Academy at Gosport." MM, 51 (February 1965): 57-59. Seen as the best naval school in Europe; founded in 1791 by Dr. William Burney; closed 1904.

2234 McDermott, Eric. "The Elder Pitt and His Admirals and Generals." Military Affairs, 20 (Summer 1956): 65-70. Re the great war administration of Lord Chatham; some now say that reputation was exaggerated.

2235 McDermott, James. Martin Frobisher: Elizabethan Privateer. New Haven: Yale UP, 2001, xv, 509 pp. Re his naval service for the Queen, best known as an explorer; this stresses his privateering operations to further his selfish interests.

2236 McDonald, R. Andrew. The Kingdom of the Isles: Scotland's Western Seaboard, c.1100-c.1336. East Linton: Tuckwell, 1997, xv, 280 pp. The history of this formative kingdom of the Western Isles led by the McSorleys, holders of the Lordship of the Isles; originally an Irish kingdom, "Scotti of Dal Riata" from County Atrim, emigrating to western Scotland; a geographical link of Scotland, Ireland, England, and Norway; title ultimately forfeited to Scotland.

2237 MacDonogh, Katherine. "The Sympathetic Ear: Napoleon, Elba and the British." HisTod, 44 (February 1994): 29-35. Contention: the British knew of and connived in the escape of Napoleon from Elba to return to power in France in the spring of 1815.

2238 MacDougall, Norman. James IV. Edinburgh: Donald, 1989, xi, 339 pp. The biography of the best known of the early Stewart kings, husband of Margaret Tudor, and his "Royal obsession, the Navy" during the late 15th and early 16th centuries, e.g., in 1506, built a fleet of 38 ships to defend Scotland; invaded England, killed at the battle of Flodden.

2239 MacDougall, Norman, ed. Scotland and War, AD 79-1918. NY: Barnes; Edinburgh: Donald, 1991, xiv, 216 pp. 9 essays by experts, e.g., MacDougall on ships of James IV, especially GREAT MICHAEL, the greatest ship in Europe; others on archaeological evidence and the Romans in Scotland.

2240 MacDougall, Philip C. The Chatham Dockyard Story. Rochester: Baggin, 1981, 1989, 2001, 189 pp. Folio size, illustrated; the history of 500 years as an industrialized center; some decline in importance after the Dutch threat ended; HMS VICTORY built in mid-18th century; closed in 1981, now a museum.

2241 -------. Chatham Past. London: Phillimore, 1999. A general history of Chatham.

2242 -------. "The Formative Years: Malta Dockyard, 1800-1815." MM, 76 (August 1990): 205-13. Napoleon had captured Malta in 1798; French expelled by Maltese-

British-Neapolitan-Portuguese forces and RN took over the dockyard which serviced the Mediterranean squadron.

2243 -------. "Hazardous Waters: Naval Dockyard Harbours during the Age of Fighting Sail." MM, 87 (February 2001): 15-29. By the late 18th-early 19th centuries, increasingly clear Royal Dockyards were located in inappropriate places, especially Woolwich and Deptford.

2244 -------. Royal Dockyards. Newton Abbot: David and Charles, 1982, 1989, 216 pp. A survey of the network of bases and dockyards within the British Isles since the Tudor era; good bibliography but not a comprehensive synthesis as touted.

2245 McEwen, W.A. and Lewis, A.H. Encyclopedia of Nautical Knowledge. Cambridge: Cornell Maritime, 1953, viii, 618 pp. Features practical, theoretical, and historical aspects; no satisfactory introduction and no mention of predecessors; no scholarly apparatus.

2246 McFarland, Alfred. Mutiny in the BOUNTY and Story of the Pitcairn Islanders. Sydney: Moore, 1884, xix, 240 pp. An older account.

2247 McFarlane, Anthony. The British in the Americas, 1480-1815. London: Longman, 1992, 1994, 1995, xiv, 365 pp. A chronological survey, beginning in the early 1480s, Bristol ships en route "Brasil"; the Cabots in the 1490s; Elizabethan adventurers; later, Cromwell's "Western Design."

2248 McFee, William. The Life of Sir Martin Frobisher. Golden Hind series. NY: Harper, 1928, xiv, 288 pp. Frobisher, 1535-1594; by an American novelist; no scholarly apparatus.

2249 McGowan, Alan P. "The Administration of the Navy under the First Duke of Buckingham, Lord High Admiral of England, 1618-1628." Bull IHR, 40 (1967): 225-27. A summary of the Julian Corbett Prize Essay; Buckingham has been condemned as inept and corrupt; not deserved as he kept close oversight, implemented reforms, e.g., welfare and health of seamen, formulated a programme of small fast ships to combat pirates of Dunkirk, and led the attack on Rhe, 1627.

2250 -------. HMS VICTORY: Her Construction, Career and Restoration. London: Chatham; Annapolis: NIP, 1999, x, 222 pp. Very large folio size, drawings by John McKay; fwd: Michael Boyce; a complete history of HMS VICTORY, built in the 1760s; in 1922, the decision to restore and role of SNR; still flagship for 2nd Sea Lord.

2251 [NRS 116]. McGowan, Alan P., ed. The Jacobean Commissions of Enquiry, 1608 and 1618. Publications of the Navy Records Society, vol. 116. London: NRS, 1971, xxx, 319 pp. After sensational scandals and corruption; published reports of the Commissions.

2252 -------. "The Royal Navy under the First Duke of Buckingham, Lord High Admiral, 1618-1628." Ph.D. diss, London, 1967. A scholarly, detailed, and thorough account of the administration.

2253 -------. The Ship. IV: The Century before Steam: The Development of the Sailing Ship, 1700-1820. London: HMSO, 1980, 60 pp. For NMM; in a series, # 4 of 10.

2254 -------. The Ship. III: Tiller and Whipstaff: The Development of the Sailing Ship, 1400-1700. London: HMSO, 1981, 59 pp. For NMM; in a series, # 3 of 10.

2255 McGrail, Sean. Ancient Boats. Shire Archaeology series. Aylesbury: Shire, 1983, 64 pp. Illustrated; a description of nautical archaeology; focus on water transport of northern and western Europe.

2256 -------. Ancient Boats in Northern Europe: The Archaeology of Water Transport to A.D. 1500. London: Longman, 1987, 1998, xxi, 321 pp. A technical handbook, details on construction, performance, different types, and sailing; extensive introduction.

2257 McGrail, Sean, ed. The Archaeology of Medieval Ships and Harbours in Northern Europe. Archaeological series, # 5. Oxford: BAR, 1979, ix, 260 pp. Proceedings from the International Symposium on Boat and Ship Archaeology, Bremerhaven, Germany, 1979.

2258 McGrail, Sean. "Cross-Channel Seamanship and Navigation in the Late First Millennium BC." Oxford J Archaeology, 2 (1983): 299-337. A review of the knowledge and skills of seamen; analysis of 9 sea routes; type of boats; describes sources, including nautical archaeology.

2259 McGrail, Sean, ed. Maritime Celts: Frisians and Saxons: Papers Presented at a Conference at Oxford in November 1988. London: British Archaelogy, 1990, x, 134 pp. 16 papers, focusing on the North Sea and English Channel, 300 BC to 800 AD; topics, e.g., Frisian domination, methods of transport, and Saxon Shore.

2260 McGrail, Sean. Studies in Maritime Archaeology. British Archaeological Reports, # 256. Oxford: Hadrian, 1997, 374 pp. Fwd: Basil Greenhill; a series of papers presented, 1975-1995, e.g., an attack on the Trustees of NMM for shutting down the Archaeological Unit.

2261 McGrath, Charles. "The Long Journey." The New Yorker (18 October 1993): 121-26. A review of The Wine-Dark Sea by Patrick O'Brian, # 16 and touted then as "the last."

2262 MacGregor, David R. The Schooner: Its Design and Development from 1600 to the Present. Annapolis: NIP, 2001, 192 pp. The Dutch first designed this sleek, elegant, romantic ship type.

2263 McGuffie, T.H. "Recruiting the Ranks of the Regular British Army during the French Wars." <u>J Society for Army Historical Research</u>, 34 (June 1956): 50-58, 123-32. A case study of Army recruiting at a crucial time, as war began in 1793; government forced to resort to levies, bounties, Volunteer Acts, crimps and a press gang; instructive as comparison.

2264 -------. <u>The Siege of Gibraltar, 1779-1783</u>. Phil: Dufour; London: Batsford, 1965, 208 pp. A detailed history of the "Great Siege."

2265 McGurk, J.N. "Armada Preparations in Kent and Arrangements Made After the Defeat, 1587-1589." <u>Archaeologia Cantiana</u>, 85 (1970): 71-93. A large force assembled, 27,000 foot and 2500 horse, to follow the Armada up the Channel; all forts inspected and prepared; army recalled from the Netherlands.

2266 MacInnes, John. "West Highland Sea-Power in the Middle Ages." <u>Trans of the Gaelic Society of Inverness</u>, 48 (1972-1974): 518-56. A rare study of a neglected subject.

2267 Macintyre, Donald G.F.W. <u>Admiral Rodney</u>. London: Davies, 1962, 280 pp. By a naval officer-writer about naval operations of World War II; George Rodney, 1719-1792; 18 untitled chapters, dependent on Callender, not researched, the bibliography is paltry.

2268 Macintyre, Donald G.F.W. and Hall, Julian, eds. <u>The Adventure of Sail, 1520-1914: An Anthology</u>. NY: Random House, 1970, 255 pp. Lavishly illustrated; a collection of readings.

2269 Macintyre, Donald G.F.W. and Bathe, Basil W. <u>The Man-of-War: A History of the Combat Vessel</u>. London: Methuen, 1969, 273 pp. Folio size, lavishly illustrated, especially with color paintings; sailing ships and steam ships.

2270 Macintyre, Donald G.F.W. <u>Sea Power in the Pacific: A History from the Sixteenth Century to the Present Day</u>. London: Barker, 1972, 281 pp. Some coverage of early years of European expansion, e.g., Portuguese, Dutch, and British, but most on World War II.

2271 -------. <u>Trafalgar: Nelson's Great Victory</u>. London: Butterworth, 1968, 80 pp. Illus: David Cobb and Maxine Reilly; a brief, popular narrative account nicely illustrated.

2272 McIntyre, Kenneth G. <u>The Secret Discovery of Australia: Portuguese Ventures 250 Years before Captain Cook</u>. Sydney: Picador, 1977, 1982, xv, 236 pp. An entry in the debate in favor of the claims of Portugal and "the Dauphin Map."

2273 McIntyre, Ruth A. "The Role of the English Merchant in the Promotion of Discovery and Colonial Enterprise, 1496-1616." Ph.D. diss, Minnesota, 1948. Merchants, e.g., from London or Bristol, financed these voyages, including privateering and pirate enterprises.

2274 McIvor, Aidan. <u>A History of the Irish Naval Service</u>. Dublin: Irish Academic, 1994, 256 pp. Also as "Mcivor"; fwd: John Moore; "this is the tale of a maritime country"; on the occasion of the 50th anniversary of establishment of a naval service for the Republic; the sequence: Celtic invaders from Britain about 2500 BC; then Picts from Scotland; 5th century, AD, St. Patrick; the famous Celtic missionaries who ventured out in extraordinary voyages; 8th century, the Vikings; then Henry II; Cromwell; William III; attempts by the French; even small craft during the Irish Civil War of the 1920s, and, finally, its own naval service.

2275 Mack, James D. <u>Matthew Flinders, 1774-1814</u>. Melbourne: Nelson, 1966, 270 pp. Protege of Cook who returned to survey Australia, confirming his reputation.

2276 Mack, William P. <u>Captain Kilburnie</u>. Annapolis: NIP, 1999, 367 pp. By the former commander, U.S. 7th Fleet, author of six naval novels set in World War II, some with his son, William P. Mack, Jr.; recent nautical fiction, the story of the rise through the ranks during the Nelsonian era of Fergus Kilburnie, a Scotsman.

2277 -------. <u>Lieutenant Christopher: A Novel of the Sea</u>. Mt. Pleasant: N&A, 1999, 320 pp. Nautical fiction, this an American privateer, Matthew Christopher, attacking British shipping, later serving with John Paul Jones.

2278 Mackanness, George, ed. <u>A Book of the BOUNTY, William Bligh and Others</u>. London: Kent; NY: Dutton, 1938, 1981, xvi, 321 pp. Intro: Gavin Kennedy; a selection of original sources, e.g., pamphlets and letters by this Australian scholar and biographer of Bligh; over 400 entries in bibliography.

2279 Mackanness, George. <u>Captain William Bligh's Discoveries and Observations in Van Dieman's Land</u>. Sydney: Ford, 1943, 1953, 51 pp. A published lecture given in October 1943.

2280 Mackanness, George, ed. <u>Fresh Light on Bligh: Some Unpublished Correspondence</u>. <u>Australian Historical Monographs</u>, # 5. Sydney: Ford, 1949, 1953, 120 pp. A collection published in pamphlet format; included 53 letters from Bligh.

2281 Mackanness, George. <u>The Life of Vice-Admiral William Bligh</u>. 2 vols. Sydney: Angus; NY: Farrar, 1931, 1936, 1951, 764 pp. Also 2 vols. in one; a substantial and authoritative biography; informative description of sources.

2282 -------. <u>Sir Joseph Banks: His Relationships with Australia</u>. Sydney: Angus, 1931, 146 pp. Banks was the scientist-naturalist on the 1st voyage of Cook; later, a publicist on natural life of the region, e.g., it was Banks who initiated the penal colony idea and facilitated the breadfruit projects.

2283 Mackay, David L. "Banks, Bligh, and Breadfruit." <u>New Zealand J History</u>, 8

(April 1974): 61-77. The background and execution of the famous breadfruit projects.

2284 -------. "Exploration and the Economic Development of the Empire, 1782-1798, with Special Reference to the Activities of Sir Joseph Banks." Ph.D. diss, London, 1969. The basis of these entries.

2285 -------. In the Wake of Cook: Exploration, Science, and Empire, 1780-1801. London: Croom; NY: St. Martin, 1985, xii, 216 pp. After the death of Cook, Banks succeeded him as activist for Admiralty sponsorship of projects; sea power and science were the motives; Banks was a primary facilitator of broad-based expansion, e.g., food for slaves of the West Indies, establishment of penal colony, development of cotton and the fur trade, and general advancement of science.

2286 McKay, John. The Armed Transport BOUNTY. The Anatomy of the Ship series, # 15. London: Conway; Annapolis: NIP, 1989, 120 pp. Folio size, 97 pages of illustrations, e.g., pictures of 2 replicas made for movies; originally BETHIA, a sailing merchant vessel; little original research.

2287 -------. The 100-Gun Ship VICTORY. The Anatomy of the Ship series. London: Conway; Annapolis: NIP, 1987, 2000, 120 pp. Typical of the series, many illustrations; other books on VICTORY, the flagship of Nelson at Trafalgar, are better; little original research.

2288 McKay, John and Coleman, Ron. The 24-Gun Frigate PANDORA, 1779. The Anatomy of the Ship series. London: Conway, 1991, 128 pp. Folio size, 300 illustrations; a veteran of the War of the American Revolution, laid up, and brought out in 1790 to search for the mutineers of BOUNTY, those recaptured being kept in a "box" on deck; then wrecked on Great Barrier Reef; in 1977, Coleman led the nautical archaeological expedition which discovered the wreck; some artifacts recovered.

2289 Mackay, Ruddock F. Admiral Hawke. Oxford: Clarendon; London: Chatham, 1965, 2002, 374 pp. By a veteran, Royal New Zealand Navy, later an academic and biographer of Fisher and Arthur Balfour; a substantial, recent biography superseding Burrows and Corbett; use of Hawk papers which he edited for NRS; Hawke at Toulon, 1744, apparently the only commander demonstrating initiative at the time of the notorious Mathews-Lestock confrontation; and, of course, Quiberon Bay of 1759.

2290 [NRS 129]. Mackay, Ruddock F., ed. The Hawke Papers: A Selection, 1743-1771. Publications of the Navy Records Society, vol. 129. Aldershot: Scolar, 1990, xxx, 521 pp. One of the great admirals of the 18th century; 2nd Cape Finisterre, blockade of Brest, Quiberon Bay, and Belle Isle.

2291 Mackay, Ruddock F. "Lord St. Vincent's Early Years, 1735-1759." MM, 76 (February 1990): 51-65. Jervis, born 1735, at age 12 to Greenwich, Anson being his patron; by age 25, captain of frigate GOSPORT.

2292 McKee, Alexander. Against the Odds: Battles at Sea, 1591-1949. London: Souvenir; Annapolis: NIP, 1991, xii, 272 pp. Illustrated; by a prolific naval writer; descriptions of 26 naval battles and commanders fighting against the odds, e.g., REVENGE, Blake, and J.P. Jones.

2293 -------. Death Raft: The Human Drama of the MEDUSA Shipwreck. NY: Scribner, 1976, 336 pp. A shipwreck achieving notoriety from a famous painting; in 1816, HMS MEDUSA, a frigate carrying passengers and led by incompetents, wrecked off the west coast of Africa; most of the 1100 persons aboard died; McKee also wrote a dramatic account of the sensational wreck of ROYAL CHARTER in 1859 off Anglesey; great loss of life, carrying gold bullion.

2294 -------. From Merciless Invaders: The Defeat of the Spanish Armada. London: Nelson; London: Souvenir, 1963, 1964, 1987, 288 pp. "A narrative of adventure"; the original supported a BBC documentary, 1954; a mediocre history of the Armada stressing eye-witness accounts; the 2nd edition elaborates on the discovery by nautical archaeologists of 9 wrecks of the Armada off the west coast of Ireland.

2295 -------. "Henry VIII as Military Commander." HisTod, 41 (June 1991): 22-29. Henry was a student of war and led land and sea campaigns; had MARY ROSE and GREAT HARRY, among others, built; conclusion: he made political mistakes but not military ones.

2296 -------. HMS BOUNTY: The Truth about the Mutiny on the BOUNTY. NY: Morrow, 1962, 222 pp. An adequate account.

2297 -------. History under the Sea. NY: Dutton; London: Hutchinson, 1968, 1969, viii, 342 pp. Folio size, many b/w illustrations; descriptions of nautical archaeological operations, e.g., at Spithead, searching for MARY ROSE, in the Mediterranean, Northwest Europe, and the Caribbean.

2298 -------. How We Found the MARY ROSE. London: Souvenir, 1982, 144 pp. Recalled a search of the 1830s and the search for ROYAL GEORGE in the 1960s; then, operations of "Mad Mac's Marauders" searching, finding, recovering, and displaying MARY ROSE, 1965-1979; 1000 persons, including Prince Charles, were involved; MARY ROSE sank in the Solent in 1545.

2299 -------. King Henry VIII's MARY ROSE: Its Fate and Future. London: Souvenir, 1973, xii, 346 pp. A narrative of the search in progress, having begun in 1965.

2300 -------. The Queen's Corsair: Drake's Journey of Circumnavigation, 1577-1580. NY: Stein; London: Souvenir, 1978, 1979, 320 pp. Re "the master thief of the unknown world"; the 1st English circumnavigation, demonstrating what a brilliant navigator Drake was; less emphasis on that and more on sensational depredations.

2301 Mackenzie, Robert Holden. The Trafalgar Roll: The Ships and the Officers. London: Greenhill; Annapolis: NIP, 1913, 1989, xviii, 336 pp. A listing of the 33 British ships and biographical entries of 850 officers of RN at Trafalgar.

2302 Mackesy, Piers G. "British Strategy in the Mediterranean, 1803-1810." D.Phil., diss, Oxford, 1954. The basis of some following entries.

2303 -------. British Victory in Egypt, 1801: The End of Napoleon's Conquest. London: Routledge, 1995, xiii, 282 pp. In a series of 4 vols. on naval-military-diplomatic-international efforts by the British to defeat the French; as the 1st phase of the Napoleonic war was ending, it was imperative to conclude the Egyptian campaign; combined operations ultimately successful for the British.

2304 -------. "Problems of an Amphibious Power: Britain against France, 1793-1815." NWCR, 30 (1978): 16-25. The British had enormous obligations: security, imperial and colonial protection, and balance of power in Europe; until 1807, various attempts at amphibious operations failed, then, the Peninsular campaign opened; the British had a base in Portugal; now the solution to the problems and success followed.

2305 -------. The War for America, 1775-1783. Cambridge: Harvard UP; London: Longman, 1964, 1993, xx, 565 pp. A classic account of British policies and operations during the American Revolution; part of a failed grand imperial strategy; a world-wide perspective.

2306 -------. The War in the Mediterranean, 1803-1810. Cambridge: Harvard UP; Westport: Greenwood, 1957, 1961, 1981, xviii, 430 pp. In a series of 4 vols.; a masterly monograph of naval, military, and diplomatic affairs; links a variety of operations and activities; downplays the significance of Trafalgar; plays up the actions of Collingwood in the Mediterranean; British naval pressure was costly for Napoleon, eliminating his fleet and forcing him to implement defensive measures.

2307 Mackie, J.D. "Scotland and the Spanish Armada." Scottish Historical Review, 12 (October 1914): 1-23. In her will, Mary, Queen of Scots left her claim of the English throne to Philip II of Spain; Scotland had no navy but much activity of merchant and pirate maritime forces; Scots did see Armada as Catholic aggression and Philip increasingly ignored Scotland.

2308 McKinney, Sam. Bligh: True Account of Mutiny aboard His Majesty's Ship BOUNTY. London: International Marine, 1989, 1993, 208 pp. On the occasion of the bicentennial; touted as a search for truth and to correct depictions of the mutiny in movies; tells the whole story elegantly; Bligh properly praised for incredible achievements of navigation; mutineers seen as pathetic in frantic efforts to hide.

2309 McLaren, P., ed. Hearts of Oak: A Collection of Royal Navy Anecdotes. Brighton: Fernhurst, 1994, 128 pp. Fwd: John Woodward; dedicated to "Jack"; to support a project to raise money for maritime charities; Britain has needed a navy since the 9th century and it is the most strategic and senior armed force; a series of stories and yarns.

2310 MacLean, Alistair. <u>Captain Cook</u>. London: Collins; NY: Doubleday, 1972, 1974, 192 pp. For juveniles by a novelist; re James Cook, 1728-1779; hagiography, no scholarly apparatus.

2311 MacLeay, Alison. <u>The Tobermory Treasure: The True Story of a Fabulous Armada Galleon</u>. London; Conway, 1986, 192 pp. Fwd: Duke of Argyll; FLORNCIA, the large Spanish galleon, built in Regusa, sank in Tobermory Bay, Isle of Mull, Inner Hebrides; extensive diving and searching, controlled and uncontrolled; little has been found.

2312 McLynn, Frank J. <u>Invasion: From the Armada to Hitler, 1588-1945</u>. NY: Routledge, 1987, vi, 170 pp. Describes a series of attempts, contending none have succeeded after 1066, e.g., Armada, Jacobites, Napoleon, and Operation Sea Lion; superficial, lapses, and gaps, e.g., William of Orange in 1688.

2313 -------. <u>Napoleon: A Biography</u>. London: Cape, 1997, 739 pp. Not "life and times" but emphasis on psychological aspects; idiosyncratic; Napoleon seen as psychosomatic; blames collapse of Amiens on British, and Hudson Lowe, in charge at St. Helena, depicted as "bad guy."

2314 -------. "Sea Power and the Jacobite Rising of 1745." <u>MM</u>, 67 (May 1981): 163-72. RN has been credited with preventing Jacobite successes; this is questioned; it did deny French threats by blockading Scotland; actually, British control of the sea only a minor irritant to Jacobite operations.

2315 -------. <u>1066: The Year of the Three Battles</u>. London: Cape, 1998, 1999, xiv, 304 pp. A review of spectacular events throughout the year; focused on personalities, e.g., Harold and William.

2316 McMillan, A.R.G. "'The Admiral of Scotland." <u>Scottish Historical Review</u>, 20 (1923): 11-18. The sea was important to the Scots and in Scottish history; but the English claimed dominance of "the 4 seas" which included that around Scotland; the 1st "Admiral" was the Earl of Orkney about 1400; in the 17th century, a "Lord High Admiral" was appointed to suppress piracy.

2317 MacMillan, Ken. "Discourse on History, Geography, and Law: John Dee and the Limits of the British Empire, 1576-1580." <u>Canadian J History</u>, 26 (April 2001): 1-25. Re the polymath, Dee, 1527-1608; formulated a rationale for the Queen advocating trade, empire, and legal claims of territory; all adopted.

2318 McNeill, John R. <u>Atlantic Empires of France and Spain: Louisbourg and Havana, 1700-1763</u>. Chapel Hill: UNCP, 1985, xvii, 329 pp. Comparative history; French and Spanish imperialists both continually threatened by British sea power, a mutual fear; by 1700 both had conceded "command of the sea" to the British; both were imperial capitals and military, commercial, demographic, and administrative centers; both were heavily and expensively fortified.

2319 McNeill, William H. The Age of Gunpowder Empires, 1450-1800. Wash: AHA, 1989, vii, 49 pp. Fwd: Michael Adas; by the eminent world historian, a succinct overview as a pamplet for the American Historical Association; a brilliant systhesis by the most noted expert.

2320 -------. Venice: The Hinge of Europe, 1081-1797. Chicago: Chicago UP, 1974, xvii, 334 pp. Emphasis on maritime expansion into the great, perhaps, the greatest political, commercial, cultural, and technological center of its day.

2321 McWhannell, D.C. "The Galleys of Argyll." MM, 88 (February 2002): 14-32. Unfortunately, no wreck finds from nautical archaeology but can identify from iconography, e.g., 78 stones with carved images of galleys in use over 800 years; these galleys were power-status symbols among the Dalriada of the West Highlands and the Isles; based on Scandinavian vessels of the Viking era.

2322 Mace, Rodney. Trafalgar Square: Emblem of Empire. London: Lawrence, 1976, 338 pp. A fascinating account of its origins and history; in 1839, a Nelson Memorial competition was won by William Railton: the single tall column with the statue by Edward Baily and reliefs on the 4 sides at the base: St. Vincent, the Nile, Copenhagen, and Trafalgar; the central location for large demonstrations and celebrations, even riots, over the decades.

2323 Madariaga, Isabel de. Britain, Russia and the Armed Neutrality of 1780: Sir James Harris's Mission to St. Petersburg during the American Revolution. New Haven: Yale UP, 1962, xiv, 496 pp. Fwd: Samuel Flagg Bemis; an outstanding study in diplomatic history; an important factor in British relations with Russia and with the Dutch who carried most of the Baltic trade, and, of course, with America.

2324 Madison, Robert D. "Cooper and the Sea: Bibliographical Note." AmNep, 57 (Fall 1997): 371-72. J.F. Cooper favored writing about the sea, 1820s-1840s; and he influenced Conrad and Melville.

2325 Maffeo, Steven E. Most Secret and Confidential: Intelligence in the Age of Nelson. London: Chatham; Annapolis: NIP, 2000, xxvii, 355 pp. Fwds: Howard Roop and Bruce Black; somewhat idiosyncratic and little primary research; interestingly, cites all the nautical fiction of Patrick O'Brian and dedicates it "inevitably" to C.S. Forester; touted as the 1st concise analysis of the approach and topic; sheds light on this neglected topic and demonstrates the importance of intelligence in naval operations; intelligence and frigates were vitally connected; a case study: the Copenhagen campaign of 1801.

2326 Magoun, Francis P. "King Alfred's Naval and Beach Battle." Modern Language Review, 37 (October 1942): 409-14. In 897, Alfred with 9 ships commanded a battle against the Danes with 6 ships, contending that this was the 1st naval battle in English history.

2327 -------. "The SUTTON HOO Ship Burial: Chronological Bibliography." Speculum, 29 (January 1954): 116-24. Discovered in digs in 1939-1940, magnificent artifacts and ship form, but no body; the most spectacular find of Western Europe; contributed to the British Museum; a bibliography of all publications about it, 1939-1952.

2328 Mahan, Alfred Thayer. The Influence of Sea Power upon the French Revolution and Empire, 1793-1812. 2 vols. Boston: Little, Brown, 1892, 1980, 1987, 709 pp. Mahan, 1840-1914, the influential American naval officer-theorist-publicist and advocate of a national strategy based on sea power; lionized by the British; this volume the sequel to the more important next entry.

2329 -------. The Influence of Sea Power upon History, 1660-1783. Boston: Little, Brown; Novato: Presidio, 1890, 1980, 1987, 557 pp. This formative treatise went through 50 editions in 6 languages, especially German and Japanese; Mahan used English history as the basis for formulating his strategy based on a blue-water fleet, "those far-distant, storm-tossed ships upon which the Grand Army never looked, stood between it and dominion of the world."

2330 -------. The Life of Nelson: The Embodiment of the Sea Power of Great Britain. 2 vols. Boston: Little, Brown; NY: Greenwood; Ithaca: Regatta; Annapolis: NIP, 1897, 1899, 1943, 1968, 2000, 2001, xxiii, 764 pp. Callender described it as the best on Nelson's service life and what it meant; Mahan had access to papers of many of the "Band of Brothers" and was supported by Laughton, Earl Nelson, and Nelson Ward, son of Horatia.

2331 -------. The Major Operations of the Navies in the War of American Independence. Boston: Little, Brown; London: Low, Marston; NY: Greenwood, 1913, 1969, xxiii, 280 pp. A survey of naval operations.

2332 -------. Sea Power in Its Relation to the War of 1812. 2 vols. Boston: Little, Brown; NY: Haskell, 1905, 1969, 879 pp. The final work in the sea power series; saw the causes as impressment and free trade; best on sea operations, including those on the Lakes.

2333 -------. Types of Naval Officers, Drawn from the History of the British Navy. London: Sampson; Boston: Little, Brown, 1902, xiv, 500 pp. A didactic approach, presenting biographical suveys of noted British naval officers, e.g., de Saumarez, Rodney, St. Vincent, Hawke, and Pellew; on didacticism, e.g., Richard Howe conceded to all demands of the mutineers of 1797 but discipline did not improve; it took St. Vincent to intervene in the Mediterranean before restoration of proper discipline.

2334 Mahon, John K. The War of 1812. Gainesville: U Fla P; NY: DaCapo, 1972, 1991, xii, 476 pp. Praise of the account of Henry Adams; Mahon researched in

British and Canadian sources; presents the most balanced account; focus on the war itself; reviews several controversies.

2335 Maihafer, Harry J. "Beginning of Longest Conflict." Military History, 7 (August 1990): 25-29. Some superficial features; the battle of Sluys, 22 June 1340, "a land battle at sea"; 200 English "civvie" [??] ships vs. French-Spanish-Genoese ships; an uneven contest; English archers overwhelmed the enemies.

2336 Maine, Rene. Trafalgar: Napoleon's Naval Waterloo. NY: Scribner, 1957, viiii, 261 pp. Trans: Rita Eldon and B.W. Robinson; a complete review of the long campaign, much detail but exaggerated conclusions; comparisons to Hitler and 1940-1941; not reliable and no scholarly apparatus.

2337 Mainwaring, Henry. The Sea-man's Dictionary: Or, an Exposition and Demonstration of All the Parts and Things Belonging to a Ship. London: Hurlock; Menston: Scolar, 1644, 1666, 1972, xii, 130 pp. The original was in 1620; the first marine dictionary in English; 17th century terms, phrases, and nautical descriptions; best as research source for definitions.

2338 Major, Albany F. "Ship Burials in Scandinavian Lands and Beliefs that Underlie Them." Folk-Lore, 35 (June 1924): 113-50. Based on archaeological and literary studies, the 1920s being early for that, also critical analysis; ship burials were not a Viking custom but that or variations were common throughout the world; an explanation of the mythology.

2339 Malcolm, Elizabeth. "The Mighty Quinn." History Ireland, 6 (Autumn 1998): 13-16. An interview presenting background about David B. Quinn, "Ireland's greatest living historian."

2340 Malcomson, Robert and Malcomson, Thomas. HMS DETROIT: The Battle for Lake Erie. Annapolis: NIP, 1990, 1991, 150 pp. During the War of 1812, the fight for hegemony of the Lakes, September 1813, e.g., a 3-hour battle on Lake Erie, HMS DETROIT vs USS LAWRENCE, re-enacted with replicas in 1988 as 175th anniversary.

2341 Malcomson, Robert. Lord of the Lakes: The Naval War on Lake Ontario, 1812-1814. London: Chatham; Annapolis: NIP, 1998, 1999, xx, 411 pp. Fwd: Donald Graves; re the struggle for hegemony on the Lakes, a theater of crucial importance; one manifestation was a shipbuilding race; careful to present U.S., British, and Canadian perspectives.

2342 -------. Warships of the Great Lakes, 1754-1834. London: Chatham, 2001, 128 pp. Technical details on warships built and operating in inland waters, rowboats to 3-deckers; also on logistics and ordnance.

2343 Malcolmson, Tom. "An Aid to Nelson's Victory?: A Description of the Harbour of Aboukir, 1798." MM, 84 (August 1998): 291-97. On the occasion of the bicentennial of the battle of the Nile, new evidence that Nelson did have access to a map, thus, an informed boldness; among papers of Sir Benjamin Hollowell-Carew at PRO was a sketch of Aboukir Bay; reviews the literature on this issue.

2344 Mallalieu, J.P.W. Extraordinary Seaman. NY: Macmillan, 1958, x, 179 pp. A short, popular biography of Cochrane, Earl of Dundonald.

2345 Mallet, Michael E. "Anglo-Florentine Commercial Relations, 1465-1491." Economic History Review, 2nd ser, 15 (December 1962): 250-65. Informative on trade, from the Mediterranean, e.g., Venice in 1420s and Florence in 1460s using galleys with destinations to Southampton and London, and to the Mediterranean, indeed to the Levant, e.g., a Bristol merchant in 1447 and 1457; describes routes and products, e.g., wool from England, alum from Italy.

2346 -------. The Florentine Galleys in the Fifteenth Century. Oxford: Clarendon, 1967, xiv, 293 pp. A description of the galleys, their voyages, and details of the trade.

2347 Mallet, Michael E. and Hale, J.R. The Military Organization of a Renaissance State: Venice, c. 1400 to 1617. Cambridge: Cambridge UP, 1984, xiv, 525 pp. An account of the creation and development, especially model institutions; features, e.g., the famous Arsenal and permanent defense forces.

2348 Malone, Joseph J. "The British Naval Stores and Forests Policy in New England, 1691-1775." Ph.D. diss, London, 1956. The basis for later entries.

2349 -------. "England and the Baltic Naval Stores Trade in the Seventeenth and Eighteenth Centuries." MM, 58 (November 1972): 375-91. Re the influence of naval stores on sea power; the primary source of naval stores was the Baltic Sea region; search for alternatives, e.g., New England; ultimately, decreasing dependence on the Baltic.

2350 -------. Pine Trees and Politics: The Naval Stores and Forest Policy in Colonial New England, 1691-1775. London: Longman; Seattle: U Wash P, 1964, 219 pp. Re logistics and sources of timber, especially white pine for masts; the Naval Stores Act of 1705 addressed the issue; a factor antagonizing colonists.

2351 Maloney, Raymond J. "Where Did the Mutiny on the BOUNTY Occur?" AmNep, 56 (Fall 1996): 383-87. Much study and interest about this incident; the log of Bligh is vague, unusual for such an expert navigator; to pursue the issue further.

2352 Maltby, William S. The Black Legend in England: The Development of Anti-Spanish Sentiment, 1558-1660. Duke Historical Publications. Durham: Duke UP, 1968, 1971, viii, 180 pp. Re myths and their consequences; increasingly prevalent was anti-Spanish sentiments in the 16th century; reviews the manifestations, e.g., anti-Catholicism, anti-Papism, denunciations of the Inquisition, the assassination of

William of Orange, and the ultimate vindication, the great victory over the Armada; contemporaneous chroniclers were notorious, e.g., Holinshed and Camden; later, Merriman and Mattingly are rare in presenting balanced views.

2353 Manning, Samuel F. New England Masts and the King's Broad Arrow. Maritime Monographs and Reports, # 42. Greenwich: NMM, 1979, 1980, iv, 40 pp. Re "the wooden economy"; as sources for masts from the Baltic became more complicated, a shift to New England; agents sent to seek sources, placing "the King's Broad Arrow," an exclusive mark on designated trees as British naval property; large fine for anyone who cut them down.

2354 Manning, Thomas D. and Walker, C.F. British Warship Names. London: Putnam, 1959, 498 pp. Fwd: Earl Mountbatten; by members of the Ship Names Committee; dictionary format, e.g., when, what, and battles.

2355 Manwaring, George E. A Bibliography of British Naval History: Biographical and Historical Guide to Printed and Manuscript Sources. London: Routledge; London: Conway, 1930, 1970, xxii, 163 pp. 6000 entries; coverage of sources and manuscripts about British naval history from earliest times to 1815 and no works beyond 1930; not comprehensive.

2356 Manwaring, George E., ed. Diary of Henry Teonage: Chaplain on Board HMS ASSISTANCE and ROYAL OAK, 1675-1679. London: Routledge, 1927, 318 pp. A diary of a chaplain.

2357 Manwaring, George E. "The Dress of the British Seaman: From the Revolution to the Peace of 1748." MM, 10 (January 1924): 31-48. During the 17th century, increasing uniformity of clothing of seamen, called "slops"; related to health and discipline; meant smarter and more business-like appearance; the dress by the 1690s, e.g., blue waistcoats, white breeches, red caps, and white neckcloths; by 1746, uniform for officers standardized.

2358 Manwaring, George E. and Dobree, Bonamy. The Floating Republic: An Account of the Mutinies at Spithead and the Nore in 1797. London: Bles; NY: Harcourt; London: Hutchinson, 1935, 1987, 1989, xi, 299 pp. An account of the mutinies but imbalance; apologetics for mutineers and exaggerated image of officers as tyrannical; little on economic issues.

2359 Manwaring, George E. The Flower of England's Garland. London: Allan, 1936, xii, 235 pp. Reprints of 7 articles, e.g., impressions of RN by foreigners, Woodes Rogers, the Ostend expedition of 1798, and "Libel of English Policy."

2360 [NRS #54 and 56]. Manwaring, George E. and Perrin, W.G., eds. The Life and Works of Sir Henry Mainwaring. 2 vols. Publications of the Navy Records Society, vol. 54 and 56. London: NRS, 1920-1921, xviii, 375 and x, 301 pp. Mainwaring, 1587-1653; a noted Jacobean pirate, admiral, and lexicographer; includes a seaman's dictionary.

2361 Manwaring, George E. My Friend the Admiral: The Life, Letters, and Journals of Rear-Admiral James Burney, FRS, the Companion of Captain Cook and Friend of Charles Lamb. London; Routledge, 1931, xvi, 313 pp. A private journal; Burney accompanied Cook on 2nd and 3rd voyages; details about events leading to the death of Cook.

2362 -------. Woodes Rogers: Privateer and Governor. Nassau: Peggs, 1928, 1957, 48 pp. Ed: Deans Peggs; originally in Seafarer's Library; re the captain who rescued "Robinson Crusoe."

2363 Maple, J.T. The Irish Sea Region, 850-1254 AD. Lawrence: U Kans P, 1985. A history of events in the region.

2364 Maples, Charles T. "Parliament's Admiral: The Parliamentary and Naval Career of Robert Rich, Second Earl of Warwick, during the Reign of Charles I." Ph.D. diss, Alabama, 1975, 310 pp. Re the naval leader of the Civil War bringing the navy over to the side of Parliament and brought it back again after it rebelled in 1648; began as privateer; later, effective against the Scots.

2365 Marcus, Geoffrey J. The Conquest of the North Atlantic. Ipswich: Boydell; NY: Oxford UP, 1980, 1981, xiv, 224 pp. An illustrated scholarly study of European exploration and settlement, e.g., Faroes, Iceland, Greenland, and North America; early voyages of Norse, Irish, Hanse, and Bristol merchants; elaboration on Vinland Map controversy.

2366 -------. "The First English Voyage to Iceland." MM, 42 (November 1956): 313-18. During the reign of Edward III, men of Blakeney to Iceland, fishers and traders; a nursery for English seamen and important in maritime development.

2367 -------. Heart of Oak: A Survey of British Sea Power in the Georgian Era. London: Oxford UP, 1975, xii, 308 pp. Re 1714-1830, a synthesis of the greatest era of British sailing warfare; features, e.g., seamanship, navigation, maritime rights, administration, supply, and Lloyds; annotated bibliography.

2368 -------. A Naval History of England. 2 vols. I: The Formative Centuries. II: The Age of Nelson: The Royal Navy, 1793-1815. London: Allen, 1961-1971, 1026 pp. Original aim was to supersede Laird Clowes; 4 volumes projected but only 2 published, e.g., III: The Empire of the Ocean, 1815-1918, never published; a plan to divide up sections: did publish Quiberon Bay, as noted below, and, apparently, he also prepared The Great Armada, not published; Henry VIII ushered in "the true beginning of the fighting navy"; Hawke credited with implementing close blockade in the West culminating in his victory at Quiberon Bay, "consummate seamanship"; details on Saunders-Wolfe "conjunct" operations against Quebec.

2369 -------. "The Navigation of the Norsemen." MM, 39 (May 1953): 112-31. Re the ability of the Norsemen to sail long distances and on a regular schedule; description of ships, how built, and how sailed, e.g., mention of tacking; navigation must have been combination of dead reckoning and nautical astronomy.

2370 -------. "Ocean Navigation of the Middle Ages: Northern Waters." D.Phil. diss, Oxford, 1955. The basis of some of these entries.

2371 -------. Quiberon Bay. British Battles series. London: Batsford, 1960, 1963, 212 pp. Establishes the broad strategy, Pitt government, Anson reforms, preliminary battles, development of the Western Squadron, the brilliant planning, seamanship, and logistical system of Hawke, and a description of the extraordinary conditions leading to the battle; appendix on hygiene and logistics.

2372 Marden, Luis. "I Found the Bones of the BOUNTY." National Geographic, 112 (December 1957): 725-89. Illustrated in color; discovery in Bounty Bay, 1957; only debris was left.

2373 Marder, Arthur J. Portrait of an Admiral: The Life and Papers of Sir Herbert Richmond. Cambridge: Harvard UP, 1952, 407 pp. Assisted by Richmond's journal, Marder produced an excellent biography of this brilliant naval officer, strategic theorist, historian, professor; critical of the Admiralty for not appreciating his skills and contributions.

2374 Margolin, Samuel G. "Guardships on the Virginia Station, 1667-1767." AmNep, 55 (Winter 1995): 19-41. The Admiralty assigned guardships on a regular basis in the 17th century in the Chesapeake area, called "the Virginia Station"; operations to stop piracy, illegal trade, unauthorized salvage, and "wrecking," all much aided by locals; study determined poor performance, e.g., timid, inept, corrupt, and unskilled commanders and inferior ships; one success: victory over Blackbeard by Lt. Maynard.

2375 -------. "Lawlessness on the Maritime Frontier of the Greater Chesapeake, 1650-1750." Ph.D. diss, William and Mary, 1992, 459 pp. The basis for the previous entry.

2376 Mariejol, Jean H. The Master of the Armada: The Life and Reign of Philip II. Alt. title: Philip II, the First Modern King. London: Hamilton; NY: Harper, 1933, 380 pp. Trans: W.B. Wells; a biography by a noted authority; details on formulating and executing his "Grand Design" against England; depicts Medina Sidonia as ignorant of the sea; his mistakes abounded, e.g., to land at Plymouth, to link up with army near Calais, and the decision to sail into the North Sea and around Scotland.

2377 Marindin, George E., ed. Our Naval Heroes. London: Murray, 1901, xvi, 385 pp. Preface: Charles Beresford; a series of 20 mini-biographies originally from United Service Magazine; Beresford a turn-of-century, outspoken, admiral-member of Parliament.

2378 Mariner's Mirror. The Complete "Mariner's Mirror" on CD-ROM. London: Chatham, 2001, 45,000 pp. For the SNR; all of this journal, 1911-2000, with 11,000 indexed articles and 2000 illustrations, available on CD-ROM.

2379 Mariner's Mirror Bibliography. Sometime in the November issue. Eds: M. Patrick, Michael Partridge, and Simon Ville; bibliography divided by subject areas, e.g., history, archaeology, biography, and voyages.

2380 The Mariners' Museum, 1930-1950: History and Guide. Museum Publications, # 20. Newport News: Mariners' Museum, 1950, viii, 264 pp. Folio size, illustrated; an important museum with an international reputation; includes some Nelson items.

2381 Marini, Alfred J. "The British Corps of Marines, 1746-1771 and the U.S. Marine Corps, 1798-1818: A Comparative Study of the Early Administration and Institutionalization of Two Modern Marine Forces." Ph.D. diss, Maine, 1979, 348 pp. A comparative study; a case study of the growth of a national bureaucracy.

2382 Maritime Dimensions of the American Revolution. Wash: Naval Historical Division, 1977, 36 pp. A series of pertinent articles, e.g., David Syrett on the impact of American victories on the British.

2383 Maritime History: A Preliminary Hand-List of the Collection in the John Carter Brown Library, Brown University: With a Special Section on Sir Francis Drake. Plus a Supplement. Providence: Brown U, 1979 and 1985, 335 and 34 pp. This library on the campus of Brown University features maritime history; 1176 entries in the former; divided by subjects, e.g., navigation and seamanship, sailing directions, shipping, health, piracy, shipwrecks, navies and warfare, and Drake.

2384 [NRS 5]. Markham, Clements R., ed. Life of Captain Stephen Martin, 1666-1740. Publications of the Navy Records Society, vol. 5. London: NRS, 1895, xl, 223 pp. Martin was active, 1686-1714, including flag captain to Admiral Sir John Leake; at battles of La Hogue and Malaga.

2385 [NRS 28]. Markham, Clements R., ed. Selections from the Correspondence of Admiral John Markham during the years, 1801-1804 and 1806-1807. Publications of the Navy Records Society, vol. 28. London: NRS, 1904, xx, 451 pp. Markham entered the navy in 1776, serving extensively in the Admiralty, e.g., First Sea Lord under St. Vincent, and during administrations of Addington and Grenville.

2386 Marks, Richard Lee. Three Men of the BEAGLE. NY: Knopf, 1991, ix, 256 pp. Re the voyage of scientific advancement sponsored by the Admiralty; the three: Darwin, FitzRoy, and "Jemmy Button," an Indian guide.

2387 Marley, David F. "A Fearful Gift: The Spanish Naval Build-up in the West Indies, 1759-1762." MM, 80 (November 1994): 403-17. A dynastic crisis for Spain meant opportunities for expansion for the British; campaigns in Martinique and Havana; later Florida added.

2388 -------. "Havana Surprised: Prelude to the British Invasion, 1762." MM, 78 (August 1992): 293-305. An alert sent from Spain was intercepted and the British attack was a complete surprise.

2389 -------. "The Last Manila Galleon." Warship (1991): 9-18. The annual galleon, Manila to Acapulco; built in the Philippines; 1764, captured and taken to England.

2390 -------. Pirates: Adventurers of the High Seas. London: Arms, 1995, 1997, 160 pp. Very large folio size, glossy color photos, and a first-rate production; an interesting account about a popular topic, e.g., Henry Morgan, filibusters, buccaneers, and privateers; bibliography especially impressive, entries in several languages.

2391 -------. Pirates and Engineers: Dutch and Flemish Adventurers in New Spain, 1607-1697. Windson: Netherlandic, 1992, 79 pp. Dutch piratical operations around Mexico.

2392 -------. Pirates and Privateers of the Americas, 1654-1699. Santa Barbara: ABC-Clio, 1994, 458 pp. Limited in time and to the Caribbean; 350 biographical entries, e.g., Dampier, Exquemeling, Kidd, and Morgan; a catch-all with little explanation.

2393 -------. Wars of the Americas: A Chronology of Armed Conflict in the New World, 1492 to the Present. Santa Barbara: ABC-Clio, 1998, xi, 722 pp. Large-format encyclopedia, Columbus to Pinochet; important reference guide.

2394 Marlow, John. Perfidious Albion: The Origin of Anglo-French Rivalry in the Levant. London: Elek, 1972, 323 pp. Covers from c. 1750-1840; each saw the other as conspiratorial; features, e.g., the French to Egypt and Syria and the British concerned about secure routes to India.

2395 Marquardt, Karl H. Captain Cook's ENDEAVOUR. The Anatomy of the Ship series. London: Conway; Annapolis: NIP, 1995, 136 pp. Extensive illustrations; the ship of the 1st voyage, 1768-1771, its history, hull, fittings, rigging; what was needed was a strong ship with much storage space, thus a collier.

2396 -------. HMS BEAGLE: Survey Ship Extraordinary. The Anatomy of the Ship series. London: Conway; Annapolis: NIP, 1997, 128 pp. Typical series product; outstanding detail and numerous drawings; the famous ship for science and exploration.

2397 Marriott, Leo. What's Left of Nelson? Shepperton: Dial, 1995, 160 pp. A short biography.

2398 Marryat, Frederick. Frank Mildmay. Classics of Nautical Fiction series. Ithaca: McBooks, 1998, 352 pp. Marryat, 1792-1848, veteran of RN from 1806, serving under Cochrane, among others; a series of naval novels, 1820s and 1830s, by "the grand ole man of the naval novel"; some are autobiographical.

2399 -------. Jacob Faithful. NY: 1873 Press, 2000.

2400 -------. The King's Own. NY: 1873 Press, 1896, 2000, 384 pp.

2401 -------. Masterman Ready: Or, the Wreck of the PACIFIC. London: Macmillan; London: Dent, 1901, 1907, viii, 340 pp.

2402 -------. Mr. Midshipman Easy. Classics of Naval Literature series. Annapolis: NIP; Ithaca: McBooks, 1836, 1906, 1990, 1998, 352 pp.

2403 -------. Peter Simple. 2 vols. London: Macmillan; London: Constable, 1902, 1925, 1929, xxx, 492 pp. Seen by some as the best.

2404 -------. Suggestions for the Abolition of the Present State of Impressment in the Naval Service. London: Richardson, 1822, 1827, 64 pp. Marryat opposed impressment and joined the campaign against it.

2405 -------. Works. 5 vols. Hartford: Andrews, 1849, 1852. A collection of 9 of the sea novels of Marryat.

2406 Marsden, Peter R.V. A Ship of the Roman Period from Blackfriars in the City of London. London: Guildhall Museum, 1966, 1967, 60 pp. About the discovery after excavation of the remains of this Roman vessel.

2407 -------. Ships and Shipwrecks. Alt. title: English Heritage Book of Ships and Shipwrecks. London: Batsford, 1997, 128 pp. Folio size, profusely illustrated; re nautical archaeology in Britain, chronological coverage from Iron Age boats; for English Heritage and the Nautical Archaeology Society; a total of 30,000 recorded sites.

2408 -------. The Wreck of the AMSTERDAM. London: Hutchinson, 1974, 1985, 206 pp. Beginning in 1969, amateurs initiated a treasure search; in 1749 a Dutch East Indiaman on her maiden voyage lost her rudder and beached near Hastings; Marsden and professionals took over; this the published report.

2409 Marsden, Reginald G. A Digest of Cases Relating to Shipping, Admiralty, and Insurance Law. London: Sweet, 1899, cxliv, 1389 pp. Extensive collection overseen and described by Marsden, 1845-1927.

2410 [NRS 49 and 50]. Marsden, Reginald G., ed. Documents Relating to the Law and Custom of the Sea. 2 vols. Publications of the Navy Records Society, vols. 49 and 50. London: NRS, 1915-1916, xl, 561 and xxxiv, 457 pp. Presentation of a series of laws passed by Parliament, typically during or after a war, concerning privateering, prizes, naval stores, the Salute, rights of neutrals, and Admiralty Courts.

2411 Marsden, Reginald G. "Early Prize Jurisdiction and Prize Law in England." EHR, 24 (October 1909): 675-97. In the 14th century, prize jurisdiction was given to admirals; the Cinque Ports gained privileges; precedents were from the practice of Oleron and Bayonne; later institions, e.g., HCA, Vice-Admiralty Courts, and letters of marque.

2412 -------. The High Court of the Admiralty in Relation to the National History, Commerce and the Colonisation of America, 1550-1650. London, Pamphlet, n.d., 26 pp. A survey of legal aspects.

2413 Marsden, Reginald G., ed. Select Pleas in the Court of the Admiralty. 2 vols. Publications of the Seldon Society, vols. 6 and 11. London: Seldon Society, 1892-1897. Description of selected cases, edited by a legal historian and expert on Admiralty law.

2414 Marsden, Reginald G. "The Vice-Admirals of the Coast." EHR, 22 and 23 (July 1907 and October 1908): 468-77 and 736-57. An ancient title of land admirals first noted in 1295; a crown appointment to defend the coasts of the kingdom, collect crown revenues, conduct maritime business, and adjudicate wreck salvage cases; the first piracy cases were in the 13th century.

2415 Marshall, J. Alan. Intelligence and Espionage in the Reign of Charles II, 1660-1685. Cambridge Studies in Early Modern British History. London: Cambridge UP, 1994, xvi, 337 pp. A history of intelligence and espionage; operations under the office of Secretary of State; use of the Post Office, codes, ciphers, spies, informers, and assassins; one case involved the plot to bring down Pepys and Deane, actually to get at the Catholic Duke of York; the system failed in 1688, as James II had little or no information about the movements of William of Orange and his Dutch troops.

2416 -------. "Sir Joseph Williamson and the Development of the Government Intelligence System in Restoration England, 1660-1680." Ph.D. diss, Lancaster, 1991. The basis of the previous entry.

2417 Marshall, John. Royal Naval Biography: Memoirs of the Services of All of the Flag Officers. 4 vols. London: Longman; NY: Gorman, 1823-1835, 1935. Marshall, 1784-1837, an enterprising officer on half-pay; a series of editions and selections in print; the memoirs supplied by the subjects themselves; historical and explanatory notes.

2418 Marshall, Michael W. Ocean Traders: From the Portuguese Discoveries to the Present Day. London: Batsford, 1989, 1990, 192 pp. Large folio size with exquisite b/w illustrations; the evolution of sailing ships, geographical discoveries, great trading nations, exploration, and the history of commerce; highly instructive and impressive.

2419 Marshall, Peter and Williams, Glyndwr, eds. The British Atlantic Empire before the American Revolution. London: Cass, 1980, vii, 130 pp. Re all aspects of the evolution of European operations in North America.

2420 Martelli, George. Jemmy Twitcher: A Life of the Fourth Earl of Sandwich, 1718-1792. London: Cape, 1962, 292 pp. Re John Montagu, 4th Earl, First Lord of the Admiralty in 1780s; much maligned, especially in DNB entry; and this biography is no better.

2421 Martin, Colin J.M. "EL GRAN GRIFON: An Armada Wreck on Fair Isle." International J Nautical Archaeology, 1 (March 1972): 59-71. Martin represents the Institute of Maritime Archaeology, University of St. Andrews; describes an expedition of 1968-1969 reporting on the search and discovery process.

2422 -------. "The Equipment and Fighting Potential of the Spanish Armada." Ph.D. diss, St. Andrews, 1983, 364 pp. The basis for these entries.

2423 -------. Full Fathom Five: Wrecks of the Spanish Armada. NY: Viking;. London: Chatto, 1974, 1975, 288 pp. The title from Shakespeare; details on searches and discoveries of 3 wrecks from the Armada ships; equally informative about developments and progress in nautical archaeology and searches for the Armada wrecks, especially in appendices by Sydney Wignall.

2424 Martin, Colin J.M. and Parker, Geoffrey. "If the Armada Had Landed." MHQ, 1 (Autumn 1988): 28-29. An exercise in counterfactual history; contends evidence that, if the forces of Parma had combined with those of the Armada, 23,000 troops could easily have marched on London; Ralegh was convinced; 4 years later, Parma in fact did march and capture Normandy in 6 days with 22,000 men.

2425 Martin, Colin J.M. "Incendiary Weapons from the Spanish Armada Wreck LA TRINIDAD VALENCERA, 1588." International J Nautical Archaeology, 23 (August 1994): 207-17. Another "find" from Armada wrecks, this one off the Donegal coast; included firepots and bombs, powerful weapons for use in close combat.

2426 -------. "LA TRINIDAD VALENCERA: An Armada Invasion Transport Lost off Donegal." International J Nautical Archaeology, 8 (February 1979): 13-38. Dives from the Derry Sub-Aqua Club; re a large Venetian merchantman; noted the cosmopolitan nature of the Armada; detailed report of the wreck site and pictures.

2427 Martin, Colin J.M., ed. Scotland's Historic Shipwrecks. London: Batsford, 1998, 128 pp. An attractive layout; 6 essays by experts in nautical archaeology describing historic wreck sites; for each, background, incident, salvage efforts, and current status, e.g., Tobermory Armada wreck, SAN JUAN DE SICILIA, 800 tons, built in Ragusa, salvage attempt in 1730s, and "a national treasure rivalling the VASA and MARY ROSE."

2428 Martin, Colin J.M. and Parker, Geoffrey. The Spanish Armada. London:

Hamilton; NY: Norton, London: Palgrave, 1988, 1999, 2003, xxi, 295 pp. An impressive recent survey with color pictures taking up where Mattingly left off; solid and balanced; to supersede "the pseudopatriotic, jingoism and speculative theorizing" which has dominated accounts; incorporates new information from Spanish archives and from nautical archaeological researches, e.g., about Armada guns, gunnery, and especially gun carriages, correcting the Michael Lewis study, and that a number of the Spanish guns had never fired at all.

2429 Martin, Colin J.M. "Spanish Armada Tonnages." MM, 63 (November 1977): 365-67. Re fresh evidence on calculation of tonnage, especially informative about the "Levant Squadron," 6 large ships built to operate in the Mediterranean, e.g., from Ragusa (3), from Venice (2), and from Tuscany (1); other evidence proves the survival rate was less than Atlantic built ships.

2430 Martin, Donald R. "Corruption and Reform in the Jacobean Navy: The Report of the Naval Commission of 1608-1609. Ph.D. diss, Miami, 1974, 319 pp. "After Elizabeth, the deluge"; the weaknesses of the regime of James I are clear from this report on the navy: officials Howard, Mansell, Trevor, and Pett all enriched themselves; James forgave them and dropped the investigation; all factors contributing to the Revolution.

2431 Martin, Frederick. The History of Lloyd's and of Marine Insurance in Great Britain. NY: Franklin, 1876, 1971, xx, 416 pp. The old standard; marine insurance was the oldest form of mutual protection, in this case, a confederation of underwriters, "Lloyd's."

2432 Martin, Ged, ed. The Founding of Australia: The Argument about Australia's Origins. Sydney: Hale, 1978, 314 pp. Essays by experts; an extensive survey of the literature and review of the debate, e.g., relief from overcrowded jails, a trading base, strategic naval resources such as flax and timber, and replacement for America, the lost colony.

2433 Martin, G.H. and Spufford, Peter, eds. The Records of the Nation: The Public Record Office, 1838-1988, the British Records Society, 1888-1988. Rochester: Boydell, 1990, viii, 312 pp. For the British Records Society; on the occasion of the 150th anniversary; 15 essays from a conference, Inner Temple, August 1988, e.g., about holdings, the Rolls and the State Papers series, and the 50- and 30-year rules.

2434 Martin, John and Romano, Dennis, eds. Venice Reconsidered: The History and Civilization of an Italian City-State, 1297-1797. Balt: JHUP, 2000, xiv, 538 pp. Noted considerable revision of views of the history of Venice.

2435 Martin, Lillian Ray. The Art and Archaeology of Venetian Boats and Ships. London: Chatham: 2001, 256 pp. 150 illustrations; brilliant use of sources, e.g., artistic depictions and excavations; focus on the sea power of medieval and Renaissance Venice.

2436 Martin, Paula. Spanish Armada Prisoners: The Story of the NUESTRA SENORA DEL ROSARIO and Her Crew, and of Other Prisoners in England, 1587-1597. Exeter Maritime Studies, # 1. Exeter: U Exeter P, 1988, xii, 113 pp. Re the 4th largest ship, 940 tons, captured by Drake; crew to Torbay, and from another ship wrecked on the South Devon coast; the disposition of these prisoners.

2437 Martineau, Gilbert. Napoleon's St. Helena. London: Murray, 1968, xiv, 241 pp. Trans: Frances Partridge; fwd: Montgomery Hyde; by the French consul at St. Helena; re the 67 months at Longwood House and the daily routine there; questions about escape plans and death; the body remained buried there for 19 years; in 1840, transferred to Paris.

2438 -------. Napoleon Surrenders. NY: St. Martin, 1971, x, 231 pp. Trans: Frances Partridge; re "the second downfall"; rushed to surrender to HMS BELLERPHON, thence to England during negotiations, thence to HMS NORTHAMPTON en route St. Helena.

2439 Martinsen, Steve. "French Sail-of-the-Line: In the Napoleonic Wars, 1792-1815." Warship (1994): 9-21. The French fleet was "ruined" by the Revolution; poor officers, strategy, and tactics; then, Napoleon rejuvenated the service, building better ships; Trafalgar was "the end of the beginning."

2440 Marx, Jenifer. Pirates and Privateers of the Caribbean. Melbourne: Krieger, 1992, x, 310 pp. Wife of Robert Marx, both being nautical archaeologists; an exhaustive overview of these "outlaws of the ocean" over 300 years on the Spanish Main and beyond; the "Golden Age" was 1692-1725; excellent bibliography.

2441 Marx, Robert F. The Battle of the Spanish Armada, 1588. London: Weidenfeld; Cleveland: World, 1965, 1968, 128 pp. By a noted nautical archaeologist and participant in replica productions and operations; a series of books, some reworked and expanded; popularized account of the Armada, anecdotal, and superficial; no scholarly apparatus.

2442 -------. The Capture of the Treasure Fleet: The Story of Piet Heyn. NY: McKay, 1977, x, 276 pp. Re the famous Spanish flota, in this case, Dutch efforts to capture; English attempted same; explanation of flota system; Dutch success in 1628; it took 5 days to unload the gold, silver, and other booty filling 1000 carts, including 100 tons of silver.

2443 -------. The History of Underwater Exploration. Alt. title: Into the Deep. NY: Van Nostrand; NY: Dover, 1978, 1990, vi, 198 pp. A survey of the discipline; some case studies, e.g., Tobermory galleon and Port Royal.

2444 -------. Pirate Port: The Story of the Sunken City of Port Royal. Cleveland: World; London: Pelham, 1967, 1968, 190 pp. An earlier, shorter account of the next entry.

2445 -------. Port Royal Rediscovered. NY: Doubleday, 1973, 304 pp. On 7 June 1692, 15 of the 25 acres of Port Royal, a florishing seaport, especially for pirates, population of 8000, were innundated in a terrible earthquake; population today about 500; nautical archaeological expeditions began in the mid-1960s; much learned and many artifacts.

2446 -------. The Treasure Fleets of the Spanish Main. Cleveland: World, 1968, 127 pp. Folio size, many pictures; an earlier version of a previous entry.

2447 Marzagalli, Silvia. Les Boulevards de la Fraude: Le Negoce maritime it le Blocus continentale, 1806-1813. Lille: Septentrion, 1999, 396 pp. The Continential System implemented by Napoleon; fresh and powerful analysis; assessment from the French perspective; one of the first economic blockades; study of 3 ports; British reacted by establishing alternate entrepots: Malta, Gibraltar, and Heligoland; conclusion: it failed but it hurt the British.

2448 Masefield, John. A Sailor's Garland: Selected and Edited. NY: Macmillan, 1906, 1924, xxxv, 372 pp. Masefield, 1878-1967, a noted literary figure editing this ancient treatise about a pilgrimage voyage; seen as superior to "Shipman" by Chaucer.

2449 -------. Sea Life in Nelson's Time. NY: Macmillan; London: Conway; Annapolis: NIP, 1905, 1925, 1937, 1971, 218 pp. Intro: Christopher Lloyd; on the occasion of the 100th anniversary of Trafalgar, Masefield, Conrad, and others were asked to write pieces; Masefield was a veteran seaman; this seen as a classic but hastily written; a shocking indictment of conditions; exaggerates by presenting the worst case, e.g., in the chapter on punishments: flogging, the gauntlet, keel-hauling, and hanging.

2450 Mason, A.E.W. The Life of Francis Drake. NY: Doubleday; London: Hodder, 1941, viii, 349 pp. By an eminent novelist; a long, popular, uncritical biography; long explanation about the game of bowls; no scholarly apparatus.

2451 Mason, Francis van Wyck. Cutless Empire. NY: Doubleday, 1949, xii, 396 pp. Nautical fiction; re the pirate Henry Morgan, 1635-1688.

2452 -------. Golden Admiral. NY: Doubleday, 1953, 1975, 340 pp. A fictional, realistic portrayal of Drake.

2453 -------. Manila Galleon. London: Hutchinson, 1961, 495 pp. Nautical fiction, attacks on Spanish treasure.

2454 Mason, H.B., ed. Encyclopedia of Ships and Shipping. 1908. Nautical dictionary; emphasis on British; details and lists of ships and biographies of prominent naval officers.

2455 Mason, Michael H., et al., eds. The British Seafarers. BBC Radio 4 series.

London: Hutchinson, 1980, 158 pp. For NMM, large folio size, profusely illustrated with impressive pictures.

2456 Mason, Micheal H. Willoughby the Immortal: An Account of the Life and Actions of Rear-Admiral Sir Nesbit Willoughby, 1777-1849: "The Hero of Mauritius. Oxford: Alden, 1969, x, 102 pp. A veteran officer during the Napoleonic wars, retired as Captain but promoted and knighted later.

2457 Massie, A.W. "Great Britain and the Defence of the Low Countries, 1744-1748." D.Phil. diss, Oxford, 1988. A scholarly study about the place of the Low Countries in British strategy.

2458 Massie, Robert K. Peter the Great: His Life and World. NY: Ballantine; NY: Wings, 1980, 1991, xi, 909 pp. Massie is a popular biographer, this on Peter who visited the West, e.g., Portsmouth in the late 1690s.

2459 Masson, Philippe. Histoire de la Marine Francaise. 2 vols. Paris: Lavauzelle, 1981-1983. A standard history of the French navy.

2460 Masson, Philippe and Muracciole, Jose. Napoleon et la Marine. Collection Premier Empire. Paris: Peyronnet, 1968, 331 pp. A biographical approach to French naval history.

2461 [NHS 6]. Masterman, Daniel M., ed. Naval History: The Sixth Symposium of the U.S. Naval Academy. Wilmington: Scholarly, 1987, 376 pp. (29-30 September 1983, USNA).

2462 Matar, Nabil I. Islam and Britain, 1558-1685. Cambridge: Cambridge UP, 1998, 1999, xi, 226 pp. Hakluyt and Purchas alluded to these connections; this account more sophisticated; "Brits turned Turk" as traders, diplomats, prisoners, and slaves; Arabic and "Saracen" influences in England; some exaggeration.

2463 Matham, George. Notes on the Character of Admiral Lord Nelson: In Relation to the Journal of Mrs. St. George. London: Ridgway, 1861, 15 pp. A journal produced several decades after Nelson.

2464 Matcham, Mary Eyre. The Nelsons of Burnham Thorpe: A Record of a Norfolk Family, 1787-1842. London: Lane, 1911, 306 pp. Dedicated to Horatio, 3rd Earl Nelson; a narrative geneaology with several chapters on the personal and domestic life of Nelson, e.g., "trouble at home" and "Merton Place."

2465 Mather, I.R. "The Role of the Royal Navy in the English Atlantic Empire, 1660-1720. " D.Phil. diss, Oxford, 1995. A quantitative study; re the scale, scope, and character of activities of RN in America and the West Indies; a database was created using Admiralty records, e.g., type of ship, where assigned, what duties, e.g., protection, regulation, convoying, and promotion of commerce.

2466 Mathew, David. "The Cornish and Welsh Pirates in the Reign of Elizabeth." EHR, 39 (July 1924): 337-48. Piracy in the West became an enterprise with investors, little patrolling, officials easily bribed, and no violence; all similar to commercial activity.

2467 Matthew, Donald J.A. The Norman Conquest. London: Batson; NY: Schocken, 1966, 336 pp. On the occasion of the 900th anniversary, a thorough and scholarly survey.

2468 Mattingly, Garrett. The Armada. Alt. title: The Defeat of the Spanish Armada. Boston: Houghton; NY: Sentry; London: Pimlico, 1959, 1965, 1983, 1988, 2000, 443 pp. Pulitzer Prize; Mattingly, 1900-1962, a great scholar of diplomacy and war; one of the best and most comprehensive accounts of the Armada; best at placing the campaign in the context of European politics and religion; opens with the execution of Mary, Queen of Scots; brilliant narrative unfolds; restrained and balanced assessments.

2469 -------. The "Invincible" Armada and Elizabethan England. Folger Booklet series. Ithaca: Cornell UP, 1963, 56 pp. For the Folger Library; illustrated; a classic summary of the event.

2470 Mauro, Frederic. L'Expansion Europeenne, 1600-1870. Novelle Clio series, # 27. Paris: U de France, 1964, 1967, 1996, 453 pp. Wide use of sources; survey of discovery and expansion of Portugal, Spain, the Dutch, England, and France; excellent bibliography.

2471 Maxwell, Kenneth. "Pirate Democray." New York Review of Books, 44 (6 March 1997):34-37. A long essay reviewing the practitioners, Drake, Morgan, Kidd, "Black Bart," and Jean Lafitte; the literature, e.g., Cordingly, Exquemeling, Burg, and Rediker; the literary approaches, e.g., Defoe, R.L. Stevenson, Lord Byron, Gilbert and Sullivan, and Verdi opera.

2472 Maxwell, Susan. "Henry Seckford: Sixteenth-Century Merchant, Courtier and Privateer." MM, 82 (November 1996): 387-97. A case study.

2473 May, Derwent. Critical Times: The History of "The Times Literary Supplement." London: HarperCollins, 2001, 606 pp. A substantial history of this outstanding periodical, the "Headquarters of Anglophone Republic of Letters; current circulation of 35,000.

2474 May, Steven W. Sir Walter Ralegh. Twayne's English Authors series. Boston: Twayne, 1989, xv, 164 pp. Emphasis on the literary contributions of Ralegh, e.g., accounts of voyages and A History of the World.

2475 May, W.E. Badges and Insignia of the British Armed Services: The Royal Navy. NY: St. Martin, 1974, ix, 367 pp. Folio size, illustrated; a survey.

2476 -------. The Boats of Men-of-War. London: Chatham, 1974, 1999, 128 pp. For NMM; illustrated; the boats of warships during the age of sail; Falconer and Blanckley describe some but disagree on some details.

2477 -------. A History of Marine Navigation. NY: Norton, 1973, xv, 280 pp. An illustrated survey; features, e.g., the practice, instruments, longitude, charts, and determining direction and speed.

2478 May, W.E. and Kennard, A.N. Naval Swords and Firearms. London: HMSO, 1962, 22 pp. A brief illustrated survey, includes personal firearms.

2479 May, W.E. and Annis, P.G.W. Swords for Sea Service. 2 vols. London: HMSO, 1970, 420 pp. Illustrations in color; presentation of the collection of NMM.

2480 Mayer, Hans E. "A Ghost Ship Called FRANKENEF: King Richard I's German Itinerary." EHR, 115 (February 2000): 135-44. In 1192, Richard was returning from the 3rd Crusade aboard FRANKENEF, Corfu to Ragusa, and was captured and held for ransom.

2481 Maynard, Kenneth. First Lieutenant. NY: St. Martin, 1985, 214 pp. Maynard, at least 4 novels about Matthew Lamb, a fictional officer of RN of the Nelson era.

2482 -------. Lamb in Command. London: Weidenfeld; NY: St.Martin, 1986, 199 pp. Features Matthew Lamb, naval hero.

2483 -------. Lamb's Mixed Fortunes. London: Weidenfeld, 1987, 193 pp. More adventures.

2484 -------. Lieutenant Lamb. NY: St.Martin, 1984, 191 pp. More adventures.

2485 Maynarde, Thomas. Sir Francis Drake: His Voyage, 1595. Publications of the Hakluyt Society, 1st ser, 4. NY: Franklin, 1849, 1970, viii, 65 pp. Ed: W.D. Cooley; a Spanish account of the attack on Puerto Rico by Drake.

2486 Mead, Hilary P. Trafalgar Signals. London: Marshall, 1936, 47 pp. Fwd: Earl Nelson; an interesting booklet; "England expects. . . ."; notes mistake about coloring Flag # 4.

2487 -------. Trinity House: Its Unique Record from the Days of Henry VIII. London: Sampson, 1947, xi, 178 pp. By a member of the Corporation and a Young Brethren; administers lighthouses and sea-marks, control of pilots and yachts; famous members: Pepys and Winston Churchill.

2488 Meicklejohn, A.P. "The Curious Obscurity of Dr. James Lind." J History of Medicine (1954): 304-10. What happened to the story of Lind?

2489 Meij, J.C.A. de. De Watergeuzen: Piraten en bevrijders. Haarlem: Fibula Van

Dishoeck, 1980, 114 pp. Re the Dutch pirates, 1560s and 1570s.

2490 Mellersh, Harold E.L. <u>Fitzroy of the BEAGLE</u>. London: Hart-Davis; NY: Mason, 1968, 307 pp. Robert Fitzroy, 1805-1865, captain on 2nd voyage sponsored by the Admiralty Meteorological Office; Fitzroy initiated the idea to take a naturalist on the voyage.

2491 Melville, Herman. <u>Billy Budd, Foretopman</u>. Alt. title: <u>Billy Budd, Sailor</u>. Chicago: U Chicago P, 1891, 1962, 433 pp. Eds: Harrison Hayford and Merton M. Sealts; a British seaman strikes an officer during the mutinies of 1797; Melville, 1819-1891, was a veteran seaman and was much influenced by the SOMERS mutiny of 1842; this a scholarly analysis using the original manuscript.

2492 -------. <u>Moby Dick</u>. NY: Norton: Chicago: Northwestern UP, 1899, 1921, 1926, 1946, 1951, 1956, 1964, 1967, 2001, viii, 504 pp. The ultimate classic story of the sea; Melville influenced by whaleship ESSEX, sunk, November 1820, by a whale.

2493 -------. <u>White-Jacket: Or, the World of a Man-of-War</u>. Boston: Page, 1850, 1892, 1950, 374 pp. Notes that discipline in USN just as strict as that in RN; graphic description of a flogging.

2494 Melvin, Frank E. <u>Napoleon's Navigation System: A Study of Trade Control during the Continental Blockade</u>. NY: Appleton, 1919, xv, 449 pp. An older, solid study.

2495 <u>The Men Who Fought with Nelson in HMS VICTORY at Trafalgar</u>. Leyland: Flemming, 1989, 144 pp. For the Nelson Society; a consolidated listing.

2496 Menard, Wilmon. "The BOUNTY Mutiny Remembered." <u>Naval History</u>, 5 (Summer 1991): 24-30. Reviews details, enormous interest, then and now, and later productions, e.g., replicas, movies, and novels; big name movie stars.

2497 Merians, Linda M., ed. <u>The Secret Malady: Venereal Disease in Eighteenth-Century Britain and France</u>. Lexington: U Ky P, 1996, 288 pp. An interdisciplinary collection of 15 papers by experts; demonstrates the growing political, social, and cultural importance of sexually transmitted diseases.

2498 [NRS 103]. Merriman, R.D., ed. <u>Queen Anne's Navy</u>. <u>Publications of the Navy Records Society</u>, vol. 103. London: NRS, 1961, xiv, 386 pp. Details on the Admiralty and Navy Board, e.g., finance, manning, dockyards, health, and convoys.

2499 [NRS 89]. Merriman, R.D., ed. <u>The Sergison, Papers, 1688-1702</u>. <u>Publications of the Navy Records Society</u>, vol. 89. London: NRS, 1950, xii, 382 pp. Charles Sergison, born 1654, a clerk at the Admiralty in the 1690s; Secretary of the Navy Board.

2500 Merriman, Roger Bigelow. The Rise of the Spanish Empire in the Old World and the New. 4 vols. I: The Middle Ages. II: The Catholic Kings. III: The Emperor. IV: Philip the Prudent. NY: Cooper, 1918-1934, 1962, 2415 pp. Merriman, 1876-1945, a Harvard professor; a standard history of Spain, e.g., vol. on Philip II, places him in international perspective; re the Armada, factors, depredations of Drake, plots to murder Elizabeth, execution of Mary, Queen of Scots, and a treaty with the Pope.

2501 Metzdorf, Robert F, ed. An Autobiographical Sketch, 1815-1842: Richard Henry Dana, Jr. Hamden: Shoe String, 1953, 119 pp. Re Dana.

2502 Meyer, Arnold O. England and the Catholic Church under Elizabeth. London: Routledge, 1916, 1967, xxxiv, 555 pp. Trans: J.R. McKee; intro: John Bossy; a broad survey of local, regional, and international implications; begins in 1558; extensive coverage of all aspects of Armada campaign; now later historians assessed it, e.g., Ranke: "the future of mankind held in the balance"; Froude: "decided the largest problems ever submitted in the history of mankind"; Laughton: "moulded the history of Europe."

2503 Meyer, Jack Allen, comp. An Annotated Bibliography of the Napoleonic Era: Recent Publications, 1945-1985. Bibliographies and Indexes in World History, # 8. Westport: Greenwood, 1987, viii, 288 pp. 1754 annotated entries, .e.g., section on naval affairs.

2504 Meyer, W.R. "English Privateering in the War of 1688 to 1697." MM, 67 (August 1981): 259-72. Use of records of HCA; to measure extent of "high" and "Channel" privateering and compare the total against the French; conclusion: 490 letters of marque issued; at no time did the scale of English privateering equal that of the French; corsairs from St. Malo alone took more prizes than all of English prizes.

2505 -------. "English Privateering in the War of Spanish Succession, 1702-1713." MM, 69 (November 1983): 435-46. Computations for the next war; HCA records noted 1622 letters of marque; 2239 prizes condemned but, as before, these were "pin-pricks" compared to the French; corsairs of Dunkirk alone exceeded all of the English.

2506 Middleton, Richard. "The British Coastal Expeditions to France, 1757-1758." J Society for Army Historical Research, 71 (Summer 1993): 74-92. Examples of the "conjunct operations" initiated by William Pitt; operations against Rochefort, St. Malo; not successful but distracted French; assessments by historians disagree: Tunstall and Fortesque.

2507 -------. "British Naval Strategy, 1755-1762." MM, 75 (November 1989): 349-67. Historians assess the strategy of William Pitt; praise for Anson.

2508 -------. "Pitt, Anson and the Admiralty, 1756-1761," History, 55 (June 1970):

189-98. After Minorca was lost the Admiralty Board was discredited; Pitt increasingly relied on Anson.

2509 -------. "The Visitation of the Royal Dockyards, 1749." MM, 77 (February 1991): 21-30. After problems of War of Austrian Succession, Anson initiated reforms, beginning a new era in administration; Baugh questioned bad state of affairs; hard to tell because sudden expansion of RN from 1750.

2510 Milford, Elizabeth. "The Navy at Peace: The Activities of the Early Jacobean Navy, 1603-1618." MM, 76 (February 1990): 23-36. A survey of activities and effectiveness of Jacobean navy after Anglo-Spanish war ended; "peacetime pursuits": patrol the "Narrow Seas," go after pirates, and conduct diplomacy.

2511 Millar, John F., ed. "A British Account of the Siege of Rhode Island, 1778." Rhode Island History, 38 (August 1979): 79-85. An account by Peter Reina, British midshipman, recounting siege operations and a battle within Newport harbor.

2512 Miller, David P. and Reill, Peter H., eds. Visions of Empire: Voyages, Botany, and Representations of Nature. Cambridge: Cambridge UP, 1996, xix, 370 pp. Proceedings from a conference, UCLA, January 1991, celebrating publication of Joseph Banks; what impact the voyages had in Europe, especially the discovery of peoples and plants, and especially the voyage of Cook and Banks; the results, e.g., 1000 new species of plants, 500 fish, 1300 fabulous drawings, Kew Gardens, and the Bligh breadfruit voyage; the role of science in exploration.

2513 Miller, Helen H. Captains from Devon: The Great Elizabethan Seafarers Who Won the Oceans for England. Chapel Hill: Algonquin, 1985, xii, 221 pp. A Devon marine "confraternity," e.g., Ralegh, "El Draque," Grenville, and several from the Hawkins family.

2514 Miller, John. James II: A Study of Kingship. Yale English Monarchs. Hove: Wayland; New Haven: Yale UP, 1978, 2000, x, 281 pp. A full biography; neither Catholic or Protestant historians have presented a balanced view; this one neglects James as practicing naval officer.

2515 Miller, Nathan. Broadsides: The Age of Fighting Sail, 1775-1815. NY: Wiley, 2000, xii, 388 pp. During the Wars of the American Revolution and the French Revolution and Napoleon; American perspective; one man dominates: Nelson; praise for nautical fiction writers, e.g., O'Brian, Forester, and Kent, but none cited in bibliography, and other gaps there.

2516 -------, Sea of Glory: A Naval History of the American Revolution. Alt. title: The Continental Navy Fights for Independence. NY: McKay; Mt. Pleasant: N&A, 1974, 1992, 2000, xi, 588 pp. Originally on the occasion of the bicentennial, a history of the Continental Navy; depredations against British by navy and privateers; expanded into global war.

2517 Milne-Tyte, Robert. Armada!: The Planning, the Battle, and After. London: Hale, 1988, 160 pp. An undistinguished account.

2518 Minchinton, Walter, ed. The Baltic Grain Trade: Five Essays. Exeter: Exter UP, 1985, 59 pp. For the Association for the History of the Northern Seas; from the 13th century, the Baltic trade, especially grain, grew in importance, e.g., Dutch, Hanse, English, French, Spanish, and Portuguese; Danzig and Amsterdam most important.

2519 -------, ed. Britain and the Northern Seas: Some Essays: Proceedings of the Fourth Conference of the Association for the History of the Northern Seas, 1985. Pontefract: Lofthouse, 1988, 179 pp. 17 papers, e.g., Anglo-Baltic trade, Hanseatic League, RN in the Baltic, British convoys in the North Sea, and French privateering.

2520 Minchinton, Walter and North, Michael. History of the Northern Seas: A Select Bibliography of Works. Exeter: Association for the Norther Seas, 1982, 1983, 1984, 1985, 1986, 1987, 48 pp. A bibliography updated annually.

2521 Minchinton, Walter. "Michael Oppenheim, 1853-1927: A Memoir." MM, 54 (February 1968): 85-93. Author of the classic, Naval Administration, founder of SNR and member of NRS; no scholarly training.

2522 Modelski, George and Thompson, William P. Seapower in Global Politics, 1494-1993. Seattle: U Wash P, 1988, xii, 380 pp. An important treatise with a global perspective; divided into chronological periods or "long cycles"; a series of states achieved world power status, e.g., Portugal, then Dutch, British, and U.S.; others, e.g., France, Spain, Russia, Germany, and Japan; recounts the rise and fall of maritime powers; creation of an empirical test of the validity.

2523 Moiret, Joseph-Marie. Memoirs of Napoleon's Egyptian Expedition, 1798-1801. London: Greenhill, 2001. Trans and ed: Rosemary Brindle, a memoir of the campaign.

2524 Moll. Kenneth. "A.T. Mahan, American Historian." Military Affairs, 27 (Fall 1963): 131-40. Mahan first recognized by the British; published 23 books and President, American Historical Association.

2525 Mollo, John, ed. Uniforms of the Royal Navy during the Napoleonic Wars. Warships of the Royal Navy series. London: Evelyn, 1965, 42 pp. Folio size, profusely illustrated; a rich and pleasing production.

2526 Monaque, Remi. "Latouche-Treville: The Admiral Who Defied Nelson." MM, 86 (August 2000): 272-84. Re Louis Rene de Latouche, 1745-1804, a French admiral; sudden death in 1804 meant Villeneuve took over before Trafalgar; in 1801, Nelson led an attack against French under Latouche at Boulogne; failure with heavy losses.

2527 Monk, Winston F. <u>Britain and the Western Mediterranean</u>. London: Hutchinson, 1953, 196 pp. A review of activity to maintain sea power; need for bases, e.g., Tangier, Minorca, Gibraltar, and Malta.

2528 Montagu, George. <u>A Refutation of the Incorrect Statements and Unjust Insinuations in Captain Brenton's "Naval History of Great Britain," as Far as the Same Refers to the Conduct of Admiral G. Montagu</u>. London: Murray, 1823, viii, 56 pp. Montagu, 1750-1829 vs. Edward Pelham Brenton, 1774-1839, and the vicissitudes of writing naval history.

2529 Montgomerie, Hastings S. <u>The Morrison Myth: A Pendant to "William Bligh and the BOUNTY": In Fact and In Fable</u>. London: private, 1935, 1938, 55 pp. An assessment of the account of James Morrison: "unworthy of belief"; one contention: "journal" was written after 1795, over 6 years after the mutiny; followed its path through the 19th and early 20th century; published in 1935.

2530 -------. <u>William Bligh and the BOUNTY in Fact and in Fable</u>. London: Williams, 1937, xiv, 308 pp. Reviews the life of Bligh, the mutiny, and bringing the mutineers back; too much attention paid to "journal" of James Morrison; the book by Barrow based on Morrison; it and others are anti-Bligh; later Bligh rehabilitated, e.g., by Mackaness and Rawson.

2531 Mood, Fulmer F. "The Influence of Robert Thorne upon English Maritime Expansion, 1527-1607." Ph.D. diss, Harvard, 1929. Re a Bristol merchant, influential propagandist for overseas empire.

2532 Moomaw, William H. "The Naval Career of Captain Hamond, 1775-1779." Ph.D. diss, Virginia, 1956, 125 pp. A scholarly survey; Captain Andrew S Hamond, 1779-1862.

2533 Moore, Alan H. "The Beginnings of the S.N.R." <u>MM</u>, 41 (1955): 267-80. Credit to L.Carr Laughton; Moore met Laughton and Dudley Macaulay at Cambridge; approached Michael Oppenheim; to nautical antiquarian society, "The Jal Society"; others joined, including J.K. Laughton, secretary of NRS, and C.N. Robinson; preliminary meetings in 1910; formed SNR and journal, <u>Mariner's Mirror</u>, published 11 January 1911.

2534 Moore, John. <u>The First Fleet Marines, 1786-1792</u>. St. Lucia: U Queensland P, 1987, viii, 345 pp. Re naval soldiers, Marines, to protect the new colony; coverage of preparation for the "Great Adventure," the voyage out, and establishment of Sydney.

2535 Moore, Ronald O. "Some Aspects of the Origins and Nature of English Piracy, 1603-1625." Ph.D. diss, Virginia, 1960, 285 pp. A scholarly study, beginning in 1603, from Cinque Ports against France, developments, crown policies to limit, Ireland, Thames; under Elizabeth, piracy became a profession; use of records of HCA.

2536 Moorehead, Alan. <u>Darwin and the BEAGLE</u>. NY: Harper; London: Hamilton, 1969, 280 pp. A survey of Darwin, his meeting with Fitzroy, and the implications.

2537 -------. <u>The Fatal Impact: The Tragic Effects of Captain Cook's Invasion of the South Pacific</u>. Alt. subtitle: <u>An Account of the Invasion of the South Pacific, 1767-1840</u>. London: Penguin; NY: Harper, 1966, 1975, 1987, xiv, 230 pp. Re the Euro-Polynesian encounter; condemnatory of Europeans and a "dark view," contending the indigenous culture was overwhelmed; also, European culture was affected; focus on Cook, Bligh, and Flinders and some literary figures, e.g., Defoe, Swift, Byron, Melville, and Gaugin.

2538 Moorhouse, Esther Hallam. <u>Lady Hamilton</u>. London: Foulis, 1912, 129 pp. Also as Esther Hallam Moorhouse Meynell; a shorter biography.

2539 -------. "Nelson as Seen in His Letters." <u>Fortnightly Review</u>, 90 (1911): 713-27. Nelson wrote much correspondence, e.g., on diplomacy, intelligence, the complicated affairs of the Kingdom of the Two Sicilies, naval operations, and domestic matters; Hallam assesses as an informed observer.

2540 -------. <u>Nelson in England: A Domestic Chronicle</u>. London: Chapman, 1913, ix, 274 pp. Concentrates on Nelson at home.

2541 -------. <u>Nelson's Lady Hamilton</u>. London: Methuen, 1906, xii, 376 pp. An extensive study including 53 portraits.

2542 -------. <u>Samuel Pepys: Administrator, Observer, Gossip</u>. London: Parsons, 1909, 1922, vii, 332 pp. An extensive biography.

2543 Morant, Philip. <u>The Tapestry Hangings of the House of Lords: Representing the Several Engagements between the English and Spanish Fleets in the Ever Memorable Year MDLXXXVIII</u>. London: Pine, 1739, 1753, 23 pp. The subtitle continues; an extraordinary publication; 16 double-page engravings of the tapestry hangings originally designed by C. Vroom for Howard of Effingham, later purchased by James I; later burned in the Parliament fire of 1834.

2544 Morgan, G.W. "The Impact of War on the Administration of the Army, Navy and Ordnance in Britain, 1739-1754." Ph.D. diss, Leicester, 1977, 491 pp. A scholarly study of the impact and consequences of the War of Austrian Succession.

2545 Morgan, J.B. and Perberdy, Philip, eds. <u>Collected Essays on Southampton</u>. Southampton: County Borough, 1958, 110 pp. A series of local studies, e.g., Barbara Turner, "Southampton as a Naval Centre, 1414-1458."

2546 Morillo, Stephen R., ed. <u>The Battle of Hastings: Sources and Interpretations</u>. <u>Warfare in History</u> series, # 1. Woodbridge: Boydell, 1996, xxxii, 230 pp. A collection of 12 "interpretative pieces" for use in the classroom, e.g., some original sources, William of Poitiers on massive preparations, e.g., 3000 ships, naval logistics, 21 scenes from the Bayeux tapestry, maps, and accounts of the battle.

2547 -------. "English Royal Warfare, 1066-1154." D.Phil. diss, Oxford, 1985. The basis for these entries.

2548 -------. Warfare under the Anglo-Norman Kings, 1066-1135. Rochester: Boydell, 1994, xii, 207 pp. Features synthesis and analysis, the nature of warfare, and the role of the king's military household; includes ships and sailors, naval combat, the "fyrd," and demobilization.

2549 Morison, Samuel Eliot. Admiral of the Ocean Sea: A Life of Christopher Columbus. Boston: Little, Brown, 1942, 893 pp. Morison, 1887-1976, Harvard professor, one of the great naval historians of the 20th century, and the official U.S. naval historian of World War II, publishing 15 vols; this the standard biography and extraordinary study of Columbus which included Morison personally sailing the routes of the voyages; praise for the navigation accomplishments of Columbus; awarded Pulitzer Prize.

2550 Morison, Samuel Eliot. Christopher Columbus, Mariner. London: Faber, 1956, 236 pp. An abridged version.

2551 -------. The European Discovery of America. 2 vols. I: The Northern Voyages, AD 500-1600. II: The Southern Voyages, 1492-1616. NY: Oxford UP, 1971-1974, 1993, 1512 pp. Extensive and comprehensive incorporating the unique Morison wit and intelligence; recounts all voyages with brilliant narrative descriptions, reviews the literature, and analyzes the controversies; disposes of "non-voyages," e.g., Phoenicians and a Welsh prince to America; begins with the Irish, then the Norse, Cabot, Frobisher, and Davis; "severe reservations" about the Vinland map; Southern ones, e.g., Columbus, Drake, Magellan, and Sebastian Cabot; awarded Bancroft Prize.

2552 -------. The Great Explorers: The European Discovery of America. NY: Oxford, 1978, 1986, 484 pp. An abridged version.

2553 -------. John Paul Jones: A Sailor's Biography. Classics of Naval Literature. Boston: Little, Brown; Annapolis: NIP, 1959, 1989, 453 pp. Intro: James Bradford; a standard biography; 2nd Pulitzer Prize.

2554 Morley, B.M. Henry VIII and Coastal Defence. London: HMSO, 1976, 42 pp. An oblong pamphlet including a map of Henrician forts and batteries along the southern coast built, 1539-1540.

2555 Morris, John E. The Welsh Wars of Edward I: A Contribution to Medieval Military History. Oxford: Oxford UP; NY: Haskell, 1901, 1969, xii, 327 pp. A formative study still a standard; details on the continued "pacification" of Wales begun by the Normans; includes blockades and provisioning of castles by sea, e.g., Conway; Madoc, leader of the Welsh.

2556 Morris, Norval. Maconochie's Gentlemen: The Story of Norfolk Island and the Roots of Modern Prison Reform. Oxford: Oxford UP, 2001, 213 pp. Alexander Maconochie, Captain, RN, supervised the development of the penal colony on Norfolk Island, east of Australia.

2557 Morris, Roger O. Atlantic Seafaring: Ten Centuries of Exploration and Trade in the North Atlantic. NY: McGraw; Camden: International Marine, 1992, 184 pp. Impressive layout featuring 150 maritime paintings; exploration and trade in the North Atlantic, including pre-Columbian voyages; techniques of sailing and navigation.

2558 -------. "HMS VICTORY and the Society for Nautical Research." MM, 76 (August 1990): 201-03. A review of the role of SNR and the history of HMS VICTORY; by 1921, in poor state and moved to # 2 dock, Portsmouth; SNR launched campaign, "Save the VICTORY Fund"; raised 80,000 pounds; some damage during World War II bombing.

2559 -------. Pacific Sail: Four Centuries of Western Ships in the Pacific. NY: McGraw; Camden: International Marine, 1987, 192 pp. Same layout as earlier entry; dazzling paintings.

2560 -------. "Surveying Ships of the Royal Navy from Cook to the Computer Age." MM, 72 (November 1986):385-414. The 1st hydrographer, 1683; chronological listing of hydrographic surveying ships.

2561 -------. "200 Years of Admiralty Charts and Surveys." MM, 82 (November 1996): 420-35. A survey by an expert; an overview.

2562 Morrison, Alfred. Catalog of the Collection of Autograph Letters and Historical Documents Formed by Alfred Morrison. 13 vols. London: Strangeway, 1883-1897. Morrison, 1821-1897, a wealthy collector; in 1919, his entire collection was auctioned by Sotheby's, 3300 lots requiring 18 days, raising 50,600 pounds.

2563 -------. The Hamilton-Nelson Papers. 2 vols. London: Private, 1893-1894, xiv, 661 pp. Some correspondence was added later, a splendid collection of original MSS.

2564 Morrison, Clifford A. "The Earl of Sandwich and British Naval Administration in the American Revolution." Ph.D. diss, Ohio State, 1950. A scholarly study; no access to Sandwich papers.

2565 Morrison, John, ed. The Age of the Galley: Mediterranean Oared Vessels since Pre-Classical Times. History of the Ship series. London: Conway, 1994, 256 pp. Folio size; from the trireme of 1200 BC through Roman ships to merchant galleys.

2566 Morriss, Roger A. "The Administration of the Royal Dockyards in England during the Revolutionary and Napoleonic Wars with Special Reference to the Period, 1801-1805." Ph.D. diss, London, 1978, 356 pp. The basis for these entries.

2567 -------. Captain Cook and His Exploration of the Pacific. Great Explorer series. London: Ticktock, 1997, 30 pp. For NMM and HM Bark ENDEAVOUR Foundation; an explanatory pamphlet.

2568 [NRS 141]. Morriss, Roger A. The Channel Fleet and the Blockade of Brest, 1793-1801. Publications of the Navy Records Society, vol. 141. Aldershot: Ashgate, 2001, 714 pp. Re the important role of the Channel fleet in the crucial blockade of Brest.

2569 -------. Cockburn and the British Navy in Transition: Admiral Sir George Cockburn, 1772-1853. Exeter: Exeter UP; Columbia: SCUP, 1997, 1998, xiii, 338 pp. Re "the man who burned the White House," a diehard reactionary who oversaw Napoleon at St. Helena, later, First Naval Lord; naval officer, 1793-1848, served under Nelson.

2570 -------. "Experience or Yarn?: The Journal of William Davidson and the Propaganda War against the Barbary States of North Africa." Archives, 23 (April 1998): 30-40. A British seaman aboard a Russian merchant ship documents piracy in North Africa, 1788-1789; shocking disclosures; content questioned but propaganda value exploited.

2571 Morriss, Roger A., comp. Guide to British Naval Papers in North America. London: Mansell, 1994, xxii, 418 pp. For NMM, assistance by Peter Bursey; bibliographical reference and assistance: answers what, where, and how re sources available in North America, e.g., government and ship records, personal papers, and artificial collections, all complementing the collections of NMM; contacted 30 libraries, e.g., Duke and Michigan University and Huntington libraries and the archives of the Hudson Bay Company in Manitoba; papers of American historians Arthur Marder and Brian Tunstall.

2572 Morriss, Roger A., et al., eds. Nelson: An Illustrated History. London: King, 1995, 176 pp. Folio size, impressively illustrated; for NMM; re his career and personality.

2573 Morriss, Roger A. Nelson: The Life and Letters of a Hero. Illustrated Letters series. London: Collins, 1996, 160 pp. Folio size, picture book format; for NMM; a brief life.

2574 -------. The Royal Dockyards during the Revolutionary and Napoleonic Wars. Leicester: Leicester UP, 1983, ix, 262 pp. Re the largest industrial enterprise in Britain for centuries; impressive study, covering up to 1815; notes advanced technological achievements and efficiency; detailed description of the dockyards, the workforce, administration, and organization.

2575 -------. "St. Vincent and Reform, 1801-1804." MM, 69 (August 1983): 269-90. A revised assessment of St. Vincent as First Lord as war resumed: conclusion: a failure because he was oblivious of the complexities of the civil sector, his personality too pushy.

2576 -------. "Samuel Bentham and the Management of the Royal Dockyards." Bull IHR, 54 (November 1981): 226-40. A naval bureaucrat, inspector-general of naval works, 1796-1807; a crucial period; improvements noted: "a great reformer."

2577 Moses, Norton H. "The British Navy and the Caribbean, 1688-1697." MM, 52 (February 1966): 13-40. During the Nine Years' War; concern about British colonies; fleet sent out, e.g., to Barbados in 1690; a series of defeats.

2578 Mountaine, William. The Seaman's "Vade-Mecum" and Defensive War at Sea. London: Conway, 1756, 1971, 270 pp. A boxed facsimile, a collection of essential documents of the 18th century; includes Maritime Dictionary, RN List, Duty of Sea Officers, Rules of Discipline, and Fighting Instructions.

2579 Mowat, Susan. "Shipping and Trade in Scotland, 1556-1830: The Records of the Scottish Admiralty Courts." MM, 83 (February 1997): 14-20. Cases from Admiralty Courts.

2580 Muckelroy, Keith, ed. Archaeology under Water: An Atlas of the World's Submerged Sites. New York: McGraw, 1980, 192 pp. Folio size, associated with the Council for Nautical Archaeology; 15 contributions by experts, e.g., Colin Martin, Robert Marx, and Jeremy Green; re techniques, approaches, and sites, e.g., SUTTON HOO, VASA, Armada wrecks, and Port Royal.

2581 Muckelroy, Keith. Maritime Archaeology. NY: Cambridge UP, 1978, x, 270 pp. An early guide.

2582 Muir, Rory. Britain and the Defeat of Napoleon, 1807-1815. New Haven: Yale UP, 1996, xiv, 466 pp. An overview of the progress in the war from the perspective of British officials, e.g., Peninsular War, Sicily, "the foolish and unnecessary" War of 1812, and surrender of Napoleon; good bibliographical essay.

2583 Munby, Alan N.L. The Cult of the Autograph Letter in England. London: Athelone, 1962, 117 pp. Re autograph collectors and collections, e.g., Pepys and, especially, Nelson, e.g., the Morrison collection including letters from Nelson to Lady Hamilton thought stolen in 1814, surfaced at Sotheby's sale in 1917, bought for 53,000 pounds.

2584 Mundy, Godfrey B. The Life and Correspondence of the Late Admiral Lord Rodney. 2 vols. London: Murray, 1830. An old study of Rodney, 1719-1792.

2585 Muntz, Hope. The Golden Warrior: A Novel of the Norman Conquest. Alt. title: The Story of Harold and William. NY: Scribner, 1949, xiii, 354 pp. Intro:

G.M. Trevelyan; dedicated to Winston Churchill; fictional account of the Norman Conquest and battle of Hastings.

2586 Murphy, Frank M. "Lloyd's of London and World Maritime Traditions." USNIP, 93 (May 1967): 79-87. A short history and description; a world center of shipping information and intelligence.

2587 Murphy, Larry E. H.L. HUNLEY Site Assessment. Santa Fe: National Park Service, 1998, xv, 198 pp. A technical report re the Confederate submarine sunk in Charleston harbor; discovered in 1995, raised, and investigated; outstanding example of the operations of nautical archaeology.

2588 Murray, Katherine M.E. The Constitutional History of the Cinque Ports. Manchester: Manchester UP, 1935, xvi, 282 pp. The background, development, and decline of these ports of the southeast with the feudal obligation to defend the coasts, 12th-15th centuries; the ship fyrd to serve 15 days per year; office of Lord Warden.

2589 Murray, Oswyn A.R. "The Admiralty." 9-part series. MM, 23-25 (January 1937-April 1939): various. By the Admiralty secretary, Murray, 1873-1936, his death before completion and published posthumously; the administrative and organizational history of the Admiralty.

2590 Muskett, Paul. "English Smuggling in the Eighteenth Century." Ph.D. diss, Open University, 1996. A scholarly study of the commercial and social aspects and the problem of policing.

2591 The Mutiny of the BOUNTY, 1789-1989: Exhibition Catalogue. Greenwich: NMM, 1989, 160 pp. Ed: Rina Prentice; a guide to the bicentennial exhibition; 12 essays incorporating the latest research and sources.

2592 The Mutiny of the BOUNTY: The Story of Captain Bligh, Seaman, Navigator, Surveyor , and the BOUNTY Mutineers. Sydney: Library of New South Wales, 1991, 104 pp. An account of Bligh, the mutiny, and the mutineers.

2593 Naish, George P.B. Nelson and Bronte: An Illustrated Guide to His Life and Times. London: HMSO, 1959, 29 pp. For NMM; an illustrated collection of Nelson materials supporting exhibitions.

2594 [NRS 100]. Naish, George P.B., ed. Nelson's Letters to His Wife and Other Documents, 1785-1831. Publications of the Navy Records Society, vol. 100. London: Routledge, 1958, 630 pp. Brilliantly edited; from papers at the Monmouth Museum; informative on personal problems and naval matters; an early "popular" volume in cooperation with Routledge.

2595 Naish, John M. "The Achievements of Captain George Vancouver: A Reassessment after 200 Years." MM, 80 (November 1994): 418-30. Vancouver,

1758-1798, protege of Cook and Admiralty explorer, leading a long voyage of exploration aboard DISCOVERY and CHATHAM, early 1790s, surveying 1000 miles of the west coast of North America, searching for the Northwest Passage, and successfully re-asserting British claims to Nootka Sound; success in avoiding scurvy; sadly, died in obscurity; to rehabilitate reputation of Vancouver.

2596 -------. The Interwoven Lives of George Vancouver, Archibald Menzies, Joseph Whidbey, and Peter Puget: Exploring the Pacific Northwest Coast. Lewiston: Mellen, 1996, 537 pp. Re the long Admiralty exploration voyage, 1791-1795.

2597 Napier, William. History of the War in the Peninsula and the South of France, 1807-1814. 5 vols. NY: AMS, 1828-1840, 1970. An oldtime standard history of this crucial campaign; balanced, too much so overly patriotic British historians claimed; controversial.

2598 Nash, M.D., ed. The Last Voyage of the GUARDIAN: Lieutenant Riou, Commander, 1789-1791. Cape Town: Van Riebeeck, 1989, 1990, xxxix, 243 pp. The supply ship for the First Fleet, a 44-gun frigate with stores and 250 convicts; struck iceberg and struggled back to Table Bay; some loss of life, but, more significantly, no 2-year food supply for Sydney which meant virtual starvation there.

2599 Nash, Michael, ed. The Nelson Masks: Official Interim Report of the Portsmouth Symposium. Holylake: Marine, 1993, 19 pp. For the Royal Naval Museum and 1805 Club; proceedings of a symposium, Royal Naval Museum, October 1992; examination of the evidence re 3 Nelson masks; presenters: White, Walker, Hull, and Green.

2600 -------, ed. Santa Cruz, 1797: Being a Hitherto Unpublished Spanish Diary. North Walsham: Nelson Society, 1984. An account of the attack by Nelson and RN.

2601 Nash, Michael. "Southey's Nelson: Early and Collectable Editions." Trafalgar Chronicle, 1 (1991): 36-54. Describes personal life of Southey and traces publication history from publication in 1813; seldom out-of-print; between 150 and 200 editions; most informative is 1922, edited by Callender who presents corrections, e.g., Nelson and Neopolitan rebellions.

2602 Naslund, Sena J. Ahab's Wife: Or, the Star-Gazer: A Novel. NY: Morrow, 1999, xix, 668 pp. Inspired by Moby Dick by Melville; the story from the perspective of a female.

2603 Natharius, Edward W. "The Maritime Powers and Sweden, 1698-1702." Ph.D. diss, Indiana, 1957, 280 pp. Britain and Holland active in Baltic trade, e.g., naval stores vital for the British; diplomacy of William III, creating Anglo-Dutch alliance vs the Danes; Peter the Great intervenes; became more complicated.

2604 National Maritime Museum. Catalogue of the Library of the National

Maritime Museum. 5 vols. I: Travels. II: Biography. III: Atlases and Cartography. IV: Piracy and Privateering. V: The Middle Ages. London: HMSO, 1971-1976, 1560 pp. The catalogue of the library; thousands of annotated entries; promises more to follow.

2605 The Naval Chronicle: The Contemporary Record of the Royal Navy at War. 40 vols. Published twice a year, 1799-1818, 20,000 pp. Eds: John M'Arthur and Joyce Gold; no index. See Norman Hurst, ed., published privately c.1990. Abridgement, 5 vols. I: 1793-1798. xiii, 365 pp. II: 1798-1804. vii, 374 pp. III: 1804-1806. viii, 376 pp. IV: 1807-1810. vii, 407 pp. V: 1811-1815. vii, 374 pp. London: Chatham, 1998-1999, xlii, 1896 pp.; has index. Ed: Nicholas Tracy; contained details of all aspects of naval activities, professional discussion, mini-biographies including the autobiography by Nelson, intelligence, anecdotes, poetry, battle of Trafalgar (Vol. XIV and XV).

2606 [NHS # 16]. Naval History Symposium. Projected for 2003, USNA.

2607 [NHS # 17]. Naval History Symposium. Projected for 2005, USNA. Projected cooperation with Trafalgar 200 and culmination of Nelson Decade activities.

2608 Naval Review. A journal. London, 1912-present. An in-house, members-only journal sponsored by the then Naval Society; by ambitious and far-sighted naval officers with the aim of stimulating study and discussion of pertinent issues and problems; among the founders and early contributors was Herbert Richmond.

2609 Neal, Larry. "The Cost of Impressment during the Seven Years' War."MM, 64 (February 1978): 45-56. Calculated assessments; financial costs were large but less than claimed at the time.

2610 Neale, Jonathan. The Cutlass and the Lash: Mutiny and Discipline in Nelson's Navy. London: Pluto, 1985, xvi, 208 pp. Purposely does not consider the mutinies of 1797, to be in a later study; investigates "industrial relations" from Marxist perspective; links discipline, punishment, forms of resistance, and mutiny as related.

2611 -------. "Forecastle and Quarterdeck: Protest, Discipline and Mutiny in the Royal Navy, 1793-1814." Ph.D. diss, Warwick, 1990, 554 pp. The basis of the previous entry, admittedly completed later, and less Marxist orientation.

2612 Neale, William J. Gentleman Jack: A Naval Story. 3 vols. London, 1837, 1841. Neale,1812-1893, writer of nautical fiction; similar to Marryat and they had a fistfight in Trafalgar Square, Marryat striking him with a cane, claiming he libelled Admiral Troubridge.

2613 -------. History of the Mutiny of Spithead and the Nore: With an Enquiry into Its Origin and Treatment: And Suggestions for the Prevention of Future Discontent in the Royal Navy. London, 1842. Obviously, an emotional issue; use of journalistic sources; accused of being careless with the facts.

2614 -------. Paul Periwinkle, or The Pressgang. 3 vols. London: Tegg, 1841, 640 pp. Long, nautical fiction-adventure "embellished by 40 etchings by 'Phiz'" which resemble Hogarth.

2615 Needham, Jack. Modelling Ships in Bottles. Wellingborough: Stephens, 1972, 1973, 1985, 1987, 160 pp. Fwd: Alan Villiars; for the serious hobbyist; popular interest.

2616 Neill, Peter. American Sea Writing: A Literary Anthology. NY: Library of America, 2000, xxi, 671 pp. Fwd: Nathaniel Philbrick; selections, including pertinent ones about Britain, e.g., the murder of Cook and the inspiration for "The Tempest" by Shakespeare.

2617 Nelson, Arthur. The Tudor Navy: The Ships, Men, and Organisation, 1485-1603. London: Brassey; Annapolis: NIP, 2000, xvi, 224 pp. A recent illustrated survey.

2618 Nelson, George H. "Contraband Trade under the Asiento, 1730-1739." AHR, 51 (October 1945): 55-67. Asiento, attached to a treaty, was the monopoly for supplying slaves to Spanish America; British merchants, the South Sea Company, and RN were involved; used as a screen for illegal trade; Spanish "Garda" attempted suppression; became a cause of the War of Jenkins's Ear.

2619 Nelson, Horatio. The Letters of Lord Nelson to Lady Hamilton. 2 vols. London: Lovewell, 1814, 1905, 1907, ix, 152 pp. Ed: Douglas Sladen; 61 letters; for a long time, these were considered stolen, then declared forgeries; finally to Dr. Thomas Pettitrew.

2620 -------. "A Sketch of My Life." The Naval Chronicle, 3, (January-June 1800. The "autobiography" of Nelson, a memoir he submitted to The Naval Chronicle.

2621 Nelson, James L. By Force of Arms. Revolution at Sea series, # 1. NY: Pocket; NY: Hall, 1996, 1997, 467 pp. Another contribution to nautical fiction; American colonial-revolution period.

2622 Nelson, Paul D. "British Conduct of the American Revolutionary War: A Review of Interpretations." J American History, 65 (December 1978): 623-53. A historiographical survey; reviews various causes, e.g., poor strategic planning, inferior and incompetent bureaucrats, officials, military, and naval officers, and lack of army-navy cooperation.

2623 "Nelson Biography Project." Royal Naval Museum, Portsmouth. RNM coordinating a plan for completing a new biography as the culmination of the Nelson Decade Project in 2005.

2624 "The Nelson Decade" Bicentennial Commemoration, 1995-2005. Launched, 21 October 1995; sponsored by the Official Nelson Commemorations Committee

(ONCC) with representatives from the Nelson Society, the 1805 Club, the Royal Naval Museum, Portsmouth, and the Society for Nautical Research; to commemorate and celebrate; events, e.g., St. Vincent, Santa Cruz, the Nile, Copenhagen (2001), Napoleon's Invasion Plans (2002), and, ultimately, 21 October 2005, Trafalgar; Trafalgar 200; Colin White, chair.

2625 Nelson and His Navy: Nelson and Trafalgar, the Multimedia Story. CD-ROM, 1996, 1 disc. "To sail with Nelson," e.g., battles and model of HMS VICTORY; more promised.

2626 Nelson's Last Diary and the Prayer before Trafalgar: A Facsimile. London: Seeley, 1971, 80 pp. Intro: Oliver Warner; a contribution to "Nelsoniana"; includes 3 texts, his notebook of the campaign, the prayer, and his last letter to Lady Hamilton.

2627 Nester, William R. Britain, France, and the Imperial Struggle for North America, 1607-1775. 2 vols. I: The Great Frontier War, 1607-1755. II: The First Global War, 1756-1775. Westport: Praeger, 2000, xxii, 634 pp. An ambitious effort centered around the Seven Years' War, analyzing in detail the preliminaries, context, events, and consequences; synthesis of research and interpretations.

2628 Nettels, Curtis. "England and the Spanish-American Trade, 1680-1715." J Modern History, 3 (March 1931): 1-32. Crucial was acquistion of Jamaica in 1655, to be the main base; other factors: asiento, the trade monopoly, and piracy-privateering; all leading to the War of Spanish Succession.

2629 Neumann, J. "Hydrographic and Ship-Hydrodynamic Aspects of the Norman Invasion, 1066." Anglo-Norman Studies, 11 (1988): 221-44. A fascinating reconstruction using sources from chroniclers, the Bayeux tapestry, and other contemporaneous observations to determine hydrographic factors, e.g., tides, tidal streams, weather, and winds, as of late September 1066, e.g., winds "unfavorable" for crossing for 15 days, then shift, 27-28 September, permitting the crossing, but, still, ship losses recorded.

2630 Neville-Singleton, P.A. and Payne, Anthony. Richard Hakluyt and His Books: An Interim Census of Surviving Copies of Hakluyt's "Divers Voyages" and "Principal Navigations". London: Hakluyt Society, 1996, 1997, 76 pp. A description of the dispositions of rare copies of originals.

2631 The New Dictionary of National Biography. London: Oxford UP, forthcoming in 2004 or 2005. Ed: H.C.G. Matthew, replaced at his death by Brian Harrison; 36,000 new essays and 14,000 entries to be rewritten; a massive project in process; touted as "revised, enlarged, illustrated, and modernized."

2632 Newbolt, Henry. The Year of Trafalgar: Being an Account of the Battle and of the Events Which Led Up to It. London: Murray, 1905, xvi, 244 pp. On the occasion of the centennial; Newbolt incorporates 26 poems and ballads, including his own; reviews the literature, lamenting so many errors; observations about "the New Navalism" and the "cult of Nelson."

2633 Newhall, Richard A. The English Conquest of Normandy, 1416-1424: A Study in Fifteenth-Century Warfare. New Haven: Yale UP; NY: Russell, 1924, 1971,xvii, 367 pp. Broad coverage of a limited period of the Hundred Years' War, e.g., the conquest, finances, organization, logistics, and materiel; featuring Edward III, the Black Prince, and Henry V.

2634 Newton, Arthur P., ed. The Great Age of Discovery. NY: Franklin, 1932, 1969 1970, xi, 230 pp. A series of lectures by experts, University of London, 1931, e.g., the 3 great explorers: Cabot, Columbus, and Vespucci; J.Williamson on circumnavigation and E.G.R. Taylor on northern passages, the "predestined" role of English explorers.

2635 Nicholl, Charles. The Creation of the Map: A Journey to El Dorado. Chicago: U Chicago P; London: Vintage, 1995, 1996, xii, 398 pp. Reconstruction of the voyage led by Raleigh, 1595, in travelogue format; 4 ships and 250 men to Venezuala.

2636 Nicholson, Ian. Log of Logs: A Catalogue of Logs, Journals, Shipboard Diaries, Letters, and All Forms of Voyage Narratives, 1788 to 1988, for Australia, New Zealand, and Surrounding Oceans. Aranda: Roebuck Society, 1989, x, 630 pp. For the Australian Association for Maritime History; a reference guide, alphabetical order by ship name; all types of ships included, e.g., warships and explorers.

2637 Nicholson, Joyce. Man against Mutiny: The Story of Vice-Admiral William Bligh. London: Butterworth, 1961, 95 pp. A short, undistinguished biography.

2638 Nicol, John. The Life and Adventures of John Nicol, Mariner. NY: Farrar; Melbourne: Text; Edinburgh: Canongate, 1822, 1936, 1997, 214 pp. Ed: Tim Flannery; Nicol, 1755-1825, extraordinary reminiscences of 25 years of life on the lower deck of the late 18th century, e.g., in RN, to China, to Hawaii in 1st ship after death of Cook, in Second Fleet to Australia, St. Vincent, the Nile, fled from a press gang, and denied a pension.

2639 Nicolas, Nicholas Harris. The Dispatches and Letters of Vice-Admiral Lord Nelson. 7 vols. London: Colburn; London: Chatham, 1844-1846, 1996-1997, 3900 pp. Dedicated to HRH, Prince Albert; Nicolas, 1799-1848, collected 3500 dispatches and letters; nothing equivalent for any other figure in British naval history; indispensable Nelsoniana; letters cover 1777-1895 and placed in strict chronological order; unable to acquire letters from widows of Clarke and M'Arthur; notes by Nicolas very informative; much praised by Nelson scholars; important reprint of late 1990s.

2640 -------. History of the Battle of Agincourt and the Expedition of Henry V. NY: Barnes, 1827, 1832, 1970, xvi, 404 pp. An informative history of the campaign with emphasis on the army.

2641 -------. A History of the Royal Navy from the Earliest Times to the Wars of the French Revolution. 2 vols. London: Bentley, 1847, 1004 pp. An ambitious project to supplement James with broader coverage; plan for 9 vols., but cut short by the death of Nicolas, age 49; begins with Julius Caesar and up to 1422; later supplemented by Laird Clowes who contended Nicolas would have needed 15 to 20 vols.

2642 Nicolas, Nicholas Harris, ed. Roll of Arms of the Reign of Edward the Second. London: Pickering, 1829, 166 pp. A contribution to the heraldry of Britain.

2643 -------, ed. Roll of Arms of the Reigns of Henry III and Edward III. London: Pickering, 1829, viii, 67 pp. A contribution to the heraldry of Britain, 13th and 14th centuries.

2644 Nicolas, Paul Harris. Historical Record of the Royal Marine Forces. 2 vols. London: Boone, 1845, 774 pp. A chronological survey of military actions involving the marines up to 1842.

2645 Nicolle, David C. Medieval Warfare Source Book: Warfare in Western Christendom. London: A&A; NY: Sterling, 1996, 320 pp. The first of projected 2-vol. comprehensive reference guide, 5th-14th centuries; curious organization; list of sources; covers naval warfare but as afterthought; the Frisians of 7th and 8th centuries were best known sailors; for the Normans, "guardians of the sea" were Cinque Ports; by 13th century, French galleys from Ruen and Genoese galleys dominated.

2646 -------. The Venetian Empire, 1200-1670. Osprey Men-at-Arms series, #210. London: Osprey, 1989, 48 pp. Sea warfare in the Mediterranean and nearby.

2647 Noble, William M. Huntingdonshire and the Spanish Armada: Edited from Original Manuscripts. London: Stock, 1896, viii, 61 pp. A collection of accounts of dubious origin, e.g., Tilbury speech of Elizabeth, statistics on 191 English and 130 Spanish ships, and, re Medina-Sidonia as "not only incompetent but knew of his incompetence."

2648 Nolan, John S. "English Operations around Brest, 1594." MM, 81 (August 1995): 259-74. Re amphibious operations during Anglo-Spanish war; an expedition invading Brittany to counteract Spanish preparations there.

2649 -------. "The Muster of 1588." Albion, 23 (Fall 1991): 387-407. Questions view of Parker and others that land forces, Trained Bands and General Muster, were unprepared for Spanish landing; recounts "the Great Muster" of 1588 plus system of forts and defenses created by Henry VIII and "early warning system" of beacons; all would have been formidable.

2650 Nordhoff, Charles and Hall, James Norman. The BOUNTY Trilogy. I: Mutiny on the BOUNTY. II: Men against the Sea. III: Pitcairn's Island. Boston: Little, Brown, 1932, 1934, 1936, 1947, 1960, 1962, 1982, 1985, 691 pp. A full, popularized, illustrated version incorporating fictionalized narratives; re the voyage, mutiny, longboat journey, HMS PANDORA, mutineers to Pitcairn, and their fate; the basis for a popular movie; many editions and others in foreign languages.

2651 North, Jonathan, ed. The Napoleon Options: Alternative Decisions of the Napoleonic Wars. Mechanisburg: Stackpole, 2000, 221 pp. Increasingly popular, counterfactual history with a description at the end of each telling what actually occurred; 11 attempts; at decisive moments, e.g., French invasion of Ireland succeeds and Napoleon in Egypt succeeds.

2652 Norway, Arthur H. History of the Post Office Packet Service: Between the Years 1793-1815. London: Macmillan, 1895, 312 pp. Accumulating a sizeable force of sea vessels and services.

2653 Novak, Maximilian E. Daniel Defoe: Master of Fiction. Oxford: Oxford UP, 2001, 756 pp. An extensive, comprehensive account of his life and career; 547 items attributed to Defoe.

2654 Nuttall, Zelia, ed. New Light on Drake: A Collection of Documents Relating to His Voyage of Circumnavigation, 1577-1580. Publications of the Hakluyt Society, 2nd ser, # 34. London: Hakluyt Society; NY: Kraus, 1914, 1967, xcii, 443 pp. A collection of Spanish documents including accounts of prisoners of Drake; informative and enlightening.

2655 Oakeshott, Walter F. Founded upon the Seas: A Narrative of Some English Maritime and Overseas Enterprises during the Period 1550 to 1616. Freeport: Libraries, 1942, 1973, xi, 200 pp. Narrative accounts of exploits of Tudor and Jacobean seamen, e.g., search for Northeast Passage, John Lloyd, John Cabot, Armada, expeditions to the West Indies, Drake to Cadiz, and Raleigh formulates new tactics.

2656 Oakley, Gilbert. The History of the Rod and Other Corporal Punishments. London: Walton, 1964, 304 pp. Flouts dubious credentials in "Psychology," poorly organized, overdramatized, and no scholarly apparatus; graphic descriptions of punishments; stimulating masochistic-sadistic impulses.

2657 Oakley, Stewart P. War and Peace in the Baltic, 1560-1790. War in Context series. NY: Routledge, 1992, 1993, xvii, 222 pp. The scene of frequent conflicts; rise and fall of Sweden, rise of Russia, increasing interests of Dutch, British, and French.

2658 O'Beirne, T.L. Considerations of the Principles of Naval Discipline and Naval Courts-Martial. . . . on Admiral Keppel and Sir Hugh Palliser Are Compared. London: Debrett, 1781, 192 pp. A contemporaneous account of a famous confrontation.

2659 Obeyesekere, Gananath. <u>The Apotheosis of Captain Cook: European Mythmaking in the Pacific</u>. Honolulu: Bishop Museum; Princeton: Princeton UP, 1992, xvii, 251 pp. A complex, condemnatory, and passionate treatise on mythmaking, Eurocentrism, global violence, and, most curious, Sri Lankan nationalism; the use of history itself as a tool of domination; Cook murdered 14 February 1779; speculates about erratic behavior and "destructive side" of Cook.

2660 O'Brian, Patrick. <u>Blue at the Mizzen</u>. NY: Norton, 1999, 262 pp. Jack Aubrey-Stephen Maturin, # 20. Series of 20 nautical novels of the Nelson era. New York: London: Collins or HarperCollins; New York: Norton, 1969-1999, various reprints. O'Brian, 1914-2000, died, January 2000; first novel, 1952; first sea story, 1956; in his novels he incorporates all of the following: life aboard ship, naval operations, politics, navigation, gunnery, tactics, intelligence, medicine, language, the natural world, food and drink, music and musical instruments, calculation of prize money, legitimate historical events and persons, e.g., service under Nelson at the Nile, language, recreations, furniture, ideas, and manners; better than C.S. Forester, closest comparison to Marryat and Jane Austen; the strengths are minute details about seamanship and all aspects of the world of the early nineteenth century, the Nelson era; preparing novel # 21 at time of death; <u>New York Times</u>: "the greatest historical novels ever written"; 3 ½ million copies in print; born: Richard Patrick Russ, Buckinghamshire, England; author of biographies: <u>Pablo Ruiz Picasso: A Biography</u>. 1976, 1994, 511 pp. and <u>Joseph Banks</u>. London, Harvill, 1987, 1993, 328 pp. Aubrey-Maturin Novels Association, Newsletter with 40,000 circulation; Gunroom Forum, e-mail chat room; 2 CDs of chamber music; cookbooks, and glossaries.

2661 -------. <u>The Commodore</u>. 1994, 252 pp. Jack Aubrey-Stephen Maturin, # 17.

2662 -------. <u>Desolation Island</u>. 1978, 276 pp. Jack Aubrey-Stephen Maturin, # 5.

2663 -------. <u>The Far Side of the World</u>. 1984, 371 pp. Jack Aubrey-Stephen Maturin, # 10.

2664 -------. <u>The Fortune of War</u>. 1979, 279 pp. Jack Aubrey-Stephen Maturin, # 6.

2665 O'Brian, Patrick. <u>The Golden Ocean: A Novel</u>. London: Hart-Davis; NY: Norton, 1956, 1957, 1994, 316 pp. Nautical fiction, 1st novel; re an Irish midshipman Peter Palafox on the voyage of circumnavigation by Anson, 1740s.

2666 -------. <u>HMS SUPRISE</u>. 1973, 318 pp. Jack Aubrey-Stephen Maturin, # 3.

2667 -------. <u>The Hundred Days</u>. 1998, 281 pp. Jack Aubrey-Stephen Maturin, # 19.

2668 -------. <u>The Ionian Mission</u>. 1981, 346 pp. Jack Aubrey-Stephen Maturin, # 8.

2669 O'Brian, Patrick. <u>Joseph Banks: A Life</u>. London: Harvill; Boston: Godine, 1987, 1993, 328 pp. Banks was a naturalist and longtime President of the Royal Society; links with many naval figures, e.g., Cook, Bligh, and Flinders.

2670 -------. <u>The Letter of Marque</u>. 1988, 284 pp. Jack Aubrey-Stephen Maturin, # 12.

2671 -------. <u>Master and Commander</u>. 1969, 384 pp. Jack Aubrey-Stephen Maturin, # 1.

2672 -------. <u>The Mauritius Command</u>. 1977, 268 pp. Jack Aubrey-Stephen Maturin, # 4.

2673 O'Brian, Patrick. <u>Men-of-War: Life in Nelson's Navy</u>. NY: Norton; London: Collins, 1974, 1995, 96 pp. Beautifully illustrated, assisted by NMM; a companion to the Jack Aubrey-Stephen Maturin novels; chapters include ships, guns, ship's company, life at sea, and songs.

2674 -------. <u>The Nutmeg of Consolation</u>. 1991, 315 pp. Jack Aubrey-Stephen Maturin, # 14.

2675 -------. <u>Post Captain</u>. 1972, 413 pp. Jack Aubrey-Stephen Maturin, # 2.

2676 O'Brian, Patrick. <u>The Rendezvous and Other Stories</u>. NY: Norton, 1995, 250 pp. Selections from the early works of O'Brian, 1950s to 1974; 27 short stories with formats similar to the Jack Aubrey-Stephen Maturin novels.

2677 -------. <u>The Reverse of the Medal</u>. 1986, 256 pp. Jack Aubrey-Stephen Maturin, # 11.

2678 -------. <u>The Surgeon's Mate.</u> 1980, 314 pp. Jack Aubrey-Stephen Maturin, # 7.

2679 -------. <u>The Thirteen-Gun Salute</u>. 1989, 319 pp. Jack Aubrey-Stephen Maturin, # 13.

2680 -------. <u>Treason's Harbor</u>. 1983, 320 pp. Jack Aubrey-Stephen Maturin, # 9.

2681 -------. <u>The Truelove</u>. 1992, 256 pp. Jack Aubrey-Stephen Maturin, # 15.

2682 -------. <u>The Wine-Dark Sea</u>. 1993, 251 pp. Jack Aubrey-Stephen Maturin, # 16.

2683 -------. <u>The Yellow Admiral</u>. 1996, 261 pp. Jack Aubrey-Stephen Maturin, # 18.

2684 O'Bryne, William R. <u>A Naval Biographical Dictionary: Comprising the Life and Services of Every Living Officer in Her Majesty's Navy from the Rank of</u>

Admiral of the Fleet to that of Lieutenant, Inclusive. 2 vols. London: Murray, 1849, 1988, 2000, 1400 pp. Names and details of service from the Navy List of 1845; many were active during the Nelson era; details on 20 fleet actions, 1793-1840.

2685 Observations on the Preparation and Discipline of the British Navy with Suggestions for a Better System. London: Dalton, 1837, 29 pp. A pamphlet describing the current and past system and calling for reform.

2686 O'Connell, Daniel P. The Influence of Law on Sea Power. Manchester: Manchester UP; Annapolis: NIP, 1975, 1976, xv, 204 pp. Fwds: B.A. Wortley and Peter Gretton; a treatise on the international law of the sea supported by case studies which were mostly from the 20th century; Mahan ignored theses topic, e.g., blockade, right of transit, the territorial sea, the sea bed, and coercive sea power.

2687 Odintz, Mark F. "The British Officer Corps, 1754-1783." 2 vols. Ph.D. diss, Michigan, 1988, 660 pp. Prosopography; a biographical study of 394 officers, 1767-1783; most from landed classes and other summary details; instructive about the officer corps, albeit, army.

2688 Oertling, Thomas J. Ships' Bilge Pumps: A History of Their Development, 1500-1900. Studies in Nautical Archaeology, # 2. College Station: Texas A&M UP; London: Chatham, 1996, xvii, 105 pp. Re the evolution of bilge pumps, various types.

2689 Oglesby, John C.M. "War at Sea in the West Indies, 1737-1748." Ph.D. diss, Washington, 1963, 293 pp. Focus on international rivalry, Spain, France, and Britain; demonstrated the extreme importance of the area.

2690 Ohlmeyer, Jane H. "Irish Privateers during the Civil War, 1642-1650." MM, 76 (May 1990): 119-33. Reviews operations and losses, e.g., capture of a Spanish treasure ship in 1647 and the brutal treatment of the crew; the campaign of Cromwell in 1649 ended Irish privateering.

2691 Ohrelius, Bengt. VASA, the King's Ship. Phil: Chilton; London: Cassell, 1959, 1962, 1963, 124 pp. Trans: Maurice Michael; re the extraordinary Swedish ship which capsized on its maiden voyage in Stockholm harbor, 1628, recently salvaged; informative about early 17th century warships.

2692 Oko, Adolph S. Francis Drake and New Albion. Reprint from California Society Quarterly, June 1964. Report on evidence of the landfall of Drake in 1579, not in San Francisco Bay, but 25 miles WNW of Point Reyes, "Drake's Cove" and "Drake's Bay"; the famous "plate of brass" was discovered in 1933, a fake.

2693 Oldham, W. "The Administration of the System of Transportation of British Convicts, 1763-1793." Ph.D. diss, London, 1933. A scholarly study.

2694 Oleson, Tryggvi J. Early Voyages and Northern Approaches, 1000-1632.

Toronto: McClelland, 1964, xii, 211 pp. To support the Canadian Centenary; themes, e.g., Icelandic Sagas, Vinland, Greenland, mythical voyages, Madoc, St. Brendan, Cabot, Frobisher, and the search for the Northwest Passage.

2695 Oliver, Douglas. Return to Tahiti: Bligh's Second Breadfruit Voyage. Honolulu: Hawaii UP, 1988, 1989, xx, 281 pp. Re the successful voyage of the early 1790s.

2696 Ollard, Richard L. Cromwell's Earl: A Life of Edward Monatgu, 1st Earl of Sandwich. London: HarperCollins, 1994, xviii, 283 pp. A close colleague of Cromwell, cousin to Pepys, colonel in the New Model Army, and Admiral in 3 naval wars.

2697 -------. "Greenwich." HisTod, 5 (November 1955): 777-84. A survey of the founding and development of the naval hospital.

2698 -------. Man of War: Sir Robert Holmes and the Restoration Navy. London: Hodder, 1969, 240 pp. Dedicated to Michael Lewis; Holmes, 1622-1692; a scholarly biography; a Royalist officer serving under Rupert; led naval operations in 2nd and 3rd Dutch wars.

2699 -------. Pepys: A Biography. London: Hodder: NY: Holt; London: Sinclair, 1974, 1975, 1978, 1984, 1991, 418 pp. An excellent, 1-vol. biography elegantly written; illustrated with paintings and drawings; informative on the professionalization of naval officers.

2700 Ollivier, Blaise. Eighteenth-Century Shipbuilding: Remarks on the Navies of the English and the Dutch, 1737. London: Boudriot, 1992, viii, 384 pp. Trans: David Roberts; by a French naval architect who studied shipbuilding among the English and Dutch; wrote this report of his experience; informative on sailing warship shipbuilding; obviously not the case at this time that French ship design was superior.

2701 Oman, Carola. Britain against Napoleon. Alt. title: Napoleon at the Channel. London: Faber; NY: Doubleday, 1942, xii, 316 pp. Oman, 1897-1978, actually, Lady Carola Mary Anne Lenanton, a noted Nelson scholar and daughter of Charles Oman, the great military historian; this a survey of the campaigns and operations; an obvious comparative situation at the time: Napoleon and Hitler preparing invasion.

2702 -------. Lord Nelson. Brief Lives series. NY: Macmillan; London: Collins; Hamden: Archon, 1954, 1968, 1970, 160 pp. A short, popular version of her standard biography; informative note on sources, no index.

2703 -------. Nelson. NY: Doubleday: London: Hodder; London: Greenhill, 1946, 1947, 1950, 1967, 1996, 816 pp. Intro: Stephen Howarth; seen as "a masterpiece," the standard, and the most extensive of the older biographies; best on personal life and career; others are better on naval and diplomatic matters; a worthy successor to

Southey; excellent bibliographical survey; describes Nelson monuments.

2704 -------. Sir John Moore. London: Hodder, 1953, xvi, 700 pp. Moore, 1761-1809, the standard biography of the commander of the assault force of the Egyptian campaign of 1801.

2705 Oman, Charles. A History of the Art of War in the Middle Ages. 2 vols. I: AD 378-1278. II: 1278-1485. Oxford: Oxford UP; Ithaca: Cornell UP; Novato: Presidio, 1885, 1898, 1924, 1953, 1990, 1992, 1082 pp. Revised: John Beeler; Sir Charles Oman, 1860-1946; Lothian Prize at Oxford; the great military classic; traditional military history with emphasis on battles and tactics; now out of date.

2706 -------. A History of the Art of War in the Sixteenth Century. London: Methuen; Novato: Presidio, 1937, 1987, 1999, xiv, 784 pp. A classic surevey of military science, a sequel to the previous entry; encyclopedic on battles.

2707 -------. A History of the Peninsular War. 7 vols. Oxford: Clarendon; London: Greenhill, 1902-1930, 1980, 1995-1997, 4545 pp. A massive history, chronological format, each volume covers about a year, 1807-1814; the standard recently reprinted.

2708 O'Meara, Barry E. Napoleon at St. Helena. Alt. title: Napoleon in Exile. 2 vols. Paris: Foundation; London: Bentley; NY: AMS, 1822, 1853, 1888, 1969, 1993. Originally in French; recounts the period, 1815-1821; Napoleon a prisoner and the responsibility of RN.

2709 O'Melinn, Liam S. "The English West Indies and the English Civil War." Ph.D. diss, Yale, 1991, 439 pp. British planters on Barbados and elsewhere hoped to stay out of Civil War but were openly loyal to Charles I; Parliament upset and sent a fleet and colonies overwhelmed, a situation that remained unchanged later.

2710 Oppenheim, Michael. A History of the Administration of the Royal Navy, 1509-1660. London: Lane; Brookfield: Gover, 1896, 1961, 1988, xiii, 411 pp. Intro: Kenneth Andrews; further vols. planned but not published; has remained the standard on the 16th and 17th centuries despite some errors and an anti-government bias.

2711 [NRS 8]. Oppenheim, Michael, ed. Naval Accounts and Inventories of the Reign of Henry VII, 1485-1488 and 1495-1497. Publications of the Navy Records Society, vol. 8. London: NRS, 1896, lvi, 349 pp. Records of "the Kyngis Shipps," e.g., accounts of expenses, e.g., construction of the dry dock at Portsmouth; origin of the bounty system.

2712 [NRS 22, 23, 43, 45, and 47]. Oppenheim, Michael, ed. The Naval Tracts of of Sir William Monson in Six Books. 5 vols. Publications of the Navy Records Society, vols. 22, 23, 43, 45, and 47. London: NRS, 1902-1914, lxvi, 395, viii, 395, x, 443, x, 444, and xii, 370 pp. Informative introductions by Oppenheim; a series of narratives describing operations during the Anglo-Spanish War, e.g., those of Drake and Hawkins; others about private adventurers and their prizes; Monson was later "Admiral of the Narrow Seas."

2713 Orde, Denis A. Nelson's Mediterranean Command: Concerning Pride, Preference, and Prize Money. London: Pentland, 1997, xiv, 228 pp. Illustrated; re events and personalities of officers and commanders of British forces in the Mediterranean, e.g., Jervis, Nelson, mutinies, threats of invasion; includes feuds among the commanders.

2714 Ormrod, D.J. "Anglo-Dutch Commerce, 1700-1760." Ph.D. diss, Cambridge, 1977. A scholarly study of this important competition.

2715 Ortiz-Sotelo, J. "Peru and the British Naval Station, 1808-1839." Ph.D. diss, St. Andrews, 1998. A case study of a RN station, in this case to protect British interests in the Pacific; primary responsibility was to British merchants; time of independence meant more pressures and threats.

2716 O'Sullivan, Dan. The Age of Discovery, 1400-1550. London: Longman, 1984, viii, 136 pp. A general overview; chapters on Prince Henry, Spain, and England, e.g., the Cabots and the role of Bristol and its merchants; little documentation about Cabots, not even clear which, John or Sabastian, did which.

2717 Owen, David R. and Tolley, Michael C. Courts of Admiralty in Colonial America: The Maryland Experience, 1634-1776. Durham: Carolina Academic, 1995, xxxiii, 421 pp. A case study of Vice-Admiralty Courts; study of 150 cases; primary duty to enforce Navigation Acts; also shipping contracts and wages of seamen; after Revolution, little change, thus a precedent for U.S. Admiralty Courts.

2718 Owen, J.H. War at Sea under Queen Anne, 1702-1708. NY: Macmillan; Cambridge: Cambridge UP, 1938, xii, 316 pp. Recounts naval operations in the War of Spanish Succession; a series of tactical disasters; Prince George, husband of Anne, LHA until his death in 1708, then Anne took over; Rooke and Shovell also; former captured Gibraltar.

2719 Owens, W.R. and Furbank, P.N., eds. Political and Economic Writings of Daniel Defoe. 8 vols. London: Chatto, 2000, 3200 pp. The 1st of a series of publications for all of the works of Defoe, projected to be 44 vols. and to take 7 years; Defoe an apologist for 1688 and 1714 and for the "Protestant" cause.

2720 Ozveren, Y. Eyup. "Shipbuilding, 1590-1790." Review, 23 (2000): 1-86. A special edition on 1 of 3 premier industrial productions, introduced by Immanuel Wallerstein; for warships, the Venetians began from the Venice Arsenal; Ragusans challenged, then Portuguese, Spanish, Dutch, French, and English; timber-related activities: tar-processing, sailcloth, and cordage.

2721 Paasch, Heinrich. Paasch's Illustrated Marine Dictionary. Maritime Classics series. London: Conway; NY: Lyons, 1885, 1997, 408 pp. Nautical dictionary, glossary of nautical terms including French and German equivalents.

2722 Pack, A. J. The Man Who Burned the White House: Admiral Sir George Cockburn, 1772-1853. Annapolis: NIP, 1987, 288 pp. A full biography; reviews his career, e.g., acolyte for Nelson, admiral at age 40, "Predator of the Chesapeake," gaoler of Napoleon, MP and First Naval Lord.

2723 -------. Nelson's Blood: The Story of Naval Rum. Havant: Mason, 1982, 1983, 196 pp. Fwd: Terence Lewin; daily rum ration named for Vernon, "Old Grogram" or "Nelson's Blood"; high point in mid-19th century; officially abolished 31 July 1970; 300 years of tradition.

2724 Pack, S.W.C. Admiral Lord Anson: The Story of Anson's Voyage and Naval Events of His Day. London: Cassell, 1960, xviii, 262 pp. The 1st of the great 18th century admirals; circumnavigation in the 1740s, taking Manila galleon and other booty, thence to Admiralty and MP; credited as "Father of the Navy" and able administrator.

2725 -------. The WAGER Mutiny. London: Redman, 1964, 256 pp. An incident on Anson's circumnavigation of 1740s; WAGER turned back at Cape Horn and wrecked, mutiny, and murder of Captain; later court martial of those who returned to England; no convictions.

2726 Padfield, Peter. Armada: A Celebration of the Four Hundredth Anniversary of the Defeat of the Spanish Armada, 1588-1988. Annapolis: NIP; London: Gollancz, 1988, 208 pp. By the prolific popular naval historian; large folio size, profusely illustrated; based on his interests and experience which includes sailing in replicas, best on guns and ships; use of term "defeat" no longer politically, or historically, correct.

2727 -------. Broke of the SHANNON. London: Hodder, 1968, 246 pp. A popular biography.

2728 -------. Guns at Sea. London: Evelyn; NY: St. Martin, 1972, 1973, 320 pp. Folio size, profusely illustrated; a survey from earliest times to the present, focusing on the technical and the tactical.

2729 -------. Maritime Supremacy and the Opening of the Western Mind: Naval Campaigns that Shaped the Modern World, 1588-1782. London: Murray; NY: Overlook, 1999, vii, 340 pp. Illustrated; thesis: maritime supremacy was the key to Western hegemony and that a factor of political, economic, social, and naval developments; key was set of decisive battles; begins with Armada, yet Dutch were actually the 1st, then to British, and later to Americans; other important battles, e.g., Sole Bay, Finisterre, and the Saints.

2730 -------. Nelson's War. London: Hart-Davis, 1976, 200 pp. The war of 1793-

1815 was the great turning point of history, the beginning of Pax Britannica.

2731 -------. Tides of Empire: Decisive Naval Campaigns in the Rise of the West. 2 vols. I: 1481-1654. II: 1654-1763. London: Routledge, 1979-1982, 546 pp. Fwd: Ian Jacob; projected 4 vols., only 2 published; combination of expansionism and imperialism; the "tide" sequence: Portugal, Spain, the Dutch, and Britain; themes, e.g., monopolistic trade, piracy, privateering, war, plunder, and destruction; superficial, not scholarly.

2732 Pagano de Divitiis, Gigliola. English Merchants in Seventeenth-Century Italy. NY: Cambridge UP, 1997, xv, 202 pp. Trans: Stephen Parkin; a manifestation of the shift of European finance center from the Mediterranean to the North; Italian shipping, e.g., from Genoa, Venice, and Florence to Amsterdam and London; all facilitated by dominance of the English navy and use of armed forces to promote trade; English gains due to war and privateering.

2733 Paine, Ralph D. The Fight for a Free Sea: A Chronicle of the War of 1812. Chronicles of America series. New Haven: Yale UP, 1920, xii, 235 pp. The stereotypical American bias; chapters, e.g., "On to Canada," Navy in Blue Water, Matchless Frigates, and Peace with Honor; and some excerpts, e.g., "the greatest armed conflict of all time," "a victory," and the war cry: "Free Trade and Sailors' Rights"; and bibliographical assessments, e.g., A. Mahan: "the final word"; T. Roosevelt: "spirited and accurate"; and William James: "irritating reading," "glaring inaccuracies," and "his venomous hatred of Americans."

2734 Palmer, A.J. "The 'Military Revolution' Afloat: The Era of the Anglo-Dutch Wars and the Transition to Modern Warfare at Sea." War in History, 4 (1997): 123-49. An extended article incorporating the debate over "the Military Revolution" into a phase of naval warfare.

2735 Palmer, Micheal A. "Lord Nelson: Master of Command." NWCR, 41 (Winter 1988): 105-16. Mahan said, within Nelson could be found all that was right with RN; precipitated a revolution in naval warfare; the "Nelson Touch" and "Band of Brothers"; and, from Sam Slick: "that cripple-gaited, one-eyed, one-armed little naval critter."

2736 -------. "'The Soul's Right Hand': Command and Control in the Age of Fighting Sail, 1652-1827." J Military History, 61 (October 1997): 679-706. An assessment of Fighting Instructions and line-of-battle; from 1653, that was the standard fighting formation despite problems of command and control; the result was a series of indecisive confrontations; then Vernon, Anson, Hawke, Rodney, and, especially, Nelson altered it, favoring decentralized command.

2737 Palmer, M.A.J. "Sir John's Victory: The Battle of Cape St. Vincent Reconsidered." MM, 77 (February 1991): 31-46. Lamented "some curious deficiencies in the English account"; to reconsider, e.g., look at log of HMS VICTORY, the flagship; much detail on early phase; Nelson's action was a brilliant move but breaking the line was not new; the victory was great for the time: invasion threat ended and a psychological defeat for Spain.

2738 Palmer, Roy, ed. The Valiant Sailor: Sea Songs and Ballads and Prose Passages Illustrating Life on the Lower Deck in Nelson's Navy. The Resources of Music series. London: Cambridge UP, 1973, 64 pp. Extensively researched; nautical songs and ballads demonstrating the view of the lower deck: appalling conditions, floating prisons; also about bravery, loyalty, and beauty.

2739 Palmer, Roy. The Water Closet: A New History. Newton Abbot: David and Charles, 1973, 141 pp. A colorful history of this necessary facility.

2740 Palmer, Sarah and William, Glyndwr, eds. Charted and Uncharted Waters: Proceedings of a Conference on the Study of British Maritime History, 8-11 September 1981, Queen Mary College, London. London: NMM, 1982, viii, 260 pp. 12 outstanding papers from experts, most for the post-1815 period; pertinent, e.g., J.S. Bromley on Admiralty reforms of the lower deck and Conrad Dixon on victualling and diet of seamen; very informative and essential reading.

2741 Palmer, Sarah. Politics, Shipping and the Repeal of the Navigation Laws. Manchester: Manchester UP, 1990, 1991, x, 209 pp. Re protection of shipping interests in British history accomplished for 200 years, 1650s-1850s, by the Navigation Acts; recalled the rationale: maritime power and national defense depended on the ability to man the navy with skilled seamen, which, in turn, relied on the merchant marine as supply or "nursery" of seamen.

2742 Paluka, Frank. The Three Voyages of Captain Cook. Princeton: Beta Phi Mu, 1974, 80 pp. An elegant production with concise narrative describing essentials of the 3 voyages, all supported by excellent bibliographical footnotes.

2743 Panzac, Daniel. "Armed Peace in the Mediterranean, 1736-1739: A Comparative Survey of the Navies." MM, 84 (February 1998): 41-55. In analyzing the naval situation in the Mediterranean prior to the beginning of a long war; tables on size, age, firepower, crew size, pay, budgets, diet, and shipbuilding capacity of warships: Venice, Ottoman Empire, Britain, France, and Spain.

2744 Pares, Richard. Colonial Blockade and Neutral Rights, 1739-1763. Oxford: Clarendon, 1938, vii, 323 pp. During the period between the War of Austrian Succession and the Seven Years' War, British policies toward neutrals and commerce; related was the issue of privateering and the Rule of 1753.

2745 -------. "The Manning of the Royal Navy in the West Indies, 1702-1763." Trans RHS, 4th ser, 20 (1937): 31-60. For Britain and France, a problem of manning for naval operations in the West Indies; problems due to attractions to privateers and the merchant marine, plus disease and climate; forced to resort to press gangs and even the use of POWs.

2746 -------. War and Trade in the West Indies, 1739-1763. Oxford: Clarendon; London: Cass, 1936, 1963, xi, 631 pp. During 2 major wars, the West Indies seen as most valuable; focus not on battles but on crucial diplomatic crises, 1739-1741 and 1761-1762; war seen as social institution; a critique of "drum and trumphet" military history.

2747 Paret, Peter, ed. Makers of Modern Strategy: From Machiavelli to the Nuclear Age. Princeton: Princeton UP, 1986, vii, 941 pp. An update of a classic of 1943, 28 essays by experts on the making of modern strategy, e.g., on Vauban, Mahan, and Brodie.

2748 Parker, Geoffrey and Thompson, I.A.A. "The Battle of Lepanto, 1571: The Costs of Victory." MM, 64 (February 1978): 13-22. Lepanto often linked to and compared with the Armada; this detailed calculations on costs of the Holy League, Spain, Venice, and the Papacy, in confronting the Turks in the late 16th century; conclusion: Lepanto and its costs did nothing to improve security against the Turks.

2749 Parker, Geoffrey. "The DREADNOUGHT Revolution of Tudor England." MM, 82 (August 1996): 269-300. An analysis of the performance of gunnery during the Armada campaign; Spanish suffered losses but most due to non-English factors, plus, among other limiting factors, 2-wheeled gun carriages; for the English, not one reference to structural damage from Spanish gunnery; summary of reasons for English success.

2750 -------. The Grand Strategy of Philip II. New Haven: Yale UP, 1998, xxvi, 446 pp. On the occasion of the quadricentennial of his death; revision: Philip did formulate a grand strategy, a conclusion contrary to those of Braudel, Kennedy, and Kamen, among others; Philip ruled the 1st global empire and had excellent communications; admittedly, strategic errors.

2751 -------. "If the Armada Had Landed." History, 61 (1976): 358-68. Counterfactual speculation; from a paper given at an Armada symposium, 1974.

2752 -------. The Military Revolution: Military Innovation and the Rise of the West, 1500-1800. NY: Cambridge UP, 1987, 1988, 1996, xix, 265 pp. The Lees Knowles Lectures; a detailed and controversial analysis of the superiority of European military developments; based on the thesis of Michael Roberts; conclusion: the military revolution in Europe permitted Europeans to defeat larger native forces all over the world and gain hegemony; included chapters on naval warfare, trade, and colonial developments

2753 -------. Philip II. London: Hutchinson; Boston: Little, Brown, 1978, 1979, xix, 234 pp. A solid, up-to-date biography by a noted authority.

2754 Parker, Geoffrey, ed. The Thirty Years' War. NY: Routledge, 1984, 1997, xliii, 340 pp. Essays by experts, e.g., Simon Adams, John Elliott, and Michael Roberts, providing comprehensive coverage, e.g., preliminaries, the indecisive phase, and "total war" phase, concluding with "myth, legend, and history."

2755 Parker, Geoffrey. "Why the Armada Failed." HisTod, 38 (May 1988): 26-33 and MHQ, 1 (Autumn 1988): 18-27. An analysis by an expert and prolific scholar; noted advent of massive new research results, e.g., from nautical archaeology and Spanish archives.

2756 Parker, John. Books to Build an Empire: A Bibliographical History of English Overseas Interests to 1620. Amsterdam: Israel, 1965, 1966, vii, 290 pp. A survey of 267 titles, a literature dealing with overseas propaganda, navigation, and travel; features, e.g., Cabot, Caxton, role of Bristol, and, especially, the Richard Hakluyts.

2757 Parker, John, ed. Merchants and Scholars: Essays in the History of Exploration and Trade. Minneapolis: Minn UP, 1965, vi, 258 pp. Dedicated to the memory of J.F. Bell; essays by experts, e.g., Helen Wallis, Frank Gillis, David Quinn, and Paul Bamford.

2758 Parkin, Ray. HM Bark ENDEAVOUR: Her Place in Australian History. Melbourne: Melbourne UP; London: Gazelle, 1997, xi, 467 pp. A superb boxed set production profusely illustrated; the 1st Pacific voyage; origins, details, and schematics of ENDEAVOUR, plus the human story, e.g., re scurvy and the delightful analysis of wildlife in ship's biscuits by Joseph Banks; a replica was built and sailed in the 1990s.

2759 Parkinson, C. Northcote. Britannia Rules: The Classic Age of Naval History, 1793-1815. London: Weidenfeld; Stroud: Sutton, 1977, 1996, ix, 199 pp. A detailed story of British preparations for war with France, Admiralty organization, operations, dockyards, health matters, tactics, and battles.

2760 -------. Dead Reckoning. London: Murray, 1978, 276 pp. Nautical fiction; hero is Guernseyman, Richard Delancey.

2761 -------. The Devil to Pay. London: Murray, 1973. Nautical fiction; another Delancey novel.

2762 -------. Edward Pellew, Viscount Exmouth: Admiral of the Red. London: Methuen; London: Chatham 1934, 2002, 478 pp. The Julian Corbett Prize, 1935; biography of the renowned frigate captain and model for naval leadership.

2763 -------. The Fireship. London: Murray, 1975, 187 pp. Nautical fiction; hero is Guernseyman, Richard Delancey.

2764 -------. "Greenwich Historians." Fortnightly Review, 160 (December 1946): 432-36. A tribute to Geoffrey Callender who died 6 November 1946; saw him in "apostolic succession": Corbett, Laughton, Callender, and Michael Lewis; the "Greenwich School" of historians.

2765 -------. The Guernseyman. Ithaca: McBooks, 2001, 208 pp. The first of the Richard Delancey nautical fiction works.

2766 -------. The Life and Times of Horatio Hornblower. Boston: Little, Brown; London: Penguin; Stroud: Sutton, 1970, 1973, 1996, 304 pp. Seemingly a formal biography of a prominent and successful naval figure based on discovery of new material; presented as serious and scholarly biography, following closely the story line of the 11 Hornblower novels by C.S. Forester; Times Literary Supplement, 9 July 1971, treated it as non-fiction biography.

2767 -------. Portsmouth Point: The Navy in Fiction. Liverpool: Liverpool UP; London: Hodder, 1948, 154 pp. An anthology of passages, quotes from 35 naval novels, two from 1805; from the "school of Captain Marryat"; Marryat influenced by Tobias Smollett; elsewhere, Parkinson created hero-seaman: Richard Delancey.

2768 Parkinson, C. Northcote, ed. Samuel Walters, Lieutenant, RN. Liverpool: Liverpool UP, 1949. For the Liverpool NRS; publication of a manuscript-journal covering 1797-1810.

2769 Parkinson, C. Northcote. So Near, So Far. London: Murray. More nautical fiction.

2770 -------. Touch and Go. London: Murray; Series #5, Ithaca: McBrooks, 1977, 2003, 272 pp. Nautical fiction; Richard Delancey novel.

2771 -------. Trade in the Eastern Seas, 1793-1813. London: Cambridge UP; NY: Kelley, 1937, 1966, xii, 434 pp. Laments neglect of maritime history which is essential to understand English history; actually, trade and war in the East, e.g., naval protection and RN.

2772 Parkinson, C. Northcote, ed. The Trade Winds: A Study of British Overseas Trade during the French Wars, 1793-1815. London: Allen, 1948, 336 pp. Intro: William James; essays by experts on different trades, insurance, ports, seamen, health, and RN.

2773 Parkinson, C. Northcote. War in the Eastern Seas, 1793-1815. London: Allen, 1954, 477 pp. A monograph on a neglected aspect of sea power.

2774 -------. "War and Trade in the Far East, 1803-1815." Ph.D. diss, London, 1935. The basis of some of these entries.

2775 Parkinson, Roger. The Peninsular War. Wordsworth Military Library series. London: Hart-Davis, 1973, 2000, 208 pp. A recent reprint of a general survey.

2776 Parkinson, Sydney. A Journal of a Voyage to the South Seas: In His Majesty's Ship the ENDEAVOUR: Faithfully Transcribed. London: Caliban, 1784, 1984, xxiv, 212 pp. A reprint of the original journal with excellent illustrations.

2777 Parks, George B. "Richard Hakluyt and the English Voyages." Ph.D. diss, Columbia, 1928 pp. The basis of the next entry.

2778 -------. Richard Hakluyt and the English Voyages. NY: American Geographic; NY: Ungar, 1928, 1930, 1961, xix, 288 pp. Ed: James Williamson; the definitive biography; there are two Hakluyts, one a minister, ward and cousin to the younger, a lawyer; the elder, essentially the first professional geographer.

2779 Parry, Henry. Minutes of the Proceedings at a Court Martial: Assembled for the Trial of Captain John Mountray of HM Ship RAMILLES; Respecting the Cause, Circumstances, and Capture, of the Convoy under His Charge, on the 9th of August Last, by the Enemy's Fleet. London: Fielding; NY: Arno, 1781, 1969, 170 pp. By the clerk; the proceedings of this court martial consisting of Admiral Rowley and 11 Captains held at Jamaica; findings: guilty; punishment: dismissed the service.

2780 Parry, J.H. The Age of Reconnaissance: Discovery, Exploration and Settlement, 1450 to 1650. Berkeley: U Cal P; NY: Praeger, 1963, 1969, 1981; xvi, 366 pp. One of a trilogy; this on the conditions, story, and fruits of discovery; themes, e.g., commerce, ships, shipbuilding, navigation, and fighting capacity.

2781 -------. The Discovery of the Sea. NY: Dial; Berkeley: U Cal P, 1974, 1975, 1981, xvii, 302 pp. Third of the trilogy; a survey of geography and maritime history.

2782 -------. The Establishment of the European Hegemony, 1415-1715: Trade and Exploration in the Age of the Renaissance. NY: Harper, 1961, 1966, 176 pp. How and why Europe achieved hegemony, e.g., the tools of empire: ships, guns, and charts.

2783 -------. Romance of the Sea. Wash: National Geographic, 1981, 312 pp. Very large folio size with beautiful color photos, some double page, a masterpiece; history of seafaring, e.g., the Vikings, the Portuguese, Magellan, Nelson, life on the lower deck, piracy, and whaling.

2784 -------. The Spanish Seaborne Empire. History of Human Society. Berkeley: U Cal P; NY: Penguin, 1966, 1973, xxiv, 338 pp. A standard history of Spanish imperial developments, 15th-19th centuries; an important contribution by a preeminent scholar.

2785 -------. Trade and Dominion: The European Overseas Empires in the Eighteenth Century. NY: Praeger, 1971, xvii, 408 pp. Second of the trilogy; traces the development of European empires, e.g., ships, sailors, charts, navigators, and areas of conflict.

2786 Parsons, George S. Nelsonian Reminiscences: Leaves from Memory's Log. Sailors' Tales series. London: Chatham, 1843, 1905, 1998, 332 pp. Ed: W.H. Long; Parsons, 1783-1854; an eyewitness account of naval service, 1795-1810, e.g., with

Nelson during his controversial time at Naples.

2787 Pastor, Xavier. The Ships of Christopher Columbus: SANTA MARIA, NINA, and PINTA. The Anatomy of the Ship series. Annapolis: NIP, 1992, 128 pp. On the occasion of the 500th anniversary, 240 illustrations; typical ships of the 15th century, caravels; poor content and narrow focus; replicas of SANTA MARIA, 1892, 1927, and 1964; all 3, 1992.

2788 The Patrick O'Brian 1995 Calander. Rockville: Kramer, 1995. Calendar format; illustrations, paintings of book covers, by Geoff Hunt.

2789 Patterson, A. Temple. A History of Southampton, 1700-1914. 3 vols. Southampton: Southampton UP, 1966-1975. An extensive survey; Southampton was a very important port, commercial and naval, in past times.

2790 [NRS 108 and 111]. Patterson, A. Temple, ed. The Jellicoe Papers. 2 vols. Publications of the Navy Records Society, vols. 108 and 111. London: NRS, 1966-1968, viii, 315 and xvi, 497 pp. From the papers of Jellicoe, commander during the battle of Jutland and, later, First Sea Lord; over 60 pages on the controversy about Jutland; informative about the writing of the official history by Corbett.

2791 Patterson, A. Temple. The Naval Mutiny at Spithead, 1797. Portsmouth Papers, # 5. Portsmouth: City Council, 1968, 15 pp. The result of discontent on the lower deck, exaggerated because in the midst of a major war; Spithead between Portsmouth and the Isle of Wight, a large anchorage area.

2792 -------. The Other Armada: The Franco-Spanish Attempt to Invade Britain in 1779. NY: Barnes; Manchester: Manchester UP, 1960, ix, 247 pp. During the War of American Independence; British forces were abroad and a superior enemy fleet was present, yet the operation failed; French overextended financially.

2793 Patterson, Benton Rain. Harold and William: The Battle for England, 1064-1066. NY: Cooper Square, 2001, xxiv, 209 pp. A review of the conflict between them; illustrations from the Bayeux tapestry.

2794 Paviot, Jacques. The Naval Policies of the Dukes of Burgundy, 1384-1482. Lille: Lille UP, 1995, 387 pp. Follows these policies of 4 consecutive Dukes; a naval build-up in the Channel and North Sea; how each Duke pursued naval policies, especially re England, e.g., Philip the Bold planned an invasion in the 1380s but his successor was more conciliatory.

2795 -------. "La Politique Navale des Ducs de Bourgogue, 1384-1482." Ph.D. diss, Sorbonne, 1993, 387 pp. The basis of the previous entry.

2796 Pawson, Michael and Buisseret, David. Port Royal, Jamaica. Oxford: Clarendon, 1975, xv, 204 pp. The English came to Jamaica, late 1650s, as part of the Western Design of Cromwell; established privateering and, later, a naval, base;

then, the earthquake of 1692; archaeological evidence is informative.

2797 Payne, J. Memoir of the Life of Admiral Lord Nelson. Norwich: Payne, (1801?). A pamphlet format, a very early published account of Nelson by a "neighbor."

2798 Pearman, Robert. The Cadogans at War, 1783-1862: The Third Earl Cadogan and His Family. London: Haggerston, 1990, 208 pp. Service at age 12 aboard INDEFATIGABLE, famous frigate of Edward Pellew; follows career of naval officer and life aboard ship; noted observing Nelson Column construction in Trafalgar Square.

2799 Pears, Edwin. "The Spanish Armada and the Ottoman Porte." EHR, 31 (July 1893): 439-66. Clearly, English relations and contacts with the Eastern Mediterranean increased in the 16th century, an English consul to Chios since 1513; Elizabeth officially sought assistance from the Turks, citing commercial and religious grounds; attack the Spanish to divert them; however, Lepanto and a war with Persia deterred the Turks from lending aid to England.

2800 Pearsall, Alan W.H. "The Royal Navy and Trade Protection, 1688-1714." Renaissance and Modern Studies, 30 (1989): 109-23. A survey of this essential and formative series of operations.

2801 -------. The Second Dutch War, 1665-1667. London: HMSO, 1967. A NMM pamphlet supporting an exhibition.

2802 Pearson, Michael P., et al. "Three Men and a Boat: SUTTON HOO and the East Saxon Kingdom." Anglo-Saxon England, 22 (1993). An article reviewing the findings.

2803 Pearson, W.H. "Hawkesworth's Alterations." J Pacific History, 7 (1972): 45-72. Part of the ongoing controversy about publication of journals of exploration voyages, in this case, the 1st voyage of Cook; John Hawkesworth tampered with the original documents; the motives and rationales were more complex than previously thought.

2804 Peck, Linda L. Court Patronage and Corruption in Early Stuart England. Boston: Hyman, 1990, 1991, 1993, xii, 319 pp. Re instances of corruption, e.g., in the administration of the navy, the second largest department; features, e.g., public and private interests overlapped, bribery, sale of offices, the Pett family, and ship money.

2805 Peddie, John. Alfred: Warrior King. NY: Sutton, 1999, xv, 224 pp. Folio size, slick production with drawings and colored pictures; analysis of military aspects, e.g., Viking raids, inshore and river estuary battles, and his "newly founded navy" with ships "of superior size."

2806 -------. Invasion: The Roman Invasion of Britain in the Year 43 and the Events Leading to Their Occupation of the West Country. Alt. title: Conquest. NY: St. Martin, 1987, 1997, xv, 214 pp. Incorporates new archaeological evidence; during reign of Claudius, 45,000 men and 15,000 animals would have required over 900 ships; shipping described; thence 3 routes inland, to Lincoln, to the Midlands, and to the Southwest; emphasis on the latter.

2807 Pengelly, Colin A. The First BELLERPHON. London: Baker, 1966, 303 pp. Preface: Christopher Lloyd; design by Slade who also designed HMS VICTORY; BELLERPHON, 1st of '74s, two decks, launched 1786; at Glorious 1st of June, the Nile, Trafalgar, carried Napoleon to NORTHAMPTON, thence to St. Helena, convict hulk, and broken up in 1836.

2808 Penn, Christopher D. The Navy under the Early Stuarts and Its Influence on English History. Manchester: Faith, 1913, 1970, xvi, 302 pp. After 1603, terms used: deterioration, corruption, malpractice, and chaos; features, e.g., Buckingham, Algiers expedition, Cadiz, Re, La Rochelle, and ship money; the Commonwealth meant rehabilitation plus Blake, Monck, Penn, and Lawson.

2809 Pennell, C.R., ed. Bandits at Sea: A Pirates Reader. NY: NYUP, 2001, ix, 351 pp. An anthology about pirates and piracy.

2810 -------, ed. Piracy and Diplomacy in Seventeenth-Century North Africa: The Journal of Thomas Baker, English Consul in Tripoli, 1677-1685. London: Associated UP, 1989, 261 pp. Baker died, 1720; informative introduction; summary of relationships, English, Dutch, French, and North Africa; the English concluded a treaty and were less bothered.

2811 Pennington, L.E., ed. The Purchas Handbook: Studies of the Life, Times and Writings of Samuel Purchas, 1577-1626. 2 vols. Publications of the Hakluyt Society, 2nd ser, # 185 and 186. London: Hakluyt Society, 1997, xxiv, 811 pp. Purchase was an Anglican cleric who saw himself as successor to the Hakluyts; compiled a 4-vol. collection, 1625, but inferior to earlier works; extensive introduction.

2812 Penrose, Boies. Travel and Discovery in the Renaissance, 1420-1620. Cambridge: Cambridge UP; Cambridge: Harvard UP, 1952, 1971, xvi, 369 pp. A survey of European expansion to non-European areas, e.g., the Portuguese, Columbus, Magellan, the Dutch, the English, the search for Passages, Northeast and Northwest; good survey of the literature.

2813 Penrose, Charles V. A Friendly Address to the Seamen of the British Navy. London: Liddell, 1820, 16 pp. A pamphlet of advice by Sir Charles Penrose; one observer assessed it as "a gross whitewash."

2814 -------. Observations on Corporal Punishment, Impressment and Other Matters Relative to the Present State of HM Royal Navy. London: Bodmin, 1824, 66 pp. A treatise making observations about the 2 most pressing issues of the day re naval reform.

2815 Pepys, Samuel. Catalogue of the Pepys Library of Magdalene College. 5 vols. Woodbridge: Brewer, 1989-1994. Ed: David McKitterick; 7 vols. planned; a catalogue for 114 vols. of papers; Pepys prepared some of it himself and Pepys began to prepare to write a history of the navy; listings by topics, e.g., maps, drawings, music, and ballads.

2816 -------. Concise Pepys Diary. Wordsworth Classic in World Literature. London: Wordsworth, 1997, 800 pp. An abridged version in print.

2817 -------. Diary. Various number of vols. London: Bell; NY: Harper; Berkeley: U Cal P, 1825, 1893-1899, 1926, 1970-1983, 1995. Eds: Richard Braybrooke, H.B. Wheatley, Robert Latham, and William Matthews; covers 1660-1669, Pepys, age 26-36; a great piece of modern literature; Latham-Matthews edition latest and best: 11 vols., basically, 1 vol. per year, 1660-1669, plus Companion and Index vols.

2818 -------. Letters and the Second Diary of Samuel Pepys. London: Dent, 1932, 1933, xxiv, 456 pp. Ed: R.G. Howarth; less significant than the classic covering the 1660s; most are private letters, e.g., to Evelyn; "second" diary covers 9 years, later in his career.

2819 Perez-Reverte, Arturo. The Nautical Chart. London: Picador, 2002, 466 pp. Trans: Margaret sayers; nautical fiction by a Spanish novelist; chasing and sinking a pirate ship in the 18th century; map indicating location of this sunken treasure ship.

2820 Perkins, Bradford, ed. The Causes of the War of 1812: National Honor or National Interest? NY: Holt, 1962, 124 pp. Essays, e.g., Henry Adams, J. Pratt, R. Horsman, and George Dangerfield; subjects, e.g., varied interpretations, mixed motives, complex causes, and contrasting arguments.

2821 Perkins, Roger and Douglas-Morris, K.J. Gunfire in Barbary: Admiral Lord Exmouth's Battle with the Corsairs of Algiers in 1816. Havant: Mason, 1982, 200 pp. Definitive on a neglected topic; Pellew, the noted frigate captain, was commander of this Anglo-Dutch expedition, bombarding Algiers and suppressing White Christian slavery.

2822 Perrett, Bryan. The Real Hornblower: The Life of Admiral of the Fleet Sir James Alexander Gordon, GCB: Last Governor of the Royal Naval Hospital, Greenwich. Annapolis: NIP; London: Arms, 1997, 160 pp. Clearly, in his book on the War of 1812, Forester was impressed with the exploits of Gordon; inspiration for nautical fiction mentioned throughout; Gordon to RN, age 11, and up to Admiral of the Fleet; among exploits, captured Alexandria and attacked Baltimore, total of 75 years in RN; Hornblower designation not convincing.

2823 [NRS 51]. Perrin, William G., ed. The Autobiography of Phineas Pett.

Publications of the Navy Records Society, vol. 51. London: NRS, 1918, civ, 244 pp. Pett, 1570-1638; probably written in sections and stops abruptly, 1638; Pepys copied the MSS; emphasis on the development of shipwrights; many details supplied by Perrin.

2824 [NRS 65]. Perrin, William G., ed. Boteler's Dialogues. Publications of the Navy Records Society, vol. 65. London: NRS, 1929, xl, 341 pp. Re Nathaniel Butler, born 1577, a name which evolved into Boteler; early voyages to Virginia and the West Indies.

2825 Perrin, William G. British Flags: Their Early History, and Their Development at Sea. Cambridge: Cambridge UP, 1922, xii, 207 pp. Illustrated in color: Herbert Vaughn; the standard for this subject; 1st used in 17th century.

2826 [NRS 62, 90, and 96]. Perrin, William G. and Lloyd, Christopher, eds. The Keith Papers: Selected from the Letters and Papers of Admiral Viscount Keith. 3 vols. Publications of the Navy Records Society, vols. 62, 90, and 96. London: NRS, 1927-1956, 492, xii, 422, and xx, 394 pp. Various papers covering his career, 1772-1815; official documents and correspondence.

2827 Perrin, William G. "The Lord High Admiral and the Board of Admiralty." MM, 12 (April 1926): 117-44. The title was first used under Henry VIII; Buckingham raised it to its highest level and it declined after his death; went into Commission; informative on naval titles originating in the 13th century.

2828 [NRS 63]. Perrin, William G., ed. The Naval Miscellany. Publications of the Navy Records Society, vol. 63. London: NRS, 1928, xii, 483 pp. The 3rd of these miscellany volumes, e.g., operations of 1666, the Channel Fleet of 1779, some Nelson letters, instructions to Cook, and a description of the bombardment of Copenhagen of 1807.

2829 -------. Nelson's Signals: The Evolution of the Signal Flags. London: HMSO, 1908, 40 pp. A pamphlet published by the Admiralty when Perrin discovered an old signal book of 1804; determined which flags Nelson used at Trafalgar.

2830 Perroy, Edouard. The Hundred Years War. Bloomington: Ind UP; NY: Capricorn, 1945, 1959, 1965, 384 pp. Intro: David Douglas; actually written while in Gestapo jail; scholarship of 50 years; the old standard and a good 1-vol. study.

2831 Perry, Thomas M. The Discovery of Australia: The Charts and Maps of the Navigators and Explorers. Melbourne: Nelson, 1982, 159 pp. Folio size, illustrated with maps and charts; details of their origins, development, and use.

2832 Peters, Marie. The Elder Pitt. London: Longman, 1998, xiii, 284 pp. The long-awaited revision on Pitt; concluded Pitt subject to violent shifts; powerful while he controlled House of Commons and less when he went to Lords as Chatham; no sign of "Plan" and certainly not founder of British Empire; 2 bouts with manic depression, late 1760s and mid 1770s.

2833 -------. "The Myth of William Pitt, Earl of Chatham, Great Imperialist. Part I: Pitt and Imperial Expansion, 1738-1763. II: Chatham and Imperial Reorganization, 1763-1778." J Imperial and Commonwealth History, 21 and 22 (January 1993 and September 1994): 31-74 and 393-431. An extensive critical analysis and historiographical essay; a revisionist conclusion about Britain and British expansion in the 18th century, correcting "myths" about Pitt, e.g., there was no "plan" and Pitt was not the "great imperialist"; survey of biographical literature, e.g., Basil Williams, Corbett, Tunstall, Robertson, Plumb, Middleton, Namier, and Brewer.

2834 Petersen, Charles W. "English and Danish Naval Strategy in the Seventeenth Century." Ph.D. diss, Maine, 1975, 362 pp. Danish fleet developed to entice English into alliance but repeated failures to exploit hurt; leaders opted for Dutch and French and English retaliated.

2835 Petersson, Lennarth. Rigging Period Ship Models: A Step-by-Step Guide to the Intricacies of Square-Rig. London: Chatham, 2000, 128 pp. 400 drawings; the latest and ultimate guide for 18th century SOTL, e.g., requirements: 1000 blocks, miles of rigging, and acres of canvas.

2836 Petrides, Anne and Downs, Jonathan, eds. Sea Soldier: An Officer of Marines with Duncan, Nelson, Collingwood, and Cockburn: The Letters and Journals of Major T. Marmaduke Wybourn, RM, 1797-1813. Tunbridge Wells: Parapress, 2000, xi, 212 pp. A series of original papers; unfortunately, mostly personal items in letters to sisters; claims best material "lost in the post."

2837 Petrie, Donald A. The Prize Game: Lawful Looting on the High Seas in the Days of Fighting Sail. Annapolis: NIP, 1999, xiii, 217 pp. A comprehensive survey, explaining origins, distinctions between piracy and privateering, development, rules of the sea, prize courts, and decline; follows 5 case studies.

2838 Pettigrew, Thomas J. Memoirs of the Life of Vice-Admiral Lord Viscount Nelson. 2 vols. London: Boone, 1849, xxxvi, 1169 pp. By a naval surgeon, "Dr. Pettigrew"; a controversial "biography" allegedly based on letters of dubious origin held by Lady Hamilton; Laughton dubbed it "School for Scandal"; yet, he did know the truth about Horatia; generated much correspondence in The Times.

2839 Pfitzer, Gregory M. Samuel Eliot Morison's Historical World: In Quest of a New Parkman. Boston: Northeastern UP, 1991, 367 pp. Less biography than apologetics; a spectacular career as professor, sailor, biographer, official historian, and New England patriarch with 2 Pulitzer Prizes.

2840 Philbrick, Nathaniel. In the Heart of the Sea: The Tragedy of the Whaleship ESSEX. NY: HarperCollins, 2000, 302 pp. An award-winning bestseller; the Nantucket whaleship attacked and sunk by a whale in the Pacific, 20 November 1820; the incident was the inspiration for Moby Dick by Herman Melville.

2841 Philbrick Thomas. <u>James Fenimore Cooper and the Development of American Sea Fiction</u>. Cambridge: Harvard UP, 1961, xi, 329 pp. Cooper, 1789-1851, famous American writer of nautical fiction; influenced by Smollett and Marryat.

2842 Phillips, Carla Rahn. "The Evolution of Spanish Ship Design from the 15th to the 18th century." <u>AmNep</u>, 53 (Fall 1993): 229-38. Recent research in the Spanish archives; the transition to global voyaging was a dynamic period; the products were remarkably successful at fulfilling required functions.

2843 -------. <u>Six Galleons for the King of Spain: Imperial Defense in the Early Seventeenth Century</u>. Balt: JHUP, 1986, xiv, 318 pp. In 1620s, 6 galleons were built for the Crown; much detail of all aspects of the process, including descriptions of the infrastructure of Spanish "industry" demonstrating viability and progress, not "decline."

2844 Phillips, Cecil E. Lucas. <u>Cromwell's Captains</u>. London: Heinemann, 1938, ix, 426 pp. A series of biograhical studies, e.g., Hampden, Skippon, Blake, and Lambert.

2845 Phillips, C.W. "The SUTTON HOO Ship Burial." <u>MM</u>, 26 (October 1940): 346-55. An early announcement and description by the director of the "dig," estimated from about 630.

2846 Phillips, Edward J. "The Establishment of a Navy in Peter the Great's Russia: The Azov Fleet, 1688-1714." Ph.D. diss, North Carolina, 1990, 306 pp. The basis of the next entry.

2847 -------. <u>The Founding of Russia's Navy: Peter the Great and the Azov Fleet, 1688-1714</u>. Westport: Greenwood, 1995, ix, 214 pp. Peter captured Azov in 1696, the impetus for expanding his navy and the Great Embassy to Western Europe to gain technological expertise, e.g., at Portsmouth dockyard.

2848 Phillips, Gervase. <u>Anglo-Scots Wars, 1513-1550: A Military History</u>. <u>War in History</u> series. Woodbridge: Boydell, 1999, 291 pp. An account of warfare in early modern Europe; most on army operations but navies were required for transport, logistics, shore bombardment, and amphibious operations, e.g., 13 individual ships mentioned and Hertford-led campaign of 1544 from Newcastle bypassing Scottish strongholds involved a 200-ship armada landing 16,000 men; conclusion: Anglo-Scottish warfare looked ahead to the military revolution, not back to medieval times.

2849 Phillips, I. Lloyd. "The Evangelical Administrator: Sir Charles Middleton at the Navy Board, 1778-1790." D.Phil. diss, Oxford, 1974. A scholarly study of administration during this crucial period.

2850 Phillips, Lawrence. "The Abolition of the Rum Ration." <u>USNIP</u>, 96 (July

1970): 86-88. On the occasion of its abolition, details about the rum ration for RN over the years, e.g., 95.5 degrees proof, consisting of percentages of Demerara, Trinidad, and other: 60, 30, 10, respectively; 1/8 pint daily; began 1731, Vernon diluted it and the name "grog"; reduced by ½ in 1825 and again in 1850, the year it was abolished in USN.

2851 Phillips-Birt, Douglas H.C. A History of Seamanship. NY: Doubleday, 1971, vii, 319 pp. Profusely illustrated in color; a general survey for popular consumption; photos of navigation instruments, chronometers, and lighthouses.

2852 Phillipson, David J. Band of Brothers: Boy Seamen in the Royal Navy, 1800-1956. Stroud: Sutton; Annapolis: NIP, 1996, 1997, x, 150 pp. The "boy" rating from officer's servant of the 18th century; this about formal training at HMS GANGES and description of service life and daily routine; anecdotal; "Band of Brothers" inappropriate title; better title: "coming of age in the post-World War II RN."

2853 -------. Smuggling: A History, 1700-1970. Newton Abbot: David and Charles, 1973, 155 pp. A supreficial survey; re revenue cutters.

2854 Pierson, Peter O. Commander for the Armada: The Seventh Duke of Medina Sidonia. New Haven: Yale UP, 1989, 304 pp. The Duke, 1549-1615, was called up after the death of Santa Cruz; has not had a good press but rehabilitated by Williamson and Mattingly; a veteran commander who would lead creditably again; much on Armada.

2855 Pilgrim, Donald G. "The Uses and Limitations of French Naval Power in the Reign of Louis XIV: The Administration of the Marquis de Seignelay, 1683-1690." Ph.D. diss, Brown, 1969, 440 pp. An assessment of the times, e.g., the problems and limitations of naval development; French failure to follow-up the victory of Beachy Head is a case in point.

2856 Pincus, Steven C.A. Protestantism and Patriotism: Ideologies and the Making of English Foreign Policy, 1650-1668. Cambridge: Cambridge UP, 1995, 1996, 506 pp. A curious and complex study of religion, politics, foreign policy, ecnomics, the 1st and 2nd Anglo-Dutch wars, and the impact of ideology; ironic that both were Protestant, republican, highly cultured, and commercial competitors, so, strange that two wars would occur; look to internal political situations at the time, e.g., Puritanism and revolution, state of monarchy in both countries at the moment, and pure obstinancy.

2857 -------. "Protestantism and Patriotism: Ideologies and the Making of English Foreign Policy, 1650-1665." Ph.D. diss, Harvard, 1990. The basis of the previous entry.

2858 Pistono, Stephen P. "Henry IV and the English Privateers." EHR, 90 (April 1975): 322-30. Succession in 1399; problems of piracy in the Channel; evidence to support "school for seaman" thesis; Henry dependent on West Country pirates for "naval forces"; several named, e.g., Prince of Isle of Wight, Pay of Poole, and Hawley of Dartmouth.

2859 Pitch, Anthony S. The Burning of Washington: The British Invasion of 1814. Annapolis: NIP, 1998, 2000, xv, 298 pp. A narrative and limited account of campaigns against Alexandria, Washington, and Baltimore; no analysis.

2860 Pivka, Otto von. Navies of the Napoleonic Era. Newton Abbot: David and Charles; NY: Hippocrene, 1980, 272 pp. See companion Armies of. . . .; a concise account, e.g., national navies, ships, men, and engagements; many lists, e.g., losses.

2861 Platt, Colin. Medieval Southampton: The Port and Trading Community, AD 1000-1600. London: Routledge, 1973, xvi, 309 pp. A medieval entrepot, especially for wool and wine; important center for foreign merchants, especially from Italy and Gascony.

2862 Plowden, Alison. Armada 1588. London: English Heritage, 1988, 26 pp. Ed: Rick Nisbet; folio size, colorful pamphlet; a brief summary.

2863 -------. The Elizabethan Secret Service. NY: St. Martin; London: Harvester, 1991, xix, 158 pp. A lively, informative, and stimulating narrative re Elizabethan intrigue, espionage, conspiracies, spies, and double agents; describes an advanced intelligence network.

2864 Pocock, Tom. Battle for Empire: The Very First World War, 1756-1763. London: O'Mara, 1998, 272 pp. Pocock, born 1925, descendant of Nicholas Pocock, painter of Nelson and author of several books on Nelson; a popular narrative of the Seven Years' War; emphasis on foreign campaigns, e.g., in India, North America, the Caribbean, and Southeast Asia.

2865 -------. Captain Marryat: Seaman, Writer, and Adventurer. London: Chatham, 2000, 256 pp. Demonstrates what a professional naval officer can do on half-pay in peacetime; one of the most popular English writers of the 19th century; a great storyteller, direct progenitor of Forester and O'Brian; humorous and critic of Admiralty.

2866 -------. Horatio Nelson. London: Bodley; NY: Knopf, 1987, 1988, 1994, xx, 364 pp. A "warts and all" biography, e.g., his vanity, greed, and cruelty to his wife; bibliography lists 38 other biographies plus this 3rd one by Pocock.

2867 -------. "Lord Nelson: A Selected Bibliography." Naval History, 4 (Summer 1990): 64-66. Noted at least 200 biographies; Oliver Warner praised.

2868 -------. Nelson and the Campaign in Corsica. The Nelson 2005 Commemoration series, # 1. Hoylake: 1805 Club, 1994, iv, 26 pp. First in a series of commemorative pamphlets.

2869 -------. <u>Nelson and His World</u>. NY: Viking; London: Thames, 1968, 1974, 142 pp. Folio size with pictures and drawings; focus on places Nelson went and persons close to him.

2870 -------. <u>Nelson's Women</u>. London: Deutsch, 1999, x, 278 pp. Fills a gap and insightful, e.g., mother, 3 he pursued unsuccessfully, wife, mistress, and daughter.

2871 Pocock, Tom, ed. <u>Remember Nelson: The Life of Captain Sir William Hoste</u>. London: Collins, 1833, 1977, 256 pp. A memoir originally edited by the widow of Hoste, plus additional information from Pocock; Hoste was famous for displaying that signal before his battles, e.g., Lissa in 1811.

2872 Pocock, Tom. <u>Sailor King: The Life of King William IV</u>. London: Sinclair, 1991, xv, 254 pp. William was king in the 1830s, this biography stresses his early life in RN, 1779-1790, as sailor-prince.

2873 -------. <u>A Thirst for Glory: The Life of Admiral Sir Sidney Smith</u>. London: Aurum; NY: Random House, 1996, 1998, 261 pp. William Sydney Smith, 1764-1840, was a well-known, heroic, impulsive naval officer disliked by some of his peers, e.g., Nelson, Pellew, Collingwood, and Wellington; even Napoleon called him "half mad"; "hot dog" might be a descriptive term today; a review of his many exploits, e.g., distinguished himself at Toulon, captured Acre, and escaped from a Paris jail.

2874 -------. <u>The Young Nelson in the Americas</u>. London: Collins, 1980, 241 pp. Nelson commanded a frigate at age 21 and served extensively in the Caribbean; already distinguishing himself at this early age.

2875 Pohl, Frederick J. <u>Atlantic Crossings before Columbus</u>. NY: Norton, 1961. Notes the likelihood that adventurous Europeans other than the Norse reached America in the Middle Ages.

2876 -------. <u>Prince Henry Sinclair: His Expedition to the New World in 1398</u>. NY: Crown, 1974, 230 pp. Contention: Zeno documents indicate Sinclair, Earl of Orkney, also known as Prince Zichmni, led an expedition to the New World; Morison doubts it; various crossings by Irish, Norse, Bretons, Basques, and Portuguese, but few records.

2877 Pollington, Stephen. <u>The Warrior's Way: England in the Viking Age</u>. Wash: Kramer; NY: Sterling, 1989, 1990, 192 pp. Illustrated; re Viking attacks against the Anglo-Saxons, 9th-11th centuries, e.g., famous battle of Maldon, 991, in New Forest area: a Viking fleet of 93 ships, all depicted in a poem.

2878 Pollitt, Ronald L. "Beaucracy and the Armada: The Administrator's Battle." <u>MM</u>, 60 (May 1974): 119-32. Role of administration under Elizabeth neglected; a major contribution to English victory over the Armada, e.g., strategic planning by the Privy Council, provisions for materiel, financing, manning, maintenance, and equipping.

2879 -------. "Contingency Planning and the Defeat of the Spanish Armada." AmNep, 45 (Winter 1984): 25-32. English success was facilitated by government officials who planned and prepared; establishment of intelligence networks; as early as 1584, decision on strategy to prevent landing by the Spanish; praise for "naval bureaucratic prowess."

2880 -------. "The Elizabethan Navy Board: A Study in Administrative Revolution." Ph.D. diss, Northwestern, 1968, 347 pp. Henry VIII created the naval bureaucracy in 1546; Hawkins and Howard advanced it; a decisive contribution to the victory over the Armada.

2881 Pool, Bernard. "Lord Barham: A Great Naval Administrator." HisTod, 15 (May 1965): 347-54. Sir Charles Middleton, 1st Baron Barham, 1726-1813, First Lord after 1805.

2882 -------. Navy Board Contracts, 1660-1832: Contract Administration under the Navy Board. London: Longman; Hamden: Archon, 1966, 158 pp. The Board was responsible for shipbuilding, supply, refit, and repair, effectively running one of the largest industries in the world; a detailed description of the contract system; no records available about private yards.

2883 -------. "Pepys and the Thirty Ships." HisTod, 20 (July 1970): 489-95. Re the shipbuilding programme of 1677, Pepys seeing it as his major accomplishment; saw Pepys as the greatest administrator of the navy.

2884 Poolman, Kenneth. Guns Off Cape Ann: The Story of the SHANNON and the CHESAPEAKE. London: Evans; Chicago: Rand, 1961, 1962, 175 pp. Based on, and, apparently, only on, the Court of Inquiry for USS CHEAPEAKE, no chapter titles, no scholarly apparatus; only details on disposition of the 7 courts martial; not satisfactory.

2885 -------. The SPEEDWELL Voyage: A Tale of Piracy and Mutiny in the Eighteenth Century. Annapolis: NIP; NY: Berkley, 1999, 2001, viii, 192 pp. A 22-gun privateer in 1718, to harrass the Spanish; into the Pacific, many crises, e.g., 2 mutinies and shipwreck, replaced by Spanish prizes; also incident of shooting an albatross, an inspiration for Coleridge.

2886 Pope, Dudley. Admiral. London: Seeker. Nautical fiction; during the Restoration period, in Jamaica; Ned Yorke series #2; hero-seaman, Edward Yorke.

2887 -------. At Twelve Mr. Byng Was Shot. Phil: Lippincott, 1962, 375 pp. The prolific Pope, a veteran of the merchant marine who lives on a yacht, RAMAGE; about 20 novels with Nicholas Ramage as hero set in the Nelson era; at least 3 with Edward Yorke, a buccaneer reminiscent of Henry Morgan, set in mid-17th century; this work on Byng; in March 1757, Admiral John Byng was executed on his own quarterdeck, the charge: failure to pursue the enemy during a battle off Minorca; a sensational episode.

2888 -------. The Black Ship. Phil: Lippincott, 1963, 1964, 367 pp. Much detail re the sensational case of the frigate HERMIONE, Captain Hugh Pigot, September 1797; a violent mutiny, 10 of 14 officers killed, and the ship was sailed to a Spanish port where it was turned over to the enemy; the issue seemed to be oppressive officers; later, a bold cutting-out operation recovered her; as was the case with BOUNTY, many of the mutineers were hunted down and hanged.

2889 -------. Buccaneer. London: Seeker. Nautical fiction; Ned Yorke series #1.

2890 -------. Corsair. London: Seeker. Nautical fiction; Ned Yorke series # 4.

2891 -------. The Devil Himself: The Mutiny of 1800. London: Seeker, Ithaca: McBooks, 1987, 2003, 186 pp. Much detail re the sensational case of the frigate DANAE, 14 March 1800; the crew took her to Brest and turned her over to the French; the issue seemed to be the evils of impressment; 45 mutineers, only a few were ever caught; the captain and loyal members of the crew were exchanged and he was exonerated at court martial; the title comes from the file name in the French archives.

2892 -------. England Expects: Nelson and the Trafalgar Campaign. Alt. title: Decision at Trafalgar. Phil: Lippincott; London: Chatham, 1959, 1960, 1998, 1999, 381 pp. A review of the entire campaign; much focus on Nelson; the title comes from the famous signal by Nelson just before the battle..

2893 -------. Galleon. London: Seeker, 1986, 258 pp. Nautical fiction; Ned Yorke serie #3; in the Caribbean; buccaneers against the Spanish in the 17th century.

2894 -------. Governor Ramage. London: Alison, 1973, 1975, 2000, 340 pp. Nicholas Ramage novel, # 4.

2895 -------. The Great Gamble: Nelson at Copenhagen. London: Weidenfeld, 1972, 2001, xiii, 579 pp. Impressive documentation, including Danish sources; an overview of why the British fleet was in the Baltic, the diplomatic activities, and the battle including an explanation of the famous signal from Parker to break off action; Nelson acknowledged it and continued the battle; Nelson believed Russia was the real enemy; contrasts dynamic Nelson and plodding Hyde Parker.

2896 -------. Guns: From the Invention of Gunpowder to the Twentieth Century. London: Weidenfeld; NY: Delacorte, 1965, 254 pp. A survey, including naval ordnance.

2897 -------. Harry Morgan's Way: The Biography of Sir Henry Morgan, 1635-1684. Alt. title: The Buccaneer King. London: Seeker; NY: Dodd, 1977, xx, 379 pp. Morgan had a spectacular career; rose to leadership at Port Royal, president of the Admiralty Court, and knighted by Charles II; then leader of the buccaneers, elected "admiral" of the Brethren of the Coast; sacking Spanish towns and bases.

2898 -------. Life in Nelson's Navy. London: Allen; Annapolis: NIP; London: Chatham, 1981, 1987, 1996, 2001, 296 pp. A social history describing conditions and a typical day.

2899 -------. Ramage: A Novel. Phil: Lippincott; London: Fontana, 1965, 1975, 1979, 2000, 302 pp. Nicholas Ramage, # 1.

2900 -------. The Ramage Touch. 1979, 1980, 284 pp. Nicholas Ramage, # 10.

2901 -------. Ramage and the Dido. 1989, 1990. Nicholas Ramage, # 18.

2902 -------. Ramage and the Drum Beats. 1967, 1973, 270 pp. Nicholas Ramage, # 2.

2903 -------. Ramage and the Freebooters. 1969, 1970, 1977, 1996, 384 pp. Nicholas Ramage, # 3.

2904 -------. Ramage and the Guillotine. 1975, 1988, 286 pp. Nicholas Ramage, # 6.

2905 -------. Ramage and the Rebels: A Novel. 1978, 1979, 1985, 1996, 2001, 287 pp. Nicholas Ramage, # 9.

2906 -------. Ramage and the Renegades. 1981, 1982, 2002. Nicholas Ramage, # 12.

2907 -------. Ramage and the Saracens. London: Alison, 1988, 1990, 1997, 258 pp. Nicholas Ramage, # 17.

2908 -------. Ramage at Trafalgar. London: Alison, 1986, 214 pp. Nicholas Ramage, # 16.

2909 -------. Ramage's Challenge. 1985, 1886, 262 pp. Nicholas Ramage, # 15.

2910 -------. Ramage's Devil. 1982, 1983, 1996. Nicholas Ramage, # 13.

2911 -------. Ramage's Diamond. 1976, 2001. Nicholas Ramage, # 7.

2912 -------. Ramage's Mutiny. London: Alison; London: Fontana, 1977, 1978, 2001, 255 pp. Nicholas Ramage, # 8.

2913 -------. Ramage's Prize: A Novel. London: Alison, 1974, 1982, 2000, 344 pp. Nicholas Ramage, # 5.

2914 -------. Ramage's Signal. 1980, 1981. Nicholas Ramage, # 11.

2915 -------. Ramage's Trial. London: Seeker, 1984, 284 pp. Nicholas Ramage, # 14.

2916 Pope, Peter E. The Many Landfalls of John Cabot. Toronto: Toronto UP, 1997, xii, 244 pp. Cabot, 1450-1499, a native of Venice and explorer operating from Bristol; several voyages into the North Atlantic in the 1490s, never returning from a voyage in 1797; an important study.

2917 Pope, Stephen. Hornblower's Navy: Life at Sea in the Age of Nelson. London: Orion, 1998, 111 pp. Massive folio size with spectacular colored illustrations; touts Hornblower as the most enduring military hero in British fiction and James Alexander Gordon as the "real Hornblower"; much on life and conditions at sea in this era.

2918 Popham, Hugh. A Damned Cunning Fellow: The Eventful Life of Rear-Admiral Sir Home Popham, 1762-1820. Cornwall: Old Ferry, 1991, 268 pp. The life of a brilliant maverick; invented a method of signalling and formulated a maritime dictionary.

2919 Porter, Andrew N., ed. The Atlas of British Overseas Expansion. NY: Simon, 1991, x, 279 pp. 140 maps depicting voyages from the late 15th century to the present, e.g., early ones from Bristol, Frobisher, Ralegh, and Cook.

2920 Porter, Bernard. Plots and Paranoia: A History of Political Espionage in Britain, 1790-1988. Boston: Unwin; London: Routledge, 1989, 1992, 288 pp. A study of domestic spying with scholarly documentation; conclusion: no evidence of an ongoing government intelligence agency; noted a "black chamber" from late 16th century, the use of spies for internal and external threats; by the 1820s, the police handled these matters.

2921 Porter, Frances. A Sense of History: A Commemorative Publication of John Cawte Beaglehole, O.M., about James Cook's Landing Sites in New Zealand. Wellington: Government, 1978, 90 pp. For the New Zealand Historical Places Trust; a commemoration to Beaglehole; a systematic process to identify and mark Cook landing sites; Cook spent 100 days in the 1770s.

2922 Postan, M.M. "The Costs of the Hundred Years' War." Past and Present, 27 (April 1964): 34-53. Statistical details and analysis of manpower and logistical costs of the campaigns in France, e.g., the largest was Crecy-Calais, 32,000 combatants, Agincourt, 15,000 requiring 1500 naval vessels; especially expensive were naval forces, e.g., warships, barges, and transports.

2923 Potter, E.B. and Nimitz, Chester W. Sea Power: A Naval History. NY: Prentice-Hall, 1961, 1981, 932 pp. A standard textbook for naval history courses and for reference; covers 2000 years.

2924 [NRS 105]. Powell, John R. and Timings, E.K., eds. Documents Relating to the Civil War, 1642-1648. Publications of the Navy Records Society, vol. 105. London: NRS, 1963, xiv, 430 pp. Chronological coverage, year by year; the RN was decisive for the Parliamentary victory.

2925 [NRS 76]. Powell, John R., ed. The Letters of Robert Blake: Together with Supplementary Documents. Publications of the Navy Records Society, vol. 76. London: NRS, 1937, xxiii, 501 pp. Correspondence of Blake, e.g., pursuit of Rupert and the First Dutch War.

2926 Powell, John R. The Navy in the English Civil War. Hamden: Archon, 1962, xviii, 240 pp. Intro: C.V. Wedgwood; a definitive study of the role of the navy in the Civil War; early support for Parliament was decisive; key personalities were Warwick, Batten, and Blake; Laughton and others had insisted the navy was passive and neutral; not so.

2927 -------. Robert Blake: General-at-Sea. London: Collins; NY: Crane, 1972, 352 pp. A definitive biography; best on his naval career.

2928 -------. Robert Blake: General-at-Sea. Bridgwater: Bridgwater Booklets, 1933, 50 pp. A succinct assessment.

2929 [NRS 112]. Powell, John R. and Timings, E.K., eds. The Rupert and Monck Letter Book, 1666: Together with Supporting Documents. Publications of the Navy Records Society, vol. 112. London: NRS, 1969, x, 307 pp. Recounts operations during the 2nd Dutch War, e.g., battles of St. James Day and 4 Days.

2930 Powell, John W.D. The Bristol Privateers and Ships of War. Bristol: Arrowsmith, 1930, xx, 412 pp. Accumulated records of 900 ships of 3 types: King's ships, private ships of war functioning under letters of marque, and merchantmen, e.g., in 1346, a fleet of 738 ships was mobilized for the Crecy-Calais campaign and 20 Bristol vessels in the Armada campaign.

2931 Powell, Michael. Spithead: The Navy's Anvil. Winchester: Redan, 1977, 60 pp. Illustrates with aerial photos the extensive fortifications to defend Portsmouth, the Solent, and Spithead, e.g. 623 guns.

2932 Powell, Mike. 1784: The Battle of Mudeford. London: Natula, 1993, 72 pp. Re an incident, a revenue cutter patrolling to discourage illegal running of contraband from France; customs officers killed by smugglers.

2933 Powell, W.R. "The Administration of the Navy and the Stannaries, 1189-1216." EHR, 71 (April 1956): 177-88. Instances of accumulation of naval forces and corresponding "naval administration"; Richard I assembled a fleet, perhaps as many as 150 ships, for the Third Crusade; John formulated a scheme for allocating revenues from the stannaries, a tax on tin smelting, to the navy without passing through the Exchequer; further instances of naval expansion: 1205-1206 and 1210s.

2934 Power, D'Arcy. "Amputation: The Operation on Nelson in 1797." <u>The British J of Surgery</u>, 19 (1932): 345-51. A description of the medical aspects.

2935 Power, Eileen and Postan, M.M., eds. <u>Studies in English Trade in the Fifteenth Century</u>. NY: Barnes, 1933, 1966, xx, 435 pp. A series of essays by experts presenting the fundamentals of trade of the 15th century, the century of transformation, from medieval England, isolated and intensely local, to England of the Tudor and Stuart age of world-wide connections and imperial designs, e.g., Power on the wool trade, the oldest, largest, and foremost of all branches of English commerce, the trade going to the clothmaking towns of the Netherlands and Italy; Carus-Wilson on the Iceland trade; and Postan on relations with the Hanse.

2936 Powers, Stephen T. "The Decline and Extinction of American Naval Power, 1781-1787." Ph.D. diss, Notre Dame, 1965, 294 pp. In the 1780s, naval affairs deteriorated due to financial problems; the navy was liquidated and no funds were allocated by the Continental Congress.

2937 Powicke, M.R. <u>Military Obligation in Medieval England: A Study in Liberty and Duty</u>. Oxford: Clarendon, 1962, 263 pp. The focus is on knight's service and military obligations, e.g., the fyrd.

2938 Powley, Edward B. <u>The English Navy in the Revolution of 1688</u>. Cambridge: Cambridge UP, 1920, 1928, 1929, viii, 188 pp. Fwd: Earl Jellicoe; a rare study of the navy during the revolution; the forces of William of Orange vs. Lord Dartmouth and the English navy.

2939 -------. "The Naval Side of King William's War: Opening Phase, November 1688 to December 1689." D.Phil. diss, Oxford, 1961. The basis of these entries.

2940 -------. <u>The Naval Side of King William's War: 16/26 November 1688-14 June 1690</u>. London: Baker; Hamden: Anchor, 1972, 392 pp. Fwd: Arthur Bryant; Powley died in 1968; covers the landing of William at Torbay to his victory at the Boyne; strategy against France, in the Mediterranean, and against Ireland, e.g., Bantry Bay and operations up to Beachy Head.

2941 Poynter, F.N.L., ed. <u>The Journal of James Yonge, 1647-1721: Plymouth Surgeon</u>. London: Longman, 1963, 1965, 247 pp. Dedicated to J.J. Keevil; an edition of this 17th-century journal, e.g., the siege of Algiers and capture and imprisonment by the Dutch.

2942 Prentice, Rina. <u>A Celebration of the Sea: The Decorative Art Collections of the National Maritime Museum</u>. London: HMSO, 1994, xii, 120 pp. 300 photos of objects, selections from the largest collection of art objects with nautical association in the world, e.g., glass, pottery, porcelain, silver, gold, textiles, wood, mugs, scrimshaw, trophies, and paintings; notable Nelson relics.

2943 Press, Jonathan. <u>The Merchant Seamen of Bristol, 1747-1789</u>. Bristol:

Historical Association, 1976, 23 pp. A local history pamphlet, more than the title suggests, e.g., conditions, wages, impressment, and privateers.

2944 Prest, Wilfrid. <u>Albion Ascendant: English History, 1660-1815</u>. <u>Short Oxford History of the Modern World</u>. Oxford: Oxford UP, 1998, xiv, 363 pp. A recent, solid, scholarly survey which focuses on the unique state-building; the process of creating a political system and ruling order; from an insignificant offshore island to superstate.

2945 Preston, Antony. <u>History of the Royal Navy</u>. London: Hamlyn; NY: Bison, 1983, 192 pp. Folio size, illustrated; a popular survey beginning with the Spanish Armada and through the Falklands/Malvinas campaign.

2946 Preston, Antony, ed. <u>Mahan's "Influence of Sea Power upon History, 1660-1805</u>." Novato: Presidio, 1890, 1987, 256 pp. An interesting combination, an abridgement of the 1st volume and 45 pp. from the 2nd.

2947 Prestwich, Michael. <u>Armies and Warfare in the Middle Ages: The English Experience</u>. New Haven: Yale UP, 1996, ix, 396 pp. An extensively illustrated, scholarly synthesis, e.g., army organization, strategy, tactics, naval forces, and logistics, especially the 13th and 14th centuries.

2948 -------. "Edward I's Wars and Their Financing, 1294-1307." D.Phil. diss, 1968. The basis of these entries.

2949 Prestwich, Michael, ed. <u>Thirteenth-Century England</u>. Vol. VI. Woodbury: Boydell, 1997. From a journal published every 2 years; see article by John Gillingham, "Richard I, Galley-Warfare, and Portsmouth: The Beginnings of the Royal Navy" (pp. 1-15); informative on 12th century naval warfare.

2950 Prestwich, Michael. <u>The Three Edwards: War and State in England, 1272-1377</u>. London: Weidenfeld; London: Methuen, 1980, 1981, 336 pp. A neglected century and the 3 kings; their problems and warfare, e.g., against Scotland and the Hundred Years' War.

2951 -------. <u>War, Politics and Finance under Edward I</u>. London: Faber, 1972, 317 pp. Re the mobilization and direction of resources for a series of campaigns, e.g., vs. Wales, Scotland, and Flanders; retention of Gascony.

2952 Price, Anthony. <u>The Eyes of the Fleet: A Popular History of Frigates and Frigate Captain, 1793-1815</u>. London: Hutchinson, 1990, 1996, 298 pp. Price, author of spy novels, turns in this dubious effort in history during the age of sail; curious claim and presentation: frigates and their captains outperformed any fictional depictions; odd selection of 5 frigate captains: Pellew, Pigot (HERMOINE), Cochrane (claimed as the greatest), Hoste, Broke, and, Horatio Hornblower, the latter being the most unusual choice; many digressions; no primary research.

2953 Pringle, Patrick. Jolly Roger: The Story of the Great Age of Piracy. London: Museum, 1953, 294 pp. A popular survey; bibliography dated.

2954 Pritchard, James S. Anatomy of a Naval Disaster: The 1746 French Expedition to North America. Montreal: McGill-Queens UP, 1995, 1996, 344 pp. The Louisbourg campaign to recover French imperial ambitions; a series of disasters; no reconnaissance, no intelligence, no maps, delays, violent weather, disease, and no contact with Anglo-American enemies; intensively researched and informative about the bureaucracy of the ancien regime.

2955 -------. "Fir Trees, Financiers, and the French Navy during the 1750s." Canadian J History, 23 (December 1988): 337-54. Elaboration and revision of the Bamford thesis; logistics only one problem, others being administration, finance, and corrupt contractors.

2956 -------. Louis XV's Navy: A Study of Organization and Administration. London: McGill-Queens UP, 1987, xiv, 285 pp. A brilliant administrative history of the French navy comparable to Baugh; patterns of growth and decline, mostly the latter; deterioration not the fault of administrators and officials but decreased funding.

2957 Proctor, David. Music of the Sea. London: HMSO, 1992, x, 150 pp. For NMM; a comprehensive description of songs, shanties, airs, pipes, and bands; international coverage.

2958 Prynne, M.W. "Henry V's GRACE DIEU." MM, 54 (May 1968): 115-28. Detailed description of what was the largest warship in Northern Europe for centuries; launched 1418 and burned 1439; most of career at anchor in the Hamble.

2959 Pryor, Felix, ed. The Faber Book of Letters: Letters Written in the English Language. London: Faber, 1988, xvi, 319 pp. A collection of letters, some newly discovered, e.g., from Nelson to Emma of January 1800, plus subsequent ones; definitely love letters.

2960 Pryor, John H. Commerce, Shipping and Naval Warfare in the Medieval Mediterranean. London: Variorum, 1987, x, 338 pp. A collection of 7 articles, e.g., transportation of horses during the Crusades and an architectural history of these transport ships.

2961 -------. "The Naval Architecture of Crusader Transport Ships: A Reconstruction of Some Archetypes for Round-Hulled Sailing Ships." MM, 70. 3 parts. (May-November 1984): 171-219, 275-92, and 363-86. Ships furnished by Genoa, Venice, and Marsailles; details on design, rigging, equipment, and boats.

2962 -------. "Transportation of Horses by Sea during the Era of the Crusades: Eighth Century to 1285 AD." MM, 68. 2 parts. (February and May 1982): 9-27 and 103-25. The era was characterized by conflicts between Byzantium and the

Crusaders; also, Normans to Sicily in 1038 and 1061.

2963 Pugh, Ellen and Pugh, David. Brave His Soul: The Story of Prince Madog of Wales and His Discovery of America in 1170. NY: Dodd, 1970, 144 pp. Interesting but nothing new on this Welsh prince; legendary exploits; not convincing.

2964 Pugh, P.D.G. Nelson and His Surgeons: Nelson Chirurgiique: Being an Account of the Illnesses and Wounds Sustained by Lord Nelson and His Relationship with the Surgeons of the Day. Edinburgh: Livingstone, 1968, 68 pp. Fwd: H.J. Burrows; by a Surgeon Commander, RN; to support an exhibition, Royal Naval Hospital, Haslar, April 1967; a fascinating overview of the health of Nelson throughout his lifetime; details on wounds and diseases plus a list of 25 surgeons consulted by Nelson.

2965 Pugh, Philip G. "Of Strategy and Money." Warship (1989): 17-21. Pugh published an extensive study on the post-1815 RN; this article expands that earlier to the 16th century; collected data and computes costs of warships and naval operations over time.

2966 Puleston, William D. Mahan: The Life and Work of Captain Aflred Thayer Mahan, USN. New Haven: Yale UP, 1939, 380 pp. A solid study.

2967 Pullen, Hugh F. The SHANNON and the CHESAPEAKE. Toronto: McClelland, 1970, xix, 174 pp. A account of the famous engagement.

2968 Purchas, Samuel. Hakluyt Posthumus or Purchas, His Pilgrimage. 20 vols. Glasgow, MacLehose, 1615, 1625, 1905-1907. Purchas, 1577-1626, self-appointed successor to Richard Hakluyt the Younger, continuing to gather accounts of "pilgrimes" and to publish some of which the Hakluyts collected but did not publish, e.g., the circumnavigation of Drake and records of the East India Company.

2969 Purves, Libby. "Plymouth Ho!" In Britain (February 1992): 7-12. A popular account of the seafaring tradition, e.g., Drake, Cook, Darwin, and Plymouth Hoe.

2970 Puype, Jan-Piet. "Guns and Their Handling at Sea in the Seventeenth Century: A Dutch Point of View." J Ordnance Society, 1 (1990): 11-24. Basic information and details, e.g., bronze vs. iron cannon, heavy gun carriages, types of rope, and processes of moving, aiming, and firing naval guns.

2971 Quand Voguaient les Galeres. Paris: Quest-France, 1990, 319 pp. An important and informative history of oar- and sail-powered galleys from earliest times through the 18th century, e.g., Venice, Malta, and France.

2972 Quill, Humphrey. John Harrison: The Man Who Found Longitude. London: Baker, 1966, xiv, 255 pp. Fwd: Richard Woolley; an excellent biography of the chronometer maker.

2973 Quinn, David B. "Columbus and the North: England, Iceland, and Ireland." William and Mary Quarterly, 3rd ser, 49 (January 1992): 278-97. Quinn, 1909-2002, was doyen of historians of medieval and early modern English maritime expansionism; notes gaps in the early life of Columbus after he left Genoa; possibly, in 1477, to England and Ireland, and even Iceland.

2974 -------. Drake's Circumnavigation of the Globe: A Review: The Fifteenth Harte Lecture, University of Exeter, 1980. Exeter: Exeter UP, 1981, 14 pp. Reevaluates Drake in light of recent evidence; gaining experience in seamanship in the 1560s and 1570s.

2975 -------. England and the Discovery of America, 1481-1620: From the Bristol Voyages of the Fifteenth Century to the Pilgrim Settlement at Plymouth. New York: Knopf, 1974, xliv, 497 pp. 8 related essays, a comprehensive survey of the role of the English in the discovery, exploration, and settlement of North America, e.g., contends Bristol seamen were first to America in 1481, even before Cabot; that the English produced the first viable plan for community settlement; assessment of the Vinland Map, and the reaction of all to this by Spain.

2976 Quinn, David B. and Ryan, A.N. England's Sea Empire, 1550-1642. Boston: Allen, 1983, 256 pp. A comprehensive survey of this formative period, the development of English naval power and expanison of commerce and overseas colonization by noted experts; the initiatives were by private adventurers seeking profits and power, all supported by officials; the most important study combining these factors: development of naval power and expansion of overseas exploration, trade, and settlement; brilliant introductory bibliographical essay.

2977 Quinn, David B. and Quinn, Alison, M., eds. The English New England Voyages, 1602-1608. Publications of the Hakluyt Society. London: Hakluyt Society, 1983, xxiv, 580 pp. Accounts of discovery voyages, e.g., sponsored by the Plymouth Division of the Virginia Company; also roles of London, Bristol, and Exeter.

2978 Quinn, David B. European Approaches to North America, 1450-1640. Aldershot: Ashgate: 1998, vii, 341 pp. A collection of 15 articles, 4 not previously published; covers a variety of issues; somewhat dated.

2979 -------. Explorers and Colonies: America, 1500-1625. Ronceverte: Hambledon, 1990, xii, 449 pp. 25 essays on exploration, cartography, and leaders, e.g., Drake, Richard Hakluyt, Purchas, and Gilbert.

2980 Quinn, David B., ed. The Hakluyt Handbook. 2 vols. Publications of the Hakluyt Society, 2nd ser, vols. 144 and 145. London: Hakluyt Society, 1974, xxxix, 706 pp. Dedicated to R.A. Skelton; a commemoration of the Hakluyt Society, founded in 1846 to honor Richard Hakluyt the Younger, 1552-1616; a comprehensive guide with essays by primary authorities, e.g., George Naish, Helen Wallis, J.H. Parry, K.R. Andrews, and D.F. Lach.

2981 -------, ed. <u>The Last Voyages of Thomas Cavendish, 1591-1592</u>. Chicago: Chicago UP, 1975, ix, 165 pp. For the Newberry Library; Cavendish, 1560-1592; this account written in 1593; another circumnavigation by an Elizabethan sea adventurer.

2982 -------, ed. <u>New American World: A Documentary History of North America to 1612</u>. 5 vols. London: Macmillan, 1979, cxl, 2200 pp. Extensive coverage, e.g., III. on English plans for Roanoke and New England and part of IV. on the search for the Northwest Passage.

2983 Quinn, David B. <u>North America from Earliest Discovery to First Settlements</u>. NY: Harper, 1971, 1977, xvii, 621 pp. A survey of exploration of North America to 1612; early contacts, e.g., Spain, Portugal, England, and France.

2984 -------. <u>Raleigh and the British Empire</u>. London: Hodder; NY: Macmillan: London: Penguin, 1947, 1962, 1973, xiii, 284 pp. Re the exploits of Raleigh, e.g., the Lost Colony, Irish Plantation, refounding of Virginia, and the Guiana "gamble."

2985 Quinn, David B., ed. <u>The Roanoke Voyages, 1584-1590: Documents to Illustrate the English Voyages to North America under the Patent Granted by Walter Raleigh in 1584</u>. 2 vols. <u>Publications of the Hakluyt Society</u>, 2nd ser, vols. 104 and 105. London: Hakluyt Society, 1955-1967, xxxii, 1036 pp. Accounts of voyages along the coast of North Carolina; Quinn notes this as one of the most important of all of the exploratory voyages.

2986 Quinn, David B. <u>Sebastian Cabot and Bristol Exploration</u>. Bristol: Historical Association, 1968, 1993, 40 pp. Sets the Cabot voyages in context.

2987 -------. <u>Sir Francis Drake as Seen by His Contemporaries</u>. Providence: JCB Library, 1996, xvi, 96 pp. For the Hakluyt Society; comp: Burton Edwards; selections; a bibliography of holdings about Drake at the JCB Library.

2988 -------. "Spanish Armada Prisoners' Escape from Ireland." <u>MM</u>, 70 (May 1984): 117-18. Re Cuellar and his escape to Scotland; others were held for ransom by Sir William Fitzwilliam.

2989 Quinn, David B., ed. <u>The Voyages and Colonizing Enterprises of Sir Humphrey Gilbert</u>. 2 vols. <u>Publications of the Hakluyt Society</u>, 2nd ser, vols. 83 and 84. London: Hakluyt Society, 1940. Gilbert, 1539-1583; a collection of all known accounts of his voyages and settlements of the 1570s and 1580s; as with Raleigh, an example of poor planning which would inevitably fail.

2990 Quinn, Rory, <u>et al</u>. "The INVINCIBLE (1758) Site: An Integrated Geophysical Assessemnt." <u>International J Nautical Archaeology</u>, 27 (May 1998): 126-38. Originally, L'INVINCIBLE '74, a French 3rd rate, captured in 1747, the design considered a model and copied; lost off Portsmouth in 1758; in 1980s and 1990s, a systematic excavation and geophysical survey described in detail.

2991 Quintrell, Brian. "Charles I and His Navy in the 1630s." Seventeenth Century, 3 (Autumn 1988): 159-79. Charles was attracted to ships and his navy; 11 new ships built; but, compared to Cromwell, a failure; the fleet immediately went over to Parliament in 1642.

2992 Quirk, Ronald J. Literature as Introspection: Spain Confronts Trafalgar. NY: Lang, 1998, 89 pp. A fascinating study of literary and artistic references and reactions in Spain during the 19th century after the battle of Trafalgar, 1805; a kind of evolution: minimizing the impact, outrage, hand-wringing, retaliation, revenge, a curious respect for and praise of Nelson and related blaming of Napoleon, and much anti-French venom.

2993 Raban, Jonathan, ed. The Oxford Book of the Sea. NY: Oxford UP, 1992, xviii, 524 pp. An anthology of English works, e.g., the Hakluyts, Purchas, Defoe, Anson, Falconer, and S.E. Morison.

2994 Raban, Peter. "The Profits of Privateering: A Guernsey Fleet, 1756-1762." MM, 80 (August 1994): 298-311. A case study demonstrating good and bad aspects, e.g., cruising in the Channel meant intelligence information to RN and assisted in blockade operations, but not profitable.

2995 Rabb, Theodore K. "The Bayeux Tapestry: Artist on War." MHQ, 9 (Summer 1997): 80-85. Depicts the battle of Hastings, 14 October 1066; images of preliminaries, events of battles, and aftermath, all incorporated, even Halley's Comet.

2996 Rackham, Oliver. Trees and Woodland in the British Landscape. Archaeology in the Field series. London: Dent, 1976, 1977, 1990, 204 pp. A history of the disposition and management of the woodlands from prehistoric times; corrective to Albion: excessive reliance on complaints to the Admiralty about shipbuilding problems; but, in fact, naval shipbuilding continued to use British wood except for masts into the 19th century; "no war was lost due to want of shipping"; the contract price was unchanged during the 18th century.

2997 Rae, Julia and Peel, Alwyn, eds. Captain James Cook ENDEAVOUR: Commemorating the Visit of Cook's Ship the ENDEAVOUR, 1997. London: Stepney, 1997, 118 pp. A survey of the career of Cook before 1768, e.g., Whitby, the Pool of London, Wapping, the Seven Years' War, and surveying the coast of Canada and Newfoundland.

2998 Rae, Julia. From Whitby to Wapping: The Story of the Early Years of Captain James Cook. London: Stepney, 1991, 39 pp. An earlier version of the previous entry; under her original name, Julia Hunt.

2999 Raine, David F. Sir George Somers: A Man and His Times. Bermuda: Pompano, 1984, 189 pp. Re an important explorer-colonizer of the 16th century linked to an extraordinary circle, e.g., the Hawkins, Grenville, Raleigh, and Gilbert.

3000 Rainey, John R. "The Defense of Calais, 1436-1477." Ph.D. diss, Rutgers, 1987, 284 pp. An account of English development of Calais in the 15th century; a major point of contact with the continent.

3001 Raleigh, Walter. The History of the World. Phil: Temple UP, 1614, 1971, 418 pp. Ed: C.A. Partrides; written by Raleigh, 1554-1618, when he was in the Tower; a history and his perspectives on issues of his time; an important literary work.

3002 -------. The Last Fight of the REVENGE. London: Gibbings, c. 1615, 1908, 129 pp. Ed: Henry Newbolt; the account by Raleigh.

3003 Ralfe, James. The Naval Biography of Great Britain: Consisting of Historical Memoirs during the Reign of George III. 4 vols. London: Whitmore; Boston: Gregg, 1828, 1972. Recounting the naval careers of the officers of RN; about 30 per volume, e.g., Rodney, Hawke, Hood, Duncan, St. Vincent, and Nelson.

3004 Ramsay, G.D. "The Smugglers' Trade: A Neglected Aspect of English Commercial Development." Trans RHS, 5th ser, 2 (1952): 131-57. A significant share of English foreign trade was credited to smugglers and that endured up through the 18th century despite customs agents and coastguards.

3005 Randles, W.G.L. Geography, Cartography and Nautical Science in the Renaissance: The Impact of the Great Discoveries. Variorum Collected Studies. Aldershot: Ashgate, 2000, xii, 354 pp. A collection of 9 of the papers of Randles; these discoveries of the 15th and 16th centuries transformed concepts of the world.

3006 [NRS 128 and 132]. Ranft, Bryan M., ed. The Beatty Papers: Selections from the Private and Official Correspondence of Admiral of the Fleet Earl Beatty. 2 vols. Publications of the Navy Records Society, vols. 128 and 132. London: Scolar, 1989-1993, xxiv, 592 and xxiv, 496 pp. Extensive papers acquired by NMM in 1981; informative on the career of Beatty; details on relations and various debates with Jellicoe, e.g., how to deploy the powerful 5th Battle Squadron; development of his strategic and tactical thought; disposition of Fleet Air Arm.

3007 Ranft, Bryan M. "The Significance of the Political Career of Samuel Pepys." J Modern History, 24 (December 1952): 368-75. Informative on the complexities of the relationships of Pepys to the King and House of Commons; his role as advocate for the navy; issues, e.g., the Medway incident, wages of seamen, and administration of the Admiralty.

3008 [NRS 99]. Ranft, Bryan M., ed. The Vernon Papers. Publications of the Navy Records Society, vol. 99. London: NRS, 1958, xii, 599 pp. Vernon, 1684-1757; correspondence on strategy, administration, and discipline; introduced "grog."

3009 Rankin, Hugh F. The Golden Age of Piracy. NY: Holt, 1969, xv, 173 pp. An undistinguished survey.

3010 Rasor, Eugene L. The Battle of Jutland: A Bibliography. Bibliographies of Battles and Leaders series, vol. 7. Westport: Greenwood, 1991, xiv, 178 pp., 538 annotated entries. Same format as over a dozen historiographical-bibliographical surveys for Greenwood Press.

3011 -------. "British Naval History: A Survey of Recent Developments." International Social Sciences Review, 76 (2001): 44-65. A historiographical survey of recent literature and developments.

3012 -------. British Naval History since 1815: A Guide to the Literature. Military History Bibliographies series. NY: Garland , 1990, xxii, 841 pp. Series ed: Robin Higham; the "prequel" to this work; a comprehensive historiographical and bibliographical survey of 3125 academic and printed materials, including monographs, secondary works, dissertations, government publications, and important articles, on the maritime and naval history of Great Britain since 1815; items published since 1960.

3013 -------. The Falklands/Malvinas Campaign: A Bibliography. Bibliographies of Battles and Leaders series, vol. 6. Westport: Greenwood, 1991, xvi, 196 pp., 554 annotated entries; incorporates aspects at time of and after the discovery and various conflicts involving Britain, Spain, and France.

3014 -------. "The Problem of Discipline in the Mid-Nineteenth-Century Royal Navy." Ph.D. diss, Virginia, 1972, 312 pp. The basis of some of these entries.

3015 -------. Reform in the Royal Navy: A Social History of the Lower Deck, 1850-1880. Hamden, CT: Archon, 1975, 210 pp. A monograph describing and analyzing a series of significant reforms instituted by the Admiralty to improve conditions and life among the enlisted constitutency of the Royal Navy during the late nineteenth century; presents background of ongoing controversies, e.g., impressment, punishments, and conditions on the lower deck.

3016 -------. The Spanish Armada of 1588: Historiography and Annotated Bibliography. Bibliographies of Battles and Leaders series, vol. 9. Westport: Greenwood, 1993, xviii, 278 pp., 1125 annotated entries; long historiographical essay critically analyzing and integrating the literature about the Armada.

3017 -------. The TITANIC: Historiography and Annotated Bibliography. Bibliographies and Indexes in World History series, vol. 53. Westport: Greenwood, 2001, xvi, 238 pp., 674 annotated entries, a total of 930 items described; a general interest, reference, and research guide to the important literature and cultural factors associated with the TITANIC; in three parts: a historiographical narrative, a series of descriptive lists, and an annotated bibliography.

3018 Rathbone, Philip. Paradise Merton: The Story of Nelson and the Hamiltons at Merton Place. London: Private, 1973, 12 pp. From a lecture to the Merton Historical Society; all changed now, located near the present South Wimbledon

Underground Station, an ancient Priory; Nelson and Lord and Lady Hamilton lived there, 1801-1805 (Hamilton died in 1803); sold in 1808 and again in 1815, then vacant and finally pulled down.

3019 Rattigan, Terence. "Bequest to the Nation: A Play." London: West End Theater, 1969. Began as a TV script, "Nelson: A Study in Miniature," 1966; depicts Nelson-Emma relationship during their last time together, August-September 1805, seen through the eyes of nephew, George Matcham.

3020 Raudzens, George. Empires: Europe and Globalization, 1492-1788. Stroud: Sutton, 1999, x, 214 pp. Fwd: Jeremy Black; a synthesis summarizing European oceanic expansion and creation of a global network, all facilitated by the development of the fully-rigged, cannon-armed oceanic vessel; reviews the sequence of powers; factors: maritime expansion, trade, colonization, and warfare.

3021 -------. "Military Revolution or Maritime Evolution?: Military Superiorities or Transportation Advantages as Main Causes of European Colonial Conquest to 1788." J Military History, 63 (July 1999): 631-42. A contribution to the ongoing debate: was it ship and gun technology, diseases, or oceanic transport monopoly; reviews Levathes, Diamond, Cipolla, Mahan, Albion, Graham, Parry, Scammell, Modelski, and Kennedy.

3022 Raven, G.J.A. and Rodger, N.A.M., eds. Navies and Armies: The Anglo-Dutch Relationship in War and Peace, 1688-1988. Edinburgh: Donald, 1990, x, 118 pp. Proceedings from a conference, the tercentenary of the Glorious Revolution, June 1988, at the Royal Naval College of Holland; 7 essays, e.g., Rodger on the British view of the Anglo-Dutch alliance and de Moor on the disruptive relations in the Far East.

3023 Rawlinson, H.G. "The Flanders Galleys: Some Notes on Seaborne Trade between Venice and England, 1327-1532." MM, 12 (April 1926): 145-68. Details on an annual trade cycle; English-Venetian trade relations began during the Crusades; earliest galley fleet to England via Gibraltar, 1317; to Southampton and London.

3024 Rawson, Geoffrey. Bligh of the BOUNTY. London: Allan, 1930, 1934, 244 pp. An older, balanced biography; 60 pages on the mutiny on the BOUNTY.

3025 Rawson, Geoffrey, comp. Letters from Lord Nelson. London: Staples; London: Dent, 1949, 1960, 486 pp. Notes by Michael Lewis; an extensive collection of letters.

3026 Rawson, Geoffrey. Matthew Flinders' Narrative of His Voyage in the Schooner FRANCIS, 1798. London: Golden Cockerel, 1946, 100 pp. Illustrations by John Wright; an account of the voyage.

3027 Rawson, Geoffrey, ed. Nelson's Letters from the Leeward Islands and Other

Original Documents in the Public Record Office and the British Museum. London: Golden Cockerel; London: Dent, 1953, 1960, 73 pp. Letters from Nelson; enlightening on his activities in the West Indies in 1780s.

3028 Rawson, Geoffrey. PANDORA's Last Voyage. London: Longman, 1963, vii, 165 pp. Reviews the mutiny and subsequent events related to the mutineers; Bligh, the hero, and Fletcher Christian, the villain; the search by PANDOA, a police mission to capture the wicked desperado, Christian, and his pirate gang; its fate.

3029 Raymond, R.J. "Privateers and Privateering off the Irish Coast in the Eighteenth Century." Irish Sword, 13 (Summer 1977): 60-69. Enlightening on privateering practices, seen as warfare on the cheap; a curious form called "reprisals"; Irish seamen involved in operations for and against the French.

3030 Razzell, Edward and Razzell, Peter, eds. The English Civil War: A Contemporary Account. 5 vols. London: Caliban, 1996, xxx, 1847 pp. Preface: Christopher Hill; edited reports of the Venetian ambassador from Calendar of State Papers, Venetian; enlightening on political, commercial, and naval activities, e.g., mutinies and operations of Monck and Blake.

3031 Rea, Lorna. The Spanish Armada. NY: Putnam, 1933, 175 pp. An undistinguished account.

3032 Read, Conyers. "Queen Elizabeth's Seizure of the Duke of Alva's Pay-Ships." J Modern History, 5 (December 1933): 443-64. By the preeminent Tudor historian, biographer of Walsingham and Burghley; an incident with fateful consequences; in November 1568, 5 Spanish ships sought refuge from weather and privateers into English ports where all were confiscated, e.g., wool and 155 chests of money and treasure, part of which was to pay the army of Alva; contributed to deteriorating Anglo-Spanish relations.

3033 Read, J. Gordon. "National Museums and Galleries on Merseyside." Perspectives, 29 (April 1991): 8-9. Description of this unique combination of ports, museums, and archive centers, e.g., dock registers, Cook expeditions, and maritime record centers.

3034 Real, Christopal. El Corsario Drake y el Imperio Espanol. Madrid: Editora Nacional, 1941, 1942, 273 pp. The Spanish perspective on Drake.

3035 Reddie, James. "On Manning the Navy." JRUSI, 61 (1967): 279-362. A long discussion reviewing the problem and summarizing efforts at reform.

3036 Redgrave, M.O. "Wellington's Logistical Arrangements in the Peninsular War, 1809-1814." Ph.D. diss, London. In 2001, noted as forthcoming; presents useful detail of the logistical situation.

3037 Rediker, Marcus B. Between the Devil and the Deep Blue Sea: Merchant

Seamen, Pirates, and the Anglo-American Maritime World, 1700-1750. Cambridge: Cambridge UP, 1987, xv, 325 pp. An extensive scholarly study and Marxist analysis; important and controversial; focus on practices of discipline, command, punishment, piracy, mutinies, and 60 cases before HCA; describes the "social world" of the pirates.

3038 -------. "Society and Culture among Anglo-American Deep Sea Sailors, 1700-1750." Ph.D. diss, Pennsylvania, 1982, 374 pp. The basis for the previous entry.

3039 -------. "'Under the Banner of King Death': The Social World of Anglo-American Pirates, 1716 to 1726." William and Mary Quarterly, 38 (April 1981):203-27. Elaboration on these entries.

3040 Reed, Joseph W. English Biography in the Early Nineteenth Century, 1801-1838. New Haven: Yale UP, 1966, xi, 180 pp. A literary study including a chapter on "Southey's Nelson"; assessed as widely read although factually inaccurate; other assessments, e.g., Callender, Oman, and Mahan.

3041 Reed, Philip. Modelling Sailing Men-of-War. London: Chatham, 2000, 128 pp. A step-by-step manual for model builders; 400 illustrations.

3042 Rees, Sian. The Floating Brothel: The Extraordinary True Story of an Eighteenth-Century Ship and Its Cargo of Female Convicts. London: Headline, 2001, 248 pp. The account of a specific voyage, 247 women transported to New South Wales aboard LADY JULIANA in 1789; most were convicted of petty crimes; presents details of shipboard life; well researched but too speculative and overdramatized.

3043 Regan, Geoffrey. The Guinness Book of Naval Blunders. Enfield: Guinness, 1993, vi, 186 pp. Folio size, colored illustrations; collects every conceivable gaff and exaggerates the outcomes; chapter titles, e.g., lunatic admirals, price of admiralty, and that sinking feeling; case studies, e.g., Medway, Beachy Head, Toulon, and the Armada of 1779; individual ships, e.g., WHITE SHIP, MARY ROSE, ROYAL GEORGE, and VASA.

3044 -------. Lionhearts: Saladin, Richard I, and the Era of the Third Crusade. London: Constable; NY: Walker, 1998, 1999, xxv, 254 pp. Coverage of events of the 1180s, the "Holy War" involving Jerusalem and Acre.

3045 Reid, W.S. Stanford. "Sea-Power in the Anglo-Scottish War, 1296-1328." MM, 46 (February 1960): 7-22. Ships and naval forces were the principal means of transport and providing logistics, e.g., Edward I during the 1290s and 1300s; the Scots were successful in resisting English expansion, partly due to sea power, e.g., Scottish galleys were effective on occasion.

3046 Reitan, Earl A. Politics, War, and Empire: The Rise of Britain to a World Power, 1688-1792. Arlington Heights: Ill. State UP, 1994, ix, 185 pp. Presents the transformation of Britain from a minor to a world power; emphasis of politics, diplomacy, and war; Pitt the Elder a contributor.

3047 Reston, James, Jr. <u>Warriors of God: Richard the Lionheart and Saladin the Third Crusade</u>. London: Faber; NY: Doubleday, 2001, xx, 364 pp. A recent study of the great antagonists of the 3rd Crusade; overly popularized.

3048 Reynolds, Clark G. <u>Command of the Sea: The History and Strategy of Maritime Empires</u>. 2 vols. plus <u>Supplement</u>. I: <u>To 1815</u>. II: <u>Since 1815</u>. Supp: <u>Set of Strategic Maps</u>. NY: Morrow, 1974, 1983, 694 pp. An excellent survey by a noted expert; focus on developments in strategy; broad based and balanced; excellent introduction and bibliography.

3049 -------. <u>History and the Sea: Essays on Maritime Strategy</u>. Columbia: USCP, 1989, viii, 232 pp. 10 essays, a synthesis on maritime strategy, especially on sea-oriented empires; assessment of Mahan, "the great savant of sea power."

3050 -------. <u>Navies in History</u>. Annapolis: NIP, 1998, xi, 267 pp. An overview of naval history; world-wide coverage beginning about 2000 BC; occasional supportive essays of elaboration, e.g., the 4-Days Battle, "fleet-in-being," lower deck, and Trafalgar.

3051 -------. "Traders: The Maritime World." <u>Wilson Quarterly</u>, 11 (Summer 1987): 95-111. A survey of maritime empires, e.g., Egypt, Minoa, Athens, Rome, Venice, especially dominant, Genoa, Pisa, Florence, Spain, Portugal, the Dutch, and Britain.

3052 Rice, E.E., ed. <u>The Sea and History</u>. Stroud: Sutton, 1996, xiii, 165 pp. A series of lectures, Wolfson College, Oxford University, 1995, e.g., on nautical archaeology, Sean McGrail on the ship, and John Keegan on the rise of British imperialism and naval mastery.

3053 Richardson, William. <u>A Mariner of England: An Account of the Career of William Richardson from Cabin Boy in the Merchant Service to Warrant Officer in the Royal Navy, 1780-1819</u>. London: Conway; Annapolis: NIP, 1908, 1970, 317 pp. Ed: Spencer Childers; a memoir of service on the lower deck, 13 years in the merchant service, 26 years in RN; twice "pressed" and critic of "flogging round the fleet."

3054 Richey, Michael. "E.G.R. Taylor and the Vinland Map." <u>J Navigation</u>, 53 (May 2000): 193-205. The Taylor Lecture, Royal Geographical Society, November 1999; re the reaction of Taylor upon the announcement by Yale University about the Vinland Map; she insisted it was a forgery.

3055 Richmond, C.F. "English Naval Power in the Fifteenth Century." <u>History</u>, 52 (Februrary 1967): 1-15. The only late medieval king to undertake long-term naval activity was Henry V, during the late 1410s, a fleet of 30 ships patrolling the

Channel in war against France; then long pause, 1422-1480.

3056 -------. "The Keeping of the Seas during the Hundred Years' War, 1422-1440." History, 49 (October 1964): 283-98. During the 1420s, the King's Ships were sold off; defense of the Channel and territories in France dependent on private individuals; no royal navy.

3057 -------. "Royal Administration and the Keeping of the Seas, 1422-1485." D.Phil. diss, Oxford, 1963. The basis of the previous entries.

3058 Richmond, Herbert W. Amphibious Warfare in British History. Historical Association Pamphlet, # 119. Exeter: Wheaton, 1941, 31 pp. Admiral Sir Herbert Richmond, 1871-1946, influential naval strategist, historian, intellectual, and professor; a short survey of several types of amphibious operations, a total of 12 case studies, e.g., Drake in the West Indies in the 1580s, Pocock at Havana, 1762, and failure by Vernon at Cartagena, 1741.

3059 -------. Invasion of Britain: An Account of Plans, Attempts, and Counter-measures from 1586 to 1918. London: Methuen, 1941, 81 pp. For the Historical Association; a contemporaneous threat prompts a review, e.g., attempts by Spain, France, and Germany; discussion of "legend" that England was saved by the wind from the Armada; refuted by J. Laughton, Corbett, and Holland Rose.

3060 -------. "The Naval Officer in Fiction." Essays and Studies by Members of the English Association, 30 (1945): 7-25. A review of examples, e.g., Marryat being a class by itself.

3061 -------. "The Navy and Its Records from the Armada to Trafalgar." MM, 24 (January 1938): 68-81. An address by Richmond to the Navy Records Society, a tribute to John Laughton and Julian Corbett; Laughton initiated methods of modern research on naval history; Laughton influenced Mahan.

3062 -------. The Navy in India, 1763-1783. London: Benn, 1921, 1931, 432 pp. An assessement by a prominent historian.

3063 -------. The Navy in the War of 1739-1748. 3 vols. Cambridge: Cambridge UP, 1920, 845 pp. An intensively researched and detailed study of this formative period; efforts at amphibious operations usually failed and France had similar problems.

3064 [NRS 42]. Richmond, Herbert W., ed. Papers Relating to the Loss of Minorca in 1756. Publications of the Navy Records Society, vol. 42. London: NRS, 1913, xl, 224 pp. After the execution of Byng, an investigation of the circumstances and background of the Minorca imbroglio.

3065 Richmond, Herbert W. "Sir Julian Corbett: Died 21 September 1922." History, 7 (January 1923): 274-75. A serious loss to naval history; Corbett responsible for raising the level to new heights; emphasis on the interdependence of land and sea operations.

3066 -------. Statesmen and Sea Power: The Navy as an Instrument of Policy, 1558-1727. Oxford: Clarendon; Cambridge: Cambridge UP, 1946, 1953, 404 pp. Ed: E.A. Hughes; the Ford Lectures at Oxford, 1943; when Elizabeth came to the throne, threats from Spain, the Dutch, and France, thus, a need for a navy; review of 250 years to Rule Britannia.

3067 Rickard, Suzanne, ed. George Barrington's Voyage to Botany Bay. London: Continuum, 2001, 181 pp. A convicted criminal, to a convict hulk, then to New South Wales in the Third Fleet voyage; reformed in Australia and became a government official.

3068 Ridd, Stephen, ed. Julius Caesar in Gaul and Britain. History Eyewitness series. Austin: Raintree, 1995, 48 pp. Excerpts from the account by Caesar.

3069 Riley, James C. "Mortality on Long Distance Voyages in the Eighteenth Century." J Economic History, 41 (September 1981): 651-56. A detailed study of voyages of 84 vessels in the 1730s; 8 months or longer of the Dutch East India Company; mortality data of 17,092 persons; conclusions: rates were higher than time on land.

3070 Risse, Guenter B. "Britainnia Rules the Seas: The Health of Seamen, Edinburgh, 1791-1800." J History Medicine, 43 (1988): 426-46. Some diseases originate from causes peculiar to sea life; pioneers, e.g., Lind, Blane, and Trotter; use of hospital records to determine the incidence of disease.

3071 Ritchie, George S. The Admiralty Chart: British Naval Hydrography in the Nineteenth Century. London: Hollis; Edinburgh: Pentland, 1967, 1995, 388 pp. By the Hydrographer of the Navy; accurate and detailed; describes naval surveys.

3072 Ritchie, Robert C. Captain Kidd and the War against the Pirates. Cambridge: Harvard UP, 1986, 1989, vii, 306 pp. A scholarly survey presenting the rationale for the rise of buccaneering; pirates, e.g., Kidd, Blackbeard, and Morgan.

3073 Rivington, Francis C. and Rivington, John. Life of Horatio, Lord Viscount Nelson. London, 1822. A collection of accounts, e.g., the original Southey article in Quarterly Review, 1810.

3074 Rixson, Denis. The West Highland Galley. Edinburgh: Berling, 1998, xvi, 237 pp. Galleys of the Hebrides beginning in the 6th century; depictions in heraldry, jewelry, pub signs, grave stones, and graffiti; sadly, no archaeological finds; included Vikings, Picts, Irish, Scots, and Lords of the Isles.

3075 Roberts, John C. de V. Devon and the Armada. East Wittering: Gooday, 1988, 282 pp. An account of regional responses; on the occasion of the

Quadricentennial.

3076 Roberts, Keith. <u>Pavane</u>. London: Gollancz, 1968, 1984, viii, 279 pp. Historical fiction; counterfactual: the Spanish Armada succeeded, Queen Elizabeth assassinated, July 1588, Spanish occupied England; Guises encouraged in France and defeated Valois; Holy League prevailed, Protestants quashed.

3077 Roberts, Kenneth L. <u>Arundel</u>. NY: Doubleday, 1968, 412 pp. Roberts, 1885-1957; nautical fiction; from War of 1812, threats to invade Canada.

3078 -------. <u>Boon Island</u>. Hanover: UP of New England, 1955, 1996, 373 pp. Nautical fiction; this on pirates.

3079 -------. <u>Captain Caution: A Chronicle of Arundel</u>. NY: Doubleday, 1960, 310 pp. Nautical fiction; War of 1812.

3080 -------. <u>Northwest Passage</u>. 2 vols. NY: Doubleday, 1937, 1938, 709 pp. Several editions in foreign languages; Rogers Rangers fiction, focus of 18th century.

3081 Roberts, Michael. <u>Essays in Swedish History</u>. Minneapolis: U Minn P; London: Weidenfeld, 1966, 1967, ix, 358 pp. Includes the famous "the Military Revolution, 1560-1660" essay of 1956 which generated much debate.

3082 [NRS 9]. Roberts, William R. and Sweetman, Jack, eds. <u>New Interpretations in Naval History: Selected Papers from the Ninth Naval History Symposium Held at the U.S. Naval Academy, 18-20 October 1989</u>. Annapolis: NIP, 1991, xxii, 389 pp.

3083 [NHS 15] Roberts, William R., ed. <u>[Papers from the Fifteenth Naval History Symposium]</u>. (12-13 September 2001, USNA). CANCELLED.

3084 Robertson, F.W. "The Rise of a Scottish Navy, 1460-1513." Ph.D. diss, Edinburgh, 1934. A scholarly study.

3085 Robertson, Frederick L. <u>The Evolution of Naval Armament</u>. London: Storey, 1921, 1968, ix, 307 pp. A survey of developments in naval gunnery; incorporates ships, guns, and propulsion.

3086 Robertson, Jillian. <u>The Captain Cook Myth</u>. Sydney: Angus, 1981. Emphasis on Cook in Australia.

3087 Robertson, John W. <u>The Harbor of St. Francis: Francis Drake Lands Latitude 38 Degrees North</u>. San Francisco: Robertson, 1926, 119 pp. The local perspective in California of the events known.

3088 Robinson, Arthur H.W. <u>Marine Cartography in Britain: A History of the Sea Chart to 1855</u>. Leicester: Leicester UP, 1961, 1962, 222 pp. Fwd: John Edgell; Richard Hakluyt called for charts in the 16th century; eventually RN proceeded to survey with goals of national defense, reducing shipwrecks, and establishing aids to navigation; the Hydrographic Office was established in 1795.

3089 Robinson, Charles Napier and Leyland, John. The British Tar in Fact and Fiction: The Poetry, Pathos, and Humour of the Sailor's Life. NY: Harper, 1909, 1911, 520 pp. Robinson, Commander, RN, on life of officers and enlisted, 15th to 18th centuries; anectodal, careless crediting sources; themes, e.g., discipline, impressment, and sea stories.

3090 Robinson, Dwight E. "Secret of British Power in the Age of Sail: Admiralty Records of the Coasting Fleet." AmNep, 48 (Winter 1988): 5-21. A new and closer look at the coastal fleet, larger and more important than previously considered, e.g., Davis underestimated its extent and the coal trade was ignored; vital for development of industry and for manning the navy; the register of seamen was the source of impressment operations, both for exemptions and manning.

3091 Robinson, Gregory. The Elizabethan Ship. London: Longman, 1956, 58 pp. Illustrated by P.A. Jobson; a survey.

3092 -------. "A Forgotten Life of Sir Francis Drake." MM, 7 (January 1921): 10-18. Revision on Drake; too much glorification and myth; critical of Callender; assessments, e.g., a "courageous plunderer," absconded and sought prizes at crucial time during Armada, and Doughty affair revived.

3093 -------. "The GREAT HARRY." MM, 20 (January 1934): 85-92. Re HENRY GRACE A DIEU, larger than previously believed.

3094 -------. "The Seventeenth-Century Frigate." MM, 15 (July 1929): 271-81. Discussion of various configurations.

3095 -------. "The Trial and Death of Thomas Doughty." MM, 7 (September 1921): 271-82. A reply to Callender who exaggerates character of Drake; apologist for Doughty.

3096 Robinson, William. Jack Nastyface: Memoirs of an English Seaman. London: Wayland; Annapolis: NIP, 1836, 1973, 2002, 157 pp. Intro: Oliver Warner; a classic about the lower deck, 1805-1811; fought at Trafalgar; confirms general adoration of Nelson; denounces "torturing punishments" and "the unnatural and uncivilized custom of impressment."

3097 Robison, S.S. and Robison, M.L. A History of Naval Tactics from 1530 to 1930: The Evolution of Tactical Maxims. Annapolis: NIP, 1942, xxiii, 956 pp. An extensive survey, including tactical doctrine of England, the Dutch, France, and America; reviews series of battles and warships; begins with capture of a Turkish dromon off Beirut in 1191 by galleys of Richard I; learned much from Italian shipwrights.

3098 Robson, John. <u>Captain Cook's World: Maps of the Life and Voyages of James Cook, RN</u>. London: Chatham; Auckland: Random House, 2000, 212 pp. A geographic perspective on Cook and his exploits.

3099 Robson, L.L. <u>The Convict Settlers of Australia: A Enquiry into the Origins and Character of the Convicts Transported to New South Wales and Van Dieman's Land, 1787-1852</u>. Melbourne: Melbourne UP, 1965, 1970, 1973, 1976, xi, 257 pp. A statistical analysis of 163,000 convicts (estimates: 124,000 males and 25,000 females), e.g., origins, reasons, settlement, and subsequent life of these "founding felons."

3100 Roche, T.W.E. <u>The Golden Hind</u>. NY: Praeger, 1973, xiv, 200 pp. Completed by Neville Williams; Drake's ship, a replica to be built in North Devon and to sail from Plymouth to San Francisco in 1974.

3101 Roddis, Louis H. <u>James Lind: Founder of Nautical Medicine</u>. NY: Schuman; London: Heinemann, 1950, 1952, xi, 177 pp. Re "the Hippocrates of Nautical Medicine," e.g., the conquest of scurvy and developer of tropical medicines; to Royal Hospital at Haslar.

3102 Rodger, A.B. <u>The War of the Second Coalition, 1798 to 1801: A Strategic Commentary</u>. Oxford: Clarendon, 1964, viii, 312 pp. Ed: Christopher Duffy; a serious time for Britain, just after the great mutinies; includes the Egyptian campaign, "the chase," and the battle of the Nile.

3103 Rodger, N.A.M. The Admiralty. <u>Offices of State</u> series. London: Terence, 1979, 179 pp. Rodger, 1949-___, formerly at the Public Record Office, then NMM, thence to Exeter University; a comprehensive survey of the Admiralty, its officals, civil and professional; supersedes Gardiner and Murray; first permanent administration under Henry VIII, Board created in 17th century; role of Pepys.

3104 -------. <u>The Armada in the Public Records</u>. London: HMSO, 1988, iv, 76 pp. For the PRO; a description of sources available and their contents.

3105 -------. <u>Articles of War: The Statutes which Governed Our Fighting Navies, 1661, 1749 and 1886</u>. London: Mason, 1982, 61 pp. The origins from 1661 and changes, e.g., 1749, 1886, and 1957; provides for the governing of RN.

3106 -------. "Cnut's Geld and the Size of Danish Ships." <u>EHR</u>, 110 (April 1995): 392-403. Initial information from <u>Anglo-Saxon Chronicle</u>, a "geld" from Harthacnut in 1040 to pay for the fleet; records provide details about ships, number, size, and manpower of Danish ships.

3107 -------. "The Development of Broadside Gunnery, 1450-1650." <u>MM</u>, 82 (August 1996): 301-24. The origins, credited to the English by Corbett and others, are more complicated; need to look at developments in ship rigging, gunnery, and the broadside; look to Venice in the 15th century, the first to mount heavy guns at sea.

3108 -------. "Elizabethan Naval Gunnery." MM, 61 (November 1975): 353-54. Details gleaned from ordnance receipts and issues, a register of 1572; more revision of Lewis's "Armada Guns."

3109 -------. The Insatiable Earl: A Life of John Montagu, 4th Earl of Sandwich, 1718-1792. London: HarperCollins, 1993, 1994, xviii, 425 pp. Whig historians destroyed his reputation: corrupt and responsible for the loss of the American colonies, his mistress murdered on the steps of the Admiralty, and, of course, the "sandwich"; 20 years as 1st Lord; hardworking, effective, and a determined administrator; a brilliant biographical study.

3110 -------. A Naval History of Britain. ___ vols. London: HarperCollins. I: The Safeguard of the Sea, 600-1649, 1997, 1998, xxviii, 691 pp. II: A Great Liberty, 1649-1815. London: Harper, 1997-____. The first multi-volume history of the Royal Navy since Clowes, sponsored by NMM, NRS, SNR, and Exeter University, Vol I, 1997; Vol. II projected 2003 or 2004; subsequent vols. forthcoming; a brilliant systhesis incorporating the latest literature and intrepretations from all perspectives and all levels by the preeminent and prolific naval scholar of the day; on the best seller list and available in paperback; coverage of England, Wales, Ireland, "the Western Isles," and Scotland; brings in the nation and the navy, administration, finance, social aspects, and traditional battles and ships; no "Royal Navy" during the period covered by vol. I.

3111 [NRS 125]. Rodger, N.A.M., ed. The Naval Miscellany. Publications of the Navy Records Society, vol. 125. London: Allen, 1984, xiv, 546 pp. The 5th vol. in the series; a voyage of the Earl of Warwick, management of the dockyards in the 1670s, Benbow's "last fight," operations against Copenhagen, and the Dardanelles campaign.

3112 Rodger, N.A.M. Naval Records for Genealogists. PRO Handbook, # 22. London: HMSO, 1984, 1988, 1989, ix, 220 pp. A comprehensive description of the public records and a guide on how to use them; not Royal Marines and nothing from Tudor and earlier periods.

3113 Rodger, N.A.M. "The Naval Service of the Cinque Ports." EHR, 111 (June 1996): 636-51. Those "powerful and privileged towns" of the Southeast coast; origins as a transport service to Normandy; heyday in the 13th century.

3114 -------. "The Norman Invasion of 1066." MM, 80 (November 1994): 459-63. The invasion is a complex story; must transport large army of cavalry, then land and provide time for recovery and preparation; needed at least 4 horses per knight; that came to 8 to 12,000.

3115 -------. "Recent Books on the Royal Navy of the Eighteenth Century." J Military History, 63 (July 1999): 683-703. The literature of the 1st great age of naval history, since 1960, broader coverage, e.g., privateering, dockyards, logistics, conferences, and proceedings; reviews a number of important works.

3116 -------. "Stragglers and Deserters from the Royal Navy during the Seven Years' War." Bull IHR, 57 (1984): 54-73. Masefield depicts floating concentration camps, Jack Tar, beaten and broken; Baugh and others have presented a more correct picture, more complicated.

3117 -------. The Wooden World: An Anatomy of the Georgian Navy. Annapolis: NIP; London: Collins, 1986, 1988, 445 pp. The standard on the lower deck in the 18th century; significant contrast from depictions of Marcus Rediker, not cited in extensive bibliography; focus on period, 1740-1775; "wooden world" was a society in minature; the RN, the largest industrial unit in the world at the time.

3118 Rodgers, S."The Symbolism of Ship Launching in the Royal Navy." D.Phil. diss, Oxford, 1983, 695 pp. Traces the tradition and ceremony.

3119 Rodgers, William L. Naval Warfare under Oars: 4th to 16th Centuries: A Study of Strategy, Tactics, and Ship Design. Annapolis: NIP, 1939, 1940, 1967, 1970, xiii, 358 pp. A narrative survey; coverage, e.g., Romans, Vikings, the Crusades, Italian naval wars, and later naval wars involving Spain, France, and England; concludes with the Armada.

3120 Rodriguez-Salgado, M.J., ed. Armada, 1588-1988: An International Exhibition to Commemorate the Spanish Armada, National Maritime Museum, Greenwich, 20 April-4 September 1988: The Official Catalogue. London: Penguin, 1988, 295 pp. In coordination with the staff of NMM; the exhibition moved on to the Ulster Museum, Belfast, 12 October 1588-8 January 1989; a massive exhibition in 16 sections, the largest ever for NMM; incorporates politics, personalities, art, culture, and technology of the 16th century and artifacts from the shipwrecks; over 400 items from other countries, e.g., Spain, Austria, the Vatican, and the U.S.

3121 Rodriguez-Salgado, M.J. and Adams, Simon, eds. England, Spain and the Gran Armada, 1585-1604: Essays from the Anglo-Spanish Conferences, London and Madrid, 1988. NY: Barnes: Edinburgh: David, 1990, 1991, xv, 308 pp. Papers by expert scholars from Britain and Spain; topics, e.g., the Anglo-Spanish war as a continuation of the Wars of the Roses, Elizabethan naval warfare, a clash between 2 different military systems, and an enlightening comparison of the endurance and survivability of Mediterranean-built and Atlantic-built Spanish ships.

3122 Rodriguez-Salgado, M.J. "The Spanish Story of the 1588 Armada Reassessed." Historical J, 33 (June 1990): 461-78. A historiographical survey, especially of Spanish works; incorporation of the intensive archival research among Spanish sources encouraged in Spain; confirms the revised view that the Armada campaign was not so decisive for the Spanish nor the English.

3123 Rogers, Clifford J. "The Military Revolution of the Hundred Years' War." J

Military History, 57 (April 1993): 241-78. Reviews contributions to the debate, e.g., Roberts, Parker, Duffy, and Lynn; but neglect of earlier period, the Hundred Years' War.

3124 Rogers, Clifford J., ed. The Military Revolution Debate. Boulder: Westview, 1995, 404 pp. Includes a dozen essays, old and new, reviewing the great debate over the "Military Revolution" which has been raging for 40 years; covers the late middle ages to the industrial age; issues, e.g., the process of state building, changes in technology, land and naval warfare, and the rise of the West.

3125 Rogers, Clifford J. War Cruel and Sharp: English Strategy under Edward III, 1327-1360. Warfare in History series. Woodbridge: Boydell, 2000, xviii, 458 pp. Reviews the military and political strategies; covers series of campaigns and battles, e.g., siege of Berwick, invasion of 1346, siege of Calais, and battles of Sluys and Winchelsea.

3126 Rogers, Clifford J., ed. The Wars of Edward III: Sources and Interpretations. Warfare in History series. Rochester: Boydell, 2000, xxvii, 382 pp. In 2 parts, sources and articles by experts; issues, e.g., causes, strategy, and the role of Scotland; but neglects war at sea and most is obsolete.

3127 Rogers, Hugh C.B. Generals-at-Sea: Naval Operations during the English Civil War and the Anglo-Dutch Wars. Bromley: Galago, 1992, xii, 161 pp. Illustrated with 28 paintings from NMM; touted the origins of the modern navy during this time, sponsored by Parliament; the hierarchy of command was created; the Articles of War and Fighting Instructions; Generals, e.g., Blake, Monck, Sandwich, Richard Deane, Rupert, Penn, and Holmes.

3128 -------. Troopships and Their History. London: Seeley, 1963, 223 pp. British transport of soldiers, 17th-20th centuries, e.g., the first, to Tangier in 1660, and other combined operations; noted crowding and health consequences.

3129 Rogers, John G. Origins of Sea Terms. Boston: Nimrod, 1984, xv, 215 pp. For Mystic Seaport Museum; a survey.

3130 Rogers, Nicholas. Crowds, Culture, and Politics in Georgian Britain. Oxford: Clarendon, 1998, xii, 291 pp. By protege of Georges Rude; 9 essays on collective protest, e.g., resistance to impressment and acquittal of Admiral Keppel in 1779.

3131 Rogers, P.G. The Dutch in the Medway. Oxford: Oxford UP, 1970, 192 pp. Depicts the "catastrophe" of 1667, comparable to Majuba Hill and Singapore; the plan of de Witt; much detail on before, during, and after, even "celebration" of 1967; nicely illustrated.

3132 Rogers, Woodes. A Cruising Voyage Round the World. Boston: Smith; London: Lintot, 1712, 1726, xix, 428 pp. An account by Woodes Rogers who died about 1730.

3133 Rogozinski, Jan. Honour among Thieves: Captain Kidd, Henry Every and the Pirate Republic of Libertalia. London: Conway, 2001, 324 pp. An authoritative account of this island run by pirates, the original "Treasure Island."

3134 -------. Pirates!: Brigands, Buccaneers, and Privateers in Fact, Fiction and Legend: An A-Z Encyclopedia. NY: DeCapo, 1995, 1996, xvi, 398 pp. Over 1000 entries; cultural and media emphasis, e.g., art, poems, fiction, exploits, history, and movies.

3135 Roland, Alex F. "A Triumph of Natural Magic: The Development of Undersea Warfare in the Age of Sail, 1571-1865." Ph.D. diss, Duke, 1974, 266 pp. The basis of the next entry.

3136 -------. Undersea Warfare in the Age of Sail. Bloomington: Ind UP, 1977, 1978, 237 pp. Re the development of underwater vessels and weapons; based on advances in science and technology, e.g., underwater charges to break keel, mines, and torpedoes.

3137 Roosevelt, Theodore. The Naval War of 1812. Classics of Naval Literature NY: Putnam; NY: DaCapo; Annapolis: NIP, 1882, 1894, 1968, 1987, 1999, xxxviii, 486 pp. Intro: Edward Eckert; an extensive history by the future president; presents American perspective and critical of James, J.F. Cooper, and British interpretations; still considered as a major source.

3138 Roscoe, E.S. A History of the English Prize Court. London: Lloyds, 1924, 115 pp. Fwd: Henry Duke; describes the procedures in the court and a series of case studies; jurisdiction was first recognized in 1360; the basis became The Black Book of the Admiralty; American Prize Law followed the English tradition.

3139 Rose, J. Holland. Hood and the Defence of Toulon. Cambridge: Cambridge UP, 1922, vi, 175 pp. Rose, 1855-1942, theVere Harmsworth Professor of Naval History, Cambridge; a campaign early in the War of the French Revolution; Sidney Smith played important role.

3140 -------. "Napoleon and Seapower." Cambridge Historical J, 1 (1924): 138-57. An assessment; the French navy suffered badly from the Revolution; Napoleon had little appreciation of seapower but came to appreciate some aspects, e.g., Continental System and earlier grandiose plans for invasion of Egypt, Ireland, and England, all foiled; the British enjoyed a history and tradition of great seamen who led the Admiralty and formulated doctrines.

3141 -------. "The State of Nelson's Fleet before Trafalgar." MM, 8 (March 1922): 75-81. Re the Mediterranean Squadron, 1803-1805, its condition and the health of its seamen; blockade operations for 22 months, then to West Indies and back; virtually no health problems.

3142 -------. "Was the Failure of the Spanish Armada Due to Storms?" Proceedings of the British Academy, 22 (1936): 207-44. Laughton, Corbett, and even Ranke had answered "yes"; not so, the wind actually favored Spain on 5 occasions.

3143 Rose, Susan."Bayonne and the King's Ships, 1204-1420." MM, 86 (May 2000): 140-47. Port for Aquitaine and Gascony; noted for shipwrights and pirates; a number of English Crown ships built there.

3144 -------. "Islam versus Christendom: The Naval Dimension, 1000-1600." J Military History, 63 (July 1999): 561-78. Because Western scholars neglect Arabic sources, underestimation of Moslem naval forces and operations; look at Saladin and his successors and, later, the Ottomans.

3145 -------. Medieval Naval Warfare. Warfare in History series. London: Routledge, 2002, 176 pp. Coverage of strategy, tactics, dangers, difficulties, especially, Italian states, England, and France.

3146 [NRS 123]. Rose, Susan, ed. The Navy of the Lancastrian Kings: Accounts and Inventories of William Soper, Keeper of the King's Ships, 1422-1427. Publications of the Navy Records Society, vol. 123. London: Allen, 1982, xx, 288 pp. Informative on the administration and logistics of RN of 15th century during reigns of Henry V and VI; interim measures after the decline of the Cinque Ports.

3147 Rosenberg, Max. The Building of Perry's Fleet on Lake Erie, 1812-1813. Harrisburg: Pennslyvania Historical, 1950, 1968, viii, 72 pp. A history of the operation.

3148 [NRS 113]. Roskill, Stephen W., ed. Documents Relating to the Naval Air Service, 1909-1918. Publications of the Navy Records Society, vol. 113. London: NRS, 1969, xxii, 790 pp. Noted as "Vol. I," but no subsequent volumes; re the background, early frustrations, war operations, and post-war controversies, 1908-1918.

3149 Roskill, Stephen W. The Strategy of Sea Power: Its Development and Application. London: Collins, 1962, 1986, 288 pp. The Lees-Knowles Lecture, Cambridge; fwd: John Fieldhouse; intro: Geoffrey Till; analyzes the invasion question from Tudor times.

3150 Ross, Steven T. Quest for Victory: French Military Strategy, 1792-1799. Canbury: Barnes, 1973, 320 pp. Survey of the making and executing of French strategy.

3151 Rosselli, John. Lord William Bentinck and the British Occupation of Sicily, 1811-1814. Cambridge: Cambridge UP, 1956, 220 pp. The British intervened to protect Mediterranean bases, especially after Naples was captured; alternative base.

3152 Roth, Milton. Ship Modelling from Stem to Stern. Blue Ridge: TAB, 1988, viii, 280 pp. A guide and handbook.

3153 Rowbotham, W.B. "The Algerine War in the Time of Charles II." JRUSI, 109 (May, August, November 1964): 160-68, 253-62, and 350-56. A campaign to suppress piracy from the ports of North Africa, Tripoli, Tunis, Algiers, and Sallee, in the 1670s and 1680s.

3154 [NRS 87]. Rowbotham, W.B., ed. The Naval Brigades of the Indian Mutiny, 1857-1858. Publications of the Navy Records Society, vol. 87. London: NRS, 1947, xvi, 304 pp. Describes operations of Naval Brigades in India assembled after the Mutiny of 1857.

3155 -------. "Soldiers and Seaman's Wives and Children in H.M. Ships." MM, 47 (February 1961): 42-48. In the 18th century, especially in 1793, a shortage of seamen; the Army was called upon to fill in with soldiers; interestingly, some brought their "wives" and children from marriages "on the strength"; a kind of regimental housing.

3156 Rowe, Violet A. Sir Henry Vane the Younger: A Study in Political and Administrative History. London: Athlone, 1970, xiii, 298 pp. Fwd: C.V. Wedgwood; re the brilliant and unscrupulous Parliamentary leader during the 1640s; instrumental in building up the navy, first as a member of the Admiralty Committee and then as an Admiralty Commissioner.

3157 Rowse, A.L. Exhibition of the Historical Relics of Sir Francis Drake. London, 1952. The catalogue of the exhibition: "Sir Francis Drake and the British Enterprise," July 1952.

3158 -------. The Expansion of Elizabethan England. Harper Torchbook. NY: Harper; NY: St. Martin, 1955, 1965, 1972, 450 pp. A detailed narrative of the expansion; essential was sea power; the history of RN as a continuous force begins with the Tudors; much on the significance of the Armada campaign and subsequent operations.

3159 -------. Sir Richard Grenville and the REVENGE: An Elizabethan Hero. Boston: Houghton, 1937, 365 pp. Seen as an aspect to the growth of the navy; Grenville took on a whole fleet.

3160 -------. "Sir Richard Grenville's Place in English History." Proceedings of the British Academy, 43 (1957): 79-95. The Raleigh Lecture; Grenville was assistant to Raleigh during the Virginia voyages.

3161 -------. Sir Walter Ralegh: His Family and Private Life. NY: Harper, 1962, xii, 348 pp. A good modern biography.

3162 Royen, Paul C. van, et al., eds. "Those Emblems of Hell"?: European Sailors and the Maritime Labour Market, 1570-1870. St. John's: IMEHA, 1997, xii, 362 pp. A collection of essays, general surveys of sailors of nations, e.g., for England, Peter Earle, for Britain, Sarah Palmer, and for Scotland, Gordon Jackson, plus 7 others; a curious title and rigid structure.

3163 Ruddock, Alwyn A. "The Earliest Records of the High Court of the Admiralty, 1515-1558." Bull IHR, 22 (November 1949): 139-51. Some case studies from the earliest records, e.g., unauthorized privateers and piracy in the Channel.

3164 -------. Italian Merchants and Shipping in Southampton, 1270-1600. Southampton: University College, 1950, 1951, xii, 300 pp. An Italian enclave developed; acted as bankers for the Crown; wool trade; from Genoa, Venice, and Florence; declined in 16th century.

3165 -------. "Italian Trading Fleets in Medieval England." History, 29 (1944): 192-202. English trade with the Mediterranean; Italian merchant fleets developed alternatives to Eastern caravan, overland trade; merchant galleys, then, later, the carrack, demonstrating advances in shipbuilding; Venice, Genoa, and Florence; trade to Southampton, Sandwich, and London ports; items, e.g., wool, spices, silks, carpets, perfumes, and jewels.

3166 -------. "John Day of Bristol and the English Voyages across the Atlantic before 1497." Geographical J, 132 (June 1966): 225-32. From an extant letter, Day made voyage across the Atlantic; Day, a London merchant admitted to the Bristol Staple in 1494; did Bristol men discover America before Columbus?

3167 -------. "The Trinity House at Deptford in the Sixteenth Century." EHR, 65 (October 1950): 458-76. Most records destroyed; seen as "the cradle of the Royal Navy"; a corporation with master and bretheren; control over pilots and navigation of the Thames; other Trinity Houses in other ports.

3168 Rule, Margaret. The MARY ROSE: The Excavation and Raising of Henry VIII's Flagship. London: Conway, 1982, 1983, 240 pp. Fwd: Prince of Wales; lost in 1545, MARY ROSE was discovered by diver Alexander McKee in 1970; support from Prince Charles, Duke of Edinbugh, and Earl Mountbatten; 1979-1982, 25,000 dives; ultimately raised and now in special museum, Portsmouth Naval Base.

3169 Rumble, Alexander R., ed. The Reign of Cnut: King of England, Denmark and Norway. Studies in the Early History of Britain. London: Leicester UP, 1994, xviii, 340 pp. Several articles by prominent authorities, e.g., on military developments: 2 types of forces, house earls and lithsmen; at sea, a paid fleet of lithsmen

3170 Runyan, Timothy J. "The American Neptune: A Half Century of Maritime History." AmNep, 51 (Winter 1991): 45-48. By an editor; interest in a journal expressed in 1939, leading to quarterly journal, 1st issue, January 1941; S.E. Morison was instrumental.

3171 -------. "The English Navy in the Reign of Edward III." Ph.D. diss, Maryland, 1972, 292 pp. The basis for these entries.

3172 -------. "Ships and Fleets in Anglo-French Warfare, 1337-1360." AmNep, 46 (Spring 1986): 91-99. During the Hundred Years' War, a naval conflict in the Channel; extensive use of naval transport, e.g., for campaigns of Crecy and Poitiers; collected data on 1291 ships, 325 identified by type and 31 as King's Ships; during the reign of Edward III, 1327-1377, an embryonic navy came into being; an official clerk of the King's Ships; battles of Sluys (vs French) of 1340 and L'Espagnols sur Mer (vs Spanish) of 1350; maritime Law of Oleron adopted and Vice Admiralty Courts created.

3173 -------. "Ships and Mariners in Late Medieval England." J British Studies, 16 (Spring 1977): 1-17. Describes records which provide important information.

3174 Runyan, Timothy J., ed. Ships, Seafaring and Society: Essays in Maritime History. Detroit: Wayne State UP, 1987, xvi, 366 pp. For the Great Lakes Historical Society; 20 essays from NAOSH of 1987, e.g., Runyan on Royal Fleets in medieval England, Miller on naval stores from the Baltic, and Dye on American prisoners during the War of 1812.

3175 Russell, Edward F. Knight of the Sword: The Life and Letters of Admiral Sir William Sidney Smith. London: Gollancz, 1964, 224 pp. By Lord Russell of Liverpool; Smith, 1764-1840; the 1st modern biography.

3176 Russell, Jack. Gibraltar Besieged, 1779-1783. London: Heinemann, 1965, xi, 308 pp. Recounts a long siege.

3177 -------. Nelson and the Hamiltons. NY: Simon; London: Blond, 1969, 1972, 448 pp. Nelson met the Hamiltons in 1793 when he was 35 years old; much use of correspondence and much detail.

3178 Russell, Percy. Dartmouth: History of the Port and Town. British Cities series. London: Batsford, 1950, vii, 184 pp. Enlightening on activities on the Channel coast.

3179 Russell, Peter E. The English Intervention in Spain and Portugal in the Time of Edward III and Richard II. Oxford: Oxford UP, 1955, xxiv, 611 pp. Broad-based research; English interventions, mostly by sea, in ancient Spanish kingdoms, e.g., Castile, Navarre, Aragon, Portugal, and Gascony; French also involved; galley fleets; Edward III consulted with Genoa re galley warfare; series of naval attacks along English coast; describes typical galley of 13th and 14th centuries.

3180 -------. Prince Henry "The Navigator": A Life. New Haven: Yale UP, 2000, x, 448 pp. A solid, scholarly study; revisionist; Henry was half English-Plantagenet; downgrades his contributions, debunks the legends of nautical expertise.

3181 Russell, William Clark. Horatio Nelson and the Naval Supremacy of England: A Biography. Heroes of the Nations series. London: Abbott; NY: Putnam, 1890, 1923, xiv, 357 pp. A biography; most extensive on battles.

3182 -------. The Life of Admiral Lord Collingwood. London: Methuen, 1895, xv, 271 pp. An older biography.

3183 -------. The Life of Nelson in a Series of Episodes. London: Christian Knowledge Society, 1905, 274 pp. A biography with a message.

3184 Russell, William Clark, ed. Nelson's Words and Deeds: A Selection from the Dispatches and Correspondence of Horatio Nelson. London: Low, 1890, vii, 224 pp. An anthology from documents.

3185 Russell, William Clark. Pictures from the Life of Nelson. London: Bowden, 1897, xxvii, 301 pp. A series of illustrations re Nelson.

3186 -------. Sailors' Language: A Collection of Sea-Terms and Their Definitions. London: Low, 1883, xvi, 164. The contribution of Russell to the nautical dictionary.

3187 -------. William Dampier. English Men of Action series. London: Macmillan, 1889, 1916, 192 pp. An older biography.

3188 Rutter, Owen, ed. The Court Martial of the BOUNTY Mutineers. Notable British Trials series. London: Hodge, 1931, x, 202 pp. The court martial of 12-18 September 1792, the 10 defendants included Peter Heywood; preceded by the PANDORA court martial; 4 executed.

3189 -------, ed. John Fryer of the BOUNTY: Notes on His Career Written by His Daughter Mary Ann. London: Golden Cockerel, 1939. Fryer, 1752-1817, was Master of BOUNTY; loyal to Bligh but they hated each other; a postscript to the account of the BOUNTY launch.

3190 -------, ed. The Journal of James Morrison, Boatswain's Mate of the BOUNTY, Describing the Mutiny and Subsequent Misfortunes of the Mutineers, Together with an Account of the Island of Tahiti. London: Golden Cockerel, 1935, 242 pp. The original journal from Mitchell Library, Sydney; probably written later after the shipwreck of PANDORA.

3191 Rutter, Owen. The True Story of the Mutiny in the BOUNTY. London: Newnes, 1936, 185 pp. Details on the background for the voyage, the mutiny, the voyage of the launch, and disposition of BOUNTY and the mutineers; less sympathy for Bligh, more for Christian.

3192 -------. Turbulent Journey: A Life of William Bligh, Vice-Admiral of the Blue. London: Nicholson, 1936, 279 pp. A biography; no introduction; Bligh was no sadist, nor deliberately or wantonly cruel.

3193 Ryan, Anthony N. "The Causes of the British Attack upon Copenhagen in 1807." EHR, 68 (January 1953): 37-55. The controversial attack on this neutral country; a consequence of the Tilsit Agreement; to prevent Danish fleet from aiding

Napoleon.

3194 -------. "The Defence of British Trade with the Baltic, 1808-1813." EHR, 74 (July 1959): 443-66. Re an extensive operation by RN to maintain British trade and counter the Continental System; trade included essential naval stores and masts.

3195 -------. "'God of His Mercy Keep Us from Sickness': Disease and Defeat in the Age of Francis Drake." Bull Liverpool Medical History Society, 3 (July 1990): 26-32. Describes situation of health and disease at sea in 16th century.

3196 -------. "The Navy at Copenhagen in 1807." MM, 39 (August 1953): 201-10. Lord Gambier led a land and sea attack.

3197 [NRS 110]. Ryan, Anthony N., ed. The Saumarez Papers: Selections from the Baltic Correspondence of Vice-Admiral Sir James Saumarez, 1808-1812. Publications of the Navy Records Society, vol. 110. London: NRS, 1968, xxvi, 287 pp. Details on his Baltic campaigns when his flagship was HMS VICTORY; bombarded Copenhagen in 1807; Saumarez was one of Nelson's captains, not always a favorite; at the Saints and the Nile but not Trafalgar.

3198 Ryan, Simon. The Cartographic Eye: How Explorers Saw Australia. London: Cambridge UP, 1996, xi, 235 pp. "The antipodes in the European imagination"; scientific and literary methodogy of exploration.

3199 Rystad, Goran, et al., eds. In Quest of Trade and Security: The Baltic in Power Politics, 1500-1990. Lund: Lund UP, 1994, 334 pp. A collection of papers by experts, e.g., competition among the English, Dutch, Swedes, and Danes; scholars, e.g., Andrew Lambert, Jan Glete, and Stewart Oakley.

3200 Sacks, David Harris. "Trade, Society and Politics in Bristol, c. 1500-c. 1640." Ph.D. diss, Harvard, 1977. 3 vols. The basis of the following entries.

3201 -------. Trade, Society and Politics in Bristol, 1500-1640. 2 vols. NY: Garland, 1985, vii, 982 pp. The history of Bristol, especially its role in commerce, exploration, and politics.

3202 -------. The Widening Gate: Bristol and the Atlantic Economy, 1450-1700. Berkeley: U Cal P, 1991, xxvi, 464 pp. A fantastic production, an elegant and highly sophisticated analysis of the role of Bristol in the process of social, political,and cultural change leading to the modern Western economy; Bristol from leading medieval commercial center to bustling Atlantic entrepot; links to Gascony were at first contributory, then, after its loss and after the Hundred Years' War, Bristol diversified into luxury goods and voyages of exploration; trade with Spain and the Mediterranean; John Cabot departed here in 1497; he and others searched for the Northwest Passage, among other things.

3203 Saddington, D.B. "The Origin and Nature of the German and British Fleets."

Britannia, 21 (1990): 223-32. Back to time of 1st Roman incursions of 55 and 54 BC; Julius Caesar summoned 80 transports from the region; heavy losses due to storms.

3204 Sadlier, Michael. Excursions in Victorian Bibliography. London: Cox, 1922, 240 pp. A selection of 8 literary figures, e.g., Frederick Marryat and Herman Melville.

3205 Sahlins, Marshall. Historical Metaphors and Mythical Realities: Structure in the Early History of the Sandwich Islands Kingdom. Ann Arbor: U Mich P, 1981, viii, 84 pp. Re "structural anthropology" seen as "a radical opposition to history" or history as myth, epic, and cosmic travelogue; the case study: the apotheosis of Captain Cook.

3206 -------. How "Natives" Think: About Captain Cook, For Example. Chicago: U Chicago P, 1995, 288 pp. Elaboration of the previous entry and debate with Gananath Obeyesekere; a debate among anthropologists; passionate, witty, and learned; the basis of Hawaiian perceptions of Cook.

3207 -------. Islands of History. Chicago: U Chicago P, 1985, xix, 180 pp. The original work setting off the debate with Obeyesedere; how Hawaiians viewed Cook

3208 Sainsbury, A.B. The Centenary of the Navy Records Society, 1893-1993. London: SNR, 1993. Presents the history of NRS.

3209 -------. "The Origins of the Society for Nautical Research." MM, 80 (November 1994): 450-58. The story of the making of the association; J.K. Laughton had founded the Navy Records Society in 1893; his son, L.G. Carr Laughton, SNR, in 1910.

3210 St. Vincent 200: The Proceedings of the Bicentennial International Naval Conference, Portsmouth, 15 February 1997. Portsmouth: Joint Sponsors, 1998. The published proceedings, all sponsored by SNR, the Nelson Society, and the 1805 Club; an event in the Nelson Decade.

3211 Sainty, John C., comp. Office Holders in Modern Britain: Admiralty Officials, 1660-1870. London: Athlone, 1975, 161 pp. Vol. IV in the series sponsored by IHR; a comprehensive listing.

3212 Salt, Henry S. The Flogging Craze: A Statement of the Case against Corporal Punishment. London: Allen, 1916, 158 pp. For the Humanitarian League; fwd: George Greenwood; a critique, history, and plea to abolish; calls England "the stronghold of the flogging cult."

3213 Salt, S.P. "Sir Simonds D'Ewes and the Levying of Ship Money, 1635-1640." Historical J, 37 (June 1994): 253-88. The seemingly ambiguous role of D'Ewes, Sheriff of Suffolk, responsible for collecting Ship Money, and his campaign opposing the levy.

3214 Sandahl, Bertil. Middle English Sea Terms. 3 vols. Cambridge: Harvard UP, 1951-1982. A detailed reference work; the complex nautical terminology on medieval ships; reprints essential documents, some in Latin, Norman French, and Early English; volumes divided: hulls, masts, spars, and sails, and standing and running rigging.

3215 Sanderson, Michael W.B. "English Naval Strategy and Maritime Trade in the Caribbean, 1793-1802." Ph.D. diss, London, 1968. A scholarly study of the West Indies during the War of the French Revolution.

3216 Sanderson, Michael W.B., ed. National Maritime Museum Catalogue of the Library. 2 vols. London: HMSO, 1968-1970, 977 pp. An extensive listing of the holdings by categories, e.g., reference, biographies, and Navy Lists.

3217 Sanderson, Michael W.B. Sea Battles: A Reference Guide. Middletown: Wesleyan UP, 1975, 199 pp. A guide to 250 naval battles in alphabetical order; includes maps, plans, and bibliographies, all preceded by a chronology; the 1st for Britain is Dover of 1217, then Sluys of 1340, and on through World War II.

3218 Sands, John O. Yorktown's Captive Fleet. Charlottesville: UP of Va, 1983, xii, 267 pp. For Mariner's Museum; a survey; combines conventional research with nautical archaeology.

3219 Sandstrom, Mangus. "VASA under Attack." Nature (21 February 2002). A report recounting current concerns, e.g., chemical attacks, sulfuric acid, on the wood; details of the museum and increasing interest from the public.

3220 Sanger, Ernest. Englishmen at War: A Social History in Letters. Stroud: Sutton, 1993, x, 370 pp. Fwd: Anthony Farrar-Hockley; an extensive collection of letters; recounts appalling conditions and harsh treatment, especially at sea, and especially through the 18th century; naval events, e.g., Quiberon Bay and the Saints.

3221 Saul, Norman E. "Russia and the Mediterranean, 1797-1807." Ph.D. diss, Columbia, 1965, 305 pp. The basis for the next entry.

3222 -------. Russia and the Mediterranean, 1797-1807. Chicago: Chicago UP, 1970, xii, 268 pp. Russia played an important diplomatic and military role here; fleet entered to counter French threat in Italy and, especially, to Malta; joint fleet operations with British, Austrian, and Turkish forces; withdrew after Tilsit.

3223 Saunders, Andrew. English Heritage Book of Channel Defences. London: Batsford, 1997, 128 pp. A handsome publication, illustrated; defense structures along the coast built from the 15th through the 20th centuries, e.g., Dartmouth Castle of the 1480s, Dover Castle, naval bases, and coastal fortifications.

3224 Saunders, David. <u>Britain's Maritime Memorials and Mementoes</u>. Sparkford: Stephens, 1996, 183 pp. Personal search and visit to 1400 memorials throughout the British Isles, e.g., commemorating ship disasters, lifeboat losses, and incidents associated with wars.

3225 Saunders, Roy. <u>The Raising of the VASA: The Rebirth of a Swedish Galleon</u>. London: Oldbourne, 1962, 88 pp. Similar to MARY ROSE, describes the discovery, search, and recovery.

3226 Savary des Bruslons, Jacques. <u>Universal Dictionary of Trade and Commerce</u>. 2 vols. London: Knapton; NY: Kells, 1707, 1751, 1755, 1757, 1774, 1971. Trans: M. Postlethwayt; an original French dictionary; contains much pertinent information, e.g., countries, ports, and commodities.

3227 Saville, Martin. <u>Hornblower's Ships: Their History and Their Models</u>. London: Conway, 2001, 128 pp. Profusely illustrated; based on the 11 scale-models used to film the Hornblower TV-mini-series; by the model coordinator.

3228 Savours, Ann. <u>The Search for the North West Passage</u>. London: Chatham, 1999, xxii, 320 pp. A historical survey of the British efforts, from the late 16th through the mid-20th centuries, e.g., Frobisher, Hudson, Baffin, Cook, and Barrow, but not Cabot.

3229 Sawers, Larry. "The Navigation Acts Revisited." <u>Economic History Review</u>, 45 (May 1992): 262-84. Summarizes the debate among historians about the consequences of the Acts; some claim a cause of the American Revolution, others not; Sawers favors former.

3230 Sawyer, P.H. <u>Kings and Vikings: Scandinavia and Europe, AD 700-1100</u>. London: Methuen, 1982, x, 192 pp. Known variously as Northmen, Danes, and Vikings; until 11th century, raids by exiles, then shift to native rulers; details of ships and "fleets"; conclusion: depredations exaggerated; the Vikings were no more violent and brutal than the English, Franks, and Friscians.

3231 Saxby, Richard. "The Blockade of Brest in the French Revolutionary War." <u>MM</u>, 78 (February 1992): 25-35. A neglected topic; a dilemma for the British, laxness or concentration at Brest.

3232 -------. "Lord Bridport and the Spithead Mutiny." <u>MM</u>, 79 (May 1993): 170-78. Bridport negotiated with the delegates; afterwards, they sent a letter of appreciation.

3233 Scammell, Geoffrey V. "The English in the Atlantic Islands, c. 1450-1650." <u>MM</u>, 72 (August 1986): 295-317 pp. The islands were Azores, Canaries, Cape Verges, Madeira, and Sao Tome; supply for trans-Atlantic voyages; Anglo-Spanish arrangements for English use and favorite operations for English privateers; Bristol had a special relationship here.

3234 -------. "European Seamanship in the Great Age of Discovery." MM, 68 (August 1982): 357-76. From 1400-1600, developments in navigation and ship design; contributions to the founding of the first global maritime empires; conclusion: at this time ships were the most advanced technological vessels but remained at the mercy of nature.

3235 -------. "Manning the English Merchants Service in the Sixteenth Century." MM, 56 (May 1970): 131-54. The tendency was to overman because of anticipation of losses; meant much manpower required.

3236 -------. Ships, Oceans and Empire: Studies in European Maritime and Colonial History, 1400-1750. Aldershot: Variorum, 1995, viii, 278 pp. A collection of 14 of his essays over 35 years of study, e.g., English merchant shipping, the Hakluyts, manning problems, and navigation acts.

3237 -------. "The Sinews of War: Manning and Provisioning English Fighting Ships, c. 1550-1650." MM, 73 (November 1987): 351-67. The rise of England as the foremost maritime power; corresponding development of grandiose naval pretentions in the Channel and North Sea; the consequence: an insatiable demand for seamen and consistent under-manning of ships.

3238 -------. The World Encompassed: The First European Maritime Empires, c.800-1650. London: Methuen; Berkeley: U Cal P, 1981, xvi, 538 pp. During this period, unparralleled expansion of Western Europeans, e.g., Vikings, Hanse, Venetians, Genoese, Portuguese, Spanish, Dutch, English, and French.

3239 Scarlett, Bernard. Shipminder: The Story of Her Majesty's Coastguard. London: Pelham, 1971, 1972, 206 pp. Origins in the 17th century as coast watchers, emergency, and anti-smuggling force, evolving into a naval reserve.

3240 Schaeffer, Robert K. "The Chains of Bondage Broke: The Proletarianization of Seafaring Labor, 1600-1800." Ph.D. diss, SUNY, Binghamton, 1984, 469 pp. An obvious Marxist agenda; the Atlantic maritime states exploited their sailors, merchant and government; their lot worsened, e.g., impressment, discipline, coersion, and reduced costs, all comparable to galley slaves of earlier times; but, late 18th century mutinies reversed the trend to a free-wage system.

3241 Schaeper, Thomas J. John Paul Jones and the Battle off Flamborough Head: A Reconsideration. NY: Lang, 1989, viii, 125 pp. By a French historian;focused on actions and contributions of various French supporters and captains, even Landais who fired on Jones; various corrections.

3242 Schama, Simon. A History of Britain. ___ vols. I: At the Edge of the World?, 3000-AD 1603. II: The British Wars, 1603-1776. London: BBC; NY: Hyperion, 2000-2001, 415 and 544 pp. A recent "cosmic" approach in the Churchill-Bryant-Sceptered Isle traditon; 2 vols. thus far; illustrated; supports 6-hour BBC-TV programme; general synthesis; recognition of contributions of "the 4 nations."

3243 Schilder, Gunter. <u>Australia Unveiled: The Share of the Dutch Navigators in the Discovery of Australia</u>. Amsterdam: Orbis, 1975, xii, 424 pp. Trans: Olaf Richter; Dutch navigators of early 17th century, especially Dutch vessel DUYFKEN, 1606; search for <u>terra Australis</u>.

3244 Schneid, Frederick C. <u>Napoleon's Grand Strategy</u>. NY: Westview. In 2000, noted as forthcoming.

3245 Schoenfeld, Maxwell P. "The Restoration Seaman and His Wages." <u>AmNep</u>, 25 (October 1965): 278-87. Documents the neglect and dishonesty of officials concerning wages of seamen; no change in the amount over centuries, wage tickets depreciated, wages not paid, and the violence associated with impressment; conclusion: "seamen suffered an endemic state of discouragement."

3246 Schom, Alan. <u>Napoleon Bonaparte: A Life</u>. NY: HarperCollins, 1997, xxii, 888 pp. A recent, solid biography with emphasis on military exploits; part of an obvious bicentenary series, this for the seizure of power of 1799; others anticipated through 2021.

3247 -------. <u>One Hundred Days: Napoleon's Road to Waterloo</u>. NY: Atheneum; London: Penguin, 1992, 1994, xv, 398 pp. A substantial account, from Elba to St. Helena, including the voyage aboard HMS NORTHUMBERLAND.

3248 -------. <u>Trafalgar: Countdown to Battle, 1803-1805</u>. NY: Atheneum; London: Joseph, 1990, 1992, x, 421 pp. A survey of the long campaign culminating in Trafalgar; role of Admiral Cornwallis and his campaign of blockading the French coast has been neglected; this fills that gap.

3249 Schreiber, Roy E. "Captain Cook Revisited." <u>Northern Mariner</u>, 11 (April 2000): 69-74. An up-to-date review of some literature, e.g., Beaglehole and the Sahlins-Obeyesekere debate.

3250 -------. <u>The Fortunate Adversities of William Bligh</u>. NY: Lang, 1991, 257 pp. Full coverage of his career, 3 mutinies in the navy and one as governor, New South Wales, yet he reaped promotions and honors, e.g., to Admiral and FRS; conclusion: Bligh was talented and lucky; his accusatory language got him into trouble.

3251 Schumacher, Henry. <u>Nelson's Last Love</u>. London: Hutchinson, n.d., 320 pp. A curious work; 39 untitled chapters, 36 illustrations, 23 of Lady Hamilton; others, Napoleon, Nelson, Horatia, Sir William Hamilton, Merton Place, Naples and its monarchs.

3252 Schur, Nathan. <u>Napoleon in the Holy Land</u>. London: Greenhill, 1999, 224 pp. The Egyptian campaign, to destroy the Ottoman Empire, and then, perhaps, the Persian, and on to India, even, beyond; but all ends at Acre; British marines assisted by RN captured his siege train, meaning disaster for Napoleon.

3253 Schurman, Donald M. The Education of a Navy: The Development of British Naval Strategic Thought, 1867-1914. Chicago: U Chicago P: NY: Krieger, 1965, 1984, 222 pp. The formative period of naval history and the formulation of strategy; on the Colomb brothers, Mahan, J.K. Laughton, Richmond, and Corbett.

3254 -------. Julian S. Corbett, 1854-1922: Historian of British Maritime Policy from Drake to Jellicoe. London: RHS, 1981, xii, 216 pp. An authoratative biography of Corbett, many seeing him as the most influential formulator of modern naval strategic thought; author of several naval histories of early modern British naval history.

3255 Schurz, William L. The Manila Galleon. NY: Dutton, 1939, 1959, 453 pp. Re Spanish maritime commerce, 1565-1815, an annual cruise, Manila to Acapulco; 4 captured by the English, 1587, 1709, 1743, and 1762.

3256 Scorza, Thomas J. In the Time before Steamships: "Billy Budd," The Limits of Politics and Modernity. DeKalb: North Ill UP, 1979, 256 pp. An esoteric treatise: "Billy Budd" was a critique of the whole of modern politics by Melville.

3257 Scott, George R. The History of Corporal Punishment: A Survey of Flagellation in Its Historical, Anthropological and Sociological Aspects. Alt. title: Flagellation. London: Torchstream; London: Tallis, 1948, 1968, 261 pp. An overly popularized, sensationalized, even dubious, survey.

3258 Scott, H.M. "The Importance of Bourbon Naval Reconstruction to the Strategy of Choiseul after the Seven Years' War." International History Review, 1 (January 1979): 17-35. After the Peace of Paris of 1763, French minister, Duke of Choiseul, planned rejuvenation of the French and Spanish navies.

3259 -------. "Sir Joseph Yorke, Dutch Politics and the Origins of the Fourth Anglo-Dutch War." Historical J, 31 (September 1988): 571-89. Re the preliminaries to the war, 1780-1784, which began over neutral rights and trade competition; the British ambassador exacerbated the situation.

3260 -------. "The Second Hundred Years' War, 1689-1815: Review Article." Historical J, 35 (June 1992): 442-69. Featured 13 books on Anglo-French relations, 4 of which were by Jeremy Black; and 6 wars; among gaps, need for biography of Rodney.

3261 Scott, J.R. "Pay-List of the Kentish Forces Raised to Resist the Spanish Armada." Archaeologyia Cantiana, 11 (1877): 388-91. Discovery of this document; informative.

3262 Scott, Walter F. "The Naval Chaplain in Stuart Times." D.Phil. diss, Oxford, 1935. A scholarly study of the naval chaplaincy.

3263 Scragg, D.G., ed. The Battle of Maldon. Manchester: Manchester UP, 1981,

110 pp. A poem presenting an account of the battle, Viking invasion defended by the English, Blackwater River in Essex; fact or fiction?

3264 Seager, Robert. <u>Alfred Thayer Mahan: The Man and His Letters</u>. Annapolis: NIP, 1977, 750 pp. A particilarly balanced account of Mahan, even iconoclastic; Mahan a genius and mediocrity.

3265 Seager, Robert and Maguire, Doris D., eds. <u>Letters and Papers of Alfred Thayer Mahan</u>. 3 vols. Annapolis: NIP, 1975, lii, 2336 pp. Enlightening on the personal and intellectual development of Mahan.

3266 Seaver, Kirsten A. <u>The Frozen Echo: Greenland and the Exploration of North America, c. AD 1000-1500</u>. Stanford: Stanford UP, 1996, xvi, 407 pp. Vikings to Greenland as early as 8th century; study of so-called West and East Settlements, voyages of John and Sebastian Cabot, role of Bristol merchants, and Vinland Map; some not convinced.

3267 Seel, Graham E. <u>The English Wars and Republic, 1637-1660</u>. London: Routledge, 1999, viii, 139 pp. A review of the issues leading to the rebellion, e.g., Ship Money, seen as a successful tax measure; most paid it.

3268 Seitz, Don C. <u>Paul Jones: His Exploits in English Seas during 1778-1780: Contemporary Accounts Collected from English Newspapers with a Complete Bibliography</u>. NY: Dutton, 1917, v, 327 pp. Local historical accounts of the operations.

3269 Selement, George. "Impressment and the American Merchant Marine, 1782-1812: An American View." <u>MM</u>, 59 (November 1973): 409-18. A survey of the issues; a serious dispute; clearly, British seamen were deserting to American ships and that increased when the Anglo-French war began in 1793; never really resolved but British did not renew the practice.

3270 Sellar, Walter C. and Yeatman, Robert J. <u>1066 and All of That: A Memorable History of England</u>. NY: Dutton; London: Sutton, 1931, 1993, 123 pp. A delightful, but, unfortunately, dated, satire on how graduate students were taught about English history.

3271 Seller, John. <u>The Sea Gunner</u>. Rotherfield: Boudriot, 1691, 1994, xvi, 234 pp. Intro: A.B. Caruana; a contemporaneous guide and reference manual.

3272 Sells, Arthur L, ed. <u>The Memoirs of James II: His Campaigns as Duke of York, 1652-1660</u>. Bloomington: Ind UP, 1962, 301 pp. Accounts of his campaigns.

3273 Senior, Clive M. "An Investigation of the Activities and Importance of English Pirates, 1603-1640." Ph.D. diss, Bristol, 1973. The basis of the next entry.

3274 -------. <u>A Nations of Pirates: English Piracy in Its Heyday</u>. Newton Abbot:

David and Charles, 1976, 166 pp. English piracy during the 1st half of the 17th century; founded on operations against Spain in the previous century; some motivated to recoup previous losses; estimate of 500 ships operating in 1608; age ended when Buckingham made LHA.

3275 Senior, William. "Drake and the Suit of John Doughty." MM, 7 (October 1921): 291-97. Re a case brought by brother, John, re the Thomas Doughty affair; suit failed.

3276 -------. Naval History in the Law Courts: A Selection of Old Maritime Cases. London: Longman, 1927, 114 pp. 10 chapters on various cases, e.g., Thomas Doughty and a trial of 11 pirates.

3277 -------. "The Navy as Penitentiary." MM, 16 (October 1930): 313-18. A review of the practice of sending criminals to RN.

3278 Sephton, Jim H. [SOVEREIGN OF THE SEAS]. In 2000, noted as forthcoming; re the spectacular warship designed by Phineas Pett, launched at Woolwich in 1637.

3279 Servies, James A., ed. The Log of HMS MENTOR, 1780-1781: A New Account of the British Navy at Pensacola. Pensacola: UP Fla, 1982, xi, 207 pp. Intro: Robert Rea; Britain gained West Florida earlier; 18-gun sloop scuttled by own crew after long siege.

3280 Setton, Kenneth M. "The Norman Conquest." National Geographic, 130 (August 1966): 206-51. Includes a reproduction of the Bayeux Tapestry, 231 feet long; depicts ships and naval operations.

3281 The 1766 Navy List. Bishop Norton: Ancholme, 2001, 200 pp. Ed: E.C. Coleman; a "snapshot" of the RN in the 18th century: all ships, officers, chaplains, and members of the various boards.

3282 Severin, Timothy. The Brendan Voyage. NY: McGraw; Norwalk: Easton, 1978, 1989, 2000, viii, 292 pp. A personal chronicle of the voyage by Severin, May 1976-June 1977, in small, oxhide boat, replica of that of Irish monks of the 6th century; to Hebrides, Faroes, Iceland, and Greenland; beautiful color pictures.

3283 -------. In Search of "Moby Dick": Quest for the White Whale. NY: Basic, 2000, 212 pp. A native of Ireland; sets out to "find" Moby Dick, recounts tragedy of ESSEX; Melville had made whaling voyages, knew about ESSEX; Severin then set out on 6000 mile quest, participates in hunt for sperm whales in Far East.

3284 Severn, Derek. "Nelson's Hardy." HisTod, 27 (August 1977): 505-12. Re Vice Admiral Sir Thomas Hardy, flag captain, HMS VICTORY; one of "band of brothers"; later to American Station and 1st Sea Lord.

3285 Seward, Desmond. The Hundred Years' War: The English in France, 1337-1453. London: Constable; NY: Penguin, 1978, 2001, 296 pp. A survey noted for its clarity; some coverage about ships and naval operations, e.g., Sluys, French invasion threats, and hiring of Genoese expertise in galleys.

3286 Sewell, William K. "Tudor English Contacts with North Americans, 1497-1603." Ph.D. diss, Ball State, 1971, 301 pp. Re Cabot and "capture" of 3 American natives; later voyages sponsored by Tudor monarchs, e.g., Frobisher who also brought natives back; also Drake, Raleigh, Davis, and Gilbert; increasing alienation of natives.

3287 Seymour, Michael. "Warships' Names of the English Republic, 1649-1659." MM, 76 (November 1990): 317-24. Information about the increase of the navy during the interregnum; used against Royalists and French privateers; initiated a professional civil service, gunboat diplomacy; names of ships highly symbolic, e.g., PRINCE, LIBERTY, UNITY, WARWICK, and COMMONWEALTH; names changed at Restoration.

3288 Shankland, Peter. Beware of Heroes: Admiral Sir Sidney Smith's War against Napoleon. London: Kimber, 1975, x, 240 pp. Re the grandiose plan to conquer the Orient; RN had withdrawn and Malta would be the initial base; in the event, it was Smith who perceived his intentions and stopped Napoleon; historians have underrated Smith, just as Napoleon did.

3289 Shannon, David. Nelsoniana, 1805-1905: An Anthology of Notes and Queries from T.P.'s Weekly Magazine in 1905, the Year of the Trafalgar Centenary. Hertford: Nelson Society, 1999, 51 pp. A delightful collections from anecdotes taken from the weekly magazine of T.P. O'Connor.

3290 [NHS 1]. Shapack, Arnold R., ed. Proceedings Naval History Symposium: The Navy in an Age of Change and Crisis: Some Challenges and Responses of the Twentieth Century. Annapolis: NIP, 1973, 92 pp. (May 1972, USNA).

3291 Shapiro, Harry L. The Heritage of the BOUNTY: The Story of Pitcairn Through Six Generations. NY: Simon, 1936, xvi, 329 pp. Traces the descendants, Anglo-Polynesians.

3292 Shapiro, Samuel. Richard Henry Dana, Jr., 1815-1882. East Lansing: Mich State UP, 1961, 251 pp. A biography of the sea fiction writer.

3293 Sharp, Andrew. The Discovery of Australia. Oxford: Clarendon, 1963, 388 pp. Re the relative lateness of this discovery; search for "Java the Great."

3294 Shaw, A.G.L. Convicts and the Colonies: A Study of Penal Transportation from Great Britain and Ireland to Australia and Other Parts of the British Empire. London: Faber; Melbourne: Melbourne UP, 1966, 1977, 399 pp. The story of the penal transportation system; various areas considered, e.g., America, South Africa, and, finally, the choice, Australia.

3295 Shaw, J.J. Sutherland. "The Hospital Ship, 1608-1740" <u>MM</u>, 22 (October 1936): 422-26. An aspect of the development of a professional, balanced navy; GOODWILL of 1608.

3296 Sheehy, David. "Old Man of the Sea: An Interview with John de Courcy Ireland." <u>History Ireland</u>, 5 (Winter 1997): 12-14. The longtime Oxford professor; goal to raise consciousness about maritime traditions in Ireland.

3297 Sheldon, Matthew. <u>Guide to the Manuscript Collection of the Royal Naval Museum</u>. Portsmouth: RNM, 1997, iv, 77. A guide to the holdings by the Curator of Manuscripts.

3298 Shenk, Robert. <u>Guide to Naval Writing</u>. Annapolis: NIP, 1990, 1997, xviii, 374 pp. A guide to technical and professional writing; USN featured.

3299 Sherbourne, J.W. "The Battle of La Rochelle and the War at Sea, 1372-1375." <u>Bull IHR</u>, 42 (May 1969): 17-29. 23 June 1372, 14 English ships overwhelmed by 12 Castillian galleys; conclusion: not so decisive loss for England as some claim; control of Channel uneffected.

3300 -------. "The Hundred Years' War: The English Navy Shipping and Manpower, 1369-1389." <u>Past and Present</u>, 37 (1967): 163-75. N. Nicolas was last to study naval forces during the Hundred Years' War and appreciated the important contribution of naval forces; early phase, Castile allied with France; details on finance, impressment, Cinque Ports, transports, and King's Ships.

3301 -------. <u>The Port of Bristol in the Middle Ages</u>. Bristol: Historical Association, 1965, 30 pp. A short survey.

3302 -------. <u>War, Politics and Culture in Fourteenth-Century England</u>. NY: Hambledon, 1994, xvi, 200 pp. Ed: Anthony Tuck; a collection of 11 articles by Sherbourne; most about English land and naval forces during mid-14th century; 6 on navy.

3303 Sherrard, Owen A. <u>A Life of Emma Hamilton</u>. London: Sidgwick, 1927, xi, 345 pp. Lady Hamilton, 1765-1815; a review of her life.

3304 -------. <u>A Life of Lord St. Vincent</u>. London: Allen, 1933, iv, 253 pp. A review of his life.

3305 Sherry, Frank. <u>Raiders and Rebels: The Golden Age of Piracy</u>. NY: Hearst, 1986, 399 pp. Features 1690s-1720s, "the most intense outbreak of seaborne banditry ever recorded."

3306 <u>Shipbuilding Timber for the British Navy: Parliamentary Papers, 1729-1792</u>.

Providence: JCB Library, 1993, 200 pp. Intro: R.J.B. Knight; official Parliamentary studies of strategic materials and forests.

3307 Shipman, Joseph C. <u>William Dampier: Seaman Scientist</u>. Lawrence: U Kans P, 1962, 63 pp. A successful privateer vs. the Spanish; capture of Manila galleon worth 200,000 pounds; accounts of voyages became very popular; honored by Royal Society.

3308 Shomette, Donald G. and Haslach, Robert D. <u>Raid on America: The Dutch Naval Campaign of 1672-1674</u>. Columbia: USCP, 1988, xiii, 386 pp. A neglected aspect from the 3rd Anglo-Dutch War; effective Dutch amphibious operations along coast, e.g., NY, NJ, and the Chesapeake.

3309 Shore, Henry N. "The Navy in the Peninsular War." <u>JRUSI</u> (1912, 1913, and 1914): various. A series of 15 articles on this.

3310 -------. <u>Smuggling Days and Smuggling Ways</u>. London: Allan, 1892, 256 pp. Focus on operations in the Channel, late 18th and early 19th centuries; led to formation of Coastguard.

3311 Short, K.R.M. "That Hamilton Woman." <u>Historical J Film, Radio, TV</u>, 11 (1991). A famous propaganda film released in 1941; dramatized threat of invasion, purposely comparing 1805 and 1941 and encouraging American support and participation; directed by Alexander Korda, Lawrence Olivier as Nelson and Vivian Leigh as Emma.

3312 Shrubb, R.E.A. and Sainsbury, A.B., eds. <u>The Royal Navy Day by Day</u>. Fontwell: Centaur, 1979, viii, 392 pp. Fwd: Terence Lewin; 400 illustrations; by officers of RN; a day by day diary noting naval events over past 700 years; informative on naval heritage.

3313 Sichel, Walter S. <u>Emma Lady Hamilton: From New and Original Sources and Documents</u>. London: Constable, 1905, 1907, xxiii, 552 pp. A comprehensive biography but lacks balance; claims new evidence and correspondence.

3314 -------. <u>Memoirs of Emma, Lady Hamilton, the Friend of Lord Nelson and the Court of Naples</u>. NY: Collier, 1910, 422 pp. Focus on the time the Hamiltons were in Naples.

3315 Siddall, Abigail T., ed. <u>Actes du 7e Colloque International d'Histoire Militaire: International Colloquy on Military History (7th: 1982: Washington, D.C., 25-30 July 1982)</u>. Manhattan: Sunflower UP, 1984, xxi, 522 pp. See essay, "Lord Anson: Sailor-Statesman or Not?" by A.W.H. Pearsall.

3316 Sigwart, Emil E. <u>The Royal Fleet Auxiliary: Its Ancestry and Affiliations, 1600-1968</u>. London: Coles, 1969, ix, 221 pp. Aspects of naval logistics, supply, victualling, and fuelling at sea, e.g., some reforms of Pepys.

3317 Silke, John J. Kinsale: The Spanish Intervention in Ireland at the End of the Elizabethan Wars. Liverpool: Liverpool UP, 1970, xiv, 208 pp. Fwd: D.B. Quinn; use of Spanish archives; Spanish coordination with army of Hugh O'Neill; Spanish occupation of Kinsale in 1601; plan to overawe England after long war.

3318 Silverberg, Robert. The Longest Voyage: Circumnavigators in the Age of Discovery. Cleveland: Bobbs-Merrill; Athens: Ohio UP, 1972, 1997, 536 pp. Recounts the great voyages,e.g., Magellan, Drake, Cavendish, etc.

3319 Simmons, Joe J. Those Vulgar Tubes: External Sanitary Accommadations aboard European Ships of the Fifteenth through the Eighteenth Centuries. Studies in Nautical Archaeology. London: Chatham; College Station: Texas A&M UP, 1997, 1998, 112 pp. Illustrated; the issue of disposal of human wastes at sea during the age of sail.

3320 Simms, Brendan. "Britain and Napoleon: Review Article." Historical J, 41 (September 1998): 885-94. 5 books reviewed, all broad-based, global perspectives, e.g., Anglo-French naval strategy after Trafalgar; French shift to guerre de course to get at Britain by sea and British unable to get at France by land and the latter stages of the French Egyptian campaign.

3321 Simon, Fray Pedro. [In Spanish] Biography of Drake, "the English Pirate". 1627. An almost contemporaneous biograhical study of Drake from Spanish sources; focus on voyage to West Indies, 1585-1586.

3322 Simpson, Colin. Emma: The Life of Lady Hamilton. London: Head, 1983, 224 pp. A popular biography; emphasis on Naples.

3323 [NRS 130]. Simpson, Michael, ed. Anglo-American Naval Relations, 1917-1919. Publications of the Navy Records Society, vol. 130. Aldershot: Scolar, 1991, xviii, 648 pp. Related to the entry of the U.S. into World War I; antisubmarine warfare; operations with the Grand Fleet, and the great mine barrage.

3324 [NRS 140]. Simpson, Michael, ed. The Cunningham Papers. I: The Mediterranean Fleet, 1939-1942. Publications of the Navy Records Society, vol. 140. Aldershot: Ashgate, 1999, xxxviii, 634 pp. 4 sections and a biographical sketch of Admiral of the Fleet Viscount Cunningham of Hyndhope, 1883, 1963, a World War II admiral, some seeing him as the Nelson of the 20th century; 2nd vol. anticipated.

3325 [NRS 134]. Simpson, Michael and Somerville, John, eds. The Somerville Papers. Publications of the Navy Records Society, vol. 134. Aldershot: Scolar, 1995. Papers of this noted admiral of World War II.

3326 Simpson, Richard F. "The Naval Career of Admiral Sir George Pocock, K.B., 1743-1763." Ph.D. diss, Indiana, 1951, 423 pp. A scholarly study.

3327 Singer, Charles J., et al., eds. A History of Technology. 6 vols. Oxford: Clarendon, 1954, 1967. The standard, a massive product; re naval history, e.g., shipbuilding, gunnery, navigation, military technology, and cartography.

3328 Singh, Simon. The Code Book: The Evolution of Secrecy from Mary Queen of Scots to Quantum Cryptography. NY: Doubleday, 1999, xiii, 402 pp. Informative on intelligence, dynastic plots, and preliminaries leading to the Spanish Armada; Walsingham needed proof that Mary was directly involved in a plot to assassinate Elizabeth; broke codes, exposing Babington Plot.

3329 Sire, H.J.A. The Knights of Malta. New Haven: Yale UP, 1994, xiii, 305 pp. Folio size, many illustrations; re the Orders of St. John and Knights Hospitallers evolved into Knights of Malta, 1530-1798.

3330 Siri, Eros Nicola. Cochrane: el Lord aventurero. Buenos Aires: Distar, 1979, 178 pp. An Argentine writer of this biography of this Latin American hero-British naval officer and peer.

3331 Sjovold, Thoreif. The OSEBERG Find and Other Viking Ship Finds. Oslo: Oslo UP, 1963, 1976, 80 pp. Trans: Mary Fjeld; a survey of Viking ship finds, 3 notable ones; informative on medieval shipbuilding and sailing.

3332 Skaggs, David C. "Aiming at the Truth: James Fenimore Cooper and the Battle of Lake Erie." J Military History, 59 (April 1995): 237-56. An assessment of his account in his History of the U.S. Navy.

3333 Skaggs, David C. and Altoff, Gerard. A Signal Victory: The Lake Erie Campaign, 1812-1813. Annapolis: NIP, 1997, x, 244 pp. Great Lakes operations; race to build fleets; then, a 3-hour battle, 10 September 1813, Perry vs. Barclay; American victory; little influence on the war.

3334 Skaggs, David C. and Nelson, Larry L., eds. The Sixty Years' War for the Great Lakes, 1754-1814. Lansing: Mich State UP, 2001, 656 pp. A recent survey of the long term; military and naval operations; incorporates political, economic, and social aspects.

3335 Skallerup, Harry R. Books Afloat and Ashore: A History of Books, Libraries, and Reading among Seamen during the Age of Sail. Hamden: Shoe String, 1974, xii, 277 pp. Re use of books by officers and seamen, especially American and British; list of books.

3336 Skelton, R.A. The Cabot Voyages and Bristol Discovery under Henry VII. Cambridge: Cambridge UP, 1962, xvi, 332 pp. Skelton, 1906-1970, the premier historian of exploration; this on voyages of the Cabots.

3337 -------. Captain James Cook: After Two Hundred Years. London: BM, 1969, 32 pp. A bicentennial commemoration address to the Hakluyt Society, July 1969.

3338 -------. "Captain James Cook as Hydrographer." MM, 40 (May 1954): 91-119. Focus on the achievements of Cook as surveyor; process of selection of Cook to lead exploration voyages.

3339 Skelton, R.A., ed. Charts and Views Drawn by Cook and His Officers and Reproduced from the Original Manuscripts. Cambridge: Hakluyt Society, 1955. 68 facsimile illustrations.

3340 Skelton, R.A., comp. Prince Henry the Navigator and Portuguese Maritime Enterprise: Catalogue of an Exhibition at the British Museum, September-October 1960. London: BM, 1960, 166 pp. Illustrated; the quincentennial of his death; emphasis on contributions to nautical science and cartography; 326 items described.

3341 Skelton, R.A., et al. The Vinland Map and the Tartar Relation. New Haven: Yale UP, 1965, 1995, lxiii, 291 pp. Fwd: Alexander Victor; intro: George Painter; the Vinland Map dated from 1440 and published for the first time in 1965; generated much debate; edition of 1995 reaffirms claim of authenticity.

3342 Sladen, Douglas B.W. The Spanish Armada: A Ballad of 1588. London: Griffith; NY: Cassell, 1888, 1891, 22 pp. A tribute on the tricentennial celebrating "our glorious victory."

3343 Sleeswyk, Andre W. "The liao and the Displacement of Ships in the Ming Navy." MM, 82 (February 1996): 3-13. To determine comparisons; 1405-1433, 7 voyages to Africa and Arabia; total crews of 27,000; about 50 large ships, "Treasure Ships"; some confusion about size and displacement; liao probably meant a half ton of displacement.

3344 Smith, Bernard W. and Wheeler, Alwyne, eds. The Art of First Fleet and Other Early Australian Drawings. New Haven: Yale UP, 1988, 288 pp. Luxurious production, 241 color plates; by a prominent Australian art historian on the occasion of the Australian Bicentennial; artists aboard the First Fleet and others.

3345 Smith, Bernard W. European Vision of the South Pacific, 1768-1850: A Study in the History of Art and Ideas. Oxford: Clarendon; New Haven: Yale UP, 1960, 1969, 1985, 384 pp. Folio size with exquisite colored pictures and drawings; arts, science, intellectual development and perceptions, cultural taste, noble savage, European reactions to the Cook voyages, and aspects of the Enlightenment are prominent themes.

3346 -------. Imagining the Pacific: In the Wake of the Cook Voyages. New Haven: Yale UP, 1992, xi, 262 pp. A collection of essays; re imagining and imaging; before photography, how peoples, places, flora, and fauna were depicted; focus on the ship's artists during the 3 Cook voyages, e.g., influenced the writings of Coleridge.

3347 Smith, Bertie W. HMS VICTORY: Nelson's Flagship at Trafalgar. London; Blackie, 1939, 223 pp. A descriptive account.

3348 [NRS 77 and 81]. Smith, David Bonner, ed. <u>The Barrington Papers: Selected from the Letters and Papers of Admiral the Hon. Samuel Barrington</u>. 2 vols. <u>Publications of the Navy Records Society</u>, vols. 77 and 81. London: NRS, 1937-1941, viii, 464 and xxxii, 374 pp. To RN, 1740; reviews his career; attainment of flag rank.

3349 Smith, David Bonner. "Drake's Prayer. <u>MM</u>, 36 (January 1950): 86-87. A search for the prayer, its origins, the myth associated with it, and later citations.

3350 [NRS 55 and 61]. Smith, David Bonner, ed. <u>The Letters of Admiral of the Fleet the Earl St. Vincent Whilst First Lord of the Admiralty, 1801-1804</u>. 2 vols. <u>Publications of the Navy Records Society</u>, vol. 55 and 61. London: NRS, 1922-1927, viii, 380 and viii, 604 pp. Separate sections by regions and fleets, e.g., Baltic, North Sea, Channel, Mediterranean, and West Indies; on administration of the Admiralty and the Royal Marines.

3351 Smith, David Bonner. "More Light on Bligh and the BOUNTY." <u>MM</u>, 23 (April 1937): 210-28. Several new studies in 1936; each account makes the mutiny more interesting; most important is the journal of Bligh.

3352 -------. "The Naval Mutinies of 1797." <u>MM</u>, 21 and 22 (October 1935 and January 1936): 428-49 and 65-86. An extensive bibliographical essay; reprints pertinent Admiralty documents.

3353 [NRS 82]. Smith, David Bonner, ed. <u>Recollections of My Sea Life from 1808 to 1830 by Captain John Harvey Boteler, RN</u>. <u>Publications of the Navy Records Society</u>, vol. 82. London: NRS, 1942, xvii, 255 pp. Reviews his naval career; recollections written in 1883, he died in 1885.

3354 [NRS 83, 84, and 85]. Smith, David Bonner, ed. <u>Russian War</u>. 3 vols. <u>Publications of the Navy Records Society</u>, vols. 83, 84, and 85. London: NRS, 1943-1945, viii, 434, viii, 414, and vi, 462 pp. Recounts naval operations, year by year, in the Baltic and Black Seas.

3355 [NRS 95]. Smith, David Bonner and Lumby, E.W.R., eds. <u>The Second China War, 1856-1860</u>. <u>Publications of the Navy Records Society</u>, vol. 95. London: NRS, 1954, xxiv, 413 pp. Naval operations in the Far East.

3356 -------. "Some Remarks about the Mutiny of the BOUNTY." <u>MM</u>, 22 (April 1936): 200-37. Noted an expanding interest and additional information.

3357 Smith, Dwight L. <u>The War of 1812: An Annotated Bibliography</u>. <u>Wars of the U.S.</u>, # 3. NY: Garland, 1985, xxiv, 340 pp. Other than the Civil War, the most hotly debated American war; the Canadians were caught in the middle; 1393 annotated entries; includes section on the war at sea.

3358 Smith, Graham. <u>King's Cutters: The Revenue Service and the War against</u>

Smuggling. London: Conway, 1983, 190 pp. Folio size, illustrated; a history.

3359 Smith, Hillas. The English Channel: A Celebration of the Channel's Role in England's History. Upton-upon-Severn: Images, 1994, 191 pp. A history from 55 BC with Julius Caesar; other features, e.g., Cinque Ports, Anglo-Dutch Wars, "the Ditch" keeping back Napoleon, and Nelson.

3360 Smith, John. A Sea Grammar. Alt. title: The Sea-Mans Grammar and Dictionary. . . . The English Experience, # 5. NY: DaCapo, 1626, 1627, 1691, 1968, 1970, 171 pp. Ed: Kermit Goell; by Captain John Smith, 1580-1631, Governor of Virginia; contribution to nautical dictionary; frequent republication.

3361 Smith, Marilyn G. The King's Yard: An Illustrated History of the Halifax Dockyard. Halifax: Nimbus, 1985, 56 pp. The HQ of the North American Station; a history.

3362 Smith, Myron J. and Weller, Robert C. Sea Fiction Guide. Metuchen: Scarecrow, 1976, xxiv, 256 pp. Fwd: Ernest Eller; 2525 entries; sea fiction from 1700 to the present; James Fenimore Cooper "invented the sea story"; others, e.g., Marryat, Conrad, Melville, Kent, Parkinson, O'Brian, Forester, and dozens more.

3363 Smith, Ralph. The Dragon in New Albion. Boston: Little, Brown, 1953. Pseud: S.H. Paxton; nautical fiction; the "dragon" is Drake on the Spanish Main.

3364 Smith, Richard W. "Mahan's Historical Method." USNIP, 90 (January 1964): 49-51. Recounts career development; 1870s and 1880s, took up academic studies of sea power based on historical accounts; ;1883, to USNWC; developed lectures which were collected and published: ISPUH (1890) and ISPUFR (1892); finally, President of American Historical Association (1902).

3365 Smith, Robert D., ed. British Naval Armaments: Conference Proceedings I. London: Royal Armouries, 1989, 101 pp. Also includes Conference II; a series of papers, e.g., "Guns from the Sea" and "The Effect of Guns on Ship Design and Tactics."

3366 Smith, Robert H. The Naval Institute Guide to Maritime Museums of North America. Annapolis: NIP, 1990, xviii, 388 pp. A directory and information on location and holdings for 300 museums, e.g., Vancouver and Key West.

3367 Smith, Roger C. "Vanguard of Empire: Fifteenth- and Sixteenth-Century Ship Technology in the Age of Discovery." Ph.D. diss, Texas A&M, 1989, 330 pp. The basis of the next entry.

3368 -------. Vanguard of Empire: Ships of Exploration in the Age of Columbus. Oxford: Oxford UP, 1993, xii, 316 pp. For the quincentennial; covers 1430-1530, emphasis on Iberian peninsula achievements; the result was permanent change globally; facilitation, e.g., boxed compass, protolan charts, and sailing directions.

3369 Smith, Simon. "Piracy in Early British America." HisTod, 46 (May 1996): 29-37. Review of myth and legend; in literature, e.g., Defoe, Stevenson, Lord Byron; Port Royal.

3370 Smith, Steven R.B. "The Institute of Historical Research, 1971-1996: Its Third Quarter-Century." Historical Research, 69 (June 1996): 181-93. Description of the institution, its services, and significance.

3371 Smoler, Frederic P. "Emeute: Mutiny and the Culture of Authority in the Victorian Navy." Ph.D. diss, Columbia, 1994, 403 pp. An analysis of the rhetoric and reality of discipline, the culture of authority, and the history of mutinies in RN.

3372 Smollett, Tobias. The Adventures of Roderick Random. London: Dent; NY: Dutton, 1748, 1927, 1931, 1964, xx, 428 pp. An influential 18th century novel emphasizing horrific conditions on the lower deck, e.g., impressment, "a claustrophobic hell," and details of the circumnavigation of Anson.

3373 Smout, T.C. "The Overseas Trade of Scotland with Particular Reference to the Baltic and Scandinavian Trade, 1660-1707." Ph.D. diss, Cambridge, 1959. Use of Sound Toll Registers in Denmark; documents 300 ships in Scot-Baltic trade.

3374 Smout, T.C., ed. Scotland and the Sea. Edinburgh: Donald, 1992, vii, 232 pp. 11 essays from a seminar, University of St. Andrews, 1991; features, e.g., Roman transport for invasions of Scotland, Jacobitism and the sea, and Scottish pirates.

3375 Smyth, Alfred P. "The Anglo-Saxon Chronicle: Questions Old English History and Historians." Historian, 49 (Spring 1996): 2-7. A historiographical analysis and critique of this famous source; early link to Alfred; survey of assessments by historians, e.g., biographies of Alfred by Asser, Stenton, Davis, and Whitelock.

3376 -------. King Alfred the Great. London: Oxford UP, 1995, xxv, 744 pp. The first scholarly biography since 1902; Stenton claimed Arthur originated English navy; analysis and critique; controversial.

3377 -------. Scandinavian Kings in the British Isles, 850-880. Oxford Historical Monographs. Oxford: Oxford UP, 1977, x, 307 pp. A survey of operations and acitivities, e.g., invasions by Danes and Vikings; to Northumbria, York, Ireland, Dublin, and the Hebrides.

3378 Smyth, William H. The Sailor's Word-Book [of 1867]. London: Conway, 1867, 1991, vi, 744 pp. An alphabetical digest of 14,000 nautical terms; in 1836 proto-JRUSI called for updating Falconer; Smyth died in 1865 and E. Belcher completed the effort.

3379 Snedeker, James. A Brief History of Courts-Martial. Annapolis: NIP, 1954, 65 pp. Informative on the background and development.

3380 Snow, Elliot, ed. The Sea, the Ship and the Sailor: Tales of Adventure from Log Books and Original Narratives. Salem: Marine Research, 1925, 353 pp. A collection or anthology, e.g., Charles Barnard and John Nicol.

3381 Snow, Richard. "An Author I'd Walk the Plank For." NY Times Book Review (January 1991). An introduction of Patrick O'Brian to American audiences; announcement that Norton would publish the series; Collins began publishing in Britain in 1970.

3382 Snowden, Keith. The Adventurous Captain Cook: The Life and Voyages of James Cook, RN, FRS. Pickering: Castleden, 1999, 68 pp. A short biography in a series on explorers.

3383 Snyder, Frank M. "Patrick O'Brian's Aubrey-Maturin Novels." NWCR, 47 (Summer 1994): 128-31. Re nautical fiction of the Nelson era; nominates as the best of all; based on actual events.

3384 Snyder, Henry L. "Queen Anne versus the Junto: The Effort to Place Orford at the Head of the Admiralty in 1709." Huntington Library Quarterly, 35 (Autumn 1972): 323-42. One in a series of political crises during the reign; Whigs pressured appointment; crisis said to have weakened Admiralty.

3385 Sobel, Dava and Andrewes, William J.H. The Illustrated Longitude. NY: Walker, 1998, 216 pp. Over 200 illustrations, 110 in color added to the next entry; praised by Patrick O'Brian.

3386 Sobel, Dava. Longitude: The True Story of a Lone Genius Who Solved the Greatest Scientific Problem of His Time. NY: Walker; London: Fourth Estate, 1995, 1996, viii, 184 pp. Award-winning and best-seller; in 1707, a British naval squadron making a landfall went aground on Scilly Islands, 2000 died; Parliament established the Board of Longitude and offered 20,000 pounds to anyone who could solve the problem; John Harrison, 1693-1776, eventually collected, but competition emerged from Rev. Mevil Maskelyne, Astronomer Royal; also see Umberto Eco and Kristen Lippincott.

3387 Sokol, A.E. "Nelson and the Russian Navy." Military Affairs, 13 (Fall 1949): 129-37. Naval encounters and naval diplomacy in the Mediterranean, 1790s.

3388 Solley, George C. and Steinbaugh, Eric, eds. Moods of the Sea: Masterworks of Sea Poetry. Annapolis: NIP, 1981, xix, 300 pp. An anthology, .e.g,, Kipling, Wordsworth, Keats, and Donne.

3389 Solley, George C., et al., eds. Short Stories of the Sea. Annapolis: NIP, 1984, viii, 566 pp. An anthology in 5 sections, e.g., Kipling, Forester, Stevenson, and Conrad.

3390 Sondhaus, Lawrence. "Napoleon's Shipbuilding Program at Venice and the

Struggle for Naval Mastery in the Adriatic, 1806-1814." J Military History, 53 (October 1989): 349-62. Clearly, after Trafalgar, Napoleon continued to challenge British seapower.

3391 Sontag, Susan. The Volcano Lover: A Romance. London: Farrar, 1992, 415 pp. Fiction; the first kiss: "a fat lady and the short man with one arm"; William Hamilton studied volcanoes; the arrival of Nelson at Naples was a volcano of sorts.

3392 Soto, Jose Luis Casado. Los Barcos Espanoles del Siglo XVIy la Gran Armada de 1588. Instituto de Historia y Cultura Naval, Serie Gran Armada, no. IV. Madrid: San Martin, 1988, 406 pp. A product of the opening and exploiting of Spanish archives and contribution to quadricentennial; clarifies details on Spanish ships and shipbuilding; conclusion: not a Spanish disaster and not a great English victory.

3393 Sottas, Jules. "An Atlas of Drake's Last Voyage." MM, 2 (May 1912): 135-42. Drake had settled down in Plymouth in the early 1590s, then, off to West Indies with John Hawkins aboard 27 ships to attack the Spanish; both died; atlas found in French archives.

3394 Souhami, Diana. Selkirk's Island: The True and Strange Adventure of the Real Robinson Crusoe. London: Weidenfeld; NY: Harcourt, 2001, 246 pp. Re Alexander Selkirk, marooned on Juan Fernadez Island for 4 years; details on his life before and after; Defoe incorporated the story in Robinson Crusoe.

3395 Sousa, Philip de. Seafaring and Civilization: Maritime Perspectives on World History. Maritime Perspectives on World History. London: Profile, 2001, xvi, 224 pp. Illustrated; a broad study incorporating navigation, trade, empire, religion, food, and health; global perspectives.

3396 Southey, Robert. The Life of Nelson. 2 vols. Classics of Naval Literature. London: Murray; London: Macdonald; NY: Dutton; Annapolis: NIP, 1813, 1814, 1825, 1830, 1844, 1877, 1897, 1902, 1916, 1922, 1953, 1973, 1990, xlii, 371 pp. Eds: John Gibbings, David Hannay, Geoffrey Callender, E.R.H. Harvey, Robert Madison, Carola Oman, Henry Newbolt, Alan Palmer, and Eric Grove. Southey, 1774-1843, sometime Poet Laureate; this biography was seen as one of the most successful of all time; most of the editors correct errors and present background of Southey and of Nelson, e.g., Callender, 1922, is one of the best.

3397 Southey, Robert and Bell, Robert. Lives of the British Admirals. 5 vols. London: Longman; London: Methuen, 1833-1848, 1895, 1904, 2006 pp. A series of mini-biograhies, e.g., Howard, Hawkins, Drake, and Cavendish; dated but interesting.

3398 Southey, Robert. "Review of Works on Nelson." Quarterly Review, 3 (February 1810): 219-62. Review of Clarke, Charnock, Bowyer, and Harrison; basis for the later successful biography.

3399 Southworth, John Van Duyn. War at Sea. 3 vols. in 4 books. I: The Ancient Fleets. II: The Age of Sail. III. The Age of Steam, 2 parts. NY: Twayne, 1967-1970, 1100 pp. History of naval warfare; focus on battles, personalities, and ships; superficial.

3400 Southworth, Samuel A., ed. Great Raids in History: From Drake to Desert One. London: Spellmount; NY: Sarpeden, 1997, 1998, xiv, 338 pp. Recounts 19 of these efforts at "irregular warfare," successes and failures, e.g., Drake at Cadiz.

3401 Spavens, William. The Narrative of William Spavens: A Chatham Pensioner by Himself. Sailors' Tales series. London: Chatham, 1796, 1998, 192 pp. Intro: N.A.M. Rodger; an autobiography of a seaman on the lower deck; eyewitness to Quiberon Bay.

3402 Spear, John W.E. "British Naval Reform, 1745-1763." Ph.D. diss, California, Riverside, 1974, 335 pp. Research in Admiralty records; several important reforms resulting in improved performance later in the century.

3403 Speck, W.A. [Life of Robert Southey]. In 2001, noted as in preparation.

3404 -------. "Robert Southey, Lord Macaulay and the Standard of Living Controversy." History 86 (October 2001): 467-77. From a series of contributions to The Quarterly Review, a conservative journal, and The Edinburgh Review, a radical journal, a literary "debate" on contemporary issues.

3405 Spectorsky, A.C., ed. The Book of the Sea. NY: Appleton, 1954, xxii, 488 pp. An anthology, e.g., Alan Villiers, Cook, Dampier, Hakluyt, Purchas, Masefield, and Conrad.

3406 Spence, Richard T. The Privateering Earl: George Clifford, 3rd Earl of Cumberland, 1558-1605. Stroud: Sutton, 1995, xv, 256 pp. Biography of Elizabethan landowner, courtier, privateer, and commander of a squadron during the Armada campaign; joint ventures including the Queen against Spain, 1586-1602.

3407 Spinney, J. David. "The DANA Mutiny." MM, 42 (February 1956): 38-53. From Admiralty records; mutiny in March 1800.

3408 -------. "The HERMIONE Mutiny." MM, 41 (May 1955): 123-36. A notorious mutiny, 1797, and the search and capture of the mutineers.

3409 -------. Rodney. Annapolis: NIP; London: Allen, 1969, 484 pp. A detailed biography; famous for innovative tactic of breaking the line; volatile personality; other issues, e.g., nepotism, creditors, and questionable operational decisions; ambivalent about Rodney.

3410 -------. "Rodney and the Saints: A Reassessment." MM, 68 (November 1982):

377-86. From a lecture, bicentennial in 1982 at NMM; 1782 seen as high-point; perhaps more credit to Rodney for restoring discipline and high professional standards than for breaking the line.

3411 [NRS 10]. Spont, M.Alfred, ed. Letters and Papers Relating to the War with France, 1512-1513. Publications of the Navy Records Society, vol. 10. London: NRS, 1897, xlviii, 218 pp. Early in the reign of Henry VIII, ambitious but failed expansionist naval operations against France.

3412 Spotswood-Green, William. "Armada Ships on the Kerry Coast." Proceedings of the Royal Irish Academy, 27 (1908-1909). An older account of Armada shipwrecks.

3413 Squire, J.C., ed. If, or History Rewritten. Alt. title: It It Had Happened Otherwise: Lapses into Imaginary History. London: Longman; NY: Kennikat, 1931, 1964, 379 pp. Early examples of counterfactual history; several prominent persons contribute, e.g., Winston Churchill on Gettysburg and G.K. Chesterton, "If Don John of Austria Had Married Mary Queen of Scots," the latter meaning alternatives to the Armada.

3414 Stacey, C.P. "Another Look at the Battle of Lake Erie." Canadian Historical Review, 39 (March 1958): 41-51. Overlooked has been the logistical issue; Americans built stronger squadron from scratch, whereas British too dependent on supply from overseas.

3415 -------. Quebec, 1759: The Siege and the Battle. Toronto: Macmillan, 1959, 210 pp. For the bicentennial; an assessment by the official Canadian Army historian.

3416 Stalkartt, Marmaduke. Naval Architecture, 1787. Rotherfield: Boudriot, 1781, 1803, 1991, iv, 231 pp. Folio size; a spectacular production-reprint including 14 large plates; a selection of ships, e.g., yacht, sloop, 44-gun ship, 74-gun ship, and frigate.

3417 Stamp, Tom and Stamp, Cordelia. James Cook, Maritime Scientist. Whitby: Caedmon, 1978, 1993, xiv, 159 pp. A biography; on his early years and local influence; Cook self-taught.

3418 Stanford, Peter M. "The Work of Sir Julian Corbett in the DREADNOUGHT Era." USNIP, 77 (January 1951): 61-71. Corbett was a brilliant writer and theorist on strategy.

3419 Stanley, Jo, ed. Bold in Her Breeches: Women Pirates across the Ages. London: Pandora, 1996, xvii, 283 pp. A series of essays; legends of piratical women, e.g., Artemisia, Alfhild, and Grace O'Malley.

3420 Stark, Suzanne J. Female Tars: Women Aboard Ship in the Age of Sail.

London: Constable; Annapolis: NIP, 1996, xii, 207 pp. Use of Admiralty records and muster books; instances of women aboard ships of RN, 1660s-1800s, e.g., prostitutes, "seamen's wives," wives of warrant officers, and women in male disguise; shoddy research but fills a gap.

3421 -------. "Sailors' Pets in the Royal Navy in the Age of Sail." AmNep, 51 (Spring 1991): 77-82. Some case studies, e.g., goat of Captain Cook (for milk for tea of officers), cats (to keep down rats), dogs, and cattle (for fresh meat); "Bounce," famous dog of Cuthbert Collingwood.

3422 -------. "Women at Sea in the Royal Navy in the Age of Sail." AmNep, 57 (Spring 1997): 101-20. Most were wives of warrant officers who could live aboard, a custom of the 17th-19th centuries; few prostitutes actually remained aboard when underway.

3423 Starkey, David J. British Privateering Enterprise in the Eighteenth Century. Exeter Maritime Studies, # 4. Exeter: Exeter UP, 1990, 344 pp. Re privateering, its scale, character, and significance; informative and comprehensive; a major contribution.

3424 -------. "British Privateering, 1702-1783, with Particular Reference to London." Ph.D. diss, Exeter, 1985. A scholarly study, the basis of these entries.

3425 -------. "The Economy and Military Significance of British Privateering, 1702-1783." J Transport History, 3rd ser, 9 (March 1988): 50-59. A vital supplement to 18th century warfare; clearly defined in maritime law; not piracy because of letters of marque, commissions, and prize adjudication.

3426 Starkey, David J., et al, eds. Pirates and Privateers: New Perspectives on the War on Trade in the Eighteenth and Nineteenth Centuries. Exeter: Exeter UP, 1997, xii, 268 pp. Extensive studies in maritime predation; 14 papers from a conference, Middleburg, Zeeland, 1991; host city once a major base for privateers.

3427 Starr, Chester G. The Influence of Sea Power on Ancient History. NY: Oxford UP, 1988, 1989, 105 pp. A corrective to Mahan; Mahan had distorted concepts of sea power; not applicable to ancient times.

3428 -------. The Roman Imperial Navy, 31 BC-AD 324. Cambridge: Heffer; Westport: Greenwood, 1941, 1960, xv, 228 pp. Includes provincial fleets and their operations; in the north, the fleet was "classis Britannica" to assure communication across the Channel; transports, galleys, lighthouses, and British bases.

3429 Starr, Walter A. "Drake Landed in San Francisco Bay in 1579: The Testimony of the Plate of Brass." California Historical Society Quarterly, 41 (September 1962): 1-29. A summary account, photos and maps; plate found in 1936 and authenticated.

3430 Statham, Edward P. Privateers and Privateering. NY: Pott; London: Hutchinson, 1910, 382 pp. A collection of true stories.

3431 Stearns, Stephen J. "The Caroline Military System, 1625-1627: The Expeditions to Cadiz and Re." Ph.D. diss, California, Berkeley, 1967, 419 pp. Campaigns of Charles I and Buckingham, but serious problems then and later, e.g., obstinate Parliament, poor logistics, late pay, and increasing opposition to authority.

3432 Stebbing, William. Sir Walter Ralegh: A Biography. Oxford: Clarendon; NY: Lemma, 1891, 1899, 1972, xxvi, 413 pp. His exploits, e.g., during the Armada; excellent bibliography.

3433 Steckley, George F. "Litigious Mariners: Wage Cases in the Seventeenth-Century Admiralty Court." Historical J, 42 (June 1999): 315-46. A study of selected wage cases over 16 years in the 17th century; appeals to Admiralty court; contrary to Rediker and Davis, seamen could expect to win appeals; conclusion: 60,000 won their cases in the 17th century.

3434 Steel, Anthony. "Anthony Merry and the Anglo-American Dispute about Impressment, 1803-1806." Cambridge Historical J, 9 (1949): 331-51. Elaboration on impressment issue; the British never claimed the right to impress non-Britons, but interpretation was "once a British subject, always a British subject"; 1792-1812, about 10,000 impressed; no mention in peace negotiations and treaty.

3435 -------. "Impressment in the Monroe-Pinkney Negotiation, 1806-1807." AHR, 57 (1951): 352-69. Assessment of impressment as issue; not vital for the British, vital for the Americans, especially after CHESAPEAKE-LEOPARD affair.

3436 Steele, Colin. English Interpretaters of the Iberian New World from Purchas to Stevens: A Bibliographical Study, 1603-1726. Oxford: Dolphin, 1975, 206 pp. Descriptive entries of literature, much translated from Spanish and Portuguese, so as to stimulate travel and colonization, e.g., Hakluyts, Purchas, and Stevens.

3437 Steer, D. Michael. "The Blockade of Brest and the Victualling of the Western Squadron, 1793-1805." MM, 76 (November 1990): 307-16. A series of problems were reduced in importance by a determined operation to maintain fresh provisions for the Western Squadron; developed by St. Vincent based at Plymouth; costly but effective.

3438 Steffy, John R. Wooden Ship Building and the Interpretation of Shipwrecks. College Station: Texas A&M UP, 1994, xii, 314 pp. Super-folio size profusely illustrated; findings from studies in nautical archaeology; synthesis of the best knowledge.

3439 Stein, Stanley J. and Stein, Barbara H. Silver, Trade and War: Spain and America in the Making of Early Modern Europe. Balt: JHUP, 2000, ix, 351 pp. The transition to capitalism, the bridge between medieval and modern, the pivotal role of Spain, and the basis: American silver; re silver mining in New Spain and Peru, especially, 1519-1665, creating a global economy.

3440 Steinberg, Jonathan. "The Copenhagen Complex." J Contemporary History, 1 (July 1966): 23-46. Alleged German fear, especially in the 1890s, of another British "Copenhagening," i.e., unprovoked, surprise attack of the fledgling German fleet as had happened to Denmark in 1807.

3441 Steiner, Dale. Historical Journals: A Handbook for Writers and Reviewers. Santa Barbara: ABC-Clio, 1981, x, 214 pp. A reference guide to journals; includes a directory.

3442 Steller, Georg W. Journal of a Voyage with Bering, 1741-1742. Stanford: Stanford UP, 1988, 259 pp. The Danish explorer for Russia; to the Northwest coast.

3443 Stenton, Frank M. The Bayeux Tapestry: A Comprehensive Survey. NY: Phaidon, 1957, 182 pp. Folio size, describing the tapestry with illustrations; an outstanding work.

3444 -------. William the Conqueror and the Rule of the Normans. NY: Putnams; NY: Barnes, 1908, 1925, 1966, xii, 518 pp. An old standard; background to the Norman Conquest, then details of the year 1066; noted that the "English navy" was "miserably ineffective"; Norman fleet ready by August and waiting for favorable wind.

3445 Stenuit, Robert. Treasures of the Armada. Newton Abbot: David and Charles, 1972, 1974, 282 pp. Trans: Francine Barker; 12,000 artifacts from nautical archaeological expeditions to GIRONA, an Armada wreck off the coast of Ireland; displayed in the Ulster Museum.

3446 Stephens, Matthew. Hannah Snell: The Secret Life of a Female Marine, 1723-1792. Sutton: Ship Street, 1997, 63 pp. A case study.

3447 Stephenson, Donald F. Admiral Collingwood and the Problems of the Naval Blockade after Trafalgar. Gateshead: Royal Grammar School, Newcastle, 1948, x, 38 pp. Fwd: the Headmaster; a pamphlet; about a beloved graduate, commended for his superb seamanship and professional excellence; most of his 50-year naval career on remote blockade service.

3448 Sternlicht, Sanford V. C.S. Forester. Twayne's English Authors series. Boston: Twayne, 1981, 177 pp. Re Cecil Lewis Troughton Smith, 1899-1966; adopted pen name, C.S. Forester in 1921; created the indomitable superhero, Hornblower, escapist fiction.

3449 Stevens, William O. and Westcott, Allan. A History of Sea Power. NY: Doubleday, 1920, 1937, 1942, 467 pp. A longtime textbook for naval academies; much on history of RN but episodic.

3450 Stevenson, Robert Louis. The Black Arrow. London: Interlink, 2001, 224 pp. Fiction; occasion of a shipwreck during the time of the Wars of the Roses; intrigue.

3451 Stewart, James. "The Press Gangs of the Royal Navy." USNIP, 86 (October 1960): 81-87. A history of the Impress Service and the manning problem for RN; sanctioned by Parliament.

3452 Stewart, Jean C. The Sea Our Heritage. London: Rowan, 1993, 1995, 304 pp. A popular survey with an agenda; traces rise and fall of British sea power; now, need for government action to revive maritime interests.

3453 Stewart, John. Maida: A Forgotten Victory. Bishop Auckland: Pentland, 1997, 82 pp. The first British land victory of the Napoleonic Wars, 1806; an army transported from Sicily by forces commanded by Sidney Smith; recovered the Kingdom of Naples.

3454 Stewart, Richard W. "Arms and Politics: The Supply of Arms in England, 1585-1625." Ph.D. diss, Yale, 1986, 426 pp. The basis of the next entry.

3455 -------. The English Ordnance Office, 1585-1625: A Case Study in Bureaucracy. Royal Historical Society Study, vol. 73. Woodbridge: Boydell, 1996, x, 181 pp. Responsible for procurement, storage, and supply of arms and armaments to all armed forces; a bureaucracy in transition.

3456 Stitt, F.B. "Admiral Anson at the Admiralty, 1744-1762." Staffordshire Studies, 4 (1991-1992): 35-76. The Anson Lecture, 14 November 1990, 250th anniversary of the circumnavigation; details of the voyage and more extensive coverage of years at Admiralty and his reforms.

3457 Stocker, Constance H.D. Naples in 1799: An Account of the Revolution of 1799 and the Rise and Fall of the Parthenopean Republic. London: Murray, 1903, xviii, 438 pp. A passionate indictment of the Bourbons, the Hamiltons, and Nelson toward the Neapolitan republicans.

3458 Stokesbury, James L. Navy and Empire. NY: Morrow, 1983, 430 pp. A survey over 400 years of the rise of RN; superficial and anecdotal, a rehash of Mahanian concepts; excellent bibliographical essay.

3459 Stone, Lawrence. "The Armada Campaign of 1588." History, 29 (September 1944): 120-43. A summary; "England emerged inglorious but undefeated."

3460 Stone, Lawrence, ed. An Imperial State at War: Britain from 1689 to 1815. London: Routledge, 1994, ix, 372 pp. Essays from a colloquium, Princeton, November 1990; scholarly reaction to John Brewer, Sinews of Power, 1989, e.g., Brewer, Daniel Baugh, Linda Colley, and Nicholas Canny; re the military-fiscal state and the Atlantic maritime empire.

3461 Storey, Mark. Robert Southey: A Life. London: Oxford UP, 1997, xv, 405 pp. A recent biography, called one of the most enigmatic figures in English literature.

3462 Stout, Neil R. The Royal Navy in America, 1760-1775: A Study of Enforcement of British Colonial Policy in the Era of the American Revolution. Annapolis: NIP, 1973, ix, 227 pp. Re the operations of the North American Squadron, 1760-1775, to enforce colonial policies, e.g., Stamp Act, Sugar Act, and Townshend Acts.

3463 -------. "The Royal Navy in American Waters, 1760-1775." Ph.D. diss, Wisconsin, 1962. The basis of the previous entry.

3464 Strachan, Hew. "The British Way in Warfare Revisited." Historical J, 26 (1983): 447-61. A survey of recent British military historians, e.g., Howard, Kennedy, Terraine, and Barnett; debate over continental or maritime emphasis.

3465 Strachey, William. History of Travell into Virginia Britania. Publications of the Hakluyt Society, ser 2, vol. 103. London: Hakluyt Society, 1953, 221 pp. Eds: Louis Wright and Virginia Freund; voyages from 1584-1609, 8 British expeditions after 2 by Gilbert, which failed; Strachey was Secretary of the Virginia Company, recalling his experiences and presenting his "agenda."

3466 Stradling, Robert A. The Armada of Flanders: Spanish Maritime Policy and European War, 1568-1668. Cambridge: Cambridge UP, 1992, 328 pp. Through naval operations, Spain is determined to maintain European hegemony; this "armada" based at Dunkirk and the new "frigate" is featured; operations and victories against the Dutch, English, and French; complements Geoffrey Parker, The Army of Flanders, 1972.

3467 -------. Europe and the Decline of Spain: A Study of the Spanish System, 1580-1720. London: Allen, 1981, 232 pp. A summary of the debate; an excellent bibliographical survey.

3468 -------. Spain's Struggle for Europe, 1598-1668. London: Hambledon, 1994, xxv, 303 pp. A collection of articles; Spanish conspiracy in England in the 1660s; Spanish support and encouragement of Dunkirk privateers, 1621-1648.

3469 -------. The Spanish Monarchy and Irish Mercenaries: The Wild Geese in Spain, 1618-1668. Blackrock, Irish Academic, 1994, 219 pp. A neglected topic: Catholic Irishmen fighting in European wars, especially thousands recruited by Spain for Army of Flanders.

3470 Strang, Robert and Stead, Richard. A Mariner of England: A Story of the Reign of Queen Elizabeth. London: Frowde, 1908,1910, 160 pp. Pseud: George H. Ely and C.J. L'Estrange; fiction re Drake.

3471 Strathmann, Ernest A. "Ralegh Plans His Last Voyage." MM, 50 (November

1964): 261-70. From the Tower, Raleigh touted a voyage to Guiana, promising rich rewards for King and country.

3472 -------. Sir Walter Ralegh: A Study in Elizabethan Skepticism. NY: Columbia UP; NY: Octagon, 1951, 1973, ix, 292 pp. A biography placing Raleigh in context in his times.

3473 Street, Lucie. An Uncommon Sailor: A Portrait of Sir William Penn: English Naval Supremacy. Oxford: Kensal, 1986, 172 pp. Penn, 1621-1670, the father of the founder of Pennsylvania; an admiral contributing to naval reform and active in Anglo-Dutch Wars.

3474 Strickland, Matthew, ed. Anglo-Norman Warfare: Studies in Late Anglo-Saxon and Anglo-Norman Military Organization and Warfare. Rochester: Boydell, 1992, xxiii, 277 pp. A collection of articles supported by an informative introduction and useful bibliography, e.g., Nicholas Hooper, "Some Observations on the Navy in Late Anglo-Saxon England"; Alfred was "founder of the Royal Navy," creating "new model" ships and achieving victories in 875, 882, and 885; later re Cnut and his 60 ships and Harold who failed to stop 3 invasions of England in 1066.

3475 -------. "Military Technology and Conquest: The Anomaly of Anglo-Saxon England." Anglo-Norman Studies, 19 (1997): 353-82. From the Battle Conference of 1996; an assessment of military and naval forces in 1066, the latter "a crucial dimension"; purpose was to transport troops, not fight battles; Harold prepared a fleet to oppose the Norman invasion and stationed it off the Isle of Wight; but forced to demobilize when time expired.

3476 Struzik, Edward and Beedell, Mike. Northwest Passage: The Quest for an Arctic Route to the East. Toronto: Porter, 1991, viii, 152 pp. Folio size with fabulous photos; for the Canadian Geographic Society; reviews the various searches over the centuries, many sponsored by RN.

3477 Stuart, Vivian and Eggleston, George T. His Majesty's Sloop-of-War DIAMOND ROCK. London: Hale, 1978, 206 pp. Fwd: Ernest Eller; informative about the origin of the name; a rock formation southwest of Martinique where a battle took place; an event frustrating Napoleonic invasion attempts.

3478 Sturdy, David. Alfred the Great. London: Constable, 1995, x, 268 pp. A recent biographical study aimed "to debunk myths"; Alfred seen as the greatest of the pre-conquest kings and much glorified by the Victorians; re "founder of the Royal Navy" and other myths and legends; good review of the literature.

3479 Styles, Showell. Admiral of England. London: Faber, 1976, 189 pp. Styles, 1908-____, prolific writer of fact and fiction; at least 30 novels aimed more at the juvenile level, e.g., heroics of Michael Fitton and Septimus Quinn, and others based upon fact with fictional additions; this one an account of the life and career of

Clowdisley Shovell, notorious commander of the fleet which ran aground off the Scilly Isles, October 1707, 2000 died; the inspiration for development of the chronometer.

3480 -------. The Admiral's Fancy. NY: Longman, 1958, 1974, 278 pp. Fiction re Emma Hamilton.

3481 -------. The Baltic Convoy. London: Faber, 1979, 1981, 189 pp. Nautical fiction.

3482 -------. A Case for Mr. Fiddle. London: Hamilton, 1969, 92 pp. Nautical fiction.

3483 -------. The Frigate Captain. London: Faber; NY: Vanguard, 1954, 1956, 261 pp. Nautical fiction re Thomas Cochrane.

3484 -------. Gentleman Johnny. NY: Macmillan, 1962, 1963, 243 pp. Nautical fiction re John Burgoyne.

3485 -------. Gun-Brig Captain. London: Kimber, 1987, 192 pp. Nautical fiction re Fitton, this time commander of HMS CRACKER, providing logistical support for Wellington's army in the Peninsular campaign.

3486 -------. HMS CRACKER. London: Kimber, 1988, 188 pp. Nautical fiction re Fitton, involved in support of the Peninsular campaign.

3487 -------. A Kiss for Captain Hardy. London: Faber, 1979, 1981, 188 pp. Nautical fiction re Thomas Hardy, 1769-1839, flag-captain to Nelson; last words of Nelson: "Kiss me, Hardy."

3488 -------. Land from the Sea. London: Faber, 1952, 262 pp. Nautical fiction re the Peninsular campaign; portrait of Lord Castlereagh.

3489 -------. The Lee Shore. London: Kimber, 1986, 173 pp. Nautical fiction re espionage and adventure during 1810.

3490 -------. The Malta Frigate. NY: Walker; London: Kimber, 1983, 1986, 189 pp. Nautical fiction re the French occupation of Malta, 1798-1800.

3491 -------. Midshipman Quinn. London: Beaver, 1957, 1961, 1968, 1976, 190 pp. Nautical fiction.

3492 -------. The Midshipman Quinn Collection. Bathgate: Bethlehem, 1999, 598 pp. Nautical fiction; a combination of 4 Quinn pieces.

3493 -------. Midshipman Quinn and Denise the Spy. NY: Vanguard, 1957, 1999, 182 pp. Fiction re the hero Septimus Quinn, this one of FURY at Trafalgar.

3494 -------. <u>Mr. Fitton and the Black Legion</u>. London: Hale, 1994. Nautical fiction.

3495 -------. <u>Mr. Fitton at the Helm</u>. London: Hale, 1998, 190 pp. Nautical fiction; Fitton and privateers in the Caribbean.

3496 -------. <u>Mr. Fitton in Command</u>. London: Hale, 1995, 174 pp. Nautical fiction.

3497 -------. <u>Mr. Fitton's Commision</u>. London: Faber, 1977, 1979, 1981, 190 pp. Nautical fiction.

3498 -------. <u>Mr. Fitton's Hurricane</u>. London: Hale, 2000, 204 pp. Nautical fiction.

3499 -------. <u>Mr. Fitton's Prize</u>. London: Hale, 1993, 190 pp. Nautical fiction.

3500 -------. <u>Mr. Nelson's Ladies</u>. London: Faber, 1953, 238 pp. Format of historical romance, accurately depicting the early career of Nelson; re Susan Barrow, Lady Parker, Chetuma, Virginie Simpson, Rose Andrews, Mrs. Mountray, Fanny Nisbet, and Bellona.

3501 -------. <u>Mutiny in the Caribbean</u>. London: Kimber, 1984, 191 pp. Nautical fiction.

3502 -------. <u>Nelson's Midshipman</u>. London: Hale, 1991, 192 pp. Nautical fiction.

3503 -------. <u>Path of Glory</u>. London: Faber, 1951, 284 pp. Nautical fiction; re fictionalized exploits of Admiral Sir Sidney Smith.

3504 -------. <u>Quinn of the FURY</u>. NY: Vanguard, 1958, 1961, 200 pp. Nautical fiction re Septimus Quinn.

3505 -------. <u>Quinn at Trafalgar</u>. NY: Vanguard, 1965, 148 pp. Nautical fiction; a young midshipman in RN in the battle of Trafalgar.

3506 -------. <u>The Sea Officer</u>. NY: Macdonald, 1962, 272 pp. Nautical fictional re Edward Pellew, Viscount Exmouth.

3507 -------. <u>Sea Road to Camperdown</u>. London: Faber, 1968, 1976, 190 pp. Nautical fiction re Admiral Adam Duncan, commander at the battle of Camperdown, 1797.

3508 -------. <u>A Ship for Mr. Fitton</u>. London: Hale, 1991, 190 pp. Nautical fiction.

3509 -------. <u>Stella and the Fireships</u>. London: Kimber, 1985, 190 pp. Nautical fiction re operational exploits of William Bissell, rival-in-love of Lord Cochrane; all vs. the French fleet at Rochefort.

3510 -------. <u>A Sword for Mr. Fitton</u>. London: Faber, 1975, 1981, 188 pp. Nautical fiction re exploits in the Caribbean.

3511 -------. "Vincey Joe" at Quiberon. London: Faber; London: Sphere, 1971, 1976, 157 pp. Nautical fiction.

3512 Sugden, John. "Lord Cochrane: Naval Commander, Radical, Inventor (1775-1860): A Study of His Early Career, 1775-1818." Ph.D. diss, Sheffield, 1981. A scholarly biographical study.

3513 -------. Sir Francis Drake. London: Barrie; NY: Holt, 1990, 1991, 1996, xii, 355 pp. A recent biography based on new evidence; synthesis and demythologizing.

3514 Sullivan, F.B. "The Naval Schoolmaster during the Eighteenth Century and the Early Nineteenth Century." MM, 62 (November 1976): 311-26. A formal program ordering formal scholars to ships of RN, 1712-1824; at least 394 schoolmasters; over 1000 warrants issued; disagrees with Michael Lewis who deemed the program a failure.

3515 Sumida, Jon T. Inventing Grand Strategy and Teaching Command: The Classic Works of Alfred Thayer Mahan Reconsidered. Balt: JHUP, 1997, 1998, 2000, xix, 164 pp. After a critical reading of all of the writings of Mahan, Sumida concludes that the ideas and theories of Mahan were more sophisticated; treatises were presented at a variety of levels to suit different audiences, e.g., the American public at large and officers of the Naval War College; J.K. Laughton seen as mentor of Mahan.

3516 -------. "New Insights from Old Books: The Case of Alfred Mahan." NWCR, 54 (Summer 2001): 100-11. A re-reading of the works of Mahan, 20 of them; conclusion: Mahan has been misunderstood, e.g., naval-military cooperation, naval supremacy, and higher education of naval officers.

3517 [NRS 124]. Sumida, Jon T., ed. The Pollen Papers: The Privately Circulated Printed Works of Arthur Hungerford Pollen, 1901-1916. Publications of the Navy Records Society, vol. 124. London: Allen, 1984, xv, 400 pp. Publication of details of the sensational Pollen case concerning gunnery and fire control before World War I.

3518 Sumption, Jonathan. The Hundred Years' War. ___ vols. I: Trial by Battle. II: Trial by Fire. London: Faber; Phil: U Penn P, 1990-1999, xxiii, 1339 pp. More volumes promised and 80 years still to cover; an ambitious project based on the broadest coverage, e.g., England, France, Scotland; analytical presenting background, details, and anecdotes with occasional exaggeration; some naval aspects, e.g., Sluys and siege of Calais; blurb compares it to Gibbon.

3519 Supple Barry. The Royal Exchange Assurance: A History of British Insurance, 1720-1970. Cambridge: Cambridge UP, 1970, xxii, 584 pp. A history, e.g, marine insurance.

3520 Suster, Gerald, ed. John Dee: Essential Readings. Wellingborough: Crucible, 1986, 157 pp. Dee, 1527-1608, a noted intellectual throughout Europe; wrote treatise on navigation.

3521 "SUTTON HOO Ship Burial." Antiquity, 14 (March 1940): 6-87. Entire issue devoted to this recent find; series of essays about the search, discovery, property situation, excavation efforts, intervention of the war, and descriptions of some artifacts.

3522 Swales, Robin J.W. "The Ship Money Levy of 1628." Bull IHR, 50 (November 1977): 164-76. Actually an extension of an older tax; contributions from inland and coastal towns to support the navy.

3523 Swanson, Bruce. Eighth Voyage of the Dragon: A History of China's Quest for Seapower. Annapolis: NIP, 1982, xiv, 348 pp. Early chapters re Ming Dynasty executing a maritime strategy; beginning in 1405, naval expeditions into Indian Ocean involving "treasure ships"; c. 2000 ships over next 16 years.

3524 Swanson, Carl E. "American Privateering and Imperial Warfare, 1739-1748." William and Mary Quarterly, 3rd ser, 42 (July 1985): 357-82. Began with historiographical survey of the literature; some say it was not important, some say it ended fast; Gwyn and Baugh stress attraction of prize money for naval officers; Jameson, Pares, and Bromley most informative; Newport was center; during this period, privateering played a leading role and made major contribution to British sea power against Spain and France; created data base from Admiralty Court records.

3525 -------. Predators and Prizes: American Privateering and Imperial Warfare, 1739-1748. Columbia: USCP, 1991, xvii, 299 pp. Privateering from the North American colonies of the British; a qualitative and quantitative analysis; determination that it was expansive and was economically and militarily significant; it virtually eliminated the overseas trade of France and Spain; database of 3973 entries for "prize" actions; some limitations in historical understanding.

3526 -------. "Predators and Prizes: Privateering in the British Colonies during the War of 1739-1748." Ph.D. diss, Western Ontario, 1979. The basis of these entries.

3527 -------. "The Profitability of Privateering: Reflections on British Colonial Privateers during the War of 1739-1748." AmNep, 42 (January 1982): 36-56. The British mobilized private investors to arm, equip, and man privately owned vessels to operate against enemy commerce; Mahan downplayed this practice and other historians ignored it; formulated a Privateer Data File; conclusion: profitable for investors and financially attractive for crews, as much as 6 times the wage rate for RN.

3528 Swanton, Michael J. "King Alfred's Ships: Text and Context." Anglo-Saxon England, 28 (1999): 1-22. Descriptions from Anglo-Saxon Chronicle; how reliable is the source?; Alfred ordered "long-ships" and his son assembled a fleet of 100 ships; other references to ships of Danes and Frisians.

3529 Sweetman, Jack, ed. The Great Admirals: Command at Sea, 1587-1945. Annapolis: NIP, 1997, xxvi, 535 pp. 19 biographical essays by naval historians; only those who led in battle, e.g., Drake, Tromp, Blake, Hawke, and Nelson; 6 British, 4 American, 2 Japanese, 2 Dutch, etc., and 1 from 16th, 4 from 17th, and 2 from 18th centuries; authors, e.g., Tony Ryan, William Cogar, Gerald Jordan, and Clark Reynolds.

3530 [NHS 10]. Sweetman, Jack, et al., eds. New Interpretations in Naval History: Selected Papers from the Tenth Naval History Symposium. Annapolis: NIP, 1993, xx, 419 pp. (11-13 September 1991, USNA).

3531 Sykes, Percy M. A History of Exploration from the Earliest Times to the Present Day. NY: Harper, 1935, 1950, 1961, xiv, 374 pp. Intro: John Wright; a general survey.

3532 Symcox, Geoffrey. The Crisis of French Sea Power, 1688-1697: From the "Guerre d'escadre" to "Guerre de course". The Hague: Nijhoff, 1974, xii, 267 pp. Re the crisis of fleet warfare and the shift to war against commerce; 1st encouraged by success at Beachy Head in 1690, then, precipitous decline; heroic age of Jean Bart and corsairs of Dunkirk and St. Malo.

3533 [NHS 4]. Symonds, Craig L. and Bartlett, Merrill, eds. New Aspects of Naval History: Selected Papers Presented at the Fourth Naval History Symposium, USNA, 25-26 October 1979. Balt: N&A, 1981, xv, 398 pp.

3534 [NHS 14]. Symonds, Craig L, ed. [Papers from the Fourteenth Naval History Symposium]. (September 1999, USNA). Noted as forthcoming.

3535 Symons, Thomas, ed. "Meta Incognita": A Discourse of Discovery: Martin Frobisher's Arctic Expeditions, 1576-1578. 2 vols. Quebec: Canadian Museum, 1999, xliv, 636 pp. A series of essays by noted scholars, e.g., Ian Friel, David Quinn, Ann Savours, and David Waters; re Arctic and other voyages, e.g., Martin Frobisher of the 1570s; biographical sketches of Frobisher and the ubiquitous John Dee.

3536 Syndenham, M.J. "The Anxieties of an Admiral: Lord Dartmouth and the Revolution of 1688." HisTod, 12 (1962): 714-20. Dartmouth was a pivotal naval figure, veteran of the 3rd Anglo-Dutch War.

3537 Syrett, David. "Admiral Rodney, Patronage, and the Leeward Island Squadron, 1780-1782." MM, 85 (November 1999): 411-20. Re other aspects of the personality and professional activities of Rodney, e.g., gambling, nepotism, vindictiveness, and "interest."

3538 -------. "American and British Naval Historians and the American Revolutionary War, 1875-1980." AmNep, 42 (July 1982):179-92. The American Revolution was part of a world-wide conflict and one of the great naval wars; J.K. Laughton influenced Mahan who became the model; unfortunate, because some was mere propaganda; Lloyd condemned Mahan; praise for Piers Mackesy.

3539 [NRS 139]. Syrett, David, ed. The Battle of the Atlantic and Signal Intelligence: U-Boat Situations and Trends, 1941-1945. Publications of the Navy Records Society, vol. 139. Aldershot: Ashgate, 1998, xl, 628 pp. Presentation of 333 documents chronologically; formerly secret details about how intelligence was acquired and utilized.

3540 Syrett, David. "The British Landing at Havana: An Example of an Eighteenth-Century Combined Operation." MM, 55 (August 1969): 325-31. Re a model for 18th century tactics and techniques of amphibious warfare.

3541 -------. "Christopher Atkinson and the Victualling Board, 1775-1782." Historical Research, 69 (June 1996): 129-42. Re the grain merchants of London and corrupt contracting, especially a notorious case of monopoly and overcharging.

3542 Syrett, David and Dinardo, R.L., eds. The Commissioned Sea Officers of the Royal Navy, 1660-1815. Occasional Publication of the Navy Records Society, # 1. London: Scolar, 1994, xi, 485 pp. A reference guide, a project begun by David Bonner Smith; complete and authoritative list of officers of RN, 1660-1815.

3543 Syrett, David. "HM Storeship PROPOISE, 1780-1783." AmNep, 49 (Spring 1989): 91-95. A former Swedish merchant ship converted to a store ship, 18-61 pound guns added.

3544 -------. "Home Waters or America?: The Dilemma of British Naval Strategy in 1778." MM, 77 (November 1991): 365-77. The responsibilities of RN expanded during the late 1770s as France, Spain, and the Dutch joined in the American war; no continental allies, no strategic options, and what to do?

3545 -------. "Lord George Germain and the Navy Board in Conflict: The ADAMANT and ARWIN GALLEY Dispute, 1777." Bull IHR, 38 (November 1965): 163-71. Re the problem of logistical transport across Atlantic; valuable storeship captured, creating serious crisis.

3546 -------. "The Methodology of British Amphibious Operations during the Seven Years' and American Wars." MM, 58 (August 1972): 269-80. Several instances of the best cooperation, e.g., Louisbourg, Quebec, Havana, New York, and South Carolina.

3547 -------. "The Navy Board's Administration of the Maritime Logistics of the British Forces during the American War, 1775-1783." Ph.D. diss, London, 1965. The basis of these entries.

3548 -------. "Nelson's Uncle: Captain Maurice Suckling, RN." MM, 88 (February 2002): 33-40. Suckling, born in 1726, a grand-nephew of Robert Walpole, to the RN, 1739; "interest" and patronage benefitted Nelson who first served on the ship of Suckling beginning in 1770; later "advanced" the career of Nelson.

3549 -------. "The Ordnance Board Charters Shipping, 1755-1762." J Society of Army Historical Research, 77 (Spring 1999): 9-18. Supplying men, munitions, and supplies during the Seven Years' War; re the Board of Ordnance.

3550 -------. The Organization of British Trade Convoys during the American War, 1775-1783." MM, 62 (May 1976): 169-82. The British were determined to protect the vital trade to America and organized a series of convoys; not a popular system but it proved to be effective.

3551 -------. "'This Penurious Old Reptile': Rear-Admiral James Gambier and the American War." Historical Research, 74 (February 2001): 63-76. The commander, RN forces in New York, American Revolution; deemed incompetent; politics and patronage involved.

3552 -------. "The Role of the Royal Navy in the Napoleonic Wars after Trafalgar, 1805-1814." NWCR, 32 (September 1979): 71-84. The primary responsibility was supply to the Peninsular campaign; thus, an unbroken series of victories.

3553 -------. The Royal Navy in European Waters during the American Revolutionary War. Studies in Maritime History. Columbia: USCP, 1998, xi, 213 pp. The story of too many obligations and not enough resources; the authorities assumed the American rebellion could be put down rapidly; forced to abandon the Mediterranean; poor leadership was one factor.

3554 -------. The Royal Navy in North American Waters, 1775-1783. Aldershot: Scolar, 1989, x, 250 pp. The RN was overwhelmed at the beginning and never recovered; no effective strategy; the French threat meant maintenance of a large fleet in home waters; an excellent overview.

3555 -------. Shipping and the American War, 1775-1783: A Study of British Transport Organization. NY: Oxford UP, 1970, vi, 274 pp. Re the structure, personnel, and methods of RN to maintain an adequate and efficient supply of shipping of all descriptions.

3556 [NRS 114]. Syrett, David, ed. The Siege and Capture of Havana, 1762. Publications of the Navy Records Society, vol. 114. London: NRS, 1970, xxxvi, 355 pp. A significant amphibious operation, the largest of a series during the Seven Years' War.

3557 Syrett, David. "The Victualling Board Charters Shipping, 1739-1748." International J Maritime History, 9 (June 1997): 57-67. The expanding obligations of the board as the RN increased in size; resorted to chartering vessels; some details on organization and administration.

3558 -------. "The Victualling Board Charters Shipping,1 1775-1782." Historical Research, 68 (June 1995): 212-24. A dramatic expansion of RN from 35 to 100 thousand men meant greater demands all around, especially shipping to North America, but more expensive.

3559 -------. "The West India Merchants and the Conveyance of the King's Troops to the Caribbean, 1779-1782." J Society Army Historical Research, 45 (Autumn 1967): 169-71. Utilization of armed transports by the Navy Board to send troops to America; 1779-1782, cost-saving and strategically beneficial arrangement to contract with West Indian merchants to convey troops, a total of 8500 men so transferred.

3560 Taillemite, E. and Guillaume, P. Tourville et Beveziers. Etudes D'Histoire Maritime, # 2. Paris, 1992, 96 pp. A French account of the campaign leading to the battle of Beachy Head or Beveziers, July 1690, a French victory over the English and Dutch.

3561 Talbott, John E. The Pen and Ink Sailor: Charles Middleton and the King's Navy, 1778-1813. London: Cass, 1998, xvi, 172 pp. Re Lord Barham, Admiralty official and adviser to William Pitt, the Younger, First Lord, and reformer, e.g., coppering ship bottoms, the carronade, and administrative improvements.

3562 -------. "The Rise and Fall of the Carronade." HisTod, 39 (August 1989): 24-30. Introduced during the regime of Lord Barham, a short, fat, effective, ship gun used at close range during the late 18th century; built by the Carron Company.

3563 [NRS 26, 27, 36, 57, and 60]. Tanner, J.R., ed. A Descriptive Catalogue of the Naval MSS. in the Pepysian Library at Magdalene College, Cambridge. 5 vols. Publications of the Navy Records Society, vols. 26, 27, 36, 57, and 60. London: NRS, 1903-1926, xii, 452, xxxviii, 455, liv, 458, cxxviii, 725, and xx, 513 pp. Dedicated to the "Memorary of Samuel Pepys, A Great Public Servant"; Pepys collected enormous amounts of Admiralty papers, apparently with the intent of writing a history; Pepys effectively took over in 1673 when the Duke of York was forced out after passage of the Test Act; an exhaustive source covering the 1670s to 1700.

3564 [NRS 7]. Tanner, J.R., ed. Discourses of the Navy, 1638 and 1659 by John Hollond, also, 1660 by Robert Slyngesbie. Publications of the Navy Records Society, vol. 7. London: NRS, 1896, lxxxiv, 419 pp. Dedicated to J.R. Seeley; Hollond was clerk to Joshua Downing in the 1620s and coverage of the Civil War period; tracts on abuses; some expose of corruption.

3565 Tanner, J.R. Mr. Pepys: An Introduction to the Diary, Together with a Sketch of His Later Life. London: Bell, 1925, xv, 308 pp. By a Pepysian expert; a survey.

3566 Tanner, J.R., ed. <u>Pepys' Memoirs of the Royal Navy, 1679-1688</u>. NY: Haskell, 1906, 1971, xx, 140 pp. The diary carried him to age 36 but he lived almost twice that long and contined service as Secretary to the Admiralty; a description of those years.

3567 Tanner, J.R., ed. <u>Private Correspondence</u>. 2 vols. and <u>Further Correspondence</u>. London: Bell, 1926-1929, xliv, 382, 392, and xxi, 381 pp. Collections of the extensive correspondence of Samuel Pepys, covering 1662-1703.

3568 Tanner, J.R. <u>Samuel Pepys and the Royal Navy</u>. Cambridge: Cambridge UP, 1920, 1971, 83 pp. The Lees Knowles Lectures, November 1919; in 4 lectures, reviews themes, e.g., administration, finance, victualling, ships, guns, personnel, and discipline.

3569 Taylor, A.B., <u>et al.</u>, eds. <u>A Rutter of the Scottish Seas</u>. <u>Maritime Monographs and Reports</u>, # 44. London: NMM, 1980, ix, 80 pp. Developed during the Anglo-Scottish wars of the 1540s by a Franco-Scottish school of navigators.

3570 Taylor, A.H. "The Battle of Trafalgar." <u>MM</u>, 36 (October 1950): 281-321 pp. Prepared in 1936; includes pull-out illustrations; an extensive description of the battle.

3571 -------. "Galleon into Ship of the Line." 3 parts. <u>MM</u>, 44 and 45 (1958 and 1959): 267-85, 14-24, and 100-14. During the mid-17th century, battle experience and ship designers, especially during the interregnum, made for changes which would remain through Trafalgar in 1805.

3572 -------. "William Bligh at Camperdown." <u>MM</u>, 23 (October 1937): 417-34. As commanding officer of HMS DIRECTOR, Bligh kept the most extensive journal of the battle.

3573 Taylor, Eva G.R. <u>The Haven-Finding Art: A History of Navigation from Odysseus to Captain Cook</u>. London: Hollis, 1956, xii, 295 pp. Fwd: K.S.B. Collins; succinct, authoritative, and informative; by the premier expert on the history of navigation; details about pertinent factors, e.g., wind, tides, currents, fogs, sea patterns, the compas, charts, rutters, and solving longitude.

3574 -------. <u>Late Tudor and Early Stuart Geography, 1583-1650: A Sequel to Tudor Geography, 1485-1583</u>. London: Methuen, 1934, ix, 322 pp. This, the sequel; both about the background of geographical thought and nautical theory; re voyages of exploration and trade; persons of note, e.g., Dee, Hakluyt, Purchas; over 2000 entries in this bibliography plus others in the "prequel."

3575 -------. "Master John Dee, Drake and the Straits of Anian." <u>MM</u>, 15 (April 1929): 125-30. Dee wrote extensively about expansion; anticipated the voyages of Drake.

3576 Taylor, Eva G.R., ed. The Original Writings and Correspondence of the Two Richard Hakluyts. 2 vols. Publications of the Hakluyt Society, ser 2, vols. 76 and 77. London: Hakluyt Society, 1935, xxiv, 516 pp. Extensive selections and informative introductions.

3577 Taylor, Eva G.R. Tudor Geography, 1485-1583. London: Methuen, 1930, ix, 290 pp. This and the sequel constitute the definitive history of this crucial and formative period in English and global developments.

3578 Taylor, F. "Some Manuscripts of the 'Libelle of Englyshe Polycye'." Bull John Rylands Library, 24 (October 1940): 376-418. "Policy of Keeping the Sea" originated from 1436; "Libelle" or "little book" was the earliest known treatise on economic and political geography in English: Hakluyt printed it later.

3579 Taylor, George R., ed. The War of 1812: Past Justifications and Present Interpretations. Problems in American Civilization series. Lexington: Heath, 1963, xii, 114 pp. A collection of accounts and ranges of interpretations in this "Problems" series.

3580 Taylor, Gordon C. The Sea Chaplains: A History of the Chaplains of the Royal Navy. Oxford: Oxford Illustrated, 1978, xx, 602 pp. Fwd: Prince Charles; a history from the Crusades to the Cod war of the 1970s; demonstrates the important role of religion in the history of RN.

3581 Taylor, Ivan E. Samuel Pepys. English Authors series. NY: Twayne, 1967, 1989, xiv, 128 pp. Pepys famous for his diary presenting his daily routine of the 1660s.

3582 Taylor, Joan D.P. and Cleere, Henri, eds. Roman Shipping and Trade: Britain and the Rhine Provinces. London: Council for British Archaeology, 1978, viii, 86 pp. 11 papers from a symposium, University of Kent, Canterbury, January 1977; descriptions of the shipping, operations, and products.

3583 Taylor, S.A.G. The Western Design: An Account of Cromwell's Expedition to the Caribbean. Kingston: Institute of Jamaica; London: Solstice, 1965, 1969, xii, 243 pp. Details on the expedition of the 1650s, capture of Jamaica "by accident," and guerrilla warfare.

3584 Tedder, Arthur W. The Navy of the Restoration: From the Death of Cromwell to the Treaty of Breda. London: Cornmarket, 1916, 1970, x, 234 pp. An important stage in the development of RN; issues, e.g, administration, discipline, and the 2nd Dutch War.

3585 Teitler, Gerke. The Genesis of the Professional Officers' Corps. Beverly Hills: Sage, 1974, 1977, 246 pp. Trans: C.N. Ter Heide-Lopy; originally in Dutch; a sociological analysis; origins of professional officer corps, for the navy, Britain in the 18th century, the army, Prussia in the 19th century.

3586 Temperley, Harold W.V. "The Causes of the War of Jenkins' Ear, 1739." Trans RHS, 3rd ser, 3 (1909): 197-236. This distinguished historian reviews the issues leading to the Anglo-Spanish war.

3587 Temple, Richard C. and Penzer, N.M., eds. The World Encompassed and Analogous Contemporary Documents Concerning Sir Francis Drake's Circumnavigation of the World. London: Argonaut, 1926, lxv, 235 pp. Primary sources of the 16th century by and related to Drake.

3588 Tench, Watkin. Sydney's First Four Years: Being a Report. . . . Sydney: Library of Australian History; Melbourne: Text, 1789, 1979, 1996, xxx, 364 pp. Intro: L.F. Fitzharding; ed: Tim Flannery; various titles; a contemporaneous survey of the origins and development of the settlement; the 11 ships of the First Fleet to New South Wales, including Captain Watkin Tench of the Marines.

3589 Tenenti, Alberto. Piracy and the Decline of Venice, 1580-1615. Berkeley: U Cal P; London: Longman, 1961, 1967, xviii, 210 pp. Trans: Janet Pullan; a comprehensive study of decline of Venice as a great sea power and international entrepot; presents causes, e.g., Barbary corsairs, other pirates, Portuguese developing an alternate route to the East, and "the final blow" from Northern fleets, especially the English; Philip II had requisitioned Venetian ships during the Anglo-Spanish war and the English then felt free to attack Venetian commerce; English and Dutch ships were equipped for trade and war, so they were pirates more ruthless than any others.

3590 Terraine, John. Trafalgar: Eye-Witness Accounts Compiled by John Westwood. NY: Mason; London: Sidgwick, 1975, 1976, 205 pp. Small folio, illustrated in color; a selection of accounts.

3591 Thomas, David A. Battles and Honours of the Royal Navy. London: Cooper, 1999, 362 pp. Summaries of all battle honors of RN and Royal Marines from the Armada to the Falklands; each engagement described in detail, updating the next entry.

3592 -------. A Companion to the Royal Navy. London: Harrap, 1988, xviii, 443 pp. A reference work "from the beginnings in the 1660s"; names, badges, battles, and honors.

3593 -------. The Illustrated Armada Handbook. London; Harrap, 1988, vi, 218 pp. Folio size, illustrated in color; a collection of data, e.g., participants, guns, losses, and further reading; superficial.

3594 Thomas, Donald. Cochrane: Britannia's Last Sea-King. Alt. subtitle: England's Sea Wolf. London: Deutsch; London: Cassell; Annapolis, NIP 1978, 1999, 2002, 384 pp. "Hero of a hundred fights" and versatile, e.g., inventor, war planner, disputes over prize money, and accused of unscrupulous politics; not the final word; popularized approach.

3595 Thomas, James H. "Jack Tar, Mr. Sawbones, and the Local Community: The Impact of Haslar Hospital, Gosport, 1750-1800." Hatcher Review, 3 (1988): 291-302. A local study.

3596 -------. "Peter the Great and the Quest for Knowledge: The Great Embassy to Western Europe, 1697-1698." Portsmouth Papers. Nelson Birthday Lecture, Portsmouth Public Library, 26 September 1998. The Embassy of 1697-1698, Peter with party of 250 officials; details on itinerary across Europe, e.g., study of shipbuilding in the Netherlands and January-May 1698 to England; spent time with William III who presented Peter with a warship; to Portsmouth.

3597 Thomas, Pascoe. Journal of a Voyage to the South Seas. 1745. An account of Anson's circumnavigation voyage.

3598 Thomazi, Auguste A. Napoleon el ses marins. Paris: Berger, 1950, vi, 316 pp. A Fench account assessing Napoleon and the sea.

3599 Thompson, Edgar K. "Note on Keelhauling." MM, 58 (May 1972): 171-72. Originating in the Dutch navy, in vogue in RN until the mid-19th century, also in French and Egyptian navies, but not USN; abolished in 1853.

3600 -------. "R.N. Hirsute History." MM, 61 (February 1975): 72. A summary of shaving practices for officers; compulsary and strictly enforced.

3601 -------. "Saga of a Mutineer." MM, 53 (May 1967): 171-78. From the notorious HERMOINE mutiny of 1797.

3602 Thompson, I.A.A. "The Appointment of the Duke of Medina Sidonia to the Command of the Spanish Armada." Historical J, 12 (1969): 197-216. Santa Cruz died, February 1588, and Philip called up Medina Sidonia; rehabilitation of his reputation.

3603 -------. "The Armada and Administrative Reform: The Spanish Council of War in the Reign of Philip II." EHR, 82 (October 1967): 698-725. A study of the process of war and administrative change in the development of the modern state.

3604 -------. "Spanish Armada Guns." MM, 61 (November 1975): 355-74. An estimated 4000 guns were present, yet relatively little damage occurred; revision of study by Michael Lewis; specific corrections of Lewis figures; conclusion: Spanish at decisive disadvantage in firepower, thus, were unable to win in a sea battle on whatever terms.

3605 Thompson, Julian. The Royal Marines: From Sea Soldiers to a Special Force. London: Sidgwick, 2000, xv, 699 pp. Formed in 1664 by Charles II, then known as "the Admiral's Regiment" for the then LHA, James, Duke of York; duties included boarding parties and as snippers operating from the rigging with special targets: enemy officers.

3606 Thomson, George M. Sir Francis Drake. NY: Morrow; London: Deutsch, 1972, 1988, x, 358 pp. Sees Drake as "an inspired guerrilla leader"; popular approach; incorporates latest studies.

3607 Thomson, Janice E. Mercenaries, Pirates, and Sovereigns: State-Building and Extraterritorial Violence in Early Modern Europe. Princeton: Princeton UP, 1994, x, 219 pp. A sociological analysis based on developments in international law, state-building, and sovereignty; piracy and privateering seen in the context of changing state sovereignty; traces origins and presents examples, e.g., analysis of non-state violence, began during Hundred Years' War, England the first to use letters of marque, and piracy and privateering became confused.

3608 Thomson, Keith S. HMS BEAGLE: The Story of Darwin's Ship. London: Norton, 1995, 320 pp. Beautiful drawings by Townsend Moore; a "biography" of this famous ship of exploration; places the voyage in historical context; another hydrographic expedition sponsored by the Admiralty; a total of 3 major voyages.

3609 Thorne, Ian D.P. "Fisher: The Greatest Admiral since Nelson." Army Quarterly and Defence J, 127 (1997): 168-70. A new biography prompted this comparison; not convincing.

3610 Thornton, Micheal J. Napoleon after Waterloo. Stanford: Stanford UP, 1968, xiv, 241 pp. Traces his itinerary, e.g., to the coast seeking asylum, surrender to HMS BELLERPHON, to Torbay, transfer to HMS NORTHUMBERLAND commanded by Cockburn, and 2-month voyage to St. Helena.

3611 Thorpe, Lewis G.M. The Bayeux Tapestry and the Norman Invasion. London: Folio Society, 1973, 110 pp. Folio size, displaying the entire tapestry; some controversy about origins and when produced; conclusion: commissioned by Odo, executed in Canterbury, finished in 1077, in 6 sections, 8 colors of wool weave, and originally hung in Bayeux Cathedral.

3612 Thring, Theodore, et al. A Treatise on the Criminal Law of the Navy. Alt. title: Manuel of Naval Law and Court Martial Procedure. London: Stevens, 1861, 1877, 1901, 1912, 529 pp. Eds: C.E. Gifford and J.E.R. Stephens; various titles; an unofficial guide; presents background and history.

3613 Throckmorton, Peter, ed. History from the Sea: Shipwrecks and Archaeology, from Homer's "Odyssey" to the TITANIC. Alt. title: The Sea Remembers. Boston: Little, Brown; London: Beazley, 1970, 1987, 240 pp. An outstanding introductory guide to nautical archaeology; essays by experts; reviews a series of finds.

3614 Thrower, Norman J.W., ed. Sir Francis Drake and the Famous Voyage, 1577-1580: Essays Commemorating the Quadricentennial of Drake's Circumnavigation of the Earth. Berkeley: U Cal P, 1984, xix, 214 pp. 8 papers from an international conference, June 1979; papers, e.g., Helen Wallis, J.H. Parry, David Waters, David Quinn, Kenneth Andrews, and Ben Draper.

3615 Thrower, Norman J.W. The Three Voyages of Edmond Halley in the PARAMORE, 1698-1701. 2 vols. Publications of the Hakluyt Society, 2nd ser, vols. 156 and 157. London; Hakluyt Society, 1980-1981. Pepys praised Halley for combining science and practical navigation; the first of the scientific exploration voyages; published treatises on trade winds and meteorological charts; edited Newton's Principia.

3616 Thrower, W.R. Life at Sea in the Age of Sail. Chichester: Phillimore, 1972, 1976, 190 pp. By an eminent medical doctor; examines the social and medical conditions of life at sea from medieval times.

3617 [NRS 91]. Thursfield, H.G., ed. Five Naval Journals, 1789-1817. Publications of the Navy Records Society, vol. 91. London: NRS, 1951, xiv, 400 pp. Journals of Mangin, Cullen, Wilson, Abbot, and Cumby; covers from 1789-1812.

3618 Thursfield, James R. Nelson and Other Naval Studies. London: Murray, 1909, xxxix, 384 pp. A series of essays for the centennial of Trafalgar; explanations, e.g., Nelson Touch, "Nelson and Bronte," and the biography by Mahan; other studies.

3619 Thrush, Andrew. "The Navy under Charles I, 1625-1642." Ph.D. diss, London, 1990. The basis of the next entries.

3620 -------. "The Ordnance Office and the Navy, 1625-1640." MM, 77 (November 1991): 339-54. It has had a bad press and not deserved; primary sources indicate productive and efficient operations despite reduced funding and staff.

3621 -------. "In Pursuit of the Frigate, 1603-1640." Historical Research, 64 (February 1991): 29-45. Julian Corbett Prize Essay, 1988; complaints of poor performance of ships of RN, especially against French privateers; led to design of fast, light warship; copied a Dutch design.

3622 Tignor, Robert L., ed. Napoleon in Egypt: Al-Jabarti's Chronicle of the French Occupation, 1798. Leiden: Brill; Princeton: Wiener, 1975, 1993, 186 pp. Translated from the Arabic; an account of the campaign.

3623 Till, Geoffrey, ed. Seapower: Theory and Practice. London: Cass, 1994, 216 pp. Papers from an international conference, Yale, 1993; papers, e.g., Jan Breemer on the burden of Trafalgar, that decisive battle which subsequent commanders sought to repeat and Till on maritime power.

3624 Tilley, John A. and Crane, Thomas. The British Navy and the American Revolution. Studies in Maritime History. Columbia: USCP, 1987, xviii, 332 pp. Observed the mediocrety of British political and naval leaders; too limited, little on obligations of RN elsewhere and successes, e.g., saving Florida; good bibliography.

3625 Tilton, W.F. "Lord Burghley on the Spanish Armada." AHR, 2 (October 1896): 93-98. An excerpt of observations by Burghley; religion in the forefront;

England must surpass Catholic Spain in piety as well as sailing and fighting.

3626 -------. Die Katastrophe der Spanischen Armada, 32 Juli-8 August 1588. Freiburg, 1894, viii, 150 pp. A German study, exhaustively researched.

3627 Tincey, John. The Armada Campaign 1588. Osprey Elite series, # 15. London: Osprey, 64 pp. A handbook from a popular publisher.

3628 Tinniswood, J.T. "English Galleys, 1272-1377." MM, 35 (October 1949): 276-315. A programme of Edward I to build 12 ships and 24 galleys to take on Crusade; galleys, 120 oars each, costs to be provided by 26 towns; only 12 galleys completed.

3629 Todd, Malcolm. Roman Britain, 55 BC-AD 400: The Province beyond Ocean. Fontana History of England. London: Fontana; NY: Humanities; Oxford: Blackwell, 1981, 1997, 1999, 304 pp. A general survey in depth; recalled earliest known voyage, Pytheas of Massilia, 4th century BC, in search of tin, to St. Michael's Mount; no certain trace exists of 2 invasions by Caesar.

3630 Tomlinson, H.C. Guns and Government: The Ordnance Office under the Later Stuarts. London: RHS, 1979, xiii, 268 pp. An administrative history; the process of professionalization; time of expanding army into the first "standing army" and the navy, by 1714, the largest in Europe; contribution of Pepys, evolution from personal assistant to public official.

3631 -------. "The Ordnance Office and the Navy, 1660-1714." EHR, 90 (January 1975): 19-39. An indepth analysis of the office, its administration, and its effectiveness; why it had problems, e.g., mismanagement, lack of facilities, failure to convoy, embezzlement, and technical backwardness.

3632 Toohey, John. Captain Bligh's Portable Nightmare: From BOUNTY to Safety. NY: Harcourt, 2000, vii, 211 pp. What might have been; an imaginative account of events before, during, and after the mutiny, especially life on the launch; to rehabilitate Bligh.

3633 Tourquist, Carl C. The Naval Campaigns of Count de Grasse during the American Revolution, 1781-1783. 1942. Trans: Amandus Johnson. An obscure account of the role of de Grasse during that decisive campaign resulting in Yorktown and surrender of the British.

3634 Tours, Hugh. The Life and Letters of Emma, Lady Hamilton. London: Gollancz, 1963, 288 pp. Blurb: to provide a true, balanced picture of her life based on her letters; poor bibliography.

3635 Tracy, Nicholas. Attack on Maritime Trade. London: Macmillan; Toronto: U Toronto P, 1991, ix, 277 pp. Maritime strategy, the combination of shipping, colonies, and navy, was decisive, said Mahan; it began with piracy, then, reprisals, letters of marque, the right of war, the declaration of war, and belligerent rights, and economic warfare.

3636 -------. "The Capture of Manila, 1762." MM, 55 (August 1969): 311-23. One of the conjunct operations of "Pitt's Plan."

3637 [NRS 136]. Tracy, Nicholas, ed. The Collective Naval Defence of the Empire, 1900-1940. Publications of the Navy Records Society, vol. 136. Aldershot: Ashgate, 1997, liv, 706 pp. Collective defense of the British Empire; major complications for centralized control; weaknesses were revealed, e.g., the fall of Singapore.

3638 -------. "The Falkland Islands Crisis of 1770: Use of Naval Force." EHR, 90 (January 1975): 40-75. A crisis, Britain vs. Family Compact, Bourbons of France and Spain; forces mobilized for war.

3639 -------. "The Gunboat Diplomacy of the Government of George Grenville, 1764-1765: The Honduras, Turks Island, and Gambian Incidents." Historical J, 17 (December 1974): 711-31. Grenville faces 3 crises of the 1760s using a combination of naval forces and diplomacy, vs. France and Spain.

3640 -------. Manila Ransomed: The British Assault on Manila in the Seven Years' War. Exeter: Exeter UP, 1995, xvi, 158 pp. In the 1760s at the end of the war, the British turned from France to Spain, Havana and Manila; demonstrated amphibious capabilities; both returned at end of the war.

3641 -------. Navies, Deterrence, and American Independence: Britain and Seapower in the 1760s and 1770s. Vancouver: U British Columbia P, 1988, x, 207 pp. Re maritime aspects of the American Revolution, British strategic systems, security policies, and application of available naval forces, e.g., against France, Spain, both intent on revenge, and Sweden, and the Turks.

3642 -------. Nelson's Battles: The Art of Victory in the Age of Sail. London: Chatham, 1996, 224 pp. Fwd: David Brown; not a biography but focus on special features of Nelson, the "Nelson Touch": tactical innovation, charismatic leadership, and devotion to duty; the 4 "greats": St. Vincent, the Nile, Copenhagen, and Trafalgar; over 200 illustrations.

3643 -------. "The Royal Navy as an Instrument in British Foreign Relations between the Peace of Paris and the War of the American Revolution." Ph.D. diss, Southampton, 1972. The basis of these entries.

3644 -------. "Sir Robert Calder's Action." MM, 77 (August 1991): 259-70. Calder's force achieved a tactical victory on 22 July 1805 but decided not to follow-up the next day; a court martial decided that was a mistake and censored him; preliminary to Trafalgar.

3645 Tranie, Jean and Carmigniani, J.C. Napoleon's War in Spain: The French Peninsular Campaigns, 1807-1814. London: Arms, 1982, 191 pp. Large folio size, profusely illustrated; fwd: David Chandler; trans: Janet Mallender and John Clements; from the notes and manuscripts of Commandant Henry Lachouque; year-by-year coverage, 1807-1814; Napoleon himself came, November 1808-January 1809, to no avail.

3646 Trease, Geoffrey. Samuel Pepys and His World. London: Thames, 1972, 128 pp. Folio size, profusely illustrated; his dominance of the navy but nothing new.

3647 Treneer, Anne. The Sea in English Literature: From Beowulf to Donne. London: Hodder, 1926, xvii, 299 pp. Compares Beowulf to Odyssey, also Hakluyt, poems on the Armada, and glorification of Drake in the 17th century.

3648 Trevelyan, Raleigh. Sir Walter Raleigh. London: Lane, 2001, 416 pp. A recent biography using new material, e.g., from Spanish archives.

3649 Trevor-Roper, Hugh R., ed. The Age of Expansion: Europe and the World, 1559-1660. NY: McGraw-Hill, 1968, 360 pp. A series of essays edited by this preeminent historian, now Lord Dacre.

3650 Trollope, Charles. "The Guns of the Queen's Ships during the Armada Campaign." J of Ordnance Society, 6 (1994): 22-38. Nautical archaeology concentrated on Spanish wrecks and Spanish guns; nothing on English guns; an reform effort was in progress led by William Wynter; to standardize gun calibers and lengths and improve performance of powder.

3651 -------. "Two Culverins from the REVENGE," J Ordnance Society, 9 (1997): 49-53. The famous ship of Grenville, 1591, lost in a battle with Spain; the Spanish repaired it but it wrecked at Terceira; some guns recovered.

3652 Trotter, Thomas. Medicina Nautica: An Essay on the Diseases of Seamen. 3 vols. London: Longman, 1797-1803. Describes "environmental" reforms on the lower deck and achievements of Lind and Blane.

3653 Trulsson, Sven G. British and Swedish Policies and Strategies in the Baltic after the Peace of Tilsit in 1807: A Study of Decision-Making. Lund: Liber Laromedel, 1976, 175 pp. Tilsit meant great strategic changes in the area crucial to British interests and logistics; bombardment of Danish fleet at Copenhagen; looked to reactions of Russia, Sweden, Norway, and France.

3654 Tuchman, Barbara W. The First Salute: A View of the American Revolution. NY: Knopf, 1988, xiii, 347 pp. To demonstrate the role of sea power in the American Revolution; how the Dutch and the French intervened; but superficial and mushy narrative.

3655 Tucker, Glenn. Poltroons and Patriots: A Popular Account of the War of

1812. 2 vols. Indianapolis: Bobs-Merrill, 1954, 812 pp. Extensive coverage of the origins, causes, issues, and operations of the war, e.g., impressment, American citizenship laws, and the burning of Washington; anecdotal and strictly from the American perspective.

3656 Tucker, Spencer C., ed. Naval Warfare: An International Encyclopedia. 3 vols.. Denver: ABC-Clio, 2002, cxxx, 1231 pp. A mamouth undertaking, 1500 entries in 3 hardback vols; over 155 contributors; a comprehensive encyclopedia.

3657 Tucker, Spencer C. and Reuter, Frank T. Injured Honor: The CHESAPEAKE-LEOPARD Affair, June 22, 1807. Annapolis: NIP, 1996, 288 pp. A ship-vs-ship confrontation off the Virginia Capes; the issue was recovery of alleged British deserters; much fascinating detail and presentation of international implications; preliminary to the War of 1812; review of the aftermath and consequences, e.g., cool heads of civilian leaders on both sides prevented war and issue of punishment of the American Captain Barron precipitated 7 duels; weak on British perspective.

3658 Tucker, Spencer C. The Jeffersonian Gunboat Policy. Studies in Maritime History. Columbia: USCP, 1993, xiii, 265 pp. The response to demands for a naval force by America, 172 gunboats; enforcement of blockade after CHESAPEAKE-LEOPARD affair; but poor quality and recruitment problems contributed to overall failure.

3659 Tunstall, Brian. Naval Warfare in the Age of Sail: The Evolution of Fighting Tactics, 1650-1815. London: Conway; Annapolis: NIP, 1990, x, 278 pp. Ed: Nicholas Tracy; the son-in-law of Julian Corbett furthered his studies, focusing on tactical theories and naval history; edited and published by Tracy; important reference work on British and French naval battles.

3660 Tunstall, W.C.Brian. The Anatomy of Neptune: From King Henry VIII to the Present Day. London: Routledge, 1936, 374 pp. An anthology of prose and verse, e.g., plunder operations of Drake, the Armada, and an incident in China.

3661 [NRS 67, 68, and 70]. Tunstall, W.C. Brian, ed. The Byng Papers: Selected from the Letters and Papers of Admiral Sir George Byng, First Viscount Trorrington and His Son, Admiral the Hon. John Byng. 3 vols. Publications of the Navy Records Society, vols. 67, 68, and 70. London: NRS, 1930-1932, lxxxiv, 265, xxx, 373, and liv, 404 pp. The father a successful naval commander and First Lord and the son, victim of the sensational execution; recounts operations during the War of Spanish Succession, e.g., in the Mediterranean and the Channel.

3662 Tunstall, W.C.Brian. Catalogue of the Corbett Papers. Bedford: Foundry, 1958, 45 pp. Eds: P.M. Stanford and D.M. Schurman; papers, e.g., correspondence with Jacky Fisher, Richmond, J.K. Laughton, and L.G. Carr Laughton.

3663 -------. Flights of Naval Genius. London: Allan, 1930, 299 pp. Mini-biographies, e.g., Howe, Rodney, S. Smith, and Camelford.

3664 -------. Nelson. Brief Lives. NY: Macmillan, 1933, 1950, 143 pp. A short biography with bibliography.

3665 -------. The Realities of Naval History. London: Allen, 1936, 224 pp. To be a textbook for naval cadets, to replace and "refute all the foolishness in Callender's Sea Kings."

3666 Turk, Richard W. The Ambiguous Relationship: Theodore Roosevelt and Alfred Thayer Mahan. Westport: Greeenwood, 1987, viii, 183 pp. A review of their relationship and correspondence; a kind of mutual admiration which turned strained; "refought the War of 1812."

3667 Turley, Hans. "Piracy, Identity, and Desire in Captain Singleton."Eighteenth-Century Studies, 31 (Winter 1997): 194-214. Touted as "proto-modern and psychological"; interprets characters in Defoe novel on pirates as having a homoerotic relationship.

3668 -------. Rum, Sodomy and the Lash" Piracy, Sexuality, and Masculine Identity. NY: NYUP, 1999, ix, 199 pp. A study of piracy from the perspective of sexuality; look at "Captain Singleton" character of Defoe and pirate history of Charles Johnson; in the former, a homoerotic relationship; in English literature, pirates had "unnatural" desires; romantic anti-heroes; assessment of Christopher Hill, Burg, Rediker, and Ritchie.

3669 Turnbull, A. "The Administration of the Royal Navy, 1660-1673." Ph.D. diss, Hull, 1975. A scholarly study.

3670 Turner, F.C. James II. NY: Macmillan, 1948, 544 pp. A sound and sober study.

3671 Turner, H. Dan T. The Cradle of the Navy: The Story of the Royal Hospital School at Greenwich and at Holbrook, 1694-1988. London: Phillimore; York: Sessions, 1980, 1990, xiii, 186 pp. Fwd: Brian Brown; the charter of 1694 founded by William and Mary; architect was Christopher Wren; at peak, 2700 sailors in residence; other institutions, e.g., chapel, Painted Hall, Queen's House, Royal Naval College, and Old Boys Association.

3672 Turner, Stephen Francis. "Cultural Encounter, Aesthetics, and the Limits of Anthropology: Captain Cook and the Maori." Ph.D. diss, Cornell, 1995, 242 pp. Late 18th century contact, Cook and Maori of New Zealand, living in "a state of nature"; but Maori contradicted Enlightenment image of noble savages; links to "capitalism."

3673 Turner, W.J. Carpenter. "The Building of the GRACEDIEU, VALENTINE and FALCONER, 1416-1420." MM, 40 (February 1954): 55-72. Henry V added several ships to his navy; a description of the largest, GRACEDIEU.

3674 Turquan, Joseph and D'Auriac, Jules. Une Adventurierre de haut vol: Lady Hamilton et la Revolution de Naples. Paris: Paul, 1913, 1914, 376 pp. Re "the Great Adventuress" and events at Naples.

3675 Tushingham, Eric and Mansfield, Clifford. Nelson's Flagship at Copenhagen: HMS ELEPHANT: The Men, the Ship, the Battle. Portsmouth: Nelson Society, 2001, 192 pp. Details about a favorite ship of Nelson's.

3676 Tute, Warren. Cochrane: A Life of Admiral the Earl of Dundonald. London: Cassell, 1965, 278 pp. A good biography of this extraordinary figure.

3677 -------. The True Glory: The Story of the Royal Navy over a Thousand Years. London: Macdonald; NY: Harper, 1983, 288 pp. Begins in 896 AD, the contributions of King Alfred; coverage of Trinity House and the Royal Marines; Rodney receives short shrift; likes Mountbatten and Chatfield.

3678 Twells, John. Nelson: The Golden Orb: A Sonnet History: [A Life and Sonnet Sequence]. Darley Abbey: Ownart, 1995, unpaged, c. 85 pp. 218 sonnet couplets in 7 chronological parts following the life of Nelson; Elizabethan sonnet form; includes short bibliography.

3679 Twitchett, Eric G. Life of a Seaman: Thomas Cochrane, 10th Earl of Dundonald. London: Wishart, 1931, 288 pp. An older biography.

3680 Tyacke, Sarah, et al., eds. Sir Francis Drake: An Exhibition to Commemorate Francis Drake's Voyage around the World, 1577-1580. London: British Museum, 1977, 128 pp. Intro: Helen Wallis; to commemorate quadricentennial; exhibition originally at British Museum, thence to Oakland Museum, summer of 1979.

3681 Tyrrell, John. "Weather and Warfare: Bantry 1796 Revisited." History Ireland, 4 (Winter 1996): 34-38. Re a French invasion force from Brittany headed for Bantry Bay, December 1796, arranged by Theobald Wolfe Tone; reconstruction of weather maps, "synoptic reconstruction," the time of the Little Ice Age; weather drove the French away; another try in 1798.

3682 Tyson, Blake. "Oak for the Navy: A Case Study, 1700-1703." Trans Cumberland and Westmorland Antiquarian and Archaeological Society, 87 (1987): 117-26. Concern about stocks and future supplies led to census of trees on crown lands in 1663; records cover 1690-1708.

3683 Ubaldini, Petrucci. Comentario Della Impresa Fatta Contra del re Catholica L'Anno 1588. London: British Museum, 1589, 1894, 36 pp. Folio size; by a Florentine teaching Italian in England, seen as the 1st historian of the Armada campaign; narrative description drawn up for Drake.

3684 -------. La Disfatta Della Flotta Spagnola (1588): Due "Commentari" Autografi Inediti." Firenze: Olschki, 1988, 155 pp. A contemporaneous description of the Armada campaign.

3685 -------. Lord Howard of Effingham and the Spanish Armada. London, c.1590, 1919, 35 pp. Interviewed Howard; also wrote account of Armada campaign.

3686 Ubbelohde, Carl. The Vice-Admiralty Courts and the American Revolution. Chapel Hill: UNCP, 1960, 242 pp. For the Institute of Early American History and Culture; in North America, Vice-Admiralty courts opened in 1764, first in Halifax, expanding to 11 courts; covered all maritime matters, e.g., wrecks, smuggling, privateers, navigation acts, and prize courts; colonists complained.

3687 Uden, Grant. British Ships and Seamen: A Short History. 2 vols. London: Macmillan, 1969, 184 pp. A short survey.

3688 Uden, Grant and Cooper, Richard. A Dictionary of British Ships and Seamen. NY: St. Martin, 1980, 591 pp. Items of naval history and maritime heritage

3689 Unger, Richard W. "Alfred Thayer Mahan, Ship Design, and the Evolution of Sea Power in the Late Middle Ages." International History Review, 19 (August 1997): 505-21. Points out gaps and misunderstandings of Mahan "philosophizing" about this period; he was unaware of technological advances.

3690 -------. The Art of Medieval Technology: Images of Noah the Shipbuilder. New Brunswick: Rutgers UP, 1991, xviii, 168 pp. The iconography of Noah and shipbuilding persisted during this period; plus 77 illustrations, unpaged.

3691 Unger, Richard W., ed. Cogs, Caravels and Galleons: The Sailing Ship, 1000-1650. Conway's History of the Ship series. London: Conway, 1994, 188 pp. The 8th of 12 vols. in this series; large folio, illustrated; descriptions of the ships, their evolution and development, navigation, and trade routes.

3692 Unger, Richard W. Dutch Shipbuilding before 1800: Ships and Guilds. Amsterdam: Van Gorcum, 1978, xii, 216 pp. Informative on this crucial phase in the development of ships.

3693 -------. The Ship in the Medieval Economy, 600-1600. London: Helm, 1980, 304 pp. Describes the changes in ship design and construction; highly technical and detailed; much information from nautical archaeology and maritime museums; thesis: ship development was a significant contribution to the expansion of Europe throughout the world and that innovation was due to economic pressures.

3694 Unger, Richard W., ed. Ships and Shipping in the North Sea and Atlantic, 1400-1800. Variorum Collected Studies. Oxford: Ashgate, 1998, xii, 316 pp. 20 essays; informative of developments in shipbuilding and ships for all states of the region, e.g., information from paintings, especially extraordinary detail in Dutch paintings.

3695 Unger, Richard W. "Northern Ships and the Late Medieval Economy." AmNep, 53 (Fall 1993): 247-53. Maritime developments in the Mediterranean and Iberia have overshadowed those in this area; look again; demographic shift from south to north; themes, e.g., Vikings, Irish, Cabot and son, Norman fishermen, and voyages from Bristol.

3696 -------. "The Tonnage of Europe's Merchant Fleets, 1300-1800." AmNep, 52 (Fall 1992): 247-61. Statistical estimates of the relative size of fleets over time, e.g., comparisons of English, Dutch, German, French, and Spanish-Portuguese: largest in 1570 and 1670, the Dutch; in 1780, English, then French, then Dutch.

3697 -------. "Warships and Cargo Ships in Medieval Europe." Technology and Culture, 22 (April 1981): 233-52. By the 16th century, 2 distinct vessel types, warship and cargo ship, and no longer interchangeable; no distinctions as the galley declined and the cog increased, 11th-13th centuries; yet, still, even in the middle ages, there were distinctions.

3698 Unsworth, Barry. Losing Nelson. NY: Doubleday, 1999, 338 pp. Nautical fiction; a curious and stimulating novel; Charles Cleasby recreates and re-enacts great victories of Nelson; increasingly, his own life is interconnected with Nelson; an obsession; all quite different from Forester, O'Brian, et al.

3699 Unsworth, Michael, ed. Military Periodicals: United States and Selected International Journals and Newspapers. Westport: Greenwood, 1990, xlii, 404 pp. A reference guide to scholarly military and naval literature, e.g., USNIP, JRUSI, Armed Forces and Society, Jane's, but not MM.

3700 Unwin, Rayner. The Defeat of John Hawkins: A Biography of His Third Slaving Voyage. NY: Macmillan, 1960, 319 pp. Touted as a biography of a voyage, the voyage of 1567-1568; re Hawkins, the most original, patient and self-effacing seaman of Elizabethan times; marked a decisive change in naval strategy and in Anglo-Spanish relations; ship, JESUS OF LUBECK.

3701 Upcott, John D. Sir Francis Drake and the Beginnings of English Sea Power. Junior History series. NY: Putnam, 1927, 185 pp. For juveniles; Drake and his naval exploits, e.g., the Plymouth Hoe incident of 19 July 1588 and the circumnavigation.

3702 Urdang, Laurence. Historical Nautical Dictionary. Project of the Society for Nautical Research. In the Chairman's Report of August 2001, noted as in progress and forthcoming; no date specified.

3703 Usher, Roland G. "The Civil Administration of the British Navy during the American Revolution." Ph.D. diss, Michigan, 1943, 566 pp. Re the civil administration of RN, 1770-1785; problem areas were victualling, manning, dockyards, and the transport service; conclusion: charges of corruption and maladministration not true; civil administration not the cause of the loss of the war.

3704 Usherwood, Stephen and Usherwood, Elizabeth. The Counter Armada, 1596: The Journal of the MARY ROSE. Annapolis: NIP, 1983, 176 pp. From the diary of George Carew, captain of MARY ROSE, one of 120 Anglo-Dutch ships commanded by Howard and Essex to Cadiz; the campaign deteriorated into pillaging.

3705 Usherwood, Stephen. The Great Enterprise: The History of the Spanish Armada. London: Bell, 1982, 192 pp. Presents a selection of documents; calls it "the first world war."

3706 -------. "The Siege of Toulon, 1793." HisTod, 22 (January 1972): 17-24. The first campaign of RN in the French Revolutionary War.

3707 Vagts, Alfred. Landing Operations: Strategy, Psychology, Tactics, Politics, from Antiquity to 1945. Harrisburg: Military Service, 1946, 1952, viii, 831 pp. A good general survey and chronological accounts of amphibious landings, e.g., Saxon, Viking, Norman, pirates, Spanish, Vauban, Conjunct Operations, invasion scares, Quebec, and others in modern times.

3708 Vale, Brian. "Appointment, Promotion and 'Interest' in the British South American Squadron, 1821-1823." MM, 88 (February 2002): 61-68. The "great slump" after 1815, e.g., ships in commission down, 713 to 134, personnel from 140,000 to 23,000; a case-study: the impact on the careers of officers in one squadron; Admiraly policy meant half of promotions from midshipment due to "interest" and half due to former service; an enlightening study.

3709 -------. "The Creation of the Imperial Brazillian Navy, 1822-1823." MM, 57 (January 1971): 63-88. 1st of 3 articles; describes the circumstances and process of gaining independence from Portugal; Brazillian navy formed; British ships and crew recruited, including Cochrane as commander, already a hero from similar exploits in Chile and Peru.

3710 -------. A Frigate of King George: Life and Duty on a British Man-of-War. London: Tauris; NY: Palgrave, 2001, xi, 204 pp. Description of life aboard DORIS, a frigate assigned to the South American squadron in the early 1820s; focus on career developments of the officers.

3711 -------. Independence or Death: British Sailors and Brazilian Independence, 1822-1825. NY: St. Martin, 1996, x, 219 pp. A war of liberation against Portugal; Cochrane and British seamen led Brazilian naval forces successfully against the Portuguese and rebellion in the northeast.

3712 -------. "Lord Cochrane in Brazil: Prize Money, Politics and Rebellion, 1824-1825." MM, 59 (May 1973): 135-59. 3rd of 3 articles; Cochrane led Brazillian naval forces, expelling the Portuguese army and navy; then, complications: he demanded tangible rewards such as prize money; controversy ensued, Cochrane left for London but a warrant for his arrest forced him to go to Greece.

3713 -------. "Lord Cochrane in Brazil: The Naval War of Independence, 1823." MM, 57 (November 1971): 415-42. 2nd of 3 articles; Cochrane with many British sailors led a Brazillian naval defeat of Portuguese forces, capturing 70 ships.

3714 -------. A War betwixt Englishmen: Brazil against Argentina on the River Plate, 1825-1830. NY: St. Martin, 2000, xi, 275 pp. A continuation, again with British officers and seamen, a third of the Brazilian and two-thirds of the Argentine forces; this the Cisplatine War resulting in stalemate and creation of Uruguay; unfortunately, only sources from British archives.

3715 Vale, Malcolm G.A. English Gascony, 1399-1453: A Study of War, Government and Politics during the Later Stages of the Hundred Years' War. Oxford: Oxford UP, 1970, xii, 271 pp. Re English territory in southwest France acquired by marriage in the 13th century and lost at the end of the war in 1453; the English built a string of "barbicans" for defense along the coasts from Calais to the Channel Islands around to Brittany and down to Bayonne; then, a series of expeditionary forces against the French, leading to bankruptcy in the 1440s.

3716 Vale, V. "Clarendon, Coventry, and the Sale of Naval Offices, 1660-1668." Cambridge Historical J, 12 (1956): 107-25. Coventry, secretary to LHA, Duke of York, and Commissioner of the Navy Board, accused by Clarendon and sent to the Tower.

3717 Valle, James E. Rocks and Shoals: Naval Discipline in the Age of Fighting Sail. Annapolis: NIP, 1980, 1996, 352 pp. A lengthy treatise about the development and execution of naval discipline policies, this for the USN; origins and tradition were based on British practices.

3718 Vancouver, George. A Voyage of Discovery to the North Pacific Ocean and Round the World, 1791-1795. 4 vols. Publications of the Hakluyt Society, 2nd ser, vol. 165. London: Hakluyt Society, 1798, 1984, 1795 pp. A boxed set; ed: W. Kaye Lamb; Vancouver, trained by Cook, leading his own voyage during the 1790s to Nootka Sound to reclaim territory in a dispute with Spain and search for the Northwest Passage, thence to Australia; indicative of increasing international competition: Britain, Spain, Russia, and the U.S.; an authoritative account.

3719 Van der Merwe, Pieter. Nelson: An Illustrated History. Great Leader series. Tunbridge Wells: Addax, 1995, 31 pp. A short biography sponsored by the NMM.

3720 Van der Vat, Dan. Stealth at Sea: The History of the Submarine. Boston: Houghton; London: Weidenfeld, 1994, 1995, x, 374 pp. Re efforts at underwater warfare, beginning in 1465 with a Nuremberg inventor; in 1578; an English inventor, William Bourne, and David Bushnell of the 1770s; later Fulton, Hunley, and Holland; simplistic, journalistic, and superficial.

3721 Van der Voort, P.J. The Pen and the Quarter Deck: The Life and Works of Captain Frederick Chamier, RN. London: Leiden UP, 1972, 173 pp. A parallel career and rival of Marryat; they met in 1831; a series of 2nd-rate novels; very detailed and tedious presentation of an undistinguished naval officer and writer.

3722 Van Foreest, H.A. and Weber, R.E.J. De Vierdaagse Zeeslag, 11-14 Juni 1666. Amsterdam: Nord-Hollandsche, 1984, 222 pp. A standard account of the 4-Days Battle.

3723 Versteeg, Dingman. The Sea Beggars: Liberators of Holland from the Yoke of Spain. NY: Continental, 1901, 339 pp. Dutch seamen, first as freebooters, then as patriots, setting off the 80 Years' War in 1568; harrassment of Spanish treasure fleets and commerce.

3724 Villiers, Alan J. The Battle of Trafalgar: Lord Nelson Sweeps the Sea. Battle Books series. NY: Macmillan, 1965, 96 pp. Juvenile literature with many illustrations; a good description of the battle.

3725 -------. Captain James Cook. Alt. title: Captain Cook: The Seamen's Seaman. NY: Scribner; London: Hodder; London: Penguin, 1967, 1969, 307 pp. By an Australian professional sailing ship seaman who has retraced the voyages of Cook; calls Cook the greatest sailing ship sailor there ever was; an excellent biography.

3726 -------. The Western Ocean: The Story of the North Atlantic. London: Museum, 1957, 288 pp. A survey of the explorers, e.g., Phoenicians, Vikings, Portuguese, the Spanish Main, the Roanoke mystery, and Jamestown.

3727 Villiers, Patrick. Les Corsaires du Littoral, Dunkerque, Calais, Boulogne, de Philippe II a Louis XIV, 1568-1713, de la guerre de 80 ans a la guerre de succession d'Espagne. Paris: UP Septentrion, 2000, 358 pp. Illustrated; focus on the history of Dunkirk, 16th-18th centuries, an important port, first for piracy, then systematic, government-sponsored privateering, e.g., the high point under Jean Bart.

3728 Vincent, Howard P., ed. Twentieth-Century Interpretations of "Billy Budd": A Collection of Critical Essays. NY: Prentice-Hall, 1970, 112 pp. Essays by W.H. Auden, Albert Camus, and E.M. Forster, among others; on Melville and on naval life.

3729 Vine, Francis T. Caesar in Kent: The Landing of Julius Caesar and His Battles with the Ancient Britons. London: Stock, 1886, 1887, 248 pp. An informative description of the routes followed by Caesar and his Roman force in 55 BC; Boulogne to Deal and, again, in 54 BC, probably as far as Chertsey.

3730 Wagner, Anthony R. Drake in England. Hanover: Historical Society, 1963, 1970, 119 pp. From a descendant; re Sir Francis Drake, "the most illustrious bearer of the name in Devon"; more on Drake family from the 14th century on.

3731 Wagner, Henry R. Sir Francis Drake's Voyage around the World. San Francisco: Howell, 1926, x, 543 pp. A description of the circumnavigation, its planning, execution, and aftermath.

3732 Wahlroos, Sven. Mutiny and Romance in the South Seas: A Companion to the BOUNTY Adventure. Topsfield: Salem, 1989, 497 pp. A bicentennial publication by a psychologist; a detailed narrative of the voyage; includes a psychoanalytical study of Bligh and a BOUNTY encyclopedia.

3733 Waite, Richard A. "Sir Home Riggs Popham: A Biography." Ph.D. diss, Harvard, 1945. A scholarly biography.

3734 Walcott, Derek. The BOUNTY. London: Faber, 1997, 78 pp. A collection of 60 poems by a Nobel Prize winner; an allusion to BOUNTY.

3735 Walder, David. Nelson: A Biography. NY: Dial; London: Hamilton, 1977, 1978, xxii, 538 pp. A good biography supplemented by a good bibliographical survey.

3736 Waldman, Milton. Sir Walter Raleigh. Golden Hind series. NY: Harper, 1928, 253 pp. A biography in a series.

3737 Walker, Bryce S. and the Editors of Time-Life Books. The Armada. The Seafarers series. Alexandria: Time-Life, 1971, 1981, 176 pp. Folio size, color illustrations; a narrative history covering preliminary events, causes, operations, and recent nautical archaeological finds.

3738 Walker, Charles F. Young Gentlemen: The Story of Midshipmen from the Seventeenth Century to the Present Day. London: Longman, 1938, 257 pp. A history of this pre-officer class.

3739 Walker, Ian W. Harold: The Last Anglo-Saxon King. Stroud: Sutton, 2000, xxix, 258 pp. Many illustrations; a comprehensive overview of Harold Godwinson and close relatives.

3740 Walker, Richard J.B. "The Nelson Portraits." JRUSI, 143 (August 1998): 61-64. Describes media glorifying Nelson, 1798-1805.

3741 Walker, Richard J.B. and Boileau, John. The Nelson Portraits: An Iconography of Horatio Viscount Nelson. Portsmouth: Royal Naval Museum, 1998, xx, 316 pp. 140 illustrations, 40 in color; media produced between 1798-1805 glorifying Nelson, e.g., portraits, medals, cartoons, and prints; recepient of the Anderson Medal of SNR.

3742 Wallace, Willard M. Sir Walter Raleigh. Princeton: Princeton UP, 1959, xiv,

334 pp. A standard biography; opens with Raleigh leading attack on Cadiz in 1596, partly as revenge for his cousin, Richard Grenville.

3743 Wallis, Helen. "Did the Portuguese Discover Australia?" HisTod, 38 (March 1988): 30-35. Reviews what is known: Terra Australis Incognitaz noted from the 16th century; the "antipodean continent" confirmed by Cook; but as early as 1540, Portuguese charts displayed Java-la-Grande.

3744 -------. The Voyage of Sir Francis Drake Mapped in Silver and Gold. Berkeley: Bancroft Library, 1979, 29 pp. To support an exhibition; the map had originally been kept secret after the circumnavigation; details on later information.

3745 Walrond, Mary L. Launching Out into the Deep: An Account of the Mission to Seamen (or The Pioneers of a Noble Effort). London: SPCK, 1904, 210 pp. A history of these missions.

3746 Walsh, John E. Night on Fire: The First Complete Account of John Paul Jones's Greatest Battle. NY: McGraw, 1978, viii, 185 pp. The battle of Flamborough Head of 1779.

3747 Walter, Chaplin R. Anson's Voyage Around the World in the Years 1740-1744. Santa Barbara: Narrative, 2001, 445 pp. A recent account.

3748 Walton, Timothy R. The Spanish Treasure Fleets. Sarasota, Pineapple, 1994, xiv, 256 pp. Over 2 centuries, production of silver and gold and Spanish treasure fleets from America to Europe altered the world economy; includes findings from nautical archaeological expeditions.

3749 Warden, William. Letters Written in HMS NORTHUMBERLAND and St. Helena. London: Private, 1816, 1817, viii, 215 pp. Warden, 1777-1849, was surgeon of NORTHUMBERLAND; conversations with Napoleon aboard and for several months on St. Helena.

3750 Ware, Chris. The Bomb Vessel: Shore Bombardment Ships in the Age of Sail. Conway Ship Types series. London: Conway, 1994, 112 pp. Many illustrations including 70 schematics of ship plans; ships in RN, 1687-1854.

3751 Wareham, T.N.R. "The Frigate Captains of the Royal Navy, 1793-1815." Ph.D. diss, Exeter, 1999. The basis for the next entry.

3752 -------. The Star Captains: Frigate Command in the Napoleonic Wars. London: Chatham, 2001, 256 pp. Accounts of 200 "star" frigate commanders demonstrating the role and deployment of frigates; these captains seen as the genuine elite of RN at that time; conclusion: for frigate captains, performance was more important than "interest" for getting ahead; these "stars" were favorite characters for novelists, e.g., Marryat, Forester, and O'Brian.

3753 Warkentin, Germaine, ed. <u>Critical Issues in Editing Exploration Texts</u>. Toronto: U Toronto P, 1996, vi, 150 pp. A philological approach; reviews renowned editors, e.g., Henige, Wallis, and the Quinns; themes, e.g., details on how editors of the journals of Cook operated and critical analysis of the Hakluyts.

3754 Warlow, Ben. <u>The Purser and His Men: A Short History of the Supply and Secretariat Branch of the Royal Navy</u>. Salisbury: Erskine, 1984, 116 pp. Fwd: W.A. Higgins; a definitive history of this branch; chronological coverage; features, e.g., dress of sailors and identifying symbols, discipline regulations, pay, victualling, and rations.

3755 Warner, Oliver. <u>The Battle of the Nile</u>. <u>British Battles</u> series. London: Batsford, 1960, 184 pp. Warner, 1903-1976, prolific naval historian of the Nelson and other eras; a good account; synthesis of the literature.

3756 -------. <u>The British Navy: A Concise History</u>. London: Thames, 1975, 191 pp. Folio size; dedicated to Arthur Marder; a good synthesis; RN begins with the Tudors.

3757 -------. <u>Captain Cook and the South Pacific</u>. London: Cassell, 1963, 1964, 153 pp. Juvenile literature, profusely illustrated; stresses contribution of the Admiralty to exploration, hydrography, and science.

3758 -------. <u>Captain Marryat: A Rediscovery</u>. London: Constable, 1953, 210 pp. Captures the freshness and love of life of Marryat; he served under Cochrane, who was his model for fiction.

3759 -------. "The Character of Collingwood." <u>USNIP</u>, 95 (June 1969): 63-71. Collingwood, 1748-1810; enlightening on his character and career.

3760 -------. <u>Command of the Sea: Great Fighting Admirals from Hawke to Nimitz</u>. London: Cassell, 1976, 196 pp. A series of biographical sketches, e.g., Hawke, Saunders, Suffren, and Bougainville.

3761 -------. "The Court-Martial of Sir Robert Calder, 1805." <u>HisTod</u>, 19 (December 1969): 863-68. In July 1805, a battle with the Franco-Spanish fleet of Villeneuve; reprimanded in the court martial.

3762 -------. <u>Emma Hamilton and Sir William</u>. London: Chatto, 1960, 223 pp. A general survey, including relations with Nelson.

3763 -------. <u>English Maritime Writing: Hakluyt to Cook</u>. London: Longman, 1958, 35 pp. For the British Council and National Book League; in a bibliographical series, this one covering the 15th-18th centuries; in addition to the subtitle, Dampier, Defoe, and Anson.

3764 -------. <u>The Glorious First of June</u>. <u>British Battles</u> series. London: Batsford,

1961, 184 pp. Excellent coverage of the battle of 1794, Howe vs. Villaret-Joyeuse; more on strategic implications.

3765 -------. Great Seamen: From Drake to Cunningham. London: Bell, 1961, 226 pp. Biographical essays, e.g., Drake, Anson, Hawke, Howe, Cook, and Nelson.

3766 -------. Hero of the Restoration: A Life of General George Monck, First Duke of Albemarle, KG. London: Jarrolds, 1936, 288 pp. A good biography.

3767 -------. "HMS VICTORY, 1765-1965." HisTod, 15 (May 1965): 306-11. On the occasion of the bicentennial of the launch at Chatham, the 7th VICTORY; details on design, dimensions, restoration, and current status.

3768 -------. An Introduction to British Marine Painting. London: Batsford, 1948, 48 pp. A good survey, e.g., the Thames Group, war artists, Pocock, Turner, Constable, and Whistler.

3769 -------. Joseph Conrad. Men and Books series. London: Longman, 1950, 1951. Noted recent revival of interest; his sea experiences and appreciation of the sea.

3770 -------. The Life and Letters of Vice-Admiral Lord Collingwood. NY: Oxford UP, 1968, xix, 276 pp. Dedicated to NRS and SNR; contemporary of Nelson, later C-in-C, Mediterranean; emphasis on duty.

3771 -------. Lord Nelson: A Reading Guide. London: Caravel, 1955, 31 pp. A historiographical survey of 68 works on Nelson; "Nelsoniana"; Laughton wrote the entry in DNB; favorite topics, e.g., Lady Hamilton and treatment of Neapolitan Jacobins; also describes prominent portraits.

3772 -------. Nelson. London: Follett, 1975, 231 pp. Folio size, profusely illustrated; intro: Elizabeth Longford; a fresh assessment; features the Nelson Touch and Band of Brothers.

3773 Warner, Oliver and Nimitz, Chester W. Nelson and the Age of Fighting Sail. London: Cassell; NY: Harper, 1963, 153 pp. Folio size, profusely illustrated; juvenile literature; a good survey.

3774 Warner, Oliver. Nelson's Battles. London: Batsford; Newton Abbot: David and Charles, 1965, 1971, 254 pp. Includes the Nile, Copenhagen, and Trafalgar.

3775 -------. A Portrait of Lord Nelson. London: Chatto: London: Viking, 1958, 1988, 408 pp. Many see this as the best of the works of Warner and Warner the best of the post-World War II historians of the Nelson era; lists portraits.

3776 -------. The Sea and the Sword: The Baltic, 1630-1945. London: Cape; NY: Morrow, 1964, 1965, xiv, 319 pp. A survey of the strategic significance of the Baltic, dominated by Sweden in the 17th and Russia in subsequent centuries.

3777 -------. Trafalgar. British Battles series. NY: Macmillan, 1959, 1966, 184 pp. A detailed description of the battle.

3778 -------. Victory: The Life of Lord Nelson. Boston: Little, Brown, 1958, xviii, 393 pp. Intro: Nicholas Monsarrat; on the occasion of the bicentennial of his birth; reviews all the tributes, monuments, and commemorations; includes his "autobiography."

3779 Washburn, Wilcomb E., ed. Proceedings of the Vinland Map Conference, Smithsonian Institution, 1966. Chicago: U Chic P, 1971, 185 pp. For the Newberry Library and in memory of R.A. Skelton, 1906-1970; 11 essays from the conference; the debate over the authenticity; the claim: the only pre-Columbus map showing North America; assessments varied wildly.

3780 Waters, David W. The Art of Navigation in England in Elizabethan and Early Stuart Times. New Haven: Yale UP; Greenwich: NMM, 1958, 1978, xxxix, 696 pp. Fwd: Earl Mountbatten; a history of advances in navigation, e.g., stars, exploration, determination of latitude and longitude, instruments, tables, charts, and aids.

3781 -------. "The Elizabethan Navy and the Armada Campaign." MM, 35 (April 1949): 90-138. Extensively illustrated; discussion of the issues of English victory and Spanish defeat.

3782 -------. The Elizabethan Navy and the Armada of Spain. Maritime Monographs, # 17. Greenwich: NMM, 1975, viii, 102 pp. A series of papers supported by original documents and extensively illustrated, e.g., the orders of Philip II to Medina Sidonia and a quantitative and qualitative assessment of the forces of each side.

3783 -------. "The English Pilot: English Sailing Directions and Charts and the Rise of English Shipping, 16th to 18th centuries." J Navigation, 42 (September 1989): 317-53. The Eva Taylor Lecture, December 1988; in the 1580s, English expansion was facilitated by "waggoners" or "English Pilots" or "Mariners Mirrour," the 1st sailing directions; the English were dependent on the Dutch.

3784 Waters, David W., ed. The Rutters of the Sea: The Sailing Directions of Pierre Garcie. New Haven: Yale UP, 1967, xv, 478 pp. Fwd: Henry Taylor; the 1st printed sailing directions, the equivalent of Admiralty Pilots.

3785 Watkins, T.H. "Sir Joseph Banks: The Greening of the Empire." National Geographic, 190 (November 1996): 28-53. A general descriptive account of his contributions, e.g., collections from his voyage with Cook and the advancement of natural science.

3786 Watson, Boog. "Diary of a Naval Surgeon, 1793-1828." Bull History of Medicine (1972): 131-49. An informative, eye-witness description by Surgeon Thomas Robertson of medical advances and punishments, e.g., Robertson intervened after 125 lashes during a punishment which was to have been 400 lashes, mutinies during 1797, and the state of medical knowledge, e.g., 75 years after Lind, still no awareness of the cure for scurvy.

3787 Watson, Harold F. The Sailor in English Fiction and Drama, 1550-1800. NY: Columbia UP; NY: AMS, 1931, 1966, v, 241 pp. Divides into 3 chronological periods; reviews novels and plays; limited coverage.

3788 Watson, Michael E.C. "Appropriating Empire: The British North American Vice-Admiralty Judges, 1697-1775." Ph.D. diss, Western Ontario, 1997, 344 pp. A study of the judges, 1697, when the court was created, to the American Revlution; judges were influential and the courts were an important part of the legal system.

3789 Watson, Paula K. "The Commission for Victualling the Navy, the Commission for Sick and Wounded Seamen and Prisoners of War and the Commission for Transport, 1702-1714." Ph.D. diss, London, 1965. A scholarly study based on Commission reports.

3790 Watt, James, et al., eds. Starving Sailors: The Influence of Nutrition upon Naval and Maritime History: Proceedings of an International Symposium, 16-18 April 1980. Greenwich: NMM, 1981, xi, 212 pp. A series of papers by naval historians, nutrition experts, and medical specialists; conclusion: poor nutrition led to physical and mental problems, e.g., insufficient vitamin C causing scurvy; interesting that Pepys was informed that a good diet meant high morale and less problems; theory that Cook himself contacted infection causing deterioration of health and judgment.

3791 Watts, Anthony J. Pictorial History of the Royal Navy. 2 vols. I: 1816-1880. II: 1880-1914. London: Allan, 1970-1971, 288 pp. An illustrated history.

3792 -------. The Royal Navy: An Illustrated History. Annapolis: NIP, 1995, 256 pp. Coverage of 200 years; over 100 photos; "from the Industrial Revolution"; little from the age of sail.

3793 Watts, Christopher T. and Watts, Michael J. My Ancestor Was a Merchant Seaman: How Can I Find Out More about Him? London: Society of Genealogists, 1986, 1991, 84 pp. A reference guide to records and archives, e.g., Lloyd's, Trinity House, LHA, Prize Courts, and NMM.

3794 Watts, Philip. "Notes on the Preservation of HMS VICTORY and Her Restoration to the Trafalgar Condition." MM, 9 (April 1923): 98-103. On the earlier centennial of Trafalgar, a call for restoration; search for original drawings; a report on the project.

3795 Webb, J., et al. The Spirit of Portsmouth: A History. Chichester: Shopwyke, 1989, 212 pp. A history of Portsmouth aimed at the local population.

3796 Webb, John. Horatio Admiral Lord Nelson: Was He a Freemason. London: Allen, 2001, 62 pp. No question mark in subtitle and numerous errors in the narrative and illustrations; answer: not proven.

3797 Webb, Paul. "The Frigate Situation of the Royal Navy, 1793-1815." MM, 82 (February 1996): 28-40. Details about these "maids of all work," "eyes of the fleet," convoy escorts, and intelligence gathering; noted the lament of Nelson in the Mediterranean; statistical data.

3798 -------. "The Rebuildling and Repair of the Fleet, 1783-1793." Bull IHR, 50 (November 1977): 194-209. Explanations about the deterioration during the interwar period; maintenance programmes due to Middleton and Sandwich; conclusion: more attention, support, and funding than previously admitted.

3799 -------. "Seapower in the Ochakov Affair of 1791." International History Review, 2 (January 1980): 13-33. Compared to earlier pre-war preparation of the navy, Pitt was determined to maintain the fleet, and it was done: by 1793, 100 SOTL were ready, a record.

3800 Webb, William. Coastguard!: An Official History of HM Coastguard. London: HMSO, 1976, 196 pp. Fwd: Prince of Wales; prior to official founding in 1822, a force developed to prevent smuggling; later a reserve for RN.

3801 Webster, Graham. The Roman Invasion of Britain. London: Batsford, 1980, 224 pp. During the period of the Celts and Roman invasions, e.g., Julius Caesar.

3802 Wedgwood, C.V. The Thirty Years' War. New Haven: Yale UP; NY: Doubleday; NY: Smith, 1938, 1961, 1967, 520 pp. By the preeminent 17th-century historian; one of the best surveys of the war.

3803 Weider, Ben and Forschufvud, Sten. Assassination at St. Helena Revisited. NY: Wiley, 1978, 1995, 555 pp. Fwd: David Chandler; Weider, sometime President, International Napoleon Society; support for the theory of poisoning by arsenic; included tests by toxicologists.

3804 Weil, Alethea J. The Navy of Venice. London: Murray, 1910, xvi, 370 pp. An older history.

3805 Weinberger, Caspar. "The Nelson Touch." Nelson Dispatch, 2 (July 1987): 217. By the former American Cabinet minister knighted by Prime Minister Thatcher; a Nelson enthusiast.

3806 Weir, Michael. "English Naval Activities, 1242-1243." MM, 58 (February 1972): 85-92. During the reign of Henry III; attempt to recover French lands, e.g., Gascony; use of navies; Henry turned to the Cinque Ports; in the end, English efforts failed.

3807 -------. "The Preparation for War in Medieval England, 1199-1307." Ph.D. diss, Brown, 1970, 344 pp. A major transformation of the nature of war; the end of feudal practices and the increasing use of mercenaries.

3808 Weller, Jac. "Gibraltar: Monument to Seapower." USNIP, 97 (October 1972): 27-33. British control in the 18th and 19th centuries effectively forced division of French and Spanish fleets into 2 parts.

3809 Wells, David F. "The Trial of Admiral Keppel, 1779: A Study of Political Opposition to the North Ministry." Ph.D. diss, Kentucky, 1957, 204 pp. The trial of Admiral Keppel; the result of Keppel-Palliser dispute which deteriorated into a partisan conflict; Keppel acquitted.

3810 Wells, John. The Royal Navy: An Illustrated Social History. Stroud: Sutton, 1994, 306 pp. A history emphasizing modern developments; illustrated but not a picture book; more a sociological analysis; the navy as community; anecdotal.

3811 Wells, Roger A.E. Insurrection: The British Experience, 1795-1803. Gloucester: Stroud, 1983, xiv, 312 pp. Presented a mass movement of working-class revolutionaries, e.g., execution of 6 after an alleged attempt to kill the king in 1802; chapter on naval mutinies of 1797, depicted as occurring in a background of multi-dimensional political crisis.

3812 Welsh, William J. and Skaggs, David C., eds. War on the Great Lakes: Essays Commemorating the 175th Anniversary of the Battle of Lake Erie. Kent: Kent State UP, 1991, vi, 154 pp. A series of essays from a symposium, 9-11 September 1988, about the battle, campaigns, and the War of 1812, e.g., W.A.B. Douglas, Harold Langley, and Christoper McKee.

3813 Wernham, R.B. After the Armada: Elizabethan England and the Struggle for Western Europe, 1588-1595. Oxford: Clarendon, 1984, xxix, 613 pp. The 2nd of a definitive trilogy; continuation of his study of England, foreign and domestic issues; survey of the situation on the Continent; France out, Spain still viable and expansive, and England exhausted and tired; threats from Scotland; court vs. country; and the war at sea continued.

3814 -------. Before the Armada: The Emergence of the English Nation, 1485-1588. NY: Harcourt; London: Cape, 1966, 1972, 448 pp. The 1st of the 3; the standard analysis of all aspects of politics, grand strategy, and international relations in the century leading up to the Armada; the best survey of Tudor foreign policy.

3815 [NRS 127]. Wernham, R.B., ed. The Expedition of Sir John Norris and Sir Francis Drake to Spain and Portugal, 1589. Publications of the Navy Records Society, vol. 127. Aldershot: Smith, 1988, lxvi, 380 pp. To follow-up after the Armada; resources of Crown exhausted, so investors contributed; much potential but a glorious failure.

3816 Wernham, R.B. "Queen Elizabeth and the Portuguese Expedition of 1589." EHR, 65 (January and April 1951): 1-26 and 194-218. Drake and John Norris led a counter-armada, but failure; traditional blame to parsimony of Elizabeth; fresh evidence: Elizabeth supplied extra funds and victualling plus enthusiastic support, so cannot blame her.

3817 -------. The Return of the Armadas: The Later Years of the Elizabethan War against Spain, 1595-1603. Oxford: Clarendon, 1994, 452 pp. The 3rd of the trilogy; further operations, e.g., the last and fatal voyage of Drake and Hawkins, 1595; another Spanish Armada, 1596, again scattered by "Protestant" wind; the persistent problem was Ireland.

3818 West, Jenny W. Gunpowder, Government and War in the Mid-Eighteenth Century. RHS Studies in History, # 63. Woodbridge: Boydell, 1991, xiii, 242 pp. A brilliant monograph, the study of military/naval logistics and government policy, especially during the Seven Years' War; private firms supplied gunpowder; never ran out but continuous shortages and RN most effected; looks at administration, logistics, and distribution: conclusion: the Ordnance Office functioned effectively but some problems of transport and communication.

3819 -------. "The Supply of Gunpowder to the Ordnance Office in the Mid-Eighteenth Century, with Specific Reference to Supply, Distribution, and Legislation during the Seven Years' War." Ph.D. diss, London, 1986. The basis for the previous entry.

3820 West, John. A Captain in the Navy of Queen Anne. Then and There series. London: Longman, 1970, viii, 98 pp. Re Edmund Lechmere and experiences in the War of Spanish Succession; includes his exercise book.

3821 West, Richard. The Life and Strange Surprising Adventures of Daniel Defoe. London: HarperCollins, 1997, xvi, 427 pp. Chronological treatment; activist radical after Restoration; secret agent, journalist, novelist, and great tour; no mention of Johnson or pirates.

3822 Westcott, Allan, ed. Mahan on Naval Warfare: Selections from the Writings of Rear Admiral Alfred T. Mahan. Boston: Little, Brown, 1941, 372 pp. Selections from writings.

3823 Whaley, Leigh Ann. The Impact of Napoleon, 1800-1815: An Annotated Bibliography. Lanham: Scarecrow, 1997, xiii, 209 pp. A useful survey of the literature, 480 annotated entries; over 400,000 works have appeared on Napoleon, estimated over 250,000 biographies since 1821; 38 are selected here.

3824 Wheatley, Keith. National Maritime Museum Guide to Maritime Britain. Exeter: Webb, 1990, 1991, 208 pp. Folio size with color pictures; fwd: Duke of Edinburgh; divides British Isles into 10 areas; 430 important places, e.g., docks, preserved ships, nautical archaeological sites, and associations, e.g., MARY ROSE,

Albert Docks, HMS VICTORY, SNR, NRS, and Hakluyt Society.

3825 Wheeler, Dennis A. "The Influence of the Weather during the Camperdown Campaign of 1797." MM, 77 (February 1991): 47-54. An extensive description of the background leading up to the battle, e.g., a French invasion threat, the "fickle" weather, the mutinies, and actions of the Dutch.

3826 Wheeler, H.F.B. and Broadley, A.M. Napoleon and the Invasion of England: The Story of the Great Terror. 2 vols. London: Lane, 1908. The various plans and schemes of Napoleon.

3827 Wheeler, James S. The Making of a World Power: War and the Military Revolution in Seventeenth-Century England. Stroud: Sutton, 1999, vii, 280 pp. Pushes crucial period of transition and expansion back to early and mid-17th century, the wars of Charles I and Civil War; all demanded new methods of finance and administration; costs increased dramatically; beginnings of standing army, professional navy, and sufficient financing; also aspect of state-building.

3828 -------. "Navy Finance, 1649-1660." Historical J, 39 (June 1996): 457-66. A new kind of military force emerged, the New Model Army, the Ship Money fleet, and finances to support them.

3829 -------. "Prelude to Power: The Crisis of 1649 and the Foundation of English Naval Power." MM, 81 (May 1995): 148-55. The debate over the Military Revolution; Britain was transformed during the Civil War, especially 1649-1651; to sustain a standing army and professional navy.

3830 White, Arnold and Moorhouse, E. Hallam. Nelson and the Twentieth Century. London: Cassell, 1905, xvi, 340 pp. A centennial publication, to apply Nelson and Nelsonian values to the present; fostered "cult of Nelson" and "New Navalism"; J.K. Laughton proved Lady Hamilton deserved no consideration; the Cabinet was correct; even if the situation were to be reviewed again in 2005, the same conclusion must be reached.

3831 White, Colin S. The Battle of Cape St. Vincent, 14 February 1797. Nelson 2005: Commemorative Series, # 2. A publication for the Nelson Decade.

3832 White, Colin S., ed. Collection Edition of Nelson Letters. London: NMM. Forthcoming, see later entry; White to be Nelson Research Fellow, NMM, during final years of Nelson Decade; this to be complete and comprehensive collection.

3833 White, Colin S., ed. The Nelson Companion. Stoud: Sutton; Annapolis: NIP, 1995, 1997, xiv, 228 pp. For the Royal Naval Museum; 8 essays supported by 102 illustrations, e.g., White on "The Immortal Memory," Pocock on Nelson sites worldwide, and Nash on top 20 biographies.

3834 White, Colin S. The Nelson Encyclopedia. London; Chatham, 2002, 288 pp.

A recent comprehensive sourcebook; a publication for the bicentennial of death of Nelson; lavish and well researched.

3835 White, Colin S., ed. The Nelson Legend. Portsmouth. By the then Chief Curator, Royal Naval Museum; reviews the myths and legends.

3836 White, Colin S. "The Nelson Letters Project." MM, 87 (November 2001): 476-78. A description by the editor-director of this ambitious project to collect and publish all correspondence by Nelson, a feature of the Nelson Decade; noted that 550 unpublished letters have already been found; more are anticipated.

3837 -------. 1797: Nelson's Year of Destiny. Stroud: Sutton, 1998, 2001, 274 pp. Folio size, illustrated; for the Royal Naval Museum; a feature of the Nelson Decade; St. Vincent and Santa Cruz.

3838 White, David. The Frigate DIANA. The Anatomy of the Ship series. Annapolis: NIP, 1988, 120 pp. Folio size, 312 illustrations; British warship built in 1793.

3839 White, Donald A. "Litus Saxonicum": The British Saxon Shore in Scholarship and History. Madison: State Historical Society, 1961, 122 pp. Re the Saxon Shore, the series of forts defending southeast England.

3840 White, D. Fedotoff. "The Russian Navy in Trieste during the Wars of the Revolution and Empire." American Slavic and East European Review, 6 (December 1947): 25-41. Russian naval forces into the Mediterranean to attack France; frigates blockading Ancona in 1800; Nelson and Hamiltons departing Naples; threat of French attack, so Russian squadron conveyed them and others, including the Queen of Naples, in safety to Trieste.

3841 White, Joshua. Memoirs of the Professional Life of Horatio Nelson, Viscount and Baron Nelson. London: Cunder, 1806, xii, 347 pp. The work of a contemporaneous bookseller; of little value other than an early work.

3842 Whitehead, Bertrand T. Brags and Boasts: Propaganda in the Year of the Armada. Stroud: Sutton, 1994, xiv, 226 pp. Folio size; a survey of "media" of the 16th century, e.g., broadsides; England and Spain launched propaganda campaigns almost a year beforehand; much perpetuated as myth which was enhanced by the Victorians, e.g., Black Legend, game of bowls of Drake, Tilbury speech of Elizabeth, and the "Invincible" Armada.

3843 Whitehill, Walter M. New England Blockade in 1814: The Journal of Henry Napier, Lieutenant in HMS NYMPHE. Salem: Peabody Museum, 1939. A first-hand description of blockading.

3844 Whitehorne, Joseph A. The Battle of Baltimore, 1814. Balt: N&A, 1997, 262 pp. Re the British Chesapeake campaign; Baltimore seen as "a nest of pirates"; an excellent account; the British lost this one.

3845 -------. While Washington Burned: The Battle for Fort Erie, 1814. Balt: N&A, 1993, x, 227 pp. A comprehensive description; plans and operations, invasion, siege, and finale.

3846 Whiteley, W.H. "The British Navy and the Siege of Quebec, 1775-1776." Canadian Historical Review, 61 (March 1980): 3-27. The British army and navy were not always effective during this period; an exception was the defense of Quebec, unsuccessfully besieged by American forces; RN broke through and relieved the fortress; praise for Sandwich by George III.

3847 Whitfield, Peter. New Found Lands: Maps in the History of Exploration. Discoveries in Geography series. London: BL; NY: Routledge, 1998, viii, 200 pp. Folio size, illustrated with map collection of BL; the role of cartography in exploration; interesting division into periods: lure of the East, 1250-1550, New World, 1490-1630, Pacific and Australia, 1520-1800, and continents explored, 1500-1900; not scholarly.

3848 Whiting, J.R.S. The Enterprise of England: The Spanish Armada. NY: St. Martin; Gloucester: Sutton, 1988, 248 pp. A quadricentennial publication; incorporates new evidence and latest interpretations, demythologizing in the process; illustrations include facsimile playing cards depicting the Armada defeat.

3849 Wibberley, Leonard P.O. The King's Beard. NY: Ariel, 1952, 198 pp. Juvenile, nautical fiction; re the raid of Drake on Cadiz, "singeing the King of Spain's beard."

3850 Wickwire, Franklin B. "Admiralty Secretaries and the British Civil Service." Hungtington Library Quarterly, 23 (May 1965): 235-54. Praise for civil servants of the 18th century; series of distinguished administrators devoted to improving RN.

3851 Wickwire, Mary B. "Lord Sandwich and the King's Ships: A Study of British Naval Administration, 1771-1782." Ph.D. diss, Yale, 1963. A scholarly appraisal of Sandwich.

3852 Wiggs, J.L. "The Seaborne Trade of Southampton in the Second Half of the Sixteenth Century." Ph.D. diss, Southampton, 1955. Actually Mrs. J.L. Thomas; a scholarly study of this formative period of international trade.

3853 Wignall, Sydney. In Search of Spanish Treasure: A Diver's Story. Newton Abbot: David and Charles, 1982, 252 pp. Reviews a number of projects of nautical archaeology, e.g.. off Irish coast, Fair Isle, the search for REVENGE, and for the lead coffin of Drake off Panama.

3854 -------. The Spanish Armada Salvage Expedition. Privately printed, 1968. A progress report about 7 years work of nautical archaeology on SANTA MARIA DE

LA ROSA.

3855 Wilcox, Leslie A. Mr. Pepys' Navy. NY: Barnes; London: Bell, 1966, 1968, ix, 189 pp. A day-by-day reconstruction of developments in RN after the Restoration; illustrated with drawings by the author.

3856 Wilder, Patrick A. The Battle of Sackett's Harbour: and the Struggle for Lake Ontario. Balt: N&A, 1994, 300 pp. Crucial events of the War of 1812; an American victory to dominate the area of the Niagara River and Lakes Ontario and Erie.

3857 Wilkinson, Clennell. "British Politics, Government and the Navy, 1763-1778." Ph.D. diss, East Anglia, 1997. Re peacetime administration and politics; why did the navy decline?; conducted a computer analysis of records of maintenance and building; conclusion: Sandwich was blamed but he implemented proper reforms; real causes were international tensions, changes in dockyard practices, and unusual climate conditions.

3858 Wilkinson, Clennell A. Nelson. London: Harrap, 1931, ix, 322 pp. Illustrated; one of the most popular biographies; many anecdotes, humanizing Nelson, repeating all of the myths, e.g., Nelson and the polar bear, climbing the pear tree, and knowing no fear; much on his health which was never good.

3859 -------. Prince Rupert, the Cavalier. London: Lippincott, 1935, 259 pp. A biography of the great Royalist naval commander.

3860 -------. William Dampier. Alt. title: Dampier: Explorer and Buccaneer. NY: Harper; London: Lane, 1929, xii, 257 pp. A biography.

3861 Wilkinson, Clive. "The Earl of Egmont and the Navy, 1763-1766." MM, 84 (1998): 418-35. The basis for a forthcoming book; informative about the navy in the 18th century

3862 Wilkinson, Cuthbert S. The Wake of the BOUNTY: An Attempt to Prove that Fletcher Christian Was the Original of the "Ancient Mariner". London: Cassell, 1953, xiii, 200 pp. A curious conglomeration; Bligh vs. Christian; the brilliance of Bligh to have navigated 4000 miles in an open launch; Christian as the model for "the Ancient Mariner" by Coleridge; also brings in "The Island" by Lord Byron; important that BOUNTY mutiny was "the greatest" and led by "the greatest of mutineers," yet, there is no biography; "Awake Bold Bligh! The foe is at the gate."

3863 Wilkinson-Latham, Robert. The Royal Navy, 1790-1970. Osprey Men-at-Arms series. London: Osprey, 1977, 40 pp. The typical Osprey oversize pamphlet format; focus on the development of naval uniforms of RN.

3864 Willan, T.S. The Early History of the Russia Company, 1553-1603. Manchester: Manchester UP, 1956, ix, 295 pp. An aspect of the search for a Northeast Passage; also, Spanish-Portuguese "monopolies" not applicable; serious challenges: cold, ice, and fog; Sebastian Cabot involved; charter of company in 1555.

3865 -------. "Some Aspects of English Trade with the Levant in the Sixteenth Century." EHR, 70 (July 1955): 399-410. Anglo-Turkish relations and trade in the Levant early in the 16th century; meant competition with the French; ships of Venice and Genoa may have been used; trade ceased later in the century.

3866 Willard, James F. and Morris, William A., eds. The English Government at Work, 1327-1336. Cambridge: Harvard UP, 1940, 475 pp. A series of essays, e.g., A.E. Prince on the army and the navy; re the navy, administration, "Masters of the King's Ships," captains and crews; calls it "the royal navy."

3867 Willasey-Wilsey, A.P. "The Royal Marines." USNIP, 91 (November 1965): 64-70. A short history for its tricentennial; formed in 1664 by Charles II; later the emphases were maintenance of discipline and amphibious operations.

3868 Willcox, William B. "The British Road to Yorktown: A Study in Divided Command." AHR, 52 (October 1946): 1-35. The overall strategy of the British has been neglected, overshadowed by Franco-American cooperation; an example of the failure of army-navy cooperation.

3869 -------. "Rhode Island in British Strategy, 1780-1781." J Modern History, 17 (December 1945): 304-31. Re the role of sea power in the American Revolution; the British were past masters with a long series of victories, e.g., Louisbourg, Quebec, and Gibraltar; French established a base at Newport; assisted in the dominance at Yorktown; the French prevailed and Britain suffered a debacle.

3870 Williams, Coleman O. "The Role of the British Navy in the Helder Campaign, 1799." Ph.D. diss, Auburn, 1985. A scholarly study, an Anglo-Russian effort to liberate the Batavian Republic from France; analysis showed RN operations were creditable; the campaign was a failure.

3871 Williams, David M. "The Progress of Maritime History, 1953-1993. J Transport History, 3rd ser, 14 (September 1993): 126-41. A survey and assessment of the status and development of interest; conclusion: increased interest: books, societies, media, and museums, e.g., MARY ROSE, VICTORY, SNR, NRS, British and International Commissions, and academic programmes at St. Andrews and Exeter.

3872 Williams, Glyndwr. The British Search for the Northwest Passage in the Eighteenth Century. London: Longman, 1962, xvi, 306 pp. For the Royal Commonwealth Society; Williams, 1933-___, the premier historian for the age of exploration; this study: beginning in the early 16th century, a search for access to the West, e.g., initiatives from Bristol merchant, Robert Thorne; Frobisher made 3 voyages later in the century; Davis and Hudson.

3873 -------. "Commodore Anson and the Acapulco Galleon." HisTod, 17 (August 1967): 525-32. Anson, an important reformer at the Admiralty; earlier, an expedition to the Pacific; especially dramatic was his capture of the Manila-Acapulco galleon near the Philippines; established his fame and fortune.

3874 [NRS 109]. Williams, Glyndwr, ed. Documents Relating to Anson's Voyage Round the World, 1740-1744. Publications of the Navy Records Society, vol. 109. London: NRS, 1967, xiv, 303 pp. Recounts the capture of the Manila galleon with booty unsurpassed in the history of RN; details on the Walter narrative.

3875 Williams, Glyndwr. The Expansion of Europe in the Eighteenth Century: Overseas Rivalry, Discovery and Exploitation. London: Blandford, 1966, x, 309 pp. Competition among the European powers, Spain, Portugal, the Dutch, England, and France; an outstanding bibliographical essay.

3876 -------. The Great South Sea: English Voyages and Encounter, 1570-1750. New Haven: Yale UP, 1997, xvi, 300 pp. Describes English interests and operations as an obsession; dreams to repeat the adventures and riches achieved by Drake and Anson, much encouraged by propaganda and fiction, e.g., by Hakluyts, Swift, and Defoe.

3877 -------. The Prize of All the Oceans: The Triumph of Anson's Voyage Round the World. London: HarperCollins; NY: Viking, 1999, 2001, xxi, 264 pp. Details on the famous circumnavigation, 1740-1744; discussion of implications and consequences, e.g., only 188 of 1900 men survived and prize disputes lasted into late 1740s.

3878 -------. "Seamen and Philosophers in the South Seas in the Age of Captain Cook." MM, 65 (February 1979): 3-22. The Eva Taylor Lecture; re philosophical implications of these expeditions overseas; created a "Pacific craze" related to advances in science, concepts of the noble savage, and descriptions of unspoiled territories.

3879 Williams, Glyndwr and Frost, Alan, eds. "Terra Australis" to Australia. Melbourne: Oxford UP, 1988, xviii, 242 pp. Focus on historical cartography; supported by 145 plates, many in color; began with the Portuguese and Dutch pursuing Java la Grande; Dampier and later explorations; all part of Australian bicentennial sponsored by the Australian Academy of the Humanities.

3880 Williams, Glyndwr. "'To Make Discoveries of Countries Hitherto Unknown': The Admiralty and Pacific Exploration in the Eighteenth Century." MM, 82 (February 1996): 14-27. The Caird Lecture at NMM; voyages advancing science and exploration were officially sponsored, e.g., Cook and Vancouver in the 18th century; Anson and Sandwich made important contributions.

3881 Williams, J.E.D. From Sails to Satellites: The Origin and Development of Navigational Science. NY: Oxford UP, 1992, 1993, 1994, xii, 310 pp. A broad, comprehensive study; descriptions of instruments, compasses, and chronometers; some gaps and not scholarly.

3882 Williams, Jay. The Spanish Armada. Horizon Caravel Book. NY: Harper, 1966, 153 pp. Folio size with color illustrations; an adequate survey; good on background and implications.

3883 Williams, M.J. "The Naval Administration of the Fourth Earl of Sandwich, 1771-1782." D.Phil. diss, Oxford, 1962. A scholarly study.

3884 Williams, Neville J. All the Queen's Men: Elizabeth and Her Courtiers. London: Weidenfeld, 1972, 272 pp. Over a dozen top ministers, advisers, and nobles are presented, e.g., Cecil, Leicester, Walsingham, Sydney, Essex, Raleigh, and Lord Howard.

3885 -------. Captains Outrageous: Seven Centuries of Piracy. London: Barrie, 1961, xii, 243 pp. Insists this is about lawbreakers, pirates; privateers operated under a commission but, on occasion, it was difficult to distinguish; begins in 1200 and continuing for centuries to recent times in the China Seas; pirates operated from the Cinque Ports and they seemed to be immune as long as they fulfilled obligations to the Crown; later "Queen's Ships" meant a pirate navy.

3886 -------. Contraband Cargoes: Seven Centuries of Smuggling. London: Longman; Hamden: Shoe String, 1959, 1961, xiv, 301 pp. Begins with 1272, smuggling increasingly seen as a recognized profession, its heyday seen as the period, 1713-1775, finally superseded by free trade and a new morality; in England, smuggling arose when the Customs and Excise Duties were instituted in the 13th century by Edward I, thus, to avoid taxes.

3887 -------. The Sea Dogs: Privateers, Plunder and Piracy in the Elizabethan Age. London: Weidenfeld, 1975, 278 pp. Re the exploits of the Sea Dogs, e.g., operating from Corfe Castle on the Isle of Purbeck, and from Bristol; some personalities, e.g., Sebastian Cabot, John Hawkins, and Drake.

3888 Williams, Norman L. Sir Walter Raleigh. Balt: Penguin, 1962, 1965, 276 pp. A creditable popular biography.

3889 Williams, Patrick. Armada. London: Tempus, 2000. A recent survey, placing it in European context and presenting experiences of seamen on both sides.

3890 Williams, Ronald. The Lords of the Isles: The Clan Donald and the Early Kingdom of the Scots. London: Hogarth, 1984, xxvi, 270 pp. Re the Great Lords of the Isles of the Western Highlands and Hebrides and the Dalraida; in the early 6th century, 3 Gaelic clans of Ireland landed, establishing the Albain kingdom of Dalraida; Romans called them "Scotti" and they later gave their name to the kingdom of Scotland; nothing here on naval power.

3891 Williamson, James A. The Age of Drake. The Pioneer Histories series. London: Black, 1938, 1946, 1952, 1960, 1965, viii, 399 pp. An older, broad survey by this long-lived and prolific historian of English exploration and expansion; features, e.g., expansion, Hawkins, Drake, circumnavigation, the Armada, to the Far East, the Cabots, and the Hakluyts.

3892 -------. "Books on Drake." History, 12 (1927): 310-21. A good review article.

3893 -------. The Cabot Voyages and Bristol Discovery under Henry VII with the Cartography of the Voyages. Publications of the Hakluyt Society. Cambridge: Cambridge UP, 1962, xvi, 332 pp. Re little-known voyages from Bristol of the 1480s to the 1510s; supported by a series of documents.

3894 -------. Cook and the Opening of the Pacific. Teach Yourself History series. London: Hodder, 1946, 1948, xii, 251 pp. The field was vast, the progress slow, and the problem remained unsolved until the late 18th century; Dampier to Bougainville; recounts the voyages of Cook who cleared up all the major uncertainties.

3895 -------. The English Channel: A History. Cleveland: World, 1959, 1960, 381 pp. A history of the Channel in 18 chapters up through World War II; the scope is the English shore and the activities upon it; features, e.g., the Romans landed at "the tin islands," a Roman lighthouse at Dover, numerous invasions, Cinque Ports, the Tudors and a real navy, Drake's game of bowls, the Armada, and other events.

3896 -------. Hawkins of Plymouth: A New History of Sir John Hawkins and of the Other Members of His Family Prominent in Tudor England. London: Black, 1949, 1969, xii, 348 pp. Re the family of overseas adventurers; in 3 parts, Hawkins to America in the 1560s, as administrator of the navy, and contributor to maritime expansion; others were William, the elder, sons William and John, and Richard.

3897 -------. Maritime Enterprise, 1485-1558. Oxford: Oxford UP, 1913, 1941, 1972, 416 pp. Re discovery and trade; includes a chapter on the navy.

3898 Williamson, James A., ed. The Observations of Sir Richard Hawkins. London: Argonaut, 1628, 1933. A reprint from the original text; the son of John, Richard having less interest in the sea, but much on Elizabethan sea-practice.

3899 Williamson, James A. The Ocean in English History: Being the Ford Lectures, 1939-1940. Oxford: Oxford UP, 1941, 208 pp. Published lectures covering the 15th throuogh the 18th centuries; the "Oceanic Interest" as a formative influence on modern England; reviews the propagandists, e.g., Thomas More, the Hakluyts, Purchas, and Raleigh.

3900 -------. A Short History of British Expansion. 2 vols. I: The Old Colonial Empire. II: The Modern Empire and Commonwealth. NY: St. Martin, 1922, 1930, 1936, 1945, 1967, x, 886 pp. Later editions ed: Donald Southgate; an excellent survey; chapters on armed trade and reprisals and the Spanish war.

3901 -------. Sir Francis Drake. Brief Lives, # 1. London: Collins, 1957, 1961, 1966, 160 pp. A short biography.

3902 -------. Sir John Hawkins: The Time and the Man. Oxford: Clarendon; Westport: Greenwood, 1927, 1970, xii, 542 pp. A standard biography, rehabilitating him from the image of "enriching himself . . . and Admiralty official whose integrity was suspected"; for Williamson, Hawkins was "a major contributor to naval administration."

3903 -------. The Voyages of the Cabots and the English Discovery of North America under Henry VII and Henry VIII. London: Argonaut; NY: DaCapo, 1929, 1970, 1971, xiii, 290 pp. Narrative, documents, and cartographical material; assesses the Cabots.

3904 -------. The Voyages of John and Sebastian Cabot. Historical Association Pamphlet, # 106. London: Bell, 1937, 19 pp. A short survey; admits much not known about the Cabots.

3905 Willis, Garry. Venice: Lion City: The Religion of Empire. NY: Simon, 2001, 415 pp. Copious illustrations from art history; Venice, with the most sophisticated and advanced fleet in Europe; created by the noted Venice Arsenal; longtime dominance of the Mediterranean.

3906 Willmoth, Frances, ed. Flamsteed's Stars: New Perspectives on the Life and Work of the First Astromomer Royal, 1664-1719. Woodbridge: Boydell, 1997, xiv, 271 pp. Proceedings of a conference, NMM, October 1995; Flamsteed set the standard for Greenwich Observatory for 300 years.

3907 Wilson, Angus. [Anglo-Saxon Attitudes]. London: Secker, 1956, 1957, 1960, 412 pp. A Scandinavian piece later turned into a TV movie adapted by Andrew Davies; a novel based on SUTTON HOO; mysterious discoveries in a royal tomb at "Melpham"; mixed Christian and pagan, secular and sacred.

3908 Wilson, Charles H. Profit and Power: England and the Dutch Wars. London: Longman, 1957, 169 pp. The series of wars of the late 17th century were fought over trade and sea power.

3909 Wilson, Charles H. and Procter, David, eds. 1688: The Seaborne Alliance and Diplomatic Revolution: Proceedings of an International Symposium, National Maritime Museum, Greenwich, 5-6 October 1988. Greenwich: NMM, 1989, 176 pp. Fwd: Prince of Wales; on the occasion of the tercentennial of the Glorious Revolution; 12 essays from the symposium, e.g., Jonathan Israel on economic factors and the revolution, Jaap Bruijn on the Dutch navy, C.R. Boxer on Anglo-Dutch animosity, and Alan McGowan on the influence of Dutch shipbuilding on the English.

3910 Wilson, Derek A. The World Encompassed: Francis Drake and His Great Voyage, 1577-1580. NY: Harper; London: Hamilton, 1977, 1999, xiii, 240 pp. On the occasion of the quadricentennial; a chronological narrative of the circumnavigation; 5 ships proceeded with much secrecy, then and later; a complicated political and diplomatic background.

3911 Wilson, Ian. The Columbus Myth: Did Men of Bristol Reach America before Columbus? London: Simon, 1991, xvi, 240 pp. Investigates whether there was a Columbus-Bristol connection, even a Cabot-Columbus connection; problem of disparity of sources: much on Columbus, little on Bristol and the Cabots.

3912 Wilson, Jenny. "Sir Walter Ralegh's History of the World: Its Purpose and Political Significance." Historian, 59 (Autumn 1998): 10-15. In 1608-1609, Raleigh wrote this while in the Tower; details on content.

3913 Wilson, Kathleen. "Empire, Trade and Popular Politics in Mid-Hanoverian Britain: The Case of Admiral Vernon." Past and Present, 121 (November 1988): 74-109. In the war of 1739-1740, a series of British defeats; Vernon reversed that, becoming a hero; he had political status and influence; critic of Walpole government.

3914 Wilson, Leonard G. "The Clinical Definition of Scurvy and the Discovery of Vitamin C." J History of Medicine and Allied Science, 30 (January 1975): 40-60. The story of scurvy and experiments to eliminate it.

3915 Wilson, Timothy. Flags at Sea: A Guide to the Flags Flown at Sea by British and Some Foreign Ships. London: HMSO; Annapolis: NIP, 1986, 1999, 140 pp. Many illustrations; signalling flags of Britain, France, and the U.S., 16th century to the present; from the collection at NMM.

3916 Winfield, Rif. The 50-Gun Ship. London: Chatham, 1997, 128 pp. The size less than SOTL, began as Flemish privateer and adopted by RN; 123 tables and illustrations; masts, rigging, crew, stores, and accounts of actions.

3917 Winklareth, Robert J. Naval Shipbuilders of the World: From the Age of Sail to the Present Day. London: Chatham, 2000, 384 pp. A history; the evolution of naval shipbuilding, then chapters on nations; the 1st true warship was the war galley about the 8th century BC; included the navy of Alfred built to protect against the Danes; others were Richard II, Henry V, and Henry VIII; superficial.

3918 Winnefeld, James A. "A Voyage through Modern Naval Fiction." NWCR, 49 (Spring 1996): 120-25. Prioritizes: O'Brian, Monsarrat, Wouk, Forester, McKenna, and earlier, Cooper, Melville, and Conrad; the Ramage series of Pope falls short; Tom Clancy characters lack depth; favorite is The Caine Mutiny.

3919 Winship, G.P. John Cabot and the Study of Sources. Wash: American Historical Association, 1898, 41 pp. A guide to the sources; analysis of various sources; to enlighten and clarify complex and disputed accounts.

3920 Winslow, Richard E. <u>Wealth and Honour: Portsmouth during the Golden Age of Privateering, 1775-1815</u>. Portsmouth: Marine Society, 1988, xx, 304 pp. Portsmouth, New Hampshire; extensive coverage of operations of privateers during 3 wars; not scholarly, not balanced, and exaggerated but informative on the regional perspective.

3921 Winton, John. <u>An Illustrated History of the Royal Navy</u>. London: Salamander, 2000, 2002, 224 pp. By the prolific writer of naval history; for the Royal Naval Museum, a history from earliest times; profusely illustrated; not scholarly.

3922 -------. <u>The Naval Heritage of Portsmouth</u>. Southampton: Ensign, 1989, 229 pp. A history from the earliest nautical associations to the present; many illustrations.

3923 -------. <u>Sir Walter Ralegh</u>. London: Joseph, 1975, 352 pp. A popular biography; many illustrations; no scholarly apparatus.

3924 Winton-Clare, C. "A Shipbuilder's War." <u>MM</u>, 29 (July 1943): 139-48. Re the Lakes during the War of 1812, a unique situation; makes the point that a single ship built could shift the balance; superiority of RN elsewhere meant nothing here.

3925 Wintringham, Thomas H. <u>Mutiny: Being a Survey of Mutinies from Spartcus to Invergordon</u>. NY: Fortuny, 1936, 355 pp. An analysis of mutinies and chapters on prominent ones, e.g., 1797, India in 1857, avoiding one at Portsmouth in 1918-1919, and Invergordon in 1931.

3926 Wissolik, Richard D. <u>The Bayeux Tapestry: A Critical Annotated Bibliography with Cross-References and Summary Outlines of Scholarship, 1729-1990</u>. Greensburg: Eadmer, 1990, xii, 74 pp. An extensive annotated bibliography and analysis.

3927 Wiswall, F.L. <u>The Development of Admiralty Jurisdiction and Practice since 1800: An English Study with American Comparisons</u>. NY: Cambridge UP, 1970, xxvii, 223 pp. The Yorke Prize; not a history but a study of maritime jurisdiction and practice of Admiralty Courts, e.g., Prize Court decisions and the interaction between English and American courts.

3928 Witherby, C.T. <u>The Battle of Bonchurch</u>. Upper Bonchurch: Private, 1962, 22 pp. A local history of the French amphibious attack on the south coast of the Isle of Wight.

3929 Withey, Lynne. <u>Voyages of Discovery: Captain Cook and the Exploration of the Pacific</u>. NY: Morrow; Berkeley: U Cal P, 1987, 1989, 512 pp. During the period of the last great European-initiated age of exploration and discovery; noted the expansive popularity of accounts of these voyages and contributions to the advancement of science; the voyages of Cook studied plant and animal life and customs.

3930 Wood, Gerold A. The Discovery of Australia. London: Macmillan, 1922, 1969, 541 pp. Revised: J.C. Beaglehole; fwd: O.H.K. Spate; the old standard updated by the preeminent expert.

3931 Wood, Ian and Lund, Niels, eds. People and Places in Northern Europe, 500-1600: Essays in Honour of Peter Hayes Sawyer. Woodbridge: Boydell, 1991, xxii, 248 pp. A festschrift for the great historian of the Viking era; see Wood on SUTTON HOO, presenting several competing candidates for the person in the ship burial.

3932 Wood, James P. The Queen's Most Honorable Pirate. NY: Harper, 1961, 184 pp. Nautical fiction, re Drake.

3933 Wood, William C.H. Elizabethan Sea-Dogs: A Chronicle of Drake and His Companions. New Haven: Yale UP, 1918, 1920, xi, 252 pp. Blurb: command of the sea was won during this period under the leadership of Drake; unfortunate that Mahan began in the 17th century; should have been a century earlier; the first modern admirals known as "sea-dogs."

3934 Woodfine, Philip L. Britannia's Glories: The Walpole Ministry and the 1739 War with Spain. Rochester: Boydell, 1998, 279 pp. For the Royal Historical Society; by the winner of the Julian Corbett Prize; a neglected war, Anglo-Spanish of 1739; deteriorating Anglo-Spanish relations through the 1730s; important role and contribution of the press and control of public opinion; economic objectives dominated military and naval planning.

3935 -------. "The War of Jenkins' Ear: A New Voice in the Wentworth-Vernon Debate." J Society Army Historical Research, 65 (Summer 1967): 67-91. A neglected British war; some contemporaneous accounts of operations; Tobias Smollett was a participant.

3936 Woodley, Alfred E. Fire Over England. NY: Doubleday, 1936, 305 pp. Nautical fiction, re the Armada.

3937 Woodman, Richard. Baltic Mission. NY: Sheridan, 1986, 2000, 211 pp. Woodman,1944-___; nautical fiction of the Nelson era and other naval topics; veteran of Trinity House; "hero" is Nathaniel Drinkwater, this the 7th in the series; in the Mariner's Library Fiction Classics series.

3938 -------. Beneath the Aurora. London: Murray, 1995, 247 pp. The 12th Drinkwater novel.

3939 -------. The Bomb Vessel. NY: Walker, 1984, 1986, 2000, 216 pp. The 4th Drinkwatere novel; re battle of Copenhagen.

3940 -------. A Brig of War. London: Murray, 1998, 2001, 308 pp. The 3rd Dringwater novel; plan by Napoleon to invade meant expansion of operations into the Mediterranean Sea.

3941 -------. The Corvette. London: Murray, 1985, 1987, 2000, 232 pp. The 5th Drinkwater novel; re protection of the Hull whaling fleet, operations in the Arctic.

3942 -------. The Darkening Sea. NY: Sheridan, 2000.

3943 -------. Ebb Tide. A Nathaniel Drinkwater Novel. London: Murray, 1998, 230 pp. The 14th Drinkwater novel.

3944 -------. 1805. London: Murray, 1985, 209 pp. The 6th Drinkwater novel; meets Villeneuve.

3945 -------. An Eye of the Fleet: A Nathaniel Drinkwater Novel. London: Murray, 1981, 2001, 185 pp. The 1st Drinkwater novel.

3946 -------. Flying Squadron. London: Murray, 1992, 1999, 250 pp. The 11th Drinkwater novel.

3947 -------. The History of the Ship: The Comprehensive Story of Seafaring from the Earliest Times to the Present. London: Conway, 1997, 352 pp. Large folio size, illustrated; a summary of The History of the Ship, 12-vol. series; covers a vast field.

3948 -------. In Distant Waters. London: Murray, 1988, 2000, 246 pp. The 8th Drinkwater novel; commander of a frigate operating in the Pacific off North America discouraging Spanish and Russian expansion.

3949 -------. Keepers of the Sea: A History of the Yachts and Tenders of Trinity House. Lavenham: Dalton, 1983, ix, 190. Re Trinity House, the institution which tends lighthouses and navigation aids.

3950 -------. A King's Cutter. London: Murray, 1997, 2001, 212 pp. The 2nd Drinkwater novel; Lt. of KESTREL conveying secret agents to France.

3951 -------. A Private Revenge. London: Murray, 1989, 1999, 247 pp. The 9th Drinkwater novel; escorts convoy of East Indiamen to Far East.

3952 -------. The Sea Warriors: Fighting Captains and Frigate Warfare in the Age of Nelson. NY: Carroll, 2001, 384 pp. A general survey of a favorite topic.

3953 -------. The Shadow of the Eagle. London: Murray, 1997, 260 pp. The 13th Drinkwater novel; intrigue to free Napoleon after his first abdication.

3954 -------. Under False Colours. London: Murray, 1990, 1999, 260 pp. The 10th Drinkwater novel.

3955 [Wars of the French Revolution and Napoleon, 1793-1815, vol. V]. Woodman, Richard, ed. The Victory of Seapower: Winning the Napoleonic War, 1806-1814. Chatham Pictorial Histories series, co-sponsored by the National Maritime Museum, Greenwich. London: Chatham; Annapolis: NIP, 1998, 192 pp. 5th in the spectacular series, folio size, profusely illustrated.

3956 Woodrooffe, Thomas. Vantage at Sea: England's Emergence as an Oceanic Power. London: Faber; NY: St. Martin, 1958, 301 pp. The rise of the English; features, e.g., Bristol merchants sponsor exploration war with Spain, "beyond the line," Spanish Main, Spanish treasure, the Cadiz raid, and the Armada.

3957 Woodward, F.W. Plymouth's Defences: A Short History. Ivybridge: Woodward, 1990, 63 pp. A regional assessment; the history of Plymouth and sea power; includes dockyard at Devonport.

3958 Woodward, Ralph L. Robinson Crusoe's Island: A History of the Juan Fernandez Islands. Chapel Hill: UNCP, 1969, 267 pp. The famous island 360 miles due west of central Chile; discovered in 1574; once a penal colony; Alexander Selkirk, aka Robinson Crusoe, was marooned there.

3959 Wordsworth, William. Character of the Happy Warrior: A Poem. NY: Hobby, 1913, 1915, 36 pp. For the Medici Society; re the character of Nelson.

3960 Wren, Melvin C. "London and the Twenty Ships, 1626-1627." AHR, 55 (1950): 321-35. Increasing political and financial crisis during the reign of Charles I; war with Spain and Parliament refused sufficient funding; search for alternate sources; order of 20 "impressed" ships with "impressed" crews led to increasing opposition; a step toward rebellion.

3961 Wright, Charles and Fayle, C. Ernest. A History of Lloyd's: From the Founding of Lloyd's Coffee House to the Present Day. London: Macmillan, 1928, xxi, 475 pp. On the occasion of opening a new building; Lloyd's was a leader of commercial, naval, and social history; featured insurance and Lloyd's List; origins in the 16th century; "old" and "new" Lloyd's.

3962 Wright, Irene A., ed. Documents Concerning English Voyages to the Caribbean and the Spanish Main, 1569-1580. Publications of the Hakluyt Society, 2nd ser, vol. 71. London: Hakluyt Society, 1932, lxiv, 348 pp. Documents from Archives of the Indies, Seville; re operations of Drake.

3963 Wright, Irene A., ed. Further English Voyages to Spanish America, 1583-1594. Publications of the Hakluyt Society, 2nd ser, vol. 99. London: Hakluyt Society, 1951, xciii, 314 pp. A continuation of the previous entry.

3964 Wright, Irene A., ed. Spanish Documents Concerning English Voyages to the Caribbean, 1527-1568: Selected from the Archives of the Indies, Seville. Publications of the Hakluyt Society, 2nd ser, vol. 62. London: Hakluyt Society,

1929, x, 167 pp. A continuation.

3965 Wright, J.L. Anglo-Spanish Rivalry in North America. Athens: U Ga P, 1971, xiii, 257 pp. A concise summary, an overview in 2 parts: 1492-1763 and 1783-1821; features, e.g., English "intrusion" of any form seen by Spain as illegal, Florida, Virginia, and Carolina; War of Jenkins's Ear.

3966 Wright, W.H.K. "The Armada Tercentenary Exhibition." Western Antiquary, 8 (1888): 1-9, 33-41, and 67-69. A description of the tercentennial exhibition.

3967 -------. Britain's Salamis: Or, the Glorious Fight of 1588: An Historical Lecture. Plymouth: Westcott, 1888, 56 pp. On the occasion of the tercentennial.

3968 -------. Catalogue of the Exhibition of Armada and Elizabethan Relics Held in the Grand Saloon of the Theatre Royal, Drury Lane, London: Opened October 24, 1888. Plymouth: Westcott, 1888. An exhibition on the occasion of the tercentennial.

3969 -------. The Plymouth Hoe: Its Scenery and Historical Association. Plymouth: Duprez, 1872, 16 pp. A local history.

3970 -------. The Spanish Armada: A Descriptive Historical Poem. Plymouth: Friend, 1874, 1887, 32 pp. To support the reproductions of the tapestries by Pine.

3971 Wroth, Lawrence C. The Way of the Ship: An Essay on the Literature of Navigational Science. Portland: Southworth, 1937, xii, 91 pp. By the librarian of the John Carter Brown Library to support an exhibition; based on the holdings there; charts, sailing directions, instruments, astronomical calculations, Mercator, and the chronometer of Harrison.

3972 Wyatt, H.V. "James Lind and the Prevention of Scurvy." Medical History, 20 (October 1976): 433-38. A response to R.E. Hughes, who responded to Wyatt; a debate over Lind, his methods, and his accomplishments; Lind used the scientific method, controlled chemical trials.

3973 Yardley, B.C. "The Political Career of George Villiers, Second Duke of Buckingham, 1628-1687." D.Phil. diss, Oxford, 1989. Re the son of the minister of James I; later very influential after the Restoration; anti-Duke of York, anti-Pepys, and anti-Deane.

3974 Yonge, Charles D. The History of the British Navy: From the Earliest Period to the Present Time. 3 vols. London: Bentley, 1863, 1866, 1524 pp. An extensive and early history of RN.

3975 Youings, Joyce, ed. Ralegh in Exeter, 1985: Privateering and Colonisation in the Reign of Elizabeth I: Papers, Conference at Exeter University, 3-4 May 1985. Exeter Studies in History, # 10. Exeter: UP Exeter, 1985, 127 pp. On the occasion of the quadricentennial of the settlement of English people in North America, an expedition from Plymouth in 1585 sponsored by Ralegh; Grenville to Roanoke Island; papers, e.g., Friel on the 3-masted ship and Quinn on the lost colonists.

3976 Young, George. Life and Voyages of James Cook. London, 1836. By Rev. Young of Whitby; a local perspective on Cook.

3977 Young, Michael B. Servility and Service: The Life and Work of Sir John Coke. RHS Studies in History, # 45. Woodbridge: Boydell, 1986, xii, 300 pp. Re RN during the era of Buckingham; Coke being Commissioner and Deputy Treasurer of the Navy; naval performance was bad.

3978 -------. "Sir John Coke, 1563-1644." Ph.D. diss, Harvard, 1971. The basis of the previous entry.

3979 Yturriaga, Jose Antonio de. "Attitudes in Ireland Towards the Survivors of the Spanish Armada." Irish Sword, 17 (Summer 1990): 244-54. Clarification of the disposition of Spanish seamen from ship wrecks along the west Irish coast; casualties of ships and men have been exaggerated; conclusion: 26 ships wrecked, 6000 men affected, 3750 drowned, 1100 executed by English, 400 killed by Irish, and 750 survived, most returning to Spain via Scotland.

3980 Zahadieh, Nuala. "'A Frugal, Prudential and Hopeful Trade': Privateering in Jamaica, 1655-1689." J Imperial and Commonwealth History, 18 (May 1990): 145-68. The English in the Caribbean; accounts of piracy and privateering; focus on business aspects, e.g., the role of plunder, source of funds for the colonists, small capital outlay, and quick return.

3981 -------. "Trade, Plunder and Economic Development in Early English Jamaica, 1655-1689." Ph.D. diss, London, 1984. The basis for the previous entry.

3982 Ziebarth, Marilyn, ed. "The Francis Drake Controversy: His California Anchorage, June 17-July 3, 1579." California Historical Quarterly, 53 (Fall 1974): 197-292 pp. Presentation of the extensive debate; journal noted "a faire and good baye" and anchored for 36 days; 3 possible locations described.

3983 Zimmerman, James F. Impressment of American Seamen. NY: Columbia UP; NY: Kennikat, 1925, 1966, 279 pp. A review of the issue and its significance before, during, and after the American Revolution; the British ceased actions against Americans after the War of 1812 but never renounced the policy; conclusion: significance has been exaggerated, more an issue of national honor and pride.

3984 Zins, Henryk. England and the Baltic in the Elizabethan Era. Manchester: Manchester UP, 1967, 1972, ix, 347 pp. Trans: H.C. Stevens; in Polish; the earliest commercial expansion of the English was to the Baltic and North; competition with the Dutch and Germans; products were naval stores and cloth; some Marxist rhetoric.

3985 Zuckerman, Arnold. "Disease and Ventilation in the Royal Navy: The Woodenship Years." Eighteenth-Century Life, 11 (November 1987): 77-89. Re the unhealthy state of life in sailing ships; in the 18th century, efforts to force ventilate; some claimed scurvy due to bad air; Lind and Blane proved otherwise.

3986 -------. "Scurvy and Ventilation of Ships in the Royal Navy: Samuel Sutton's Contribution." Eighteenth-Century Studies, 10 (Winter 1976): 222-34. Sutton invented a device to remove foul air but not the solution.

3987 Zulueta, Julian de. "Health and Military Factors in Vernon's Failure at Cartagena." MM, 77 (1992): 127-41. Use of Spanish sources; the failure of Vernon attributed to health problems; Vernon blamed for laxness on that issue; Nelson later appreciated the problem.

3988 -------. "Trafalgar: The Spanish View." MM, 66 (November 1980): 293-318. Secret report of 1793 on state of the navy in Spanish archives; admitted English gun carriages superior leading to more rapid rate of fire; shipbuilders more influenced by French warship designers; Spanish concern that English ships could stay at sea longer; Trafalgar meant end of Spanish role in sea power.

ADDENDUM

NOTE OF EXPLANATION:

As noted earlier, the moment a draft of a historiographical-bibliographical work is completed, it becomes obsolete. Inevitably, new and additional works come to the attention of the author. In the case of English/British Naval History to 1815, a long interval of several months intervened between submission of a final draft and the acceptance of the manuscript. Only then was it possible to proceed with the final steps, the making of the Author Index and the Subject Index.

The 136 annotated bibliographical entries in this Addendum, items numbered **3989** to **4124**, are new and additional works which came to the attention of the author in that interval of several months. It was not possible to incorporate them into Part I, the Historiographical Narrative Section. They are added here for the purpose of making this work as up-to-date as possible.

3989 Abels, Richard P. and Bachrach, Bernard S., eds. The Normans and Their Adversaries: Essays in Memory of C. Warren Hollister. Warfare in History # 12. Rochester: Boydell, 2001, 232 pp. A tribute to Hollister, the authority on feudal institutions and military-naval aspects; a series of essays by experts, e.g., on Harold as war lord and on the failures of the Anglo-Saxons.

3990 Apestegui, Cruz. Pirates of the Caribbean: Buccaneers, Privateers, Freebooters and Filibusters, 1493-1720. London: Conway, 2002, 233 pp. Folio format, lavishly illustrated; exploiting and contributing to revived interest in pirates of the Caribbean, especially in the entertainment media of North America.

3991 Austin, Paul Britten. 1815: The Return of Napoleon. Mechanicsburg: Stackpole, 2002, 336 pp. An account of the dramatic return and resumption of power for the hundred days in 1815; featured eyewitness accounts.

3992 Barker, Simon. The Ship: Retracing Cook's ENDEAVOUR Voyage. London: BBC, 2001. A publication in support of a BBC-TV series; following the famous voyage of 1768.

3993 Bienkowski, Lee. Admirals in the Age of Nelson. Annapolis: NIP, 2002. Sketches of the great British admirals of the late 18th century, e.g., Howe, Duncan, and Duckworth.

3994 Black, Jeremy. European Warfare, 1494-1660. London: Routledge, 2002, xii, 244 pp. A prequel in a 2-vol. series; typically well done by this prolific expert on European military history; 4 sections on land warfare and individual sections on overseas expansion and on naval developments, all in a global context; includes a synthesis and analysis of "the Military Revolution" debate.

3995 Block, Leo. To Harness the Wind: A Short History of the Development of Sails. Annapolis: NIP, 2003, 164 pp. The history of sails from 6000 BC.

3996 "The Boundless Deep": The European Conquest of the Oceans, 1450-1840. Providence: JCB Library, 2003. The Exhibition Catalogue of pertinent holdings from the John Carter Brown Library for an exhibition at the Newport, RI Art Museum, 27 April-27 July 2003.

3997 The BOUNTY Mutiny: William Bligh and Edward Christian. Penguin Classic series. NY: Penguin, 2001, 224 pp. Ed: R.D. Madison; a collection of all of the relevant documents, e.g., the narrative of Bligh, proceedings of the courts martial, and accusations and apologetics of Edward Christian.

3998 Brooks, Richard. The Royal Marines, 1664 to the Present. L: Constable, 2002, 340 pp. On the occasion of the 200th anniversary when "Royal" was added; a popular history; not scholarly and error prone.

3999 Burg, B.R., ed. Gay Warriors: A Documentary History from the Ancient World to the Present. NY: NYUP, 2002, viii, 299 pp. By the noted authority on this subject; contributions from notables, e.g., Walt Whitman, Herman Melvile, Siegfried Sassoon, T.E. Lawrence, Arthur Gilbert, and Burg; use of trial proceedings, e.g., courts martial of the RN, and personal diaries.

4000 Bushhovitch, Paul. Peter the Great: The Struggle for Power, 1671-1725. Cambridge: Cambridge UP, 2002. A new biography.

4001 Callo, Joseph. Nelson in the Caribbean: The Hero Emerges, 1784-1787.

Annapolis: NIP, 2002, 230 pp. An account of the early naval career of Nelson; commander of HMS BOREAS in the Caribbean, a captain at the age of 25 years; some operations alienated American colonists there; a timely publication; Admiral Callo, USNR-Ret., is an Amerian enthusiast.

4002 Clifford, Barry. The Lost Fleet. NY: HarperCollins, 2002, 304 pp. Nautical archaeology; accounts of recovering pirate wrecks; descriptions of the original maritime disasters during the golden age of piracy.

4003 Coetzee, J.M. Foe. London: Penguin, 1986, 157 pp. A modern sequel to Daniel Defoe, Robinson Crusoe; the title being the original name of Defoe, "Foe."

4004 Coleman, Terry. The Nelson Touch: The Life and Legend of Horatio Nelson. Oxford: Oxford UP, 2002, xix, 424 pp. A well-researched, scholarly presentation, "warts and all"; "to tease out the man from the legend"; portrays personalities and events in a lively manner.

4005 Collingridge, Venessa. Captain Cook: A Legend under Fire. Guilford: Lyons, 2002, 376 pp. By a TV journalist; a curious but delightful approach; to recreate the life of Cook, the greatest cartographer and navigator of the age.

4006 Conley, Mary A. "From Jack Tar to Union Jack: Images and Identities of British Naval Men, 1870-1918." Ph.D. diss, Boston College, 2000. Although covering a later era, most enlightening on life on the lower deck and about the life of naval sailors ashore, e.g., Portsmouth.

4007 Conway, Stephen. The British Isles and the War of American Independence. Oxford: Oxford UP, 2000, xi, 407 pp. A recent judicious and comprehensive analysis of empire and its demise in the 18th century.

4008 Cordingly, David. Heroines and Harlots: Women at Sea in the Age of Sail. London: Macmillan, 2002, 334 pp. A surprising number of women went to sea during this period; limited to Anglo-American instances; includes women in seaports, press gangs, and women who routinely accompanied their husbands.

4009 Courtney, Nicholas. Gale Force 10: The Life and Legacy of Admiral Beaufort, 1774-1857. London: Review, 2002, xii, 340 pp. Re Francis Beaufort, 1774-1857, Hydrographer of the Navy, 1829-1846; veteran of the Glorious First of June as signals officer for Admiral Lord Howe; in 1806 as captain of HMS WOOLWICH, estimated the force of the wind according to a scale, 0 through 13, the Beaufort Wind Scale.

4010 Cowley, Robert, ed. More What If?: Eminent Historians Imagine What Might Have Been. London: Macmillan, 2002, 427 pp. Further examples of counter-factual history; a series of essays and speculations by noted authorities, e.g., an alternative result to the battle of Hastings of 1066 and a healthy Napoleon III in 1870.

4011 Cunliffe, Barry. The Extraordinary Voyage of Pythias the Greek. NY: Walker, 2002, 179 pp. The noted archaeologist searched for evidence of a cruise from Marseilles to the British Isles about 330 BC in search for tin and amber, a legend concerning Pythias.

4012 Dash, Mike. Batavia's Graveyard. London. An account of a mutiny in 1629 off the west coast of Australia, an East Indiaman; vivid details of a bloody episode.

4013 Defoe, Daniel. The King of Pirates. London: Hesperus, 2002, 112 pp. Foreword: Peter Ackroyd; an account of pirate living by the famous Defoe.

4014 Delgado, James P. Lost Warships: An Archaeological Tour of War at Sea. London: Conway, 2001. By the director of the Vancouver Maritime Museum; a survey of nautical archaeology focusing on warships.

4015 Dickenson, H.W. "The Portsmouth Naval Academy, 1733-1806." MM, 89 (February 2003): 17-30. A naval school to prepare officers; provision for 40 boys age 13-16, focusing on navigation, fortification, and gunnery; clearly rehabilitates the effectiveness and quality of the institution, comparing it with Eton, Westminster, and Harrow in the 18th century; Lloyd and Lewis had attacked it.

4016 Disney, Anthony and Booth, Emily, eds. Vasco da Gama and the Linking of Europe and Asia. Oxford: Oxford UP, 2000, viii, 504 pp. A formative voyage from the Portuguese explorer.

4017 Donachie, David. The Devil's Own Luck. Ithaca: McBook, 2001, 302 pp. Nautical fiction; about Harry Ludlow, a privatersman, this covering 1793 and the first of a series.

4018 -------. The Dying Tide. Ithaca: McBook, 2001, 384 pp. Nautical fiction; again, Harry Ludlow, privateersman; this covering 1794 and the second of the series.

4019 -------. An Element of Chance. Ithaca: McBook, 2002, 448 pp. Nautical fiction; this again about Harry Ludlow, privateersman; covering 1795 and the fourth of the series.

4020 -------. A Game of Bones. Ithaca: McBook, 2002, 352 pp. Nautical fiction; this again about Harry Ludlow, privateersman; the sixth in the series.

4021 -------. A Hanging Matter. Ithaca: McBook, 2001, 416 pp. Nautical fiction; this again about Harry Ludlow, privateersman; covering 1794 and the third in the series.

4022 -------. On Making Tide. Ithaca: McBook, 2003. Nautical fiction; the first of a projected three volumes on Nelson and Emma Hamilton, two people fated for each other.

4023 -------. The Nelson and Emma Trilogy. Ithaca: McBooks, 2003. Noted as forthcoming in the McBooks catalogue of 2003.

4024 -------. The Scent of Betrayal. Ithaca: McBook, 2002, 448 pp. Nautical fiction; this featuring Harry Ludlow, privateersman, the fifth in a series.

4025 Donaldson, D.W. "Port Mahon, Minorca: The Preferred Naval Base for the English Fleet in the Mediterranean in the Seventeenth Century." MM, 88 (November 2002): 423-36. In the strategic picture of the western Mediterranean, Port Mahon offered a large natural harbor, the favorite of the English; the biggest threat was from the Barbary pirates; the origins for the English were back to the 14th century and trade between Italian states and Southampton and London.

4026 Druett, Joan. In the Wake of Madness. NY: Algonquin, 2003. Another mutiny incident, albeit occurring in December 1842 and aboard the whaling ship SHARON; a possible influence on the writings of Herman Melville; this included the murder of the captain, Howes Norris.

4027 Dudley, Wade G. Drake. Brassey's Military Profiles series. Wash: Brassey. In 2003, noted as forthcoming; a new biography of Drake.

4028 -------. Splintering the Wooden Walls: The British Blockade of the United States, 1812-1815. Annapolis: NIP, 2003, xii, 229 pp. A reassessment of naval siege warfare.

4029 Dunmore, Spencer. Lost Subs: From the HUNLEY to the KURSK, the Greatest Submarines Ever Lost--and Found. Cambridge: DaCapo, 2002, 176 pp. Large folio format, handsomely produced; included because of contributions to nautical archaeology; the project concerning raising and displaying HUNLEY is particularly important; the latest information.

4030 Elliott, J.H. Imperial Spain, 1469-1716. NY: St. Martin; London: Penguin, 1963, 1967, 2003, 424 pp. Sir John Elliott is the leading authority on this period of Spanish history, including, of course, the Spanish Armada; a new introduction.

4031 Erskine, David, ed. August Hervey's Journal: The Adventures Afloat nd Ashore of a Naval Casanova. London: Chatham, 1953, 2002, 349 pp. A journal covering 1746-1759 about his private life and thoughts composed years later; enlightening about the diplomacy practiced by captains of the RN; Hervey was in Lisbon at the time of the earthquake of 1755; observations about the demise of Admiral Byng.

4032 Esdaile, Charles. The Peninsular War: A New History. London: Penguin, 2002, xxxi, 564 pp. A recent and brilliant reappraisal of this key campaign; puts it all in the international perspective; especially contributory in tracing the impact and consequences on Spain and Portugal, then and later; an extensive bibliography.

4033 Feldbaek, Ole. <u>The Battle of Copenhagen, 1801: Nelson's Historic Victory</u>. Annapolis: NIP; Barnsley: Pen and Sword, 2002, 272 pp. A recent account of one of Nelson's greatest victories; on the occasion of the bicentennial, an event of the Nelson Decade.

4034 Fitz-Enz, David G. <u>The Final Invasion: Plattsburgh, the War of 1812's Most Decisive Battle</u>. NY: Cooper Square, 2001, 271 pp. In the Lake Champlain Valley, the British vs. the French had fought there in the Seven Years' War, now it was British vs. Americans, 11 September 1814; the British squadron was annihilated and the British abandoned the land campaign; not a good account, e.g., lacks understanding of the sea and error-prone.

4035 Fleming, Feargus. <u>Ninety Degrees North: The Quest for the North Pole</u>. NY: Grove, 2002, 470 pp. A history of the exploration of the Arctic; the quest for the North Pole emerged out of the obsession with the Northwest Passage.

4036 Foster, George. <u>Voyage Round the World</u>. 2 vols. Honolulu: Hawaii UP, 2000, xlvii, 860 pp. Eds: Nicholas Thomas and Oliver Berghof; focus on the 2nd voyage of Captain Cook, 1772-1775; an excellent review of the literature, e.g., the Cook-Forster friction over the authorized account.

4037 Friedenbert, Zachery B. <u>Medicine under Sail</u>. London: Chatham; Annapolis: NIP, 2002, 248 pp. A general survey; focus on injuries, diseases, and death at sea; noted Thomas Woodall of the 17th century as "the father of marine medicine" and St. Vincent as more contributory in this area than was Nelson; extensive bibliography.

4038 Friel, Ian. <u>Maritime History of Britain and Ireland</u>. London: British Museum, 2003. A review focusing on technological advances from medieval times to the present.

4039 Fry, Michael. <u>The Scottish Empire</u>. Edinburgh: Birlinn, 2001, xxvi, 580 pp. A survey of the achievements of the Scots in empire, formal and informal; characteristics included rigid and strict Presbyterians and many as missionaries, especially to India; Rosebery was a later imperialist-Scot.

4040 Gerson, Noel B. [pseud. for Paul Lewis]. <u>The Nelson Touch</u>. NY: Holt, 1960, 287 pp. A popularized version describing the special achievements of Nelson.

4041 Goodwin, Peter. <u>Nelson's Ships: A History of the Vessels in Which He Served, 1771-1805</u>. London: Conway, 2002, 328 pp. Color illustrations; total of 25 ships upon which Nelson served from HMS RAISONABLE to HMS VICTORY; a chapter for each.

4042 Gough, Barry M. <u>Fighting Sail on Lake Huron and Georgian Bay: The War of 1812 and Its Aftermath</u>. Annapolis: NIP, 2002, xxi, 215 pp. A major contribution, presenting a neglected phase of the campaigns in the area of the Great Lakes during the War of 1812; details on how the British utilized small scale naval operations; actually, bitter competition of the British, Canadians, Americans, and Native Americans for primacy of the region; one consequence was the final boundary between the U.S. and Canada.

4043 Guilmartin, John F. Galleons and Galleys. London: Cassell, 2002, 224 pp. A recent survey by the noted authority.

4044 Hansen, Brooks. The Monsters of St. Helena. NY: Farrar, 2003, 306 pp. A fictional account which incorporates details of the Napoleonic incarceration, e.g., French court intrigue and ghosts.

4045 Harland, John. Ships and Seamanship: The Maritime Prints of J.J. Baugean. Annapolis: NIP, 2001, 208 pp. Beautifully illustrated; by a recognized British authority on the age of sail.

4046 Harvie, David. Limeys: The True Story of One Man's War against Ignorance, the Establishment and the Deadly Scurvy. Stroud: Sutton , 2002, vi, 314 pp. A dramatic story, crediting the Scottish surgeon James Lind; a comprehensive history of all aspects of the malady, the search for a cure, the struggle for acceptance of the theory about citrus juice, and the identification of Vitamin C in the 20th century.

4047 Hattendorf, John B. and Unger, Richard W., eds. War at Sea in the Middle Ages and the Renaissance. Rochester: Boydell, 2002, 272 pp. A survey of naval warfare in these early times; see Hattendorf on theories of naval power, Timothy Runyan on maritime technology in the Hundred Years' War, Ian Friel on oars, sails, and guns, and N.A.M. Rodger on Atlantic naval warfare in the 16th century.

4048 Hattendorf, John B. The Boundless Deep: The European Conquest of the Oceans, 1450 to 1840: Catalogue of an Exhibition of Rare Books, Maps, Charts, Prints, and Manuscripts Relating to Maritime History from the John Carter Brown Library. Providence: J.C. Brown Library, 2003. Profusely illustrated; the catalogue of the exhibition presented at the Newport, RI, Art Museum, 27 April-27 July 2003; featured over 220 individual items, including books, maps, and manuscripts.

4049 Hayward, Joel. For Good and Glory: Lord Nelson and His Way of War. Annapolis: NIP, 2003, 256 pp. A thematic approach to the life of Nelson, e.g., sections on tactics, operations, doctrine, command, and leadership.

4050 Heidler, David S. and Heidler, Jeanne T. The War of 1812. Greenwood Guides to Historic Events, 1500-1900 series. Westport: Greenwood, 2002, 256 pp. An informative guide to the war, placing it in historical and social context, e.g., a timeline.

4051 Hicks, Brian and Kropf, Schuyler. Raising the HUNLEY. NY: Ballantine, 2002. A case study of recent nautical archaeology; journalists from Charleston tell to story of the H.L. HUNLEY, Confederate submarine; more pertinent is the extensive description of the recovery and preservation processes.

4052 Hitchcock, R.F. "Cavendish's Last Voyage: John Jane's Narrative of the Voyage of DESIRE." MM, 89 (February 2003): 4-16. The 3rd article in a series, this about a 140-ton flagship of circumnavigation, 1586-1588; details of subsequent voyages; Jane was a supercargo.

4053 Hobson, Rolf and Kristiansen, Tom, eds. Navies in Northern Waters, 1721-2000. Naval Policy and History series. London: Cass, 2004, 256 pp. A collection of pertinent articles; various challenges to Britain by northern European powers and the U.S.

4054 Hopton, Richard. The Battle of Maida, 1806: Fifteen Minutes of Glory. London: Cooper, 2002, 197 pp. A short battle in the Mediterranean; a campaign in Calabria; the British to defend Sicily; Royal Navy under command of Sir John Stuart put 5000 British troops ashore; vs. 5000 French; other nationalities participated; British casualties: 44; French: 700.

4055 Horden, Peregrine and Purcell, Nicholas. The Corrupting Sea: A Study of Mediterranean History. Oxford: Blackwell, 2000, xiv, 761 pp. A substantial tome and a second volume is projected; an innovative approach: "microecological"; in the tradition of Rostovtzeff, Pirenne, and, especially, Braudel; "one constant piracy" but even that "facilitates exchange," and is, thus, a "good thing."

4056 Horwitz, Tony. Blue Latitudes: Boldly Going Where Captain Cook Has Gone. London: Bloomsbury; NY: Holt, 2002, 480 pp. Publication sensation, a best seller; a combination of biography and travel book; following all three voyages of Cook with commentary, e.g., Cook is hated by Hawaiians, a symbol of all that is wrong in its society, and where does Cook fit into the postcolonial world?; author spent some time on replica of ENDEAVOUR; note subtitle and link to Gene Roddenberry, Captain Kirk, and the ENTERPRISE; reference to the Captain Cook Society.

4057 -------. "A Week before the Mast: Our Far-Flung Correspondents." New Yorker (22 July 2002): 42-55. Recounsted voyage around the world of the replica, HM Bark ENDEAVOUR; series of volunteers as crew.

4058 Howard, Ian. "Swein Forkbeard's Invasion of England." Ph.D. diss, Manchester, 2000. Recounted a less publicized invasion.

4059 Hughes, Lindsey. Peter the Great: A Biography. New Haven: Yale UP, 2002, 304 pp. A recent biography.

4060 Johnson, Paul. Napoleon. Penguin Lives Biography series. NY: Penguin, 2002, xii, 190 pp. Focus on Napoleon as a historical figure; judgmental and idiosyncratic: Napoleon:"an ogre surrounded by trolls," e.g., Talleyrand and Fouche; one legacy seen: "the totalitarian state of the 20th century"; not only attacked Napoleon, but the European Union and biographers, e.g., Scott, Belloc, Hardy, and Carlyle; in a review, David Chandler summed up: "tasteless tittle-tattle."

4061 Jongste, Jan A.F. de and Veenendaal, A.J., eds. Antonie Heinsius and the Dutch Republic, 1688-1714: Politics, Finance, and War. The Hague: Institute, 2002. A series of essays by experts; a history at the time of William III; see Hattendorf on Anglo-Dutch cooperation in coalition warfare at sea.

4062 Kamen, Henry. Spain's Road to Empire: The Making of a World Power, 1492-1763. London: Lane, 2002, xxviii, 608 pp. An extensive analysis of the formative period of Spanish imperial expansion.

4063 Kelsey, Harry. Sir John Hawkins: Queen Elizabeth's Slave Trader. New Haven: Yale UP, 2003, 384 pp. A recent popular biography of this leading Tudor naval leader.

4064 Kent, Alexander. Man of War. Ithaca: McBooks, 2003. Nautical fiction; # 26 in the Richard Bolitho series.

4065 Knox, MacGregor and Murray, Williamson, eds. The Dynamics of Military Revolution, 1300-2050. Cambridge: Cambridge UP, 2001, xiv, 203 pp. Assessments by experts, e.g., Dennis Showalter, Holger Herwig, Knox, John Lynn, and Clifford Rogers; topics, e.g., the French Revolution, 17th century France, and 14th century England.

4066 Lambert, Andrew. TRINCOMALEE: The Last of Nelson's Frigates. London: Chatham, 2002, 192 pp. Lavishly illustrated; details of frigates, notably this one, the class Nelson lamented as essential and in too short supply; this one built in 1817 of teak in Bombay; design from a captured French frigate; restored in 1987 at Hartlepool.

4067 Lavery, Brian. Horatio Lord Nelson. NY: New York UP, 2003. The formal announcement of publication of item # **2075**, one of the Nelson Decade biographies.

4068 Lawlor, Laurie. Magnificent Voyage: An American Adventure on Captain James Cook's Final Expedition. NY: Holiday, 2003. Fiction for juveniles; profusely illustrated and numerous charts; the voyage in search of the Northwest Passage; a "journal" of John Ledyard.

4069 Lawson, M.K. The Battle of Hastings, 1066. Charleston: Tempus, 2002, 287 pp. A recent and authoritative synthesis and definitive account; assessment of the sources, e.g., the Bayeux Tapestry.

4070 LeQuesne, Leslie P. Nelson Commemorated in Glass Pictures. Woodbridge: Antique, 2002, 103 pp. From the 18th-century process called "mezzotint," transfer black and white images onto glass and paint colors; most were produced within 6 months after his death; another contribution in support of the Nelson Decade.

4071 Lincoln, Margarette. Representing the Royal Navy: British Sea Power, 1750-1815. Aldershot: Ashgate, 2002, 240 pp. For NMM; a study of the Royal Navy in the cultural context, e.g., race, gender, and war and peace; again, Nelson era highlighted.

4072 Linebaugh, Peter and Rediker, Marcus. The Many-Headed Hydra: Sailors, Slaves, Commoners, and the Hidden History of the Revolutionary Atlantic. Boston: Beacon, 2000, 433 pp. A survey of lower-deck history in the Marxist-sociological tradition; "from the underdog's view" and a global history perspective; life in the wooden world was multiethnic and a phase of globalization.

4073 Loades, David M. and Knighton, C.S. Letters from the MARY ROSE. Stroud: Sutton, 2002. In association with the MARY ROSE Trust; publication of surviving letters from crew members.

4074 The London Gazette. An official publication of the Crown-Government of Britain since the mid-17th century, touted as the oldest continuously published newspaper; official notices, honors, and awards are announced; included to demonstrate another outlet for publication of aspects of naval interest, among others.

4075 Lundy, Derek. The Way of a Ship: A Square-Rigger Voyage in the Last Days of Sail. NY: Ecco, 2003, 352 pp. A quasi-fictional recreation of a voyage of BEARA HEAD, a merchant sailing ship during the 1880s; informative on the timelessness of conditions, superstitions, weather, and other common factors.

4076 McCaffery, Lloyd. Ships in Minature: The Classic Manual for Ship Modelers. London: Conway, 2002, 144 pp. A recent guide.

4077 McGrail, Sean. Boats of the World: From the Stone Age to Medieval Times. Oxford: Oxford UP, 2002, 480 pp. Nautical archaeology; history of water transport based on evidence from "finds" and much iconographics; a wide context.

4078 -------. "The Sea and Archaeology." Historical Research, 76 (February 2003): 1-17. From a paper presented at the Anglo-American Historians Conference, "The Sea," July 2001; a general survey, 40,000 years of seafaring, no direct evidence before 8000 BC; a need to fill gaps.

4079 Mack, William P. Commodore Kilburnie. Annapolis: NIP, 2002, 256 pp. Nautical fiction; another in the Kilburnie, the Scotsman in Nelson's navy.

4080 "Master and Commander: The Far Side of the World. Movie. Twentieth-Century Fox production; directed by Peter Weir, starring Russell Crowe as Jack Aubrey and Paul Bettany as Stephen Maturin. The first film production of a Patrick O'Brian novel; to cost $135 million; in process during 2003.

4081 Menzies, Gavin. 1421: The Year China Discovered the World. London: Transworld; NY: Bantam, 2002, 520 pp. Spectacular claims; Chinese sailors led by Zheng He exploring the world; "to the end of the earth to collect tribute," survivors returning in 1423; contends the voyage included the Americas, Australia, and the Arctic and that signs included wrecks, Asian chickens in Peru, and plants; some reviewers are dubious.

4082 Milton, Giles. Samurai William: The Englishman Who Opened Japan. NY: Farrar, 2003, 352 pp. Re William Adams, an English navigator sailing for the Dutch; in a 5-ship fleet from Rotterdam, June 1598, to Japan via Pacific route in 1600; gained concessions for Dutch and English; annual memorialzation at burial site near Yokosuka to this day.

4083 Moffat, Hugh. Ships and Shipyards of Ipswich, 1700-1970. Suffolk: Malthouse, 2002, 192 pp. Profusely illustrated; origins as early as 1294; included galleys for the King's Navy

4084 Monaque, Remi. "Was Nelson Killed by Robert Guillemard?" MM, 88 (November 2002): 469-72. By a French scholar; from the "Notes" section; Nelson fell at 1:15 PM, 21 October 1805, dying in 3:40 PM; VICTORY broke at line at 12:04; shots from the tops of French SOTL, REDOUTABLE; Nelson was in dress uniform with all medals; French marksman Robert Guillemard probably fired the fatal shot.

4085 The National Nelson Catalogue. An online catalogue of all collections related to Nelson, public and private; cooperation of numerous agencies and associations; projected for 2005, the culmination of the Nelson Decade.

4086 Needle, Jan. A Fine Boy for Killing. Ithaca: McBooks, 2000. Nautical fiction, the first of the William Bentley series.

4087 -------. The Wicked Trade. Ithaca: McBooks, 2001, 382 pp. The second of the William Bentley series; re a midshipman of the Impress Service of the RN.

4088 Nicastro, Nicholas. Between Two Fires: A Novel of John Paul Jones. Ithaca: McBook, 2002, 368 pp. Nautical fiction; the second of three novels about Jones; in this case commanding a squadron bitterly divided and operating in enemy waters.

4089 -------. The Eighteenth Captain: A Novel of John Paul Jones. Ithaca: McBook, 2001. Nautical fiction; the first of three novels about Jones.

4090 The Official Nelson Celebrations Committee (ONCC). "The Nelson Touch: A Vision for the Trafalgar Bicentennial." London: ONCC, 2002, 4 pp. Publication about organization, participants, sponsors, plans, and events; ONCC: patron: The Earl Nelson; representation: NMM, RNM, HMS VICTORY, Flagship Portsmouth, the Monmouth Museum, Lloyds Nelson Collection, SNR, the 1805 Club, the Nelson Society, and the Norfolk Nelson Museum; plans: the Trafalgar Festival, a national and international programme, e.g., an extravaganza at Albert Hall, Trafalgar Night Dinners, exhibitions, stamps, scholarly projects, "the Virtual Nelson," and "the Nelson Road Show"; not listed: International Festival of the Sea (IFOS), Portsmouth, Bank Holiday Weekend, August, e.g., tall ships return and raising original foretopsail, HMS VICTORY.

4091 Pocock, Tom. [The Period after the Battle of Trafalgar]. Noted in the summer of 2002 as forthcoming. Focus on the friends and proteges of Nelson, e.g., Collingwood, Sydney Smith, and Hoste.

4092 -------. The Terror before Trafalgar: Nelson and the Secret War. London: Murray, 2002. A review of the 4 years leading up to the battle of Trafalgar; focus on espionage, the secret war, and new weapons; an account of the failed Boulogne expedition led by Nelson.

4093 Porter, Andrew N., ed. Bibliography of Imperial, Colonial, and Commonwealth History since 1600. Royal Historical Society Bibliography. Oxford: Oxford UP, 2002, xx, 1060 pp. A recent extensive compilation.

4094 Riding, Christine. "The Fatal Raft." HisTod, 53 (February 2003): 38-44. Re "The Raft of the MEDUSA," the famous painting by Theodore Gericault, depicting the horrors of the notorious maritime disaster of July 1816 of the French frigate MEDUSA off the west coast of Africa; the scandal became associated with negligence, betrayal, mutiny, slaughter, and cannibalism.

4095 Robson, Martin. "British Intervention in Portugal, 1793-1808." Historical Research, 76 (February 2003): 93-107. Intervention began with limited aims related to the war with France; use of bases, e.g., Lisbon and the Tagus, for expedition forces.

4096 Rodger, N.A.M. "Honour and Duty at Sea, 1660-1815." Historical Research, 75 (November 2002): 425-47. A discussion of the changing concepts of honor and duty among sea officers during the long 18th century; honor: a gentleman's virtue; duty: most noted among the rising middle class.

4097 -------. A Naval History of Britain. Vol. II: A Great Liberty, 1648-1815. London: HarperCollins. Noted: manuscript to publisher in 2003; anticipated publication in 2004; new list of sponsors: the Anderson Fund of SNR, NRS, Exeter University, and the Fischer Foundation; Rodger now at the University of Exeter.

4098 -------. Training or Education: A Naval Dilemma over Three Centuries. Oxford University/ Navy Defence Studies. Oxford: Oxford UP, 2001. The Hudson Lecture for 2001.

4099 Rose, Susan. "Anchoring and Mooring: An Examination of English Maritime Practice before c.1650." MM, 89 (May 2003): 151-66. An analysis of the practice in earliest times; begins with the Laws of Oleron and other legal documents; looks a facilities and equipment, charts, rutters, and pilot books, and nautical dictionaries, e.g., Manwayring and Falconer.

4100 Rudick, Michael, ed. The Poems of Sir Walter Ralegh: A Historical Edition. Tempe: Arizona Center, 1999, lxxviii, 239 pp. After extensive searching, publication of collected poems.

4101 Schneid, Frederick C. Napoleon's Italian Campaign, 1805-1815. Westport: Praeger, 2002, xviii, 228 pp. Fills some gaps about later campaigns of Napoleon in Italy; purely military history and overly detailed; unfortunately nothing on British-French battle of Maida, a victory for a British expeditionary force inferior to the French.

4102 Selincourt, Aubrey de. The Book of the Sea: An Anthology. London: Chatham, 1961, 2002, xxiv, 376 pp. A reprint of an earlier work; complements The Oxford Book of the Sea, 1992.

4103 Severin, Tim. In Search of Robinson Crusoe. NY: Basic, 2002, 333 pp. Another of the fascinating searches of Severin.

4104 Shenk, Robert, ed. Authors at Sea: Modern American Writers Remember Their Naval Service. Annapolis: NIP, 1990, 1997, xii, 318 pp. Excerpts from noted American literary figures recalling their naval service.

4105 Smith, E. Nautisk Ord Book. Stockholm: Literatim, 1914, 2000, 518 pp. A nautical dictionary in Swedish but with English and German translations; comparative analyses.

4106 Southam, Brian. Jane Austin and the Navy. NY: Hambledon, 2001, xiv, 384 pp. Two of her novels depict naval connections: Mansfield Park, 1814, and Persuasion, 1818.

4107 Stirland, A.J. Raising the Dead: The Skeleton Crew of King Henry VIII's Great Ship, the MARY ROSE. Chichester: Wiley, 2000, xviii, 183 pp. Ms. Stirland investigated the men who were manning MARY ROSE at the time she sank, 179 men or 43% of the regular crew; informative on the Tudor navy and its personnel.

4108 Stockwin, Julian. Artemis. London: Hodder, 2002, 374 pp. Nautical fiction; set during the Napoleonic wars; re Thomas Paine Kydd of the RN.

4109 -------. Kydd. London: Hodder, 2001, 373 pp. Nautical fiction; one of projected 11-volume series from the perspective of the lower deck during the Napoleonic wars; Kydd from pressed landsman to admiral; definitely not up to standard of O'Brian.

4110 Sullivan, F.B. "The Evolution and Development of Education in the Royal Navy, 1702-1902." Ph.D. diss, Reading, 1974. A scholarly study.

4111 Syrett, David. "The Navy Board and Transports for Cartagena, 1740." War in History, 9 (April 2002): 127-42. By the prolific naval historian; the movement of British troops and supplies in the first large transatlantic amphibious operation; the Navy Board was responsible; chartered merchant ships.

4112 Takahashi, Daisuke. In Search of Robinson Crusoe. NY: Cooper Square, 2002, 229 pp. Trans: Juliet Carpenter; from the Japanese; following in the footsteps of Robinson Crusoe.

4113 Till, Geoffrey, ed. The Development of British Naval Thinking: Essays in Memory of Bryan Ranft. Naval Policy and History series. London: Cass, 2004, 256 pp. A series of essays by leading naval historians covering the last 3 centuries; the development of organized naval thought; commemorating Professor Ranft.

4114 Tomalin, Claire. Samuel Pepys: The Unequalled Self. London: Viking, 2002, lviii, 512 pp. Pepys was fascinated with himself and an appealing and complex individual; a focus on the Pepys of the diary; his public career was problematical: a hypocrit who taking bribes, seducer, abusive, and autocratic.

4115 Tracy, Nicholas, ed. The Age of Sail: The Annual of the Historic Sailing Ship. London: Conway; Annapolis: NIP, 2002, 208 pp. An new annual begun in 2002, this the first volume; to publicize all aspects of maritime warfare.

4116 The Trafalgar Conference. A projected conference planned by ONCC; participants to be historians and writers; international: especially British, French, Spanish; focus on the campaign of Trafalgar, 1802-1805.

4117 Trafalgar 200. The year of celebrations and events planned by ONCC: see entry on ONCC above.

4118 Turner, Gerand L'E. Elizabethan Instrument Makers: The Origins of the London Trade in Precision Instrument Making. Oxford: Oxford UP, 2000, xiv, 305 pp. By the foremost authority; a catalogue describing 103 instruments beginning in the 1540s, e.g., instruments for navigation, surveying, and astronomy.

4119 Vincent, Edgar. Nelson: Love and Fame. New Haven: Yale UP, 2003, 656 pp. A recent full-length biography of the favorite hero of the British; the late 18th and early 19th century was a good time for heroes; St. Paul's Cathedral was turned into a Pantheon; their state funerals exceeded those of the royals.

4120 Wathen, B. "Making Drake: The Cultural Construction of Sir Francis Drake from the Late Sixteenth Century to the Present." Ph.D. diss, Exeter, 2001. Presents 400 years of cultural production; ways of construction of representations of Drake.

4121 Williams, Glyndwr. Voyages of Delusion: The Search for the Northwest Passage in the Age of Reason. London: HarperCollins, 2002, xx, 467 pp. Re the elusive Northwest Passage, a "maritime philosopher's stone" in the 18th century;

focus on the irrationality.

4122 Williams, P. "Piracy and Naval Conflict in the Mediterranean, 1590-1620." D.Phil. diss, Oxford, 2001. Was there distinction between piracy and official operations?; galleys as corsairs; privateering operations furthered the development of galley warfare; participants: Ottoman Empire, Venice, Genoa, Tuscany, Savoy, and Malta; this Mediterranean system collapsed in the 1620s.

4123 Woolley, Benjamin. The Queen's Conjurer: The Science and Magic of Dr. Dee. NY: Holt, 2001, 394 pp. Re John Dee and Queen Elizabeth in the 16th century.

4124 Zacks, Richard. The Pirate Hunter: The True Story of Captain Kidd. NY: Theia, 2002, 426 pp. Again, were there distinctions between piracy and privateering?; Kidd was commissioned by the Royal Navy to hunt down piracy; bounties offered by the East India Company; documentary evidenc discovered about 1910; later, Kidd was disowned, tried, and executed.

Appendix I.

Pertinent Masters Degree Theses

1) Brown, J.W. "British Privateering during the Seven Years' War, 1756-1763." MA thesis, Exeter, 1978.

2) Buchanan, E.A. "Early Maritime Scotland, 10,000 BC to AD 1018: With Emphasis on the Importance of Water to Man and the Landscape." M.Phil thesis, St. Andrews, 1996.

3) Clark, S. "English Naval Strategy during the Anglo-Scottish Wars of the 1540s." M.Phil thesis, Strathclyde, 1991.

4) Colgate, Hugh. "Trincomalee and the East India Squadron, 1746-1844." MA thesis, London, 1959.

5) Curry, J. "English Sea-Chaplains in the Royal Navy, 1577-1684." MA thesis, Bristol, 1855.

6) Farrands, H.A. "British Naval Administration, with Emphasis on the Navy and Ordnance Board, 1763-1783." M.Phil. thesis, London, 1984.

7) Goodman, Warren H. "The Origins of the War of 1812: A Critical Examination of Historical Interpretations." MA thesis, Duke, 1940.

8) Gunn, A. "The West Highland Galley from Carvings on Late Medieval Gravestones." MA thesis, Glasgow, 1986.

9) Hall, A.T. "The Employment of Naval Forces in the Reign of Edward III." MA thesis, Leeds, 1955.

10) Hill, J.A. "The Role of the Lord Warden in the Administration of the Cinque Ports in the Sixteenth Century." MA thesis, Kent, 1996.

11) Hughes, Quentin. "The British and the Mediterranean: A Study of the Defence of Her Naval Stations." MA thesis, Liverpool, 1980.

12) Hurd, D.G.E. "Some Aspects of the Attempts of the Government to Suppress Piracy during the Reign of Elizabeth I." MA thesis, London, 1961.

13) Konstam, R.A. "Naval Artillery to 1550: Its Design, Evolution and Employment." MA thesis, St. Andrews, 1987.

14) Lewis, P.N. "The Wars of Richard I in the West." M.Phil. thesis, London, 1977.

15) MacDougall, Philip C. "Chatham: The Social of the Royal Dockyard, 1770-1801." M.Phil. thesis, Open University, 1983.

16) Malkin, H.C. "The Life and Times of Admiral Rodney." MA thesis, London, 1956.

17) Neale, Jonathan. "Discipline and Mutiny in the Royal Navy, 1793-1803." MA thesis, Warwick, 1984.

18) Oprey, C. "Schemes for the Reform of Naval Recruitment, 1793-1815." MA thesis, Liverpool, 1961.

19) Ryan, Anthony N. "The Copenhagen Expedition, 1807." MA thesis, Liverpool, 1951.

20) Sainsbury, A.B. "The Life and Career of Admiral Sir John Duckworth." M.Phil. thesis, London, 1984.

21) Starkey, David J. "Liverpool Privateering, 1702-1783." MA thesis, Exeter, 1979.

22) Steer, Michael. "The Blockade of Brest and the Royal Navy, 1793-1805." MA thesis, Liverpool, 1971.

23) Tanner, I. :Henry VII's Expedition to France of 1492: A Study of Its Financing, Organisation and Supply." MA thesis, Keele, 1988.

24) Taylor, Roy. "Manning the Royal Navy: The Reform of the Recruiting System, 1847-1861." MA thesis, London, 1954.

25) Webb, Paul. "The Navy and British Diplomacy, 1783-1793." M.Litt. thesis, Cambridge, 1971.

26) Yerxa, Donald R. "Admiral Samuel Graves and the Falmouth Affair: A Case Study in British Imperial Pacification, 1775." MA thesis, Maine, 1974.

Appendix II.

Publications of the Navy Records Society

1. Laughton, John Knox, ed. State Papers Relating to the Defeat of the Spanish Armada. 2 vols. Publications of the Navy Records Society, vols. 1 and 2. London: NRS, 1894-1895, 1900, 1981, lxxxiv, 365 and vi, 418 pp.
2. See vol. 1, 1895, 1900.
3. Hannay, David, ed. Letters Written by Sir Samuel Hood, 1781-1783. Publications of the Navy Records Society, vol. 3. London: NRS, 1895, xlvii, 170 pp.
4. Brassey, T.A., ed. An Index to James' "Naval History," 1886 Edition: Prepared by C.G. Toogood. Publications of the Navy Records Society, vol. 4. London: NRS, 1895, vi, 188 pp.
5. Markham, Clements R., ed. Life of Captain Stephen Martin, 1666-1740. Publications of the Navy Records Society, vol. 5. London: NRS, 1895, xl, 223 pp.
6. Laughton, John Knox and Sulivan, J.Y.F., eds. Journal of Rear-Admiral Bartholonew James, 1752-1828. Publications of the Navy Records Society, vol. 6. London: NRS, 1896, xxvi, 402 pp.
7. Tanner, J.R., ed. Discourses of the Navy, 1638 and 1659 by John Hollond, also, 1660 by Robert Slyngesbie. Publications of the Navy Records Society, vol. 7. London: NRS, 1896, lxxxiv, 419 pp.
8. Oppenheim, Michael, ed. Naval Accounts and Inventories of the Reign of Henry VII, 1485-1488 and 1495-1497. Publications of the Navy Records Society, vol. 8. London: NRS, 1896, lvi, 349 pp.
9. Browning, Oscar, ed. The Journal of Sir George Rooke: Admiral of the Fleet, 1700-1702. Publications of the Navy Records Society, vol. 9. London: NRS, 1897, xlvi, 272 pp.
10. Spont, M.Alfred, ed. Letters and Papers Relating to the War with France, 1512-1513. Publications of the Navy Records Society, vol. 10. London: NRS, 1897, xlviii, 218 pp.

11. Corbett, Julian S., ed. Papers Relating to the Navy during the Spanish War, 1585-1587. Publications of the Navy Records Society, vol. 11. London: NRS, 1898, xlix, 363 pp.

12. Hamilton, R. Vesey, ed. Letters and Papers of Admiral of the Fleet Sir Thomas Byam Martin, GCB. 3 vols. Publications of the Navy Records Society, vols. 12, 19, and 24. London: NRS, 1898-1903, xxiv, 384, xvii, 416, and xxii, 399 pp.

13. Gardiner, Samuel R. and Atkinson, C.T., eds. Letters and Papers Relating to the First Dutch War, 1652-1654. 6 vols. Publications of the Navy Records Society, vols. 13, 17, 30, 37, 41, and 66. London: NRS, 1899-1930, xx, 431, xx, 507, xviii, 452, xiv, 396, xvi, 429, and xiv, 379 pp.

14. Leyland, John, ed. Dispatches and Letters Relating to the Blockade of Brest, 1803-1805. 2 vols. Publications of the Navy Records Society, vols. 14 and 21. London: NRS, 1898-1902, lxvi, 369 and lvi, 390 pp.

15. Bridge, Cyrian A.G., ed. History of the Russian Fleet during the Reign of Peter the Great: By a Contemporary Englishman, 1724. Publications of the Navy Records Society, vol. 15. London: NRS, 1899, xxvv, 161 pp.

16. Jackson, T. Sturges, ed. Logs of the Great Sea Fights, 1794-1805. 2 vols. Publications of the Navy Records Society, vols. 16 and 18. London: NRS, 1899-1900, xvi, 342 and vi, 343 pp. 1900.

17. See vol. 13, 1900.

18. See vol. 16, 1900.

19. See vol. 12, 1898.

20. Laughton, John Knox, ed. The Naval Miscellany. Publications of the Navy Records Society, vol. 20. London: NRS, 1902, xii, 463 pp.

21. See vol. 14., 1902.

22. Oppenheim, Michael, ed. The Naval Tracts of of Sir William Monson in Six Books. 5 vols. Publications of the Navy Records Society, vols. 22, 23, 43, 45, and 47. London: NRS, 1902-1914, lxvi, 395, viii, 395, x, 443, x, 444, and xii, 370 pp.

23. See vol. 22, 1902.

24. See vol. 12, 1905.

25. Gutteridge, H.C., ed. Nelson and the Neapolitan Jacobins: Documents Relating to the Suppression of the Jacobin Revolution at Naples, June 1799. Publications of the Navy Records Society, vol. 25. London: NRS, 1903, cxvii, 347 pp.

26. Tanner, J.R., ed. A Descriptive Catalogue of the Naval MSS. in the Pepysian Library at Magdalene College, Cambridge. 5 vols. Publications of the Navy Records Society, vols. 26, 27, 36, 37, and 60. London: NRS, 1903-1926, xii, 452, xxxviii, 455, liv, 458, cxxviii, 725, and xx, 513 pp.

27. See vol. 26, 1904.

28. Markham, Clements R., ed. Selections from the Correspondence of Admiral John Markham during the years, 1801-1804 and 1806-1807. Publications of the Navy Records Society, vol. 28. London: NRS, 1904, xx, 451 pp.

29. Corbett, Julian S., ed. <u>Fighting Instructions, 1530-1816</u>. <u>Publications of the Navy Records Society</u>, vol. 29. London: NRS, 1905, xvi, 366 pp.

30. See vol. 13, 1906.

31. Hamilton, R. Vesey and Laughton, John Knox, eds. <u>Recollections of James Anthony Gardner, Commander, RN, 1775-1814</u>. <u>Publications of the Navy Records Society</u>, vol. 31. London: NRS, 1906, xxii, 287 pp.

32. Laughton, John Knox, ed. <u>Letters and Papers of Charles, Lord Barham, Admiral of the Red Squadron, 1758-1813</u>. 3 vols. <u>Publications of the Navy Records Society</u>, 32, 38, and 39. London: NRS, 1907-1911, lxvi, 422, xxii, 438, and xl, 413 pp.

33. Firth, Charles H., ed. <u>Naval Songs and Ballads</u>. <u>Publications of the Navy Records Society</u>, vol. 33. London: NRS, 1908, cxxiv, 387 pp.

34. Corbett, Julian S., ed. <u>Views of the Battles of the Third Dutch War</u>. <u>Publications of the Navy Records Society</u>, vol. 34. London: NRS.

35. Corbett, Julian S., ed. <u>Signals and Instructions, 1776-1794: With Addenda to Vol. 29</u>. <u>Publications of the Navy Records Society</u>, vol. 35. London: NRS, 1908, xvi, 403 pp.

36. See vol. 26, 1909.

37. See vol. 13, 1910.

38. See vol. 32, 1910.

39, See vol. 32, 1911.

40. Laughton, John Knox, ed. <u>The Naval Miscellany</u>. <u>Publications of the Navy Records Society</u>, vol. 40. London: NRS, 1912, x, 430 pp.

41. See vol. 13, 1912.

42. Richmond, H.W., ed. <u>Papers Relating to the Loss of Minorca in 1756</u>. <u>Publications of the Navy Records Society</u>, vol. 42. London: NRS, 1913, xl, 224 pp.

43. See vol. 22, 1913.

44. Grant, James, ed. <u>The Old Scots Navy from 1689 to 1710</u>. <u>Publications of the Navy Records Society</u>, vol. 44. London: NRS, 1914, lx, 448 pp.

45. See vol. 22, 1913.

46. Corbett, Julian S. and Richmond, H.W., eds. <u>Private Papers of George, Second Earl Spencer, First Lord of the Admiralty, 1794-1801</u>. 4 vols. <u>Publications of the Navy Records Society</u>, vols. 46, 48, 58, and 59. London: NRS, 1913-1924, xxiv, 417, vi, 518, xvi, 401, and viii, 320 pp.

47. See vol. 22, 1914.

48. See vol. 46, 1914.

49. Marsden, Reginald G., ed. <u>Documents Relating to the Law and Custom of the Sea</u>. 2 vols. <u>Publications of the Navy Records Society</u>, vols. 49 and 50. London: NRS, 1915-1916, xl, 561 and xxxiv, 457 pp.

50. See vol. 49, 1916.

51. Perrin, William G., ed. <u>The Autobiography of Phineas Pett</u>. <u>Publications of the Navy Records Society</u>, vol. 51. London: NRS, 1918, civ, 244 pp.

52. Callender, Geoffrey, ed. The Life of Sir John Leake, Rear-Admiral of Great Britain by Stephen Martin-Leake. 2 vols. Publications of the Navy Records Society, vol. 52 and 53. London: NRS, 1920, clviii, 334 and x, 490 pp.

53. See vol. 52, 1920.

54. Manwaring, G.E. and Perrin, W.G., eds. The Life and Works of Sir Henry Mainwaring. 2 vols. Publications of the Navy Records Society, vol. 54 and 56. London: NRS, 1920-1921, xviii, 375 and x, 301 pp.

55. Smith, David Bonner, ed. The Letters of Admiral of the Fleet the Earl St. Vincent Whilst First Lord of the Admiralty, 1801-1804. 2 vols. Publications of the Navy Records Society, vol. 55 and 61. London: NRS, 1922-1927, viii, 380 and viii, 604 pp.

56. See vol. 54, 1921.

57. See vol. 26, 1923.

58. See vol. 46, 1924.

59. See vol. 46, 1924.

60. See vol. 26, 1926.

61. See vol. 55, 1927.

62. Perrin, William G. and Lloyd, Christopher, eds. The Keith Papers: Selected from the Letters and Papers of Admiral Viscount Keith. 3 vols. Publications of the Navy Records Society, vols. 62, 90, and 96. London: NRS, 1927-1956, 492, xii, 422, and xx, 394 pp.

63. Perrin, William G., ed. The Naval Miscellany. Publications of the Navy Records Society, vol. 63. London: NRS, 1928, xii, 483 pp.

64. Anderson, R.C., ed. The Journal of Edward Montagu, First Earl of Sandwich, Admiral and General at Sea, 1659-1665. Publications of the Navy Records Society, vol. 64. London: NRS, 1929, 329 pp.

65. Perrin, William G., ed. Boteler's Dialogues. Publications of the Navy Records Society, vol. 65. London: NRS, 1929, xl, 341 pp.

66. See vol. 13, 1930.

67. Tunstall, W.C. Brian, ed. The Byng Papers: Selected from the Letters and Papers of Admiral Sir George Byng, First Viscount Trorrington and His Son, Admiral the Hon. John Byng. 3 vols. Publications of the Navy Records Society, vols. 67, 68, and 70. London: NRS, 1930-1932, lxxxiv, 265, xxx, 373, and liv, 404 pp.

68. See vol. 67, 1931.

69. Barnes, G.R. and Owen, J.H., eds. The Private Papers of John, Earl of Sandwich, First Lord of the Admiralty, 1771-1782. 4 vols. Publications of the Navy Records Society, vols. 69, 71, 75, and 78. London: NRS, 1932-1938, xxx, 456, xiv, 394, x, 333, and xii, 446 pp.

70. See vol. 67, 1932.

71. See vol. 69, 1933.

72. Jones, G. Pitcairn, ed. Piracy in the Levant, 1827-1828: Selected from the Papers of Admiral Sir Edward Codrington, KCB. Publications of the Navy Records Society, vol. 72. London: NRS, 1934, xxxvi, 325 pp.

73. Chappell, Edwin, ed. The Tangier Papers of Samuel Pepys. Publications of the Navy Records Society, vol. 73. London: NRS, 1935, liv, 372 pp.

74. Bullock, J.G., ed. The Tomlinson Papers: Selected from the Correspondence and Pamphlets of Captain Robert Tomlinson, RN and Vice-Admiral Nicholas Tomlinson. Publications of the Navy Records Society, vol. 74. London: NRS, 1935, xxx, 400 pp.

75. See vol. 69, 1936.

76. Powell, J.R., ed. The Letters of Robert Blake: Together with Supplementary Documents. Publications of the Navy Records Society, vol. 76. London: NRS, 1937, xxiii, 501 pp.

77. Smith, David Bonner, ed. The Barrington Papers: Selected from the Letters and Papers of Admiral the Hon. Samuel Barrington. 2 vols. Publications of the Navy Records Society, vols. 77 and 81. London: NRS, 1937-1941, viii, 464 and xxxii, 374 pp.

78. See vol. 69, 1938.

79. Anderson, R.C., ed. The Journals of Sir Thomas Allin, 1660-1678. 2 vols. Publications of the Navy Records Society, vols. 79 and 80. London: NRS, 1939-1940, xiv, 309 and lii, 272 pp.

80. See vol. 79, 1940.

81. See vol. 77, 1941.

82. Smith, David Bonner, ed. Recollections of My Sea Life from 1808 to 1830 by Captain John Harvey Boteler, RN. Publications of the Navy Records Society, vol. 82. London: NRS, 1942, xvii, 255 pp.

83. Smith, David Bonner, ed. Russian War. 3 vols. Publications of the Navy Records Society, vols. 83, 84, and 85. London: NRS, 1943-1945, viii, 434, viii, 414, and vi, 462 pp.

84. See vol. 83, 1944.

85. See vol. 83, 1945.

86. Anderson, R.C., ed. Journals and Narratives of the Third Dutch War. Publications of the Navy Records Society, vol. 86. London: NRS, 1946, vi, 421 pp.

87. Rowbotham, W.B., ed. The Naval Brigades of the Indian Mutiny, 1857-1858. Publications of the Navy Records Society, vol. 87. London: NRS, 1947, xvi, 304 pp.

88. Cranmer-Byng, J.L., ed. Pattee Byng's Journal, 1718-1720. Publications of the Navy Records Society, vol. 88. London: NRS, 1950, xxxii, 311 pp.

89. Merriman, R.D., ed. The Sergison, Papers, 1688-1702. London: NRS, 1950, xii, 382 pp.

90. See vol. 62, 1950.

91. Thursfield, H.G., ed. Five Naval Journals, 1789-1817. Publications of the Navy Records Society, vol. 91. London: NRS, 1951, xiv, 400 pp.

92. Lloyd, C. Christopher, ed. The Naval Miscellany. Publications of the Navy Records Society, vol. 92. London: NRS, 1952, xii, 502 pp.

93. Lewis, Michael A., ed. A Narrative of Professional Adventures by Sir William Henry Dillon, Vice-Admiral of the Red. 2 vols. Publications of the Navy Records Society, vols. 93 and 97. London: NRS, 1953-1956, xxxiv, 468 and xxix, 407 pp.

94. Graham, Gerald S., ed. The Walker Expedition to Quebec, 1711. Publications of the Navy Records Society, vol. 94. London: NRS, 1953, xx, 430 pp.

95. Smith, David and Lumby, E.W.R., eds. The Second China War, 1856-1860. Publications of the Navy Records Society, vol. 95. London: NRS, 1954, xxiv, 413 pp.

96. See vol. 62, 1955.

97. See vol. 93, vol. 1956.

98. Hughes, Edward, ed. The Private Correspondence of Admiral Lord Collingwood. Publications of the Navy Records Society, vol. 98. London: NRS, 1956, 348 pp.

99. Ranft, Bryan M., ed. The Vernon Papers. Publications of the Navy Records Society, vol. 99. London: NRS, 1958, xii, 599 pp.

100. Naish, George P.B., ed. Nelson's Letters to His Wife and Other Documents, 1785-1831. Publications of the Navy Records Society, vol. 100. London: Routledge, 1958, 630 pp.

101. Lloyd, Christopher and Anderson, R.C., eds. A Memoir of James Trevenen, 1760-1790. Publications of the Navy Records Society, vol. 101. London: NRS, 1959, xiv, 250 pp.

102. Kemp, P.K., ed. The Papers of Admiral Sir John Fisher. 2 vols. Publications of the Navy Records Society, vols. 102 and 106. London: NRS, 1955-1964, xxviii, 411 and xii, 472 pp.

103. Merriman, R.D., ed. Queen Anne's Navy. Publications of the Navy Records Society, vol. 103. London: NRS, 1961, xiv, 386 pp.

104. Graham, Gerald S. and Humphreys, R.A., eds. The Navy and South America, 1807-1823: Correspondence of the Commanders-in-Chief. . . . Dedicated to Sir Charles Webster. Publications of the Navy Records Society, vol. 104. London: NRS, 1962, xxxiv, 394 pp.

105. Powell, J.R. and Timings, E.K., eds. Documents Relating to the Civil War, 1642-1648. Publications of the Navy Records Society, vol. 105. London: NRS, 1963, xiv, 430 pp.

106. See vol. 102, 1964.

107. Lloyd, Christopher, ed. The Health of Seamen: Selections from the Works of Dr. James Lind, Sir Gilbert Blane, and Dr. Thomas Trotter. Publications of the Navy Records Society, vol. 107. London: NRS, 1965, viii, 319 pp.

108. Patterson, A.T., ed. The Jellicoe Papers. 2 vols. Publications of the Navy Records Society, vols. 108 and 111. London: NRS, 1966-1968, viii, 315 and xvi, 497 pp.

109. Williams, Glyndwr, ed. Documents Relating to Anson's Round the World, 1740-1744. Publications of the Navy Records Society, vol. 109. London: NRS, 1967, xiv, 303 pp.

110. Ryan, A.N., ed. The Saumarez Papers: Selections from the Baltic Correspondence of Vice-Admiral Sir James Saumarez, 1808-1812. Publications of the Navy Records Society, vol. 110. London: NRS, 1968, xxvi, 287 pp.

111. See vol. 108, 1968.

112. Powell, J.R. and Timings, E.K., eds. The Rupert and Monck Letter Book, 1666: Together with Supporting Documents. Publications of the Navy Records Society, vol. 112. London: NRS, 1969, x, 307 pp.

113. Roskill, Stephen W., ed. Documents Relating to the Naval Air Service, 1909-1918. Publications of the Navy Records Society, vol. 113. London: NRS, 1969, xxii, 790 pp.

114. Syrett, David, ed. The Siege and Capture of Havana, 1762. Publications of the Navy Records Society, vol. 114. London: NRS, 1970, xxxvi, 355 pp.

115. Lumby, E.W.R., ed. Policy and Operations in the Mediterranean, 1912-1914. Publications of the Navy Records Society, vol. 115. London: NRS, 1970, xvi, 481 pp.

116. McGowan, Alan P., ed. The Jacobean Commission of Enquiry, 1608 and 1618. Publications of the Navy Records Society, vol. 116. London: NRS, 1971, xxx, 319 pp.

117. Halpern, Paul G., ed. The Keyes Papers. 3 vols. Publications of the Navy Records Society, vols. 117, 121, and 122. London: NRS, 1972-1981, xxiv, 547, xiv, 468, and xvi, 398 pp.

118. Gwyn, Julian, ed. The Royal Navy and North America: The Warren Papers, 1736-1752. Publications of the Navy Records Society, vol. 118. London: NRS, 1973, xlvi, 464 pp.

119. Bromley, John Selwyn, ed. The Manning of the Royal Navy: Selected Public Pamphlets, 1693-1873. Publications of the Navy Records Society, vol. 119. London: NRS, 1976, li, 409 pp.

120. Baugh, Daniel A., ed. Naval Administration, 1715-1750. Publications of the Navy Records Society, vol. 120. London: NRS, 1977, xvi, 523 pp.

121. See vol. 117, 1980.

122. See vol. 117, 1981.

123. Rose, Susan, ed. The Navy of the Lancastrian Kings: Accounts and Inventories of William Soper, Keeper of the King's Ships, 1422-1427. Publications of the Navy Records Society, London: Allen, 1982, xx, 288 pp.

124. Sumida, Jon T., ed. The Pollen Papers: The Privately Circulated Printed Works of Arthur Hungerford Pollen, 1901-1916. Publications of the Navy Records Society, vol. 124. London: Allen, 1984, xv, 400 pp.

125. Rodger, N.A.M., ed. The Naval Miscellany. Publications of the Navy Records Society, vol. 125. London: Allen, 1984, xiv, 546 pp.

126. Halpern, Paul G., ed. The Royal Navy in the Mediterranean, 1915-1918. Publications of the Navy Records Society, vol. 126. London: NRS, 1987, xvi, 623 pp.

127. Wernham, R.B., ed. The Expedition of Sir John Norris and Sir Francis Drake to Spain and Portugal, 1589. Publications of the Navy Records Society, vol. 127. Aldershot: Smith, 1988, lxvi, 380 pp.

128. Ranft, Bryan M., ed. The Beatty Papers: Selections from the Private and Official Correspondence of Admiral of the Fleet Earl Beatty. 2 vols. Publications of the Navy Records Society, vols. 128 and 132. London: Scolar, 1989-1993, xxiv, 592 and xxiv, 496 pp.

129. Mackay, Ruddock F., ed. The Hawke Papers: A Selection, 1743-1771. Publications of the Navy Records Society, vol. 129. Aldershot: Scolar, 1990, xxx, 521 pp.

130. Simpson, Michael, ed. Anglo-American Naval Relations, 1917-1919. Publications of the Navy Records Society, vol. 130. Aldershot: Scolar, 1991, xviii, 648 pp.

131. Hattendorf, John B., Knight, R.J.B., Pearsall, A.W.H., Rodger, N.A.M., and Till, Geoffrey, eds. British Naval Documents, 1204-1960. Publications of the Navy Records Society, Vol. 131. Aldershot: Scolar, 1993, 1196 pp.

132. See vol. 128, 1993.

133. Latham, Robert, ed. Samuel Pepys and the Second Dutch War: Pepy's Navy White Book and Brooke House Papers. Publications of the Navy Records Society, vol. 133. London: Scolar, 1995, xxxix, 488 pp.

134. Simpson, Michael and Somerville, John, eds. The Somerville Papers. Publications of the Navy Records Society, vol. 134. Aldershot: Scolar, 1995, xxv, 696 pp.

135. Grainger, John D, ed. The Royal Navy on the River Plate, 1806-1807. Publications of the Navy Records Society, vol. 135. Aldershot: Scolar, 1996, xiv, 384 pp.

136. Tracy, Nicholas, ed. The Collective Naval Defence of the Empire, 1900-1940. Publications of the Navy Records Society, vol. 136. Aldershot: Ashgate, 1997, liv, 706 pp.

137. Grove, Eric, ed. The Defeat of the Enemy Attacks on Shipping, 1939-1945. Publications of the Navy Records Society, vol. 137. Aldershot: Ashgate, 1997, xc, 380 pp.

138. Lavery, Brian, ed. Shipboard Life and Organisation, 1731-1815. Publications of the Navy Records Society, vol. 138. London: Ashgate, 1998, 682 pp.

139. Syrett, David, ed. The Battle of the Atlantic and Signal Intelligence: U-Boat Situations and Trends, 1941-1945. Publications of the Navy Records Society, vol. 139. Aldershot: Ashgate, 1998, xl, 621 pp.

141. Morriss, Roger, ed. The Channel Fleet and the Blockade of Brest, 1793-1801. Publications of the Navy Records Society, vol. 141. Aldershot: Ashgate, 2001, xii, 700 pp.

142. Lambert, Nicholas, ed. <u>The Submarine Service, 1900-1918</u>. <u>Publications of the Navy Records Society</u>, vol. 142. Aldershot: Ashgate, 2001, xliv, 397 pp.

___. Lambert, Andrew, ed. <u>The Papers of Sir John Knox Laughton</u>. <u>Publications of the Navy Records Society</u>, vol. ___. London: NRS. In 2001, noted as forthcoming.

___. Hattendorf, John B., ed. <u>The Journal of Admiral Sir George Rooke, 1700-1704</u>. <u>Publications of the Navy Records Society</u>, vol. ___. London: NRS. In 2000, noted as in progress and forthcoming.

___. Beeler, John F., ed. <u>The Papers of Admiral Alexander Milne</u>. <u>Publications of the Navy Records Society</u>, vol. ___. London: NRS. In 2001, noted as in progress and forthcoming.

Author – Person Index

Note: The nature of the historiographical-bibliographical survey is different from that of the traditional narrative history, monograph, and biography. There are two indexes which follow, Author-Person and Subject. Because persons incorporated in this survey are authors and, on occasion, participants and subjects of works, all persons have been included in the Author-Person Index. All other items, not persons, are included in the Subject Index. In the Author-Person Index all male monarchs, for example, kings, emporers, and princes, have been collected in one place, "Kings, Emperors, and Dynasties," placed alphabetically after "King"; similarly, Queens have been incorporated alphabetically under "Queens."

In the Author-Person Index, regular type numbers indicate page numbers; bold type numbers indicate entry numbers in the Annotated Bibliography Section.

Abbott, John L., 307; **1**

Abell, Westcott S., 269; **2**

Abels, Richard P., 68; **3-5**

Abernathy, George, 141

Acerra, Martine, 139, 236; **6, 7**

Acton, Harold, 169; **8**

Aczel, Amir D., 319; **9**

Adair, E.R., 242; **10**

Adam, Frank, 344; **11**

Adams, Henry, 149, 151; **12**

Adams, John, 307

Adams, Randolph G., 134; **13**

Adams, Simon L., 103, 196; **14-17**

Adams, Thomas R., 16; **18**

Adamson, Jack H., 195; **19**

Addington, Larry H., 259; **20, 21**

Addis, Charles P., 171; **22**

Aiken William A., 37; **23**

Aker, Raymond, 194; **24**

Alban, J.R., 87; **25**

Albert, Marvin H., 188; **26**

Albion, Robert G., 4, 15, 41, 48, 51, 157, 235, 271; **27-31**

Alden, Dauril, 48; **32**

Alderman, Clifford L., 350; **33**

Aldous, Tony, 274; **34**

Aldridge, David D., 36, 84; **35, 36**

Alexander, Christopher, 28; **37**

Subject Index